CORPORATE ADVISORY ●MANAGEMENT CONSULTING

Deloitte Ross
Tohmatsu

280 NOT OUT
THE HISTORY OF
SUN ALLIANCE AND CRICKET

It all began in 1710 when a partnership of 24 members formed the Sun Insurance Company in London. Just 13 years after the first recorded "Genuine Eleven a Side Cricket Match" in Sussex in 1697, and 34 years before the publication of the first edition of "The Laws Of Cricket" in 1744.

Today Sun Alliance is the oldest continuously operating insurance company in the world with total assets in excess of $25 billion.

The first life insurance policy in Australia was written by the British office of the Alliance Assurance Company in 1833. This same company merged to form the Sun Alliance of today, opening an office in Australia that same year, 30 years after the first recorded cricket game in Australia in 1803.

SUN ALLIANCE
AUSTRALIA GROUP

In 1839, the Phoenix insurance company (another company forming part of todays Group) opened its doors in Australia, 1 year after the founding of the famous Melbourne Cricket Club in 1838. And in 1879, 1 year following the historic defeat of the MCC by the first Australian touring side in 1878, the Sun insurance company began operations in Australia.

This close association has seen the Sun Alliance group of companies grow to encompass all of Australia, with an extensive branch network of offices providing a wide range of insurance products to suit the individual.

SUN ALLIANCE
AUSTRALIA GROUP

STATE BRANCHES:

New South Wales
22 Bridge Street
Sydney 2000
Ph: (02) 233 9000
Fax: (02) 233 9876

Western Australia
41 St. Georges Terrace
Perth 6000
Ph: (09) 325 8733
Fax: (09) 220 1214

Queensland
12 Creek Street
Brisbane 4000
Ph: (07) 229 6133
Fax: (07) 221 7893

South Australia
45 Grenfell Street
Adelaide 5000
Ph: (08) 210 5111
Fax: (08) 212 6891

Tasmania
39 Murray Street
Hobart 7000
Ph: (002) 23 1400
Fax: (002) 31 1231

Victoria
34 Queen Street
Melbourne 3000
Ph: (03) 618 8111
Fax: (03) 618 8118

THE  ABC AUSTRALIAN CRICKET ALMANAC

EDITED BY PHILIP DERRIMAN
STATISTICS BY ROSS DUNDAS

1990

an
ABC
BOOK

Published by ABC Enterprises for the
AUSTRALIAN BROADCASTING CORPORATION
20 Atchison Street (Box 8888) Crows Nest NSW 2065

First published 1990

National Library of Australia
Cataloguing-in-Publication entry

ABC Australian cricket almanac 1990.

ISBN 0 7333 0064 2.

1. Cricket – Australia. 2. Cricket – Australia – Records.
I. Derriman, Philip, 1943-   . II. Title: Australian
cricket almanac 1990. III. Title: Australian Broadcasting
Corporation Australian cricket almanac 1990.

796.3580994

Edited by Stuart Neal
Designed by Howard Binns-McDonald
Cover photography by Paul Austin—Five Star, Sydney
Set in 9/10 pt. Highland by Midland Typesetters, Victoria
Printed and bound in Australia by Australian Print Group, Victoria

10.6-1999

EDITOR'S NOTE

IN THIS FIRST EDITION OF THE ABC AUSTRALIAN CRICKET ALMANAC, the Three Australian Players of the Year and the Three Sheffield Shield Players of the Year were chosen by a panel of six ABC cricket commentators. The commentators who kindly agreed to be part of the panel were Jim Maxwell of Sydney, Tim Lane of Melbourne, Gerry Collins of Brisbane, Roger Wills of Adelaide, Trevor Jenkins of Perth and Neville Oliver of Hobart. Some explanation is needed here of the selection criteria. The Three Australian Players of the Year were chosen from players who had represented Australia in the year under review, May 1989 to April 1990, on the basis of their performances in the national side. The Three Sheffield Shield Players of the Year were chosen from all cricketers on the basis of their performances in Shield matches in the 1989-90 season. Although cricketers who had played for Australia during the season, either in Tests or limited-over matches, were not excluded, effectively the players considered by the panel had to have played Shield cricket for *most* of the season.

A great many people outside the ABC provided enormous help in the compilation of this almanac, and for this the ABC offers thanks. Some of the people around Australia whose invaluable contribution the editor would like to acknowledge are, in no special order: Ken Jacobs, Richard Hickman, David Lemon, Brian Hughes, Tony Mann, Richard Watson, Denis O'Dea, Brian Sweetapple, John Wood, Grantley Evans, Ray Sutton, Peter Binns, Denis Broad, Geoff Hickman, Don Howard, Virginia Iredale, John Harris, Peter Spence, Jenny Condello, Max Walters, Ronald Cardwell, Ed Parker, Don Marsdon, Neil Ballard, Bob Hooper, Kevin Connor, Don Woon, Ian Sturgess, Ron Williams, Ralph Wiese, Phil Ridings, Lindsay Hassett, James Rodgers, Keith Miller, Bob Spence, Steve Bernard, Ted Richardson, Neville Jones, Cliff Winning, Warren Saunders and Tony Gifford. Special thanks are owed, too, to Greg McKie, who compiled the reports on junior cricket, Erica Sainsbury, who compiled the report on women's cricket, and Ric Finlay, who provided expert advice.

This first edition of the almanac is distinguished by an article by Sir Donald Bradman. As well as being the greatest of all Australian cricketers, Sir Donald is one of the game's clearest thinkers, and the ABC is deeply appreciative of his contribution.

CONTENTS

GENERAL STATISTICS

THE GAME
IN REVIEW

by SIR DONALD BRADMAN AC

I AM INFORMED THAT THE ABC intends to produce a book titled *The ABC Australian Cricket Almanac* and I have been honoured by a request to contribute an article. This I do with pleasure. I am mindful of the valued participation of the ABC in radio broadcasts of cricket in my early days. On my first tour of England in 1930 I was, of course, a player—not a listener—but many were the stories told to me by Australian fans who were enthralled by the broadcasts and who actually believed the sound of bat on ball was real, not synthetic. Those events now sound antiquated but they paved the way for the wonderful radio and television which now provide so much enjoyment to vast audiences.

For a variety of reasons the game of cricket lends itself to the production of literature. The most famous of all cricket publications is, of course, *Wisdens Cricketer's Almanac*, the 1990 edition of which is the 127th. So its genesis dates back to 1864. A complete set of *Wisdens* is now rare and commands a very high price. Whereas the first edition was comparatively small, my latest copy runs to 1,264 pages, of which no less than 28 are devoted to obituaries during the previous year, and 44 to the births and deaths of cricketers. The latter category originally covered all those who had played first class cricket but has perforce been reduced of late by the elimination of certain categories of lesser importance. In addition, *Wisden* contains a full list of the cricketers who have played in Tests since 1877. The births and deaths are of males with, I think, only one exception—namely Mrs HM Grace (mother of WG, EM and GF) born July 18, 1812, died July 25, 1884, a touching tribute to the memory of the mother of the world's most famous cricketing son, Dr WG Grace, who died in 1915. I am sure the ABC does not intend to challenge the size and content of *Wisden* but it does intend producing a prestige publication which will occupy a prominent place in the libraries of all Australian cricket lovers.

The literature that is churned out every year about cricket is quite incredible. Sometimes I think the value of statistics is a bit overwhelming and the number of Tests being played these days, compared with the number when I was a youth, is making comparisons somewhat insignificant. For instance, runs made or wickets taken must obviously relate to the number of matches played and a cricketer may now participate in more Test matches in a year than some illustrious performers of yesteryear did in a lifetime. The most meaningful statistic left is probably a batting or bowling average because it gets far less distorted by volume. But statistics of any kind fascinate the cricket lover.

I doubt if today's era is producing the quality literature produced by Sir Neville Cardus, AA Thomson and a few other writers, but this seems to be dictated by the mode of modern living. No longer can a writer be given two columns in the morning paper—he is required to produce a tabloid report circumscribed by both space and time. Nevertheless there are many extremely good writers who contribute handsomely when they are given time for reflection and many biographies in recent years have been splendid.

There is far more coaching today than ever before and whilst I remain of the opinion that genius is a God-given gift—not a product of coaching—it must be admitted that we are seeing a vast number of very good young players and the general standard of play has probably improved. The great batsmen of my generation had a wider range of shots than the best players of today, especially off the back foot. And in saying that I am thinking of men like Charlie Macartney, Stan McCabe and Denis Compton. One reason may well be the questionable tendency of modern players to use much heavier bats— 3 lbs (1.4 kg) as against say 2 lbs 4 ozs (1 kg)—which pander to the forward pendulum stroke but inhibit the cut and pull shots. These heavy weapons demand a strong physique and not everyone is as powerful as Clive Lloyd.

There is certainly no leg spin bowler today within cooee of the quality of Grimmett or O'Reilly. The demise of the leg spinner is one of the tragedies of modern cricket. Why has it happened? One reason certainly is that accuracy and inexpensive leg spin cannot be developed without years of experience and the time is no longer available, especially in one-day cricket where runs per over mostly exceed in importance the value of wickets taken. Richie Benaud became a great leg spinner. But how many people realise that his first two tours of England yielded a mere 10 Test wickets at an average of 50? With confidence, foresight and patience the selectors stuck by him and by 1961 he was a Test winner. On the other side of the ledger I wonder how many realise that Stan McCabe was picked to go to England in 1930 without ever having scored a century in first-class cricket, whereas last summer in Australia a young South Australian batsman made several centuries but couldn't force his way into the Test XI.

I am proud to think I have been part of the first-class cricket scene for well over 60 years, during which time I have been fortunate enough to rub shoulders with most of the great players and administrators who created history. It has been a fascinating experience. Whereas the Test match-playing countries were originally only Australia and England, and they contested the first 30 Tests from 1877 to 1888, South Africa entered the fray in March 1889. Her first Test was played at Port Elizabeth and the English captain was Charles Aubrey Smith (later knighted), commonly known by the nickname of 'Round-the-corner Smith' because of the angled run he took coming in to bowl. In 1932 I played against him in a game in Hollywood where he captained the local side, and although he is now deceased I revere his memory as a grand and very lovable character.

Today the Test countries include the West Indies, India, Pakistan, Sri Lanka and New Zealand, with other applicants in the wings.

Sadly, for reasons which had nothing to do with cricket, South Africa had to withdraw. It will be a red-letter day for cricket devotees when circumstances enable South Africa to once again take her place. Meanwhile there is comforting evidence that South Africa is still producing players of the highest quality.

As a player I look back with pride and satisfaction, believing that my interpretation of cricket on the field contributed to the welfare and health of the game as well as maximising spectator enjoyment. To administration I devoted countless hours but my success or failure in this field cannot be measured, not least because I failed to achieve many of the things I espoused. It is interesting to look back and re-read my first contribution to *Wisden* as a writer in the 1939 edition. For instance, I warned of the intrusion of other forms of entertainment impinging on cricket's popularity, and the critical area of finance. I played in a Test match at Melbourne in 1937 which attracted 350 534 spectators. Imagine what a gate of that magnitude would do for the Australian Cricket Board today. The treasurer would have a coronary.

A repetition of such a crowd will remain a dream from now on, largely because of the increasing public demand for speed, action and entertainment. The latter is now to some extent provided through the one-day limited-over games. Distasteful as it may be to some old cricket diehards I re-assert what I wrote in the 1986 *Wisden* under the heading of 'Whither Cricket Now?', namely 'if there is a threat to the survival of the game of cricket, that threat lies in the first-class arena. One-day cricket, especially day-night cricket, is here to stay'. The answer lies simply in my forecast over 60 years ago of the need to cater for the demands of the modern generations.

Other matters I touched on included the quality of pitches. Significantly, in English county cricket there is now a point penalty against a county if it produces a sub-standard pitch. I advocated a change in the lbw law which duly came to pass. It has been largely successful in forcing players to attempt to hit the ball and not just 'pad up', but has been nullified to some extent by batsmen cultivating forward play to an excessive degree, thereby reducing the variety and quality of strokes off the back foot. I feel sure we have not seen the last alteration in the lbw law.

I advocated an eight-ball over and remain convinced that the public would prefer eight balls rather than six. The latter remains in use primarily because of the obstinate refusal of England to listen to Australia's arguments. Our proposal has never been given an extended and adequate trial in England. My plea for modern scoreboards has been answered to the extent that our modern electronic marvels give a surfeit of information, sometimes to the great embarrassment of a hapless umpire who has given a wrong judgment on a run out. I now go further and support the use of the electronic eye to determine a run out decision, and probably stumpings. It would be perfectly simple to implement. From what I have read a majority of umpires have spoken up against this viewpoint but why they should do so remains a mystery to me. It would not only bring justice (as it now does on the race tracks of the world), it would also lessen the umpire's responsibility. He must, of course, remain the exclusive arbiter on lbw decisions but they are in a different category because they are a matter of opinion, not fact.

Another matter of relative unimportance that worries me is the question of light appeals. At one time there was a condition that only the batting side could appeal against the light and appeals were limited to one per session of play. In my view this worked perfectly. But now the umpires, for some inexplicable reason, are empowered to 'offer the light'. Whether they do it per medium of light meters or simply by observation, I think it is quite wrong for umpires to intervene in this way without appeal. I have never yet seen an occasion when the light was 'offered' and the batsmen refused. It would be far better to go back to the situation once extant that play should only be suspended 'when the conditions are so bad that it is unreasonable or dangerous for it to continue'. The rights of the spectators should not be overlooked, but sadly I don't think they are given enough weight. As a player I loved nothing better than to bat without a cap under dull, overcast conditions. Providing there is an adequate sightboard I found an even dull light much kinder than bright sunlight. I am reminded of the Yorkshireman who was in Australia watching a match when the players came off because of the light. He turned to his neighbour and inquired why the players were coming off. On being told it was because the light was not good enough he retorted, 'My friend, if we couldn't play in this light in Sheffield we would never start a match, let alone finish it.'

Another of the problems confronting modern legislators is the question of bouncers. Prior to 1932 they were not a serious problem. Their use during the 1932/3 season in conjunction with a packed leg-side field, led to the introduction of a rule virtually banning 'bodyline' by restricting the on-side fielders to a maximum of two behind square leg. The law was also amended giving the umpire power to intervene if he thought the bowler was trying to intimidate the striker, the ultimate penalty being that the bowler had to be taken off and not allowed to bowl again in the same innings. That law just simply has not worked. I think the reasons are (a) that umpires are reluctant to exercise a moral judgment as to the intent of the bowler and (b) the severity of the penalty. In regard to (b) can we really expect a local umpire in an emotional and volatile situation at a critical stage of a Test match to ban the local hero for the rest of the innings?

There is no simple answer to the problem. But I would point out that in one-day cricket the bowling of a bouncer which rises head-high is negated by the call of no ball. Umpires don't hesitate to invoke the penalty and so it works. The judgment becomes one of fact—not a moral issue. The sanction does not prevent the bowler continuing but does prevent him profiting from his tactics. As he can't get a batsman out from such a delivery, as the striker can score runs with impunity, and as the ball does not count in the over, the bowler quickly sees the light. There are many people who believe the bowling of bouncers (within reason) in Test cricket should not be banned because they are a legitimate weapon in the hands of a fast bowler, they test the courage of batsmen, and they often result in strokes of great skill and excitement. I understand such a view. Indeed as a batsman (bodyline excluded) I welcomed this type of contest. But as things stand some bowlers exploit the weakness in the law to the very limit of tolerance and I think both players and public would prefer to see helmets being worn as a precaution rather than a necessity. I was particularly pleased that Terry Alderman met with such success on his last English tour because he seldom used the bouncer but relied on swing, cut and accuracy to achieve results. His performance was an object lesson.

There are occasionally circumstances of light and weather when I think umpires are too severe in their judgment as to whether play shall continue or even take place at all. May I remind readers of a piece of history. Cricket was originally played under conditions where the pitch and ground, as a whole, were at the mercy of the weather. That was the case when Australia toured England in 1902. In the fourth Test at Manchester Australia won the toss and batted on a pitch which had been exposed to the elements, as had been the bowler's footholds. The latter were so wet and slippery that England's fast bowler Lockwood could not be used until the score was 129 and England had to open the bowling with two slow bowlers. The legendary Victor Trumper made his famous century before lunch and Australia's total at the adjournment was 173 for 1. Contrast that with the first Test between Australia and England at Brisbane in 1936. Playing conditions then provided for the pitch to be uncovered but the bowler's footholds had to be protected. Australia had to bat on a 'sticky' and were all out for 58 in less than 13 overs, with fast bowlers Allen (5 for 36) and Voce (4 for 16) from dry firm footholds hurling their thunderbolts into a wet pitch. The best slow left-hand spinner in the world at that time, Hedley Verity, who had taken 14 wickets in one day at Lord's against Australia in 1934, was not given even one over. Without at this stage engaging in an argument about covered or uncovered pitches, my purpose in emphasising this contrast is that umpires should not suspend play because playing conditions are difficult or inconvenient, but only if they are well nigh unplayable. The interests of the viewing public should be taken into account.

There are other cricket laws which could do with scrutiny or are crying out for revision, such as, for instance, the front-foot no-ball law, which in my view is a disaster. The original no-ball law required the bowler to deliver the ball with one foot on the ground behind the bowling crease. That was interpreted sensibly by umpires as meaning 'in the process of delivering the ball' and I can't remember any complaint about the law until after World War II—which means it proved adequate for over 200 years. Then some enterprising fellow with a high-speed slow-motion camera produced film to show that certain bowlers—Ray Lindwall was one of the prime targets—had a very long drag and clearly had the ball in hand after the back foot had crossed the bowling crease. This evidence apparently goaded the MCC into action and in 1947 it altered the law and made it read that the offending foot had to be behind the bowling crease 'at the instant of delivery'. The new wording was manna from heaven for the photographers who now proceeded to show that almost every bowler offended under the new wording. The words 'instant of delivery' were absolutely precise, and instead of interpreting the law with common sense as meaning 'in the process of delivering the ball', the umpires now found themselves *directed* to adjudicate on that split fraction of a second as the ball left the hand.

The change in the wording was utterly stupid because no umpire can possibly watch simultaneously the hand and the foot. To get around the new absurdity, a sensible and reasonable measure of control was adopted whereby the umpire, in the case of draggers, was empowered to use a disc or marker which was placed at a sufficient distance behind the bowling crease to offset the bowler's drag, the disc in effect becoming the bowling crease. As evidence of the effectiveness of this measure I would point out that in my 1948 tour of England, Ray Lindwall was my principle fast bowler, yet in the whole five Tests, the no-balls debited against the Australian bowlers in each Test, averaged just under 3.

A further complication reared its head about this time when a handful of bowlers appeared to combine excessive drag with a doubtful bowling action. I know that certain English batsmen linked drag and throw as related evils. Cure one, they said, you cure the other. Despite an affinity in one particular case, they were not necessarily bed fellows. Two of the longest draggers were Ray Lindwall and Fred Trueman and both had perfect bowling actions with no semblance of a throw. Indeed the 'throwing' problem was completely eradicated by a change in the definition of a throw, a change brought about mainly through suggestions which emanated from discussions between my late friend Sir George Allen and me. The new wording was totally unrelated to the position of the feet or to drag. Despite undeniable evidence that the drag was well under control there remained opponents of the law who magnified certain minor and quite unimportant flaws concerning the use of the disc and finally, after a short period of experimentation, MCC altered the law to make the deciding criterion the position of the front foot as it related to the *batting* crease—not the bowling crease—the latter now becoming utterly redundant.

The new law made an absolute mockery of one which had stood the test of time for over two centuries. Bowlers could now place both feet clearly ahead of the defunct bowling crease. Many proceeded to do so, and still do. So long as the bowler's front foot was not over the *batting* crease he was in the clear. One of the original complaints, the fact that he had the ball in his hand after the back foot crossed the bowling crease, which virtually every bowler did and still does, was ignored. Australia's legislators were almost totally opposed to the MCC decision. In due course I was stunned to be told by a gentleman who was at the fatal meeting when the change was approved, that in response to a query, members present were informed that Australia supported the change. This may well have influenced the vote and was, of course, untrue.

Sadly the pro-front footers won the day. They had eliminated drag and made it irrelevant. But they were short-sighted because in curing one evil they had not perceived that they were creating a worse problem. Alec Bedser, a strong advocate in favour of judgment via the back foot, makes the cogent point that bowlers, at the point of delivery, need to be concentrating on where to pitch the ball. The last thing they need is to be distracted, even subconsciously, by having to worry about where the front foot is going to land. Alec feels this is very important, especially for up and coming young bowlers just learning their trade. Front-foot jurisdiction in its technical application is wrong and detracts from the development of a rhythmic and fluent action.

When the West Indians were last in Australia they bowled a plethora of no-balls from which hardly a run was made off the bat because the batsmen mostly played at the ball before they heard the belated front foot no-ball call. The West Indians failed to bowl their required 90 overs a day (and were heavily fined) primarily because no-balls are not counted in the overs. Ninety six-ball overs equal 540 balls. But 540 balls, of which 36 are called no-balls, come to only 84 overs. The situation was really farcical. In one Sheffield Shield match last season the fielding side conceded no less than 56 no-balls—top score for the innings. All of this is bad enough but is not nearly so bad as the problem confronting umpires. They must wait until the front foot hits the ground before making a call. There is often a split second before the umpire makes his decision and by the time he looks up, the ball from fast bowlers has sometimes reached the striker. The time during which the umpire must make an adjudication on a leg before or caught behind, a fraction of a second, is markedly reduced. Officially, umpires are reluctant to complain. Unofficially, many of them admit that mistakes are sometimes made and are caused by this wretched law. There are other problems with the law but space limitations prevent me going into them in detail.

Ever since this law came in I have worked unceasingly (but so far without success) to have it changed to the original back-foot determination, and almost without exception I believe I have the support in Australia of players, ex-players, umpires, administrators, and, for sure, the general public. The matter is important and it is high time the MCC admitted the present situation is totally unsatisfactory and made a change acceptable to all Test match-playing countries.

Another current hot potato is the number of overs to be bowled in a day. MCC has been trying to grapple with this problem for a long time. Press reports of the recent Test series in the West Indies indicate that both sides virtually ignored the official recommendations. The fight must go on. There is something radically wrong when the players of today can't bowl even 90 overs a day whereas those of the 1920s had no difficulty in getting through nearer 120. This is hardly value for those who pay to watch.

I have unashamedly used this ABC publication as a forum for expressing my personal views, knowing some of them to be controversial. Though I no longer hold any administrative position and therefore do not take part in the making of decisions, I retain a passionate desire to see cricket being played under rules and conditions which are not only the right ones practically and technically for those who play, but also create the maximum simplicity and enjoyment for spectators.

I am now an old man but am not one of those who thinks everything was better 'in my day'. I hope and believe I am still able to discern good from bad with a detached mind. Against the views perhaps held by a majority of the oldies I like one-day cricket. Despite its anomalies and weaknesses it forces players to get on with the game. Not all the strokes played are out of the coaching manual but they are exciting. The standard of fielding has improved enormously—cricket under lights with the white ball is wonderful and fascinating—the public are entertained and they see results in one day. That in no sense detracts from the truth that Test matches, played at the right tempo and in the right spirit, are still the pinnacle of skill. I hope the future will embrace and make the best of both types of entertainment.

I trust this ABC publication will play its part in the future development of our great game which is a way of life for so many people.

A YEAR
OF CRICKET

AT THE END OF THE 1989-90 SEASON, Australia could look back on its most successful twelve months in international cricket since the mid-1970s. It had overwhelmed England in a six-Test series, it had defeated Sri Lanka and Pakistan in two shorter series, it had beaten the same two countries convincingly in the Benson and Hedges World Series tournament, and it had won all five matches against New Zealand and India in the Rothmans Cup series in New Zealand. Its loss to New Zealand in the single Test played there in March 1990 was certainly a blemish on the record and, in fact, it was Australia's first defeat in 15 Tests. But the match was played on a rain-affected pitch, so to some extent the result could be considered an aberration.

Although some are reserving final judgment on this Australian team until it is tested in a wider arena, nobody could deny it was a more competitive, more efficient and more confident side than the teams which Australia fielded during the lean years of the mid and late 1980s. The Australian revival in 1989 was essentially a batting-led revival. In Mark Taylor, Australia gained a highly competent and productive opening batsman, who gave the Australian innings new solidity. Dean Jones and Steve Waugh were not new to the Australian team, of course, but their talent had not bloomed so fully before— even if Waugh's batting did lose some of its bloom before the summer was over. With Allan Border, who scored with remarkable consistency, and David Boon, who, against New Zealand in Perth, played one of the great innings of the season, these players provided a powerful and well-rounded batting combination. It was a measure of Australia's newly acquired batting strength that players such as Darren Lehmann and Mark Waugh could not find a place in the Test team. Tom Moody was brought into the side to replace the injured Geoff Marsh and scored a Test century against Sri Lanka, but was dropped two Tests later. Rarely has Australia been able to omit such talented batsmen as these.

The Australian bowling attack generally did what was expected of it, and in the Ashes Tests it achieved almost bewildering success against a strangely submissive England. But it was basically a pace attack, and its pace bowlers—Terry Alderman, Carl Rackemann, Geoff Lawson and Merv Hughes—were for the most part seasoned performers whose time at the top must be limited. If the Australian team has any cause for concern about the future, it is that there are no obvious replacements for them in sight. It is true, of course, that fast bowlers tend to come to the fore rapidly: the scarcely known Sheffield Shield bowler of one season can become the successful Test bowler in the next. This has happened before, and it may happen again.

On the other hand, there was a promising array of young spin bowlers around the country, including leg-spin bowlers. Trevor Hohns retired after the Ashes tour and on the whole Peter Sleep had a disappointing season, but Victoria's young leg-spinner, Peter McIntyre, bowled encouragingly well, and New South Wales's new leg-spinner, Adrian Tucker, began his first-class career in impressive fashion. Those who feared Australia's proud tradition of leg-spin bowling might be in danger of dying out altogether will be heartened by the presence in the first-class game of these two young bowlers. Of the off-spinners, it was Peter Taylor who received the call from the selectors, but Greg Matthews bowled with considerable success, too. It remains to be seen whether Tim May can fully overcome his injury problems.

Australia's selectors appeared to make an unfortunate error by fielding an all-pace attack in the Test against New Zealand at Perth, which they immediately repeated in the following Test against Sri Lanka in Brisbane. On several occasions in the 1980s Australia's selectors opted for an all-pace attack in Australia, generally without success, and now it has failed as a selection policy twice again. Quite apart from all this, an all-pace attack plainly makes for monotonous, tedious and therefore inferior cricket. It is to be hoped the national selectors will not choose one again.

THE
BRADMAN
MUSEUM

THE BRADMAN MUSEUM AT BOWRAL, which opened in October 1989, is in a number of ways a unique development. From the outset, the museum's organisers insisted the museum was not intended to be merely a shrine to the famous player it was named after, and this has proved to be true. If anything, the Bradman Museum has concentrated more on the present and future than it has on the past. Junior coaching clinics have been run there, the first of the annual Bradman Scholarships to Oxford has been awarded, and a match on the adjacent Bradman Oval in Bowral between the touring England side and a Bradman XI in December 1990 has been arranged.

On the other hand, Sir Donald Bradman and his achievements remain the museum's focal point. Clearly, without the Bradman connection and the drawing power of the Bradman name, the project would never have got off the ground and would certainly not have attracted the extraordinarily generous support which it received from Australia's business community. Sir Donald had nothing to do with the project in its initial stages, but he was persuaded to lend his support to it. He allowed the Bradman Museum Trust to use his name, and he donated some of his cricketing souvenirs as museum exhibits, including his 1947-48 Australian blazer, a New South Wales cap, pads, long whites, photographs, a painting, a sculpture and several trophies. He made another big personal contribution by travelling with Lady Bradman to New South Wales for the museum's inauguration. First, he attended and spoke at a dinner at Sydney's Regent Hotel on October 13, at which the Prime Minister, Mr Bob Hawke, formally launched the Bradman Scholarships scheme. About 650 people were present, including the president of the MCC, Sir Denys Roberts, who had flown from London for the occasion and whose humourous speech at the dinner was a classic of its kind. On the following day, Sir Donald and Lady Bradman attended the opening of the museum at Bowral, which attracted a crowd of about 4,000 people. Sir Donald spoke again, this time in nostalgic vein about his early years at Bowral. In the absence of the New South Wales Premier, Mr Nick Greiner, who was ill, Lady Bradman declared the museum open. Afterwards, at his own suggestion, Sir Donald spent nearly two hours in the museum pavilion signing autographs for a seemingly endless queue of admirers.

The museum trust's founding chairman was Bruce Collins, QC, a cricket-loving Sydney barrister who has a home at Bowral. Mr Collins was the driving force behind the entire project. He planned and oversaw the construction of the first stage of the museum complex, the pavilion, and he personally led a remarkably successful fund-raising drive to finance the building of the museum, the purchase of museum exhibits, the running of the coaching clinics and the establishment of the Bradman scholarships scheme. As he envisaged it, the purpose of the Bradman Museum was to present Sir Donald's career as an inspiration to young cricketers and to foster the sport generally. 'What we're doing, I suppose, is using Don Bradman's life as an example of what someone who came from a country town, without the benefit of influence or family connections, could achieve,' he said.

The public's early response to the Bradman Museum has been encouraging. Although work on the project's second stage, the museum itself, was not expected to start until mid-1990, the complex was visited in the first six months by almost 25 000 people, some of them visitors from England and other cricketing countries. It was always an aim of the Bradman Museum Trust to establish Bradman Oval as an important cricketing venue and, accordingly, the ground has been upgraded with the help of the local shire council. The wicket square has been relaid with Bulli-type soil, an in-ground watering system in the outfield has been installed, and a traditional picket fence and a new scoreboard were to be erected by mid-1990. It is expected that the England touring side will be only one of a number of visiting teams to play at Bowral in 1990-91.

The winner of the first Bradman Scholarship was Geoffrey Lovell of Sydney, an engineering graduate and first-grade cricketer.

PLAYERS
OF THE YEAR

Terry Alderman

Bowlers do not often see their efforts so generously rewarded as Terry Alderman's swing bowling was in England in 1989. His success was to some extent a product of perseverence. In the Ashes series in England in 1981, Alderman was Australia's most successful bowler, taking 42 wickets in 6 Tests. In the following year he badly injured his shoulder grappling with a spectator who invaded the field at Perth, and in the years which followed he struggled to recover his best form. When he joined Kim Hughes's Australians on their tours of South Africa in the mid-1980s, it seemed Alderman's Test career was probably over. But Alderman persisted, and in 1989 he regained his position at the head of the Australian attack, a position he had last held eight years before. As well as being a personal triumph, Alderman's success represented a victory for the art of bowling. In an age when most pace bowlers have sought to blast out batsmen with speed, Alderman achieved the same results with skill and guile. His outstanding performance will have been an inspiration to young swing bowlers everywhere.

Terry Alderman

Test	Date	Opponent	Venue	Ovrs	Md	Rns	Wk	NB	W	Balls	Mds	Runs	Wkt	Avrge	NB	W	Stk/rt	RPO
1	8/6/89	England	Leeds	37.0	7	107	5	3	—	222	7	107	5	21.40	3	—	44.40	2.89
1	8/6/89	England	Leeds	20.0	7	44	5	3	—	342	14	151	10	15.10	6	—	34.20	2.65
2	22/6/89	England	Lord's	20.5	4	60	3	1	—	467	18	211	13	16.23	7	—	35.92	2.71
2	22/6/89	England	Lord's	38.0	6	128	6	—	—	695	24	339	19	17.84	7	—	36.58	2.93
3	6/7/89	England	Birmingham	26.3	6	61	3	5	—	854	30	400	22	18.18	12	—	38.82	2.81
4	27/7/89	England	Manchester	25.0	13	49	—	—	—	1004	43	449	22	20.41	12	—	45.64	2.68
4	27/7/89	England	Manchester	27.0	7	66	5	4	—	1166	50	515	27	19.07	16	—	43.19	2.65
5	10/8/89	England	Nottingham	19.0	2	69	5	9	—	1280	52	584	32	18.25	25	—	40.00	2.74
5	10/8/89	England	Nottingham	16.0	6	32	2	4	—	1376	58	616	34	18.12	29	—	40.47	2.69
6	24/8/89	England	The Oval	27.0	7	66	5	10	—	1538	65	682	39	17.49	39	—	39.44	2.66
6	24/8/89	England	The Oval	13.0	3	30	2	3	—	1616	68	712	41	17.37	42	—	39.41	2.64
7	24/11/89	New Zealand	Perth	25.4	7	73	3	2	—	1770	75	785	44	17.84	44	—	40.23	2.66
7	24/11/89	New Zealand	Perth	32.0	14	59	1	—	—	1962	89	844	45	18.76	44	—	43.60	2.58
8	8/12/89	Sri Lanka	Brisbane	40.0	13	81	5	3	—	2202	102	925	48	19.27	48	—	45.88	2.52
9	16/12/89	Sri Lanka	Hobart	23.0	2	71	2	1	—	2340	104	996	50	19.92	49	—	46.80	2.55
9	16/12/89	Sri Lanka	Hobart	30.0	12	48	—	3	—	2520	116	1044	50	20.88	52	—	50.40	2.49
10	12/1/90	Pakistan	Melbourne	19.0	6	30	3	6	—	2634	122	1074	53	20.26	58	—	49.70	2.45
10	12/1/90	Pakistan	Melbourne	33.5	6	105	5	4	—	2837	128	1179	58	20.33	62	—	48.91	2.49
11	3/2/90	Pakistan	Sydney	33.5	10	65	5	1	—	3040	138	1244	63	19.75	63	—	48.25	2.46
12	15/3/90	New Zealand	Wellington	29.0	9	46	4	1	—	3214	147	1290	67	19.25	64	—	47.97	2.41
12	15/3/90	New Zealand	Wellington	14.0	8	27	—	—	—	3298	155	1317	67	19.66	64	—	49.22	2.40

◀ **Dean Jones** • **Terry Alderman** • **Mark Taylor**

Dean Jones

By the end of the summer of 1989-90 Dean Jones was sometimes described as the world's number one batsman in limited-overs cricket. Indeed, it was possible to argue he was the world's most in-form batsman in any kind of cricket, for no batsman in the previous year had dominated bowlers so completely as Jones. At times he looked quite unstoppable, and perhaps the outstanding feature of his batting was the extraordinary ease with which he handled the best of bowlers, Wasim Akram and Richard Hadlee included. Success tends to breed success, and this was true in Jones's case for a special reason: each success seemed to add to his confidence. The Dean Jones of 1989 and early 1990 could not have been less like the highly strung young batsman of three years before, who seemed to arrive at the crease in a state of agitation. Now, Jones arrived at the crease with the assurance of a batsman who *knows* he will score runs. It will not be easy for him to maintain his superb form of 1989 and 1990, but if he does he will certainly add a new dimension to Australia's batting.

Dean Jones

Test	Inn	Date	Opponent	Venue	Pos	H/O	Fielder	Bowler	Runs	Ttl Runs	Avrge
1	1	8/6/89	England	Leeds	5	Cgt	Russell RC	Newport PJ	79	79	79.00
1	2	8/6/89	England	Leeds	5	NO			40	119	119.00
2	3	22/6/89	England	Lord's	5	Lbw		Foster NA	27	146	73.00
2	4	22/6/89	England	Lord's	5	Cgt	Russell RC	Foster NA	0	146	48.67
3	5	6/7/89	England	Birmingham	5	Cgt	(S)Foley I	Fraser ARC	157	303	75.75
4	6	27/7/89	England	Manchester	5	Bwd		Botham IT	69	372	74.40
5	7	10/8/89	England	Nottingham	5	Cgt	Gower DI	Fraser ARC	22	394	65.67
6	8	24/8/89	England	The Oval	5	Cgt	Gower DI	Small GC	122	516	73.71
6	9	24/8/89	England	The Oval	5	Bwd		Capel DJ	50	566	70.75
7	10	24/11/89	New Zealand	Perth	5	Lbw		Morrison DK	99	665	73.89
8	11	8/12/89	Sri Lanka	Brisbane	5	Lbw		Labrooy GF	15	680	68.00
8	12	8/12/89	Sri Lanka	Brisbane	4	Cgt	Ramanayeke CPH	De Silva PA	23	703	63.91
9	13	16/12/89	Sri Lanka	Hobart	5	Cgt	Tillekeratne HP	Ratnayeke RJ	3	706	58.83
9	14	16/12/89	Sri Lanka	Hobart	6	NO			118	824	68.67
10	15	12/1/90	Pakistan	Melbourne	5	Cgt	Salim Yousuf	Imran Khan	0	824	63.38
10	16	12/1/90	Pakistan	Melbourne	5	Lbw		Wasim Akram	10	834	59.57
11	17	19/1/90	Pakistan	Adelaide	5	Cgt	Wasim Akram	Imran Khan	116	950	63.33
11	18	19/1/90	Pakistan	Adelaide	4	NO			121	1071	71.40
12	18	3/2/90	Pakistan	Sydney	5	did not bat			—	1071	71.40
13	19	15/3/90	New Zealand	Wellington	5	Cgtt	Wright JG	Snedden MC	20	1091	68.19
13	20	15/3/90	New Zealand	Wellington	6	Lbw		Morrison DK	0	1091	64.18

Mark Taylor

Mark Taylor has established himself so firmly as one of Australia's most productive run-makers that it is easy to forget he is still a relative newcomer to international cricket. He was by no means assured of a place in the Australian side at the start of the 1989 tour of England and, in fact, he began the tour so shakily that in mid-May the commentator Henry Blofeld observed that 'Taylor's lack of runs is beginning to be a worry.' A few days later, Taylor opened the batting against Somerset at Taunton. He started uncertainly, playing and missing several times, and was dropped when he was 8. But he hung on and with great determination fought on to make 97. That innings was a turning point. From then on Taylor feared no bowler. He proceeded to produce runs in such volume that a failure by him to make a half-century surprised. Above all, Taylor looked a supremely *competent* player. His technique was sound, and he batted sensibly with confidence and composure. To opposing bowlers, he no doubt appeared a most formidable obstacle, for his bat seemed unusually broad. There is every chance he will remain a formidable obstacle for some time to come.

Mark Taylor

Test	Inn	Date	Opponent	Venue	Pos	H/O	Fielder	Bowler	Runs	Ttl Runs	Avrge
1	1	8/6/89	England	Leeds	2	Lbw		Foster NA	136	136	136.00
1	2	8/6/89	England	Leeds	1	Cgt	Broad BC	Pringle DR	60	196	98.00
2	3	22/6/89	England	Lord's	2	Lbw		Foster NA	62	258	86.00
2	4	22/6/89	England	Lord's	1	Cgt	Gooch GA	Foster NA	27	285	71.25
3	5	6/7/89	England	Birmingham	2	Stp	Russell RC	Emburey JE	43	328	65.60
3	6	6/7/89	England	Birmingham	1	Cgt	Botham IT	Gooch GA	51	379	63.17
4	7	27/7/89	England	Manchester	1	Stp	Russell RC	Emburey JE	85	464	66.29
4	8	27/7/89	England	Manchester	2	NO			37	501	71.57
5	9	10/8/89	England	Nottingham	2	Stp	Russell RC	Cook NGB	219	720	90.00
6	10	24/8/89	England	The Oval	2	Cgt	Russell RC	Igglesden AP	71	791	87.89
6	11	24/8/89	England	The Oval	1	Cgt	Russell RC	Small GC	48	839	83.90
7	12	24/11/89	New Zealand	Perth	1	Cgt	Wright JG	Morrison DK	9	848	77.09
8	13	8/12/89	Sri Lanka	Brisbane	2	Cgt	Wickremasinghe AGD	Ramanayeke CPH	9	857	71.42
8	14	8/12/89	Sri Lanka	Brisbane	1	Lbw		Ramanayeke CPH	164	1021	78.54
9	15	16/12/89	Sri Lanka	Hobart	2	Cgt	Tillekeratne HP	Ratnayake RJ	23	1044	74.57
9	16	16/12/89	Sri Lanka	Hobart	1	Cgt	Gurusinha AP	De Silva PA	108	1152	76.80
10	17	12/1/90	Pakistan	Melbourne	2	Cgt	Aaqib Javed	Imran Khan	52	1204	75.25
10	18	12/1/90	Pakistan	Melbourne	1	Cgt	Aamer Malik	Tauseef Ahmed	101	1305	76.76
11	19	19/1/90	Pakistan	Adelaide	2	Lbw		Imran Khan	77	1382	76.78
11	20	19/1/90	Pakistan	Adelaide	1	Cgt	(S)Saeed Anwar	Mushtag Ahmed	59	1441	75.84
12	21	3/2/90	Pakistan	Sydney	1	NO			101	1542	81.16
13	22	15/3/90	New Zealand	Wellington	1	Lbw		Morrison DK	4	1546	77.30
13	23	15/3/90	New Zealand	Wellington	2	Lbw		Hadlee RJ	5	1551	73.86

AUSTRALIAN TOUR OF ENGLAND AND EUROPE 1989

IN ENGLAND IN 1989 the Australians performed creditably against the county elevens, lost narrowly a series of three one-day matches against England and were resoundingly victorious in a six-match Test series. Their success in the Tests took almost everyone by surprise. Before the tour began the general expectation was that Australia would struggle to hold its own, even against the relatively weak Test side which England seemed likely to field. Instead, the Australians inflicted on England one of the most comprehensive defeats in the history of Anglo-Australian cricket. Australia won four of the six Tests and, but for the weather, would almost certainly have won them all. The Australians gained the upper hand on the first day of the first Test, and they retained the upper hand right through the series, until the last day of the last Test. Indeed, it is hard to think of any Ashes series in the past which was more one-sided than this one.

Various explanations have been offered for the remarkable improvement in the performance of the Australians in 1989. Some suggested that the Australians achieved their victories largely by default—that they were really an average team which out-classed a second-rate opponent—and it is certainly true that the teams fielded by England in 1989 were unusually weak, both in batting and bowling. Yet this can only have been part of the equation. The chief reason Australia dominated the series was a newly acquired strength in batting. This new strength was drawn from a number of sources. The enormous difference Mark Taylor made to the team was obvious enough from the scorebook, and by the end of the series few doubted that a new Australian champion had arrived on the scene. Steve Waugh's two great innings in the first two Tests showed he had at last come of age as a batsman, fulfilling the high hopes many people had of him since he first appeared for New South Wales. Dean Jones's batting, too, attained a new stature. He continued to bat with exuberance, but the exuberance now seemed to be controlled. Allan Border did not score a century in the series, but the consistency with which he scored half-centuries (he made six of them in only nine Test innings) showed he was still the mainspring of Australia's batting. David Boon's performances tended to be over-shadowed by the more spectacular deeds of his team-mates, but he nevertheless had a fine series, scoring 442 runs at an average of 55. Of the batsmen, Geoff Marsh alone failed to shine, yet he still made a grand entry in the record books by virtue of the 329-run opening stand he shared with Taylor in the fifth Test. Together, these six batsmen formed a highly effective combination, blending solidity with flair in about the right proportions.

Australia's bowlers enjoyed as much success as its batsmen, although in their case the success could not be attributed to the emergence of new talent. The most successful Australian bowlers, Terry Alderman and Geoff Lawson, were old campaigners. Both had played off and on for Australia throughout the 1980s, and if they excelled on this occasion it was because they made the most of conditions which suited them. Alderman, in particular, bowled with great skill. His wonderful achievement of taking 41 wickets in the series at an average of 17.37 made some people wonder later what other great feats he might have performed if he had played more of his cricket in England. At the same time, it must be said that England's batsmen often made the task of taking their wickets look a good deal easier than it ought to have been.

1989 Australian Tour of England

Date		Venue	Opponent	Result
May	5*	West Bromwich	League Cricket Conference XI	Won by 165 runs
May	7*	Arundel	Lavinia, Duchess of Norfolk XI	Won by 120 runs
May	9*	Hove	Sussex	Lost by 4 wkts
May	11*	Lord's	MCC	Won by 101 runs
May	13	Worcester	Worcestershire	Lost by 3 wkts
May	17	Taunton	Somerset	Drawn
May	20	Lord's	Middlesex	Won by 3 wkts
May	25*	Manchester	England	Lost by 95 runs
May	27*	Nottingham	England	Tied
May	29*	Lord's	England	Won by 6 wkts
May	31	Birmingham	Warwickshire	Drawn
Jun	3	Derby	Derbyshire	Won by 11 runs
Jun	8	Leeds	ENGLAND	Won by 210 runs
Jun	14	Manchester	Lancashire	Won by 9 wkts
Jun	17	Northampton	Northamptonshire	Won by 272 runs
Jun	22	Lord's	ENGLAND	Won by 6 wkts
Jly	1	Neath	Glamorgan	Drawn
Jly	6	Birmingham	ENGLAND	Drawn
Jly	15*	Scotland	Glasgow	Won by 97 runs
Jly	17*	Trowbridge	Minor Counties	Won by 27 runs
Jly	19	Southampton	Hampshire	Drawn
Jly	22	Bristol	Gloucestershire	Won by an inns & 146 runs
Jly	27	Manchester	ENGLAND	Won by 9 wkts
Aug	2	Nottingham	Nottinghamshire	Won by 196 runs
Aug	5	Leicester	Leicestershire	Won by 9 wkts
Aug	10	Nottingham	ENGLAND	Won by an inns & 180 runs
Aug	16	Canterbury	Kent	Drawn
Aug	19	Chelmsford	Essex	Won by 150 runs
Aug	24	The Oval	ENGLAND	Drawn

* Denotes not first-class

League Cricket Conference XI v Australians
Not First-Class—50-over Match
West Bromwich Dartmouth
May 5 1989
Toss: Australians
Result: Australians won by 165 runs

Against an attack which included the Indian Test spin bowler Maninder Singh and the Australian Simon O'Donnell, Dean Jones (170) and Geoff Marsh (101) scored a welter of runs in this opening match, and Jones, in particular, looked in fine touch. Replying to the huge Australian total of 3 for 326, the home side managed only 5 for 161 in its 55 overs, O'Donnell remaining not out 52 at the end.

Australians

Batsman	How Out	Ttl
GR Marsh (c)	c Moseley b McMillan	101
MA Taylor	c McMillan b Trotter	23
DM Jones	c Samarasekera b Moseley	170
TM Moody	not out	7
MRJ Veletta	not out	2
SR Waugh	did not bat	
IA Healy (+)	did not bat	
GD Campbell	did not bat	
TV Hohns	did not bat	
MG Hughes	did not bat	
CG Rackemann	did not bat	
SUNDRIES: B. 6 LB. 10 W. 3 NB. 4		23
TOTAL	3 wkts for 326	
F/W: 65 299 318		

Bowler	O	M	R	Wkts
Moseley	11	1	27	1
Trotter	11	1	30	1
Maninder Singh	10	—	88	—
O'Donnell	10	—	53	—
McMillan	11	—	72	1
Samarasekera	2	—	40	—
Overs:	55.0			

League Cricket Conference XI

Batsman	How Out	Ttl
B Knowles (c)	b Hughes	7
J Foster	c Healy b Hughes	0
MAR Samarasekera	b Campbell	0
PR Oliver	lbw Waugh	31
M Ingham	not out	56
BM McMillan	c Waugh b Rackemann	2
SP O'Donnell	not out	52
D Borthwick (+)	did not bat	
EA Moseley	did not bat	
K Trotter	did not bat	
Maninder Singh	did not bat	
SUNDRIES: B. 7 LB. 0 W. 4 NB. 2		13
TOTAL	5 wkts for 161	
F/W: 2 7 9 48 55		

Bowler	O	M	R	Wkts
Hughes	11	4	39	2
Campbell	7	—	27	1
Rackemann	11	3	35	1
Waugh	7	—	17	1
Hohns	11	3	18	—
Moody	8	1	18	—
Overs:	55.0			

Umpires: B Turner & J Potts

Duchess of Norfolk's XI v Australians
Not First-Class—50-over Match
Arundel
May 7 1989
Toss: Duchess of Norfolk's XI
Result: Australians won by 120 runs

The Australians gave an exciting display of high-powered batting while compiling their total of 6 for 314 in 50 overs. David Boon scored his 114 off 103 balls, hitting 10 fours and 2 sixes, and Tom Moody his 72 off 66 balls. Moody hit 4 big sixes. Allan Border and Steve Waugh, who were both appearing at the crease for the first time on tour, also made runs. The home side was restricted to a total of 5 for 194, Merv Hughes finishing with the fine figures of 2 for 23 off 10 overs.

Australians

Batsman	How Out	Ttl
DC Boon	retired hurt	114
MA Taylor	lbw Agnew	3
TM Moody	b Waller	72
AR Border (c)	c Boon b Needham	66
MRJ Veletta	c Whitticase b Parsons	8
SR Waugh	not out	44
TJ Zoehrer (+)	c Willey b Taylor	1
MG Hughes	c Agnew b Taylor	1
GF Lawson	not out	2
TBA May	did not bat	
TM Alderman	did not bat	
SUNDRIES: B. 1 LB. 1 W. 0 NB. 1		3
TOTAL		6 wkts for 314

F/W: 29 177 238 272 278 283

Bowler	O	M	R	Wkts
Agnew	8	—	38	1
Taylor	9	—	42	2
Parsons	7	—	49	1
Willey	7	—	56	—
Waller	10	—	66	1
Needham	9	—	61	1
Overs:	50.0			

Duchess of Norfolk's XI

Batsman	How Out	Ttl
P Willey	c Boon b May	39
MP Speight	b Hughes	35
DI Gower (c)	lbw Hughes	9
TJ Boon	c Moody b Waugh	37
A Needham	c Hughes b Waugh	8
P Whitticase (+)	not out	26
CT Radley	not out	13
GJ Parsons	did not bat	
LB Taylor	did not bat	
JP Agnew	did not bat	
CE Waller	did not bat	
SUNDRIES: B. 1 LB. 4 W. 1 NB. 1		7
TOTAL		5 wkts for 194

F/W: 88 101 106 142 159

Bowler	O	M	R	Wkts
Alderman	6	1	17	—
Lawson	9	—	23	—
Waugh	9	1	52	2
Hughes	10	2	23	2
May	10	2	43	1
Border	4	—	26	—
Veletta	2	—	5	—
Overs:	50.0			

Umpires: C Cook & JG Langridge

Sussex v Australians
Not First-Class—55-over Match
Hove
May 9 1989
Toss: Australians
Result: Sussex won by 4 wkts

The Australians received their first setback of the tour, losing by 4 wickets. Batting first on an unpredictable pitch, the Australians were dismissed for 154 in 44.3 overs. Steve Waugh was the only successful batsman. He played with assurance for his 86, in one over hitting the Victorian Tony Dodemaide for 16 runs. Dean Jones suffered a depressed fracture of the cheekbone when he tried to hook the medium-pacer Tony Pigott, although he later returned to bat. Sussex proceeded cautiously in pursuit of the small Australian total, and did not pass it until the 48th over. Carl Rackemann, who took 3 wickets, was the most successful of the Australian bowlers.

Australians

Batsman	How Out	Ttl
MA Taylor	c Moores b Pigott	0
MRJ Veletta	c Moores b Pigott	2
SR Waugh	c Parker b Babington	86
DM Jones	lbw Clarke	19
GR Marsh (c)	run out	0
TJ Zoehrer (+)	b CM Wells	11
TV Hohns	b Babington	6
TBA May	lbw Dodemaide	9
GD Campbell	c Moores b Dodemaide	2
TM Alderman	b CM Wells	2
CG Rackemann	not out	1
SUNDRIES: B. 2 LB. 3 W. 4 NB. 7		16
TOTAL		154

F/W: 0 22 44 67 89 106 114 128 150 154

Bowler	O	M	R	Wkts
Pigott	9	3	20	3
Dodemaide	11	—	59	2
CM Wells	9	1	25	2
Babington	8.3	—	30	2
Clarke	7	1	15	1
Overs:	44.3			

Sussex

Batsman	How Out	Ttl
AM Green	c Veletta b Rackemann	0
DM Smith	lbw Waugh	22
PWG Parker (c)	lbw Rackemann	48
AP Wells	c Taylor b Rackemann	17
CM Wells	run out	1
IJ Gould	c Taylor b May	12
AIC Dodemaide	not out	17
ACS Pigott	not out	28
AM Babington	did not bat	
AR Clarke	did not bat	
P Moores (+)	did not bat	
SUNDRIES: B. 5 LB. 4 W. 1 NB. 3		13
TOTAL	6 wkts for 158	

F/W: 1 40 93 100 104 114

Bowler	O	M	R	Wkts
Alderman	11	3	25	—
Rackemann	11	—	30	3
Campbell	8.5	1	35	—
Waugh	4	—	17	1
May	11	3	33	1
Hohns	2	—	9	—
Overs:	47.5			

Umpires: R Julian & PB Wight

MCC v Australians
Not First-Class—55-over Match
Lord's
May 11 1989
Toss: Australians
Result: Australia won by 101 runs

A huge opening partnership by David Boon and Geoff Marsh set up Australia's easy victory. The pair put on 277 for the first wicket, the highest opening partnership ever scored in a one-day match in England. Boon lorded it over the MCC attack. He scored his 166 off 165 balls, hit 3 sixes and 19 fours, and raced far ahead of his partner, Geoff Marsh, who took 141 balls to reach his century. The MCC began well in reply and at one stage was 1 for 141, but thereafter the innings began to go to pieces, and the last wicket fell in the 49th for 208. Mike Gatting batted well for 86, while Steve Waugh was the best of the bowlers with 3 wickets.

Australians

Batsman	How Out	Ttl
DC Boon	c Fraser b Cowdrey	166
GR Marsh	c Ellison b Cowdrey	102
TM Moody	c Marks b Cowdrey	14
MG Hughes	c Carr b Cowdrey	6
AR Border (c)	not out	1
MRJ Veletta	not out	1
SR Waugh	did not bat	
IA Healy (+)	did not bat	
GF Lawson	did not bat	
GD Campbell	did not bat	
TM Alderman	did not bat	
SUNDRIES: B. 1 LB. 9 W. 7 NB. 2		19
TOTAL	4 wkts for 309	

F/W: 277 295 307 307

Bowler	O	M	R	Wkts
Ellison	11	1	61	—
Fraser	11	1	53	—
Watkinson	11	2	46	—
Cowdrey	11	—	60	4
Marks	8	—	63	—
Carr	3	—	16	—
Overs:	55.0			

MCC

Batsman	How Out	Ttl
GD Mendis	c Veletta b Campbell	52
JD Carr	lbw Alderman	23
MW Gatting (c)	c (s)May b Hughes	86
NH Fairbrother	b Campbell	0
MR Ramprakash	lbw Waugh	1
CS Cowdrey	c Healy b Hughes	5
M Watkinson	b Waugh	5
PR Downton (+)	b Lawson	15
VJ Marks	b Waugh	0
RM Ellison	not out	2
ARC Fraser	c Hughes b Lawson	0
SUNDRIES: B. 2 LB. 6 W. 5 NB. 6		19
TOTAL		208

F/W: 43 141 141 145 180 180 192 192 202 208

Bowler	O	M	R	Wkts
Alderman	8	—	41	1
Hughes	11	1	37	2
Campbell	11	—	47	2
Lawson	7.5	1	37	2
Waugh	11	1	38	3
Overs:	48.5			

Umpires: HD Bird & KE Palmer

Worcestershire v Australians
Worcester
May 13, 14 1989
Toss: Australians
Result: Worcestershire won by 3 wkts

This was the first first-class match of the tour, so Worcestershire's victory in two days was an embarrassment for the Australians, notwithstanding the fact that the inferior pitch had a big bearing on the outcome. Worcestershire needed only three bowlers and 30.5 overs to dismiss the Australians for 103, Phil Newport taking 6 for 43. Worcestershire passed the Australian total with 6 wickets in hand, only to be all out for 146. Allan Border (48) and Steve Waugh (63) helped revive Australian hopes in the second innings, and Worcestershire needed 163 to win. Two wickets fell early, but Graeme Hick (43) and Ian Botham (42) kept the innings intact, and Worcestershire made the necessary runs with 3 wickets to spare. The Australians were later criticised for declining a request to play a one-day match against Worcestershire the next day, which was originally scheduled as the third day of the match.

Australians

Batsman	First Innings How Out	Ttl		Second Innings How Out	Ttl
GR Marsh	c Rhodes b Radford	21	(2)	c Hick b Newport	0
MA Taylor	c Rhodes b Pridgeon	6	(1)	c D'Oliveira b Newport	11
TM Moody	c Rhodes b Newport	9		c Botham b Newport	9
AR Border (c)	c Hick b Newport	8		b Newport	48
MRJ Veletta	c Radford b Newport	0		c Rhodes b Newport	2
SR Waugh	c Rhodes b Newport	0		lbw Botham	63
IA Healy (+)	not out	25		b Radford	26
TV Hohns	lbw Newport	3		c Rhodes b Radford	6
GF Lawson	c Illingworth b Radford	8		b Radford	17
MG Hughes	lbw Radford	2		c Botham b Radford	3
TM Alderman	c Pridgeon b Newport	6		not out	3
SUNDRIES: B. 0 LB. 8 W. 0 NB. 7		15		B. 4 LB. 7 W. 3 NB. 3	17
TOTAL		103			205

F/W: 10 34 56 56 56 64 67 82 89 103

F/W: 6 17 27 33 130 169 169 198 202 205

Bowler	O	M	R	Wkts	Bowler	O	M	R	Wkts
Radford	11	2	32	3	Radford	28.2	8	58	4
Pridgeon	9	1	20	1	Newport	27	4	84	5
Newport	10.5	2	43	6	Botham	10	3	18	1
Overs:	30.5				Pridgeon	9	2	34	—
					Overs:	74.2			

Worcestershire

Batsman	First Innings How Out	Ttl	Second Innings How Out	Ttl
TS Curtis	c Healy b Hughes	46	lbw Alderman	8
GJ Lord	c Border b Alderman	0	lbw Lawson	12
GA Hick	c Marsh b Waugh	13	c Border b Waugh	43
DB D'Oliveira	c Healy b Waugh	1	c Veletta b Waugh	4
IT Botham (c)	c Taylor b Alderman	39	c Healy b Alderman	42
SJ O'Shaughnessy	b Lawson	4	c Healy b Alderman	7
SJ Rhodes (+)	c Taylor b Lawson	18	b Alderman	16
PJ Newport	b Alderman	3	not out	5
RK Illingworth	c Border b Alderman	0	not out	12
NV Radford	not out	6		
AP Pridgeon	c Taylor b Lawson	0		
SUNDRIES: B. 3 LB. 6 W. 5 NB. 2		16	B. 3 LB. 7 W. 0 NB. 4	14
TOTAL		146	7 wkts for 163	

F/W: 7 66 68 68 104 124 132 132 146 146

F/W: 20 22 65 86 109 142 145

28

Bowler	O	M	R	Wkts	Bowler	O	M	R	Wkts
Alderman	14	4	33	4	Alderman	17	4	61	4
Lawson	14.4	1	50	3	Lawson	18.4	6	44	1
Hughes	11	4	31	1	Waugh	6	—	25	2
Waugh	6	1	23	2	Hughes	4	1	23	—
Overs:	45.4				Overs:	45.4			

Umpires: JW Holder & DR Shepherd

Somerset v Australians
Taunton
May 17, 18, 19 1989
Toss: Somerset
Result: Drawn

Australia's first innings total of 8 declared for 339 restored confidence in the Australians' batting generally, and in the batting of Mark Taylor in particular, who, after several previous failures, struggled at first but eventually played himself into form with an innings of 97. David Boon made 61, Mike Veletta 46 and Tim Zoehrer 48. Carl Rackemann broke through Somerset's top order, taking 3 wickets in 13 balls, and Somerset's batting did not recover. The home side was all out for 140, Tim May taking three of the wickets. Richard Harden was Somerset's top scorer with 45. Geoff Marsh and Taylor both scored half-centuries in Australia's second innings, which Allan Border chose to close at 3 for 144, giving Somerset a day to score 344 for victory. That target proved to be beyond the Somerset batsmen, who nevertheless managed to draw the match with honour, Jimmy Cook scoring 57 and Peter Roebuck a gritty 100 not out. Tim May, who was expected to lead the Australian attack on the last day, did not take a wicket.

Australians

Batsman	First Innings How Out	Ttl		Second Innings How Out	Ttl
GR Marsh	c Burns b Jones	10	(2)	c Jones b Unwin	57
MA Taylor	c Burns b Rose	97	(1)	c Bartlett b Roebuck	58
DC Boon	c Burns b Unwin	61			
TM Moody	c Bartlett b Unwin	17	(5)	not out	2
AR Border (c)	c Burns b Unwin	0			
MRJ Veletta	c Burns b Mallender	46			
TJ Zoehrer (+)	lbw Jones	48			
TBA May	not out	13			
GD Campbell	b Mallender	10			
MG Hughes	not out	21	(3)	not out	15
CG Rackemann	did not bat		(4)	c Roebuck b Unwin	0
SUNDRIES: B. 0 LB. 7 W. 1 NB. 8		16		B. 4 LB. 7 W. 0 NB. 1	12
TOTAL	8 wkts dec	339		3 wkts dec	144
F/W: 32 142 174 177 203 290 294 315				F/W: 119 129 134	

Bowler	O	M	R	Wkts	Bowler	O	M	R	Wkts
Jones	21	2	83	2	Jones	5	—	15	—
Mallender	20	5	55	2	Mallender	6	1	25	—
Foster	16	2	49	—	Rose	6	1	18	—
Rose	16	5	45	1	Unwin	12	1	43	2
Unwin	24	5	73	3	Foster	4	—	17	—
Roebuck	7	1	27	—	Roebuck	4	1	15	1
Overs:	104.0				Overs:	37.0			

▶

29

Somerset

First Innings			Second Innings	
Batsman	*How Out*	*Ttl*	*How Out*	*Ttl*
SJ Cook	c Veletta b Rackemann	11	lbw Hughes	57
PM Roebuck	c Boon b Hughes	13	not out	100
RJ Bartlett	c Taylor b Rackemann	0	c Campbell b Border	18
CJ Tavare (c)	c Veletta b Rackemann	6	b Hughes	43
RJ Harden	c Border b May	45	not out	4
ND Burns (+)	run out	27		
GD Rose	c Boon b Hughes	0		
NA Mallender	c Boon b May	0		
AN Jones	c Taylor b May	15		
PD Unwin	not out	4		
DJ Foster	b Campbell	6		
SUNDRIES: B. 2 LB. 6 W. 2 NB. 3		13	B. 1 LB. 4 W. 2 NB. 6	13
TOTAL		140	3 wkts for 235	
F/W: 19 19 25 48 108 112 112 112 133 140			F/W: 111 154 230	

Bowler	*O*	*M*	*R*	*Wkts*	*Bowler*	*O*	*M*	*R*	*Wkts*
Rackemann	13	3	33	3	Rackemann	14	6	29	—
Campbell	9.4	1	25	1	Campbell	12	5	26	—
May	28	15	48	3	Hughes	15	4	44	2
Hughes	16	7	26	2	May	21	5	63	—
Overs:	66.4				Border	25	8	55	1
					Moody	7	2	13	—
					Overs:	94.0			

Umpires: DJ Constant & MJ Kitchen

Middlesex v Australians
Lord's
May 20, 21, 22 1989
Toss: Middlesex
Result: Australians by 3 wkts

The Australians demonstrated impressive batting strength in defeating a well equipped Middlesex side by 3 wickets. Having dismissed Middlesex for 245, the Australians declared at 2 for 233 in reply, Geoff Marsh making his third century of the tour and Tom Moody 60 not out. Batting again, Middlesex got to 3 for 159, but fine bowling by Geoff Lawson produced a late collapse on the morning of the third day, and Middlesex was all out for 227. Mike Gatting, who had top-scored with 65 in the first innings, top-scored again with 79. To win, the Australians had to score 240 in a possible 73 overs, which they just managed to do. David Boon (86) and Allan Border (77) were the leaders in the run chase.

Middlesex

First Innings			Second Innings	
Batsman	*How Out*	*Ttl*	*How Out*	*Ttl*
JD Carr	b Moody	22	b Lawson	13
DL Haynes	lbw Alderman	13	c Boon b Alderman	12
MW Gatting (c)	lbw Lawson	65	b Lawson	79
RO Butcher	c Alderman b Rackemann	31	lbw Alderman	21
MR Ramprakash	not out	46	c Healy b Alderman	33
PR Downton (+)	lbw Lawson	8	c Taylor b Lawson	6
JE Emburey	c Veletta b Alderman	4 (8)	b Lawson	0
NF Williams	lbw Rackemann	28 (7)	not out	36
SP Hughes	b Rackemann	0	hit wicket b Lawson	5

Batsman	How Out	Ttl	How Out	Ttl
ARC Fraser	lbw Rackemann	0	lbw Hohns	3
NG Cowans	b Hohns	17	b Rackemann	0
SUNDRIES: B. 0 LB. 8 W. 1 NB. 2		11	B. 4 LB. 10 W. 0 NB. 5	19
TOTAL		245		227

F/W: 17 60 112 142 154 162 216 216 216 245

F/W: 26 26 76 159 177 177 177 204 226 227

Bowler	O	M	R	Wkts	Bowler	O	M	R	Wkts
Alderman	15	6	31	2	Alderman	21	2	73	3
Lawson	22	5	59	2	Lawson	19	7	48	5
Rackemann	21	5	85	4	Moody	3	1	3	—
Moody	6	1	10	1	Rackemann	11.5	1	39	1
Hohns	17.5	5	52	1	Hohns	13	3	36	1
Overs:	81.5				Border	3	—	14	—
					Overs:	70.5			

Australians

First Innings   **Second Innings**

Batsman	How Out	Ttl	How Out	Ttl
GR Marsh	not out	100	(8) not out	12
MA Taylor	c Ramprakash b Williams	35	(6) st Downton b Emburey	24
DC Boon	c Ramprakash b Hughes	20	(1) b Fraser	86
TM Moody	not out	60	(7) c Butcher b Emburey	7
MRJ Veletta	did not bat		(2) lbw Cowans	7
AR Border (c)	did not bat		(3) b Fraser	77
IA Healy (+)	did not bat		(4) c Downton b Fraser	2
TV Hohns	did not bat		(5) c Downton b Fraser	7
GF Lawson	did not bat		not out	5
CG Rackemann	did not bat			
TM Alderman	did not bat			
SUNDRIES: B. 4 LB. 11 W. 2 NB. 1		18	B. 5 LB. 7 W. 0 NB. 4	16
TOTAL	2 wkts dec	233	7 wkts for	243

F/W: 67 111

F/W: 17 163 169 190 191 201 234

Bowler	O	M	R	Wkts	Bowler	O	M	R	Wkts
Cowans	14	3	40	—	Cowans	13	2	35	1
Fraser	17	4	42	—	Fraser	30.3	5	89	4
Hughes	11	5	41	1	Williams	8	1	23	—
Emburey	20	7	49	—	Emburey	21	4	84	2
Williams	12	1	35	1	Overs:	72.3			
Gatting	4	—	11	—					
Overs:	78.0								

Umpires: HD Bird & BJ Meyer

Yorkshire v Australians
Not First-Class—55-over Match
Headingley, Leeds
May 23 1989
Toss: Australians
Result: Australia won by 109 runs

David Boon continued his run of heavy scoring with a splendid innings of 172, his third century of the tour, which was scored off 157 balls and included 3 sixes. Boon so dominated the Yorkshire attack that for much of his innings he appeared able to score at will. The other successful Australian batsman was Dean Jones, who was batting for the first time since having his cheekbone broken at Hove two weeks before. He began tentatively but later began playing fluently, and he faced only 101 balls while making his unbeaten 89. Yorkshire did not at any stage look likely to approach Australia's total of 3 for 297, and was all out in the 49th over for 188. The leg-spinner Trevor Hohns played in the match, and although he took only 1 wicket for 62 in 11 overs, he did bowl Martyn Moxon, who top-scored with 55. David Bairstow made 46.

Australians

Batsman	How Out	Ttl
DC Boon	b Sidebottom	172
GR Marsh	c & b Pickles	14
DM Jones	not out	89
SR Waugh (+)	b Jarvis	13
TJ Zoehrer (+)	not out	1
AR Border (c)	did not bat	
TM Moody	did not bat	
TV Hohns	did not bat	
MG Hughes	did not bat	
GD Campbell	did not bat	
CG Rackemann	did not bat	
SUNDRIES: B. 0 LB. 3 W. 3 NB. 2		8
TOTAL	3 wkts for 297	

F/W: 66 250 283

Bowler	O	M	R	Wkts
Sidebottom	11	1	64	1
Jarvis	11	1	62	1
Pickles	11	2	48	1
Carrick	11	1	47	—
Hartley	4	1	31	—
Byas	3	—	18	—
Moxon	4	—	24	—
Overs:	55.0			

Yorkshire

Batsman	How Out	Ttl
MD Moxon	b Hohns	55
AA Metcalfe	b Hughes	2
RJ Blakey	c Zoehrer b Campbell	2
K Sharp	b Rackemann	6
D Byas	c Zoehrer b Moody	13
DL Bairstow (+)	c Moody b Waugh	46
SN Hartley	c Marsh b Moody	5
P Carrick (c)	c Zoehrer b Waugh	17
A Sidebottom	b Waugh	2
PW Jarvis	c Zoehrer b Jones	15
CS Pickles	not out	5
SUNDRIES: B. 5 LB. 1 W. 1 NB. 13		20
TOTAL		188

F/W: 11 16 23 86 90 105 144 163 179 188

Bowler	O	M	R	Wkts
Campbell	8	2	14	1
Hughes	6	—	11	1
Rackemann	6	—	31	1
Waugh	9	1	41	3
Moody	8	2	23	2
Hohns	11	—	62	1
Jones	0.2	—	0	1
Overs:	48.2			

Umpires: JH Hampshire & NT Plews

Texaco Trophy matches, played on May 25, 27 and 29, 1989.
For details, see section on Texaco Trophy series.

Warwickshire v Australians
Edgbaston, Birmingham
May 31 June 1, 2 1989
Toss: Australians
Result: Drawn

Dean Jones and Tom Moody gave Warwickshire's rather inadequate attack a prolonged battering as the Australians amassed a first innings total of 3 declared for 444. Jones's innings of 248, his highest in first-class cricket, was quite spectacular. He was at the crease for only 331 minutes and he hit 12 sixes—an all-time record for an Australian in a first-class match. He and Moody, who finished with 144 not out, put on 198 runs in the session between lunch and tea, Jones scoring 96 of them. It later emerged that Jones had a finger in his left hand broken during his innings. Warwickshire was restricted to 235 in reply, mainly because of fine bowling by Trevor Hohns, who took 4 for 87. Asif Din made 50 and Geoff Humpage 58. Choosing to bat again instead of enforcing the follow-on, the Australians hurried to 4 for 195 before declaring just before lunch on the final day, Mark Taylor and Allan Border both making half-centuries. Warwickshire successfully batted out the remaining time, finishing with 3 for 105.

Australians

Batsman	First Innings How Out	Ttl		Second Innings How Out	Ttl
DC Boon	lbw b Merrick	0			
MA Taylor	st Humpage b Pierson	30	(1)	c Moles b Munton	67
DM Jones	c (s)Steer b Asif Din	248			
TM Moody	not out	144			
TJ Zoehrer (+)	did not bat		(2)	lbw Benjamin	0
AR Border (c)	did not bat		(3)	c Moles b Munton	69
TV Hohns	did not bat		(4)	b Asif Din	14
MG Hughes	did not bat		(5)	not out	27
GD Campbell	did not bat		(6)	not out	8
TBA May	did not bat				
GF Lawson	did not bat				
SUNDRIES: B. 0 LB. 14 W. 0 NB. 8		22		B. 0 LB. 10 W. 0 NB. 0	10
TOTAL		3 wkts dec 444			4 wkts dec 195
F/W: 0 95 444				F/W: 4 134 153 173	

Bowler	O	M	R	Wkts	Bowler	O	M	R	Wkts
Merrick	22	4	107	1	Merrick	8	—	23	—
Benjamin	14	2	81	—	Benjamin	7	1	31	1
Munton	21	6	85	—	Pierson	22	7	51	—
Pierson	27	5	98	1	Munton	21	7	60	2
Twose	3	—	23	—	Asif Din	3	—	20	1
Asif Din	6.4	—	36	1	Overs:	61.0			
Overs:	93.4								

Warwickshire

Batsman	First Innings How Out	Ttl		Second Innings How Out	Ttl
AJ Moles	lbw Hughes	14		lbw Campbell	9
JD Ratcliffe	b Hughes	6		c Moody b Hohns	17
Asif Din	b Hohns	50		lbw Lawson	38
ARK Pierson	c Zoehrer b Campbell	4			
TA Lloyd (c)	c Campbell b Lawson	22			
GW Humpage (+)	b Hohns	58			
DA Banks	c Lawson b Campbell	28	(4)	not out	18
RG Twose	c (s)McNamara b Hohns	17	(5)	not out	15

▶

33

Batsman	How Out	Ttl	How Out	Ttl
TA Merrick	b Campbell	0		
JE Benjamin	not out	8		
TA Munton	b Hohns	3		
SUNDRIES: B. 10 LB. 10 W. 1 NB. 4		25	B. 0 LB. 7 W. 0 NB. 1	8
TOTAL		235		3 wkts for 105

F/W: 20 23 33 97 131 182 220 220 231 235   F/W: 15 66 84

Bowler	O	M	R	Wkts	Bowler	O	M	R	Wkts
Hughes	19	5	62	2	Hughes	5	3	8	—
Campbell	18	4	41	3	Campbell	7	3	15	1
Hohns	27.3	4	87	4	Hohns	14	2	45	1
Lawson	7	1	20	1	Lawson	11	3	30	1
Border	6	3	5	—	Overs:	37.0			
Overs:	77.3								

Umpires: R Palmer & NT Plews

Derbyshire v Australians
Derby
June 3, 4, 5 1989
Toss: Derbyshire
Result: Australia by 11 runs

Three wickets in quick succession by Carl Rackemann in the closing minutes of the match enabled the Australians to convert an impending defeat by Derbyshire to a narrow outright victory. Although an unpredictable pitch made batting difficult for both sides, the chief reason for the low scoring appeared to be poor batting. The Australians made 200, to which Derbyshire replied with 228. Derbyshire's captain, Kim Barnett, made 76, which, as it proved, was the only half-century scored in the match. In their second innings, the Australian batsmen had even less success than before and were all out for 180 late on the second day of the match. Ian Healy top scored with 39. So Derbyshire needed just 153 runs to win, and at lunch on the final day it was 7 for 122, 31 runs short of victory. After lunch, the score had moved on to 7 for 129 when Rackemann made his crucial intervention. The last wicket fell at 141. Australia won by 11 runs.

Australians

First Innings   Second Innings

Batsman	How Out	Ttl		How Out	Ttl
GR Marsh	c Maher b Base	34	(2)	b Malcolm	27
MA Taylor	c Bowler b Malcolm	5	(1)	c Morris b Base	28
DC Boon	c Bowler b Base	34		c (s) Newman b Malcolm	6
SR Waugh	c Maher b Mortensen	14		c Bishop b Base	9
AR Border (c)	b Base	17		c Roberts b Mortensen	9
TM Moody	c Roberts b Base	0		c Maher b Bishop	34
TV Hohns	b Malcolm	11	(8)	lbw Bishop	2
IA Healy (+)	c Roberts b Mortensen	30	(7)	c Maher b Malcolm	39
GD Campbell	c Barnett b Mortensen	31		c Maher b Malcolm	11
CG Rackemann	not out	0		b Bishop	5
TM Alderman	lbw Mortensen	0		not out	5
SUNDRIES: B. 6 LB. 11 W. 5 NB. 2		24		B. 0 LB. 5 W. 3 NB. 1	9
TOTAL		200			180

F/W: 18 74 79 92 93 123 137 193 200 200   F/W: 41 47 64 77 78 149 153 159 164 180

Bowler	O	M	R	Wkts	Bowler	O	M	R	Wkts
Bishop	14	2	44	—	Bishop	15	4	32	3
Malcolm	13	2	50	2	Malcolm	18.3	1	68	4
Mortensen	12.4	—	40	4	Base	13	3	41	2
Base	12	—	49	4	Mortensen	8	—	34	1
Overs:	51.4				Overs:	54.3			

Derbyshire

First Innings		Second Innings	
Batsman	**How Out** **Ttl**	**How Out**	**Ttl**
KJ Barnett (c)	c Taylor b Campbell 76	b Campbell	23
PD Bowler	lbw Alderman 4	c Healy b Campbell	9
BJM Maher (+)	c Boon b Waugh 17	c Taylor b Alderman	0
JE Morris	c Healy b Rackemann 7	c Taylor b Campbell	34
B Roberts	run out 31	c Border b Alderman	1
SC Goldsmith	c Healy b Campbell 31	c Border b Alderman	0
R Sharma	c Alderman b Waugh 28	not out	37
IR Bishop	c Moody b Alderman 4	b Alderman	10
OH Mortensen	c Border b Alderman 0	c Taylor b Rackemann	1
SJ Base	c Healy b Rackemann 7	c Taylor b Rackemann	6
DE Malcolm	not out 4	c Healy b Rackemann	4
SUNDRIES: B.5 LB.2 W.1 NB.11	19	B.4 LB.7 W.2 NB.3	16
TOTAL	228		141

F/W: 31 106 110 129 181 182 188 198 224 228

F/W: 31 32 34 35 35 90 122 129 137 141

Bowler	O	M	R	Wkts	Bowler	O	M	R	Wkts
Alderman	18	6	38	3	Alderman	21	5	32	4
Rackemann	17	2	60	2	Rackemann	13	3	36	3
Waugh	11.2	2	35	2	Campbell	16	1	44	3
Campbell	18	3	70	2	Waugh	13	5	18	—
Moody	5	1	18	—	Overs:	63.0			
Overs:	69.2								

Umpires: JH Hampshire & KE Palmer

FIRST TEST

England v Australia
Headingley
June 8, 9, 10, 12, 13 1989
Toss: England
Result: Australia won by 210 runs

Both sides chose to go into this Test without a spin bowler, a decision both came to regret before the match was half over. Asked to bat by the England captain, David Gower, the Australians rarely appeared threatened by England's pace bowlers as they amassed a total of 7 declared for 601. Mark Taylor looked confident and compact while scoring his first Test century, but the innings which excited the spectators' imagination was Steve Waugh's brilliant 177 not out. Again, Waugh displayed his peculiar gift of scoring rapidly without haste. Dean Jones and Allan Border made half-centuries, and the innings was unexpectedly rounded off by a vigorous 71 by Merv Hughes. England had virtually no chance now of winning the match, but its batsmen set about building a total big enough to ensure England did not lose. At 2 for 195, they seemed well on the way to doing this, but then wickets fell steadily, and England was all out for 430,

Allan Lamb top scoring with 125. Having failed to force the follow-on, the Australians rattled up 230 quick runs before declaring. At lunch on the final day, England was 1 for 67 and apparently assured of saving the match, but its batting collapsed in the afternoon, giving Australia victory by the substantial margin of 210. For the second time in the match, Terry Alderman took 5 wickets. It was Australia's first Test win at Headingley since 1964.

Australia

First Innings / Second Innings

Batsman	How Out	Ttl	Balls		How Out	Ttl	Balls
GR Marsh	lbw DeFreitas	16	63	(2)	c Russell b Foster	6	22
MA Taylor	lbw Foster	136	315	(1)	c Broad b Pringle	60	112
DC Boon	c Russell b Foster	9	24		lbw b DeFreitas	43	95
AR Border (c)	c Foster b DeFreitas	66	118		not out	60	76
DM Jones	c Russell b Newport	79	172		not out	40	33
SR Waugh	not out	177	242				
IA Healy (+)	c & b Newport	16	31				
MG Hughes	c Russell b Foster	71	105				
GF Lawson	not out	10	13				
GD Campbell	did not bat						
TM Alderman	did not bat						
SUNDRIES: B. 0 LB. 13 W. 1 NB. 7		21	1083		B. 2 LB. 5 W. 9 NB. 5	21	338
TOTAL	7 wkts dec 601				3 wkts dec 230		
F/W: 44 57 174 273 411 441 588					F/W: 14 97 129		

Bowler	O	M	R	Wkts	NB	W	Bowler	O	M	R	Wkts	NB	W
DeFreitas	45.3	8	140	2	—	—	Foster	19	4	65	1	—	5
Foster	46	14	109	3	—	1	DeFreitas	18	2	76	1	2	—
Pringle	33	5	123	—	4	—	Pringle	12.5	1	60	1	3	4
Newport	39	5	153	2	3	—	Newport	5	2	22	—	—	—
Gooch	9	1	31	—	—	—	Overs:	54.5					
Barnett	6	—	32	—	—	—							
Overs:	178.3												

England

First Innings / Second Innings

Batsman	How Out	Ttl	Balls		How Out	Ttl	Balls
GA Gooch	lbw Alderman	13	46		lbw Hughes	68	118
BC Broad	b Hughes	37	74		lbw Alderman	7	12
KJ Barnett	lbw Alderman	80	118		c Taylor b Alderman	34	46
AJ Lamb	c Boon b Alderman	125	205		c Boon b Alderman	4	6
DI Gower (c)	c Healy b Lawson	26	38		c Healy b Lawson	34	44
RA Smith	lbw Alderman	66	132		c Border b Lawson	0	3
DR Pringle	lbw Campbell	6	15		c Border b Alderman	0	27
PJ Newport	c Boon b Lawson	36	73		c Marsh b Alderman	8	27
RC Russell (+)	c Marsh b Lawson	15	33		c Healy b Hughes	2	22
PAJ DeFreitas	lbw Alderman	1	6	(11)	b Hughes	21	18
NA Foster	not out	2	5	(10)	not out	1	16
SUNDRIES: B. 5 LB. 7 W. 1 NB. 10		23	745		B. 4 LB. 3 W. 0 NB. 5	12	339
TOTAL		430				191	
F/W: 35 81 195 243 323 338 392 421 424 430					F/W: 17 67 77 134 134 153 153 166 170 191		

Bowler	O	M	R	Wkts	NB	W	Bowler	O	M	R	Wkts	NB	W
Alderman	37	7	107	5	3	—	Alderman	20	7	44	5	3	—
Lawson	34.5	6	105	3	—	1	Lawson	11	2	58	2	—	—
Campbell	14	—	82	1	6	—	Campbell	10	—	42	—	2	—
Hughes	28	7	92	1	—	—	Hughes	9.2	2	36	3	—	—
Waugh	6	2	27	—	1	—	Border	5	3	4	—	—	—
Border	2	1	5	—	—	—	Overs:	55.2					
Overs:	121.5												

Umpires: DR Shepherd & JW Holder

12th Men: JE Emburey (England) & TM Moody (Australia)

Lancashire v Australians
Old Trafford, Manchester
June 14, 15, 16 1989
Toss: Lancashire
Result: Australians by 9 wkts

The Australians bowled their way to a comfortable win, dismissing Lancashire twice for modest totals of 184 and 185. Geoff Lawson was the most successful bowler in the first innings with 4 wickets, and Greg Campbell in the second with five. The Australians made 288 in their first innings after Lancashire's West Indian-born fast bowler, Patrick Patterson, disposed of Mike Veletta and David Boon, each for a duck, reducing Australia to 2 for 1. Geoff Marsh (46), Tom Moody (74), Dean Jones (59) and Steve Waugh (42) ensured the Australians achieved its big first-innings lead. The Australians needed to make only 82 in their second innings to win, which they did with the loss of only 1 wicket, but they had to endure a barrage of bouncers by Patterson and Wasim Akram, the second of whom was warned for intimidatory bowling.

Lancashire

Batsman	First Innings How Out	Ttl	Second Innings How Out	Ttl
GD Mendis	c Zoehrer b Waugh	25	c Zoehrer b Campbell	28
NJ Speak	c Marsh b Waugh	26	b Lawson	12
AN Hayhurst	c Zoehrer b Campbell	40	b Campbell	13
NH Fairbrother (c)	c Moody b Lawson	49	c Zoehrer b Lawson	2
TJ Jesty	c Zoehrer b Lawson	0	c Moody b Campbell	12
Wasim Akram	c & b Lawson	0	c Veletta b Campbell	2
WK Hegg (+)	c Moody b Lawson	0	c & b Hohns	23
JD Fitton	c & b May	2	c Hohns b Waugh	44
I Folley	b Campbell	8	c Marsh b Campbell	27
PJ Martin	c Jones b May	16	c Hohns b Lawson	4
BP Patterson	not out	4	not out	1
SUNDRIES: B.1 LB.7 W.0 NB.6		14	B.0 LB.8 W.0 NB.9	17
TOTAL		184		185

F/W: 54 55 136 136 136 144 154 156 166 184

F/W: 39 43 46 60 64 94 101 172 179 185

Bowler	O	M	R	Wkts	Bowler	O	M	R	Wkts
Lawson	17	2	44	4	Lawson	18	4	48	3
Campbell	12	2	48	2	Campbell	20.2	4	54	5
Waugh	9	2	28	2	May	12	3	32	—
Hohns	8	3	27	—	Hohns	9	2	30	1
May	15.3	6	29	2	Waugh	5	1	13	1
Overs:	61.3				Overs:	64.2			

Australians

Batsman	First Innings How Out	Ttl		Second Innings How Out	Ttl
GR Marsh (c)	b Patterson	46	(2)	not out	27
MRJ Veletta	c Speak b Patterson	0	(1)	c Martin b Wasim Akram	22
DC Boon	c Hegg b Patterson	0		not out	23
TM Moody	b Fitton	74			
DM Jones	c Hegg b Martin	59			
SR Waugh	c Fitton b Folley	42			
TJ Zoehrer (+)	b Folley	30			
TV Hohns	c Folley b Patterson	12			
TBA May	not out	0			
GD Campbell	b Wasim Akram	0			
GF Lawson	c Hegg b Wasim Akram	0			
SUNDRIES: B.0 LB.0 W.0 NB.11		25		B.0 LB.0 W.0 NB.12	12
TOTAL		288		1 wkt for 84	

F/W: 1 1 128 147 227 245 285 285 288 288

F/W: 51

►

Bowler	O	M	R	Wkts	Bowler	O	M	R	Wkts
Patterson	16	4	48	4	Patterson	4	—	16	—
Martin	17	3	46	1	Wasim Akram	8	2	21	1
Hayhurst	5	1	14	—	Martin	4	—	15	—
Wasim Akram	12.3	2	35	2	Folley	4	—	19	—
Fitton	18	2	59	1	Fitton	3.3	1	13	—
Folley	17	3	72	2	Overs:	23.3			
Overs:	85.3								

Umpires: DGL Evans & AA Jones

Northamptonshire v Australians
Northampton
June 17, 18, 19 1989
Toss: Australia
Result: Australians by 272 runs

The Australians had an easy victory in a match which from first to last was an uneven contest. The feature of the Australians' first-innings total of 329 was Allan Border's innings of 135, his first century of the tour. David Boon made 54 and Geoff Marsh 32. The home team was dismissed for 180 in reply, Merv Hughes taking five of the wickets in the space of 27 balls. Wayne Larkins provided lone resistance to the Australian bowlers, scoring 84. In their second innings, the Australians declared at 5 for 229 early on the third day, Mark Taylor having made 69 and Jones 68 not out. The home side thus had the job of trying to bat until stumps to save the match, but Terry Alderman took three early wickets and Steve Waugh finished off the tail. Northamptonshire was all out for 106. The Australians won by 272 runs.

Australians

First Innings			Second Innings		
Batsman	How Out	Ttl	How Out		Ttl
GR Marsh	c Lamb b Penberthy	32	lbw Walker		9
MA Taylor	c Noon b Penberthy	28	c Penberthy b Robinson		69
DC Boon	b Cook	54	c Noon b Robinson		22
AR Border (c)	st Noon b Cook	135			
DM Jones	c (s)Wild b Penberthy	7	not out		68
SR Waugh	lbw Cook	13	b Davis		2
IA Healy (+)	c Larkins b Cook	20	(4)	c Noon b Davis	39
MG Hughes	b Cook	12	(7)	not out	12
TBA May	c Cook b Bailey	4			
GD Campbell	c Felton b Bailey	2			
TM Alderman	not out	4			
SUNDRIES: B. 0 LB. 9 W. 0 NB. 9		18	B. 0 LB. 4 W. 0 NB. 4		8
TOTAL		329	5 wkts dec		229

F/W: 62 77 204 217 254 299 319 320 324 329

F/W: 30 99 110 197 209

Bowler	O	M	R	Wkts	Bowler	O	M	R	Wkts
Davis	11	1	45	—	Davis	9	1	29	2
Walker	11	—	64	—	Walker	17	1	57	1
Robinson	16	2	39	—	Penberthy	10	—	28	—
Penberthy	15	1	56	3	Bailey	8	—	29	—
Cook	30	8	76	5	Cook	14	3	43	—
Bailey	15.2	4	40	2	Robinson	8	1	33	2
Overs:	98.2				Fordham	1	—	6	—
					Overs:	67.0			

Northamptonshire

Batsman	How Out	Ttl	How Out	Ttl
A Fordham	lbw Alderman	4	lbw Alderman	0
W Larkins	c Taylor b Waugh	84	c Hughes b Campbell	21
NA Felton	c Healy b Hughes	26	lbw Alderman	1
RJ Bailey	c Healy b Hughes	2	b May	17
AL Penberthy	c Boon b Hughes	0	lbw Alderman	0
WM Noon (+)	c Marsh b Hughes	0	lbw Hughes	37
NGB Cook	b Hughes	2	lbw Waugh	14
WW Davis	c Marsh b Waugh	24	b Waugh	0
A Walker	not out	14	not out	0
MA Robinson	c Alderman b May	1	b Waugh	0
AJ Lamb (c)	absent injured			
SUNDRIES: B. 9 LB. 9 W. 1 NB. 4		23	B. 5 LB. 10 W. 0 NB. 1	16
TOTAL		180		106

F/W: 4 66 78 82 82 88 125 161 180

F/W: 8 22 24 24 53 104 106 106 106

Bowler	O	M	R	Wkts	Bowler	O	M	R	Wkts
Alderman	10	3	35	1	Alderman	6	3	10	3
Campbell	3	—	15	—	Campbell	8	1	31	1
Hughes	11	2	37	5	May	6	1	17	1
May	15.3	1	35	1	Hughes	8	2	23	1
Waugh	11	1	40	2	Waugh	4.5	1	10	3
Overs:	50.3				Overs:	32.5			

Umpires: DO Oslear & RA White

SECOND TEST

England v Australia
Lord's
June 22, 23, 24, 26, 27 1989
Toss: England
Result: Australia won by 6 wickets

Batting first, England's batsmen were intent on redeeming themselves after their second-innings failure at Headingley, but by lunch on the first day England was again in trouble. Among the top-order batsmen, only Graham Gooch (60) and David Gower (57) made a decent showing against the Australian pace bowlers, and if it had not been for a gritty innings of 64 by Jack Russell, batting at eight, England might have made barely 200. England's total, 286, was not big, although on the Lord's pitch it seemed possibly big enough. But England's bowlers could not prevent Australia compiling another huge total. Mark Taylor made a half-century and David Boon a fine innings of 94, and once more Steve Waugh occupied centre stage with a splendid innings of 152 not out. In the end, though, it was Geoff Lawson's unexpected 74 which enabled Australia to pass 500. The situation called for highly disciplined batting by England to save the match, but again the top order wickets fell cheaply. A partnership of 139 between Gower and Robin Smith offered England some hope, but after Gower was out for a typically elegant 106 there was no more substantial resistance, although Smith went on to make a defiant 96. Alderman took 6 wickets in this innings, raising his total from two Tests to 19. It was clear only rain could prevent Australia scoring the 118 it needed for victory, and the rain did not come.

England

First Innings				Second Innings		
Batsman	How Out	Ttl	Balls	How Out	Ttl	Balls
GA Gooch	c Healy b Waugh	60	123	lbw Alderman	0	3
BC Broad	lbw Alderman	18	45	b Lawson	20	30
KJ Barnett	c Boon b Hughes	14	24	c Jones b Alderman	3	21
MW Gatting	c Boon b Hughes	0	1	lbw Alderman	22	82
DI Gower (c)	b Lawson	57	62	c Border b Hughes	106	198
RA Smith	c Hohns b Lawson	32	36	b Alderman	96	206
JE Emburey	b Alderman	0	2 (8)	not out	36	96
RC Russell (+)	not out	64	115 (7)	c Boon b Lawson	29	65
NA Foster	c Jones b Hughes	16	51	lbw Alderman	4	2
PW Jarvis	c Marsh b Hughes	6	14	lbw Alderman	5	16
GR Dilley	c Border b Alderman	7	51	c Boon b Hughes	24	64
SUNDRIES: B. 0 LB. 9 W. 0 NB. 3		12	523	B. 6 LB. 6 W. 0 NB. 2	14	782
TOTAL		286			359	

F/W: 31 52 58 131 180 185 191 237 253 286

F/W: 0 18 28 84 223 274 300 304 314 359

Bowler	O	M	R	Wkts	NB	W	Bowler	O	M	R	Wkts	NB	W
Alderman	20.5	4	60	3	1	—	Alderman	38	6	128	6	—	—
Lawson	27	8	88	2	—	—	Lawson	39	10	99	2	2	—
Hughes	23	6	71	4	—	—	Hughes	24	8	44	2	—	—
Waugh	9	3	49	1	2	—	Border	9	3	23	—	—	—
Hohns	7	3	9	—	—	—	Hohns	13	6	33	—	—	—
Overs:	86.5						Waugh	7	2	20	—	—	—
							Overs:	130.0					

Australia

First Innings				Second Innings		
Batsman	How Out	Ttl	Balls	How Out	Ttl	Balls
GR Marsh	c Russell b Dilley	3	14 (2)	b Dilley	1	12
MA Taylor	lbw Foster	62	162 (1)	c Gooch b Foster	27	61
DC Boon	c Gooch b Dilley	94	189	not out	58	121
AR Border (c)	c Smith b Emburey	35	62	c (s) Sims b Foster	1	10
DM Jones	lbw Foster	27	31	c Russell b Foster	0	4
SR Waugh	not out	152	249	not out	21	40
IA Healy (+)	c Russell b Jarvis	3	30			
MG Hughes	c Gooch b Foster	30	52			
TV Hohns	b Emburey	21	38			
GF Lawson	c Broad b Emburey	74	94			
TM Alderman	lbw Emburey	8	39			
SUNDRIES: B. 0 LB. 11 W. 0 NB. 8		19	960	B. 3 LB. 4 W. 0 NB. 4	11	248
TOTAL		528		4 wkts for 119		

F/W: 6 151 192 221 235 265 331 381 511 528

F/W: 9 51 61 67

Bowler	O	M	R	Wkts	NB	W	Bowler	O	M	R	Wkts	NB	W
Dilley	34	3	141	2	7	—	Dilley	10	2	27	1	4	—
Foster	45	7	129	3	—	—	Foster	18	3	39	3	—	—
Jarvis	31	3	150	1	—	—	Jarvis	9.2	—	38	—	—	—
Emburey	42	12	88	4	1	—	Emburey	3	—	8	—	—	—
Gooch	6	2	9	—	—	—	Overs:	40.2					
Overs:	158.0												

Umpires: HD Bird & NT Plews

12th Men: ARC Fraser (England) & GD Campbell (Australia)

Oxford & Cambridge Universities v Australians
Not First-Class—35-over Match
Oxford
Jun 28 1989
Toss: Australians
Result: Australians won by 99 runs

The Australians scored faster than a run per ball to compile 5 for 215, and most of its top order batsmen made runs. Geoff Marsh scored 73, Tom Moody 47 not out, Mike Veletta 42 and Mark Taylor, batting at three, 33. The Combined Universities' response was rather feeble—116 runs for the loss of 4 wickets. Trevor Hohns was the best of the Australian bowlers, taking three of the four wickets. Carl Rackemann, returning to active service after knee surgery, bowled 7 economical overs but failed to take a wicket.

Australians

Batsman	How Out	Ttl
GR Marsh (c)	c Crawley b Hester	73
MRJ Veletta	c Edwards b Crawley	42
MA Taylor	b Pyman	33
TM Moody	not out	47
DM Jones	c Atkinson b Pyman	9
IA Healy	run out	1
TJ Zoehrer (+)	did not bat	
TV Hohns	did not bat	
MG Hughes	did not bat	
GD Campbell	did not bat	
CG Rackemann	did not bat	
SUNDRIES: B. 0 LB. 5 W. 5 NB. 0		10
TOTAL	5 wkts for 215	

F/W: 105 153 160 197 215

Bowler	O	M	R	Wkts
Henderson	6	—	39	—
Hester	7	1	47	1
Crawley	7	—	27	1
Edwards	6	—	41	—
Atherton	2	—	21	—
Pyman	7	—	35	2
Overs:	35.0			

Oxford & Cambridge Universities

Batsman	How Out	Ttl
SP James	not out	43
R Heap	c Marsh b Campbell	4
MA Atherton (c)	c Rackemann b Hohns	20
DA Hagan	b Hohns	16
JCM Atkinson	c & b Hohns	0
AM Crawley	not out	13
RJ Turner (+)	did not bat	
IM Henderson	did not bat	
ED Hester	did not bat	
RA Pyman	did not bat	
PG Edwards	did not bat	
SUNDRIES: B. 4 LB. 11 W. 5 NB. 0		20
TOTAL	4 wkts for 116	

F/W: 17 53 86 86

Bowler	O	M	R	Wkts
Campbell	6	—	26	1
Rackemann	7	1	15	—
Moody	7	1	20	—
Hohns	7	—	14	3
Hughes	6	—	19	—
Veletta	1	—	2	—
Taylor	1	—	5	—

Umpires: JH Harris & MJ Kitchen

Glamorgan v Australians
Neath
July 1, 2, 3, 4 1989
Toss: Australians
Result: Drawn

The Australians had only slightly the better of a match in which Glamorgan's batsmen were able to score heavily against an understrength Australian attack. Batting first, the Australians made the most of the short boundaries and were 4 for 373 at the end of the first day, Mike Veletta having batted throughout the day for an unbeaten 134 and Allan Border having scored a bright 91. Next day, after Allan Border declared at the overnight score, Glamorgan batted in spirited style and was able to declare late in the afternoon at 5 for 301. Glamorgan had an opening partnership of 107, which was broken when off-spinner Tim May bowled Alan Butcher for 54. Glamorgan's captain, Hugh Morris, made 94 and Matthew Maynard 42. May (1 for 61) and Carl Rackemann (1 for 67) were both recovering from injuries, and Trevor Hohns (2 for 44) proved the most impressive of the bowlers. Australia declared again in its second innings at 5 for 216, leaving Glamorgan to bat out the hours remaining. Veletta confirmed his return to form with a second innings score of 83, while Dean Jones made 56.

Australians

First Innings				Second Innings	
Batsman	How Out	Ttl		How Out	Ttl
GR Marsh	c Maynard b Barwick	21	(2)	c Holmes b Dennis	33
MRJ Veletta	not out	134	(1)	c Maynard b Smith	83
DM Jones	lbw Watkin	37		c Smith b Shastri	56
TM Moody	lbw Smith	29			
AR Border (c)	c Maynard b Watkin	91			
SR Waugh	not out	34			
IA Healy (+)	did not bat		(4)	c Metson b Dennis	13
TV Hohns	did not bat		(5)	b Smith	15
TBA May	did not bat		(6)	not out	10
MG Hughes	did not bat				
CG Rackemann	did not bat				
SUNDRIES: B. 4 LB. 12 W. 4 NB. 7		27		B. 1 LB. 3 W. 0 NB. 2	6
TOTAL		4 wkts dec 373			5 wkts dec 216
F/W: 45 117 168 319				F/W: 61 156 182 196 216	

Bowler	O	M	R	Wkts	Bowler	O	M	R	Wkts
Watkin	24	5	81	2	Watkin	14	2	36	—
Dennis	28	8	69	—	Dennis	25	4	65	2
Barwick	16	2	41	1	Smith	18.2	2	66	2
Shastri	4	—	20	—	Cann	1	—	8	—
Smith	18	3	75	1	Holmes	6	—	21	—
Cann	4	1	22	—	Shastri	2	—	16	1
Holmes	12	—	49	—	Overs:	66.2			
Overs:	106.0								

Glamorgan

First Innings				Second Innings	
Batsman	How Out	Ttl		How Out	Ttl
AR Butcher	b May	54		c Veletta b Waugh	14
H Morris (c)	c Border b Hohns	94		b Moody	5
MJ Cann	c Healy b Rackemann	3		b Waugh	5
MP Maynard	b Waugh	42		c & b Rackemann	26
RJ Shastri	st Healy b Hohns	10	(7)	not out	44
GC Holmes	not out	26	(5)	lbw Waugh	0

Batsman	How Out	Ttl	How Out	Ttl
I Smith	not out	61	(6) not out	38
CP Metson (+)	did not bat			
SR Barwick	did not bat			
SJ Dennis	did not bat			
SL Watkin	did not bat			
SUNDRIES: B. 0 LB. 9 W. 0 NB. 2		11	B. 0 LB. 1 W. 0 NB. 2	3
TOTAL	5 wkts dec	301	5 wkts for	135
F/W: 107 128 184 209 211			F/W: 18 20 30 30 66	

Bowler	O	M	R	Wkts	Bowler	O	M	R	Wkts
Hughes	15	5	42	—	Waugh	10	2	32	3
Rackemann	15	1	67	1	Moody	9	2	32	1
Waugh	21	3	61	1	Rackemann	9	1	31	1
Moody	4	—	17	—	May	9	2	39	—
May	16	5	61	1	Overs:	37.0			
Hohns	20	6	44	2					
Overs:	91.0								

Umpires: B Leadbeater & KJ Lyons

THIRD TEST

England v Australia
Edbgaston
July 6, 7, 8, 10, 11 1989
Toss: Australia
Result: Drawn

Ian Botham returned to the England side for this Test, and there was some hope in the England camp that his presence might help restore the home side's sagging confidence. Choosing to bat first, Australia found the going rather harder than in the first two Tests, and, in fact, only one batsman, Dean Jones, bettered 50. Jones's dashing yet disciplined 157 was the mainstay of the Australia's innings, which climbed to 424. In ordinary circumstances, this might have seemed a winning total, but so many hours' play had been lost because of rain that the Australian innings did not end until the fourth day. This meant that if Australia were to win it would have to compel England to follow on, so interest was now centred on whether England's batsmen could scrape together the 225 needed to avoid this. England began disastrously, crashing to 5 for 75, but Ian Botham (46) and Jack Russell (42) steadied the innings, and England had crept up to 215 when the ninth wicket fell. The last two batsmen, Paul Jarvis and Graham Dilley, thus had to make 10 to avoid the follow-on, which they managed to do, despite a desperate effort by the Australians to remove them. With a first-innings lead of 182, Australia might still have sought victory by scoring quick runs and putting England in again, but the captain, Allan Border, playing safe, preferred to bat out time.

Australia

First Innings					Second Innings			
Batsman	*How Out*	*Ttl*	*Balls*		*How Out*		*Ttl*	*Balls*
GR Marsh	lbw Botham	42	134	(2)	b Jarvis		42	86
MA Taylor	st Russell b Emburey	43	99	(1)	c Botham b Gooch		51	148
DC Boon	run out	38	109		not out		22	112
AR Border (c)	b Emburey	8	22					
DM Jones	c (s)Folley b Fraser	157	295					
SR Waugh	b Fraser	43	54					
IA Healy (+)	b Fraser	2	12	(4)	not out		33	45
MG Hughes	c Botham b Dilley	2	16					
TV Hohns	c Gooch b Dilley	40	98					
GF Lawson	b Fraser	12	28					
TM Alderman	not out	0	8					
SUNDRIES: B. 0 LB. 20 W. 0 NB. 17		37	875		B. 4 LB. 4 W. 0 NB. 2		10	391
TOTAL		424			2 wkts for 158			

F/W: 88 94 105 201 272 289 299 391 421 424

F/W: 81 109

Bowler	O	M	R	Wkts	NB	W	Bowler	O	M	R	Wkts	NB	W
Dilley	30	3	123	2	12	—	Dilley	10	4	27	—	—	—
Jarvis	23	4	82	—	—	—	Fraser	12	—	29	—	2	—
Fraser	33	8	63	4	5	—	Emburey	20	8	37	—	—	—
Botham	26	5	75	1	—	—	Jarvis	6	1	20	1	—	—
Emburey	29	5	61	2	—	—	Gooch	14	5	30	1	—	—
Overs:	141.0						Curtis	3	—	7	—	—	—
							Overs:	65.0					

England

First Innings

Batsman	*How Out*	*Ttl*	*Balls*
GA Gooch	lbw Lawson	8	33
TS Curtis	lbw Hughes	41	81
DI Gower (c)	lbw Alderman	8	26
CJ Tavare	c Taylor b Alderman	2	9
KJ Barnett	c Healy b Waugh	10	21
IT Botham	b Hughes	46	110
RC Russell (+)	c Taylor b Hohns	42	131
JE Emburey	c Boon b Lawson	26	58
ARC Fraser	run out	12	29
GR Dilley	not out	11	63
PW Jarvis	lbw Alderman	22	31
SUNDRIES: B. 1 LB. 2 W. 0 NB. 11		14	592
TOTAL		242	

F/W: 17 42 47 75 75 171 171 185 215 242

Bowler	O	M	R	Wkts	NB	W
Alderman	26.3	6	61	3	5	—
Lawson	21	4	54	2	—	—
Waugh	11	3	38	1	5	—
Hughes	22	4	68	2	1	—
Hohns	16	8	18	1	—	—
Overs:	96.3					

Umpires: HD Bird & JW Holder

12th Men: RJ Blakey (England) & MRJ Veletta (Australia)

Scotland v Australians
Not First-Class—55-over Match
Glasgow
July 15 1989
Toss: Scotland
Result: Australians by 97 runs

Mike Veletta and Tom Moody each made 101, thus enabling the Australians to compile the sizeable total of 7 for 307 in their 55 overs. Scotland began well with an opening stand of 90, but wickets fell steadily after that, despite the fact that the Australians used no fewer than 10 bowlers. Scotland was 9 for 210 at the end, giving the visitors victory by 97 runs.

Australians

Batsman	How Out	Ttl
DC Boon	c Govan b Brown	19
MRJ Veletta	c Haggo b Brown	101
TM Moody	b Moir	101
DM Jones	b Moir	36
TJ Zoehrer (+)	lbw Moir	2
AR Border (c)	b Moir	4
SR Waugh	not out	23
MG Hughes	b Moir	0
TBA May	not out	7
GD Campbell	did not bat	
CG Rackemann	did not bat	
SUNDRIES: B. 4 LB. 5 W. 0 NB. 5		14
TOTAL	7 wkts for 307	

F/W: 38 212 258 265 274 287 287

Bowler	O	M	R	Wkts
Moir	11	3	33	5
Brown	11	—	68	2
Goram	6	—	30	—
Smith	11	—	53	—
Henry	11	—	70	—
Govan	5	—	44	—
Overs:	55.0			

Scotland

Batsman	How Out	Ttl
IL Philip	lbw May	24
BMW Patterson	lbw May	70
RG Swan (c)	c Jones b Border	8
AL Goram	b May	4
O Henry	lbw Moody	3
MJ Smith	st Zoehrer b Boon	24
DL Snodgrass	c Jones b Campbell	3
DR Brown	b Campbell	2
JW Govan	not out	32
DJ Haggo	st Zoehrer b Veletta	7
JD Moir	not out	14
SUNDRIES: B. 0 LB. 14 W. 4 NB. 1		19
TOTAL	9 wkts for 210	

F/W: 90 105 115 118 134 152 156 158 184

Bowler	O	M	R	Wkts
Rackemann	10	2	48	—
Campbell	8	—	30	2
Waugh	2	—	17	—
Hughes	9	1	23	—
May	11	1	21	3
Moody	6	2	15	1
Border	3	—	8	1
Jones	2	—	5	—
Boon	2	—	7	1
Veletta	2	—	22	1
Overs:	55.0			

Umpires: P Brown & A Woods

Minor Counties v Australians
Not First-Class—55-over Match
Trowbridge
July 17 1989
Toss: Australians
Result: Australians by 27 runs

Geoff Marsh (110) and David Boon (61) were the leading scorers in an unhurried Australian innings which ended at 4 for 229 after 55 overs. Marsh's opening partner, Mike Veletta, who had found his best form in previous matches, had his right little finger broken by a rising delivery and retired hurt for 3. After looking for a time as if they might achieve an upset victory over the Australians, Minor Counties were bowled out in 54 overs for 202. The Australians thus won by 27 runs.

Australians

Batsman	How Out	Ttl
GR Marsh (c)	c Evans b Taylor	110
MRJ Veletta	retired hurt	3
MA Taylor	c Folland b Conn	11
TM Moody	c Greenswood b Conn	1
DC Boon	c Priestly b Taylor	61
IA Healy (+)	not out	25
TV Hohns	not out	2
GF Lawson	did not bat	
TM Alderman	did not bat	
GD Campbell	did not bat	
CG Rackemann	did not bat	
SUNDRIES: B. 1 LB. 4 W. 9 NB. 2		16
TOTAL	4 wkts for 229	

F/W: 37 41 187 211

Bowler	O	M	R	Wkts
Green	11	1	46	—
Taylor	11	2	50	2
Conn	11	1	34	2
Greenswood	11	4	22	—
Evans	7	—	50	—
Plumb	4	1	22	—
Overs:	55.0			

Minor Counties

Batsman	How Out	Ttl
SG Plumb (c)	lbw Alderman	0
GK Brown	b Hohns	31
NA Folland	b Campbell	51
I Cockbain	b Rackemann	28
TA Lester	not out	37
N Priestly (+)	b Campbell	1
S Greenswood	hit wicket b Campbell	17
RA Evans	b Lawson	10
IE Conn	b Lawson	0
RC Green	b Alderman	3
MR Taylor	c Alderman b Lawson	7
SUNDRIES: B. 0 LB. 10 W. 2 NB. 5		17
TOTAL		202

F/W: 6 84 115 131 132 156 178 178 183 202

Bowler	O	M	R	Wkts
Alderman	10	1	43	2
Lawson	10	1	30	3
Hohns	11	1	30	1
Rackemann	11	—	35	1
Campbell	11	2	45	3
Moody	1	—	9	—
Overs:	54.0			

Umpires: P Adams & DJ Halfyard

Hampshire v Australians
Southampton
July 19, 20, 21 1989
Toss: Australians
Result: Drawn

In the first innings, the Australian batting again proved too strong for county bowling, and the captain, Geoff Marsh, was able to declare at 6 for 343. David Boon and Steve Waugh made centuries, and Mark Taylor and Tim Zoehrer were both out in the 40s. Hampshire responded with 6 declared for 275, an innings built around an undefeated century by MCJ Nicholas. Tim May had been outshone recently by the leg-spinner Trevor Hohns, but on this occasion he took 2 wickets and Hohns none. Australia's batsmen were not so impressive in their second innings and were all out for 246. The total included a dynamic innings of 67 by Steve Waugh, who hit a six and 13 fours and scored his half-century off only 30 balls. With so little time left, however, the runs did not have much meaning, and the Hampshire openers played out the 38 overs bowled to them in their second innings.

Australians

First Innings				Second Innings	
Batsman	**How Out**	**Ttl**		**How Out**	**Ttl**
GR Marsh (c)	c Parks b Jefferies	15	(2)	c Smith b Andrew	5
MA Taylor	run out	46	(1)	lbw Maru	38
DC Boon	c Terry b James	103		c & b Jefferies	24
SR Waugh	c & b Andrew	112		lbw Maru	67
TM Moody	c Smith b Nicholas	7		c & b Maru	5
TJ Zoehrer (+)	b Andrew	42		c James b Maru	1
TV Hohns	not out	2		not out	58
TBA May	did not bat			lbw James	7
CD Campbell	did not bat			c Nicholas b Maru	15
GF Lawson	did not bat			c Parks b Connor	7
CG Rackemann	did not bat			c Nicholas b Connor	11
SUNDRIES: B. 1 LB. 9 W. 0 NB. 6		16		B. 0 LB. 5 W. 0 NB. 3	8
TOTAL	6 wkts dec	343			246
F/W: 22 124 242 261 324 343				F/W: 29 57 115 145 147 147 168	
				189 212 246	

Bowler	O	M	R	Wkts	Bowler	O	M	R	Wkts
Andrew	14.5	3	60	2	Andrew	10	—	68	1
Jefferies	15	2	59	1	Connor	14.1	1	68	2
Connor	15	2	51	—	Maru	23	10	44	5
Maru	21	2	85	—	Smith	2	—	3	—
James	14	4	39	1	Jefferies	11	1	26	1
Nicholas	9	—	39	1	James	9	—	32	1
Overs:	88.5				Overs:	69.1			

▶

Hampshire

First Innings

Batsman	How Out	Ttl
VP Terry	lbw Lawson	19
CL Smith	c Boon b May	32
KD James	c Boon b May	5
RA Smith	c Zoehrer b Rackemann	9
MCJ Nicholas (c)	not out	102
JR Wood	c Zoehrer b Waugh	65
RJ Parks (+)	c Marsh b Waugh	0
ST Jefferies	not out	28
SJW Andrew	did not bat	
CA Connor	did not bat	
RJ Maru	did not bat	
SUNDRIES: B.7 LB.6 W.0 NB.2		15
TOTAL		6 wkts dec 275

F/W: 56 56 71 77 220 220

Second Innings

Batsman	How Out	Ttl
	not out	28
	not out	49
	B.4 LB.0 W.0 NB.0	4
		0 wkts for 81

F/W:

Bowler	O	M	R	Wkts	Bowler	O	M	R	Wkts
Lawson	21	8	55	1	Lawson	6	3	13	—
Rackemann	20	4	79	1	Campbell	6	2	8	—
May	24	10	52	2	Rackemann	10	1	29	—
Waugh	7	1	28	2	May	3	—	4	—
Hohns	13	7	23	—	Hohns	10	3	15	—
Campbell	7	2	25	—	Waugh	3	2	8	—
Overs:	92.0				Overs:	38.0			

Umpires: VA Holder & DS Thompsett

Gloucestershire v Australians
Bristol
July 22, 23 1989
Toss: Gloucestershire
Result: Australians by an inns & 146 runs

Gloucestershire was no match for a confident Australian team playing at peak form, and it lost the match by an innings and 146 runs in two days. Batting first, the home side passed 100 with the loss of only 3 wickets but a tail-end collapse, in which 5 wickets were lost for 12 runs, restricted it to a total of 200. Terry Alderman and Greg Campbell each took 4 wickets. The Australians were 3 for 101 in reply when Mark Taylor and Dean Jones came together, and the next wicket did not fall until the total was 328. Taylor made 141, becoming the first Australian on the tour to score 1,000 first-class runs, and Jones thumped a very fast 167 not out, in the course of which he scored 106 in a session of play. Gloucestershire, now needing to bat for more than a day to save the match, began its second innings soundly enough, and was 1 for 54 when Geoff Lawson took the first of a remarkable series of wickets. In 29 balls, Lawson dismissed six Gloucestershire batsmen, and the home side, thus routed, was all out for 92. Lawson's figures were 6 for 30 from 13 overs.

Gloucestershire

First Innings

Batsman	How Out	Ttl
AJ Wright	b Alderman	0
IP Butcher	lbw Alderman	0
JW Lloyds	c Border b Hughes	46
CWJ Athey (c)	c Marsh b Campbell	34
KM Curran	c Healy b Campbell	46

Second Innings

How Out	Ttl
lbw Lawson	21
c Taylor b Alderman	8
c Boon b Lawson	36
c Boon b Lawson	0
c Taylor b Lawson	4

Batsman	How Out	Ttl	How Out	Ttl
MW Alleyne	b Lawson	22	c Healy b Lawson	0
RC Russell (+)	lbw Alderman	16	c Marsh b Lawson	9
VS Greene	c Healy b Alderman	4	lbw Campbell	1
MJC Ball	b Campbell	4	b Hohns	4
DA Graveney	not out	1	not out	1
KBS Jarvis	b Campbell	0	lbw Campbell	0
SUNDRIES: B. 12 LB. 7 W. 0 NB. 8		27	B. 0 LB. 0 W. 0 NB. 8	8
TOTAL		200		92

F/W: 1 22 78 108 137 188 188 193 197 200

F/W: 15 54 58 72 72 81 87 87 91 92

Bowler	O	M	R	Wkts	Bowler	O	M	R	Wkts
Alderman	13	3	39	4	Alderman	7	—	31	1
Lawson	13	3	55	1	Lawson	13	5	30	6
Campbell	13.1	4	47	4	Hughes	6	1	26	—
Hughes	10	1	33	1	Campbell	2	1	1	2
Hohns	6	3	7	—	Hohns	1	—	4	1
Overs:	55.1				Overs:	29.0			

Australians

First Innings

Batsman	How Out	Ttl
MA Taylor	c Ball b Alleyne	141
GR Marsh	lbw Greene	5
DC Boon	c Athey b Graveney	16
AR Border (c)	c & b Ball	25
DM Jones	not out	167
IA Healy (+)	c Lloyds b Jarvis	21
TV Hohns	lbw Greene	2
MG Hughes	c Athey b Jarvis	14
GD Campbell	c Athey b Jarvis	3
GF Lawson	c Wright b Graveney	22
TM Alderman	st Russell b Lloyds	0
SUNDRIES: B. 2 LB. 9 W. 3 NB. 8		22
TOTAL		438

F/W: 28 54 101 328 353 364 385 389 437 438

Bowler	O	M	R	Wkts
Greene	20	1	65	2
Jarvis	25	7	77	3
Alleyne	13	2	60	1
Athey	9	3	27	—
Graveney	26	3	112	2
Ball	15	1	64	1
Lloyds	4.2	—	22	1
Overs:	112.2			

Umpires: B Dudleston & MJ Harris

FOURTH TEST

England v Australia
Old Trafford
July 27, 28, 29, 31 August 1 1989
Toss: England
Result: Australia won by 9 wickets

This Test offered England its last real chance of making a contest of the series and, accordingly, a determined effort was expected from the home side—particularly its batsmen. But with Graham Gooch's dismissal 49 minutes into the match England began yet another notorious decline. Wickets fell in steady succession, yet one batsman, Robin Smith, stood firm. His dedicated 143 saved the England innings from becoming a complete disaster. Geoff Lawson headed the bowling list with 6 wickets, followed by the leg-spinner, Trevor Hohns, with 3. Australia easily passed England's total of 260, although for once no Australian scored a century. Three made more than 80, however, including Steve Waugh, the last batsman out, who fell at 92 playing a rash stroke trying to keep the strike. Australia was 187 ahead and poised to grab victory if England's batsmen failed again. They did fail, even more disastrously than before. Five wickets fell for 38, and six for 59. Jack Russell was now joined by John Emburey, and the two batsmen halted the collapse with a dogged partnership lasting nearly four hours. Emburey was eventually out for 64 and Russell went on to make an undefeated 128. They had spared England the indignity of an innings defeat, but Australia won the match and the Ashes.

England

First Innings				Second Innings		
Batsman	How Out	Ttl	Balls	How Out	Ttl	Balls
GA Gooch	b Lawson	11	32	c Alderman b Lawson	13	23
TS Curtis	b Lawson	22	103	c Boon b Alderman	0	2
RT Robinson	lbw Lawson	0	9	lbw Lawson	12	28
RA Smith	c Hohns b Hughes	143	285	c Healy b Alderman	1	8
DI Gower (c)	lbw Hohns	35	51	c Marsh b Lawson	15	40
IT Botham	b Hohns	0	6	lbw Alderman	4	23
RC Russell (+)	lbw Lawson	1	11	not out	128	294
JE Emburey	lbw Hohns	5	34	b Alderman	64	183
NA Foster	c Border b Lawson	39	68	b Alderman	6	28
ARC Fraser	lbw Lawson	2	9	c Marsh b Hohns	3	32
NGB Cook	not out	0	10	c Healy b Hughes	5	11
SUNDRIES: B. 0 LB. 2 W. 0 NB. 0		2	618	B. 0 LB. 6 W. 2 NB. 5	13	672
TOTAL		260			264	
F/W: 23 23 56 132 140 147 158 232 252 260				F/W: 10 25 27 28 38 59 201 223 255 264		

Bowler	O	M	R	Wkts	NB	W	Bowler	O	M	R	Wkts	NB	W
Alderman	25	13	49	—	—	—	Lawson	31	8	81	3	1	2
Lawson	33	11	72	6	—	—	Alderman	27	7	66	5	4	—
Hughes	17	6	55	1	—	—	Hohns	26	15	37	1	—	—
Hohns	22	7	59	3	—	—	Hughes	14.4	2	45	1	—	—
Waugh	6	1	23	—	—	—	Border	8	2	12	—	—	—
Overs:	103.0						Waugh	4	—	17	—	—	—
							Overs:	110.4					

Australia

First Innings					Second Innings		
Batsman	How Out	Ttl	Balls		How Out	Ttl	Balls
MA Taylor	st Russell b Emburey	85	180	(2)	not out	37	83
GR Marsh	c Russell b Botham	47	100	(1)	c Robinson b Emburey	31	92
DC Boon	b Fraser	12	40		not out	10	23
AR Border (c)	c Russell b Foster	80	267				
DM Jones	b Botham	69	142				
SR Waugh	c Curtis b Fraser	92	175				
IA Healy (+)	lbw Foster	0	1				
TV Hohns	c Gower b Cook	17	64				
MG Hughes	b Cook	3	6				
GF Lawson	b Fraser	17	31				
TM Alderman	not out	6	12				
SUNDRIES: B. 5 LB. 7 W. 1 NB. 6		19	1018		B. 0 LB. 0 W. 0 NB. 3	3	198
TOTAL		447			1 wkt for 81		
F/W: 135 143 154 274 362 362 413 423 423 447					F/W: 62		

Bowler	O	M	R	Wkts	NB	W	Bowler	O	M	R	Wkts	NB	W
Foster	34	12	74	2	—	—	Foster	5	2	5	—	—	—
Fraser	36.5	4	95	3	6	—	Fraser	10	—	28	—	3	—
Emburey	45	9	118	1	—	—	Emburey	13	3	30	1	—	—
Cook	28	6	85	2	—	—	Cook	4.5	—	18	—	—	—
Botham	24	6	63	2	—	1	Overs:	32.5					
Overs:	167.5												

Umpires: BJ Meyer & JH Hampshire

12th Men: PW Jarvis (England) & GD Campbell (Australia)

Nottinghamshire v Australians
Trent Bridge, Nottingham
August 2, 3, 4 1989
Toss: Australians
Result: Australians by 196 runs

The Australians continued their triumphant march through England's counties with another resounding victory over their old foe, Nottinghamshire. To begin with, Nottinghamshire was entitled to be satisfied with dismissing the tourists for 284, the smallest total they had compiled in the first innings of a first-class match in two months. Dean Jones had made 82 and David Boon 76. Nottinghamshire made 195 in reply, FD Stephenson top-scoring with 47 and Merv Hughes took 5 wickets. The Australians regained their appetite for runs in the second innings, which they closed at 4 for 255, David Boon remaining 102 not out. Under pressure from an Australian attack seeking an outright victory, Nottinghamshire's batting crumbled in the second innings, and the home side was all out for 148, thus losing the match by 196 runs. Derek Randall top scored with 48. Carl Rackemann, with 5 for 65, was Australia's leading wicket-taker, but Tim May was extremely successful, too, with 4 for 43.

Australians

Batsman	First Innings How Out	Ttl	Second Innings How Out	Ttl
GR Marsh (c)	c Newell b Cooper	16	lbw Stephenson	66
MA Taylor	c French b Millns	33	lbw Cooper	30
DC Boon	c Johnson b Millns	76	not out	102
DM Jones	b Hemmings	82	st French b Afford	22
TM Moody	c Newell b Hemmings	7	st French b Afford	11
SR Waugh	not out	46	not out	13
TJ Zoehrer (+)	run out	0		
MG Hughes	b Millns	0		
TBA May	c Robinson b Millns	1		
GD Campbell	lbw Cooper	7		
CG Rackemann	b Cooper	2		
SUNDRIES:	B. 0 LB. 12 W. 0 NB. 2	14	B. 6 LB. 5 W. 0 NB. 0	11
TOTAL		284	4 wkts dec	255

F/W: 55 55 210 226 228 228 228 242 266 284

F/W: 73 120 165 205

Bowler	O	M	R	Wkts	Bowler	O	M	R	Wkts
Stephenson	10	4	16	—	Stephenson	10	3	12	1
Millns	25	5	86	4	Millns	14	2	53	—
Cooper	17.3	7	47	3	Cooper	9	2	25	1
Hemmings	17	4	48	2	Hemmings	20.4	3	86	—
Afford	13	2	75	—	Afford	19	4	68	2
Overs:	82.3				Overs:	72.4			

▶

Nottinghamshire

First Innings						Second Innings				
Batsman	How Out	Ttl				How Out	Ttl			
P Pollard	c Zoehrer b Hughes	35				c Jones b Rackemann	11			
M Newell	b Hughes	12				lbw Hughes	4			
RT Robinson (c)	c Zoehrer b Rackemann	37	(5)			b May	5			
P Johnson	c Zoehrer b Hughes	0				c Taylor b Rackemann	23			
DW Randall	c Rackemann b Hughes	0	(3)			c (s) Healy b May	48			
BN French (+)	c Zoehrer b May	20				c Marsh b May	9			
FD Stephenson	b May	47				c Taylor b Rackemann	13			
EE Hemmings	lbw Rackemann	4				c Zoehrer b Rackemann	6			
KE Cooper	c Zoehrer b Hughes	9				c Marsh b Rackemann	10			
DJ Millns	not out	7				c (s) Healy b May	9			
JA Afford	c Boon b May	9				not out	3			
SUNDRIES: B. 1 LB. 10 W. 1 NB. 3		15				B. 4 LB. 1 W. 0 NB. 2	7			
TOTAL		195					148			

F/W: 44 67 67 67 116 117 149 179 179 195

F/W: 15 27 86 89 102 103 116 126 135 148

Bowler	O	M	R	Wkts		Bowler	O	M	R	Wkts
Hughes	20	8	38	5		Hughes	9	4	35	1
Campbell	12	2	34	—		Rackemann	18	3	65	5
May	16	6	40	3		May	10.4	1	43	4
Waugh	5	2	13	—		Overs:	37.4			
Rackemann	11	3	59	2						
Overs:	64.0									

Umpires: DJ Constant & K Taylor

Leicestershire v Australians
Leicester
August 5, 6, 7 1989
Toss: Leicestershire
Result: Australians by 9 wkts

The Australian bowlers made short work of the home side's batsmen in their first innings. Leicestershire was all out for 157, succumbing to the pace of Geoff Lawson (4 for 38) and Carl Rackemann (3 for 19). The England captain, David Gower, was one of the failed batsmen. Dropped from the first ball he faced, he survived to make only 9. Mark Taylor made 70, but otherwise the Australian top order did not function as efficiently as usual. It was left to Ian Healy and Trevor Hohns, batting at six and seven, to push the score well beyond Leicestershire's. They had a partnership of 146, after which the Australian innings ended abruptly at 305. The West Indian pace bowler Winston Benjamin, took a hat-trick and finished with the outstanding figures of 7 for 54. In the second innings, the Leicestershire batsmen, including David Gower, who top-scored with 46, improved on their previous performance, but their total of 243 left the Australians in need of only 96 runs to win, which they scored with the loss of only 1 wicket.

Leicestershire

First Innings			Second Innings	
Batsman	How Out	Ttl	How Out	Ttl
TJ Boon	c Moody b Lawson	14	c Healy b Rackemann	20
NE Briers	c Healy b Rackemann	15	b Rackemann	41
DI Gower (c)	c Moody b Lawson	9	st Healy b May	46
JJ Whitaker	b Lawson	6	lbw Lawson	17
L Potter	c Healy b Rackemann	41	b Lawson	18

Batsman	How Out	Ttl	How Out	Ttl
PN Hepworth	c Marsh b Hohns	6	c Healy b Hughes	9
WKM Benjamin	lbw Rackemann	0	b May	14
PA Nixon (+)	b May	24	lbw Hohns	17
JP Agnew	c Border b Lawson	30	c Lawson b Hohns	39
PM Such	b May	1 (11)	not out	2
LB Taylor	not out	0 (10)	b Hohns	0
SUNDRIES: B. 1 LB. 4 W. 0 NB. 6		11	B. 2 LB. 10 W. 0 NB. 8	20
TOTAL		157		243

F/W: 27 39 45 49 62 63 117 156 157 157

F/W: 70 93 133 158 160 176 182 237 237 243

Bowler	O	M	R	Wkts	Bowler	O	M	R	Wkts
Lawson	15	5	38	4	Lawson	17	9	30	2
Hughes	14	3	48	—	Rackemann	11	2	41	2
Rackemann	10	2	19	3	May	29	7	79	2
Hohns	18	9	26	1	Hughes	9	2	18	1
May	10.1	2	21	2	Border	3	—	14	—
Overs:	67.1				Hohns	5.2	—	49	3
					Overs:	74.2			

Australians

First Innings

Second Innings

Batsman	How Out	Ttl	How Out	Ttl
MA Taylor	lbw Benjamin	70		
GR Marsh	c Whitaker b Taylor	22 (1)	not out	27
TM Moody	c Boon b Benjamin	6 (2)	c Potter b Taylor	36
AR Border (c)	b Benjamin	0 (3)	not out	22
SR Waugh	b Agnew	7		
IA Healy (+)	not out	73		
TV Hohns	c Nixon b Benjamin	95		
MG Hughes	lbw Benjamin	7		
TBA May	c Potter b Benjamin	0		
GF Lawson	b Benjamin	0		
CG Rackemann	b Agnew	4		
SUNDRIES: B. 4 LB. 15 W. 0 NB. 2		21	B. 8 LB. 5 W. 0 NB. 1	14
TOTAL		305	1 wkt for 99	

F/W: 50 88 88 109 139 285 300 300 300 305

F/W: 52

Bowler	O	M	R	Wkts	Bowler	O	M	R	Wkts
Benjamin	23	6	54	7	Benjamin	6	3	7	—
Agnew	23	3	64	2	Agnew	7	—	39	—
Taylor	14	1	49	1	Taylor	7	1	31	1
Such	24	4	77	—	Such	6	2	9	—
Potter	10	—	42	—	Boon	0.5	—	0	—
Overs:	94.0				Overs:	26.5			

Umpires: JD Bond & PJ Eele

FIFTH TEST

England v Australia
Trent Bridge
August 10, 11, 12, 14 1989
Toss: Australia
Result: Australia won by an innings & 180 runs

Several England players were not considered for this Test because
they had agreed to join a rebel tour of South Africa, and Graham
Gooch had stood down voluntarily while he tried to regain his form.
So England went into the match with a few new players who, it

was hoped, might give the home side fresh impetus. But England's hopes were crushed on the first day when the Australian openers Mark Taylor and Geoff Marsh batted until stumps in an epic partnership which, when Marsh was out next day for 138, totalled 329. The stand broke many records, including the 78-year-old record for an opening partnership in Anglo-Australian Tests. Taylor pushed on to a score of 219, and Allan Border finally called a halt when Australia was 6 for 602. England's batsmen again faced the task of batting for a draw, and again the task proved beyond them. Terry Alderman disposed of three England batsmen before the score passed 14, and England was all out for 255, Alderman again having taken 5 wickets. Robin Smith alone kept England's colours aloft with a thunderous innings of 101, scored off only 150 balls. England was thus 347 behind on the first innings, a position which its batsmen apparently judged as hopeless, for their second innings was virtually a capitulation. England was all out for 167, giving Australia victory by an innings and 180 runs.

Australia

First Innings

Batsman	How Out	Ttl	Balls
GR Marsh	c Botham b Cook	138	382
MA Taylor	st Russell b Cook	219	461
DC Boon	st Russell b Cook	73	182
AR Border (c)	not out	65	144
DM Jones	c Gower b Fraser	22	35
SR Waugh	c Gower b Malcolm	0	8
IA Healy (+)	b Fraser	5	13
TV Hohns	not out	19	44
GF Lawson	did not bat		
MG Hughes	did not bat		
TM Alderman	did not bat		
SUNDRIES: B. 6 LB. 23 W. 3 NB. 29		61	1269
TOTAL	6 wkts dec	602	

F/W: 329 430 502 543 553 560

Bowler	O	M	R	Wkts	NB	W
Fraser	52.3	18	108	2	12	—
Malcolm	44	2	166	1	15	2
Botham	30	4	103	—	—	1
Hemmings	33	9	81	—	—	—
Cook	40	10	91	3	—	—
Atherton	7	—	24	—	2	—
Overs:	206.3					

England

	First Innings				Second Innings		
Batsman	How Out	Ttl	Balls		How Out	Ttl	Balls
TS Curtis	lbw Alderman	2	16	(2)	lbw Alderman	6	10
MD Moxon	c Waugh b Alderman	0	3	(5)	b Alderman	18	48
MA Atherton	lbw Alderman	0	2		c & b Hohns	47	127
RA Smith	c Healy b Alderman	101	150		b Hughes	26	44
DI Gower (c)	c Healy b Lawson	11	26	(1)	b Lawson	5	6
RC Russell (+)	c Healy b Lawson	20	63		b Lawson	1	14
EE Hemmings	b Alderman	38	83		lbw Hughes	35	48
ARC Fraser	b Hohns	29	55		b Hohns	1	9
IT Botham	c Waugh b Hohns	12	49		absent injured		
NGB Cook	not out	2	15	(9)	not out	7	27
DE Malcolm	c Healy b Hughes	9	15	(10)	b Hughes	5	9
SUNDRIES: B. 0 LB. 18 W. 0 NB. 13		31	477		B. 3 LB. 6 W. 1 NB. 6	16	342
TOTAL		255				167	

F/W: 1 1 14 37 119 172 214 243 244 255

F/W: 5 13 67 106 114 120 134 160 167

Bowler	O	M	R	Wkts	NB	W
Alderman	19	2	69	5	9	—
Lawson	21	5	57	2	1	—
Hohns	18	8	48	2	—	—
Hughes	7.5	—	40	1	2	—
Waugh	11	4	23	—	1	—
Overs:	76.5					

Bowler	O	M	R	Wkts	NB	W
Alderman	16	6	32	2	4	—
Lawson	15	3	51	2	—	—
Hughes	12.3	1	46	3	2	—
Hohns	12	3	29	2	—	1
Overs:	55.3					

Umpires: BJ Meyer & NT Plews

12th Men: JG Thomas (England) & TBA May (Australia)

Kent v Australians
Canterbury
August 16, 17, 18 1989
Toss: Kent
Result: Drawn

The Australians were in some trouble in their first innings at 3 for 35, but a partnership of 183 between Dean Jones and David Boon placed the visitors in a commanding position. Boon made 86 and Jones 128, and the Australians were later able to declare at 8 for 356. Kent's opening bowler, Danny Kelleher, took 4 for 82. In reply, Kent lost two early wickets, but the opener Simon Hinks kept the side more or less together with a fine innings of 85, and Kent was able to push on to 191. Compelled to bat again, Kent showed much more resistance in its second innings. Its captain, Mark Benson, made 106, an innings which frustrated Australian attempts to secure an outright victory. At the end, Kent was still hanging on at 9 for 237.

Australians

First Innings

Batsman	How Out	Ttl
MA Taylor	c Farbrace b Kelleher	14
GR Marsh (c)	lbw Kelleher	2
DC Boon	c Farbrace b Ealham	86
TM Moody	b Kelleher	14
DM Jones	c Kelleher b Davis	128
SR Waugh	b Kelleher	1
TJ Zoehrer (+)	st Farbrace b Dobson	32
TV Hohns	not out	39
TBA May	c Davis b Dobson	24
GD Campbell	not out	0
CG Rackemann	did not bat	
SUNDRIES: B. 0 LB. 8 W. 0 NB. 8		16
TOTAL	8 wkts dec	356

F/W: 17 18 35 218 228 281 311 353

Bowler	O	M	R	Wkts
Kelleher	26.1	7	82	4
Ealham	24	5	92	1
Fleming	19	3	55	—
Davis	21	3	75	1
Dobson	12	—	44	2
Overs:	102.1			

▶

Kent

First Innings

Batsman	How Out	Ttl		How Out (Second Innings)	Ttl
SG Hinks	b May	85		c Zoehrer b Moody	16
MR Benson (c)	lbw Rackemann	3		c Waugh b Campbell	106
RF Pienaar	c Taylor b Rackemann	0	(4)	b May	7
TR Ward	c Zoehrer b Waugh	32	(5)	c Marsh b Moody	36
JI Longley	c Hohns b Campbell	10	(6)	lbw Moody	0
MV Fleming	b Campbell	7	(7)	lbw Moody	0
MC Dobson	lbw Campbell	2	(8)	c Waugh b Rackemann	33
P Farbrace (+)	lbw May	35	(9)	c Moody b Rackemann	1
MA Ealham	c Boon b May	7	(10)	not out	4
DJM Kelleher	c Hohns b Campbell	8	(11)	not out	12
RP Davis	not out	0	(3)	c Taylor b May	11
SUNDRIES: B. 0 LB. 1 W. 0 NB. 1		2		B. 4 LB. 6 W. 0 NB. 1	11
TOTAL		191		9 wkts for 237	

F/W: 7 11 63 82 98 106 173 178 191 191

F/W: 42 63 81 149 149 149 217 219 219

Bowler	O	M	R	Wkts	Bowler	O	M	R	Wkts
Rackemann	10	3	39	2	Campbell	18	7	46	1
Campbell	23.1	5	78	4	Rackemann	20	7	36	2
Waugh	7	1	29	1	Moody	21	11	30	4
May	15	5	40	3	May	29	10	42	2
Hohns	2	1	4	—	Hohns	23	7	60	—
Overs:	57.1				Jones	1	—	13	—
					Overs:	112.0			

Umpires: B Hassan & K Taylor

12th Men: GF Lawson (Australia) & Kent not named

Essex v Australians
Chelmsford
August 19, 20, 21 1989
Toss: Australians
Result: Australians by 150 runs

The Australians won their last county match by the substantial margin of 150 runs, although the result was to some extent contrived. Batting first, the visitors once again were able to close their first innings after several fine individual performances. David Boon made 151, Tom Moody 80, Dean Jones 70 and Allan Border 40, and Australia declared at 7 for 387. Essex responded with several fine individual performances, too—Graham Gooch's 58, Paul Prichard's 86 and an unbeaten century by Steve Waugh's brother Mark, who was playing a season of county cricket. Essex declared at 6 for 290 and, accepting the challenge, the Australians raced to 2 for 258 and declared again. The highlight of the Australian innings was a dashing century by Steve Waugh, which outdid even his brother's earlier performance. Steve Waugh faced only 101 balls and sped from 50 to 100 with only 15 scoring shots, two of them big sixes. Tom Zoehrer supported him with 93. Essex lost its first 3 wickets for 40, and although Prichard (52) and Mark Waugh (57) revived the innings for a time, the home side was dismissed for 205.

Australians

Batsman	First Innings How Out	Ttl		Second Innings How Out	Ttl
DC Boon	c Hardie b Childs	151			
TJ Zoehrer	c Waugh b Lever	13	(1)	lbw Shahid	93
TM Moody	b Shahid	80	(4)	not out	13
SR Waugh	lbw Childs	1	(3)	not out	100
AR Border (c)	st Garnham b Shahid	40			
DM Jones	st Garnham b Childs	70			
IA Healy (+)	not out	6	(2)	b Waugh	45
MG Hughes	c Garnham b Waugh	6			
GF Lawson	did not bat				
TBA May	did not bat				
GD Campbell	did not bat				
SUNDRIES: B. 1 LB. 4 W. 4 NB. 11		20		B. 5 LB. 1 W. 0 NB. 1	7
TOTAL	7 wkts dec	387		2 wkts dec	258
F/W: 21 188 189 237 370 376 387				F/W: 89 220	

Bowler	O	M	R	Wkts	Bowler	O	M	R	Wkts
Lever	17	4	43	1	Lever	13	1	56	—
Topley	12	1	40	—	Topley	11	2	48	—
Waugh	20	3	68	1	Waugh	7	—	40	1
Stephenson	5	—	30	—	Childs	12	1	53	—
Gooch	7	—	49	—	Shahid	9.1	1	53	1
Childs	18	2	69	3	Stephenson	1	—	2	—
Shahid	14	2	83	2	Overs:	53.1			
Overs:	93.0								

Essex

Batsman	First Innings How Out	Ttl		Second Innings How Out	Ttl
GA Gooch (c)	c Border b Hughes	58		b Lawson	21
JP Stephenson	lbw Lawson	3		b Hughes	3
N Shahid	b Lawson	0	(8)	c Jones b May	10
PJ Prichard	c Healy b Lawson	86	(5)	lbw Lawson	52
ME Waugh	not out	100	(6)	c Jones b Hughes	57
N Hussain	c Border b Hughes	14	(4)	b Hughes	31
BR Hardie	c Border b Zoehrer	9	(3)	b Hughes	8
MA Garnham (+)	not out	1	(7)	lbw Lawson	1
TD Topley	did not bat			c Lawson b Hughes	9
JK Lever	did not bat			c Campbell b May	0
JH Childs	did not bat			not out	1
SUNDRIES: B. 6 LB. 8 W. 0 NB. 5		19		B. 0 LB. 10 W. 0 NB. 2	12
TOTAL	6 wkts dec	290			205
F/W: 36 36 110 200 232 287				F/W: 20 34 40 87 169 175 193 193 193 205	

Bowler	O	M	R	Wkts	Bowler	O	M	R	Wkts
Lawson	18	6	52	3	Lawson	15	4	40	3
Hughes	20	4	69	2	Hughes	17.4	5	64	5
Campbell	14	3	51	—	Campbell	7	—	41	—
May	11	2	45	—	May	17	5	50	2
Moody	8	1	28	—	Overs:	56.4			
Border	7	1	22	—					
Zoehrer	5	—	9	1					
Boon	1	1	0	—					
Overs:	84.0								

Umpires: MJ Harris & AGT Whitehead

12th Men: TM Alderman (Australia) & Essex not named

SIXTH TEST

England v Australia
Kennington Oval
August 24, 25, 26, 28, 29 1989
Toss: Australia
Result: Drawn

Perhaps reasoning that England had nothing else to lose, England's selectors made several experimental changes, while the same Australian eleven took the field for the fifth match in a row. Batting first, Australia again scored more than 400—a total which comprised several good innings and one great one, played by Dean Jones. Jones faced 180 balls, hit 17 boundaries, scored 122 runs and gave a superb display of attacking strokeplay. The pressure was on England's batsmen in this final Test to try to regain some lost pride, and much attention was focused, in particular, on Graham Gooch's return to the team. Gooch went for 0, however, starting a collapse which reduced England to 6 for 98. A ninth-wicket partnership of 73 between Gladstone Small and Nick Cook saved England from the follow-on, so if Australia was to win its batsmen would have to score runs quickly. To begin with there was no urgency in the Australian batting, and Allan Border was not prepared to declare until lunch on the final day, by which time Australia was 402 ahead. Australia did not have enough time to win the match, but its bowlers were able to embarrass England's batsmen one last time, dismissing four of them before the total passed 67. Altogether, more than a day's play was lost during the match because of rain, and this certainly saved England from defeat.

Australia

First Innings

Batsman	How Out	Ttl	Balls		Second Innings How Out	Ttl	Balls
GR Marsh	c Igglesden b Small	17	62	(2)	lbw Igglesden	4	13
MA Taylor	c Russell b Igglesden	71	125	(1)	c Russell b Small	48	120
DC Boon	c Atherton b Small	46	90		run out	37	107
AR Border (c)	c Russell b Capel	76	157		not out	51	74
DM Jones	c Gower b Small	122	180		b Capel	50	79
SR Waugh	b Igglesden	14	28		not out	7	12
IA Healy (+)	c Russell b Pringle	44	44				
TV Hohns	c Russell b Pringle	30	62				
MG Hughes	lbw Pringle	21	42				
GF Lawson	b Pringle	2	8				
TM Alderman	not out	6	10				
SUNDRIES: B. 1 LB. 9 W. 0 NB. 9		19	808		B. 2 LB. 7 W. 0 NB. 13	22	405
TOTAL		468			4 wkts dec 219		

F/W: 48 130 149 345 347 386 409 447 453 468

F/W: 7 100 101 189

Bowler	O	M	R	Wkts	NB	W	Bowler	O	M	R	Wkts	NB	W
Small	40	8	141	3	—	—	Small	20	4	57	1	—	—
Igglesden	24	2	91	2	8	—	Igglesden	13	1	55	1	9	—
Pringle	24.3	6	70	4	1	—	Capel	8	—	35	1	—	—
Capel	16	2	66	1	—	—	Pringle	16	—	53	—	4	—
Cook	25	5	78	—	—	—	Cook	6	2	10	—	—	—
Atherton	1	—	10	—	—	—	Overs:	63.0					
Gooch	2	1	2	—	—	—							
Overs:	132.3												

58

England

First Innings					Second Innings		
Batsman	*How Out*		*Ttl*	*Balls*	*How Out*	*Ttl*	*Balls*
GA Gooch	lbw Alderman		0	3	c & b Alderman	10	34
JP Stephenson	c Waugh b Alderman		25	66	lbw Alderman	11	23
MA Atherton	c Healy b Hughes		12	34	b Lawson	14	47
RA Smith	b Lawson		11	19	not out	77	99
DI Gower (c)	c Healy b Alderman		79	120	c Waugh b Lawson	7	24
DJ Capel	lbw Alderman		4	3	c Taylor b Hohns	17	50
RC Russell (+)	c Healy b Alderman		12	13	not out	0	6
DR Pringle	c Taylor b Hohns		27	90			
GC Small	c Jones b Lawson		59	97			
NGB Cook	c Jones b Lawson		31	102			
AP Igglesden	not out		2	23			
SUNDRIES: B. 2 LB. 7 W. 1 NB. 13			23	570	B. 0 LB. 1 W. 1 NB. 5	7	283
TOTAL			285		5 wkts for 143		
F/W: 1 28 47 80 84 98 169 201 274 285					F/W: 20 27 51 67 138		

Bowler	*O*	*M*	*R*	*Wkts*	*NB*	*W*	*Bowler*	*O*	*M*	*R*	*Wkts*	*NB*	*W*
Alderman	27	7	66	5	10	—	Alderman	13	3	30	2	3	—
Lawson	29.1	9	85	3	—	1	Lawson	15.1	2	41	2	1	1
Hughes	23	3	84	1	3	—	Hughes	8	2	34	—	1	—
Hohns	10	1	30	1	—	—	Hohns	10	2	37	1	—	—
Waugh	3	—	11	—	—	—	Overs:	46.1					
Overs:	92.1												

Umpires: HD Bird & KE Palmer

12th Men: VP Terry (England) & TBA May (Australia)

Tour Statistics

1989 Australian First-Class Averages

Batsman	M	Inn	NO	Runs	HS	50	100	Avrge	Ct/St
DM Jones	14	20	3	1510	248	8	5	88.82	8
SR Waugh	16	24	8	1030	177*	3	4	64.38	6
MA Taylor	17	30	1	1669	219	10	3	57.55	23
DC Boon	17	28	5	1306	151	8	3	56.78	21
AR Border	16	22	4	979	135	9	1	54.39	18
MRJ Veletta	5	8	1	294	134*	1	1	42.00	6
TM Moody	12	20	4	564	144*	3	1	35.25	8
GR Marsh	18	33	4	934	138	2	2	32.21	17
IA Healy	14	19	4	442	73*	1	—	29.47	35/2
TJ Zoehrer	7	9	—	259	93	1	—	28.78	16/-
TV Hohns	15	18	4	393	95	2	—	28.07	8
MG Hughes	15	16	4	246	71	1	—	20.50	1
GF Lawson	14	12	2	174	74	1	—	17.40	4
TBA May	10	8	3	59	24	—	—	11.80	1
GD Campbell	11	10	2	87	31	—	—	10.88	3
TM Alderman	11	10	6	38	8	—	—	9.50	5
CG Rackemann	8	6	1	22	11	—	—	4.40	2

Bowler	M	Overs	Mdns	Runs	Wkts	Avrge	5wi	10m	Best
TJ Zoehrer	7	5.0	—	9	1	9.00	—	—	1/9
TM Alderman	11	411.2	104	1095	70	15.64	6	1	6/128
GF Lawson	14	522.3	140	1447	69	20.97	3	—	6/30
CG Rackemann	8	223.5	47	747	32	23.34	1	—	5/65
SR Waugh	16	176.1	39	571	23	24.83	—	—	3/10
TM Moody	12	63.0	19	151	6	25.17	—	—	4/30
MG Hughes	15	399.0	102	1242	47	26.43	3	—	5/37
TBA May	10	287.5	86	740	28	26.43	—	—	4/43
GD Campbell	11	250.2	50	824	30	27.47	1	—	5/54
TV Hohns	15	321.4	108	809	26	31.12	—	—	4/87
AR Border	16	68.0	21	154	1	154.00	—	—	1/55
DM Jones	14	1.0	—	13	—	—	—	—	—
DC Boon	17	1.0	1	0	—	—	—	—	—

1989 Australia v England Test Averages

Batsman	M	Inn	NO	Runs	HS	50	100	Avrge	Ct/St
SR Waugh	6	8	4	506	177*	1	2	126.50	4
MA Taylor	6	11	1	839	219	5	2	83.90	5
AR Border	6	9	3	442	80	6	—	73.67	5
DM Jones	6	9	1	566	157	3	2	70.75	4
DC Boon	6	11	3	442	94	3	—	55.25	9
TV Hohns	5	5	1	127	40	—	—	31.75	3
GR Marsh	6	11	—	347	138	—	1	31.55	5
GF Lawson	6	5	1	115	74	1	—	28.75	—
MG Hughes	6	5	—	127	71	1	—	25.40	—
TM Alderman	6	4	3	20	8	—	—	20.00	2
IA Healy	6	7	1	103	44	—	—	17.17	14/-
GD Campbell	1	—	—	—	—	—	—	—	—

Bowler	M	Overs	Mdns	Runs	Wkts	Avrge	5wi	10m	NB	W	Best
TM Alderman	6	269.2	68	712	41	17.37	6	1	42	—	6/128
TV Hohns	5	134.0	53	300	11	27.27	—	—	—	1	3/59
GF Lawson	6	277.1	68	791	29	27.28	1	—	5	5	6/72
MG Hughes	6	189.2	41	615	19	32.37	—	—	9	—	4/71
SR Waugh	6	57.0	15	208	2	104.00	—	—	9	—	1/38
GD Campbell	1	24.0	—	124	1	124.00	—	—	8	—	1/82
AR Border	6	24.0	9	44	—	—	—	—	—	—	—

1989 England v Australia Test Averages

Batsman	M	Inn	NO	Runs	HS	50	100	Avrge	Ct/St
AJ Lamb	1	2	—	129	125	—	1	64.50	—
RA Smith	5	10	1	553	143	3	2	61.44	1
GC Small	1	1	—	59	59	1	—	59.00	—
RC Russell	6	11	3	314	128*	1	1	39.25	14/4
EE Hemmings	1	2	—	73	38	—	—	36.50	—
DI Gower	6	11	—	383	106	2	1	34.82	4
JE Emburey	3	5	1	131	64	1	—	32.75	—
KJ Barnett	3	5	—	141	80	1	—	28.20	—
NGB Cook	3	5	3	45	31	—	—	22.50	—
PJ Newport	1	2	—	44	36	—	—	22.00	1

Batsman	M	Inn	NO	Runs	HS	50	100	Avrge	Ct/St
GR Dilley	2	3	1	42	24	—	—	21.00	—
BC Broad	2	4	—	82	37	—	—	20.50	2
GA Gooch	5	9	—	183	68	2	—	20.33	4
MA Atherton	2	4	—	73	47	—	—	18.25	1
JP Stephenson	1	2	—	36	25	—	—	18.00	—
NA Foster	3	6	2	68	39	—	—	17.00	1
IT Botham	3	4	—	62	46	—	—	15.50	3
TS Curtis	3	5	—	71	41	—	—	14.20	1
PW Jarvis	2	3	—	33	22	—	—	11.00	—
PAJ DeFreitas	1	2	—	22	21	—	—	11.00	—
MW Gatting	1	2	—	22	22	—	—	11.00	—
DR Pringle	2	3	—	33	27	—	—	11.00	—
DJ Capel	1	2	—	21	17	—	—	10.50	—
ARC Fraser	3	5	—	47	29	—	—	9.40	—
MD Moxon	1	2	—	18	18	—	—	9.00	—
DE Malcolm	1	2	—	14	9	—	—	7.00	—
RT Robinson	1	2	—	12	12	—	—	6.00	1
CJ Tavare	1	1	—	2	2•	—	—	2.00	—
AP Igglesden	1	1	1	2	2•	—	—	—	1

Bowler	M	Overs	Mdns	Runs	Wkts	Avrge	5wi	10m	NB	W	Best
NA Foster	3	167.0	42	421	12	35.08	—	—	—	6	3/39
ARC Fraser	3	144.2	30	323	9	35.89	—	—	28	—	4/63
JE Emburey	3	152.0	37	342	8	42.75	—	—	1	—	4/88
AP Igglesden	1	37.0	3	146	3	48.67	—	—	17	—	2/91
GC Small	1	60.0	12	198	4	49.50	—	—	—	—	3/141
DJ Capel	1	24.0	2	101	2	50.50	—	—	—	—	1/35
NGB Cook	3	103.5	23	282	5	56.40	—	—	—	—	3/91
DR Pringle	2	86.2	12	306	5	61.20	—	—	8	4	4/70
GR Dilley	2	84.0	12	318	5	63.60	—	—	23	—	2/123
PAJ DeFreitas	1	63.3	10	216	3	72.00	—	—	2	—	2/140
GA Gooch	5	31.0	9	72	1	72.00	—	—	—	—	1/30
IT Botham	3	80.0	15	241	3	80.33	—	—	—	2	2/63
PJ Newport	1	44.0	7	175	2	87.50	—	—	3	—	2/153
PW Jarvis	2	69.2	8	290	2	145.00	—	—	—	—	1/20
DE Malcolm	1	44.0	2	166	1	166.00	1	1	15	2	1/166
EE Hemmings	1	33.0	9	81	—	—	—	—	—	—	—
KJ Barnett	3	6.0	—	32	—	—	—	—	—	—	—
MA Atherton	2	8.0	—	34	—	—	—	—	2	—	—
TS Curtis	3	3.0	—	7	—	—	—	—	—	—	—

Centuries for Australia

Total	Batsman	Team	Venue
248	DM Jones	Warwickshire	Edgbaston
219	MA Taylor	England	Nottingham
177•	SR Waugh	England	Leeds
167•	DM Jones	Gloucestershire	Bristol
157	DM Jones	England	Birmingham
152•	SR Waugh	England	Lord's
151	DC Boon	Essex	Chelmsford
144•	TM Moody	Warwickshire	Edgbaston
141	MA Taylor	Gloucestershire	Bristol
138	GR Marsh	England	Nottingham
136	MA Taylor	England	Leeds
135	AR Border	Northamptonshire	Northampton
134•	MRJ Veletta	Glamorgan	Neath
128	DM Jones	Kent	Canterbury
122	DM Jones	England	The Oval
112	SR Waugh	Hampshire	Southampton
103	DC Boon	Hampshire	Southampton
102•	DC Boon	Nottinghamshire	Nottingham
100•	GR Marsh	Middlesex	Lord's
100•	SR Waugh	Essex	Chelmsford

Centuries against Australia

Total	Batsman	Team	Venue
143	RA Smith	England	Manchester
128•	RC Russell	England	Manchester
125	AJ Lamb	England	Leeds
106	DI Gower	England	Lord's
106	MR Benson	Kent	Canterbury
102•	MCJ Nicholas	Hampshire	Southampton
101	RA Smith	England	Nottingham
100•	PM Roebuck	Somerset	Taunton
100•	ME Waugh	Essex	Chelmsford

Best Innings Bowling Performance For Australia

Wkts	Bowler	Team	Venue
6/30	GF Lawson	Gloucestershire	Bristol
6/72	GF Lawson	England	Manchester
6/128	TM Alderman	England	Lord's
5/37	MG Hughes	Northamptonshire	Northampton
5/38	MG Hughes	Nottinghamshire	Nottingham
5/44	TM Alderman	England	Leeds
5/48	GF Lawson	Middlesex	Lord's
5/54	GD Campbell	Lancashire	Manchester
5/64	MG Hughes	Essex	Chelmsford
5/65	CG Rackemann	Nottinghamshire	Nottingham
5/66	TM Alderman	England	Manchester
5/66	TM Alderman	England	The Oval
5/69	TM Alderman	England	Nottingham
5/107	TM Alderman	England	Leeds

Best Innings Bowling Performance Against Australia

Wkts	Bowler	Team	Venue
7/54	WKM Benjamin	Leicestershire	Leicester
6/43	PJ Newport	Worcestershire	Worcester
5/44	RJ Maru	Hampshire	Southampton
5/76	NGB Cook	Northamptonshire	Northampton
5/84	PJ Newport	Worcestershire	Worcester

Highest Wicket Partnerships For Australia

Wkt	Total	Batsmen	Team	Venue
1st	329	GR Marsh, MA Taylor	England	Nottingham
2nd	220	TJ Zoehrer, SR Waugh	Essex	Chelmsford
3rd	349	DM Jones, TM Moody	Warwickshire	Birmingham
4th	227	MA Taylor, DM Jones	Gloucestershire	Bristol
5th	138	DM Jones, SR Waugh	England	Leeds
6th	146	IA Healy, TV Hohns	Leicestershire	Leicester
7th	147	SR Waugh, MG Hughes	England	Leeds
8th	92	DM Jones, TV Hohns	England	Birmingham
9th	130	SR Waugh, GF Lawson	England	Lord's
10th	24	GF Lawson, TM Alderman	England	Manchester

Highest Wicket Partnerships Against Australians

Wkt	Total	Batsmen	Team	Venue
1st	107	AR Butcher, H Morris	Glamorgan	Neath
2nd	75	KJ Barnett, BJM Maher	Derbyshire	Derby
3rd	114	KJ Barnett, AJ Lamb	England	Leeds
4th	90	PJ Prichard, ME Waugh	Essex	Chelmsford
5th	143	MCJ Nicholas, JR Wood	Hampshire	Southampton
6th	96	IT Botham, RC Russell	England	Birmingham
7th	142	RC Russell, JE Emburey	England	Manchester
8th	74	RA Smith, NA Foster	England	Manchester
9th	73	GC Small, NGB Cook	England	The Oval
10th	45	GR Dilley, JE Emburey	England	Lord's

Century Wicket Partnerships For Australia

Wkt	Total	Batsmen	Team	Venue
3rd	349	DM Jones, TM Moody	Warwickshire	Birmingham
1st	329	GR Marsh, MA Taylor	England	Nottingham
4th	227	MA Taylor, DM Jones	Gloucestershire	Bristol
4th	196	AR Border, DM Jones	England	The Oval
4th	183	DC Boon, DM Jones	Kent	Canterbury
2nd	167	DC Boon, TM Moody	Essex	Chelmsford
3rd	155	DC Boon, DM Jones	Nottinghamshire	Nottingham
4th	151	MRJ Veletta, AR Border	Glamorgan	Neath
7th	147	SR Waugh, MG Hughes	England	Leeds
2nd	146	DC Boon, AR Border	Middlesex	Lord's
6th	146	IA Healy, TV Hohns	Leicestershire	Leicester
2nd	145	MA Taylor, DC Boon	England	Lord's
5th	138	DM Jones, SR Waugh	England	Leeds
1st	135	MA Taylor, GR Marsh	England	Manchester
5th	133	DC Boon, DM Jones	Essex	Chelmsford
2nd	130	MA Taylor, AR Border	Warwickshire	Birmingham
9th	130	SR Waugh, GF Lawson	England	Lord's
3rd	127	GR Marsh, TM Moody	Lancashire	Manchester
3rd	127	DC Boon, AR Border	Northamptonshire	Northampton

Wkt	Total	Batsmen	Team	Venue
3rd	122*	GR Marsh, TM Moody	Middlesex	Lord's
4th	120	AR Border, DM Jones	England	Manchester
1st	119	MA Taylor, GR Marsh	Somerset	Taunton
3rd	118	DC Boon, SR Waugh	Hampshire	Southampton
3rd	117	MA Taylor, AR Border	England	Leeds
2nd	110	MA Taylor, DC Boon	Somerset	Taunton
2nd	102	MA Taylor, DC Boon	Hampshire	Southampton
4th	101*	AR Border, DM Jones	England	Leeds
2nd	101	MA Taylor, DC Boon	England	Nottingham

Century Wicket Partnerships Against Australia

Wkt	Total	Batsmen	Team	Venue
5th	143	MCJ Nicholas, JR Wood	Hampshire	Southampton
7th	142	RC Russell, JE Emburey	England	Manchester
5th	139	DI Gower, RA Smith	England	Lord's
3rd	114	KJ Barnett, AJ Lamb	England	Leeds
1st	107	AR Butcher, H Morris	Glamorgan	Neath
1st	101	SJ Cook, PM Roebuck	Somerset	Taunton

Australia First-Class Tours of England

Results for Australia

Season	Games	W	L	D	T	Captain
1878	15	7	4	4	—	DW Gregory
1880	10	5	2	3	—	WL Murdoch
1882	33	18	4	11	—	WL Murdoch
1884	31	17	7	7	—	WL Murdoch
1886	37	9	7	21	—	HJH Scott
1888	37	17	13	7	—	PS McDonnell
1890	34	10	16	8	—	WL Murdoch
1893	31	14	10	7	—	JM Blackham
1896	34	20	6	8	—	GHS Trott
1899	35	16	3	16	—	J Darling
1902	38	22	2	14	—	J Darling
1905	35	15	3	17	—	J Darling
1909	37	11	4	22	—	MA Noble
1912	36	9	8	19	—	SE Gregory
1919	28	12	4	12	—	HL Collins
1921	34	21	2	11	—	WW Armstrong
1926	33	9	1	23	—	HL Collins
1930	31	11	1	18	1	WM Woodfull
1934	30	13	1	16	—	WM Woodfull
1938	29	15	2	12	—	DG Bradman
1945	6	1	2	5	—	AL Hassett
1948	31	23	—	8	—	DG Bradman
1953	33	16	1	16	—	AL Hassett
1956	31	9	3	19	—	IW Johnson
1961	32	13	1	18	—	R Benaud
1964	30	11	3	16	—	RB Simpson
1968	25	8	3	14	—	WM Lawry
1972	26	11	5	10	—	IM Chappell
1975	15	8	2	5	—	IM Chappell
1977	22	5	4	13	—	GS Chappell
1980	5	1	2	2	—	GS Chappell
1981	17	3	3	11	—	KJ Hughes
1985	20	4	3	13	—	AR Border
1989	20	12	1	7	—	AR Border
Total	941	398	133	409	1	

Australia in England

Opponent	Venue	First Game	Games	W	L	D	T
ENGLAND	The Oval	Sep 6 1880	30	5	13	12	—
	Manchester	Jly 11 1884	25	5	7	13	—
	Lord's	Jly 21 1884	29	11	5	13	—
	Nottingham	Jun 1 1899	16	5	3	8	—
	Leeds	Jun 29 1899	20	6	6	8	—
	Birmingham	May 29 1902	8	1	3	4	—
	Sheffield	Jly 3 1902	1	1	—	—	—
Total			129	34	37	58	—

Continued

Opponent	Venue	First Game	Games	W	L	D	T
AER Gilligan's XI	Hastings	Sep 2 1964	1	1	—	—	—
A Shaw's XI	Leeds	Sep 11 1882	1	1	—	—	—
	The Oval	Sep 18 1882	1	—	—	1	—
Total			2	1	—	1	—
A Shrewsbury's XI	Holbeck	Sep 10 1888	1	—	1	—	—
	Manchester	Sep 13 1888	1	—	1	—	—
	Nottingham	Jun 26 1893	1	—	1	—	—
Total			3	—	3	—	—
A Staffordshire's XI	Stoke-on-Trent	Jly 3 1890	1	1	—	—	—
Cambridge & Oxford Uni's	Portsmouth	Aug 27 1888	3	—	—	3	—
	Leyton	Aug 7 1890	1	—	—	1	—
	Oxford	Jun 14 1972	1	1	—	—	—
Total			5	1	—	4	—
Cambridge University	Lord's	Jly 22 1878	1	—	1	—	—
	Cambridge	May 29 1882	23	15	1	7	—
	Portsmouth	Aug 17 1882	1	—	1	—	—
	Hove	Aug 25 1884	1	1	—	—	—
	Leyton	Aug 23 1886	2	—	—	2	—
Total			28	16	3	9	—
CB Fry's XI	Wicklow, Ireland	Sep 12 1912	1	—	1	—	—
CE De Trafford's XI	Crystal Palace	May 18 1896	1	1	—	—	—
CI Thornton's XI	Chiswick Park	Jly 2 1886	1	—	—	1	—
	Surrey	May 7 1888	1	1	—	—	—
	Scarborough	Sep 4 1893	8	—	3	5	—
Total			10	1	3	6	—
Combined Services	Kingston	Sep 5 1953	1	1	—	—	—
Derbyshire	Derby	May 17 1880	17	11	1	5	—
	Chesterfield	Jun 23 1926	10	5	—	5	—
Total			27	16	1	10	—
Earl De La Warr's XI	Bexhill	Jly 30 1896	1	—	1	—	—
England XI	Derby	Aug 14 1882	1	—	—	1	—
	Harrogate	Sep 23 1882	3	2	—	1	—
	Birmingham	May 26 1884	3	2	—	1	—
	Huddersfield	Jly 3 1884	1	—	—	1	—
	Stoke-on-Trent	Jly 26 1886	2	1	—	1	—
	Lord's	Sep 19 1886	4	2	—	2	—
	Hastings	Aug 3 1888	3	2	—	1	—
	Crystal Palace	Aug 23 1888	1	—	1	—	—
	Manchester	Sep 18 1890	2	—	1	1	—
	Eastbourne	May 18 1899	3	2	1	—	—
	Truro	Jly 7 1899	1	1	—	—	—
	Bradford	Jun 26 1902	1	1	—	—	—
	Bournemouth	Aug 31 1905	1	1	—	—	—
	Blackpool	Aug 12 1909	3	1	—	2	—
	Norwich	Aug 27 1912	1	—	—	1	—
	Folkestone	Sep 1 1926	4	—	—	4	—
	Scarborough	Sep 10 1930	4	2	1	1	—
	Sheffield	Jun 23 1945	1	—	1	—	—
Total			39	17	5	17	—
Essex	Leyton	May 14 1896	14	5	2	7	—
	Southend	Aug 21 1919	9	8	1	—	—
	Chelmsford	May 16 1934	6	3	—	3	—
	Ilford	Jun 17 1972	1	—	—	1	—
Total			30	16	3	11	—

Opponent	Venue	First Game	Games	W	L	D	T
Gentlemen of England	Chelsea	Jun 17 1878	1	—	1	—	—
	Scarborough	Sep 9 1878	1	—	—	1	—
	The Oval	Jun 22 1882	3	2	—	1	—
	Lord's	May 29 1884	11	6	2	3	—
	Crystal Palace	May 4 1905	1	—	—	1	—
Total			17	8	3	6	—
Gentlemen of Scotland	Edinburgh	Sep 16 1880	1	1	—	—	—
GN Wyatt's XI	Portsmouth	Aug 19 1886	1	1	—	—	—
Glamorgan	Swansea	Jly 30 1921	14	3	2	9	—
	Cardiff	May 20 1961	2	—	—	2	—
	St Helens	May 14 1977	1	—	—	1	—
	Neath	Jly 20 1985	2	—	—	2	—
Total			19	3	2	14	—
Gloucestershire	Clifton	Sep 5 1878	8	3	1	4	—
	Cheltenham	Aug 18 1884	13	8	1	4	—
	Perth	Jly 10 1890	7	4	—	3	—
	Bristol	Jun 8 1921	15	8	—	6	1
Total			43	23	2	17	1
Hampshire	Southampton	Jly 6 1896	24	12	1	11	—
HK Foster's XI	Heraford	Jly 16 1919	1	—	—	1	—
Hurst Park Club	East Molesey	Sep 11 1890	1	—	1	—	—
I Zingari	Scarborough	Sep 7 1882	2	1	—	1	—
Kent	Canterbury	Aug 7 1882	30	12	6	12	—
	Maidstone	Jly 28 1890	1	1	—	—	—
	Gravesend	Jun 22 1893	1	1	—	—	—
Total			32	14	6	12	—
Lancashire	Manchester	Aug 15 1878	34	14	3	17	—
	Liverpool	Aug 27 1896	9	4	1	4	—
Total			43	18	4	21	—
Lancashire & Yorkshire	Manchester	Jun 26 1909	1	—	—	1	—
	Hull	Jly 29 1909	1	—	—	1	—
Total			2	—	—	2	—
Leicestershire	Leicester	Jly 13 1896	23	10	1	12	—
Leverson-Gower's XI	Scarborough	Sep 5 1945	2	1	—	1	—
Liverpool & Districts	Liverpool	Jly 31 1882	5	3	—	2	—
London County	Crystal Palace	May 5 1902	1	—	—	1	—
Lord Londesborough's XI	Scarborough	Sep 2 1886	5	1	2	2	—
Lord March's XI	Chichester	Jun 28 1886	1	1	—	—	—
Lord Sheffield's XI	Uckfield	May 12 1884	5	2	2	1	—
L Robinson's XI	Attleborough	May 14 1919	2	—	—	2	—
MCC	Lord's	May 27 1878	34	14	6	14	—
Middlesex	Lord's	Jun 20 1878	29	16	—	13	—
Midlands Counties XI	Birmingham	Jun 18 1896	2	1	1	—	—
Minor Counties	Stoke-on-Trent	May 23 1953	2	2	—	—	—
MR Bamford's XI	Staffordshire	Sep 7 1909	1	—	—	1	—

Continued

Opponent	Venue	First Game	Games	W	L	D	T
Northamptonshire	Northampton	Aug 17 1905	21	13	1	7	—
North of England	Manchester	Sep 14 1882	7	3	2	2	—
	Nottingham	Sep 1 1884	1	—	1	—	—
	Leeds	Sep 1 1890	1	1	—	—	—
	Birmingham	Jun 2 1926	1	—	—	1	—
Total			10	4	3	3	—
Nottinghamshire	Nottingham	May 20 1878	35	11	8	16	—
Oxford University	Oxford	May 15 1882	23	17	1	5	—
	Leyton	Jun 11 1888	1	1	—	—	—
	Portsmouth	Jun 19 1899	1	1	—	—	—
Total			25	19	1	5	—
Players of England	The Oval	Sep 2 1878	5	2	2	1	—
	Chelsea	Sep 11 1878	1	—	—	1	—
	Crystal Palace	Sep 27 1880	1	1	—	—	—
	Sheffield	Jun 30 1884	2	1	1	—	—
	Nottingham	Jun 21 1886	1	—	—	1	—
	Bradford	Sep 6 1886	1	—	—	1	—
	Lord's	Jun 19 1890	2	1	1	—	—
	Leyton	Jly 9 1896	1	1	—	—	—
	Harrogate	Sep 1 1902	1	1	—	—	—
Total			15	7	4	4	—
Players of the North	Bradford	Sep 20 1880	1	—	—	1	—
President's MCC XI	Lord's	Aug 19 1964	2	—	—	2	—
Rest of the World XI	Lord's	Aug 31 1968	1	1	—	—	—
Scotland	Edinburgh	Jun 30 1902	7	2	—	5	—
Second Class Counties	Birmingham	Aug 21 1893	1	1	—	—	—
SH Cochran's XI	Wicklow, Ireland	Sep 17 1909	1	—	—	1	—
Somerset	Taunton	Aug 21 1882	22	13	—	9	—
	Bath	Jly 13 1905	4	1	1	2	—
Total			26	14	1	11	—
SOUTH AFRICA	Manchester	May 28 1912	1	1	—	—	—
	Lord's	Jly 15 1912	1	1	—	—	—
	Nottingham	Aug 5 1912	1	—	—	1	—
Total			3	2	—	1	—
South of England	Chichester	Jun 26 1882	1	1	—	—	—
	Gravesend	Aug 28 1884	2	1	—	1	—
	The Oval	Sep 11 1884	3	1	2	—	—
	Hove	Sep 9 1886	1	—	—	1	—
	Hastings	Sep 16 1886	14	4	3	7	—
	Eastbourne	May 21 1896	1	1	—	—	—
	Crystal Palace	May 8 1899	1	—	—	1	—
	Bournemouth	Sep 12 1902	1	1	—	—	—
	Portsmouth	Sep 4 1919	1	1	—	—	—
	Bristol	May 26 1926	1	—	—	1	—
Total			26	10	5	11	—
Surrey	The Oval	Jun 3 1878	49	19	9	21	—
Surrey & Middlesex	The Oval	Sep 2 1912	1	—	1	—	—
Sussex	Hove	Aug 29 1878	32	14	2	16	—
The Lyric Club	Barnes	Jly 31 1890	1	—	1	—	—
The Orleans Club	Twickenham	Jly 8 1878	2	—	—	2	—
The Services	Portsmouth	May 14 1921	1	1	—	—	—

Opponent	Venue	First Game	Games	W	L	D	T
The United XI	Tunbridge Wells	Aug 31 1882	1	—	—	1	—
TN Pearce's XI	Scarborough	Sep 5 1956	4	4	—	—	—
Warwickshire	Birmingham	Aug 3 1896	22	9	1	12	—
Wembly Park XI	Wembly Park	Jun 8 1896	1	1	—	—	—
WG Grace's XI	Crystal Palace	Jly 20 1899	1	—	—	1	—
WH Laverton's XI	Wiltshire	May 15 1890	1	—	1	—	—
Worcestershire	Worcester	Jly 10 1902	19	10	1	8	—
Yorkshire	Huddersfield	May 30 1878	4	1	—	3	—
	Sheffield	Jly 1 1878	23	6	4	13	—
	Dewsbury	Jun 10 1880	2	1	—	1	—
	Bradford	Jun 6 1882	20	8	1	11	—
	Middlesborough	Jly 20 1882	1	1	—	—	—
	Leeds	Jly 10 1893	4	1	1	2	—
	Scarborough	Jly 2 1977	1	—	—	1	—
Total			55	18	6	31	—
Total in England			941	398	133	409	1

TEXACO TROPHY
Limited-overs Series

Australia lost this three match series on a count-back, but it did have the satisfaction of finishing the series on top. Australia and England won one match each and tied the other, but because England lost fewer wickets in the tied match the result counted in its favour. The two teams proved to be evenly matched, with the result that two of the games were closely contested and there was much entertaining play. Ground attendances were high and, commercially, the series was a big success.

TEXACO TROPHY – GAME 1
England v Australia
Old Trafford, Manchester
May 25 1989
Toss: England
England won by 95 runs

England batted first and made 9 for 231, only a moderately good score in a 55-over contest. Several England batsmen made promising starts but none went on to play a big innings. Graham Gooch top scored with an unusually cautious 52. The Australians started so badly in reply, losing three early wickets, that they never seemed likely to approach the England total. They were all out for 136 in the 48th over, a feeble effort which made some observers wonder if a one-sided series lay ahead.

England

Batsman	How Out	Ttl	Balls	Mins	4s	6s
GA Gooch	c Jones b Border	52	111	134	4	—
DI Gower (c)	c Healy b Rackemann	36	33	49	5	1
MW Gatting	c Boon b Waugh	3	12	20	—	—
AJ Lamb	b Lawson	35	59	80	—	—
RA Smith	c & b Alderman	35	40	41	4	—
IT Botham	c Boon b Lawson	4	12	9	—	—
DR Pringle	lbw b Waugh	9	18	40	—	—
SJ Rhodes (+)	b Lawson	8	16	16	—	—
PAJ DeFreitas	not out	17	20	33	—	—
JE Emburey	b Rackemann	10	11	14	—	—
NA Foster	not out	5	3	4	—	—
SUNDRIES: B. 0 LB. 12 W. 3 NB. 2		17	335	229	13	1
TOTAL	9 wkts for 231					

F/W: 55 70 125 161 167 179 190 203 220

Bowler	O	M	R	Wkts	NB	W
Alderman	11	2	38	1	1	—
Lawson	11	1	48	3	—	1
Rackemann	10	1	33	2	—	—
Waugh	11	1	45	2	1	2
Moody	8	—	37	—	—	—
Border	4	—	18	1	—	—
Overs:	55.0					

Australia

Batsman	How Out	Ttl	Balls	Mins	4s	6s
GR Marsh	c Rhodes b Emburey	17	78	101	1	—
DC Boon	b DeFreitas	5	9	15	—	—
DM Jones	c Rhodes b Foster	4	15	15	1	—
AR Border (c)	b Foster	4	6	7	1	—
SR Waugh	c Smith b DeFreitas	35	74	81	2	—
TM Moody	b Emburey	24	38	43	—	—
MRJ Veletta	lbw Pringle	17	31	32	1	—
IA Healy (+)	c Emburey b Foster	10	20	22	1	—
GF Lawson	c DeFreitas b Emburey	0	1	2	—	—
CG Rackemann	b Botham	6	9	20	—	—
TM Alderman	not out	0	2	2	—	—
SUNDRIES: B. 1 LB. 9 W. 4 NB. 0		14	283	175	7	—
TOTAL		136				

F/W: 8 13 17 64 85 115 119 120 136 136

Bowler	O	M	R	Wkts	NB	W
Foster	10	3	29	3	—	2
DeFreitas	8	3	19	2	—	—
Pringle	8	2	19	1	—	1
Botham	10.1	1	28	1	—	1
Emburey	11	—	31	3	—	—
Overs:	47.1					

Umpires: JW Holder & NT Plews

Man of Match: PAJ DeFreitas

TEXACO TROPHY – GAME 2
England v Australia
Trent Bridge, Nottingham
May 27 1989
Toss: England
Australia won by 6 wkts

Batting first again, England lost just 5 wickets yet managed to score only a modest 226. Allan Lamb played a superb innings, scoring 100 not out at the rate of almost a run per ball. An interesting feature of the Australian bowling was that Tim May, the off-spinner, was the most economical bowler, conceding only 35 runs from 11 overs. Each of the five top Australian batsmen made a good start, but none managed to build on it. Steve Waugh looked in fine form when he was run out for 43, a mishap which probably cost Australia the match. In an exciting last over, the Australians had to score 7 to win but managed only 6, tying the match with a bye off the last ball.

England

Batsman	How Out	Ttl	Balls	Mins	4s	6s
GA Gooch	c Jones b Alderman	10	35	45	—	—
DI Gower (c)	b Waugh	28	59	88	3	—
MW Gatting	b May	37	76	104	3	—
AJ Lamb	not out	100	105	140	9	—
RA Smith	st Healy b May	3	9	6	—	—
IT Botham	run out	8	15	17	—	—
DR Pringle	not out	25	32	51	2	—
SJ Rhodes (+)	did not bat					
PAJ DeFreitas	did not bat					
JE Emburey	did not bat					
NA Foster	did not bat					
SUNDRIES: B. 0 LB. 14 W. 1 NB. 0		15	331	230	17	—
TOTAL	5 wkts for 226					

F/W: 30 57 119 123 138

Bowler	O	M	R	Wkts	NB	W
Alderman	9	2	38	1	—	—
Lawson	11	—	47	—	—	—
Rackemann	11	1	37	—	—	1
Waugh	11	1	47	1	—	—
May	11	1	35	2	—	—
Moody	2	—	8	—	—	—
Overs:	55.0					

Australia

Batsman	How Out	Ttl	Balls	Mins	4s	6s
DC Boon	b Botham	28	35	61	2	—
GR Marsh	lbw Emburey	34	87	91	3	—
DM Jones	b Emburey	29	47	52	3	—
AR Border (c)	c Rhodes b Pringle	39	58	65	3	—
SR Waugh	run out	43	61	79	5	—
TM Moody	run out	10	7	12	—	1
IA Healy (+)	not out	26	28	50	—	—
GF Lawson	c Gooch b Foster	1	5	12	—	—
TBA May	b DeFreitas	2	3	8	—	—
CG Rackemann	not out	0	1	1	—	—
TM Alderman	did not bat					
SUNDRIES: B. 1 LB. 6 W. 7 NB. 0		14	332	227	16	1
TOTAL	8 wkts for 226					

F/W: 59 81 116 153 174 205 218 225

Bowler	O	M	R	Wkts	NB	W
Foster	11	2	44	1	—	2
DeFreitas	11	—	48	1	—	2
Pringle	11	1	38	1	—	1
Botham	11	—	42	1	—	2
Emburey	11	—	47	2	—	—
Overs:	55.0					

Umpires: HD Bird & JH Hampshire

Man of Match: AJ Lamb

TEXACO TROPHY – GAME 3
England v Australia
Lord's
May 29 1989
Toss: England
Match Tied

Opening for England, Graham Gooch played a superb innings, scoring 136 from only 162 balls. England made 123 before losing its first wicket and 180 before losing its second, at which point Australia looked almost out of contention. England was 7 for 278 at the end of its 55 overs, a total which, to judge from their previous form, seemed beyond the reach of the Australians. If Australia was to win, at least one Australian needed to play a sterling innings, and Geoff Marsh proved to be the man for the occasion. He batted right through the Australian innings for 111 not out, scoring runs steadily at one end while more attacking batsmen (most notably Allan Border and Steve Waugh) battered the bowling at the other. Again, the result was decided in the last over, Australia winning with three balls to spare.

England

Batsman	How Out	Ttl	Balls	Mins	4s	6s
GA Gooch	b Alderman	136	162	229	11	—
DI Gower (c)	c Veletta b Moody	61	100	127	6	—
MW Gatting	run out	18	31	46	2	—
AJ Lamb	lbw b Alderman	0	1	3	—	—
RA Smith	b Rackemann	21	22	37	1	—
IT Botham	not out	25	11	21	3	1
PAJ DeFreitas	c Rackemann b Alderman	0	2	2	—	—
DR Pringle	run out	0	1	2	—	—
SJ Rhodes (+)	not out	1	1	3	—	—
JE Emburey	did not bat					
NA Foster	did not bat					
SUNDRIES: B. 0 LB. 14 W. 2 NB. 0		16	331	241	23	1
TOTAL	7 wkts for 278					

F/W: 123 180 182 239 266 266 268

Bowler	O	M	R	Wkts	NB	W
Alderman	11	2	36	3	—	1
Rackemann	11	—	56	1	—	—
Lawson	11	—	48	—	—	1
Waugh	11	—	70	—	—	—
May	6	—	33	—	—	—
Moody	5	—	21	1	—	—
Overs:	54.3					

Australia

Batsman	How Out	Ttl	Balls	Mins	4s	6s
GR Marsh	not out	111	162	217	7	1
DC Boon	lbw Foster	19	17	21	3	—
DM Jones	c Gower b Emburey	27	67	71	2	—
AR Border (c)	b Pringle	53	46	70	5	—
SR Waugh	c Gooch b Foster	35	32	41	—	2
TM Moody	not out	6	4	6	—	—
MRJ Veletta (+)	did not bat					
TBA May	did not bat					
GF Lawson	did not bat					
CG Rackemann	did not bat					
TM Alderman	did not bat					
SUNDRIES: B. 0 LB. 18 W. 9 NB. 1		28	328	217	17	3
TOTAL	4 wkts for 279					

F/W: 24 84 197 268

Bowler	O	M	R	Wkts	NB	W
DeFreitas	11	1	50	—	—	—
Foster	11	—	57	2	—	2
Botham	11	—	43	—	—	4
Pringle	10.3	—	50	1	1	1
Emburey	11	—	61	1	—	2
Overs:	54.3					

Umpires: BJ Meyer & DR Shepherd

Man of Match: GR Marsh

1989 Texaco Trophy

Australia

Batsman	M	Inn	NO	Runs	HS	50	100	Avrge	Ct/St
GR Marsh	3	3	1	162	111*	—	1	81.00	—
SR Waugh	3	3	—	113	43	—	—	37.67	—
IA Healy	2	2	1	36	26*	—	—	36.00	1/1
AR Border	3	3	—	96	53	1	—	32.00	—
TM Moody	3	3	1	40	24	—	—	20.00	—
DM Jones	3	3	—	60	29	—	—	20.00	2
DC Boon	3	3	—	52	28	—	—	17.33	2
MRJ Veletta	2	1	—	17	17	—	—	17.00	1
CG Rackemann	3	2	1	6	6	—	—	6.00	1
TBA May	2	1	—	2	2	—	—	2.00	—
GF Lawson	3	2	—	1	1	—	—	0.50	—
TM Alderman	3	1	1	0	0*	—	—	—	1

Bowler	M	Overs	Mdns	Runs	Wkts	Avrge	5wi	NB	W	Best
AR Border	3	4.0	—	18	1	18.00	—	—	—	1/18
TM Alderman	3	31.0	6	112	5	22.40	—	1	1	3/36
TBA May	2	17.0	1	68	2	34.00	—	—	—	2/35
CG Rackemann	3	32.0	2	126	3	42.00	—	—	1	2/33
GF Lawson	3	33.0	1	143	3	47.67	—	—	2	3/48
SR Waugh	3	33.0	2	162	3	54.00	—	1	2	2/45
TM Moody	3	15.0	—	66	1	66.00	—	—	—	1/21

England

Batsman	M	Inn	NO	Runs	HS	50	100	Avrge	Ct/St
AJ Lamb	3	3	1	135	100*	—	1	67.50	—
GA Gooch	3	3	—	198	136	1	1	66.00	2
DI Gower	3	3	—	125	61	1	—	41.67	1
RA Smith	3	3	—	59	35	—	—	19.67	1
MW Gatting	3	3	—	58	37	—	—	19.33	—
IT Botham	3	3	1	37	25*	—	—	18.50	—
PAJ DeFreitas	3	2	1	17	17*	—	—	17.00	1
DR Pringle	3	3	1	34	25*.	—	—	17.00	—
JE Emburey	3	1	—	10	10	—	—	10.00	1
SJ Rhodes	3	2	1	9	8	—	—	9.00	3/-
NA Foster	3	1	1	5	5*	—	—	—	—

Bowler	M	Overs	Mdns	Runs	Wkts	Avrge	5wi	NB	W	Best
NA Foster	3	32.0	5	130	6	21.67	—	—	6	3/29
JE Emburey	3	33.0	—	139	6	23.17	—	—	2	3/31
DR Pringle	3	29.3	3	107	3	35.67	—	1	3	1/19
PAJ DeFreitas	3	30.0	4	117	3	39.00	—	—	2	2/19
IT Botham	3	32.1	1	113	2	56.50	—	—	7	1/28

AUSTRALIANS IN EUROPE

The Netherlands v Australians
Not First-Class
The Hague
Sep 2 1989
Toss: Australians
Result: Australians won by 57 runs

Australians

Batsman	How Out	Ttl
DC Boon	b Holland	82
MRJ Veletta	c & b Aponso	16
DM Jones	c Vos b Lubbers	6
TM Moody	b Lubbers	2
AR Border (c)	c Jansen b Lubbers	7
SR Waugh	b Jansen	34
TJ Zoehrer	c Ruskamp b Bakker	6
IA Healy (+)	c Lifmann b Jansen	7
TBA May	not out	31
GF Lawson	run out	15
CG Rackemann	did not bat	
SUNDRIES: B. 2 LB. 4 W. 0 NB. 1		7
TOTAL	9 wkts for 213	

F/W: 66 77 87 95 147 155 161 181 213

Bowler	O	M	R	Wkts
Jansen	11	1	48	2
Bakker	12	3	43	1
Aponso	12	2	33	1
Lubbers	12	1	63	3
Holland	3	—	20	1
Overs:	50.0			

The Netherlands

Batsman	How Out	Ttl
E Gouka	c Boon b Rackemann	2
GJAF Aponso	c Healy b Rackemann	11
RE Lifmann	st Healy b May	18
NE Clarke	c Veletta b Moody	21
P Holland	c Veletta b Jones	24
R Gomes	st Healy b Zoehrer	19
SW Lubbers (c)	c Moody b Zoehrer	2
R Vos	c Veletta b Jones	13
C Ruskamp (+)	st Healy b Zoehrer	1
F Jansen	not out	9
PJ Bakker	not out	20
SUNDRIES: B. 0 LB. 3 W. 11 NB. 2		16
TOTAL	9 wkts for 156	

F/W: 3 23 54 62 96 98 110 119 129

Bowler	O	M	R	Wkts
Lawson	6	2	12	—
Rackemann	6	—	23	2
Moody	6	1	17	1
May	10	1	20	1
Zoehrer	10	3	33	3
Jones	9	1	39	2
Boon	3	1	9	—
Overs:	50.0			

Umpires: R Dukker & WJ van Wijk

12th Men: J Donelan (The Netherlands) & MA Taylor Australia)

The Netherlands v Australians
Not First-Class
The Hague
Sep 3 1989
Toss: The Netherlands
Result: Australians won by 4 wkts

The Netherlands

Batsman	How Out	Ttl
E Gouka	c Border b Rackemann	14
GJAFF Aponso	c Taylor b Rackemann	7
RE Lifmann	run out	13
NE Clarke	b May	5
SW Lubbers (c)	c May b Zoehrer	30
R Gomes	run out	16
RP Lefebvre	c Healy b Border	0
A van Lomwell	c Waugh b Border	12
C Ruskamp (+)	not out	24
F Jansen	not out	18
PJ Bakker	did not bat	
SUNDRIES: B. 3 LB. 2 W. 9 NB. 1		15
TOTAL	8 wkts for 154	

F/W: 22 27 45 48 95 95 95 120

Bowler	O	M	R	Wkts
Lawson	5	2	4	—
Rackemann	7	1	18	2
Moody	10	—	23	—
May	10	2	32	1
Zoehrer	10	2	32	1
Border	8	1	40	2
Overs:	50.0			

Australians

Batsman	How Out	Ttl
MRJ Veletta	run out	25
MA Taylor	c Lubbers b Bakker	0
DM Jones	c Lubbers b Bakker	0
TM Moody	c Lefebvre b Bakker	61
AR Border (c)	c Bakker b Lefebvre	4
SR Waugh	c Ruskamp b Jansen	23
TJ Zoehrer	not out	9
IA Healy (+)	not out	0
GF Lawson	did not bat	
TBA May	did not bat	
CG Rackemann	did not bat	
SUNDRIES: B. 0 LB. 7 W. 2 NB. 1		10
TOTAL	6 wkts for 132	

F/W: 4 6 65 81 120 124

Note: Target reduced to 130 from 42 overs due to rain

Bowler	O	M	R	Wkts
Jansen	8.2	2	28	1
Bakker	9	3	20	3
Aponso	10	—	46	—
Lefebvre	10	4	24	1
Gomes	1	—	7	—
Overs:	38.2			

Umpires: ED Oha & JO Wilts

12th Men: R Vos (The Netherlands) & DC Boon (Australia)

Denmark v Australians
Not First-Class
Brondby Stadium
Sep 5 1989
Toss: Denmark
Result: Australians won by 45 runs

Australians

Batsman	How Out	Ttl
MA Taylor	b Mortensen	10
DC Boon	run out	48
DM Jones	b Henriksen	35
TM Moody	c Mikkelsen b Butt	53
SR Waugh	b Henriksen	8
MRJ Veletta (+)	b Mortensen	17
AR Border (c)	run out	2
CG Rackemann	b Mortensen	0
TJ Zoehrer	c & b Butt	8
TBA May	run out	2
GF Lawson	not out	4
SUNDRIES: B. 0 LB. 3 W. 1 NB. 0		4
TOTAL		191

F/W: 24 81 133 153 163 170 171 182 186 191

Bowler	O	M	R	Wkts
Mortensen	10	2	15	3
Thomsen	5	—	27	—
Butt	9	1	45	2
Henriksen	10	—	41	2
Mikkelsen	3	1	30	—
Strandvig	3	—	30	—
Overs:	40.0			

Denmark

Batsman	How Out	Ttl
P Jensen	b May	29
J Jensen	b Rackemann	6
T Jensen	c Moody b Zoehrer	26
S Mikkelsen	c Rackemann b Moody	0
A Ahead	c Zoehrer b Moody	1
S Henriksen (c)	st Veletta b May	48
O Mortensen	run out	5
A Butt	c Veletta b Taylor	9
S Thomsen	c (s)Healy b Taylor	9
N Bindsley (+)	not out	0
C Strandvig	not out	0
SUNDRIES: B. 5 LB. 3 W. 4 NB. 1		13
TOTAL	9 wkts for 146	

F/W: 38 38 44 56 72 111 135 146 146

Bowler	O	M	R	Wkts
Lawson	4	—	13	—
Rackemann	7	1	29	1
May	8	—	15	2
Moody	9	1	21	2
Zoehrer	7	—	26	1
Jones	3	—	27	—
Border	1	—	3	—
Taylor	1	—	4	2
Overs:	40.0			

Umpires: NO Bjerregaard & Bo Bluitgen

12th Men: JC Neilsen (Denmark) & IA Healy (Australia)

Denmark v Australians
Not First-Class
Slegelse Stadium
Sep 6 1989
Toss: Australians
Result: Australians won by 54 runs

Australians

Batsman	How Out	Ttl
DC Boon	c Bindsley b Thomsen	5
MA Taylor	c Mikkelsen b Thomsen	22
DM Jones	b Henriksen	56
TM Moody	c & b Henriksen	70
SR Waugh	c Henriksen b Mikkelsen	20
MRJ Veletta (+)	c Henriksen b Mortensen	6
AR Border (c)	run out	24
CG Rackemann	run out	4
IA Healy	not out	7
TBA May	b Mortensen	2
GF Lawson	run out	3
SUNDRIES: B. 2 LB. 2 W. 0 NB. 0		4
TOTAL		223

F/W: 7 42 131 166 173 185 210 210 216 223

Bowler	O	M	R	Wkts
Mortensen	10	2	27	2
Thomsen	9	2	56	2
Mikkelsen	10	—	65	1
Nielsen	2	—	29	—
Henriksen	8.1	—	42	2
Overs:	39.1			

Denmark

Batsman	How Out	Ttl
P Jensen	run out	15
J Jensen	b Rackemann	18
T Jensen	st Veletta b May	3
S Mikkelsen	run out	8
A Ahead	not out	77
S Henriksen (c)	c Rackemann b Border	12
O Mortensen	c Moody b Border	1
A Butt	c Boon b Jones	21
S Thomsen	st Veletta b Boon	7
N Bindsley (+)	not out	1
JC Nielsen	did not bat	
SUNDRIES: B. 1 LB. 4 W. 1 NB. 0		6
TOTAL	8 wkts for	169

F/W: 34 37 40 58 76 81 132 166

Bowler	O	M	R	Wkts
Lawson	4	1	8	—
Rackemann	6	—	19	1
May	8	2	23	1
Moody	4	1	14	—
Jones	8	—	51	1
Border	6	—	30	2
Boon	2	—	10	1
Taylor	1	—	6	—
Healy	1	—	3	—
Overs:	40.0			

Umpires: JC Hansen & J Petersen

12th Men: C Stradvig (Denmark) & TJ Zoehrer (Australia)

NEHRU CUP
Limited-overs
Series
OCTOBER-NOVEMBER 1989

Pakistan won the competition, played at various venues in India from October 15 to November 1, 1989, by narrowly defeating the West Indies before a crowd of 70 000 in an exciting final at Calcutta. Set the formidable task of scoring 274 to win, the Pakistanis achieved their goal with one ball to spare. It was a disappointing result for the West Indians, who had begun the tournament badly, losing to Australia and Sri Lanka in their first two matches, but had recovered to make the final. For the Pakistanis, it was a confirmation of their high world ranking. In their semi-final matches, Pakistan had beaten England by six wickets and the West Indies had beaten India by eight wickets.

The Australians' failure to make the semi-finals brought to an abrupt end the run of success they had been enjoying. Altogether, Australia won only two of its five Nehru Cup matches, yet it might still have made the semi-finals on the strength of a superior run rate if Pakistan had not beaten India. A review of the five matches shows that Australia's batsmen performed creditably enough but that their bowlers generally found the going difficult. For instance, Australia scored 247 against India and 242 against England yet lost both matches. The Australians also failed to hold a number of catches which, with hindsight, might have been considered crucial. A highlight of the Australian batting was Allan Border's innings of 84 not out in the match against England. He faced only 44 balls yet hit 5 sixes and 8 fours. Border said at the end of the tournament that Steve Waugh's inability to bowl because of a back injury had upset the rhythm of the team.

NEHRU CUP – GAME 1
England v Sri Lanka
Feroz Shah Kotla, Delhi
Oct 15 1989
Toss: England
England won by 5 wkts

Sri Lanka _____ 193 (48.3) PA De Silva 80, PAJ DeFreitas 3/38
England _____ 5/196 (48.4) RS Smith 81*, AJ Lamb 52

Man of Match: RA Smith

NEHRU CUP – GAME 2
Australia v England
Lal Bahadur Shastri Stadium, Hyderabad
Oct 19 1989
Toss: Australia
England won by 7 wkts

Australia

Batsman	How Out	Ttl
DC Boon	c Gooch b Fraser	0
GR Marsh	c Lamb b Small	54
DM Jones	run out	50
PL Taylor	not out	36
AR Border (c)	not out	84
SR Waugh	did not bat	
SP O'Donnell	did not bat	
IA Healy (+)	did not bat	
GF Lawson	did not bat	
TBA May	did not bat	
TM Alderman	did not bat	
SUNDRIES: B. 0 LB. 6 W. 4 NB. 8		18
TOTAL	3 wkts for 242	

F/W: 0 108 122

Bowler	O	M	R	Wkts	NB	W
Fraser	10	2	48	1	—	1
Pringle	10	3	42	—	4	—
Small	10	—	55	1	—	2
Capel	8	—	39	—	4	1
Gooch	10	3	35	—	—	—
Hemmings	2	—	17	—	—	—
Overs:	50.0					

England

Batsman	How Out	Ttl
GA Gooch (c)	lbw Border	56
W Larkins	c Border b May	124
RS Smith	not out	24
AJ Lamb	b Lawson	23
AJ Stewart	not out	4
RC Russell (+)	did not bat	
DR Pringle	did not bat	
DJ Capel	did not bat	
GC Small	did not bat	
EE Hemmings	did not bat	
ARC Fraser	did not bat	
SUNDRIES: B. 1 LB. 9 W. 0 NB. 2		12
TOTAL	3 wkts for 243	

F/W: 185 191 234

Bowler	O	M	R	Wkts	NB	W
Alderman	7	1	28	—	—	—
Lawson	10	1	51	1	—	—
May	10	—	55	1	—	—
O'Donnell	7.3	—	27	—	2	—
Border	10	—	43	1	—	—
Taylor	3	—	29	—	—	—
Overs:	47.3					

Umpires: LH Barker & Khizar Hayat

Man of Match: W Larkins

NEHRU CUP – GAME 3
Sri Lanka v West Indies
Municipal Ground, Rajkot
Oct 19 1989
Toss: Sri Lanka
Sri Lanka won 4 wkts

West Indies —————— 9/176 (50.0) AL Logie 54*, DL Haynes 42
Sri Lanka —————— 6/180 (47.1) AP Gurusinha 66, WKM Benjamin 3/22

Man of Match: AP Gurusinha

NEHRU CUP – GAME 4
Australia v West Indies
Chidambaram Stadium, Chepauk, Madras
Oct 21 1989
Toss: Australia
Australia by 99 runs

Australia

Batsman	How Out	Ttl
GR Marsh	c DL Haynes b RC Haynes	74
DC Boon	b Benjamin	1
DM Jones	c Best b Walsh	20
AR Border (c)	c Ambrose b RC Haynes	46
SR Waugh	not out	53
SP O'Donnell	c RC Haynes b Benjamin	17
IA Healy (+)	b Benjamin	2
MG Hughes	not out	3
GF Lawson	did not bat	
TBA May	did not bat	
TM Alderman	did not bat	
SUNDRIES: B. 1 LB. 12 W. 7 NB. 5		25
TOTAL	6 wkts for 241	
F/W: 2 35 147 169 230 237		

Bowler	O	M	R	Wkts	NB	W
Ambrose	9	1	37	—	—	2
Benjamin	9	2	38	3	—	—
Walsh	10	—	50	1	2	1
Marshall	10	—	31	—	3	2
Richards	6	—	36	—	—	1
RC Haynes	6	—	36	2	—	1
Overs:	50.0					

West Indies

Batsman	How Out	Ttl
DL Haynes	run out	5
CA Best	b Alderman	0
RB Richardson	c & b Border	61
AL Logie	b O'Donnell	8
IVA Richards (c)	b Hughes	5
PJL Dujon (+)	b Border	13
RC Haynes	c Jones b Hughes	18
MD Marshall	c Alderman b Border	12
WKM Benjamin	lbw Jones	2
CEL Ambrose	not out	0
CA Walsh	b Jones	6
SUNDRIES: B. 2 LB. 3 W. 4 NB. 3		12
TOTAL		142
F/W: 2 11 36 59 86 110 122 134 134 142		

Bowler	O	M	R	Wkts	NB	W
Alderman	6	—	19	1	2	—
Lawson	7	—	18	—	—	—
Hughes	6	—	27	2	1	1
O'Donnell	6	—	19	1	—	1
Border	10	2	20	3	—	—
Jones	6.1	—	34	2	—	2
Overs:	41.1					

Umpires: SK Ghosh & JW Holder

Man of Match: AR Border

NEHRU CUP – GAME 5
England v Pakistan
Baribati Stadium, Cuttack
Oct 22 1989
Toss: Pakistan
England won by 4 wkts

Pakistan _____ 9/148 (50.0) Salim Malik 42, GA Gooch 3/19
England _____ 6/149 (43.2) AJ Lamb 42, AJ Stewart 31

Man of Match: GA Gooch

NEHRU CUP – GAME 6
India v Sri Lanka
Gujarat Stadium, Ahmedabad
Oct 22 1989
Toss: India
India won by 6 runs

India _____ 8/227 (50.0) NS Sidhu 80, JR Ratnayeke 3/35
Sri Lanka _____ 221 (49.4) AP Gurusinha 83, Kapil Dev 3/26 Prabhakar 3/34

Man of Match: NS Sidhu

NEHRU CUP – GAME 7
India v West Indies
Feroz Shah, Delhi
Oct 23 1989
Toss: India
West Indies won by 20 runs

West Indies _____ 9/196 (45.0) RB Richardson 57, IVA Richards 44, Chetan Sharma 3/46
India _____ 176 (41.4) RM Lamba 61, IVA Richards 6/41

Man of Match: IVA Richards

NEHRU CUP – GAME 8
Australia v Pakistan
Wankhede Stadium, Bombay
Oct 23 1989
Toss: Australia
Pakistan won by 66 runs

Pakistan

Batsman	How Out	Ttl
Shoaib Mohammad	c Waugh b Alderman	73
Rameez Raja	c Jones b Lawson	2
Shahid Saeed	c & b Alderman	6
Javed Miandad	c Lawson b Border	34
Salim Malik	c Boon b Alderman	15
Ijaz Ahmed	c Border b Alderman	1
Imran Khan (c)	c Healy b Hughes	8
Wasim Akram	run out	28
Akram Reza	not out	12
Abdul Qadir	not out	5
Waqar Younus	did not bat	
SUNDRIES: B. 2 LB. 11 W. 3 NB. 5		21
TOTAL	8 wkts for 205	

F/W: 10 29 101 138 140 153 154 197

Bowler	O	M	R	Wkts	NB	W
Alderman	10	3	22	4	1	—
Lawson	10	1	34	1	—	—
Hughes	9	1	29	1	1	2
O'Donnell	10	1	38	—	2	—
Taylor	6	—	37	—	1	1
Border	5	—	32	1	—	—
Overs:	50.0					

Australia

Batsman	How Out	Ttl
DC Boon	run out	0
GR Marsh	c Malik b Younus	8
DM Jones	lbw Qadir	58
AR Border (c)	c Miandad b Imran	4
SR Waugh	b Imran	0
SP O'Donnell	lbw Imran	3
PL Taylor	not out	31
IA Healy (+)	c Ijaz b Shoaib	7
MG Hughes	lbw Qadir	0
GF Lawson	b Qadir	1
TM Alderman	lbw Wasim	0
SUNDRIES: B. 4 LB. 11 W. 9 NB. 3		27
TOTAL		139

F/W: 2 46 58 58 70 104 126 134 136 139

Bowler	O	M	R	Wkts	NB	W
Wasim Akram	6.2	—	21	1	3	1
Waqar Younus	7	2	27	1	—	1
Imran Khan	8	2	13	3	—	1
Akram Reza	10	—	26	—	—	4
Abdul Qadir	9	—	27	3	—	1
Shoaib Mohammad	3	—	10	1	—	1
Overs:	43.2					

Umpires: LH Barker & PD Reporter

Man of Match: Imran Khan

NEHRU CUP – GAME 9
England v India
Green Park, Kanpur
Oct 25 1989
Toss: India
India won by 6 wkts

England _____ 7/255 (50.0) AJ Lamb 91, AJ Stewart 61, W Larkins 42
India _____ 4/259 (48.1) Chetan Sharma 101*, NS Sidhu 61

Man of Match: Chetan Sharma

NEHRU CUP – GAME 10
Australia v Sri Lanka
Fatorda Stadium, Margoa
Oct 25 1989
Toss: Australia
Australia won by 28 runs

Australia

Batsman	How Out	Ttl
GR Marsh	run out	38
DC Boon	lbw Fernando	19
DM Jones	lbw Labrooy	85
AR Border (c)	b Labrooy	26
SR Waugh	run out	2
TM Moody	b Labrooy	12
SP O'Donnell	not out	6
IA Healy (+)	run out	3
MG Hughes	not out	8
GF Lawson	did not bat	
TM Alderman	did not bat	
SUNDRIES: B. 4 LB. 10 W. 8 NB. 1		23
TOTAL	7 wkts for	222

F/W: 40 105 160 165 190 205 210

Bowler	O	M	R	Wkts	NB	W
Ratnayeke	9	1	34	—	—	3
Labrooy	10	1	38	3	—	1
Wijegunawardene	10	—	40	—	1	1
Fernando	3	—	16	1	—	1
EAR De Silva	7	—	30	—	—	—
PA De Silva	9	—	36	—	—	1
Ranatunga	2	—	14	—	—	1
Overs:	50.0					

Sri Lanka

Batsman	How Out	Ttl
RS Mahanama	lbw Alderman	5
DSBP Kuruppu (+)	b Hughes	13
AP Gurusinha	c Boon b Lawson	13
PA De Silva	b O'Donnell	96
JR Ratnayeke	run out	2
A Ranatunga (c)	c Waugh b Border	15
HP Tillekratne	c Boon b O'Donnell	24
L Fernando	c Alderman b O'Donnell	8
GF Labrooy	run out	1
EAR De Silva	not out	7
KIW Wijegunawardene	b Lawson	0
SUNDRIES: B. 2 LB. 2 W. 4 NB. 2		10
TOTAL		194

F/W: 7 21 54 74 103 166 179 182 191 194

81

Bowler	O	M	R	Wkts	NB	W
Alderman	9	1	41	1	1	1
Lawson	8.1	2	23	2	—	1
Hughes	10	—	39	1	1	—
O'Donnell	10	1	48	3	—	2
Border	10	—	39	1	—	—
Overs:	47.1					

Umpires: LH Barker & PD Reporter

Man of Match: PA De Silva

NEHRU CUP – GAME 11
Pakistan v West Indies
Burlton Park, Jullundur
Oct 25 1989
Toss: Pakistan
West Indies won by 6 wkts

Pakistan ———— 5/223 (50.0) Aamir Malik 77, Salim Malik 44*
West Indies ———— 4/226 (48.3) RB Richardson 80, IVA Richards 47*, PJL Dujon 46

Man of Match: RB Richardson

NEHRU CUP – GAME 12
Australia v India
Chinnaswamy Stadium, Bangalore
Oct 27 1989
Toss: Australia
India won by 3 wkts

Australia

Batsman	How Out	Ttl
DC Boon	c Srikkanth b Amarnath	49
GR Marsh	st More b Ajay Sharma	27
DM Jones	c More b Ajay Sharma	53
AR Border (c)	b Ajay Sharma	41
SR Waugh	c Ajay Sharma b Kapil Dev	28
GRJ Matthews	lbw Kapil Dev	5
SP O'Donnell	c (s)Shastri b Prabhakar	17
IA Healy (+)	not out	14
MG Hughes	run out	1
GF Lawson	not out	3
TM Alderman	did not bat	
SUNDRIES: B. 1 LB. 7 W. 1 NB. 0		9
TOTAL	8 wkts for 247	

F/W: 59 109 165 188 203 214 233 236

Bowler	O	M	R	Wkts	NB	W
Prabhakar	7	1	35	1	—	—
Kapil Dev	10	—	49	2	—	—
Chetan Sharma	3	—	22	—	—	—
Amarnath	10	—	43	1	—	—
Arshad Ayub	10	—	49	—	—	1
Ajay Sharma	10	—	41	3	—	—
Overs:	50.0					

82

India

Batsman	How Out	Ttl
K Srikkanth (c)	c O'Donnell b Matthews	58
RM Lamba	lbw Matthews	57
MB Amarnath	b Matthews	5
DB Vengsarkar	c Boon b Lawson	25
M Azharuddin	c & b Border	8
Ajay Sharma	c Waugh b Border	32
Kapil Dev	c Healy b Lawson	9
Chetan Sharma	not out	20
M Prabhakar	not out	16
KS More (+)	did not bat	
Arshad Ayub	did not bat	
SUNDRIES: B. 0 LB. 11 W. 7 NB. 1		19
TOTAL	7 wkts for 249	

F/W: 115 122 132 141 191 199 209

Bowler	O	M	R	Wkts	NB	W
Alderman	6	2	23	—	1	1
Lawson	10	1	39	2	—	1
Hughes	6	—	27	—	—	3
O'Donnell	5.1	—	42	—	—	—
Matthews	10	—	56	3	—	1
Border	10	—	51	2	—	1
Overs:	47.1					

Umpires: LH Barker & Khizar Hayat

Man of Match: Ajay Sharma

NEHRU CUP – GAME 13
Pakistan v Sri Lanka
KD Singh Babu Stadium, Lucknow
Oct 27 1989
Toss: Pakistan
Pakistan won by 6 runs

Pakistan ———— 6/219 (50.0) Imran Khan 84*
Sri Lanka———— 213 (49.2) PA De Silva 83, HP Tillekeratne 71

Man of Match: Imran Khan

NEHRU CUP – GAME 14
England v West Indies
Roop Sing Stadium, Gwalior
Oct 27 1989
Toss: West Indies
West Indies won by 26 runs

West Indies ———— 5/265 (50.0) DL Haynes 138*, RB Richardson 44, GC Small 3/39
England———— 8/239 (50.0) RS Smith 65, GA Gooch 59, MD Marshall 4/33

Man of Match: DL Haynes

NEHRU CUP – GAME 15
India v Pakistan
Eden Gardens, Calcutta
Oct 28 1989
Toss: India
Pakistan won by 77 runs

Pakistan ———— 7/279 (50.0) Rameez Raja 77, Aamir Malik 51
India ———— 202 (42.3) K Srikkanth 65, RM Lamba 57, Mushtaq Ahmed 3/51

Man of Match: Imran Khan

NEHRU CUP – SEMI-FINAL
India v West Indies
Wankhede Stadium, Bombay
Oct 30 1989
Toss: India
West Indies won by 8 wkts

India

Batsman	How Out	Ttl
K Srikkanth (c)	run out	1
RM Lamba	c Richardson b Walsh	29
MB Amarnath	b Walsh	15
DB Vengsarkar	c Richards b Wassh	8
M Azharuddin	c Haynes b Simmons	38
Kapil Dev	lbw Ambrose	19
Ajay Sharma	b Benjamin	15
M Prabhakar	c Richards b Marshall	4
Chetan Sharma	c Richards b Benjamin	12
KS More	not out	5
Arshad Ayub	c Marshall b Ambrose	3
SUNDRIES: B. 0 LB. 3 W. 11 NB. 2		16
TOTAL		165

F/W: 3 50 55 76 107 131 141 151 159 165

Bowler	O	M	R	Wkts
Ambrose	8.5	—	13	2
Benjamin	9	2	34	2
Walsh	10	—	39	3
Marshall	10	2	19	1
Richards	4	—	21	—
Simmons	7	—	36	1
Overs:	48.5			

West Indies

Batsman	How Out	Ttl
DL Haynes	lbw Kapil Dev	64
PV Simmons	lbw Kapil Dev	11
RB Richardson	not out	58
PJL Dujon (+)	not out	20
IVA Richards (c)	did not bat	
KLT Arthurton	did not bat	
AL Logie	did not bat	
MD Marshall	did not bat	
WKM Benjamin	did not bat	
ELC Ambrose	did not bat	
CA Walsh	did not bat	
SUNDRIES: B. 2 LB. 4 W. 3 NB. 4		13
TOTAL	2 wkts for 166	

F/W: 22 139

84

Bowler	O	M	R	Wkts
Kapil Dev	8	—	31	2
Prabhakar	4	—	21	—
Arshad Ayub	10	2	29	—
Ajay Sharma	10	2	30	—
Srikkanth	7	1	30	—
Azharuddin	3	—	17	—
Lamba	0.1	—	2	—
Overs:	42.1			

Umpires: JW Holder & PJ McConnell

Man of Match: IVA Richards

NEHRU CUP – SEMI-FINAL
England v Pakistan
Vibharba CA Stadium, Nagpur
Oct 30 1989
Toss: Pakistan
Pakistan won by 6 wkts

England

Batsman	How Out	Ttl
GA Gooch (c)	c (s)Shoaib b Younus	35
W Larkins	c & b Reza	25
RS Smith	b Qadir	55
AJ Stewart	b Younus	0
N Hussain	lbw Qadir	2
AJ Lamb	c Aamir b Qadir	6
DJ Capel	run out	20
DR Pringle	not out	21
PAJ DeFreitas	not out	4
GC Small	did not bat	
ARC Fraser	did not bat	
SUNDRIES: B. 3 LB. 20 W. 3 NB. 0		26
TOTAL	7 wkts for 194	

F/W: 44 102 103 136 144 145 184

Bowler	O	M	R	Wkts
Imran Khan	4	—	26	—
Wasim Akram	6	—	28	—
Akram Reza	5	—	28	1
Waqar Younus	6	1	40	2
Mushtaq Ahmed	3	—	19	—
Abdul Qadir	6	—	30	3
Overs:	30.0			

Pakistan

Batsman	How Out	Ttl
Rameez Raja	not out	85
Javed Miandad	b DeFreitas	17
Ijaz Ahmed	c Smith b DeFreitas	2
Imran Khan (c)	lbw Small	15
Salim Malik	c Lamb b Fraser	66
Wasim Akram	not out	0
Aamir Malik (+)	did not bat	
Abdul Qadir	did not bat	
Akram Reza	did not bat	
Mushtaq Ahmed	did not bat	
Waqar Younus	did not bat	
SUNDRIES: B. 0 LB. 10 W. 0 NB. 0		10
TOTAL	4 wkts for 195	

F/W: 26 32 69 191

▶

Bowler	O	M	R	Wkts
Fraser	6	—	58	1
DeFreitas	6	—	40	2
Capel	6	—	24	—
Pringle	5	—	33	—
Small	5.3	—	30	1
Overs:	28.3			

Umpires: RB Gupta & VK Ramaswamy
Man of Match: Rameez Raja

NEHRU CUP – FINAL
West Indies v Pakistan
Eden Gardens, Calcutta
Nov 1 1989
Toss: West Indies
Pakistan by 4 wkts

West Indies

Batsman	How Out	Ttl
DL Haynes	not out	107
PV Simmons	c Ijaz b Mushtaq	40
RB Richardson	b Reza	27
IVA Richards (c)	c Mushtaq b Imran	21
PJL Dujon (+)	c Qadir b Imran	28
AL Logie	c (s)Shoaib b Imran	14
MD Marshall	not out	10
WKM Benjamin	did not bat	
ELC Ambrose	did not bat	
RC Haynes	did not bat	
CA Walsh	did not bat	
SUNDRIES: B. 11 LB. 14 W. 1 NB. 0		26
TOTAL	5 wkts for 273	

F/W: 83 144 175 221 244

Bowler	O	M	R	Wkts
Aaqib Javed	10	2	25	—
Wasim Akram	10	1	46	—
Akram Reza	5	—	26	1
Mushtaq Ahmed	9	—	55	1
Abdul Qadir	7	—	49	—
Imran Khan	9	—	47	3
Overs:	50.0			

Pakistan

Batsman	How Out	Ttl
Aamir Malik (+)	c Dujon b Benjamin	3
Rameez Raja	c Logie b Walsh	35
Ijaz Ahmed	run out	56
Javed Miandad	c Richards b Benjamin	17
Salim Malik	c Dujon b Ambrose	71
Imran Khan (c)	not out	55
Akram Reza	run out	19
Wasim Akram	not out	6
Abdul Qadir	did not bat	
Mushtaq Ahmed	did not bat	
Aaqib Javed	did not bat	
SUNDRIES: B. 0 LB. 4 W. 10 NB. 1		15
TOTAL	6 wkts for 277	

F/W: 4 64 110 133 226 270

Bowler	O	M	R	Wkts
Ambrose	10	—	41	1
Benjamin	10	—	71	2
Marshall	10	—	43	—
Walsh	10	—	55	1
RC Haynes	3	—	21	—
Richards	6.5	—	42	—
Overs:	49.5			

Umpires: SK Ghosh & PD Reporter

Man of Match: Imran Khan

1989/90 Nehru Cup Averages

Batsman	Country	M	Inn	NO	Runs	HS	50	100	Avrge
Imran Khan	Pak	10	10	5	374	84°	3	—	74.80
RA Smith	Eng	6	6	2	244	81°	3	—	61.00
Salim Malik	Pak	11	11	2	539	102	4	1	59.89
PA De Silva	SL	5	5	—	280	96	3	—	56.00
DM Jones	Aus	5	5	—	266	85	4	—	53.20
NS Sidhu	Ind	6	6	—	314	108	2	1	52.33
DL Haynes	WI	11	11	2	455	138°	2	2	50.56
AR Border	Aus	5	5	1	201	84°	1	—	50.25
RB Richardson	WI	11	11	1	413	80	4	—	41.30
GR Marsh	Aus	5	5	—	201	74	2	—	40.20
Rameez Raja	Pak	8	8	1	280	85°	2	—	40.00
W Larkins	Eng	6	6	—	239	124	—	1	39.83
AJ Lamb	Eng	6	6	—	214	91	2	—	35.67
RM Lamba	Ind	7	7	—	249	61	3	—	35.57
Shoaib Mohammad	Pak	8	8	—	281	73	3	—	35.13
MB Amarnath	Ind	9	9	1	258	88	1	—	32.25
IVA Richards	WI	10	9	1	242	47°	—	—	30.25
K Srikkanth	Ind	10	10	—	292	65	3	—	29.20

Bowler	Country	M	Overs	Mdns	Runs	Wkts	Avrge	5wi	Best
Wasim Akram	Pak	9	78.0	5	284	17	16.71	1	5/38
Benjamin WKM	WI	9	84.0	6	381	16	23.81	—	3/22
CA Walsh	WI	11	109.0	6	412	17	24.24	—	4/25
Kapil Dev	Ind	9	79.2	5	327	13	25.15	—	3/26
Abdul Qadir	Pak	11	89.4	3	416	16	26.00	—	3/27
CEL Ambrose	WI	11	104.0	7	381	14	27.21	—	2/13
M Prabhakar	Ind	10	85.0	7	361	12	30.08	—	3/34
Arshad Ayub	Ind	10	95.0	7	396	11	36.00	—	2/27
IVA Richards	WI	10	74.3	—	377	10	37.70	1	6/41
Mushtaq Ahmed	Pak	10	82.0	5	387	10	38.70	—	3/51

Australia

Batsman	M	Inn	NO	Runs	HS	50	100	Avrge	Ct/st
DM Jones	5	5	—	266	85	4	—	53.20	2
AR Border	5	5	1	201	84°	1	—	50.25	4
GR Marsh	5	5	—	201	74	2	—	40.20	—
SR Waugh	5	4	1	83	53°	1	—	27.67	3
SP O'Donnell	5	4	1	43	17	—	—	14.33	1
DC Boon	5	5	—	69	49	—	—	13.80	4
TM Moody	1	1	—	12	12	—	—	12.00	—
IA Healy	5	4	1	26	14°	—	—	8.67	2
MG Hughes	4	4	2	12	8°	—	—	6.00	—
GRJ Matthews	1	1	—	5	5	—	—	5.00	—
GF Lawson	5	2	1	4	3°	—	—	4.00	1
TM Alderman	5	1	—	0	0	—	—	0.00	3
PL Taylor	2	2	2	67	36°	—	—	—	—
TBA May	2	—	—	—	—	—	—	—	—

Bowler	M	Overs	Mdns	Runs	Wkts	Avrge	5wi	Best
DM Jones	5	6.3	—	34	2	17.00	—	2/34
GRJ Matthews	1	10.0	—	56	3	18.67	—	3/56
TM Alderman	5	37.0	7	133	6	22.17	—	4/22
AR Border	5	45.0	2	185	8	23.13	—	3/20
GF Lawson	5	45.1	5	165	6	27.50	—	2/23
MG Hughes	4	31.0	1	122	4	30.50	—	2/27
SP O'Donnell	5	38.4	2	174	4	43.50	—	3/48
TBA May	2	10.0	—	55	1	55.00	—	1/55
PL Taylor	2	9.0	—	66	—	—	—	—

NEW ZEALAND
TOUR OF AUSTRALIA
NOVEMBER 1989

THE NEW ZEALAND TOUR WAS A SHORT ONE, lasting less than three weeks in all, but it was an important one for Australian cricket, since it provided the Australian team with its first chance since the victorious Ashes tour to test itself against another Test side. The New Zealanders began the tour under-strength (their premier bowler, Richard Hadlee, had withdrawn) and, by their own admission, under-prepared. They received further setbacks after the tour got under way when one of their most consistent batsmen, Andrew Jones, and their leading spin bowler, John Bracewell, were sidelined by injuries. So Australia went into the Test at Perth strongly favoured to win and, accordingly, the pressure was on the Australian players to perform well. For the first three days of the Test the Australians met all expectations, compiling a large total and dismissing New Zealand cheaply. The remarkable resistance of the New Zealand batsmen on the last two days, however, made Australia's all-pace attack seem less than effective. The New Zealanders emerged from the Test with an honourable draw. Their batsman Mark Greatbatch won much admiration for his courageous batting in both innings, and although their young fast bowler Chris Cairns failed to take a wicket he showed enough ability to be considered a fine prospect.

1989/90 Tour of Australia

Date	Venue	Opponent	Result for New Zealand
Nov 8*	Perth	Western Australia	Lost by 8 wkts
Nov 10	Perth	Western Australia	Drawn
Nov 17	Adelaide	South Australia	Drawn
Nov 24	Perth	Australia	Drawn

* Denotes not first-class

Western Australia v New Zealanders
Not First-Class
WACA Ground, Perth
Nov 8 1989
Toss: New Zealanders
Result: Western Australia won by 7 wkts

Western Australia won this opening fixture of the New Zealanders' tour with unexpected ease. Batting first, New Zealand could manage only 8 for 181, despite an aggressive innings of 84 by Andrew Jones. New Zealand's other successful batsman, Jeff Crowe, was not out 51. A feature of the home side's bowling was the outstanding economy of Ken MacLeay, whose 10 overs cost only 17 runs. Western Australia needed only 34.1 overs to pass the New Zealand total. Tom Moody led the run chase with an exuberant innings of 94 not out, which he scored off only 102 balls.

New Zealanders

Batsman	How Out	Ttl	Balls	Mins	4s	6s
JG Wright (c)	c Zoehrer b Alderman	1	7	8	—	—
RH Vance	c Veletta b Capes	4	16	23	—	—
AH Jones	run out	84	122	150	8	—
MD Crowe	lbw Russell	10	24	40	—	—
MJ Greatbatch	run out	6	13	22	1	—
JJ Crowe	not out	51	95	105	1	—
JG Bracewell	b Alderman	8	12	12	—	—
GK Robertson	run out	2	6	6	—	—
BP Bracewell	c Veletta b Alderman	2	8	8	—	—
DK Morrison	not out	2	3	2	—	—
W Watson	did not bat					
SUNDRIES: B. 1 LB. 3 W. 2 NB. 5		11	303	196	10	—
TOTAL	8 wkts for 181					
F/W: 2 13 48 59 147 163 169 178						

Bowler	O	M	R	Wkts	NB	W
Capes	8	1	26	1	3	—
Alderman	9	—	33	3	1	1
Russell	7	—	26	1	1	1
MacLeay	10	2	17	—	—	—
Hogan	10	—	47	—	—	—
Moody	6	—	28	—	—	—
Overs:	50.0					

Western Australia

Batsman	How Out	Ttl	Balls	Mins	4s	6s
GM Wood (c)	b JG Bracewell	48	80	121	5	—
MRJ Veletta	lbw Watson	6	18	25	1	—
TM Moody	not out	94	102	133 11	2	—
WS Andrews	lbw BP Bracewell	0	3	3	—	—
JA Brayshaw	not out	13	21	32	1	—
TJ Zoehrer (+)	did not bat					
KH MacLeay	did not bat					
TG Hogan	did not bat					
S Russell	did not bat					
PA Capes	did not bat					
TM Alderman	did not bat					
SUNDRIES: B. 3 LB. 5 W. 5 NB. 10		23	224	160	18	2
TOTAL	3 wkts for 184					
F/W: 25 138 139						

▶

Bowler	O	M	R	Wkts	NB	W
Morrison	7	—	21	—	3	1
Watson	7	—	40	1	4	3
Robertson	6	—	46	—	3	—
BP Bracewell	7	1	36	1	—	—
JG Bracewell	7.1	1	33	1	—	1
Overs:	34.1					

Umpires: RJ Evans & G Bibby

12th Men: AD Mullally (Western Australia) & IDS Smith (New Zealanders)

Western Australia v New Zealanders
WACA Ground, Perth
Nov 10, 11, 12, 13 1989
Toss: Western Australia
Result: Drawn

A watchful 87 by Martin Crowe rescued New Zealand after the tourists had slumped to 4 for 49 in their first innings. Crowe shared in two partnerships which steadied the innings—one of 49 with Jeff Crowe (25) and another of 135 with John Bracewell (86). Bruce Yardley, returning to the Western Australian side after several years' retirement, took 3 wickets for 76. In reply, the Western Australians spent nearly 10 hours compiling a total of 9 declared for 374. Western Australian captain, Graeme Wood, top scored with a patient 125 not out, and Mike Veletta made 91. With a lead of 91, Western Australia was in a position to press for victory, and on the final day New Zealand was in deep trouble at 6 for 105, but John Wright and Ian Smith joined in a counter-offensive, and their partnership of 191 carried New Zealand out of danger. Both made centuries. Wright's was a careful innings lasting more than six and a half hours, while Smith's was an explosive innings scored at better than a rate of a run per ball.

New Zealanders

First Innings					Second Innings			
Batsman	How Out		Ttl	Balls	How Out		Ttl	Balls
RH Vance	c Moody b Alderman		1	19	(2)	lbw Mullally	1	5
JG Wright (c)	c Zoehrer Mullally		3	15	(1)	not out	107	282
AH Jones	b Matthews		13	49				
MD Crowe	c Mullally b Yardley		87	225	(3)	lbw Moody	10	30
MJ Greatbatch	lbw Matthews		0	6	(6)	c (s) McPhee b Hogan	3	48
JJ Crowe	c Veletta b Yardley		25	51	(4)	c (s) MacLeay b Yardley	5	26
JG Bracewell	c Andrews b Yardley		86	117		c Zoehrer b Yardley	18	47
IDS Smith (+)	b Mullally		26	51		c Zoehrer b Moody	123	120
BP Bracewell	c Matthews b Wood		8	46	(5)	c Marsh b Moody	9	40
DK Morrison	not out		0	4	(9)	not out	0	6
W Watson	run out		0	0				
SUNDRIES: B.5 LB.16 W.8 NB.5			34	583		B.8 LB.7 W.4 NB.1	20	604
TOTAL			283			7 wkts for 296		
F/W: 5 5 47 49 98 233 267 283 283 283					F/W: 3 20 27 44 67 105 296			

90

Bowler	O	M	R	Wkts	NB	W	Bowler	O	M	R	Wkts	NB	W
Mullally	21	5	48	2	2	5	Mullally	25	3	74	1	—	4
Alderman	9	3	11	1	2	—	Moody	28.1	11	89	3	—	—
Moody	16	4	43	—	—	—	Matthews	4.5—	9	—	1	—	
Matthews	17	2	52	2	1	3	Yardley	24	10	56	2	—	—
Yardley	22	4	76	3	—	—	Hogan	17	8	46	1	—	—
Hogan	10	1	32	—	—	—	Andrews	1	—	7	—	—	—
Wood	0.4—	0	1	—	—		Overs:	100.0					
Overs:	95.4												

Western Australia

First Innings

Batsman	How Out	Ttl	Balls
GR Marsh	c MD Crowe b Morrison	2	23
MRJ Veletta	c MD Crowe b JG Bracewell	91	243
TM Moody	lbw Morrison	34	45
GM Wood (c)	not out	125	341
WS Andrews	lbw Morrison	21	49
TJ Zoehrer (+)	c BP Bracewell b Morrison	3	7
TG Hogan	c JJ Crowe b BP Bracewell	47	86
CD Matthews	c Jones b JG Bracewell	28	39
B Yardley	c BP Bracewell b JG Bracewell	3	7
AD Mullally	lbw JG Bracewell	0	2
TM Alderman	did not bat		
SUNDRIES: B. 4 LB. 8 W. 1 NB. 7		20	
TOTAL	9 wkts dec	374	842

F/W: 8 65 203 238 242 326 369 373 374

Bowler	O	M	R	Wkts	NB	W
Morrison	27	4	71	4	6	—
Watson	45	9	122	—	1	1
BP Bracewell	32	8	88	1	—	—
JG Bracewell	34	5	81	4	—	—
Overs:	138.0					

Umpires: PJ McConnell & TA Prue

12th Men: KH MacLeay (Western Australia) & GK Robertson (New Zealanders)

South Australia v New Zealanders
Adelaide Oval, Adelaide
Nov 17, 18, 19, 20 1989
Toss: New Zealanders
Result: Drawn

The Adelaide pitch again proved a comfortable one for batsmen, and the match ended inconclusively in a high-scoring draw. South Australia's captain, David Hookes, was reported afterwards to have irritated the New Zealanders by batting down to the last man instead of declaring, and the New Zealanders' response was to occupy the crease for well over eleven hours while accumulating a total of 7 declared for 445. Glenn Bishop top-scored for South Australia with an enterprising 173, his third successive century against touring New Zealand teams, while Darren Lehmann played aggressively for 80. The Crowe brothers, Martin and Jeff, both scored centuries for New Zealand. Martin Crowe's careful innings was his fiftieth first-class century. South Australia batted for a little less than two hours in its second innings, and the young New Zealand fast bowler Chris Cairns took both wickets which fell, making his total four for the match.

South Australia

First Innings

Batsman	How Out	Ttl	Balls		How Out	Ttl	Balls
AMJ Hilditch	lbw Snedden	33	58	(2)	c JJ Crowe b Cairns	32	55
GA Bishop	b Watson	173	310	(1)	not out	26	96
PC Nobes	b Snedden	58	104		b Cairns	2	9
DW Hookes (c)	c Greatbatch b Snedden	8	16		not out	3	11
DS Lehmann	c Cairns b Patel	80	130				
PR Sleep	c Cairns b Watson	0	3				
JC Scuderi	not out	75	100				
DS Berry (+)	c JJ Crowe b Cairns	7	30				
PW Gladigau	lbw Cairns	0	8				
PJS Alley	lbw Patel	1	14				
DW Clarke	c Greatbatch b Patel	9	22				
SUNDRIES: B. 1 LB. 10 W. 0 NB. 4		15	795		B. 0 LB. 1 W. 0 NB. 3	4	171
TOTAL		459			2 for 67		

F/W: 72 212 223 343 343 386 402 416 429 459

F/W: 55 59

Bowler	O	M	R	Wkts	NB	W	Bowler	O	M	R	Wkts	NB	W
Morrison	22	3	90	—	—	—	Morrison	3	1	12	—	—	—
Cairns	31	4	108	2	1	—	Watson	6	—	12	—	3	—
Watson	25	4	103	2	—	—	Snedden	11	3	20	—	—	—
Snedden	26	3	85	3	—	—	Cairns	8	2	22	2	—	—
Patel	27.4	8	62	3	—	—	Overs:	28.0					
Overs:	131.4												

New Zealanders

First Innings

Batsman	How Out	Ttl	Balls
RH Vance	c Hookes b Alley	65	172
JG Wright (c)	lbw Alley	23	96
MJ Greatbatch	c Berry b Gladigau	36	53
MD Crowe	c Bishop b Alley	143	322
DN Patel	c Alley b Sleep	20	70
JJ Crowe	not out	109	279
IDS Smith (+)	lbw Sleep	4	15
CL Cairns	b Hilditch	39	92
MC Snedden	did not bat		
DK Morrison	did not bat		
W Watson	did not bat		
SUNDRIES: B. 0 LB. 5 W. 0 NB. 1		6	1099
TOTAL	7 wkts for 445		

F/W: 57 114 141 188 345 350 445

Bowler	O	M	R	Wkts	NB	W
Gladigau	33	10	82	1	—	—
Clarke	33	14	70	—	—	—
Scuderi	38	18	67	—	1	—
Alley	26	10	78	3	—	—
Sleep	49	13	131	2	—	—
Hilditch	4	—	12	1	—	—
Overs:	183.0					

Umpires: AR Crafter & DJ Harper

12th Men: BD Williams (South Australia) & GK Robertson (New Zealanders)

TEST

Australia v New Zealand
WACA Ground, Perth
Nov 24, 25, 26, 27, 28 1989
Toss: New Zealand
Result: Drawn

The Australian selectors appeared to tempt fate by choosing an all-pace attack for this match, and their choice eventually proved questionable. Having won the toss and sent Australia in, New Zealand was soon reminded that pace bowlers could no longer count on easy wickets on the Perth pitch. David Boon's double century was an inspired innings, scored off only 326 balls, and the first double century ever scored in a Test at Perth. Dean Jones played with a mixture of caution and aggression, and was in no trouble until his dismissal for 99 with the first ball after a drinks break. It was the ninth time in nine Tests that Australia exceeded 400 in its first innings—a record for any country—and New Zealand faced the prospect of batting for three days to save the match. The Australian pace bowlers made short work of the New Zealanders in their first innings, dismissing them in a little over a day and forcing them to follow-on. Wickets fell early in their second innings, too, and it looked as if Australia might win with a day to spare. But Mark Greatbatch, the top scorer in the first innings, dug in again, frustrating the Australian bowlers for 10 hours 55 minutes. His endurance allowed New Zealand to escape with a draw—and it raised serious doubts about the penetration of the Australian pace bowlers on a good batting wicket.

Australia

First Innings

Batsman	How Out	Ttl	Balls
MA Taylor	c Wright b Morrison	9	29
DC Boon	c Wright b Snedden	200	326
TM Moody	c Smith b Snedden	61	135
AR Border (c)	b Morrison	50	118
DM Jones	lbw Morrison	99	192
SR Waugh	c Greatbatch b Snedden	17	48
IA Healy (+)	c JJ Crowe b Patel	28	45
MG Hughes	c Wright b Snedden	16	32
GF Lawson	b Morrison	1	6
CG Rackemann	not out	15	35
TM Alderman	did not bat		
SUNDRIES: B. 1 LB. 9 W. 2 NB. 13		25	966
TOTAL	9 dec for 521		

F/W: 28 177 316 361 395 449 489 490 521

Bowler	O	M	R	Wkts	NB	W
Morrison	39.1	8	145	4	3	—
Cairns	12	2	60	—	—	—
Snedden	42	10	108	4	5	—
Watson	37	7	118	—	5	2
Patel	28	5	80	1	—	—
Overs:	158.1					

New Zealand

First Innings

Batsman	How Out	Ttl	Balls	Second Innings How Out	Ttl	Balls
JG Wright (c)	b Rackemann	34	110	c Border b Lawson	3	16
RH Vance	b Alderman	4	22	c Alderman b Rackemann	8	34
MJ Greatbatch	c Healy b Hughes	76	139	not out	146	485
MD Crowe	lbw Alderman	62	139	c Taylor b Moody	30	89
DN Patel	c Boon b Hughes	0	4	lbw Alderman	7	26
JJ Crowe	c Healy b Rackemann	7	58	lbw Hughes	49	115
IDS Smith (+)	c Lawson b Hughes	11	17	c Border b Hughes	0	1
CL Cairns	c Healy b Hughes	1	9	lbw Hughes	28	6
MC Snedden	not out	13	35	not out	33	142
DK Morrison	c Border b Lawson	3	22			
W Watson	lbw Alderman	4	7			
SUNDRIES: B. 1 LB. 6 W. 4 NB. 5		16	562	B. 0 LB. 14 W. 0 NB. 4	18	975
TOTAL		231		7 for 322		

F/W: 28 84 173 178 191 204 206 212 226 231

F/W: 11 11 79 107 189 189 234

▶

Bowler	O	M	R	Wkts	NB	W	Bowler	O	M	R	Wkts	NB	W
Alderman	25.4	7	73	3	2	—	Alderman	32	14	59	1	—	—
Lawson	22	5	54	1	—	4	Lawson	38	12	88	1	1	—
Rackemann	20	4	39	2	2	—	Rackemann	31	21	23	1	3	—
Hughes	20	7	51	4	1	—	Hughes	36	8	92	3	—	—
Moody	4	1	6	—	—	—	Moody	17	6	23	1	—	—
Border	1	—	1	—	—	—	Border	5	2	17	—	—	—
Overs:	92.4						Jones	3	2	6	—	—	—
							Overs:	162.0					

Umpires: PJ McConnell & RJ Evans

12th Men: GD Campbell (Australia) & GK Robertson (New Zealand)

Tour Statistics

1989/90 New Zealanders First-Class Averages

Batsman	M	Inn	NO	Runs	HS	50	100	Avrge	Ct/St
MD Crowe	3	5	—	332	143	2	1	66.40	2
MJ Greatbatch	3	5	1	261	146*	1	1	65.25	3
JG Bracewell	1	2	—	104	86	1	—	52.00	—
JJ Crowe	3	5	1	195	109*	—	1	48.75	4
JG Wright	3	5	1	170	107*	—	1	42.50	3
IDS Smith	3	5	—	164	123	—	1	32.80	1/-
CL Cairns	2	3	—	68	39	—	—	22.67	2
RH Vance	3	5	—	79	65	1	—	15.80	—
AH Jones	1	1	—	13	13	—	—	13.00	1
DN Patel	2	3	—	27	20	—	—	9.00	—
BP Bracewell	1	2	—	17	9	—	—	8.50	2
DK Morrison	3	3	2	3	3	—	—	3.00	—
W Watson	3	2	—	4	4	—	—	2.00	—
MC Snedden	2	2	2	46	33*	—	—	—	—
GK Robertson			did not play a first-class game on tour						

Bowler	M	Overs	Mdns	Runs	Wkts	Avrge	5wi	10m	NB	W	Best
JG Bracewell	1	34.0	5	81	4	20.25	—	—	—	—	4/81
MC Snedden	2	79.0	16	213	7	30.43	—	—	8	—	4/108
DN Patel	2	55.4	13	142	4	35.50	—	—	—	—	3/62
DK Morrison	3	91.1	16	318	8	39.75	—	—	9	—	4/71
CL Cairns	2	51.0	8	190	4	47.50	—	—	1	—	2/22
BP Bracewell	1	32.0	8	88	1	88.00	—	—	—	—	1/88
W Watson	3	113.0	20	355	2	177.50	—	—	9	3	2/103

1989/90 Australia v New Zealand Test Averages

Batsman	M	Inn	NO	Runs	HS	50	100	Avrge	Ct/St
DC Boon	1	1	—	200	200	—	1	200.00	1
DM Jones	1	1	—	99	99	1	—	99.00	—
TM Moody	1	1	—	61	61	1	—	61.00	—
AR Border	1	1	—	50	50	1	—	50.00	3
IA Healy	1	1	—	28	28	—	—	28.00	3/-
SR Waugh	1	1	—	17	17	—	—	17.00	—
MG Hughes	1	1	—	16	16	—	—	16.00	—
MA Taylor	1	1	—	9	9	—	—	9.00	1
GF Lawson	1	1	—	1	1	—	—	1.00	1
CG Rackemann	1	1	1	15	15*	—	—	—	—
TM Alderman	1	—		—	—	—	—	—	1

Bowler	M	Overs	Mdns	Runs	Wkts	Avrge	5wi	10m	NB	W	Best
MG Hughes	1	56.0	15	143	7	20.43	—	—	1	—	4/51
CG Rackemann	1	51.0	25	62	3	20.67	—	—	5	—	2/39
TM Moody	1	21.0	7	29	1	29.00	—	—	—	—	1/23
TM Alderman	1	57.4	21	132	4	33.00	—	—	2	—	3/73
GF Lawson	1	60.0	17	142	2	71.00	—	—	1	4	1/54
AR Border	1	6.0	2	18	—	—	—	—	—	—	—
DM Jones	1	3.0	2	6	—	—	—	—	—	—	—

1989/90 New Zealand v Australia Test Averages

Batsman	M	Inn	NO	Runs	HS	50	100	Avrge	Ct/St
MJ Greatbatch	1	2	1	222	146*	1	1	222.00	1
MD Crowe	1	2	—	92	62	1	—	46.00	—
JJ Crowe	1	2	—	56	49	—	—	28.00	1
JG Wright	1	2	—	37	34	—	—	18.50	3
CL Cairns	1	2	—	29	28	—	—	14.50	—
RH Vance	1	2	—	12	8	—	—	6.00	—
IDS Smith	1	2	—	11	11	—	—	5.50	1/-
W Watson	1	1	—	4	4	—	—	4.00	—
DN Patel	1	2	—	7	7	—	—	3.50	—
DK Morrison	1	1	—	3	3	—	—	3.00	—
MC Snedden	1	2	2	46	33*	—	—	—	—

Bowler	M	Overs	Mdns	Runs	Wkts	Avrge	5wi	10m	NB	W	Best
MC Snedden	1	42.0	10	108	4	27.00	—	—	5	—	4/108
DK Morrison	1	39.1	8	145	4	36.25	—	—	3	—	4/145
DN Patel	1	28.0	5	80	1	80.00	—	—	—	—	1/80
W Watson	1	37.0	7	118	—	—	—	—	5	2	—
CL Cairns	1	12.0	2	60	—	—	—	—	—	—	—

Centuries For New Zealanders

Total	Batsman	Team	Venue
146*	MJ Greatbatch	Australia	Perth
143	MD Crowe	South Australia	Adelaide
123	IDS Smith	Western Australia	Perth
109*	JJ Crowe	South Australia	Adelaide
107*	JG Wright	Western Australia	Perth

Centuries Against New Zealanders

Total	Batsman	Team	Venue
200	DC Boon	Australia	Perth
173	GA Bishop	South Australia	Adelaide
125*	GM Wood	Western Australia	Perth

Best Innings Bowling Performance For New Zealanders

Wkts	Bowler	Team	Venue
4/71	DK Morrison	Western Australia	Perth
4/81	JG Bracewell	Western Australia	Perth
4/108	MC Snedden	Australia	Perth
4/145	DK Morrison	Australia	Perth

Best Innings Bowling Performance Against New Zealanders

Wkts	Bowler	Team	Venue
4/51	MG Hughes	Australia	Perth

Highest Partnership Records For New Zealanders

Wkt	Total	Batsmen	Team	Venue
1st	57	RH Vance, JG Wright	South Australia	Adelaide
2nd	57	RH Vance, MJ Greatbatch	South Australia	Adelaide
3rd	89	MJ Greatbatch, MD Crowe	Australia	Perth
4th	47	MD Crowe, DN Patel	South Australia	Adelaide
5th	157	MD Crowe, JJ Crowe	South Australia	Adelaide
6th	135	MD Crowe, JG Bracewell	Western Australia	Perth
7th	191	JG Wright, IDS Smith	Western Australia	Perth
8th	88*	MJ Greatbatch, MC Snedden	Australia	Perth
9th	14	MC Snedden, DK Morrison	Australia	Perth
10th	5	MC Snedden, W Watson	Australia	Perth

Century Wicket Partnerships For New Zealanders

Wkt	Total	Batsmen	Team	Venue
7th	191	JG Wright, IDS Smith	Western Australia	Perth
5th	157	MD Crowe, JJ Crowe	South Australia	Adelaide
6th	135	MD Crowe, JG Bracewell	Western Australia	Perth

Highest Partnership Records Against New Zealanders

Wkt	Total	Batsmen	Team	Venue
1st	72	AMJ Hilditch, GA Bishop	South Australia	Adelaide
2nd	149	DC Boon, TM Moody	Australia	Perth
3rd	139	DC Boon, AR Border	Australia	Perth
4th	120	GA Bishop, DS Lehmann	South Australia	Adelaide
5th	34	DM Jones, SR Waugh	Australia	Perth
6th	84	GM Wood, TG Hogan	Western Australia	Perth
7th	43	GM Wood, CD Matthews	Western Australia	Perth
8th	14	JC Scuderi, PW Gladigau	South Australia	Adelaide
9th	31	DM Jones, CG Rackemann	Australia	Perth
10th	30	JC Scuderi, DW Clarke	South Australia	Adelaide

Century Wicket Partnerships Against New Zealanders

Wkt	Total	Batsmen	Team	Venue
2nd	149	DC Boon, TM Moody	Australia	Perth
2nd	140	GA Bishop, PC Nobes	South Australia	Adelaide
3rd	139	DC Boon, AR Border	Australia	Perth
3rd	138	MRJ Veletta, GM Wood	Western Australia	Perth
4th	120	GA Bishop, DS Lehmann	South Australia	Adelaide

New Zealand First-Class Tours of Australia

Results for New Zealand

Season	Games	W	L	D	T	Captain
1898/99	2	—	2	—	—	LB Cobcroft
1913/14	4	1	2	1	—	D Reese
1925/26	4	—	1	3	—	WR Patrick
1927/28	1	—	1	—	—	TC Lowry
1937/38	3	—	3	—	—	ML Page
1953/54	3	2	—	1	—	B Sutcliffe
1961/62	3	—	2	1	—	JR Reid
1967/68	4	—	2	2	—	BW Sutcliffe
1969/70	3	—	—	3	—	GT Dowling
1970/71	1	—	—	1	—	GT Dowling
1972/73	1	—	—	1	—	BE Congdon
1973/74	9	2	5	2	—	BE Congdon
1980/81	7	1	2	4	—	GP Howarth
1982/83	2	—	—	1	1	GP Howarth
1985/86	6	2	1	3	—	JV Coney
1987/88	6	1	2	3	—	JJ Crowe
1989/90	3	—	—	3	—	JG Wright
Total	62	9	23	29	1	

New Zealand in Australia

Opponent	Venue	First Game	Games	W	L	D	T
AUSTRALIA	Melbourne	Dec 29 1973	3	—	1	2	—
	Sydney	Jan 5 1974	2	—	1	1	—
	Adelaide	Jan 26 1974	2	—	1	1	—
	Brisbane	Nov 28 1980	3	1	2	1	—
	Perth	Dec 12 1980	3	1	1	1	—
Total			13	2	6	5	—
New South Wales	Sydney	Feb 24 1899	11	—	7	4	—
Queensland	Brisbane	Dec 19 1913	6	1	2	3	—
	Bundaberg	Dec 18 1982	1	—	—	1	—
Total			7	1	2	4	—
South Australia	Adelaide	Jan 16 1914	11	1	5	5	—
Tasmania	Hobart TCA	Dec 26 1969	1	—	—	1	—
	Launceston	Jan 12 1974	2	1	—	1	—
	Devonport	Dec 18 1987	1	—	—	1	—
Total			4	1	—	3	—
Victoria	Melbourne	Feb 17 1899	10	1	3	5	1
Western Australia	Perth	Mar 5 1954	6	3	—	3	—

AUSTRALIA – THE ASHES TEAM

Back Row, l to r: Errol Alcott (Physiotherapist), Trevor Hohns, Tim May, Geoff Lawson, Carl Rackemann, Tom Moody, Merv Hughes, Terry Alderman, Greg Campbell, Mike Walsh (Scorer). Front Row, l to r: Bob Simpson (Coach), Tim Zoehrer, Mark Taylor, Dean Jones, Allan Border (Captain), Lawrie Sawle (Manager), Geoff Marsh (Vice-captain), David Boon, Steve Waugh, Mike Veletta, Ian Healy

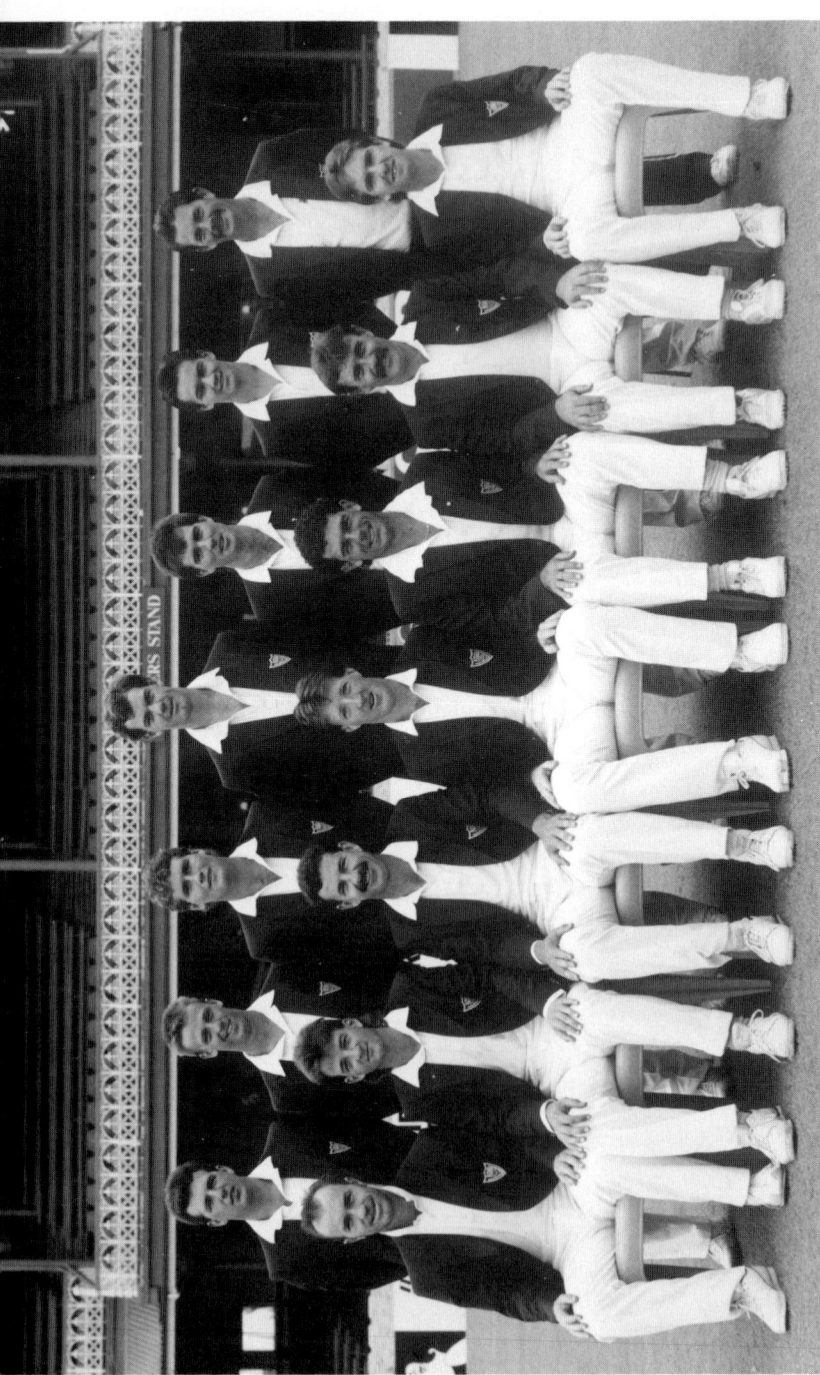

SHEFFIELD SHIELD – NEW SOUTH WALES

Back Row, l to r: Brad McNamara, Wayne Holdsworth, Phil Emery, Richard Stobo, Geoff Milliken, Adrian Tucker, Steve Nixon (Coach). Front Row, l to r: Greg Matthews, Mark Waugh, Steve Small, Geoff Lawson, Mike Whitney, Mark O'Neill, Trevor Bayliss

SHEFFIELD SHIELD – QUEENSLAND

Back Row, l to r: Stuart Law, Michael Polzin, Peter Cantrell, Brad Inwood.
Middle Row, l to r: Lindsay Trigar (Physiotherapist), Ian Healy, Stephen Storey,
Craig McDermott, Dirk Tazelaar, Richie Robinson (Coach). Front Row, l to r:
Allan Border, Greg Ritchie (Captain), Rob Kerr, Carl Rackemann

SHEFFIELD SHIELD – TASMANIA

Back Row, l to r: D O'Connor, D Gilbert, G Robertson, S Hookey, R Bennett, J Cox, L McGee (Physiotherapist). Front Row, l to r: A de Winter, R Tucker, G Campbell, D Wellham (Captain), D Boon, G Shipperd, R Soule. Absent: P McPhee, M Farrell, T Bower, T Cooley, P Faulkner

SRI LANKA
TOUR OF AUSTRALIA
NOVEMBER 1989–FEBRUARY 1990

IN THE FINAL RECKONING, the Sri Lankans lost many matches and won only a few, yet their performances on the tour confirmed their increasing strength as a cricket nation. They had more success than on their previous visit to Australia, especially in the Test arena, and they played well enough, often enough, to show that on their day they could be a match for any opposition. Their batting was full of talent, and, in particular, Aravinda de Silva's spirited performances with the bat in both Tests were among the most memorable of the summer. The Sri Lankans' bowling was obviously the weaker half of their game. Rumesh Ratnayake proved himself to be a fine bowler, and by taking 6 for 66 in the second Test he was largely responsible for giving Australian batsmen their biggest setback in more than a year. (In fact, it is necessary to go back thirteen Tests to find a lower Australian first-innings total than its 224 in this Test.) But for the most part Sri Lanka's bowling attack was not of international class, which in the one-day matches had the effect of putting immense pressure on its batsmen. Still, it is on record that Sri Lanka led Australia on the first innings in the first Test and that it held its own in the second Test until quite late in the match. Perhaps the most unfortunate feature of the Sri Lankans' tour was the second-string itinerary prepared for them from the end of the first Test to the start of the one-day internationals, and they could be excused if they found it hard maintaining their enthusiasm in the various minor matches they were called on to play.

1989/90 Sri Lankan Tour of Australia

Date	Venue	Opponent	Result for Sri Lankans
Nov 17	Canberra	New South Wales	Drawn
Nov 24	Sale	Victoria	Lost by an inns & 3 runs
Dec 1	Adelaide	South Australia	Drawn
Dec 8	Brisbane	Australia	Drawn
Dec 16	Hobart Bel	Australia	Lost by 173 runs
Dec 22*	Melbourne	Victoria	Lost by 109 runs
Dec 23*	Hastings	Victorian Country XI	Lost by 3 wkts
Dec 26*	Melbourne	Australia	Lost by 30 runs
Dec 30*	Perth	Australia	Lost by 9 wkts
Dec 31*	Perth	Pakistan	Won by 3 wkts
Jan 4*	Melbourne	Australia	Lost by 73 runs
Jan 6	Devonport	Tasmania	Drawn
Jan 10*	Adelaide	Australian Cricket Academy	Drawn
Jan 14*	Port Lincoln	South Australian Country XI	Won by 35 runs
Jan 17*	Bendigo	Australian Country XI	Drawn
Jan 21*	Coffs Harbour	New South Wales	Lost by 81 runs
Jan 23*	Grafton	New South Wales Country XI	Won by 3 wkts
Jan 26*	Rockhampton	Queensland	Drawn
Jan 28*	Rockhampton	Queensland	Lost by 5 runs
Jan 30*	Caloundra	Queensland Country XI	Won by 7 wkts
Feb 2*	Perth	Western Australia	Won by 4 wkts
Feb 4*	Perth	Western Australia	Lost by 65 runs
Feb 6*	Brookton	Western Australian Country XI	Won by 63 runs
Feb 10*	Brisbane	Pakistan	Lost by 5 wkts
Feb 15*	Hobart Bel	Pakistan	Lost by 6 wkts
Feb 17*	Adelaide	Pakistan	Lost by 23 runs
Feb 18*	Adelaide	Australia	Lost by 7 wkts

* Denotes not first-class

New South Wales v Sri Lankans
Manuka Oval, Canberra
Nov 17, 18, 19, 20 1989
Toss: Sri Lankans
Result: Drawn

In a sobering start to their Australian tour, Sri Lanka came close to losing the match outright. Having won the toss and asked New South Wales to bat, its bowlers made little impact on the New South Wales batting. Five of the first eight batsmen scored half-centuries, and New South Wales declared at lunch on the second day at 7 for 423. Because of rain and poor light, there was little further play that day, but on the third day the opener Athula Samarasekera scored a fine century and at stumps Sri Lanka was in a sound position at 3 for 217. On the last day, however, its batting collapsed, the last 6 wickets falling for 50 runs. New South Wales batted for an hour and a half and gave Sri Lanka 152 minutes to score 238 for victory. In that time, the Sri Lankans lost 7 wickets. Mike Whitney took 3 of them, as he did in the first innings, and if Geoff Lawson had not been injured and unable to bowl, Sri Lanka might have found it hard to hold out for a draw.

New South Wales

First Innings

Batsman	How Out	Ttl	Balls
SM Small	c Ratnayeke b Labrooy	36	75
MA Taylor	c Ratnayeke b Labrooy	53	69
TH Bayliss	c D Ranatunga b Labrooy	89	94
SR Waugh	c Gurusinha b Labrooy	57	68
ME Waugh	c Gurusinha b Labrooy	42	59
MD O'Neill	run out	65	118
PL Taylor	c Madurasinghe b Ratnayeke	2	10
GRJ Matthews	not out	52	123
PA Emery (+)	not out	15	59
GF Lawson (c)	did not bat		
MR Whitney	did not bat		
SUNDRIES: B. 0 LB. 9 W. 0 NB. 3		12	675
TOTAL	7 wkts dec	423	

F/W: 84 108 223 254 297 306 385

Second Innings

How Out	Ttl	Balls
not out	36	72
c Ratnayeke b A Ranatunga	28	24
lbw A Ranatunga	2	11
not out	11	31
B. 0 LB. 0 W. 1 NB. 4	5	138
2 wkts dec	82	

F/W: 54 58

Bowler	O	M	R	Wkts	NB	W
Ratnayeke	34	3	111	1	1	—
Labrooy	31	2	141	5	2	—
Madurasinghe	22	—	83	—	—	—
A Ranatunga	13	—	36	—	—	—
Samarasekera	1	—	15	—	—	—
Jayasuriya	3	—	14	—	—	—
De Silva	8	2	14	—	—	—
Overs:	112.0					

Bowler	O	M	R	Wkts	NB	W
Ratnayeke	9	2	38	—	4	1
Gurusinha	4	—	23	—	—	—
A Ranatunga	7	—	17	2	—	—
Madurasinghe	2	—	4	—	—	—
Overs:	22.0					

Sri Lankans

First Innings

Batsman	How Out	Ttl	Balls
D Ranatunga	c Emery b Whitney	56	231
MAR Samarasekera	c Emery b Matthews	133	258
AP Gurusinha	c & b O'Neill	8	36
PA De Silva	c Emery b Whitney	30	52
AGD Wickremasinghe	b Whitney	0	17
A Ranatunga (c)	lbw Lawson	4	11

Second Innings

How Out	Ttl	Balls
lbw Whitney	0	1
b Whitney	0	6
c Matthews b PL Taylor	45	92
c SR Waugh b Whitney	2	6
(9) not out	4	10
c Matthews b PL Taylor	18	25

Batsman	How Out	Ttl	Balls	How Out	Ttl	Balls
HP Tillekeratne	lbw Lawson	0	3	(5) lbw ME Waugh	5	66
ST Jayasuriya	lbw ME Waugh	27	37	(7) not out	27	20
JR Ratnayeke	lbw ME Waugh	1	13	(8) c Emery b O'Neill	12	16
MAWR Madurasinghe	not out	4	15			
GF Labrooy	absent injured					
SUNDRIES: B. 0 LB. 4 W. 0 NB. 1		5	673	B. 0 LB. 5 W. 0 NB. 1	6	242
TOTAL		268		7 wkts for 119		

F/W: 159 190 208 218 225 225 255 258 268

F/W: 0 1 9 14 59 98 113

Bowler	O	M	R	Wkts	NB	W	Bowler	O	M	R	Wkts	NB	W
Lawson	25	13	39	2	—	—	Whitney	9	2	21	3	—	—
Whitney	24	7	54	3	—	—	ME Waugh	6	1	29	1	1	—
ME Waugh	4.3	2	7	2	1	—	Matthews	11	4	32	—	—	—
PL Taylor	15	3	40	—	—	—	PL Taylor	11	3	28	2	—	—
Matthews	23	6	58	1	—	—	O'Neill	3	2	4	1	—	—
O'Neill	20	5	66	1	—	—	Overs:	40.0					
Overs:	111.3												

Umpires: IS Thomas & GE Reed

12th Men: WJ Holdsworth (New South Wales) & KIW Wijegunawardene (Sri Lankans)

Victoria v Sri Lankans
Sale City Oval, Sale
Nov 24, 25, 26, 27 1989
Toss: Victoria
Result: Victoria won by an inns & 3 runs

Victoria's overwhelming victory raised further doubts about the penetration of Sri Lanka's bowlers. Victoria lost two early wickets, but otherwise its batsmen looked untroubled by the Sri Lankan attack, and three—Jamie Siddons, Wayne Phillips and Simon O'Donnell—scored centuries in a first innings which Victoria closed on the second day at 6 for 507. O'Donnell's century, which included 3 sixes, was his first since his return to senior cricket after a serious illness. Sri Lanka's innings could hardly have begun more badly, both openers losing their wickets in the second over without scoring. The middle order staged a partial recovery, and the total was eventually pushed beyond 300, but the Sri Lankans still had to follow-on. They began the last day at 2 for 63 in their second innings, 126 behind. Their object was to bat on for a draw, but wickets fell steadily and, in the end, they failed to avoid an innings defeat by 3 runs. Victoria's young leg-spin bowler Peter McIntyre took 4 wickets.

Victoria

First Innings

Batsman	How Out	Ttl	Balls
GM Watts	b Ratnayeke	4	5
ID Frazer	c Mahanama b Ratnayeke	0	9
WN Phillips	c A Ranatunga b Jayasuriya	134	242
JD Siddons	c Wickremasinghe b Ratnayeke	113	195
GR Parker	c Mahanama b Ratnayake	8	31
SP O'Donnell (c)	st W'singhe b A Ranatunga	121	135
DW Fleming	not out	63	124
MGD Dimattina (+)	not out	32	68

▶

Batsman	How Out	Ttl	Balls
PR Reiffel	did not bat		
PW Jackson	did not bat		
PE McIntyre	did not bat		
SUNDRIES: B.0 LB.8 W.0 NB.24		32	809
TOTAL	6 wkts dec 507		

F/W: 4 7 210 233 305 443

Bowler	O	M	R	Wkts	NB	W
Ratnayeke	22	2	75	2	—	—
Ratnayeke	29	—	129	2	13	—
Wijegunawardene	20	1	109	—	5	—
EAR De Silva	22	3	70	—	4	—
PA De Silva	17	1	60	—	1	—
Jayasuriya	7	2	17	1	—	—
A Ranatunga	12	—	39	1	1	—
Overs:	129.0					

Sri Lankans

First Innings

Second Innings

Batsman	How Out	Ttl	Balls		How Out	Ttl	Balls
RS Mahanama	c Siddons b Fleming	0	8		c Frazer b O'Donnell	12	49
D Ranatunga	c Dimattina b Fleming	0	1		c Frazer b Jackson	46	173
AP Gurusinha	c Frazer b Fleming	55	138		st Dimattina b McIntyre	5	20
PA De Silva	c Fleming b O'Donnell	54	83	(5)	c Fleming b McIntyre	22	61
A Ranatunga (c)	c Dimattina b Fleming	75	115		absent injured		
EAR De Silva	c O'Donnell b McIntyre	9	36	(8)	c Parker b McIntyre	15	58
ST Jayasuriya	run out	31	38	(6)	c Dimattina b Jackson	34	38
JR Ratnayeke	not out	65	126	(7)	run out	26	40
G Wickremasinghe	lbw Reiffel	6	62	(4)	st Dimattina b McIntyre	13	171
RJ Ratnayake	c Dimattina b Reiffel	4	21	(9)	b Reiffel	4	42
KIW Wijegunawardene	b Jackson	5	24	(10)	not out	1	14
SUNDRIES: B.0 LB.5 W.1 NB.8		14	652		B.3 LB.3 W.0 NB.2	8	
TOTAL		318				186	666

F/W: 0 5 101 150 180 226 236 276 288 318

F/W: 30 47 74 96 114 144 172 184 186

Bowler	O	M	R	Wkts	NB	W	Bowler	O	M	R	Wkts	NB	W
Reiffel	28	5	61	2	3	—	Reiffel	19.1	9	22	1	1	—
Fleming	23	3	74	4	2	1	Fleming	10	2	22	—	1	—
McIntyre	23	2	104	1	—	—	O'Donnell	9	3	13	1	—	—
Jackson	20.3	8	43	1	—	—	McIntyre	39	18	56	4	—	—
O'Donnell	6	2	13	1	3	—	Jackson	31	16	59	2	—	—
Siddons	1	—	3	—	—	—	Siddons	2	1	8	—	—	—
Parker	5	1	15	—	—	—	Overs:	110.1					
Overs:	106.3												

Umpires: DW Holt & WP Sheahan

12th Men: AIC Dodemaide (Victoria) & HP Tillekeratne (Sri Lankans)

South Australians v Sri Lankans
Adelaide Oval, Adelaide
Dec 1, 2, 3, 4 1989
Toss: South Australia
Result: Drawn

This was another match in which Sri Lanka's batsmen gave a good account of themselves but in which its bowling generally looked below international standard. Play was virtually washed out on the opening day, and on the second day the Sri Lankan batsmen gave a solid display and were 5 for 274 at stumps, Asanka Gurusinha having scored a bright century. Sri Lanka chose to declare at its overnight score, and next day its bowlers were given rough treatment by the

South Australian batsmen, most notably Glenn Bishop, whose 156 was his second century in successive matches, and Darren Lehmann, who faced only 137 balls while scoring 109. The Sri Lankan bowling was later criticised for lacking discipline. Having begun the last day at 3 for 340, South Australia finally declared at 8 for 472 and gave the Sri Lankans a couple of hours' batting.

Sri Lankans

First Innings

Batsman	How Out	Ttl	Balls
RS Mahanama	b Miller	10	53
D Ranatunga	b Miller	8	35
AP Gurusinha	run out	109	229
PA De Silva	b Sleep	54	120
MAR Samarasekera	run out	26	60
HP Tillekeratne (+)	not out	23	89
ST Jayasuriya	not out	37	65
JR Ratnayeke (c)	did not bat		
CPH Ramanayake	did not bat		
GF Labrooy	did not bat		
EAR De Silva	did not bat		
SUNDRIES: B. 0 LB. 2 W. 3 NB. 2		7	651
TOTAL	5 wkts dec 274		

F/W: 16 31 155 206 220

Bowler	O	M	R	Wkts	NB	W
Gladigau	17	3	51	—	2	—
Miller	25	7	49	2	—	—
Zesers	12	4	30	—	—	—
Sleep	33	14	70	1	—	3
Francis	20	1	72	—	—	—
Hookes	1	1	0	—	—	—
Overs:	108.0					

Second Innings

How Out	Ttl	Balls
not out	56	122
lbw Miller	0	10
b Miller	10	18
run out	9	22
not out	10	44
B. 1 LB. 2 W. 0 NB. 0	3	216
3 wkts for 88		

F/W: 4 22 50

Bowler	O	M	R	Wkts	NB	W
Gladigau	10	3	17	—	—	—
Miller	10	3	30	2	—	—
Zesers	8	3	24	—	—	—
Sleep	5	2	12	—	—	—
Francis	2	—	2	—	—	—
Nobes	1	1	0	—	—	—
Overs:	36.0					

South Australia

First Innings

Batsman	How Out	Ttl	Balls
AMJ Hilditch	c Gurusinha b Ratnayeke	9	18
GA Bishop	c PA De Silva b Labrooy	156	287
PC Nobes	c Gurusinha b EAR De Silva	45	105
DW Hookes (c)	c Ratnayeke b EAR De Silva	50	78
DS Lehmann	c EAR De Silva b Ramanayeke	109	137
PR Sleep	c EAR De Silva b Labrooy	0	4
DS Berry (+)	retired hurt	17	40
AK Zesers	not out	25	55
PW Gladigau	lbw Labrooy	0	3
CR Miller	b EAR De Silva	34	38
CL Francis	did not bat		
SUNDRIES: B. 2 LB. 8 W. 0 NB. 17		27	765
TOTAL	8 wkts dec 472		

F/W: 25 115 221 361 368 414 414 472

Bowler	O	M	R	Wkts	NB	W
Ratnayeke	18	2	57	1	6	—
Labrooy	31	5	116	3	5	—
Ramanayake	25	2	103	1	1	—
EAR De Silva	35.1	7	121	3	4	—
PA De Silva	8	—	35	—	1	—
Jayasuriya	6	—	30	—	—	—
Overs:	123.1					

Umpires: AR Crafter & IR Berry

12th Men: BD Williams (South Australia) & MAWR Madurasinghe (Sri Lankans)

Australia v Sri Lanka
Brisbane Cricket Ground, Brisbane
Dec 8, 9, 10, 11, 12 1989
Toss: Sri Lanka
Result: Drawn

Sent in to bat on an uncertain pitch, Australia was in early trouble at 2 for 27, but Tom Moody (106) and Allan Border (56) halted the Sri Lankan advance with a partnership of 158 which did not end until the second morning. Moody's innings was a marvel of concentration, for it was interrupted six times by rain on the first day. Steve Waugh later batted carefully for 60, but for the first time in ten Tests Australia failed to make 400 in its first innings, Graeme Labrooy finishing with the fine bowling figures of 5 for 133. From the start, Sri Lanka's batsmen looked unthreatened by Australia's all-pace attack, and by stumps on the third day, when Sri Lanka was 6 for 275, Australia already had cause to regret the selectors' failure to include a spin bowler. On the fourth day, the Sri Lankans achieved a moral victory by leading Australia on the first innings, and one or two Australian bowlers gave unfortunate displays of frustration. Aravinda de Silva's robust innings of 167 included 17 fours and a six, but the Sri Lankans made such slow progress generally, occupying the crease for nearly twelve hours, that there was little hope of a result. The Australians were therefore content to bat out the remaining eight hours of play, and Mark Taylor used the occasion to add to his already impressive record with a highly competent innings of 164.

Australia

First Innings — Second Innings

Batsman	How Out	Ttl	Balls		How Out	Ttl	Balls
DC Boon	c Samarasekera b Labrooy	0	8	(5)	lbw Ramanayake	26	62
MA Taylor	c W'singhe b Ramanayake	9	24	(1)	lbw Ramanayake	164	334
TM Moody	c Wickremasinghe b Labrooy	106	179		c A Ranatunga b EAR De Silva	30	78
AR Border (c)	c A Ranatunga b Labrooy	56	109				
DM Jones	lbw Labrooy	15	26	(4)	c Ramanayake b PA De Silva	23	45
SR Waugh	c A Ranatunga b Ramanayake	60	99	(5)	b Gurusinha	57	147
IA Healy (+)	lbw Gurusinha	21	55	(6)	not out	26	52
MG Hughes	run out	25	19	(8)	not out	23	38
GF Lawson	c Wickremasinghe b Labrooy	22	25				
CG Rackemann	not out	5	23	(7)	b Gurusinha	0	2
TM Alderman	c PA De Silva b Gurusinha	18	31				
SUNDRIES:	B. 1 LB. 8 W. 0 NB. 21	30	598		B. 5 LB. 4 W. 0 NB. 17	26	758
TOTAL		367			6 wkts for 375		

F/W: 1 27 185 197 210 247 295 339 339 367

F/W: 60 124 167 316 324 324

Bowler	O	M	R	Wkts	NB	W
Ratnayeke	8.5	1	17	—	2	—
Labrooy	31.1	5	133	5	11	—
Ramanayake	26	2	101	2	8	—
A Ranatunga	13	1	49	—	—	—
EAR De Silva	8	1	21	—	—	—
Gurusinha	8.3	1	37	2	—	—
Overs:	95.3					

Bowler	O	M	R	Wkts	NB	W
Labrooy	24	4	69	—	6	—
Ramanayake	28	3	81	2	9	—
EAR De Silva	39	8	112	1	—	—
Gurusinha	10	3	31	2	—	—
A Ranatunga	6	—	25	—	—	—
PA De Silva	15	2	45	1	2	—
Mahanama	1	—	3	—	—	—
Overs:	123.0					

Sri Lanka

First Innings

Batsman	How Out	Ttl	Balls
RS Mahanama	lbw Alderman	5	29
D Ranatunga	c Waugh b Lawson	40	121
AP Gurusinha	c Healy b Rackemann	43	104
EAR De Silva	b Alderman	22	128
PA De Silva	c Lawson b Rackemann	167	361
A Ranatunga (c)	lbw Hughes	25	63
MAR Samarasekera	c Moody b Rackemann	18	33
JR Ratnayeke	lbw Hughes	56	138
AGD Wickremasinghe	c Boon b Hughes	2	9
GF Labrooy	lbw Alderman	1	8
CPH Ramanayake	not out	10	15
SUNDRIES: B. 0 LB. 23 W. 2 NB. 4		29	1008
TOTAL		418	

F/W: 10 80 114 148 201 238 382 386 391

Bowler	O	M	R	Wkts	NB	W
Alderman	40	13	81	3	4	—
Lawson	33	10	51	1	—	1
Rackemann	30.3	6	88	3	—	—
Hughes	39	8	123	3	—	1
Moody	16	8	15	—	—	—
Border	7	—	36	—	—	—
Jones	1	—	1	—	—	—
Overs:	166.3					

Umpires: AR Crafter & CD Timmins

12th Men: GD Campbell (Australia) & HP Tillekeratne (Sri Lanka)

SECOND TEST

Australia v Sri Lanka
Bellerive Oval, Hobart
Dec 16, 17, 18, 19, 20 1989
Toss: Sri Lanka
Result: Australia by 173 runs

Although Australia ended up winning by 173, the match was closely contested until the last hour of play. As in the first Test, Sri Lanka won the toss and sent Australia in, and its bowlers again had early success. Rumesh Ratnayake, returning to the side after an injury, took 4 wickets before lunch, a blow from which Australia did not really recover. If it had not been for Peter Sleep's resolute innings of 47 not out the Australian total might have been embarrassingly low. In 44 minutes batting on the first day, the Sri Lankans lost 3 wickets, and next day, despite resistance by Roshan Mahanama (85) and Aravinda de Silva (75), they were all out for 216, 8 runs behind. Australia began its second innings shakily, losing 2 wickets for 10, but on the third and fourth days the strength of its batting was displayed in full. Three players—Mark Taylor, Dean Jones and Steve Waugh—made centuries, the first time three Australians had done this in the second innings of a Test since 1920-21. Waugh was particularly severe on the bowling, taking only 177 balls to score 134. Having declared at 5 for 513, Australia had 10 hours to dismiss the Sri Lankans, but the batsmen proved defiant, and by the afternoon of the last day it seemed the Sri Lankans might yet hold out for a draw. A late collapse, however, brought the match to a sudden end. Aravinda de Silva's 72 in the second innings sealed for him the Man of the Match and Man of the Series awards.

Australia

First Innings

Batsman	How Out	Ttl	Balls		How Out	Ttl	Balls
DC Boon	c Mahanama b Ratnayake	41	73	(2)	c Ratnayake b Labrooy	0	1
MA Taylor	c Tillekeratne b Ratnayake	23	46	(1)	c Gurusinha b PA De Silva	108	211
TM Moody	c Gurusinha b Ratnayake	6	13		c Tillekeratne b Ratnayake	5	18
AR Border (c)	c EAR De Silva b Ratnayeke	24	34	(5)	b PA De Silva	85	151
DM Jones	c Tillekeratne b Ratnayeke	3	2	(6)	not out	118	178
SR Waugh	c Tillekeratne b Labrooy	16	24	(7)	not out	134	177
PR Sleep	not out	47	125				
IA Healy (+)	c Tillekeratne b Gurusinha	17	47				
MG Hughes	b EAR De Silva	27	43	(4)	c Gurusinha b Ratnayake	30	44
GD Campbell	c Mahanama b Ratnayake	6	38				
TM Alderman	b Ratnayake	0	1				
SUNDRIES: B. 0 LB. 7 W. 1 NB. 6		14	446		B. 2 LB. 5 W. 4 NB. 22	33	780
TOTAL		224			5 dec for 513		

F/W: 50 68 83 89 112 123 166 207 224 224

F/W: 1 10 77 240 253

Bowler	O	M	R	Wkts	NB	W	Bowler	O	M	R	Wkts	NB	W
Ratnayeke	15	2	39	1	2	—	Labrooy	22	3	100	1	3	—
Labrooy	19	3	61	1	—	—	Ratnayeke	35	5	123	2	6	4
Ratnayake	19.4	2	66	6	4	—	Ratnayeke	19	1	86	—	4	—
Ramanayake	4	—	21	—	—	—	EAR De Silva	21	2	83	—	1	—
Gurusinha	6	—	20	1	—	1	PA De Silva	18	1	65	2	4	—
EAR De Silva	9	6	10	1	—	—	Ramanayake	10	—	49	—	4	—
Overs:	72.4						Overs:	125.0					

Sri Lanka

First Innings

Batsman	How Out	Ttl	Balls		How Out	Ttl	Balls
RS Mahanama	c Healy b Sleep	85	229		lbw Campbell	5	7
D Ranatunga	c Moody b Alderman	2	7		c Healy b Hughes	45	123
AP Gurusinha	c Taylor b Alderman	0	7		c (s)Tucker b Hughes	20	62
EAR De Silva	c Border b Campbell	2	4	(8)	b Campbell	50	189
PA De Silva	lbw Campbell	75	130	(4)	c Campbell b Sleep	72	133
A Ranatunga (c)	c Moody b Sleep	21	53	(5)	c Jones b Hughes	38	91
HP Tillekeratne (+)	c Taylor b Sleep	0	11	(6)	c Waugh b Sleep	6	21
JR Ratnayeke	c Taylor b Hughes	9	11	(7)	c Healy b Campbell	75	187
GF Labrooy	b Hughes	11	28		b Hughes	5	12

Batsman	How Out	Ttl	Balls	How Out	Ttl	Balls
CPH Ramanayake	not out	4	23	not out	2	15
RJ Ratnayake	c Border b Hughes	0	5	lbw Hughes	5	15
SUNDRIES: B. 0 LB. 4 W. 0 NB. 3		7	508	B. 9 LB. 12 W. 0 NB. 4	25	855
TOTAL		216			348	

F/W: 11 15 18 146 188 192 193 201 216 216

F/W: 6 53 94 187 187 208 332 337 337 348

Bowler	O	M	R	Wkts	NB	W	Bowler	O	M	R	Wkts	NB	W
Alderman	23	2	71	2	1	—	Alderman	30	12	48	—	3	—
Campbell	23	9	41	2	—	—	Campbell	33	8	102	3	1	—
Hughes	21.4	6	68	3	—	—	Sleep	36	16	73	2	—	—
Sleep	10	4	26	3	—	—	Hughes	31.4	8	88	5	—	—
Waugh	6	3	6	—	2	—	Moody	2	—	9	—	—	—
Overs:	83.4						Jones	4	2	5	—	—	—
							Border	5	4	2	—	—	—
							Overs:	141.4					

Umpires: SG Randell & LJ King

12th Men: CG Rackemann (Australia) & ST Jayasuriya (Sri Lanka)

Victoria v Sri Lankans
Not First-Class – 50-over Match
Melbourne Cricket Ground, Melbourne
Dec 22 1989
Toss: Victoria
Result: Victoria by 109 runs

Unexpectedly feeble batting by the Sri Lankans enabled Victoria to score a substantial victory. A rapid century by the Victorian opening batsman Gary Watts, scored off 134 balls, was the basis of his side's large total. Replying, Sri Lanka was 4 for 108 when the loss of 3 wickets for 1 run virtually ended its hopes.

Victoria

Batsman	How Out	Ttl	Balls	Mins	4s	6s
GM Watts	c Samarasekera b W'wardene	111	134	179	6	—
WG Ayres	c & b Wijegunawardene	14	29	43	—	—
GR Parker	c W'wardene b A Ranatunga	35	61	65	1	—
WN Phillips	c W'wardene b Ramanayake	26	34	52	—	—
JD Siddons	not out	27	23	50	1	—
SP O'Donnell (c)	c Samarasekera b W'wardene	19	16	20	2	—
AIC Dodemaide	c D Ranatunga b Ramanayake	5	5	5	—	—
PR Reiffel	run out	8	5	6	—	—
MGD Dimattina (+)	did not bat					
DW Fleming	did not bat					
PW Jackson	did not bat					
SUNDRIES: B. 2 LB. 3 W. 4 NB. 3		12	307	213	10	—
TOTAL	7 wkts for 257					

F/W: 31 101 178 204 235 243 257

Bowler	O	M	R	Wkts	NB	W
Ratnayake	10	1	52	—	—	2
Ramanayake	10	1	47	2	1	1
Wijegunawardene	10	—	55	3	1	1
A Ranatunga	7	—	30	1	—	—
EAR De Silva	10	—	45	—	—	—
PA De Silva	3	—	23	—	1	—
Overs:	50.0					

▶

105

Sri Lankans

Batsman	How Out	Ttl	Balls	Mins	4s	6s
RS Mahanama	c Dimattina b Fleming	7	18	22	1	—
D Ranatunga	b Jackson	25	73	99	—	—
AP Gurusinha	run out	0	0	3	—	—
PA De Silva	b O'Donnell	32	31	33	4	—
A Ranatunga (c)	c Reiffel b Phillips	45	50	101	2	1
MAR Samarasekera	lbw Dodemaide	9	24	25	1	—
HP Tillekeratne (+)	c Dimattina b Dodemaide	0	2	2	—	—
EAR De Silva	run out	0	2	4	—	—
CPH Ramanayake	not out	15	40	44	—	—
RJ Ratnayake	c Dimattina b Jackson	0	4	5	—	—
KIW Wijegunawardene	b O'Donnell	3	11	9	—	—
SUNDRIES: B.0 LB.9 W.0 NB.3		12	255	178	8	1
TOTAL		148				

F/W: 12 14 58 81 108 108 109 143 144 148

Bowler	O	M	R	Wkts	NB	W
Reiffel	6	—	23	—	—	—
Fleming	7	2	23	1	—	—
O'Donnell	6	—	17	2	1	—
Dodemaide	10	2	29	2	—	—
Jackson	10	—	26	2	—	—
Phillips	3	—	21	1	—	—
Overs:	42.0					

Umpires: RC Bailhache & WP Sheahan

12th Men: ID Frazer (Victoria) & ST Jayasuriya (Sri Lankans)

Victorian Country XI v Sri Lankans
Not First-Class - 50-over Match
RM Hooper Oval, Hastings
Dec 23 1989
Toss: Sri Lankans
Result: Victorian Country XI by 3 wkts

A second-string Sri Lankan team gave a disappointing batting performance, scoring only 174 off 49 overs. Terry Doyle, a pace bowler from Langwarren, took 3 for 38 in 9 overs. Four of the Victorian Country players made sound starts without going on to play a big innings—Robert Bedford of Karingal, who scored 38, including 2 sixes, Lindsay Wulf of Ferntree Gully 30, Kevin Bartholomew of Toora 22 and John Hille of Frankston 20. In the end, Victorian Country managed to score the required runs with just two balls to spare.

Sri Lankans

Batsman	How Out	Ttl	Balls	Mins	4s	6s
JR Ratnayeke (c)	c Bedford b Doyle	4	4	5	1	—
MAR Samarasekera	c Cooper b Jackson	19	29	40	3	—
HP Tillekeratne	c Hille b Jackson	3	17	27	—	—
ST Jayasuriya	c Cooper b Doyle	4	7	3	—	—
AP Gurusinha	c Cooper b Lillico	28	64	100	2	—
ACD Wickremasinghe (+)	c Reed b Bedford	53	102	131	4	—
EAR De Silva	c Rolland b Lillico	3	13	14	—	—
CPH Ramanayake	b Reed	5	12	11	—	—
RJ Ratnayake	c Jackson b Doyle	30	31	31	2	2
MAWR Madurasinghe	run out	10	18	30	—	—
KIW Wijegunawardene	not out	1	1	5	—	—
SUNDRIES: B.0 LB.5 W.7 NB.2		14	298	201	12	2
TOTAL		174				

F/W: 4 26 32 32 100 116 129 132 168 174

Bowler	O	M	R	Wkts	NB	W
Doyle	9	2	38	3	1	1
Jackson	10	2	22	2	—	4
Johnson	8	2	27	—	—	—
Reed	10	—	33	1	—	—
Lillico	10	—	37	2	—	2
Bedford	2	—	12	1	1	—
Overs:	49.0					

Victorian Country XI

Batsman	How Out	Ttl	Balls	Mins	4s	6s
G Cooper	c Jayasuriya b Ratnayeke	11	40	45	—	—
J Hille	c (s)Silva b De Silva	20	45	57	3	—
K Bartholomew (+)	c Samarasekera b Jayasuriya	22	46	60	4	—
L Wulf	c Tillekeratne b Gurusinha	30	67	87	1	—
R Bedford	c Samarasekera b M'singhe	38	54	66	2	2
D Rolland	lbw Gurusinha	12	23	31	1	—
S Johnson (c)	not out	4	9	25	—	—
T Doyle	b De Silva	8	14	13	1	—
S Reed	not out	8	6	7	1	—
R Jackson	did not bat					
J Lillico	did not bat					
SUNDRIES: B. 4 LB. 10 W. 8 NB. 1		23	304	199	13	2
TOTAL	7 wkts for 176					

F/W: 32 38 75 123 152 153 166

Bowler	O	M	R	Wkts	NB	W
Ratnayeke	7	—	12	1	—	4
Ramanayake	5	—	22	—	1	1
De Silva	10	2	29	2	—	—
Wijegunawardene	6	1	21	—	—	2
Madurasinghe	10	2	30	1	—	—
Jayasuriya	5	—	25	1	—	—
Gurusinha	6.4	—	23	2	—	1
Overs:	49.4					

Umpires: J Northfield & M Rolfe

12th men: M Grange (Victorian Country XI) & Sri Lankans not named

Australia v Sri Lanka
Melbourne Cricket Ground, Melbourne
December 26, 1989
Limited-overs International
Result: Australia by 30 runs

For details see section on Benson and Hedges World Series matches.

Australia v Sri Lanka
WACA Ground, Perth
December 30, 1989
Limited-overs International
Result: Australia by 9 wkts

For details see section on Benson and Hedges World Series matches.

Pakistan v Sri Lanka
WACA Ground, Perth
December 31, 1989
Limited-overs International
Result: Sri Lanka by 3 wkts

For details see section on Benson and Hedges World Series matches.

Australia v Sri Lanka
Melbourne Cricket Ground, Melbourne
January 4, 1990
Limited-overs International
Result: Australia by 73 runs

For details see section on Benson and Hedges World Series matches.

Tasmania v Sri Lankans
Devonport Oval, Devonport
Jan 6, 7, 8 1990
Toss: Sri Lankans
Result: Drawn

As it had several times before on the tour, Sri Lanka chose to field after winning the toss, and in this case the strategy was unsuccessful. David Boon launched a furious assault on the bowling and his captain, Dirk Wellham, was able to declare at tea on the first day at 1 for 201. Boon played a remarkable innings, scoring 101 runs between lunch and tea, and Sri Lanka used eight bowlers in a vain attempt to contain him. The Sri Lankans, too, scored briskly, declaring at 6 for 207 at lunch next day. Tasmania declared on the third and last day at 8 for 238, setting the Sri Lankans the task of scoring 242 runs at 3.67 an over to win. For a time the Sri Lankans were ahead of this run rate, but after Aravinda de Silva's dismissal for 39 the steam went out of the run chase, and both sides agreed to end the match at 6pm when no result seemed possible. The last day's play was marred by a clash on the field between de Silva and Rod Tucker, for which de Silva was later reported to have apologised.

Tasmania

Batsman	First Innings How Out		Ttl	Balls	Second Innings How Out		Ttl	Balls
RJ Bennett	c EAR De Silva b Ramanayake		9	28	c M'singhe b EAR De Silva		60	123
G Shipperd	not out		57	172				
DC Boon	not out		133	164	(9) not out		25	48
J Cox					(3) c Labrooy b Madurasinghe		31	69
DM Wellham (c)					(5) b Madurasinghe		27	45
RJ Tucker					(4) b Ramanayake		10	13
GR Robertson					(6) c Kalpage			
RE Soule (+)					b Madurasinghe		39	80
GD Campbell					(2) c W'singhe b Ratnayake		4	11
DR Gilbert					(10) not out		5	12
TJ Cooley					(8) lbw Ramanayake		7	33
SUNDRIES:	B. 0 LB. 0 W. 4 NB. 7		11	369	B. 6 LB. 4 W. 0 NB. 10		20	471
TOTAL	1 wkt dec 210				8 wkts for 238			
F/W: 18					F/W: 11 61 75 138 138 162 178 216			

Bowler	O	M	R	Wkts	NB	W	Bowler	O	M	R	Wkts	NB	W
Labrooy	9	1	32	—	—	—	Ramanayake	25	4	96	2	7	—
Ratnayake	12	2	27	—	—	1	Ratnayake	9	1	18	1	—	—
Ramanayake	11	2	39	1	6	1	Tillekeratne	2	—	10	—	—	—

Bowler	O	M	R	Wkts	NB	W	Bowler	O	M	R	Wkts	NB	W
Kalpage	1	—	6	—	—	—	Madurasinghe	29	5	80	4	—	—
EAR De Silva	13	2	45	—	1	—	EAR De Silva	13	—	24	1	3	—
Madurasinghe	7	—	40	—	—	—	Overs:	75.0					
PA De Silva	2	1	8	—	—	—							
Jayasuriya	4	1	13	—	—	—							
Overs:	59.0												

Sri Lankans

First Innings — Second Innings

Batsman	How Out	Ttl	Balls	How Out	Ttl	Balls
MAR Samarasekera	c Robertson b Gilbert	3	9	c Cox b Cooley	11	21
ADG Wickremasinghe	hit wicket b Gilbert	24	53	b Gilbert	1	19
HP Tillekeratne	b Tucker	74	134	b Campbell	35	72
ST Jayasuriya	c Shipperd b Campbell	2	6 (8)	c Cooley b Robertson	13	22
EAR De Silva	not out	66	103 (5)	lbw Gilbert	34	75
CPH Ramanayake	c Soule b Tucker	3	3 (7)	not out	16	90
GF Labrooy	c Soule b Tucker	0	1 (9)	not out	26	49
R Kalpage	not out	10	13 (6)	c Cooley b Robertson	0	6
PA De Silva (c)			(4)	hit wicket b Campbell	39	30
MAWR Madurasinghe	did not bat					
NLK Ratnayake	did not bat					
SUNDRIES:	B. 9 LB. 6 W. 0 NB. 10	25	322	B. 8 LB. 6 W. 1 NB. 10	25	384
TOTAL	6 wkts dec	207		7 wkts for	200	

F/W: 5 61 63 166 172 172

F/W: 14 17 83 121 122 139 156

AGD Wickremasinghe (Wicket-keeper)

Bowler	O	M	R	Wkts	NB	W	Bowler	O	M	R	Wkts	NB	W
Gilbert	14	3	51	2	1	—	Gilbert	13	1	44	2	4	—
Cooley	11	2	44	—	8	—	Cooley	9	3	45	1	3	1
Campbell	13	3	43	1	—	—	Tucker	8	1	26	—	2	—
Robertson	5	1	6	—	—	—	Campbell	16	4	44	2	1	—
Tucker	9	—	48	3	1	—	Robinson	16	6	27	2	—	—
Overs:	52.0						Overs:	62.0					

Umpires: P Clark & B Knight

12th Men: PI Faulkner (Tasmania) & A Ranatunga (Sri Lankans)

Australian Cricket Academy v Sri Lankans
Not First-Class
Adelaide Oval, Adelaide
Jan 11, 12 1990
Toss: Australian Cricket Academy
Result: Drawn

Sent in, the Sri Lankans were dismissed in 52 overs for 103, the Port Hedland bowler Brendan Julian taking 4 for 14. Undisciplined batting appeared the main reason for this poor performance. Although the pitch had some moisture, it did not give any special advantage to the bowlers. Julian's bowling figures were impressive, especially in the light of the fact that he had hardly bowled for two months because of an injury. In reply, the academy team displayed batting strength in depth, compiling a total of 348. Six of its players made 30 or more, the leading scorers being Craig White of Bendigo, who made 84, Cameron Williamson of Adelaide, who made 54, and Michael Slater from Wagga, who scored 43 runs from 50 balls, including 7 fours. The Sri Lankans made the Academy bowlers work harder in their second innings, and at the end of the match, shortened from three to two days, were 1 for 117.

Sri Lankans

First Innings   Second Innings

Batsman	How Out	Ttl	Balls		How Out	Ttl	Balls
JR Ratnayeke (c)	c Williams b Mack	13	41	(3)	not out	39	64
AGD Wickremasinghe	c Williams b Mack	6	27		c & b Mack	4	7
AP Gurusinha	c Williams b Julian	17	38	(1)	not out	66	76
HP Tillekeratne	run out	8	43				
PA De Silva	c Clarke b Julian	0	1				
EAR De Silva	c Hills b Julian	2	9				
RS Kalpage	c Auty b Julian	1	8				
CPH Ramanayake	c Hills b Mack	3	37				
MAWR Madurasinghe	not out	35	64				
NLK Ratnayeke	c Williamson b Auty	10	39				
KIW Wijegunawardene	c Williamson b Clarke	3	8				
SUNDRIES: B. 0 LB. 4 W. 0 NB. 1		5	315		B. 0 LB. 6 W. 0 NB. 2	8	147
TOTAL		103			1 wkt for 117		

F/W: 20 21 40 40 47 49 50 61 94 103   F/W: 15
AGD Wickremasinghe (Wicket-keeper)

Bowler	O	M	R	Wkts	NB	W		Bowler	O	M	R	Wkts	NB	W
Alley	5	2	6	—	—	—		Mack	5	—	26	1	—	—
Mack	14	5	38	3	—	—		Alley	7	—	37	—	2	—
Clarke	15.2	7	19	1	—	—		Williamson	5	—	23	—	—	—
Julian	10	3	14	4	1	—		Julian	3	—	14	—	—	—
Auty	8	2	22	1	—	—		Bevan	2	—	10	—	—	—
Overs:	52.2							Auty	2	1	1	—	—	—
								Overs:	24.0					

Aust. Academy

First Innings

Batsman	How Out	Ttl	Balls
MJ Slater	c PA De Silva b Kalpage	43	50
DF Hills	c Gurusinha b Kalpage	15	40
C White	c Ramanayake b Madurasinghe	84	158
MG Bevan	b Kalpage	2	9
BP Julian	c W'singhe b M'singhe	32	42
CB Williamson	lbw Madurasinghe	54	108
JM Williams	st W'singhe b M'singhe	39	64
C Auty	c W'singhe b M'singhe	8	27
DA Clarke	c PA De Silva b Kalpage	36	46
PJS Alley	lbw PA De Silva	6	12
CD Mack	not out	4	13
SUNDRIES: B. 9 LB. 6 W. 0 NB. 10		25	569
TOTAL		348	

F/W: 57 60 64 113 228 274 296 297 318 348

Bowler	O	M	R	Wkts	NB	W
Ramanayake	10	—	46	—	4	—
Ratnayeke	11	3	39	—	—	—
Madurasinghe	41	7	95	5	—	—
Kalpage	10.2	1	47	4	—	—
PA De Silva	12	—	60	1	1	—
Wijegunawardene	8	—	46	—	5	—
Overs:	92.2					

Umpires: MP Brien SJ Davis

12th Men: MP Hay (Aust. Cricket Academy) & GF Labrooy (Sri Lankans)

South Australian Country XI v Sri Lankans
Not First-Class
Centenary Oval, Port Lincoln
Jan 14 1990
Toss: South Australian Country XI
Result: Sri Lankans by 35 runs

South Australian Country looked to have a good chance of winning this match after it dismissed Sri Lanka for 170. Simon Fuchs, an eighteen-year-old leg-spinner from Port Pirie, worried the Sri Lankan batsmen with accurate bowling and finished with the excellent figures of 5 for 47 off 15 overs. South Australian Country's innings began badly, but between them Darren Jackson from Whyalla and John Mosey from Robertstown raised the total to 55 runs short of victory with 7 wickets in hand. Jackson made 45 and Mosey 35 but their dismissals in quick succession proved to be the start of a collapse in which South Australian Country lost its last 7 wickets for only 20 runs.

Sri Lankans

Batsman	How Out	Ttl	Balls	Mins	4s	6s
RS Mahanama	c Jackson b Penna	37	49	54	4	—
MAR Samarasekera	c Penna b Lindner	14	35	50	1	—
AP Gurusinha	c Gutsche b Fuchs	9	23	34	1	—
A Ranatunga (c)	c Hayles b Penna	0	1	5	—	—
ST Jayasuriya	c Penna b Fuchs	28	68	60	2	—
AGD Wickremasinghe (+)	c Penna b Fuchs	18	40	54	1	—
RJ Ratnayake	c Parsons b Fuchs	17	31	1	—	—
CPH Ramanayake	c Andrenacci b May	34	28	43	2	—
MAWR Madurasinghe	c Gutsche b May	4	5	5	—	—
NLK Ratnayake	c Penna b Fuchs	2	15	20	—	—
KIW Wijegunawardene	not out	2	6	11	—	—
SUNDRIES: B. 2 LB. 1 W. 0 NB. 2		5				
TOTAL		170	301	188 11		

F/W: 47 53 55 72 102 120 129 133 148 170

Bowler	O	M	R	Wkts	NB	W
May	11	2	54	2	2	—
Penna	9	1	37	2	—	—
Lindner	14	2	29	1	—	—
Fuchs	15	3	47	5	—	—
Overs:	50.0					

South Australian Country XI

Batsman	How Out	Ttl	Balls	Mins	4s	6s
G Tee	b Ramanayake	2	3	1	—	—
D Hayles	c Samarasekera b Ranatunga	13	24	60	—	—
L Andrenacci	c Samarasekera b Ramanayake	13	40	42	—	—
D Jackson	c Samarasekera b Jayasuriya	45	99	93	3	—
J Mosey	b Madurasinghe	35	67	86	3	1
P Parsons	b Jayasuriya	1	8	7	—	—
C Penna (c)	c W'singhe b Jayasuriya	0	5	8	—	—
R Gutsche (+)	not out	11	18	31	—	—
S Fuchs	c W'singhe b Madurasinghe	4	23	14	—	—
S Lindner	c W'singhe b Madurasinghe	1	7	6	—	—
T May	not out	0	0	1	—	—
SUNDRIES: B. 2 LB. 3 W. 0 NB. 5		10	305	179	6	1
TOTAL	9 wkts for 135	135				

F/W: 2 25 36 115 116 116 118 127 134 135

▶

Bowler	O	M	R	Wkts	NB	W
Ramanayake	7	1	20	2	2	—
NLK Ratnayake	5	—	12	—	1	—
RJ Ratnayake	4	1	10	—	1	—
Ranatunga	9	1	26	1	—	—
Madurasinghe	16	4	38	3	—	—
Wijegunawardene	3	1	17	—	1	—
Jayasuriya	6	3	7	3	—	—
Overs:	50.0					

Umpires: AR Crafter & IR Berry

12th Men: M Cameron (S.Aust. Country XI) & Sri Lankans – not named

Australian Country XI v Sri Lankans
Not First-Class
Queen Elizabeth Oval, Bendigo
Jan 17, 18, 19 1990
Result: Drawn

The country players more than held their own in this drawn match. Batting first, the Sri Lankans were restricted to a total of 234 by a combination of tight bowling and fine catching. Australian Country's leading wicket-taker was the pace bowler Eugene Nix of the ACT, who took 4 for 62. Only one Sri Lankan batsman made a half-century—Athula Samarasekera, who opened the batting and scored a brisk 51. In reply, Australian Country declared at 9 for 238. The opener Terry Oliver of Mackay scored 59, which helped give his side a sound start, but none of the other top-order batsmen was able to get going, and Australian Country was only 190 when the ninth wicket fell. But the side's captain, Terry Waldron, of Western Australia, batting at nine, and the last man in, Colin Crouch of Queanbeyan, made an undefeated partnership of 48 to gain the first innings lead. They did have some good fortune, however. Waldron, who made 51 not out, was dropped three times. The Sri Lankans closed their second innings at 9 for 175 just before tea on the third day, setting Australian Country the task of scoring 4.5 runs an over to win. But the country players could not manage the scoring rate, and the exciting finish which had been expected did not eventuate.

Sri Lankans

First Innings			Second Innings		
Batsman	How Out	Ttl		How Out	Ttl
D Ranatunga	run out	32	(2)	c Nix b Wrigley	0
MAR Samarasekera	c Wrigley b Crouch	51	(1)	c Phillips b Nix	83
AP Gurusinha	c Wrigley b Nix	38	(3)	c Beaumont b Crouch	4
HP Tillekeratne	c Waldron b Nix	0	(4)	c Waldron b Wrigley	8
A Ranatunga (c)	c Waldron b Wrigley	38	(6)	not out	54
ST Jayasuriya	c Scuderi b Gerhard	0	(5)	b Wrigley	4
AGD Wickremasinghe	c Kelaher b Crouch	28		c Wrigley b Nix	1
EAR De Silva	c Kelaher b Nix	22		c Phillips b Gerhard	11
GF Labrooy	st Waldron b Gerhard	12		b Gerhard	0
MAWR Madurasinghe	b Nix	2		c Nix b Gerhard	0
KIW Wijegunawardene	not out	0			
SUNDRIES: B. 3 LB. 6 W. 0 NB. 2		11		B. 6 LB. 3 W. 0 NB. 1	10
TOTAL		234		9 dec for 175	

F/W: 80 88 99 145 154 180 204 227 229 234

F/W: 4 31 62 76 123 125 171 175 175

AGD Wickremasinghe (Wicket-keeper)

Bowler	O	M	R	Wkts	NB	W	Bowler	O	M	R	Wkts	NB	W
Crouch	20	5	59	2	1	—	Crouch	15	3	37	1	—	—
Wrigley	15	2	44	1	—	—	Wrigley	12	2	51	3	—	—
Nix	22.4	5	62	4	1	—	Nix	12	4	32	2	1	—
Gerhard	20	5	55	2	—	—	Gerhard	12	2	42	3	—	—
Kelaher	2	—	5	—	—	—	Kelaher	2	1	4	—	—	—
Overs:	79.4						Overs:	53.0					

Aust. Country XI

First Innings / Second Innings

Batsman	How Out	Ttl	How Out	Ttl
T Oliver	lbw De Silva	59	b Wijegunawardene	7
G Phillips	run out	10	c Jayasuriya b Madurasinghe	29
M Kelaher	c W'singhe b A Ranatunga	24	lbw Madurasinghe	17
S Scuderi	c W'singhe b Labrooy	10	not out	25
P Evans	lbw Madurasinghe	20	(6) b Madurasinghe	3
G Beaumont	c Gurusinha b Madurasinghe	14	(7) not out	3
T Waldron (+)	not out	51		
P Gerhard	b Madurasinghe	13		
J Wrigley	c Gurusinha b Madurasinghe	0	(5) st W'singhe b Jayasuriya	8
E Nix	lbw Labrooy	0		
C Crouch	not out	8		
SUNDRIES:	B. 8 LB. 9 W. 1 NB. 11	29	B. 0 LB. 7 W. 0 NB. 1	8
TOTAL	9 wkts dec 238		5 for 100	

F/W: 29 93 113 115 152 157 189 189 190

F/W: 10 53 72 89 92

Bowler	O	M	R	Wkts	NB	W	Bowler	O	M	R	Wkts	NB	W
Labrooy	22	4	62	2	5	1	Wijegunawardene	9	1	30	1	1	—
Wijegunawardene	10.1	2	24	—	2	—	Gurusinha	8	1	13	—	—	—
EAR De Silva	26	8	48	1	3	—	Madurasinghe	6	1	24	3	—	—
Madurasinghe	21	4	51	4	1	—	Jayasuriya	5	—	26	1	—	—
A Ranatunga	9	1	36	1	—	—	Overs:	28.0					
Overs:	88.1												

Umpires: G Cole & B Murton

New South Wales v Sri Lankans
Not First-Class
Brelsford Park, Coffs Harbour
Jan 21 1990
Toss: New South Wales
Result: New South Wales won by 81 runs

Sri Lanka was no match on the day for a New South Wales team performing near to its peak. Choosing to bat first, the home side found run-making easy on a small ground and against an attack weakened by the absence of the injured pace bowlers Rumesh Ratnayake and Graeme Labrooy. Steve Small's 101 earned him the Man of the Match award. Trevor Bayliss's 97 not out was scored off only 93 balls and included 5 sixes. New South Wales's total of 4 for 262 meant the Sri Lankans needed to score at 5.26 an over, and their top-order batsmen put them ahead of the rate. At 3 for 134 in the 25th over, the Sri Lankans were well placed to push on to the target, but their batsmen continued to take risks, and the wickets fell rapidly. With more than 9 overs still to be bowled, Sri Lanka was all out for 181, having lost its last 7 wickets for 47 runs.

New South Wales

Batsman	How Out	Ttl	Balls	Mins	4s	6s
SM Small	c Samarasekera b Gurusinha	101	115	173	5	1
PA Emery (+)	c Jayasuriya b PA De Silva	31	74	85	1	—
TH Bayliss	not out	97	93	113	2	5
MD O'Neill	c Samarasekera b Gurusinha	11	14	16	—	—
ME Waugh	b Gurusinha	8	5	5	—	1
BE McNamara	not out	1	3	2	—	—
GRJ Matthews	did not bat					
PH Marks	did not bat					
GF Lawson (c)	did not bat					
RM Stobo	did not bat					
WJ Holdsworth	did not bat					
SUNDRIES: B. 1 LB. 8 W. 2 NB. 2		13	304	199	8	7
TOTAL	4 wkts for 262					

F/W: 74 197 242 259

Bowler	O	M	R	Wkts	NB	W
Ratnayeke	8	—	40	—	—	1
Ramanayake	10	1	39	—	2	—
Wijegunawardene	6	—	36	—	—	—
Ranatunga	9	1	42	—	—	—
EAR De Silva	6	—	34	1	—	1
PA De Silva	4	—	24	—	—	—
Gurusinha	7	—	38	3	—	—
Overs:	50.0					

Sri Lankans

Batsman	How Out	Ttl	Balls	Mins	4s	6s
RS Mahanama	c Lawson b Holdsworth	12	21	31	1	—
MAR Samarasekera	b Lawson	44	40	47	3	2
AP Gurusinha	c Stobo b Matthews	39	51	65	4	—
PA De Silva	run out	43	54	80	3	1
A Ranatunga (c)	st Emery b Matthews	2	3	9	—	—
HP Tillekeratne (+)	c Waugh b Matthews	17	33	51	1	—
ST Jayasuriya	c Waugh b Matthews	3	16	12	—	—
JR Ratnayeke	lbw O'Neill	2	3	3	—	—
EAR De Silva	not out	8	22	22	—	—
CPH Ramanayake	b O'Neill	1	3	3	—	—
KIW Wijegunawardene	c Waugh b O'Neill	1	7	8	—	—
SUNDRIES: B. 2 LB. 4 W. 3 NB. 0		9	253	172	12	3
TOTAL	181					

F/W: 44 57 118 134 151 159 162 176 177 181

Bowler	O	M	R	Wkts	NB	W
Lawson	6	—	33	1	—	1
Holdsworth	7	—	37	1	—	1
Waugh	5	—	26	—	—	—
Stobo	4	—	21	—	—	1
Matthews	10	—	22	4	—	—
O'Neill	9.4	1	36	3	—	—
Overs:	41.4					

Umpires: IS Thomas & AG Marshall

12th Men: GS Milliken (New South Wales) & MAWR Madurasinghe (Sri Lankans)

New South Wales Country XI v Sri Lankans
Not First-Class
McKittrick Park, Grafton
Jan 23 1990
Toss: New South Wales Country XI
Result: Sri Lankans won by 3 wkts

The outfield was heavy, and runs did not come easily for either team. Batting first, the country side in its 50 overs scored only 9 for 162. Its premier batsman, Mark Curry of Newcastle, hit 2 sixes and offered hope of accelerating the scoring rate, so his dismissal for 40 was costly to his team. Another moderately successful country batsman was Eric Higgins of Gloucester, who made 29. The Sri Lankan batsmen had to work hard to score the necessary runs and, in fact, did not reach their target until the 49th over. John Frame, a leg-spinner from Grafton, had the excellent figures of 3 for 15 from 9 overs.

New South Wales Country XI

Batsman	How Out	Ttl	Balls	Mins	4s	6s
G Arms	c W'wardene b Ratnayeke	5	19	29	—	—
G Ryan	c Tillekeratne b W'wardene	15	53	80	2	—
E Higgins	c Mahanama b Jayasuriya	29	72	56	2	—
M Curry	c Madurasinhge b Ratnayeke	40	57	73	1	2
D Willis	b Jayasuriya	19	20	57	2	—
J Frame	b Jayasuriya	2	8	12	—	—
R Merlo	run out	15	24	29	1	—
M Christie	c Mahanama b Jayasuriya	11	23	19	—	—
C Hamilton	run out	0	11	14	—	—
S Bridges	not out	6	14	17	—	—
G Hooper	not out	8	4	9	—	1
SUNDRIES: B. 0 LB. 4 W. 3 NB. 5		12	305	202	8	3
TOTAL	9 wkts for 162					

F/W: 10 46 76 108 119 121 137 147 148

Bowler	O	M	R	Wkts	NB	W
Ratnayeke	9	1	19	2	2	2
Ramanayake	6	—	21	—	2	—
Wijegunawardene	6	1	13	1	—	—
A Ranatunga	9	2	33	—	1	—
Madurasinghe	10	2	36	—	—	—
Jayasuriya	10	—	36	4	—	1
Overs:	50.0					

Sri Lankans

Batsman	How Out	Ttl	Balls	Mins	4s	6s
MAR Samarasekera	c & b Christie	26	19	17	3	1
D Ranatunga	run out	9	44	55	—	—
HP Tillekeratne (+)	c Bridges b Frame	46	105	134	1	—
AP Gurusinha	c Merlo b Christie	12	16	30	—	1
A Ranatunga (c)	c Higgins b Frame	1	3	9	—	—
RS Mahanama	c Higgins b Christie	44	62	76	3	—
ST Jayasuriya	c & b Frame	3	21	24	—	—
JR Ratnayeke	not out	12	19	33	1	—
CPH Ramanayake	not out	0	4	3	—	—
MAWR Madurasinghe	did not bat					
KIW Wijegunawardene	did not bat					
SUNDRIES: B. 4 LB. 2 W. 4 NB. 2		12	293	194	8	2
TOTAL	7 wkts for 165					

F/W: 28 50 51 59 132 137 160

Bowler	O	M	R	Wkts	NB	W
Hooper	7.1	—	46	—	1	1
Christie	10	3	25	3	1	1
Hamilton	9	2	28	—	—	1
Frame	9	2	15	3	—	—
Curry	5	—	18	—	—	—
Willis	8	—	27	—	—	1
Overs:	48.1					

Umpires: K Pye & K Bourke

12th Men: M Pigg (New South Wales Country XI) & Sri Lankans – not named

Queensland v Sri Lankans
Not First-Class
Rockhampton Cricket Ground, Rockhampton
Jan 26, 27 1990
Toss: Queensland
Result: Drawn

The teams scarcely had time to bat through an innings each in this two-day match, which predictably ended in a draw. The fragility of Sri Lanka's batting was exposed on the first day when the side was dismissed in less than two sessions of play for 129. The outstanding Queensland bowler was eighteen-year-old Michael Kasprowicz, who took 5 for 29 and hit the stumps three times. The Queenslanders then batted until after tea on the second day, when they were all out for 291. The opener Peter Cantrell, who made 105, was the mainstay of the innings. Sri Lanka had barely begun its second innings when the match ended.

Sri Lankans

First Innings

Batsman	How Out	Ttl	Balls		Second Innings How Out	Ttl	Balls
MAR Samarasekera	b Kasprowicz	6	17				
D Ranatunga	b Kasprowicz	5	10		not out	11	42
HP Tillekeratne (+)	c Kerr b Kasprowicz	13	31				
A Ranatunga (c)	c Smart b Storey	35	47				
RS Mahanama	c Storey b Polzin	12	17	(1)	not out	14	36
ST Jayasuriya	c Storey b Kasprowicz	15	42				
JR Ratnayeke	b Kasprowicz	10	28				
EAR De Silva	lbw Storey	10	32				
CPH Ramanayake	c Ritchie b Polzin	6	38				
MAWR Madurasinghe	not out	1	15				
KIW Wijegunawardene	run out	3	3				
SUNDRIES: B. 1 LB. 4 W. 3 NB. 5		13	280		B. 3 LB. 0 W. 0 NB. 0 3		78
TOTAL		129			0 wkts for 28		
F/W: 12 13 36 52 92 99 110 122 126 129					F/W:		

Bowler	O	M	R	Wkts	NB	W	Bowler	O	M	R	Wkts	NB	W
McDermott	8	1	33	—	3	—	Kasprowicz	3	—	8	—	—	—
Kasprowicz	13	2	29	5	—	3	Polzin	3	1	4	—	—	—
Polzin	11	2	30	2	—	—	Healy	4	1	9	—	—	—
Foley	2	—	14	—	1	—	Ritchie	2	2	0	—	—	—
Storey	10.1	6	16	2	1	—	Law	1	—	4	—	—	—
Cantrell	1	—	2	—	—	—	Overs:	13.0					
Overs:	45.1												

Queensland

First Innings

Batsman	How Out	Ttl	Balls
GI Foley	lbw Ramanayake	51	131
PE Cantrell	run out	105	235
RB Kerr	st Tillekeratne b M'singhe	15	55
SG Law	c Tillekeratne b M'singhe	4	12
CB Smart	b De Silva	17	24
SC Storey	c Madurasinghe b De Silva	40	51
GM Ritchie (c)	c & b De Silva	0	6
IA Healy (+)	c Madurasinghe b De Silva	28	52
CJ McDermott	st Tillekeratne b De Silva	4	12
MA Polzin	run out	0	10
MS Kasprowicz	not out	15	10
SUNDRIES: B. 3 LB. 8 W. 0 NB. 1		12	598
TOTAL		291	
F/W: 133 171 179 186 207 212 248 257 270 291			

Bowler	O	M	R	Wkts	NB	W
Ratnayeke	10	1	26	—	—	—
Ramanayake	19	4	35	1	—	—
Wijegunawardene	9	1	39	—	1	—
A Ranatunga	6	1	17	—	—	—
De Silva	22.2	6	52	5	—	—
Madurasinghe	29	6	90	2	—	—
Jayasuriya	4	—	21	—	—	—
Overs:	99.2					

Umpires: CA Bertwistle & MT Musch

12th Men: BP Inwood (Queensland) & AGD Wickremasinghe (Sri Lankans)

Queensland v Sri Lankans
Not First-Class
Rockhampton Cricket Ground, Rockhampton
Jan 28 1990
Toss: Queensland
Result: Queensland won by 5 runs

Sri Lanka's tactical approach appeared to cost them this match. Whereas the Queensland batsmen paced themselves, using all the 49 overs available to score 7 for 195, the Sri Lankans batted with excessive haste and were all out in 41 overs, only 6 runs short of their target. Geoff Foley, who scored 65, was the only batsman to better 30 in the Queensland innings. Typically, the Sri Lankan innings was mixture of good and bad play, but with 4 wickets and ample overs in hand and only 35 runs to get the Sri Lankans looked to be in a commanding position. At this point, though, the innings fell away, and Queensland narrowly won the match. Afterwards, the Sri Lankan captain, Arjuna Ranatunga, complained publicly about various umpire's decisions which had gone against his team.

Queensland

Batsman	How Out	Ttl	Balls	Mins	4s	6s
PE Cantrell	lbw Ranatunga	16	47	73	—	—
GI Foley	c W'wardene b M'singhe	65	118	154	3	—
GM Ritchie (c)	run out	10	15	26	—	—
RB Kerr	c & b Madurasinghe	30	48	55	2	—
SC Storey	c Gurusinha b EAR De Silva	20	24	38	1	—
CJ McDermott	c PA De Silva b EAR De Silva	8	7	10	1	—
CB Smart	not out	23	25	45	—	—
IA Healy (+)	c W'wardene b Ramanayake	8	9	16	—	—
BP Inwood	not out	1	1	2	—	—
MA Polzin	did not bat					
MS Kasprowicz	did not bat					
SUNDRIES: B. 1 LB. 13 W. 0 NB. 0		14	294	213	7	
TOTAL	7 wkts for 195					

F/W: 45 75 127 127 142 170 191

Bowler	O	M	R	Wkts	NB	W
Ramanayake	8	—	29	1	—	—
Wijegunawardene	6	—	24	—	—	—
EAR De Silva	10	—	37	2	—	—
A Ranatunga	5	1	12	1	—	—
Madurasinghe	10	—	33	2	—	—
Jayasuriya	10	—	46	—	—	—
Overs:	49.0					

▶

Sri Lankans

Batsman	How Out	Ttl	Balls	Mins	4s	6s
MAR Samarasekera	c Inwood b Kasprowicz	36	38	58	4	—
HP Tillekeratne (+)	c Healy b McDermott	0	3	5	—	—
AP Gurusinha	c & b Foley	12	38	58	—	—
PA De Silva	c Ritchie b Cantrell	24	19	47	2	1
A Ranatunga (c)	b Foley	8	25	25	1	—
RS Mahanama	not out	67	70	109	2	—
ST Jayasuriya	c Healy b Storey	13	35	40	—	—
EAR De Silva	b McDermott	13	10	19	1	—
CPH Ramanayake	lbw McDermott	0	2	2	—	—
MAWR Madurasinghe	c Ritchie b Inwood	6	7	21	1	—
KIW Wijegunawardene	run out	1	1	7	—	—
SUNDRIES: B. 4 LB. 5 W. 1 NB. 0		10	248	200	11	1
TOTAL		190				

F/W: 1 50 50 75 93 130 161 161 184 190

Bowler	O	M	R	Wkts	NB	W
McDermott	9	2	18	3	—	—
Polzin	7	1	45	—	—	—
Foley	7	1	39	2	—	—
Kasprowicz	6	—	29	1	—	1
Cantrell	4	2	11	1	—	—
Storey	7	1	33	1	—	—
Inwood	1	—	6	1	—	—
Overs:	41.0					

Umpires: CA Bertwistle & MT Musch

12th Men: SG Law (Queensland) & AGD Wickremasinghe (Sri Lankans)

Queensland Country XI v Sri Lankans
Not First-Class
Caloundra
Jan 30 1990
Toss:
Result: Sri Lankans won by 7 wkts

Queensland Country did well to make 7 for 188 in 45 overs, but its bowlers were unable to contain the Sri Lankan batsmen, who scored the runs required in less than 36 overs. Sam Scuderi of Ingham, the brother of Joe Scuderi, and Andrew Walsh, originally from Wollongong but now based in Ipswich, each scored 44. Scuderi is regarded in Queensland cricket circles as a player of exceptional talent, but he looked a little out of touch on this occasion, no doubt because he had played so little cricket at the senior level. Sri Lanka's batsmen scored at a hectic rate from the outset, as if they were hoping for an early finish. The crowd of about 3000 was smaller than expected, and this was blamed partly on a radio station's announcement on the morning of the match that play would not start until after lunch.

Queensland Country XI

Batsman	How Out	Ttl	Balls	Mins	4s	6s
E Harris	lbw Ramanayake	10	19	28	1	—
T Oliver	b EAR De Silva	21	31	55	3	—
S Scuderi	c Jayasuriya b Madurasinghe	44	94	115	3	—
A Walsh	c W'wardene b M'singhe	44	59	81	3	1
L Schulte	lbw Madurasinghe	2	6	7	—	—
B Spanner	not out	24	24	36	1	—
C White	c Ramanayake b PA De Silva	9	14	14	1	—

Batsman	How Out	Ttl	Balls	Mins	4s	6s
B Murphy	st W'singhe b EAR De Silva	27	16	18	—	3
B Bauer	not out	1	1	1	—	—
G Hogan	did not bat					
P Hutchinson	did not bat					
SUNDRIES: B. 2 LB. 3 W. 0 NB. 1		6	264	177	12	4
TOTAL	7 wkts for 188					
F/W: 28 36 119 125 125 147 187						

Bowler	O	M	R	Wkts	NB	W
Ramanayake	7	2	27	1	1	—
Wijegunawardene	6	1	21	—	—	—
EAR De Silva	9	4	20	2	—	—
A Ranatunga	6	—	26	—	—	—
Jayasuriya	4	—	21	—	—	—
Madurasinghe	9	1	32	3	—	—
PA De Silva	4	—	36	1	—	—
Overs:	45.0					

Sri Lankans

Batsman	How Out	Ttl	Balls	Mins	4s	6s
MAR Samarasekera	c Hogan b Hutchinson	75	86	128	9	1
D Ranatunga	lbw Hutchinson	8	19	26	1	—
AP Gurusinha	c Murphy b Bauer	54	82	92	6	—
PA De Silva	not out	27	22	25	3	—
ST Jayasuriya	not out	6	13	24	—	—
A Ranatunga (c)	did not bat					
AGD Wickremasinghe (+)	did not bat					
EAR De Silva	did not bat					
CPH Ramanayake	did not bat					
MAWR Madurasinghe	did not bat					
KIW Wijegunawardene	did not bat					
SUNDRIES: B. 6 LB. 5 W. 6 NB. 3		20	222	147	19	1
TOTAL	3 wkts for 190					
F/W: 33 153 153						

Bowler	O	M	R	Wkts	NB	W
Hutchinson	9	—	41	2	3	1
Hogan	5	—	28	—	—	—
White	9	1	40	—	—	2
Bauer	8.3	1	47	1	—	3
Schulte	1	—	7	—	—	—
Spanner	3	—	16	—	—	—
Overs:	35.3					

Umpires: R Christenson & W Mateson

Western Australia v Sri Lankans
Not First-Class
WACA Ground, Perth
Feb 2 1990
Toss: Western Australia
Result: Sri Lankans by 4 wkts

Arriving at the crease when Western Australia was in trouble at 3 for 20, Wayne Andrews proceeded to play a controlled and finally unbeaten innings which was largely responsible for the advancement of the home side's total beyond 200. His 103 not out was scored off 127 balls, although he hit only five boundaries. Ravi Ratnayeke prevented a last-minute surge of scoring by taking 2 wickets in the last over of the innings, the 48th. Sri Lanka lost one wicket before the side had scored and later slipped to 4 for 68. Hashan Tillekeratne, who made a cautious 68, and Roshan Mahanama, who made a rapid

65, then stopped the slide with a partnership of 101. Sri Lanka raced to victory in the 47th over. In the end, Ravindran Ratnayeke ensured the victory was obtained with balls to spare by scoring 10 runs off the 4 balls he faced. Tom Hogan was treated roughly, having 47 runs hit off his 8 overs.

Western Australia

Batsman	How Out	Ttl	Balls	Mins	4s	6s
MW McPhee	c Tillekeratne b Labrooy	5	15	29	—	—
DJ Ramshaw	run out	0	5	12	—	—
JA Brayshaw	b Ratnayake	7	33	40	—	—
GM Wood	c A Ranatunga b Gurusinha	18	50	81	—	—
WS Andrews (c)	not out	103	127	160	5	—
BP Julian	c & b Madurasinghe	23	26	33	2	—
TG Hogan	b Ratnayake	33	42	70	1	—
MB Palmer (+)	b Ratnayeke	0	1	1	—	—
RS Russell	not out	1	1	2	—	—
PA Capes	did not bat					
CD Mack	did not bat					
SUNDRIES: B. 0 LB. 5 W. 6 NB. 3		14	300	216	8	—
TOTAL	7 wkts for 204					

F/W: 6 6 20 66 108 202 202

Bowler	O	M	R	Wkts	NB	W
Labrooy	3	—	5	1	—	1
Ratnayake	10	1	37	3	2	1
Ramanayake	10	—	44	—	1	1
A Ranatunga	10	—	39	—	—	3
Gurusinha	7	—	32	1	—	—
Madurasinghe	6	—	31	1	—	—
PA De Silva	2	—	11	—	—	—
Overs:	48.0					

Sri Lankans

Batsman	How Out	Ttl	Balls	Mins	4s	6s
D Ranatunga	c Palmer b Capes	0	2	1	—	—
HP Tillekeratne (+)	c Palmer b Russell	68	122	196	5	—
AP Gurusinha	c Hogan b Mack	12	36	30	—	—
PA De Silva	c Ramshaw b Russell	19	25	32	3	—
A Ranatunga (c)	c Wood b Julian	6	14	21	1	—
RS Mahanama	c Mack b Capes	65	68	83	4	—
ST Jayasuriya	not out	10	19	27	1	—
RJ Ratnayake	not out	10	4	6	2	—
CPH Ramanayake	did not bat					
MAWR Madurasinghe	did not bat					
GF Labrooy	did not bat					
SUNDRIES: B. 0 LB. 6 W. 9 NB. 1		16	290	204	16	—
TOTAL	6 wkts for 206					

F/W: 0 20 49 68 169 191

Bowler	O	M	R	Wkts	NB	W
Capes	9.3	1	32	2	—	5
Mack	10	1	28	1	—	1
Julian	10	1	43	1	—	1
Russell	9	—	50	2	1	2
Hogan	8	—	47	—	—	—
Overs:	46.3					

Umpires: TA Prue & RA Emerson

12th Men: AD Mullally (Western Australia) & Sri Lankans - not named

Western Australia v Sri Lankans
Not First-Class
WACA Ground, Perth
Feb 4 1990
Toss: Western Australia
Result: Western Australia by 65 runs

Western Australia reversed the result of the match against Sri Lanka two days before by dismissing the tourists in the 41st over for a mere 143. Batting first, the Western Australians played steadily for a total of 6 for 208. Again, the Sri Lankans failed to get through the required number of overs, and the match was shortened to 48 overs. Western Australia's successful batsmen were Mark McPhee, who was run out for 68, and Graeme Wood, who was unbeaten on 71. In reply, the Sri Lankans lost their first wicket for 0, then moved to 1 for 43 before the collapse of its innings began. Thereafter, wickets fell steadily. This was partly to the credit of the Western Australian bowlers, but the Sri Lankans accelerated the collapse by running themselves out. Three of Sri Lanka's top six batsmen lost their wickets in this way.

Western Australia

Batsman	How Out	Ttl	Balls	Mins	4s	6s
DJ Ramshaw	c D Ranatunga b Ramanayake	15	45	60	2	—
MW McPhee	run out	68	103	150	5	—
GM Wood	not out	71	102	150	2	—
JA Brayshaw	b EAR De Silva	22	33	31	—	—
TJ Zoehrer (+)	c (s)W'singhe b EAR De Silva	7	6	5	1	—
WS Andrews (c)	b EAR De Silva	2	2	1	—	—
BP Julian	c NLK Ratnayake b Ramanayake	3	6	10	—	—
KH MacLeay	not out	2	4	5	—	—
CD Matthews	did not bat					
CD Mack	did not bat					
AD Mullally	did not bat					
SUNDRIES: B. 1 LB. 7 W. 8 NB. 2		18	301	212	10	—
TOTAL	6 wkts for 208					

F/W: 46 133 169 179 182 197

Bowler	O	M	R	Wkts	NB	W
RJ Ratnayake	10	1	34	—	—	2
NLK Ratnayake	8	—	31	—	—	—
Ramanayake	9	1	33	2	2	1
A Ranatunga	10	1	46	—	—	2
EAR De Silva	10	—	45	3	—	—
Gurusinha	1	—	11	—	—	—
Overs:	48.0					

Sri Lankans

Batsman	How Out	Ttl	Balls	Mins	4s	6s
MAR Samarasekera	c Wood b Mullally	0	5	3	—	—
HP Tillekeratne (+)	c MacLeay b Matthews	23	48	56	3	—
AP Gurusinha	run out	11	31	57	1	—
PA De Silva	run out	14	20	28	2	—
A Ranatunga (c)	lbw Matthews	2	3	5	—	—
ST Jayasuriya	run out	24	45	60	2	—
D Ranatunga	c Zoehrer b Mullally	8	14	19	2	—
EAR De Silva	c & b Julian	15	53	78	1	—
CPH Ramanayake	b Julian	1	11	16	—	—
RJ Ratnayake	c Mullally b Mack	16	35	40	1	—
NLK Ratnayake	not out	1	2	4	—	—
SUNDRIES: B. 0 LB. 7 W. 17 NB. 4		28	267	191	12	—
TOTAL		143				

F/W: 0 43 48 54 67 91 106 109 142 143

▶

Bowler	O	M	R	Wkts	NB	W
Mullally	10	1	21	2	—	6
Mack	8.4	1	32	1	3	5
MacLeay	10	1	25	—	—	3
Matthews	6	1	33	2	—	2
Julian	6	1	25	2	1	1
Overs:	40.4					

Umpires: RJ Evans & GJ Bibby

12th Men: MB Palmer (Western Australia) & Sri Lankans – not named

Western Australia Country XI v Sri Lankans
Not First-Class
Brookton
Feb 6 1990
Toss: Western Australia Country XI
Result: Sri Lankans won by 63 runs

The Brookton pitch played reasonably well, so it could not be blamed for the low scoring in this match. Batting first, the Sri Lankans were all out for 173 in 37.1 overs, Aravinda de Silva dominating the innings with a score of 96. In reply, Western Australia Country could manage only 110 before it was all out in the 36th over. Peter Shine of Bunbury made 29 and Mike Knuckey of Geraldton 22. The match was played in a social atmosphere which perhaps detracted from the Sri Lankans' performance.

Sri Lankans

Batsman	How Out	Ttl	Balls	Mins	4s	6s
D Ranatunga	c Shine b Menasse	4	48	53	—	—
AGD Wickremasinghe (+)	c Waldron b Obst	3	9	16	—	—
AP Gurusinha	c Waldron b Obst	2	3	2	—	—
PA De Silva	st Waldron b Menasse	96	82	100	10	3
A Ranatunga (c)	c Waldron b Francis	6	7	12	—	—
ST Jayasuriya	st Waldron b Menasse	3	12	11	—	—
EAR De Silva	not out	32	55	66	4	—
MAWR Madurasinghe	run out	2	6	8	—	—
RJ Ratnayake	c Shine b Rowe	1	2	4	—	—
NLK Ratnayake	c Waldron b Wyllie	4	3	2	—	—
KIW Wijegunawardene	b Rowe	1	3	3	—	—
SUNDRIES: B. 2 LB. 8 W. 7 NB. 2		19	230	147	14	3
TOTAL		173				

F/W: 8 10 51 73 86 148 158 165 169 173

Bowler	O	M	R	Wkts	NB	W
Obst	6	—	23	2	2	1
Morris	6	1	13	—	—	3
Francis	9	—	35	1	—	—
Menasse	9	—	53	3	—	—
Rowe	6.1	—	33	2	—	—
Wyllie	1	—	6	1	—	—
Overs:	37.1					

Western Australia Country XI

Batsman	How Out	Ttl	Balls	Mins	4s	6s
D Wyllie	c W'singhe b RJ Ratnayake	0	1	1	—	—
L Bowyer	c PA De Silva b RJ Ratnayake	4	18	31	—	—
P Shine	c W'singhe b W'ardene	29	54	83	3	—
M Knuckey	c W'singhe b Ramanayake	22	20	26	2	—
T Waldron (c) (+)	b EAR De Silva	17	38	71	—	1
R Waterman	b Ramanayake	2	6	5	—	—
R Menasse	c & b EAR De Silva	7	29	33	—	—
P Rowee	c NLK Ratnayake b M'singhe	13	28	25	—	—

▶

Batsman	How Out	Ttl	Balls	Mins	4s	6s
D Francis	not out	5	18	6	—	—
M Obst	b NLK Ratnayake	0	2	1	—	—
G Morris	stp W'singhe b M'singhe	0	2	3	—	—
SUNDRIES: B. 0 LB. 6 W. 5 NB. 0		11	216	162	5	1
TOTAL		110				

F/W: 0 24 56 65 68 90 95 109 109 110

Bowler	O	M	R	Wkts	NB	W
RJ Ratnayake	5	—	23	2	—	4
NLK Ratnayake	4	—	10	—	—	1
KIW Wijegunawardene	6	—	17	1	—	—
Ramanayake	7	1	26	2	—	—
Madurasinghe	8.1	1	20	2	—	—
EAR De Silva	5	—	8	2	—	—
Overs:	35.1					

Umpires: W Reynolds & D Johnson

12th Men: B Higgins (WA Country) & Sri Lankan—not named

Pakistan v Sri Lanka
Brisbane Cricket Ground, Brisbane
February 10, 1990
Limited-overs International
Result: Pakistan won by 5 wkts

For details see section on Benson and Hedges World Series matches.

Pakistan v Sri Lanka
Bellerive Oval, Hobart
February 15, 1990
Limited-overs International
Result: Pakistan won by 6 wkts

For details see section on Benson and Hedges World Series matches.

Pakistan v Sri Lanka
Adelaide Oval, Adelaide
February 17, 1990
Limited-overs International
Result: Pakistan won by 27 runs

For details see section on Benson and Hedges World Series matches.

Australia v Sri Lanka
Adelaide Oval, Adelaide
February 18, 1990
Limited-overs International
Result: Australia won by 7 wkts

For details see section on Benson and Hedges World Series matches.

Tour Statistics

1989/90 Sri Lankan First-Class Averages

Batsman	M	Inn	NO	Runs	HS	50	100	Avrge	Ct/St
PA De Silva	6	10	—	524	167	4	1	52.40	2
JR Ratnayeke	5	7	1	244	75	3	—	40.67	4
CPH Ramanayake	4	5	4	35	16*	—	—	35.00	1
ST Jayasuriya	4	7	2	171	37*	—	—	34.20	—
MAR Samarasekera	4	7	1	201	133	—	1	33.50	1
EAR De Silva	5	7	1	198	66*	2	—	33.00	4
AP Gurusinha	5	9	—	295	109	1	1	32.78	7
A Ranatunga	4	6	—	181	75	1	—	30.17	4
RS Mahanama	4	7	1	173	85	2	—	28.83	4
HP Tillekeratne	4	7	1	143	74	1	—	23.83	5/-
D Ranatunga	5	9	—	197	56	1	—	21.89	1
GF Labrooy	5	5	1	43	26*	—	—	10.75	1
R Kalpage	1	2	1	10	10*	—	—	10.00	1
RJ Ratnayake	2	4	—	13	5	—	—	3.25	1
KIW Wijegunawardene	1	2	1	6	5	—	—	6.00	—
AGD Wickremasinghe	4	7	1	50	24	—	—	8.33	5/1
MAWR Madurasinghe	2	1	1	4	4*	—	—	—	2
NLK Ratnayake	1	—	—	—	—	—	—	—	—

Bowler	M	Overs	Mdns	Runs	Wkts	Avrge	5wi	10wm	NB	W	Best
AP Gurusinha	5	28.3	4	111	5	22.20	—	—	—	1	2/31
RJ Ratnayake	2	83.4	7	318	10	31.80	1	—	23	4	6/66
GF Labrooy	5	167.1	23	652	15	43.47	2	—	27	—	5/133
NLK Ratnayake	1	21.0	3	45	1	45.00	—	—	—	1	1/18
MAWR Madurasinghe	2	60.0	5	207	4	51.75	—	—	—	—	4/80
A Ranatunga	4	51.0	1	166	3	55.33	—	—	1	—	2/17
CPH Ramanayake	4	129.0	13	490	8	61.25	—	—	35	1	2/81
ST Jayasuriya	4	20.0	3	74	1	74.00	—	—	1	—	1/17
PA De Silva	6	68.0	7	227	3	75.66	—	—	8	—	2/65
EAR De Silva	5	160.1	29	486	6	81.00	—	—	13	—	3/121
JR Ratnayeke	5	125.5	13	423	5	84.60	—	—	19	1	2/75
R Kalpage	1	1.0	—	6	—	—	—	—	—	—	—
KIW Wijegunawardene	1	20.0	1	109	—	—	—	—	5	—	—
MAR Samarasekera	4	1.0	—	15	—	—	—	—	—	—	—
HP Tillekeratne	4	2.0	—	10	—	—	—	—	—	—	—
RS Mahanama	4	1.0	—	3	—	—	—	—	—	—	—

1989/90 Australia v Sri Lanka Test Averages

Batsman	M	Inn	NO	Runs	HS	50	100	Avrge	Ct/St
SR Waugh	2	4	1	267	134*	2	1	89.00	2
MA Taylor	2	4	—	304	164	—	2	76.00	3
AR Border	2	3	—	165	85	2	—	55.00	2
DM Jones	2	4	1	159	118*	—	1	53.00	1
TM Moody	2	4	—	147	106	—	1	36.75	3
MG Hughes	2	4	1	105	30	—	—	35.00	—
IA Healy	2	3	1	64	26*	—	—	32.00	4/-
GF Lawson	1	1	—	22	22	—	—	22.00	1
DC Boon	2	4	—	67	41	—	—	16.75	1
TM Alderman	2	2	—	18	18	—	—	9.00	—
GD Campbell	1	1	—	6	6	—	—	6.00	1
CG Rackemann	1	2	1	5	5*	—	—	5.00	—
PR Sleep	1	1	1	47	47*	—	—	—	—

Bowler	M	Overs	Mdns	Runs	Wkts	Avrge	5wi	10wm	NB	W	Best
PR Sleep	1	46.0	20	99	5	19.80	—	—	—	—	3/26
MG Hughes	2	92.2	22	279	11	25.36	1	—	—	1	5/88
GD Campbell	1	56.0	17	143	5	28.60	—	—	1	—	3/102
CG Rackemann	1	30.3	6	88	3	29.33	—	—	—	—	3/88
TM Alderman	2	93.0	27	200	5	40.00	—	—	8	—	3/81
GF Lawson	1	33.0	10	51	1	51.00	—	—	—	1	1/51
AR Border	2	12.0	4	38	—	—	—	—	—	—	—
DM Jones	2	5.0	2	6	—	—	—	—	—	—	—
TM Moody	2	18.0	8	24	—	—	—	—	—	—	—
SR Waugh	2	6.0	3	6	—	—	—	—	2	—	—

1989/90 Sri Lanka v Australia Test Averages

Batsman	M	Inn	NO	Runs	HS	50	100	Avrge	Ct/St
PA De Silva	2	3	—	314	167	2	1	104.67	1
JR Ratnayeke	2	3	—	140	75	2	—	46.67	—
RS Mahanama	2	3	—	95	85	1	—	31.67	2
D Ranatunga	2	3	—	87	45	—	—	29.00	—
A Ranatunga	2	3	—	84	38	—	—	28.00	3
EAR De Silva	2	3	—	74	50	1	—	24.67	1
AP Gurusinha	2	3	—	63	43	—	—	21.00	3
MAR Samarasekera	1	1	—	18	18	—	—	18.00	1
GF Labrooy	2	3	—	17	11	—	—	5.67	—
HP Tillekeratne	1	2	—	6	6	—	—	3.00	5/-
RJ Ratnayake	1	2	—	5	5	—	—	2.50	1
AGD Wickremasinghe	1	1	—	2	2	—	—	2.00	3/-
CPH Ramanayake	2	3	3	16	10*	—	—	—	1

Bowler	M	Overs	Mdns	Runs	Wkts	Avrge	5wi	10wm	NB	W	Best
AP Gurusinha	2	24.3	4	88	5	17.60	—	—	—	1	2/31
RJ Ratnayake	1	54.4	7	189	8	23.63	1	—	10	4	6/66
PA De Silva	2	33.0	3	110	3	36.67	—	—	6	—	2/65
GF Labrooy	2	96.1	15	363	7	51.86	1	—	20	—	5/133
CPH Ramanayake	2	68.0	5	252	4	63.00	—	—	21	—	2/81
EAR De Silva	2	77.0	17	226	2	113.00	—	—	1	—	1/10
JR Ratnayeke	2	42.5	4	142	1	142.00	—	—	8	—	1/39
RS Mahanama	2	1.0	—	3	—	—	—	—	—	—	—
A Ranatunga	2	19.0	1	74	—	—	—	—	—	—	—

Centuries For Sri Lankans

Total	Batsman	Team	Venue
167	PA De Silva	Australia	Brisbane
133	MAR Samarasekera	New South Wales	Canberra
109	AP Gurusinha	South Australia	Adelaide

Centuries Against Sri Lankans

Total	Batsman	Team	Venue
164	MA Taylor	Australia	Brisbane
156	GA Bishop	South Australia	Adelaide
134	WN Phillips	Victoria	Sale
134*	SR Waugh	Australia	Hobart
133*	DC Boon	Tasmania	Devonport
121	SP O'Donnell	Victoria	Sale
118*	DM Jones	Australia	Hobart
113	JD Siddons	Victoria	Sale
109	DS Lehmann	South Australia	Adelaide
108	MA Taylor	Australia	Hobart
106	TM Moody	Australia	Brisbane

Best Innings Bowling Performance Sri Lankans

Wkts	Bowler	Team	Venue
5/141	GF Labrooy	New South Wales	Canberra

Best Innings Bowling Performance Against Sri Lankans

Wkts	Bowler	Team	Venue
5/88	MG Hughes	Australia	Hobart

Highest Partnership Records For Sri Lankans

Wkt	Total	Batsmen	Team	Venue
1st	159	D Ranatunga, MAR Samarasekera	New South Wales	Canberra
2nd	70	D Ranatunga, AP Gurusinha	Australia	Brisbane
3rd	124	AP Gurusinha, PA De Silva	South Australia	Adelaide
4th	128	RS Mahanama, PA De Silva	Australia	Hobart
5th	53	PA De Silva, A Ranatunga	Australia	Brisbane
6th	54*	HP Tillekeratne, ST Jayasuriya	South Australia	Adelaide
7th	144	PA De Silva, JR Ratnayeke	Australia	Brisbane
8th	44*	CPH Ramanayake, GF Labrooy	Tasmania	Devonport
9th	15	GF Labrooy, CPH Ramanayake	Australia	Hobart
10th	30	JR Ratnayeke, KIW Wijegunawardene	Victoria	Sale

Century Wicket Partnerships For Sri Lankans

Wkt	Total	Batsmen	Team	Venue
1st	159	D Ranatunga, MAR Samarasekera	New South Wales	Canberra
7th	144	PA De Silva, JR Ratnayeke	Australia	Brisbane
4th	128	RS Mahanama, PA De Silva	Australia	Hobart
3rd	124	AP Gurusinha, PA De Silva	South Australia	Adelaide
7th	124	JR Ratnayeke, EAR De Silva	Australia	Hobart
4th	103	HP Tillekeratne, EAR De Silva	Tasmania	Devonport

Highest Partnership Records Against Sri Lankans

Wkt	Total	Batsmen	Team	Venue
1st	84	SM Small, MA Taylor	New South Wales	Canberra
2nd	192*	G Shipperd, DC Boon	Tasmania	Devonport
3rd	203	WN Phillips, JD Siddons	Victoria	Sale
4th	149	MA Taylor, SR Waugh	Australia	Brisbane
5th	72	GR Parker, SP O'Donnell	Victoria	Sale
6th	260*	DM Jones, SR Waugh	Australia	Hobart
7th	79	MD O'Neill, GRJ Matthews	New South Wales	Canberra
8th	58	AK Zesers, CR Miller	South Australia	Adelaide
9th	22*	DC Boon, GD Campbell	Tasmania	Devonport
10th	28	CG Rackemann, TM Alderman	Australia	Brisbane

Century Wicket Partnerships Against Sri Lankans

Wkt	Total	Batsmen	Team	Venue
6th	260*	DM Jones, SR Waugh	Australia	Hobart
3rd	203	WN Phillips, JD Siddons	Victoria	Sale
2nd	192*	G Shipperd, DC Boon	Tasmania	Devonport
4th	163	MA Taylor, AR Border	Australia	Hobart
3rd	158	TM Moody, AR Border	Australia	Brisbane
4th	149	MA Taylor, SR Waugh	Australia	Brisbane
4th	140	GA Bishop, DS Lehmann	South Australia	Adelaide
6th	138	SP O'Donnell, DW Fleming	Victoria	Sale
3rd	115	TH Bayliss, SR Waugh	New South Wales	Canberra
3rd	106	GA Bishop, DW Hookes	South Australia	Adelaide

Sri Lankan First-Class Tours of Australia

Results for Sri Lanka

Season	Games	W	L	D	T	Captain
1982/83	2	—	—	2	—	LRD Mendis
1984/85	1	1	—	—	—	LRD Mendis
1987/88	3	—	1	2	—	RS Madugalle
1989/90	6	—	2	4	—	A Ranatunga
Total	12	1	3	8	—	

Sri Lankans in Australia

Opponents	Venue	First Game	Games	W	L	D	T
Australia	Perth	Feb 12 1988	1	—	1	—	—
	Brisbane	Dec 8 1989	1	—	—	1	—
	Hobart Bel	Dec 16 1989	1	—	1	—	—
Total			3	—	2	1	—
New South Wales	Sydney	Feb 10 1983	1	—	—	1	—
	Canberra	Nov 17 1989	1	—	—	1	—
Total			2	—	—	2	—
South Australia	Adelaide	Dec 1 1989	1	—	—	1	—
Tasmania	Devonport	Feb 14 1983	2	—	—	2	—
	Hobart Bel	Jan 23 1988	1	—	—	1	—
Total			3	—	—	3	—
Victoria	Melbourne	Feb 6 1988	1	—	—	1	—
	Sale	Nov 24 1989	1	—	1	—	—
Total			2	—	1	1	—
Western Australia	Perth	Dec 31 1984	1	1	—	—	—

PAKISTAN TOUR OF AUSTRALIA
DECEMBER 1989–FEBRUARY 1990

WHEN THE PAKISTANIS ARRIVED in Australia they were widely regarded as one of the strongest cricket teams in the world—perhaps *the* strongest after the West Indians. When they left three months later after a tour which was consistently unsuccessful, that reputation was considerably diminished. Despite their many failures in Australia, however, nobody doubted that Imran Khan's Pakistanis were a team of fine cricketers. They simply hadn't played well as a team in Australia, and since the tour ended there must have been much self-examination in Pakistan to try to isolate the reason.

It was apparent, even to an outsider, that there were serious, debilitating problems within the Pakistani team. The most telling evidence of this was not so much the Pakistanis' poor performances on the field (although these were certainly evidence of a kind) but rather the many unpleasant incidents on the field which blighted the tour. Of these, none was less pleasant than the silly decision by the Pakistanis to stage a walk-off during their match against Victoria in protest at an umpire's ruling. This was surely the action of a team low in morale and lacking purpose. There was another clue in the Pakistanis' play itself: they fielded badly—invariably a sign of a team unhappy with itself. In fact, at the end of the tour Imran Khan nominated poor catching and the repeated failures of his top order batsmen as primary factors in his team's defeat in the Test series (by one Test to nil) and in the limited-overs competition.

If the Pakistanis had any cause for consolation, it was the outstanding performances of individual players, and no player was more outstanding than Wasim Akram, who convinced many Australians during the tour that he was indeed the world's premier all-rounder. Compared with the bowling of all other Test bowlers seen in Australia during the summer, Akram's was in a class of its own. The Australian opener Mark Taylor, who had faced the best of the West Indian pace bowlers in the past year, rated Akram the finest bowler he had faced in a Test match. Akram bowled fast, he bowled with control, he swung the ball both ways (with little change of action, according to Mark Taylor) and he was always hostile, always probing. If any one delivery in all the matches he played were to be chosen as representative of his skill, it might well be the ball with which he bowled Steve Waugh in the first final of the World Series. It was a fast, in-swinging delivery of full pitch, which began outside off stump and hit leg. Akram's batting, too, had both quality and power, and it seemed surprising that he batted as far down the order (usually at number 8) as he did. The fluency and power of his driving, in particular, were exceptional.

Imran Khan was not the force he had been on previous tours, but he kept picking up useful wickets and his batting was as sound, if not quite so dynamic, as ever. For instance, his scores in the Tests were 3, 45, 13, 136 and 82 not out, which gave him a series average of 69.75. He was always the hardened campaigner, and nowhere did he demonstrate that better than in the last qualifying match of the World Series against Australia. Bowling the last over of the match, Imran had to prevent Australia scoring a mere 4 runs for victory, seemingly an impossible task. In a remarkable display of coolness under pressure, Imran took 2 wickets, restricted Australia to scoring only a leg bye, and consequently won the match for Pakistan.

Javed Miandad appeared to have lost none of his marvellous skill, yet he did not make the impact most people expected him to make on this tour. Often he began playing what seemed likely to become a big innings, but somehow the big innings did not follow. His scores in the Tests indicate this—3, 65, 52, 21 and 49. Whatever the full story behind Abdul Qadir's early return to Pakistan, his absence proved to be a great pity, not only for Pakistani supporters who looked to him for match-winning performances but for Australian supporters, too, for they were deprived of the engaging spectacle of a world class leg-spinner in combat.

1989/90 Pakistan Tour of Australia

Date	Venue	Opponent	Result for Pakistan
Dec 27	Perth	Western Australia	Lost by an inns & 78 runs
Dec 31*	Perth	Sri Lanka	Lost by 3 wkts
Jan 3*	Melbourne	Australia	Lost by 7 wkts
Jan 6	Brisbane	Queensland	Drawn
Jan 12	Melbourne	Australia	Lost by 92 runs
Jan 19	Adelaide	Australia	Drawn
Jan 26	Melbourne	Victoria	Lost by 59 runs
Jan 31*	Canberra	Prime Minister's XI	Lost by 81 runs
Feb 3	Sydney	Australia	Drawn
Feb 10*	Brisbane	Sri Lanka	Won by 5 wkts
Feb 11*	Brisbane	Australia	Lost by 67 runs
Feb 13*	Sydney	Australia	Won by 5 wkts
Feb 15*	Hobart Bel	Sri Lanka	Won by 6 wkts
Feb 17*	Adelaide	Sri Lanka	Won by 23 runs
Feb 20*	Sydney	Australia	Won by 2 runs
Feb 23*	Melbourne	Australia	Lost by 7 wkts
Feb 25*	Sydney	Australia	Lost by 69 runs

* Denotes not first-class

SHEFFIELD SHIELD – WESTERN AUSTRALIA

Back Row, l to r: Mark McPhee, Darrin Ramshaw, Chris Mack, Steve Russell, Tom Moody, Brendon Julian, Ken MacLeay and James Brayshaw. Front Row, l to r: Graham McKenzie (Assistant Coach), Mike Veletta, Peter Capes, Terry Alderman, Geoff Marsh (Captain), Wayne Andrews (Vice Captain), Tom Hogan, Chris Matthews and Daryl Foster (Coach)

SHEFFIELD SHIELD – VICTORIA

Standing, l to r: S Warne, S Prescott, N Strong, T Amalfi, W A Phillips, C Bradley, W Ayres, D Emerson, G Parker. Middle: R McCarthy, J Sutherland, C Bustard, D Welch, R Herman, P Reiffel, D Hickey, M Hughes, L Stonehouse, D Fleming. Seated, l to r: P Jackson, M Dimattina, J Siddons, I Redpath (Coach), T Dodemaide, WN Phillips, P Smith, G Watts. Absentees: S O'Donnell (Captain), D Jones, I Frazer, L Herbert, C Ingram, P McIntyre, M Osborne, D Saker, D Walker, P Young

AUSTRALIA – WOMEN

Back Row, l to r: Peter Bakker (Coach), Sally Griffiths, Salley Moffat, Debbie Wilson, Zoe Goss, Katherine Raymont, Andrea Macauley, Melissa Papworth, Meg McIntyre (Physiotherapist). Front Row, l to r: Denise Annetts, Belinda Haggett, Christina Matthews, Lyn Larsen, Karen Brown, Jo Broadbent, Ailsa Rowell, Christine Brierley (Manager)

1st GRADE PREMIERS – GORDON, SYDNEY

Back Row, l to r: David Evans (Manager/Scorer), Warwick Adlam, Ross Toohey, John Davison, Richard Stobo, Mark Aldridge, Peter Rowley-Bates, Michael Cant, Paul McLean. Front Row, l to r: Geoff Hickman, Kevin Roberts, Mark O'Neill, Stephen Day (Captain), Phil Emery, Adam Gilchrist, Jamie Bray

Western Australia v Pakistanis
WACA Ground, Perth
Dec 27, 28, 29 1989
Toss: Western Australia
Result: Western Australia by an inns & 78 runs

Pakistan began its tour on a low note, losing to Western Australia by an innings and 78 runs in just over two days. Western Australia batted first, and on an apparently inoffensive pitch, compiled 9 declared for 398. Tom Moody missed a century by 7 runs, and Wayne Andrews and Mike Veletta both scored half-centuries. In reply, the Pakistanis had moved without mishap to 37 when the fast bowler Chris Matthews came on at first change, bowling with the wind. An hour and a quarter later, the Pakistanis had lost all 10 wickets, and Matthews had the exceptional figures of 7 for 22 off 8.3 overs. There was nothing in the pitch or the conditions to explain Pakistan's collapse, which was widely attributed to poor batting. Made to follow-on, Pakistan showed little improvement in its second innings. The opener Shoaib Mohammad (40) played a gritty innings, but other top order batsmen went cheaply. Then, as if in desperation, Saleem Yousuf (78) and the captain, Abdul Qadir (51), made a savage assault on the bowling. Yousuf hit 14 fours and Qadir 4 sixes. A late collapse though, brought the match to an early end.

Western Australia

First Innings

Batsman	How Out	Ttl	Balls
JA Brayshaw	c Yousuf b Aaqib	23	50
MRJ Veletta	c Yousuf b Qadir	51	99
TM Moody	c Maqsood b Ghauri	93	108
GM Wood (c)	c Ijaz b Waqar	1	14
WS Andrews	c Shoaib b Maqsood	80	108
TJ Zoehrer (+)	b Maqsood	33	49
TG Hogan	not out	41	48
KH MacLeay	c Ijaz b Ghauri	27	50
RS Russell	c Anwar b Ghauri	18	28
CD Matthews	st Yousuf b Qadir	1	3
PA Capes	not out	7	5
SUNDRIES: B. 0 LB. 9 W. 1 NB. 13		23	562
TOTAL	9 wkts dec	398	

F/W: 50 138 145 210 297 305 350 379 380

Bowler	O	M	R	Wkts	NB	W
Aaqib Javed	19	5	50	1	7	—
Waqar Younus	15	2	72	1	—	—
Maqsood Rana	15	2	57	2	—	1
Abdul Qadir	21	2	101	2	6	—
Nadeem Ghauri	18	—	94	3	—	—
Shoaib Mohammad	2	—	15	—	—	—
Overs:	90.0					

Pakistanis

First Innings				Second Innings		
Batsman	How Out	Ttl	Balls	How Out	Ttl	Balls
Aamir Malik	c Zoehrer b Matthews	19	45	c Veletta b Capes	0	6
Shoaib Mohammad	b Matthews	30	46	c (s) Ramshaw b Hogan	40	125
Mansoor Akhtar	lbw Matthews	0	1	c Wood b Capes	20	62
Saeed Anwar	c Wood b Russell	0	9	c Brayshaw b Capes	11	13
Ijaz Ahmed	lbw Matthews	3	15	lbw Matthews	27	43
Salim Yousuf (+)	c Veletta b Russell	18	26	c Russell b Capes	78	112

▶

129

Batsman	How Out	Ttl	Balls	How Out	Ttl	Balls
Abdul Qadir (c)	c MacLeay b Matthews	0	3	c Zoehrer b MacLeay	51	40
Aaqib Javed	c Zoehrer b Russell	0	4	b Capes	0	1
Nadeem Ghauri	b Matthews	1	3 (11)	not out	0	2
Waqar Younus	not out	1	5	c Zoehrer b MacLeay	3	5
Maqsood Rana	b Matthews	0	4 (9)	b Capes	7	12
SUNDRIES: B. 1 LB. 1 W. 1 NB. 0		3	161	B. 0 LB. 6 W. 0 NB. 2	8	421
TOTAL		75			245	

F/W: 41 45 46 51 68 68 69 70 74 75

F/W: 0 53 77 79 142 216 234 241 245 245

Bowler	O	M	R	Wkts	NB	W	Bowler	O	M	R	Wkts	NB	W
Capes	5	2	17	—	—	—	Capes	18	3	92	6	2	—
MacLeay	6	—	24	—	—	—	MacLeay	12	7	18	2	—	—
Matthews	8.3	2	22	7	—	1	Matthews	12.4	1	37	1	—	—
Russell	7	4	10	3	—	—	Russell	11	2	29	—	—	—
Overs:	26.3						Hogan	12	2	54	1	—	—
							Moody	3	1	7	—	—	—
							Brayshaw	0.2	—	2	—	—	—
							Overs:	69.0					

Umpires: TA Prue & GJ Bibby

12th Men: DJ Ramshaw (Western Australia) & Tauseef Ahmed (Pakistanis)

Pakistan v Sri Lanka
WACA Ground, Perth
December 31, 1989
Limited-overs International
Result: Sri Lanka won by 3 wkts

For details see section on Benson and Hedges World Series matches.

Australia v Pakistan
Melbourne Cricket Ground, Melbourne
January 3, 1990
Limited-overs International
Result: Australia won by 7 wkts

For details see section on Benson and Hedges World Series matches.

Queensland v Pakistanis
Brisbane Cricket Ground, Brisbane
Jan 6, 7, 8, 9 1990
Toss: Queensland
Result: Drawn

After losing the first three matches of their tour, the Pakistanis must have been anxious to do well against Queensland, but things went badly for them at first. Sent in, Pakistan struggled to make 257. Javed Miandad (77) batted with assurance, but for the most part the Pakistanis appeared to be searching for form. Mick Polzin, brought into the team at the last minute when Craig McDermott withdrew, made the most of the opportunity by taking 5 for 56. The wicket-keeper, Ian Healy, had a hand in five dismissals, one of them a smart stumping. Queensland replied resoundingly with 8 declared for 436, an innings dominated by a partnership of 225 between young Geoff Foley, who made a determined 155—a record score by an Australian on debut against a touring side—and Greg Ritchie, whose 123 was his twentieth first-class century. The Pakistani fieldsmen dropped eight catches. With more than a day to go, the Pakistanis looked in danger of another defeat, but in their second innings their batsmen lifted their performance generally, obtaining valuable match practice for the coming Test. One serious concern was the poor form of leg-spinner Abdul Qadir, who injured a finger in this match.

Pakistanis

First Innings

Batsman	How Out	Ttl	Balls	How Out	Ttl	Balls
Aamir Malik	c Healy b Polzin	5	21	c Ritchie b Polzin	14	39
Shoaib Mohammad	c Foley b Polzin	13	23	c Clifford b Polzin	52	102
Mansoor Akhtar	c Healy b Rackemann	14	51	b Cantrell	74	111
Javed Miandad	st Healy b Storey	77	157 (5)	not out	55	123
Saeed Anwar	c Healy b Polzin	28	63 (6)	c Smart b Carew	25	45
Ijaz Ahmed	c Smart b Storey	44	77 (4)	c Polzin b Cantrell	35	46
Imran Khan (c)	c Healy b Carew	20	77	c Law b Foley	21	32
Salim Yousuf (+)	not out	35	105	not out	21	48
Abdul Qadir	b Carew	0	4			
Waqar Younus	c Clifford b Polzin	1	6			
Aaqib Javed	c Clifford b Polzin	0	13			
SUNDRIES: B. 1 LB. 11 W. 0 NB. 8		20	597	B. 2 LB. 3 W. 0 NB. 5 10		546
TOTAL		257		6 wkts for 307		

F/W: 20 26 57 109 191 192 246 250 257 257

F/W: 28 115 165 194 233 266

Second Innings

Bowler	O	M	R	Wkts	NB	W	Bowler	O	M	R	Wkts	NB	W
Polzin	24	8	56	5	—	—	Polzin	18	3	60	2	—	—
Carew	16	5	43	2	—	—	Carew	21	6	65	1	—	—
Rackemann	21	4	47	1	4	—	Rackemann	9	2	22	—	—	—
Storey	17	6	45	2	3	—	Storey	15	4	67	—	1	—
Cantrell	12	1	40	—	—	—	Cantrell	14	3	46	2	—	—
Foley	8	1	14	—	1	—	Foley	10	—	28	1	4	—
Overs:	98.0						Law	2	—	13	—	—	—
							Healy	1	—	1	—	—	—
							Overs:	90.0					

Queensland

First Innings

Batsman	How Out	Ttl	Balls
PE Cantrell	c Qadir b Waqar	19	47
GI Foley	c Yousuf b Aaqib	155	406
SG Law	c Imran b Qadir	30	87
GM Ritchie (c)	c Yousuf b Aamir	123	195
PS Clifford	b Aamir	1	12
CB Smart	lbw Aaqib	11	19
SC Storey	c Aaqib b Anwar	54	105
IA Healy (+)	b Anwar	25	87
MA Polzin	not out	0	4
CG Rackemann	did not bat		
PJ Carew	did not bat		
SUNDRIES: B. 0 LB. 12 W. 1 NB. 5		18	962
TOTAL	8 wkts dec 436		

F/W: 35 105 330 332 349 356 434 436

Bowler	O	M	R	Wkts	NB	W
Imran Khan	34	6	80	—	—	—
Aaqib Javed	34	11	79	2	3	1
Waqar Younus	28	4	89	1	—	—
Abdul Qadir	32.2	6	80	1	—	—
Shoaib Mohammad	2	1	4	—	—	—
Aamir Malik	14	1	57	2	2	—
Saeed Anwar	14.5	1	35	2	—	—
Overs:	159.1					

Umpires: CD Timmins & PD Parker

12th Men: BP Inwood (Queensland) & Tauseef Ahmed (Pakistanis)

FIRST TEST

Australia v Pakistan
Melbourne Cricket Ground, Melbourne
Jan 12, 13, 14, 15, 16 1990
Toss: Pakistan
Result: Australia by 92 runs

Australia won this Test largely because its batsmen were better able to handle difficult batting conditions. Imran Khan won the toss and sent Australia in, having decided the pitch would favour his seam bowlers. This proved to be true, and the Australian openers, Mark Taylor (52) and Geoff Marsh (30), did well to put on 90 for the first wicket. The worth of their opening stand became apparent when it was followed at once by a collapse, at the end of which Australia had lost 4 wickets for 8 runs. Australia slipped further to 6 for 148, but then Peter Sleep (23) and Ian Healy (48) prevented complete disintegration of the innings with a seventh-wicket partnership of 53. Wasim Akram, who bowled superbly and took 6 for 62, deserved most of the credit for restricting Australia to a total of 223. The Pakistanis thus had an opportunity to bat themselves into a commanding position, but from the outset they floundered against the Australian pace attack, and in just under five hours the Pakistani innings was over. Not one batsman reached 20, and the small total, 107, meant Australia led by 116. Australia's second innings was dominated by Mark Taylor's hard-earned century and Allan Border's patient 62 not out. When Border declared at 8 for 312, Pakistan had to score 429 for victory or bat just over 10 hours for a draw. Javed Miandad's dismissal late on the fourth day for 65 left Pakistan 4 for 134 and seemed to rule out any chance of its saving the match. But on the last day Ijaz Ahmed led such a determined fight for survival that in the afternoon it seemed Australia might be denied victory after all. Ijaz batted for seven and a half hours for his 121, and in the end Australia achieved its victory with only 22 minutes to spare. The Test was marred by an on-field altercation between the captains and recriminations afterwards about the number of bouncers bowled by both sides.

Australia

First Innings

Batsman	How Out	Ttl	Balls		How Out	Ttl	Balls
GR Marsh	c Yousuf b Akram	30	125	(2)	c Akram b Aaqib	24	82
MA Taylor	c Aaqib b Imran	52	144	(1)	c Aamir b Tauseef	101	240
DC Boon	lbw Akram	0	1		run out	21	45
AR Border (c)	c Miandad b Akram	24	76		not out	62	184
DM Jones	c Yousuf b Imran	0	1		lbw Akram	10	11
SR Waugh	c Yousuf b Aaqib	20	35		c Yousuf b Akram	3	3
PR Sleep	lbw Akram	23	74		b Akram	0	1
IA Healy (+)	c Shoaib b Aaqib	48	81		c Ijaz b Akram	25	37
MG Hughes	c Mansoor b Akram	8	12		c Mansoor b Akram	32	50
TM Alderman	c Aamir b Akram	0	2		not out	1	19
CG Rackemann	not out	0	2				
SUNDRIES: B. 0 LB. 9 W. 0 NB. 9		18	553		B. 2 LB. 10 W. 1 NB. 20	33	672
TOTAL		223			8 wkts for 312		

Second Innings

F/W: 90 90 98 98 131 148 201 223 223 223

F/W: 73 116 204 216 220 220 260 305

132

Bowler	O	M	R	Wkts	NB	W
Imran Khan	18	6	53	2	—	—
Wasim Akram	30	9	62	6	8	—
Aaqib Javed	22.1	7	47	2	—	—
Waqar Younus	12	3	27	—	1	—
Tauseef Ahmed	8	1	25	—	—	—
Overs:	90.1					

Bowler	O	M	R	Wkts	NB	W
Wasim Akram	41.4	12	98	5	11	—
Aaqib Javed	21	1	55	1	5	—
Imran Khan	8	2	21	—	1	—
Waqar Younus	22	4	68	—	3	1
Tauseef Ahmed	16	3	58	1	—	—
Overs:	108.4					

Pakistan

First Innings

Batsman	How Out	Ttl	Balls
Aamir Malik	lbw Alderman	7	30
Shoaib Mohammad	c Healy b Alderman	6	14 (3)
Mansoor Akhtar	c Taylor b Rackemann	5	18 (2)
Javed Miandad	c Healy b Alderman	3	48
Ijaz Ahmed	c Taylor b Hughes	19	33
Imran Khan (c)	c Alderman b Rackemann	3	29
Salim Yousuf (+)	c Taylor b Hughes	16	36
Wasim Akram	c Healy b Hughes	6	9
Tauseef Ahmed	not out	9	94
Waqar Younus	lbw Sleep	18	85
Aaqib Javed	c Healy b Rackemann	0	9
SUNDRIES: B.1 LB.4 W.0 NB.10		15	405
TOTAL		107	

F/W: 12 20 20 44 44 65 71 71 106 107

Second Innings

How Out	Ttl	Balls
c Taylor b Hughes	0	20
c Boon b Hughes	10	39
lbw Alderman	14	50
lbw Waugh	65	100
c Marsh b Hughes	121	331
lbw Alderman	45	111
lbw Alderman	38	66
c Taylor b Sleep	6	14
not out	14	65
lbw Alderman	4	27
lbw Alderman	0	16
B.1 LB.7 W.2 NB.9	19	839
	336	

F/W: 4 23 31 134 218 219 303 328 333 336

Bowler	O	M	R	Wkts	NB	W
Alderman	19	6	30	3	6	—
Rackemann	21.5	8	32	3	2	—
Hughes	17	7	34	3	2	—
Sleep	8	5	6	1	—	—
Overs:	65.5					

Bowler	O	M	R	Wkts	NB	W
Hughes	42	14	79	3	1	—
Rackemann	38	13	67	—	4	1
Alderman	33.5	6	105	5	4	—
Sleep	21	7	64	1	—	1
Waugh	3	—	13	1	—	—
Overs:	137.5					

Umpires: PJ McConnell & RJ Evans

SECOND TEST

Australia v Pakistan
Adelaide Oval, Adelaide
Jan 19, 20, 21, 22, 23 1990
Toss: Pakistan
Result: Drawn

In this absorbing contest, Pakistan at first looked to be sinking to defeat and then, after a spirited recovery, found itself in a position to win. It was probably fitting, therefore, that the match ended in a draw, with honours for the two sides about even. The first day belonged to Australia. The Pakistanis batted first on what seemed a good wicket, yet by 5.37 pm they were all out for 257. It was a poor batting performance under the circumstances, although Carl Rackemann (4 for 40) and Greg Campbell (3 for 79), replacing the injured Terry Alderman, deserved credit for keeping the Pakistani batsmen under pressure. Javed Miandad and Wasim Akram batted aggressively and both scored 52, the latter's performance being briefly soured by a physical clash with Merv Hughes. Australia advanced to a comfortable first innings lead on the third day, thanks largely to yet another half-century by Mark Taylor and a century by Dean Jones. Akram (5 for 100) again bowled with hostility and skill. By

133

stumps on the third day, Pakistan's top order had been routed by Hughes, and at 4 for 73, still 11 behind Australia, its position was desperate. On the fourth day, however, Imran Khan (136) and Akram (123) turned the match around with marvellous batting. Akram's innings, in particular, was memorable for its immensely powerful drives. Pakistan declared next morning, hopeful of bowling Australia out on a pitch taking spin. Australia needed to score 304 off a minimum of 78 overs to win, but the loss of 2 wickets before lunch forced them to abandon that hope. The redoubtable Mark Taylor (59) and Dean Jones, scoring his second century in the match, kept the Pakistani spin bowlers at bay.

Pakistan

First Innings / Second Innings

Batsman	How Out	Ttl	Balls	How Out	Ttl	Balls
Shoaib Mohammad	lbw Hughes	43	85	c Healy b Hughes	0	4
Rameez Raja	c PL Taylor b Campbell	9	16	c Waugh b Hughes	2	17
Salim Yousuf (+)	lbw Rackemann	38	42	c MA Taylor b Hughes	1	9
Javed Miandad	c Healy b Campbell	52	95 (6)	c PL Taylor b Hughes	21	114
Ijaz Ahmed	c Marsh b Border	28	79 (4)	c PL Taylor b Hughes	4	4
Salim Malik	c Healy b Hughes	11	22 (8)	not out	65	105
Imran Khan (c)	c Healy b Rackemann	13	49 (5)	b PL Taylor	136	361
Wasim Akram	c Border b Campbell	52	68 (7)	b Campbell	123	195
Tauseef Ahmed	c Healy b Rackemann	0	2	c Healy b Rackemann	18	54
Mushtaq Ahmed	c Healy b Rackemann	0	1	b PL Taylor	4	5
Waqar Younus	not out	1	2			
SUNDRIES: B. 4 LB. 4 W. 1 NB. 1		10	461	B. 4 LB. 5 W. 1 NB. 3	13	868
TOTAL		257		9 wkts dec	387	

F/W: 27 91 95 166 187 187 241 251 251 257

F/W: 0 2 7 22 90 281 316 380 387

Bowler	O	M	R	Wkts	NB	W	Bowler	O	M	R	Wkts	NB	W
Hughes	18	5	63	2	—	—	Hughes	32	9	111	5	2	1
Campbell	21.3	2	79	3	1	1	Campbell	29	5	83	1	—	—
PL Taylor	12	—	57	—	—	—	Rackemann	37	11	85	1	1	—
Rackemann	21	3	40	4	—	—	PL Taylor	41.5	13	94	2	—	—
Border	4	—	10	1	—	—	Border	4	—	5	—	—	—
Overs:	76.3						Overs:	143.5					

Australia

First Innings / Second Innings

Batsman	How Out	Ttl	Balls	How Out	Ttl	Balls
GR Marsh	c Yousuf b Akram	13	30			
MA Taylor	lbw Imran	77	193 (1)	c (s) Anwar b Mushtaq	59	106
DC Boon	lbw Akram	29	83 (2)	c Rameez b Akram	5	10
AR Border (c)	b Younus	13	37 (3)	c Yousuf b Younus	8	24
DM Jones	c Akram b Imran	116	239 (4)	not out	121	205
SR Waugh	lbw Akram	17	47 (5)	b Tauseef	4	38
IA Healy (+)	c (s) Maqsood b Younus	12	27 (6)	c (s) Aamir b Tauseef	27	94
PL Taylor	run out	33	144 (7)	c Shoaib b Tauseef	1	19
MG Hughes	not out	6	9 (8)	not out	2	6
GD Campbell	lbw Akram	0	3			
CG Rackemann	b Akram	0	1			
SUNDRIES: B. 0 LB. 12 W. 0 NB. 13		25	813	B. 0 LB. 3 W. 0 NB. 3	6	502
TOTAL		341		6 wkts for	233	

F/W: 82 113 156 188 216 328 328 341 341 341

F/W: 9 33 106 129 213 229

Bowler	O	M	R	Wkts	NB	W	Bowler	O	M	R	Wkts	NB	W
Wasim Akram	43	10	100	5	7	—	Wasim Akram	11	3	29	1	1	—
Waqar Younus	26	4	66	2	3	—	Waqar Younus	14	4	42	1	—	—
Mushtaq Ahmed	23	4	69	—	—	—	Tauseef Ahmed	32	6	80	3	1	—
Imran Khan	27	6	61	2	3	—	Mushtaq Ahmed	25	5	72	1	1	—
Tauseef Ahmed	14	1	33	—	—	—	Shoaib Mohammad	1	—	7	—	—	—
Overs:	133.0						Overs:	83.0					

Umpires: AR Crafter & LJ King

12th Men: PR Sleep (Australia) & Maqsood Rana (Pakistan)

Victoria v Pakistanis
Melbourne Cricket Ground, Melbourne
Jan 26, 27, 28 1990
Toss: Victoria
Result: Victoria won by 59 runs

This was an unhappy match for the Pakistanis in several respects. They lost it by 59 runs and they created a regrettable incident on the first day by walking off the field. The reason for this extraordinary action was umpire Robin Bailache's decision to rule the leg-spinner Mushtaq Ahmed out of the attack after formally warning him three times in one over for running on the pitch. Claiming he had not been told of the second warning, Pakistan's captain, Rameez Raja, sent for the team's manager, Intikhab Alam, who at 2.46 pm led the Pakistanis off the field. A settlement was arrived at hurriedly by the match referee, Ken Jacobs, as a result of which Mushtaq was considered to have received only two warnings, and play resumed at 3.19 pm. Victoria's reliable opener Gary Watts (102) and Simon O'Donnell (69) helped the home side to a total of 313. Pakistan replied with 233. In their second innings, the Victorians were at a loss against the off-spinner Tauseef Ahmed (5 for 42) and were bundled out for 173. The Pakistanis thus needed to score 254 to win, but in another disappointing batting display they were all out for 194. Peter McIntyre took 5 for 53, one of the best performances by an Australian leg-spinner in recent years.

Victoria

Batsman	How Out	Ttl	Balls	How Out	Ttl	Balls
	First Innings			Second Innings		
GM Watts	lbw Younus	102	221	c Ijaz b Tauseef	70	127
SS Prescott	c Anwar b Ghauri	10	93	b Younus	2	7
WN Phillips	c Anwar b Mushtaq	4	16	b Tauseef	16	39
JD Siddons	c Ghauri b Mushtaq	17	25	not out	22	45
WG Ayres	b Ghauri	24	65	lbw Aaqib	9	30
SP O'Donnell (c)	c Ijaz b Younus	69	90 (7)	lbw Tauseef	16	13
AIC Dodemaide	c Aamir b Ghauri	16	41 (8)	c Mushtaq b Tauseef	15	31
PR Reiffel	not out	18	98 (9)	c Aamir b Mushtaq	0	2
MGD Dimattina (+)	lbw Younus	0	1 (6)	c Yousuf b Aaqib	1	11
DW Fleming	c Yousuf b Ghauri	11	23	c Ijaz b Mushtaq	0	10
PE McIntyre	c Mushtaq b Aaqib	20	64	c Anwar b Tauseef	6	12
SUNDRIES: B. 12 LB. 3 W. 0 NB. 7		22	737	B. 3 LB. 10 W. 0 NB. 3	16	327
TOTAL		313			173	

F/W: 51 56 91 142 218 257 259 259 280 313

F/W: 21 67 110 113 119 134 141 149 167 173

Bowler	O	M	R	Wkts	NB	W	Bowler	O	M	R	Wkts	NB	W
Waqar Younus	25	1	84	3	1	—	Waqar Younus	6	—	27	1	—	—
Aaqib Javed	11	3	43	1	5	—	Aaqib Javed	14	3	53	2	3	—
Nadeem Ghauri	40	16	59	4		—	Nadeem Ghauri	10	4	21	—	—	—
Tauseef Ahmed	24	5	58	—	—	—	Tauseef Ahmed	18.5	7	42	5	—	—
Mushtaq Ahmed	21	7	54	2	1	—	Mushtaq Ahmed	5	2	17	2	—	—
Overs:	121.0						Overs:	53.5					

Pakistanis

Batsman	How Out	Ttl	Balls	How Out	Ttl	Balls
	First Innings			Second Innings		
Rameez Raja	c Dimattina b Reiffel	4	6 (4)	c O'Donnell b Reiffel	9	12
Shoaib Mohammad	c Siddons b Reiffel	9	15	lbw Fleming	7	11
Aamir Malik	c Fleming b Reiffel	53	82 (1)	c (s) Frazer b Reiffel	8	17

▶

135

Batsman	How Out	Ttl	Balls		How Out	Ttl	Balls
Ijaz Ahmed	lbw Dodemaide	36	82	(5)	c Reiffel b McIntyre	24	28
Salim Yousuf (+)	c Siddons b Reiffel	3	18	(7)	c & b McIntyre	11	28
Saeed Anwar	c Dimattina b Dodemaide	23	36	(6)	c Prescott b O'Donnell	44	48
Mushtaq Ahmed	c Prescott b Dodemaide	32	77	(8)	c Dodemaide b McIntyre	15	25
Tauseef Ahmed	c Prescott b Fleming	36	93	(3)	b McIntyre	22	86
Waqar Younus	b Fleming	23	41		c Ayres b McIntyre	14	30
Nadeem Ghauri	c Siddons b Fleming	0	1		c O'Donnell b Dodemaide	19	50
Aaqib Javed	not out	1	7		not out	9	36
SUNDRIES: B.0 LB.6 W.0 NB.7		13	458		B.0 LB.4 W.0 NB.8	12	363
TOTAL		233				194	

F/W: 5 36 108 111 114 144 184 224 224 233

F/W: 12 16 31 68 120 133 136 151 174 194

Bowler	O	M	R	Wkts	NB	W	Bowler	O	M	R	Wkts	NB	W
Reiffel	20	5	62	4	7	—	Reiffel	18	4	79	2	8	—
Fleming	17.4	4	63	3	—	—	Fleming	7	3	21	1	—	—
O'Donnell	6	—	23	—	—	—	McIntyre	22	7	53	5	—	—
McIntyre	12	4	31	—	—	—	O'Donnell	10	2	33	1	—	—
Dodemaide	19	6	48	3	—	—	Dodemaide	1.5	1	4	1	—	—
Overs:	74.4						Overs:	58.5					

Umpires: RC Bailhache & WP Sheahan

12th Men: ID Frazer (Victoria) & Maqsood Rana (Pakistan)

Prime Minister's XI v Pakistanis
Manuka Oval, Canberra
Jan 31 1990
Toss: Prime Minister's XI
Result: Prime Minister's XI by 81 runs

A match which traditionally has been a light-hearted fixture ended on a sour note when the Pakistanis, seeing no hope of winning, chose to bat out their 50 overs defensively. The last two batsmen, Salim Yousuf and Waqar Younus, were heckled by spectators as they left the field, and even the Prime Minister, Mr Bob Hawke, expressed regret at the Pakistanis' negative approach. The Prime Minister's XI was given a flying start by Jamie Cox (66 off 92 balls) and Mike Veletta (50 off 43), but the most warmly received innings was played by Michael Bevan, originally from Canberra, who batted fluently for 74, scored off 84 balls, and was later named Man of the Match. It was clear several Pakistani batsmen would have to play big innings if Pakistan was to better the Prime Minister's XI's total, 8 for 266, but the top-order batsmen lost their wickets cheaply, and when Pakistan slumped to 7 for 120 the match virtually ceased to be a contest. It was then that Yousuf and Waqar began their long, slow partnership which so annoyed the crowd, and they were still together after 50 overs. Allan Border acknowledged the match had become a farce by bowling all ten fieldsmen. Pakistan was without several first-ranked players, but its defeat by 87 runs was nevertheless its sixth in eight tour matches.

Prime Minister's XI

First Innings

Batsman	How Out	Ttl	Balls	Mins	4s	6s
J Cox	lbw Ghauri	66	92	122	5	—
MRJ Veletta	c Anwar b Ghauri	50	43	75	7	—
ME Waugh	c Anwar b Tauseef	4	8	8	—	—
DS Lehmann	run out	4	8	10	—	—
MG Bevan	c Tauseef b Aaqib	74	84	110	6	—
AR Border (c)	c Ijaz b Mushtaq	14	20	19	1	—
TJ Zoehrer (+)	c Tauseef b Mushtaq	6	8	10	1	—
SC Storey	b Shoaib	19	28	45	1	—
JC Scuderi	not out	8	6	10	1	—
DW Fleming	not out	1	2	3	—	—
WJ Holdsworth	did not bat					
SUNDRIES: B. 1 LB. 8 W. 9 NB. 2		20	299	212	22	—
TOTAL	9 wkts for 266					

F/W: 88 104 113 156 178 187 244 256

Bowler	O	M	R	Wkts	NB	W
Waqar Younus	10	—	57	—	1	3
Aaqib Javed	9	—	45	1	1	6
Nadeem Ghauri	10	—	58	2	—	—
Tauseef Ahmed	10	—	47	1	—	—
Mushtaq Ahmed	10	—	46	2	—	—
Shoaib Mohammad	1	—	6	1	—	—
Overs:	50.0					

Pakistanis

First Innings

Batsman	How Out	Ttl	Balls	Mins	4s	6s
Aamir Malik	lbw Holdsworth	4	4	1	—	
Shoaib Mohammad	c Border b Waugh	33	89	2	—	
Rameez Raja	c Waugh b Scuderi	20	3	2	—	
Ijaz Ahmed	c Fleming b Waugh	15	27	2	—	
Saeed Anwar	run out	16	13	—	—	
Salim Yousuf (+)	not out	54	85	4	—	
Mushtaq Ahmed	c (s)Wade b Border	8	15	—	—	
Tauseef Ahmed	c Waugh b Storey	0	4	—	—	
Waqar Younus	not out	28	54	2	1	
Nadeem Ghauri	did not bat					
Aaqib Javed	did not bat					
SUNDRIES: B. 0 LB. 2 W. 4 NB. 1		7	210	13	1	
TOTAL	7 wkts for 185					

F/W: 4 54 78 89 97 119 120

Bowler	O	M	R	Wkts	NB	W
Holdsworth	5	—	28	1	—	1
Fleming	6	1	21	—	—	3
Scuderi	7	—	26	1	—	—
Waugh	5	—	13	2	1	—
Storey	10	1	23	1	—	—
Border	8	2	18	1	—	—
Veletta	3	—	12	—	—	—
Lehmann	3	—	19	—	—	—
Cox	2	—	12	—	—	—
Bevan	1	—	9	—	—	—
Overs:	50.0					

Umpires: LJ King & G Davidson

12th Men: M Wade (Prime Minister's XI) & Salim Malik (Pakistanis)

THIRD TEST

Australia v Pakistan
Sydney Cricket Ground
Feb 3, 4, 5, 6, 7, 8 1990 (*No play 3, 4, 6—Test Match extended into 6th day*)
Toss: Australia
Result: Drawn

Heavy rain washed out three days of this Test, and although the authorities took the unusual step of adding a day to the fixture a result never seemed likely. The Test was scheduled to start on Saturday, 3 February, but when no play was possible on the first two days it was decided to extend the match to Thursday. The Test finally got under way at 12.14pm on Monday, the Pakistanis having been sent in to bat on an unpredictable pitch. Its batsmen were in trouble at once, and 3 wickets fell before the total advanced beyond 20. Javed Miandad had by this time come to the crease and, hampered by a back injury, he batted with extreme caution in recognition of the difficult conditions. After more than three hours, he reached 49, but then spent 40 minutes without scoring before giving a catch to the gully. This left the Pakistanis at 5 for 110 at stumps, and on Tuesday they moved on slowly to a final innings total of 199. Terry Alderman, vice-captain for the match in place of the injured Geoff Marsh, took 5 wickets for the thirteenth time in his Test career. Imran Khan played an unusually defensive innings of 82 not out. Play was washed out again on Wednesday, leaving the Australians one day of batting on Thursday. Mark Taylor spent the day scoring another century, his fourth Test century of the summer, and Australia was 2 for 176 when the match ended. Alderman was named Man of the Match.

Pakistan

First Innings

Batsman	How Out	Ttl	Balls
Aamir Malik	c Healy b Alderman	7	36
Rameez Raja	c & b Hughes	0	5
Shoaib Mohammad	lbw Alderman	9	20
Javed Miandad	c Jones b Hughes	49	158
Ijaz Ahmed	c MA Taylor b Rackemann	8	51
Imran Khan (c)	not out	82	203
Wasim Akram	c MA Taylor b Alderman	10	29
Salim Yousuf (+)	c Jones b Rackemann	6	44
Tauseef Ahmed	b Alderman	0	16
Waqar Younus	c Veletta b Hughes	16	12
Nadeem Ghauri	b Alderman	0	2
SUNDRIES: B. 1 LB. 7 W. 0 NB. 4		12	576
TOTAL		199	

F/W: 2 15 20 51 106 128 154 160 191 199

Bowler	O	M	R	Wkts	NB	W
Alderman	33.5	10	65	5	1	—
Hughes	31	16	70	3	2	—
Rackemann	22	8	33	2	1	—
PL Taylor	8	1	23	—	—	—
Overs:	94.5					

Australia

First Innings

Batsman	How Out	Ttl	Balls
MA Taylor	not out	101	227
MRJ Veletta	lbw Younus	9	46
TM Moody	c Aamir b Tauseef	26	58
AR Border (c)	not out	27	65
DM Jones	did not bat		
SR Waugh	did not bat		
IA Healy (+)	did not bat		
PL Taylor	did not bat		
MG Hughes	did not bat		
CG Rackemann	did not bat		
TM Alderman	did not bat		
SUNDRIES: B. 4 LB. 5 W. 0 NB. 4		13	396
TOTAL	2 wkts for 176		

F/W: 33 106

Bowler	O	M	R	Wkts	NB	W
Wasim Akram	10	3	29	—	3	—
Imran Khan	17	2	32	—	1	—
Tauseef Ahmed	19	3	62	1	—	—
Nadeem Ghauri	8	1	20	—	—	—
Waqar Younus	9	4	21	1	—	—
Ijaz Ahmed	2	—	3	—	—	—
Overs:	65.0					

Umpires: AR Crafter & PJ McConnell

12th Men: DS Lehmann (Australia) & Mushtaq Ahmed (Pakistan)

Pakistan v Sri Lanka   Brisbane Cricket Ground, Brisbane, February 10, 1990
Limited-overs international
Result: Pakistan won by 5 wickets

For details see section on Benson and Hedges World Series matches.

Australia v Pakistan
Brisbane Cricket Ground, Brisbane
February 11, 1990
Limited-overs International
Result: Australia won by 67 runs

For details see section on Benson and Hedges World Series matches.

Australia v Pakistan
Sydney Cricket Ground, Sydney
February 13, 1990
Limited-overs International
Result: Pakistan won by 5 wkts

For details see section on Benson and Hedges World Series matches.

Pakistan v Sri Lanka
Bellerive Oval, Hobart
February 15, 1990
Limited-overs International
Result: Pakistan won by 6 wkts

For details see section on Benson and Hedges World Series matches.

Pakistan v Sri Lanka
Adelaide Oval, Adelaide
February 17, 1990
Limited-overs International
Result: Pakistan won by 27 runs

For details see section on Benson and Hedges World Series matches.

Australia v Pakistan
Sydney Cricket Ground, Sydney
February 20, 1990
Limited-overs International
Result: Pakistan won by 2 runs

For details see section on Benson and Hedges World Series matches.

Australia v Pakistan
Melbourne Cricket Ground, Melbourne
February 23, 1990
Limited-overs International—FIRST FINAL
Result: Australia won by 7 wkts

For details see section on Benson and Hedges World Series matches.

Australia v Pakistan
Sydney Cricket Ground, Sydney
February 25, 1990
Limited-overs International—SECOND FINAL
Result: Australia won by 69 runs

For details see section on Benson and Hedges World Series matches.

Tour Statistics

1989/90 Pakistanis First-Class Averages

Batsman	M	Inn	NO	Runs	HS	50	100	Avrge	Ct/St
Salim Malik	1	2	1	76	65*	1	—	76.00	—
Javed Miandad	4	7	1	322	77	4	—	53.67	1
Imran Khan	4	7	1	320	136	1	1	53.33	1
Wasim Akram	3	5	—	197	123	1	1	39.40	2
Ijaz Ahmed	6	11	—	349	121	—	1	31.73	6
Salim Yousuf	6	11	2	265	78	1	—	29.44	12/1
Saeed Anwar	3	6	—	131	44	—	—	21.83	4
Mansoor Akhtar	3	6	—	127	74	1	—	21.17	2
Shoaib Mohammad	6	11	—	219	52	1	—	19.91	3
Tauseef Ahmed	4	7	2	99	36	—	—	19.80	—
Abdul Qadir	2	3	—	51	51	1	—	17.00	1
Mushtaq Ahmed	2	4	—	51	32	—	—	12.75	2
Aamir Malik	5	9	—	113	53	1	—	12.56	5
Waqar Younus	6	9	2	81	23	—	—	11.57	—
Nadeem Ghauri	3	5	1	20	19	—	—	5.00	1
Rameez Raja	3	5	—	24	9	—	—	4.80	1
Maqsood Rana	1	2	—	7	7	—	—	3.50	1
Aaqib Javed	4	7	2	10	9*	—	—	2.00	2

Bowler	M	Overs	Mdns	Runs	Wkts	Avrge	5wi	10m	NB	W	Best
Saeed Anwar	3	14.5	1	35	2	17.50	—	—	—	—	2/35
Wasim Akram	3	135.4	37	318	17	18.71	3	1	30	—	6/62
Nadeem Ghauri	3	76.0	21	194	7	27.71	—	—	—	—	4/59
Aamir Malik	5	14.0	1	57	2	28.50	—	—	2	—	2/57
Maqsood Rana	1	15.0	2	57	2	28.50	—	—	—	1	2/57
Tauseef Ahmed	4	131.5	26	358	10	35.80	1	—	1	—	5/42
Aaqib Javed	4	121.1	30	327	9	36.33	—	—	23	1	2/47
Mushtaq Ahmed	2	74.0	18	212	5	42.40	—	—	2	—	2/17
Waqar Younus	6	157.0	26	496	10	49.60	—	—	8	1	3/84
Abdul Qadir	2	53.2	8	181	3	60.33	—	—	6	—	2/101
Imran Khan	4	104.0	22	247	4	61.75	—	—	5	—	2/53
Ijaz Ahmed	6	2.0	—	3	—	—	—	—	—	—	—
Shoaib Mohammad	6	5.0	1	26	—	—	—	—	—	—	—

1989/90 Australia v Pakistan Test Averages

Batsman	M	Inn	NO	Runs	HS	50	100	Avrge	Ct/St
MA Taylor	3	5	1	390	101*	3	2	97.50	8
DM Jones	3	4	1	247	121*	—	2	82.33	2
AR Border	3	5	2	134	62*	1	—	44.67	1
IA Healy	3	4	—	112	48	—	—	28.00	12/-
TM Moody	1	1	—	26	26	—	—	26.00	—
MG Hughes	3	4	2	48	32	—	—	24.00	1
GR Marsh	2	3	—	67	30	—	—	22.33	2
PL Taylor	2	2	—	34	33	—	—	17.00	3
DC Boon	2	4	—	55	29	—	—	13.75	1
PR Sleep	1	2	—	23	23	—	—	11.50	—
SR Waugh	3	4	—	44	20	—	—	11.00	1
MRJ Veletta	1	1	—	9	9	—	—	9.00	1
TM Alderman	2	2	1	1	1*	—	—	1.00	1
CG Rackemann	3	2	1	0	0*	—	—	0.00	—
GD Campbell	1	1	—	0	0	—	—	0.00	—

Bowler	M	Overs	Mdns	Runs	Wkts	Avrge	5wi	10m	NB	W	Best
SR Waugh	3	3.0	—	13	1	13.00	—	—	—	—	1/13
AR Border	3	8.0	—	15	1	15.00	—	—	—	—	1/10
TM Alderman	2	86.4	22	200	13	15.38	2	—	11	—	5/65
MG Hughes	3	140.0	51	357	16	22.31	1	—	7	1	5/111
CG Rackemann	3	139.5	43	257	10	25.70	—	—	8	1	4/40
PR Sleep	1	29.0	12	70	2	35.00	—	—	—	1	1/6
GD Campbell	1	50.3	7	162	4	40.50	—	—	1	1	3/79
PL Taylor	2	61.5	14	174	2	87.00	—	—	—	—	2/94

1989/90 Pakistan v Australia Test Averages

Batsman	M	Inn	NO	Runs	HS	50	100	Avrge	Ct/St
Salim Malik	1	2	1	76	65*	1	—	76.00	—
Imran Khan	3	5	1	279	136	1	1	69.75	—
Wasim Akram	3	5	—	197	123	1	1	39.40	2
Javed Miandad	3	5	—	190	65	2	—	38.00	1
Ijaz Ahmed	3	5	—	180	121	—	1	36.00	1
Salim Yousuf	3	5	—	99	38	—	—	19.80	6
Tauseef Ahmed	3	5	2	41	18	—	—	13.67	—
Shoaib Mohammad	3	5	—	68	43	—	—	13.60	2
Waqar Younus	3	4	1	39	18	—	—	13.00	—
Mansoor Akhtar	1	2	—	19	14	—	—	9.50	2
Aamir Malik	2	3	—	14	7	—	—	4.67	3
Rameez Raja	2	3	—	11	9	—	—	3.67	1
Mushtaq Ahmed	1	2	—	4	4	—	—	2.00	—
Aaqib Javed	1	2	—	0	0	—	—	0.00	1
Nadeem Ghauri	1	1	—	0	0	—	—	0.00	—

Bowler	M	Overs	Mdns	Runs	Wkts	Avrge	5wi	10m	NB	W	Best
Wasim Akram	3	135.4	37	318	17	18.71	3	1	30	—	6/62
Aaqib Javed	1	43.1	8	102	3	34.00	—	—	5	—	2/47
Imran Khan	3	70.0	16	167	4	41.75	—	—	5	—	2/53
Tauseef Ahmed	3	89.0	14	258	5	51.60	—	—	1	—	3/80
Waqar Younus	3	83.0	19	224	4	56.00	—	—	7	1	2/66
Mushtaq Ahmed	1	48.0	9	141	1	141.00	—	—	1	—	1/72
Shoaib Mohammad	3	1.0	—	7	—	—	—	—	—	—	—
Nadeem Ghauri	1	8.0	1	20	—	—	—	—	—	—	—
Ijaz Ahmed	3	2.0	—	3	—	—	—	—	—	—	—

141

Centuries for Pakistanis

Total	Batsman	Team	Venue
136	Imran Khan	Australia	Adelaide
123	Wasim Akram	Australia	Adelaide
121	Ijaz Ahmed	Australia	Melbourne

Centuries Against Pakistanis

Total	Batsman	Team	Venue
155	GI Foley	Queensland	Brisbane
123	GM Ritchie	Queensland	Brisbane
121°	DM Jones	Australia	Adelaide
116	DM Jones	Australia	Adelaide
102	GM Watts	Victoria	Melbourne
101	MA Taylor	Australia	Melbourne
101°	MA Taylor	Australia	Sydney

Best Innings Bowling Performance For Pakistanis

Wkts	Bowler	Team	Venue
6/62	Wasim Akram	Australia	Melbourne
5/42	Tauseef Ahmed	Victoria	Melbourne
5/98	Wasim Akram	Australia	Melbourne
5/100	Wasim Akram	Australia	Adelaide

Best Innings Bowling Performance Against Pakistanis

Wkts	Bowler	Team	Venue
7/22	CD Matthews	Western Australia	Perth
6/92	PA Capes	Western Australia	Perth
5/53	PE McIntyre	Victoria	Melbourne
5/56	MA Polzin	Queensland	Brisbane
5/65	TM Alderman	Australia	Sydney
5/105	TM Alderman	Australia	Melbourne
5/111	MG Hughes	Australia	Adelaide

Highest Partnership Records For Pakistanis

Wkt	Total	Batsmen	Team	Venue
1st	41	Aamir Malik, Shoaib Mohammad	Western Australia	Perth
2nd	87	Shoaib Mohammad, Mansoor Akhtar	Queensland	Brisbane
3rd	72	Aamir Malik, Ijaz Ahmed	Victoria	Melbourne
4th	103	Javed Miandad, Ijaz Ahmed	Australia	Melbourne
5th	84	Ijaz Ahmed, Imran Khan	Australia	Melbourne
6th	191	Imran Khan, Wasim Akram	Australia	Adelaide
7th	54	Imran Khan, Salim Yousuf	Queensland	Brisbane
"	54	Imran Khan, Wasim Akram	Australia	Adelaide
8th	64	Salim Malik, Tauseef Ahmed	Australia	Adelaide
9th	31	Imran Khan, Waqar Younus	Australia	Sydney
10th	20	Nadeem Ghauri, Aaqib Javed	Victoria	Melbourne

Century Wicket Partnerships For Pakistanis

Wkt	Total	Batsmen	Team	Venue
6th	191	Imran Khan, Wasim Akram	Australia	Adelaide
4th	103	Javed Miandad, Ijaz Ahmed	Australia	Melbourne

Highest Partnership Records Against Pakistanis

Wkt	Total	Batsmen	Team	Venue
1st	90	GR Marsh, MA Taylor	Australia	Melbourne
2nd	88	MRJ Veletta, TM Moody	Western Australia	Perth
3rd	225	GI Foley, GM Ritchie	Queensland	Brisbane
4th	65	TM Moody, WS Andrews	Western Australia	Perth
5th	87	WS Andrews, TJ Zoehrer	Western Australia	Perth
6th	112	DM Jones, PL Taylor	Australia	Australia
7th	78	SC Storey, IA Healy	Queensland	Brisbane
8th	45	AR Border, MG Hughes	Australia	Melbourne
9th	21	PR Reiffel, DW Fleming	Victoria	Melbourne
10th	33	PR Reiffel, PE McIntyre	Victoria	Melbourne

Wkt	Total	Batsmen	Team	Venue
3rd	225	GI Foley, GM Ritchie_____	Queensland	Brisbane
6th	112	DM Jones, PL Taylor _____	Australia	Adelaide

Pakistan First-Class Tours of Australia

Results for Pakistan

Season	Games	W	L	D	T	Captain
1964/65_____	4	—	—	4	—	Hanif Mohammad
1972/73_____	8	2	5	1	—	Intikhab Alam
1976/77_____	5	1	2	2	—	Mushtaq Mohammad
1978/79_____	4	1	1	2	—	Mushtaq Mohammad
1981/82_____	8	2	2	4	—	Javed Miandad
1983/84_____	11	3	3	5	—	Imran Khan
1988/89_____	1	—	—	1	—	Imran Khan
1989/90_____	6	—	3	3	—	Imran Khan
Total	**47**	**9**	**16**	**22**	**—**	

Pakistanis Tours of Australia

Opponents	Venue	First Game	Games	W	L	D	T
AUSTRALIA	Melbourne _____	Dec 4 1964	6	2	3	2	—
	Adelaide _____	Dec 22 1972	3	—	1	3	—
	Sydney_____	Jan 6 1973	3	1	2	1	—
	Perth_____	Mar 24 1979	3	—	3	—	—
	Brisbane _____	Nov 27 1981	2	—	1	1	—
Total			**20**	**3**	**10**	**7**	**—**
Combined XI	Launceston _____	Dec 18 1972	1	—	—	1	—
New South Wales	Sydney_____	Dec 11 1964	3	—	—	3	—
	Canberra_____	Mar 3 1979	1	—	—	1	—
Total			**4**	**—**	**—**	**4**	**—**
Queensland	Brisbane _____	Nov 27 1964	6	1	—	5	—
South Australia	Adelaide _____	Dec 18 1983	4	1	—	3	—
Tasmania	Hobart TCA_____	Dec 15 1972	2	2	—	—	—
	Launceston _____	Jan 1 1982	1	1	—	—	—
Total			**3**	**3**	**—**	**—**	**—**
Victoria	Melbourne _____	Nov 24 1972	4	1	2	1	—
Western Australia	Perth _____	Nov 18 1972	5	—	4	1	—

BENSON & HEDGES WORLD SERIES

DECEMBER 1989–FEBRUARY 1990

AUSTRALIA DOMINATED this series of limited-overs inter-nationals, winning eight of the ten matches it played and beating Pakistan by two matches to nil in the final series. The Australians played throughout as an extremely professional unit. They batted with confidence and purpose, they bowled with control, and their fielding was a class above the fielding of both their opponents. Their success reflected well on the captaincy of Allan Border, who throughout the series gave an impression of being in command of events. One shortcoming was the indifferent form of Steve Waugh, in recent years a key player for Australia in limited-overs cricket, but this was more than compensated for by the new soundness which Mark Taylor gave the Australian top order, the fine form of Tom Moody and the outstanding consistency of Dean Jones, who during the series shone brighter than any other Australian batsman.

As a team, the Pakistanis rarely performed at the level expected of them, yet there were many fine individual performances, most notably by Wasim Akram, Imran Khan and Saeed Anwar. While the Sri Lankans finished the series with a poor record on paper, their batting occasionally rose to impressive heights. Indeed, there was enough talent in the Sri Lankan line-up to ensure that the Australians and the Pakistanis never entered a match against them without apprehension.

BENSON AND HEDGES WORLD SERIES – GAME 1
Australia v Sri Lanka
Melbourne Cricket Ground, Melbourne
Dec 26 1989
Toss: Sri Lanka
Attendance: 45 012
Result: Australia won by 30 runs

Although in the end the Australians won comfortably, at several stages during the match it looked as if they might not have scored enough runs to win against a Sri Lankan side potentially strong in batting. Sent in, the Australians paid the price for some undisciplined batting and slumped to 5 for 120. After 40 overs, they were 5 for 150 and by no means sure of making 200. In the remaining 8.5 overs, however, Dean Jones (85 not out) and Simon O'Donnell (57 not out) thrashed the bowling and Australia added another 78 before the innings was cut short by rain. The Sri Lankans got off to a good start in reply, and its first three batsmen all made runs. Sri Lanka was 4 for 161 and in sight of victory when the innings collapsed with such suddenness that the last 6 wickets fell for only 37 runs. Simon O'Donnell took 4 for 36, which, after his earlier success with the bat, earned him the Man of the Match award.

Australia

Batsman	How Out	Ttl	Balls	Mins	4s	6s
MA Taylor	c & b Ratnayeke	11	25	22	—	1
GR Marsh	c PA De Silva b Ranatunga	38	82	102	2	—
DC Boon	c Jayasuriya b Ratnayake	11	19	29	—	—
DM Jones	not out	85	89	144	4	1
AR Border (c)	c Samarasekera b Ranatunga	11	15	14	1	—
SR Waugh	c Tillekeratne b Ranatunga	5	7	11	—	—
SP O'Donnell	not out	57	60	67	3	1
IA Healy (+)	did not bat					
PL Taylor	did not bat					
MG Hughes	did not bat					
GD Campbell	did not bat					
SUNDRIES: B. 0 LB. 6 W. 2 NB. 2		10	297	197	10	3
TOTAL	5 wkts for 228					

F/W: 17 42 88 106 120

Bowler	O	M	R	Wkts	NB	W
Labrooy	9	—	40	—	—	—
Ratnayeke	9	1	47	1	2	—
Ratnayake	9.5	—	43	1	—	2
Ranatunga	10	2	41	3	—	—
EAR De Silva	10	—	42	—	—	—
Gurusinha	1	—	9	—	—	—
Overs:	48.5					

Sri Lanka

Batsman	How Out	Ttl	Balls	Mins	4s	6s
RS Mahanama	c Border b Waugh	36	67	94	3	—
MAR Samaresekera	c Hughes b O'Donnell	30	50	62	2	—
A Ranatunga (c)	c Healy b O'Donnell	55	70	111	3	—
PA De Silva	c Border b PL Taylor	9	10	13	1	—
ST Jayasuriya	c Campbell b Hughes	3	5	11	—	—
AP Gurusinha	c O'Donnell b PL Taylor	22	40	42	—	—
HP Tillekeratne (+)	c Healy b O'Donnell	11	23	37	—	—
JR Ratnayeke	run out	0	2	2	—	—
EAR De Silva	not out	13	17	29	—	—
GF Labrooy	b O'Donnell	6	2	2	—	1
RJ Ratnayake	c Healy b Hughes	0	1	2	—	—
SUNDRIES: B. 0 LB. 6 W. 4 NB. 3		13	287	207	9	1
TOTAL		198				

F/W: 59 85 101 109 161 169 169 190 197 198

Bowler	O	M	R	Wkts	NB	W
Hughes	9.2	—	41	2	1	3
Campbell	10	2	36	—	1	—
O'Donnell	9	1	36	4	1	—
Waugh	6	—	26	1	—	—
PL Taylor	10	1	36	2	—	1
Border	3	—	17	—	—	—
Overs:	47.2					

Umpires: CD Timmins & LJ King

Man of Match: SP O'Donnell

12th Men: TM Alderman (Australia) & KIW Wijegunawardene (Sri Lanka)

BENSON AND HEDGES WORLD SERIES – GAME 2
Australia v Sri Lanka
WACA Ground, Perth
Dec 30 1989
Toss: Sri Lanka
Attendance: 22 150
Result: Australia won by 9 wkts

Sri Lanka's batsmen performed creditably, scoring 203 from 48 overs, but its bowlers proved almost entirely ineffective, and Australia won by 9 wickets with nearly 9 overs to spare. Terry Alderman, who had been rested in the first one-day match against Sri Lanka four days before, was back in the side and in superb form. He conceded only 25 runs in his 10 overs and took 3 wickets. If it had not been for the extremely tight bowling by Alderman and Simon O'Donnell, the Sri Lankans would have been able to set Australia a much bigger target. The Australian batsmen were on top from the outset. Mark Taylor went for 37 when the score was 87, but that was the Sri Lankan bowlers' only success. Altogether, their performance was an inferior one. Apart from failing to take wickets or contain the batsmen, they bowled 11 wides and 11 no-balls. Geoff Marsh was named Man of the Match for his steady innings of 80 not out.

Sri Lanka

Batsman	How Out	Ttl	Balls	Mins	4s	6s
RS Mahanama	lbw Alderman	27	45	64	5	—
MAR Samarasekera	c Alderman b Hughes	5	8	12	1	—
AP Gurusinha	c Healy b Alderman	0	3	3	—	—
HP Tillekeratne (+)	c Jones b O'Donnell	13	44	68	—	—
PA De Silva	c Border b Campbell	4	5	5	1	—
A Ranatunga (c)	not out	71	106	139	7	—
ST Jayasuriya	c Healy b O'Donnell	13	16	32	—	—
RJ Ratnayeke	lbw Alderman	25	50	55	2	—
GF Labrooy	b Waugh	1	5	4	—	—
RJ Ratnayake	c Waugh b O'Donnell	19	21	26	1	1
KIW Wijegunawardene	did not bat					
SUNDRIES: B. 0 LB. 8 W. 15 NB. 2		25	303	212	17	1
TOTAL	9 wkts for 203					

F/W: 8 9 50 56 60 100 162 167 203

Bowler	O	M	R	Wkts	NB	W
Hughes	10	—	35	1	—	5
Alderman	10	2	25	3	—	1
Campbell	10	2	54	1	2	2
O'Donnell	9	1	36	3	—	6
Waugh	9	—	45	1	—	1
Overs:	48.0					

Australia

Batsman	How Out	Ttl	Balls	Mins	4s	6s
GR Marsh	not out	80	136	188	5	—
MA Taylor	c Tillekeratne b W'wardene	37	50	80	6	—
DC Boon	not out	49	73	106	5	—
AR Border (c)	did not bat					
DM Jones	did not bat					
SR Waugh	did not bat					
IA Healy (+)	did not bat					
MG Hughes	did not bat					
SP O'Donnell	did not bat					
GD Campbell	did not bat					
TM Alderman	did not bat					
SUNDRIES: B. 0 LB. 16 W. 11 NB. 11		38	259	188	16	—
TOTAL	1 wkt for 204					

F/W: 87

146

Bowler	O	M	R	Wkts	NB	W
Labrooy	10	1	46	—	—	3
Ratnayeke	7.5	—	51	—	3	3
Ratnayake	10	—	37	—	4	5
Wijegunawardene	7	—	33	1	4	—
Ranatunga	4	—	21	—	—	—
Overs:	38.5					

Umpires: AR Crafter & RJ Evans

Man of Match: GR Marsh

12th Men: PL Taylor (Australia) & EAR De Silva (Sri Lanka)

BENSON AND HEDGES WORLD SERIES – GAME 3
Pakistan v Sri Lanka
WACA Ground, Perth
Dec 31 1989
Toss: Pakistan
Attendance: 10 000
Result: Sri Lanka won by 3 wkts

After losing twice to Australia in four days, the Sri Lankans lifted their game and beat the Pakistanis with 9 balls to spare. The Sri Lankan bowlers could take little credit for the victory, however. They again wasted runs and balls, bowling 11 wides and 3 no-balls, which had much to do with their failure (for which the team was later fined) to bowl more than 47 overs. The match having thus been reduced to a 47-over contest, Pakistan's total of 222 appeared a substantial one, yet the Sri Lankans passed it without the usual last-minute scramble for runs. Opening the innings, Athula Samarasekera batted aggressively for 60, and his role in setting Sri Lanka on course for victory earned him the Man of the Match award. The Pakistani bowlers made their task of containing the Sri Lankans much harder by bowling 10 wides and 6 no-balls.

Pakistan

Batsman	How Out	Ttl	Balls	Mins	4s	6s
Aamir Malik (+)	b Ratnayeke	69	122	167	2	—
Shoaib Mohammad	b Ratnayeke	9	30	42	2	—
Mansoor Akhtar	run out	13	33	46	—	—
Saeed Anwar	run out	33	36	54	3	—
Javed Miandad	c Samarasekera b Labrooy	43	43	58	1	—
Imran Khan (c)	c & b Labrooy	32	25	30	2	—
Ijaz Ahmed	not out	3	4	10	—	—
Wasim Akram	run out	0	0	1	—	—
Abdul Qadir	not out	0	0	1	—	—
Waqar Younus	did not bat					
Aaqib Javed	did not bat					
SUNDRIES: B. 1 LB. 5 W. 11 NB. 3		20	293	211	10	—
TOTAL	7 wkts for 222					

F/W: 27 51 118 151 206 220 221

Bowler	O	M	R	Wkts	NB	W
Labrooy	10	1	43	2	1	3
Ratnayeke	10	2	33	2	2	—
Wijegunawardene	7	—	27	—	—	—
Ratnayake	9	—	54	—	—	2
Ranatunga	4	—	18	—	—	3
Gurusinha	7	—	41	—	—	3
Overs:	47.0					

147

Sri Lanka

Batsman	How Out	Ttl	Balls	Mins	4s	6s
RS Mahanama	not out	19	32	41	—	—
MAR Samaresekera	c Aaqib b Qadir	60	89	124	8	—
HP Tillekeratne (+)	c Aamir b Akram	1	11	18	—	—
AP Gurusinha	b Waqar	37	50	82	5	—
PA De Silva	c Imran b Akram	40	57	93	3	—
A Ranatunga (c)	run out	0	0	2	—	—
ST Jayasuriya	c Aamir b Imran	24	41	53	—	—
JR Ratnayeke	c Anwar b Imran	2	5	6	—	—
RJ Ratnayake	not out	1	3	7	—	—
GF Labrooy	did not bat					
KIW Wijegunawardene	did not bat					
SUNDRIES: B. 1 LB. 22 W. 10 NB. 6		39	288	218	16	—
TOTAL	7 wkts for 223					

F/W: 8 103 120 124 179 205 211

Bowler	O	M	R	Wkts	NB	W
Wasim Akram	10	1	37	2	2	1
Aaqib Javed	10	—	45	—	1	1
Waqar Younus	8	1	44	1	2	5
Imran Khan	9.3	1	40	2	—	3
Abdul Qadir	8	—	34	1	1	—
Overs:	45.3					

Umpires: AR Crafter & PJ McConnell

Man of Match: MAR Samaresekera

12th Men: Tauseef Ahmed (Pakistan) & MAWR Madurasinghe (Sri Lanka)

BENSON AND HEDGES WORLD SERIES – GAME 4
Australia v Pakistan
Melbourne Cricket Ground, Melbourne
Jan 3 1990
Toss: Pakistan
Attendance: 52 813
Result: Australia won by 7 wkts

A crowd of 52 813 came to see this first encounter between the teams
tipped to dominate the summer's limited-overs international cricket.
Those hoping to see a hard-fought contest were disappointed, for
the match proved to be a walk-over for the Australians, who
performed efficiently in all departments. By contrast, the Pakistanis
looked stale and out of form. Their batsmen began well enough,
putting on 56 for the first wicket, but they were kept under pressure
by the pace and accuracy of Carl Rackemann and Merv Hughes,
who conceded only 21 runs and 16 runs respectively in the 10 overs
each of them bowled. Afterwards, the Pakistani innings steadily fell
apart, the last 9 wickets falling for only 105 runs. In reply, Australia
had early problems, losing 2 wickets for 17, but the problems ended
when Allan Border arrived at the crease. He played a commanding
innings of 69 not out, which won him the Man of the Match award,
and with Steve Waugh (31 not out) he saw Australia to victory with
fully 9 overs to spare.

Pakistan

Batsman	How Out	Ttl	Balls	Mins	4s	6s
Aamir Malik (+)	c Healy b Alderman	23	65	87	1	—
Shoaib Mohammad	c Healy b Rackemann	22	58	92	2	—
Mansoor Akhtar	b Taylor	32	42	56	—	—
Saeed Anwar	c Marsh b Taylor	3	11	12	—	—
Imran Khan (c)	c Hughes b O'Donnell	39	62	99	—	—
Ijaz Ahmed	run out	3	11	9	—	—
Wasim Akram	c Taylor b Rackemann	8	17	25	—	—
Abdul Qadir	c Border b Alderman	1	5	4	—	—
Maqsood Rana	run out	5	13	11	—	—
Nadeem Ghauri	not out	7	13	14	—	—
Aaqib Javed	run out	1	5	6	—	—
SUNDRIES: B. 0 LB. 8 W. 8 NB. 1		17	302	222	3	—
TOTAL		161				

F/W: 56 59 67 107 115 136 138 148 156 161

Bowler	O	M	R	Wkts	NB	W
Hughes	10	3	16	—	—	—
Alderman	10	2	31	1	—	2
Rackemann	10	2	21	3	1	—
O'Donnell	9	—	43	1	—	6
Taylor	10	—	36	2	—	—
Waugh	1	—	6	—	—	—
Overs:	50.0					

Australia

Batsman	How Out	Ttl	Balls	Mins	4s	6s
DC Boon	b Ghauri	39	66	91	1	—
GR Marsh	c Aamir b Akram	3	8	8	—	—
DM Jones	b Aaqib	2	15	15	—	—
AR Border (c)	not out	69	103	139	8	—
SR Waugh	not out	31	56	72	3	—
SP O'Donnell	did not bat					
IA Healy (+)	did not bat					
PL Taylor	did not bat					
MG Hughes	did not bat					
CG Rackemann	did not bat					
TM Alderman	did not bat					
SUNDRIES: B. 7 LB. 8 W. 2 NB. 1		18	248	164	12	—
TOTAL	3 wkts for 162					

F/W: 6 17 81

Bowler	O	M	R	Wkts	NB	W
Wasim Akram	10	1	24	1	1	—
Aaqib Javed	8	—	30	1	—	2
Maqsood Rana	2	—	11	—	—	—
Imran Khan	7	—	29	—	—	—
Nadeem Ghauri	10	3	30	1	—	—
Abdul Qadir	4	—	23	—	—	—
Overs:	41.0					

Umpires: LJ King & SG Randell

Man of Match: AR Border

12th Men: MA Taylor (Australia) & Tauseef Ahmed (Pakistan)

BENSON AND HEDGES WORLD SERIES – GAME 5
Australia v Sri Lanka
Melbourne Cricket Ground, Melbourne
Jan 4 1990
Toss: Australia
Attendance: 33 029
Result: Australia won by 73 runs

Australia recovered from an early batting collapse to inflict another heavy defeat on the Sri Lankans. Batting first, Australia slumped to 4 for 46 before Dean Jones and Simon O'Donnell arrested the decline. Although hampered by a knee injury, Jones played sensibly for 69, and after O'Donnell's departure he was given valuable support by Ian Healy, who made 33. Nevertheless, Australia finished with the barely moderate total of 202, which seemed well within reach of the Sri Lankans, who in their previous match against Australia had scored 203 in 48 overs. To begin with, things went well for the Sri Lankan batsmen. At 4 for 121, they had reason to feel optimistic about the outcome. Then the off-spinner Peter Taylor took three wickets, and the Sri Lankan innings was suddenly in disarray. The collapse continued and, remarkably, Sri Lanka lost its last 6 wickets for 8 runs.

Australia

Batsman	How Out	Ttl	Balls	Mins	4s	6s
MA Taylor	c Tillekeratne b Ratnayeke	16	30	37	1	—
GR Marsh	c Tillekeratne b Labrooy	9	25	34	1	—
DM Jones	run out	69	98	130	2	—
AR Border (c)	c Jayasuriya b Ratnayake	10	16	13	—	—
SR Waugh	c Tillekeratne b Ratnayake	0	5	8	—	—
SP O'Donnell	c Ranatunga b Ratnayeke	36	78	75	1	—
IA Healy (+)	c & b Labrooy	33	32	53	1	—
PL Taylor	not out	16	15	26	1	—
MG Hughes	not out	0	1	1	—	—
CG Rackemann	did not bat					
TM Alderman	did not bat					
SUNDRIES: B. 5 LB. 5 W. 3 NB. 0		13	300	192	7	—
TOTAL	7 wkts for 202					

F/W: 28 28 42 46 128 163 201

Bowler	O	M	R	Wkts	NB	W
Labrooy	10	—	46	2	—	2
Ratnayeke	8	1	24	1	—	—
Ratnayake	10	2	44	3	—	1
EAR De Silva	10	—	29	—	—	—
Ranatunga	2	—	13	—	—	—
PA De Silva	10	—	36	—	—	—
Overs:	50.0					

Sri Lanka

Batsman	How Out	Ttl	Balls	Mins	4s	6s
RS Mahanama	lbw Rackemann	27	44	68	2	—
MAR Samaresekera	lbw Alderman	6	17	13	—	—
HP Tillekeratne (+)	c Healy b Hughes	38	72	110	2	—
PA De Silva	lbw O'Donnell	4	12	14	—	—
A Ranatunga (c)	b PL Taylor	39	62	86	2	—
AP Gurusinha	st Healy b PL Taylor	8	20	28	—	—
RJ Ratnayake	c Hughes b PL Taylor	1	3	6	—	—
ST Jayasuriya	b Alderman	0	3	5	—	—
JR Ratnayeke	c O'Donnell b Alderman	2	7	13	—	—
EAR De Silva	run out	1	2	2	—	—
GF Labrooy	not out	1	5	6	—	—
SUNDRIES: B. 0 LB. 1 W. 1 NB. 0		2	247	180	6	—
TOTAL		129				

F/W: 8 49 58 101 121 125 125 125 127 129

150

Bowler	O	M	R	Wkts	NB	W
Hughes	8	1	20	1	—	—
Alderman	9	1	29	3	—	—
Rackemann	8	—	19	1	—	—
O'Donnell	7	1	24	1	—	1
PL Taylor	9	—	36	3	—	—
Overs:	41.0					

Umpires: CD Timmins & SG Randell

Man of Match: DM Jones

12th Men: DC Boon (Australia) & MAWR Madurasinghe (Sri Lanka)

BENSON AND HEDGES WORLD SERIES – GAME 6
Pakistan v Sri Lanka
Brisbane Cricket Ground, Brisbane
Feb 10 1990
Toss: Pakistan
Attendance: 4697
Result: Pakistan won by 5 wkts

The Sri Lankans went into the match without three of their pace bowlers, Graeme Labrooy, Ravi Ratnayeke and Kapila Wijegunawardene, all of whom were injured, so their performance under the circumstances was creditable. In sweltering conditions, Pakistan won the match with 18 balls to spare, but it took a high-speed century by Ijaz Ahmed, later named Man of the Match, to secure the victory. Batting first, the Sri Lankans lost only five wickets while compiling 253. There seemed a reasonable chance this would prove a winning total, but the Sri Lankan bowlers did not take enough wickets to put the Pakistani batsmen under pressure. Ijaz scored his 102 not out off 101 balls, hitting nine fours and one six. It was the Pakistanis' first win in ten tour matches.

Sri Lanka

Batsman	How Out	Ttl	Balls	Mins	4s	6s
MAR Samarasekera	c Ijaz b Aaqib	10	25	37	—	—
HP Tillekeratne (+)	c Ijaz b Mushtaq	61	127	154	3	—
AP Gurusinha	st Yousuf b Mushtaq	88	108	133	5	2
RJ Ratnayake	b Tauseef	31	27	36	2	1
PA De Silva	c Younus b Tauseef	32	21	26	—	2
RS Mahanama	not out	4	4	8	—	—
A Ranatunga (c)	not out	1	1	1	—	—
ST Jayasuriya	did not bat					
EAR De Silva	did not bat					
CPH Ramanayake	did not bat					
NLK Ratnayake	did not bat					
SUNDRIES: B. 1 LB. 14 W. 7 NB. 4		26	313	200	10	5
TOTAL	5 wkts for 253					

F/W: 25 163 191 236 251

Bowler	O	M	R	Wkts	NB	W
Wasim Akram	10	1	39	—	2	3
Aaqib Javed	10	1	39	1	1	1
Imran Khan	7	—	30	—	—	—
Waqar Younus	5	—	27	—	1	3
Tauseef Ahmed	10	—	48	2	—	—
Mushtaq Ahmed	8	—	55	2	—	—
Overs:	50.0					

Pakistan

Batsman	How Out	Ttl	Balls	Mins	4s	6s
Rameez Raja	c Gurusinha b Ramanayake	12	27	45	—	—
Salim Yousuf (+)	b EAR De Silva	52	73	96	6	—
Ijaz Ahmed	not out	102	101	150	9	1
Javed Miandad	c Jayasuriya b PA De Silva	39	64	61	1	—
Salim Malik	c Tillekeratne b Gurusinha	14	13	19	—	—
Imran Khan (c)	c Mahanama b NLK Ratnayake	15	13	14	2	—
Wasim Akram	not out	3	3	2	—	—
Tauseef Ahmed	did not bat					
Mushtaq Ahmed	did not bat					
Waqar Younus	did not bat					
Aaqib Javed	did not bat					
SUNDRIES: B. 0 LB. 7 W. 9 NB. 1		17	294	196	18	1
TOTAL	5 wkts for 254					

F/W: 45 114 193 228 251

Bowler	O	M	R	Wkts	NB	W
RJ Ratnayake	9	1	39	—	1	2
NLK Ratnayake	7	—	39	1	—	2
Ramanayake	5.2	—	25	1	—	—
Ranatunga	3	—	22	—	—	—
EAR De Silva	10	—	47	1	—	—
Gurusinha	6.4	—	40	1	—	5
PA De Silva	6	—	35	1	—	—
Overs:	47.0					

Umpires: CD Timmins & RJ Evans

Man of Match: Ijaz Ahmed

12th Men: Shoaib Mohammad (Pakistan) & MAWR Madurasinghe (Sri Lanka)

BENSON AND HEDGES WORLD SERIES – GAME 7
Australia v Pakistan
Brisbane Cricket Ground, Brisbane
Feb 11 1990
Toss: Pakistan
Attendance: 19 874
Result: Australia won by 67 runs

Australia's victory was set up by Tom Moody's spectacular innings of 89, scored off 82 balls. He hit four big sixes, one of which nearly hit the press box. The importance of Moody's innings was that he played it as an opening batsman, thereby giving Australia a rapid start. This allowed later batsmen to carry the total to 300, a record for limited-overs matches in Brisbane. Realising that to win they must score rapidly from the outset, the Pakistanis launched a frantic assault on the bowling, and after 15 overs had scored 91. But the price they paid for their aggression was a steady loss of wickets, and they were all out in 39.1 overs. Fine outfielding by the Australians, including a running catch by Dean Jones and two outstanding run-out throws, by Steve Waugh and Moody, played an important part in the dismissal of the Pakistanis. The win ensured Australia a place in the finals with three matches to spare.

Australia

Batsman	How Out	Ttl	Balls	Mins	4s	6s
MA Taylor	b Tauseef	66	88	121	5	—
TM Moody	lbw Mushtaq	89	82	106	4	4
DM Jones	run out	32	41	47	1	1
AR Border (c)	c Yousuf b Wasim Akram	26	30	50	1	—

▶

Batsman	How Out	Ttl	Balls	Mins	4s	6s
SR Waugh	c Malik b Mushtaq	13	16	11	2	—
SP O'Donnell	not out	31	28	32	2	—
IA Healy (+)	not out	22	20	26	1	—
PL Taylor	did not bat					
MG Hughes	did not bat					
CG Rackemann	did not bat					
TM Alderman	did not bat					
SUNDRIES: B. 3 LB. 13 W. 4 NB. 1		21	305	199	16	5
TOTAL	5 wkts for 300					

F/W: 154 176 222 241 246

Bowler	O	M	R	Wkts	NB	W
Wasim Akram	10	1	43	1	1	1
Imran Khan	10	—	54	—	—	1
Aaqib Javed	10	—	54	—	—	1
Tauseef Ahmed	10	—	57	1	—	—
Mushtaq Ahmed	10	—	76	2	—	1
Overs:	50.0					

Pakistan

Batsman	How Out	Ttl	Balls	Mins	4s	6s
Javed Miandad	c Waugh b Alderman	18	18	21	2	—
Salim Yousuf (+)	c MA Taylor b Hughes	7	6	12	1	—
Saeed Anwar	c Jones b Rackemann	37	24	41	4	—
Rameez Raja	c PL Taylor b O'Donnell	9	17	24	1	—
Ijaz Ahmed	run out	27	32	51	2	—
Imran Khan (c)	c Border b Rackemann	82	89	118	4	—
Salim Malik	run out	27	26	33	1	—
Wasim Akram	b Rackemann	8	7	1	1	—
Mushtaq Ahmed	c MA Taylor b Rackemann	11	14	18	1	—
Tauseef Ahmed	run out	1	3	5	—	—
Aaqib Javed	not out	0	2	2	—	—
SUNDRIES: B. 2 LB. 2 W. 1 NB. 1		6	238	173	17	—
TOTAL		233				

F/W: 20 37 66 77 132 192 206 228 233 233

Bowler	O	M	R	Wkts	NB	W
Alderman	5	—	39	1	—	—
Hughes	7	—	39	1	—	1
Rackemann	8.1	—	44	4	—	—
O'Donnell	8	—	43	1	1	—
PL Taylor	7	—	41	—	—	—
Border	4	—	23	—	—	—
Overs:	39.1					

Umpires: RJ Evans & TA Prue

Man of Match: TM Moody

12th Men: DS Lehmann (Australia) & Shoaib Mohammad (Pakistan)

BENSON AND HEDGES WORLD SERIES – GAME 8
Australia v Pakistan
Sydney Cricket Ground, Sydney
Feb 13 1990
Toss: Pakistan
Attendance: 29 810
Result: Pakistan won by 5 wkts

After a fortnight's heavy rain in Sydney, the SCG pitch proved sluggish and unpredictable, and both sides struggled to score runs. Tom Moody, opening the batting for Australia, fell victim to the conditions in the third over, bowled by a ball of less than knee height. Mark Taylor, Dean Jones, Steve Waugh and later Allan Border each spent a reasonable time at the crease, but none scored easily off deliveries which generally kept low and came on to the bat slowly. Several of them lost their wickets in desperate attempts to accelerate the scoring—Taylor by swishing wildly and Jones and Border by foolish run outs. Pakistan's batsmen appeared to handle the conditions more efficiently, although more than half-way through their innings they were behind Australia both in terms of wickets lost and runs scored. But steady batting by Imran Khan and brilliant hitting by Wasim Akram added 56 runs in the last 7.5 overs, and Pakistan won the match with nine balls to spare.

Australia

Batsman	How Out	Ttl	Balls	Mins	4s	6s
MA Taylor	b Imran	23	77	91	1	—
TM Moody	b Akram	3	13	18	—	—
DM Jones	run out	54	89	112	3	—
SR Waugh	c Miandad b Shoaib	28	64	64	—	—
SP O'Donnell	b Imran	3	7	19	—	—
AR Border (c)	run out	22	31	38	—	—
IA Healy (+)	b Akram	11	16	26	—	—
PL Taylor	not out	3	6	10	—	—
CJ McDermott	run out	0	1	2	—	—
CG Rackemann	did not bat					
TM Alderman	did not bat					
SUNDRIES: B. 0 LB. 13 W. 3 NB. 2		18	304	194	4	—
TOTAL	8 wkts for 165					

F/W: 8 68 110 123 125 153 164 165

Bowler	O	M	R	Wkts	NB	W
Wasim Akram	10	2	21	2	—	2
Waqar Younus	10	1	36	—	2	1
Aaqib Javed	7	—	28	—	—	—
Nadeem Ghauri	10	1	23	—	—	—
Imran Khan	10	1	30	2	—	—
Shoaib Mohammad	3	—	14	1	—	—
Overs:	50.0					

Pakistan

Batsman	How Out	Ttl	Balls	Mins	4s	6s
Saeed Ahmed	b McDermott	27	30	40	3	1
Shoaib Mohammad	c McDermott b O'Donnell	9	57	80	—	—
Ijaz Ahmed	b O'Donnell	3	13	19	—	—
Javed Miandad	lbw Alderman	29	54	92	1	—
Imran Khan (c)	not out	56	106	123	5	—
Salim Malik	c Border b PL Taylor	0	4	10	—	—
Wasim Akram	not out	34	30	37	5	—
Salim Yousuf (c)	did not bat					
Waqar Younus	did not bat					
Aaqib Javed	did not bat					
Nadeem Ghauri	did not bat					
SUNDRIES: B. 3 LB. 4 W. 0 NB. 2		9	294	204	14	1
TOTAL	5 wkts for 167					

F/W: 32 38 43 102 111

Bowler	O	M	R	Wkts	NB	W
Alderman	10	2	29	1	—	—
McDermott	8	1	35	1	1	—
O'Donnell	9.3	1	32	2	1	—
Rackemann	8	1	24	—	—	—
PL Taylor	9	1	26	1	—	—
Border	4	—	14	—	—	—
Overs:	48.3					

Umpires: TA Prue & RJ Evans

Man of Match: Imran Khan

12th Men: DS Lehmann (Australia) & Mushtaq Ahmed (Pakistan)

BENSON AND HEDGES WORLD SERIES – GAME 9
Pakistan v Sri Lanka
Bellerive Oval, Hobart
Feb 15 1990
Toss: Pakistan
Attendance: 3323
Result: Pakistan won by 6 wkts

Sri Lanka had to win this match to have any real hope of making the finals and, accordingly, much was expected of its batting, the stronger half of its game. The Pakistani captain, Imran Khan, won the toss, and the Sri Lankans were made to bat first on a lively, bouncy pitch. Both openers went cheaply, but Sri Lanka's other recognised batsmen were building a promising total when, at 4 for 151, Arjuna Ranatunga was caught on the boundary for 42. This proved to be the start of a batting collapse in which the last 6 wickets fell for only 44 runs. Sri Lanka was all out in the 48th over for 195, which meant that to stay in the game its bowlers had to take early Pakistani wickets. In fact, the Pakistani batsmen had little trouble scoring the necessary runs in 48.3 overs. Opener Rameez Raja saw his team home to victory with an innings of 116 not out, and was later named Man of the Match.

Sri Lanka

Batsman	How Out	Ttl	Balls	Mins	4s	6s
MAR Samarasekera	lbw Younus	7	24	28	1	—
DSBP Kuruppu	c Yousuf b Younus	1	10	11	—	—
AP Gurusinha	b Younus	59	86	131	5	—
HP Tillekeratne (+)	b Imran Khan	19	46	48	2	—
EAR De Silva	c & b Aaqib	5	9	12	—	—
A Ranatunga (c)	c Akram b Ghauri	42	50	47	1	2
RS Mahanama	c Yousuf b Ghauri	24	28	37	1	—
PA De Silva	b Younus	1	9	10	—	—
RJ Ratnayake	c Yousuf b Akram	14	26	30	1	—
GF Labrooy	c (s)Mushtaq b Aaqib	2	8	12	—	—
KIW Wijegunawardene	not out	0	4	4	—	—
SUNDRIES: B. 0 LB. 10 W. 9 NB. 2		21	300	190	11	2
TOTAL		195				

F/W: 6 25 62 79 151 152 158 188 193 195

Bowler	O	M	R	Wkts	NB	W
Wasim Akram	9	2	23	1	—	4
Imran Khan	10	—	28	1	—	—
Waqar Younus	10	2	39	4	2	3
Aaqib Javed	8.5	—	44	2	—	2
Nadeem Ghauri	10	—	51	2	—	—
Overs:	47.5					

Pakistan

Batsman	How Out	Ttl	Balls	Mins	4s	6s
Rameez Raja	not out	116	150	198	8	—
Saeed Anwar	b Ratnayake	17	30	41	—	—
Ijaz Ahmed	lbw Wijegunawardene	1	5	4	—	—
Javed Miandad	c EAR De Silva b W'wardene	42	90	111	—	—
Salim Malik	run out	3	5	12	—	—
Salim Yousuf (+)	not out	10	15	25	1	—
Imran Khan (c)	did not bat					
Wasim Akram	did not bat					
Waqar Younus	did not bat					
Aaqib Javed	did not bat					
Nadeem Ghauri	did not bat					
SUNDRIES: B. 1 LB. 4 W. 4 NB. 0		9	295	198	9	—
TOTAL	4 wkts for 198					

F/W: 46 53 158 166

▶

Bowler	O	M	R	Wkts	NB	W
Labrooy	9	—	41	—	—	2
Ratnayake	9.3	—	47	1	—	2
Wijegunawardene	10	1	34	2	—	—
Ranatunga	10	—	37	—	—	—
EAR De Silva	10	—	34	—	—	—
Overs:	48.3					

Umpires: SG Randell & LJ King

Man of Match: Rameez Raja

12th Men: Mushtaq Ahmed (Pakistan) & ST Jayasuriya (Sri Lanka)

BENSON AND HEDGES WORLD SERIES – GAME 10
Pakistan v Sri Lanka
Adelaide Oval, Adelaide
Feb 17 1990
Toss: Sri Lanka
Attendance: 3854
Result: Pakistan won by 27 runs

Runs were scored in such extravagant quantities that by the end of the day the two teams had amassed 603 between them—the highest aggregate ever compiled in an international 50-over match. The fact only 11 wickets fell while all these runs were being scored was a further indication of the dominance of bat over ball. The wicket played easily and the two sides made full use of the short square boundaries, but there was also much spectacular strokeplay, particularly by Pakistani opener Saeed Anwar. Statistically, his innings was exceptional. He hit 6 sixes while scoring 126 from 99 balls, and he took only 87 balls to reach his century. Anwar and Rameez Raja, who went on to make 107 not out, put on 202 for the first wicket. In reply, the Sri Lankans played what in most circumstances would have been a match-winning innings of 8 for 288, Roshan Mahanama top-scoring with 72. The loss ruled out any chance of Sri Lanka making the finals.

Pakistan

Batsman	How Out	Ttl	Balls	Mins	4s	6s
Saeed Anwar	b EAR De Silva	126	99	132	8	6
Rameez Raja	not out	107	159	202	3	—
Salim Malik	c Ratnayake b EAR De Silva	25	25	34	1	—
Wasim Akram	b Ratnayake	34	23	34	1	2
Imran Khan (c)	not out	1	1	1	—	—
Javed Miandad	did not bat					
Ijaz Ahmed	did not bat					
Salim Yousuf (+)	did not bat					
Waqar Younus	did not bat					
Aaqib Javed	did not bat					
Nadeem Ghauri	did not bat					
SUNDRIES: B. 5 LB. 10 W. 4 NB. 3		22	307	202	13	8
TOTAL	3 wkts for 315					
F/W: 202 252 314						

Bowler	O	M	R	Wkts	NB	W
Labrooy	10	—	56	—	3	2
Ratnayake	10	1	38	1	—	1
Wijegunawardene	4	—	38	—	—	—
Ranatunga	10	—	50	—	—	—
PA De Silva	4	—	30	—	—	—
EAR De Silva	9	—	57	2	—	—
Gurusinha	3	—	31	—	—	1
Overs:	50.0					

Sri Lanka

Batsman	How Out	Ttl	Balls	Mins	4s	6s
DBSP Kuruppu (+)	run out	37	58	64	2	—
MAR Samarasekera	c Akram b Aaqib	24	34	42	4	—
PA De Silva	run out	22	18	27	1	1
A Ranatunga (c)	c Malik b Aaqib	64	72	107	—	2
AP Gurusinha	c Miandad b Ghauri	16	17	22	2	—
RS Mahanama	run out	72	81	97	2	—
RJ Ratnayake	b Younus	3	5	7	—	—
GF Labrooy	b Younus	12	13	16	—	—
EAR De Silva	not out	3	6	12	—	—
HP Tillekeratne	not out	5	6	6	—	—
KIW Wijegunawardene	did not bat					
SUNDRIES: B. 1 LB. 21 W. 6 NB. 2		30	310	204	11	3
TOTAL	8 wkts for 288					

F/W: 55 90 94 123 251 258 271 280

Bowler	O	M	R	Wkts	NB	W
Wasim Akram	10	—	49	—	—	1
Waqar Younus	10	1	35	2	1	2
Aaqib Javed	10	—	57	2	—	2
Nadeem Ghauri	8	—	54	1	1	—
Imran Khan	10	—	60	—	—	—
Ijaz Ahmed	2	—	11	—	—	1
Overs:	50.0					

Umpires: AR Crafter & SG Randell

Man of Match: Saeed Anwar

12th Men: Mushtaq Rana (Pakistan) & ST Jayasuriya (Sri Lanka)

BENSON AND HEDGES WORLD SERIES – GAME 11
Australia v Sri Lanka
Adelaide Oval, Adelaide
Feb 18 1990
Toss: Sri Lanka
Attendance: 16 827
Result: Australia won by 7 wkts

Almost as if they had exhausted themselves by their frantic run chase of the previous day, the Sri Lankan batsmen performed indifferently. Carl Rackemann struck early with two wickets, reducing Sri Lanka to 2 for 21, and the tourists did not manage to recover. Aravinda de Silva did attempt a spirited counter-attack, scoring 39 off only 29 balls, but his departure when the score was 81 seemed to end the Sri Lankans' hopes of compiling a winning total. They were all out in the 41st over for 158, a poor effort compared with their valiant performance a day earlier. The Australians passed that total with predictable ease, Dean Jones top-scoring with 80 not out and being named Man of the Match. This was the Sri Lankans' last match in Australia, and they were no doubt disappointed to end their tour on a low note.

Sri Lanka

Batsman	How Out	Ttl	Balls	Mins	4s	6s
DBSP Kuruppu (+)	c Alderman b Rackemann	12	17	26	—	—
MAR Samarasekera	c Healy b Rackemann	1	13	17	—	—
AP Gurusinha	c Healy b Campbell	20	34	68	—	—
PA De Silva	b Alderman	39	29	30	3	3
A Ranatunga (c)	c Healy b Campbell	1	7	6	—	—
HP Tillekeratne	b Campbell	3	13	29		

Batsman	How Out	Ttl	Balls	Mins	4s	6s
ST Jayasuriya	c MA Taylor b Border	31	67	87	1	—
EAR De Silva	b O'Donnell	7	18	28	—	—
RJ Ratnayake	run out	31	39	38	3	—
MAWR Madurasinghe	c PL Taylor b Border	1	8	5	—	—
KIW Wijegunawardene	not out	1	5	5	—	—
SUNDRIES: B. 1 LB. 5 W. 1 NB. 4		11	250	174	7	3
TOTAL		158				

F/W: 10 21 68 70 81 88 106 150 155 158

Bowler	O	M	R	Wkts	NB	W
Alderman	7	—	30	1	3	—
Rackemann	9	—	48	2	—	—
Campbell	7	1	31	3	—	—
O'Donnell	7	—	19	1	1	—
PL Taylor	8	1	22	—	—	1
Border	2.4	1	2	2	—	—
Overs:	40.4					

Australia

Batsman	How Out	Ttl	Balls	Mins	4s	6s
MA Taylor	c Madurasinghe b EAR De Silva	23	54	72	3	—
DM Jones	not out	80	120	149	5	—
TM Moody	c Kuruppu b Gurusinha	5	19	18	—	—
AR Border (c)	b Madurasinghe	29	35	43	3	—
SR Waugh	not out	11	14	16	1	—
SP O'Donnell	did not bat					
IA Healy (+)	did not bat					
PL Taylor	did not bat					
GD Campbell	did not bat					
CG Rackemann	did not bat					
TM Alderman	did not bat					
SUNDRIES: B. 7 LB. 2 W. 2 NB. 0		11	242	149	12	—
TOTAL	3 wkts for	159				

F/W: 67 78 134

Bowler	O	M	R	Wkts	NB	W
Ratnayake	7	1	20	—	—	1
Wijegunawardene	7	—	34	—	—	1
Gurusinha	7	—	16	1	—	—
EAR De Silva	10	—	37	1	—	—
Madurasinghe	6	—	27	1	—	—
Jayasuriya	3	—	16	—	—	—
Overs:	40.0					

Umpires: PJ McConnell & AR Crafter

Man of Match: DM Jones

12th Men: CJ McDermott (Australia) & NLK Ratnayake (Sri Lanka)

BENSON AND HEDGES WORLD SERIES – GAME 12
Australia v Pakistan
Sydney Cricket Ground, Sydney
Feb 20 1990
Toss: Pakistan
Attendance: 24 581
Result: Pakistan won by 2 runs

In a close, exciting finish, Pakistan defeated Australia by 2 runs after Imran Khan, bowling the last over of the match, performed the outstanding feat of bowling a maiden. At the start of Imran's over, Australia needed to score only 4 runs for victory, but instead it lost 2 wickets in the over and managed to score only one run—a leg bye. This was the last of the preliminary matches, and Pakistan's victory meant it could enter the finals with confidence. Batting first, Pakistan was given a strong start by its top order batsmen, although the innings fell away later. The Pakistani total, 220, seemed within the Australian batsmen's reach, but Australia lost wickets steadily and was generally under pressure. However, powerful hitting in the last few overs by Simon O'Donnell restored Australia to what seemed a winning position, and at the start of the final over the Pakistanis looked to have little chance of preventing an Australian victory. O'Donnell, who earlier had bowled with great economy, was named Man of the Match.

Pakistan

Batsman	How Out	Ttl	Balls	Mins	4s	6s
Rameez Raja	c Moody b Alderman	3	13	11	—	—
Saeed Anwar	c SR Waugh b Campbell	43	36	62	6	1
Salim Malik	c Moody b Rackemann	67	86	127	4	—
Imran Khan (c)	c MA Taylor b Alderman	56	98	123	3	1
Ijaz Ahmed	c SR Waugh b O'Donnell	9	18	20	—	—
Salim Yousuf (+)	lbw O'Donnell	5	9	9	—	—
Aamir Malik	b Campbell	14	22	25	1	—
Mushtaq Ahmed	not out	17	17	23	—	—
Waqar Younus	run out	0	2	7	—	—
Tauseef Ahmed	not out	1	2	1	—	—
Aaqib Javed	did not bat					
SUNDRIES: B. 0 LB. 0 W. 2 NB. 3		5	303	210	14	2
TOTAL	8 wkts for 220					

F/W: 4 74 161 176 184 196 207 218

Bowler	O	M	R	Wkts	NB	W
Alderman	9	2	46	2	1	—
Rackemann	10	—	45	1	1	1
Campbell	9	—	46	2	—	1
O'Donnell	10	—	32	2	1	—
PL Taylor	7	—	28	—	—	—
Border	4	—	23	—	—	—
Overs:	49.0					

Australia

Batsman	How Out	Ttl	Balls	Mins	4s	6s
MA Taylor	c Yousuf b Younus	29	25	29	4	—
TM Moody	st Yousuf b Anwar	74	111	162	5	—
DM Jones	c Ijaz b Aaqib	10	13	14	1	—
AR Border (c)	b Tauseef	26	52	62	3	—
SR Waugh	st Younus b Mushtaq	3	10	9	—	—
PL Taylor	c Imran b Mushtaq	14	28	30	—	—
SP O'Donnell	lbw Imran	39	37	48	2	1
IA Healy (+)	run out	8	9	9	—	—
GD Campbell	not out	4	13	31	—	—
CG Rackemann	b Imran	0	2	2	—	—
TM Alderman	not out	0	1	3	—	—
SUNDRIES: B. 0 LB. 5 W. 6 NB. 0		11	301	204	15	1
TOTAL	9 wkts for 218					

F/W: 44 58 122 127 159 169 192 218 218

Bowler	O	M	R	Wkts	NB	W
Imran Khan	7	1	28	2	—	—
Waqar Younus	7	—	40	1	—	5
Aaqib Javed	9	—	39	1	—	1
Aamir Malik	3	—	12	—	—	—
Tauseef Ahmed	10	—	33	1	—	—
Mushtaq Ahmed	10	1	46	2	—	—
Saeed Anwar	3	—	15	1	—	—
Overs:	49.0					

Umpires: PJ McConnell & LJ King

Man of Match: SP O'Donnell

12th Men: ME Waugh (Australia) & Shoaib Mohammad (Pakistan)

FIRST FINAL

BENSON AND HEDGES WORLD SERIES
Australia v Pakistan
Melbourne Cricket Ground, Melbourne
Feb 23 1990
Toss: Australia
Attendance: 55 205
Result: Australia won by 7 wkts

Fine weather having been forecast, the Melbourne pitch was left uncovered on the eve of the match, but rain fell overnight, and the dampened pitch made batting extremely difficult for the first 20 overs. Accordingly, Pakistan, which lost the toss and had to bat first, found itself at an absurd disadvantage. Its leading batsmen floundered in the conditions, and the first 6 wickets fell for only 77 runs. It was then that Wasim Akram set upon the bowling and, with a lusty innings of 86, saved the Pakistani innings from complete disaster. He faced only 76 balls, and hit 3 sixes. But it was obvious Pakistan's final total, 162, would be difficult to defend on a batting strip which had been improving steadily, although the loss of two early Australian wickets offered the Pakistanis some hope. A short time later, Akram bowled Steve Waugh with an in-swinging yorker, and it seemed Australia might have a fight on its hands. But Dean Jones (83 not out) and Allan Border (44 not out) saw Australia through to an easy victory without further alarm. The match, rendered one-sided by the pitch, was a let-down for the 55 205 spectators.

Pakistan

Batsman	How Out	Ttl	Balls	Mins	4s	6s
Saeed Anwar	c & b Alderman	2	5	11	—	—
Rameez Raja	c Healy b O'Donnell	1	7	7	—	—
Salim Malik	c Alderman b Campbell	39	47	77	6	—
Javed Miandad	c Healy b Rackemann	2	26	39	—	—
Imran Khan (c)	c Healy b Rackemann	1	24	30	—	—
Ijaz Ahmed	lbw O'Donnell	7	34	46	—	—
Wasim Akram	c PL Taylor b Campbell	86	76	113	5	3
Salim Yousuf	c Rackemann b PL Taylor	4	22	21	—	—
Tauseef Ahmed	c PL Taylor b Campbell	10	43	44	—	—
Waqar Younus	b Alderman	0	1	7	—	—
Nadeem Ghauri	not out	3	4	4	—	—
SUNDRIES: B. 0 LB. 3 W. 3 NB. 1		7	289	204	11	3
TOTAL		162				

F/W: 2 8 46 50 50 77 96 153 159 162

Bowler	O	M	R	Wkts	NB	W
Alderman	8.5	2	26	2	—	—
O'Donnell	10	2	29	2	1	—
Rackemann	10	5	32	2	—	—
Campbell	9	1	39	3	—	2
PL Taylor	10	—	33	1	—	1
Overs:	47.5					

Australia

Batsman	How Out	Ttl	Balls	Mins	4s	6s
MA Taylor	c Yousuf b Younus	13	38	36	—	—
TM Moody	c Yousuf b Akram	4	13	14	—	—
DM Jones	not out	83	135	160	3	1
SR Waugh	b Akram	13	32	50	1	—
AR Border (c)	not out	44	61	87	2	—
SP O'Donnell	did not bat					
IA Healy (+)	did not bat					
PL Taylor	did not bat					
GD Campbell	did not bat					
CG Rackemann	did not bat					
TM Alderman	did not bat					
SUNDRIES: B. 0 LB. 3 W. 1 NB. 2		6	279	175	6	1
TOTAL	3 wkts for 163					

F/W: 9 23 54

Bowler	O	M	R	Wkts	NB	W
Wasim Akram	10	—	30	2	2	—
Imran Khan	9	—	32	—	—	—
Waqar Younus	9	—	26	1	—	—
Nadeem Ghauri	9	—	27	—	—	—
Tauseef Ahmed	8.5	—	45	—	—	1
Overs:	45.5					

Umpires: PJ McConnell & AR Crafter

12th Men: ME Waugh (Australia) & Mushtaq Ahmed (Pakistan)

SECOND FINAL

BENSON AND HEDGES WORLD SERIES
Australia v Pakistan
Sydney Cricket Ground, Sydney
Feb 25 1990
Toss: Australia
Attendance: 34 443
Result: Australia won by 69 runs

Pakistan failed to produce the big effort with the bat which it needed to win, and the result—an Australian victory by 69 runs—proved to be an anti-climax. Australia's first four batsmen set up the victory, Mark Taylor top-scoring with 76. Dean Jones's 46, following his 83 not out in the first final, later earned him the title Player of the Final Series. An interesting feature of the Australian batting line-up was the inclusion of Mark Waugh in place of his brother Steve, who had been dropped after a number of indifferent performances. Mark Waugh, making his first appearance of the season for Australia, was run out for 14. Set a target of 256 to win, Pakistan chose to bat Wasim Akram at number 3, apparently in the hope that he would accelerate the run rate early. Akram scored 36 off 30 balls, including a six and 6 fours, and his dismissal by a smart stumping proved a fatal blow for Pakistan. Thereafter, wickets tumbled until Pakistan was in a hopeless position at 8 for 132. Salim Yousuf (59) staged a late rally, but the innings lasted only 45 overs.

Australia

Batsman	How Out	Ttl	Balls	Mins	4s	6s
MA Taylor	c Younus b Mushtaq	76	120	154	4	—
TM Moody	st Younus b Ghauri	44	63	82	4	—
DM Jones	run out	46	53	76	1	—
AR Border (c)	not out	34	35	50	2	—
ME Waugh	run out	14	14	14	1	—
SP O'Donnell	c Yousuf b Imran	3	9	9	—	—
IA Healy (+)	c Anwar b Mushtaq	15	11	8	—	—
PL Taylor	not out	3	3	11	—	—
GD Campbell	did not bat					
CG Rackemann	did not bat					
TM Alderman	did not bat					
SUNDRIES: B. 1 LB. 11 W. 6 NB. 2		20	308	205	12	—
TOTAL	6 wkts for 255					

F/W: 84 179 183 207 214 231

Bowler	O	M	R	Wkts	NB	W
Wasim Akram	10	—	42	—	—	4
Imran Khan	10	—	43	1	1	—
Waqar Younus	10	—	48	—	1	2
Nadeem Ghauri	10	—	45	1	—	—
Mushtaq Ahmed	10	—	65	2	—	—
Overs:	50.0					

Pakistan

Batsman	How Out	Ttl	Balls	Mins	4s	6s
Saeed Anwar	c Healy b O'Donnell	5	11	7	—	—
Rameez Raja	lbw Alderman	0	1	10	—	—
Wasim Akram	st Healy b PL Taylor	36	30	47	6	1
Salim Malik	b Alderman	15	23	29	2	—
Javed Miandad	run out	11	35	51	—	—
Imran Khan (c)	c MA Taylor b Campbell	1	15	24	—	—
Ijaz Ahmed	b PL Taylor	29	45	58	1	—
Salim Yousuf (+)	c Moody b O'Donnell	59	75	30	6	—
Mushtaq Ahmed	c Healy b PL Taylor	0	2	1	—	—
Waqar Younus	not out	20	29	38	—	1
Nadeem Ghauri	c Campbell b O'Donnell	4	8	8	—	—
SUNDRIES: B. 0 LB. 2 W. 2 NB. 2		6	274	182	15	2
TOTAL		186				

F/W: 6 6 52 62 72 76 132 132 176 186

Bowler	O	M	R	Wkts	NB	W
Alderman	7	1	28	2	1	1
O'Donnell	6	1	38	3	—	1
PL Taylor	10	1	43	3	—	—
Rackemann	8	1	20	—	—	—
Campbell	7	—	21	1	1	—
Border	7	—	34	—	—	—
Overs:	45.0					

Umpires: PJ McConnell & AR Crafter

Player of Finals: DM Jones

12th Men: SR Waugh (Australia) & Shoaib Mohammad (Pakistan)

Benson and Hedges World Series Statistics

1989/90 Benson and Hedges World Series – Leading Averages

Batsman	Country	M	Inn	NO	Runs	HS	50	100	Avrge
DM Jones	Aus	10	9	3	461	85*	5	—	76.83
Rameez Raja	Pak	7	7	2	248	116*	—	2	49.60
A Ranatunga	SL	8	8	2	273	71*	3	—	45.50
AR Border	Aus	10	9	3	271	69*	1	—	45.17
SP O'Donnell	Aus	10	6	2	169	57*	1	—	42.25
RS Mahanama	SL	7	7	2	209	72	1	—	41.80
Imran Khan	Pak	10	9	2	283	82	3	—	40.43

Batsman	Country	M	Inn	NO	Runs	HS	50	100	Avrge
TM Moody	Aus	6	6	—	219	89	2	—	36.50
Wasim Akram	Pak	9	8	2	209	86	1	—	34.83
MA Taylor	Aus	9	9	—	294	76	2	—	32.67
Saeed Anwar	Pak	9	9	—	293	126	—	1	32.56
AP Gurusinha	SL	8	8	—	250	88	2	—	31.25
Ijaz Ahmed	Pak	10	9	2	184	102*	—	1	26.29
Javed Miandad	Pak	8	7	—	184	43	—	—	26.29
Salim Malik	Pak	8	8	—	190	67	1	—	23.75
HP Tillekeratne	SL	8	8	1	151	61	1	—	21.57
PA De Silva	SL	8	8	—	155	40	—	—	19.38

Bowler	Country	M	Overs	Mdns	Runs	Wkts	Avrge	5wi	NB	W	Best
SP O'Donnell	Aus	10	84.3	7	332	20	16.60	—	6	14	4/36
TM Alderman	Aus	9	75.5	12	283	16	17.69	—	5	4	3/25
CG Rackemann	Aus	8	71.1	9	253	13	19.46	—	2	1	3/31
GD Campbell	Aus	6	52.0	6	227	10	22.70	—	4	5	3/31
PL Taylor	Aus	9	80.0	4	301	12	25.08	—	—	3	3/36
MG Hughes	Aus	5	44.2	4	151	5	30.20	—	1	9	2/41
Mushtaq Ahmed	Pak	4	38.0	1	242	8	30.25	—	—	1	2/46
Waqar Younus	Pak	8	69.0	5	295	9	32.78	—	9	21	4/39
Wasim Akram	Pak	9	89.0	8	308	9	34.22	—	8	16	2/21
Nadeem Ghauri	Pak	6	57.0	4	230	5	46.00	—	1	—	2/51
Imran Khan	Pak	10	89.3	3	374	8	46.75	—	1	4	2/28
Aaqib Javed	Pak	8	72.5	1	336	7	48.00	—	2	10	2/44
RJ Ratnayake	SL	8	74.2	5	322	6	53.67	—	5	15	3/44

Australia

Batsman	M	Inn	NO	Runs	HS	50	100	Avrge	Ct/st
DM Jones	10	9	3	461	85*	5	—	76.83	2
DC Boon	3	3	1	99	49*	—	—	49.50	—
AR Border	10	9	3	271	69*	1	—	45.17	6
GR Marsh	4	4	1	130	80*	1	—	43.33	1
SP O'Donnell	10	6	2	169	57*	1	—	42.?5	2
TM Moody	6	6	—	219	89	2	—	36.50	3
PL Taylor	9	4	3	36	16*	—	—	36.00	5
MA Taylor	9	9	—	294	76	2	—	32.67	5
IA Healy	10	5	1	89	33	—	—	22.25	16/2
SR Waugh	9	8	2	104	31*	—	—	17.33	3
ME Waugh	1	1	—	14	14	—	—	14.00	—
CJ McDermott	1	1	—	0	0	—	—	0.00	1
CG Rackemann	8	1	—	0	0	—	—	0.00	—
GD Campbell	6	1	1	4	4*	—	—	—	2
MG Hughes	5	1	1	0	0*	—	—	—	4
TM Alderman	9	1	1	0	0*	—	—	—	5

Bowler	M	Overs	Mdns	Runs	Wkts	Avrge	5wi	NB	W	Best
SP O'Donnell	10	84.3	7	332	20	16.60	—	6	14	4/36
TM Alderman	9	75.5	12	283	16	17.69	—	5	4	3/25
CG Rackemann	8	71.1	9	253	13	19.46	—	2	1	4/44
GD Campbell	6	52.0	6	227	10	22.70	—	4	5	3/31
PL Taylor	9	80.0	4	301	12	25.08	—	—	3	3/36
MG Hughes	5	44.2	4	151	5	30.20	—	1	9	2/41
CJ McDermott	1	8.0	1	35	1	35.00	—	1	—	1/35
SR Waugh	9	16.0	—	77	2	38.50	—	—	1	1/26
AR Border	10	24.4	1	113	2	56.50	—	—	—	2/2

Pakistan

Batsman	M	Inn	NO	Runs	HS	50	100	Avrge	Ct/st
Rameez Raja	7	7	2	248	116*	—	2	49.60	—
Imran Khan	10	9	2	283	82	3	—	40.43	2
Aamir Malik	3	3	—	106	69	1	—	35.33	3
Wasim Akram	9	8	2	209	86	1	—	34.83	2
Saeed Anwar	9	9	—	293	126	—	1	32.56	2
Salim Yousuf	8	6	1	137	59	2	—	27.40	8/4
Javed Miandad	8	7	—	184	43	—	—	26.29	2
Ijaz Ahmed	10	9	2	184	102*	—	1	26.29	3
Salim Malik	8	8	—	190	67	1	—	23.75	2
Mansoor Akhtar	2	2	—	45	32	—	—	22.50	—
Mushtaq Ahmed	4	3	1	28	17*	—	—	14.00	—
Nadeem Ghauri	6	3	2	14	7*	—	—	14.00	—
Shoaib Mohammad	3	3	—	40	22	—	—	13.33	—

▶

Batsman	M	Inn	NO	Runs	HS	50	100	Avrge	Ct/St
Waqar Younus	8	3	1	20	20*	—	—	10.00	2
Tauseef Ahmed	4	3	1	12	10	—	—	6.00	—
Maqsood Rana	1	1	—	5	5	—	—	5.00	—
Abdul Qadir	2	2	1	1	1	—	—	1.00	—
Aaqib Javed	8	2	1	1	1	—	—	1.00	2

Bowler	M	Overs	Mdns	Runs	Wkts	Avrge	5wi	NB	W	Best
Shoaib Mohammad	3	3.0	—	14	1	14.00	—	—	—	1/14
Saeed Anwar	9	3.0	—	15	1	15.00	—	—	—	1/15
Mushtaq Ahmed	4	38.0	1	242	8	30.25	—	—	1	2/46
Waqar Younus	8	69.0	5	295	9	32.78	—	9	21	4/39
Wasim Akram	9	89.0	8	308	9	34.22	—	8	16	2/21
Tauseef Ahmed	4	38.5	—	183	4	45.75	—	—	1	2/48
Nadeem Ghauri	6	57.0	4	230	5	46.00	—	1	—	2/51
Imran Khan	10	89.3	3	374	8	46.75	—	1	4	2/28
Aaqib Javed	8	72.5	1	336	7	48.00	—	2	10	2/44
Abdul Qadir	2	12.0	—	57	1	57.00	—	1	—	1/34
Ijaz Ahmed	10	2.0	—	11	—	—	—	—	1	—
Maqsood Rana	1	2.0	—	11	—	—	—	—	—	—
Aamir Malik	3	3.0	—	12	—	—	—	—	—	—

Sri Lanka

Batsman	M	Inn	NO	Runs	HS	50	100	Avrge	Ct/St
A Ranatunga	8	8	2	273	71*	3	—	45.50	1
RS Mahanama	7	7	2	209	72	1	—	41.80	1
AP Gurusinha	8	8	—	250	88	2	—	31.25	1
HP Tillekeratne	8	8	1	151	61	1	—	21.57	5/1
PA De Silva	8	8	—	155	40	—	—	19.38	1
MAR Samarasekera	8	8	—	143	60	1	—	17.88	2
DSBP Kuruppu	3	3	—	50	37	—	—	16.67	1
RJ Ratnayake	8	8	1	100	31	—	—	14.29	1
ST Jayasuriya	6	5	—	71	31	—	—	14.20	3
EAR De Silva	6	5	2	25	13*	—	—	8.33	1
JR Ratnayeke	4	4	—	29	25	—	—	7.25	1
GF Labrooy	6	5	1	22	12	—	—	5.50	2
MAWR Madurasinghe	1	1	—	1	1	—	—	1.00	1
KIW Wijegunawardene	5	2	2	1	1*	—	—	—	—
CPH Ramanayake	1	—	—	—	—	—	—	—	—
NLK Ratnayake	1	—	—	—	—	—	—	—	—

Bowler	M	Overs	Mdns	Runs	Wkts	Avrge	5wi	NB	W	Best
CPH Ramanayake	1	5.2	—	25	1	25.00	—	—	—	1/25
MAWR Madurasinghe	1	6.0	—	27	1	27.00	—	—	—	1/27
JR Ratnayeke	4	34.5	4	155	4	38.75	—	7	3	2/33
NLK Ratnayake	1	7.0	—	39	1	39.00	—	—	2	1/39
RJ Ratnayake	8	74.2	5	322	6	53.67	—	5	15	3/44
KIW Wijegunawardene	5	35.0	1	166	3	55.33	—	4	2	2/34
EAR De Silva	6	59.0	—	246	4	61.50	—	—	—	2/57
A Ranatunga	8	43.0	2	202	3	67.33	—	—	3	3/41
GF Labrooy	6	58.0	2	272	4	68.00	—	4	12	2/43
AP Gurusinha	8	24.4	—	137	2	68.50	—	—	9	1/16
PA De Silva	8	20.0	—	101	1	101.00	—	—	—	1/35
ST Jayasuriya	6	3.0	—	16	—	—	—	—	—	—

AUSTRALIAN
TOUR OF
NEW ZEALAND
JANUARY–FEBRUARY 1990

THE SHORT TOUR OF NEW ZEALAND proved a bitter-sweet experience for the Australians. After demonstrating again their mastery of the limited-overs game with resounding victories over New Zealand and India in the Rothman's Cup series, they succumbed ingloriously to New Zealand in the single Test. The defeat was Australia's first in 15 Tests and the first since the end of 1988. The Australians were entitled to blame the rain-affected pitch for much of their misfortune in this match, so it would be wrong to read too much into their defeat, although the Australian bowlers' ineffectiveness on the final day of the Test called into question again the adequacy of their attack. In particular, the lack of a spin bowler of Test quality was again evident. Merv Hughes did not play in the Test, and his inclusion in the touring side after knee surgery must be counted among the more curious selections of the summer.

Before the Test at Wellington, Australia and New Zealand were the only teams in the world to have gone a year without being defeated in a Test. After New Zealand emerged from this match with its record intact, it had some grounds to claim a high place in the international rankings. As in the Test in Perth at the start of the season, the New Zealanders showed that above all they are highly competitive in the Test match environment. The fact they won the Test in Wellington so handsomely without their premier batsman, Martin Crowe, made their achievement all the greater.

1989/90 Australian Tour of New Zealand

Date	Venue	Opponent	Result
Mar 3*	Christchurch	India	Won by 18 runs
Mar 4*	Christchurch	New Zealand	Won by 150 runs
Mar 8*	Hamilton	India	Won by 7 wkts
Mar 10*	Auckland	New Zealand	Won on run rate
Mar 11*	Auckland	New Zealand	Won by 8 wkts
Mar 15	Wellington	New Zealand	Lost by 9 wkts

* Denotes not first-class

ROTHMAN'S CUP
Limited-overs Series

Australia demonstrated a clear superiority over New Zealand and India at the limited-overs game by winning all five matches it played in this triangular tournament, three of them by overwhelming margins. For the most part, its victories were set up by strong batting performances. On only one occasion—when the Australians made 9 for 187 against India in their opening competition match—did their batting falter, and on this occasion their bowlers met the challenge by bowling India out for 169. In its other four matches Australia had totals of 8 for 244 and 6 for 239 when batting first and totals of 3 for 212 and 2 for 164 when batting second. The outstanding Australian batsman was again Dean Jones, who attained exceptional heights of batsmanship in the limited-overs context. In the four matches he played his scores were 32, 107, 59 and 102 not out, and in the last of these innings, in particular, he batted with the abandon of a man in supreme form. Carl Rackemann was the most effective of the bowlers, his best figures being 3 wickets for 22 runs in 10 overs in the final against New Zealand. In the four matches he played, he conceded runs at the rate of only 3.23 an over. Merv Hughes, on the other hand, proved unusually expensive, conceding 64 runs from the 11 overs he bowled in the competition, which did nothing to answer questions which had been raised about his selection for the tour so soon after a knee operation.

Neither of Australia's opponents played with consistency, and each of them was shown to be liable to batting failures. New Zealand's Richard Hadlee did not prove to be nearly so threatening with the ball as expected and, although he twice took Dean Jones's wicket in the three matches he bowled to him, Jones certainly emerged on top from this renewed encounter with his rival. On the other hand, Hadlee was in fine batting form, and played a couple of hard-hitting innings.

ROTHMAN'S INTERNATIONAL SERIES – GAME 1
New Zealand v India
Carisbrook, Dunedin
Mar 1 1990
Toss: New Zealand
New Zealand won by 108 runs

A century by Martin Crowe, advanced to the position of opening batsman, set up New Zealand's unexpectedly easy victory. Crowe played a highly competent innings on a pitch of low and uncertain bounce. Three New Zealand wickets had fallen for 66 when Crowe was joined by Ken Rutherford. The pair raised the total to 218 before Crowe was out for only his second century in limited-overs internationals. Rutherford (78 not out) saw New Zealand through to 6 for 246—a large total for an innings shortened to 47 overs by rain. So the target set for the Indian batsmen was a daunting one, and this probably contributed to the rapid disintegration of their innings. At 2 for 57, the Indians lost 4 wickets for 9 runs and thereafter defeat was inevitable. New Zealand's victory followed 11 consecutive losses to India in limited-overs matches. The Indian team's manager, Bishan Bedi, later criticised his team for lacking application.

New Zealand_____ 6/246 (47.0) MD Crowe 104, KR Rutherford 78*
India _____ 138 (32.1) WV Raman 32, SA Thomson 3/19, DK Morrison 3/43

Man of Match: MD Crowe

ROTHMAN'S INTERNATIONAL SERIES – GAME 2
Australia v India
Lancaster Park, Christchurch
Mar 3 1990
Toss: Australia
Result: Australia won by 18 runs

Fine bowling by Terry Alderman, who was named Man of the Match, and three outstanding catches in the outfield enabled the Australians to emerge victors from a match they had looked likely to lose. Batting first, the Australians appeared to have trouble making runs on the slow pitch, and several of them lost their wickets after frantic attempts to score. No batsman went on to play a dominant innings, and Allan Border top scored with a mere 37. Towards the end of the innings Ian Healy hit a breezy 25, including a six, which helped raise the score to 187, although this hardly seemed a winning total. But the Indian batsmen struggled against Australia's opening attack of Alderman and Carl Rackemann, and after 12 overs had lost 3 for 23. India recovered to be within sight of victory at 6 for 154, but in another collapse lost their last 4 wickets for 15 runs. The Indian innings lasted only 45 overs.

Australia

Batsman	How Out	Ttl	Balls	Mins	4s	6s
MA Taylor	st More b Hirwani	10	48	51	1	—
DC Boon	run out	22	52	78	1	—
DM Jones	c Manjrekar b Hirwani	32	42	57	1	—
AR Border (c)	run out	37	50	60	1	1
SR Waugh	c Manjrekar b Kapil Dev	10	28	38	—	—
SP O'Donnell	lbw Ajay Sharma	12	17	22	1	—
IA Healy (+)	run out	25	27	36	1	1
PL Taylor	not out	18	28	42	—	—
GD Campbell	c More b Kapil Dev	0	3	2	—	—
CG Rackemann	c Kapil Dev b Prabhakar	6	9	14	—	—
TM Alderman	did not bat					
SUNDRIES: B. 0 LB. 8 W. 4 NB. 3		15	304	208	6	2
TOTAL	9 wkts for 187					

F/W: 31 51 92 119 123 140 170 172 187

Bowler	O	M	R	Wkts	NB	W
Kapil Dev	10	—	29	2	2	2
Prabhakar	10	3	35	1	1	1
Wassan	10	—	36	—	—	—
Hirwani	10	2	39	2	—	—
Ajay Sharma	10	—	40	1	—	1
Overs:	50.0					

India

Batsman	How Out	Ttl	Balls	Mins	4s	6s
VB Chandrasekhar	c Waugh b Alderman	8	19	28	—	—
WV Raman	c MA Taylor b Alderman	2	6	8	—	—
SV Manjrekar	c Healy b Rackemann	6	24	41	—	—
DB Vengsarkar	c Jones b Campbell	35	56	71	6	—
M Azharuddin (c)	c Alderman b PL Taylor	26	61	81	2	—
Ajay Sharma	lbw O'Donnell	15	27	37	2	—
Kapil Dev	c Jones b Alderman	27	32	42	2	—
M Prabhakar	c Waugh b Rackemann	21	33	42	3	—
KS More (+)	c Campbell b Alderman	8	8	17	1	—
A Wassan	b Alderman	4	11	14	—	—
ND Hirwani	not out	1	1	1	—	—
SUNDRIES: B. 4 LB. 2 W. 3 NB. 7		16	278	200	16	—
TOTAL		169				

F/W: 5 14 23 75 98 110 154 155 167 169

167

Bowler	O	M	R	Wkts	NB	W
Alderman	10	2	32	5	—	2
Rackemann	9	—	27	2	1	1
Campbell	8	—	29	1	5	—
O'Donnell	8	—	36	1	1	—
PL Taylor	10	2	39	1	—	—
Overs:	45.0					

Umpires: RL McHarg & BL Aldridge

Man of Match: TM Alderman

12th Man: SR Waugh (Australia)

ROTHMAN'S INTERNATIONAL SERIES – GAME 3
New Zealand v Australia
Lancaster Park, Christchurch
Mar 4 1990
Toss: Australia
Result: Australia won by 150 runs

The very magnitude of the Australians' victory was remarkable. They won not only by 150 runs but with nearly 25 overs to spare after New Zealand's batting fell to pieces in astonishing fashion. Batting first, the Australians had lost opener Geoff Marsh early, but then David Boon and Dean Jones put on 145 runs in a partnership which virtually decided the outcome of the match. Boon scored 67 off 89 balls, and Jones went on to score his fourth century in limited-over internationals, an innings which earned him the Man of the Match award. Simon O'Donnell hit two sixes in a late flurry of scoring, including a fine hit off Richard Hadlee. New Zealand began well enough, but collapsed sensationally, losing its last 8 wickets for only 15 runs. Simon O'Donnell led the rout, taking 5 for 13. From an Australian viewpoint, the only disappointing feature of the play was the failure of Steve Waugh, who looked out of touch during his brief innings. For Martin Crowe, standing in for John Wright, who was ill, it was an unhappy debut as New Zealand captain.

Australia

Batsman	How Out	Ttl	Balls	Mins	4s	6s
DC Boon	c Crowe b Larsen	67	89	124	5	—
GR Marsh	c Smith b Hadlee	2	5	2	—	—
DM Jones	b Hadlee	107	144	196	8	—
SR Waugh	run out	3	11	10	—	—
AR Border (c)	c Bracewell b Snedden	6	22	30	—	—
SP O'Donnell	c Jones b Snedden	20	19	16	—	2
IA Healy (+)	b Snedden	6	5	9	1	—
PL Taylor	not out	6	4	10	1	—
GD Campbell	b Morrison	2	4	2	—	—
CG Rackemann	not out	2	2	3	—	—
TM Alderman	did not bat					
SUNDRIES: B. 0 LB. 17 W. 3 NB. 3		23	305	209	15	2
TOTAL	8 wkts for 244					

F/W: 3 148 153 190 214 229 233 240

Bowler	O	M	R	Wkts	NB	W
Hadlee	10	1	43	2	2	—
Morrison	9	—	51	1	1	2
Snedden	10	2	32	3	—	1
Thomson	8	—	49	—	—	—
Larsen	10	—	32	1	—	—
Bracewell	3	—	20	—	—	—
Overs:	50.0					

New Zealand

Batsman	How Out	Ttl	Balls	Mins	4s	6s
MD Crowe	c Waugh b Rackemann	17	26	39	4	—
AH Jones	c Border b Campbell	43	67	98	5	—
MJ Greatbatch	c Healy b Rackemann	0	4	2	—	—
KR Rutherford	lbw O'Donnell	20	15	27	2	—
SA Thomson	b O'Donnell	1	9	8	—	—
GR Larsen	b O'Donnell	1	7	7	—	—
IDS Smith (+)	c Border b Campbell	3	5	7	—	—
RJ Hadlee	b Campbell	2	13	18	—	—
JG Bracewell	b O'Donnell	0	1	3	—	—
MC Snedden	c Jones b O'Donnell	0	7	9	—	—
DK Morrison	not out	0	0	1	—	—
SUNDRIES: B. 0 LB. 3 W. 3 NB. 1		7	154	118	11	—
TOTAL		94				

F/W: 39 39 79 81 87 91 92 93 94 94

Bowler	O	M	R	Wkts	NB	W
Alderman	7	1	34	—	—	1
Rackemann	6	2	27	2	—	1
Campbell	6.2	2	17	3	1	—
O'Donnell	6	—	13	5	—	—
Overs:	25.2					

Umpires: RL McHarg & BL Aldridge

Man of Match: DM Jones

12th Man: MA Taylor (Australia)

ROTHMAN'S INTERNATIONAL SERIES – GAME 4
New Zealand v India
Basin Reserve, Wellington
Mar 6 1990
Toss: India
India won by 1 run

The outcome of the match was decided in an exciting last over, during which the fortunes of the two sides rose and fell in turn. India had batted first and compiled a total of 221 in an innings shortened to 49 overs. Three of its top-order batsmen, including the sixteen-year-old batsman Sachin Tendulkar, made the same score, 36. The highest scorer, however, was Kapil Dev, who batted exuberantly for 46, scored off 38 balls. Despite the early loss of Martin Crowe, the New Zealanders advanced steadily towards their target, thanks to Mark Greatbatch's 53 and Ken Rutherford's 44. But from 6 for 210, New Zealand slipped to 8 for 211 at the start of the last over, which meant that to win it needed to score 11 runs off 6 balls. Richard Hadlee, who had scored 37 from 32 balls, was on strike, and Kapil Dev was the bowler. Hadlee hit two fours off the first three balls and completed one run safely off the fourth ball, but his partner, Martin Snedden, was run out trying for a second. Having thus retained the strike, Hadlee needed to score only 2 runs from the remaining two deliveries, but he was bowled by Dev's fifth ball, a yorker on the leg stump. India thus won the match by 1 run with one ball to spare.

India _____ 221 (48.2) Kapil Dev 46, M Prabhakar 39, SV Manjrekar 39
SR Tendulkar 39
New Zealand _____ 220 (48.5) RJ Hadlee 46, KR Rutherford 44, M Prabhakar 3/37

Man of Match: Kapil Dev

ROTHMAN'S INTERNATIONAL SERIES – GAME 5
Australia v India
Seddon Park, Hamilton
Mar 8 1990
Toss: India
Result: Australia won by 7 wkts

India batted well, compiling 211 for the loss of 8 wickets, but not well enough to defeat an Australian team playing close to its best form. The top order Indian batsmen, including the top scorer, Woorkeri Raman (58), were pinned down by disciplined Australian bowling, and after 40 overs India's run rate barely exceeded 3 and over. Adventurous batting in the last 10 overs—especially by Kapil Dev, whose 48 not out was scored off only 53 balls—added another 80 runs and appeared to keep India in the match. Peter Taylor, who took 3 for 31 off 10 overs, was the most effective Australian bowler, while Simon O'Donnell was roughly treated, conceding 62 runs in 9 overs. A century stand by the openers Geoff Marsh and Mark Taylor virtually ensured that the Australians would score the runs needed, which they proceeded to do with 2 overs and 7 wickets in hand. Marsh went on to score 86 and was chosen as Man of the Match. Steve Waugh played fluently for his 23 off 32 balls.

India

Batsman	How Out	Ttl	Balls	Mins	4s	6s
WV Raman	c Healy b PL Taylor	58	86	116	7	1
M Prabhakar	c MA Taylor b Hughes	7	13	22	1	—
SV Manjrekar	run out	33	70	81	1	—
M Azharuddin (c)	lbw Hughes	37	47	67	2	1
VB Chandrasekar	c Border b PL Taylor	3	10	7	—	—
Gurshanan Singh	lbw PL Taylor	4	10	9	—	—
Kapil Dev	not out	48	53	58	4	1
Ajay Sharma	c Campbell b Hughes	7	6	8	—	—
KS More (+)	run out	1	2	5	—	—
A Wassan	not out	8	4	5	1	—
ND Hirwani	did not bat					
SUNDRIES: B. 0 LB. 4 W. 0 NB. 1		5	301	195	16	3
TOTAL	8 wkts for 211					

F/W: 12 92 108 114 123 174 194 200

Bowler	O	M	R	Wkts	NB	W
Alderman	7	—	13	—	—	—
Hughes	7	—	36	3	—	—
Campbell	8	—	25	—	—	—
O'Donnell	9	1	62	—	1	—
PL Taylor	10	2	31	3	—	—
Border	9	—	40	—	—	—
Overs:	50.0					

Australia

Batsman	How Out	Ttl	Balls	Mins	4s	6s
GR Marsh	c Gurshanan b Kapil Dev	86	144	187	10	1
MA Taylor	st More b Ajay Sharma	56	90	115	8	—
SR Waugh	c Prabhakar b Hirwani	23	32	40	2	—
DC Boon	not out	24	24	35	4	—
AR Border (c)	not out	9	6	4	—	1
SP O'Donnell	did not bat					
PL Taylor	did not bat					
IA Healy (+)	did not bat					
MG Hughes	did not bat					
GD Campbell	did not bat					
TM Alderman	did not bat					
SUNDRIES: B. 4 LB. 5 W. 4 NB. 1		14	296	192	24	2
TOTAL	3 wkts for 212					

F/W: 112 158 203

Bowler	O	M	R	Wkts	NB	W
Kapil Dev	8	—	37	1	—	—
Prabhakar	8	1	29	—	1	1
Wassan	2	—	12	—	—	2
Hirwani	10	2	25	1	—	—
Raman	10	1	43	—	—	—
Ajay Sharma	10	—	57	1	—	1
Overs:	48.0					

Man of Match: GR Marsh

12th Man: DM Jones (Australia)

ROTHMAN'S INTERNATIONAL SERIES – GAME 6
New Zealand v Australia
Eden Park, Auckland
Mar 10 1990
Toss: New Zealand
Result: Australia won on run rate

Things did not go the New Zealander's way in this match, yet they might still have won if they had grasped an opportunity offered them by the weather. Batting first, Australia made the ample total of 6 for 239 in an innings shortened to 47 overs by a brief rain interruption. Further rain interruptions seemed probable, and under these circumstances batting second was a big advantage for the New Zealanders, since the match was likely to be decided by the better run rate. Despite a fine start by the openers John Wright (48) and Martin Crowe (retired hurt 51), the New Zealanders fell behind the Australian run rate. When rain and bad light ended the match after 34.5 overs, New Zealand was 2 for 167—a run rate of 4.84 an over, compared with Australia's 5.09 an over. The New Zealanders were left to wonder how different the outcome might have been if Crowe not been forced from the field with a strained thigh. Dean Jones again dominated the Australian innings, making a high speed 59. He scored his half-century off only 37 balls and was named Man of the Match. Simon O'Donnell batted powerfully for 52, hitting two sixes, and Steve Waugh (36) showed signs of a return to form.

Australia

Batsman	How Out	Ttl	Balls	Mins	4s	6s
MA Taylor	c Larsen b Thomson	17	56	63	2	—
GR Marsh (c)	c Jones b Snedden	6	16	22	1	—
DM Jones	c & b Hadlee	59	41	83	8	1
DC Boon	c Rutherford b Morrison	9	10	12	1	—
SR Waugh	c Smith b Snedden	36	62	77	2	—
SP O'Donnell	run out	52	51	55	2	2
IA Healy (+)	not out	36	31	40	2	—
PL Taylor	not out	11	16	30	—	—
MG Hughes	did not bat					
GD Campbell	did not bat					
CG Rackemann	did not bat					
SUNDRIES: B. 1 LB. 4 W. 7 NB. 1		13	283	197	18	3
TOTAL	6 wkts for 239					

F/W: 12 61 85 118 184 194

▶

Bowler	O	M	R	Wkts	NB	W
Hadlee	10	1	40	1	1	3
Snedden	9	1	45	2	—	1
Morrison	9	1	39	1	—	1
Thomson	8	—	60	1	—	1
Larsen	10	—	45	—	—	1
Rutherford	1	—	5	—	—	—
Overs:	47.0					

New Zealand

Batsman	How Out	Ttl	Balls	Mins	4s	6s
JG Wright (c)	b PL Taylor	48	49	82	9	—
MD Crowe	retired hurt	51	77	109	3	—
AH Jones	not out	26	46	76	—	—
MJ Greatbatch	c Healy b Rackemann	0	2	1	—	—
KR Rutherford	not out	29	36	49	2	—
RJ Hadlee	did not bat					
IDS Smith (+)	did not bat					
SA Thomson	did not bat					
GR Larsen	did not bat					
MC Snedden	did not bat					
DK Morrison	did not bat					
SUNDRIES: B. 0 LB. 3 W. 9 NB. 1		13	210	160	14	—
TOTAL	2 wkts for 167					
F/W: 99 115						

Bowler	O	M	R	Wkts	NB	W
Hughes	4	—	28	—	—	6
Campbell	7.5	—	37	—	1	1
O'Donnell	6	—	35	—	—	1
Rackemann	10	—	37	1	—	1
PL Taylor	7	—	27	1	—	—
Overs:	34.5					

Umpires: RS Dunne & SJ Woodward

Man of Match: DM Jones

12th Man: TM Alderman (Australia)

FINAL

ROTHMAN'S INTERNATIONAL SERIES
New Zealand v Australia
Eden Park, Auckland
Mar 11 1990
Toss: New Zealand
Result: Australia won by 8 wkts

Australia's victory in this match and therefore in the series was made memorable by Dean Jones's dynamic century, which might well have been the finest one-day innings of the summer. The New Zealanders went into the match without their leading batsman, Martin Crowe, who was injured, and they soon had cause to regret his absence. Batting first, New Zealand suffered a top order collapse, and after 16 overs it was in deep trouble at 5 for 33. Jeff Crowe and Richard Hadlee revived the innings with a partnership of 80, but it was not really enough to get New Zealand back in the match, and the home side lost its last wicket in the 50th over for 162. Hadlee's innings of 79 was a gallant one under the circumstances, scored off 92 balls.

Australia's most successful bowler was Carl Rackemann, who took 3 for 22 in 10 overs. The target of 163 was clearly well within the Australians' range, but nobody expected they would reach it so quickly or dramatically. David Boon's early dismissal brought Dean Jones to the crease at 1 for 13, and from then on Jones held sway. In a remarkable display of power batting, he scored his 102 off 90 balls and hit 5 sixes, two of them off Hadlee and two off Danny Morrison. With 10 runs to win, Jones was still 9 short of a century, but the other batsman, Allan Border, avoided scoring, allowing Jones to get his 100.

New Zealand

Batsman	How Out	Ttl	Balls	Mins	4s	6s
JG Wright (c)	c Healy b Rackemann	4	15	24	—	—
AH Jones	c Boon b Alderman	7	23	40	1	—
MJ Greatbatch	c Jones b Campbell	11	31	44	1	—
KR Rutherford	c Healy b Rackemann	2	9	14	—	—
JJ Crowe	c & b Alderman	28	60	100	2	—
GR Larsen	c Healy b O'Donnell	1	7	7	—	—
RJ Hadlee	c Boon b Rackemann	79	92	106	7	2
IDS Smith (+)	c Jones b Campbell	9	9	14	1	—
JG Bracewell	c Healy b Campbell	3	10	16	—	—
MC Snedden	c Marsh b Taylor	5	17	22	—	—
DK Morrison	not out	9	24	18	—	—
SUNDRIES: B. 0 LB. 2 W. 2 NB. 0		4	297	208	12	2
TOTAL		162				

F/W: 12 15 26 32 33 113 134 147 147 162

Bowler	O	M	R	Wkts	NB	W
Alderman	10	2	34	2	—	2
Rackemann	10	2	22	3	—	—
O'Donnell	8	3	12	1	—	—
Campbell	10	—	37	3	—	—
PL Taylor	9.2	—	50	1	—	—
Border	2	—	5	—	—	—
Overs:	49.2					

Australia

Batsman	How Out	Ttl	Balls	Mins	4s	6s
DC Boon	lbw Morrison	9	15	24	—	—
GR Marsh	b Bracewell	24	69	91	—	—
DM Jones	not out	102	90	134	6	5
AR Border (c)	not out	19	65	67	2	1
SR Waugh	did not bat					
SP O'Donnell	did not bat					
IA Healy (+)	did not bat					
PL Taylor	did not bat					
CG Rackemann	did not bat					
GD Campbell	did not bat					
TM Alderman	did not bat					
SUNDRIES: B. 0 LB. 2 W. 4 NB. 4		10	293	160	8	6
TOTAL	2 wkts for 164					

F/W: 13 81

Bowler	O	M	R	Wkts	NB	W
Hadlee	9	3	34	—	1	—
Morrison	8	—	46	1	3	3
Snedden	5	—	13	—	—	—
Larsen	7.1	1	27	—	—	1
Bracewell	10	—	42	1	—	—
Overs:	39.1					

Umpires: RS Dunne & SJ Woodward

Man of Match: DM Jones

12th Man: MA Taylor (Australia)

Rothman's International Series Statistics

1989/90 Rothman's International Series

Australia

Batsman	M	Inn	NO	Runs	HS	50	100	Avrge	Ct/st
DM Jones	4	4	1	300	107	1	2	100.00	6
AR Border	4	4	2	71	37	—	—	35.50	3
IA Healy	5	3	1	67	36*	—	—	33.50	8
DC Boon	5	5	1	131	67	1	—	32.75	2
GR Marsh	4	4	—	118	86	1	—	29.50	1
SP O'Donnell	5	3	—	84	52	1	—	28.00	—
MA Taylor	3	3	—	83	56	1	—	27.67	2
SR Waugh	5	4	—	72	36	—	—	18.00	3
CG Rackemann	4	2	1	8	6	—	—	8.00	—
GD Campbell	5	2	—	2	2	—	—	1.00	2
PL Taylor	5	3	3	35	18*	—	—	—	—
MG Hughes	2	—	—	—	—	—	—	—	—
TM Alderman	4	—	—	—	—	—	—	—	2

Bowler	M	Overs	Mdns	Runs	Wkts	Avrge	5wi	NB	W	Best
CG Rackemann	4	35.0	4	113	8	14.13	—	1	3	3/22
TM Alderman	4	34.0	5	113	7	16.14	1	—	5	5/32
GD Campbell	5	40.1	2	145	7	20.71	—	7	1	3/17
MG Hughes	2	11.0	—	64	3	21.33	—	—	6	3/36
SP O'Donnell	5	37.0	4	158	7	22.57	1	2	1	5/13
PL Taylor	5	36.2	4	147	6	24.50	—	—	—	3/31
AR Border	4	11.0	—	45	—	—	—	—	—	—

New Zealand

Batsman	M	Inn	NO	Runs	HS	50	100	Avrge	Ct/st
MD Crowe	4	4	1	190	104	1	1	63.33	3
KR Rutherford	5	5	2	173	78*	1	—	57.67	3
RJ Hadlee	4	3	—	127	79	1	—	42.33	1
JJ Crowe	2	2	—	54	28	—	—	27.00	—
JG Wright	3	3	—	75	48	—	—	25.00	1
AH Jones	5	5	1	85	43	—	—	21.25	1
MJ Greatbatch	5	5	—	77	53	1	—	15.40	1
IDS Smith	5	4	—	21	9	—	—	5.25	6
SA Thomson	4	3	—	6	3	—	—	2.00	1
MC Snedden	5	3	—	5	5	—	—	1.67	—
JG Bracewell	2	2	—	3	3	—	—	1.50	1
GR Larsen	5	3	—	2	1	—	—	0.67	1
DK Morrison	5	3	3	9	9*	—	—	—	—
SJ Roberts	1	—	—	—	—	—	—	—	—

Bowler	M	Overs	Mdns	Runs	Wkts	Avrge	5wi	NB	W	Best
DK Morrison	5	43.1	3	212	9	23.56	—	5	11	3/33
MC Snedden	5	42.0	4	168	6	28.00	—	—	5	3/32
RJ Hadlee	4	38.2	7	144	5	28.80	—	4	3	2/27
SA Thomson	4	32.0	1	175	6	29.17	—	—	6	3/19
JG Bracewell	2	13.0	—	62	1	62.00	—	—	—	1/42
GR Larsen	5	43.1	2	169	2	84.50	—	—	2	1/14
SJ Roberts	1	4.0	—	26	—	—	—	—	1	—
KR Rutherford	5	1.0	—	5	—	—	—	—	—	—

India

Batsman	M	Inn	NO	Runs	HS	50	100	Avrge	Ct/st
Kapil Dev	4	4	1	133	48*	—	—	44.33	2
M Azharuddin	4	4	—	104	37	—	—	26.00	—
SV Manjrekar	3	3	—	75	36	—	—	25.00	2
WV Raman	4	4	—	92	58	1	—	23.00	—
M Prabhakar	4	4	—	78	36	—	—	19.50	2
SR Tendulkar	2	2	—	36	36	—	—	18.00	—
A Wassan	4	4	2	32	16	—	—	16.00	1
DB Vengsarkar	3	3	—	37	35	—	—	12.33	—
KS More	4	4	—	34	23*	—	—	11.33	3
Ajay Sharma	4	4	—	37	15	—	—	9.25	1
VB Chandresekhar	1	1	—	8	8	—	—	8.00	—

Bowler	M	Overs	Mdns	Runs	Wkts	Avrge	5wi	NB	W	Best
Gursharan Singh	1	1	—	4	4	—	—	4.00	1
VS Raju	1	1	—	4	4	—	—	4.00	—
VB Chandrasekhar	2	2	—	7	4	—	—	3.50	—
N Hirwani	3	2	1	1	1*	—	—	1.00	—

Bowler	M	Overs	Mdns	Runs	Wkts	Avrge	5wi	NB	W	Best
M Prabhakar	4	38.0	6	150	6	25.00	—	2	4	3/37
Kapil Dev	4	36.5	1	160	6	26.67	—	2	3	2/29
N Hirwani	3	30.0	4	110	4	27.50	—	—	—	2/39
A Wassan	4	32.0	—	139	5	27.80	—	—	4	3/45
Ajay Sharma	4	38.0	—	182	2	91.00	—	—	3	1/40
VS Raju	1	9.0	—	38	—	—	—	—	—	—
WV Raman	4	10.0	1	43	—	—	—	—	—	—

TEST

New Zealand v Australia
Wellington
March 15, 16, 17, 18, 19 1990
Toss: Australia
Result: New Zealand won by 9 wkts

It was a pity the weather had such an important bearing on the outcome of this contest, yet there is no doubt that the New Zealanders, whose leading batsman, Martin Crowe, was unable to play, handled the conditions better. Allan Border was roundly criticised for choosing to bat on a pitch still drying after incessant rain. Although the pitch was extremely slow and the ball kept low it appeared to be a key factor in only a few dismissals in Australia's dismal first innings—most notably Mark Taylor's dismissal by a ball of shin height. Australia was all out in little more than three hours for 110. Richard Hadlee had the best bowling figures, 5 for 39, but the most serious damage was done by Danny Morrison (3 for 22) in his early spell. Having ended the first day at 0 for 18, the New Zealanders batted defensively through a rain-shortened second day and finally were all out on the third day for 202, scored off 121 overs. At one stage Martin Snedden (23) went for 94 minutes without scoring. Australia lost two wickets before stumps, but next day the nightwatchman Peter Taylor and Allan Border put on 103 for the fourth wicket, and at 3 for 194 Australia appeared to be batting its way out of trouble. Then Taylor went for 87 and Dean Jones for a duck in a highly controversial lbw dismissal. But Border was still there, and the total had moved on to 6 for 261 when in the space of a half-hour John Bracewell (6 for 85) finished off the innings with his off-spin. Although the New Zealanders needed only 178 to win, it seemed they would have to work hard for the runs when they began the final day at 0 for 4. In fact, they did it easily on a pitch which had steadily improved throughout the match, losing only one wicket. John Wright's century earned him the Man of the Match title. It was Australia's first defeat in 15 Tests.

Australia

First Innings

Batsman	How Out	Ttl	Balls
MA Taylor	lbw Morrison	4	26
GR Marsh	b Morrison	4	3
DC Boon	lbw Hadlee	0	12
AR Border (c)	lbw Morrison	1	11
DM Jones	c Wright b Snedden	20	29
SR Waugh	b Hadlee	25	75
IA Healy (+)	b Snedden	0	7
PL Taylor	c Wright b Hadlee	29	73
GD Campbell	lbw Hadlee	4	22
CG Rackemann	not out	6	20
TM Alderman	b Hadlee	4	4
SUNDRIES: B.0 LB.6 W.0 NB.7		13	282
TOTAL		110	

F/W: 4 9 9 12 38 44 70 87 103 110

Second Innings

How Out	Ttl	Balls
lbw Hadlee	5	20
c Rutherford b Bracewell	41	106
c Smith b Bracewell	12	34
not out	78	239
lbw Morrison (6)	0	2
c Greatbatch b Hadlee (7)	25	62
c Rutherford b Bracewell (8)	10	24
c Smith b Morrison (4)	87	155
b Bracewell	0	1
b Bracewell	1	1
st Smith b Bracewell	1	8
B.0 LB.6 W.0 NB.3	9	661
	269	

F/W: 27 54 91 194 194 232 261 261 267 269

Bowler	O	M	R	Wkts	NB	W
Hadlee	16.2	5	39	5	2	—
Morrison	10	4	22	3	—	—
Snedden	15	2	33	2	5	—
Rutherford	2	—	8	—	—	—
Bracewell	2	1	2	—	—	—
Overs:	45.2					

Bowler	O	M	R	Wkts	NB	W
Hadlee	25	3	70	2	1	—
Morrison	24	8	58	2	2	—
Snedden	25	5	46	—	—	—
Bracewell	34.2	11	85	6	—	—
Jones	1	—	4	—	—	—
Overs:	109.2					

New Zealand

First Innings

Batsman	How Out	Ttl	Balls
TJ Franklin	c Marsh b PL Taylor	28	113
JG Wright (c)	c Healy b Alderman	36	149
AH Jones	c & b Border	18	69
MC Snedden	b Alderman	23	122
MJ Greatbatch	c Healy b PL Taylor	16	59
KR Rutherford	c Healy b PL Taylor	12	24
JJ Crowe	lbw Alderman	9	44
RJ Hadlee	lbw Campbell	18	33
IDS Smith (+)	c MA Taylor b Campbell	1	4
JG Bracewell	not out	19	68
DK Morrison	c MA Taylor b Alderman	12	44
SUNDRIES: B.2 LB.5 W.0 NB.3		10	729
TOTAL		202	

F/W: 48 89 89 111 123 150 151 152 171 202

Second Innings

How Out	Ttl	Balls
c Healy b Campbell	18	87
not out	117	197
not out	33	99
B.2 LB.10 W.0 NB.1	13	383
1 wkt for 181		

F/W: 53

Bowler	O	M	R	Wkts	NB	W
Alderman	29	9	46	4	1	—
Rackemann	32	17	42	—	—	—
PL Taylor	33	19	44	3	—	—
Campbell	21	3	51	2	2	—
Border	6	3	12	1	—	—
Overs:	121.0					

Bowler	O	M	R	Wkts	NB	W
Alderman	14	8	27	—	—	—
Rackemann	15	4	39	—	1	—
PL Taylor	11	3	39	—	—	—
Campbell	7	2	23	1	—	—
Jones	6	3	14	—	—	—
Border	10.4	5	27	—	—	—
Overs:	63.4					

Umpires: SJ Woodward & RS Dunne

12th Men: SA Thomson (New Zealand) & MG Hughes (Australia)

Tour Statistics

Australian Test Averages

Batsman	M	Inn	NO	Runs	HS	50	100	Avrge	Ct/St
AR Border	1	2	1	79	78*	1	—	79.00	1
PL Taylor	1	2	—	116	87	1	—	58.00	—
SR Waugh	1	2	—	50	25	—	—	25.00	—
GR Marsh	1	2	—	45	41	—	—	22.50	1
DM Jones	1	2	—	20	20	—	—	10.00	—
CG Rackemann	1	2	1	7	6*	—	—	7.00	—
DC Boon	1	2	—	12	12	—	—	6.00	—
IA Healy	1	2	—	10	10	—	—	5.00	4/-
MA Taylor	1	2	—	9	5	—	—	4.50	2
TM Alderman	1	2	—	5	4	—	—	2.50	—
GD Campbell	1	2	—	4	4	—	—	2.00	—

Bowler	M	Overs	Mdns	Runs	Wkts	Avrge	5wi	10m	NB	W	Best
AR Border	1	16.4	8	39	1	39.00	—	—	—	—	1/12
GD Campbell	1	28.0	5	74	3	24.67	—	—	2	—	2/51
PL Taylor	1	44.0	22	83	3	27.67	—	—	—	—	3/44
TM Alderman	1	43.0	17	73	4	18.25	—	—	1	—	4/46
CG Rackemann	1	47.0	21	81	—	—	—	—	1	—	—
DM Jones	1	6.0	3	14	—	—	—	—	—	—	—

New Zealand Test Averages

Batsman	M	Inn	NO	Runs	HS	50	100	Avrge	Ct/St
JG Wright	1	2	1	153	117*	—	1	153.00	2 —
AH Jones	1	2	1	51	33*	—	—	51.00	— —
TJ Franklin	1	2	—	46	28	—	—	23.00	— —
MC Snedden	1	1	—	23	23	—	—	23.00	— —
RJ Hadlee	1	1	—	18	18	—	—	18.00	— —
MJ Greatbatch	1	1	—	16	16	—	—	16.00	1 —
KR Rutherford	1	1	—	12	12	—	—	12.00	2 —
DK Morrison	1	1	—	12	12	—	—	12.00	— —
JJ Crowe	1	1	—	9	9	—	—	9.00	— —
IDS Smith	1	1	—	1	1	—	—	1.00	2 1
JG Bracewell	1	1	1	19	19*	—	—	—	— —

Bowler	M	Overs	Mdns	Runs	Wkts	Avrge	5wi	10m	NB	W	Best
MC Snedden	1	40.0	7	79	2	39.50	—	—	5	—	2/33
DK Morrison	1	34.0	12	80	5	16.00	—	—	2	—	3/22
JG Bracewell	1	36.2	12	87	6	14.50	1	—	—	—	6/85
RJ Hadlee	1	41.2	8	109	7	15.57	1	—	3	—	5/39
AH Jones	1	1.0	—	4	—	—	—	—	—	—	—
KR Rutherford	1	2.0	—	8	—	—	—	—	—	—	—

Australian First-Class Tours of New Zealand

Results for Australia

Season	Touring Team	Games	W	L	D	T	Captain
1883/84	Tasmania	4	—	3	1	—	JG Davis
1889/90	New South Wales	5	4	—	1	—	J Davis
1893/94	New South Wales	7	4	1	2	—	J Davis
1895/96	New South Wales	5	3	1	1	—	LT Cobcroft
1896/97	Australia	5	3	1	1	—	OC Hitchcock
1904/05	Australia	4	3	—	1	—	MA Noble
1909/10	Australia	6	5	—	1	—	WW Armstrong
1913/14	Australia	8	6	—	2	—	A Sims
1920/21	Australia	9	6	—	3	—	VS Ransford
1923/24	New South Wales	6	5	—	1	—	CG Macartney
1924/25	Victoria	6	1	1	4	—	ER Mayne
1927/28	Australia	6	4	—	2	—	VY Richardson
1945/46	Australia	5	5	—	—	—	WA Brown
1949/50	Australia	5	3	—	2	—	WA Brown
1956/57	Australia	7	5	—	2	—	ID Craig

▶

Season	Touring Team	Games	W	L	D	T	Captain
1959/60	Australia	6	2	—	4	—	ID Craig
1966/67	Australia	9	1	2	6	—	LE Favell
1969/70	Australia	8	2	—	6	—	SC Trimble
1973/74	Australia	7	2	1	4	—	IM Chappell
1976/77	Australia	6	5	—	1	—	GS Chappell
1981/82	Australia	5	1	1	3	—	GS Chappell
1985/86	Australia	5	1	1	3	—	AR Border
1989/90	Australia	1	—	1	—	—	AR Border
Total		**135**	**71**	**13**	**41**	**—**	

Australia in New Zealand

Opponent	Venue	First Game	Games	W	L	D	T
NEW ZEALAND	Wellington	Mar 29 1946	5	1	1	3	—
	Christchurch	Mar 8 1974	4	1	1	2	—
	Auckland	Mar 22 1974	4	2	2	—	—
Total			**13**	**4**	**4**	**5**	**—**
Auckland	Auckland	Jan 30 1890	17	11	—	6	—
Canterbury	Christchurch	Feb 7 1884	20	11	4	5	—
Central Districts	New Plymouth	Mar 23 1957	3	1	—	2	—
	Palmerston North	Mar 12 1960	2	—	—	2	—
	Nelson	Feb 8 1977	1	1	—	—	—
Total			**6**	**2**	**—**	**4**	—
Hawke's Bay	Napier	Jan 24 1894	3	2	—	1	—
	Nelson	Feb 18 1914	1	1	—	—	—
Total			**4**	**3**	**—**	**1**	—
Minor Associations	Wellington	Mar 8 1921	1	1	—	—	—
New Zealand Under 23s	Napier	Mar 2 1970	1	1	—	—	—
New Zealand XI	Christchurch	Feb 15 1894	10	3	1	6	—
	Wellington	Dec 26 1896	9	4	1	4	—
	Dunedin	Mar 6 1914	5	3	—	2	—
	Auckland	Mar 27 1914	7	3	—	4	—
	New Plymouth	Mar 3 1967	1	—	1	—	—
Total			**32**	**13**	**3**	**16**	**—**
North Island	Wellington	Feb 19 1894	1	1	—	—	—
	Napier	Feb 22 1982	1	—	—	1	—
Total			**2**	**1**	**—**	**1**	**—**
Northern Districts	Hamilton	Mar 21 1967	5	3	—	2	—
NZCC President's XI	Christchurch	Mar 6 1982	1	—	—	1	—
Otago	Dunedin	Feb 1 1884	18	12	1	5	—
Southland	Invercargill	Mar 16 1921	1	—	—	1	—
Wellington	Wellington	Feb 21 1890	14	9	1	4	—
Total in New Zealand			**135**	**71**	**13**	**51**	**—**

Australian Test Cricketers May 1989–April 1990

Batsman	M	Inn	NO	Runs	HS	50	100	Avrge	Ct/St
MA Taylor	13	23	2	1551	219	8	6	73.86	19
DM Jones	13	20	3	1091	157	4	5	64.18	7
SR Waugh	13	19	5	884	177*	3	3	63.14	7
AR Border	13	20	6	870	85	11	—	62.14	12
DC Boon	12	22	3	776	200	3	1	40.84	12
TM Moody	4	6	—	234	106	1	1	39.00	3
PL Taylor	3	4	—	150	87	1	—	37.50	3
PR Sleep	2	3	1	70	47*	—	—	35.00	—
TV Hohns	5	5	1	127	40	—	—	31.75	3
GR Marsh	9	16	—	459	138	—	1	28.69	7
MG Hughes	12	14	3	296	71	1	—	26.91	1
GF Lawson	8	7	1	138	74	1	—	23.00	2
IA Healy	13	17	2	317	48	—	—	21.13	37/-
MRJ Veletta	1	1	—	9	9	—	—	9.00	1
CG Rackemann	6	7	4	27	15*	—	—	9.00	—
TM Alderman	12	10	4	44	18	—	—	7.33	4
GD Campbell	4	4	—	10	6	—	—	2.50	1

Bowler	M	Overs	Mdns	Runs	Wkts	Avrge	5wi	10m	NB	W	Best
TM Alderman	12	549.4	155	1317	67	19.66	8	1	64	—	6/128
PR Sleep	2	75.0	32	169	7	24.14	—	—	—	1	3/26
MG Hughes	12	477.4	129	1394	53	26.30	2	—	17	2	5/88
TV Hohns	5	134.0	53	300	11	27.27	—	—	—	1	3/59
CG Rackemann	6	268.2	95	488	16	30.50	—	—	14	1	4/40
GF Lawson	8	370.1	95	984	32	30.75	1	—	6	10	6/72
GD Campbell	4	158.3	29	503	13	38.69	—	—	12	1	3/79
PL Taylor	3	105.5	36	257	5	51.40	—	—	—	—	3/44
TM Moody	4	39.0	15	53	1	53.00	—	—	—	—	1/23
SR Waugh	13	66.0	18	227	3	75.67	—	—	11	—	1/13
AR Border	13	66.4	23	154	2	77.00	—	—	—	—	1/10
DM Jones	13	14.0	7	26	—	—	—	—	—	—	—

SHARJAH TOUR
Limited-overs
Series
APRIL–MAY 1990

AUSTRALASIA CUP

Australia and Pakistan, the two most fancied teams in this tournament at Sharjah, duly contested the final, which Pakistan won by 36 runs. The key to Pakistan's success throughout the tournament proved to be the fiery bowling of its pace bowlers, Waqar Younus and Wasim Akram, who between them caused opposing batsmen many problems. Younus took 6 for 26 against Sri Lanka and followed this with 5 for 20 against New Zealand, a performance which was largely responsible for New Zealand's dismissal for only 74.

The Australians produced several fine individual performances during the tournament, and until their defeat in the final they had, as a team, swept all before them. If their loss to Pakistan in the final could be attributed to any single factor, it was the simultaneous failure of two key batsmen, Dean Jones and Allan Border. Simon O'Donnell set a new record for the fastest half-century in international limited-overs cricket scoring 50 off 18 balls in the match against Sri Lanka.

QUALIFYING MATCHES

Australia won both its Group A qualifying matches comfortably, defeating New Zealand by 63 runs and Bangladesh by 7 wickets and with 24.2 overs to spare.

In the first of these matches, Mark Taylor was run out for 60 and David Boon, batting at four, made an unbeaten 92, allowing Australia to reach a total of 5 for 258. The New Zealand top order collapsed under the pressure of having to keep up the run rate, and the side could manage only 7 for 195 in the 50 overs. It was Allan Border who started the collapse. He took 3 for 25 in six overs.

In the one-sided match against Bangladesh, the Australian bowlers restricted Bangladesh to 8 for 134 in 50 overs. Facing such a small total, the Australian captain, Allan Border, changed the batting order, opening with O'Donnell and Ian Healy. Peter Taylor batted at four and top-scored with 54 not out.

AUSTRALASIA CUP—GAME 1
India v Sri Lanka
Sharjah
Apr 25 1990
Result: Sri Lanka won by 3 wkts

India_____ 8-241 (50.0) M Azharuddin 108, NS Sidhu 64, JR Ratnayeke 3/31
Sri Lanka _____ 7-242 (49.2) A Ranatunga 85*, PA De Silva 34, JR Ratnayeke 32

Man of Match: A Ranatunga

AUSTRALASIA CUP—GAME 2
Australia v New Zealand
Sharjah
Apr 26 1990
Toss: New Zealand
Result: Australia won by 63 runs

Australia

Batsman	How Out	Ttl
GR Marsh	c Smith b Snedden	26
MA Taylor	run out	60
DM Jones	c Morrison b Snedden	1
DC Boon	not out	92
SR Waugh	run out	34
AR Border (c)	c Bracewell b Morrison	34
SP O'Donnell	not out	3
PL Taylor	did not bat	
IA Healy (+)	did not bat	
CG Rackemann	did not bat	
TM Alderman	did not bat	
SUNDRIES: B. 0 LB. 6 W. 2 NB. 0		8
TOTAL:		5 wkts for 258

F/W: 67 73 115 196 247

Bowler	O	M	R	Wkts
Morrison	10	1	51	1
Millmow	10	—	57	—
Snedden	10	1	31	2
Bracewell	10	—	47	—
Priest	7	—	43	—
Rutherford	3	—	23	—
Overs:	50.0			

New Zealand

Batsman	How Out	Ttl
JG Wright (c)	c Marsh b Alderman	0
MD Crowe	b PL Taylor	41
AH Jones	b O'Donnell	15
MJ Greatbatch	b Border	37
KR Rutherford	c & b Border	20
IDS Smith (+)	c Marsh b Border	2
JG Bracewell	not out	36
MW Priest	b Alderman	15
MC Snedden	not out	13
JP Millmow	did not bat	
DK Morrison	did not bat	
SUNDRIES: B. 0 LB. 11 W. 4 NB. 1		16
TOTAL		7 wkts for 195

F/W: 10 26 91 121 127 129 166

▶

181

Bowler	O	M	R	Wkts
Alderman	10	—	46	2
Rackemann	7	—	27	—
O'Donnell	10	3	27	1
Waugh	7	—	32	—
PL Taylor	10	—	27	1
Border	6	1	25	3
Overs:	50.0			

Man of Match: DC Boon

AUSTRALASIA CUP—GAME 3
Pakistan v India
Sharjah
Apr 27 1990
Toss: India
Result: Pakistan won by 26 runs

Pakistan ————— 9-235 (50.0) Salim Yousuf 62, Saeed Anwar 37, Javed Miandad 37
India————— 209 (46.3) M Azharuddin 78*, K Srikkanth 35, Waqar Younus 4/42

Man of Match: Waqar Younus

AUSTRALASIA CUP—GAME 4
New Zealand v Bangladesh
Sharjah
Apr 28 1990
Toss: New Zealand
Result: New Zealand won by 161 runs

New Zealand ————— 4-338 (50.0) JG Wright 93, AH Jones 93, MD Crowe 69
Bangladesh ————— 5-177 (50.0) Azhur Shantu 54, Akram Khan 33

Man of Match: JG Wright

AUSTRALASIA CUP—GAME 5
Pakistan v Sri Lanka
Sharjah
Apr 29 1990
Toss: Sri Lanka
Result: Pakistan won by 90 runs

Pakistan ————— 8-311 (50.0) Ijaz Ahmed 89, Javed Miandad 75, JR Ratnayeke 3/65
Sri Lanka ————— 221 (47.4) DBSP Kuruppu 41, Waqar Younus 6/26

Man of Match: Waqar Younus

AUSTRALASIA CUP—GAME 6
Australia v Bangladesh
Sharjah
Apr 30 1990
Toss: Bangladesh
Result: Australia won by 7 wkts

Bangladesh

Batsman	How Out	Ttl
Azhar Hussain Shantu	c Healy b Hughes	5
Zahid Razzak	c Healy b Campbell	4
Akram Hussain Khan	c Marsh b O'Donnell	13
Gazi Ashraf Lipu	b PL Taylor	18
Minhazul Abedin Nanu	c Healy b PL Taylor	0
Faruque Ahmed	lbw Waugh	6
Amin-ul-Islam	not out	41
Enam-ul-Haque	c Jones b Waugh	18
Nazir Ahmed	b O'Donnell	3
JA Taluder	not out	7
Ghulam Nowsher	did not bat	
SUNDRIES: B. 2 LB. 7 W. 8 NB. 2		19
TOTAL	8 wkts for 134	
F/W: 10 12 33 47 50 59 107 121		

Bowler	O	M	R	Wkts	NB	W
Hughes	10	3	15	1	2	1
Campbell	10	1	32	1	—	4
O'Donnell	10	1	34	2	—	1
Waugh	10	2	22	2	—	2
PL Taylor	10	2	22	2	—	—
Overs:	50.0					

Australia

Batsman	How Out	Ttl
SP O'Donnell	c Ashraf b Abedin	20
IA Healy (+)	c Azhar b Nowsher	34
DM Jones	c Faruque b Abedin	19
PL Taylor	not out	54
MG Hughes	not out	10
GR Marsh	did not bat	
MA Taylor	did not bat	
DC Boon	did not bat	
AR Border (c)	did not bat	
SR Waugh	did not bat	
GD Campbell	did not bat	
SUNDRIES: B. 0 LB. 1 W. 1 NB. 1		3
TOTAL	3 wkts for 140	
F/W: 50 57 102		

Bowler	O	M	R	Wkts
Nowsher	6	—	27	1
Taludar	4	—	20	—
Azhar Hussain	7	1	26	—
Minhazul Abedin	6	—	43	2
Amin-ul-Islam	1.4	—	16	—
Enam-ul-Haque	1	—	7	—
Overs:	25.4			

Man of Match: PL Taylor

SEMI-FINALS

In the first semi-final, the Pakistani pace bowlers routed the New Zealanders, dismissing them for a mere 74 in 31.1 overs. Waqar Younus, who took 5 for 20, was the main destroyer, and he was later named Man of the Match. The Pakistanis needed only 15.4 overs to score the required runs.

In the second semi-final, the Australian batsmen scored runs in profusion against a Sri Lankan attack which appeared quite powerless to prevent them. Dean Jones made 117 not out, but his innings was overshadowed by Simon O'Donnell's spectacular 74. O'Donnell faced only 29 balls and hit 6 sixes and 4 fours. He made 50 off only 18 balls, a record in international cricket. In reply to Australia's 3 for 332, the Sri Lankans were all out in 45.4 overs for 218.

AUSTRALASIA CUP—GAME 7
Pakistan v New Zealand
Sharjah
May 1 1990
Result: Pakistan won by 8 wkts

New Zealand———— 74 (31.1) AH Jones 47, Waqar Younus 5/20
Pakistan———————2-77 (15.4) Salim Malik 31°, Salim Yousuf 25

Man of Match: Waqar Younus

AUSTRALASIA CUP—GAME 8
Australia v Sri Lanka
Sharjah
May 2 1990
Result: Australia won by 114 runs

Australia

Batsman	How Out	Ttl
GR Marsh	c Kuruppu b Ratnayeke	68
MA Taylor	st Kuruppu b Madurasinghe	27
DM Jones	not out	117
SP O'Donnell	b Ramanayake	74
DC Boon	not out	30
AR Border (c)	did not bat	
SR Waugh	did not bat	
IA Healy (+)	did not bat	
PL Taylor	did not bat	
CG Rackemann	did not bat	
TM Alderman	did not bat	
SUNDRIES: B.5 LB.6 W.5 NB.0		16
TOTAL	3 wkts for 332	

F/W: 35 172 278

Bowler	O	M	R	Wkts	NB	W
Ratnayeke	10	—	70	1	—	—
Ratnayake	10	—	55	—	—	2
Madurasinghe	10	—	32	1	—	—
Ramanayake	10	—	82	1	—	2
EAR De Silva	5	—	34	—	—	1
Gurusinha	5	—	48	—	—	—
Overs:	50.0					

Sri Lanka

Batsman	How Out	Ttl
DBSP Kuruppu	c Marsh b Alderman	14
MAR Samaresekera	lbw Alderman	25
HP Tillekeratne	st Healy b Border	76
PA De Silva	c Marsh b Taylor	19
A Ranatunga (c)	c Rackemann b Waugh	26
JR Ratnayeke	run out	4
RJ Ratnayake	c Border b PL Taylor	8
EAR De Silva	c Healy b Border	9
CPH Ramanayake	c Waugh b O'Donnell	18
MAWR Madurasinghe	not out	9
AP Gurusinha	absent injured	
SUNDRIES: B. 1 LB. 6 W. 3 NB. 0		10
TOTAL		218

F/W: 25 43 77 124 135 150 174 206 218

Bowler	O	M	R	Wkts	NB	W
Alderman	7	—	35	2	—	1
Rackemann	10	—	51	—	—	1
PL Taylor	10	1	28	2	—	—
O'Donnell	5.4	—	19	1	—	—
Waugh	7	—	36	1	—	1
Border	6	—	42	2	—	—
Overs:	45.4					

Man of Match: DM Jones

FINAL

AUSTRALASIA CUP
Australia v Pakistan
Sharjah
May 4 1990
Toss: Pakistan
Result: Pakistan won by 36 runs

Batting first, the Pakistanis began a little unsteadily and were at one stage 4 for 109, but Salim Malik restored the innings with a fine 87 and in the final overs Wasim Akram hit 49 off 35 balls. This late burst of scoring pushed Pakistan on to the substantial total of 7 for 266. Australia began well enough in reply, and its first wicket did not fall until the total was 60. This brought Dean Jones to the wicket, a batsman who, under the circumstances, Australia relied on heavily. But Jones was bowled by Waqar Younus for 0, and immediately afterwards Border was out lbw to Younus for 2. Australia had slipped to 3 for 64, but all was not yet lost. A fine innings of 64 by Steve Waugh enabled Australia to fight its way back into the match, and at 5 for 207 Australia appeared to have victory within range. At this point, however, the loss of the wickets of Waugh and Peter Taylor virtually sealed Australia's fate. Wasim Akram delivered the coup de grace, dismissing the last three batsmen with a hat-trick.

Pakistan

Batsman	How Out	Ttl
Saaed Anwar	c Healy b Rackemann	40
Salim Yousuf	lbw Alderman	5
Javed Miandad	c Healy b Waugh	14
Salim Malik	c Border b PL Taylor	87
Ijaz Ahmed	c Healy b Rackemann	20
Imran Khan (c)	c Healy b Rackemann	2
Mansoor Rana	run out	10
Wasim Akram	not out	49
Mushtaq Ahmed	not out	17
Waqar Younus	did not bat	
Aaquib Javed	did not bat	
SUNDRIES: B. 3 LB. 10 W. 9 NB. 0		22
TOTAL	7 wkts for 266	

F/W: 40 54 80 109 154 179 207

Bowler	O	M	R	Wkts	NB	W
Alderman	5	1	22	1	—	2
Hughes	10	—	55	—	—	1
Rackemann	10	—	49	3	—	2
O'Donnell	10	—	66	—	—	2
Waugh	5	—	22	1	—	1
PL Taylor	10	—	39	1	—	1
Overs:	50.0					

Australia

Batsman	How Out	Ttl
DC Boon	run out	37
MA Taylor	run out	52
DM Jones	b Younus	0
AR Border (c)	lbw Younus	1
SR Waugh	c Aaquib b Mushtaq	64
SP O'Donnell	c Ijaz b Mushtaq	33
PL Taylor	c Anwar b Mushtaq	9
IA Healy (+)	not out	12
MG Hughes	b Akram	9
CG Rackemann	b Akram	0
TM Alderman	b Akram	0
SUNDRIES: B. 0 LB. 10 W. 3 NB. 0		13
TOTAL		230

F/W: 62 62 64 133 187 207 207 230 230 230

Bowler	O	M	R	Wkts	NB	W
Wasim Akram	8.5	—	45	3	—	1
Aaquib Javed	7	—	27	—	—	1
Waqar Younus	8	—	38	2	—	—
Mushtaq Ahmed	10	1	48	3	—	1
Imran Khan	7	—	28	—	—	—
Saeed Anwar	6	—	34	—	—	—
Overs:	46.5					

Man of Match: Wasim Akrim

Australasia Cup Statistics

1989/90 Australasia Cup
Australia

Batsman	M	Inn	NO	Runs	HS	50	100	Avrge	Ct/St
DC Boon	4	3	2	159	92*	1	—	159.00	—
PL Taylor	4	2	1	63	54*	1	—	63.00	—
SR Waugh	4	2	—	98	64	1	—	49.00	1
GR Marsh	3	2	—	94	68	1	—	47.00	5
MA Taylor	4	3	—	139	60	2	—	46.33	—
IA Healy	4	2	1	46	34	—	—	46.00	8/1
DM Jones	4	4	1	137	117*	—	1	45.67	1

Batsman	M	Inn	NO	Runs	HS	50	100	Avrge	Ct/St
SP O'Donnell	4	4	1	130	74	1	—	43.33	—
MG Hughes	2	2	1	19	10*	—	—	19.00	—
AR Border	4	2	—	35	34	—	—	17.50	3
CG Rackemann	3	1	—	0	0	—	—	0.00	1
TM Alderman	3	1	—	0	0	—	—	0.00	—
GD Campbell	1	—	—	—	—	—	—	—	—

Bowler	M	Overs	Mdns	Runs	Wkts	Avrge	5wi	Best
AR Border	4	12.0	1	67	5	13.40	—	3/25
PL Taylor	4	40.0	3	116	6	19.33	—	2/22
TM Alderman	3	22.0	1	103	5	20.60	—	2/35
SR Waugh	4	29.0	2	112	4	28.00	—	2/22
GD Campbell	1	10.0	1	32	1	32.00	—	1/32
SP O'Donnell	4	35.4	4	146	4	36.50	—	2/34
CG Rackemann	3	27.0	—	127	3	42.33	—	3/49
MG Hughes	2	20.0	3	70	1	70.00	—	1/15

Pakistan

Batsman	M	Inn	NO	Runs	HS	50	100	Avrge	Ct/St
Wasim Akram	3	2	1	60	49*	—	—	60.00	0
Salim Malik	4	4	1	151	87	1	—	50.33	0
Ijaz Ahmed	4	3	—	141	89	1	—	47.00	2
Javed Miandad	4	3	—	126	75	1	—	42.00	1
Salim Yousuf	4	4	—	138	62	1	—	34.50	7/1
Saeed Anwar	4	4	—	120	40	—	.	30.00	3
Imran Khan	4	4	1	41	18	—	—	13.67	1
Waqar Younus	4	2	1	9	7*	—	—	9.00	—
Mansoor Rana	2	2	—	15	10	—	—	7.50	—
Sajjad Akbar	2	1	—	5	5	—	—	5.00	—
Abdul Qadir	1	1	—	1	1	—	—	1.00	—
Zakir Khan	1	1	1	2	2*	—	—	—	—
Mushtaq Ahmed	3	2	2	21	17*	—	—	—	—
Aaquib Javed	4	1	1	0	0*	—	—	—	2

Bowler	M	Overs	Mdns	Runs	Wkts	Avrge	5wi	Best
Waqar Younus	4	37.0	3	126	17	7.41	2	6/26
Wasim Akram	3	23.2	1	90	6	15.00	—	3/45
Mushtaq Ahmed	3	22.1	3	101	6	16.83	—	3/48
Sajjad Akbar	2	10.0	1	45	2	22.50	—	2/45
Zakir Khan	1	9.4	—	41	1	41.00	—	1/41
Imran Khan	4	16.0	2	52	1	52.00	—	1/17
Aaquib Javed	4	30.0	2	108	2	54.00	—	1/22
Saeed Anwar	4	16.0	—	83	—	—	—	—
Abdul Qadir	1	7.0	—	44	—	—	—	—
Mansoor Rana	2	1.0	—	7	—	—	—	—

India

Batsman	M	Inn	NO	Runs	HS	50	100	Avrge	Ct/St
M Azharuddin	2	2	1	186	108	1	1	186.00	—
NS Sidhu	2	2	—	64	64	1	—	32.00	—
M Prabhakar	2	2	1	29	27	—	—	29.00	—
K Srikkanth	2	2	—	54	35	—	—	27.00	—
SR Tendulkar	2	2	—	30	20	—	—	15.00	1
SV Manjrekar	1	1	—	10	10	—	—	10.00	—
Sanjeev Sharma	2	2	1	7	5	—	—	7.00	—
WV Raman	1	1	—	7	7	—	—	7.00	—
RJ Shastri	2	2	—	12	9	—	—	6.00	1
Kapil Dev	2	2	—	9	8	—	—	4.50	1
KS More	2	2	—	6	4	—	—	3.00	3/1
A Kumble	2	1	—	0	0	—	.	0.00	—

Bowler	M	Overs	Mdns	Runs	Wkts	Avrge	5wi	Best
RJ Shastri	2	20.0	1	66	3	22.00	—	2/36
M Prabhakar	2	20.0	1	106	3	35.33	—	2/55
A Kumble	2	20.0	—	75	2	37.50	—	1/33
Sanjeev Sharma	2	20.0	1	115	3	38.33	—	2/63
Kapil Dev	2	14.2	1	74	1	74.00	—	1/44
K Srikkanth	2	5.0	—	19	—	—	—	—

Sri Lanka

Batsman	M	Inn	NO	Runs	HS	50	100	Avrge	Ct/St
A Ranatunga	3	3	1	149	85*	1	—	74.50	1
HP Tillekeratne	3	3	—	119	76	1	—	39.67	2
DBSP Kuruppu	2	2	—	55	41	—	—	27.50	1/1
RJ Ratnayake	3	3	1	49	26	—	—	24.50	1
MAR Samaresekera	3	3	—	68	29	—	—	22.67	2
CPH Ramanayake	1	1	—	18	18	—	—	18.00	—
PA De Silva	3	3	—	53	34	—	—	17.67	1
JR Ratnayeke	3	3	—	45	32	—	—	15.00	—
AP Gurusinha	3	2	—	30	21	—	—	15.00	1
USH Karnain	2	2	—	15	14	—	—	7.50	—
EAR De Silva	3	2	—	9	9	—	—	4.50	—
ST Jayasuriya	1	1	—	4	4	—	—	4.00	—
MAWR Madurasinghe	3	2	2	10	9*	—	—	—	1

Bowler	M	Overs	Mdns	Runs	Wkts	Avrge	5wi	Best
JR Ratnayeke	3	30.0	—	166	7	23.71	—	3/31
USH Karnain	2	12.0	1	61	2	30.50	—	2/43
MAWR Madurasinghe	3	20.0	—	72	2	36.00	—	1/32
PA De Silva	3	10.0	—	63	1	63.00	—	1/63
RJ Ratnayake	3	29.0	—	151	2	75.50	—	2/44
AP Gurusinha	3	11.0	—	82	1	82.00	—	1/34
CPH Ramanayake	1	10.0	—	82	1	82.00	—	1/82
A Ranatunga	3	9.0	—	59	—	—	—	—
EAR De Silva	3	19.0	—	129	—	—	—	—

New Zealand

Batsman	M	Inn	NO	Runs	HS	50	100	Avrge	Ct/St
AH Jones	3	3	—	155	93	1	—	51.67	—
JG Bracewell	3	2	1	40	36*	—	—	40.00	2
MD Crowe	3	3	—	115	69	1	—	38.33	1
JG Wright	3	3	—	94	93	1	—	31.33	1
KR Rutherford	3	3	1	50	30*	—	—	25.00	—
MG Greatbatch	3	3	—	73	37	—	—	24.33	—
MW Priest	1	1	—	15	15	—	—	15.00	—
MC Snedden	3	2	1	14	13*	—	—	14.00	—
SA Thomson	2	2	1	12	8*	—	—	12.00	1
IDS Smith	3	2	—	2	2	—	—	1.00	1
DK Morrison	3	1	—	0	0	—	—	0.00	1
JP Millmow	3	1	1	0	0*	—	—	—	—

Bowler	M	Overs	Mdns	Runs	Wkts	Avrge	5wi	Best
MC Snedden	3	17.0	3	49	3	16.33	—	2/31
JP Millmow	3	25.0	—	120	4	30.00	—	2/22
KR Rutherford	3	6.0	—	35	1	35.00	—	1/12
JG Bracewell	3	20.0	—	79	1	79.00	—	1/32
DK Morrison	3	20.0	1	102	1	102.00	—	1/51
MW Priest	1	7.0	—	43	—	—	—	—
MD Crowe	3	0.4	—	5	—	—	—	—
AH Jones	3	6.0	1	20	—	—	—	—
SA Thomson	2	14.0	2	41	—	—	—	—

Bangladesh

Batsman	M	Inn	NO	Runs	HS	50	100	Avrge	Ct/St
Enam-ul-Haque	2	2	1	31	18	—	—	31.00	—
Akram Hussain Khan	2	2	—	46	33	—	—	23.00	1
Azhar Hussain Shantu	3	3	—	67	54	1	—	22.33	1
Nurul Abedin	1	1	—	18	18	—	—	18.00	1
Gazi Ashraf Lipu	1	1	—	18	18	—	—	18.00	1
Faruque Ahmed	1	1	—	6	6	—	—	6.00	1
Zahid Razzak	2	2	—	8	4	—	—	4.00	—
Nazir Ahmed	2	1	—	3	3	—	—	3.00	—
Minhazul Abedin Nanu	1	1	—	0	0	—	—	0.00	—
JA Taluder	1	1	1	7	7*	—	—	—	—
Amin-ul-Islam Bulbul	2	2	2	71	41*	—	—	—	—
Ghulam Nowsher	2	—	—	—	—	—	—	—	—
Ghulam Faruque Suru	1	—	—	—	—	—	—	—	—
Jahangir Badshah	1	—	—	—	—	—	—	—	1

Bowler	M	Overs	Mdns	Runs	Wkts	Avrge	5wi	Best
Nurul Abedin	1	7.0	—	39	2	19.50	—	2/39
Minhazul Abedin Nanu	1	6.0	—	43	2	21.50	—	2/43
Ghulam Faruque Suru	1	4.3	—	28	1	28.00	—	1/28
Ghulam Nowsher	2	16.0	—	82	2	41.00	—	1/27
Azhar Hussain Shantu	3	14.3	1	81	—	—	—	—
Zahid Razzak	2	10.0	—	72	—	—	—	—
Amin-ul-Islam Bulbul	2	3.4	—	37	—	—	—	—
Enam-ul-Haque	2	1.0	—	7	—	—	—	—
Jahangir Badshah	1	9.0	—	62	—	—	—	—
JA Taluder	1	4.0	—	20	—	—	—	—

AUSTRALIAN LIMITED-OVERS AVERAGES MAY 1989—JUNE 1990

Player	M	Inn	NO	Runs	HS	50	100	Avrge	Ct/St
PL Taylor	19	10	8	165	54*	1	—	82.50	5
DM Jones	21	20	5	1094	117*	9	3	72.93	10
DC Boon	15	14	4	457	92*	2	—	45.70	6
GR Marsh	14	13	1	415	86	3	—	34.58	7
AR Border	21	18	5	448	69*	1	—	34.46	14
MA Taylor	16	15	—	516	76	5	—	34.40	7
SP O'Donnell	22	16	4	409	74	3	—	34.08	3
TM Moody	7	7	—	231	89	2	—	33.00	3
IA Healy	22	13	4	226	36*	—	—	25.11	34/3
SR Waugh	21	17	2	304	64	1	—	20.27	10
ME Waugh	1	1	—	14	14	—	—	14.00	—
MG Hughes	12	6	3	28	10*	—	—	9.33	4
GRJ Matthews	1	1	—	5	5	—	—	5.00	—
GF Lawson	3	2	1	4	3*	—	—	4.00	1
GD Campbell	12	3	1	6	4*	—	—	3.00	4
CG Rackemann	15	4	1	8	6	—	—	2.67	2
TM Alderman	19	3	1	0	0*	—	—	0.00	8
CJ McDermott	1	1	—	0	0	—	—	0.00	1

Player	M	Overs	Mdns	Runs	Wkts	Avrge	5wi	NB	W	Best
TM Alderman	19	156.5	24	585	33	17.73	1	8	14	5/32
GRJ Matthews	1	10.0	0	56	3	18.67	—	—	1	3/56
GF Lawson	3	28.1	4	96	5	19.20	—	—	2	2/23
CG Rackemann	15	133.1	13	493	24	20.54	—	3	7	4/44
GD Campbell	12	102.1	9	404	18	22.44	—	11	6	3/17
SP O'Donnell	22	182.2	17	764	34	22.47	1	10	19	5/13
PL Taylor	19	162.2	11	601	24	25.04	—	1	5	3/31
SR Waugh	21	45.0	2	189	6	31.50	—	—	3	2/22
AR Border	21	72.4	2	347	11	31.55	—	—	1	3/25
MG Hughes	12	100.2	8	380	11	34.55	—	3	21	3/38
CJ McDermott	1	8.0	1	35	1	35.00	—	1	—	1/35

SHEFFIELD SHIELD

FROM A PURELY CRICKETING POINT OF VIEW, it was disappointing that a Sheffield Shield season so closely contested over a period of five months should have ended in such an unequal contest in the final. The huge margin by which New South Wales defeated Queensland in this match was nevertheless a measure of New South Wales's strength in 1989-90. Only a state with great depth of talent could afford to leave a current Australian player out of its eleven, as New South Wales did in the Shield final, when it made Peter Taylor twelfth man. For the Queenslanders, who ran second in the competition for the thirteenth time, the disappointment must have been intense. They were, however, clearly the second-best team in the competition.

Although a precise comparison was not available, crowds at Shield matches during the season seemed generally a little down on the season before, when, it must be admitted, attendances were unusually high. On the other hand, it was apparent that the competition held the interest of cricket followers in Australia throughout the season. A pleasing feature of recent Shield seasons has been the establishment of a stratum of senior players who are apparently no longer in strong contention for national selection yet whose personal reputation gives the competition much added prestige. They included players such as David Hookes of South Australia, Greg Ritchie of Queensland and Dirk Wellham of Tasmania. It is to be hoped such players continue to enhance the Shield competition by their presence.

Queensland v Victoria
Brisbane Cricket Ground, Brisbane
Oct 25, 26, 27, 28 1989
Toss: Queensland
Result: Drawn
Points: Queensland 2 & Victoria 0

Queensland took first innings points from a drawn match highlighted by fine performances by the Queensland opening batsman Peter Cantrell and the Victorian opening batsman Gary Watts. Cantrell's patient innings, the highest of his career so far, was the mainstay of his side's batting. His runs were scored in 459 minutes off 362 balls. Earlier, the Queensland fast bowlers Carl Rackemann and Craig McDermott were largely responsible for restricting Victoria to the moderate total of 235. Queensland lost a couple of early wickets, but Cantrell steadied the home side's innings, and the Queenslanders were not dismissed until the afternoon of the third day. With a lead of 82, there seemed little chance then that Queensland could obtain an outright victory, and Watts, redeeming himself after a first innings duck, put the matter beyond doubt with an undefeated 162. The match ended a half-hour early when it was clear no result was possible.

Victoria

First Innings / Second Innings

Batsman	How Out	Ttl	Balls	How Out		Ttl	Balls
GM Watts	c Barsby b McDermott	0	7	not out		162	355
ID Frazer	c Barsby b Rackemann	5	39	c Cantrell b McDermott		7	46
WN Phillips	c Law b Polzin	52	91	c Anderson b Tazelaar	(4)	2	19
JD Siddons (c)	c Law b Inwood	71	129	lbw Rackemann	(5)	5	14
GR Parker	c Kerr b Rackemann	37	136	c Polzin b Cantrell	(6)	75	198
PW Young	c Anderson b Rackemann	7	57	not out	(7)	0	0
AIC Dodemaide	c Anderson b Rackemann	9	31				
MGD Dimattina (+)	b Tazelaar	7	34	b Polzin	(3)	6	61
PR Reiffel	not out	8	37				
DJ Hickey	c Ritchie b McDermott	2	11				
PE McIntyre	b McDermott	2	7				
SUNDRIES:	B. 0 LB. 9 W. 0 NB. 13	35	579	B. 0 LB. 5 W. 0 NB. 11		27	693
TOTAL		235		5 wkts for 284			

F/W: 0 41 83 162 192 201 214 220 231 235

F/W: 19 69 74 98 284

Bowler	O	M	R	Wkts	NB	W	Bowler	O	M	R	Wkts	NB	W
McDermott	20.2	7	54	3	8	—	McDermott	23	3	72	1	11	—
Tazelaar	24	7	35	1	—	—	Tazelaar	19	5	32	1	—	—
Polzin	13	4	27	1	—	—	Rackemann	19	5	37	1	—	—
Rackemann	20	4	53	4	5	—	Polzin	16	4	41	1	—	—
Cantrell	10	2	48	—	—	—	Cantrell	22	6	64	1	—	—
Inwood	7	3	9	1	—	—	Inwood	15	7	33	—	—	—
Overs	94.2						Overs:	114.0					

Queensland

First Innings

Batsman	How Out	Ttl	Balls
TJ Barsby	b Dodemaide	18	13
PE Cantrell	c Watts b Parker	125	362
RB Kerr	lbw Hickey	4	9
GM Ritchie (c)	c Dimattina b Young	56	115
MA Polzin	c Frazer b McIntyre	29	67
SG Law	c McIntyre b Hickey	24	58
BP Inwood	lbw Dodemaide	19	36
PW Anderson (+)	c & b Dodemaide	0	8
CJ McDermott	b Parker	26	57
D Tazelaar	c Hickey b Dodemaide	0	6
CG Rackemann	not out	1	9
SUNDRIES:	B. 0 LB. 5 W. 0 NB. 5	15	740
TOTAL		317	

F/W: 29 34 123 183 232 273 273 303 304 317

Bowler	O	M	R	Wkts	NB	W
Hickey	29.3	5	118	2	3	—
Dodemaide	45	17	76	4	1	—
Reiffel	3.3	1	6	—	1	—
McIntyre	20	6	56	1	—	—
Young	9	—	26	1	—	—
Parker	15.3	4	30	2	—	—
Overs:	122.3					

Umpires: PD Parker & CD Timmins

12th Men: SC Storey (Queensland) & DW Fleming (Victoria)

Western Australia v Tasmania
WACA Ground, Perth
Nov 1, 2, 3, 4 1989
Toss: Western Australia
Result: Drawn
Points: Western Australia 0 & Tasmania 2

Tasmania might well have won this match outright if its batsmen had not taken so long to secure its big first innings lead. The Western Australians had chosen to bat first and had begun their innings disastrously, losing their first five wickets before lunch for 51. Most of the damage was done by the Tasmanian opening bowlers, Dave Gilbert and Greg Campbell. When the home side lost its eighth wicket for 113 it seemed the Western Australians might be all out before tea, but the tail-end batsmen, especially Tom Hogan, showed unexpected resistance, and Western Australia managed a respectable 215. The Tasmanians batted laboriously in reply, taking 400 minutes to pass the Western Australian total. They eventually declared at 6 for 478 when the opener Greg Shipperd reached a marathon 200, scored in 708 minutes. Shipperd shared a partnership of 222 with Jamie Cox, who made 101. In hope of an outright victory, Gilbert struck again with three quick Western Australian wickets, but in the end the Tasmanians ran out of time.

Western Australia

First Innings

Batsman	How Out	Ttl	Balls		How Out	Ttl	Balls
GR Marsh	c Shipperd b Gilbert	5	7	(2)	lbw Gilbert	9	23
MRJ Veletta	c Robertson b Campbell	8	29	(1)	c Soule b Gilbert	4	4
TM Moody	b Gilbert	6	4		c Tucker b Gilbert	41	69
GM Wood (c)	c Boon b De Winter	36	81	(5)	run out	44	140
WS Andrews	c De Winter b Campbell	7	30	(6)	lbw Gilbert	77	194
TJ Zoehrer (+)	b Campbell	0	1	(7)	c Wellham b Robertson	23	72
KH MacLeay	c Boon b De Winter	27	81	(8)	not out	9	69
TG Hogan	not out	58	131	(9)	not out	28	51
PA Capes	c De Winter b Campbell	5	13				
AD Mullally	c & b Gilbert	34	71	(4)	c (s)O'Connor b Gilbert	0	3
TM Alderman	b Tucker	18	24				
SUNDRIES: B. 0 LB. 6 W. 3 NB. 1		11	472		B. 9 LB. 6 W. 1 NB. 7	30	625
TOTAL		215			7 wkts for 265		

F/W: 9 17 35 51 51 77 104 113 184 215

F/W: 4 29 29 80 143 208 228

Bowler	O	M	R	Wkts	NB	W	Bowler	O	M	R	Wkts	NB	W
Gilbert	24	4	82	3	—	—	Gilbert	23	9	47	5	—	—
Campbell	19	5	38	4	—	1	De Winter	25	1	100	—	7	1
Robertson	7	2	16	—	—	—	Robertson	26	6	58	1	—	—
De Winter	21	2	60	2	1	2	Campbell	23	8	40	—	—	—
Tucker	7	2	13	1	—	—	Tucker	6	2	5	—	—	—
Overs:	78.0						Overs:	103.0					

Tasmania

First Innings

Batsman	How Out	Ttl	Balls
SG Hookey	c Zoehrer b Capes	0	11
G Shipperd	not out	200	571
DR Gilbert	c Zoehrer b Mullally	6	32
DC Boon	c Moody b Hogan	63	110
J Cox	b Alderman	101	277
RJ Tucker	st Zoehrer b Hogan	54	57
DM Wellham (c)	c & b Alderman	11	23
GR Robertson	not out	21	26

Continued

Batsman	How Out	Ttl	Balls
RE Soule (+)	did not bat		
AJ De Winter	did not bat		
GD Campbell	did not bat		
SUNDRIES: B. 7 LB. 6 W. 1 NB. 4		22	1107
TOTAL	6 wkts dec 478		

F/W: 0 17 110 322 403 438

Bowler	O	M	R	Wkts	NB	W
Capes	30	10	71	1	—	—
Alderman	38	14	96	2	3	—
Mullally	37	10	112	1	1	1
MacLeay	31.4	12	70	—	—	—
Moody	20	8	37	—	—	—
Hogan	27	5	79	2	—	—
Overs:	183.4					

Umpires: TA Prue & RJ Evans

12th Men: JA Brayshaw (Western Australia) & DFG O'Connor (Tasmania)

Queensland v South Australia
Brisbane Cricket Ground, Brisbane
Nov 3, 4, 5, 6 1989
Toss: Queensland
Result: Queensland won by 6 wkts
Points: Queensland 6 & South Australia 0

For the most part this was an evenly contested match, yet Queensland won it comfortably in the end. Sent in by the Queensland captain, Greg Ritchie, the South Australians worked hard against an effective pace attack to compile 239. In reply, the Queenslanders started badly, but a century by Allan Border, who hit a six as well as 16 fours, enabled the home side to gain a 36 run lead. The South Australians were still hopeful of winning outright, and David Hookes and Darren Lehmann had scored 89 in a lively partnership when Lehmann was ruled lbw. It was the start of a mid-order collapse. From 3 for 168, the South Australians slumped to 6 for 168 and were all out on the last ball of the third day for 248. Queensland thus needed to make 213 on the final day to win, a task it accomplished easily, thanks to an opening stand of 173 by Peter Cantrell and Robbie Kerr. Despite a minor batting collapse near the end, Queensland won the match with an hour and a quarter to spare.

South Australia

First Innings				Second Innings		
Batsman	How Out	Ttl	Balls	How Out	Ttl	Balls
BD Williams	c Healy b Rackemann	28	82	b Rackemann	17	58
AMJ Hilditch	b McDermott	14	37	c Border b McDermott	0	1
PC Nobes	c Border b Rackemann	46	88	c Healy b Rackemann	30	72
DW Hookes (c)	c Healy b Inwood	39	56	c McDermott b Rackemann	67	95
DS Lehmann	c Ritchie b Tazelaar	15	14	lbw Storey	35	69
PR Sleep	lbw McDermott	52	165	c Kerr b Storey	0	1
JC Scuderi	c Border b Tazelaar	0	3	c Cantrell b McDermott	39	45
DS Berry (+)	c Healy b Rackemann	6	64	c Healy b Tazelaar	10	51
PW Gladigau	c Border b Rackemann	5	15	not out	18	16
PJS Alley	not out	3	35	lbw McDermott	0	2
CR Miller	c Kerr b McDermott	4	7	lbw Inwood	7	15
SUNDRIES: B. 0 LB. 5 W. 0 NB. 11		27	566	B. 4 LB. 1 W. 0 NB. 10	25	425
TOTAL		239			248	

F/W: 35 78 143 145 161 161 194 204 233 239

F/W: 3 56 79 168 168 168 217 221 221 248

Bowler	O	M	R	Wkts	NB	W	Bowler	O	M	R	Wkts	NB	W
McDermott	25.3	7	69	3	4	—	McDermott	19	4	69	3	6	—
Tazelaar	28	4	76	2	6	—	Tazelaar	20	3	72	1	4	—
Rackemann	21	5	39	4	—	—	Rackemann	15	5	34	3	—	—
Cantrell	3	—	12	—	—	—	Cantrell	4	1	14	—	—	—
Inwood	4	1	14	1	—	—	Inwood	4.1	1	12	1	—	—
Storey	11	5	24	—	1	—	Storey	7	—	42	2	—	—
Overs:	92.3						Overs:	69.1					

Queensland

Batsman	First Innings How Out	Ttl	Balls		Second Innings How Out	Ttl	Balls
PE Cantrell	c(s)Bishop b Sleep	51	167	(2)	c Williams b Miller	85	198
RB Kerr	c Sleep b Miller	0	7	(1)	c Lehmann b Miller	86	176
SG Law	lbw Miller	2	10		c Berry b Miller	1	10
AR Border	not out	144	277	(5)	not out	19	35
GM Ritchie (c)	run out	0	1	(4)	b Miller	2	12
BD Inwood	c Nobes b Scuderi	15	56		not out	12	33
IA Healy (+)	c Berry b Scuderi	0	6				
SC Storey	run out	46	70				
CJ McDermott	c Sleep b Miller	6	16				
D Tazelaar	c Berry b Miller	0	3				
CG Rackemann	c Berry b Gladigau	1	9				
SUNDRIES: B. 0 LB. 2 W. 0 NB. 4		10	622		B. 0 LB. 6 W. 0 NB. 1	8	464
TOTAL		275			4 wkts for 213		

F/W: 4 10 123 123 176 178 256 270 270 275

F/W: 173 175 177 188

Bowler	O	M	R	Wkts	NB	W	Bowler	O	M	R	Wkts	NB	W
Gladigau	30	11	70	1	2	—	Gladigau	16	4	42	—	1	—
Miller	23	6	67	4	—	—	Miller	20	8	46	4	—	—
Alley	14	2	48	—	1	—	Alley	7	2	19	—	—	—
Scuderi	29	10	50	2	1	—	Sleep	17	2	44	—	—	—
Sleep	7	—	38	1	—	—	Scuderi	3	—	12	—	—	—
Overs:	103.0						Williams	4	1	15	—	—	—
							Hookes	8.1	—	28	—	—	—
							Hilditch	2	1	1	—	—	—
							Overs:	77.1					

Umpires: PD Parker & CD Timmins

12th Men: MA Polzin (Queensland) & GA Bishop (South Australia)

South Australia v New South Wales
Adelaide Oval, Adelaide
Nov 10, 11, 12, 13 1989
Toss: South Australia
Result: Drawn
Points: South Australia 2 & New South Wales 0

The Adelaide pitch proved a generous provider of runs for both sides in this match, yet the South Australian captain, David Hookes, was uncertain of it at the outset, for having won the toss he asked New South Wales to bat. At the end of the first day, this seemed a calamitous mistake. Mark Taylor, showing the same capacity for heavy scoring he had displayed in England a few months before, was 144 not out and his side 3 for 303. Next day, Taylor advanced to 199 and Mark Waugh to 172 before New South Wales declared at 7 for 516. This seemed more than enough to assure first innings points, and when South Australia lost its first 4 wickets for only 90 New South Wales had its sights on outright victory. Then Darren

Lehmann joined Hookes in a partnership which turned the match around. Together, they put on 200 before Hookes went for 99. Lehmann, 19 years old and an exceptionally robust batsman, went on to make 228, scored off only 318 balls. South Australia edged past New South Wales for first innings points, leaving the visitors to bat out the remaining four hours.

New South Wales

First Innings

Batsman	How Out	Ttl	Balls
SM Small	b Alley	23	38
MA Taylor	c Hookes b Sleep	199	371
TH Bayliss	c Berry b Gladigau	36	79
SR Waugh	c Nobes b Alley	22	33
ME Waugh	c Berry b Gladigau	172	301
MD O'Neill	b Alley	36	61
GRJ Matthews	lbw Alley	6	30
PA Emery (+)	not out	6	14
GF Lawson (c)	did not bat		
MR Whitney	did not bat		
WJ Holdsworth	did not bat		
SUNDRIES: B. 0 LB. 10 W. 2 NB. 2		16	927
TOTAL	7 wkts dec 516		
F/W: 50 128 159 422 494 504 516			

Second Innings

How Out	Ttl	Balls
st Berry b Sleep	79	179
c Berry b Alley	30	49
not out	48	144
(4) not out	16	25
B. 0 LB. 4 W. 0 NB. 1	6	397
2 for 179		
F/W: 58 153		

Bowler	O	M	R	Wkts	NB	W
Gladigau	27	2	109	2	2	—
Miller	33	7	114	—	—	1
Alley	31.5	8	98	4	—	1
Scuderi	28	6	76	—	—	—
Sleep	34	2	109	1	—	—
Overs:	153.5					

Bowler	O	M	R	Wkts	NB	W
Gladigau	17	2	60	—	1	—
Alley	11	3	32	1	—	—
Hookes	10	2	24	—	—	—
Sleep	22	5	50	1	—	—
Hilditch	6	2	9	—	—	—
Overs:	66.0					

South Australia

First Innings

Batsman	How Out	Ttl	Balls
BD Williams	c Taylor b Whitney	9	24
AMJ Hilditch	c ME Waugh b Whitney	44	67
PC Nobes	run out	30	44
DS Berry (+)	c Bayliss b Matthews	4	13
DW Hookes (c)	lbw Whitney	99	154
DS Lehmann	c Whitney b O'Neill	228	318
PR Sleep	lbw ME Waugh	31	82
JC Scuderi	c Small b Whitney	43	86
PW Gladigau	b Whitney	2	18
PJS Alley	not out	5	22
CR Miller	c Holdsworth b O'Neill	0	3
SUNDRIES: B. 2 LB. 12 W. 0 NB. 5		24	831
TOTAL		519	
F/W: 27 76 90 90 290 388 474 494 519 519			

Bowler	O	M	R	Wkts	NB	W
Lawson	27	3	87	—	—	—
Whitney	34	3	125	5	3	—
Holdsworth	20	—	93	—	1	—
Matthews	35	7	117	1	—	—
O'Neill	15.4	1	65	2	—	—
ME Waugh	5	1	18	1	1	—
Bayliss	1	1	0	—	—	—
Overs:	137.4					

Umpires: AR Crafter & DJ Harper

12th Men: GA Bishop (South Australia) & PL Taylor (New South Wales)

Victoria v Tasmania
Junction Oval, St Kilda
Nov 10, 11, 12, 13 1989
Toss: Tasmania
Result: Drawn
Points: Victoria 0 & Tasmania 2

Again, Tasmania had to settle for first innings points after looking to have a good chance of winning outright. Batting first, the Victorians were given a good start by their openers, Gary Watts and Ian Frazer, who put on 134 for the first wicket. But then the Tasmanian pace bowler Greg Campbell swept through the Victorian middle order, taking 6 for 80, and the home side was out for 259. The Tasmanian batsmen replied with a solid performance down the list, the feature of which was another fine innings by young Jamie Cox. Having scored his maiden Sheffield Shield century in the previous match, Cox was out here for 99, falling to Simon O'Donnell's slower ball. Tasmania made 381, and at stumps on the third day Victoria was 0-9, still 113 behind. Wickets fell steadily next day, and just after tea, when Victoria was 7-119, a Tasmanian victory looked likely. But in a fighting stand lasting 92 minutes Tony Dodemaide and Merv Hughes held out for a draw.

Victoria

First Innings

Batsman	How Out	Ttl	Balls	How Out	Ttl	Balls
GM Watts	c Soule b Campbell	67	122	c Soule b De Winter	23	64
ID Frazer	c Robertson b Campbell	71	197	lbw Gilbert	4	23
WN Phillips	c Shipperd b Campbell	32	132	c Soule b Tucker	16	49
JD Siddons	c De Winter b Robertson	17	73	run out	9	68
DM Jones	c De Winter b Campbell	5	20	c Campbell b Tucker	19	66
SP O'Donnell (c)	c Robertson b Campbell	16	41	c Wellham b Campbell	10	43
AIC Dodemaide	c Soule b Gilbert	1	13	not out	30	157
MGD Dimattina (+)	c Soule b Campbell	1	13	b Robertson	5	38
MG Hughes	c Robertson b Gilbert	20	47	not out	22	77
PE McIntyre	b Gilbert	6	19			
DJ Hickey	not out	2	1			
SUNDRIES: B.2 LB.6 W.0 NB.6*		21	678	B.8 LB.7 W.6 NB.1	23	585
TOTAL		259		7 for 161		

F/W: 134 163 208 211 218 223 250 250 257 259
F/W: 15 49 49 86 89 103 119
Note: One leg-bye from a no-ball from Campbell

Bowler	O	M	R	Wkts	NB	W	Bowler	O	M	R	Wkts	NB	W
Gilbert	26.1	5	71	3	2	—	Gilbert	22	6	32	1	—	—
Campbell	33	8	80	6	3	—	Campbell	24	9	41	1	—	—
Robertson	30	9	52	1	—	—	De Winter	13	4	34	1	1	6
De Winter	14	5	23	—	—	—	Tucker	23	10	27	2	—	—
Tucker	9	2	25	—	1	—	Robertson	15	9	12	1	—	—
Overs:	112.1						Overs:	97.0					

Tasmania

First Innings

Batsman	How Out	Ttl	Balls
RJ Bennett	c Watts b McIntyre	35	136
G Shipperd	b Hickey	29	99
J Cox	b O'Donnell	99	273
RJ Tucker	c Dimattina b Hickey	54	126
DM Wellham (c)	c Dimattina b Hughes	5	28
DFG O'Connor	c Dimattina b Hickey	43	97
GR Robertson	run out	42	129
RE Soule (+)	c Hughes b McIntyre	4	16
AJ De Winter	b Hughes	28	49
GD Campbell	b Hughes	1	12

Continued

Batsman	How Out	Ttl	Balls
DR Gilbert	not out	4	16
SUNDRIES: B. 2 LB. 19 W. 4 NB. 6		37	981
TOTAL		381	

F/W: 78 100 180 197 281 315 325 369 371 381

Bowler	O	M	R	Wkts	NB	W	Bowler
Hughes	38	13	68	3	—	—	
Hickey	32	4	89	3	5	4	
Dodemaide	23	5	59	—	—	—	
McIntyre	46.5	13	95	2	—	—	
O'Donnell	18	3	42	1	1	—	
Jones	4	2	7	—	—	—	
Overs:	161.5						

Umpires: RC Bailhache & LJ King

12th Men: GR Parker (Victoria) & TD Bower (Tasmania)

Victoria v Western Australia
Junction Oval, St Kilda
Nov 17, 18, 19, 20 1989
Toss: Victoria
Result: Drawn
Points: Victoria 2 & Western Australia 0

Victoria gained a crucial advantage by winning the toss, for Western Australia had to bat on an inferior wicket which favoured pace bowlers. The result was a batting disaster for the Western Australians, who were bundled out in 48 overs for 133. Only one of them, Wayne Andrews, who scored a brisk 51, offered much resistance. The Victorian who made the most of the conditions was nineteen-year-old fast bowler Damien Fleming, who, in his first-class debut, finished with 6 for 37. Batting proved easier on the second and third days, and Victoria declared at 8 for 297 in hope of an outright win. Western Australia began the final day at 2 for 56, still 108 runs behind, so a Victorian victory was on the cards, but the Victorian bowlers were frustrated again by Wayne Andrews, who defied them for 4 hours 31 minutes while making 103. In the end, the Victorians needed to score 81 to win, but their frantic run chase ended 25 runs short of the target.

Western Australia

First Innings / Second Innings

Batsman	How Out	Ttl	Balls		How Out	Ttl	Balls
MRJ Veletta	c McIntyre b Fleming	2	12	(2)	b Dodemaide	13	93
GR Marsh	c Dimattina b Fleming	13	75	(1)	c Dimattina b Fleming	9	22
TM Moody	c Dimattina b Fleming	4	18		c Watts b Fleming	30	86
KH MacLeay	c Watts b Fleming	2	5	(7)	c Dodemaide b O'Donnell	13	53
PA Capes	c Dodemaide b Fleming	9	38	(9)	c Hughes b Dodemaide	10	35
GM Wood (c)	c Parker b Hughes	20	27	(4)	c Frazer b Hughes	0	8
WS Andrews	c Parker b O'Donnell	51	68	(5)	c Dimattina b O'Donnell	103	225
TJ Zoehrer (+)	b Fleming	7	10	(6)	run out	27	74
TG Hogan	lbw O'Donnell	10	21	(8)	b Hughes	9	16
AD Mullally	c & b O'Donnell	2	7		not out	2	14
B Yardley	not out	7	7		c Watts b O'Donnell	10	18
SUNDRIES: B. 2 LB. 3 W. 1 NB. 0		6	288		B. 3 LB. 10 W. 0 NB. 2	18	644
TOTAL		133				244	

F/W: 3 11 13 34 39 57 66 104 110 133

F/W: 13 56 60 60 114 175 191 230 232 244

Note: 1 leg-bye from a no-ball

▶

Bowler	O	M	R	Wkts	NB	W
Hughes	12	5	27	1	—	—
Fleming	18	5	37	6	—	1
O'Donnell	11	4	40	3	—	—
Dodemaide	7	—	24	—	—	—
Overs:	48.0					

Bowler	O	M	R	Wkts	NB	W
Hughes	25	8	72	2	1	—
Fleming	25	7	57	2	—	—
O'Donnell	18	6	28	3	1	—
McIntyre	19	5	53	—	—	—
Dodemaide	17	7	20	2	—	—
Jones	3	2	1	—	—	—
Overs:	107.0					

Victoria

Batsman	How Out	Ttl	Balls	How Out	Ttl	Balls
	First Innings			Second Innings		
GM Watts	lbw Mullally	0	1	run out	21	24
ID Frazer	b Capes	90	309			
WN Phillips	c Zoehrer b Moody	18	53 (2)	lbw Capes	1	3
DM Jones	c Marsh b Mullally	49	155 (3)	not out	27	31
GR Parker	c Zoehrer b Moody	22	78			
SP O'Donnell (c)	b Mullally	39	45 (4)	not out	5	4
AIC Dodemaide	b Moody	6	41			
MGD Dimattina (+)	b Hogan	19	40			
MG Hughes	not out	19	35			
DW Fleming	not out	0	10			
PE McIntyre	did not bat					
SUNDRIES: B. 6 LB. 7 W. 0 NB. 11		35	767	B. 1 LB. 1 W. 0 NB. 0	2	62
TOTAL	8 wkts dec	297			2 wkts for 56	

F/W: 0 47 162 207 211 254 264 279

F/W: 10 44

Bowler	O	M	R	Wkts	NB	W
Mullally	37	12	74	3	4	—
MacLeay	22	11	34	—	—	—
Capes	23	3	74	1	7	—
Moody	24	3	57	3	—	—
Yardley	15	4	29	—	—	—
Hogan	5	3	16	1	—	—
Overs:	126.0					

Bowler	O	M	R	Wkts	NB	W
Mullally	5.2	—	25	—	—	—
Capes	5	—	29	1	—	—
Overs:	10.2					

Umpires: RC Bailhache & LJ King

12th Men: JD Siddons (Victoria) & RS Russell (Western Australia)

Tasmania v Queensland
Bellerive Oval, Hobart
Nov 17, 18, 19, 20 1989
Toss: Queensland
Result: Drawn
Points: Tasmania 0 & Queensland 2

The outcome of the match showed that Queensland's captain, Greg Ritchie, made the right decision when he asked Tasmania to bat, yet the matter remained in doubt until the third day. The Tasmanians struggled against the Queensland pace attack, at one stage slumping to 5 for 125, and they were probably pleased to finish with 262. Queensland's most successful bowler was Dirk Tazelaar, number three in the pace attack, who took 6 for 48. On an increasingly slow pitch Queensland's batsmen made heavy work of trying to exceed the Tasmanian total, and Ritchie was the only top-order batsman to get runs. It was left to Ian Healy, batting at eight, to ensure Queensland gained first innings points by scoring a breezy 81 not out. At stumps on the third day, Tasmania was 1 for 83. It was clear the final day's play would have no bearing on the result, but David Boon used the opportunity to find form for the coming Test against New Zealand by scoring his 31st first-class century.

Tasmania

First Innings

Batsman	How Out	Ttl	Balls
RJ Bennett	c Healy b McDermott	0	1
G Shipperd	c Cantrell b Tazelaar	42	122
DC Boon	c Kerr b Tazelaar	14	29
J Cox	c Healy b Rackemann	18	38
RJ Tucker	b Storey	30	86
DM Wellham (c)	lbw Tazelaar	35	166
GR Robertson	lbw Tazelaar	53	108
RE Soule (+)	c Healy b Tazelaar	4	15
AJ De Winter	b McDermott	2	21
GD Campbell	not out	9	27
DR Gilbert	c Healy b Tazelaar	22	33
SUNDRIES: B. 3 LB. 8 W. 0 NB. 11		33	646
TOTAL		262	

F/W: 0 17 56 106 125 209 219 224 236 262

Second Innings

How Out	Ttl	Balls
c Trimble b Tazelaar	3	12
c Ritchie b Tazelaar	72	280
c Trimble b Tazelaar	100	222
b Rackemann	1	15
not out	9	36
(7) not out	19	47
(6) b Storey	7	22
(5) lbw Rackemann	0	1
B. 3 LB. 6 W. 0 NB. 5	19	635
6 wkts dec	230	

(8) RJ Tucker | (7) DM Wellham | (6) GR Robertson | (5) AJ De Winter

F/W: 6 172 177 177 197 204

Bowler	O	M	R	Wkts	NB	W
McDermott	32	8	93	2	5	—
Tazelaar	28.5	11	48	6	2	—
Rackemann	19	4	65	1	4	—
Inwood	5	2	12	—	—	—
Storey	19	6	25	1	—	—
Cantrell	2	—	8	—	—	—
Overs:	105.5					

Bowler	O	M	R	Wkts	NB	W
McDermott	17	—	63	—	1	—
Tazelaar	25	5	54	3	3	—
Rackemann	30	8	50	2	1	—
Inwood	10	6	10	—	—	—
Storey	15	4	28	1	—	—
Cantrell	8	2	16	—	—	—
Overs:	105.0					

Queensland

First Innings

Batsman	How Out	Ttl	Balls
PE Cantrell	c Soule b Tucker	23	70
RB Kerr	c Boon b Campbell	28	52
SG Law	lbw Gilbert	14	62
GM Ritchie (c)	c De Winter b Gilbert	52	212
GS Trimble	c Soule b Tucker	39	140
BP Inwood	c Soule b Gilbert	6	30
SC Storey	c Soule b Robertson	20	61
IA Healy (+)	not out	81	110
CJ McDermott	c (S)O'Connor b Gilbert	15	40
D Tazelaar	lbw Campbell	0	11
CG Rackemann	c Robertson b Campbell	9	20
SUNDRIES: B. 0 LB. 11 W. 3 NB. 1		16	808
TOTAL		303	

F/W: 45 70 72 144 154 183 205 246 261 303

Second Innings

How Out	Ttl	Balls
(2) not out	13	67
(1) not out	18	59
B. 0 LB. 0 W. 0 NB. 0	0	126
0 wkts for	31	

F/W:

Bowler	O	M	R	Wkts	NB	W
Gilbert	35	8	76	4	—	—
Campbell	32	8	74	3	—	—
De Winter	19	5	48	—	1	3
Tucker	27	10	42	2	—	—
Robertson	21	5	52	1	—	—
Overs:	134.0					

Bowler	O	M	R	Wkts	NB	W
De Winter	8	2	17	—	—	—
Tucker	5	2	5	—	—	—
Wellham	4	1	6	—	—	—
Robertson	3	1	3	—	—	—
Cox	1	1	0	—	—	—
Overs:	21.0					

Umpires: SG Randell & DR Close

12th Men: DFG O'Connor (Tasmania) & MA Polzin (Queensland)

New South Wales v Queensland
Newcastle International Sports Ground, Newcastle
Dec 1, 2, 3, 4 1989
Toss: Queensland
Result: New South Wales won by 32 runs
Points: New South Wales 6 & Queensland 2

Queensland seemed assured of winning this low-scoring match until the last day. Sent in to bat, New South Wales struggled to make 211 against a sustained pace attack led by Craig McDermott, who took 6 for 77. Not one New South Wales batsman made a half-century. The young New South Wales fast bowler Wayne Holdsworth led a spirited counter-attack, dismissing two Queenslanders before a run had been scored and finishing with 5 for 71. He was largely responsible for restricting Queensland's lead to 48. Batting again, New South Wales's leading batsmen all failed to make runs, Mark O'Neill being the only player to better 50. New South Wales's total of 211, the same as in the first innings, left Queensland requiring 164 to win. At the start of the final day, Queensland was 0 for 9 and needing only another 155. Then wickets started to fall. The Queenslanders slipped to 5 for 54, rallied briefly, then were all out for 131. In an extraordinary reversal, the home side had won by 32 and given the Queenslanders their first setback of the season. Complaints about several umpires' rulings were reported from the Queensland camp.

New South Wales

First Innings

Batsman	How Out	Ttl	Balls	How Out	Ttl	Balls
SM Small	lbw Rackemann	48	54	b McDermott	2	8
MA Taylor	c Healy b McDermott	46	123	lbw Tazelaar	15	49
TH Bayliss	c Border b Rackemann	6	24	lbw Rackemann	21	42
SR Waugh	lbw McDermott	2	5	c Healy b Rackemann	13	18
ME Waugh	c Healy b McDermott	46	99	c Tazelaar b Rackemann	18	34
MD O'Neill	c Trimble b Rackemann	24	79	b McDermott	69	145
PL Taylor	c Border b McDermott	5	14	c Smart b Rackemann	33	70
PA Emery (+)	not out	11	29	c Cantrell b McDermott	1	53
GF Lawson (c)	c Cantrell b McDermott	0	4	not out	13	14
MR Whitney	retired hurt	0	4	absent injured		
WJ Holdsworth	b McDermott	0	5 (10)	c Healy b Tazelaar	0	14
SUNDRIES: B. 0 LB. 4 W. 0 NB. 9*		23		B. 0 LB. 4 W. 0 NB. 11	26	447
TOTAL		211	440			

F/W: 81 102 113 118 191 191 205 209 211

F/W: 6 46 46 63 88 174 193 198 211

* One leg-bye from a no-ball from McDermott

Bowler	O	M	R	Wkts	NB	W	Bowler	O	M	R	Wkts	NB	W
McDermott	23.5	7	77	6	6	—	McDermott	19	4	65	3	4	—
Tazelaar	15	4	49	—	2	—	Tazelaar	17.5	1	48	2	6	—
Rackemann	20	6	37	3	1	—	Rackemann	17	2	51	4	1	—
Storey	10	—	39	—	—	—	Cantrell	13	4	22	—	—	—
Cantrell	3	1	5	—	—	—	Storey	2	—	16	—	—	—
Overs:	71.5						Border	4	2	5	—	—	—
							Overs:	72.5					

Queensland

Batsman	How Out	Ttl	Balls		How Out	Ttl	Balls
	First Innings				Second Innings		
PE Cantrell	b Holdsworth	0	2	(2)	c Holdsworth b PL Taylor	30	127
RB Kerr	lbw Holdsworth	11	27	(1)	lbw Holdsworth	12	31
CB Smart	c Emery b Holdsworth	0	2		lbw Lawson	3	11
SC Storey	c Bayliss b O'Neill	30	120	(7)	c Emery b PL Taylor	20	55
IA Healy (+)	c Emery b ME Waugh	66	74	(8)	c ME Waugh b PL Taylor	17	22
AR Border	c Emery b Holdsworth	34	72	(4)	lbw Lawson	5	13
GM Ritchie (c)	c Bayliss b PL Taylor	42	107	(5)	c Emery b ME Waugh	7	22
GS Trimble	c Emery b Lawson	11	36	(6)	c (s)SR Waugh b ME Waugh	0	2
CJ McDermott	c MA Taylor b PL Taylor	37	53		c & b Lawson	23	17
D Tazelaar	c Emery b Holdsworth	6	25		c ME Waugh b PL Taylor	1	10
CG Rackemann	not out	0	3		not out	4	8
SUNDRIES:	B. 4 LB. 14 W. 0 NB. 2	22	521		B. 1 LB. 6 W. 0 NB. 1	9	318
TOTAL		259				131	

F/W: 0 0 27 117 117 183 205 223 259 259

F/W: 24 37 43 54 54 83 90 107 115 131

Bowler	O	M	R	Wkts	NB	W	Bowler	O	M	R	Wkts	NB	W
Holdsworth	18.3	—	71	5	—	—	Holdsworth	11	1	40	1	—	—
Lawson	24	10	43	1	—	—	Lawson	12.5	4	21	3	—	—
PL Taylor	22	8	53	2	—	—	ME Waugh	15	5	34	2	1	—
ME Waugh	10	1	31	1	2	—	PL Taylor	14	4	29	4	—	—
O'Neill	12	2	43	1	—	—	Overs:	52.5					
Overs:	86.3												

Umpires: IS Thomas & GE Reed

12th Men: GRJ Matthews (New South Wales) & BP Inwood (Queensland)

Tasmania v Victoria
Launceston Oval, Launceston
Dec 1, 2, 3, 4 1989
Toss: Victoria
Result: Drawn
Points: Tasmania 0 & Victoria 2

On a good batting pitch, both sides exceeded 400 in what developed into a closely contested struggle for first innings points. Victoria batted first and advanced with apparent ease to its big total, thanks largely to adventurous batting by Dean Jones and Simon O'Donnell, both of whom scored centuries. O'Donnell, the Victorian captain, declared an hour before stumps on the second day, apparently in hope of breaking through the Tasmanian batsmen quickly, but it soon became clear the Tasmanians were intent on outlasting and outscoring their opponents. Greg Shipperd played a typically stubborn innings, taking more than eight hours to score 100, and Rod Tucker hit an entertaining century which contained 10 boundaries. At 8 for 408, only 17 runs short of the Victorian total, the Tasmanians seemed likely to attain their goal, but then lost their last two wickets in seven balls. It was a disappointing result for the Tasmanians, who had to bat one man short after their captain, Dirk Wellham, became ill.

Victoria

First Innings

Batsman	How Out	Ttl	Balls		How Out	Ttl	Balls
GM Watts	c O'Connor b Campbell	18	68		c Tucker b Robertson	11	53
ID Frazer	lbw Gilbert	1	3		not out	16	77
WN Phillips	c Cox b Robertson	14	53	(4)	not out	2	11
JD Siddons	c Cox b Robertson	57	100				
DM Jones	b Gilbert	149	257				
SP O'Donnell (c)	c Bennett b De Winter	104	201				
MGD Dimattina (+)	lbw Campbell	19	51				
MG Hughes	c Campbell b De Winter	1	8				
DW Fleming	c O'Connor b Campbell	1	8				
PW Jackson	not out	14	30				
PE McIntyre	not out	15	37	(3)	b De Winter	0	2
SUNDRIES:	B. 4 LB. 4 W. 2 NB. 11	32	816		B. 0 LB. 0 W. 4 NB. 0	4	143
TOTAL	9 wkts dec	425			2 wkts for	33	

F/W: 1 32 48 142 334 392 393 395 395

F/W: 27 28

Bowler	O	M	R	Wkts	NB	W	Bowler	O	M	R	Wkts	NB	W
Gilbert	27	5	87	2	7	—	Gilbert	5	2	6	—	—	—
Campbell	36	7	114	3	2	—	Campbell	3	1	7	—	—	—
Robertson	24	6	66	2	—	—	Robertson	9	4	6	1	—	—
Tucker	22	7	58	—	—	—	De Winter	7	2	14	1	—	4
De Winter	23	4	86	2	2	2	Overs:	24.0					
O'Connor	2	—	6	—	—	—							
Overs:	134.0												

Tasmania

First Innings

Batsman	How Out	Ttl	Balls
RJ Bennett	c Frazer b Jones	47	162
G Shipperd	c Dimattina b Jackson	100	424
J Cox	c McIntyre b Jackson	45	75
RJ Tucker	b Jackson	118	235
DFG O'Connor	lbw McIntyre	5	24
GR Robertson	lbw Fleming	13	40
RE Soule (+)	c Watts b McIntyre	22	34
AJ De Winter	run out	33	58
GD Campbell	lbw O'Donnell	2	28
DR Gilbert	not out	0	2
DM Wellham (c)	absent ill		
SUNDRIES:	B. 10 LB. 10 W. 0 NB. 2	24	1082
TOTAL		409	

F/W: 80 159 268 289 322 357 389 408 409

Bowler	O	M	R	Wkts	NB	W
Hughes	30	8	50	—	—	—
Fleming	25	11	60	1	2	—
Jackson	56	16	103	3	—	—
McIntyre	53	11	130	2	—	—
Jones	7	1	25	1	—	—
O'Donnell	8.3	4	21	1	—	—
Overs:	179.3					

Umpires: SG Randell & DR Close

12th Men: TJ Cooley (Tasmania) & AIC Dodemaide (Victoria)

Victoria v South Australia
Melbourne Cricket Ground, Melbourne
Dec 8, 9, 10, 11 1989
Toss: South Australia
Result: Victoria won by 4 wkts
Points: Victoria 6 & South Australia 0

Victoria won outright on the very last ball of the match, a fitting end to an enthralling contest. Choosing to bat first, South Australia was rescued from early trouble by Darren Lehmann, who came to the crease when his side was 3 for 45 and proceeded to play an outstanding innings. Displaying both great power and delicate touch, Lehmann scored 128 and enabled his team to compile 246. Given a solid start by its opening batsmen, Victoria replied with 293, so South Australia began its second innings 47 behind. At stumps on the third day, South Australia was 3 for 150—103 ahead—and intent on winning outright. But it lost its last seven wickets on the final day for only 76 runs, and Victoria began its second innings needing to score 180 from 53 overs to win. A minor batting collapse reduced Victoria to 5 for 110 and revived South Australian hopes, but Simon O'Donnell, who finished with 50 not out, led the final charge to victory. One consolation for South Australia was the pleasing form of Tim May, who took 5 wickets on his return after months of injury.

South Australia

Batsman	First Innings How Out	Ttl	Balls		Second Innings How Out	Ttl	Balls
GA Bishop	c Siddons b Dodemaide	20	68	(2)	c O'Donnell b McIntyre	69	145
AMJ Hilditch	c O'Donnell b Fleming	3	7	(1)	c Parker b Fleming	14	19
PC Nobes	b Fleming	0	17		c Dimattina b Dodemaide	37	102
DW Hookes (c)	c Watts b O'Donnell	18	32		run out	23	86
DS Lehmann	lbw Dodemaide	128	203		c McIntyre b Reiffel	9	36
PR Sleep	c Parker b Dodemaide	3	20		c Dimattina b Reiffel	13	40
JC Scuderi	c Watts b McIntyre	21	58		run out	33	70
DS Berry (+)	c Dimattina b McIntyre	0	9		c Phillips b Reiffel	17	73
PJS Alley	c Siddons b Dodemaide	0	1	(10)	b Fleming	0	5
TBA May	not out	35	109	(9)	lbw Reiffel	0	11
CR Miller	c O'Donnell b Reiffel	5	32		not out	0	4
SUNDRIES:	B. 2 LB. 7 W. 0 NB. 2	13	556		B. 0 LB. 3 W. 0 NB. 4	11	591
TOTAL		246				226	

F/W: 6 12 45 51 58 124 136 137 222 246

F/W: 19 115 131 151 176 177 224 226 226 226

Bowler	O	M	R	Wkts	NB	W	Bowler	O	M	R	Wkts	NB	W
Reiffel	23.2	7	63	1	1	—	Reiffel	20	4	43	4	2	—
Fleming	14	2	32	2	1	—	Fleming	10.5	2	31	2	—	—
Dodemaide	15	2	54	4	—	—	McIntyre	31	7	77	1	—	—
O'Donnell	15	6	35	1	—	—	Dodemaide	24	4	51	1	1	—
McIntyre	24	9	50	2	—	—	O'Donnell	12	3	21	—	1	—
Phillips	1	—	3	—	—	—	Overs:	97.5					
Overs:	92.2												

Victoria

First Innings				Second Innings		
Batsman	How Out	Ttl	Balls	How Out	Ttl	Balls
GM Watts	lbw Hilditch	55	163	lbw Alley	29	37
ID Frazer	c Berry b May	59	209	c Berry b Scuderi	6	23
WN Phillips	c Bishop b May	5	20	c Alley b Sleep	33	100
JD Siddons	c Nobes b May	14	18	c Bishop b May	33	37
GR Parker	lbw Miller	18	98	lbw May	3	5
SP O'Donnell (c)	c Hilditch b Miller	47	111	not out	50	74
AIC Dodemaide	c & b Sleep	38	75	lbw Miller	7	32
MGD Dimattina (+)	lbw Miller	0	6	not out	8	13
DW Fleming	c Berry b Miller	4	21			
PR Reiffel	not out	19	51			
PE McIntyre	lbw Sleep	4	13			
SUNDRIES: B. 0 LB. 12 W. 0 NB. 9		30	785	B. 0 LB. 5 W. 0 NB. 3	11	321
TOTAL		293		6 wkts for 180		

F/W: 122 135 142 155 219 236 240 258 283 293

F/W: 30 46 103 106 110 142

Bowler	O	M	R	Wkts	NB	W	Bowler	O	M	R	Wkts	NB	W
Alley	13	2	43	—	—	—	Miller	10	2	50	1	—	—
Miller	28	11	59	4	—	—	Scuderi	6	1	21	1	1	—
Scuderi	21	4	54	—	3	—	Alley	6	2	12	1	—	—
May	42	11	89	3	6	—	May	20	4	62	2	2	—
Sleep	18.2	7	30	2	—	—	Sleep	11	—	30	1	—	—
Hilditch	4	3	5	1	—	—	Overs:	53.0					
Hookes	3	2	1	—	—	—							
Overs:	129.2												

Umpires: DW Holt & LJ King

12th Men: PW Jackson (Victoria) & PW Gladigau (South Australia)

New South Wales v Victoria
Lavington Sports Club Ground, Albury
Dec 15, 16, 17, 18 1989
Toss: Victoria
Result: Drawn
Points: New South Wales 2 & Victoria 0

New South Wales seemed sure to win with two hours to go but was denied victory in the end by stubborn Victorian batting. Sent in by the Victorian captain, Simon O'Donnell, New South Wales was dismissed shortly after lunch on the second day for 307. Victoria was on course to pass this total when its tail collapsed after lunch on the third day, the last three wickets falling in the space of seven balls. New South Wales's leading bowler was again young Wayne Holdsworth. Seeing a chance of outright victory, New South Wales stepped up its scoring rate in the second innings. It was 4 for 143 at stumps and declared at 5 for 226 a half-hour before lunch on the final day after Mark Waugh reached his century. The declaration gave Victoria an outside chance of victory—it had at least 69 overs to score 274—but wickets fell rapidly, and just before tea Victoria was 7 for 73. Wayne Phillips was still there, however, and after tea the Victorians held out with great determination for a draw, losing only one more wicket.

New South Wales

First Innings

Batsman	How Out	Ttl	Balls
SM Small	c Siddons b O'Donnell	47	105
GS Milliken	c Dimattina b O'Donnell	19	66
TH Bayliss	c Reiffel b Fleming	47	71
MD O'Neill	c Fleming b McIntyre	47	129
ME Waugh	c O'Donnell b Dodemaide	4	24
BE McNamara	c Parker b O'Donnell	11	63
GRJ Matthews	b O'Donnell	56	175
PL Taylor	c Siddons b Fleming	15	49
PA Emery (+)	b McIntyre	16	69
CF Lawson (c)	c Phillips b McIntyre	14	7
WJ Holdsworth	not out	0	0
SUNDRIES: B. 0 LB. 12 W. 1 NB. 9		31	758
TOTAL		307	

F/W: 64 105 151 167 191 199 241 293 303 307

Second Innings

How Out	Ttl	Balls
b Reiffel	2	6
c Dimattina b Reiffel	10	24
c Watts b Reiffel	56	127
lbw Dodemaide	0	6
not out	100	186
(7) not out	11	20
(6) b Fleming	29	46
B. 0 LB. 3 W. 1 NB. 7	18	415
5 dec for 226		

F/W: 2 34 49 139 197

Bowler	O	M	R	Wkts	NB	W
Reiffel	24	4	67	—	5	—
Fleming	23	8	62	2	4	1
Dodemaide	33	5	68	1	—	—
McIntyre	23.4	5	55	3	—	—
O'Donnell	20	7	38	4	—	—
Siddons	1	—	5	—	—	—
Overs:	124.4					

Bowler	O	M	R	Wkts	NB	W
Reiffel	15	2	62	3	6	—
Fleming	12	3	43	1	—	1
Dodemaide	15.5	3	56	1	1	—
McIntyre	17	3	48	—	—	—
O'Donnell	8	3	14	—	—	—
Overs:	67.5					

Victoria

First Innings

Batsman	How Out	Ttl	Balls
GM Watts	c Emery b O'Neill	50	77
ID Frazer	lbw Lawson	8	39
WN Phillips	st Emery b O'Neill	44	117
JD Siddons	c & b O'Neill	36	35
GR Parker	lbw Holdsworth	29	104
SP O'Donnell (c)	c Waugh b Holdsworth	9	28
PR Reiffel	b Matthews	27	145
AIC Dodemaide	c O'Neill b Holdsworth	27	89
MGD Dimattina (+)	c Small b Holdsworth	14	39
PE McIntyre	run out	0	0
DW Fleming	not out	0	0
SUNDRIES: B. 5 LB. 3 W. 0 NB. 4		16	673
TOTAL		260	

F/W: 25 75 125 154 171 182 234 258 258 260

Second Innings

How Out	Ttl	Balls
c Matthews b Holdsworth	4	8
lbw Matthews	31	80
(7) not out	78	162
c Milliken b Lawson	0	3
(3) lbw Lawson	4	16
(5) c Lawson b Holdsworth	8	18
(9) not out	12	54
(6) lbw Matthews	8	39
(8) b Matthews	0	1
(9) c Waugh b Matthews	11	56
B. 2 LB. 2 W. 1 NB. 0	5	437
8 wkts for 161		

F/W: 5 16 16 35 54 73 73 109

Bowler	O	M	R	Wkts	NB	W
Lawson	19	7	33	1	—	—
Holdsworth	28	7	97	4	—	—
Waugh	15	4	39	—	4	—
O'Neill	30	9	51	3	—	—
Taylor	9	2	13	—	—	—
Matthews	8	3	10	1	—	—
McNamara	3	—	9	—	—	—
Overs:	112.0					

Bowler	O	M	R	Wkts	NB	W
Holdsworth	17	1	57	2	—	—
Lawson	13	3	31	2	—	1
O'Neill	15	3	35	—	—	—
Matthews	18	12	13	4	—	—
Taylor	8	3	20	—	—	—
Waugh	1	—	1	—	—	—
Overs:	72.0					

Umpires: IS Thomas & DR Hair

12th Men: PH Marks (New South Wales) & PW Jackson (Victoria)

Western Australia v South Australia
WACA Ground, Perth
Dec 15, 16, 17, 18 1989
Toss: South Australia
Result: Drawn
Points: Western Australia 2 & South Australia 0

The play was dominated by Geoff Marsh's triple century and his record-breaking partnership with Mike Veletta. Marsh's 355 was a record score for Western Australia and the Veletta-Marsh partnership of 431 was the highest opening partnership in Sheffield Shield history. Ironically, Veletta and Marsh went to the crease at the invitation of the South Australian captain, David Hookes, who had won the toss. At the end of the first day the Western Australians were 0 for 283, and they batted until tea on the second day, declaring then at 3 for 565. Marsh, who had been out of cricket for two weeks with a broken toe, scored his runs off only 545 balls and hit 53 fours and 2 sixes. In pursuit of the huge West Australian total, two South Australians, Paul Nobes and Michael Bevan, scored maiden Sheffield Shield centuries, and at the end of the third day South Australia was 6 for 327, but the innings folded quickly next day. It was then up to South Australia, following on, to bat out the remaining four hours, but Darren Lehmann created some late excitement with a high-powered innings of 48, scored off only 31 balls.

Western Australia

First Innings

Batsman	How Out	Ttl	Balls
MRJ Veletta	c Bishop b Hookes	150	364
GR Marsh	not out	355	545
CD Matthews	b Hookes	2	9
DJ Ramshaw	c Berry b Cladigau	11	33
GM Wood (c)	not out	26	62
WS Andrews	did not bat		
JA Brayshaw	did not bat		
TJ Zoehrer (+)	did not bat		
KH MacLeay	did not bat		
PA Capes	did not bat		
AD Mullally	did not bat		
SUNDRIES: B. 1 LB. 10 W. 0 NB. 5		21	1013
TOTAL	3 wkts dec 565		

F/W: 431 452 489

Bowler	O	M	R	Wkts	NB	W
Gladigau	42	10	126	1	2	—
Miller	28	6	100	—	—	—
Scuderi	31	9	103	—	3	—
May	38	9	126	—	—	—
Hookes	27	5	89	2	—	—
Bevan	2	—	10	—	—	—
Overs:	168.0					

South Australia

First Innings / Second Innings

Batsman	How Out	Ttl	Balls		How Out	Ttl	Balls
GA Bishop	lbw Matthews	22	58	(2)	c & b MacLeay	27	57
AMJ Hilditch	b Capes	20	74	(1)	not out	62	196
DS Berry (+)	lbw Matthews	0	4				
PC Nobes	c Wood b Matthews	124	234	(3)	b Matthews	59	83
DW Hookes (c)	lbw Capes	0	10				
DS Lehmann	b Capes	0	5	(4)	b Matthews	48	31
MG Bevan	c Zoehrer b Mullally	114	282	(5)	b Marsh	2	29
JC Scuderi	c Zoehrer b Capes	38	91	(6)	not out	0	8
TBA May	c Ramshaw b Mullally	15	33				
PW Gladigau	c Brayshaw b Mullally	1	8				
CR Miller	not out	3	1				
SUNDRIES: B. 1 LB. 4 W. 0 NB. 12		29	800		B. 0 LB. 5 W. 0 NB. 2	9	404
TOTAL		366			4 wkts for 207		

F/W: 46 46 59 63 63 284 340 362 363 366

F/W: 50 129 191 207

206

Bowler	O	M	R	Wkts	NB	W
Capes	34	7	109	4	5	—
MacLeay	40	16	77	—	—	—
Matthews	18	3	62	3	4	—
Mullally	20.2	2	83	3	—	—
Brayshaw	8	4	8	—	3	—
Andrews	11	2	22	—	—	—
Overs:	131.2					

Bowler	O	M	R	Wkts	NB	W
Matthews	16	4	42	2	1	—
MacLeay	15	3	40	1	—	—
Brayshaw	5	1	23	—	1	—
Capes	3	—	14	—	—	—
Mullally	12	5	31	—	—	—
Andrews	11	3	47	—	—	—
Zoehrer	3	1	4	—	—	—
Marsh	2	1	1	1	—	—
Overs:	67.0					

Umpires: IS Thomas & DR Hair

12th Men: TG Hogan (Western Australia) & PJS Alley (South Australia)

Queensland v New South Wales
Brisbane Cricket Ground, Brisbane
Dec 29, 30, 31 Jan 1 1990
Toss: New South Wales
Result: Queensland won by 5 wkts
Points: Queensland 6 & New South Wales 2

New South Wales lost the match, but its skipper, Geoff Lawson, won admiration for the enterprising captaincy which prevented the match from ending in a draw. Batting first, New South Wales compiled 367 at the rate of almost a run per minute. Trevor Bayliss, who made 115, and Mark Waugh, who made 60, batted with particular aggression. Queensland was all out for 265 on the third day, 102 behind New South Wales, and the New South Wales batsmen began chasing runs to try to force an outright victory. The price they paid for the haste was a batting collapse in the hour before stumps, which left them at 7 for 146. A Queensland victory had now become a possibility, yet Lawson went ahead with his plan to win outright. He declared next day at 8 for 201, setting Queensland the task of scoring 304 from 76 overs. Led by Rob Kerr, who scored a dashing 123, Queensland performed the feat with time to spare, although Wayne Holdsworth's retirement from the field with a strained side took the edge off the New South Wales attack.

New South Wales

First Innings

Batsman	How Out	Ttl	Balls	How Out	Ttl	Balls
SM Small	c Storey b Rackemann	75	124	c Cantrell b Storey	28	93
GS Milliken	lbw McDermott	1	16	b Rackemann	11	25
TH Bayliss	c Barsby b Cantrell	115	168	c Clifford b Tazelaar	47	62
MD O'Neill	run out	37	91	not out	64	103
ME Waugh	b McDermott	60	68	c Smart b Storey	4	10
BE McNamara	c Cantrell b Storey	18	51	c Anderson b Rackemann	2	15
GRJ Matthews	lbw McDermott	23	38	st Anderson b Storey	13	12
PA Emery (+)	c Kerr b Rackemann	16	34	c Anderson b Storey	2	4
GJ Rowell	c Ritchie b Rackemann	1	8	c Ritchie b McDermott	9	49
GF Lawson (c)	c Clifford b Rackemann	0	3	not out	10	12
WJ Holdsworth	not out	0	4			
SUNDRIES: B. 0 LB. 3 W. 0 NB. 9		21	605	B. 2 LB. 7 W. 0 NB. 1	11	385
TOTAL		367		8 dec for 201		

F/W: 11 167 234 261 312 321 349 357 367 367

F/W: 19 87 100 104 115 132 138 174

207

Bowler	O	M	R	Wkts	NB	W	Bowler	O	M	R	Wkts	NB	W
McDermott	23.2	4	94	3	6	—	McDermott	14	4	54	1	1	—
Tazelaar	20	1	78	—	3	—	Rackemann	21	5	55	2	—	—
Rackemann	25	7	69	4	—	—	Tazelaar	11	2	32	1	—	—
Cantrell	20	6	75	1	—	—	Cantrell	8	—	32	—	—	—
Storey	10	3	41	1	—	—	Storey	10	5	19	4	—	—
Barsby	1	—	7	—	—	—	Overs:	64.0					
Overs:	99.2												

Queensland

	First Innings				Second Innings		
Batsman	How Out	Ttl	Balls		How Out	Ttl	Balls
PE Cantrell	c Waugh b Rowell	17	71	(2)	c Matthews b Lawson	81	138
RB Kerr	c Waugh b Rowell	5	20	(3)	run out	123	192
TJ Barsby	c Milliken b Rowell	6	39	(1)	c Milliken b Lawson	2	19
GM Ritchie (c)	c Emery b O'Neill	44	106		c Emery b Lawson	5	8
PS Clifford	c McNamara b Holdsworth	75	185		b McNamara	28	29
CB Smart	run out	58	219	(7)	not out	6	10
SC Storey	lbw Holdsworth	3	10	(6)	not out	53	42
PW Anderson (+)	c & b Lawson	4	7				
CJ McDermott	b Lawson	0	1				
D Tazelaar	c Waugh b Matthews	28	68				
CG Rackemann	not out	8	22				
SUNDRIES: B. 1 LB. 9 W. 1 NB. 3		17	748		B. 0 LB. 6 W. 1 NB. 0	7	438
TOTAL		265			5 wkts for 305		

F/W: 17 29 32 124 186 192 201 201 246 265
F/W: 9 175 181 224 270

Bowler	O	M	R	Wkts	NB	W	Bowler	O	M	R	Wkts	NB	W
Holdsworth	23	5	72	2	1	—	Holdsworth	10	2	28	—	—	—
Lawson	27	10	43	2	—	—	Lawson	19	3	67	3	—	—
Rowell	23	9	41	3	—	—	Rowell	8	—	45	—	—	1
Matthews	26	8	57	1	—	—	Matthews	21.5	—	98	—	—	—
Waugh	9	2	26	—	2	1	O'Neill	5	—	23	—	—	—
O'Neill	16	7	16	1	—	—	Waugh	5	—	14	—	—	—
Overs:	124.0						McNamara	4	—	24	1	—	—
							Overs:	72.5					

Umpires: CA Bertwistle & AJ McQuillan

12th Men: SG Law (Queensland) & PH Marks (New South Wales)

New South Wales v Western Australia
Sydney Cricket Ground, Sydney
Jan 6, 7, 8, (No play 9) 1990
Toss: Western Australia
Result: Drawn
Points: New South Wales 2 & Western Australia 0

After withstanding several early shocks, Western Australia went on to make 262. Geoff Lawson did the early damage. In his sixth over he had Geoff Marsh lbw for 5—his 300th Sheffield Shield wicket—and two balls later he dismissed Tom Moody without scoring. In his next over, Lawson bowled Graeme Wood for 0, his third wicket in seven deliveries. Western Australia was in deep trouble at 3 for 20, but the opener Mike Veletta, having been dropped earlier, held the innings together with tenacious batting, eventually carrying his bat and making 110. New South Wales looked to be making easy work at first of exceeding the Western Australian total. Given a good start by Mark Taylor (67) and Steve Small (70), it was at one stage 2 for 197 and ended the second day at 5 for 243. But next day it lost its last five wickets for 21 more runs, only just managing to take a first innings lead. Western Australia had made a solid start to its second innings before rain washed out the last day's play.

Western Australia

First Innings

Batsman	How Out	Ttl	Balls
GR Marsh	lbw Lawson	5	34 (2)
MRJ Veletta	not out	110	289 (1)
TM Moody	c Small b Lawson	0	2
GM Wood (c)	b Lawson	0	7
WS Andrews	c MA Taylor b Matthews	34	57
TJ Zoehrer (+)	c & b Matthews	0	14
TG Hogan	c Emery b ME Waugh	18	77
RS Russell	c ME Waugh b Lawson	7	25
PA Capes	c Emery b Stobo	22	73
TM Alderman	c Lawson b ME Waugh	11	16
B Yardley	b Stobo	27	25
SUNDRIES: B. 0 LB. 10 W. 2 NB. 8		28	619
TOTAL		262	

F/W: 16 16 20 78 80 137 150 204 219 262

Second Innings

How Out	Ttl	Balls
not out	36	146
c Emery b Lawson	0	1
not out	66	144
B. 0 LB. 1 W. 1 NB. 1	4	291
1 wkt for 106		

F/W: 0

Bowler	O	M	R	Wkts	NB	W
Lawson	27	12	51	4	1	1
Stobo	22.2	6	73	2	1	—
ME Waugh	11	1	58	2	6	1
PL Taylor	22	11	35	—	—	—
Matthews	20	9	35	2	—	—
Overs:	102.2					

Bowler	O	M	R	Wkts	NB	W
Lawson	14	5	27	1	1	1
Stobo	8	4	11	—	—	—
O'Neill	16	9	28	—	—	—
Matthews	8	1	27	—	—	—
PL Taylor	2	—	12	—	—	—
ME Waugh	0.1	—	0	—	—	—
Overs:	48.1					

New South Wales

First Innings

Batsman	How Out	Ttl	Balls
SM Small	b Hogan	70	124
MA Taylor	c & b Russell	67	146
TH Bayliss	c Russell b Yardley	28	87
SR Waugh	b Hogan	33	40
ME Waugh	b Alderman	31	70
MD O'Neill	c Veletta b Yardley	0	8
GRJ Matthews	not out	16	58
PL Taylor	lbw Alderman	0	4
PA Emery (+)	lbw Alderman	5	38
GF Lawson (c)	b Alderman	0	2
RM Stobo	c Capes b Alderman	0	4
SUNDRIES: B. 3 LB. 10 W. 1 NB. 0		14	581
TOTAL		264	

F/W: 140 150 197 242 242 246 246 264 264 264

Bowler	O	M	R	Wkts	NB	W
Capes	18	5	48	—	—	1
Alderman	26.4	10	62	5	—	—
Russell	15	2	55	1	—	—
Yardley	14	8	37	2	—	—
Hogan	23	5	49	2	—	—
Overs:	96.4					

Umpires: IS Thomas & DR Hair

12th Men: BE McNamara (New South Wales) & AD Mullally (Western Australia)

South Australia v Victoria
Adelaide Oval, Adelaide
Jan 6, 7, 8, 9 1989
Toss: Victoria
Result: Drawn
Points: South Australia 0 & Victoria 2

Adelaide Oval's second Sheffield Shield match produced more heavy scoring. Six of the nine Victorians who batted in the first innings made 50 or more, the highest scorer being Jamie Siddons, who played an entertaining innings of 159 in a little more than five hours. When Victoria declared at 8 for 500, it was the third time in a row that 500 or more had been scored in a completed innings at Adelaide. South Australia made a good start in reply. Andrew Hilditch, who was expected to be twelfth man before David Hookes was injured, batted with determination to make 102. At 2 for 139 he was joined by Darren Lehmann, who at once began a furious assault on the bowling. In an innings which lasted only 141 minutes, Lehmann scored 125 from only 126 balls, hitting 18 fours. But once the Lehmann-Hilditch partnership was broken wickets fell rapidly, and South Australia finished 90 behind. Victoria's early second innings declaration could not prevent the match ending in a draw, and both captains later criticised the docility of the Adelaide pitch.

Victoria

Batsman	How Out	Ttl	Balls		How Out	Ttl	Balls
GM Watts	c Bishop b Miller	0	7		lbw Miller	22	49
ID Frazer	c George b Miller	8	28		run out	47	110
WN Phillips	lbw Scuderi	73	188		lbw Scuderi	14	39
JD Siddons	b Scuderi	159	236	(5)	not out	78	83
DM Jones	c Berry b George	65	75	(6)	not out	49	46
SP O'Donnell (c)	st Berry b May	50	76				
PR Reiffel	c Berry b George	0	11				
AIC Dodemaide	c Lehmann b Sleep	73	162				
MG Hughes	not out	60	71				
MGD Dimattina (+)	did not bat			(4)	b Miller	8	33
PE McIntyre	did not bat						
SUNDRIES: B. 1 LB. 10 W. 1 NB. 0		12	854		B. 0 LB. 4 W. 0 NB. 0	4	360
TOTAL	8 wkts dec 500				4 dec for 222		

F/W: 13 14 221 291 311 313 389 500

F/W: 27 48 73 122

Bowler	O	M	R	Wkts	NB	W	Bowler	O	M	R	Wkts	NB	W
George	27	7	95	2	—	—	George	6	1	33	—	—	—
Miller	35	6	101	2	—	—	Miller	24	6	72	2	—	—
Scuderi	30	7	81	2	—	1	Scuderi	18	3	51	1	—	—
May	34	3	144	1	—	—	Sleep	7	—	41	—	—	—
Sleep	15	1	67	1	—	—	Hilditch	5	—	21	—	—	—
Hilditch	1	—	1	—	—	—	Overs:	60.0					
Overs:	142.0												

South Australia

Batsman	How Out	Ttl	Balls		How Out	Ttl	Balls
GA Bishop	b O'Donnell	35	62	(2)	c Dimattina b Reiffel	3	3
AMJ Hilditch	b Reiffel	102	277	(1)	c Jones b O'Donnell	37	91
PC Nobes	lbw Reiffel	42	58		b O'Donnell	89	74
DS Lehmann	c Siddons b Dodemaide	125	126		run out	22	17
MG Bevan	st Dimattina b McIntyre	6	14		not out	8	64
PR Sleep (c)	lbw Hughes	3	12		not out	16	60
JC Scuderi	c McIntyre b Reiffel	28	31				
DS Berry (+)	b O'Donnell	6	15				
TBA May	not out	18	37				
SPG George	c Siddons b Hughes	0	5				
CR Miller	b Reiffel	13	20				
SUNDRIES: B. 6 LB. 10 W. 0 NB. 8		32	657		B. 2 LB. 3 W. 0 NB. 3	11	309
TOTAL	410				4 wkts for 186		

F/W: 81 139 308 322 333 351 367 377 380 410

F/W: 6 127 152 159

Bowler	O	M	R	Wkts	NB	W	Bowler	O	M	R	Wkts	NB	W
Hughes	26	2	97	2	—	—	Hughes	9	2	36	—	—	—
Reiffel	22.1	1	78	4	4	—	Reiffel	4	—	42	1	3	—
McIntyre	17	3	90	1	—	—	McIntyre	19	3	65	—	—	—
O'Donnell	21	5	58	2	1	—	O'Donnell	17	6	31	2	—	—
Dodemaide	16	4	51	1	3	—	Jones	2	—	7	—	—	—
Jones	6	2	20	—	—	—	Overs:	51.0					
Overs:	108.1												

Umpires: AR Crafter & DJ Harper

12th Men: BD Williams (South Australia) & DW Fleming (Victoria)

Queensland v Western Australia
Brisbane Cricket Ground, Brisbane
Jan 19, 20, 21, 22 1990
Toss: Western Australia
Result: Drawn
Points: Queensland 2 & Western Australia 0

Queensland gained first innings points from a match which failed to develop into an engaging contest. Batting first, the Queenslanders occupied the crease for nearly two days while making 449. The former New South Wales batsman Peter Clifford top-scored with 114, and Chris Smart pushed a catch to short mid-wicket when 2 runs short of a century. Chris Matthews, with 5 wickets, was the most successful of the Western Australian bowlers. The Western Australians never looked likely to bat themselves to a first innings lead. Several of them made promising starts, most notably Tom Moody (59) and Tim Zoehrer (48), but none was able to play the big innings which Western Australia probably needed to pass the Queensland total. At 7 for 227, the Western Australians looked vulnerable, but an innings of 51 by the number 9 batsman Matthews removed the danger of outright defeat, and the final day's play was of little consequence.

Queensland

First Innings

Batsman	How Out	Ttl	Balls		How Out	Ttl	Balls
GI Foley	c Zoehrer b Matthews	37	147	(2)	c Mullally b Matthews	11	40
PE Cantrell	c Veletta b Matthews	69	251	(1)	c Hogan b Capes	6	15
GM Ritchie (c)	c Zoehrer b Russell	15	24	(4)	b Matthews	83	121
RB Kerr	c Veletta b Capes	4	30	(3)	b Hogan	58	139
PS Clifford	c (s)Brayshaw b Matthews	114	230				
CB Smart	c (s)Brayshaw b Matthews	98	302				
SC Storey	c Veletta b Russell	0	1	(5)	not out	11	22
PW Anderson (+)	c Mullally b Hogan	44	58				
CJ McDermott	c Veletta b Mullally	20	20	(6)	not out	6	15
MA Polzin	not out	4	23				
MS Kasprowicz	lbw Matthews	0	1				
SUNDRIES: B. 0 LB. 29 W. 11 NB. 2		44	1087		B. 5 LB. 5 W. 0 NB. 4	18	352
TOTAL		449			4 wkts dec 193		

F/W: 89 109 130 175 323 328 392 421 449 449
F/W: 14 35 171 179

Bowler	O	M	R	Wkts	NB	W	Bowler	O	M	R	Wkts	NB	W
Capes	31	2	86	1	1	—	Capes	10	3	25	1	2	—
Mullally	41	8	104	1	—	9	Matthews	12	2	43	2	1	—
Russell	30	7	72	2	—	1	Mullally	15	3	38	—	—	—
Matthews	40.3	13	72	5	1	1	Hogan	10	1	34	1	—	—
Hogan	30	6	77	1	—	—	Russell	11	3	43	—	1	—
Moody	3	3	0	—	—	—	Overs:	58.0					
Andrews	4	1	9	—	—	—							
Overs:	179.3												

Western Australia

First Innings

Batsman	How Out	Ttl	Balls		How Out	Ttl	Balls
MW McPhee	c Cantrell b Foley	19	80	(2)	not out	35	85
MRJ Veletta	b McDermott	23	85				
TM Moody	lbw Polzin	59	114				
GM Wood (c)	c (s)Law b Polzin	39	78				
WS Andrews	c Anderson b McDermott	31	46	(1)	c Anderson b Polzin	31	48
TJ Zoehrer (+)	c (s)Robinson b Polzin	48	86				
TG Hogan	c (s)Law b McDermott	0	3				
RS Russell	c (s)Robinson b McDermott	6	13	(3)	not out	14	47

Continued

Batsman	How Out	Ttl	Balls	How Out	Ttl	Balls
CD Matthews	b Cantrell	51	74			
PA Capes	not out	15	35			
AD Mullally	did not bat					
SUNDRIES: B. 0 LB. 3 W. 0 NB. 28		59	614	B. 0 LB. 1 W. 0 NB. 0	1	180
TOTAL	9 wkts dec	350		1 wkt for 81		
F/W: 45 71 169 176 213 213 227 297 350				F/W: 74		

Bowler	O	M	R	Wkts	NB	W	Bowler	O	M	R	Wkts	NB	W
McDermott	27	6	97	4	16	—	Ritchie	8	1	26	—	—	—
Polzin	20	3	58	3	—	—	Foley	9	1	29	—	—	—
Kasprowicz	14	2	71	—	—	—	Polzin	7	3	13	1	—	—
Foley	17	7	45	1	3	—	Kasprowicz	6	2	12	—	—	—
Cantrell	8.4	1	36	1	—	—	Overs:	30.0					
Storey	11	—	40	—	—	—							
Overs:	97.4												

Umpires: AJ McQuillan & CD Timmins

12th Men: SG Law (Queensland) & JA Brayshaw (Western Australia)

Tasmania v South Australia
Devonport Oval, Devonport
Jan 19, 20, 21, 22 1990
Toss: Tasmania
Result: South Australia won by 5 wkts
Points: South Australia 6 & Tasmania 0

With hindsight it is clear Tasmania began sliding to defeat when its batting failed on the first day. Tasmania looked for a while as if it might make a sizeable score when, with only two wickets down, Richard Bennett and Rod Tucker took the total past 100, but Bennett was run out when the total was 112, and thereafter wickets fell in steady succession. The South Australians had little trouble advancing past the Tasmanian total, David Hookes making a resounding return to the team with 139. The 6 wickets taken by Dave Gilbert took his tally for the season to an impressive 28. Batting again, the Tasmanians barely improved on their first innings performance. Although five of their first six batsmen reached 20, not one went on to make a half-century, and Tasmania was all out before lunch on the final day. South Australia needed only 121 runs to win but lost 5 wickets scoring them. This was Dirk Wellham's fifteenth Shield match as Tasmanian captain and the first he had lost outright.

Tasmania

First Innings

Batsman	How Out	Ttl	Balls	How Out	Ttl	Balls
RJ Bennett	run out	55	143	c Lehmann b Miller	2	15
G Shipperd	b Miller	4	19	lbw May	21	61
J Cox	b Owen	5	29	c Berry b Scuderi	21	55
RJ Tucker	b May	58	157	c Berry b Owen	49	94
DM Wellham (c)	c Berry b Scuderi	2	7	lbw May	38	119
SG Hookey	c Hookes b May	4	19	lbw Scuderi	47	80
PI Faulkner	c Hookes b Miller	0	13	lbw Miller	12	60
GR Robertson	run out	0	1	b Owen	27	69
RE Soule (+)	b Owen	47	84	st Berry b May	2	22
DR Gilbert	lbw Scuderi	19	63	c Berry b Scuderi	22	31
TJ Cooley	not out	4	9	not out	0	3
SUNDRIES: B. 3 LB. 8 W. 0 NB. 10		31	544	B. 0 LB. 9 W. 0 NB. 11	31	609
TOTAL		229			272	
F/W: 15 36 112 125 142 147 147 152 225 229				F/W: 8 46 48 144 154 216 220 237 272 272		

Bowler	O	M	R	Wkts	NB	W	Bowler	O	M	R	Wkts	NB	W
Miller	16	3	45	2	—	—	Miller	23	7	71	2	—	—
Owen	11	1	30	2	—	—	Owen	18	5	49	2	—	—
Scuderi	25.4	8	55	2	2	—	May	37	11	99	3	7	—
May	33	10	77	2	8	—	Scuderi	23.3	7	44	3	4	—
Hookes	3	1	11	—	—	—	Overs:	101.3					
Overs:	88.4												

South Australia

First Innings

Batsman	How Out	Ttl	Balls	How Out	Ttl	Balls
GA Bishop	lbw Tucker	19	51 (2)	lbw Cooley	3	4
AMJ Hilditch	c Soule b Gilbert	18	74 (1)	lbw Gilbert	26	95
PC Nobes	lbw Robertson	52	97	b Tucker	39	58
DW Hookes (c)	c Tucker b Gilbert	139	246	lbw Tucker	0	2
DS Lehmann	c Soule b Gilbert	34	32	b Tucker	10	29
MG Bevan	lbw Gilbert	0	1	not out	9	23
JC Scuderi	c Soule b Gilbert	1	7	not out	13	35
DS Berry (+)	b Gilbert	38	96			
TBA May	c Wellham b Gilbert	1	14			
CJ Owen	c Faulkner b Robertson	16	69			
CR Miller	not out	3	11			
SUNDRIES: B. 9 LB. 5 W. 0 NB. 23		60	698	B. 1 LB. 6 W. 0 NB. 7 21		246
TOTAL		381		5 wkts for 121		

F/W: 54 74 154 215 215 221 319 331 372 381   F/W: 4 76 76 96 96

Bowler	O	M	R	Wkts	NB	W	Bowler	O	M	R	Wkts	NB	W
Gilbert	33	2	127	7	12	—	Gilbert	13	2	40	1	4	—
Faulkner	17	4	37	—	—	—	Cooley	4	1	16	1	3	—
Cooley	20	2	66	—	11	—	Robertson	7	1	17	—	—	—
Tucker	17	2	56	1	—	—	Tucker	14.5	3	36	3	—	—
Robertson	25.2	7	81	2	—	—	Faulkner	1	—	5	—	—	—
Overs:	112.2						Overs:	39.5					

Umpires: SG Randell & DR Close

12th Men: DFG O'Connor (Tasmania) & SP George (South Australia)

Tasmania v New South Wales
Bellerive Oval, Hobart
Jan 26, 27, 28, 29 1990
Toss: Tasmania
Result: Tasmania won by 4 wkts
Points: Tasmania 6 & New South Wales 0

For the second time in a month the New South Wales captain, Geoff Lawson, gambled on winning outright by making a generous declaration, and for the second time the gamble failed. Tasmania achieved victory on the fifth ball of the last over when Gavin Robertson hit the winning runs. The result was a little hard on New South Wales, which had the better of the contest for most of the four days and, in fact, lost only 9 wickets in the match. New South Wales had declared at 7 for 454 soon after its two century-makers, Steve Waugh (196) and Greg Matthews (117), were out. Waugh's score was the highest of his first-class career. Intent on first innings points, the Tasmanians batted slowly and deliberately, taking 163 overs to make their 456—46 overs more than New South Wales. The outstanding exception was Jamie Cox, who scored a hard-hitting 175. In an attempt to make a match of it, New South Wales declared after rattling up 2 for 220, leaving the Tasmanians to make 219 in 41 overs. Another bright century by Cox enabled them to just do it.

New South Wales

Batsman	How Out	Ttl	Balls	How Out	Ttl	Balls
	First Innings			**Second Innings**		
SM Small	c Soule b McPhee	33	74	c Soule b Robertson	86	135
MA Taylor	b McPhee	16	40	c Bennett b McPhee	19	59
TH Bayliss	c Cooley b Robertson	34	71	not out	75	108
SR Waugh	c Soule b Robertson	196	268	not out	26	43
ME Waugh	c Soule b Gilbert	0	6			
MD O'Neill	c Robertson b McPhee	19	47			
GRJ Matthews	b Robertson	117	199			
PL Taylor	not out	2	3			
PA Emery (+)	not out	0	6			
GF Lawson (c)	did not bat					
WJ Holdsworth	did not bat					
SUNDRIES:	B. 0 LB. 13 W. 0 NB. 12	37	714	B. 0 LB. 8 W. 0 NB. 3	14	345
TOTAL	7 wkts dec	454		2 wkts dec	220	

F/W: 49 72 130 130 181 452 453   F/W: 53 164

Bowler	O	M	R	Wkts	NB	W	Bowler	O	M	R	Wkts	NB	W
Gilbert	30	5	113	1	9	—	Cooley	6	1	23	—	2	—
Cooley	21	2	111	—	3	—	Gilbert	8	2	18	—	—	—
McPhee	20	1	70	3	—	—	McPhee	11	3	29	1	—	—
Robertson	35	4	107	3	—	—	Robertson	20	1	78	1	—	—
Tucker	11	1	40	—	—	—	Tucker	12	—	64	—	1	—
Overs:	117.0						Overs:	57.0					

Tasmania

Batsman	How Out	Ttl	Balls	How Out	Ttl	Balls
	First Innings			**Second Innings**		
RJ Bennett	c ME Waugh b Holdsworth	3	15 (8)	not out	0	1
G Shipperd	lbw Lawson	11	23	b PL Taylor	64	95
J Cox	c Small b PL Taylor	175	372	run out	102	95
RJ Tucker	c Emery b Holdsworth	49	93	b Lawson	2	3
DM Wellham (c)	b O'Neill	90	192	c Emery b Lawson	7	15
SG Hookey	c ME Waugh b PL Taylor	8	44 (1)	c Emery b Holdsworth	4	19
GR Robertson	c Holdsworth b Lawson	47	81	not out	19	13
RE Soule (+)	st Emery b O'Neill	20	58	b ME Waugh	6	6
DR Gilbert	c PL Taylor b Lawson	6	49			
TJ Cooley	not out	17	38			
PT McPhee	not out	5	22			
SUNDRIES:	B. 0 LB. 9 W. 0 NB. 8	25	987	B. 11 LB. 3 W. 1 NB. 0	15	247
TOTAL	9 wkts dec	456		6 wkts for	219	

F/W: 8 22 129 321 359 368 393 431 435   F/W: 23 128 143 189 192 216

Bowler	O	M	R	Wkts	NB	W	Bowler	O	M	R	Wkts	NB	W
Holdsworth	24	—	108	2	2	—	Lawson	13	1	46	2	—	—
Lawson	33.1	9	93	3	2	—	Holdsworth	6	—	27	1	—	—
PL Taylor	37	16	53	2	—	—	PL Taylor	11	—	71	1	—	—
ME Waugh	13	—	48	—	4	—	ME Waugh	6.5	—	42	1	—	—
Matthews	26	6	60	—	—	—	O'Neill	4	—	19	—	—	1
O'Neill	29	11	83	2	—	—	Overs:	40.5					
Bayliss	1	—	2	—	—	—							
Overs:	163.1												

Umpires: SG Randell & BT Knight

12th Men: MG Farrell (Tasmania) & RM Stobo (New South Wales)

South Australia v Western Australia
Adelaide Oval, Adelaide
Jan 26, 27, 28 1990
Toss: Western Australia
Result: South Australia won by an inns & 44 runs
Points: South Australia 6 & Western Australia 0

Even the South Australians were astonished by the scope of Western Australia's defeat. Batting first, South Australia had declared at 8 for 371—a substantial total yet by no means a huge one on the Adelaide pitch. Andrew Hilditch (100) and David Hookes (118) each scored his second century of the month, and Terry Alderman, with 4 wickets, was the most successful Western Australian bowler. The start of the Western Australian innings was delayed by rain, but nothing about the conditions could explain what followed. Having reached 23 without loss, the Western Australians collapsed to be all out for 41—their lowest total since entering the Sheffield Shield competition in 1947-48. Ten wickets fell for 18 runs in 67 minutes, and Joe Scuderi finished with 6 wickets for 6 runs off 4.2 overs. Made to follow-on, Western Australia seemed likely to avoid an innings defeat until the final session on the third day, when its last five batsmen were dismissed for only 24 runs.

South Australia
First Innings

Batsman	How Out	Ttl	Balls
GA Bishop	c & b Alderman	8	28
AMJ Hilditch	c Veletta b Yardley	100	249
PC Nobes	c Zoehrer b Capes	53	108
DW Hookes (c)	c Zoehrer b Alderman	118	151
DS Lehmann	c Zoehrer b Capes	41	64
PR Sleep	lbw Capes	7	16
JC Scuderi	lbw Alderman	2	8
DS Berry (+)	c McPhee b Alderman	0	2
SPG George	not out	16	16
CJ Owen	not out	3	17
CR Miller	did not bat		
SUNDRIES: B. 0 LB. 7 W. 0 NB. 8		23	659
TOTAL	8 wkts dec 371		

F/W: 14 127 277 328 345 352 352 352

Bowler	O	M	R	Wkts	NB	W
Alderman	25.4	5	83	4	4	—
Capes	23	7	69	3	1	—
Matthews	16	3	58	—	2	—
Yardley	29	5	105	1	1	—
Hogan	15	3	49	—	—	—
Overs:	108.4					

Western Australia
First Innings

Batsman	How Out	Ttl	Balls	How Out	Ttl	Balls
MW McPhee	b Scuderi	10	40	b Miller	23	82
MRJ Veletta	c Miller b George	13	40	lbw Miller	7	33
TM Moody	b Scuderi	6	27	lbw Scuderi	49	83
GM Wood (c)	c Berry b Miller	2	7	c Berry b Owen	12	29
WS Andrews	lbw Miller	0	3	b Hookes	89	155
TJ Zoehrer (+)	lbw Scuderi	0	1	lbw Scuderi	6	12
TG Hogan	c Berry b Miller	2	13	c Berry b George	52	117
CD Matthews	b Scuderi	0	5	not out	11	27

Continued

Batsman	How Out	Ttl	Balls	How Out	Ttl	Balls
PA Capes	c Berry b Scuderi	1	9	lbw Miller	0	7
TM Alderman	c Berry b Scuderi	0	2	b Miller	0	6
B Yardley	not out	0	0	b Miller	11	6
SUNDRIES: B. 5 LB. 0 W. 0 NB. 1		7	147	B. 0 LB. 5 W. 1 NB. 10	26	557
TOTAL		41			286	
F/W: 23 29 34 38 38 40 40 40 40 41				F/W: 18 58 83 111 129 262 263 263 268 286		

Bowler	O	M	R	Wkts	NB	W	Bowler	O	M	R	Wkts	NB	W
George	8	2	16	1	1	—	Scuderi	25	6	70	2	5	—
Miller	12	4	14	3			Miller	17	5	44	4	—	—
Scuderi	4.2	1	6	6	—	—	George	18	5	53	2	4	—
Overs:	24.2						Owen	18	2	71	1	1	1
							Sleep	8	—	34	—	1	—
							Hookes	5	1	9	1	—	—
							Overs:	91.0					

Umpires: MG O'Connell & DP Rebbeck

12th Men: MG Bevan (South Australia) & RS Russell (Western Australia)

Queensland v Tasmania
Brisbane Cricket Ground, Brisbane
Feb 2, 3, 4, 5 1990
Toss: Queensland
Result: Drawn
Points: Queensland 2 & Tasmania 0

Rain from a passing cyclone washed out almost five sessions of play on the first two days and produced treacherous batting conditions for both sides. Sent in, Tasmania was struggling at 3 for 69 when rain stopped play on the first day. There was no play next day, and when play was resumed on the third day the Queensland fast bowler Craig McDermott, bowling with considerable speed and hostility, swept through the remainder of Tasmania's batting, finishing with 8 for 44—a personal best in first-class cricket. Queensland's batsmen found the conditions just as difficult, and when their seventh wicket fell for only 85 it seemed Tasmania might yet take first innings points. But an eighth wicket partnership of 24 between McDermott and Steve Storey secured a first innings lead. On the last day, Tasmania batted until 4.40 pm before declaring, leaving Queensland no chance of victory. Scott Hookey of Tasmania hit three sixes in a high-powered innings of 116 not out, one of which cleared the Clem Jones Stand and landed in Stanley Street.

Tasmania

First Innings				Second Innings		
Batsman	How Out	Ttl	Balls	How Out	Ttl	Balls
RJ Bennett	c Ritchie b Polzin	9	32	c Polzin b Foley	44	184
G Shipperd	b McDermott	26	104	c Ritchie b McDermott	11	28
J Cox	c Clifford b McDermott	22	64	c Smart b Kasprowicz	1	24
RJ Tucker	c Anderson b McDermott	17	60	c Anderson b Foley	59	125
DM Wellham (c)	c Storey b McDermott	3	6	not out	28	90
SG Hookey	c Storey b McDermott	6	18	not out	116	110
GR Robertson	c Storey b McDermott	2	11			

Continued

Batsman	How Out	Ttl	Balls	How Out	Ttl	Balls
RE Soule (+)	c Anderson b McDermott	4	14			
GD Campbell	c Anderson b McDermott	3	17			
DR Gilbert	c Ritchie b Kasprowicz	1	12			
PT McPhee	not out	0	1			
SUNDRIES: B. 0 LB. 4 W. 0 NB. 4		12	339	B. 4 LB. 5 W. 0 NB. 3 15		561
TOTAL		105		4 dec for 274		
F/W: 21 58 69 73 83 89 99 102 105 105				F/W: 17 25 126 126		

Bowler	O	M	R	Wkts	NB	W	Bowler	O	M	R	Wkts	NB	W
McDermott	22	8	44	8	3	—	McDermott	21	8	51	1	3	—
Polzin	20	6	35	1	—	—	Polzin	14	5	25	—	—	—
Kasprowicz	8.5	2	14	1	—	—	Kasprowicz	12	4	25	1	—	—
Foley	4	1	8	—	1	—	Cantrell	10	2	25	—	—	—
Cantrell	1	1	0	—	—	—	Storey	22	5	76	—	—	—
Overs:	55.5						Foley	13	2	57	2	—	—
							Ritchie	1	—	6	—	—	—
							Overs:	93.0					

Queensland

First Innings   Second Innings

Batsman	How Out	Ttl	Balls	How Out	Ttl	Balls
GI Foley	c Shipperd b Gilbert	35	104 (2)	not out	1	45
PE Cantrell	c Soule b Campbell	8	34 (1)	not out	6	34
RB Kerr	b McPhee	6	17			
GM Ritchie (c)	c Campbell b Gilbert	11	25			
PS Clifford	c Robertson b Gilbert	4	9			
CB Smart	lbw Gilbert	1	11			
SC Storey	not out	18	40			
PW Anderson (+)	c Hookey b Campbell	5	15			
CJ McDermott	not out	7	12			
MA Polzin	did not bat					
MS Kasprowicz	did not bat					
SUNDRIES: B. 0 LB. 6 W. 0 NB. 4		14	267	B. 0 LB. 1 W. 1 NB. 0 2		79
TOTAL	7 wkts dec	109		0 wkts for 9		
F/W: 11 24 45 53 55 78 85				F/W:		

Bowler	O	M	R	Wkts	NB	W	Bowler	O	M	R	Wkts	NB	W
Gilbert	19	4	46	4	4	—	McPhee	7	5	5	—	—	1
Campbell	12.5	3	24	2	—	—	Robertson	5	4	2	—	—	—
McPhee	12	4	33	1	—	—	Hookey	1	—	1	—	—	—
Overs:	43.5						Overs:	13.0					

Umpires: CA Bertwistle & PD Parker

12th Men: MV Tooley (Queensland) & MG Farrell (Tasmania)

Victoria v New South Wales
Melbourne Cricket Ground, Melbourne
Feb 9, 10, 11, 12 1990
Toss: New South Wales
Result: Drawn
Points: Victoria 0 & New South Wales 2

New South Wales, eager for competition points to ensure a place in the Sheffield Shield final, again failed to gain outright victory after appearing to be in a winning position. Batting first, New South Wales declared late on the second day at 5 for 495. There were two century-makers—Geoff Milliken, one of the season's heaviest scorers in Sydney grade cricket, and Mark Waugh, who batted stylishly for 100 not out. The Victorian attack was without the leg-spinner Peter McIntyre, who unexpectedly had been dropped. At stumps on the second day, Victoria was already reeling at 3 for 74, and on the following day its innings crumbled, Wayne Phillips (62) alone offering resistance. New South Wales thus had four sessions of play in which to bowl out the Victorians and win the match, but in their second innings the Victorians proved much more resolute. Starting the final day at 0 for 64, they held out comfortably until stumps, losing only three wickets. Warren Ayres, who made 134 not out, was at the crease for 431 minutes.

New South Wales

First Innings

Batsman	How Out	Ttl	Balls
SM Small	c Dimattina b Reiffel	6	18
GS Milliken	c Dimattina b McCarthy	151	348
TH Bayliss	c Siddons b Jackson	90	137
MD O'Neill	b Reiffel	70	144
ME Waugh	not out	100	154
GRJ Matthews	b Dodemaide	39	83
PH Marks	not out	2	16
PA Emery (+)	did not bat		
GF Lawson (c)	did not bat		
MR Whitney	did not bat		
WJ Holdsworth	did not bat		
SUNDRIES: B. 6 LB. 15 W. 0 NB. 8		37	900
TOTAL	5 wkts dec 495		
F/W: 22 173 328 371 486			

Bowler	O	M	R	Wkts	NB	W
Reiffel	27.4	1	120	2	7	—
Fleming	23	2	84	—	1	—
Dodemaide	28	6	99	1	—	—
McCarthy	32	7	90	1	—	—
Jackson	38	8	81	1	—	—
Overs:	148.4					

Victoria

Batsman	First Innings How Out	Ttl	Balls		Second Innings How Out	Ttl	Balls
GM Watts	c Emery b Lawson	19	34		c Lawson b Matthews	68	158
ID Frazer	c Marks b Holdsworth	1	14	(4)	c Matthews b Bayliss	61	155
WN Phillips	c Small b Matthews	62	124		lbw Matthews	11	32
JD Siddons (c)	c Holdsworth b Whitney	21	33				
MGD Dimattina (+)	c Waugh b Whitney	5	32				
WG Ayres	c Waugh b Matthews	12	34	(2)	not out	134	361
AIC Dodemaide	c Emery b Whitney	10	74				
RCAM McCarthy	c Marks b O'Neill	28	90				
PR Reiffel	not out	11	69				
DW Fleming	lbw Lawson	11	37				
PW Jackson	c Waugh b Holdsworth	1	8	(5)	not out	0	9
SUNDRIES: B. 0 LB. 1 W. 0 NB. 5		11	549		B. 3 LB. 6 W. 1 NB. 6	23	715
TOTAL		192			3 wkts for 297		
F/W: 20 20 72 86 115 126 156 175 189 192					F/W: 118 148 297		

* 1 no-ball from Waugh was worth 3

Bowler	O	M	R	Wkts	NB	W	Bowler	O	M	R	Wkts	NB	W
Lawson	16	2	45	2	—	—	Holdsworth	4	—	17	—	—	—
Holdsworth	13.4	2	40	2	1	—	Lawson	17	8	25	—	—	1
Waugh	1	—	12	—	—	—	Whitney	18	4	60	—	2	—
Marks	2	—	6	—	1	—	Marks	2	—	10	—	1	—
Whitney	15	5	31	3	3	—	Matthews	38	14	95	2	1	—
Matthews	33	17	45	2	—	—	O'Neill	29	11	66	—	—	—
O'Neill	10	4	12	1	—	—	Bayliss	4	2	7	1	—	—
Overs:	90.4						Waugh	4	2	8	—	2*	—
							Small	2	2	0	—	—	—

Umpires: RC Bailhache & LJ King

12th Men: PE McIntyre (Victoria) & BE McNamara (New South Wales)

Tasmania v Western Australia
Launceston Oval, Launceston
Feb 9, 10, 11, 12 1990
Toss: Tasmania
Result: Tasmania won by 85 runs
Points: Tasmania 6 & Western Australia 0

Bold tactics by both captains enabled the match to develop into an enthralling contest. The Tasmanians batted first on a pitch already showing signs of deteriorating yet ended the first day in a sound position at 4 for 200. Greg Shipperd, who had made 200 not out against Western Australia in their previous match, top-scored again with an undefeated 132. Tasmania's captain, Dirk Wellham, declared next day at 8 for 287, and at stumps Western Australia was 3 for 138. On the third day, the Western Australian captain, Wayne Andrews, gambled on winning outright by declaring at 4 for 229, 58 behind Tasmania, and at first it seemed the gamble had paid off. Tom Hogan took 5 wickets, and Tasmania crashed to 9 for 119 at stumps. On the final day, Tasmania pushed its total up to 143, but that left the Western Australians needing only 202 for victory. At 1 for 70, they seemed on course to win, but after lunch their batting succumbed in startling fashion to the bowling of Dave Gilbert and Greg Campbell, each of whom took 4 wickets. The last wicket fell 17 minutes after tea, giving Tasmania victory by 85 runs.

Tasmania

Batsman	How Out	Ttl	Balls	How Out	Ttl	Balls
	First Innings			Second Innings		
RJ Bennett	b Mack	1	6	c Matthews b Hogan	17	66
G Shipperd	not out	132	405	c Matthews b Hogan	24	76
J Cox	c Zoehrer b Matthews	30	45	b Matthews	6	33
RJ Tucker	c Zoehrer b Mack	12	15	b Hogan	36	55
DM Wellham (c)	c Hogan b Julian	57	157	lbw Matthews	1	9
RE Soule (+)	c Brayshaw b Mack	5	70 (8)	lbw Hogan	3	12
SG Hookey	b Matthews	12	20 (6)	c Zoehrer b Matthews	0	1
GR Robertson	b Hogan	6	8 (7)	not out	33	128
GD Campbell	lbw Matthews	11	23	b Mack	5	10
DR Gilbert	not out	0	6 (11)	b Mack	9	46
PT McPhee	did not bat		(10)	lbw Hogan	3	37
SUNDRIES:	B. 3 LB. 7 W. 1 NB. 5	21	755	B. 2 LB. 2 W. 0 NB. 1	6	473
TOTAL	8 wkts dec 287			143		

F/W: 4 54 75 187 223 247 258 277

F/W: 37 50 50 60 60 96 102 109 118 143

Bowler	O	M	R	Wkts	NB	W	Bowler	O	M	R	Wkts	NB	W
Mullally	20	6	42	—	1	1	Mullally	6	1	17	—	1	—
Mack	28	5	70	3	—	—	Mack	16.5	5	27	2	—	—
Matthews	27	8	56	3	3	—	Hogan	36	16	60	5	—	—
Julian	11	3	30	1	—	—	Matthews	20	8	35	3	—	—
Hogan	27	10	61	1	—	—	Overs:	78.5					
Brayshaw	12	4	18	—	1	—							
Overs:	125.0												

Western Australia

Batsman	How Out	Ttl	Balls	How Out	Ttl	Balls
	First Innings			Second Innings		
MW McPhee	b Robertson	12	53 (2)	lbw Gilbert	37	102
MRJ Veletta	lbw Gilbert	0	6 (1)	c Soule b McPhee	5	14
GM Wood	not out	88	279	not out	47	137
WS Andrews (c)	b McPhee	48	115	c Shipperd b Gilbert	8	9

Continued

219

Batsman	How Out	Ttl	Balls	How Out	Ttl	Balls
JA Brayshaw	c Cox b Tucker	43	115	c Shipperd b Campbell	4	11
BP Julian	not out	6	13	c Soule b Campbell	1	9
TJ Zoehrer	did not bat			b Campbell	1	9
TG Hogan	did not bat			b McPhee	2	6
CD Matthews	did not bat			b Gilbert	0	8
AD Mullally	did not bat			lbw Campbell	0	8
CD Mack	did not bat			lbw Gilbert	0	1
SUNDRIES: B. 11 LB. 12 W. 1 NB. 4		32	581	B. 0 LB. 3 W. 6 NB. 1	11	314
TOTAL	4 wkts dec 229				116	

F/W: 1 36 116 205

F/W: 5 70 80 91 93 101 104 110
113 116

Bowler	O	M	R	Wkts	NB	W	Bowler	O	M	R	Wkts	NB	W
Gilbert	15	4	33	1	1	—	Campbell	15	4	21	4	1	2
Campbell	21	7	36	—	3	1	McPhee	15	5	25	2	—	—
McPhee	19	8	29	1	—	—	Robertson	11	1	37	—	—	—
Robertson	26	2	72	1	—	—	Gilbert	11	1	30	4	—	4
Tucker	15	3	36	1	—	—	Overs:	52.0					
Overs:	96.0												

Umpires: SG Randell & BT Knight

12th Men: MG Farrell (Tasmania) & PA Capes (Western Australia)

New South Wales v South Australia
Sydney Cricket Ground, Sydney
Feb 15, 16, 17, 18 1990
Toss: South Australia
Result: New South Wales won by 10 wkts
Points: New South Wales 6 & South Australia 0

The New South Welshmen at last secured the outright victory they had come close to achieving in several previous matches, and they did it in convincing style. Sent in by the South Australian captain, David Hookes, who apparently judged the wicket to be under-prepared after recent rain, New South Wales scored 376—an innings made memorable by a brilliant century by Mark Waugh. Waugh scored 137 in 3 hours 5 minutes, playing many wonderful attacking strokes, including a huge six off Peter Sleep which nearly hit the clock tower on the Members' Pavilion. Fine bowling by Geoff Lawson and Greg Matthews on the second day restricted the South Australians to a total of 204, thus compelling them to follow on. When bad light stopped play just after tea on the third day, South Australia was 5 for 179 in its second innings, only 7 runs ahead. New South Wales had been frustrated several times before in a quest for victory on the final day, but this time it sealed the match in one session, Lawson finishing with 4 wickets.

New South Wales

First Innings

Second Innings

Batsman	How Out	Ttl	Balls	How Out	Ttl	Balls
SM Small	c Hilditch b Miller	4	19	not out	16	43
GS Milliken	c Plummer b Miller	33	100	not out	15	33
TH Bayliss	lbw George	59	62			
ME Waugh	c Scuderi b Hilditch	137	185			
GRJ Matthews	c Berry b Miller	73	163			
PH Marks	lbw Miller	0	5			
PA Emery (+)	c Berry b George	9	38			
AE Tucker	c Berry b Miller	17	26			

Continued

Batsman	How Out	Ttl	Balls	How Out	Ttl	Balls
GF Lawson (c)	run out	12	24			
RM Stobo	b Miller	3	7			
MR Whitney	not out	0	0			
SUNDRIES: B.3 LB.14 W.0 NB.6		29	629	B.0 LB.0 W.2 NB.1	4	76
TOTAL		376		0 wkts for 35		
F/W: 15 108 116 312 318 337 351 367 376 376				F/W:		

Bowler	O	M	R	Wkts	NB	W	Bowler	O	M	R	Wkts	NB	W
George	25	3	95	2	6	—	George	5	2	16	—	1	—
Miller	28.5	7	83	6	—	—	Miller	5	1	13	—	—	2
Scuderi	21	5	54	—	—	—	Plummer	1.1	—	4	—	—	—
Plummer	11	3	56	—	—	—	Nobes	1	—	2	—	—	—
Hookes	1	1	0	—	—	—	Overs:	12.1					
Sleep	10	1	50	—	—	—							
Hilditch	7	1	21	1	—	—							
Overs:	103.5												

South Australia

First Innings | | | | Second Innings

Batsman	How Out	Ttl	Balls	How Out	Ttl	Balls
AMJ Hilditch	c Emery b Lawson	9	27	run out	51	148
MG Bevan	c Whitney b Matthews	64	173	c Matthews b Marks	7	35
PC Nobes	c Tucker b Lawson	25	60	c Emery b Tucker	18	58
DW Hookes (c)	c Marks b Lawson	10	11	c Whitney b Lawson	20	38
DS Lehmann	c Tucker b Stobo	9	15	c Milliken b Lawson	5	10
PR Sleep	b Matthews	14	28	c Small b Matthews	31	73
JC Scuderi	lbw Matthews	2	12	c Milliken b Lawson	52	85
NR Plummer	not out	29	118	run out	0	5
DS Berry (+)	c Emery b Whitney	27	57	not out	3	4
SP George	b Whitney	0	4 (11)	b Lawson	2	3
CR Miller	c Marks b Whitney	0	8 (10)	lbw Matthews	4	16
SUNDRIES: B.0 LB.9 W.0 NB.3		15	513	B.3 LB.2 W.0 NB.4	13	475
TOTAL		204			206	

F/W: 18 62 74 91 122 136 149 196 196 204

F/W: 29 68 102 104 121 191 196 196 203 206

Bowler	O	M	R	Wkts	NB	W	Bowler	O	M	R	Wkts	NB	W
Lawson	21	10	37	3	—	—	Lawson	13.2	5	26	4	—	—
Whitney	15.1	7	41	3	—	—	Whitney	12	3	37	—	1	—
Stobo	11	1	49	1	3	—	Marks	9	2	24	1	—	—
Waugh	3	—	13	—	—	—	Stobo	5	1	21	—	3	--
Matthews	23	9	27	3	—	—	Tucker	14	3	47	1	—	—
Tucker	12	3	28	—	—	—	Matthews	26	10	46	2	—	—
Overs:	85.1						Overs:	79.2					

Umpires: IS Thomas & DR Hair

12th Men: BE McNamara (New South Wales) & CJ Owen (South Australia)

Western Australia v Queensland
WACA Ground, Perth
Feb 16, 17, 18, 19 1990
Toss:
Result: Western Australia by an inns & 177 runs
Points: Western Australia 6 & Queensland 0

Queensland, the team placed first in the Sheffield Shield competition, was given an unexpected trouncing by Western Australia, the team placed last. The Queenslanders were in trouble at 4 for 75 but went on to compile a first innings total of 273, thanks largely to a determined century by Peter Clifford. In reply, the Western Australian batsmen made runs with remarkable ease. The opener Mark McPhee batted so aggressively on the second day that he scored 101 runs between lunch and tea. McPhee was out after tea for 113, but Mike Veletta pressed on, and at stumps the Western Australians were 1 for 286. Next day, Veletta was out eventually for 228 and Wayne Andrews for 92, and Western Australia declared at 8 for 607. Queensland began the last day at 2 for 34 in its second innings, apparently determined to hold out for a draw. But its batsmen yielded rather tamely, and Queensland lost its last 8 wickets for 123 runs in just over three hours. Thus, Western Australia had won by an innings and 177 runs—its first outright win of the season.

Queensland

Batsman	First Innings How Out	Ttl	Balls		Second Innings How Out	Ttl	Balls
PE Cantrell	c Veletta b MacLeay	10	39	(2)	lbw Matthews	8	79
GI Foley	c McPhee b MacLeay	24	60	(1)	c Zoehrer b Capes	4	13
RB Kerr	c Zoehrer b Mack	10	51		c Zoehrer b MacLeay	13	55
GM Ritchie (c)	c Zoehrer b Capes	22	54		lbw Matthews	1	6
PS Clifford	c Zoehrer b Matthews	109	234		c Zoehrer b MacLeay	21	41
MV Tooley	c Andrew b Mack	31	99	(8)	not out	17	84
SC Storey	lbw Matthews	20	79	(6)	c Veletta b Capes	6	51
PW Anderson (+)	b Mack	7	22	(7)	lbw MacLeay	0	9
MA Polzin	b Matthews	28	46		c McPhee b Capes	0	4
PJ Carew	c Julian b MacLeay	0	9		b Matthews	23	37
MS Kasprowicz	not out	0	0		c Zoehrer b Julian	49	67
SUNDRIES:	B. 1 LB. 7 W. 0 NB. 2	12	693		B. 1 LB. 6 W. 2 NB. 3	15	446
TOTAL		273				157	

F/W: 33 40 55 75 151 200 219 273 273 273
F/W: 5 34 34 43 63 65 67 67 97 157

Bowler	O	M	R	Wkts	NB	W	Bowler	O	M	R	Wkts	NB	W
Capes	26	7	74	1	1	—	Mack	16	8	25	—	—	1
Mack	28	9	81	3	—	—	Capes	16	6	32	3	2	1
Matthews	22	8	49	3	—	—	Matthews	18	4	54	3	—	—
MacLeay	24.4	10	38	3	—	—	MacLeay	16	5	22	3	1	—
Julian	4	1	13	—	1	—	Andrews	5	1	10	—	—	—
Andrews	8	4	10	—	—	—	Julian	2.3	1	7	1	—	—
Brayshaw	3	3	0	—	—	—	Overs:	73.3					
Overs:	115.4												

Western Australia

Batsman	First Innings How Out	Ttl	Balls	Second Innings How Out	Ttl	Balls
MW McPhee	st Anderson b Storey	113	135			
MRJ Veletta	c Ritchie b Polzin	228	333			
DJ Ramshaw	c Ritchie b Carew	44	151			
WS Andrews (c)	c Anderson b Polzin	92	114			
JA Brayshaw	run out	2	10			
BP Julian	c Ritchie b Polzin	9	13			
TJ Zoehrer (+)	c Anderson b Polzin	34	29			
KH MacLeay	not out	18	21			
CD Matthews	c Ritchie b Carew	40	23			
PA Capes	not out	1	2			
CD Mack	did not bat					
SUNDRIES:	B. 1 LB. 11 W. 8 NB. 3	26	831			
TOTAL		8 wkts dec 607				

F/W: 188 347 460 470 481 541 548

Bowler	O	M	R	Wkts	NB	W	Bowler	O	M	R	Wkts	NB	W
Kasprowicz	24.5	4	115	—	3	1							
Polzin	37	4	133	4	—	5							
Carew	42	8	181	2	—	1							
Foley	17	2	68	—	—	1							
Cantrell	7	—	39	—	—	—							
Storey	8	2	49	1	—	—							
Ritchie	1	—	10	—	—	—							
Overs:	136.5												

Umpires: TA Prue & RJ Evans

12th Men: TG Hogan (Western Australia) & CB Smart (Queensland)

Victoria v Queensland
Melbourne Cricket Ground, Melbourne
Mar 2, 3, 4, 5 1990
Toss: Queensland
Result: Drawn
Points: Victoria 0 & Queensland 2

A reversal in fortunes on the last day deprived Queensland of the victory which would have ensured it a place in the Sheffield Shield final. Sent in to bat on a damp pitch, the Victorians began strongly and were 2 for 184 a few minutes before tea, when Warren Ayres was run out for 93. His dismissal was followed after tea by a rapid batting collapse, and Victoria was all out next morning for 272. Queensland passed this total comfortably, its captain, Greg Ritchie, batting soundly for 167 not out, his highest Shield score. After declaring at 4 for 358, the Queenslanders quickly broke through the Victorian top order, and at the start of the last day Victoria was 97 ahead with 5 wickets left. But the Queenslanders were frustrated by determined batting by David Harris (90) and Tony Dodemaide (54), and Victoria eventually made 285, which meant the Queenslanders had to score 200 in 49 overs to win. The Queensland medium-pacer Michael Polzin took 8 for 51. In a scramble for runs, four Queenslanders were run out, and at the end Queensland was just 5 runs short of the victory target—and just one wicket from defeat.

Victoria

Batsman	How Out	Ttl	Balls	How Out	Ttl	Balls
	First Innings			Second Innings		
GM Watts (c)	c Tazelaar b McDermott	41	76	c Ritchie b McDermott	24	44
WG Ayres	run out	93	192	c McDermott b Polzin	23	61
WN Phillips	c Cantrell b Tazelaar	5	22	c Drinnen b Polzin	15	34
CE Bradley	c Foley b McDermott	46	106	c Drinnen b Polzin	0	2
SS Prescott	c Cantrell b McDermott	8	16	c Drinnen b Polzin	9	27
DA Harris	b Cantrell	30	57	lbw Polzin	90	218
AIC Dodemaide	lbw McDermott	16	50	b McDermott	54	187
RCAM McCarthy	b Tazelaar	0	7	c Ritchie b Polzin	1	15
PR Reiffel	c Drinnen b Tazelaar	1	34	c Clifford b Polzin	0	1
MGD Dimattina (+)	b McDermott	9	30	c Ritchie b Polzin	13	32
PE McIntyre	not out	0	0	not out	6	32
SUNDRIES:	B. 0 LB. 6 W. 1 NB. 8	23	590	B. 5 LB. 12 W. 1 NB. 16	50	653
TOTAL		272			285	

F/W: 87 94 184 207 208 256 257 257 268 272

F/W: 66 72 72 89 94 262 265 265 266 285

Bowler	O	M	R	Wkts	NB	W	Bowler	O	M	R	Wkts	NB	W
McDermott	27	5	99	5	2	—	McDermott	30	7	83	2	8	1
Tazelaar	19	9	32	3	4	—	Tazelaar	15	3	48	—	4	—
Polzin	9	2	21	—	—	1	Polzin	25.2	12	51	8	—	—
Storey	6	1	36	—	1	—	Cantrell	19	4	43	—	1	—
Foley	15	5	25	—	1	—	Foley	9	6	13	—	2	—
Cantrell	21	6	53	1	—	—	Storey	8	2	30	—	1	—
Overs:	97.0						Overs:	106.2					

Queensland

Batsman	How Out	Ttl	Balls	How Out	Ttl	Balls
	First Innings			Second Innings		
TJ Barsby	lbw Reiffel	28	67 (2)	b Reiffel	0	5
PE Cantrell	c Bradley b McCarthy	25	36 (1)	run out	53	80
GM Ritchie (c)	not out	167	320	b Reiffel	0	2

Continued

223

Batsman	How Out	Ttl	Balls	How Out	Ttl	Balls
GI Foley	c McIntyre b Dodemaide	34	123	run out	18	48
PS Clifford	b Reiffel	8	6	b McCarthy	14	32
SG Law	not out	66	110	c Dimattina b Dodemaide	25	33
SC Storey	did not bat			run out	22	41
PJ Drinnen (+)	did not bat			c Dimattina b McCarthy	0	5
CJ McDermott	did not bat			run out	33	36
D Tazelaar	did not bat			not out	0	1
MA Polzin	did not bat			not out	7	13
SUNDRIES: B. 4 LB. 10 W. 0 NB. 8		30	662	B. 1 LB. 18 W. 0 NB. 2	23	296
TOTAL	4 wkts dec 358			9 wkts for 195		
F/W: 45 81 162 179				F/W: 7 7 70 81 107 125 128 177 195		

Bowler	O	M	R	Wkts	NB	W	Bowler	O	M	R	Wkts	NB	W
Reiffel	24	3	94	2	2	—	Reiffel	10	2	43	2	1	—
McCarthy	27	6	81	1	1	—	Dodemaide	15	2	61	1	—	—
Dodemaide	26	5	79	1	5	—	McCarthy	15	2	43	2	1	—
McIntyre	29	8	83	—	—	—	McIntyre	9	1	29	—	—	—
Phillips	3	1	7	—	—	—	Overs:	49.0					
Overs:	109.0												

Umpires: DW Holt & WP Sheahan

12th Men: DW Fleming (Victoria) & MS Kasprowicz (Queensland)

South Australia v Tasmania
Adelaide Oval, Adelaide
Mar 2, 3, 4, 5 1990
Toss: Tasmania
Result: South Australia by 127 runs
Points: South Australia 6 & Tasmania 0

South Australia outplayed Tasmania generally to gain its third outright victory in four matches. Batting first, the South Australians felt confident enough to declare at 5 for 291 at the end of the first day. Andrew Hilditch played a dogged innings of 103 not out against a Tasmanian attack weakened by the absence of its leading wicket-taker, Dave Gilbert, who was injured. After a bad start, Tasmania recovered to be 5 for 191, but then lost its last 5 wickets for 34 to trail South Australia by 66. Seeking outright victory, the South Australians batted adventurously in their second innings and raced past 200 with the loss of only 3 wickets. Michael Bevan made 88, and Darren Lehmann 63 off 65 balls. After losing 6 wickets in 9 overs, South Australia declared in the last hour of play on the third day, setting Tasmania a target of 351 to win. It was a total Tasmania never looked likely to achieve, although Rod Tucker, who had top-scored in the first innings with 71, delayed the South Australian victory with a determined 67.

South Australia

First Innings | | | | Second Innings

Batsman	How Out	Ttl	Balls	How Out	Ttl	Balls
AMJ Hilditch	not out	103	262	lbw McPhee	2	18
MG Bevan	c Cooley b Tucker	35	65	c Robertson b McPhee	88	236
PC Nobes	c Robertson b McPhee	29	77	c Shipperd b De Winter	33	58
DW Hookes (c)	lbw De Winter	27	49	c Cooley b McPhee	38	77
DS Lehmann	lbw Cooley	9	26	b Tucker	63	65

Continued

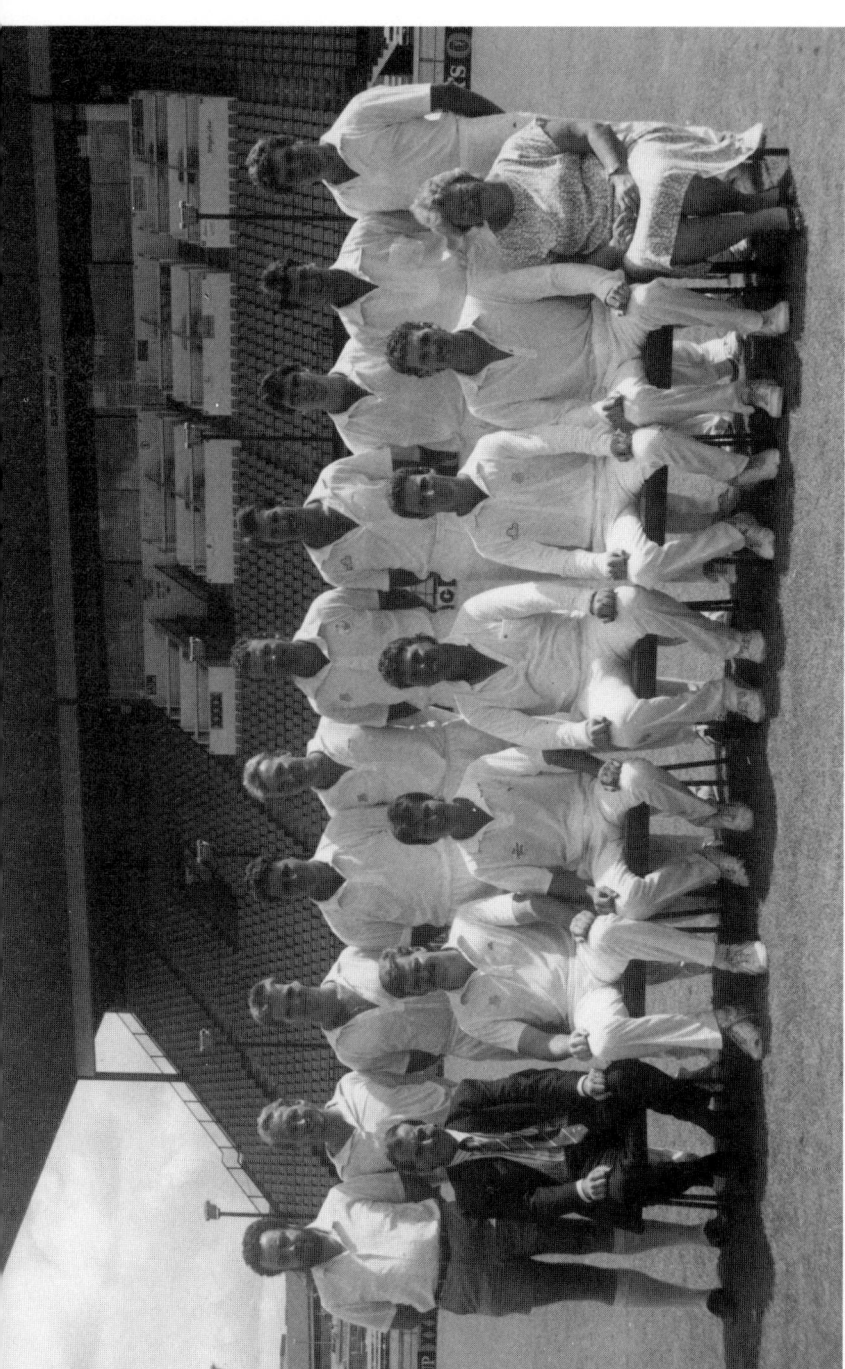

1st GRADE PREMIERS – EASTERN SUBURBS, BRISBANE

Back Row, l to r: John Thorburn (Scorer), Wayne Hayes, Ian Stenhouse, Evan Bancroft, Frank Shelley, Brian Brix, Gerry Rowan, Greg Ellis, Kent Waddell, Stephen Storey. Front Row, l to r: John Salter (President), Paul Stenhouse, Craig Jesberg, Greg Ritchie, Mal Freeman, Peter Anderson, Jean Holdway (Secretary)

A GRADE PREMIERS – STURT, ADELAIDE

Standing, l to r: M Weatherald (Coaching Co-ordinator), J Brooks, P Judd,
S Howard, J Bolton, A Meinel, S Cunningham, G McGuire, D Ritossa, D King,
J Orchard, M Barrington (Manager), D Howard (Secretary/Scorer),
I Carmichael, Seated, l to r: A Carver, R Phillips (Coach), D Scott, W Hayes
(President), W Phillips (Captain), R McGuire (Chairman), C Miller, N Clarke

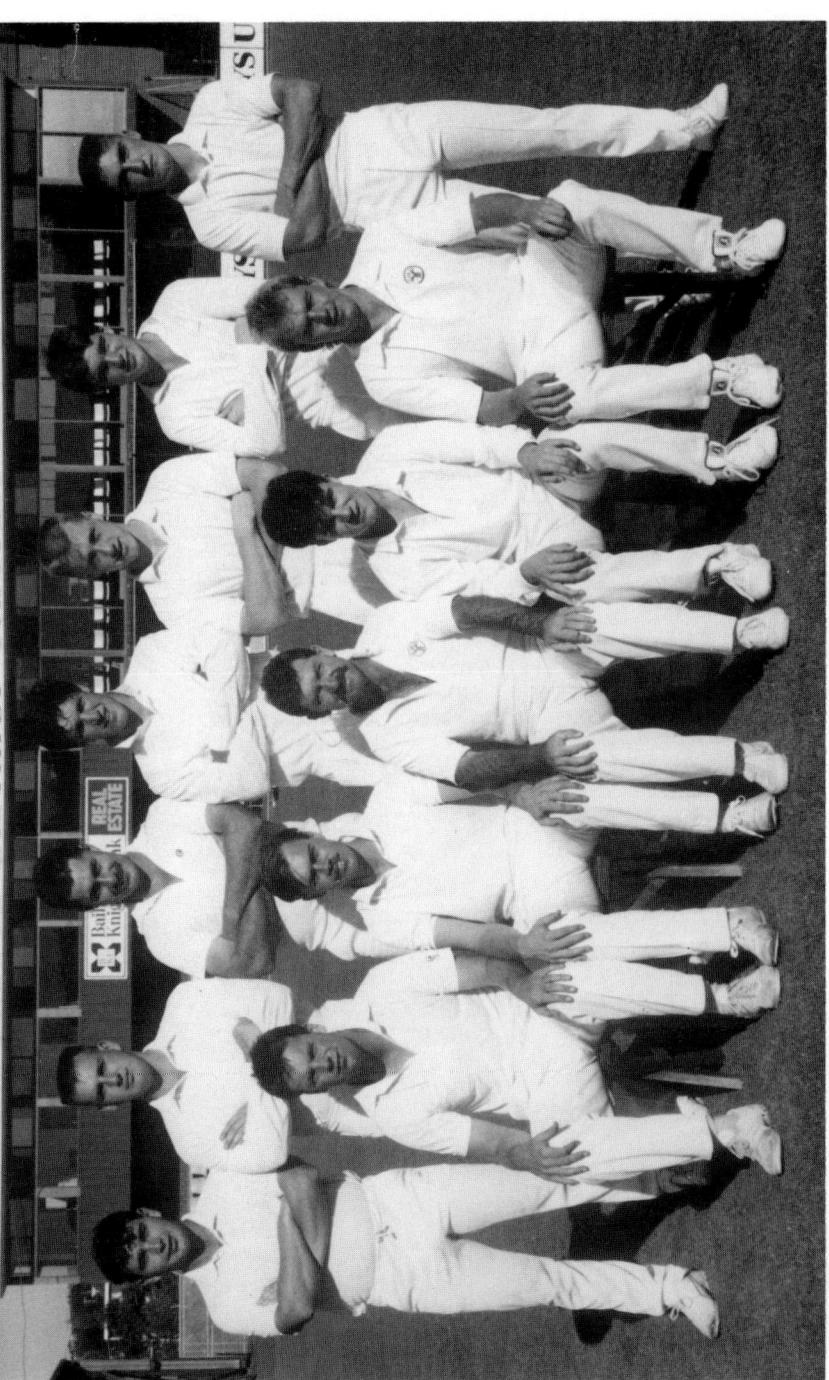

1st GRADE PREMIERS – CLARENCE, HOBART

Back Row, l to r: S Brown, A de Winter, P McPhee, M Colegrave, A Dykes, M Lee, G Cooney. Front Row, l to r: B Patterson, P Schofield, G Shipperd (Captain), D Hurd, G Campbell

NWTCA PREMIERS – SHEFFIELD

Back Row, l to r: Dion Smith, Gary Spillane, Tony Brown, Craig Boutcher, John Stevenson, Terence Sharman, Tom Howett (Scorer). Front Row, l to r: Shane Wootton, Warren Hegg, Baden Sharman, Jason Maddox, Tim Irvine.

Batsman	How Out	Ttl	Balls	How Out	Ttl	Balls
JC Scuderi	c Bennett b Tucker	40	62	b Tucker	2	10
PR Sleep	not out	23	49	c Robertson b McPhee	7	13
DS Berry (+)	did not bat			lbw McPhee	1	3
CR Miller	did not bat			not out	5	15
CJ Owen	did not bat			run out	0	5
SPG George	did not bat			not out	7	8
SUNDRIES: B. 3 LB. 5 W. 9 NB. 4		25	590	B. 7 LB. 12 W. 1 NB. 9	38	508
TOTAL	5 wkts dec 291			9 wkts dec 284		
F/W: 62 117 155 180 229				F/W: 8 79 141 245 253 270 272 273 273		

Bowler	O	M	R	Wkts	NB	W	Bowler	O	M	R	Wkts	NB	W
McPhee	29	11	66	1	1	3	McPhee	26	7	73	5	1	—
Cooley	16	3	62	1	3	—	Cooley	16	2	74	—	7	—
Tucker	14	4	40	2	—	—	Robertson	20	6	46	—	—	—
De Winter	12	1	42	1	—	6	De Winter	8	3	24	1	1	1
Robertson	25	4	67	—	—	—	Tucker	13	1	48	2	—	—
Cox	1	—	6	—	—	—	Overs:	83.0					
Overs:	97.0												

Tasmania

First Innings | Second Innings

Batsman	How Out	Ttl	Balls	How Out	Ttl	Balls
RJ Bennett	lbw Miller	1	5	lbw Miller	14	48
G Shipperd	c Bevan b Owen	15	40	lbw Owen	36	97
J Cox	lbw George	3	5	lbw Scuderi	19	55
RJ Tucker	c Berry b Miller	71	131	b Miller	67	171
DM Wellham (c)	b George	21	70	c & b Scuderi	4	16
SG Hookey	lbw Owen	42	82	c Berry b Scuderi	0	3
GR Robertson	b Scuderi	30	99	c Nobes b Scuderi	24	47
RE Soule (+)	c George b Scuderi	12	45	b Miller	0	11
AJ De Winter	c Nobes b Scuderi	2	8	c Owen b Sleep	30	50
TJ Cooley	c Hilditch b Sleep	9	18	b Owen	4	12
PT McPhee	not out	2	9	not out	5	39
SUNDRIES: B. 0 LB. 5 W. 0 NB. 6		17	512	B. 7 LB. 3 W. 0 NB. 5	20	549
TOTAL		225			223	
F/W: 3 6 43 121 121 191 200 204 221 225				F/W: 27 69 83 90 92 124 137 191 199 223		

Bowler	O	M	R	Wkts	NB	W	Bowler	O	M	R	Wkts	NB	W
George	16	3	53	2	4	—	George	14	2	37	—	2	—
Miller	18	5	40	2	—	—	Miller	22.2	6	59	3	—	—
Owen	18	6	38	2	—	—	Sleep	13	5	29	1	—	—
Scuderi	15.2	2	45	3	2	—	Scuderi	21	8	48	4	3	—
Hookes	1	1	0	—	—	—	Owen	16	6	28	2	—	—
Sleep	16	4	44	1	—	—	Hookes	5	2	12	—	—	—
Overs:	84.2						Overs:	91.2					

Umpires: AR Crafter & DJ Harper

12th Men: GA Bishop (South Australia) & MG Farrell (Tasmania)

Western Australia v New South Wales
WACA Ground, Perth
Mar 2, 3, 4, 5 1990
Toss: New South Wales
Result: Western Australia won by 156 runs
Points: Western Australia 6 & New South Wales 0

Sent in, Western Australia's batsmen denied New South Wales's pace bowlers the early wickets they were hoping for and went on to make 317. It was a solid batting performance, in which eight players scored 20 or more. New South Wales made a bright start, bringing up 50 in better than even time, but then fast bowler Chris Matthews single-handedly broke the back of the innings. Bowling with impressive speed, Matthews took six consecutive wickets in the space of 75 deliveries. Trevor Bayliss survived, however, and went on to make 101 in just over three hours. Behind by 81 on the first innings, New South Wales got back into the match by dismissing the Western Australians for 247, Geoff Lawson providing the early breakthroughs. New South Wales thus needed to make 329 to win, and it began the last day at 0 for 5. But Geoff Milliken was dismissed almost at once, which set a pattern for the day. Peter Capes took 4 for 60 as the Western Australian bowlers swept through New South Wales in just over three hours.

Western Australia

First Innings

Batsman	How Out	Ttl	Balls		How Out	Ttl	Balls
MRJ Veletta	c Waugh b Matthews	45	91	(2)	c Emery b Lawson	5	15
MW McPhee	c Matthews b Lawson	32	96	(1)	c Emery b Lawson	11	33
TM Moody	c Matthews b Lawson	63	133		c Emery b Lawson	0	1
WS Andrews (c)	b Matthews	21	45		b Waugh	59	128
JA Brayshaw	b Matthews	29	83		c Whitney b Waugh	69	153
DJ Ramshaw	c Emery b Lawson	5	26		lbw Whitney	1	13
TJ Zoehrer (+)	c Stobo b Lawson	8	18		run out	31	69
KH MacLeay	not out	53	110		c Waugh b Matthews	27	46
CD Matthews	c Emery b Stobo	41	89		c O'Neill b Whitney	10	32
PA Capes	c Emery b Matthews	0	6		c Stobo b Matthews	7	21
CD Mack	c Waugh b Matthews	0	4		not out	1	1
SUNDRIES: B. 0 LB. 5 W. 5 NB. 5		20	701		B. 5 LB. 5 W. 2 NB. 7	26	512
TOTAL		317				247	

F/W: 86 88 131 195 205 209 220 314 315 317

F/W: 13 13 22 146 155 159 214 227 244 247

Bowler	O	M	R	Wkts	NB	W	Bowler	O	M	R	Wkts	NB	W
Lawson	29	5	69	4	—	1	Lawson	15	3	32	3	—	—
Whitney	23	5	90	—	1	—	Whitney	18.4	4	56	2	1	—
Stobo	17	2	58	1	3	4	Stobo	12	1	47	—	2	2
Marks	8	2	23	—	1	—	Waugh	13	1	55	2	4	—
Matthews	37.4	14	70	5	—	—	Matthews	25	10	47	2	—	—
O'Neill	1	—	2	—	—	—	Overs:	83.4					
Overs:	115.4												

New South Wales

First Innings

Batsman	How Out	Ttl	Balls	How Out	Ttl	Balls
SM Small	c Moody b Capes	32	39	c Andrews b MacLeay	24	62
GS Milliken	c Zoehrer b Matthews	18	51	c Veletta b Capes	2	10
TH Bayliss	b MacLeay	101	146	c Zoehrer b Matthews	35	43
MD O'Neill	c MacLeay b Matthews	19	26	c Andrews b Mack	50	53
ME Waugh	c Veletta b Matthews	5	8	c Zoehrer b Capes	11	22
GRJ Matthews	c Zoehrer b Matthews	22	41	c Zoehrer b MacLeay	4	15
PH Marks	lbw Matthews	0	1	c Moody b Capes	5	36
PA Emery (+)	c Moody b Matthews	5	16	c Veletta b Capes	4	35
GF Lawson (c)	c Andrews b MacLeay	10	23	st Zoehrer b Andrews	17	27
MR Whitney	not out	1	3	st Zoehrer b Moody	0	2
WJ Holdsworth	c Veletta b MacLeay	0	3	not out	0	5
SUNDRIES: B. 0 LB. 3 W. 5 NB. 7		23	357	B. 1 LB. 5 W. 2 NB. 6	20	310
TOTAL		236			172	

F/W: 52 74 106 112 154 154 166 231 236 236

F/W: 7 71 71 83 104 147 147 172 172 172

Bowler	O	M	R	Wkts	NB	W	Bowler	O	M	R	Wkts	NB	W
Capes	11	1	52	1	4	—	Capes	15	2	60	4	5	—
Matthews	21	4	81	6	—	4	Mack	13	1	46	1	—	2
Mack	12	—	39	—	1	1	Matthews	10	2	41	1	—	—
MacLeay	14	4	61	3	2	—	MacLeay	8	3	18	2	1	—
Overs:	58.0						Andrews	4	3	1	1	—	—
Note: 1 no-ball was worth 3							Moody	0.2	—	0	1	—	—
							Overs:	50.2					

Umpires: RA Emerson & RJ Evans

12th Men: BP Julian (Western Australia) & AE Tucker (New South Wales)

New South Wales v Tasmania
Sydney Cricket Ground, Sydney
Mar 9, 10, 11 1990
Toss: Tasmania
Result: New South Wales by an inns & 156 runs
Points: New South Wales 6 & Tasmania 0

This match was crucial to New South Wales's chances in the Sheffield Shield competition, and New South Wales could hardly have won it more convincingly. The Tasmanians were unable to cope with New South Wales's spinners on a Sydney wicket which turned on the first day, and they were all out in less than three hours for 117. The young leg-spin bowler Adrian Tucker took 4 wickets and Greg Matthews 3. Tasmania's bowlers struck back on the first day, and at one stage New South Wales was 3 for 33, but a superb innings of 198 not out by Mark Waugh, supported by Mark O'Neill (71) and Phil Emery (81), transformed the match. Waugh faced only 390 balls, and he and Emery put on 224 between them, a record for the sixth wicket in New South Wales-Tasmanian Sheffield Shield matches. Waugh was 198 not out at stumps on the second day, but because showers were possible his captain, Geoff Lawson, did not risk batting on to let him make 200 and declared at the overnight score, 6 for 430. Tasmania again fell victim to spin on a turning wicket and was all out at 3.03 pm, Matthews having taken 7 for 50. Michael Farrell, making his debut for Tasmania, provided lone resistance, scoring 96.

Tasmania

Batsman	How Out (First Innings)	Ttl	Balls	How Out (Second Innings)	Ttl	Balls
MG Farrell	c Whitney b Lawson	5	22	b Matthews	96	169
G Shipperd	b Whitney	1	12	lbw Holdsworth	0	5
J Cox	lbw Holdsworth	10	23	c Emery b Matthews	4	48
RJ Tucker	b Tucker	37	75	c Holdsworth b Matthews	5	9
DM Wellham (c)	lbw Tucker	27	52	c Bayliss b Matthews	0	9
SG Hookey	c Milliken b Matthews	19	26	c Waugh b Matthews	0	5
GR Robertson	c Small b Matthews	0	18	c & b Matthews	10	30
RE Soule (+)	b Matthews	4	14	c Whitney b Tucker	2	23
DR Gilbert	c Emery b Tucker	9	11	not out	23	59
TJ Cooley	not out	0	0	c Whitney b Matthews	8	12
PT McPhee	c Bayliss b Tucker	0	1	b O'Neill	0	13
SUNDRIES:	B. 0 LB. 1 W. 0 NB. 2	5	254	B. 4 LB. 5 W. 0 NB. 0	9	382
TOTAL		117			157	

F/W: 4 12 32 82 95 103 104 113 117 117

F/W: 2 33 41 49 77 106 130 146 157 157

Bowler	O	M	R	Wkts	NB	W	Bowler	O	M	R	Wkts	NB	W
Lawson	6	2	10	1	—	—	Whitney	7	4	8	—	—	—
Whitney	9	3	26	1	2	—	Holdsworth	7	5	24	1	—	—
Holdsworth	6	1	29	1	—	—	Matthews	25	12	50	7	—	—
Matthews	12	3	26	3	—	—	Tucker	19	6	51	1	—	—
Tucker	9.5	4	25	4	—	—	O'Neill	5.5	1	15	1	—	—
Overs:	42.5						Overs:	63.5					

New South Wales

First Innings

Batsman	How Out	Ttl	Balls
SM Small	lbw Gilbert	0	11
GS Milliken	c Cox b McPhee	0	4
TH Bayliss	b Robertson	20	50
MD O'Neill	run out	71	167
ME Waugh	not out	198	390
GRJ Matthews	lbw Gilbert	5	9
PA Emery (+)	lbw McPhee	81	245
AE Tucker	not out	18	25
GF Lawson (c)	did not bat		
MR Whitney	did not bat		
WJ Holdsworth	did not bat		
SUNDRIES: B. 1 LB. 14 W. 0 NB. 11		37	901
TOTAL	6 wkts dec 430		

F/W: 2 4 33 155 161 385

Bowler	O	M	R	Wkts	NB	W
Gilbert	32	7	96	2	2	—
McPhee	36	10	83	2	1	—
Robertson	44	8	125	1	—	—
Cooley	19	1	81	—	8	—
Farrell	17	3	30	—	—	—
Overs:	148.0					

Umpires: IS Thomas & DR Hair

12th Men: BE McNamara (New South Wales) & AJ De Winter (Tasmania)

South Australia v Queensland
Adelaide Oval, Adelaide
Mar 9, 10, 11, 12 1990
Toss: South Australia
Result: Drawn
Points: South Australia 0 & Queensland 2

To ensure a place in the Sheffield Shield final, Queensland needed to gain first innings points from this match while South Australia had to win outright. As it turned out, the outcome was really determined on the first day when Queensland's bowlers, led by Craig McDermott (5 for 74), dismissed South Australia in just over five hours for 262. The highlight of South Australia's innings was Darren Lehmann's dynamic century, scored off 126 balls. Lehmann thus became at 20 years 32 days, the youngest batsman ever to score 1,000 runs in an Australian domestic season. Queensland replied with 456, an innings dominated by Greg Ritchie's 213, his highest score in first-class cricket. Queensland batted until 3.07 pm on the third day, which meant it had almost a day and a half to force the outright win which would have ensured that the Sheffield Shield final was played in Brisbane. But South Australia's batsmen—particularly David Hookes, whose 159 equalled Ian Chappell's record of 26 centuries for South Australia—played with much more assurance than in the first innings, batting through to the end of the match.

South Australia

First Innings

Batsman	How Out	Ttl	Balls
AMJ Hilditch	b Kasprowicz	4	11
MG Bevan	c Ritchie b McDermott	5	19
PC Nobes	lbw McDermott	3	11
DW Hookes (c)	b McDermott	5	3
DS Lehmann	c Polzin b Storey	100	126
JC Scuderi	c Cantrell b Polzin	21	37
PR Sleep	not out	75	174
DS Berry (+)	run out	19	44
CR Miller	c Kasprowicz b McDermott	0	6
CJ Owen	c Cantrell b McDermott	2	23
SPG George	c Drinnen b Kasprowicz	10	19
SUNDRIES: B.0 LB.4 W.1 NB.6		18	473
TOTAL		262	

F/W: 9 9 15 24 81 180 223 233 249 262

Second Innings

How Out	Ttl	Balls
b Cantrell	54	154
c Drinnen b McDermott	0	9
c & b McDermott	0	2
b Cantrell	159	245
c (s)Tazelaar b Polzin	72	163
c Barsby b Kasprowicz	24	51
not out	31	94
c (s)Robinson b Foley	16	31
c Polzin b Storey	20	39
not out	0	2
B.9 LB.8 W.0 NB.4	25	790
8 wkts for 401		

F/W: 13 13 179 276 319 340 365 399

Note: 1 no-ball from McDermott worth 3

Bowler	O	M	R	Wkts	NB	W
McDermott	21	5	75	5	5	—
Kasprowicz	15.2	—	59	2	1	—
Polzin	24	4	82	1	—	1
Cantrell	12	4	20	—	—	—
Foley	1	—	6	—	—	—
Storey	4	1	16	1	—	—
Overs:	77.2					

Bowler	O	M	R	Wkts	NB	W
McDermott	11	4	34	2	1	—
Kasprowicz	21	4	74	1	—	—
Polzin	33	7	80	1	—	—
Cantrell	33	11	92	2	1	—
Storey	17	4	76	1	—	—
Foley	10	6	17	1	2	—
Clifford	3	2	2	—	—	—
Ritchie	3	—	9	—	—	—
Overs:	131.0					

Queensland

First Innings

Batsman	How Out	Ttl	Balls
TJ Barsby	c Berry b George	27	53
PE Cantrell	b Scuderi	22	65
GI Foley	b Owen	20	49
GM Ritchie (c)	not out	213	360
PS Clifford	b Miller	30	46
SG Law	b Owen	54	110
SC Storey	c Berry b George	12	38
PJ Drinnen (+)	c & b Sleep	14	34
CJ McDermott	c Nobes b Sleep	23	79
MA Polzin	c Berry b Owen	2	14
MS Kasprowicz	c Miller b Sleep	18	31
SUNDRIES: B.3 LB.12 W.4 NB.1		21	879
TOTAL		456	

F/W: 56 73 94 129 254 283 317 382 391 456

Second Innings

How Out	Ttl	Balls

Bowler	O	M	R	Wkts	NB	W
George	23	4	89	2	—	3
Miller	24	7	60	1	—	—
Scuderi	24	5	78	1	1	—
Owen	19	5	80	3	—	1
Sleep	41.5	7	107	3	—	—
Hookes	14	3	27	—	—	—
Overs:	145.5					

Umpires: AR Crafter & PD Rebbeck

12th Men: GA Bishop (South Australia) & D Tazelaar (Queensland)

Western Australia v Victoria
WACA Ground, Perth
Mar 9, 10, 11, 12 1990
Toss: Victoria
Result: Drawn
Points: Western Australia 0 & Victoria 2

Neither team gained a clear upper hand in this match, which consequently ended in a draw, but there were several fine individual performances. In Victoria's first innings, Jamie Siddons played steadily for a century after being dropped at 14, and the Victorians ended the first day at 4 for 277. Next day, their last 6 wickets fell for 46, and Victoria was all out for 323. The Western Australians began shakily, losing several early wickets, and thereafter never really looked likely to overtake Victoria. After Tom Moody went for 0, Jamie Brayshaw survived a couple of chances to make 80, but on the third day Western Australia was all out for 279, 44 runs behind. The Victorians batted strongly in their second innings. Gary Watts rounded off a good season with another century, and Wayne Phillips made 75. Victoria eventually declared at 6 for 308 at 2.37 pm, which meant that to win the Western Australians had to score 353 off 54 overs. Although this was clearly beyond them, they made a stirring attempt to do it, and Tim Zoehrer, in particular, played a remarkable innings, scoring 103 off only 75 balls. His second 50 was scored off 24 balls. The Victorian leg-spinner Peter McIntyre took 2 of the 6 wickets which fell, making a total of 5 for the match.

Victoria

Batsman	How Out	Ttl	Balls		How Out	Ttl	Balls
GM Watts	c Moody b Hogan	42	57		c MacLeay b Matthews	108	195
WG Ayres	lbw Capes	6	15		lbw MacLeay	9	33
WN Phillips	c Brayshaw b MacLeay	29	91		st Zoehrer b Andrews	75	177
JD Siddons (c)	c Zoehrer b Hogan	124	228		c Brayshaw b Andrews	17	27
DA Harris	c Veletta b Mack	50	178		c MacLeay b Andrews	19	18
MGD Dimattina (+)	c Veletta b Capes	4	31	(7)	not out	29	74
CE Bradley	c Brayshaw b Mack	23	36	(6)	c Mack b Zoehrer	30	59
RCAM McCarthy	c Moody b Capes	0	11		not out	13	19
PR Reiffel	not out	5	41				
DW Fleming	c Zoehrer b MacLeay	12	36				
PE McIntyre	c Moody b Hogan	0	5				
SUNDRIES: B. 0 LB. 6 W. 6 NB. 8		28	729		B. 0 LB. 5 W. 1 NB. 1	8	602
TOTAL		323			6 wkts dec 308		

F/W: 35 58 102 269 277 289 296 306 322 323
F/W: 43 187 213 225 242 289

Bowler	O	M	R	Wkts	NB	W	Bowler	O	M	R	Wkts	NB	W
Capes	26	4	93	3	2	—	Capes	11	2	33	—	—	—
Mack	18	4	71	2	—	5	Mack	16	2	56	—	—	1
Hogan	20.3	3	44	3	—	—	Matthews	13	3	29	1	—	—
Matthews	28	10	64	—	1	1	MacLeay	12	2	41	1	—	—
MacLeay	21	10	20	2	2	—	Hogan	16	7	40	—	—	—
Brayshaw	6	—	25	—	3	—	Brayshaw	6	—	20	—	1	—
Overs:	119.3						Moody	11	1	32	—	—	—
							Andrews	11	2	43	3	—	—
							Zoehrer	4	1	9	1	—	—
							Overs:	100.0					

230

Western Australia

First Innings   Second Innings

Batsman	How Out	Ttl	Balls		How Out	Ttl	Balls
MRJ Veletta	b Fleming	59	118	(7)	not out	32	57
MW McPhee	c Siddons b Fleming	16	40	(1)	b Fleming	3	7
TM Moody	c Siddons b McCarthy	0	12		c Harris b Reiffel	23	38
WS Andrews (c)	c Dimattina b Fleming	3	10	(6)	c Siddons b McIntyre	4	19
JA Brayshaw	c Watts b McIntyre	80	208	(8)	not out	41	43
KH MacLeay	lbw McIntyre	1	7				
TJ Zoehrer (+)	b McIntyre	6	26	(2)	b McCarthy	103	75
TG Hogan	c (s)Dodemaide b Reiffel	19	44				
CD Matthews	not out	53	76	(5)	b McCarthy	22	29
PA Capes	c Reiffel b McCarthy	14	51	(4)	b McIntyre	3	14
CD Mack	c Siddons b Reiffel	8	24				
SUNDRIES:	B. 5 LB. 9 W. 0 NB. 3	20	616		B. 0 LB. 5 W. 0 NB. 6	17	282
TOTAL		279			6 wkts for 248		

F/W: 21 36 45 108 109 135 180 192 261 279

F/W: 7 98 137 139 154 184

Bowler	O	M	R	Wkts	NB	W	Bowler	O	M	R	Wkts	NB	W
Reiffel	27.3	7	77	2	3	—	Reiffel	15	2	75	1	4	—
Fleming	18	6	52	3	—	—	Fleming	8	1	55	1	—	—
McCarthy	23	3	70	2	—	—	McIntyre	15	2	58	2	—	—
McIntyre	32	9	63	3	—	—	McCarthy	8	—	55	2	2	—
Phillips	2	1	3	—	—	—	Overs:	46.0					
Overs:	102.3												

Umpires: TA Prue & GJ Bibby

12th Men: BP Julian (Western Australia) & AIC Dodemaïde (Victoria)

SHEFFIELD SHIELD FINAL

New South Wales v Queensland
Sydney Cricket Ground, Sydney
Mar 23, 24, 25, 26, 27 1990
Toss: Queensland
Result: New South Wales by 345 runs

This was an extremely one-sided match which consequently suffered as a spectacle, yet it attracted unusually large crowds—including a Sunday attendance of 10 295, the biggest at a Sheffield Shield match in Sydney in nearly thirty years. New South Wales gained the upper hand on the first day and held it until the match ended. There were two surprises in the home side. Peter Taylor, a current Australian player, was made twelfth man, his place being taken by the 20-year-old leg-spinner Adrian Tucker, and less than an hour before the start of play Geoff Lawson withdrew with a shoulder injury and was replaced as captain by Mark Taylor. While New South Wales went into the match with a strong spin attack, Queensland chose to rely on a four-man pace attack, and when this attack failed to break through on the first day Queensland resorted to Allan Border and Peter Cantrell to bowl spin. At stumps on the first day New South Wales was already in a commanding position at 4 for 231, with Mark Taylor not out on 107. Next day Queensland's bowlers fought back and dismissed New South Wales for 360, a smaller total than had earlier seemed likely. But Queensland lost all the ground it had regained when its batting succumbed to the spin of Adrian Tucker and Greg Matthews. Eight for 91 at stumps, Queensland was out on the third day for 103, Matthews taking 5 for 31. Despite its lead of 257, New South Wales chose to bat again, and Mark Taylor proceeded to score his second century of the match and his seventh of the season in first-class cricket. Having moved to 6 for 286 at stumps, New South Wales added another 110 runs on the fourth day before declaring, Mark Waugh having scored a fine 78 not out. Behind by 653 runs, Queensland was 4 for 156 at stumps on day four. Allan Border's dismissal for 30, beaten by Tucker's wrong'un, had been a decisive blow for the home side, which finished off the rest of the innings at 1.52 pm next day.

New South Wales

First Innings

Batsman	How Out	Ttl	Balls		How Out	Ttl	Balls
SM Small	c Law b Rackemann	75	191		b Law	58	112
MA Taylor (c)	c Healy b Tazelaar	127	307		st Healy b Border	100	181
TH Bayliss	lbw Border	25	35		c & b Rackemann	58	93
SR Waugh	c Healy b McDermott	6	24		c Healy b Rackemann	10	28
ME Waugh	c Healy b Border	3	16		not out	78	137
PA Emery (+)	b McDermott	13	45	(8)	c Tazelaar b Rackemann	11	34
MD O'Neill	c Healy b Rackemann	50	107	(6)	b Cantrell	0	6
GRJ Matthews	lbw Tazelaar	8	19	(7)	b Cantrell	19	15
AE Tucker	b Border	4	35		run out	16	28
MR Whitney	not out	15	44		c Border b Cantrell	8	20
WJ Holdsworth	b Kasprowicz	7	17				
SUNDRIES: B. 0 LB. 9 W. 0 NB. 9		27	840		B. 13 LB. 13 W. 2 NB. 5	38	654
TOTAL		360			9 wkts dec	396	

F/W: 160 194 205 220 261 272 286 309 347 360

F/W: 133 205 242 249 254 282 311 372 396

Bowler	O	M	R	Wkts	NB	W		Bowler	O	M	R	Wkts	NB	W
McDermott	38	8	102	2	4	—		McDermott	18	1	81	—	2	—
Rackemann	28	6	72	2	1	—		Tazelaar	12	—	53	—	1	—
Tazelaar	18	4	46	2	4	—		Kasprowicz	12	2	41	—	—	1
Border	24	5	44	3				Border	16	1	58	1	—	—
Kasprowicz	12.3	2	40	1	—	—		Cantrell	20.5	5	71	3	—	—
Cantrell	15	4	39	—	—	—		Rackemann	22	7	36	3	2	1
Foley	3	1	8	—	—	—		Law	3	1	16	1	—	—
Overs:	138.3							Clifford	4	1	14	—	—	—
								Overs:	107.5					

Queensland

First Innings

Batsman	How Out	Ttl	Balls		How Out	Ttl	Balls
PE Cantrell	b Whitney	0	8	(2)	st Emery b Matthews	60	166
GI Foley	c & b Matthews	0	20	(1)	c Emery b ME Waugh	10	29
GM Ritchie (c)	c Emery b Matthews	16	29	(5)	b Matthews	69	96
AR Border	b Tucker	36	76		c Emery b Tucker	34	96
PS Clifford	c Emery b ME Waugh	0	6	(6)	run out	28	73
SG Law	b Matthews	8	23	(3)	c Small b Whitney	6	15
IA Healy (+)	not out	21	63		not out	40	85
CJ McDermott	c & b Tucker	2	7		lbw ME Waugh	16	15
MS Kasprowicz	c Small b Tucker	0	1		b Whitney	1	7
D Tazelaar	lbw Matthews	0	8		c Emery b Whitney	10	22
CG Rackemann	b Matthews	9	22		c & b Matthews	17	22
SUNDRIES: B. 0 LB. 7 W. 0 NB. 2		11	263		B. 2 LB. 5 W. 0 NB. 5	17	626
TOTAL		103				308	

F/W: 0 44 49 64 72 76 76 77 95 103

F/W: 33 42 114 122 216 234 256 257 279 308

Bowler	O	M	R	Wkts	NB	W		Bowler	O	M	R	Wkts	NB	W
Whitney	8	2	24	1	1	—		Whitney	28	9	66	3	5	—
Holdsworth	5	3	16	—	—	—		Holdsworth	3	—	17	—	—	—
Matthews	16.3	5	31	5	—	—		ME Waugh	6	—	22	2	—	—
Tucker	11	4	17	3	—	—		Matthews	37.3	15	96	3	—	—
ME Waugh	3	—	8	1	1	—		Tucker	27	3	92	1	—	—
Overs:	43.3							O'Neill	2	—	8	—	—	—
								Overs:	103.3					

Umpires: AR Crafter & PJ McConnell

12th Men: PL Taylor (New South Wales) & SC Storey (Queensland)

SHEFFIELD SHIELD PLAYERS OF THE YEAR

Darren Lehmann

It wasn't so much the quantity of runs Darren Lehmann scored in the 1989-90 Sheffield Shield season which set him apart from other Shield batsmen, although the quantity was impressive enough. Rather, it was the pure aggression which characterised his batting, almost regardless of the circumstances. In Sheffield Shield matches, Lehmann made his 953 runs at the rate of 4.24 per six balls faced, a rate unmatched by any other Shield batsman in memory. By comparison, Mark Waugh, an attacking player who scored as many runs as Lehmann, had a scoring rate of 3.39 per six balls faced. Moreover, Lehmann did not ever allow caution to restrict him, for it was clear he considered attack the best means of defence. In its final match of the season against Queensland, South Australia was 2 for 9 when Lehmann came in, and slipped further to 4 for 24. Lehmann responded by hitting a century off 126 balls. He is not a graceful player, but he has a superb eye and timing and appears to abound with confidence. No serious technical faults have been detected so far, although opposing captains will surely look for them. In 1989-90, Lehmann became, at 20 years and 32 days, the youngest Australian to score 1,000 runs in a domestic season.

Game	Inn	Date	Opponent	Venue	Pos	H/O	Fielder	Bowler	Runs	Ttl Runs	Avrge
1	1	3/11/89	Queensland	Brisbane	5	Cgt	Ritchie GM	Tazelaar D	15	15	15.00
1	2	3/11/89	Queensland	Brisbane	5	Lbw		Storey SC	35	50	25.00
2	3	10/11/89	New South Wales	Adelaide	6	Cgt	Whitney MR	O'Neill MD	228	278	92.67
3	4	8/12/89	Victoria	Melbourne	5	Lbw		Dodemaide AIC	128	406	101.50
3	5	8/12/89	Victoria	Melbourne	5	Cgt	McIntyre PE	Reiffel PR	9	415	83.00
4	6	15/12/89	Western Australia	Perth	6	Bwd		Capes PA	0	415	69.17
4	7	15/12/89	Western Australia	Perth	4	Bwd		Matthews CD	48	463	66.14
5	8	6/1/90	Victoria	Adelaide	4	Cgt	Siddons JD	Dodemaide AIC	125	588	73.50
5	9	6/1/90	Victoria	Adelaide	4	RO			22	610	67.78
6	10	19/1/90	Tasmania	Devonport	5	Cgt	Soule RE	Gilbert DR	34	644	64.40
6	11	19/1/90	Tasmania	Devonport	5	Bwd		Tucker RJ	10	654	59.45
7	12	26/1/90	Western Australia	Adelaide	5	Cgt	Zoehrer TJ	Capes PA	41	695	57.92
8	13	15/2/90	New South Wales	Sydney	5	Cgt	Tucker AE	Stobo RM	9	704	54.15
8	14	15/2/90	New South Wales	Sydney	5	Cgt	Milliken GS	Lawson GF	5	709	50.64
9	15	2/3/90	Tasmania	Adelaide	5	Lbw		Cooley TJ	9	718	47.87
9	16	2/3/90	Tasmania	Adelaide	5	Bwd		Tucker RJ	63	781	48.81
10	17	9/3/90	Queensland	Adelaide	5	Cgt	Polzin MA	Storey SC	100	881	51.82
10	18	9/3/90	Queensland	Adelaide	5	Cgt	(S)Tazelaar D	Polzin MA	72	953	52.94

Mark Waugh

Just when it seemed opportunity might have passed him by, Mark Waugh had a resoundingly successful Sheffield Shield season, which raised his stocks higher than they had ever been and placed him at the door of the national side. The selectors eventually brought him into the Australian side for the last of the World Series Cup matches against Pakistan—ironically in place of his brother Steve—but in the context of the season this was really a case of too little too late. It may be said that in any season in the past ten years other than 1989-90 Mark Waugh would probably have played Test cricket for Australia. In 1989-90, Waugh seemed a more mature, more complete batsman. He still played with his characteristic blend of dash and elegance, but his batting seemed to be reinforced now by extra application and determination. As a result, runs flowed from his bat consistently and in copious quantities throughout the season. He was the leading run-getter in the Sheffield Shield competition, scoring 967 runs at the outstanding average of 80.58, and he hit five Shield centuries. If he can keep this up, the selectors will not easily resist his claims for a place in the Test side.

Game	Inn	Date	Opponent	Venue	Pos	H/O	Fielder	Bowler	Runs	Ttl Runs	Avrge
1	1	10/11/89	South Australia	Adelaide	5	Cgt	Berry DS	Gladigau PW	172	172	172.00
2	2	1/12/89	Queensland	Newcastle	5	Cgt	Healy IA	McDermott CJ	46	218	109.00
2	3	1/12/89	Queensland	Newcastle	5	Cgt	Tazelaar D	Rackemann CG	18	236	78.67
3	4	15/12/89	Victoria	Albury	5	Cgt	O'Donnell SP	Dodemaide AIC	4	240	60.00
3	5	15/12/89	Victoria	Albury	5	NO			100	340	85.00
4	6	29/12/89	Queensland	Brisbane	5	Bwd		McDermott CJ	60	400	80.00
4	7	29/12/89	Queensland	Brisbane	5	Cgt	Smart CB	Storey SC	4	404	67.33
5	8	6/1/90	Western Australia	Sydney	5	Bwd		Alderman TM	31	435	62.14
6	9	26/1/90	Tasmania	Hobart	5	Cgt	Soule RE	Gilbert DR	0	435	54.38
7	10	9/2/90	Victoria	Melbourne	5	NO			100	535	66.88
8	11	15/2/90	South Australia	Sydney	4	Cgt	Scuderi JC	Hilditch AMJ	137	672	74.67
9	12	2/3/90	Western Australia	Perth	5	Cgt	Veletta MRJ	Matthews CD	5	677	67.70
9	13	2/3/90	Western Australia	Perth	5	Cgt	Zoehrer TJ	Capes PA	11	688	62.55
10	14	9/3/90	Tasmania	Sydney	5	NO			198	886	80.55
11	15	23/3/90	Queensland	Sydney	5	Cgt	Healy IA	Border AR	3	889	74.08
11	16	23/3/90	Queensland	Sydney	5	NO			78	967	80.58

Geoff Lawson

Geoff Lawson played such an important part in New South Wales's victory in the 1989-90 Sheffield Shield competition that it is hard to imagine how the team would have won it without him. His contribution to the victory was vital in two ways. In the ten Shield matches he played he took 39 wickets at an average of 20.15. Even more important, perhaps, he led the team with flair and daring, always being ready to risk defeat in pursuit of victory, and in the process he seemed to condition his side to winning. Indeed, Lawson's adventurous captaincy had an energising influence on the Shield competition as a whole. Lawson's omission from the Test side must have been a disappointment for him personally, especially after his success in England in 1989, yet as things turned out his loss was New South Wales's gain. Although not so fiery as before, Lawson was in some ways a better and more consistent bowler than ever. He certainly had a bigger armoury, which now included an out-swinger. As captain he often gambled, but only after a careful reading of the game and always with a close eye on the odds.

Game	Date	Opponent	Venue	Inn	Ovrs	Md	Rns	Wk	NB	W	Balls	Mdns	Runs	Wkt	Avrge	NB	W	Stk/rt	RPO
1	10/11/1989	South Australia	Adelaide	2	27.0	3	87	—	—	—	162	3	87	—	—	—	—	—	3.22
2	01/12/1989	Queensland	Newcastle	2	24.0	10	43	1	—	—	306	13	130	1	130.00	—	—	306.00	2.55
2	01/12/1989	Queensland	Newcastle	4	12.5	4	21	3	—	—	383	17	151	4	37.75	—	—	95.75	2.37
3	15/12/1989	Victoria	Albury	2	19.0	7	33	1	—	—	497	24	184	5	36.80	—	—	99.40	2.22
3	15/12/1989	Victoria	Albury	4	13.0	3	31	2	—	1	575	27	215	7	30.71	—	1	82.14	2.24
4	29/12/1989	Queensland	Brisbane	2	27.0	10	43	2	—	—	737	37	258	9	28.67	—	1	81.89	2.10
4	29/12/1989	Queensland	Brisbane	4	19.0	3	67	3	—	—	851	40	325	12	27.08	—	1	70.92	2.29
5	06/01/1990	Western Australia	Sydney	1	27.0	12	51	4	1	1	1013	52	376	16	23.50	1	2	63.31	2.23
5	06/01/1990	Western Australia	Sydney	3	14.0	5	27	1	1	1	1097	57	403	17	23.71	2	3	64.53	2.20
6	26/01/1990	Tasmania	Hobart Bel	2	33.1	9	93	3	2	—	1296	66	496	20	24.80	4	3	64.80	2.30
6	26/01/1990	Tasmania	Hobart Bel	4	13.0	1	46	2	—	—	1374	67	542	22	24.64	4	3	62.45	2.37
7	09/02/1990	Victoria	Melbourne	2	16.0	2	45	2	—	—	1470	69	587	24	24.46	4	3	61.25	2.40
7	09/02/1990	Victoria	Melbourne	3	17.0	8	25	—	—	1	1572	77	612	24	25.50	4	4	65.50	2.34
8	15/02/1990	South Australia	Sydney	2	21.0	10	37	3	—	—	1698	87	649	27	24.04	4	4	62.89	2.29
8	15/02/1990	South Australia	Sydney	3	13.2	5	26	1	—	—	1778	92	675	31	21.77	4	4	57.35	2.28
9	02/03/1990	Western Australia	Perth	1	29.0	5	69	4	—	1	1952	97	744	35	21.26	4	5	55.77	2.29
9	02/03/1990	Western Australia	Perth	3	15.0	3	32	3	—	—	2042	100	776	38	20.42	4	5	53.74	2.28
10	09/03/1990	Tasmania	Sydney	1	6.0	2	10	1	—	—	2078	102	786	39	20.15	4	5	53.28	2.27

Sheffield Shield Winners - 1892/93 - 1989/90

1892/93	Victoria		1946/47	Victoria
1893/94	South Australia		1947/48	Western Australia
1894/95	Victoria		1949/50	New South Wales
1948/49	New South Wales		1950/51	Victoria
1895/96	New South Wales		1951/52	New South Wales
1896/97	New South Wales		1952/53	South Australia
1897/98	Victoria		1953/54	New South Wales
1898/99	Victoria		1954/55	New South Wales
1899/00	New South Wales		1955/56	New South Wales
1900/01	Victoria		1956/57	New South Wales
1901/02	New South Wales		1957/58	New South Wales
1902/03	New South Wales		1958/59	New South Wales
1903/04	New South Wales		1959/60	New South Wales
1904/05	New South Wales		1960/61	New South Wales
1905/06	New South Wales		1961/62	New South Wales
1906/07	New South Wales		1962/63	Victoria
1907/08	Victoria		1963/64	South Australia
1908/09	New South Wales		1964/65	New South Wales
1909/10	South Australia		1965/66	New South Wales
1910/11	New South Wales		1966/67	Victoria
1911/12	New South Wales		1967/68	Western Australia
1912/13	South Australia		1968/69	South Australia
1913/14	New South Wales		1969/70	Victoria
1914/15	Victoria		1970/71	South Australia
1915/19	No Competition		1971/72	Western Australia
1915/19	No Competition		1972/73	Western Australia
1919/20	New South Wales		1973/74	Victoria
1920/21	New South Wales		1974/75	Western Australia
1921/22	Victoria		1975/76	South Australia
1922/23	New South Wales		1976/77	Western Australia
1923/24	Victoria		1977/78	Western Australia
1924/25	Victoria		1978/79	Victoria
1925/26	New South Wales		1979/80	Victoria
1926/27	South Australia		1980/81	Western Australia
1927/28	Victoria		1981/82	South Australia
1928/29	New South Wales		1982/83*	New South Wales
1929/30	Victoria		1983/84*	Western Australia
1930/31	Victoria		1984/85*	New South Wales
1931/32	New South Wales		1985/86*	New South Wales
1932/33	New South Wales		1986/87*	Western Australia
1933/34	Victoria		1987/88*	Western Australia
1934/35	Victoria		1988/89*	Western Australia
1935/36	South Australia		1989/90*	New South Wales
1936/37	Victoria			
1937/38	New South Wales			
1938/39	South Australia			
1939/40	New South Wales			
1940/46	No Competition			

* The winner of the Sheffield since 1982/83 season has been decided by the 2 top teams at the end of the competition playing a final at the Top of the Table's home ground.

The Winners

State	First Season	Played	Won	Lost	Drawn	Ties	Abandoned
New South Wales	1892/93	565	255	143	166	1	—
Victoria	1892/93	560	213	159	184	1	3
South Australia	1892/93	558	160	252	145	1	—
Queensland	1926/27	446	104	165	173	1	3
Western Australia	1947/48	332	111	92	129	—	—
Tasmania	1977/78	105	10	42	53	—	—
Total		1283					

Sheffield Shield Placings

State	1st	2nd	3rd	4th	5th	6th	Seasons
New South Wales	40	21	16	8	3	—	88
Victoria	24	33	16	7	3	5	88
South Australia	12	17	34	8	16	1	88
Queensland	—	12	13	21	12	—	58
Western Australia	12	5	8	11	7	—	43
Tasmania	—	—	1	3	2	7	13
Total	88	88	88	58	43	13	88

1989/90 Sheffield Shield Averages

1989/90 Sheffield Shield Table

State	Played	WO	WI	LI	LO	Drw	Pts	Quotient
New South Wales	10	3	3	1	3*	—	26	1.45
Queensland	10	2	6	—	2*	—	26	0.92
South Australia	10	3	1	3	3	—	20	0.89
Tasmania	10	2	2	3	3	—	16	0.84
Western Australia	10	2	1	5	2	—:	14	0.98
Victoria	10	1	4	5	—	—	14	0.97

* received 2 points for 1st innings lead when beaten outright.

Leading Batting Averages - (Minimum - 500 Runs)

Batsman	State	M	Inn	NO	Runs	HS	50	100	Avrge
ME Waugh	NSW	11	16	4	967	198*	2	5	80.58
MA Taylor	NSW	5	9	—	619	199	1	3	68.78
TH Bayliss	NSW	11	18	2	901	115	5	2	56.31
DS Lehmann	SA	10	18	—	953	228	2	4	52.94
G Shipperd	Tas	10	17	2	788	200*	2	3	52.53
DW Hookes	SA	9	15	—	762	159	2	3	50.80
GM Ritchie	Qld	11	18	2	805	213*	4	2	50.31
JD Siddons	Vic	8	14	1	641	159	3	2	49.31
MRJ Veletta	WA	10	17	2	704	228	1	3	46.93
RJ Tucker	Tas	10	17	1	727	118	6	1	45.44
AMJ Hilditch	SA	10	18	2	663	103*	3	3	41.44
WS Andrews	WA	10	16	—	658	103	5	1	41.13
GM Watts	Vic	10	20	1	764	162*	4	2	40.21
MD O'Neill	NSW	10	15	1	556	71	6	—	39.71
PC Nobes	SA	10	18	—	709	124	4	1	39.39
SM Small	NSW	11	19	1	708	86	6	—	39.33
J Cox	Tas	10	17	—	662	175	1	3	38.94
PE Cantrell	Qld	11	19	1	674	125	6	1	37.44
WN Phillips	Vic	10	20	2	581	78*	5	—	32.28

Leading Bowling Averages - (Minimum - 20 Wkts)

Bowler	State	M	Overs	Mdns	Runs	Wkts	Avrge	5wi	10m	NB	W	Best
CG Rackemann	Qld	6	257.0	64	598	33	18.12	—	—	17	1	4/39
GF Lawson	NSW	10	346.2	102	786	39	20.15	—	—	4	5	4/26
GD Campbell	Tas	6	218.5	60	473	23	20.57	1	—	8	4	6/80
CD Matthews	WA	7	261.3	72	686	32	21.44	2	—	13	6	6/81
GRJ Matthews	NSW	10	436.3	155	950	43	22.09	3	1	1	—	7/50
DR Gilbert	Tas	9	323.1	66	904	38	23.79	2	—	41	4	7/127
CJ McDermott	Qld	10	432.0	100	1375	54	25.46	4	—	94	1	8/44
DW Fleming	Vic	6	176.5	47	513	20	25.65	1	—	8	3	6/37
CR Miller	SA	10	367.1	97	1038	40	25.95	1	—	1	3	6/83
MA Polzin	Qld	6	218.2	54	566	21	26.95	1	—	—	7	8/51
JC Scuderi	SA	10	325.5	82	848	27	31.41	1	—	25	1	6/6
D Tazelaar	Qld	7	272.4	59	703	22	31.95	1	—	39	—	6/48
PR Reiffel	Vic	7	216.1	34	770	22	35.00	—	—	39	—	4/43
WJ Holdsworth	NSW	8	196.1	27	736	21	35.05	1	—	5	—	5/71
PA Capes	WA	9	282.0	59	869	24	36.21	—	—	30	2	4/60

1989/90 Sheffield Shield Averages

Batting	State	M	Inn	NO	Runs	HS	50	100	Avrge	Ct	St
Alderman, TM	WA	3	4	—	29	18	—	—	7.25	2	—
Alley, PJS	SA	3	5	2	8	5*	—	—	2.67	1	—
Anderson, PW	Qld	5	6	—	60	44	—	—	10.00	13	2
Andrews, WS	WA	10	16	—	658	103	5	1	41.13	4	—
Ayres, WG	Vic	3	6	1	277	134*	1	1	55.40	—	—
Barsby, TJ	Qld	4	6	—	81	28	—	—	13.50	4	—
Bayliss, TH	NSW	11	18	2	901	115	5	2	56.31	5	—
Bennett, RJ	Tas	8	14	1	231	55	1	—	17.77	3	—
Berry, DS	SA	10	14	1	147	38	—	—	11.31	31	3
Bevan, MG	SA	6	12	2	338	114	2	1	33.80	1	—
Bishop, GA	SA	5	9	—	206	69	1	—	22.89	4	—
Boon, DC	Tas	2	3	—	177	100	1	1	59.00	3	—
Border, AR	Qld	3	6	2	272	144*	1	1	68.00	7	—
Bradley, CE	Vic	2	4	—	99	46	—	—	24.75	1	—
Brayshaw, JA	WA	5	7	1	268	80	2	—	44.67	5	—
Campbell, GD	Tas	6	6	1	31	11	—	—	6.20	3	—
Cantrell, PE	Qld	11	19	1	674	125	6	1	37.44	12	—

Batting	State	M	Inn	NO	Runs	HS	50	100	Avrge	Ct	St
Capes, PA	WA	9	12	2	87	22	—	—	8.70	2	—
Carew, PJ	Qld	1	2	—	23	23	—	—	11.50	—	—
Clifford, PS	Qld	7	11	—	431	114	1	2	39.18	5	—
Cooley, TJ	Tas	4	7	4	42	17*	—	—	14.00	3	—
Cox, J	Tas	10	17	—	662	175	1	3	38.94	5	—
De Winter, AJ	Tas	5	6	—	95	33	—	—	15.83	5	—
Dimattina, MGD	Vic	10	16	2	147	29*	—	—	10.50	20	1
Dodemaide, AIC	Vic	8	12	1	279	73	2	—	25.36	3	—
Drinnen, PJ	Qld	2	2	—	14	14	—	—	7.00	6	—
Emery, PA	NSW	11	15	3	209	81	1	—	17.42	34	3
Farrell, MG	Tas	1	2	—	101	96	1	—	50.50	—	—
Faulkner, PI	Tas	1	2	—	12	12	—	—	6.00	1	—
Fleming, DW	Vic	6	7	2	39	12	—	—	7.80	1	—
Foley, GI	Qld	6	11	1	199	37	—	—	19.90	1	—
Frazer, ID	Vic	8	15	1	415	90	4	—	29.64	3	—
George, SPG	SA	5	6	2	35	16*	—	—	8.75	2	—
Gilbert, DR	Tas	9	12	4	121	23*	—	—	15.13	1	—
Gladigau, PW	SA	3	4	1	26	18*	—	—	8.67	—	—
Harris, D	Vic	2	4	—	189	90	2	—	47.25	1	—
Healy, IA	Qld	4	6	3	225	81*	2	—	75.00	18	1
Hickey, DJ	Vic	2	2	1	4	2*	—	—	4.00	1	—
Hilditch, AMJ	SA	10	18	2	663	103*	3	3	41.44	3	—
Hogan, TG	WA	7	10	2	198	58*	2	—	24.75	2	—
Holdsworth, WJ	NSW	8	6	3	23	16*	—	—	7.67	5	—
Hookes, DW	SA	9	15	—	762	159	2	3	50.80	3	—
Hookey, SG	Tas	7	13	1	258	116*	1	—	21.50	1	—
Hughes, MG	Vic	4	5	3	122	60*	1	—	61.00	2	—
Inwood, BP	Qld	3	5	2	70	19	—	—	23.33	—	—
Jackson, PW	Vic	2	3	2	15	14*	—	—	15.00	—	—
Jones, DM	Vic	4	7	2	363	149	1	1	72.60	1	—
Julian, BP	WA	2	3	1	16	9	—	—	8.00	1	—
Kasprowicz, MS	Qld	5	6	1	68	49	—	—	13.60	1	—
Kerr, RB	Qld	8	13	—	360	123	2	1	27.69	5	—
Lawson, GF	NSW	10	9	2	76	17	—	—	10.86	5	—
Law, SG	Qld	6	10	2	213	66*	2	—	26.63	4	—
Lehmann, DS	SA	10	18	—	953	228	2	4	52.94	3	—
MacLeay, KH	WA	6	8	3	150	53*	1	—	30.00	4	—
Mack, CD	WA	4	4	1	9	8	—	—	3.00	1	—
Marks, PH	NSW	3	4	1	7	5	—	—	2.33	4	—
Marsh, GR	WA	4	7	2	432	355*	—	1	86.40	1	—
Matthews, CD	WA	7	10	2	230	53*	2	—	28.75	2	—
Matthews, GRJ	NSW	10	13	1	401	117	2	1	33.42	10	—
May, TBA	SA	4	5	2	69	35*	—	—	23.00	—	—
McCarthy, RCAM	Vic	3	5	1	42	28	—	—	10.50	—	—
McDermott, CJ	Qld	10	13	2	214	37	—	—	19.45	3	—
McIntyre, PE	Vic	9	9	3	33	15*	—	—	5.50	6	—
McNamara, BE	NSW	2	4	1	42	18	—	—	14.00	1	—
McPhee, MW	WA	6	11	1	311	113	—	1	31.10	3	—
McPhee, PT	Tas	5	7	4	15	5*	—	—	5.00	—	—
Miller, CR	SA	10	13	4	64	20	—	—	7.11	2	—
Milliken, GS	NSW	6	10	1	260	151	—	1	28.89	6	—
Moody, TM	WA	7	13	1	347	66*	3	—	28.92	7	—
Mullally, AD	WA	5	5	1	38	34	—	—	9.50	2	—
Nobes, PC	SA	10	18	—	709	124	4	1	39.39	6	—
Owen, CJ	SA	4	5	2	21	16	—	—	7.00	1	—
O'Connor, DFG	Tas	2	2	—	48	43	—	—	24.00	2	—
O'Donnell, SP	Vic	6	10	2	338	104	2	1	42.25	5	—
O'Neill, MD	NSW	10	15	1	556	71	6	—	39.71	3	—
Parker, GR	Vic	4	7	—	188	75	1	—	26.86	5	—
Phillips, WN	Vic	10	20	2	581	78*	5	—	32.28	2	—
Plummer, N	SA	1	2	1	29	29*	—	—	29.00	1	—
Polzin, MA	Qld	6	6	2	70	29	—	—	17.50	4	—
Prescott, SS	Vic	1	2	—	17	9	—	—	8.50	—	—
Rackemann, CG	Qld	6	8	4	49	17	—	—	12.25	1	—
Ramshaw, DJ	WA	3	4	—	61	44	—	—	15.25	1	—
Reiffel, PR	Vic	7	9	5	83	27	—	—	20.75	2	—
Ritchie, GM	Qld	11	18	2	805	213*	4	2	50.31	16	—
Robertson, GR	Tas	10	16	3	334	53	1	—	25.69	10	—
Rowell, GJ	NSW	1	2	—	10	9	—	—	5.00	—	—
Russell, RS	WA	2	3	1	27	14*	—	—	13.50	2	—
Scuderi, JC	SA	10	17	2	359	52	1	—	23.93	2	—
Shipperd, G	Tas	10	17	2	788	200*	2	3	52.53	6	—
Siddons, JD	Vic	8	14	1	641	159	3	2	49.31	11	—
Sleep, PR	SA	8	14	4	306	75*	2	—	30.60	4	—
Small, SM	NSW	11	19	1	708	86	6	—	39.33	8	—
Smart, CB	Qld	4	6	1	166	98	2	—	33.20	3	—

Continued

Batting	State	M	Inn	NO	Runs	HS	50	100	Avrge	Ct	St
Soule, RE	Tas	10	14	—	135	47	—	—	9.64	20	—
Stobo, RM	NSW	3	4	1	3	3	—	—	1.00	2	—
Storey, SC	Qld	9	13	3	261	53*	1	—	26.10	4	—
Taylor, MA	NSW	5	9	—	619	199	1	3	68.78	3	—
Taylor, PL	NSW	4	5	1	55	33	—	—	13.75	1	—
Tazelaar, D	Qld	7	9	1	45	28	—	—	5.63	3	—
Tooley, MV	Tas	1	2	1	48	31	—	—	48.00	—	—
Trimble, GS	Qld	2	3	—	50	39	—	—	16.67	3	—
Tucker, AE	NSW	3	4	1	55	18*	—	—	18.33	3	—
Tucker, RJ	Tas	10	17	1	727	118	6	1	45.44	3	—
Veletta, MRJ	WA	10	17	2	704	228	1	3	46.93	14	—
Watts, GM	Vic	10	20	1	764	162*	4	2	40.21	10	—
Waugh, ME	NSW	11	16	4	967	198*	2	5	80.58	18	—
Waugh, SR	NSW	5	8	1	308	196	—	1	44.00	1	—
Wellham, DM	Tas	10	16	2	348	90	2	—	24.86	3	—
Whitney, MR	NSW	7	6	4	24	15*	—	—	12.00	7	—
Williams, BD	SA	2	3	—	54	28	—	—	18.00	1	—
Wood, GM	WA	7	11	3	314	88*	1	—	39.25	1	—
Yardley, B	WA	3	5	2	55	27	—	—	18.33	—	—
Young, PW	Vic	1	2	1	7	7	—	—	7.00	—	—
Zoehrer, TJ	WA	10	14	—	294	103	—	1	21.00	28	4

Bowling	State	M	Overs	Mdns	Runs	Wkts	Avrge	5wi	10m	NB	W	Best
Alderman, TM	WA	3	90.2	29	241	11	21.91	1	—	7	—	5/62
Alley, PJS	SA	3	82.5	19	252	6	42.00	—	—	1	1	4/98
Andrews, WS	WA	10	54.0	16	142	4	35.50	—	—	—	—	3/43
Barsby, TJ	Qld	4	1.0	—	7	—	—	—	—	—	—	—
Bayliss, TH	NSW	11	6.0	3	9	1	9.00	—	—	—	—	1/7
Bevan, MG	SA	6	2.0	—	10	—	—	—	—	—	—	—
Border, AR	Qld	3	44.0	8	107	4	26.75	—	—	—	—	3/44
Brayshaw, JA	WA	5	40.0	12	94	—	—	—	—	9	—	—
Campbell, GD	Tas	6	218.5	60	473	23	20.57	1	—	8	4	6/80
Cantrell, PE	Qld	11	240.3	60	714	9	79.33	—	—	2	—	3/71
Capes, PA	WA	9	282.0	59	869	24	36.21	—	—	30	2	4/60
Carew, PJ	Qld	1	42.0	8	181	2	90.50	—	—	—	1	2/181
Clifford, PS	Qld	7	7.0	3	16	—	—	—	—	—	—	—
Cooley, TJ	Tas	4	102.0	12	433	2	216.50	—	—	37	—	1/16
Cox, J	Tas	10	2.0	1	6	—	—	—	—	—	—	—
De Winter, AJ	Tas	5	150.0	29	448	8	56.00	—	—	13	25	2/60
Dodemaide, AIC	Vic	8	264.5	60	698	17	41.06	—	—	11	—	4/54
Farrell, MG	Tas	1	17.0	3	30	—	—	—	—	—	—	—
Faulkner, PI	Tas	1	18.0	4	42	—	—	—	—	—	—	—
Fleming, DW	Vic	6	176.5	47	513	20	25.65	1	—	8	3	6/37
Foley, GI	Qld	6	98.0	31	276	4	69.00	—	—	9	1	2/57
George, SPG	SA	5	142.0	29	487	11	44.27	—	—	18	3	2/53
Gilbert, DR	Tas	9	323.1	66	904	38	23.79	2	—	41	4	7/127
Gladigau, PW	SA	3	132.0	29	407	4	101.75	—	—	8	—	2/109
Hickey, DJ	Vic	2	61.3	9	207	5	41.40	—	—	8	4	3/89
Hilditch, AMJ	SA	10	25.0	7	58	2	29.00	—	—	—	—	1/5
Hogan, TG	WA	7	208.3	59	509	16	31.81	1	—	—	—	5/60
Holdsworth, WJ	NSW	8	196.1	27	736	21	35.05	1	—	5	—	5/71
Hookes, DW	SA	9	77.1	18	201	3	67.00	—	—	—	—	2/89
Hookey, SC	Tas	7	1.0	—	1	—	—	—	—	—	—	—
Hughes, MG	Vic	4	140.0	38	350	8	43.75	—	—	1	—	3/68
Inwood, BP	Qld	3	45.1	20	90	3	30.00	—	—	—	—	1/9
Jackson, PW	Vic	2	94.0	24	184	4	46.00	—	—	—	—	3/103
Jones, DM	Vic	4	22.0	7	60	1	60.00	—	—	—	—	1/25
Julian, BP	WA	4	17.3	5	50	2	25.00	—	—	1	—	1/7
Kasprowicz, MS	Qld	5	126.3	22	451	6	75.17	—	—	13	2	2/59
Lawson, GF	NSW	10	346.2	102	786	39	20.15	—	—	4	5	4/26
Law, SG	Qld	6	3.0	1	16	1	16.00	—	—	—	—	1/16
MacLeay, KH	WA	6	204.2	76	421	15	28.07	—	—	6	—	3/22
Mack, CD	WA	4	147.5	34	415	11	37.73	—	—	1	10	3/70
Marks, PH	NSW	3	21.0	4	63	1	63.00	—	—	3	—	1/24
Marsh, GR	WA	4	2.0	1	1	1	1.00	—	—	—	—	1/1
Matthews, CD	WA	7	261.3	72	686	32	21.44	2	—	13	6	6/81
Matthews, GRJ	NSW	10	436.3	155	950	43	22.09	3	1	1	—	7/50
May, TBA	SA	4	204.0	48	597	11	54.27	—	—	22	—	3/89
McCarthy, RCAM	Vic	3	105.0	18	339	8	42.38	—	—	4	—	2/43
McDermott, CJ	Qld	10	432.0	100	1375	54	25.46	4	—	94	1	8/44
McIntyre, PE	Vic	9	355.3	85	952	17	56.00	—	—	—	—	3/55
McNamara, BE	NSW	2	7.0	—	33	1	33.00	—	—	—	—	1/24
McPhee, PT	Tas	5	175.0	54	413	16	25.81	1	—	3	4	5/73
Miller, CR	SA	10	367.1	97	1038	40	25.95	1	—	1	3	6/83
Moody, TM	WA	7	58.2	15	126	4	31.50	—	—	—	—	3/57
Mullally, AD	WA	5	193.4	47	526	8	65.75	—	—	7	11	3/74

Bowling	State	M	Overs	Mdns	Runs	Wkts	Avrge	5wi	10m	NB	W	Best
Nobes, PC	SA	10	1.0	—	2	—	—	—	—	—	—	—
Owen, CJ	SA	4	100.0	25	296	12	24.67	—	—	—	2	3/80
O'Connor, DFG	Tas	2	2.0	—	6	—	—	—	—	—	—	—
O'Donnell, SP	Vic	6	148.3	47	328	17	19.29	—	—	4	—	4/38
O'Neill, MD	NSW	10	190.3	58	466	11	42.36	—	—	—	—	3/51
Parker, GR	Vic	4	15.3	4	30	2	15.00	—	—	—	—	2/30
Phillips, WN	Vic	10	6.0	2	13	—	—	—	—	—	—	—
Plummer, N	SA	1	12.1	3	60	—	—	—	—	—	—	—
Polzin, MA	Qld	6	218.2	54	566	21	26.95	1	—	—	7	8/51
Rackemann, CG	Qld	6	257.0	64	598	33	18.12	—	—	17	1	4/39
Reiffel, PR	Vic	7	216.1	34	770	22	35.00	—	—	39	—	4/43
Ritchie, GM	Qld	11	13.0	1	51	—	—	—	—	—	—	—
Robertson, GR	Tas	10	353.2	80	897	15	59.80	—	—	—	—	3/107
Rowell, GJ	NSW	1	31.0	9	86	3	28.67	—	—	—	1	3/41
Russell, RS	WA	2	56.0	12	170	3	56.67	—	—	1	1	2/72
Scuderi, JC	SA	10	325.5	82	848	27	31.41	1	—	25	1	6/6
Siddons, JD	Vic	8	1.0	—	5	—	—	—	—	—	—	—
Sleep, PR	SA	8	220.1	34	673	12	56.08	—	—	1	—	3/107
Small, SM	NSW	11	2.0	2	—	—	—	—	—	—	—	—
Stobo, RM	NSW	3	75.2	15	259	4	64.75	—	—	12	6	2/73
Storey, SC	Qld	9	160.0	38	557	12	46.42	—	—	3	—	4/19
Taylor, PL	NSW	4	125.0	44	286	9	31.78	—	—	—	—	4/29
Tazelaar, D	Qld	7	272.4	59	703	22	31.95	1	—	39	—	6/48
Tucker, AE	NSW	3	92.5	23	260	10	26.00	—	—	—	—	4/25
Tucker, RJ	Tas	10	195.5	49	495	14	35.36	—	—	2	—	3/36
Waugh, ME	NSW	11	117.0	15	421	12	35.08	—	—	25	3	2/22
Waugh, SR	NSW	5	4.0	2	8	—	—	—	—	2	—	—
Wellham, DM	Tas	10	4.0	1	6	—	—	—	—	—	—	—
Whitney, MR	NSW	7	187.5	49	564	18	31.33	1	—	19	—	5/125
Williams, BD	SA	2	4.0	1	15	—	—	—	—	—	—	—
Yardley, B	WA	3	58.0	17	171	3	57.00	—	—	1	—	2/37
Young, PW	Vic	1	9.0	—	26	1	26.00	—	—	—	—	1/26
Zoehrer, TJ	WA	10	7.0	2	13	1	13.00	—	—	—	—	1/9

1989/90 AUSTRALIAN FIRST-CLASS CRICKET

1989/90 First-Class Matches

Match	Date	Venue	Team Batting 1st			Team Batting 2nd			Result
Qld v Vic	Oct 25	Brisbane	Vic	235	5-284	Qld*	317	—	Drawn
WA v Tas	Nov 1	Perth	WA*	215	7-265	Tas	6d-478	—	Drawn
Qld v SA	Nov 3	Brisbane	SA	239	248	Qld*	275	4-213	Qld by 6 wkts
Vic v Tas	Nov 10	St Kilda	Vic	259	7-161	Tas*	381	—	Drawn
SA v NSW	Nov 10	Adelaide	NSW	7d-516	2-179	S.A*	519		Drawn
WA v NZ	Nov 10	Perth	NZ	283	7-296	WA*	9d-374	—	Drawn
NSW v SL	Nov 17	Canberra	NSW	7d-423	2d-82	SL*	268	7-119	Drawn
Vic v WA	Nov 17	St Kilda	WA	133	244	Vic*	8d-297	2-56	Drawn
Tas v Qld	Nov 17	Hobart	Tas	262	6d-230	Qld*	303	0-31	Drawn
SA v NZ	Nov 17	Adelaide	SA	459	2-67	NZ*	7d-445	—	Drawn
Vic v SL	Nov 24	Sale	Vic*	6d-507	—	SL	318	186	Vic by an inns & 3 runs
Aus v NZ	Nov 24	Perth	Aus	9d-521	—	NZ*	231	7-322	Drawn
NSW v Qld	Dec 1	Newcastle	NSW	211	211	Qld*	259	131	NSW by 32 runs
Tas v Vic	Dec 1	Launceston	Vic*	9d-425	2-33	Tas	409	—	Drawn
SA v SL	Dec 1	Adelaide	SL	5d-274	3-88	SA*	8d-472	—	Drawn
Aus v SL	Dec 8	Brisbane	Aus	367	6-375	SL*	418	—	Drawn
Vic v SA	Dec 8	Melbourne	SA*	246	226	Vic	293	6-180	Vic by 4 wkts
NSW v Vic	Dec 15	Albury	NSW	307	5d-226	Vic*	260	8-161	Drawn
WA v SA	Dec 15	Perth	WA	3d-565	—	SA*	366	4-207	Drawn
Aus v SL	Dec 16	Hobart	Aus	224	5d-513	SL*	216	348	Aus by 173 runs
WA v Pak	Dec 27	Perth	WA*	9d-398	—	Pak	75	245	WA by an inns & 78 runs
Qld v NSW	Dec 29	Brisbane	NSW*	367	8d-201	Qld	285	5-305	Qld by 5 wkts
Qld v Pak	Jan 6	Brisbane	Pak	257	6-307	Qld*	8d-436	—	Drawn
NSW v WA	Jan 6	Sydney	WA*	262	1-106	NSW	264	—	Drawn
Tas v SL	Jan 6	Devonport	Tas	1d-210	8d-238	SL*	6d-207	7-200	Drawn
SA v Vic	Jan 6	Adelaide	Vic*	8d-500	4d-222	SA	410	4-186	Drawn
Aus v Pak	Jan 12	Melbourne	Aus	223	8d-312	Pak*	107	336	Aus by 92 runs
Qld v WA	Jan 19	Brisbane	Qld	449	4d-193	WA*	9d-350	1-81	Drawn

Continued

Match	Date		Venue	Team Batting 1st			Team Batting 2nd		Result
Tas v SA	Jan	19	Devonport	Tas•	229	272	SA	381 5-121	SA by 5 wkts
Aus v Pak	Jan	19	Adelaide	Pak•	257 9d-387		Aus	341 6-233	Drawn
Vic v Pak	Jan	26	Melbourne	Vic•	313	173	Pak	233 194	Vic by 59 runs
Tas v NSW	Jan	26	Hobart	NSW	7d-454 2-220		Tas•	9d-456 6-219	Tas by 4 wkts
SA v WA	Jan	26	Adelaide	SA	8d-371	—	WA•	41 286	SA by an inns & 44 runs
Qld v Tas	Feb	2	Brisbane	Tas	105 4d-274		Qld•	7d-109 0-9	Drawn
Aus v Pak	Feb	3	Sydney	Pak	199	—	Aus•	2-176 —	Drawn
Vic v NSW	Feb	9	Melbourne	NSW•	5d-495	—	Vic	192 3-297	Drawn
Tas v WA	Feb	9	Launceston	Tas•	8d-287	143	WA	4d-229 116	Tas by 85 runs
NSW v SA	Feb	15	Sydney	NSW	376 0-35		SA•	204 206	NSW by 10 wkts
WA v Qld	Feb	16	Perth	Qld	273 .157		WA•	8d-607 —	WA by an inns & 177 runs
Vic v Qld	Mar	2	Melbourne	Vic	272	285	Qld•	4d-358 9-195	Drawn
SA v Tas	Mar	2	Adelaide	. SA	5d-291 9d-284		Tas•	225 223	SA by 127 runs
WA v NSW	Mar	2	Perth	WA	317	247	NSW•	236 172	WA by 156 runs
NSW v Tas	Mar	9	Sydney	Tas•	117	157	NSW	6d-430 —	NSW by an inns & 156 runs
SA v Qld	Mar	9	Adelaide	SA•	262 8-401		Qld	456 —	Drawn
WA v Vic	Mar	9	Perth	Vic•	323 6d-308		WA	279 6-248	Drawn
NSW v Qld	Mar	23	Sydney	NSW	360 9d-396		Qld•	103 308	NSW by 345 runs

• Denotes won toss

Leading Batting Averages – (Minimum – 500 Runs)

Player	Teams	M	Inn	NO	Runs	HS	50	100	Avrge
ME Waugh	NSW	12	17	4	1009	198•	2	5	77.62
DM Jones	Vic/Aus	10	16	4	868	149	2	4	72.33
MA Taylor	NSW/Aus	12	21	1	1403	199	5	7	70.15
DS Lehmann	SA	12	20	—	1142	228	3	5	57.10
AR Border	Qld/Aus	9	15	4	621	144•	4	1	56.45
G Shipperd	Tas	11	18	3	845	200•	3	3	56.33
GR Marsh	WA/Aus	7	11	2	501	355•	—	1	55.67
TH Bayliss	NSW	12	20	2	992	115	6	2	55.11
DC Boon	TAS/Aus	8	14	2	657	200	1	3	54.75
GM Ritchie	Qld	12	19	2	928	213•	4	3	54.59
JD Siddons	Vic	10	17	2	793	159	3	3	52.87
PA De Silva	SL	6	10	—	524	167	4	1	52.40
GA Bishop	SA	7	12	1	561	173	1	2	51.00
SP O'Donnell	Vic	8	13	2	544	121	3	2	49.45
DW Hookes	SA	11	18	1	823	159	3	3	48.41
MRJ Veletta	WA	13	20	2	855	228	3	3	47.50
SR Waugh	NSW/Aus	12	19	3	704	196	3	2	44.00
RJ Tucker	Tas	11	18	1	737	118	6	1	43.35
GM Watts	Vic	12	23	1	940	162•	5	3	42.73
WS Andrews	WA	12	18	—	759	103	6	1	42.17
MD O'Neill	NSW	11	16	1	621	71	7	—	41.40
SM Small	NSW	12	21	2	780	86	6	—	41.05
AMJ Hilditch	SA	12	21	2	737	103•	3	3	38.79
PC Nobes	SA	12	21	—	814	124	5	1	38.76
J Cox	Tas	11	18	—	693	175	1	3	38.50
PE Cantrell	Qld	12	20	1	693	125	6	1	36.47
TM Moody	WA/Aus	13	21	1	708	106	5	1	35.40
WN Phillips	Vic	12	23	2	735	134	5	1	35.00

Leading Bowling Averages – (Minimum – 20 Wkts)

Player	Teams	M	Overs	Mdns	Runs	Wkts	Avrge	5w	10m	NB	W	Best
CD Matthews	WA	9	304.3	77	806	42	19.19	3	—	15	10	7/22
SP O'Donnell	Vic	8	179.3	54	410	20	20.50	—	—	7	—	4/38
CG Rackemann	Qld/Aus	12	508.2	144	1074	50	21.48	—	—	34	2	4/39
TM Alderman	WA/Aus	9	336.4	102	784	34	23.06	3	—	30	—	5/62
GF Lawson	NSW/Aus	13	464.2	142	1018	44	23.14	—	—	5	10	4/26
GRJ Matthews	NSW	11	470.3	165	1040	44	23.64	3	1	1	—	7/50
DR Gilbert	Tas	10	350.1	70	999	42	23.79	2	—	46	4	7/127
MA Polzin	Qld	7	260.2	65	682	28	24.36	2	—	—	7	8/51
GD Campbell	Tas/Aus	9	354.2	91	865	35	24.71	1	—	11	5	6/80
DW Fleming	Vic	8	234.3	59	693	28	24.75	1	—	11	4	6/37
CR Miller	SA	11	402.1	107	1117	44	25.39	1	—	1	3	6/83
CJ McDermott	Qld	10	432.0	100	1375	54	25.46	4	—	94	1	8/44
MR Whitney	NSW	8	220.5	58	639	24	26.63	1	—	19	—	5/125
MG Hughes	Vic/Aus	10	428.2	126	1129	42	26.88	2	—	9	2	5/88

Player	Teams	M	Overs	Mdns	Runs	Wkts	Avrge	5w	10m	NB	W	Best
D Tazelaar	Qld	7	272.4	59	703	22	31.95	1	—	39	—	6/48
PR Reiffel	Vic	9	301.2	57	994	31	32.06	—	—	58	—	4/43
PA Capes	WA	10	305.0	64	978	30	32.60	1	—	32	2	6/92
JC Scuderi	SA	11	363.5	100	915	27	33.89	1	—	26	1	6/6
WJ Holdsworth	NSW	8	196.1	27	736	21	35.05	1	—	5	—	5/71
AIC Dodemaide	Vic	9	285.4	67	750	21	35.71	—	—	11	—	4/54
PE McIntyre	Vic	11	451.3	116	1196	27	44.30	1	—	—	—	5/53
PR Sleep	SA/Aus	12	382.1	95	1055	22	47.95	—	—	1	4	3/26

Teams Batting Details

Teams	M	Inn	NO	Runs	HS	50	100	Avrge	Ct/St	W	D	L
Australia	6	91	15	3285	200	11	10	43.22	62/-	2	4	—
New South Wales	12	180	32	6161	199	28	13	41.63	125/3	4	5	3
New Zealanders	3	48	7	1577	146*	5	5	38.46	18/-	—	3	—
Pakistanis	6	117	12	2597	136	12	3	24.73	47/1	—	3	3
Queensland	12	190	29	5145	213*	21	9	31.96	130/4	2	7	3
South Australia	12	203	30	6166	228	21	15	35.64	70/3	3	6	3
Sri Lankans	6	102	16	2642	167	15	3	30.72	43/1	—	4	2
Tasmania	11	184	27	4915	200*	17	10	31.31	77/-	2	6	3
Victoria	12	209	35	6036	162*	29	11	34.69	104/3	3	9	—
Western Australia	12	185	28	5363	355*	21	8	34.16	106/4	3	7	2
Total	46	1509	231	43887	355*	180	87	34.34	782/19	19	27	19

Teams Bowling Details

Teams	M	Overs	Mdns	Runs	Wkts	Avrge	5wi	10m	NB	W	Best
Australia	6	1165.2	357	2821	96	29.39	4	—	47	10	5/65
New South Wales	12	1990.0	556	5478	198	27.67	5	1	73	15	7/50
New Zealanders	3	455.5	86	1421	30	47.37	—	—	27	3	4/71
Pakistanis	6	903.5	193	2605	73	35.68	4	—	77	3	6/62
Queensland	12	2148.1	512	6445	192	33.57	7	—	190	13	8/44
South Australia	12	2022.2	499	5893	149	39.55	2	—	79	13	6/6
Sri Lankans	6	939.2	108	3411	63	54.14	3	—	131	10	6/66
Tasmania	11	1676.1	383	4743	133	35.66	4	1	124	38	7/127
Victoria	12	1966.0	481	5591	171	32.70	2	—	100	8	6/37
Western Australia	12	1973.1	531	5479	173	31.67	6	—	84	43	7/22
Total	46	15240.1	3706	43887	1278	34.34	37	2	932	156	8/44

Mode of Dismissals for Batsmen

Teams	M	Inn	NO	Cght	C&B	Bwld	LBW	Stmp	RO	H/Wkt
Australia	6	91	15	49	—	11	13	—	3	—
New South Wales	12	180	32	89	2	28	19	5	5	—
New Zealanders	3	48	7	25	—	5	10	—	1	—
Pakistanis	6	117	12	72	2	14	16	1	—	—
Queensland	12	190	29	96	7	28	20	1	9	—
South Australia	12	203	30	98	3	31	32	1	8	—
Sri Lankans	6	102	16	45	1	15	16	2	5	2
Tasmania	11	184	27	80	3	39	27	3	5	—
Victoria	12	209	35	109	2	23	31	4	5	—
Western Australia	12	185	28	95	3	33	20	2	4	—
Total	46	1509	231	758	23	227	204	19	45	2

Mode of Dismissals for Bowlers

Teams	Wkts	Cght	C&B	Bwld	LBW	St	H/Wkt	RO	NB	W
Australia	96	61	1	11	23	—	—	—	47	10
New South Wales	198	116	9	31	30	3	—	9	73	15
New Zealanders	30	18	—	5	7	—	—	—	27	3
Pakistanis	73	47	—	10	13	1	—	2	77	3
Queensland	192	128	2	33	20	4	—	5	190	13
South Australia	149	67	3	33	34	3	—	9	79	13
Sri Lankans	63	43	—	9	8	1	—	2	131	10
Tasmania	133	76	1	24	26	—	2	4	124	38
Victoria	171	100	3	37	16	3	—	12	100	8
Western Australia	173	102	4	34	27	4	—	2	84	43
Total	1278	758	23	227	204	19	2	45	932	156

Extras Gained when Batting

Teams	M	Runs	Extras	Byes	Leg-Byes	NB	Wides	% Runs
Australia	6	3285	223	15	72	128	8	6.79
New South Wales	12	6161	449	29	160	124	17	7.29
New Zealanders	3	1577	94	14	48	16	16	5.96
Pakistanis	6	2597	135	15	58	57	5	5.20
Queensland	12	5145	329	23	177	55	24	6.39
South Australia	12	6166	465	52	127	149	11	7.54
Sri Lankans	6	2642	154	29	73	45	9	5.83
Tasmania	11	4915	373	65	114	100	9	7.59
Victoria	12	6036	470	52	132	147	24	7.79
Western Australia	12	5363	406	46	124	111	33	7.57
Total	46	43887	3098	340	1085	932	156	7.06

Extras Conceded when Bowling

Teams	M	Runs	Extras	Byes	Leg-Byes	NB	Wides	% Runs
Australia	6	2821	164	21	86	47	10	5.81
New South Wales	12	5478	333	43	130	73	15	6.08
New Zealand	3	1421	64	6	28	27	3	4.50
Pakistan	6	2605	174	21	73	77	3	6.68
Queensland	12	6445	571	47	142	190	13	8.86
South Australia	12	5893	320	24	128	79	13	5.43
Sri Lankans	6	3411	210	15	54	131	10	6.16
Tasmania	11	4743	478	72	139	124	38	10.08
Victoria	12	5591	390	46	160	100	8	6.98
Western Australia	12	5479	394	45	145	84	43	7.19
Total	46	43887	3098	340	1085	932	156	7.06

Highest Innings Totals

Score	Inn	Team	Opponent	Venue
8d-607	(2)	Western Australia	Queensland	Perth
3d-565	(1)	Western Australia	South Australia	Perth
9d-521	(1)	Australia	New Zealand	Perth
519	(2)	South Australia	New South Wales	Adelaide
7d-516	(1)	New South Wales	South Australia	Adelaide
5d-513	(3)	Australia	Sri Lanka	Hobart
6d-507	(1)	Victoria	Sri Lankans	Sale
8d-500	(1)	Victoria	South Australia	Adelaide
5d-495	(1)	New South Wales	Victoria	Melbourne
6d-478	(2)	Tasmania	Western Australia	Perth
8d-472	(2)	South Australia	Sri Lankans	Adelaide
459	(1)	South Australia	New Zealanders	Adelaide
9d-456	(2)	Tasmania	New South Wales	Hobart
456	(2)	Queensland	South Australia	Adelaide
7d-454	(1)	New South Wales	Tasmania	Hobart
449	(1)	Queensland	Western Australia	Brisbane
7d-445	(2)	New Zealanders	South Australia	Adelaide
8d-436	(2)	Queensland	Pakistanis	Brisbane
6d-430	(2)	New South Wales	Tasmania	Sydney
9d-425	(1)	Victoria	Tasmania	Launceston
7d-423	(1)	New South Wales	Sri Lankans	Canberra
418	(2)	Sri Lanka	Australia	Brisbane
410	(2)	South Australia	Victoria	Adelaide
409	(2)	Tasmania	Victoria	Launceston
8-401	(3)	South Australia	Queensland	Adelaide

Highest Match Totals

Runs	Wkts	Avrge	Home Team	Opponent	Venue
1349	24	56.21	Tasmania	New South Wales	Hobart
1318	26	50.69	South Australia	Victoria	Adelaide
1301	35	37.17	Australia	Sri Lanka	Hobart
1218	35	34.80	Australia	Pakistan	Adelaide
1214	19	63.89	South Australia	New South Wales	Adelaide
1167	39	29.92	New South Wales	Queensland	Sydney
1160	26	44.62	Australia	Sri Lanka	Brisbane
1158	32	36.19	Western Australia	Victoria	Perth
1138	17	66.94	Western Australia	South Australia	Perth
1138	33	34.48	Queensland	New South Wales	Brisbane
1119	28	30.96	South Australia	Queensland	Adelaide
1110	33	33.64	Victoria	Queensland	Melbourne
1074	26	41.31	Australia	New Zealand	Perth

Runs	Wkts	Avrge	Home Team	Opponent	Venue
1073	24	44.71	Queensland	Western Australia	Brisbane
1037	28	37.04	Western Australia	Queensland	Perth
1023	34	30.09	South Australia	Tasmania	Adelaide
1011	25	40.44	Victoria	Sri Lankans	Sale
1003	35	28.66	Tasmania	South Australia	Devonport
1000	24	41.67	Queensland	Pakistanis	Brisbane

Lowest Completed Innings Totals

Score	Inn	Team	Opponent	Venue
41	(2)	Western Australia	South Australia	Adelaide
75	(2)	Pakistanis	Western Australia	Perth
103	(2)	Queensland	New South Wales	Sydney
105	(1)	Tasmania	Queensland	Brisbane
107	(2)	Pakistan	Australia	Melbourne
116	(4)	Western Australia	Tasmania	Launceston
117	(1)	Tasmania	New South Wales	Sydney
131	(4)	Queensland	New South Wales	Newcastle
133	(1)	Western Australia	Victoria	St Kilda
143	(3)	Tasmania	Western Australia	Launceston

Lowest Completed Match Totals

Runs	Wkts	Avrge	Home Team	Opponent	Venue
698	28	24.93	South Australia	Western Australia	Adelaide
704	26	27.08	New South Wales	Tasmania	Sydney
718	29	24.76	Western Australia	Pakistanis	Perth
775	32	24.22	Tasmania	Western Australia	Launceston
812	38	21.37	New South Wales	Queensland	Newcastle
821	30	27.37	New South Wales	South Australia	Sydney
913	40	22.83	Victoria	Pakistanis	Melbourne
945	36	26.25	Victoria	South Australia	Melbourne
975	34	28.68	Queensland	South Australia	Brisbane
972	40	24.30	Western Australia	New South Wales	Perth
978	38	25.74	Australia	Pakistan	Melbourne

Highest Individual Totals

Batsman	Score	Team	Opponent	Venue
GR Marsh	355*	Western Australia	South Australia	Perth
DS Lehmann	228	South Australia	New South Wales	Adelaide
MRJ Veletta	228	Western Australia	Queensland	Perth
GM Ritchie	213*	Queensland	South Australia	Adelaide
G Shipperd	200*	Tasmania	Western Australia	Perth
DC Boon	200	Australia	New Zealand	Perth
MA Taylor	199	New South Wales	South Australia	Adelaide
ME Waugh	198*	New South Wales	Tasmania	Sydney
SR Waugh	196	New South Wales	Tasmania	Hobart
J Cox	175	Tasmania	New South Wales	Hobart
GA Bishop	173	South Australia	New Zealanders	Adelaide
ME Waugh	172	New South Wales	South Australia	Adelaide
PA De Silva	167	Sri Lanka	Australia	Brisbane
GM Ritchie	167*	Queensland	Victoria	Melbourne
MA Taylor	164	Australia	Sri Lanka	Brisbane
GM Watts	162*	Victoria	Queensland	Brisbane
JD Siddons	159	Victoria	South Australia	Adelaide
DW Hookes	159	South Australia	Queensland	Adelaide
GA Bishop	156	South Australia	Sri Lankans	Adelaide
GI Foley	155	Queensland	Pakistanis	Brisbane
GS Milliken	151	New South Wales	Victoria	Melbourne
MRJ Veletta	150	Western Australia	South Australia	Perth

Summary of Centuries

Venue	Matches	Centuries	100–149	150–199	200+	Innings 1st	2nd	3rd	4th
Adelaide	8	22	14	6	2	9	9	3	1
Albury	1	1	1	—	—	—	—	1	—
Brisbane	7	12	8	4	—	3	5	3	1
Canberra	1	1	1	—	—	—	1	—	—
Devonport	2	2	2	—	—	1	1	—	—

Continued

Venue	Matches	Centuries	100-149	150-199	200+	Innings 1st	2nd	3rd	4th
Hobart	3	8	6	2	—	2	1	4	1
Launceston	2	5	5	—	—	3	2	—	—
Melbourne	5	8	6	2	—	4	1	2	1
Newcastle	1	—	—	—	—	—	—	—	—
Perth	8	18	13	1	4	5	8	4	1
Sale	1	3	3	—	—	3	—	—	—
St Kilda	2	1	1	—	—	—	—	1	—
Sydney	5	6	5	1	—	3	2	1	—
Total	46	87	65	16	6	33	30	19	5

Centuries - (87)

Batsman	Score	Inns	Team	Opponent	Venue
Andrews WS	103	3	Western Australia	Victoria	St Kilda
Ayres WG	134*	3	Victoria	New South Wales	Melbourne
Bayliss TH (2)	115	1	New South Wales	Queensland	Brisbane
	101	2	New South Wales	Western Australia	Perth
Bevan MG	114	2	South Australia	Western Australia	Perth
Bishop GA (2)	173	1	South Australia	New Zealanders	Adelaide
	156	2	South Australia	Sri Lankans	Adelaide
Boon DC (3)	100	3	Tasmania	Queensland	Hobart
	200	1	Australia	New Zealand	Perth
	133*	1	Tasmania	Sri Lankans	Devonport
Border AR	144*	2	Queensland	South Australia	Brisbane
Cantrell PE	125	2	Queensland	Victoria	Brisbane
Clifford PS (2)	114	1	Queensland	Western Australia	Brisbane
	109	1	Queensland	Western Australia	Perth
Cox J (3)	101	2	Tasmania	Western Australia	Perth
	175	2	Tasmania	New South Wales	Hobart
	102	4	Tasmania	New South Wales	Hobart
Crowe JJ	109*	2	New Zealanders	South Australia	Adelaide
Crowe MD	143	2	New Zealanders	South Australia	Adelaide
De Silva PA	167	2	Sri Lanka	Australia	Brisbane
Foley GI	155	2	Queensland	Pakistanis	Brisbane
Greatbatch MJ	146*	3	New Zealand	Australia	Perth
Gurusinha AP	109	1	Sri Lankans	South Australia	Adelaide
Hilditch AMJ (3)	102	2	South Australia	Victoria	Adelaide
	100	1	South Australia	Western Australia	Adelaide
	103*	1	South Australia	Tasmania	Adelaide
Hookes DW (3)	139	2	South Australia	Tasmania	Devonport
	118	2	South Australia	Western Australia	Adelaide
	159	3	South Australia	Queensland	Adelaide
Hookey SG	116*	3	Tasmania	Queensland	Brisbane
Ijaz Ahmed	121	4	Pakistan	Australia	Melbourne
Imran Khan	136	3	Pakistan	Australia	Adelaide
Jones DM (4)	149	1	Victoria	Tasmania	Launceston
	118*	3	Australia	Sri Lanka	Hobart
	116	2	Australia	Pakistan	Adelaide
	121*	4	Australia	Pakistan	Adelaide
Kerr RB	123	4	Queensland	New South Wales	Brisbane
Lehmann DS (5)	228	2	South Australia	New South Wales	Adelaide
	109	2	South Australia	Sri Lankans	Adelaide
	128	1	South Australia	Victoria	Melbourne
	125	2	South Australia	Victoria	Adelaide
	100	1	South Australia	Queensland	Adelaide
Marsh GR	355*	1	Western Australia	South Australia	Perth
Matthews GRJ	117	1	New South Wales	Tasmania	Hobart
McPhee MW	113	2	Western Australia	Queensland	Perth
Milliken GS	151	1	New South Wales	Victoria	Melbourne
Moody TM	106	1	Australia	Sri Lanka	Brisbane
Nobes PC	124	2	South Australia	Western Australia	Perth
O'Donnell SP (2)	121	1	Victoria	Sri Lankans	Sale
	104	1	Victoria	Tasmania	Launceston
Phillips WN	134	1	Victoria	Sri Lankans	Sale
Ritchie GM (3)	123	2	Queensland	Pakistanis	Brisbane
	167*	2	Queensland	Victoria	Melbourne
	213*	2	Queensland	South Australia	Adelaide
Samarasekera MAR	133	2	Sri Lankans	New South Wales	Canberra
Shipperd G (3)	200*	2	Tasmania	Western Australia	Perth
	100	2	Tasmania	Victoria	Launceston
	132*	1	Tasmania	Western Australia	Launceston
Siddons JD (3)	113	1	Victoria	Sri Lankans	Sale
	159	1	Victoria	South Australia	Adelaide
	124	1	Victoria	Western Australia	Perth

Batsman	Score	Inns	Team	Opponent	Venue
Smith IDS	123	3	New Zealanders	Western Australia	Perth
Taylor MA	(7) 199	1	New South Wales	South Australia	Adelaide
	164	3	Australia	Sri Lanka	Brisbane
	108	3	Australia	Sri Lanka	Hobart
	101	3	Australia	Pakistan	Melbourne
	101*	2	Australia	Pakistan	Sydney
	127	1	New South Wales	Queensland	Sydney
	100	3	New South Wales	Queensland	Sydney
Tucker RJ	118	2	Tasmania	Victoria	Launceston
Veletta MRJ	(3) 150	1	Western Australia	South Australia	Perth
	110*	1	Western Australia	New South Wales	Sydney
	228	2	Western Australia	Queensland	Perth
Wasim Akram	123	3	Pakistan	Australia	Adelaide
Watts GM	(3) 162*	3	Victoria	Queensland	Brisbane
	102	1	Victoria	Pakistanis	Melbourne
	108	3	Victoria	Western Australia	Perth
Waugh ME	(5) 172	1	New South Wales	South Australia	Adelaide
	100*	3	New South Wales	Victoria	Albury
	100*	1	New South Wales	Victoria	Melbourne
	137	1	New South Wales	South Australia	Sydney
	198*	2	New South Wales	Tasmania	Sydney
Waugh SR	(2) 134*	3	Australia	Sri Lanka	Hobart
	196	1	New South Wales	Tasmania	Hobart
Wood GM	125*	2	Western Australia	New Zealanders	Perth
Wright JG	107*	3	New Zealanders	Western Australia	Perth
Zoehrer TJ	103	4	Western Australia	Victoria	Perth

Best Individual Innings Bowling Performance

Bowler	Wkts	Team	Opponent	Venue
CJ McDermott	8/44	Queensland	Tasmania	Brisbane
MA Polzin	8/51	Queensland	Victoria	Melbourne
CD Matthews	7/22	Western Australia	Pakistanis	Perth
GRJ Matthews	7/50	New South Wales	Tasmania	Sydney
DR Gilbert	7/127	Tasmania	South Australia	Devonport
JC Scuderi	6/6	South Australia	Western Australia	Adelaide
DW Fleming	6/37	Victoria	Western Australia	St Kilda
D Tazelaar	6/48	Queensland	Tasmania	Hobart
Wasim Akram	6/62	Pakistan	Australia	Melbourne
RJ Ratnayake	6/66	Sri Lanka	Australia	Hobart
CJ McDermott	6/77	Queensland	New South Wales	Newcastle
GD Campbell	6/80	Tasmania	Victoria	St Kilda
CD Matthews	6/81	Western Australia	New South Wales	Perth
CR Miller	6/83	South Australia	New South Wales	Sydney
PA Capes	6/92	Western Australia	Pakistanis	Perth

Summary of 5 Wkts in an Innings

Venue	Matches	5wi	1st	2nd	3rd	4th	Fast/Med	Slow
Adelaide	8	6	1	3	2	—	6	—
Albury	1	—	—	—	—	—	—	—
Brisbane	7	4	4	—	—	—	4	—
Canberra	1	1	1	—	—	—	1	—
Devonport	2	1	—	1	—	—	1	—
Hobart	3	3	2	—	—	1	3	—
Launceston	2	1	—	—	1	—	—	1
Melbourne	5	7	2	—	3	2	5	2
Newcastle	1	2	1	1	—	—	2	—
Perth	8	5	1	2	2	—	4	1
Sale	1	—	—	—	—	—	—	—
St Kilda	2	2	2	—	—	—	2	—
Sydney	5	5	2	2	1	—	3	2
TOTAL	46	37	16	9	9	3	31	6

Five Wickets in an Innings - (37)

Bowler	Wkts	Inns	Team	Opponent	Venue
Alderman, TM	(3) 5/62	2	Western Australia	New South Wales	Sydney
	5/105	4	Australia	Pakistan	Melbourne
	5/65	1	Australia	Pakistan	Sydney
Campbell GD	6/80	1	Tasmania	Victoria	St Kilda
Capes PA	6/92	3	Western Australia	Pakistanis	Perth

/Continued

Bowler	Wkts	Inns	Team	Opponent	Venue
Fleming DW_____	6/37	1	Victoria	Western Australia	St Kilda
Gilbert DR _____	(2) 5/47	3	Tasmania	Western Australia	Perth
	7/127	2	Tasmania	South Australia	Devonport
Hogan TG_____	5/60	3	Western Australia	Tasmania	Launceston
Holdsworth WJ ___	5/71	2	New South Wales	Queensland	Newcastle
Hughes MG _____	(2) 5/88	4	Australia	Sri Lanka	Hobart
	5/111	3	Australia	Pakistan	Adelaide
Labrooy GF _____	(2) 5/141	1	Sri Lankans	New South Wales	Canberra
	5/133	1	Sri Lanka	Australia	Brisbane
Matthews CD_____	(3) 7/22	2	Western Australia	Pakistanis	Perth
	5/72	1	Western Australia	Queensland	Brisbane
	6/81	2	Western Australia	New South Wales	Perth
Matthews GRJ _____	(3) 5/70	1	New South Wales	Western Australia	Perth
	7/50	3	New South Wales	Tasmania	Sydney
	5/31	2	New South Wales	Queensland	Sydney
McDermott CJ_____	(3) 6/77	1	Queensland	New South Wales	Newcastle
	8/44	1	Queensland	Tasmania	Brisbane
	5/99	1	Queensland	Victoria	Melbourne
	5/75	1	Queensland	South Australia	Adelaide
McIntyre PE_____	5/53	4	Victoria	Pakistanis	Melbourne
McPhee PT _____	5/73	3	Tasmania	South Australia	Adelaide
Miller CR _____	6/83	1	South Australia	New South Wales	Sydney
Polzin MA_____	(2) 5/56	1	Queensland	Pakistanis	Brisbane
	8/51	3	Queensland	Victoria	Melbourne
Ratnayake RJ ____	6/66	1	Sri Lanka	Australia	Hobart
Scuderi JC _____	6/6	2	South Australia	Western Australia	Adelaide
Tauseef Ahmed ___	5/42	3	Pakistanis	Victoria	Melbourne
Tazelaar D _____	6/48	1	Queensland	New South Wales	Hobart
Wasim Akram _____	(3) 6/62	1	Pakistan	Australia	Melbourne
	5/98	3	Pakistan	Australia	Melbourne
	5/100	2	Pakistan	Australia	Adelaide
Whitney MR_____	5/125	2	New South Wales	South Australia	Adelaide

Ten Wickets in a Match - (2)

Bowler	Wkts		Team	Opponent	Venue
Wasim Akram ____	11/160	(6/62 5/98)	Pakistan	Australia	Melbourne
GRJ Matthews ____	10/76	(3/26 7/50)	New South Wales	Tasmania	Sydney

Highest Wicket Partnerships

Wkt	Ttl	Batsmen	Team	Opponent	Venue
1st	431	MRJ Veletta, GR Marsh ____	Western Australia	South Australia	Perth
2nd	192*	DC Boon, G Shipperd____	Tasmania	Sri Lankans	Devonport
3rd	225	GI Foley, GM Ritchie ____	Queensland	Pakistanis	Brisbane
4th	263	MA Taylor, ME Waugh ____	New South Wales	South Australia	Adelaide
5th	200	DW Hookes, DS Lehmann____	South Australia	New South Wales	Adelaide
6th	271	SR Waugh, GRJ Matthews____	New South Wales	Tasmania	Hobart
7th	191	JG Wright, IDS Smith____	New Zealanders	Western Australia	Perth
8th	111*	AIC Dodemaide, MG Hughes	Victoria	South Australia	Adelaide
9th	85	DS Lehmann, TBA May ____	South Australia	Victoria	Melbourne
10th	65	GM Ritchie, MS Kasprowicz	Queensland	South Australia	Adelaide

Highest Wicket Partnerships

Wkt	Ttl	Batsmen	Team	Opponent	Venue
1st	431	MRJ Veletta, GR Marsh ____	Western Australia	South Australia	Perth
6th	271	SR Waugh, GRJ Matthews ____	New South Wales	Tasmania	Hobart
4th	263	MA Taylor, ME Waugh ____	New South Wales	South Australia	Adelaide
6th	260*	DM Jones, SR Waugh____	Australia	Sri Lanka	Hobart
3rd	225	GI Foley, GM Ritchie ____	Queensland	Pakistanis	Brisbane
6th	224	ME Waugh, PA Emery____	New South Wales	Tasmania	Sydney
6th	221	PC Nobes, MG Bevan____	South Australia	Western Australia	Perth
4th	212	G Shipperd, RJ Tucker____	Tasmania	Western Australia	Perth
3rd	207	WN Phillips, JD Siddons ____	Victoria	South Australia	Adelaide
3rd	203	WN Phillips, JD Siddons ____	Victoria	Sri Lankans	Sale
5th	200	DW Hookes, DS Lehmann____	South Australia	New South Wales	Adelaide
4th	196	ME Waugh, GRJ Matthews	New South Wales	South Australia	Sydney
2nd	192*	DC Boon, G Shipperd____	Tasmania	Sri Lankans	Devonport
5th	192	DM Jones, SP O'Donnell ___	Victoria	Tasmania	Launceston
4th	192	J Cox, DM Wellham ____	Tasmania	New South Wales	Hobart

Wkt	Ttl	Batsmen	Team	Opponent	Venue
6th	191	Imran Khan, Wasim Akram	Pakistan	Australia	Adelaide
7th	191	JG Wright, IDS Smith	New Zealanders	Western Australia	Perth
1st	188	MW McPhee, MRJ Veletta	Western Australia	Queensland	Perth
5th	186	GM Watts, GR Parker	Victoria	Queensland	Brisbane
5th	179*	GM Ritchie, SG Law	Queensland	Victoria	Melbourne

Hundred Wicket Partnerships

1st Wicket

Ttl	Batsmen	Team	Opponent	Venue
431	MRJ Veletta, GR Marsh	Western Australia	South Australia	Perth
188	MW McPhee, MRJ Veletta	Western Australia	Queensland	Perth
173	RB Kerr, PE Cantrell	Queensland	South Australia	Brisbane
160	SM Small, MA Taylor	New South Wales	Queensland	Sydney
159	D Ranatunga, A Samarasekera	Sri Lankans	New South Wales	Canberra
140	SM Small, MA Taylor	New South Wales	Western Australia	Sydney
134	GM Watts, ID Frazer	Victoria	Tasmania	St Kilda
133	SM Small, MA Taylor	New South Wales	Queensland	Sydney
122	GM Watts, ID Frazer	Victoria	South Australia	Melbourne
118	GM Watts, AG Ayres	Victoria	New South Wales	Melbourne

2nd Wicket

Ttl	Batsmen	Team	Opponent	Venue
192*	DC Boon, G Shipperd	Tasmania	Sri Lankans	Devonport
166	G Shipperd, DC Boon	Tasmania	Queensland	Hobart
166	PE Cantrell, RB Kerr	Queensland	New South Wales	Brisbane
159	MRJ Veletta, DJ Ramshaw	Western Australia	Queensland	Perth
156	SM Small, TH Bayliss	New South Wales	Queensland	Brisbane
151	GS Milliken, TH Bayliss	New South Wales	Victoria	Melbourne
149	DC Boon, TM Moody	Australia	New Zealand	Perth
144	GM Watts, WN Phillips	Victoria	Western Australia	Perth
140	GA Bishop, PC Nobes	South Australia	New Zealanders	Adelaide
121	AMJ Hilditch, PC Nobes	South Australia	Victoria	Adelaide
113	AMJ Hilditch, PC Nobes	South Australia	Western Australia	Adelaide
111	SM Small, TH Bayliss	New South Wales	Tasmania	Hobart
106*	GR Marsh, TM Moody	Western Australia	Western Australia	Sydney
105	G Shipperd, J Cox	Tasmania	New South Wales	Hobart

3rd Wicket

Ttl	Batsmen	Team	Opponent	Venue
225	GI Foley, GM Ritchie	Queensland	Pakistanis	Brisbane
207	WN Phillips, JD Siddons	Victoria	South Australia	Adelaide
203	WN Phillips, JD Siddons	Victoria	Sri Lankans	Sale
169	AMJ Hilditch, DS Lehmann	South Australia	Victoria	Adelaide
166	AMJ Hilditch, DW Hookes	South Australia	Queensland	Adelaide
158	TM Moody, AR Border	Australia	Sri Lanka	Brisbane
155	GS Milliken, MD O'Neill	New South Wales	Victoria	Melbourne
150	AMJ Hilditch, DW Hookes	South Australia	Western Australia	Adelaide
149	WG Ayres, ID Frazer	Victoria	New South Wales	Melbourne
139	DC Boon, AR Border	Australia	New Zealand	Perth
138	MRJ Veletta, GM Wood	Western Australia	New Zealanders	Perth
136	RB Kerr, GM Ritchie	Queensland	Western Australia	Brisbane
124	AP Gurusinha, PA De Silva	Sri Lankans	South Australia	Adelaide
115	TH Bayliss, SR Waugh	New South Wales	Sri Lankans	Canberra
115	ID Frazer, DM Jones	Victoria	Western Australia	St Kilda
113	MRJ Veletta, WS Andrews	Western Australia	Queensland	Perth
113	PE Cantrell, AR Border	Queensland	South Australia	Brisbane
109	G Shipperd, RJ Tucker	Tasmania	Victoria	Launceston
107	J Cox, RJ Tucker	Tasmania	New South Wales	Hobart
106	GA Bishop, DW Hookes	South Australia	Sri Lankans	Adelaide
101	RJ Bennett, RJ Tucker	Tasmania	Queensland	Brisbane

4th Wicket

Ttl	Batsmen	Team	Opponent	Venue
263	MA Taylor, ME Waugh	New South Wales	South Australia	Adelaide
212	G Shipperd, RJ Tucker	Tasmania	Western Australia	Perth
196	ME Waugh, GRJ Matthews	New South Wales	South Australia	Sydney
192	J Cox, DM Wellham	Tasmania	New South Wales	Hobart
167	JD Siddons, D Harris	Victoria	Western Australia	Perth
163	MA Taylor, AR Border	Australia	Sri Lanka	Hobart

Continued

Ttl	Batsmen	Team	Opponent	Venue
149	MA Taylor, SR Waugh _____	Australia	Sri Lanka	Brisbane
140	GA Bishop, DS Lehmann _____	South Australia	Sri Lankans	Adelaide
128	RS Mahanama, PA De Silva ___	Sri Lanka	Australia	Hobart
124	WS Andrews, JA Brayshaw ___	Western Australia	New South Wales	Perth
122	ME Waugh, MD O'Neill _____	New South Wales	Tasmania	Sydney
120	GA Bishop, DS Lehmann _____	South Australia	New Zealanders	Adelaide
112	G Shipperd, DM Wellham ____	Tasmania	Western Australia	Launceston
104	MG Bevan, DS Lehmann _____	South Australia	Tasmania	Adelaide
103	Javed Miandad, Ijaz Ahmed __	Pakistan	Australia	Melbourne
103	HP Tillekeratne, EAR De Silva	Sri Lankans	Tasmania	Devonport

5th Wicket

Ttl	Batsmen	Team	Opponent	Venue
200	DW Hookes, DS Lehmann ____	South Australia	New South Wales	Adelaide
192	DM Jones, SP O'Donnell_____	Victoria	Tasmania	Launceston
186	GM Watts, GR Parker _____	Victoria	Queensland	Brisbane
179*	GM Ritchie, SG Law _____	Queensland	Victoria	Melbourne
157	MD Crowe, JJ Crowe _____	New Zealanders	South Australia	Adelaide
148*	DM Wellham, SG Hookey ____	Tasmania	Queensland	Brisbane
148	PS Clifford, CB Smart_____	Queensland	Western Australia	Brisbane
125	GM Ritchie, SG Law _____	Queensland	South Australia	Adelaide
115	ME Waugh, GRJ Matthews ___	New South Wales	Victoria	Melbourne
100*	JD Siddons, DM Jones_____	Victoria	South Australia	Adelaide

6th Wicket

Ttl	Batsmen	Team	Opponent	Venue
271	SR Waugh, GRJ Matthews ____	New South Wales	Tasmania	Hobart
260*	DM Jones, SR Waugh _____	Australia	Sri Lanka	Hobart
224	ME Waugh, PA Emery _____	New South Wales	Tasmania	Sydney
221	PC Nobes, MG Bevan _____	South Australia	Western Australia	Perth
191	Imran Khan, Wasim Akram ___	Pakistan	Australia	Adelaide
167	D Harris, AIC Dodemaide ___	Victoria	Queensland	Melbourne
138	SP O'Donnell, DW Fleming __	Victoria	Sri Lankans	Sale
135	MD Crowe, JG Bracewell____	New Zealanders	Western Australia	Perth
133	WS Andrews, TG Hogan_____	Western Australia	South Australia	Adelaide
112	DM Jones, PL Taylor_____	Australia	Pakistan	Adelaide

7th Wicket

Ttl	Batsmen	Team	Opponent	Venue
191	JG Wright, IDS Smith _____	New Zealanders	Western Australia	Perth
144	PA De Silva, JR Ratnayeke____	Sri Lanka	Australia	Brisbane
124	JR Ratnayeke, EAR De Silva	Sri Lanka	Australia	Hobart

8th Wicket

Ttl	Batsmen	Team	Opponent	Venue
111*	AIC Dodemaide, MG Hughes	Victoria	South Australia	Adelaide

Summary of Hundred Wicket Partnerships

Team	1st	2nd	3rd	4th	5th	6th	7th	8th	9th	10th	Ttl
Australia _____	—	1	2	2	—	2	—	—	—	—	7
New South Wales _____	3	3	2	3	1	2	—	—	—	—	14
New Zealanders_____	—	—	—	—	1	1	1	—	—	—	3
Pakistanis _____	—	—	—	1	—	1	—	—	—	—	2
Queensland_____	1	1	3	—	3	—	—	—	—	—	8
South Australia_____	—	3	4	3	1	1	—	—	—	—	12
Sri Lankans _____	1	1	2	—	—	—	2	—	—	—	6
Tasmania_____	—	3	3	3	1	—	—	—	—	—	10
Victoria _____	3	1	4	1	3	2	—	1	—	—	15
Western Australia _____	2	2	2	1	—	1	—	—	—	—	8
TOTAL	10	15	22	14	10	10	3	1	—	—	85

Venue	1st	2nd	3rd	4th	5th	6th	7th	8th	9th	10th	Ttl
Adelaide _____	—	3	6	4	4	3	—	1	—	—	21
Albury _____	—	—	—	—	—	—	—	—	—	—	—
Brisbane _____	1	2	5	1	3	—	1	—	—	—	13
Canberra _____	1	—	1	—	—	—	—	—	—	—	2
Devonport _____	—	1	—	1	—	—	—	—	—	—	2
Hobart_____	—	3	1	3	—	2	1	—	—	—	10

Venue	1st	2nd	3rd	4th	5th	6th	7th	8th	9th	10th	Ttl
Launceston	—	—	1	1	1	—	—	—	—	—	3
Melbourne	2	1	2	1	2	1	—	—	—	—	9
Newcastle	—	—	—	—	—	—	—	—	—	—	—
Perth	2	3	3	3	—	2	1	—	—	—	14
Sale	—	—	1	—	—	1	—	—	—	—	2
St Kilda	1	—	1	—	—	—	—	—	—	—	2
Sydney	3	1	—	2	—	1	—	—	—	—	7
TOTAL	10	14	21	16	10	10	3	1	—	—	85

Leading First-Class Fieldsmen

Fielder	Teams	M	Ct
ME Waugh	NSW	12	18
GM Ritchie	Qld	12	17
MA Taylor	NSW/Aus	12	15
JD Siddons	Vic	10	15
MRJ Veletta	WA/Aus	12	14*
AR Border	Qld/Aus	9	13
PE Cantrell	Qld	12	12
GRJ Matthews	NSW	11	12
TM Moody	WA/Aus	13	11
GR Robertson	Tas	11	11
GM Watts	Vic	12	10

Note: Mike Veletta took a further 4 catches when wicket-keeping for Western Australia v Queensland, Brisbane.

Most Catches in an Innings

Catches	Fieldsman	Team	Opponent	Venue
4	GM Ritchie	Queensland	Western Australia	Perth
3	AR Border	Queensland	South Australia	Brisbane
3	GR Robertson	Tasmania	Victoria	St Kilda
3	JG Wright	New Zealand	Australia	Perth
3	MA Taylor	Australia	Sri Lanka	Hobart
3	ME Waugh	New South Wales	Queensland	Brisbane
3	MA Taylor	Australia	Pakistan	Melbourne
3	SC Storey	Queensland	Tasmania	Brisbane
3	ME Waugh	New South Wales	Victoria	Melbourne
3	GM Ritchie	Queensland	Victoria	Melbourne

Most Catches in a Match

Catches	Fieldsman	Team	Opponent	Venue
5	MA Taylor	Australia	Pakistan	Melbourne
4	AR Border	Queensland	South Australia	Brisbane
4	MRJ Veletta	Western Australia	New South Wales	Perth

Leading First-Class Wicket-Keepers

Wicket-Keeper	Teams	M	Ttl	Ct/St
IA Healy	Qld/Aus	11	43	41/2
PA Emery	NSW	12	41	38/3
TJ Zoehrer	WA	12	39	35/4
DS Berry	SA	12	35	32/3
MGD Dimattina	Vic	12	29	26/3
RE Soule	Tas	11	22	22/-
PW Anderson	Qld	5	15	13/2
Salim Yousuf	Pak	6	13	12/1
PJ Drinnen	Qld	2	6	6/-

Most Dismissals in an Innings

Dis.	Ct/St	Wicket-keeper	Team	Opponent	Venue
5	5/-	PA Emery	New South Wales	Queensland	Newcastle
5	4/1	IA Healy	Queensland	Pakistan	Brisbane
5	5/-	IA Healy	Australia	Pakistan	Adelaide
5	3/2	TJ Zoehrer	Western Australia	New South Wales	Perth

Most Dismissals in a Match

Dis.	Ct/St	Wicket-keeper	Team	Opponent	Venue
7	7/- ____	PA Emery	New South Wales	Queensland	Newcastle
7	7/- ____	IA Healy	Australia	Pakistan	Adelaide
7	7/- ____	TJ Zoehrer	Western Australia	Queensland	Perth
7	5/2 ____	TJ Zoehrer	Western Australia	New South Wales	Perth

1989/90 FIRST-CLASS BATTING AVERAGES

Batsman		M	Inn	NO	Runs	HS	50	100	Avrge	Ct	St
Aamir Malik	Pak	5	9	—	113	53*	1	—	12.56	5	—
Aaqib Javed	Pak	4	7	2	10	9*	—	—	2.00	2	—
Abdul Qadir	Pak	2	3	—	51	51	1	—	17.00	1	—
Alderman TM	WA/Aus	9	8	1	48	18	—	—	6.86	4	—
Alley PJS	SA	4	6	2	9	5*	—	—	2.25	2	—
Anderson PW	Qld	5	6	—	60	44	—	—	10.00	13	2
Andrews WS	WA	12	18	—	759	103	6	1	42.17	5	—
Ayres WG	Vic	4	8	1	310	134*	1	1	44.29	1	—
Barsby TJ	Qld	4	6	—	81	28	—	—	13.50	4	—
Bayliss TH	NSW	12	20	2	992	115	6	2	55.11	5	—
Bennett RJ	Tas	9	16	1	300	60	2	—	20.00	3	—
Berry DS	SA	12	16	2	171	38	—	—	12.21	32	3
Bevan MG	SA	6	12	2	338	114	2	1	33.80	1	—
Bishop GA	SA	7	12	1	561	173	1	2	51.00	5	—
Boon DC	Tas/Aus	8	14	2	657	200	1	3	54.75	6	—
Border AR	Qld/Aus	9	15	4	621	144*	4	1	56.45	13	—
Bracewell BP	NZ	1	2	—	17	9	—	—	8.50	2	—
Bracewell JG	NZ	1	2	—	104	86	1	—	52.00	—	—
Bradley CE	Vic	2	4	—	99	46	—	—	24.75	1	—
Brayshaw JA	WA	6	8	1	291	80	2	—	41.57	6	—
Cairns CL	NZ	2	3	—	68	39	—	—	22.67	2	—
Campbell GD	Tas/Aus	9	9	2	42	11	—	—	6.00	4	—
Cantrell PE	Qld	12	20	1	693	125	6	1	36.47	12	—
Capes PA	WA	10	13	3	94	22	—	—	9.40	1	—
Carew PJ	Qld	2	2	—	23	23	—	—	11.50	—	—
Clarke DA	SA	1	1	—	9	9	—	—	9.00	—	—
Clifford PS	Qld	8	12	—	432	114	1	2	36.00	7	—
Cooley TJ	Tas	5	8	4	52	17*	—	—	13.00	5	—
Cox J	Tas	11	18	—	693	175	1	3	38.50	5	—
Crowe JJ	NZ	3	5	1	195	109*	—	1	48.75	4	—
Crowe MD	NZ	3	5	—	332	143	2	1	66.40	2	—
De Silva EAR	SL	5	7	1	198	66*	2	—	33.00	4	—
De Silva PA	SL	6	10	—	524	167	4	1	52.40	2	—
De Winter AJ	Tas	5	6	—	95	33	—	—	15.83	5	—
Dimattina MGD	Vic	12	19	3	180	32*	—	—	11.25	26	3
Dodemaide AIC	Vic	9	14	1	310	73	2	—	23.85	4	—
Drinnen PJ	Qld	2	2	—	14	14	—	—	7.00	6	—
Emery PA	NSW	12	16	4	224	81	1	—	18.67	38	3
Farrell MG	Tas	1	2	—	101	96	1	—	50.50	—	—
Faulkner PI	Tas	1	2	—	12	12	—	—	6.00	1	—
Fleming DW	Vic	8	10	3	113	63*	1	—	16.14	4	—
Foley GI	Qld	7	12	1	354	155	—	1	32.18	2	—
Francis CL	SA	1	—	—	—	—	—	—	—	—	—
Frazer ID	Vic	9	16	1	415	90	4	—	27.67	6	—
George SP	SA	5	6	2	35	16*	—	—	8.75	2	—
Gilbert DR	Tas	10	13	4	128	23*	—	—	14.22	1	—
Gladigau PW	SA	5	6	1	26	18*	—	—	5.20	—	—
Greatbatch MJ	NZ	3	5	1	261	146*	1	1	65.25	3	—
Gurusinha AP	SL	5	9	—	295	109	1	1	32.78	7	—
Harris DA	Vic	2	4	—	189	90	2	—	47.25	1	—
Healy IA	Qld/Aus	11	15	4	454	81*	2	—	41.27	41	2
Hickey DJ	Vic	2	2	1	4	2*	—	—	4.00	1	—
Hilditch AMJ	SA	12	21	2	737	103*	3	3	38.79	3	—
Hogan TG	WA	9	12	3	286	58*	2	—	31.78	2	—
Holdsworth WJ	NSW	8	6	3	23	16*	—	—	7.67	5	—
Hookes DW	SA	11	18	1	823	159	3	3	48.41	4	—
Hookey SG	Tas	7	13	1	258	116*	—	1	21.50	1	—
Hughes MG	Vic/Aus	10	14	6	291	60*	1	—	36.38	3	—
Ijaz Ahmed	Pak	6	11	—	349	121	—	1	31.73	6	—
Imran Khan	Pak	4	7	1	320	136	1	1	53.33	1	—
Inwood BP	Qld	3	5	2	70	19	—	—	23.33	—	—
Jackson PW	Vic	3	3	2	15	14*	—	—	15.00	—	—
Javed Miandad	Pak	4	7	1	322	77	4	—	53.67	1	—
Jayasuriya ST	SL	4	7	2	171	37*	—	—	34.20	—	—
Jones AH	NZ	1	1	—	13	13	—	—	13.00	1	—

Batsman		M	Inn	NO	Runs	HS	50	100	Avrge	Ct	St
Jones DM	Vic/Aus	10	16	4	868	149	2	4	72.33	4	—
Julian BP	WA	2	3	1	16	9	—	—	8.00	1	—
Kalpage RS	SL	1	2	1	10	10*	—	—	10.00	1	—
Kasprowicz MS	Qld	5	6	1	68	49	—	—	13.60	1	—
Kerr RB	Qld	8	13	—	360	123	2	1	27.69	5	—
Labrooy GF	SL	5	5	1	43	26*	—	—	10.75	1	—
Law SG	Qld	7	11	2	243	66*	2	—	27.00	4	—
Lawson GF	NSW/Aus	13	11	2	99	22	—	—	11.00	7	—
Lehmann DS	SA	12	20	—	1142	228	3	5	57.10	3	—
Mack CD	WA	4	4	1	9	8	—	—	3.00	1	—
MacLeay KH	WA	7	9	3	177	53*	1	—	29.50	5	—
Madurasinghe MAWR	SL	2	1	1	4	4*	—	—	—	2	—
Mahanama RS	SL	4	7	1	173	85	2	—	28.83	4	—
Mansoor Akhtar	Pak	3	6	—	127	74	1	—	21.17	2	—
Maqsood Rana	Pak	1	2	—	7	7	—	—	3.50	1	—
Marks PH	NSW	3	4	1	7	5	—	—	2.33	4	—
March GR	WA/Aus	7	11	2	501	355*	—	1	55.67	4	—
Matthews CD	WA	9	12	2	259	53*	2	—	25.90	3	—
Matthews GRJ	NSW	11	14	2	453	117	3	1	37.75	12	—
May TBA	SA	4	5	2	69	35*	—	—	23.00	—	—
McCarthy RCAM	Vic	3	5	1	42	28	—	—	10.50	—	—
McDermott CJ	Qld	10	13	2	214	37	—	—	19.45	3	—
McIntyre PE	Vic	11	11	3	59	20	—	—	7.38	7	—
McNamara BE	NSW	2	4	1	42	18	—	—	14.00	1	—
McPhee MW	WA	6	11	1	311	113	—	1	31.10	3	—
McPhee PT	Tas	5	7	4	15	5*	—	—	5.00	—	—
Miller CR	SA	11	14	4	98	34	—	—	9.80	2	—
Milliken GS	NSW	6	10	1	260	151	—	1	28.89	6	—
Moody TM	WA/Aus	13	21	1	708	106	5	1	35.40	11	—
Morrison DK	NZ	3	3	2	3	3	—	—	3.00	—	—
Mullally AD	WA	6	6	1	38	34	—	—	7.60	3	—
Mushtaq Ahmed	Pak	2	4	—	51	32	—	—	12.75	2	—
Nadeem Ghauri	Pak	3	5	1	20	19	—	—	5.00	1	—
Nobes PC	SA	12	21	—	814	124	5	1	38.76	6	—
Owen CJ	SA	4	5	2	21	16	—	—	7.00	1	—
O'Connor DFG	Tas	2	2	—	48	43	—	—	24.00	2	—
O'Donnell SP	Vic	8	13	2	544	121	3	2	49.45	8	—
O'Neill MD	NSW	11	16	1	621	71	7	—	41.40	4	—
Parker GR	Vic	5	8	—	196	75	1	—	24.50	6	—
Patel DN	NZ	2	3	—	27	20	—	—	9.00	—	—
Phillips WN	Vic	12	23	2	735	134	5	1	35.00	2	—
Plummer NR	SA	1	2	1	29	29*	—	—	29.00	1	—
Polzin MA	Qld	7	7	3	70	29	—	—	17.50	5	—
Prescott SS	Vic	2	4	—	29	10	—	—	7.25	3	—
Rackemann CG	Qld/Aus	12	13	7	69	17	—	—	11.50	1	—
Ramanayake CPH	SL	4	5	4	35	16*	—	—	35.00	1	—
Rameez Raja	Pak	3	5	—	24	9	—	—	4.80	1	—
Ramshaw DJ	WA	3	4	—	61	44	—	—	15.25	1	—
Ranatunga A	SL	4	6	—	181	75	1	—	30.17	4	—
Ranatunga D	SL	5	9	—	197	56	1	—	21.89	1	—
Ratnayake NLK	SL	1	—	—	—	—	—	—	—	—	—
Ratnayake RJ	SL	2	4	—	13	5	—	—	3.25	1	—
Ratnayeke JR	SL	5	7	1	244	75	3	—	40.67	4	—
Reiffel PR	Vic	9	11	6	101	27	—	—	20.20	3	—
Ritchie GM	Qld	12	19	2	928	213*	4	3	54.59	17	—
Robertson GR	Tas	11	17	3	373	53	1	—	26.64	11	—
Rowell GJ	NSW	1	2	—	10	9	—	—	5.00	—	—
Russell RS	WA	3	4	1	45	18	—	—	15.00	3	—
Saeed Anwar	Pak	3	6	—	131	44	—	—	21.83	4	—
Salim Malik	Pak	1	2	1	76	65*	1	—	76.00	—	—
Salim Yousuf	Pak	6	11	2	265	78	1	—	29.44	12	1
Samarasekera MAR	SL	4	7	1	201	133	—	1	33.50	1	—
Scuderi JC	SA	11	18	3	434	75*	2	—	28.93	2	—
Shipperd G	Tas	11	18	3	845	200*	3	3	56.33	7	—
Shoaib Mohammad	Pak	6	11	—	219	52	1	—	19.91	3	—
Siddons JD	Vic	10	17	2	793	159	3	3	52.87	15	—
Sleep PR	SA/Aus	12	19	5	376	75*	—	—	26.86	4	—
Small SM	NSW	12	21	2	780	86	6	—	41.05	8	—
Smart CB	Qld	5	7	1	177	98	2	—	29.50	5	—
Smith IDS	NZ	3	5	—	164	123	—	1	32.80	1	—
Snedden MC	NZ	2	2	2	46	33*	—	—	—	—	—
Soule RE	Tas	11	15	—	139	47	—	—	9.27	22	—
Stobo RM	NSW	3	4	1	3	3	—	—	1.00	2	—
Storey SC	Qld	10	14	3	315	54	2	—	28.64	4	—
Tauseef Ahmed	Pak	4	7	2	99	36	—	—	19.80	—	—
Taylor MA	NSW/Aus	12	21	1	1403	199	5	7	70.15	15	—

Continued

Batsman		M	Inn	NO	Runs	HS	50	100	Avrge	Ct	St
Taylor PL	NSW/Aus	7	8	1	91	33	—	—	13.00	4	—
Tazelaar D	Qld	7	9	1	45	28	—	—	5.63	3	—
Tillekeratne HP	SL	4	7	1	143	74	1	—	23.83	5	—
Tooley MV	Tas	1	2	1	48	31	—	—	48.00	—	—
Trimble GS	Qld	2	3	—	50	39	—	—	16.67	3	—
Tucker AE	NSW	3	4	1	55	18*	—	—	18.33	3	—
Tucker RJ	Tas	11	18	1	737	118	6	1	43.35	3	—
Vance RH	NZ	3	5	—	79	65	1	—	15.80	—	—
Veletta MRJ	WA	13	20	2	855	228	3	3	47.50	18	—
Waqar Younus	Pak	6	9	2	81	23	—	—	11.57	—	—
Wasim Akram	Pak	3	5	—	197	123	1	1	39.40	2	—
Watson W	NZ	3	2	—	4	4	—	—	2.00	—	—
Watts GM	Vic	12	23	1	940	162*	5	3	42.73	10	—
Waugh ME	NSW	12	17	4	1009	198*	2	5	77.62	18	—
Waugh SR	NSW/Aus	12	19	3	704	196	3	2	44.00	5	—
Wellham DM	Tas	11	17	2	375	90	2	—	25.00	3	—
Whitney MR	NSW	8	6	4	24	15*	—	—	12.00	7	—
Wickremasinghe AGD	SL	4	7	1	50	24	—	—	8.33	5	1
Wijegunawardene KIW	SL	1	2	1	6	5	—	—	6.00	—	—
Williams BD	SA	2	3	—	54	28	—	—	18.00	1	—
Wood GM	WA	9	13	4	440	125*	1	1	48.89	3	—
Wright JG	NZ	3	5	1	170	107*	—	1	42.50	3	—
Yardley B	WA	4	6	2	58	27	—	—	14.50	—	—
Young PW	Vic	1	2	1	7	7	—	—	7.00	—	—
Zesers AK	SA	1	1	1	25	25*	—	—	—	—	—
Zoehrer TJ	WA	12	16	—	330	103	—	1	20.63	35	4

1989/90 FIRST-CLASS BOWLING AVERAGES

Bowler		M	Overs	Mdns	Runs	Wkts	Avrge	5	10	NB	W	Best
Aamir Malik	Pak	5	14.0	1	57	2	28.50	—	—	2	—	2/57
Aaqib Javed	Pak	4	121.1	30	327	9	36.33	—	—	23	1	2/47
Abdul Qadir	Pak	2	53.2	8	181	3	60.33	—	—	6	—	2/101
Alderman TM	WA/Aus	9	336.4	102	784	34	23.06	3	—	30	—	5/62
Alley PJS	SA	4	108.5	29	330	9	36.67	—	—	1	1	4/98
Andrews WS	WA	12	55.0	16	149	4	37.25	—	—	—	—	3/43
Barsby TJ	Qld	4	1.0	—	7	—	—	—	—	—	—	—
Bayliss TH	NSW	12	6.0	3	9	1	9.00	—	—	—	—	1/7
Bevan MG	SA	6	2.0	—	10	—	—	—	—	—	—	—
Border AR	Qld/Aus	9	70.0	14	178	5	35.60	—	—	—	—	3/44
Bracewell BP	NZ	1	32.0	8	88	1	88.00	—	—	—	—	1/88
Bracewell JG	NZ	1	34.0	5	81	4	20.25	—	—	—	—	4/81
Brayshaw JA	WA	6	40.2	12	96	—	—	—	—	9	—	—
Cairns CL	NZ	2	51.0	8	190	4	47.50	—	—	1	—	2/22
Campbell GD	Tas/Aus	9	354.2	91	866	35	24.74	1	—	11	5	6/80
Cantrell PE	Qld	12	266.3	64	800	11	72.73	—	—	2	—	3/71
Capes PA	WA	10	305.0	64	978	30	32.60	1	—	32	2	6/92
Carew PJ	Qld	2	79.0	19	289	5	57.80	—	—	—	1	2/43
Clarke DA	SA	1	33.0	14	70	—	—	—	—	—	—	—
Clifford PS	Qld	8	7.0	3	16	—	—	—	—	—	—	—
Cooley TJ	Tas	5	122.0	17	522	3	174.00	—	—	48	1	1/16
Cox J	Tas	11	2.0	1	6	—	—	—	—	—	—	—
De Silva EAR	SL	5	160.1	29	486	6	81.00	—	—	13	—	3/121
De Silva PA	SL	6	68.0	7	227	3	75.67	—	—	8	—	2/65
De Winter AJ	Tas	5	150.0	29	448	8	56.00	—	—	13	25	2/60
Dodemaide AIC	Vic	9	285.4	67	750	21	35.71	—	—	11	—	4/54
Farrell MG	Tas	1	17.0	3	30	—	—	—	—	—	—	—
Faulkner PI	Tas	1	18.0	4	42	—	—	—	—	—	—	—
Fleming DW	Vic	8	234.3	59	693	28	24.75	1	—	11	4	6/37
Foley GI	Qld	7	116.0	32	318	5	63.60	—	—	14	1	2/57
Francis CL	SA	1	22.0	1	74	—	—	—	—	—	—	—
George SP	SA	5	142.0	29	487	11	44.27	—	—	18	3	2/53
Gilbert DR	Tas	10	350.1	70	1000	42	23.81	2	—	46	4	7/127
Gladigau PW	SA	5	192.0	45	557	5	111.40	—	—	10	—	2/109
Gurusinha AP	SL	5	28.3	4	111	5	22.20	—	—	—	1	2/31
Healy IA	Qld/Aus	11	1.0	—	1	—	—	—	—	—	—	—
Hickey DJ	Vic	2	61.3	9	207	5	41.40	—	—	8	4	3/89
Hilditch AMJ	SA	12	29.0	7	70	3	23.33	—	—	—	—	1/5
Hogan TG	WA	9	248.3	70	641	18	35.61	1	—	—	—	5/60
Holdsworth WJ	NSW	8	196.1	27	736	21	35.05	1	—	5	—	5/71
Hookes DW	SA	11	78.1	19	201	3	67.00	—	—	—	—	2/89
Hookey SG	Tas	7	1.0	—	1	—	—	—	—	—	—	—
Hughes MG	Vic/Aus	10	428.2	126	1129	42	26.88	2	—	9	2	5/88
Ijaz Ahmed	Pak	6	2.0	—	3	—	—	—	—	—	—	—

Bowler		M	Overs	Mdns	Runs	Wkts	Avrge	5	10	NB	W	Best
Imran Khan	Pak	4	104.0	22	247	4	61.75	—	—	5	—	2/53
Inwood BP	Qld	3	45.1	20	90	3	30.00	—	—	—	—	1/9
Jackson PW	Vic	3	145.3	48	286	7	40.86	—	—	—	—	3/103
Jayasuriya ST	SL	4	20.0	3	74	1	74.00	—	—	—	—	1/17
Jones DM	Vic/Aus	10	30.0	11	72	1	72.00	—	—	—	—	1/25
Julian BP	WA	2	17.3	5	50	2	25.00	—	—	1	—	1/7
Kalpage R	SL	1	1.0	—	6	—	—	—	—	—	—	—
Kasprowicz MS	Qld	5	126.3	22	451	6	75.17	—	—	13	2	2/59
Labrooy GF	SL	5	167.1	23	652	15	43.47	2	—	27	2	5/133
Law SG	Qld	7	5.0	1	29	1	29.00	—	—	—	—	1/16
Lawson GF	NSW/Aus	13	464.2	142	1018	44	23.14	—	—	5	10	4/26
Mack CD	WA	4	147.5	34	415	11	37.73	—	—	1	10	3/70
MacLeay KH	WA	7	222.2	83	463	17	27.24	—	—	6	—	3/22
Madurasinghe MAWR	SL	2	60.0	5	207	4	51.75	—	—	—	—	4/80
Mahanama RS	SL	4	1.0	—	3	—	—	—	—	—	—	—
Maqsood Rana	Pak	1	15.0	2	57	2	28.50	—	—	—	1	2/57
Marks PH	NSW	3	21.0	4	63	1	63.00	—	—	3	—	1/24
Marsh GR	WA	7	2.0	1	1	1	1.00	—	—	—	—	1/1
Matthews CD	WA	9	304.3	77	806	42	19.19	3	—	15	10	7/22
Matthews GRJ	NSW	11	470.3	166	1040	44	23.64	3	1	1	—	7/50
May TBA	SA	4	204.0	48	597	11	54.27	—	—	22	—	3/89
McCarthy RCAM	Vic	3	105.0	18	339	8	42.38	—	—	4	—	2/43
McDermott CJ	Qld	10	432.0	100	1376	54	25.48	4	—	94	1	8/44
McIntyre PE	Vic	11	451.3	116	1196	27	44.30	1	—	—	—	5/53
McNamara BE	NSW	2	7.0	—	33	1	33.00	—	—	—	—	1/24
McPhee PT	Tas	5	175.0	54	413	16	25.81	1	—	3	4	5/73
Miller CR	SA	11	402.1	107	1117	44	25.39	1	—	1	3	6/83
Moody TM	WA/Aus	13	144.3	46	318	8	39.75	—	—	—	—	3/57
Morrison DK	NZ	3	91.1	16	318	8	39.75	—	—	9	—	4/71
Mullally AD	WA	6	239.4	55	648	11	58.91	—	—	9	20	3/74
Mushtaq Ahmed	Pak	2	74.0	18	212	5	42.40	—	—	2	—	2/17
Nadeem Ghauri	Pak	3	76.0	21	194	7	27.71	—	—	—	—	4/59
Nobes PC	SA	12	2.0	1	2	—	—	—	—	—	—	—
Owen CJ	SA	4	100.0	25	296	12	24.67	—	—	—	2	3/80
O'Connor DFG	Tas	2	2.0	—	6	—	—	—	—	—	—	—
O'Donnell SP	Vic	8	179.3	54	410	20	20.50	—	—	7	—	4/38
O'Neill MD	NSW	11	213.3	65	536	13	41.23	—	—	—	—	3/51
Parker GR	Vic	5	20.3	5	45	2	22.50	—	—	—	—	2/30
Patel DN	NZ	2	55.4	13	142	4	35.50	—	—	—	—	3/62
Phillips WN	Vic	12	6.0	2	13	—	—	—	—	—	—	—
Plummer NR	SA	1	12.1	3	60	—	—	—	—	—	—	—
Polzin MA	Qld	7	260.2	65	682	28	24.36	2	—	—	7	8/51
Rackemann CG	Qld/Aus	12	508.2	144	1074	50	21.48	—	—	34	2	4/39
Ramanayake CPH	SL	4	129.0	13	490	8	61.25	—	—	35	1	2/81
Ranatunga A	SL	4	51.0	1	166	3	55.33	—	—	1	—	2/17
Ratnayake NLK	SL	1	21.0	3	45	1	45.00	—	—	—	1	1/18
Ratnayake RJ	SL	2	83.4	7	318	10	31.80	1	—	23	4	6/66
Ratnayeke JR	SL	5	125.5	13	423	5	84.60	—	—	19	1	2/75
Reiffel PR	Vic	9	301.2	57	994	31	32.06	—	—	58	—	4/43
Ritchie GM	Qld	12	13.0	1	51	—	—	—	—	—	—	—
Robertson GR	Tas	11	374.2	87	930	17	54.71	—	—	—	—	3/107
Rowell GJ	NSW	1	31.0	9	86	3	28.67	—	—	—	1	3/41
Russell RS	WA	3	74.0	18	209	6	34.83	—	—	1	1	3/10
Saeed Anwar	Pak	3	14.5	1	35	2	17.50	—	—	—	—	2/35
Samarasekera MAR	SL	4	1.0	—	15	—	—	—	—	—	—	—
Scuderi JC	SA	11	363.5	100	915	27	33.89	1	—	26	1	6/6
Shoaib Mohammad	Pak	6	5.0	1	26	—	—	—	—	—	—	—
Siddons JD	Vic	10	4.0	1	16	—	—	—	—	—	—	—
Sleep PR	SA/Aus	12	382.1	95	1055	22	47.95	—	—	1	4	3/26
Small SM	NSW	12	2.0	2	0	—	—	—	—	—	—	—
Snedden MC	NZ	2	79.0	16	213	7	30.43	—	—	8	—	4/108
Stobo RM	NSW	3	75.2	15	259	4	64.75	—	—	12	6	2/73
Storey SC	Qld	10	192.0	48	669	14	47.79	—	—	7	—	4/19
Tauseef Ahmed	Pak	4	131.5	26	358	10	35.80	1	—	1	—	5/42
Taylor PL	NSW/Aus	7	212.5	64	528	13	40.62	—	—	4	—	4/29
Tazelaar D	Qld	7	272.4	59	703	22	31.95	1	—	39	—	6/48
Tillekeratne HP	SL	4	2.0	—	10	—	—	—	—	—	—	—
Tucker AE	NSW	3	92.5	23	260	10	26.00	—	—	—	—	4/25
Tucker RJ	Tas	11	212.5	50	569	17	33.47	—	—	5	—	3/36
Waqar Younus	Pak	6	157.0	26	496	10	49.60	—	—	8	1	3/84
Wasim Akram	Pak	3	135.4	37	318	17	18.71	3	1	30	—	6/62
Watson W	NZ	3	113.0	20	355	2	177.50	—	—	9	3	2/103
Waugh ME	NSW	12	131.3	20	465	15	31.00	—	—	29	3	2/7
Waugh SR	NSW/Aus	12	9.0	3	19	1	19.00	—	—	2	—	1/3
Wellham DM	Tas	11	4.0	1	6	—	—	—	—	—	—	—

Continued

253

Bowler		M	Overs	Mdns	Runs	Wkts	Avrge	5	10	NB	W	Best
Whitney MR	NSW	8	220.5	58	639	24	26.63	1	—	19	—	5/125
Wijegunawardene												
KIW	SL	1	20.0	1	109	—	—	—	—	5	—	—
Williams BD	SA	2	4.0	1	15	—	—	—	—	—	—	—
Wood GM	WA	9	0.4	—	0	1	0.00	—	—	—	—	1/0
Yardley B	WA	4	104.0	31	303	8	37.88	—	—	1	—	3/76
Young PW	Vic	1	9.0	—	26	1	26.00	—	—	—	—	1/26
Zesers AK	SA	1	20.0	7	54	—	—	—	—	—	—	—
Zoehrer TJ	WA	12	7.0	2	13	1	13.00	—	—	—	—	1/9

FAI
INSURANCE CUP

THE 1989-90 LIMITED-OVERS COMPETITION was full of interest until the semi-finals, but the final between Western Australia and South Australia was a one-sided affair whose outcome was virtually decided in the opening overs. It was a good example of how dependent the limited-overs game is, as a spectator sport, on a reasonably close finish. Western Australia won the match by 7 wickets, which was consolation for its generally disappointing showing in the Sheffield Shield competition, yet quite consistent with the sharp improvement in its play later in the season. Western Australia won every match it played in the tournament and, in fact, found itself under pressure only once, and that was in its first match against New South Wales, which it won with one ball to spare.

South Australia v Queensland
Adelaide Oval, Adelaide
Oct 21 1989
Toss: Queensland
Result: South Australia won by 5 wkts

South Australia was carried to victory with 7 balls to spare by a partnership of 81 between Darren Lehmann, who scored his 67 off 64 balls, and Peter Sleep (45 not out). Earlier, Queensland had done well to make 210 after such a bad start. Queensland lost its first 2 wickets for only 1 run, but its captain, Greg Ritchie, steadied the innings with a fine 66.

Queensland

Batsman	How Out	Ttl	Balls	Mins	4s	6s
PE Cantrell	c Hilditch b Gladigau	1	6	7	—	—
TJ Barsby	lbw Johnston	23	60	71	3	—
RB Kerr	c Berry b Gladigau	0	1	1	—	—
GM Ritchie (c)	c Williams b Scuderi	66	115	176	2	—
SG Law	c Lehmann b Alley	14	19	31	1	—
BP Inwood	c Berry b Alley	13	24	21	2	—
PW Anderson (+)	not out	63	64	82	4	1
CJ McDermott	not out	13	14	21	—	—
D Tazelaar	did not bat					
CG Rackemann	did not bat					
PJ Carew	did not bat					
SUNDRIES: B. 0 LB. 12 W. 3 NB. 1		17	303	208	12	1
TOTAL	6 wkts for 210					
F/W: 1 1 37 69 91 176						

Bowler	O	M	R	Wkts	NB	W
Johnston	10	2	26	1	—	—
Gladigau	9.3	2	27	2	—	—
Williams	10	—	40	—	—	1
Scuderi	10	—	56	1	1	1
Alley	10	—	45	2	—	1
Hookes	0.3	—	4	—	—	—
Overs:	50.0					

▶

South Australia

Batsman	How Out	Ttl	Balls	Mins	4s	6s
BD Williams	c Anderson b Rackemann	20	60	75	1	—
AMJ Hilditch	c Kerr b Inwood	61	101	150	1	—
PC Nobes	c Anderson b Carew	9	19	19	2	—
DW Hookes (c)	b Carew	1	5	4	—	—
DS Lehmann	c Inwood b McDermott	67	64	102	4	—
PR Sleep	not out	45	42	56	3	—
JC Scuderi	not out	2	4	3	—	—
DS Berry (+)	did not bat					
PW Cladigau	did not bat					
DA Johnston	did not bat					
PJS Alley	did not bat					
SUNDRIES: B. 0 LB. 3 W. 3 NB. 0		6	295	207	11	—
TOTAL	5 wkts for 211					

F/W: 48 61 63 128 209

Bowler	O	M	R	Wkts	NB	W
McDermott	9.5	2	41	1	—	—
Tazelaar	10	1	23	—	—	2
Rackemann	9	1	40	1	—	1
Cantrell	10	1	41	—	—	—
Carew	6	—	39	2	—	—
Inwood	4	—	24	1	—	—
Overs:	48.5					

Umpires: AR Crafter & IR Berry

12th Men: GA Bishop (South Australia) & AB Henschell (Queensland)

Man of Match : DS Lehmann (South Australia)

South Australia v Victoria
Adelaide Oval, Adelaide
Oct 22 1989
Toss: Victoria
Result: Victoria won by 28 runs

Victoria got off to a fine start with an opening stand of 112, which was followed immediately by a brilliant innings of 84 not out by Jamie Siddons, who faced only 60 balls. South Australia, on the other hand, began badly, losing its first 3 wickets for 17 runs, so it was a creditable achievement by later batsmen to raise the total to 232. Siddons was named Man of the Match.

Victoria

Batsman	How Out	Ttl	Balls	Mins	4s	6s
GD Watts	run out	67	118	150	5	—
ID Frazer	c Berry b Williams	47	82	125	1	—
JD Siddons (c)	not out	84	60	82	8	—
WN Phillips	b Hilditch	28	29	38	2	—
PW Young	lbw Scuderi	4	4	2	—	—
AIC Dodemaide	not out	17	11	15	—	—
MGD Dimattina (+)	did not bat					
DW Fleming	did not bat					
PR Reiffel	did not bat					
PW Jackson	did not bat					
DJ Hickey	did not bat					
SUNDRIES: B. 3 LB. 6 W. 4 NB. —		13	304	208	16	—
TOTAL	4 wkts for 260					

F/W: 112 144 218 223

1st GRADE PREMIERS – CLAREMONT-NEDLANDS, PERTH

Back Row, l to r: K Gorey, B Johnson, S Cary, N Rohr, D Lovell. Front Row, l to r: D Reeve, C Beveridge, B Whiteaker (Captain), K Coughlan (Vice Captain), R Alikhan, J Brayshaw

1st GRADE PREMIERS – RICHMOND, MELBOURNE

Back row, l to r: A W Hill (Scorer), G J Clarke, P A Quinn, P R Reiffel, P J Davies, D J Saker, R A Hodges (12th), R Ward (Masseur). Front row, l to r: D King (Manager), D A Harris, G R Parker, R J Bright (Captain/Coach), M B Quinn, G J Holland, P W Jackson

NEW SOUTH WALES, COUNTRY

Back Row, l to r: Wayne McLennan, Grant Ryan, David Willis, John Frame, Craig Hamilton, Peter Gerharn, Murray Christie, Glenn Hooper. Front Row, l to r: Ivor Erwin (Assistant Manager), Eric Higgins, Stuart Bridges, Greg Arms (Captain), Mark Curry (Vice Captain), Mark Kelaher, Ken Robson (Manager)

AUSTRALIAN CAPITAL TERRITORY

Back Row, l to r: Mick Carruthers (Vice Captain), Neil Woods, Grant Woodbridge, Justin Williams, Andrew Yates, Colin Crouch, Ken Bone, Robbie Lopes, (Fitness Adviser); Front Row, l to r: Col Kelaart (Cricket Manager), Peter Solway, Eugene Nix, Greg Irvine (Captain), Paul Evans, Darryle MacDonald, Tony Duffy (Manager)

Bowler	O	M	R	Wkts	NB	W
Johnston	10	—	52	—	—	—
Gladigau	10	2	25	—	—	1
Scuderi	10	—	71	1	—	—
Alley	10	—	40	—	—	3
Williams	7	—	46	1	—	—
Hilditch	3	—	17	1	—	—
Overs:	50.0					

South Australia

Batsman	How Out	Ttl	Balls	Mins	4s	6s
BD Williams	run out	1	7	7	—	—
AMJ Hilditch	c & b Fleming	10	23	31	—	—
PC Nobes	c & b Hickey	1	9	11	—	—
DW Hookes (c)	b Fleming	18	24	37	2	—
DS Lehmann	lbw Jackson	33	42	57	3	—
PR Sleep	c Young b Jackson	41	66	83	2	—
JC Scuderi	b Reiffel	58	68	78	2	—
DS Berry (+)	run out	28	27	44	1	—
PW Gladigau	run out	17	14	14	1	—
PJS Alley	not out	8	10	17	—	—
DA Johnston	not out	6	14	14	—	—
SUNDRIES: B. 0 LB. 5 W. 2 NB. 2		11	304	201	11	—
TOTAL	9 wkts for 232					

F/W: 2 11 17 52 85 148 185 215 217

Bowler	O	M	R	Wkts	NB	W
Hickey	10	1	48	1	—	—
Fleming	10	1	35	2	—	1
Reiffel	10	—	51	1	2	1
Jackson	10	1	37	2	—	—
Dodemaide	10	—	56	—	—	—
Overs:	50.0					

Umpires: DJ Harper & DB Rebbeck

12th Men: GA Bishop (South Australia) & GR Parker (Victoria)

Man of Match: JD Siddons (Victoria)

Western Australia v New South Wales
WACA Ground, Perth
Oct 22 1989
Toss: New South Wales
Result: Western Australia won by 4 wkts

The home side overtook New South Wales with just one ball to spare in a high scoring match. Steve Small (80) was the mainstay of the New South Wales innings, while his team-mates pushed along the scoring. Needing to score almost 5 runs an over to win, Western Australia for a time fell behind in its run chase, but Wayne Andrews (72) led a charge home to victory and was named Man of the Match.

New South Wales

Batsman	How Out	Ttl	Balls	Mins	4s	6s
J Dyson (c)	c & b Mullally	0	11	17	—	—
SM Small	b Capes	80	124	158	7	—
ME Waugh	c Zoehrer b Capes	32	47	50	3	—
D Tucker	c Zoehrer b Mullally	11	17	17	1	—
TH Bayliss	c Veletta b MacLeay	36	57	72	2	—
GL Smith	not out	24	27	40	2	—
PH Marks	not out	39	31	36	5	—
GRJ Matthews	did not bat					
PA Emery (+)	did not bat					
WJ Holdsworth	did not bat					
MR Whitney	did not bat					
SUNDRIES: B. 0 LB. 8 W. 8 NB. 5		26	314	200	20	—
TOTAL	5 wkts for 248					

F/W: 10 83 98 181 183

▶

Bowler	O	M	R	Wkts	NB	W
Mullally	10	2	56	2	4	—
MacLeay	9	1	46	1	—	5
Capes	10	—	46	2	1	2
Russell	10	1	46	—	—	1
Hogan	10	—	42	—	—	—
Andrews	1	—	4	—	—	—
Overs:	50.0					

Western Australia

Batsman	How Out	Ttl	Balls	Mins	4s	6s
P Gonnella	lbw Whitney	14	20	35	2	—
MRJ Veletta	lbw Holdsworth	31	54	64	4	—
GM Wood (c)	b Smith	50	69	91	3	—
WS Andrews	b Whitney	72	84	117	5	1
JA Brayshaw	st Emery b Matthews	4	9	9	—	—
TJ Zoehrer (+)	not out	57	54	76	8	—
KH MacLeay	c & b Waugh	6	14	23	—	—
RS Russell	not out	1	2	7	—	—
TG Hogan	did not bat					
PA Capes	did not bat					
AD Mullally	did not bat					
SUNDRIES: B. 2 LB. 10 W. 5 NB. 0		17	306	217	22	1
TOTAL	6 wkts for 252					

F/W: 37 58 129 142 202 241

Bowler	O	M	R	Wkts	NB	W
Whitney	10	—	38	2	—	1
Holdsworth	10	—	41	1	—	1
Marks	9	—	50	—	—	2
Smith	8	—	39	1	—	—
Matthews	8	—	46	1	—	1
Waugh	4.5	—	26	1	—	—
Overs:	49.5					

Umpires: RJ Evans & TA Prue

12th Men: DJ Ramshaw (Western Australia) & BE McNamara (New South Wales)

Man of Match: WS Andrews (Western Australia)

New South Wales v Tasmania
North Sydney Oval, North Sydney
Oct 28 1989
Toss: New South Wales
Result: New South Wales won by 83 runs

Batting first, New South Wales lost 5 wickets by run-outs and could manage only the moderate total of 183. So victory seemed within Tasmania's reach, but in the first over of its innings Scott Hookey was out lbw, and from then on Tasmania's batting was always in trouble. Brad McNamara, making his debut for New South Wales, was named Man of the Match after scoring 20 and taking 3 wickets for 26.

New South Wales

Batsman	How Out	Ttl	Balls	Mins	4s	6s
J Dyson (c)	c Tucker b Campbell	3	5	6	—	—
SM Small	run out	48	80	102	5	—
ME Waugh	run out	0	6	7	—	—
D Tucker	b De Winter	15	46	62	1	—
TH Bayliss	run out	18	46	43	1	—
BE McNamara	c O'Connor b Tucker	20	41	58	—	—
GL Smith	run out	37	57	60	2	—

Continued

Batsman	How Out	Ttl	Balls	Mins	4s	6s
PH Marks	c Soule b Tucker	7	12	13	—	—
PA Emery (+)	run out	8	7	14	1	—
MR Whitney	lbw Gilbert	0	1	2	—	—
WJ Holdsworth	not out	7	3	4	—	1
SUNDRIES: B. 0 LB. 15 W. 3 NB. 1		20				
TOTAL		183	304	190	10	1

F/W: 5 10 67 83 99 145 157 169 170 183

Bowler	O	M	R	Wkts	NB	W
Gilbert	10	—	33	1	1	—
Campbell	10	—	33	1	—	—
De Winter	10	3	26	1	—	2
Tucker	10	1	35	2	—	—
Robertson	10	—	41	—	—	1
Overs:	50.0					

Tasmania

Batsman	How Out	Ttl	Balls	Mins	4s	6s
SG Hookey	lbw Whitney	0	5	2	—	—
G Shipperd	b McNamara	28	87	106	2	—
J Cox	c Bayliss b Whitney	8	23	32	—	—
RJ Tucker	b Holdsworth	5	9	11	1	—
DM Wellham (c)	c Waugh b Marks	32	63	95	1	—
DFG O'Connor	b McNamara	0	1	1	—	—
GR Robertson	c McNamara b Marks	2	8	9	—	—
RE Soule (+)	b Marks	2	11	8	—	—
AJ De Winter	b McNamara	17	14	10	3	—
GD Campbell	not out	0	7	11	—	—
DR Gilbert	b Marks	0	10	8	—	—
SUNDRIES: B. 0 LB. 0 W. 4 NB. 1		6	238	153	7	—
TOTAL		100				

F/W: 0 12 17 68 68 73 79 100 100 100

Bowler	O	M	R	Wkts	NB	W
Whitney	5	—	8	2	—	—
Holdsworth	7	2	16	1	—	2
Smith	5	1	7	—	—	—
Waugh	4	—	13	—	—	—
Marks	9.5	1	30	4	—	1
McNamara	8	2	26	3	1	1
Overs:	38.5					

Umpires: IS Thomas & GE Reed

12th Men: SBJ Whitfield (New South Wales) & PI Faulkner (Tasmania)

Man of Match: BE McNamara (New South Wales)

Queensland v Victoria
Brisbane Cricket Ground, Brisbane
Oct 29 1989
Toss: Victoria
Result: Queensland by 7 wkts

This was a disappointing match for the Victorians. They were all out for 78, and their bowlers sent down 9 wides in only 24 overs. Having been set such a small target, the Queenslanders caused some surprise by batting carefully. If they had scored the necessary 79 runs in 84 balls they would have topped their group on the basis of run rates and therefore played the semi-final on their home ground. Instead, Queensland finished second behind South Australia.

Victoria

Batsman	How Out	Ttl	Balls	Mins	4s	6s
GM Watts	c Ritchie b Tazelaar	7	30	43	—	—
ID Frazer	b McDermott	5	18	18	—	—
JD Siddons (c)	c Trimble b Tazelaar	4	6	11	1	—
WN Phillips	run out	0	0	3	—	—
GR Parker	c Ritchie b Rackemann	4	11	14	—	—
PW Young	b Rackemann	1	21	26	—	—
AIC Dodemaide	b Polzin	7	31	53	1	—
MGD Dimattina (+)	c Tazelaar b Cantrell	30	89	94	—	—
RCAM McCarthy	b Inwood	5	26	25	—	—
DW Fleming	c Anderson b Inwood	2	13	19	—	—
PW Jackson	not out	2	14	15	—	—
SUNDRIES: B. 0 LB. 4 W. 5 NB. 1		11	259	165	2	—
TOTAL		78				

F/W: 11 20 22 24 27 32 45 58 68 78

Bowler	O	M	R	Wkts	NB	W
McDermott	5	—	12	1	1	—
Tazelaar	10	2	18	2	—	1
Rackemann	7	3	7	2	—	1
Inwood	10	—	20	2	—	2
Polzin	5	1	10	1	—	1
Cantrell	5.1	2	7	1	—	—
Overs:	42.1					

Queensland

Batsman	How Out	Ttl	Balls	Mins	4s	6s
PE Cantrell	lbw Dodemaide	24	54	63	3	—
TJ Barsby	b Fleming	0	8	10	—	—
SG Law	run out	37	72	79	2	—
GS Trimble	not out	6	17	36	1	—
BP Inwood	not out	0	2	3	—	—
GM Ritchie (c)	did not bat					
PW Anderson (+)	did not bat					
CJ McDermott	did not bat					
D Tazelaar	did not bat					
CG Rackemann	did not bat					
MA Polzin	did not bat					
SUNDRIES: B. 1 LB. 2 W. 9 NB. 0		12	153	94	6	—
TOTAL	3 wkts for 79					

F/W: 6 56 72

Bowler	O	M	R	Wkts	NB	W
Fleming	10	2	30	1	—	6
McCarthy	6	—	25	—	—	3
Dodemaide	6	1	13	1	—	—
Jackson	2	—	8	—	—	—
Overs:	24.0					

Umpires: AJ McQuillan & CA Bertwistle

12th Men: RB Kerr (Queensland) & DJ Hickey (Victoria)

Man of Match: D Tazelaar (Queensland)

Western Australia v Tasmania
WACA Ground, Perth
Nov 5 1989
Toss: Tasmania
Result: Western Australia won by 4 wkts

A fine innings by Tom Moody, who scored 102 not out off just 100 balls, enabled Western Australia to pass Tasmania's big total with almost three overs to spare. He was rewarded by being named Man of the Match. In its previous match Western Australia had made 6 for 252 to win, and here it made 6 for 250. A factor in Tasmania's defeat was the loss of three wickets by run-outs.

Tasmania

Batsman	How Out	Ttl	Balls	Mins	4s	6s
SG Hookey	c & b Hogan	76	117	142	7	1
DM Wellham (c)	run out	10	29	48	—	—
DC Boon	b Russell	11	17	27	2	—
J Cox	run out	25	48	41	1	1
RJ Tucker	c Russell b Alderman	54	56	60	4	—
DFG O'Connor	run out	30	31	36	2	—
AJ De Winter	not out	16	16	13	2	—
GR Robertson	not out	1	1	1	—	—
RE Soule (+)	did not bat					
TD Bower	did not bat					
GD Campbell	did not bat					
SUNDRIES: B. 4 LB. 9 W. 7 NB. 3		26	309	195	18	2
TOTAL	6 wkts for 249					

F/W: 35 61 116 148 224 246

Bowler	O	M	R	Wkts	NB	W
Capes	9	1	40	—	2	4
Alderman	10	1	45	1	1	—
Russell	8	1	40	1	—	—
MacLeay	6	—	30	—	—	2
Hogan	10	—	41	1	—	—
Moody	7	—	40	—	—	1
Overs:	50.0					

Western Australia

Batsman	How Out	Ttl	Balls	Mins	4s	6s
GR Marsh	c Soule b Robertson	38	83	93	2	—
MRJ Veletta	c O'Connor b Campbell	2	28	32	—	—
TM Moody	not out	102	100	169	6	1
GM Wood (c)	c Soule b Tucker	2	4	5	—	—
WS Andrews	c Tucker b Robertson	29	34	37	2	—
TJ Zoehrer (+)	lbw Tucker	18	27	26	2	—
TG Hogan	lbw Campbell	7	13	12	—	—
KH MacLeay	not out	15	9	20	1	—
RS Russell	did not bat					
PA Capes	did not bat					
TM Alderman	did not bat					
SUNDRIES: B. 7 LB. 11 W. 11 NB. 4		37	298	203	13	1
TOTAL	6 wkts for 250					

F/W: 16 99 104 158 195 211

Bowler	O	M	R	Wkts	NB	W
Campbell	8.2	2	32	2	1	—
Bower	9	1	36	—	—	4
De Winter	10	—	79	—	3	5
Robertson	10	—	50	2	—	1
Tucker	10	1	35	2	—	1
Overs:	47.2					

Umpires: RJ Evans & RA Emerson

12th Men: AD Mullally (Western Australia) & G Shipperd (Tasmania)

Man of Match: TM Moody (Western Australia)

FAI CUP SEMI FINAL

Western Australia v Queensland
WACA Ground, Perth
Mar 17 1990
Toss: Queensland
Result: Western Australia won by 6 wkts

Tom Moody's fine performances with both ball and bat were largely responsible for Western Australia's easy victory in this match. Batting first, the Queenslanders had scored freely against the Western Australian pace bowlers before Moody, who had not bowled for several months because of a back complaint, was brought on to bowl his medium pace. Almost at once he took the wicket of Steve Storey (23) and not long afterwards the wickets of Greg Ritchie (39) and then Geoff Foley (28). After its strong start, the Queensland innings eventually ended at 202, Peter Clifford top scoring with 52 not out. Although it was generally expected that the Queenslanders would find it hard to defend this total, nobody expected the Western Australians to win as easily as they did. Its top order batsmen, most notably Moody, scored at such a furious rate—better than a run per ball—that Western Australia passed the Queensland total in only the 33rd over. Moody, later chosen as Man of the Match, scored his 81 off only 63 balls and hit 12 fours and a six. Queensland's cause was not helped by some dissension within the team while Western Australia was batting.

Queensland

Batsman	How Out	Ttl	Balls	Mins	4s	6s
PE Cantrell	b Mack	17	41	54	1	—
SC Storey	c Brayshaw b Moody	23	58	85	—	1
CM Ritchie (c)	c Zoehrer b Moody	39	46	60	2	—
GI Foley	c Andrews b Moody	28	47	47	2	—
PS Clifford	not out	52	73	90	1	—
SG Law	lbw Matthews	7	15	17	—	—
BP Inwood	b Matthews	9	10	16	1	—
BR Stephensen	c Andrews b MacLeay	1	3	3	—	—
MS Kasprowicz	c Brayshaw b Mack	1	12	16	—	—
PJ Drinnen (+)	c Veletta b Matthews	0	2	4	—	—
D Tazelaar	run out	2	2	6	—	—
SUNDRIES: B. 1 LB. 10 W. 10 NB. 1		23	309	208	7	1
TOTAL		202				

F/W: 49 74 112 135 150 168 171 187 191 202

Bowler	O	M	R	Wkts	NB	W
Capes	8	1	21	—	1	4
MacLeay	8	—	33	1	—	2
Mack	7	—	34	2	—	2
Hogan	8	—	36	—	—	—
Moody	10	—	29	3	—	1
Matthews	9	—	38	3	—	1
Overs:	50.0					

Western Australia

Batsman	How Out	Ttl	Balls	Mins	4s	6s
MRJ Veletta	c Drinnen b Kasprowicz	52	71	133	5	—
MW McPhee	c Drinnen b Stephensen	32	46	52	7	—
TM Moody	c Drinnen b Tazelaar	81	63	54	12	1
WS Andrews (c)	c Tazelaar b Foley	11	18	17	2	—
JA Brayshaw	not out	3	9	9	—	—
KH MacLeay	not out	0	1	3	—	—
TJ Zoehrer (+)	did not bat					
CD Matthews	did not bat					
TG Hogan	did not bat					
PA Capes	did not bat					
CD Mack	did not bat					
SUNDRIES: B.1 LB.6 W.5 NB.6		24	208	138	26	1
TOTAL	4 wkts for 203					

F/W: 70 170 193 201

Bowler	O	M	R	Wkts	NB	W
Tazelaar	8	—	50	1	6	—
Kasprowicz	10	—	57	1	—	3
Stephensen	4	—	18	1	—	1
Foley	4.5	—	19	1	—	1
Inwood	3	—	29	—	—	—
Cantrell	3	—	23	—	—	—
Overs:	32.5					

Umpires: PJ McConnell & RJ Evans

12th Men: BP Julian (Western Australia) & RD Robinson (Queensland)

Man of Match: TM Moody (Western Australia)

FAI CUP SEMI FINAL

South Australia v New South Wales
Adelaide Oval, Adelaide
Mar 18 1990
Toss: South Australia
Result: South Australia won by 53 runs

A match which looked at one time to be heading for a close finish was won easily in the end by South Australia after its captain, David Hookes, achieved unexpected success bowling his left arm spin. Brisk scoring by South Australia's middle order (Hookes 45, Darren Lehmann 52 and Michael Bevan 55) ensured that South Australia compiled the substantial total of 9 for 234. Lehmann batted impressively, scoring rapidly with singles and twos yet taking no risks, but then lost his wicket in ungainly fashion, drawing away to cut a ball on his stumps and missing. After an uncertain start, New South Wales had moved to 3 for 118 in the 33rd over when Hookes claimed the extremely valuable wicket of Mark Waugh, who by then had scored 50. Having taken Waugh's wicket in his second over, Hookes continued to bowl himself and took wickets in his sixth, seventh, eighth and ninth overs. Although Greg Matthews (38) delayed South Australia's rapid advance to victory, the last New South Wales wicket fell in the 49th over. Tim May, returning to the team after his knee injury, took 1 for 32 in 10 overs. Hookes's batting and bowling success earned him the Man of the Match title.

South Australia

Batsman	How Out	Ttl	Balls	Mins	4s	6s
AMJ Hilditch	c Lawson b Holdsworth	31	52	80	5	—
DB Scott	c Emery b Whitney	9	36	41	—	—
PC Nobes	b Matthews	13	25	30	1	—
DW Hookes (c)	c Waugh b Matthews	45	55	56	1	—
DS Lehmann	b Waugh	52	60	85	1	—
MG Bevan	c Matthews b Marks	55	58	65	3	—
JC Scuderi	run out	0	5	5	—	—
DS Berry (+)	c O'Neill b Marks	7	8	12	—	—
PW Gladigau	b McNamara	4	5	7	—	—
CR Miller	not out	1	2	4	—	—
TBA May	not out	2	2	2	—	—
SUNDRIES: B. 0 LB. 5 W. 6 NB. 2		15	308	198	13	—
TOTAL	9 wkts for 234					

F/W: 25 53 62 139 186 189 217 231 231

Bowler	O	M	R	Wkts	NB	W
Lawson	7	3	9	—	—	1
Whitney	10	—	37	1	—	2
Holdsworth	5	—	31	1	—	1
Matthews	10	—	50	2	—	—
Waugh	10	—	47	1	1	1
Marks	5	—	35	2	—	1
McNamara	3	—	20	1	1	—
Overs:	50.0					

New South Wales

Batsman	How Out	Ttl	Balls	Mins	4s	6s
SM Small	lbw Gladigau	7	21	16	1	—
TH Bayliss	c Nobes b Gladigau	22	28	46	4	—
MD O'Neill	run out	1	9	11	—	—
ME Waugh	c Berry b Hookes	50	78	95	—	1
GRJ Matthews	c Scott b May	38	80	93	—	—
BE McNamara	c Gladigau b Hookes	16	29	36	—	—
PH Marks	b Hookes	5	9	10	—	—
PA Emery (+)	st Berry b Hookes	10	12	23	—	—
GF Lawson	c Hilditch b Scuderi	1	4	3	—	—
MR Whitney	st Berry b Hookes	12	17	17	—	—
WJ Holdsworth	not out	5	7	7	—	—
SUNDRIES: B. 1 LB. 9 W. 1 NB. 1		14	294	183	5	1
TOTAL		181				

F/W: 16 21 36 118 128 140 151 153 170 181

Bowler	O	M	R	Wkts	NB	W
Gladigau	10	2	29	2	—	—
Miller	10	2	32	—	—	—
Scuderi	9	—	37	1	1	1
May	10	1	32	1	—	—
Hookes	9.3	—	41	5	—	1
Overs:	48.3					

Umpires: AR Crafter & DJ Harper

12th Men: BD Williams (South Australia) & GS Milliken (New South Wales)

Man of Match: DW Hookes (South Australia)

FAI CUP FINAL

Western Australia v South Australia
WACA Ground, Perth
Mar 31 1990
Toss: Western Australia
Result: Western Australia won by 7 wkts

Western Australia's victory seemed virtually assured before the match was a half-hour old. Batting first, the South Australians lost their first wicket for 0 when Terry Alderman bowled Andrew Hilditch with the sixth ball of the match and they lost their second and third wickets in Alderman's third over. From this point, it seemed all but impossible for the South Australians to get back into the match unless one of the two young middle-order batsmen, such as Darren Lehmann and Michael Bevan, managed to play a really big innings. Neither did, although Bevan survived until the end, finishing with 23 not out. To add to South Australia's troubles, two batsmen in succession were run out. South Australia's total of 87 was its lowest ever in interstate limited-overs matches, the previous lowest having been its 97 against Queensland in 1975-76. The Western Australian batsmen seemed unlikely to encounter problems making the necessary runs, and no problems arose. They hit the winning run in only the 20th over, a premature and rather tame ending to a match which promised much excitement. Terry Alderman, who took 4 for 14, was named Man of the Match in recognition of the critical damage he did to South Australia's batting.

South Australia

Batsman	How Out	Ttl	Balls	Mins	4s	6s
AMJ Hilditch	b Alderman	0	6	4	—	—
PC Nobes	c Veletta b MacLeay	9	30	63	2	—
JC Scuderi	c Zoehrer b Alderman	5	12	13	1	—
DW Hookes (c)	c Zoehrer b Alderman	0	4	2	—	—
DS Lehmann	lbw Alderman	11	22	25	1	—
MG Bevan	not out	23	57	103	—	—
DB Scott	run out	10	25	23	1	—
DS Berry (+)	run out	10	24	20	1	—
PW Gladigau	b Matthews	0	3	2	—	—
CR Miller	c Veletta b MacLeay	4	30	31	—	—
TBA May	c Moody b Matthews	2	3	6	—	—
SUNDRIES: B. 0 LB. 6 W. 7 NB. 0		13	191	155	6	—
TOTAL		87				

F/W: 0 7 8 28 30 45 61 61 82 87

Bowler	O	M	R	Wkts	NB	W
Alderman	8	3	14	4	—	1
Capes	5	—	19	—	—	1
MacLeay	8	2	18	2	—	—
Matthews	9.5	3	16	2	—	4
Moody	4	—	14	—	—	1
Overs:	34.5					

Western Australia

Batsman	How Out	Ttl	Balls	Mins	4s	6s
MW McPhee	c Berry b Miller	25	41	50	3	—
GR Marsh (c)	not out	29	55	84	5	—
TM Moody	c May b Gladigau	8	12	11	1	—
WS Andrews	c Hookes b Miller	8	11	14	1	—
MRJ Veletta	not out	4	4	3	—	—
JA Brayshaw	did not bat					
TJ Zoehrer (+)	did not bat					
KH MacLeay	did not bat					
CD Matthews	did not bat					
PA Capes	did not bat					
TM Alderman	did not bat					
SUNDRIES: B. 0 LB. 6 W. 8 NB. 0		14	123	84	10	—
TOTAL	4 wkts for 88					

F/W: 46 67 84

Bowler	O	M	R	Wkts	NB	W
Miller	10	—	42	2	—	4
Gladigau	9.1	1	40	1	—	4
Overs:	19.1					

Umpires: TA Prue & RJ Evans

12th Men: TG Hogan (Western Australia) & SPG George (South Australia)

Man of Match: TM Alderman (Western Australia)

1989/90 FAI INSURANCE CUP

The Games

Date	Match	Venue	Batted 1st		Batted 2nd		Result
Oct 21	SA v Qld	Adelaide	Qld°	6-210	SA	5-211	SA by 5 wkts
Oct 22	SA v Vic	Adelaide	Vic°	4-260	SA	9-232	Vic by 28 runs
Oct 22	WA v NSW	Perth	NSW°	5-248	WA	6-252	WA by 4 wkts
Oct 28	NSW v Tas	Nth Sydney	NSW°	183	Tas	100	NSW by 83 runs
Oct 29	Qld v Vic	Brisbane	Vic°	78	Qld	3-79	Qld by 7 wkts
Nov 6	WA v Tas	Perth	Tas°	6-249	WA	6-250	WA by 4 wkts
Mar 17	WA v Qld	Perth	Qld°	202	WA	4-203	WA by 6 wkts
Mar 18	SA v NSW	Adelaide	SA°	9-234	NSW	181	SA by 53 runs
Mar 31	WA v SA	Perth	SA	87	WA°	3-88	WA by 7 wkts

Leading Batting Averages—(Minimum—100 Runs)

Batsman	State	M	Inn	NO	Runs	HS	50	100	Avrge
TM Moody	WA	3	3	1	191	102°	1	1	95.50
GM Ritchie	Qld	3	2	—	105	66	1	—	52.50
SM Small	NSW	3	3	—	135	80	1	—	45.00
DS Lehmann	SA	4	4	—	163	67	2	—	40.75
WS Andrews	WA	4	4	—	120	72	1	—	30.00
AMJ Hilditch	SA	4	4	—	102	61	1	—	25.50

Leading Bowling Averages—(Minimum—5 Wkts)

Bowler	State	M	Overs	Mdns	Runs	Wkts	Avrge	5wi	NB	W	Best
DW Hookes	SA	4	10.0	—	45	5	9.00	1	—	1	5/41
CD Matthews	WA	2	18.5	3	54	5	10.80	—	—	5	3/38
TM Alderman	WA	2	18.0	4	59	5	11.80	—	1	1	4/14
MR Whitney	NSW	3	25.0	—	83	5	16.60	—	—	3	2/8
PH Marks	NSW	3	23.5	1	115	6	19.17	—	—	4	4/30
PW Gladigau	SA	4	38.4	7	121	5	24.20	—	—	5	2/27

Centuries

102°	TM Moody	Western Australia v Tasmania	Perth

Five Wickets in an Innings

5/41	DW Hookes	South Australia v New South Wales	Adelaide

Highest Wicket Partnerships

Wkt	Ttl	Batsmen	Team	Opponent	Venue
1st	112	GM Watts, ID Frazer	Victoria	South Australia	Adelaide
2nd	100	MRJ Veletta, TM Moody	Western Australia	Queensland	Perth
3rd	74	JD Siddons, WN Phillips	Victoria	South Australia	Adelaide
4th	83	SM Small, TH Bayliss	New South Wales	Tasmania	Nth Sydney
5th	81	DS Lehmann, PR Sleep	South Australia	Queensland	Adelaide
6th	85	GM Ritchie, PW Anderson	Queensland	South Australia	Adelaide
7th	39°	TM Moody, KH MacLeay	Western Australia	Tasmania	Perth
8th	21	DM Wellham, AJ De Winter	Tasmania	New South Wales	Nth Sydney
9th	21	MG Bevan, CR Miller	South Australia	Western Australia	Perth
10th	13	PA Emery, WJ Holdsworth	New South Wales	Tasmania	Nth Sydney

Highest Partnerships

Wkt	Ttl	Batsmen	Team	Opponent	Venue
1st	112	GM Watts, ID Frazer	Victoria	South Australia	Adelaide
2nd	100	MRJ Veletta, TM Moody	Western Australia	Queensland	Perth
6th	85	GM Ritchie, PW Anderson	Queensland	South Australia	Adelaide
4th	83	SM Small, TH Bayliss	New South Wales	Tasmania	Nth Sydney
2nd	83	GR Marsh, TM Moody	Western Australia	Tasmania	Perth
4th	82	ME Waugh, CRJ Matthews	New South Wales	South Australia	Adelaide
5th	81	DS Lehmann, PR Sleep	South Australia	Queensland	Adelaide
4th	77	DW Hookes, DS Lehmann	South Australia	New South Wales	Adelaide
3rd	74	JD Siddons, WN Phillips	Victoria	South Australia	Adelaide
3rd	71	GM Wood, WS Andrews	Western Australia	New South Wales	Perth
1st	70	MRJ Veletta, MW McPhee	Western Australia	Queensland	Perth
6th	65°	PH Marks, GL Smith	New South Wales	Tasmania	Nth Sydney
4th	65	AMJ Hilditch, DS Lehmann	South Australia	Queensland	Adelaide
6th	63	PR Sleep, JC Scuderi	South Australia	Victoria	Adelaide
5th	60	WS Andrews, TJ Zoehrer	Western Australia	New South Wales	Perth

Wkt	Ttl	Batsmen	Team	Opponent	Venue
3rd	57	SM Small, DC Tucker	New South Wales	Tasmania	Nth Sydney
4th	54	TM Moody, WS Andrews	Western Australia	Tasmania	Perth
4th	51	G Shipperd, DM Wellham	Tasmania	New South Wales	Nth Sydney
2nd	50	PE Cantrell, SG Law	Queensland	Victoria	Brisbane

1989/90 FAI Cup Averages

Batting	State	M	Inn	NO	Runs	HS	50	100	Avrge	Ct	St
Alderman, TM	WA	2	—	—	—	—	—	—	—	—	—
Alley, PJS	SA	2	1	1	8	8°	—	—	—	—	—
Anderson, PW	Qld	2	1	1	63	63°	1	—	—	3	—
Andrews, WS	WA	4	4	—	120	72	1	—	30.00	2	—
Barsby, TJ	Qld	2	2	—	23	23	—	—	11.50	—	—
Bayliss, TH	NSW	3	3	—	76	36	—	—	25.33	1	—
Berry, DS	SA	4	3	—	45	28	—	—	15.00	5	2
Bevan, MG	SA	2	2	1	78	55	1	—	78.00	—	—
Boon, DC	Tas	1	1	—	11	11	—	—	11.00	—	—
Bower, TD	Tas	1	—	—	—	—	—	—	—	—	—
Brayshaw, JA	WA	3	2	1	7	4	—	—	7.00	2	—
Campbell, GD	Tas	2	1	1	—	0°	—	—	—	—	—
Cantrell, PE	Qld	3	3	—	42	24	—	—	14.00	—	—
Capes, PA	WA	4	—	—	—	—	—	—	—	—	—
Carew, PJ	Qld	1	—	—	—	—	—	—	—	—	—
Clifford, PS	Qld	1	1	1	52	52°	1	—	—	—	—
Cox, J	Tas	2	2	—	33	25	—	—	16.50	—	—
De Winter, AJ	Tas	2	2	1	33	17	—	—	33.00	—	—
Dimattina, MGD	Vic	2	1	—	30	30	—	—	30.00	—	—
Dodemaide, AIC	Vic	2	2	1	24	17°	—	—	24.00	—	—
Drinnen, PJ	Qld	1	1	—	0	0	—	—	0.00	3	—
Dyson, J	NSW	2	2	—	3	3	—	—	1.50	—	—
Emery, PA	NSW	3	2	—	18	10	—	—	9.00	1	1
Fleming, DW	Vic	2	1	—	2	2	—	—	2.00	2	—
Foley, GI	Qld	1	1	—	28	28	—	—	28.00	—	—
Frazer, ID	Vic	2	2	—	52	47	—	—	26.00	—	—
Gilbert, DR	Tas	1	1	—	0	0	—	—	0.00	—	—
Gladigau, PW	SA	4	2	—	21	17	—	—	10.50	1	—
Gonnella, P	WA	1	1	—	14	14	—	—	14.00	—	—
Hickey, DJ	Vic	1	—	—	—	—	—	—	—	—	—
Hilditch, AMJ	SA	4	4	—	102	61	1	—	25.50	2	—
Hogan, TG	WA	3	1	—	7	7	—	—	7.00	1	—
Holdsworth, WJ	NSW	3	2	2	12	7°	—	—	—	—	—
Hookes, DW	SA	4	4	—	64	45	—	—	16.00	1	—
Hookey, SG	Tas	2	2	—	76	76	1	—	38.00	—	—
Inwood, BP	Qld	3	3	1	22	13	—	—	11.00	1	—
Jackson, PW	Vic	2	1	1	2	2°	—	—	—	—	—
Johnston, DA	SA	2	1	1	6	6°	—	—	—	—	—
Kasprowicz, MS	Qld	1	1	—	1	1	—	—	1.00	—	—
Kerr, RB	Qld	1	1	—	0	0	—	—	0.00	1	—
Lawson, GF	NSW	1	1	—	1	1	—	—	1.00	1	—
Law, SG	Qld	3	3	—	58	37	—	—	19.33	—	—
Lehmann, DS	SA	4	4	—	163	67	2	—	40.75	1	—
MacLeay, KH	WA	4	3	2	21	15°	—	—	21.00	—	—
Mack, CD	WA	1	—	—	—	—	—	—	—	—	—
Marks, PH	NSW	3	3	1	51	39°	—	—	25.50	—	—
Marsh, GR	WA	2	2	1	67	38	—	—	67.00	—	—
Matthews, CD	WA	2	—	—	—	—	—	—	—	—	—
Matthews, GRJ	NSW	2	1	—	38	38	—	—	38.00	1	—
May, TBA	SA	2	2	1	4	2°	—	—	4.00	1	—
McCarthy, RCAM	Vic	1	1	—	5	5	—	—	5.00	—	—
McDermott, CJ	Qld	2	1	1	13	13°	—	—	—	—	—
McNamara, BE	NSW	2	2	—	36	20	—	—	18.00	1	—
McPhee, MW	WA	2	2	—	57	32	—	—	28.50	—	—
Miller, CR	SA	2	2	1	5	4	—	—	5.00	—	—
Moody, TM	WA	3	3	1	191	102°	1	1	95.50	1	—
Mullally, AD	WA	1	—	—	—	—	—	—	—	1	—
Nobes, PC	SA	4	4	—	32	13	—	—	8.00	1	—
O'Connor, DFG	Tas	2	2	—	30	30	—	—	15.00	2	—
O'Neill, MD	NSW	1	1	—	1	1	—	—	1.00	1	—
Parker, GR	Vic	1	1	—	4	4	—	—	4.00	—	—
Phillips, WN	Vic	2	2	—	28	28	—	—	14.00	—	—
Polzin, MA	Qld	1	—	—	—	—	—	—	—	—	—
Rackemann, CG	Qld	2	—	—	—	—	—	—	—	—	—
Reiffel, PR	Vic	1	—	—	—	—	—	—	—	—	—
Ritchie, GM	Qld	3	2	—	105	66	1	—	52.50	2	—

Continued

Batting	State	M	Inn	NO	Runs	HS	50	100	Avrge	Ct	St
Robertson, GR	Tas	2	2	1	3	2	—	—	3.00	—	—
Russell, RS	WA	2	1	1	1	1*	—	—	—	1	—
Scott, DB	SA	2	2	—	19	10	—	—	9.50	1	—
Scuderi, JC	SA	4	4	1	65	58	1	—	21.67	—	—
Shipperd, G	Tas	1	1	—	28	28	—	—	28.00	—	—
Siddons, JD	Vic	2	2	1	88	84*	1	—	88.00	—	—
Sleep, PR	SA	2	2	1	86	45*	—	—	86.00	—	—
Small, SM	NSW	3	3	—	135	80	1	—	45.00	—	—
Smith, GL	NSW	2	2	1	61	37	—	—	61.00	—	—
Soule, RE	Tas	2	1	—	2	2	—	—	2.00	3	—
Stephensen, BR	Qld	1	1	—	1	1	—	—	1.00	—	—
Storey, SC	Qld	1	1	—	23	23	—	—	23.00	—	—
Tazelaar, D	Qld	3	1	—	2	2	—	—	2.00	2	—
Trimble, GS	Qld	1	1	1	6	6*	—	—	—	1	—
Tucker, D	NSW	2	2	—	26	15	—	—	13.00	—	—
Tucker, RJ	Tas	2	2	—	59	54	1	—	29.50	2	—
Veletta, MRJ	WA	4	4	1	89	52	1	—	29.67	4	—
Watts, GM	Vic	2	2	—	74	67	1	—	37.00	—	—
Waugh, ME	NSW	3	3	—	82	50	1	—	27.33	3	—
Wellham, DM	Tas	2	2	—	42	32	—	—	21.00	—	—
Whitney, MR	NSW	3	2	—	12	12	—	—	6.00	—	—
Williams, BD	SA	2	2	—	21	20	—	—	10.50	1	—
Wood, GM	WA	2	2	—	52	50	1	—	26.00	—	—
Young, PW	Vic	2	2	—	5	4	—	—	2.50	1	—
Zoehrer, TJ	WA	4	2	1	75	57*	1	—	75.00	5	—

Bowling	State	M	Overs	Mdns	Runs	Wkts	Avrge	5wi	NB	W	Best
Alderman, TM	WA	2	18.0	4	59	5	11.80	—	1	1	4/14
Alley, PJS	SA	2	20.0	—	85	2	42.50	—	—	4	2/45
Andrews, WS	WA	4	1.0	—	4	—	—	—	—	—	—
Bower, TD	Tas	1	9.0	1	36	—	—	—	—	4	—
Campbell, GD	Tas	2	18.2	2	65	3	21.67	—	1	—	2/32
Cantrell, PE	Qld	3	18.1	1	71	1	71.00	—	—	—	1/7
Capes, PA	WA	4	32.0	2	126	2	63.00	—	4	11	2/46
Carew, PJ	Qld	1	6.0	—	39	2	19.50	—	—	—	2/39
De Winter, AJ	Tas	2	20.0	3	105	1	105.00	—	3	7	1/26
Dodemaide, AIC	Vic	2	16.0	1	69	1	69.00	—	—	—	1/13
Fleming, DW	Vic	2	20.0	3	65	3	21.67	—	—	7	2/35
Foley, GI	Qld	1	4.5	—	19	1	19.00	—	—	1	1/19
Gilbert, DR	Tas	1	10.0	—	33	1	33.00	—	1	—	1/33
Gladigau, PW	SA	4	38.4	7	121	5	24.20	—	—	5	2/27
Hickey, DJ	Vic	1	10.0	1	48	1	48.00	—	—	—	1/48
Hilditch, AMJ	SA	4	3.0	—	17	1	17.00	—	—	—	1/17
Hogan, TG	WA	3	28.0	—	119	1	119.00	—	—	—	1/41
Holdsworth, WJ	NSW	3	22.0	2	88	3	29.33	—	—	4	1/16
Hookes, DW	SA	4	10.0	—	45	5	9.00	1	—	1	5/41
Inwood, BP	Qld	3	17.0	1	73	3	24.33	—	—	2	2/20
Jackson, PW	Vic	2	12.0	1	45	2	22.50	—	—	—	2/37
Johnston, DA	SA	2	20.0	2	78	1	78.00	—	—	—	1/26
Kasprowicz, MS	Qld	1	10.0	—	57	1	57.00	—	—	3	1/57
Lawson, GF	NSW	1	7.0	3	9	—	—	—	—	1	—
MacLeay, KH	WA	4	31.0	3	127	4	31.75	—	—	9	2/18
Mack, CD	WA	1	7.0	—	34	2	17.00	—	—	2	2/34
Marks, PH	NSW	3	23.5	1	115	6	19.17	—	—	4	4/30
Matthews, CD	WA	2	18.5	3	54	5	10.80	—	—	5	3/38
Matthews, GRJ	NSW	2	18.0	—	96	3	32.00	—	—	1	2/50
May, TBA	SA	2	10.0	1	32	1	32.00	—	—	—	1/32
McCarthy, RCAM	Vic	1	6.0	—	25	—	—	—	—	3	—
McDermott, CJ	Qld	2	14.5	2	53	2	26.50	—	1	—	1/12
McNamara, BE	NSW	2	11.0	2	46	4	11.50	—	2	1	3/26
Miller, CR	SA	2	20.0	2	74	2	37.00	—	—	4	2/42
Moody, TM	WA	3	21.0	—	83	3	27.67	—	—	3	3/29
Mullally, AD	WA	1	10.0	2	56	2	28.00	—	4	—	2/56
Polzin, MA	Qld	1	5.0	2	10	1	10.00	—	—	1	1/10
Rackemann, CG	Qld	2	16.0	4	47	3	15.67	—	—	2	2/7
Reiffel, PR	Vic	1	10.0	—	51	1	51.00	—	2	1	1/51
Robertson, GR	Tas	2	20.0	—	91	2	45.50	—	—	2	2/50
Russell, RS	WA	2	18.0	2	86	1	86.00	—	—	1	1/40
Scuderi, JC	SA	4	29.0	—	164	3	54.67	—	2	2	1/37
Smith, GL	NSW	2	13.0	1	46	1	46.00	—	—	1	1/39
Stephensen, BR	Qld	1	4.0	—	18	1	18.00	—	—	1	1/18
Tazelaar, D	Qld	3	28.0	3	91	3	30.33	—	6	3	2/18
Tucker, RJ	Tas	2	20.0	2	70	4	17.50	—	—	1	2/35
Waugh, ME	NSW	3	18.5	—	86	2	43.00	—	1	1	1/26
Whitney, MR	NSW	3	25.0	—	83	5	16.60	—	—	3	2/8
Williams, BD	SA	2	17.0	—	86	1	86.00	—	—	1	1/46

NEW SOUTH WALES

NEW SOUTH WALES'S TEAM IN 1989-90 was by common agreement the strongest in the Sheffield Shield competition and therefore a worthy Shield champion. Indeed, some would say it was the strongest team fielded by New South Wales for a generation at least. It was a team which appeared to have everything—steady batsmen, attacking batsmen, bowlers who could bat, fast bowlers, medium-pacers, spin bowlers, a reliable wicketkeeper and an extremely enterprising captain. There was perhaps no better indication of New South Wales's strength than the abundance of New South Wales cricketers playing for other states—as many as twelve, according to one count. Yet it was only at the very end of the season that New South Wales took the lead in the Shield competition. To some extent, its failure to collect more points earlier could be explained by the willingness of its captain, Geoff Lawson, to risk defeat in the hope of gaining victory. The match against Queensland in Brisbane was an instance of this. Having led by 102 on the first innings, New South Wales declared at 8 for 201 in its second innings in the hope of bowling Queensland out again. But Wayne Holdsworth, one of its strike bowlers, left the field with an injury after bowling only 10 overs, and Queensland went on to win the match, moving eight points ahead of New South Wales on the Shield table. Lawson's positive captaincy paid off in the end, however. Moreover, it was a tonic for the Shield competition as a whole.

New South Wales's batting was the stronger half of its game, not least because its many talented players complemented each other so well. Mark Taylor, in his few appearances for the state, and Mark O'Neill gave the batting stability. O'Neill did not make big scores but he was extremely consistent, often scoring runs when they were most needed, and by the end of the season he was regarded in some quarters as technically the best batsman in the team. Not so long ago, it is odd to recall, O'Neill owed his place in the team largely to his ability to bowl leg-breaks, but in 1989-90 it was his batting which flourished, although apparently to the detriment of his bowling. Steve Small, whose career had sagged a couple of years before, was another batsman who made big advances in 1989-90. Technically, his batting still had a number of flaws, but his application and determination carried him through, and the Taylor-Small opening combination, when it operated, was invariably successful.

The Waugh brothers, Mark and Steve, batted with their customary flair. Steve Waugh played a high-speed innings of 196 against Tasmania in January, but it was his one big success of the season for New South Wales, which, admittedly, he represented only a few times. Mark Waugh had a marvellous season, scoring many runs and scoring them in fine style. His immense talent had been recognised for some years, but it was only in 1989-90 that he managed to translate his talent into consistent performance. His claims on a place in the Australian side are now so strong that New South Wales may never again have his services throughout the season.

Geoff Lawson's relegation from the Australian side to the New South Wales side during the season was no doubt a disappointment for him, but it proved to be an important plus for New South Wales, for, both as captain and bowler, he was an inspiration. There was a sad irony in the fact that, because of injury, he was not part of New South Wales's final triumph against Queensland, for he undoubtedly deserved a good deal of the credit for it. Michael Whitney was forced out of the team by injury for many weeks, and his absence may well have had something to do with the setbacks New South Wales received during the same period. Wayne Holdsworth did not meet all expectations of him in 1989-90, and his proneness to injury must be a cause of concern. Yet he bowled with great speed at times—in fact, some rate him the fastest bowler in Australia on his day—and a successful future may well await him.

The strength of New South Wales's spin attack set it apart from all other state sides. The fact New South Wales could afford to leave the Test spinner Peter Taylor out of the eleven for the Sheffield Shield final said a good deal about the depth of spinning talent available. Despite Taylor's promotion to the Australian side and his fine performance in the Test in New Zealand, it was apparent by the end of the season that Greg Matthews had established himself as the state's premier off-spinner. It was also apparent that the New South Wales selectors preferred to pair Matthews with a leg-spinner such as O'Neill or Adrian Tucker than with another off-spinner, even if he happened to be as accomplished a bowler as Taylor. Tucker was young and was clearly new to cricket at the first-class level, but he excelled in the final against Queensland, and much is expected of him in coming seasons.

Phil Emery, the wicketkeeper, batted soundly and kept wickets well, rarely missing a chance. Some flaws which were observed in his glovework early in the season appeared to have been rectified later, and by the end of the season he was keeping wickets as capably as anyone in the country.

NEW SOUTH WALES FIRST-CLASS RECORDS

Season 1989/90

Date	Venue	Opponent	Result for New South Wales
Oct 22*	Perth	Western Australia	Lost by 4 wkts
Oct 28*	North Sydney	Tasmania	Won by 83 runs
Nov 10	Adelaide	South Australia	Drawn
Nov 17	Canberra	Sri Lankans	Drawn
Dec 1	Newcastle	Queensland	Won by 32 runs
Dec 15	Albury	Victoria	Drawn
Dec 29	Brisbane	Queensland	Lost by 5 wkts
Jan 6	Sydney	Western Australia	Drawn
Jan 21*	Coffs Harbour	Sri Lankans	Won by 81 runs
Jan 26	Hobart Bel	Tasmania	Lost by 4 wkts
Feb 9	Melbourne	Victoria	Drawn
Feb 15	Sydney	South Australia	Won by 10 wkts
Mar 2	Perth	Western Australia	Lost by 156 runs
Mar 9	Sydney	Tasmania	Won by an inns & 156 runs
Mar 18*	Adelaide	South Australia	Lost by 53 runs
Mar 23	Sydney	Queensland	Won by 345 runs

* Denotes not first-class

270

1989/90 New South Wales First-Class Averages

Batsman	M	Inn	NO	Runs	HS	50	100	Avrge	Ct/St
ME Waugh	12	17	4	1009	198*	2	5	77.62	18
MA Taylor	6	11	—	700	199	2	3	63.64	3
TH Bayliss	12	20	2	992	115	6	2	55.11	5
SR Waugh	6	10	2	376	196	1	1	47.00	2
MD O'Neill	11	16	1	621	71	7	—	41.40	4
SM Small	12	21	2	780	86	6	—	41.05	9
GRJ Matthews	11	14	2	453	117	3	1	37.75	12
GS Milliken	6	10	1	260	151	—	1	28.89	6
PA Emery	12	16	4	224	81	1	—	18.67	38/3
AE Tucker	3	4	1	55	18*	—	—	18.33	3
BE McNamara	2	4	1	42	18	—	—	14.00	1
MR Whitney	8	6	4	24	15*	—	—	12.00	7
PL Taylor	5	6	1	57	33	—	—	11.40	1
GF Lawson	11	9	2	76	17	—	—	10.86	5
WJ Holdsworth	8	6	3	23	16*	—	—	7.67	5
GJ Rowell	1	2	—	10	9	—	—	5.00	—
PH Marks	3	4	1	7	5	—	—	2.33	4
RM Stobo	3	4	1	3	3	—	—	1.00	2

Bowler	M	Overs	Mdns	Runs	Wkts	Avrge	5wi	10m	NB	W	Best
TH Bayliss	12	6.0	3	9	1	9.00	—	—	—	—	1/7
GF Lawson	11	371.2	115	825	41	20.12	—	—	4	5	4/26
GRJ Matthews	11	470.3	165	1040	44	23.64	3	1	1	—	7/50
AE Tucker	3	92.5	23	260	10	26.00	—	—	—	—	4/25
MR Whitney	8	220.5	58	639	24	26.63	1	—	19	—	5/125
GJ Rowell	1	31.0	9	86	3	28.67	—	—	—	1	3/41
ME Waugh	12	131.3	20	465	15	31.00	—	—	29	3	2/7
PL Taylor	5	151.0	50	354	11	32.18	—	—	—	—	4/29
BE McNamara	2	7.0	—	33	1	33.00	—	—	—	—	1/24
WJ Holdsworth	8	196.1	27	736	21	35.05	1	—	5	—	5/71
MD O'Neill	11	213.3	65	536	13	41.23	—	—	—	—	3/51
PH Marks	3	21.0	4	63	1	63.00	—	—	3	—	1/24
RM Stobo	3	75.2	15	259	4	64.75	—	—	12	6	2/73
SM Small	12	2.0	2	0	—	—	—	—	—	—	—

New South Wales First-Class Results

Opponent	Venue	First Game	Games	W	L	D	T
Australian Rep. Teams							
Australian XI's	Sydney	Jan 12 1906	3	—	1	2	—
The Rest	Sydney	Feb 15 1907	5	2	2	1	—
AIF Team	Sydney	Jan 31 1920	1	—	1	—	—
Australian Services	Sydney	Jan 11 1946	1	1	—	—	—
Total			10	3	4	3	—
England Teams	Redfern	Jan 15 1877	1	—	—	1	—
	Sydney	Dec 9 1881	58	15	25	18	—
	Canberra	Jan 26 1980	1	—	1	—	—
	Newcastle	Nov 21 1986	1	1	—	—	—
Total			61	16	26	19	—
Indians	Sydney	Nov 7 1947	3	1	1	1	—
New Zealanders	Christchurch	Feb 15 1894	3	2	1	—	—
	Sydney	Feb 24 1899	11	7	—	4	—
	Wellington	Mar 7 1924	1	1	—	—	—
Total			15	10	1	4	—
New Zealand Provinces							
Auckland	Auckland	Jan 30 1890	5	3	—	2	—
Canterbury	Christchurch	Feb 7 1890	4	3	1	—	—
Otago	Dunedin	Feb 14 1890	4	3	—	1	—
Wellington	Wellington	Feb 21 1890	4	2	—	2	—
Hawkes Bay	Napier	Jan 24 1894	1	1	—	—	—
North Island	Wellington	Feb 19 1894	1	1	—	—	—
Total			19	13	1	5	—
Pakistanis	Sydney	Dec 11 1964	3	—	—	3	—
	Canberra	Mar 3 1979	1	—	—	1	—
Total			4	—	—	4	—

Continued

Opponent	Venue	First Game	Games	W	L	D	T
Queensland	Brisbane Ex	Apr 3 1893	10	5	1	4	—
	Sydney	Mar 24 1894	80	47	12	21	—
	Brisbane	Nov 25 1899	76	28	19	29	—
	Lismore	Dec 15 1979	1	1	—	—	—
	Newcastle	Oct 22 1981	3	1	1	1	—
Total			**170**	**82**	**33**	**55**	**—**
Qld & Vic XI	Brisbane	Nov 22 1940	1	1	—	—	—
Sri Lankans	Sydney	Feb 10 1983	1	—	—	1	—
	Canberra	Nov 17 1989	1	—	—	1	—
Total			**2**	**—**	**—**	**2**	**—**
South Africans	Sydney	Nov 18 1910	7	3	1	3	—
South Australia	Sydney	Feb 14 1890	90	59	16	15	—
	Adelaide	Dec 19 1890	88	43	31	14	—
	Newcastle	Dec 16 1983	1	1	—	—	—
Total			**179**	**103**	**47**	**29**	**—**
Tasmania	Sydney	Dec 12 1898	13	10	2	1	—
	Hobart TCA	Dec 30 1899	10	7	1	2	—
	Hobart Bel	Jan 26 1990	1	—	1	—	—
	Devonport	Mar 4 1978	4	1	—	3	—
	Launceston	Dec 29 1979	2	1	—	1	—
	Newcastle	Jan 15 1985	2	—	—	2	—
Total			**32**	**19**	**4**	**9**	**—**
Victoria	Melbourne	Mar 26 1856	110	34	51	25	—
	The Domain	Jan 15 1857	6	3	3	—	—
	Redfern	Mar 9 1871	4	2	2	—	—
	Sydney	Feb 22 1878	102	51	22	29	—
	Carlton	Dec 22 1945	1	—	—	1	—
	St Kilda	Dec 24 1955	4	1	1	1	1
	Newcastle	Dec 18 1982	2	1	—	1	—
	Albury	Dec 15 1989	1	—	—	1	—
Total			**230**	**92**	**79**	**58**	**1**
Western Australia	Perth	Mar 16 1907	44	14	16	14	—
	Fremantle	Mar 23 1907	1	—	1	—	—
	Sydney	Nov 9 1912	39	21	4	14	—
	Sydney SCG No 2	Nov 11 1966	1	—	—	1	—
	Canberra	Oct 26 1984	1	—	—	1	—
	Newcastle	Dec 2 1988	1	1	—	—	—
Total			**87**	**36**	**21**	**30**	**—**
West Indians	Sydney	Nov 21 1930	10	5	4	1	—
World XI	Sydney	Nov 12 1971	1	—	—	1	—
Zimbabwe	Harare	Mar 28 1986	4	1	—	3	—
Total for New South Wales			**835**	**385**	**222**	**227**	**1**

Most Appearances for New South Wales

Games	Player	Career	Games	Player	Career
107	SJ Rixon	1974/75–1987/88	67	RB Simpson	1952/53–1977/78
103	KD Walters	1962/63–1980/81	65	KJ O'Keeffe	1968/69–1979/80
94	J Dyson	1975/76–1988/89	63	DA Ford	1957/58–1963/64
93	BC Booth	1954/55–1968/69	59	PM Toohey	1974/75–1981/82
91	GF Lawson	1977/78–1989/90	58	H Donnan	1887/88–1900/01
87	AF Kippax	1918/19–1935/36	57	C Kelleway	1907/08–1928/29
86	R Benaud	1948/49–1963/64	57	GR Davies	1965/66–1971/72
83	W Bardsley	1903/04–1925/26	56	TW Garrett	1876/77–1897/98
82	WAS Oldfield	1919/20–1937/38	56	FA Iredale	1888/89–1901/02
81	CG Macartney	1905/06–1926/27	56	SG Barnes	1936/37–1952/53
80	SE Gregory	1889/90–1911/12	55	SJ McCabe	1928/29–1941/42
79	RB McCosker	1973/74–1983/84	55	ID Craig	1951/52–1961/62

Games	Player	Career	Games	Player	Career
78	JW Martin	1956/57–1967/68	55	MA Taylor	1985/86–1989/90
77	MA Noble	1893/94–1919/20	54	WJ O'Reilly	1927/28–1945/46
76	A Turner	1968/69–1977/78	54	DA Renneberg	1964/65–1970/71
74	TJE Andrews	1912/13–1928/29	54	LS Pascoe	1974/75–1983/84
74	GRJ Matthews	1982/83–1989/90	53	JJ Kelly	1894/95–1904/05
73	VT Trumper	1894/95–1913/14	52	AJ Hopkins	1896/97–1914/15
73	HB Taber	1964/65–1973/74	52	HL Collins	1909/10–1925/26
72	AK Davidson	1949/50–1962/63	52	PI Philpott	1954/55–1966/67
70	NC O'Neill	1955/56–1966/67	51	TM Chappell	1979/80–1984/85
69	MR Whitney	1980/81–1989/90	50	AR Morris	1940/41–1954/55
68	G Thomas	1957/58–1965/66	50	RR Lindwall	1941/42–1953/54
68	DM Wellham	1980/81–1986/87	50	KR Miller	1947/48–1955/56
68	RG Holland	1978/79–1986/87			
67	AA Mailey	1912/13–1930/31			
67	JW Burke	1948/49–1958/59			

Youngest Players on First-Class Debut for New South Wales

Player	Date of Birth	F/Class Debut	Opponent	Venue	Age on Years	Debut Days
ID Craig	Jun 12 1935	Feb 16 1952	South Australia	Sydney	16	249
RB Simpson	Feb 2 1936	Jan 23 1953	Victoria	Sydney	16	355
KD Walters	Dec 21 1945	Dec 29 1962	Queensland	Brisbane	17	8
A Cotter	Dec 3 1884	Jan 25 1902	Victoria	Sydney	17	53
VT Trumper	Nov 2 1877	Jan 5 1895	South Australia	Adelaide	17	64
A Jackson	Sep 5 1909	Nov 26 1926	Queensland	Brisbane Ex	17	82
EL Waddy	Dec 3 1879	Apr 16 1897	Queensland	Brisbane Ex	17	134
F Downes	Jun 11 1864	Dec 24 1881	Victoria	Melbourne	17	196
CNJ Oliver	Apr 24 1848	Dec 26 1865	Victoria	Melbourne	17	246
EP Barbour	Jan 27 1891	Jan 1 1909	Queensland	Sydney	17	339

Highest Innings Totals for New South Wales

Total	Opponent	Venue	Season
918	South Australia	Sydney	1900/01
839	Tasmania	Sydney	1898/99
815	Victoria	Sydney	1908/09
807	South Australia	Adelaide	1899/00
805	Victoria	Melbourne	1905/06
802	South Australia	Sydney	1920/21
786	South Australia	Adelaide	1922/23
775	Victoria	Sydney	1881/82
770	South Australia	Adelaide	1920/21
763	Queensland	Brisbane	1906/07
8d-761	Queensland	Sydney	1929/30
8d-752	Otago	Dunedin	1923/24
713	South Australia	Adelaide	1908/09
6d-713	Victoria	Sydney	1928/29
708	Victoria	Sydney	1925/26
705	Victoria	Melbourne	1925/26
691	Queensland	Brisbane	1905/06
690	South Australia	Adelaide	1919/20
686	Queensland	Sydney	1904/05
684	South Australia	Sydney	1923/24
681	South Australia	Sydney	1903/04
675	Victoria	Sydney	1913/14
8d-672	Victoria	Sydney	1933/34
661	Queensland	Brisbane	1963/64
645	Australian XI	Sydney	1924/25
642	South Australia	Sydney	1925/26
640	Queensland	Sydney	1899/00
639	Western Australia	Sydney	1925/26
639	Queensland	Sydney	1927/28
8d-629	MCC	Sydney	1929/30
624	South Australia	Adelaide	1903/04
619	MCC	Sydney	1924/25
5d-614	Tasmania	Hobart TCA	1912/13
6d-614	Queensland	Sydney	1933/34
614	Victoria	Sydney	1924/25
610	South Australia	Adelaide	1930/31
602	Queensland	Brisbane	1932/33
9d-601	South Australia	Adelaide	1964/65

Lowest Innings Totals for New South Wales

Total	Opponent	Venue	Season
37	Victoria	The Domain	1868/69
42	Victoria	Melbourne	1859/60
44	Victoria	Redfern	1872/73
44	Victoria	The Domain	1860/61
44	A Shaw's XI	Sydney	1884/85
44	Victoria	Melbourne	1859/60
49	Lord Harris's XI	Sydney	1878/79
49	Victoria	Sydney	1882/83
55	Victoria	Melbourne	1871/72
57	Victoria	Melbourne	1857/58
60	A Shaw's XI	Sydney	1884/85
62	Victoria	Melbourne	1890/91
62	South Australia	Sydney	1891/92
63	Victoria	The Domain	1858/59
63	Victoria	Sydney	1888/89
64	Queensland	Brisbane	1892/93
65	Victoria	Sydney	1882/83
66	Victoria	Sydney	1882/83
66	Victoria	Melbourne	1894/95
69	Victoria	Melbourne	1857/58
71	Queensland	Brisbane	1976/77
74	Victoria	The Domain	1860/61
74	Lord Sheffield's XI	Sydney	1891/92
74	Victoria	Melbourne	1884/85

Leading Batsmen for New South Wales

Batsman	Career	M	Inn	NO	Runs	HS	Avrge	100s
AF Kippax	1918/19–1935/36	87	135	16	8005	315*	67.25	32
J Dyson	1975/76–1988/89	94	170	17	6773	241	44.27	14
KD Walters	1962/63–1980/81	103	279	21	6612	253	41.84	19
W Bardsley	1903/04–1925/26	83	132	11	6419	235	53.04	20
RB McCosker	1973/74–1983/84	79	140	17	5998	168	48.76	19
VT Trumper	1894/95–1913/14	73	123	9	5823	292*	51.07	15
DG Bradman	1927/28–1933/34	41	69	10	5813	452*	98.52	21
MA Noble	1893/94–1919/20	77	124	10	5653	281	49.58	19
CG Macartney	1905/06–1926/27	81	123	13	5581	221	50.73	22
BC Booth	1954/55–1968/69	93	146	18	5577	177	43.57	11
NC O'Neill	1955/56–1966/67	70	115	12	5419	233	52.61	18
SE Gregory	1889/90–1911/12	80	136	8	5340	201	41.71	11
RB Simpson	1952/53–1977/78	67	116	16	5317	359	53.17	15
TJE Andrews	1912/13–1928/29	74	115	6	4869	247*	44.66	11
SG Barnes	1936/37–1952/53	56	91	4	4733	200	54.40	19
AR Morris	1940/41–1954/55	50	77	4	4660	253	63.83	17
PM Toohey	1974/75–1983/84	76	128	11	4572	158	39.08	11
SJ McCabe	1928/29–1941/42	55	89	5	4556	229*	54.23	9
G Thomas	1957/58–1965/66	68	105	7	4351	229	44.39	15
DM Wellham	1980/81–1986/87	68	111	14	4297	166	44.29	9
A Turner	1968/69–1977/78	76	142	8	4171	127	31.12	4
MA Taylor	1985/86–1989/90	55	98	3	4152	199	43.71	10
R Benaud	1948/49–1963/64	86	121	10	4116	158	37.08	9
JW Burke	1948/49–1958/59	67	105	19	3901	220	45.36	9
GRJ Matthews	1982/83–1989/90	74	111	18	3644	184	39.18	7
HL Collins	1909/10–1925/26	52	86	5	3622	282	44.71	14
KR Miller	1947/48–1955/56	50	68	6	3538	214	57.06	10
ID Craig	1951/52–1961/62	55	83	5	3379	213*	43.32	7
FA Iredale	1888/89–1901/02	56	95	4	3359	196	36.91	5
SJ Rixon	1974/75–1987/88	107	155	26	3229	128	25.03	6
JHW Fingleton	1928/29–1939/40	49	80	6	3178	160	42.94	8
ME Waugh	1985/86–1989/90	45	74	13	3121	198*	51.16	11
GR Davies	1965/66–1971/72	57	101	11	3065	127	34.05	5
C Kelleway	1907/08–1928/29	57	90	10	3031	168	37.88	10
H Donnan	1887/88–1900/01	58	102	10	3019	160*	32.81	5

Highest Individual Innings for New South Wales

Score	Batsman	Opponent	Venue	Season
452*	DG Bradman	Queensland	Sydney	1929/30
383	DW Gregory	Queensland	Brisbane	1906/07
359	RB Simpson	Queensland	Brisbane	1963/64
340*	DG Bradman	Victoria	Sydney	1928/29
321	WL Murdoch	Victoria	Sydney	1881/82
315*	AF Kippax	Queensland	Sydney	1927/28
297*	H Moses	Victoria	Sydney	1887/88

274

Score	Batsman	Opponent	Venue	Season
292*	VT Trumper	Tasmania	Sydney	1898/99
282	HL Collins	Tasmania	Hobart TCA	1912/13
281	MA Noble	Victoria	Melbourne	1905/06
277	RB Simpson	Queensland	Sydney	1967/68
271	RA Duff	South Australia	Sydney	1903/04
271*	AF Kippax	Victoria	Sydney	1925/26
264*	R Flockton	South Australia	Sydney	1959/60
263	SB Smith	Victoria	Melbourne	1982/83
260*	AF Kippax	Victoria	Melbourne	1928/29
258	DG Bradman	South Australia	Adelaide	1930/31
253	VT Trumper	New Zealand	Sydney	1898/99
253	DG Bradman	Queensland	Sydney	1933/34
253	AR Morris	Queensland	Brisbane	1951/52
253	KD Walters	South Australia	Adelaide	1964/65

Most Runs in a Season for New South Wales

Batsman	Season	M	Inn	NO	Runs	HS	50	100	Avrge
DM Wellham	1982/83	13	23	5	1205	136*	10	2	66.94
MA Taylor	1988/89	12	22	1	1174	152*	7	3	55.90
RB McCosker	1982/83	13	25	4	1153	124	9	3	54.90
DG Bradman	1928/29	7	12	4	1127	340*	2	5	140.87
RB McCosker	1974/75	10	19	1	1052	164	4	4	58.44
DG Bradman	1929/30	7	11	2	1051	452*	4	2	116.77
DG Bradman	1933/34	6	9	2	1036	253	3	4	148.00
G Thomas	1965/66	9	16	—	1024	229	2	4	64.00
J Dyson	1983/84	11	19	3	1015	241	3	3	63.44
ME Waugh	1989/90	12	17	4	1009	198*	2	5	77.62
NC O'Neill	1957/58	8	14	2	1005	233	3	4	83.75
TH Bayliss	1989/90	12	20	2	992	115	6	2	55.11
MA Taylor	1986/87	12	20	1	937	118	5	2	49.32
AF Kippax	1927/28	7	13	2	926	315*	1	4	84.18
KR Miller	1950/51	8	10	2	920	214	3	4	115.00
PS Clifford	1984/85	12	21	3	919	143	4	3	51.06

Leading Wicket Takers for New South Wales

Bowler	Career	M	Runs	Wkts	Avrge	5wi	10m	Best
GF Lawson	1977/78–1989/90	92	7714	347	22.23	13	—	6/31
AA Mailey	1912/13–1929/30	67	9246	334	27.68	28	6	8/81
WJ O'Reilly	1927/28–1945/46	54	5369	325	16.52	26	7	9/41
R Benaud	1948/49–1963/64	86	8376	322	26.01	17	4	7/18
JW Martin	1956/57–1967/68	78	8987	293	30.67	12	—	8/97
AK Davidson	1949/50–1962/63	72	5858	273	21.45	10	—	7/31
CTB Turner	1882/83–1909/10	43	4256	263	16.18	29	11	8/32
MA Noble	1893/94–1919/20	77	5379	230	23.38	13	2	7/44
RG Holland	1978/79–1986/87	68	7215	228	31.64	8	1	9/83
MR Whitney	1980/81–1989/90	69	6275	227	27.64	10	—	6/65
C Kelleway	1907/08–1928/29	57	5137	215	23.89	7	1	7/35
KJ O'Keeffe	1968/69–1979/80	65	5708	211	27.05	12	1	6/49
LS Pascoe	1974/75–1986/87	54	5292	203	26.07	9	2	8/41
DJ Colley	1969/70–1977/78	71	6513	203	32.08	6	—	6/30
RR Lindwall	1941/42–1953/54	50	4451	196	22.70	7	1	7/45
WP Howell	1894/95–1904/05	48	4698	196	23.96	11	1	9/52
DA Renneberg	1964/65–1970/71	54	5793	190	30.48	8	1	7/33
GRJ Matthews	1982/83–1989/90	74	5797	189	30.67	7	1	7/50
TR McKibbin	1894/95–1898/99	25	3822	181	21.11	17	7	9/68
A Cotter	1901/02–1913/14	38	4005	171	23.42	10	1	7/77
DW Hourn	1970/71–1981/82	44	4709	164	28.71	11	2	9/77
PI Philpott	1954/55–1966/67	52	4755	153	31.07	7	2	7/53
JD Scott	1908/09–1924/25	35	3364	150	22.42	9	1	6/48
CG Macartney	1905/06–1926/27	81	3465	148	23.41	3	—	7/85
E Evans	1874/75–1887/88	27	2169	145	14.95	15	4	7/16
HC Chilvers	1929/30–1936/37	32	3604	142	25.38	11	3	6/62
GJ Gilmour	1971/72–1979/80	42	4671	140	33.36	3	—	5/59
ST Callaway	1888/89–1895/96	33	2414	139	17.36	14	4	8/98
GE Corling	1963/64–1968/69	46	4165	129	32.28	5	—	5/44
JW Gleeson	1966/67–1972/73	35	3230	126	25.63	7	1	7/52
AJ Hopkins	1896/97–1914/15	52	3235	126	25.67	6	—	5/17
TW Garrett	1876/77–1897/98	56	2912	124	23.48	9	2	6/55
FF Johnston	1946/47–1950/51	35	3623	123	29.45	5	—	6/100
MJ Bennett	1982/83–1986/87	44	3321	122	27.22	5	—	6/32
KR Miller	1947/48–1955/56	50	3019	119	25.36	3	—	7/12
KD Walters	1962/63–1980/81	103	4166	119	35.00	5	—	7/63
HSTL Hendry	1918/19–1923/24	38	2743	105	26.12	4	1	8/33
SC Everett	1921/22–1929/30	28	2724	103	26.44	8	—	6/23
JJ Ferris	1886/87–1897/98	19	1755	102	17.20	7	1	8/84

Best Bowling in an Innings for New South Wales

Wkts	Bowler	Opponent	Venue	Season
9/41	WJ O'Reilly	South Australia	Adelaide	1937/38
9/50	WJ O'Reilly	Victoria	Melbourne	1933/34
9/52	WP Howell	Victoria	Melbourne	1902/03
9/68	TR McKibbon	Queensland	Brisbane	1894/95
9/77	DW Hourn	Victoria	Sydney	1978/79
9/83	RG Holland	South Australia	Sydney	1984/85
8/14	SW Austin	Hawke's Bay	Napier	1893/94
8/23	WJ O'Reilly	Queensland	Sydney	1939/40
8/31	ES White	South Australia	Sydney	1935/36
8/32	CTB Turner	A Shrewsbury's XI	Sydney	1886/87
8/33	HSTL Hendry	New Zealand	Wellington	1923/24
8/33	RG Holland	New Zealand	Sydney	1985/86
8/39	CTB Turner	A Shrewsbury's XI	Sydney	1887/88
8/40	CTB Turner	A Shrewsbury's XI	Sydney	1887/88
8/41	LS Pascoe	Tasmania	Hobart TCA	1981/82
8/50	RB Minnett	Victoria	Melbourne	1914/15
8/56	AL Newell	Victoria	Sydney	1897/98
8/66	TR McKibbon	South Australia	Sydney	1894/95
8/74	CTB Turner	Victoria	Sydney	1890/91
8/74	TR McKibbon	South Australia	Adelaide	1896/97
8/81	HV Hordern	Queensland	Sydney	1905/06
8/81	AA Mailey	South Australia	Sydney	1920/21
8/84	JJ Ferris	South Australia	Adelaide	1890/91
8/93	TR McKibbon	Victoria	Melbourne	1895/96
8/97	JW Martin	Victoria	Sydney	1962/63
8/98	ST Callaway	New Zealand	Christchurch	1895/96
8/109	S Cosstick	Victoria	Melbourne	1865/66
8/111	GM Pierce	South Australia	Adelaide	1892/93
8/111	TR McKibbon	Victoria	Sydney	1896/97

Best Bowling in a Match for New South Wales

Wkts	Bowler	Opponent	Venue	Season
16/79	CTB Turner	A Shrewsbury's XI	Sydney	1887/88
15/125	TR McKibbin	South Australia	Adelaide	1896/97
15/174	CTB Turner	Victoria	Sydney	1890/91
15/175	ST Callaway	New Zealand	Christchurch	1895/96
14/45	WJ O'Reilly	Queensland	Sydney	1939/40
14/59	CTB Turner	A Shaw's XI	Sydney	1886/87
14/65	ST Callaway	Wellington	Wellington	1895/96
14/73	C Lawrence	Victoria	The Domain	1862/63
14/87	TR McKibbin	Queensland	Brisbane	1894/95
14/98	WJ O'Reilly	South Australia	Adelaide	1937/38
14/189	TR McKibbin	South Australia	Sydney	1894/95
14/192	JJ Ferris	South Australia	Adelaide	1890/91
13/54	CTB Turner	A Shaw's XI	Sydney	1886/87
13/87	HV Hordern	Victoria	Sydney	1910/11
13/98	SW Austin	New Zealand	Christchurch	1893/94
13/111	WJ O'Reilly	Queensland	Brisbane	1933/34
13/115	JG Lush	MCC	Sydney	1936/37
13/152	AA Mailey	Western Australia	Sydney	1912/13
13/240	TR McKibbin	Victoria	Sydney	1896/97
13/265	GM Pierce	South Australia	Adelaide	1892/93
12/58	ST Callaway	Otago	Dunedin	1889/90
12/67	CJ Hill	Queensland	Sydney	1932/33
12/83	E Trennery	Queensland	Sydney	1919/20
12/98	HV Hordern	Tasmania	Sydney	1910/11
12/106	GL Garnsey	Queensland	Sydney	1906/07
12/111	TW Garrett	Victoria	Sydney	1885/86
12/113	DW Hourn	South Australia	Sydney	1977/78
12/113	SH Emery	Victoria	Melbourne	1909/10
12/114	WPA Crawford	Queensland	Sydney	1954/55
12/142	WJ O'Reilly	Victoria	Melbourne	1933/34
12/148	R Benaud	Western Australia	Sydney	1959/60
12/196	AA Mailey	Victoria	Melbourne	1920/21
12/220	TR McKibbin	Victoria	Melbourne	1895/96
12/248	MA Noble	AE Stoddart's XI	Sydney	1897/98

Most Wickets in a Season for New South Wales

Bowler	Season	M	Overs	Mdns	Runs	Wkts	Avrge	5wi	10m	Best
CTB Turner	1887/88	8	687.3	312	952	75	12.69	10	3	8/39
RJA Massie	1912/13	10	376.5	84	1098	60	18.30	5	2	7/110
AA Mailey	1922/23	9	303.6	21	1190	55	21.60	6	1	6/45
WJ O'Reilly	1939/40	7	246.6	52	832	55	15.12	6	2	8/23
CTB Turner	1886/87	5	356.2	178	377	53	7.11	6	3	8/32
R Benaud	1958/59	8	326.5	81	995	51	19.50	4	1	7/32
DW Hourn	1977/78	10	299.6	52	1077	49	21.98	4	1	7/71
MR Whitney	1988/89	12	410.3	100	1221	49	24.92	1	—	5/66
R Benaud	1961/62	9	323.6	97	845	47	17.97	3	—	5/30
HC Chilvers	1934/35	6	237.4	22	857	46	18.63	6	3	6/67
WJ O'Reilly	1940/41	7	205.6	46	590	46	12.82	4	—	6/60
C Kelleway	1913/14	7	249.4	76	571	45	12.68	3	1	7/35
JW Martin	1959/60	8	300.3	37	1064	45	23.64	3	—	5/67
JW Gleeson	1971/72	8	233.5	59	732	45	16.26	2	1	7/52
RG Holland	1984/85	10	490.0	155	1118	45	24.84	1	1	9/83
TR McKibbin	1896/97	4	230.1	46	655	44	14.89	5	2	8/74
GRJ Matthews	1989/90	11	470.3	165	1040	44	23.64	3	1	7/50
AA Mailey	1920/21	5	1488*	17	867	42	20.64	4	1	8/81
WJ O'Reilly	1937/38	7	240.6	71	582	42	13.85	3	1	9/41
AK Davidson	1961/62	9	225.4	52	572	42	13.61	2	—	7/31
GF Lawson	1987/88	10	336.3	102	792	42	18.86	3	—	6/31
GF Lawson	1988/89	10	373.1	104	908	42	21.62	4	—	6/36
JW Martin	1965/66	10	310.3	44	1291	41	31.48	2	—	6/44
DA Renneberg	1969/70	9	285.2	42	1074	41	26.19	2	—	6/49
GF Lawson	1989/90	11	371.2	115	825	41	20.12	—	—	4/26

Most Dismissals by Wicket-Keepers for New South Wales

Wicket-Keeper	Career	M	Cght	Stmp	Total
SJ Rixon	1974/75–1987/88	107	260	50	310
HB Taber	1964/65–1973/74	73	207	35	242
WAS Oldfield	1919/20–1937/38	82	165	106	271
DA Ford	1957/58–1963/64	63	120	57	177
RA Saggers	1939/40–1950/51	40	85	30	115
JJ Kelly	1894/95–1904/05	53	81	45	126
H Carter	1897/98–1924/25	44	81	40	121
GC Dyer	1983/84–1988/89	42	98	16	114
GS Trueman	1951/52–1953/54	24	63	19	82
AT Ratcliffe	1913/14–1924/25	35	43	26	69
SG Sismey	1938/39–1950/51	20	64	4	68
O Lambert	1950/51–1956/57	24	50	14	64
PA Emery	1987/88–1989/90	19	57	4	61

Most Dismissals in a Season for New South Wales

Wicket-Keeper	Season	M	Cght	Stmp	Total
PA Emery	1989/90	12	38	3	41
M Hendricks	1969/70	9	30	9	39
SJ Rixon	1980/81	10	35	4	39
GC Dyer	1985/86	12	31	7	38
GS Trueman	1952/53	9	24	13	37
SJ Rixon	1982/83	12	28	9	37
DA Ford	1963/64	9	21	12	33
HB Taber	1964/65	9	25	8	33
HB Taber	1965/66	10	22	11	33
HB Taber	1968/69	9	28	5	33
HB Taber	1973/74	9	31	2	33
WAS Oldfield	1934/35	7	15	17	32
HB Taber	1967/68	10	29	3	32
SJ Rixon	1976/77	9	29	3	32
SJ Rixon	1974/75	10	27	4	31
RA Saggers	1940/41	7	18	12	30
DA Ford	1958/59	10	20	10	30

Most Dismissals in a Match for New South Wales

Ttl	Ct	St	Wicket-Keeper	Opponent	Venue	Season
12	9	3	HB Taber	South Australia	Adelaide	1968/69
10	9	1	RA Saggers	Combined XI	Brisbane	1940/41
9	6	3	HL Davidson	South Australia	Sydney	1928/29
9	4	5	WAS Oldfield	West Indians	Sydney	1930/31
9	4	5	DA Ford	Victoria	Sydney	1963/64
9	8	1	HB Taber	South Australia	Sydney	1971/72

Continued

277

Ttl	Ct	St	Wicket-Keeper	Opponent	Venue	Season
8	3	5	FA Easton	Queensland	Sydney	1933/34
8	6	2	RA Saggers	Queensland	Sydney	1946/47
8	4	4	HB Taber	South Australia	Sydney	1964/65
8	6	2	M Hendricks	Victoria	Sydney	1969/70
8	5	3	M Hendricks	South Australia	Adelaide	1969/70

Most Dismissals in an Innings for New South Wales

Ttl	Ct	St	Wicket-Keeper	Opponent	Venue	Season
7	7	—	RA Saggers	Combined XI	Brisbane	1940/41
7	6	1	HB Taber	South Australia	Adelaide	1968/69
6	3	3	WAS Oldfield	West Indians	Sydney	1930/31
6	4	2	RA Saggers	Queensland	Sydney	1946/47
6	6	—	SG Sismey	Victoria	Sydney	1949/50
6	5	1	CS Trueman	Queensland	Sydney	1952/53
6	3	3	M Hendricks	South Australia	Adelaide	1969/70
5	5	—	IF Wales	South Australia	Adelaide	1890/91
5	2	3	H Davidson	South Australia	Sydney	1928/29
5	5	—	WAS Oldfield	Queensland	Brisbane	1937/38
5	5	—	DA Ford	Western Australia	Perth	1958/59
5	5	—	G Thomas	Queensland	Brisbane	1959/60
5	5	—	DA Ford	South Australia	Sydney	1959/60
5	5	—	DA Ford	Western Australia	Perth	1961/62
5	1	4	DA Ford	Victoria	Sydney	1963/64
5	2	3	HB Taber	South Australia	Sydney	1964/65
5	3	2	HB Taber	South Australia	Adelaide	1968/69
5	4	1	HB Taber	South Australia	Sydney	1971/72
5	4	1	SJ Rixon	Victoria	Sydney	1975/76
5	5	—	SJ Rixon	South Australia	Adelaide	1980/81
5	4	1	GC Dyer	Western Australia	Sydney	1985/86
5	5	—	PA Emery	Queensland	Newcastle	1989/90

Most Catches by a Fieldsman for New South Wales

Fieldsman	Career	M	Catches
R Benaud	1948/49–1963/64	86	106
RB McCosker	1973/74–1983/84	79	104
RB Simpson	1952/53–1977/78	67	102
JW Martin	1956/57–1967/68	78	83
J Dyson	1975/76–1987/88	94	78
AA Mailey	1912/13–1929/30	67	74
MA Taylor	1984/85–1989/90	55	68
MA Noble	1893/94–1919/20	77	67
BC Booth	1954/55–1968/69	93	63
G Thomas	1957/58–1965/66	68	61
GR Davies	1965/66–1971/72	57	59
A Turner	1968/69–1977/78	76	57
AK Davidson	1949/50–1962/63	72	54
KD Walters	1962/63–1980/81	103	54
KJ O'Keeffe	1968/69–1979/80	65	53
PM Toohey	1974/75–1983/84	76	53
VT Trumper	1894/95–1913/14	73	51
SE Gregory	1889/90–1911/12	80	50

Most Catches in a Season for New South Wales

Catches	Fieldsman	M	Season
21	MA Taylor	12	1988/89
19	J Dyson	9	1983/84
18	ME Waugh	10	1987/88
18	ME Waugh	12	1989/90
16	MA Taylor	12	1985/86
16	SR Waugh	8	1986/87
16	MA Taylor	10	1987/88
15	RB McCosker	11	1983/84

Most Catches in a Match for New South Wales

Ct	Fieldsman	Opponent	Venue	Season
6	R Benaud	Victoria	Melbourne	1954/55
5	J Mills	Victoria	Melbourne	1857/58
5	JL Wall	Queensland	Sydney	1923/24
5	HSTL Hendry	Victoria	Melbourne	1923/24
5	AG Chipperfield	Victoria	Sydney	1939/40
5	KJ Grieves	South Australia	Adelaide	1945/46

Ct	Fieldsman	Opponent	Venue	Season
5	RE Briggs	Victoria	Sydney	1952/53
5	JW Martin	Queensland	Brisbane	1956/57
5	GF Davies	India	Sydney	1967/68
5	RB Simpson	New Zealand	Sydney	1967/68
5	K Mackay	Victoria	Sydney	1971/72
5	RP Collins	Victoria	Melbourne	1972/73
5	J Dyson	South Australia	Sydney	1984/85
5	SR Waugh	Victoria	Sydney	1986/87
5	TH Bayliss	Queensland	Brisbane	1988/89
5	MA Taylor	Tasmania	Sydney	1988/89

Most Catches in an Innings for New South Wales

Ct	Fieldsman	Opponent	Venue	Season
5	E Evans	Lord Harris's XI	Sydney	1878/79
5	CL McCool	The Rest	Sydney	1939/40
4	JM Gregory	MCC	Sydney	1924/25
4	RV James	South Australia	Sydney	1948/49
4	RE Briggs	Victoria	Sydney	1952/53
4	JW Martin	Queensland	Brisbane	1956/57
4	BC Booth	Western Australia	Sydney	1966/67
4	RB Simpson	Western Australia	Perth	1967/68
4	KJ O'Keeffe	Victoria	Melbourne	1971/72
4	J Dyson	Western Australia	Perth	1978/79
4	SR Waugh	Victoria	Sydney	1986/87
4	RJ Tucker (Sub)	Western Australia	Sydney	1986/87
4	MA Taylor	Western Australia	Perth	1987/88

Partnership Records for New South Wales

Wkt	Ttl	Batsmen	Opponent	Venue	Season
1st	319	RB McCosker, J Dyson	Western Australia	Sydney	1980/81
2nd	378	LA Marks, KD Walters	South Australia	Adelaide	1964/65
3rd	363	DG Bradman, AF Kippax	Queensland	Sydney	1933/34
4th	325	NC O'Neill, BC Booth	Victoria	Sydney	1957/58
5th	397	W Bardsley, C Kelleway	South Australia	Sydney	1920/21
6th	332	G Thomas, NG Marks	South Australia	Sydney	1958/59
7th	255	R Benaud, G Thomas	Victoria	Melbourne	1961/62
8th	270	EP Barbour, VT Trumper	Victoria	Sydney	1912/13
9th	226	C Kelleway, WAS Oldfield	Victoria	Melbourne	1925/26
10th	307	AF Kippax, JEH Hooker	Victoria	Melbourne	1928/29

Highest Partnerships for New South Wales

Wkt	Ttl	Batsmen	Opponent	Venue	Season
5th	397	W Bardsley, C Kelleway	South Australia	Sydney	1920/21
2nd	378	LA Marks, KD Walters	South Australia	Adelaide	1964/65
3rd	363	DG Bradman, AF Kippax	Queensland	Sydney	1933/34
3rd	345	W Bardsley, JM Taylor	South Australia	Adelaide	1920/21
2nd	334	A Jackson, DG Bradman	South Australia	Adelaide	1930/31
6th	332	G Thomas, NG Marks	South Australia	Sydney	1958/59
4th	325	NC O'Neill, BC Booth	Victoria	Sydney	1957/58
2nd	323	ID Craig, RN Harvey	Queensland	Sydney	1960/61
1st	319	RB McCosker, J Dyson	Western Australia	Sydney	1980/81
4th	315	MA Noble, SE Gregory	Victoria	Sydney	1907/08
1st	308	RB Simpson, G Thomas	Western Australia	Sydney	1963/64
10th	307	AF Kippax, JEH Hooker	Victoria	Melbourne	1928/29
2nd	304	W Bardsley, MA Noble	Victoria	Sydney	1908/09
1st	298	VT Trumper, RA Duff	South Australia	Sydney	1902/03
2nd	294	WA Brown, DG Bradman	Queensland	Brisbane	1933/34
4th	293	RA Duff, MA Noble	South Australia	Sydney	1903/04
5th	286	MA Noble, SE Gregory	South Australia	Adelaide	1899/00
2nd	283	AJY Hopkins, MA Noble	South Australia	Adelaide	1908/09
3rd	280	OW Bill, AF Kippax	Queensland	Brisbane Ex	1930/31
1st	276*	RB Simpson, NC O'Neill	South Australia	Sydney	1964/65
5th	274*	RG Flockton, G Thomas	South Australia	Sydney	1959/60
3rd	272	DG Bradman, AF Kippax	Queensland	Sydney	1929/30
6th	271	SR Waugh, GRJ Matthews	Tasmania	Hobart Bel	1989/90
8th	270	EP Barbour, VT Trumper	Victoria	Sydney	1912/13
2nd	270	HL Collins, TJE Andrews	MCC	Sydney	1924/25
2nd	268	JRM Mackay, MA Noble	Victoria	Melbourne	1905/06
3rd	268	HO Rock, AF Kippax	Victoria	Sydney	1924/25
1st	267	VT Trumper, RA Duff	Victoria	Sydney	1902/03
2nd	265	AR Morris, KR Miller	MCC	Sydney	1950/51
1st	265	J Dyson, WJ Seabrook	Victoria	Melbourne	1984/85

Continued

279

Wkt	Ttl	Batsmen	Opponent	Venue	Season
5th	264	AR Morris, R Benaud	Queensland	Brisbane	1953/54
4th	264	ID Craig, WJ Watson	Western Australia	Perth	1956/57
6th	263	JM Taylor, AF Kippax	South Australia	Adelaide	1922/23
4th	263	MA Taylor, ME Waugh	South Australia	Adelaide	1989/90
2nd	262	JM Gregory, TJE Andrews	New Zealand	Sydney	1927/28
2nd	262	WPJ Donaldson, KR Miller	Western Australia	Sydney	1947/48
2nd	261	AR Morris, SG Barnes	Queensland	Sydney	1940/41
2nd	261	MA Taylor, DM Wellham	South Australia	Sydney	1986/87
5th	259	BC Francis, KD Walters	Victoria	Sydney	1971/72
6th	258	VT Trumper, FA Iredale	Tasmania	Sydney	1898/99
5th	256	CG Macartney, N Callaway	Queensland	Sydney	1914/15
7th	255	G Thomas, R Benaud	Victoria	Melbourne	1961/62
4th	254	RB Simpson, GR Davies	Queensland	Sydney	1967/68
6th	253	AF Kippax, JG Morgan	Queensland	Sydney	1927/28
2nd	253	JW Burke, RN Harvey	Queensland	Brisbane	1958/59
4th	253	DM Wellham, TM Chappell	Queensland	Sydney	1982/83
4th	251	SB Smith, PM Toohey	Victoria	Melbourne	1982/83

SYDNEY CRICKET

FIRST GRADE

Gordon won the premiership for the first time since the season of 1947-48, an outstanding performance for a team which had hung about the bottom of the competition ladder throughout the 1980s and which only a year before had finished as far down as twelfth. It took the lead in the competition after the seventh round and held it for the rest of the season, defeating Northern District in one semi-final while Balmain drew with Sutherland in the other. The final premiership places were Gordon, Balmain, Sutherland and Northern District in that order, the places being decided on points after the final match was washed out. If these four teams had anything in common it was that they performed with consistency throughout the season and that they all fielded well, which is quite possibly a formula for success in all grade cricket. It is interesting to note that only one of the four, Northern District, had been a semi-finalist the season before.

Gordon clearly owed its tremendous improvement in 1989-90 to the program of junior development which it began a few years earlier. It was not by chance, therefore, that the team had an unusual proportion of talented young players, such as the seventeen-year-old batsman Kevin Roberts, who scored 625 runs at 78.1, the eighteen-year-old all-rounder Warwick Adlam, who missed four rounds yet still took 29 wickets at 15.7, and the seventeen-year-old reserve wicket-keeper Adam Gilchrist, who as well as taking part in 15 dismissals scored 297 runs at 49.5. Jamie Bray, who scored only 193 runs in the season, was probably the only youthful Gordon player not to exceed expectations. Gordon saw little of its Sheffield Shield representatives Mark O'Neill and Phil Emery, who played only five and four grade matches respectively, although another Shield player, Richard Stobo, was available for eleven of the rounds and took 32 wickets. Taken as a whole, the team was distinguished by excellent fielding. In 1989-90, according to one estimate, Gordon players dropped fewer than half the number of catches they had dropped in previous seasons. Curiously, there was one Gordon man who spanned the two premierships—David Evans, who scored for the winning team in 1989-90 and played for it in 1947-48.

Balmain was a much improved side, too, and the appointment of the club's coach, Phil Kelleard, who moved to Balmain from Western Suburbs, clearly had a good deal to do with this. As well as coming second in the first-grade competition under his tutelage, Balmain won the club championship, having finished only tenth the season before. Balmain gained much of its new strength in 1989-90 from recruitment. For instance, Phil Marks came from Manly and scored 513 runs and took 18 wickets; Brett Neil from Parramatta made 589 runs and, with Greg Hayne, provided Balmain with the reliability at the top of the innings it had long sought; Craig Hayworth from Western Suburbs made 552 runs; and Peter March from Newcastle took 28 wickets and formed an effective partnership with Andrew Jones. Balmain had a well-balanced spin attack. Greg McLay, the off-spinner, took 33 wickets at 19.0 and Adrian Tucker, the young leg-spinner who was promoted to the Shield side towards the end of the season, took 16 wickets at 27.6.

Sutherland was an extremely young side which nevertheless had a few old heads on its shoulders, most notably the former Test batsman John Dyson, who averaged 63.8 in 11 innings, and Paul Bourke, who scored his 5,000th run in first-grade cricket in what may have been his last season. At first, Sutherland lagged behind in the competition, winning only once in the first five rounds. At this point John Dyson, who had been injured, rejoined the side as captain, and Sutherland did not lose a match thereafter. Bowling seemed to be the stronger half of Sutherland's game, and its attack was led by the medium-pacers Tony Clark and Phil Wetherall and the fast-medium bowler Glenn McGrath, an incisive bowler who in his first full season in first grade took 28 wickets at 13.1. These bowlers were assisted by a highly competent wicketkeeper, Evan Atkins, who had a part in a record 35 dismissals during the season. Sutherland had four players in the State Squad—Dyson, Rodney Davison, Darryl Mann and Justin Kenny.

Although it retained its position in the premiership's top four, Northern District had more than its share of ill fortune in 1989-90. For one thing, its two leading players, Mark Taylor and Peter Taylor, were absent for all but three grade matches each. Moreover, it was left with five drawn matches because of rain, more than any other club. One of its strengths was its array of all-rounders—there were as many as six in the team at one time—and it also acquired two fine bowlers from Sydney University, the fast bowler Darby Kuoyle and the leg-spinner Chris Elder. Neil Maxwell and Randall Green were among its most valued batsmen.

Petersham-Marrickville tied for fourth place with Northern District on the points table, but was edged into fifth place by the quotients. Petersham's fortunes have fluctuated wildly in recent years. It made the final in 1987-88, finished last in 1988-89, and then bounced back to fifth place in 1989-90. Throughout the season, it relied heavily on two players, Greg Hartshorne, who made 608 runs at 55.2, and Wayne Mulherin, who took 33 wickets at 23.7. North Sydney, which finished sixth, led the competition until Christmas and was in the top four until the last round, when it was unfortunate enough to draw with the club at the bottom of the table, Penrith, in a rain-affected match. Trevor Chappell, who made 453 runs and took 27 wickets, was again its key player, and North Sydney will feel his loss if he chooses now to retire.

What had happened to the three semi-finalists in 1988-89 which did not make the final four in 1989-90—St George, Manly and Bankstown? St George, the defending champion, slipped to the tenth place in the competition. Geoff Milliken had a marvellous season with the bat, but generally St George's batting tended to run hot and cold. Moreover, only one St George bowler, Murray Bennett, had a bowling average of less than 30. Manly, the runner-up in 1988-89, finished only seventh in 1989-90, yet it actually came very close to making the semi-finals again. It went into round fifteen on fourth place and had it scored just three more runs on the second day it would have retained that fourth place. Manly's leading players included Richard Fry, who made 731 runs, and the pace bowler Warren Evans, who in his initial full first-grade season took 35 wickets at 19.2 in only twelve rounds. Bankstown, which dropped to thirteenth place, seemed to have trouble finding satisfactory replacements for Steve Small, Wayne Holdsworth and the Waugh brothers, who were absent on Sheffield Shield duty for much of the season. Dean Waugh had a fine season, however, scoring 651 runs at 50.0. Generally, Bankstown appeared often to let itself down with poor fielding.

Three first-grade players passed important milestones during the season. Jim Robson and Greg Livingstone each scored his 6,000th run for the University of NSW and Mick O'Sullivan of Sydney University took his 600th first-grade wicket.

First Grade Points Table

Gordon 60, Balmain 54 (quotient 1.4849), Sutherland 54 (quotient 1.1969), Northern District 48 (quotient 1.3300), Petersham-Marrickville 48 (quotient 0.9796), North Sydney 46, Manly-Warringah 45, Randwick 42, Campbelltown 36, St George 36, Mosman 34, Sydney University 33, Bankstown-Canterbury 30, Western Suburbs 30, University of NSW 24, Fairfield 18, Hawkesbury 18, Waverley 18, Parramatta 12, Penrith 12.

First-Grade Batting Averages (minimum 350 runs)

	I	NO	HS	R	A
G Milliken (St George)	11	1	193	892	89.2
K Roberts (Gordon)	14	6	128*	625	78.1
G Smith (St George)	10	4	114	379	63.1
J Robson (Uni. of NSW)	14	3	112*	655	59.5
G Hartshorne (Petersham)	15	4	104	608	55.2
B McNamara (Wes Subs)	9	2	128*	366	52.2
D Kingdon (Waverley)	16	5	93*	551	50.0
D Waugh (Bankstown)	15	2	125*	651	50.0
Richard Fry (Manly)	15	0	101	731	48.7
F Jacobson (Mosman)	15	5	93*	467	46.7
R Chee Quee (Randwick)	16	0	182	730	45.6

First Grade Bowling Averages (minimum 30 wickets)

	W	R	A
D Hourn (Waverley)	37	516	13.9
A Clark (Sutherland)	36	590	16.3
A Jones (Balmain)	35	625	17.8
G Price (Hawkesbury)	31	563	18.1
W Evans (Manly)	35	674	19.2
G McLay (Balmain)	35	684	19.5
R Stobo (Gordon)	32	646	20.1
B Patman (Fairfield)	33	702	21.2
P Vilimaa (Nth District)	34	732	21.5
C Bayldon (Parramatta)	33	712	21.5

SECOND GRADE

Premiers: Manly-Warringah

Place-getters: 2. North Sydney, 3. St George, 4. Western Suburbs.

Final: Manly (1 for 100) defeated North Sydney (6 for 99) on the first innings.

Points Table: Manly-Warringah 62, North Sydney 60, St George 54 (quotient 1.3964), Western Suburbs 54 (quotient 1.1283), Parramatta 48, Fairfield 42, Penrith 40, Balmain 36, Bankstown-Canterbury 36, Northern District 36, Gordon 34, Sutherland 33, Campbelltown 30, Petersham-Marrickville 30, Sydney University 30, Waverley 30, Hawkesbury 27, Mosman 24, Randwick 24, University of NSW 12.

THIRD GRADE

Premiers: Bankstown-Canterbury

Place-getters: 2. Manly-Warringah, 3. Mosman, 4. Sydney University.

Final: Manly-Warringah (8 for 41) drew with Bankstown (4 for 21).

Points Table: Bankstown-Canterbury 60 (quotient 1.6792), Mosman 60 (quotient 1.2093), Manly-Warringah 54, Sydney University 48 (quotient 1.1119), Sutherland 48 (quotient 1.0508), Fairfield 42, Hawkesbury 42, Parramatta 42, Balmain 36, Gordon 36, North Sydney 36, Petersham-Marrickville 36, University of NSW 36, Penrith 33, Northern District 30, St George 28, Randwick 24, Western Suburbs 21, Campbelltown 12, Waverley 12.

FOURTH GRADE

Premiers: Balmain

Place-getters: 2. Sutherland, 3. Western Suburbs, 4. Penrith.

Final: washed out.

Points Table: Balmain 82, Sutherland 66, Western Suburbs 54 (quotient 1.2630), Penrith 54 (quotient 1.2151), Sydney University 43, Northern District 42, Randwick 42, Gordon 36, St George 36, University of NSW 36, Manly-Warringah 33, Fairfield 30, North Sydney 30, Parramatta 30, Mosman 24, Petersham-Marrickville 24, Bankstown-Canterbury 18, Waverley 18, Campbelltown 12, Hawkesbury 12.

FIFTH GRADE

Premiers: Parramatta

Place-getters: 2. Balmain, 3. Manly-Warringah, 4. Western Suburbs.

Final: washed out.

Points Table: Parramatta 64, Balmain 63, Manly-Warringah 61, Western Suburbs 57, Sutherland 54, Waverley 48, Penrith 46,

Bankstown-Canterbury 42, Campbelltown 42, Northern District 42, Randwick 42, St George 34, Sydney University 30, Gordon 24, North Sydney 24, University of NSW 24, Fairfield 22, Mosman 21, Hawkesbury 18, Petersham-Marrickville 12.

CLUB CHAMPIONSHIP
Winner: Balmain
Points: Balmain 1,038, Manly-Warringah 1,029, Sutherland 1,005, North Sydney 870, Gordon 848, Northern District 810, Western Suburbs 810, St George 792, Bankstown-Canterbury 768, Sydney University 735, Parramatta 722, Randwick 708, Petersham-Marrickville 700, Mosman 684, Penrith 670, Fairfield 632, Campbelltown 558, University of NSW 528, Hawkesbury 501, Waverley 474.

NEWCASTLE CRICKET

Charlestown won the Newcastle first-grade competition by defeating Wallsend in a low-scoring final at the No 1 Sports Ground, Newcastle on March 25 and 31. The victory meant Charlestown was the first club in one season to claim both the first-grade premiership and the Tom Locker Cup for winning the first-grade limited-overs competition. Wallsend was entitled to feel disappointed at losing. As defending champion, it had already won the minor premiership, finishing ahead of Charlestown on quotients. Moreover, in the final it lost the toss and was sent in to bat on a rain-affected pitch. Wallsend began reasonably well. It lost its first wicket for 0, but then its captain, Greg Geise, and the other opener, David Edwards, raised the total to 40 before Giese was out for 22, trying to hit Charlestown's spinner, Mark Curry, who had just joined the attack. It was the first of 6 wickets Curry took in the innings, which were largely responsible for the collapse of Wallsend's batting. Wallsend lost 4 wickets when the total was 70 and was all out for only 117. On the following Saturday, Charlestown was made to work hard for the runs it needed, but eventually it won with 4 wickets in hand. Geise took 3 for 37 in 22 overs of tight bowling.

Wallsend

Batsman	How Out	Ttl
D Edwards	c Bristow b Curry	16
C Russell	c and b Fowler	0
G Geise	c Gilbertson b Curry	22
C Blanch	c Brown b Bristow	17
K King	st Brown b Curry	1
W Davies	st Brown b Curry	0
R Willmott	c Curry b Winchester	17
M Waugh	c and b Curry	0
L Walker	no out	19
R Hicks	b Towers	2
S Woodbridge	b Curry	4
SUNDRIES: B.—LB. 9 NB. 10		19
Total		117

F/W: 0 40 60 70 70 70 70 92 112 117

Bowler	O	M	R	Wkts
T Towers	12	3	23	1
W Fowler	6	2	9	1
T Gilbertson	7	2	14	0
M Curry	41.2	26	31	6
T Bristow	26	15	23	1
B Winchester	7	3	8	1

Charlestown

Batsman	How Out	Ttl
S Mace	c Walker b Geise	20
D Marjoribanks	c Davies b Hicks	4
F Ross	c Waugh b Geise	24
M Curry	c Russell b Geise	3
T Bristow	c Davies b Woodbridge	12
M Hall	not out	18
B Winchester	run out	10
W Fowler	not out	19
Sundries: B. 2 LB. 6 W. 1 N.B. —		9
Total		6 for 119

F/W: 4 40 43 63 71 91

Bowler	O	M	R	Wkts
M Waugh	10	5	8	0
R Hicks	10	2	25	1
G Geise	22	7	37	3
C Blanch	8	0	28	0
R Willmott	2	2	0	0
S Woodbridge	9	5	15	1

First-grade Premiership Points Table

Wallsend 27 (1.435 quotient), Charlestown 27 (1.312 quotient), University 26, Lambton-New Lambton 25, Cardiff-Boolaroo 23, Merewether 23, Stockton 22, Newcastle City 21, Southern Lakes 21, Hamilton-Wickham 19, Belmont 18, Waratah-Mayfield 18.

Club Championship Points Table

Charlestown 505.5, University 484, Stockton 474.5, Waratah-Mayfield 462, Wallsend 443.5, Cardiff-Boolaroo 426.5, Belmont 387.5, Hamilton-Wickham 387, Merewether 382, Newcastle City 376, Southern Lakes 352, Lambton-New Lambton 350.

First-Grade Batting Averages

Batsman	Inn	NO	HS	Agg.	Avrge
G Geise (W)	7	2	145*	697	139.40
R Merlo (U)	9	3	87	486	81.00
P Ross (C)	10	2	138	513	64.13
D Willis (C-B)	9	1	100	483	60.38
M Curry (C)	7	1	151*	347	57.83
G Cooke (U)	9	3	56*	305	50.80
T Bowd (U)	8	1	151*	345	49.29
C Beatty (H-W)	11	3	113*	381	47.63
D Edwards (W)	10	1	155*	405	45.00
G Arms (W-M)	9	—	104	402	44.67

First-Grade Bowling Averages

Bowler	Overs	M	Runs	Wkts	Avrge
R Holland (S.L.)	225	49	631	41	15.39
W Fowler (C)	143.1	34	341	22	15.50
M Christie (W-M)	208	61	438	28	15.64
G Geise (W)	158	48	344	21	16.38
M Varnum (M)	141	46	340	20	17.00
B Bannister (LNL)	229	73	478	28	17.07
R Scully (W-M)	164.4	43	389	22	17.68
D Wilson (C-B)	218.4	62	461	26	17.73
C Hamilton (B)	195	43	527	29	18.17
M Waugh (W)	203	57	498	27	18.44

First-Grade Wicket-Keeping

Wicket-Keeper	Cght	Stmp	Total
P Schacht (B)	25	5	30
L Walker (W)	26	2	28
C Matthews (S.L.)	14	7	21
J Thomson (H-W)	20	—	20
P Chapman (N-C)	14	5	19
D Brown (C)	14	2	16
R Merlo (U)	16	—	16
M Caponechia (S)	15	1	16
K Palmer (W-M)	15	—	15
S Bridges (M)	10	4	14

INDIVIDUAL AWARDS

NEWCASTLE HERALD AWARDS*

The Player of the Year: Greg Geise
The Club of the Year: University

JIMMY DICKINSON MEMORIAL TROPHY

Presented by Stockton District Cricket Club for the First Grade Batting Average (min 400 runs and 5 innings):
Greg Geise (Wallsend) 697 runs, average 139.40

H HEATH CUP

Presented by Newcastle District Cricket Umpires Association for the First Grade Bowling Average (min 30 wickets):
Robert Holland (Southern Lakes) 41 wickets, average 15.39

ROY McCARTNEY TROPHY

Donated by the late Mr R McCartney for the most number of Dismissals by a Wicketkeeper in First Grade:
Peter Schacht (Belmont) 30 Dismissals
(25 caught, 5 stumped)

G HODGES MEMORIAL TROPHY

Presented by Stockton District Cricket Club for the best Under 23 Bowler in First Grade:
Murray Christie (Waratah-Mayfield) 28 wickets, average 15.64

NDCA SHIELD

Presented by the NDCA for the best Under 23 Batsman in First Grade:
Robert Merlo (University) 486 runs, average 81.00

GORDON FRASER TROPHY

Donated by the late Mr Gordon Fraser for the U23 Cricketer of the season: Robert
Merlo (University)

CLIFF JONES TROPHY*

Presented by the Newcastle District Umpires Associaiton in honour of the late
Cliff Jones for the Under 17 Player of the Season:
Greg Wallace (Hamilton-Wickham)

* Decided by umpires on a points scoring basis.

TROPHIES PRESENTED for:

1st Grade Batting Aggregate: Greg Geise 697 runs
1st Grade Bowling Aggregate: Robert Holland 41 wickets

COUNTRY CRICKET

COMBINED COUNTRY v NEW SOUTH WALES 2nd XI

The Combined Country team which played two matches against
the New South Wales 2nd XI at Albury in mid-November, 1989,
was: Craig Hamilton, Mark Kelaher, David Willis and Stuart Bridges
of Newcastle, Shane Frecklington and Glen Hooper of Orange, Peter
Gerhard of Temora, John Frame of Grafton, Anthony Le Bas of
Wollongong, Jeff Lucas of Batemans Bay, Gerard Hines of
Cootamundra and Craig Morton of Stockinbingal.

Combined Country v New South Wales 2nd XI   Lavington
Sports Club Oval, Albury, November 13, 1989
50-over match

New South Wales 2nd XI 8 for 242 (R Green 52, N Maxwell 50,
J Kenny 49; P Gerhard 4/57, G Hooper 2/35) defeated Combined
Country 8 for 143 (D Willis 36, J Frame 20; G Rowell 3/12, B
McNamara 2/26, S Prestwidge 2/46) by 99 runs.

Combined Country v New South Wales 2nd XI   Lavington
Sports Club Oval, Albury, November 14-16, 1989

Protracted batting by the New South Wales 2nd XI ruled out any
chance of a result in this match, which tailed away into a draw on
the third day. Batting first, Combined Country made 226, its principal
run-getters being M Kelaher 44, J Frame 40, A Le Bas 36, D Willis
26 and P Gerhard 26. G Rowell took 3 for 33, G McLay 3 for 57
and A Tucker 2 for 49. The New South Wales 2nd XI then occupied
the crease for 567 minutes while it compiled 378, choosing not to

declare. Its batsmen failed to score off 50 of the 147.4 overs bowled to them. Brad McNamara batted for eight hours for 186 not out, the highest score, and R Green made 54. C Hamilton had the excellent bowling figures of 5 for 72, and D Willis and P Gerhard each took 2 wickets. There was only enough time left for Combined Country to make 2 for 37 in its second innings, A Le Bas finishing with 25 not out. Combined Country was not at full strength for this match, but the country players gave a good account of themselves, especially in the field.

TOOHEYS LIMITED-OVERS COUNTRY CUP

The ACT retained the cup after withstanding a determined challenge by Newcastle in the final, which it won by 7 runs. It was the ACTs fifth win in the seven years the cup has been contested, a record which confirms Canberra's strength as a cricketing city and must further encourage the ACT in its attempt to move up to interstate competition. The cricket was again of a generally high standard, despite the poor weather which disrupted some matches. This is how contenders for the championship fared as they moved towards the finals:

Quarter Finals

Newcastle v Western Newcastle No. 1 Sportsground, Newcastle. Sent in to bat on a well-grassed pitch and in overcast conditions, Western lost wickets at alarming rate. It was 5 for 29 after 20 overs, and eventually all out for 90 in 48.2 overs—Western's smallest total since entering the competition. Joel Murphy of Bathurst top scored with 19. Murray Christie finished with the remarkable bowling figures of 3 for 6, and Mark Curry, Tim Towers and David Willis each took 2 wickets. Newcastle achieved an easy victory with 15 overs to spare, having lost only 2 wickets. Greg Arms top scored with 44 not out. Newcastle won by 8 wickets.

ACT v Southern Zone Tuross Head. Winning the toss and choosing to bat, Southern had an innings of fluctuating fortunes which ended with a total of 7 for 187. At first Southern was pinned down by accurate bowling, but its middle-order batsmen pushed the score along with bright batting. Jamie Annetts, for instance, took 23 balls to score 34 not out. Michael Walker, the top scorer, was run out for 48 and Peter Hamill was run out for 30. The ACT lost early wickets and at one point seemed in trouble at 5 for 71. Greg Irvine then led a spirited counter-attack, hitting 76 not out off 78 balls, and he and Neil Woods (58*) saw the side to victory with a 117 run partnership, a competition record for the sixth wicket. The ACT won with 35 balls to spare, and Irvine was named Man of the Match.

North West v Riverina Robins Oval, Maitland. North West was awarded the match on the strength of its superior run rate after rain brought the match to an early end. Winning the toss and batting first, Riverina was 4 for 66 but Trevor Howard of Leeton (48) and

Peter Gerhard of Temora (44) led a recovery which enabled Riverina to finish its 50 overs with a total of 9 for 204. Keith Lang of Muswellbrook was a little expensive but he still had the best bowling figures, 4 for 51 in 10 overs. Rain was threatening as North West began its innings and, foreseeing a premature end to the match, the North West batsmen set about scoring as quickly as possible. Two wickets were lost, but the score rose rapidly, and when rain ended the match after 18 overs North West was 2 for 91—a run rate of 5.06 per over. Trevor Howard was chosen as Man of the Match.

Illawarra v North Coast Figtree Oval, Wollongong. This match, twice postponed because of rain, ended in excitement when North Coast hit the winning runs with one ball to spare. Illawarra began soundly enough and was at one point 2 for 117, but Steve McCrea was out then for 53, starting a collapse which reduced Illawarra to 8 for 164. By the end of its 50 overs, Illawarra had moved on to 8 for 172, Ross Steele having taken 3 for 17 in 5 overs and Dean Rumble 2 for 27 in 10 overs. North Coast lost early wickets, recovered, then slumped again. At 7 for 148 its chances appeared to be fading, but the scramble for runs continued and when the last over began North Coast needed 8 runs to win. David Campbell scored 5 off the first 3 balls, and then Dean Rumble scored 3 off the fourth. It was North Coast's first victory in the competition. Eric Higgings, who top scored for North Coast with 54, was Man of the Match.

Semi-Finals

ACT v North West Manuka Oval, Canberra. ACT owed its victory in this match largely to fine bowling performances by Greg Irvine and John Bull, who caused a collapse of the North West innings just when the North West batsmen looked to be advancing towards a large total. Having won the toss and chosen to bat, North West lost both openers cheaply, but Grant Ryan of Glen Innes (73) and Chris Barrington of Tamworth (34) put on 82 runs between them. The total had reached 2 for 103 when Irvine dismissed Barrington, and thereafter North West's batsmen seemed to struggle. Wickets fell steadily, and after 50 overs North West was 9 for 160. As it often had before, the ACT began shakily, losing 5 wickets for 63 Bull and Irvine steadied the innings with a 92 run partnership. Irvine went for 35, but Bull was undefeated on 51 when, at 6 for 161, ACT won the match with 12.3 overs to spare. Bull was Man of the Match.

North Coast v Newcastle Oxley Oval, Port Macquarie. North Coast won the toss and sent Newcastle in, probably reasoning that it needed to gain the upper hand quickly to have a chance of winning, but the gamble did not pay off and it lost the match. Newcastle, having denied the bowlers the early breakthrough they were seeking, went on to compile a large total of 4 for 241 off its 50 overs. No fewer than 91 runs were added in the last 10 overs. Greg Arms made 83 and Mark Curry 58 not out. Terry Baldwin (44) and Mark Van Eppen began the North Coast innings in promising fashion, but the loss of the first wicket at 67 was followed at once by the loss of three others. Scott Stuckey, who hit 2 sixes and made a quick 37, produced a brief flurry of scoring, but North Coast lagged far behind the required run rate, and at the end of 50 overs was 9 for 174. Newcastle thus won by 67 runs, and Mark Curry was named Man of the Match.

Final

ACT v Newcastle
Manuka Oval, Canberra
February 18, 1990

The two sides were old rivals, so it seemed fitting that the match was so closely contested. The ACT won by 7 runs, but it was not until the last over of the match that the outcome was settled. Having won the toss, the ACT's skipper, Greg Irvine, unexpectedly chose to bat—a decision which the home side must have regretted when the ACT had slipped to 3 for 14. Michael Frost (44) rescued the innings from its immediate problems, and Irvine (54) restored it further with a well-made 54. Even so, the ACT was all out for 176 in 44.2 overs, a total which appeared within Newcastle's range. After a poor start, Newcastle's two most reliable batsmen in the competition, Greg Arms and Mark Curry, put on 71 runs between them, and at 2 for 90 Newcastle was favoured to win. From this point onwards, however, wickets fell steadily until Newcastle was 9 for 157—20 runs short of victory. The last two batsmen, Tim Towers and Stuart Bridges, batted sensibly and appeared to be closing on their target when Bridges was run out trying for a second run. John Bull, who took 4 for 25 in 9 overs, was Man of the Match.

ACT

Batsman	How Out	Ttl
G Woodbridge	b Willis	0
A Yates	b Christie	3
M Frost	run out	44
P Solway	c Arms b Willis	0
P Evans	c Daly b Hamilton	21
J Bull	b Curry	14
G Irvine (c)	b Christie	54
D McDonald	c Curry b Christie	9
E Nix	b Christie	1
K Bone	c Christie b Towers	10
C Crouch	not out	2
SUNDRIES: B.1 LB. 8 W. 9 NB. —		18
Total (44.2 overs)		176

F/W: 1 10 14 44 93 97 156 162 169 176

Bowler	O	M	R	Wkts
M Christie	9	1	27	4
D Willis	9	1	29	2
T Towers	8.2	0	41	1
C Hamilton	9	0	56	1
M Curry	9	2	19	1

Newcastle

Batsman	How Out	Ttl
G Arms (c)	c Evans b Bull	48
A Daly	b Crouch	4
P Dyson	c Woodbridge b Crouch	2
M Curry	lbw b Bone	51
D Willis	c Evans b Bull	0
G McNeil	b Bull	16
R Merlo	c Bone b Bull	5
M Christie	c Evans b Irvine	12
C Hamilton	b Crouch	0
S Bridges	run out	14
T Towers	not out	7
SUNDRIES: B. — LB. 6 W. 2 NB. 2		10
Total (45.1 overs)		169

F/W: 13 19 90 98 124 132 136 139 157 169

Bowler	O	M	R	Wkts
C Crouch	10	0	39	3
E Nix	9	0	34	0
K Bone	9	1	29	1
G Irvine	6	1	22	1
J Bull	9	1	25	4
D McDonald	2.1	0	14	0

Combined Country Under-24s v Sydney Under-21s   Bankstown Oval, February 6-8, 1990

Because of rain, this match was abandoned without a ball being bowled. The Combined Country team was: Robert Merlo (captain), Newcastle; John Frame, Grafton; Murray Christie, Newcastle; Geoff Cooke, Newcastle; Anthony Daly, Newcastle; Paul Dyson, Newcastle; Mark Garland, Yass; Brad Newman, Illawarra; Richard Nind, Lismore; Anthony Parker, Newcastle; Scott Smith, ACT; and Frank Weymouth, Orange. The manager was Ken Clifford of Newcastle.

QUEENSLAND

AFTER THE SHEFFIELD SHIELD FINAL, many commentators expressed surprise at the fact that Queensland had lost a Shield final yet again. The truth is Queensland had done very well even to get into the final. Compared with other Queensland teams of recent years, this was not a particularly strong one, and it was certainly not as strong as the Queensland teams which came so close to winning the Shield in the mid-1980s. Its batting tended to be unreliable, especially in the top order, and its bowling attack, although led by a top-class fast bowler in outstanding form, Craig McDermott, was not a well balanced one. So the 1989-90 Queenslanders were entitled to feel satisfied accomplishing as much as they did, which was to lead the competition table until the very last qualifying match.

Queensland's problems really began near the top of its batting. Rob Kerr, a batsman of undoubted ability, had a generally poor season by his own standards, averaging only 27.69 in the eight Shield matches he played. Indeed, the past few seasons have been disappointing for Kerr. Not only has he slipped from contention for the Australian side, but he missed out on the Queensland captaincy which some thought would be offered to him and he is no longer the force in the side's batting which he used to be. This may be because he is concentrating more on a career outside the game, but whatever the reason, the failure of such a talented batsman to play at his best certainly had a bearing on Queensland's fortunes in 1989-90. Another talented batsman, Stuart Law, has yet to meet the high expectations his admirers hold of him, averaging only 27.00 in the seven matches he played. It seemed he neither maintained concentration nor chose his strokes as well as he might have, although these are both skills which are acquired with experience. On the other hand, Peter Cantrell advanced faster than anyone expected, and by the end of the season he had established himself as a regular opening batsman. Cantrell scored 693 runs at 36.47. Geoff Foley had a marvellous debut for Queensland in January, opening the batting against Pakistan and scoring 155. He, too, appeared to have earned a regular place near the top of the order (in fact, he opened the batting again in the Shield final) by the end of the season. Yet the general point may be made that Queensland was not given the sound starts which any team probably needs to win the Sheffield Shield.

Greg Ritchie was the mainstay of Queensland's batting. He scored 928 runs at the impressive average of 54.59, and he did it despite having to cope with the considerable pressures which the Queensland captaincy imposed on him. This was, remember, his first full season as captain, and while his captaincy was sometimes criticised and he was blamed for making one or two tactical errors, on the whole he appeared to manage the task efficiently. This was certainly the opinion which prevailed where it really mattered, in and around the Queensland team. The former New South Welshman, Peter

Clifford, returned to the Queensland side half-way through the season and batted well enough to secure a regular place. In the eight matches he played, he scored 432 runs at a creditable average of 36.00. The batsman on top of the averages was Allan Border, who scored 272 runs at 68.00. But Border played only three matches, so Queensland benefited little from his skill.

Craig McDermott was not only the side's most successful bowler but probably its outstanding player. He took 54 wickets at an average of 25.46 in the ten Shield matches he played, the fourth highest wicket aggregate in the history of the competition. McDermott bowled as fast and as well as he did in his heyday (in fact, some thought he had never bowled faster than he did against Western Australia in Brisbane), and it was not easy to see why the Australian selectors continued to overlook him. This was no doubt disappointing for McDermott personally, but it was fortunate for Queensland, which could hardly have done without him. Carl Rackemann played only seven state matches, but he took 34 wickets at the excellent average of 19.62, the best of any Queensland bowler.

The other pace bowlers Dirk Tazelaar (22 wickets at 31.95), Mick Polzin (28 wickets at 24.36) and young Michael Kasprowicz supported McDermott capably, each of them shining on occasions, but it was the lack of a quality spin bowler which was the Queensland attack's chief inadequacy. Peter Cantrell's off-spin was generally ineffective, which may well have been the price he paid for the improvement in his batting. He took just 11 wickets at the rather daunting average of 72.73. Steve Storey performed a little better (14 wickets at 47.79) without ever filling the role of a front-line bowler. Nevertheless, it did seem surprising that the tour selectors, Greg Ritchie, Allan Border and Richie Robinson, chose to make him twelfth man for the final in Sydney, where his spin bowling had a better chance than anywhere of being successful. Indeed, the need for Queensland to take a spinner into the match seemed so pressing beforehand that there was even speculation the leg-spinner Trevor Hohns might be persuaded to emerge from retirement to play. Hohns had appeared in one A grade match during the season, but was clearly never in consideration. Still, it is interesting to speculate how much closer the result might have been if by some chance Hohns had been able to play for Queensland in the final at Sydney.

QUEENSLAND FIRST-CLASS RECORDS

Season 1989/90

Date	Venue	Opponent	Result for Queensland
Oct 21*	Adelaide	South Australia	Lost by 5 wkts
Oct 25	Brisbane	Victoria	Drawn
Oct 29*	Brisbane	Victoria	Won by 7 wkts
Nov 3	Brisbane	South Australia	Won by 6 wkts
Nov 17	Hobart	Tasmania	Drawn
Dec 1	Newcastle	New South Wales	Lost by 32 runs
Dec 29	Brisbane	New South Wales	Won by 5 wkts
Jan 6	Brisbane	Pakistan	Drawn

Continued

Date		Venue	Opponent	Result for Queensland
Jan	19	Brisbane	Western Australia _____	Drawn
Jan	26*	Rockhampton	Sri Lanka _____	Drawn
Jan	28*	Rockhampton	Sri Lanka _____	Won by 5 runs
Feb	2	Brisbane	Tasmania _____	Drawn
Feb	16	Perth	Western Australia _____	Won by an inns & 177 runs
Mar	2	Melbourne	Victoria _____	Drawn
Mar	9	Adelaide	South Australia _____	Drawn
Mar	17*	Perth	Western Australia _____	Lost by 6 wkts
Mar	23	Sydney	New South Wales _____	Lost by 345 runs

* Denotes not first-class

1989/90 Queensland First-Class Averages

Batsman	M	Inn	NO	Runs	HS	50	100	Avrge	Ct/St
AR Border	3	6	2	272	144*	—	1	68.00	7
IA Healy	5	7	3	250	81*	2	—	62.50	22/2
GM Ritchie	12	19	2	928	213*	4	3	54.59	17
MV Tooley	1	2	1	48	31	—	—	48.00	—
PE Cantrell	12	20	1	693	125	6	1	36.47	12
PS Clifford	8	12	—	432	114	1	2	36.00	4
GI Foley	7	12	1	354	155	—	1	32.18	2
CB Smart	5	7	1	177	98	2	—	29.50	5
SC Storey	10	14	3	315	54	2	—	28.64	4
RB Kerr	8	13	—	360	123	2	1	27.69	5
SG Law	7	11	2	243	66*	2	—	27.00	4
BP Inwood	3	5	2	70	19	—	—	23.33	—
CJ McDermott	10	13	2	214	37	—	—	19.45	3
MA Polzin	7	7	3	70	29	—	—	17.50	5
GS Trimble	2	3	—	50	39	—	—	16.67	3
MS Kasprowicz	5	6	1	68	49	—	—	13.60	1
TJ Barsby	4	6	—	81	28	—	—	13.50	4
CG Rackemann	7	8	4	49	17	—	—	12.25	1
PJ Carew	2	2	—	23	23	—	—	11.50	—
PW Anderson	5	6	—	60	44	—	—	10.00	13/2
PJ Drinnen	2	2	—	14	14	—	—	7.00	6
D Tazelaar	7	9	1	45	28	—	—	5.63	3

Bowler	M	Overs	Mdns	Runs	Wkts	Avrge	5wi	10m	NB	W	Best
CG Rackemann	7	1722	70	667	34	19.62	—	—	21	1	4/39
MA Polzin	7	1562	65	682	28	24.36	2	—	—	7	8/51
CJ McDermott	10	2592	100	1376	54	25.48	4	—	94	1	8/44
AR Border	3	264	8	107	4	26.75	—	—	—	—	3/44
SG Law	7	30	1	29	1	29.00	—	—	—	—	1/16
BP Inwood	3	271	20	90	3	30.00	—	—	—	—	1/9
D Tazelaar	7	1636	59	703	22	31.95	1	—	39	—	6/48
SC Storey	10	1152	48	669	14	47.79	—	—	7	—	4/19
PJ Carew	2	474	19	289	5	57.80	—	—	—	1	2/43
GI Foley	7	696	32	318	5	63.60	—	—	14	1	2/57
PE Cantrell	12	1599	64	800	11	72.73	—	—	2	—	3/71
MS Kasprowicz	5	759	22	451	6	75.17	—	—	13	2	2/59
GM Ritchie	12	78	1	51	—	—	—	—	—	—	—
PS Clifford	8	42	3	16	—	—	—	—	—	—	—
IA Healy	5	6	—	1	—	—	—	—	—	—	—
TJ Barsby	4	6	—	7	—	—	—	—	—	—	—

Queensland First-Class Cricket Records

Opponent	Venue	First Game	Games	W	L	D	T
Australian Rep. Teams							
AIF Team	Brisbane _____	Jan 24 1920	1	—	—	1	—
Australian Services	Brisbane _____	Jan 18 1946	1	—	—	1	—
Total			2	—	—	2	—
England Teams	Brisbane Ex _____	Dec 7 1894	4	—	3	1	—
	Brisbane _____	Nov 27 1903	20	3	8	9	—
Total			24	3	11	10	—
India	Brisbane _____	Nov 21 1947	3	1	1	1	—

Opponent	Venue	First Game	Games	W	L	D	T
New South Wales	Brisbane Ex	Apr 3 1893	10	1	5	4	—
	Sydney	Mar 24 1894	80	12	47	21	—
	Brisbane	Nov 25 1899	76	19	28	29	—
	Lismore	Dec 15 1979	1	—	1	—	—
	Newcastle	Oct 22 1981	3	1	1	1	—
Total			170	33	82	55	—
New Zealand	Wellington	Dec 26 1896	1	—	1	—	—
	Brisbane	Dec 19 1913	6	2	1	3	—
	Bundaberg	Dec 18 1982	1	—	—	1	—
Total			8	2	2	4	—
New Zealand Provinces							
Auckland	Auckland	Dec 22 1896	1	—	—	1	—
Hawke's Bay	Napier	Dec 31 1896	1	1	—	—	—
Canterbury	Christchurch	Jan 8 1897	1	1	—	—	—
Otago	Napier	Jan 15 1897	1	1	—	—	—
Total			4	3	—	1	—
Pakistan	Brisbane	Nov 27 1964	6	—	1	5	—
South Africa	Brisbane	Nov 25 1910	4	1	1	2	—
South Australia	Brisbane	Jan 14 1899	54	21	13	20	—
	Adelaide	Dec 26 1923	60	11	29	19	1
	Brisbane Ex	Jan 23 1926	5	2	3	—	—
Total			119	34	45	39	1
Tasmania	Launceston	Feb 25 1978	5	1	1	3	—
	Brisbane	Dec 15 1978	10	4	—	6	—
	Hobart TCA	Dec 8 1979	2	1	—	1	—
	Devonport	Feb 19 1982	3	1	—	2	—
	Hobart Bel	Nov 17 1989	1	—	—	1	—
Total			21	7	1	13	—
Victoria	Brisbane	Jan 31 1903	60	19	18	23	—
	Melbourne	Dec 16 1904	52	7	34	11	—
	Brisbane Ex	Jan 31 1920	5	1	2	2	—
	Carlton	Dec 14 1945	1	—	1	—	—
	St Kilda	Dec 9 1955	4	2	1	1	—
	Geelong	Feb 26 1981	2	1	—	1	—
	Wangaratta	Nov 21 1986	1	—	—	1	—
Total			125	30	56	39	—
Western Australia	Perth	Mar 24 1894	40	6	20	14	—
	Brisbane	Feb 6 1948	37	9	6	22	—
Total			77	15	26	36	—
West Indians	Brisbane	Jan 10 1931	8	1	3	4	—
	Townsville	Jan 11 1987	1	—	—	1	—
Total			9	1	3	5	—
World XI	Brisbane	Nov 19 1971	1	—	1	—	—
Total for Queensland			573	130	230	212	1

Most Appearances for Queensland

Games	Player	Career	Games	Player	Career
133	SC Trimble	1959/60–1975/76	62	KC Wessels	1979/80–1985/86
109	KD Mackay	1946/47–1963/64	61	GS Chappell	1973/74–1983/84
109	TV Hohns	1972/73–1988/89	59	AR Border	1980/81–1989/90
96	JA Maclean	1968/69–1978/79	58	KA Archer	1946/47–1956/57
95	GM Ritchie	1980/81–1989/90	58	JJ McLaughlin	1949/50–1962/63
94	ATW Grout	1946/47–1965/66	58	JRF Duncan	1964/65–1970/71
91	PJP Burge	1952/53–1967/68	57	EC Bensted	1923/24–1936/37
89	PH Carlson	1969/70–1980/81	57	GS Trimble	1982/83–1989/90

Continued

Games	Player	Career	Games	Player	Career
87	G Dymock	1971/72–1981/82	55	TR Veivers	1958/59–1967/68
87	RB Kerr	1981/82–1989/90	55	MF Francke	1971/72–1985/86
86	D Tallon	1933/34–1953/54	54	FC Thompson	1912/13–1933/34
78	RB Phillips	1979/80–1985/86	53	JD Bratchford	1952/53–1959/60
71	VN Raymer	1940/41–1956/57	53	GR Reynolds	1955/56–1963/64
70	RK Oxenham	1911/12–1936/37	52	PJ Allan	1959/60–1968/69
68	JR Thomson	1974/75–1985/86	51	RE Rogers	1935/36–1948/49
68	JN Maguire	1977/78–1988/89	51	CJ McDermott	1983/84–1989/90
67	GG Cook	1931/32–1947/48	50	WA Brown	1936/37–1949/50
67	DFE Bull	1956/57–1967/68	50	AH Carrigan	1945/46–1951/52
64	AB Henschell	1981/82–1988/89	50	B Fisher	1954/55–1967/68
63	CG Rackemann	1979/80–1989/90			

Youngest Players on First-Class Debut for Queensland

Player	Date of Birth	F/Class Debut	Opponent	Venue	Age on Years	Debut Days
GA Bourne	Apr 21 1913	Dec 18 1930	Victoria	Melbourne	17	241
D Tallon	Feb 17 1916	Dec 1 1933	Victoria	Brisbane	17	288
JA Downey	Feb 4 1895	Nov 23 1912	New South Wales	Brisbane	17	292
JM Govan	Dec 30 1914	Oct 28 1932	Victoria	Brisbane	17	303
MS Kasprowicz	Feb 10 1972	Jan 19 1990	Western Australia	Brisbane	17	344

Highest Innings Totals for Queensland

Total	Opponent	Venue	Season
687	New South Wales	Brisbane	1930/31
613	New South Wales	Brisbane	1963/64
590	New South Wales	Sydney	1927/28
9d-589	Western Australia	Brisbane	1953/54
577	New South Wales	Sydney	1926/27
7d-575	Victoria	Brisbane	1938/39
8d-574	New South Wales	Sydney	1956/57
8d-573	South Australia	Adelaide	1945/46
561	Victoria	Brisbane	1953/54
3d-548	Western Australia	Brisbane	1963/64
547	South Australia	Adelaide	1960/61
542	Tasmania	Launceston	1984/85
540	South Africa	Brisbane	1952/53
539	Victoria	Brisbane	1985/86
4d-536	Victoria	St Kilda	1982/83
528	New South Wales	Brisbane	1935/36
7-525	Victoria	Melbourne	1966/67
523	Victoria	Wangaratta	1986/87
6d-517	New South Wales	Sydney	1964/65
5d-510	Victoria	Melbourne	1938/39
9d-506	New South Wales	Brisbane	1925/26
504	Victoria	Brisbane	1931/32
503	Western Australia	Brisbane	1964/65
501	New South Wales	Brisbane	1938/39

Lowest Innings Totals for Queensland

Total	Opponent	Venue	Season
40	Victoria	Brisbane	1902/03
49	Victoria	Melbourne	1936/37
52	Western Australia	Perth	1982/83
54	Victoria	Brisbane	1932/33
59	New South Wales	Brisbane	1903/04
65	Victoria	Melbourne	1957/58
65	Victoria	Melbourne	1969/70
73	New South Wales	Brisbane	1896/97
74	Victoria	Melbourne	1932/33

Leading Batsmen for Queensland

Batsman	Career	M	Inn	NO	Runs	HS	Avrge	100s
SC Trimble	1959/60–1975/76	133	246	14	9465	252*	40.79	24
PJP Burge	1952/53–1967/66	91	150	14	7627	283	56.08	24
KD Mackay	1946/47–1963/64	109	175	26	6875	223	46.14	16
GM Ritchie	1980/81–1989/90	95	152	12	6266	213*	44.76	15
GS Chappell	1973/74–1983/84	61	99	13	5905	194	68.66	21
RB Kerr	1981/82–1989/90	87	150	8	5538	201*	39.00	14
KC Wessels	1979/80–1985/86	62	107	3	5419	249	52.10	18
AR Border	1980/81–1989/90	59	98	17	4846	194	59.83	13
D Tallon	1933/34–1953/54	86	153	8	4355	193	30.03	6
TV Hohns	1972/73–1988/89	109	178	29	4189	103	28.11	1
PH Carlson	1969/70–1980/81	89	157	14	4144	110*	28.98	5
FC Thompson	1912/13–1933/34	54	99	9	3966	275*	44.06	10
JA Maclean	1968/69–1978/79	96	166	20	3652	156	25.01	2
GR Reynolds	1955/56–1963/64	53	87	9	3626	203*	46.48	12
GG Cook	1931/32–1947/48	67	123	9	3428	169*	30.05	3
RE Rogers	1935/36–1948/49	51	95	1	3382	181	35.97	8
ATW Grout	1946/47–1965/66	94	147	9	3351	119	24.28	3
DFE Bull	1956/57–1967/68	67	116	7	3292	167*	30.20	5
TR Veivers	1958/59–1967/68	55	92	12	3092	137	38.65	3
LPD O'Connor	1912/13–1929/30	43	82	5	3084	196	40.05	8
RK Oxenham	1911/12–1936/37	70	129	16	3082	162*	27.27	4
JJ McLaughlin	1949/50–1962/63	58	99	12	2931	146	33.68	4
AH Carrigan	1945/46–1951/52	50	87	6	2883	169	35.59	4
GS Trimble	1982/83–1989/90	57	95	8	2881	138*	37.42	4
MF Kent	1974/75–1981/82	49	85	10	2812	171	37.49	6
AB Henschell	1981/82–1988/89	64	104	16	2693	162	30.60	5
KA Archer	1946/47–1956/57	58	102	7	2665	118	28.05	2
EC Bensted	1923/24–1936/37	57	107	8	2663	155	26.89	3
BA Courtice	1982/83–1987/88	57	81	6	2639	144	35.18	4
RB Phillips	1979/80–1985/86	78	115	26	2618	111	29.41	1
AD Ogilvie	1974/75–1979/80	42	76	5	2579	194	36.32	8
CL McCool	1945/46–1952/53	47	82	9	2327	172	31.87	3
VN Raymer	1940/41–1956/57	71	116	23	2193	85	23.58	—
WD Rowe	1912/13–1930/31	47	87	8	2022	147	25.59	3

Highest Individual Innings for Queensland

Score	Batsman	Opponent	Venue	Season
283	PJP Burge	New South Wales	Brisbane	1963/64
275*	FC Thompson	New South Wales	Brisbane	1930/31
253	CW Andrews	New South Wales	Sydney	1934/35
252*	SC Trimble	New South Wales	Sydney	1963/64
249	KC Wessels	Victoria	St Kilda	1982/83
242*	PJP Burge	New South Wales	Sydney	1964/65
240	PJP Burge	South Australia	Adelaide	1960/61
223	KD Mackay	Victoria	Brisbane	1953/54
220	KC Wessels	Tasmania	Devonport	1981/82
220	SC Trimble	South Australia	Adelaide	1964/65
215	WA Brown	Victoria	Brisbane	1938/39
213*	GM Ritchie	South Australia	Adelaide	1989/90
212*	KP Ziebell	Victoria	Melbourne	1966/67
210	PJP Burge	Victoria	Brisbane	1956/57
207	WH Buckle	Western Australia	Brisbane	1964/65
205*	PJP Burge	Western Australia	Brisbane	1963/64
203	KD Mackay	New South Wales	Sydney	1955/56
203*	GR Reynolds	South Australia	Adelaide	1957/58
201*	RB Kerr	South Australia	Brisbane	1984/85

Most Runs in a Season for Queensland

Batsman	Season	M	Inn	NO	Runs	HS	50	100	Avrge
GS Chappell	1973/74	8	14	2	1178	180	4	5	98.16
KC Wessels	1981/82	11	18	—	1094	220	3	5	60.77
AD Ogilvie	1977/78	10	20	2	1084	194	2	6	60.22
SC Trimble	1963/64	9	14	2	1006	252*	2	5	83.83
WA Brown	1938/39	6	10	1	990	215	5	3	110.00
KC Wessels	1985/86	12	20	1	957	167	3	3	50.37
GS Chappell	1980/81	8	12	2	954	194	3	4	95.40
MF Kent	1980/81	11	20	4	941	171	5	2	58.81
KC Wessels	1982/83	8	15	—	939	249	2	4	62.60
GM Ritchie	1989/90	12	19	2	928	213*	4	3	54.49
SC Trimble	1964/65	9	16	1	924	220	2	3	61.60
GM Ritchie	1983/84	7	12	1	905	196	6	3	82.27

Leading Wicket-Takers for Queensland

Bowler	Career	M	Runs	Wkts	Avrge	5wi	10m	Best
JR Thomson	1974/75–1985/86	86	8668	349	24.83	17	3	7/27
G Dymock	1971/72–1981/82	87	8304	309	26.87	8	—	6/79
RK Oxenham	1911/12–1936/37	70	5236	231	22.66	10	2	6/45
CG Rackemann	1979/80–1989/90	63	5795	224	25.87	7	1	7/49
CJ McDermott	1983/84–1989/90	51	5538	209	26.49	13	1	8/44
PJ Allen	1959/60–1968/69	52	5085	199	25.55	11	3	10/61
LJ Johnson	1946/47–1952/53	48	4613	191	24.15	14	1	7/43
VN Raymer	1940/41–1956/57	71	6131	191	32.09	6	1	7/100
JN Maguire	1977/78–1988/89	68	6203	191	32.48	8	1	6/48
CL McCool	1945/46–1952/53	47	5984	189	31.66	15	1	7/74
JRF Duncan	1964/65–1970/71	58	5856	186	31.48	7	1	8/55
TV Hohns	1972/73–1988/89	109	7637	181	42.19	5	1	6/56
MF Francke	1971/72–1985/86	55	5167	167	30.94	7	1	6/62
D Tazelaar	1985/86–1989/90	44	4227	150	28.18	6	1	6/48
KD Mackay	1946/47–1963/64	109	4787	134	35.72	5	—	5/15
AR Dell	1970/71–1974/75	39	3498	131	26.70	6	1	6/17
GG Cook	1931/32–1947/48	67	4392	124	35.41	2	—	6/94
JD Bratchford	1952/53–1959/60	53	3537	120	29.47	3	—	6/57
B Fisher	1954/55–1967/68	50	3668	116	31.62	4	—	6/41
RG Paulsen	1966/67–1971/72	44	4407	116	37.99	4	—	7/73
RR Lindwall	1954/55–1959/60	34	2732	115	23.75	6	—	7/92
JRE Mackay	1959/60–1966/67	47	3660	115	31.82	3	—	5/56
OJ Morgan	1965/66–1969/70	37	3266	113	28.90	6	—	6/42
TR Veivers	1958/59–1967/68	55	3785	104	36.39	2	—	5/63
WT Walmsley	1954/55–1958/59	28	3073	102	30.12	3	—	6/56

Best Bowling in an Innings for Queensland

Wkts	Bowler	Opponent	Venue	Season
10/61	PJ Allan	Victoria	Melbourne	1965/66
8/35	R Wilson	Auckland	Auckland	1896/97
8/44	CJ McDermott	Tasmania	Brisbane	1989/90
8/51	CB Barstow	New South Wales	Brisbane	1910/11
8/51	MA Polzin	Victoria	Melbourne	1989/90
8/55	JRF Duncan	Victoria	Melbourne	1970/71
8/60	PM Hornibrook	New South Wales	Brisbane	1921/22
8/148	BJ Flynn	New South Wales	Brisbane	1953/54
7/27	JR Thomson	Western Australia	Brisbane	1984/85
7/31	PJ Allan	Victoria	Brisbane	1968/69
7/33	JR Thomson	New South Wales	Brisbane	1976/77
7/42	PH Carlson	Western Australia	Brisbane	1979/80
7/43	LJ Johnson	New South Wales	Brisbane	1949/50
7/43	LJ Johnson	Western Australia	Brisbane	1951/52
7/45	PJ Allan	New South Wales	Sydney	1968/69
7/49	CG Rackemann	South Australia	Brisbane	1982/83
7/51	JW McAndrew	New South Wales	Brisbane	1914/15
7/54	CJ McDermott	New South Wales	Newcastle	1987/88
7/58	CR Smith	Victoria	Melbourne	1951/52
7/58	JR Thomson	Victoria	Brisbane	1979/80
7/59	MA Polzin	South Australia	Brisbane	1986/87
7/60	LJ Johnson	South Australia	Adelaide	1946/47
7/62	RG Archer	Western Australia	Perth	1952/53
7/70	WT Evans	South Australia	Brisbane	1898/99
7/73	RG Paulsen	South Australia	Brisbane	1966/67
7/74	CL McCool	Australian Services	Brisbane	1945/46
7/76	WW Hall	Victoria	Brisbane	1961/62
7/83	SW Ayres	New South Wales	Brisbane	1919/20
7/86	JA Ellis	Victoria	Brisbane	1940/41
7/88	SW Ayres	New South Wales	Brisbane	1920/21
7/92	RR Lindwall	South Australia	Adelaide	1958/59
7/98	JA Downey	Victoria	Brisbane	1912/13
7/100	VN Raymer	South Australia	Adelaide	1953/54
7/106	CL McCool	South Australia	Adelaide	1945/46
7/114	LJ Johnson	South Australia	Adelaide	1947/48
7/127	BJ Flynn	South Australia	Brisbane	1952/53
7/128	CL McCool	Western Australia	Perth	1948/49
7/194	WM Kay	New South Wales	Sydney	1920/21

Best Bowling in a Match for Queensland

Wkts	Bowler	Opponent	Venue	Season
13/110	PJ Allan	New South Wales	Sydney	1968/69
13/125	JRF Duncan	Victoria	Melbourne	1970/71

Wkts	Bowler	Opponent	Venue	Season
12/56	PJ Allan	Victoria	Brisbane	1968/69
12/63	AR Dell	New Zealand	Brisbane	1973/74
12/112	JR Thomson	New South Wales	Brisbane	1976/77
12/114	CB Barstow	New South Wales	Brisbane	1910/11
11/72	RK Oxenham	New South Wales	Brisbane	1924/25
11/97	R Wilson	Auckland	Auckland	1896/97
11/97	PM Hornibrook	New South Wales	Brisbane	1921/22
11/103	M Polzin	South Australia	Brisbane	1986/87
11/107	CG Rackemann	South Australia	Brisbane	1982/83
11/116	TV Hohns	New South Wales	Sydney	1978/79
11/176	CL McCool	Australian Services	Brisbane	1945/46
11/184	FM Francke	South Australia	Adelaide	1972/73
11/218	BJ Flynn	South Australia	Brisbane	1952/53
11/240	BJ Flynn	New South Wales	Brisbane	1953/54
10/73	PH Carlson	New South Wales	Brisbane	1978/79
10/80	D Tazelaar	Victoria	St Kilda	1988/89
10/85	LJ Johnson	New South Wales	Brisbane	1949/50
10/92	CB Barstow	New Zealand	Brisbane	1913/14
10/104	RK Oxenham	South Australia	Brisbane	1933/34
10/110	CJ McDermott	New South Wales	Newcastle	1987/88
10/120	JR Thomson	Western Australia	Perth	1975/76
10/122	JN Maguire	Western Australia	Perth	1983/84
10/124	PJ Allan	Victoria	Melbourne	1965/66
10/136	WW McGlinchy	New Zealand	Wellington	1896/97
10/138	CS Griffiths	New South Wales	Brisbane	1923/24
10/142	JR Thomson	Victoria	Brisbane	1979/80
10/160	VN Raymer	Western Australia	Brisbane	1947/48
10/236	A Hurwood	New South Wales	Sydney	1929/30

Most Wickets in a Season for Queensland

Bowler	Season	M	Overs	Mdns	Runs	Wkts	Avrge	5wi	10m	Best
CJ McDermott	1986/87	11	377.4	51	1213	54	22.46	5	—	6/89
CJ McDermott	1989/90	10	432.0	100	1375	54	25.46	4	—	8/44
JR Thomson	1983/84	12	373.5	64	1361	48	28.35	1	—	5/85
PJ Allan	1968/69	9	245.3	48	753	46	16.36	5	2	7/31
C Tazelaar	1987/88	11	375.0	92	1036	46	22.52	3	—	6/52
JN Maguire	1984/85	12	461.1	104	1273	46	27.67	3	—	6/48
G Dymock	1974/75	9	275.6	42	972	45	21.60	1	—	5/48
G Dymock	1973/74	8	268.2	47	912	44	20.72	—	—	4/47
WW Hall	1961/62	8	203.5	30	871	43	20.25	4	—	7/76
G Dymock	1977/78	10	326.6	42	1073	42	25.54	1	—	6/79
CG Rackemann	1984/85	11	408.0	96	1095	42	26.07	1	—	6/54
JR Thomson	1985/86	12	372.3	49	1385	42	32.98	2	—	6/72

Most Dismissals by a Wicket-Keeper for Queensland

Wicket-Keeper	Career	M	Cght	Stmp	Total
JA Maclean	1968/69–1978/79	96	317	29	346
ATW Grout	1946/47–1965/66	94	229	64	293
D Tallon	1933/34–1953/54	86	180	85	265
RB Phillips	1979/80–1985/86	78	250	13	263
LD Cooper	1958/59–1967/68	34	84	18	102

Most Dismissals in a Season for Queensland

Wicket-Keeper	Season	M	Cght	Stmp	Total
RB Phillips	1984/85	12	55	1	56
RB Phillips	1983/84	12	45	3	48
JA Maclean	1977/78	10	44	1	45
JA Maclean	1968/69	9	36	6	42
RB Phillips	1985/86	12	41	1	42

Most Dismissals in a Match for Queensland

Ttl	Ct	St	Wicket-Keeper	Opponent	Venue	Season
12	9	3	D Tallon	New South Wales	Sydney	1938/39
9	4	5	D Tallon	Victoria	Brisbane	1938/39
9	9	—	JA Maclean	Victoria	Melbourne	1977/78
9	8	1	RB Phillips	New Zealand	Bundaberg	1982/83
8	4	4	D Tallon	New South Wales	Brisbane	1938/39
8	4	4	D Tallon	New South Wales	Brisbane	1945/46
8	6	2	D Tallon	Western Australia	Perth	1950/51
8	8	—	ATW Grout	New South Wales	Sydney	1955/56

Continued

299

Ttl	Ct	St	Wicket-Keeper	Opponent	Venue	Season
8	3	5	ATW Grout	South Australia	Brisbane	1956/57
8	8	—	ATW Grout	Western Australia	Brisbane	1959/60
8	8	—	JA Maclean	New South Wales	Sydney	1968/69
8	8	—	JA Maclean	Victoria	Brisbane	1968/69
8	8	—	JA Maclean	Victoria	Brisbane	1969/70
8	6	2	JA Maclean	New South Wales	Sydney	1975/76
8	8	—	RB Phillips	New South Wales	Sydney	1983/84
8	8	—	RB Phillips	Victoria	Brisbane	1984/85
8	8	—	RB Phillips	New South Wales	Sydney	1984/85
8	8	—	RB Phillips	South Australia	Brisbane	1985/86
8	8	—	IA Healy	Victoria	Melbourne	1987/88

Most Dismissals in an Innings for Queensland

Ttl	Ct	St	Wicket-Keeper	Opponent	Venue	Season
8	8	—	ATW Grout	Western Australia	Brisbane	1959/60
7	3	4	D Tallon	Victoria	Brisbane	1938/39
7	7	—	JA Maclean	Victoria	Melbourne	1977/78
7	6	1	RB Phillips	New Zealand	Brisbane	1982/83
6	1	5	D Tallon	MCC	Brisbane	1935/36
6	3	3	D Tallon	New South Wales	Brisbane	1938/39
6	4	2	D Tallon	New South Wales	Sydney	1938/39
6	5	1	D Tallon	New South Wales	Sydney	1938/39
6	6	—	ATW Grout	New South Wales	Sydney	1955/56
6	6	—	JA Maclean	Victoria	Melbourne	1972/73
6	5	1	RB Phillips	New South Wales	Sydney	1985/86
5	5	—	LPD O'Connor	Victoria	Melbourne	1928/29
5	4	1	D Tallon	Victoria	Brisbane	1935/36
5	4	1	D Tallon	South Australia	Adelaide	1945/46
5	5	—	D Tallon	New South Wales	Brisbane	1947/48
5	3	2	D Tallon	Western Australia	Perth	1950/51
5	2	3	ATW Grout	Western Australia	Brisbane	1953/54
5	1	4	ATW Grout	Western Australia	Brisbane	1956/57
5	2	3	ATW Grout	South Australia	Brisbane	1956/57
5	5	—	LD Cooper	South Australia	Brisbane	1962/63
5	5	—	ATW Grout	South Australia	Adelaide	1963/64
5	5	—	ATW Grout	South Australia	Adelaide	1964/65
5	5	—	LD Cooper	New South Wales	Brisbane	1967/68
5	4	1	JA Maclean	West Indians	Brisbane	1968/69
5	3	2	JA Maclean	New South Wales	Sydney	1968/69
5	5	—	JA Maclean	Victoria	Melbourne	1971/72
5	4	1	JA Maclean	South Australia	Adelaide	1972/73
5	3	2	JA Maclean	New South Wales	Sydney	1975/76
5	5	—	JA Maclean	England XI	Brisbane	1978/79
5	5	—	RB Phillips	South Australia	Brisbane	1979/80
5	5	—	RB Phillips	New Zealand	Brisbane	1980/81
5	5	—	RB Phillips	Tasmania	Brisbane	1980/81
5	5	—	RB Phillips	New South Wales	Sydney	1983/84
5	5	—	RB Phillips	Victoria	Brisbane	1984/85
5	5	—	RB Phillips	New South Wales	Sydney	1984/85
5	5	—	RB Phillips	Tasmania	Brisbane	1985/86
5	5	—	IA Healy	Victoria	Melbourne	1987/88
5	4	1	IA Healy	Pakistan	Brisbane	1989/90

Most Catches by a Fieldsman for Queensland

Fieldsman	Career	M	Catches
RB Kerr	1981/82–1989/90	87	82
SC Trimble	1959/60–1975/76	133	79
PJP Burge	1952/53–1967/68	91	77
AR Border	1980/81–1989/90	59	65
VN Raymer	1940/41–1956/57	71	61
GS Chappell	1973/74–1982/83	49	60
PH Carlson	1969/70–1980/81	89	57
CL McCool	1945/46–1952/53	47	54

Most Catches in a Season for Queensland

Catches	Fieldsman	M	Season
18	IT Botham	11	1987/88
17	GM Ritchie	12	1989/90
16	Majid Khan	9	1973/74
16	RB Kerr	12	1983/84

Catches	Fieldsman	M	Season
15	MF Kent	10	1980/81
15	GS Trimble	11	1987/88
14	CL McCool	8	1951/52
14	MF Kent	9	1974/75
13	RG Archer	7	1953/54
13	GS Chappell	6	1982/83
13	KC Wessels	12	1985/86
13	RB Kerr	12	1986/87
13	RB Kerr	11	1987/88
13	PE Cantrell	10	1988/89

Most Catches in a Match for Queensland

Ct	Fieldsman	Opponent	Venue	Season
6	JF Sheppard	New South Wales	Brisbane	1914/15
5	VN Raymer	West Indians	Brisbane	1951/52
5	RG Archer	South Australia	Adelaide	1954/55
5	KD Mackay	Western Australia	Brisbane	1962/63
5	JN Langley	England XI	Brisbane	1979/80
5	GS Chappell	South Australia	Brisbane	1982/83
5	GS Chappell	England XI	Brisbane	1982/83
5	KC Wessels	South Australia	Brisbane	1985/86
5	GS Trimble	Tasmania	Launceston	1986/87
5	PS Clifford	New South Wales	Brisbane	1986/87
5	IT Botham	Victoria	Brisbane	1987/88
5	RB Kerr	Tasmania	Launceston	1987/88

Most Catches in an Innings for Queensland

Ct	Fieldsman	Opponent	Venue	Season
6	JF Sheppard	New South Wales	Brisbane	1914/15
5	KC Wessels	South Australia	Brisbane	1985/86
4	RJ Hartigan	New South Wales	Sydney	1906/07
4	PM Hornibrook	South Australia	Brisbane	1929/30
4	VN Raymer	West Indians	Brisbane	1951/52
4	RG Archer	South Australia	Adelaide	1954/55
4	FR Crane	South Australia	Brisbane	1966/67
4	RB Kerr	South Australia	Adelaide	1985/86
4	GS Trimble	Tasmania	Launceston	1986/87
4	IT Botham	Victoria	Brisbane	1987/88
4	GM Ritchie	Western Australia	Perth	1989/90

Partnership Records for Queensland

Wkt	Ttl	Batsmen	Opponent	Venue	Season
1st	388	KC Wessels, RB Kerr	Victoria	St Kilda	1982/83
2nd	243	GR Reynolds, JJ McLaughlin	South Australia	Adelaide	1957/58
3rd	304	KC Wessels, GM Ritchie	Tasmania	Devonport	1981/82
4th	295	PJP Burge, TR Veivers	South Australia	Brisbane	1962/63
5th	231	KD Mackay, RG Archer	Victoria	Brisbane	1953/54
"	231	AR Border, GS Trimble	Victoria	Brisbane	1987/88
6th	238	R Macdonald, OW Cowley	Hawke's Bay	Napier	1896/97
7th	335	CW Andrews, EC Bensted	New South Wales	Sydney	1934/35
8th	146	TV Hohns, G Dymock	Victoria	Melbourne	1978/79
9th	152*	ATW Grout, WT Walmsley	New South Wales	Sydney	1956/57
10th	105*	WT Walmsley, JE Freeman	New South Wales	Brisbane	1957/58

Highest Partnerships for Queensland

Wkt	Ttl	Batsmen	Opponent	Venue	Season
1st	388	KC Wessels, RB Kerr	Victoria	St Kilda	1982/83
7th	335	CW Andrews, EC Bensted	New South Wales	Sydney	1934/35
1st	331	BA Courtice, RB Kerr	Tasmania	Brisbane	1984/85
3rd	304	KC Wessels, GM Ritchie	Tasmania	Devonport	1981/82
4th	295	PJP Burge, TR Veivers	South Australia	Brisbane	1962/63
3rd	295	KD Mackay, PJP Burge	South Australia	Adelaide	1960/61
1st	289	RB Kerr, BA Courtice	Victoria	Melbourne	1983/84
1st	265	WA Brown, GG Cook	New South Wales	Sydney	1938/39
4th	256*	PJP Burge, GM Bizzell	Western Australia	Brisbane	1963/64
1st	256	SC Trimble, GR Reynolds	South Australia	Adelaide	1963/64
2nd	243	GR Reynolds, JJ McLaughlin	South Australia	Adelaide	1957/58
6th	238	R Macdonald, OW Cowley	Hawke's Bay	Napier	1896/97
1st	232	KC Wessels, RB Kerr	New Zealand	Bundaberg	1982/83
5th	231	KD Mackay, RG Archer	Victoria	Brisbane	1953/54

Continued

Wkt	Ttl	Batsmen	Opponent	Venue	Season
5th	231	AR Border, GS Trimble	Victoria	Brisbane	1987/88
3rd	225	GI Foley, GM Ritchie	Pakistan	Brisbane	1989/90
2nd	224	GR Reynolds, JJ McLaughlin	Western Australia	Brisbane	1959/60
4th	223	FC Thompson, LE Oxenham	New South Wales	Sydney	1925/26
2nd	217	MJ Walters, AD Ogilvie	New South Wales	Brisbane	1977/78
4th	215	GS Chappell, MF Kent	Victoria	Brisbane	1975/76
2nd	214	GR Reynolds, KD Mackay	South Australia	Brisbane	1958/59
6th	211	TR Veivers, JD Bratchford	South Australia	Brisbane	1959/60
5th	210	GG Cook, GW Baker	New South Wales	Brisbane	1938/39
5th	210	MF Kent, PH Carlson	Pakistan	Brisbane	1976/77
3rd	210	KC Wessels, AR Border	South Australia	Adelaide	1985/86
4th	209	GJ Cosier, PH Carlton	New South Wales	Brisbane	1978/79
3rd	206	RB Kerr, AR Border	New South Wales	Newcastle	1987/88
2nd	205	GR Reynolds, SC Trimble	South Australia	Adelaide	1959/60
4th	201	GS Chappell, AR Border	New South Wales	Brisbane	1980/81
2nd	200	MF Kent, GS Chappell	South Australia	Adelaide	1980/81

BRISBANE CRICKET

FIRST-GRADE

The first-grade competition, which for two-thirds of the season looked as if it might be won by any number of clubs, eventually came to be dominated by Eastern Suburbs. A review of the first-grade points table, round by round, shows how this dominance was achieved. Wynnum-Manly led the competition after rounds one and two, Valley after rounds three and four, Northern Suburbs after five, Wynnum-Manly again after rounds six and seven, and Easts for the final five rounds. Easts then defeated Sandgate-Redcliffe in a semi-final and Toombul in the final. So in all respects the season ended satisfactorily for Easts. The club was not once beaten outright and was beaten on the first innings only three times, although on one of these occasions it went on to win outright. Easts had Greg Ritchie as captain and players such as Steve Storey, Peter Anderson, who was also Easts' coach, the all-rounder Craig Jesberg (whose bowling and batting proved decisive in the final against Toombul), and the Australian Under-19 batsman Ian Stenhouse. This was the first season Anderson coached Easts, and it could hardly have been more successful for him. As well as the first-grade premiership, Easts won the Club Championship and had four teams competing in the finals, two of which won premierships.

Toombul was a young side which performed consistently throughout the season. Peter Clifford scored many runs for the club before he became a regular in the Sheffield Shield side, and the pace bowler Bob McGhee led the attack. Toombul's batting line-up also included Peter Skuse, the captain of the Queensland Under-19 team, who scored his maiden first-grade century, 101, in the semi-final against Northern Suburbs. Northern Suburbs had more prominent players than any club and, accordingly suffered more from the loss of players to the State side. The team list included players such as Rob Kerr, Craig McDermott, Ian Healy, Mick Polzin, Steve Monty and Brad Inwood.

Sandgate-Redcliffe was one of the youngest sides in the competition. In fact, at 27 Eric Massey was its oldest player. Sandgate-

Redcliffe's hopes in the finals received a serious setback when its leading wicket-taker, the fast bowler Brendan Buckley, injured his back playing for a Queensland 2nd XI against a Queensland Country XI and as a result could not play in round 12 of the competition or in the finals. Buckley, it may be noted, headed the first-grade bowling averages. Trevor Barsby was Sandgate-Redcliffe's outstanding batsman. Although he missed a couple of rounds because of Sheffield Shield commitments, he still managed to break his own club record with an aggregate of 697 runs, scored at an average of 69.70. In his first season with Sandgate-Redcliffe, Peter Goggin established himself as one of the club's leading batsman, scoring 630 runs at 57.27.

Wynnum-Manly was a team with a strong batting line-up which included players such as Peter Cantrell, Mark Gaskell, Wayne Broad and Mark Tooley, although it had not such a strong bowling attack. As we have seen, Wynnum-Manly led the competition for much of the first half of the season, but it tailed off in the second half and just missed out on making the semi-finals. In fact, in its last six games it had only one first-innings victory.

Points Table

Club	Total
Eastern Suburbs	131.41
Toombul	119.30
Northern Suburbs	117.76
Sandgate-Redcliffe	115.17
Wynnum-Manly	114.27
South Brisbane	104.66
Western Suburbs	103.73
Valley	103.47
University	97.30
Colts	63.05

Semi-Finals—Eastern Suburbs 275 (I Stenhouse 91, P Anderson 60*, K Waddell 49; B Greevey 4/68, T Ryan 3/49) defeated Sandgate-Redcliffe 170 (C Jesberg 4/83, S Storey 3/47).

Toombul 7 for 221 (P Skuse 101, B Sheehan 66; P Charles 5/72) defeated Northern Suburbs 220 (G O'Hara 52*; B Hohns 5/47, S Williams 3/66).

FINAL
Eastern Suburbs v Toombul   Brisbane Cricket Ground, Brisbane, March 24-25 and 31-April 1, 1990
Result: Eastern Suburbs won by an innings and 26 runs

Easts took a grip on this match on the first day when its bowlers dismissed Toombul for 112 on a pitch which gave help, although not excessively, to the faster bowlers. Two bowlers were mainly responsible for Toombul's misfortune—Brian Brix, who began the batting collapse by taking three early wickets, reducing Toombul to 3 for 28, and Craig Jesberg who disposed of the remaining batsmen almost single-handedly, finishing with 6 for 38. Toombul looked to its opening bowlers, Bob McGhee and Scott Williams, to restrict Easts to a total small enough to allow Toombul to get back into the match, and by the end of the second day they had done this successfully, for Easts was then 7 for 130. On the third day, however, the all-rounder Jesberg and the number nine batsman Brix, who had both been so successful with the ball, shared a 134 run eighth-wicket partnership which effectively ended Toombul's hopes. Easts went on to make 299, and at the end Jesberg was not out 115. Brix made 53. Toombul's main wicket-takers were Williams (6 for 90) and McGhee (4 for 84). By stumps on the last day, Toombul was 4 for 102 in its second innings and so faced a struggle on the last day to avoid an innings defeat. It was Jesberg again who proved their undoing. He took· another 4 wickets, making five for the innings and 11 for the match. Toombul was all out for 160. Easts won by an innings and 26 runs.

Toombul *First Innings*

Batsman	How Out	Ttl
B Sheehan	b Jesberg	20
B Elder	c and b Brix	7
P Skuse	c P Stenhouse b Brix	7
D Millard	c Waddell b Brix	0
B Hohns	c I Stenhouse b Jesberg	8
R Lawrence	c P Stenhouse b Jesberg	3
A Knight	b P Stenhouse	4
A O'Hara	c Anderson b Jesberg	27
S Williams	c Stenhouse b Jesberg	12
R McGhee	not out	12
M Francke	b Jesberg	7
Sundries		5
Total		112

F/W: 14 28 28 38 46 51 53 83 95 112

Bowler	O	M	R	Wkts
P Stenhouse	16	4	34	1
B Brix	16	5	37	3
C Jesberg	22.2	6	38	6

Eastern Suburbs *First Innings*

Batsman	How Out	Ttl
K Waddell	lbw b McGhee	29
F Shelley	c Sheehan b McGhee	17
G Ellis	c Sheehan b McGhee	22
M Freeman	c Knight b Williams	8
I Stenhouse	b Williams	5
P Anderson	lbw b McGhee	7
C Jesberg	not out	115
P Stenhouse	c O'Hara b Williams	1
B Brix	b Williams	53
G Ritchie	c Skuse b Williams	7
H Hayes	lbw b Williams	2
Sundries		33
Total		299

F/W: 49 58 77 87 98 98 129 263 287 299

Bowler	O	M	R	Wkts
R McGhee	41	21	84	4
S Williams	22	3	90	6
A Knight	17	2	43	0
B Hohns	6	0	31	0
M Franke	12	3	31	0
P Clifford	2	0	11	0

Toombul

Second Innings

Batsman	How Out	Ttl
B Sheehan	c Storey b Brix	12
B Elder	run out	14
P Skuse	c Ellis b Stenhouse	24
P Clifford	c Anderson b Jesberg	1
B Hohns	c Anderson b Brix	26
R Lawrence	not out	11
A Knight	c Anderson b Jesberg	22
A O'Haraa	c Brix b Jesberg	7
S Williams	run out	14
R McGhee	lbw b Jesberg	10
M Franke	c Ellis b Jesberg	5
Sundries		14
Total		160

F/W: 17 51 52 53 107 107 123 138 154 160

Bowler	O	M	R	Wkts
P Stenhouse	12	2	29	1
B Brix	13	2	72	2
C Jesberg	10	5	36	5
S Storey	5	4	6	0
W Hayes	6	3	10	0
M Freeman	3	2	3	0
G Ritchie	1	1	0	0

First Grade Batting Averages

Batsman	Inn	NO	HS	Runs	Avrge
P Clifford (Toombul)	11	2	136	717	79.66
T Barsby (Sandgate-Redcliffe)	12	2	170	697	69.70
M Freeman (Eastern Suburbs)	15	5	107*	626	62.60
M Tooley (Wynnum-Manly)	13	3	117*	612	61.20
C Smart (Western Suburbs)	12	4	139*	475	59.37
P Goggin (Sandgate-Redcliffe)	15	4	144	630	57.27
B Henschell (Valley)	13	5	181	555	55.50
B Inwood (Northern Suburbs)	11	2	123	483	53.66
S Law (Valley)	9	2	87	362	51.71

First Grade Bowling Averages

Bowler	Overs	Mdns	Runs	Wkts	Avrge
B Buckley (Sandgate-Redcliffe)	200	46	677	35	19.34
D Cottee (Valley)	165	34	476	23	20.69
P Charles (Northern Suburbs)	167	44	469	22	21.31
W Hayes (Eastern Suburbs)	181.3	62	433	20	21.65
S Carty (University)	247	77	588	26	22.61
M Mainhardt (Northern Suburbs)	245	54	712	31	22.96
B Stephensen (Western Suburbs)	236.5	59	671	29	23.13
P Carew (Valley)	273	71	748	32	23.37
R McGhee (Toombul)	268.5	62	775	32	24.21
C Jesberg (Eastern Suburbs)	233.5	56	746	30	24.86

SECOND GRADE

Premiers: Toombul

Points table: Toombul 146.90, University 140.73, Valley No 2 139.14, South Brisbane 133.22, Northern Suburbs 132.07, Wynnum-Manly 118.50, Valley No 1 107.44, Eastern Suburbs 100.76, Western Suburbs 94.89, Sandgate-Redcliffe 84.03.

Final: Toombul 384 (I Venamore 102, S Wheeler 86; C White 3/78, G Atthow 3/70) defeated University 364 (A Walduck 59, W Ledger 58, A Brandon 54, D Mullins 50, R Trewatha 47; C Holding 6/135, S Becky 4/122) on the first innings.

THIRD GRADE
Premiers: South Brisbane
Points table: South Brisbane 148.53, Eastern Suburbs 133.46, Toombul 129.88, Western Suburbs No 1 123.07, University 121.85, Valley 114.29, Wynnum-Manly 102.04, Western Suburbs No 2 90.74, Sandgate-Redcliffe 66.21, Northern Suburbs 54.39.
Final: South Brisbane 9 for 278 (B Lunt 94; A Skuse 4/92, E Gourley 3/77) defeated Toombul 233 (A Jenkinson 128, S Stower 43; B Lunt 4/60, J O'Keefe 3/71) on the first innings.

FOURTH GRADE
Premiers: South Brisbane
Points table: Eastern Suburbs 191.41, South Brisbane No 2 165.47, Valley 143.22, Wynnum-Manly 135.40, Sandgate-Redcliffe 131.34, Toombul 97.74, South Brisbane No 1 96.90, University 95.31, Northern Suburbs 83.85, Western Suburbs 73.72.
Final: South Brisbane 241 (J Short 82, B Hoy 53; G White 4/62) defeated Eastern Suburbs 117 (G Farrally 7/38) and 85 (G Farrally 5/30, M Chessells 5/49) by an innings and 39 runs.

FIFTH GRADE
Premiers: Eastern Suburbs
Points table: Sandgate-Redcliffe 159.40, University No 2 150.25, University No 1 147.75, Eastern Suburbs 130.48, South Brisbane 122.46, Valley 117.45, Northern Suburbs 104.73, Wynnum-Manly 86.35, Western Suburbs 77.98, Toombul 52.36.
Final: Eastern Suburbs 234 (J Jesberg 71; J Hall 5/63) and 2 for 246 (D Keane 86, A Dosen 45°) defeated University 112 (D Donovan 43; P Knight 4/36, M Wissman 3/8) on the first innings.

UNDER-18
Premiers: Sandgate-Redcliffe
Points table: Sandgate-Redcliffe 141.91, Eastern Suburbs 116.41, Valley 109.98, Western Suburbs 104.55, Wynnum-Manly 87.11, South Brisbane 85.61, Toombul 76.96, Northern Suburbs 52.66.
Final: Sandgate-Redcliffe 218 (A Mills 43, M Goggin 41; B Nowak 4/65, P Hine 3/47) defeated Eastern Suburbs 96 (B Hintz 3/22, D McCreadie 2/18, D Huddle 2/20) on the first innings.

CLUB CHAMPIONSHIP

Points Table

Eastern Suburbs	935.34
University	850.49
South Brisbane	830.32
Valley	815.17
Sandgate-Redcliffe	813.23
Wynnum-Manly	757.94
Toombul	742.44
Western Suburbs	665.60
Northern Suburbs	663.22

COUNTRY CRICKET

Colts Match—North Queensland v South Queensland
Harrup Park, Mackay, October 14-15, 1989.

Batting first, South Queensland scored freely on a placid wicket, making 8 for 283 by the end of the allotted 60 overs. The two openers, David Bidgood and Jason Tickner, both of Toowoomba, gave their side an excellent start with a partnership of 67. Tickner was out first, for 33, and Bidgood went on to make 46. South Queensland's highest scorer was Troy Dixon of Caloundra, who batted in fine style and eventually retired at 77. He hit 9 fours and 2 sixes. There was a final acceleration of the scoring rate by the wicketkeeper, Steven Nitz, who hit the ball powerfully and made a quick 45. North Queensland lost early wickets, and when Steven Butcher of Townsville came to the crease the score was 3 for 32. With Andrew Harris (51), also from Townsville, Butcher saw North Queensland out of its immediate crisis and then pressed on, finishing with 106 not out at the end of the 60 overs. North Queensland's total was 8 for 227—56 behind. On the second day each side was allotted a 50-over innings, and the South Queensland batsmen were once more on top of the bowling, scoring 6 for 231 from the 50 overs. Bidgood (38) and Tickner (22) again began the innings soundly, but the batsman of the day was Brad Spanner of Toowoomba, whose entertaining innings came to an unfortunate end when he was run out for 99. Spanner hit 10 fours and 2 sixes, but his aggression was best demonstrated by the fact that he scored 99 of the 132 runs added to the total while he was at the crease. North Queensland was pinned down in its second innings, scoring only 6 for 159 off its 50 overs. A Farquahson was the most successful of the bowlers with 3 wickets for 40, although he conceded these runs in only 8 overs.

Metropolitan Colts v Country Colts   Toombul Oval, Brisbane,
October 23-24-25, 1989

Country's bowlers had Metropolitan in serious trouble at 6 for 137, but a high-risk innings of 98 by the No. 8 batsman Mark Thompson turned the match around and enabled Metropolitan to compile 357, a substantial total. Thompson's adventurous approach is evident from the fact that his last scoring shot, played while he was in the 90s, was a six. Country's most impressive bowler was Bevan Bauer from Bundaberg, who took 5 for 75 in 23.3 overs. Country's innings was shortened by rain and ended with the score at 7 for 282. Andrew Harris of Townsville played a controlled innings of 83, and Troy Dixon of Caloundra made 60. As the wet weather closed in Brad Spanner hit 41 and the wicketkeeper Brad Ruddell of Mackay remained 32 not out. There were six country players in the Queensland Colts side chosen after this match—Andrew Harris, Troy Dixon, Brad Spanner, Brad Ruddell, Bevan Bauer and Darren Lehmann (twelfth man).

COUNTRY CUP

The results of this tournament, sponsored again by Forex, were:
Townsville defeated Cairns by 87 runs on October 4, 1989
Mackay defeated Rockhampton by 42 runs on October 11, 1989
Gladstone drew with Biloela in a washed-out match on November 9, 1989
Maryborough defeated Bundaberg by 29 runs on December 13, 1989
Ipswich defeated Gold Coast by 52 runs on January 17, 1990
Sunshine Coast defeated Gympie by 39 runs on February 7, 1990
Eastern Downs defeated Western Downs by 107 runs on February 27, 1990

A combined side was chosen afterwards from teams competing in the Country Cup to represent the Queensland Country Cricket Association in two one-day matches against a Queensland 2nd XI under lights at Bundaberg on March 6 and 7, 1990. The results of these two matches were:

QCCA v Queensland 2nd XI   Salter Oval, Bundaberg, March 6, 1990
50-over match

Batting first, QCCA found scoring difficult against an accurate attack and compiled a total of 7 for 175 in its 50 overs. Terry Oliver, who was run out for 61, top-scored for the country team, followed by the opener Kerry Munster, who made 39. The Queensland 2nd XI began shakily in reply, losing 3 wickets for 31, but Trent Ryan (29) and Peter Goggin (49) steadied the innings, and following batsmen closed rapidly on the country team's total, which it passed in just 41.3 overs. Brett Henschell remained not out 37.

QCCA v Queensland 2nd XI   Salter Oval, Bundaberg, March 7, 1990
50-over match

The QCCA's bowlers all received rough treatment from the Queensland 2nd XI batsmen in an innings which produced 8 for 274 in 50 overs. Rob Kerr (69) and Steve Monty (98) put on 151 for the first wicket, and the second wicket did not fall until the total was 205. Monty, who lost his wicket by a run out, scored his 98 runs off only 108 balls. Russell Dennis, who took 3 wickets, was the most successful bowler as well as the most economical, although even he had 46 runs scored off his 10 overs. The country team made a poor start in reply, slipping to 4 for 37, and it was not allowed to recover. Grant Stallard (51), Brett Ramsbottom (47) and Terry Oliver (36) all performed well against the Queensland 2nd XI attack, but it was not enough, and the QCCA team was all out in the 46th over for 160. Craig Jesberg, with 3 wickets for 28 in 10 overs, was the most effective bowler.

South Queensland v North Queensland   Rockhampton Cricket Ground, Rockhampton, November 18, 1989
50-over match

North Queensland 4 for 203 (E Harris 73, T Oliver 37, S Scuderi 22; P Hutchinson 2/57) defeated South Queensland 9/201 (A Walsh 58, R Peterson 28 not out, B Murphy 27, W Short 24; J Wilson 4/33) by 7 wickets. This match decided the Forex Cup.

South Queensland v North Queensland   Rockhampton Cricket Ground, Rockhampton, November 19, 1989
50-over match

South Queensland 9 for 199 (R Staff retired 55, M Verrenkamp 51, A Walsh 22, W Short 20; A Watson 3/13, B Oches 2/35, J Wilson 2/40) played North Queensland 126 (T Oliver retired 34, S Scuderi retired 28, W Green retired 24). This match served as a selection trial for the national country championships in Bendigo.

COUNTRY WEEK

Twenty senior teams and six colts teams competed in the tournament, which was held at various grounds in Brisbane from December 27 to 30, 1989. The senior competition was won by Beaudesert, which consequently won $1,000 in prize money.

Queensland Country v Sri Lanka   Caloundra Oval, Caloundra, January 30, 1990
45-over match

The combined country team chosen for this match was, in batting order: E Harris, T Oliver, S Scuderi, A Walsh, L Schulte, B Spanner, C White, B Murphy, B Bauer, P Hutchin, G Hogan. Sri Lanka won with more than 10 overs to spare. For details of the match see the section covering the Sri Lankan tour.

SOUTH AUSTRALIA

SOUTH AUSTRALIA CAME CLOSER TO ULTIMATE success in the Sheffield Shield competition in 1989-90 than was generally appreciated. If it had gained an outright win in its last match of the season, against Queensland, it would have contested the Shield final in Adelaide, where it was invariably successful. The team's chief failing in 1989-90 was that it was rarely able to repeat this success at other grounds. In fact, South Australia earned Shield points from only one of its five away matches—and that was against Tasmania at Devonport, where, significantly, the opposition had little home-ground advantage. As it happened, South Australia's last, crucial match against Queensland was played at Brisbane, and South Australia lost it on the first innings, thus finishing third on the Shield table with 20 points. It acquired those points from three outright wins and one first innings lead.

It could be said generally of South Australia in 1989-90 that it was a team strong in batting but relatively weak in bowling, and at the heart of its bowling problems was Tim May's absence through injury. May played only four Shield matches for South Australia and was never fully fit. Even when he took the field in the FAI Insurance Cup semi-final at the end of the season he appeared to have trouble bowling his 10 overs. May's absence from the bowling crease for so much of the season not only meant South Australia was without its most highly accomplished bowler, but it appeared to affect the performance of the team's other spin bowler, Peter Sleep. Sleep and May had always bowled well as a pair, and without May to comple-ment him Sleep was not as effective as he had been in previous seasons. In 10 matches for South Australia he took only 15 wickets, a disappointing record for a bowler who at the start of the season was rated the leading leg-spinner in the country.

With its spin attack thus depleted, South Australia had to rely heavily on its pace bowlers, Colin Miller and Joe Scuderi, who between them took 71 of the 135 wickets which fell to South Australian bowlers during the season. Miller, a former Victorian, was consistently impressive and easily led the wicket aggregates with 44, including a best performance of 6 for 83. Playing his first full season for South Australia, Miller bowled at only moderate speed, but he had fine control and swung the ball with skill. Scuderi took 27 wickets, which, in view of the fact he was not always fully fit, was a creditable performance. Phil Alley, the young fast bowler from the Cricket Academy, did not quite find his feet at the state level, taking 9 wickets in the four matches he played, but he left nobody in doubt that he is a bowler of potential.

South Australia's batting line-up was one of the strongest in the competition. It had consistent performers at the top of the order in Andrew Hilditch and Paul Nobes, who were followed by two highly talented stroke-players in David Hookes and Darren Lehmann. Lehmann was one of the outstanding players in the competition, scoring 1,142 runs at an average of 57.10. It was not so much the quantity of runs he made which set Lehmann apart, however, but rather the controlled aggression of his batting. Throughout the season, Lehmann scored runs at a quite startling speed, which he appeared able to maintain irrespective of the circumstances of the match. He is likely to leave a big gap in South Australia's batting in the 1990-91 season following his move to Victoria in the off-season.

David Hookes batted with his usual flair and led the side with flair, too. Not all his gambles as captain paid off, but he was always intent on winning matches, and his positive attitude to the game no doubt had the effect of steeling his players. Indeed, Hookes's spirited captaincy raised the interest level of the Shield competition as a whole. With the bat he was extremely successful, particularly on his favourite ground, Adelaide Oval. He hit three centuries and scored 823 runs at an average of 48.41. It is a remarkable fact that, despite his infrequent appearances for Australia in recent years, Hookes's stature in the game is almost unmatched.

Hilditch did all that was expected of him as an opener, scoring 737 runs at an average of 38.79. Batting at number three, Paul Nobes was equally consistent, scoring 814 runs at 38.76. In the second half of the season Michael Bevan was brought into the side as an opener, and although he impressed everyone with the quality of his batting he had only limited success. Altogether, he made 338 runs at an average of 33.80. The truth is Bevan did not really seem suited to the task of opening the innings, and he might well have proved more successful batting down the order. The best of him, it was clear, is yet to be seen.

SOUTH AUSTRALIAN FIRST-CLASS RECORDS

Season 1989/90

Date	Venue	Opponent	Result for South Australia
Oct 21*	Adelaide	Queensland	Won by 5 wkts
Oct 22*	Adelaide	Victoria	Lost by 28 runs
Nov 3	Brisbane	Queensland	Lost by 6 wkts
Nov 10	Adelaide	New South Wales	Drawn
Nov 17	Adelaide	New Zealand	Drawn
Dec 1	Adelaide	Sri Lanka	Drawn
Dec 8	Melbourne	Victoria	Lost by 4 wkts
Dec 15	Perth	Western Australia	Drawn
Jan 6	Adelaide	Victoria	Drawn
Jan 19	Devonport	Tasmania	Won by 5 wkts
Jan 26	Adelaide	Western Australia	Won by an inns & 44 runs
Feb 15	Sydney	New South Wales	Won by 10 wkts
Mar 2	Adelaide	Tasmania	Won by 127 runs
Mar 9	Adelaide	Queensland	Drawn
Mar 18*	Adelaide	New South Wales	Won by 53 runs
Mar 31*	Perth	Western Australia	Lost by 7 wkts

* Denotes not first-class)

1989/90 South Australian First-Class Averages

Batsman	M	Inn	NO	Runs	HS	50	100	Avrge	Ct/St
DS Lehmann	12	20	—	1142	228	3	5	57.10	3
GA Bishop	7	12	1	561	173	1	2	51.00	5
DW Hookes	11	18	1	823	159	3	3	48.41	4
AMJ Hilditch	12	21	2	737	103°	3	3	38.79	3
PC Nobes	12	21	—	814	124	5	1	38.76	6
MG Bevan	6	12	2	338	114	2	1	33.80	1
NR Plummer	1	2	1	29	29°	—	—	29.00	1
JC Scuderi	11	18	3	434	75°	2	—	28.93	2
PR Sleep	10	16	4	306	75°	2	—	25.50	4
TBA May	4	5	2	69	35°	—	—	23.00	—
BD Williams	2	3	—	54	28	—	—	18.00	1
DS Berry	12	16	2	171	38	—	—	12.21	32/3
CR Miller	11	14	4	98	34	—	—	9.80	2
DA Clarke	1	1	—	9	9	—	—	9.00	—
SP George	5	6	2	35	16°	—	—	8.75	2
CJ Owen	4	5	2	21	16	—	—	7.00	1
PW Gladigau	5	6	1	26	18°	—	—	5.20	—
PJS Alley	4	6	2	9	5°	—	—	2.25	2
AK Zesers	1	1	1	25	25°	—	—	—	—
CL Francis	1	—	—	—	—	—	—	—	—

Bowlers	M	Overs	Mdns	Runs	Wkts	Avrge	5wi	10m	NB	W	Best
AMJ Hilditch	12	29.0	7	70	3	23.33	—	—	—	—	1/5
CJ Owen	4	100.0	25	296	12	24.67	—	—	—	2	3/80
CR Miller	11	402.1	107	1117	44	25.39	1	—	1	3	6/83
JC Scuderi	11	263.5	100	915	27	33.89	1	—	26	1	6/6
PJS Alley	4	108.5	29	330	9	36.67	—	—	1	1	4/98
SP George	5	142.0	29	487	11	44.27	—	—	18	3	2/53
TBA May	4	204.0	48	597	11	54.27	—	—	22	—	3/89
PR Sleep	10	307.1	63	886	15	59.07	—	—	1	3	3/107
DA Hookes	11	78.1	19	201	3	67.00	—	—	—	—	2/89
PW Gladigau	5	192.0	45	557	5	111.40	—	—	10	—	2/109
MG Bevan	6	2.0	—	10	—	—	—	—	—	—	—
DW Clarke	1	33.0	14	70	—	—	—	—	—	—	—
CL Francis	1	22.0	1	74	—	—	—	—	—	—	—
PC Nobes	12	2.0	1	2	—	—	—	—	—	—	—
NR Plummer	1	12.1	3	60	—	—	—	—	—	—	—
BD Williams	2	4.0	1	15	—	—	—	—	—	—	—
AK Zesers	1	20.0	7	54	—	—	—	—	—	—	—

South Australian First-Class Records

Opponent	Venue	First Game	Games	W	L	D	T
Australian Rep. Teams							
Australian XI's	Adelaide	Nov 23 1888	1	1	—	—	—
Australian Services	Adelaide	Dec 29 1945	1	—	—	1	—
Total			2	1	—	1	—
England Teams	Adelaide	Oct 28 1887	49	5	22	22	—
	Unley	Mar 27 1903	1	1	—	—	—
Total			50	6	22	22	—
India	Adelaide	Oct 24 1947	5	2	2	1	—
New South Wales	Sydney	Feb 14 1890	90	16	59	15	—
	Adelaide	Dec 19 1890	88	31	43	14	—
	Newcastle	Dec 16 1983	1	—	1	—	—
Total			179	47	103	29	—
New Zealand	Adelaide	Jan 16 1914	11	5	1	5	—
Queensland	Brisbane	Jan 14 1899	54	13	21	20	—
	Adelaide	Dec 26 1923	60	29	11	19	1
	Brisbane Ex	Jan 23 1926	5	3	2	—	—
Total			119	45	34	39	1
Pakistan	Adelaide	Dec 18 1983	4	—	1	3	—
South Africa	Adelaide	Nov 5 1910	7	1	4	2	—

Opponent	Venue	First Game	Games	W	L	D	T
Sri Lanka	Adelaide ———— Dec 1 1989		1	—	—	1	—
Tasmania	Adelaide ———— Nov 10 1877		15	8	1	6	—
	Hobart TCA ———— Jan 3 1957		3	2	—	1	—
	Devonport ———— Nov 3 1979		4	2	—	2	—
	Launceston ———— Feb 12 1982		4	2	—	2	—
	Hobart Bel ———— Nov 18 1988		1	—	—	1	—
Total			27	14	1	12	—
Victoria	East Melbourne ——— Nov 12 1880		2	—	2	—	—
	Adelaide ———— Apr 1 1881		93	33	42	18	—
	Melbourne ———— Feb 3 1906		89	14	52	23	—
	St Kilda ———— Jan 21 1946		4	1	1	2	—
	Geelong ———— Mar 7 1981		2	—	—	2	—
Total			190	48	97	45	—
Western Australia	Adelaide ———— Mar 17 1893		47	19	13	15	—
	Perth ———— Apr 3 1899		47	13	20	14	—
	Fremantle ———— Feb 3 1906		3	—	—	3	—
Total			97	32	33	32	—
West Indies	Adelaide ———— Dec 5 1930		12	4	3	5	—
World XI	Adelaide ———— Dec 17 1971		1	1	—	—	—
Total for South Australia			705	206	301	197	1

Most Appearances for South Australia

Games	Player	Career	Games	Player	Career
143	LE Favell	1951/52–1969/70	72	MG Waite	1930/31–1945/46
124	HN Dansie	1949/50–1966/67	72	GA Bishop	1982/83–1989/90
122	PR Sleep	1976/77–1989/90	69	RA Hamence	1935/36–1950/51
115	DW Hookes	1975/76–1989/90	64	G Giffen	1877/78–1903/04
109	IM Chappell	1961/62–1979/80	63	WB Phillips	1977/78–1988/89
105	CV Grimmett	1924/25–1940/41	61	CJ Pinch	1950/51–1959/60
104	VY Richardson	1918/19–1937/38	60	JC Lill	1955/56–1965/66
98	PL Ridings	1937/38–1956/57	60	NJN Hawke	1960/61–1967/68
94	BN Jarman	1955/56–1968/69	57	GS Chappell	1966/67–1972/73
91	AA Mallett	1967/68–1980/81	57	GR Attenborough	1972/73–1980/81
89	KG Cunningham	1960/61–1973/74	55	GRA Langley	1945/46–1956/57
87	C Hill	1892/93–1922/23	55	JW Wilson	1950/51–1957/58
81	AMJ Hilditch	1982/83–1989/90	54	Alfred James	1889/90–1905/06
80	AJ Woodcock	1967/68–1978/79	53	TW Wall	1924/25–1935/36
78	CW Walker	1928/29–1940/41	53	RJ Inverarity	1979/80–1984/85
77	TJ Jenner	1967/68–1976/77	51	GB Hole	1950/51–1957/58
76	JC Reedman	1887/88–1908/09	51	JE Nash	1970/71–1980/81
74	WM Darling	1975/76–1985/86	50	PK Lee	1925/26–1934/35

Youngest Players on First-Class Debut for South Australia

Player	Date of Birth	F/Class Debut	Opponent	Venue	Age on Years	Debut Days
C Hill	Mar 18 1877	Mar 27 1893	Western Australia	Adelaide	16	9
AH Jarvis	Oct 19 1860	Nov 10 1877	Tasmania	Adelaide	17	22
SP George	Oct 20 1970	Nov 20 1987	Queensland	Adelaide	17	31
AK Zesers	Mar 11 1967	Nov 22 1984	Tasmania	Adelaide	17	256
DS Lehmann	Feb 5 1970	Dec 11 1987	Victoria	Melbourne	17	309
RA Parker	Feb 23 1916	Feb 10 1934	Western Australia	Adelaide	17	353

Highest Innings Totals for South Australia

Total	Opponent	Venue	Season
7d-821	Queensland	Adelaide	1939/40
688	Tasmania	Adelaide	1935/36
673	Tasmania	Adelaide	1987/88
9d-649	MCC	Adelaide	1970/71
7d-644	Queensland	Adelaide	1934/35
3d-643	Tasmania	Adelaide	1986/87
8d-642	Queensland	Adelaide	1935/36

Continued

313

Total	Opponent	Venue	Season
8d-614	Western Australia	Adelaide	1929/30
612	Western Australia	Adelaide	1925/26
610	Victoria	Melbourne	1939/40
603	New South Wales	Adelaide	1946/47
8d-600	New South Wales	Adelaide	1938/39
590	Victoria	Adelaide	1909/10
7d-588	New South Wales	Adelaide	1967/68
582	Queensland	Brisbane	1898/99
582	Queensland	Adelaide	1928/29
582	Victoria	Adelaide	1928/29
579	Queensland	Adelaide	1926/27
576	New South Wales	Adelaide	1900/01
575	New South Wales	Adelaide	1935/36
9d-575	Western Australia	Perth	1970/71
573	South Africans	Adelaide	1963/64
569	New South Wales	Adelaide	1912/13
569	Victoria	Melbourne	1935/36
6d-565	Victoria	Adelaide	1935/36
562	Victoria	Adelaide	1891/92
557	Queensland	Brisbane	1938/39
4d-552	Queensland	Adelaide	1981/82
9d-551	New South Wales	Adelaide	1981/82
543	Victoria	Adelaide	1919/20
536	Victoria	Adelaide	1947/48
534	New South Wales	Adelaide	1986/87
528	New South Wales	Adelaide	1965/66
524	MCC	Adelaide	1928/29
521	Victoria	Adelaide	1951/52
7d-520	Victoria	Melbourne	1983/94
519	New South Wales	Sydney	1907/08
519	New South Wales	Adelaide	1989/90
518	Victoria	Adelaide	1924/25
8d-518	Indians	Adelaide	1947/48
515	Victoria	Melbourne	1940/41
510	Victoria	Melbourne	1988/89
508	New South Wales	Adelaide	1929/30
508	Queensland	Brisbane	1960/61
7d-507	Western Australia	Adelaide	1981/82
506	New South Wales	Adelaide	1988/89
505	Queensland	Brisbane	1927/28
500	New South Wales	Adelaide	1926/27
500	Queensland	Adelaide	1969/70

Lowest Completed Innings Totals for South Australia

Total	Opponent	Venue	Season
23	Victoria	East Melbourne	1882/83
27	New South Wales	Sydney	1955/56
47	New South Wales	Sydney	1940/41
51	Victoria	Adelaide	1880/81
54	Victoria	Melbourne	1886/87
54	Western Australia	Perth	1905/06
56	Western Australia	Perth	1959/60
61	New South Wales	Adelaide	1906/07
66	Queensland	Brisbane	1965/66
68	Victoria	Melbourne	1931/32
69	New South Wales	Sydney	1979/80
72	Queensland	Brisbane	1930/31
73	Victoria	Melbourne	1892/93
75	Queensland	Brisbane	1953/54

Leading Batsmen for South Australia

Batsman	Career	M	Inn	NO	Runs	HS	Avrge	100s
LE Favell	1951/52–1969/70	143	258	5	9656	164	38.16	23
DW Hookes	1975/76–1989/90	115	198	10	9254	306*	49.22	26
IM Chappell	1961/62–1979/80	109	188	18	8873	205*	52.19	26
C Hill	1892/93–1922/23	87	160	9	8027	365*	53.15	24
VY Richardson	1918/19–1937/38	104	188	7	7898	231	42.53	21
HN Dansie	1949/50–1966/67	124	228	9	7543	185	34.44	18
PR Sleep	1976/77–1989/90	122	204	35	6039	146*	35.73	13
DG Bradman	1935/36–1948/49	44	63	8	5753	369	104.60	25
PL Ridings	1937/38–1956/57	98	168	17	5622	186*	37.23	9
AMJ Hilditch	1982/83–1989/90	81	146	9	5580	230	40.73	13

Batsman	Career	M	Inn	NO	Runs	HS	Avrge	100s
KG Cunningham	1960/61–1973/74	89	153	14	5144	203	37.00	9
GA Bishop	1982/83–1989/90	72	131	6	4818	224*	38.54	10
G Giffen	1877/78–1903/04	64	114	7	4667	271	43.61	11
AJ Woodcock	1967/68–1978/79	80	143	4	4403	141	31.67	5
WM Darling	1975/76–1985/86	74	185	21	4246	134	25.89	7
RA Hamence	1935/36–1950/51	69	116	7	4244	173	38.93	11
WB Phillips	1977/78–1988/89	63	113	8	4173	260	39.74	10
GS Chappell	1966/67–1972/73	57	100	10	4133	156*	45.92	11
CJ Pinch	1950/51–1959/60	61	110	7	4090	146*	39.70	12
JC Lill	1955/56–1965/66	60	112	4	4087	176	37.84	8
AJ Richardson	1918/19–1926/27	45	85	4	3745	280	46.23	11
BN Jarman	1955/56–1968/69	94	158	16	3447	196	24.27	3
GB Hole	1950/51–1957/58	51	94	10	3401	226	40.48	9
DRA Gehrs	1902/03–1920/21	49	92	6	3387	170	39.38	13
CL Badcock	1934/35–1940/41	40	65	7	3282	325	56.58	12
HC Nitschke	1929/30–1934/35	41	77	3	3159	172	42.68	9
JC Reedman	1887/88–1908/09	76	141	8	3068	113	23.06	1
MG Waite	1930/31–1945/46	72	114	10	3011	137	28.95	1
AR Lonergan	1929/30–1934/35	39	72	3	3002	159	43.50	9
JJ Lyons	1884/85–1899/00	47	88	2	2980	145	34.65	8
DE Pritchard	1918/19–1931/32	49	89	2	2963	167	34.05	6
CV Grimmett	1924/25–1940/41	105	163	27	2723	71*	20.02	—
GB Stevens	1952/53–1958/59	38	71	6	2720	259*	41.84	7
G St A Sobers	1961/62–1963/64	26	45	2	2707	251	62.95	10
JE Nash	1970/71–1980/81	51	97	5	2624	134	28.52	3
J Darling	1893/94–1907/08	42	77	3	2571	210	34.74	3
RJ Inverarity	1979/80–1984/85	53	90	15	2514	126	33.52	3
GRA Langley	1945/46–1956/57	55	92	15	2369	160*	30.76	4
RE Mayne	1906/07–1914/15	37	70	1	2336	142	33.85	3
MD Haysman	1982/83–1987/88	35	63	6	2309	172	40.50	5
TJ Jenner	1967/68–1976/77	77	117	19	2169	86	22.13	—
FT Hack	1898/99–1908/99	38	73	2	2138	158*	30.11	3
IM McLachlan	1960/61–1963/64	31	55	3	2120	188*	40.76	8
N Claxton	1898/99–1909/10	39	73	3	2090	199*	29.43	1
NJN Hawke	1960/61–1967/68	60	95	26	2067	141*	29.95	1
GW Harris	1920/21–1930/31	34	64	3	2054	183	33.67	3
LD Duldig	1940/41–1952/53	36	68	5	2027	121*	32.17	1

Most Runs in a Season for South Australia

Batsman	Season	M	Inn	NO	Runs	HS	50	100	Avrge
BA Richards	1970/71	10	13	2	1538	356	3	6	139.81
DG Bradman	1939/40	8	13	3	1448	267	4	5	144.80
DW Hookes	1987/88	11	20	1	1149	132	7	4	60.47
DS Lehmann	1989/90	12	20	—	1142	228	3	5	57.10
G St A Sobers	1963/64	9	14	—	1128	195	2	6	80.57
DG Bradman	1937/38	8	14	2	1095	246	4	5	91.25
DW Hookes	1982/83	8	15	—	1080	146	5	4	72.00
WM Darling	1981/82	9	17	3	1011	134	6	3	72.21
G St A Sobers	1962/63	10	18	2	1006	196	5	3	62.87
IM Chappell	1965/66	9	17	2	983	134	4	4	65.53
GA Bishop	1985/86	11	21	1	965	224*	2	3	48.25
IM Chappell	1973/74	9	18	1	947	141*	7	3	55.70
AMJ Hilditch	1983/84	10	17	1	937	230	3	3	58.56
AMJ Hilditch	1987/88	11	20	1	922	185	5	2	48.53
GB Stevens	1958/59	9	17	—	916	259*	3	3	53.88

Highest Individual Innings for South Australia

Score	Batsman	Opponent	Venue	Season
369	DG Bradman	Tasmania	Adelaide	1935/36
365*	C Hill	New South Wales	Adelaide	1900/01
357	DG Bradman	Victoria	Melbourne	1935/36
356	BA Richards	Western Australia	Perth	1970/71
325	CL Badcock	Victoria	Adelaide	1935/36
306*	DW Hookes	Tasmania	Adelaide	1986/87
280	AJ Richardson	MCC	Adelaide	1922/23
271	G Giffen	Victoria	Adelaide	1891/92
271	CE Pellew	Victoria	Adelaide	1919/20
271*	CL Badcock	New South Wales	Adelaide	1938/39
267	DG Bradman	Victoria	Melbourne	1939/40
260	WB Phillips	Queensland	Adelaide	1981/82
259*	GB Stevens	New South Wales	Sydney	1958/59

Score	Batsman	Opponent	Venue	Season
251*	DG Bradman	New South Wales	Adelaide	1939/40
251	GStA Sobers	New South Wales	Adelaide	1961/62
246	DG Bradman	Queensland	Adelaide	1937/38
243	DW Hookes	New South Wales	Adelaide	1985/86
237	G Giffen	Victoria	Melbourne	1890/91
236	CL Badcock	Queensland	Adelaide	1939/40
234	WB Phillips	Tasmania	Adelaide	1983/84
233	DG Bradman	Queensland	Adelaide	1935/36
232	AJ Richardson	Queensland	Adelaide	1926/27
231	VY Richardson	MCC	Adelaide	1928/29
230	AMJ Hilditch	Victoria	Melbourne	1983/84
228	DS Lehmann	New South Wales	Adelaide	1989/90
227	AJ Richardson	Western Australia	Adelaide	1925/26
226	GB Hole	Queensland	Adelaide	1953/54
225	DG Bradman	Queensland	Adelaide	1938/39
224	BA Richards	MCC	Adelaide	1970/71
224*	GA Bishop	Tasmania	Adelaide	1985/86
213	ARC McLean	Queensland	Adelaide	1949/50
213*	WB Phillips	Tasmania	Adelaide	1986/87
210	J Darling	Queensland	Brisbane	1898/99
210	RV James	Queensland	Adelaide	1947/48
209*	DG Bradman	Western Australia	Perth	1939/40
206*	C Hill	New South Wales	Sydney	1895/96
205	G Giffen	New South Wales	Adelaide	1893/94
205	C Hill	New South Wales	Adelaide	1909/10
205*	IM Chappell	Queensland	Brisbane	1963/64
203	G Giffen	GF Vernon's XI	Adelaide	1887/88
203	VY Richardson	Victoria	Adelaide	1932/33
203	KG Cunningham	Victoria	Adelaide	1971/72
202*	AB Shiell	MCC	Adelaide	1965/66
202	GA Bishop	New Zealanders	Adelaide	1985/86
200	C Hill	AE Stoddart's XI	Adelaide	1897/98
200*	AJ Richardson	MCC	Adelaide	1924/25

Leading Wicket Takers for South Australia

Bowler	Career	M	Runs	Wkts	Avrge	5wi	10m	Best
CV Grimmett	1924/25-1940/41	105	16566	668	24.79	62	16	9/180
G Giffen	1877/78-1903/04	64	9597	412	23.29	47	17	9/91
AA Mallett	1967/68-1980/81	91	9534	390	24.44	20	2	7/57
PR Sleep	1976/77-1989/90	122	10381	264	39.32	6	—	8/133
TJ Jenner	1967/68-1976/77	77	7733	259	29.85	12	1	7/127
E Jones	1892/93-1902/03	47	6498	248	26.20	23	4	8/157
G Noblet	1945/46-1952/53	49	4457	236	18.88	13	2	7/29
NJN Hawke	1960/61-1967/68	60	5803	211	27.50	12	4	8/61
GR Attenborough	1972/73-1980/81	57	6170	193	31.96	8	2	7/90
FA Ward	1935/36-1940/41	38	5044	187	26.97	12	2	7/62
JW Wilson	1950/51-1957/58	55	5746	182	31.57	6	—	6/55
TW Wall	1924/25-1935/36	53	5209	178	29.26	3	1	10/36
WJ Whitty	1908/09-1925/26	43	5678	178	31.89	8	1	7/66
RM Hogg	1975/76-1983/84	39	3601	165	21.82	10	2	7/53
EW Freeman	1964/65-1973/74	44	3932	150	26.21	5	2	8/47
TBA May	1984/85-1989/90	45	5313	148	35.90	6	—	7/93
PK Lee	1925/26-1934/35	50	4186	146	28.67	6	—	5/23
AK Zesers	1984/85-1989/90	45	4323	142	30.44	4	—	7/87
W Prior	1974/75-1984/85	48	4608	138	33.39	6	1	6/41
G St A Sobers	1961/62-1963/64	26	3565	137	26.02	8	—	7/110
DJ Sincock	1960/61-1965/66	35	4775	134	35.63	10	1	7/48
JR Hammond	1969/70-1980/81	46	3550	124	28.62	5	—	6/54
JN Crawford	1909/10-1913/14	22	2864	120	23.86	11	3	8/66
MG Waite	1930/31-1945/46	72	4238	120	35.31	1	—	5/42
RJ Inverarity	1979/80-1984/85	53	3604	118	30.54	5	—	7/86
B Dooland	1945/46-1957/58	29	4108	118	34.81	5	—	6/97
AJ Richardson	1918/19-1926/27	45	4583	117	39.17	2	—	5/52
JPF Travers	1895/96-1906/07	36	3659	116	31.54	5	1	9/30
NL Williams	1919/20-1928/29	33	4593	116	39.59	8	3	6/40
JC Reedman	1887/88-1908/09	76	3657	114	32.07	6	1	7/54
AW Wright	1905/06-1920/21	29	3266	106	30.81	7	1	7/66
Alfred Jarvis	1889/90-1905/06	54	4031	106	38.02	2	—	6/114

Most Wickets in a Season for South Australia

Bowler	Season	M	Overs	Mdns	Runs	Wkts	Avrge	5wi	10m	Best
CV Grimmett	1939/40	8	398.6	53	1459	63	23.15	7	3	6/57
G Giffen	1894/95	6	454.3	85	1277	59	21.64	9	4	8/77
CV Grimmett	1929/30	8	364.3	33	1524	58	26.27	6	2	7/136
CV Grimmett	1933/34	8	317.7	53	1101	55	20.01	6	1	7/57
J Garner	1982/83	8	403.2	131	976	55	17.74	4	2	7/78
E Jones	1897/98	6	401.1	90	1100	54	20.37	8	3	7/80
G Noblet	1952/53	8	353.5	68	814	52	15.65	4	—	6/39
G St A Sobers	1962/63	10	384.3	49	1355	51	26.56	4	—	7/110
G St A Sobers	1963/64	9	411.4	50	1441	51	28.25	2	—	6/71
CV Grimmett	1932/33	8	338.0	37	1251	50	25.02	5	1	7/86
FA Ward	1935/36	8	315.6	62	1047	50	20.94	3	—	6/47
AA Mallett	1971/72	8	300.6	71	908	50	18.16	3	1	7/58
CV Grimmett	1934/35	7	276.6	35	1043	49	21.28	5	3	9/180
AA Mallett	1972/73	8	318.7	89	893	49	18.22	3	—	5/41
RHD Sellers	1963/64	9	344.7	45	1365	48	28.43	3	1	5/49
AA Mallett	1979/80	10	472.4	144	1140	48	23.75	2	—	5/67
AK Zesers	1986/87	11	499.0	161	1108	47	23.57	2	—	7/67
AA Mallett	1975/76	10	344.0	66	1035	45	23.00	1	—	5/68

Best Bowling in an Innings for South Australia

Wkts	Bowler	Opponent	Venue	Season
10/36	TW Wall	New South Wales	Sydney	1932/33
9/30	JPF Travers	Victoria	Melbourne	1900/01
9/55	J Quilty	Victoria	Adelaide	1881/82
9/67	H Hay	Lord Hawke's XI	Unley	1902/03
9/91	G Giffen	Victoria	Adelaide	1885/86
9/96	G Giffen	Victoria	Adelaide	1891/92
9/147	G Giffen	Victoria	Adelaide	1892/93
9/180	CV Grimmett	Queensland	Adelaide	1934/35
8/36	J Bevan	Tasmania	Adelaide	1877/78
8/47	EW Freeman	New Zealanders	Adelaide	1967/68
8/57	CV Grimmett	New South Wales	Adelaide	1927/28
8/61	NJN Hawke	New South Wales	Sydney	1967/68
8/64	EW Freeman	New South Wales	Adelaide	1970/71
8/65	G Giffen	Victoria	Adelaide	1887/88
8/66	JN Crawford	Victoria	Adelaide	1912/13
8/77	G Giffen	New South Wales	Adelaide	1894/95
8/83	G Giffen	Victoria	Adelaide	1886/87
8/86	CV Grimmett	Victoria	Adelaide	1923/24
8/109	G Giffen	New South Wales	Adelaide	1894/95
8/110	G Giffen	Victoria	Adelaide	1885/86
8/110	G Giffen	Victoria	Adelaide	1902/03
8/133	PR Sleep	Victoria	Melbourne	1978/79
8/157	E Jones	New South Wales	Sydney	1896/97
8/287	G Giffen	New South Wales	Adelaide	1899/00

Best Bowling in a Match for South Australia

Wkts	Bowler	Opponent	Venue	Season
17/201	G Giffen	Victoria	Adelaide	1885/86
16/166	G Giffen	Victoria	Adelaide	1891/92
16/186	G Giffen	New South Wales	Adelaide	1894/95
16/289	CV Grimmett	Queensland	Adelaide	1934/35
15/185	G Giffen	Victoria	Adelaide	1902/03
14/59	J Bevan	Tasmania	Adelaide	1877/78
14/125	G Giffen	Victoria	Adelaide	1887/88
14/237	E Jones	AE Stoddart's XI	Adelaide	1897/98
13/93	G Giffen	AC MacLaren's XI	Adelaide	1901/02
13/105	EW Freeman	New South Wales	Adelaide	1970/71
13/122	AA Mallett	Western Australia	Adelaide	1971/72
13/135	CV Grimmett	Queensland	Brisbane	1932/33
13/149	JC Reedman	Victoria	Melbourne	1904/05
13/159	G Giffen	Victoria	Melbourne	1888/89
12/82	NJN Hawke	Western Australia	Perth	1961/62
12/104	RM Hogg	Queensland	Adelaide	1982/83
12/127	A Travers	Victoria	Melbourne	1900/01
12/127	TW Wall	New South Wales	Sydney	1932/33
12/142	D Sincock	Victoria	Adelaide	1964/65
12/147	G Giffen	Victoria	Adelaide	1893/94
12/150	G Giffen	New South Wales	Sydney	1891/92
12/182	K Horsnell	Victoria	Melbourne	1953/54
12/187	G Giffen	Victoria	Melbourne	1886/87

Continued

317

Wkts	Bowler	Opponent	Venue	Season
12/191	G Giffen	New South Wales	Adelaide	1892/93
12/192	G Giffen	Victoria	Melbourne	1890/91
12/195	NL Williams	Queensland	Adelaide	1923/24
12/206	E Jones	Victoria	Melbourne	1896/97
12/234	NL Williams	Victoria	Adelaide	1926/27

Most Dismissals by a Wicket-Keeper for South Australia

Wicket-Keeper	Career	M	Cght	Stmp	Total
BN Jarman	1955/56–1968/69	94	234	65	299
CW Walker	1928/29–1940/41	78	139	113	252
GRA Langley	1945/46–1956/57	55	130	30	160
KJ Wright	1980/81–1983/84	40	110	12	122
TJ Robertson	1977/78–1979/80	32	82	12	94
M Hendricks	1970/71–1974/75	32	68	11	79
AH Jarvis	1877/78–1900/01	42	47	31	78
RP Blundell	1964/65–1970/71	24	64	13	77
WB Phillips*	1977/78–1988/89	63	71	5	76
DB Yagmich	1974/75–1976/77	20	49	12	61
JR Ducker	1952/53–1962/63	30	48	12	60
AM Ambler	1920/21–1925/26	22	28	29	57
DJ Kelly	1984/85–1986/87	19	47	6	53

* Includes 21 catches when not keeping wicket in 1986/87 & 1988/89

Most Dismissals in a Season for South Australia

Wicket-Keeper	Season	M	Cght	Stmp	Total
TJ Robertson	1978/79	11	29	8	37
BN Jarman	1961/62	10	21	16	37
CW Walker	1939/40	8	19	17	36
BN Jarman	1963/64	9	22	13	35
BN Jarman	1966/67	8	31	4	35
DS Berry	1989/90	12	32	3	35
CW Walker	1936/37	8	17	15	32
KJ Wright	1981/82	9	30	2	32
PW Anderson	1988/89	12	30	2	32
M Hendricks	1971/72	9	24	6	30

Most Dismissals in a Match for South Australia

Ttl	Ct	St	Wicket-Keeper	Opponent	Venue	Season
10	7	3	BN Jarman	New South Wales	Adelaide	1961/62
9	4	5	GB Inkster	Victoria	Melbourne	1926/27
9	3	6	CW Walker	New South Wales	Sydney	1939/40
8	3	5	CW Walker	New South Wales	Sydney	1928/29
8	3	5	GRA Langley	Victoria	Adelaide	1950/51
8	5	3	JR Ducker	Queensland	Adelaide	1952/53
8	8	—	BN Jarman	South Africans	Adelaide	1963/64
8	5	3	BN Jarman	Western Australia	Adelaide	1966/67
8	7	1	DB Yagmich	Victoria	Adelaide	1974/75
8	8	—	KJ Wright	Victoria	St Kilda	1982/83
8	8	—	KJ Wright	Western Australia	Perth	1982/83

Most Dismissals in an Innings for South Australia

Ttl	Ct	St	Wicket-Keeper	Opponent	Venue	Season
6	4	2	GB Inkster	Victoria	Melbourne	1926/27
6	2	4	CW Walker	New South Wales	Sydney	1939/40
6	5	1	GRA Langley	Queensland	Brisbane	1947/48
6	5	1	BN Jarman	Victoria	Melbourne	1956/57
6	5	1	BN Jarman	New South Wales	Adelaide	1961/62
6	5	1	RP Blundell	Queensland	Brisbane	1969/70
6	4	2	TJ Robertson	New South Wales	Adelaide	1978/79
6	6	—	KJ Wright	Western Australia	Perth	1982/83
5	2	3	AM Ambler	Victoria	Melbourne	1923/24
5	2	3	AM Ambler	Queensland	Adelaide	1923/24
5	4	1	GB Inkster	Western Australia	Adelaide	1926/27
5	2	3	CW Walker	Victoria	Adelaide	1936/37
5	5	—	CW Walker	New South Wales	Adelaide	1938/39
5	5	—	GRA Langley	Queensland	Brisbane	1948/49
5	2	3	GRA Langley	Victoria	Adelaide	1950/51
5	3	2	GRA Langley	New South Wales	Adelaide	1951/52
5	4	1	JR Ducker	Queensland	Adelaide	1952/53

Ttl	Ct	St	Wicket-Keeper	Opponent	Venue	Season
5	5	—	BN Jarman	Victoria	Adelaide	1958/59
5	4	1	BN Jarman	Queensland	Brisbane	1960/61
5	2	3	BN Jarman	Queensland	Brisbane	1963/64
5	5	—	BN Jarman	New South Wales	Adelaide	1965/66
5	2	3	BN Jarman	Western Australia	Adelaide	1966/67
5	4	1	DB Yagmich	Victoria	Adelaide	1974/75
5	5	—	KJ Wright	Victoria	St Kilda	1982/83
5	5	—	KJ Wright	Western Australia	Perth	1983/84
5	5	—	DJ Kelly	Victoria	Adelaide	1984/85

Most Catches by a Fieldsman for South Australia

Fieldsman	Career	M	Catches
IM Chappell	1961/62–1979/80	109	133
VY Richardson	1918/19–1937/38	104	128
DW Hookes	1975/76–1989/90	115	127
PR Sleep	1976/77–1989/90	122	78
LE Favell	1951/52–1969/70	143	75
G Giffen	1877/78–1903/04	64	67
AJ Woodcock	1967/68–1978/79	80	67
JC Reedman	1887/88–1908/09	76	65
GS Chappell	1966/67–1972/73	57	63
KG Cunningham	1960/61–1973/74	89	62
C Hill	1892/93–1922/23	87	61
TJ Jenner	1967/68–1976/77	77	59
CV Grimmett	1924/25–1940/41	105	58
GA Bishop	1982/83–1989/90	72	56
PL Ridings	1937/38–1956/57	98	54
JC Lill	1955/56–1965/66	60	54
DE Pritchard	1918/19–1931/32	49	51
MG Waite	1930/31–1945/46	72	51

Most Catches in a Season for South Australia

Catches	Fieldsman	M	Season
20	GS Chappell	9	1970/71
18	EW Freeman	7	1971/72
18	DW Hookes	11	1987/88
18	DW Hookes	12	1988/89
16	G St A Sobers	9	1963/64
16	IM Chappell	7	1968/69
16	IM Chappell	6	1971/72
16	IM Chappell	9	1975/76
15	JC Lill	9	1963/64
15	DW Hookes	8	1985/86
15	GA Bishop	11	1984/85
15	DW Hookes	10	1986/87

Most Catches in a Match for South Australia

Ct	Fieldsman	Opponent	Venue	Season
7	EW Freeman	Western Australia	Adelaide	1971/72
6	AJ Woodcock	Western Australia	Adelaide	1968/69
6	GS Chappell	MCC	Adelaide	1970/71
6	DJ Rolfe	Tasmania	Devonport	1979/80
5	CE Pellew	New South Wales	Adelaide	1914/15
5	MG Waite	Victoria	Melbourne	1936/37
5	MG Waite	Queensland	Adelaide	1939/40
5	GB Hole	Victoria	Melbourne	1952/53
5	IM Chappell	New South Wales	Adelaide	1975/76
5	IM Chappell	Queensland	Adelaide	1975/76
5	DW Hookes	New South Wales	Sydney	1982/83
5	MD Haysman	Tasmania	Adelaide	1983/84
5	AMJ Hilditch	Victoria	Adelaide	1984/85

Most Catches in an Innings for South Australia

Ct	Fieldsman	Opponent	Venue	Season
4	JC Reedman	New South Wales	Adelaide	1895/96
4	DE Pritchard	Victoria	Adelaide	1929/30
4	MG Waite	Victoria	Melbourne	1936/37
4	B Dooland	New South Wales	Adelaide	1946/47
4	AB Shiell	Western Australia	Perth	1965/66
4	KG Cunningham	New South Wales	Adelaide	1968/69

Continued

Ct	Fieldsman	Opponent	Venue	Season
4 _____	EW Freeman	Western Australia	Adelaide	1971/72
4 _____	IM Chappell	Queensland	Brisbane	1972/73
4 _____	IM Chappell	MCC	Adelaide	1974/75
4 _____	AMJ Hilditch	Victoria	Adelaide	1984/85

Partnership Records for South Australia

Wkt	Ttl	Batsmen	Opponent	Venue	Season
1st	313 _____	LT Gun, AJ Richardson	Western Australia	Adelaide	1925/26
2nd	308 _____	BA Richards, IM Chappell	Western Australia	Perth	1970/71
3rd	356 _____	DG Bradman, RA Hamence	Tasmania	Adelaide	1935/36
4th	462* _____	DW Hookes, WB Phillips	Tasmania	Adelaide	1986/87
5th	281 _____	CL Badcock, MG Waite	Queensland	Adelaide	1939/40
6th	255 _____	GStA Sobers, BN Jarman	Western Australia	Perth	1963/64
7th	183 _____	WC Alexander, JW Rymill	Victoria	Melbourne	1925/26
8th	192 _____	C Hill, WF Giffen	Stoddart's XI	Adelaide	1894/95
9th	232 _____	C Hill, EA Walkley	New South Wales	Adelaide	1900/01
10th	104 _____	L Michael, EI Pynor	Victoria	Adelaide	1949/50

Highest Partnerships for South Australia

Wkt	Ttl	Batsmen	Opponent	Venue	Season
4th	462* _____	DW Hookes, WB Phillips	Tasmania	Adelaide	1986/87
3rd	356 _____	DG Bradman, RA Hamence	Tasmania	Adelaide	1935/36
1st	313 _____	LT Gun, AJ Richardson	Western Australia	Adelaide	1925/26
2nd	308 _____	BA Richards, IM Chappell	Western Australia	Perth	1970/71
2nd	299 _____	EL Bowley, JT Murray	Queensland	Adelaide	1923/24
4th	297 _____	GA Bishop, PR Sleep	New Zealanders	Adelaide	1985/86
1st	281 _____	LE Favell, JP Causby	New South Wales	Adelaide	1967/68
5th	281 _____	CL Badcock, MG Waite	Queensland	Adelaide	1939/40
1st	269 _____	GA Bishop, AMJ Hilditch	New South Wales	Sydney	1986/87
5th	268 _____	RG Lloyd, IM McLachlan	Queensland	Adelaide	1960/61
5th	264 _____	DW Hookes, MD Haysman	Victoria	St Kilda	1982/83
1st	256 _____	AJ Richardson, VY Richardson	MCC	Adelaide	1922/23
2nd	255 _____	VY Richardson, DE Pritchard	MCC	Adelaide	1928/29
1st	255 _____	VY Richardson, HC Nitschke	Queensland	Adelaide	1934/35
6th	255 _____	GStA Sobers, BN Jarman	Western Australia	Perth	1963/64
3rd	253 _____	C Hill, DRA Gehrs	Victoria	Adelaide	1909/10
4th	253 _____	IM McLachlan, GStA Sobers	South Africans	Adelaide	1963/64
1st	250* _____	BA Richards, AJ Woodcock	MCC	Adelaide	1970/71
4th	240 _____	G StA Sobers, IM McLachlan	Western Australia	Adelaide	1962/63
3rd	238 _____	AR Lonergan, CL Badcock	Queensland	Adelaide	1934/35
2nd	235 _____	BA Richards, IM Chappell	MCC	Adelaide	1970/71
2nd	234 _____	G Giffen, JJ Lyons	New South Wales	Sydney	1891/92
9th	232 _____	C Hill, EA Walkley	New South Wales	Adelaide	1900/01
2nd	232 _____	RJ Craig, RV James	Queensland	Adelaide	1947/48
2nd	229 _____	EL Bowley, JT Murray	Queensland	Adelaide	1923/24
1st	228 _____	WM Darling, WB Phillips	Pakistanis	Adelaide	1981/82
2nd	227 _____	WB Phillips, MD Haysman	Tasmania	Adelaide	1983/84
1st	226 _____	RJ Craig, RD Niehuus	Indians	Adelaide	1947/48
3rd	222 _____	AJ Richardson, VY Richardson	MCC	Adelaide	1924/25
6th	221 _____	PC Nobes, MG Bevan	Western Australia	Perth	1989/90
3rd	219 _____	GB Stevens, CJ Pinch	Western Australia	Adelaide	1956/57
3rd	218 _____	AMJ Hilditch, MD Haysman	Victoria	Melbourne	1983/84
6th	215 _____	GS Chappell, BN Jarman	Western Australia	Adelaide	1967/68
3rd	215 _____	KP Harris, DW Hookes	Western Australia	Perth	1982/83
6th	214 _____	MD Haysman, RJ Inverarity	Western Australia	Perth	1984/85
3rd	213 _____	LE Favell, L Duldig	New South Wales	Adelaide	1951/52
4th	213 _____	MAJ Sargent, RG Lloyd	Queensland	Brisbane	1960/61
1st	210 _____	CL Badcock, RA Parker	Victoria	Adelaide	1935/36
2nd	207 _____	LE Favell, HN Dansie	Western Australia	Adelaide	1958/59
2nd	205 _____	JT Murray, GW Harris	Victoria	Adelaide	1924/25
4th	204 _____	AJ Handrickan, DW Hookes	New South Wales	Adelaide	1976/77
3rd	204 _____	JJ Crowe, JR Inverarity	New South Wales	Adelaide	1981/82
4th	203 _____	DG Bradman, CL Badcock	New South Wales	Adelaide	1938/39
3rd	203 _____	PL Ridings, RA Hamence	MCC	Adelaide	1946/47
3rd	202 _____	J Darling, G Giffen	Queensland	Brisbane	1898/99
3rd	202 _____	DE Pritchard, VY Richardson	New South Wales	Sydney	1924/25
2nd	202 _____	AJ Richardson, LT Gun	Queensland	Adelaide	1926/27
3rd	202 _____	DG Bradman, CL Badcock	Queensland	Adelaide	1938/39
2nd	202 _____	LE Favell, KG Cunningham	Victoria	Adelaide	1966/67
1st	201 _____	GW Harris, VY Richardson	Queensland	Adelaide	1928/29
3rd	201 _____	CL Badcock, RA Hamence	Victoria	Melbourne	1940/41
5th	200 _____	DW Hookes, DS Lehmann	New South Wales	Adelaide	1989/90

ADELAIDE CRICKET

A GRADE

A championship closely contested during the qualifying matches and then in the finals was ultimately won by Sturt, which defeated West Torrens by three wickets in the final. It was Sturt's first premiership in the A-grade competition since 1978-79, while West Torrens has not won it since 1961-62. During the season Sturt had a close contest with two other clubs, Glenelg and Salisbury, for places on the points table, and the three were never far apart on the ladder. At the end of the qualifying matches, Glenelg headed the points table, followed by, in order, Sturt, Salisbury and West Torrens. In the semi-finals on March 17 and 18, West Torrens (8 for 306) upset Glenelg (304), and Sturt (246) defeated Salisbury (232).

By and large, teams in Adelaide's A-grade competition tended to be strong in batting, and Sturt was one of the strongest. James Orchard was especially consistent, scoring 881 runs at an average of 48.94, a record aggregate for the club, and he played an important part in Sturt's success in the finals, in particular, scoring 82 in the semi-final and 94 in the final. It was fortunate for Sturt that he was able to represent the club right through the season, although Sturt may not be so fortunate in the coming season, since Orchard is likely to be a contender for the state side. Darryl Scott was another reliable batsman for Sturt, while Colin Miller bowled with great success in the matches for which he was available. Scott, who scored 609 runs at 35.82 and headed Sturt's wicket aggregates with 37 wickets at 17.59, was awarded Sturt's President's Trophy as the club's most outstanding player. Glenelg, the minor premiers, was a strong side all round, which lost only four of its fourteen matches. Its leading players were Andrew Hilditch, Michael Bevan and Peter Gladigau. Salisbury, the defending champion, appeared to have slipped a little, which may be simply because, as an aging team, it is passing through the normal cycle of success. Its best-known players were Darren Lehmann and Glenn Bishop.

The success of West Torrens was the surprise of the competition. It was a young side which early in the season struggled to win matches, but which finished impressively and is likely to be a force in the competition for several seasons to come. West Torrens no longer had the services of David Hookes, who had transferred to East Torrens, but it did have Paul Nobes, who averaged 59.55 in the matches he played.

Glenelg's pace bowler Peter Gladigau won the Bradman Medal for the best and fairest player in the competition; Tim Nielsen of West Torrens won the CW Walker Award for wicketkeeping; and Brenton Opperman won the Talbot Smith Award for fielding.

Points Table A Grade

Club	Match Pts	Performance Pts	Total
Glenelg	100	71.20	171.20
Sturt	100	66.55	166.55
Salisbury	80	74.65	154.65
West Torrens	80	76.07	151.07
Woodville	80	62.87	142.87
University	75	67.41	142.41
Kensington	75	61.63	136.63
Adelaide	60	62.46	122.46
East Torrens	55	65.05	120.05
Prospect	55	60.73	115.73
Port Adelaide	50	61.97	111.97
Tea Tree Gully	45	64.50	109.50

FINAL
Sturt v West Torrens
Adelaide Oval, Adelaide
March 24-25, 1990
100-over match
Result: Sturt won by 3 wickets

Batting first, West Torrens was able to bat out its 100 overs, but it did not make as many runs as it would have liked, and the credit for that must go to the Sturt bowlers Colin Miller, Darryl Scott and Scott Cunningham, who kept the Torrens batsmen in check. Miller and Scott, for instance, each bowled 30 overs yet conceded only 65 and 67 runs respectively. For West Torrens, D Cassidy (53) was the only batsman to make a half-century. Tim Nielsen made 44, and four others made promising starts but were not able to advance beyond the 20s. Sturt's opening batsmen, James Orchard and Darryl Scott, made 85 between them in only 20 overs before the fall of the first wicket, a fine start which other batsmen built on. In fact, six of Sturt's first seven batsmen made 20 or more, including Scott (47) and Andy Meinel (30). Orchard played the dominant innings, though, and when he was out for 94 in the 61st over Sturt was within sight of victory at 3 for 200. West Torrens's hopes were revived when Sturt lost two more wickets to be 5 for 209 after 67 overs, but Peter Judd (26) and Andrew Carver (23) halted the collapse and saw Sturt almost all the way to victory. At the end, Sturt had made 7 for 265 in 87.4 overs, winning with more than 12 overs to spare.

West Torrens

Batsman	How Out	Ttl
P Nobes	c Judd b Scottt	28
P Clark	c Cunningham b Miller	13
D Cassidy	b Miller	53
M Howell	lbw b Cunningham	20
T Nielsen	c Scott b Miller	44
J Pyke	b Scott	26
R Vincent	c Phillips b Miller	4
K Frick	c Judd b Miller	19
S George	b Scott	20
C Mack	not out	11
R Nicholls	run out	4
Sundries		20
Total		262

Bowler	O	M	R	Wkts
C Miller	30	8	65	5
D Ritossa	11	2	37	0
D Scott	30	12	67	3
S Cunningham	17	6	41	1
G Gulliver	12	1	38	0

Sturt

Batsman	How Out	Ttl
D Scott	b Mack	47
J Orchard	c Nicholls b Pyke	94
W Phillips	c Frick b George	22
A Meinel	run out	30
J Brooks	c Nielsen b Cassidy	0
P Judd	lbw b Nobes	26
A Carver	c Nielsen b Nicholls	23
C Miller	not out	1
S Cunningham	not out	5
Sundries		17
Total		7 for 265

Bowler	O	M	R	Wkts
S George	23	3	68	1
C Mack	20	2	68	1
R Nicholls	8.4	0	36	1
J Pyke	8	2	26	1
D Cassidy	27	10	56	1
P Nobes	1	1	0	1

Batting Averages—A Grade

Batsman	Avge
M Bevan (Glenelg)	85.43
M May (Kensington)	60.85
P Nobes (West Torrens)	59.55
A Hilditch (Glenelg)	55.33
A Watson (University)	54.69
J Williams (Woodville)	50.14
J Orchard (Sturt)	48.94
D Hookes (East Torrens)	47.80
M Faull (Tea Tree Gully)	47.07
K Vowles (Port Adelaide)	44.40

Bowling

Bowler	Avge
L Cleggett (Salisbury)	12.56
P Gladigau (Glenelg)	14.29
C Miller (Sturt)	14.75
C Owen (Woodville)	15.51
A Zesers (Prospect)	16.73
A Rolton (Glenelg)	17.00
P Pasculli (Adelaide)	17.44
D Scott (Sturt)	17.48
M Gladigau (Glenelg)	17.63
M. Forster	18.19

B GRADE

Adelaide won the premiership, defeating Prospect in the final. The scores were: Adelaide 9/267, Prospect 124. In the semi finals Adelaide (386) defeated Sturt (236) and Prospect (7/352) defeated Kensington (163)

Points Table

Club	Match Pts	Performance Pts	Total
Kensington	130	71.45	201.45
Adelaide	115	76.16	191.16
Sturt	100	68.91	168.91
Prospect	95	68.68	163.68
Glenelg	70	65.24	135.24
East Torrens	65	65.07	130.07
Port Adelaide	65	61.44	126.44
Salisbury	55	61.59	116.59
Tea Tree Gully	50	64.93	114.93
West Torrens	40	63.03	103.03
University	45	55.71	100.71
Woodville	30	61.86	91.86

C GRADE

Elizabeth won the competition, defeating Sturt in the final. The scores were Elizabeth 136 and 9/159, Sturt 103. In the semi-finals, Elizabeth (116 and 5/108) defeated Prospect (114 and 109) and Sturt (211) defeated Adelaide (148).

Points Table

Club	Match Pts	Performance Pts	Total
Elizabeth	105	60.70	165.70
Adelaide	100	54.75	154.75
Sturt	85	57.93	142.93
Prospect	80	57.49	137.49
Glenelg	75	53.69	128.69
Tea Tree Gully	70	57.43	127.43
Salisbury	70	51.40	121.40
Adelaide University	60	59.12	119.12
Flinders University	50	58.08	108.08
Kensington	40	58.97	98.97
West Torrens	40	56.40	96.40
East Torrens	40	52.88	92.88
Port Adelaide	35	50.21	85.21
South Districts	20	50.48	70.48
Woodville	25	41.46	66.96

D GRADE

Adelaide won the competition, defeating Prospect in the final. The scores were: Adelaide 6/260, Prospect 258. In the semi-finals, Prospect (9/225) defeated University (213) and Adelaide (5/167) defeated Kensington (159).

Points Table

Club	Match Pts	Performance Pts	Total
Adelaide	105	57.16	162.16
University	100	58.42	158.42
Prospect	90	60.93	150.93
Kensington	85	66.88	151.88
Glenelg	95	53.07	148.97
Sturt	80	55.31	135.31
Salisbury	70	55.42	125.42
East Torrens	55	57.17	112.17
Elizabeth	55	49.56	104.56
West Torrens	50	53.56	103.56
Flinders University	50	50.04	100.04
Tea Tree Gully	35	44.00	79.00
Port Adelaide	35	43.72	78.72
South Districts	15	50.88	65.88
Woodville	15	46.03	61.03

CLUB CHAMPIONSHIP

Adelaide won the competition for the third year in succession. The final points table was:

Club	Grade A	Grade B	Grade C	Grade D	Total
Adelaide	122.46	191.16	154.75	162.16	630.53
Sturt	166.55	168.91	142.93	135.31	613.70
Kensington	136.63	201.45	98.97	151.88	588.93
Glenelg	171.20	135.24	128.69	148.97	584.10
Prospect	115.73	163.68	137.49	150.93	567.83
University	142.41	100.71	119.12	158.42	520.66
Salisbury	154.65	116.59	121.40	125.42	518.06
East Torrens	120.05	130.07	92.88	112.17	455.17
West Torrens	151.07	103.03	96.40	103.56	454.06
Tea Tree Gully	109.50	114.93	127.43	79.00	430.86
Port Adelaide	111.97	126.44	85.21	78.72	402.34
Woodville	142.87	91.86	66.96	61.03	362.72

COUNTRY CRICKET

Although country cricket in South Australia continued to be played at a high standard—as demonstrated by the Combined Country side's impressive showing against a strong SACA XI—the standard of the pitches it was played on remained generally poor. The enduring problem is the lack of turf wickets. Riverland still has the only all-turf competition in the State, with turf pitches at Renmark, Berri, Barmera, Loxton, Loxton North and Waikerie. Elsewhere, turf pitches are relatively rare. Towns fortunate enough to have them include Port Pirie, Whyalla, Wudinna, Port Lincoln, Strathalbyn, Encounter Bay, Ashbourne, Pinnaroo and Mt Gambier, where a new turf pitch has been laid recently. This shortage of turf wickets is undoubtably the most serious problem with which country cricket in South Australia has to contend, although, as country cricket officials long ago found, it is not a simple problem to deal with.

Members of the Country Committee of the SACA in the 1989-90 season were: Don Woon of Loxton (country-co-ordinator), Dick Harvey of Broken Hill (Barrier League delegate), Peter Penna of Modbury (Eyre Peninsula), Don Molineux of Tarlee (Lower North), Graham Madden of Loxton (Murray Districts), Peter Haddrick of Naracoorte (South East), Athol Payne of Cambrai (Southern), John Nankivell of Minlaton (Yorke Peninsula) and Ian Rogers of Quorn (Upper North), who was later replaced by Fred Freeman of Wilmington.

COUNTRY CARNIVAL

The Harry Meyer Shield was contested in Adelaide from February 5 to 14, 1990, by teams from the eight country zones. Each side played 55-over matches against all other seven teams in the competition in a round-robin tournament. Barrier won the Harry

Meyer Shield in a carnival so closely contested that the three top place-getters finished within 2 points of each other. The final points table was:

Barrier	81.00
South East	79.48
Murray Districts	79.35
Lower North	67.95
Yorke Peninsula	67.91
Upper North	59.93
Eyre Peninsula	47.37
Southern	24.09

A 15-year-old batsman from Broken Hill, Jeff Vaughan, who played for Barrier, won the CLB Starr trophy as the player of the series. The Upper North batsman Chris Richards, from Whyalla, headed the batting aggregates with 397 runs, and Bill Slee of Broken Hill, who played for Barrier, headed the bowling aggregates with 18 wickets. The fielding trophy was won by Greg Stephenson of Geranium, who played for Murray Districts.

SACA XI-Combined Country Match
Result: SACA XI won by 3 wickets with 6 balls in hand.

At the end of the Country Carnival, a combined team was chosen from the eight zones to play what was essentially a city team. The country team was: Peter Mattey of Terowie (Lower North), Robbie Ellis of Mt Gambier (South East), David Burtenshaw of Renmark (Murray Districts), Simon Fuchs of Port Pirie (Upper North), Richie Gutsche of Curramulka (Yorke Peninsula), Greg Hanckel of Jamestown (Lower North), Chris Richards of Whyalla (Upper North), John Robins of Bute (Yorke Peninsula), Bill Slee of Broken Hill (Barrier), John Mosey of Robertson (Lower North) and Jeff Vaughan of Broken Hill (Barrier). Peter Mattey was captain and Robbie Ellis vice-captain.

The 55-over match was played at the Adelaide No 2 ground on February 15. Although it was won by the city team, the country players gave a good account of themselves, especially the two teenagers Jeff Vaughan, who was fifteen years old, and Richie Gutsche, who was eighteen. Both were playing their first representative match. Vaughan, a tall, erect batsman, played an outstanding innings. He batted with fluency and his driving, in particular, was impressive. Gutsche, the wicketkeeper, came in when Combined Country was in desperate trouble at 6 for 48. Together, the two young players halted the collapse and gradually got on top of the bowling. They were still there after 55 overs, having put on 146 runs between them. Vaughan made 100 not out and Gutsche 53 not out.

Combined Country

Batsman	How Out	Ttl
R Ellis	c Thompson b Heidrich	23
G Hanckel	run out	7
C Richards	lbw b Carpenter	3
J Vaughan	not out	100
P Mattey (c)	lbw b Pasculli	1
J Mosey	b Heidrich	2
J Robins	b Pasculli	0
R Gutsche	not out	53
Sundries		5
Total		6 for 194

Bowler	O	M	R	Wkts
S Carpenter	11	0	54	1
A Zesers	12	1	28	0
A Heidrich	6	3	9	2
P Pasculli	13	2	44	2
G Yates	11	1	39	0
W Phillips	2	0	17	0

SACA XI

Batsman	How Out	Ttl
G Lewis	c Mosey b Slee	20
J Orchard	c Fuchs b Slee	23
D Scott	run out	1
W Phillips (c)	c Burtenshaw b Robins	33
G Yates	c Gursche b Robins	45
R Thompson	c Vaughan b Fuchs	43
W Smith	b Burtenshaw	6
A Heidrich	not out	23
A Zesers	not out	2
Sundries		6
Total		7 for 202

Bowler	O	M	R	Wkts
W Slee	13	2	46	2
J Robins	13	0	71	2
D Burtenshaw	13	1	34	1
S Fuchs	11	0	41	1
J Mosey	4	1	4	0

TASMANIA

STATISTICALLY, TASMANIA ended the Sheffield Shield season exactly as it had ended the previous season—with two outright wins and two first innings leads. Yet the 1989-90 team did appear to be a better rounded and a stronger combination than the team of 1988-89. Even without Greg Campbell, who was absent for much of the season playing for Australia, Tasmania's attack was certainly better balanced, not least because of the presence in the side of a quality spin bowler, Gavin Robertson. The batting seemed also to have been strengthened by young talent coming to the fore, most notably of Rod Tucker, Jamie Cox and the 21-year-old opener Michael Farrell, who made his debut for Tasmania in the last match of the season and, against New South Wales's spin bowlers on a spinning Sydney pitch, scored 96 of a total of 157 in Tasmania's second innings.

It serves no real purpose to reflect on what might have been, yet it is clear that if Tasmania had pressed home the advantage in its opening two matches it would have begun the season with two outright wins. In the first match, the Tasmanian bowlers had Western Australia in deep trouble at 8 for 113 but were then frustrated by the tail-enders, who raised the total to 215. The Tasmanians compiled a big total in reply, 6 declared for 478, but they took so long to make the runs their bowlers simply did not have enough time to force an outright victory, although it must be admitted several close umpiring decisions went against them. In their next match, against Victoria, the Tasmanians were in a winning position on the last day but again could not finish off the tail. It was two and a half months before Tasmania registered any further Sheffield Shield points. Then, it had two stirring outright victories. In late January, Tasmania beat New South Wales outright at Hobart with one ball to spare. Two weeks later at Launceston it won outright against Western Australia by bowling out the Western Australians in their second innings for 116. This victory raised Tasmania to second place on the Sheffield Shield points table, and it may be noted that this was as late as mid-February. But these were the last points Tasmania was to earn.

Dave Gilbert was the side's outstanding bowler, taking 42 wickets in the season, equalling the Tasmanian record. This was despite the fact that an ankle injury prevented him bowling in the second last match of the season, against South Australia, and that in the last match he was compelled to bowl off five paces. For much of the season Gilbert appeared to bowl faster than ever before, and it seemed he had a positive approach to the game generally. Greg Campbell bowled with success in the few matches he played, and it is no coincidence that he played in three of the four matches from which Tasmania gained points. Campbell was sorely missed in Tasmania's last two matches, in particular, when the team was striving to make the Shield final. Gavin Robertson, the young off-spinner, showed much promise, often worrying opposing batsmen with the extra bounce he was able to obtain from the pitch.

Tasmania's premier batsman, David Boon, played only two Sheffield Shield matches, so for most of the season the batting burden was borne by the veteran Greg Shipperd and the young players Rod Tucker and Jamie Cox. Tucker was remarkably consistent with the bat, bettering 50 seven times in 18 innings, yet only once did he go on to make a century. On the other six occasions he was out for, in order, 54, 54, 58, 59, 71 and 67. This is the record of a batsman yet to master the technique of playing a big innings, and when Tucker does master it he is likely to score many runs. As it was, he averaged 43.35 for the season. Cox's form fell away late in the season, when it seemed he was experiencing a return of footwork problems, but he played several big innings which stamped him as a batsman of calibre. He had his finest moment in the match against New South Wales in January, when he scored a century in each innings, hitting 3 sixes and 9 fours in the second of them. Greg Shipperd began the season on an extremely high note with a double century, albeit a slow one, and he scored another two centuries before the season was over. Dirk Wellham had a generally disappointing season with the bat, yet as team leader and strategist he again proved effective. The wicketkeeper Richard Soule did not have nearly as good a season as he would have liked, either with bat or gloves.

Tasmania continued to be criticised occasionally for not fielding enough Tasmanian-bred players, and it is certainly true the team had an abundance of players originally from the mainland. Only four of these, though, had been recruited by Tasmania's state cricket authorities—Dirk Wellham, Dave Gilbert, Greg Shipperd and Gavin Robertson. The others—Rod Tucker, Scott Hookey, Don O'Connor and Peter McPhee—had either gone to Tasmania of their own accord or had been invited to play there by individual clubs. In any case, Tasmania's two internationals, David Boon and Greg Campbell, are both home-bred, and so is Jamie Cox. The indications are that the state's pool of native talent is growing wider and deeper. In Hobart alone 29 players will be included in the 1990/91 training squad. It is doubtful if 29 players in the whole of the state would have qualified for the squad a few years ago.

Yet Tasmania remains stuck with its own peculiarly Tasmanian problem—the lack of a home ground. Home matches were shared among three of the state's cities—Hobart, Launceston and Devonport—and as a result the Tasmanian team was largely deprived of a home ground advantage. It would not be surprising if moves are made to base the Tasmanian team at Bellerive Oval now that it has gained Test Match status.

TASMANIAN FIRST-CLASS RECORDS

Season 1989/90

Date	Venue	Opponent	Result for Tasmania
Oct 28*	North Sydney	New South Wales _____	Lost by 83 runs
Nov 1	Perth	Western Australia _____	Drawn
Nov 6*	Perth	Western Australia _____	Lost by 4 wkts
Nov 10	St Kilda	Victoria _____	Drawn
Nov 17	Hobart Bel	Queensland _____	Drawn
Dec 1	Launceston	Victoria _____	Drawn
Jan 6	Devonport	Sri Lankans _____	Drawn
Jan 19	Devonport	South Australia _____	Lost by 5 wkts
Jan 26	Hobart Bel	New South Wales _____	Won by 4 wkts
Jan 31*	Toowoomba	Toowoomba _____	Lost by 5 wkts
Feb 2	Brisbane	Queensland _____	Drawn
Feb 9	Launceston	Western Australia _____	Won by 85 runs
Mar 2	Adelaide	South Australia _____	Lost by 127 runs
Mar 9	Sydney	New South Wales _____	Lost by an inns & 156 runs

* Denotes not first-class

1989/90 Tasmanian First-Class Averages

Batsman	M	Inn	NO	Runs	HS	50	100	Avrge	Ct/St
DC Boon	3	5	2	335	133*	1	2	111.67	3
G Shipperd	11	18	3	845	200*	3	3	56.33	7
MG Farrell	1	2	—	101	96	1	—	50.50	—
RJ Tucker	11	18	1	737	118	6	1	43.35	3
J Cox	11	18	—	693	175	1	3	38.50	5
GR Robertson	11	17	3	373	53	1	—	26.64	11
DM Wellham	11	17	2	375	90	2	—	25.00	3
DFG O'Connor	2	2	—	48	43	—	—	24.00	2
SG Hookey	7	13	1	258	116*	1	1	21.50	1
RJ Bennett	9	16	1	300	60	2	—	20.00	3
AJ De Winter	5	6	—	95	33	—	—	15.83	5
DR Gilbert	10	13	4	128	23*	—	—	14.22	1
TJ Cooley	5	8	4	52	17*	—	—	13.00	5
RE Soule	11	15	—	139	47	—	—	9.27	22/-
GD Campbell	7	7	2	36	11	—	—	7.20	3
PI Faulkner	1	2	—	12	12	—	—	6.00	1
PT McPhee	5	7	4	15	5*	—	—	5.00	—

Bowler	M	Overs	Mdns	Runs	Wkts	Avrge	5wi	10m	NB	W	Best
GD Campbell	7	247.5	67	561	26	21.54	1	—	9	4	6/80
DR Gilbert	10	350.1	70	1000	42	23.79	2	—	46	4	7/127
PT McPhee	5	175.0	54	413	16	25.81	1	—	3	4	5/73
RJ Tucker	11	212.5	50	569	17	33.47	—	—	5	—	3/36
GR Robertson	11	274.2	87	930	17	54.71	—	—	—	—	3/107
AJ De Winter	5	150.0	29	448	8	56.00	—	—	13	25	2/60
TJ Cooley	5	122.0	17	522	3	174.00	—	—	40	1	1/16
J Cox	11	2.0	1	6	—	—	—	—	—	—	—
MG Farrell	1	17.0	3	30	—	—	—	—	—	—	—
PI Faulkner	1	18.0	4	42	—	—	—	—	—	—	—
SG Hookey	7	1.0	—	1	—	—	—	—	—	—	—
DFG O'Connor	2	2.0	—	6	—	—	—	—	—	—	—
DM Wellham	11	4.0	1	6	—	—	—	—	—	—	—

Tasmanian First-Class Cricket Records

Opponent	Venue	First Game	Games	W	L	D	T
Australian Rep. Teams							
Australian XI's	Launceston _____	Feb 27 1926	5	—	4	1	—
	Hobart TCA _____	Mar 24 1926	7	—	4	3	—
Australian Services	Hobart TCA _____	Jan 25 1946	1	—	—	1	—
Total			13	—	8	5	—
England Teams	Hobart TCA _____	Jan 25 1904	14	—	8	6	—
	Launceston _____	Jan 29 1904	11	—	8	3	—
Total			25	—	16	9	—

Opponent	Venue	First Game	Games	W	L	D	T
Indians	Hobart TCA	Jan 10 1948	4	1	1	2	—
	Launceston	Jan 15 1948	1	—	—	1	—
Total			5	1	1	3	—
New South Wales	Sydney	Dec 12 1898	13	2	10	1	—
	Hobart TCA	Dec 30 1899	10	1	7	2	—
	Devonport	Mar 4 1978	4	—	1	3	—
	Launceston	Dec 29 1979	2	—	1	1	—
	Newcastle	Jan 15 1985	2	—	—	2	—
	Hobart Bel	Jan 26 1990	1	1	—	—	—
Total			32	4	19	9	—
New Zealanders	Hobart TCA	Dec 26 1969	1	—	—	1	—
	Launceston	Jan 12 1974	2	—	1	1	—
	Devonport	Dec 18 1987	1	—	—	1	—
Total			4	—	1	3	—
New Zealand Provinces							
Otago	Dunedin	Feb 1 1884	2	—	1	1	—
Canterbury	Christchurch	Feb 7 1884	2	—	2	—	—
Total			4	—	3	1	—
Pakistanis	Hobart TCA	Dec 15 1972	2	—	2	—	—
	Launceston	Jan 1 1982	1	—	1	—	—
Total			3	—	3	—	—
Queensland	Launceston	Feb 25 1978	5	1	1	3	—
	Brisbane	Dec 15 1978	10	—	4	6	—
	Hobart TCA	Dec 8 1979	2	—	1	1	—
	Devonport	Feb 19 1982	3	—	1	2	—
	Hobart Bel	Nov 17 1989	1	—	—	1	—
Total			21	1	7	13	—
South Australia	Adelaide	Nov 10 1877	15	1	8	6	—
	Hobart TCA	Jan 3 1957	3	—	2	1	—
	Devonport	Nov 3 1979	4	—	2	2	—
	Launceston	Feb 12 1982	4	—	2	2	—
	Hobart Bel	Nov 18 1988	1	—	—	1	—
Total			27	1	14	12	—
South Africans	Launceston	Jan 17 1911	4	—	3	1	—
	Hobart TCA	Jan 20 1911	2	—	1	1	—
Total			6	—	4	2	—
Sri Lankans	Devonport	Feb 14 1983	2	—	—	2	—
	Hobart Bel	Jan 23 1988	1	—	—	1	—
Total			3	—	—	3	—
Victoria	Launceston	Feb 11 1851	28	7	12	9	—
	South Yarra	Mar 29 1852	1	—	1	—	—
	Hobart LRG	Mar 4 1858	1	—	1	—	—
	Melbourne	Feb 12 1869	34	6	19	9	—
	East Melbourne	Jan 1 1889	1	—	1	—	—
	Hobart TCA	Jan 8 1890	25	6	13	6	—
	South Melbourne	Mar 15 1932	1	1	—	—	—
	Richmond	Mar 14 1933	1	—	1	—	—
	St Kilda	Jan 22 1957	4	—	1	3	—
	Geelong	Feb 19 1962	1	—	1	—	—
	Devonport	Jan 8 1983	4	—	1	3	—
	Carlton	Nov 15 1984	1	—	—	1	—
Total			102	20	51	31	—
Western Australia	Hobart TCA	Jan 24 1930	3	—	—	3	—
	Perth	Oct 29 1977	11	—	7	4	—
	Devonport	Jan 27 1979	4	1	3	—	—
	Launceston	Feb 17 1984	2	1	—	1	—
	Hobart Bel	Feb 6 1988	2	—	1	—	—
Total			22	2	11	9	—

Continued

331

Opponent	Venue	First Game	Games	W	L	D	T
West Indians	Launceston ———— Dec 20 1930		4	—	4	—	—
	Hobart TCA ———— Dec 24 1930		5	—	1	4	—
	Devonport———— Dec 14 1984		1	—	—	1	—
	Hobart Bel— Dec 19 1988		1	—	—	1	—
Total			11	—	5	6	—
World XI	Launceston ———— Dec 22 1971		1	—	1	—	—
Total for Tasmania			279	29	144	106	—

Most Appearances for Tasmania

Games	Player	Career
83	DC Boon	1978/79–1989/90
77	RD Woolley	1977/78–1987/88
56	SL Saunders	1979/80–1988/89
56	RE Soule	1983/84–1989/90
49	BF Davison	1979/80–1987/88
49	DJ Buckingham	1983/84–1988/89
42	PI Faulkner	1982/83–1989/90
41	M Ray	1982/83–1985/86
35	GTH James	1928/29–1945/46
35	PM Clough	1980/81–1983/84
33	ROG Morrisby	1931/32–1951/52
33	GA Hughes	1986/87–1988/89
31	RL Brown	1984/85–1986/87
30	AO Burrows	1923/24–1936/37

Youngest Players on First-Class Debut for Tasmania

Player	Date of Birth	F/Class Debut	Opponent	Venue	Age on Debut Years	Days
CL Badcock	Apr 10 1914	Feb 17 1930	Victoria	Melbourne	15	313
FE Headlam	Jun 20 1897	Mar 6 1914	Victoria	Launceston	16	259
H Hale	Mar 27 1867	Feb 1 1884	Otago	Dunedin	16	311
ROG Morrisby	Jan 12 1915	Dec 25 1931	Victoria	Hobart TCA	16	347
RE Soule	Sep 5 1966	Dec 16 1983	Pakistanis	Hobart TCA	17	102
LW Richardson	Sep 5 1911	Jan 18 1929	MCC	Hobart TCA	17	135
AC Newton	Apr 6 1894	Feb 16 1912	Victoria	Launceston	17	316
DH Thollar	Feb 13 1919	Jan 9 1937	MCC	Launceston	17	330
DC Boon	Dec 29 1960	Dec 15 1978	Queensland	Brisbane	17	351

Highest Innings Totals for Tasmania

Total	Opponent	Venue	Season
592	South Australia	Adelaide	1987/88
526	Queensland	Brisbane	1986/87
9d-507	Queensland	Brisbane	1984/85
9d-505	Queensland	Hobart TCA	1979/80
8d-487	South Australia	Adelaide	1984/85
481	Queensland	Launceston	1987/88
6d-478	Western Australia	Perth	1989/90
458	Indians	Launceston	1947/48
9d-456	New South Wales	Hobart Bel	1989/90
8d-450	Victoria	Melbourne	1983/84
8d-450	Victoria	Melbourne	1983/84
448	Victoria	Melbourne	1912/13
446	Victoria	Launceston	1930/31
436	Victoria	Hobart TCA	1911/12
429	New South Wales	Hobart TCA	1985/86
429	Victoria	Launceston	1933/34
9d-428	Victoria	Melbourne	1988/89
425	Victoria	Hobart TCA	1980/81
420	New South Wales	Hobart TCA	1899/00
8d-409	New South Wales	Newcastle	1984/85
409	Victoria	Launceston	1989/90
8d-407	Western Australia	Hobart TCA	1985/86
405	Queensland	Devonport	1981/82
405	Queensland	Brisbane	1988/89

Lowest Completed Innings Totals for Tasmania

Total	Opponent	Venue	Season
18	Victoria	Melbourne	1868/69
25	Victoria	Hobart LRG	1857/58
33	Victoria	Launceston	1857/58
36	Victoria	Melbourne	1870/71
39	Victoria	Hobart TCA	1889/90
40	Otago	Dunedin	1883/84
47	Otago	Dunedin	1883/84
48	Victoria	Melbourne	1914/15
49	New South Wales	Sydney	1910/11
50	Victoria	Melbourne	1890/91
51	Victoria	Hobart LRG	1857/58
59	Canterbury	Christchurch	1883/84
62	Victoria	Launceston	1857/58
64	Victoria	Hobart TCA	1903/04
65	Victoria	Launceston	1952/53
65	Victoria	South Yarra	1851/52
65	South Australia	Adelaide	1961/62
65	Victoria	Launceston	1948/49
66	MCC	Hobart TCA	1928/29
67	Victoria	East Melbourne	1888/89
72	South Australia	Adelaide	1877/78

Leading Batsmen for Tasmania

Batsman	Career	M	Inn	NO	Runs	HS	Avrge	100s
DC Boon	1978/79–1989/90	83	146	10	5974	227	43.93	16
RD Woolley	1977/78–1987/88	77	139	16	4488	144	36.48	7
BF Davison	1979/80–1987/88	49	88	10	3440	173	44.10	9
DJ Buckingham	1983/84–1988/89	49	85	7	2612	150	33.49	5
GA Hughes	1986/87–1988/89	33	59	2	2153	147	37.77	2
SL Saunders	1979/80–1988/89	56	78	10	1978	138*	29.09	4
M Ray	1982/83–1985/86	41	73	2	1899	94	26.75	—
ROG Morrisby	1931/32–1951/52	33	62	6	1774	130	31.68	1
PI Faulkner	1982/83–1989/90	42	65	10	1706	100	31.02	1
RJ Hawson	1898/99–1913/14	27	54	8	1705	199*	37.06	2
EJK Burn	1883/84–1909/10	25	49	4	1385	119	30.77	2
RE Soule	1983/84–1989/90	56	85	15	1348	99	19.26	—
EAC Windsor	1890/91–1911/12	24	44	1	1341	90	31.92	—
GW Goodman	1978/79–1985/86	29	51	3	1328	123	27.66	1
RJ Tucker	1988/89–1989/90	18	30	4	1285	118	49.42	1
JA Atkinson	1927/28–1933/34	22	42	5	1273	144*	34.40	2
RV Thomas	1933/34–1950/51	24	45	1	1268	125	28.81	1
CL Badcock	1929/30–1933/34	19	37	4	1267	274	38.39	4
DC Green	1924/25–1936/37	25	44	2	1265	150*	30.11	2
G Shipperd	1988/89–1989/90	20	30	5	1227	200*	49.08	4
RJ Bennett	1984/85–1989/90	27	49	4	1131	110	25.13	1
RJ Jeffrey	1979/80–1981/82	20	37	3	1128	198	33.17	2
AC Newton	1911/12–1933/34	27	49	5	1117	117	25.38	1
CJ Eady	1889/90–1907/08	19	35	2	1106	116	33.51	3
KJ Bradshaw	1984/85–1987/88	25	46	4	1083	121	28.50	2
J Hampshire	1967/68–1978/79	14	27	4	1079	147	46.91	3
AO Burrows	1923/24–1936/37	30	54	3	1043	69	20.45	—
MD Taylor	1987/88–1988/89	19	29	—	1125	216	38.79	2

Most Runs in a Season for Tasmania

Batsman	Season	M	Inn	NO	Runs	HS	50	100	Avrge
BF Davison	1983/84	11	20	4	1036	171*	4	4	64.75
MD Taylor	1987/88	12	22	—	1003	216	5	2	45.59
G Shipperd	1989/90	11	18	3	845	200*	3	3	56.33
BF Davison	1980/81	7	13	1	824	173	3	4	68.67
CL Badcock	1933/34	5	10	1	803	274	1	4	89.22
DC Boon	1987/88	7	13	1	790	143	4	3	65.83
GA Hughes	1987/88	12	22	1	754	147	4	1	35.90
RJ Tucker	1989/90	11	18	1	737	118	6	1	43.35
RD Woolley	1984/85	11	16	2	717	144	5	1	51.21
GA Hughes	1988/89	11	18	1	711	126	5	1	41.82
J Cox	1989/90	11	18	1	693	175	1	3	38.50
GA Hughes	1986/87	10	19	1	688	96	7	—	38.22
DJ Buckingham	1985/86	10	18	1	687	121	4	1	40.41
DC Boon	1982/83	12	18	1	682	115	3	2	40.12
DC Boon	1985/86	9	18	—	677	172	1	2	37.61
DJ Buckingham	1987/88	11	20	1	668	126	1	3	35.16

Continued

Batsman	Season	M	Inn	NO	Runs	HS	50	100	Avrge
DC Boon	1983/84	11	19	—	667	227	4	1	35.11
GW Goodman	1984/85	10	18	1	659	123	5	1	38.76
M Ray	1983/84	11	20	—	654	94	4	—	32.70
PI Faulkner	1983/84	11	19	6	615	84*	6	—	47.31

Highest Individual Innings for Tasmania

Score	Batsman	Opponent	Venue	Season
274	CL Badcock	Victoria	Launceston	1933/34
227	DC Boon	Victoria	Melbourne	1983/84
216	MD Taylor	South Australia	Adelaide	1987/88
200*	RB Kanhai	Victoria	Melbourne	1969/70
200*	G Shipperd	Western Australia	Perth	1989/90
199*	RJ Hawson	Victoria	Melbourne	1912/13
198	RF Jeffery	Queensland	Hobart TCA	1979/80
196	DC Boon	New South Wales	Hobart TCA	1985/86
180*	WT Walmsley	Indians	Launceston	1947/48
175	J Cox	New South Wales	Hobart Bel	1989/90
173	BF Davison	Victoria	Hobart TCA	1980/81
172	DC Boon	Queensland	Launceston	1986/87
171*	BF Davison	Victoria	Hobart TCA	1983/84
166	MD Taylor	South Australia	Devonport	1987/88
164	MR Thomas	Australian Services	Hobart TCA	1945/46
156+	BF Davison	Queensland	Brisbane	1983/84
155*	G Shipperd	Victoria	Melbourne	1988/89
152*	BF Davison	Western Australia	Perth	1983/84
150*	DC Green	Victoria	Launceston	1932/33
150	DJ Buckingham	Western Australia	Perth	1986/87

Leading Wicket-Takers for Tasmania

Bowler	Career	M	Runs	Wkts	Avrge	5wi	10m	Best
EAC Windsor	1890/91–1911/12	24	3557	126	28.23	10	3	7/95
PM Clough	1980/81–1983/84	35	3511	115	30.53	5	—	8/95
CJ Eady	1889/90–1907/08	19	2241	109	20.56	12	5	8/34
TJ Cowley	1948/49–1961/62	24	2403	76	31.62	2	1	6/55
RL Brown	1984/85–1986/87	41	3363	84	40.03	2	1	7/80
PI Faulkner	1982/83–1989/90	42	3860	83	46.51	—	—	4/37
GTH James	1928/29–1945/46	35	3169	82	38.65	2	—	6/96
AO Burrows	1923/24–1936/37	30	2251	76	29.62	3	—	5/35
DR Gilbert	1988/89–1989/90	19	2018	68	29.68	3	—	7/127
SL Saunders	1979/80–1988/89	55	3888	67	58.03	1	—	5/114
SWL Putman	1930/31–1938/39	20	2138	62	34.48	3	—	7/102
GD Campbell	1986/87–1989/90	19	1886	62	30.39	4	—	6/80
AC Newton	1911/12–1933/34	27	2215	56	39.55	—	—	4/36
LJ Nash	1929/30–1931/32	17	1630	51	31.96	3	—	7/50
PA Blizzard	1979/80–1984/85	27	4193	51	43.67	—	—	4/62

Most Wickets in a Season for Tasmania

Bowler	Season	M	Overs	Mdns	Runs	Wkts	Avrge	5wi	10m	Best
PM Clough	1983/84	11	404.5	83	1320	42	31.43	3	—	8/95
DR Gilbert	1989/90	10	350.1	70	1000	42	23.79	2	—	7/127
PM Clough	1982/83	12	414.1	91	1089	41	26.56	2	—	6/53
RL Brown	1985/86	10	384.2	62	1365	41	33.29	1	1	7/80
BP Patterson	1984/85	10	376.0	51	1359	37	36.72	2	—	5/67
FD Stephenson	1981/82	7	229.5	57	630	36	17.50	3	1	6/19
MA Holding	1982/83	9	371.4	93	946	36	26.28	2	—	7/59
GD Campbell	1988/89	11	426.0	89	1209	36	33.58	3	—	5/44
RL Brown	1984/85	10	255.4	41	1083	29	37.34	—	—	4/46
SJ Milosz	1986/87	11	362.0	66	1216	27	45.04	2	—	6/153
DR Gilbert	1988/89	9	325.1	49	1019	26	39.19	1	—	5/88
GD Campbell	1989/90	7	247.5	67	561	26	21.54	1	—	6/80
RJ McCurdy	1980/81	7	224.5	42	773	25	30.92	1	—	7/91

Best Bowling in an Innings for Tasmania

Wkts	Bowler	Opponent	Venue	Season
8/31	W Brown	Victoria	Hobart LRG	1857/58
8/34	CJ Eady	Victoria	Melbourne	1895/96
8/82	WS Hird	South Australia	Hobart TCA	1952/53
8/95	PM Clough	Western Australia	Launceston	1983/84
7/42	W Brown	Victoria	Hobart LRG	1857/58

Wkts	Bowler	Opponent	Venue	Season
7/42	H Hale	Canterbury	Christchurch	1883/84
7/50	LJ Nash	South Africans	Hobart TCA	1931/32
7/57	CJ Eady	Victoria	Melbourne	1897/98
7/59	J Simmons	Queensland	Brisbane	1978/79
7/59	MA Holding	Victoria	Devonport	1982/83
7/66	CJ Eady	Victoria	Hobart TCA	1898/99
7/72	CJ Eady	Victoria	Hobart TCA	1906/07
7/80	RL Brown	South Australia	Adelaide	1985/86
7/83	NV Diprose	Victoria	Hobart TCA	1950/51
7/95	EAC Windsor	South Africans	Hobart TCA	1910/11
7/102	SWL Putman	Victoria	Melbourne	1934/35
7/127	DR Gilbert	South Australia	Devonport	1989/90
7/128	WW Davis	Queensland	Brisbane	1985/86

Best Bowling in a Match for Tasmania

Wkts	Bowler	Opponent	Venue	Season
15/73	W Brown	Victoria	Hobart LRG	1857/58
13/185	CJ Eady	Victoria	Hobart TCA	1906/07
12/63	CJ Eady	Victoria	Melbourne	1895/96
12/129	CJ Eady	Victoria	Hobart TCA	1898/99
12/161	CJ Eady	Victoria	Melbourne	1897/98
11/99	CJ Eady	New South Wales	Hobart TCA	1904/05
11/183	RL Brown	South Australia	Adelaide	1985/86
10/46	FB Stephenson	Victoria	Melbourne	1981/82
10/92	TJ Cowley	Victoria	Launceston	1953/54
10/100	W Henty	Victoria	South Yarra	1851/52
10/169	WW Davis	Queensland	Brisbane	1985/86
10/196	EA Windsor	Victoria	Launceston	1911/12
10/204	CJ Eady	New South Wales	Hobart TCA	1899/00
10/212	EAC Windsor	South Africans	Hobart TCA	1910/11
10/226	AC Facy	Victoria	Hobart TCA	1908/09
10/244	EAC Windsor	Victoria	Melbourne	1907/08

Most Dismissals by a Wicket-Keeper for Tasmania

Wicket-Keeper	Career	M	Cght	Stmp	Total
RD Woolley	1977/78–1987/88	77	126	15	141
RE Soule	1983/84–1989/90	56	117	5	122
GC Hudson	1959/60–1961/62	8	28	6	34
CN Parry	1931/32–1933/34	15	17	15	32
PG Henty	1922/23–1928/29	7	16	8	24
N Dodds	1898/99–1907/08	12	17	6	23
J Gardiner	1935/36–1948/49	13	14	6	20

Note: RD Woolley's 141 dismissals includes 12 catches when not keeping wicket in 1985/86, 1986/87 and 1987/88.

Most Dismissals in a Season for Tasmania

Wicket-Keeper	Season	M	Cght	Stmp	Total
RD Woolley	1982/83	12	39	2	41
RD Woolley	1984/85	11	26	2	28
RE Soule	1987/88	12	25	3	28
RE Soule	1985/86	10	23	—	23
RE Soule	1986/87	11	21	2	23
RE Soule	1989/90	11	22	—	22
RE Soule	1988/89	11	21	—	21

Most Dismissals in a Match for Tasmania

Ttl	Ct	St	Wicket-Keeper	Opponent	Venue	Season
9	8	1	RE Soule	New Zealanders	Devonport	1987/88
7	5	2	PG Henty	New South Wales	Sydney	1927/28
7	7	—	RD Woolley	Sri Lankans	Devonport	1982/83
7	7	—	RD Woolley	Western Australia	Perth	1982/83

Most Dismissals in an Innings for Tasmania

Ttl	Ct	St	Wicket-Keeper	Opponent	Venue	Season
6	5	1	GC Hudson	West Indians	Launceston	1960/61
6	6	—	RE Soule	South Australia	Launceston	1986/87
5	3	2	PG Henty	New South Wales	Sydney	1927/28
5	5	—	B Brownlow	Victoria	St Kilda	1956/57

Continued

Ttl	Ct	St	Wicket-Keeper	Opponent	Venue	Season
5	5	—	RD Woolley	Western Australia	Perth	1982/83
5	5	—	RD Woolley	Queensland	Brisbane	1984/85
5	5	—	RE Soule	New South Wales	Sydney	1985/86
5	4	1	RE Soule	Western Australia	Devonport	1986/87
5	5	—	RE Soule	New Zealanders	Devonport	1987/88

Most Catches by a Fieldsman for Tasmania

Fieldsman	Career	M	Catches
DC Boon	1978/79–1988/89	83	59
M Ray	1982/83–1985/86	41	40
J Hampshire	1967/68–1978/79	14	31
SL Saunders	1979/80–1988/89	56	30
DJ Buckingham	1983/84–1988/89	49	30
AW Rushford	1922/23–1936/37	23	29
RJ Hawson	1898/99–1913/14	27	28
BF Davison	1979/80–1987/88	49	28
JA Atkinson	1927/28–1933/34	22	27
GTH James	1928/29–1945/46	35	27

Most Catches in a Season for Tasmania

Catches	Fieldsman	M	Season
16	M Ray	11	1984/85
12	RO Butcher	12	1982/83
10	M Ray	11	1983/84
10	GR Robertson	11	1989/90

Most Catches in a Match for Tasmania

Ct	Fieldsman	Opponent	Venue	Season
7	JA Atkinson	Victoria	Melbourne	1928/29
5	EE Rodwell	Victoria	Launceston	1953/54
4	DC Boon	Victoria	Hobart TCA	1980/81
4	DB Robinson (Sub)	West Indians	Hobart TCA	1981/82
4	SM Small	Victoria	St Kilda	1982/83
4	RO Butcher	New South Wales	Hobart TCA	1982/83
4	M Ray	New South Wales	Launceston	1984/85

Most Catches in an Innings for Tasmania

Ct	Fieldsman	Opponent	Venue	Season
4	JA Atkinson	Victoria	Melbourne	1928/29
4	LA Cuff	MCC	Hobart TCA	1928/29
4	EE Rodwell	Victoria	Launceston	1953/54
4	DC Boon	Victoria	Hobart TCA	1980/81
4	DB Robinson (Sub)	West Indians	Hobart TCA	1981/82
4	RO Butcher	New South Wales	Hobart TCA	1982/83

Partnership Records for Tasmania

Wkt	Ttl	Batsmen	Opponent	Venue	Season
1st	195	DC Boon, EJ Harris	Queensland	Brisbane	1986/87
2nd	210*	G Shipperd, DC Boon	Sri Lankans	Devonport	1989/90
3rd	183	RJ Hawson, DC Paton	Victoria	Hobart TCA	1908/09
4th	258	MD Taylor, DJ Buckingham	South Australia	Adelaide	1987/88
5th	176	RD Woolley, DJ Buckingham	South Australia	Adelaide	1985/86
6th	213	BF Davison, RD Woolley	South Australia	Adelaide	1980/81
7th	203*	BF Davison, PI Faulkner	Western Australia	Perth	1983/84
8th	148	BF Davison, PI Faulkner	South Australia	Adelaide	1983/84
9th	148	HC Smith, AC Newton	Victoria	Launceston	1921/22
10th	122	WG Ward, N Dodds	Victoria	Hobart TCA	1898/99

Highest Partnerships

Wkt	Ttl	Batsmen	Opponent	Venue	Season
4th	258	MD Taylor, DJ Buckingham	South Australia	Adelaide	1987/88
6th	213	BF Davison, RD Woolley	South Australia	Adelaide	1980/81
4th	212	G Shipperd, RJ Tucker	Western Australia	Perth	1989/90
2nd	210*	G Shipperd, DC Boon	Sri Lankans	Devonport	1989/90
2nd	203	RJ Hawson, DG Paton	Victoria	Hobart TCA	1911/12
7th	203*	BF Davison, PI Faulkner	Western Australia	Perth	1983/84

Wkt	Ttl	Batsmen	Opponent	Venue	Season
2nd	197	LJ Nash, DC Green	Victoria	Launceston	1930/31
1st	195	DC Boon, EJ Harris	Queensland	Brisbane	1986/87
2nd	192*	DC Boon, G Shipperd	Sri Lankans	Devonport	1989/90
4th	192	J Cox, DM Wellham	New South Wales	Hobart Bel	1989/90
6th	188	MD Taylor, PI Faulkner	South Australia	Devonport	1987/88
7th	184	JL Hudson, F Chancellor	Victoria	Hobart TCA	1908/09
3rd	183	RJ Hawson, DG Paton	Victoria	Hobart TCA	1908/09
1st	182	GW Goodman, RF Jeffery	Queensland	Hobart TCA	1979/80
3rd	181	N Jelich, GA Hughes	New South Wales	Newcastle	1986/87
5th	176	RD Woolley, DJ Buckingham	South Australia	Adelaide	1985/86
2nd	175	CL Badcock, RA Ferrall	Victoria	Launceston	1933/34
4th	175	RJ Tucker, DW Wellham	South Australia	Adelaide	1988/89
4th	174	DC Boon, BF Davison	Victoria	Hobart TCA	1980/81
7th	172*	RD Woolley, J Simmons	Western Australia	Devonport	1978/79
3rd	171	M Ray, SM Small	Pakistanis	Hobart TCA	1983/84
7th	169	KJ Bradshaw, PI Faulkner	Queensland	Brisbane	1984/85
2nd	167	G Shipperd, DC Boon	Queensland	Hobart Bel	1989/90
3rd	166	DC Boon, MD Taylor	New South Wales	Sydney	1987/88
2nd	166	G Shipperd, DC Boon	Queensland	Hobart Bel	1989/90
2nd	165	CL Badcock, RA Ferrall	Victoria	Melbourne	1933/34
2nd	163	CJ Eady, AJ Douglas	Victoria	Hobart TCA	1894/95
1st	163	RV Thomas, ROG Morrisby	Victoria	Melbourne	1937/38
5th	158	DC Boon, DA Smith	South Australia	Devonport	1979/80
2nd	154	CWB Martin, HO Smith	South Africans	Launceston	1910/11
3rd	154	JS Wilkinson, SJ Howard	MCC.C.	Hobart TCA	1974/75
1st	150	GW Goodman, M Ray	West Indians	Devonport	1984/85

Toowoomba v Tasmania
Not First-Class
Gold Park, Toowoomba
Jan 31 1990
Result: Toowoomba won by 5 wkts

Tasmania

Batsman	How Out	Ttl
RJ Bennett	not out	103
SG Hookey	c Staff b Dennis	15
MG Farrell	c Staff b Teys	0
DM Wellham (c)	c Staff b Teys	3
RJ Tucker	c Walls b Brunner	22
RE Soule (+)	b Black	38
GR Robertson	c Staff b Teys	1
G Shipperd	b Teys	1
GD Campbell	not out	7
DR Gilbert	did not bat	
PT McPhee	did not bat	
SUNDRIES: B. 6 LB. 6 W. 8 NB. 2		22
TOTAL	7 wkts for 212	

F/W: 26 27 35 81 176 179 185

Bowler	O	M	R	Wkts
Teys	10	2	37	4
Dennis	10	—	47	1
Farquharson	3	—	16	—
Brunner	7	1	29	1
Ryle	10	—	43	—
Black	10	—	28	1
Overs:	50.0			

Toowoomba

Batsman	How Out	Ttl
R Staff	c Hookey b Campbell	4
N Fowler	c Bennett b Campbell	3
L Mason	run out	51

Continued

Batsman	How Out	Ttl
I Walls	c Shipperd b Robertson	54
B Spanner	not out	48
M Ryle	c Tucker b Farrell	27
P Teys	not out	6
R Dennis	did not bat	
A Farquharson	did not bat	
R Brunner	did not bat	
I Black	did not bat	
SUNDRIES: B. 1 LB. 8 W. 4 NB. 8		21
TOTAL	5 wkts for 214	

F/W: 9 12 113 135 198

Bowler	O	M	R	Wkts
McPhee	9	1	28	—
Campbell	4	—	11	2
Gilbert	4	—	16	1
Robertson	11	1	48	1
Farrell	10	1	49	1
Hookey	2	—	11	—
Tucker	6	1	38	—
Soule	3	—	4	—
Overs:	46.3			

HOBART CRICKET

Clarence won the first-grade competition for the third year in a row and did it convincingly, finishing a clear points leader after the qualifying rounds and defeating New Town in the semi-final and Brighton in the final. Indeed, this was Clarence's seventh win in nine seasons since 1981-82. (Its two unsuccessful seasons since then were 1985-86 and 1986-87, when University won.) Based on the eastern shore of the Derwent River, Clarence is the club in the Hobart competition most closely approximating a district club, and it appears to have drawn strength from having a home base. It managed to win this season despite being without two leading players, Greg Shipperd and Greg Campbell, for much of the season while they were playing for Tasmania or, in Campbell's case, Australia. Two other Clarence players made appearances for Tasmania—Peter McPhee, who got into the State side half-way through the season, and Allister de Winter.

The losing finalist, Brighton, was competing in the competition for only the third season, so it did well to advance as far as it did. It finished third on the table behind South Hobart-Sandy Bay, also in its third season, which was generally expected to beat Brighton in the semi-final. This semi-final was therefore generally a disappointing match for South Hobart-Sandy Bay, not least because two of its key batsmen, Dirk Wellham and Don O'Connor, were out without scoring. The fourth semi-finalist, New Town, could console itself with the knowledge that it had now advanced to the semi-finals for the fourth time in four years. New Town's leading player, Rod Tucker, was absent on Sheffield Shield duty for most of the season.

The Clarence all-rounder Andrew Dykes topped the batting averages with the help of five not outs, scoring 436 runs at 87.20.

Dykes, who is only eighteen years old, scored two centuries. The highest batting aggregate was recorded by Alan Simpson of Brighton, a Number 3 batsman who scored 686 runs at 62.36. A Clarence player topped the bowling averages, too—Peter McPhee, who took 35 wickets at 18.51 before he was promoted to the Tasmanian side. McPhee and North Hobart's left-arm orthodox spinner Tony Judd, who also took 35 wickets, were the leading wicket-takers in the competition.

The TCA medal was won by Neil Lenham of Brighton.

Points Table at end of qualifying rounds

Clarence	57
South Hobart-Sandy Bay	51
Brighton	51
New Town	51
Glenorchy	45
North Hobart	39
University	33
Kingborough	9

Semi-Finals

Brighton 6 for 221 (Alan Simpson 72, Rod Rehlberg 54) defeated South Hobart-Sandy Bay 220 (Stuart Saunders 49, Nick Allanby 44; Don Gardner 3/40).

Clarence 210 (Allister de Winter 81, Andrew Dykes 31; Andrew Saballus 3/51, Keith Bradshaw 3/33) defeated New Town 158 (Keith Bradshaw 57, Roly Hyatt 40; Peter McPhee 5/61, Allister de Winter 4/73).

FINAL

Clarence v Brighton
Bellerive Oval, Hobart
March 24-25, 1990
Result: Clarence won by 106 runs

Clarence outplayed Brighton on both days of the match and, accordingly, had a comfortable win. Batting first, Clarence looked in some difficulty at 5 for 110, but Duncan Hurd (83) and Andrew Dykes (64), both teenagers, restored the innings with a partnership of 122, and Clarence went on to make 9 for 301 in 112 overs, its maximum allowance. Brighton's innings began so badly that before it was a half-hour old any hope Brighton had of winning the match had all but faded. It lost wickets in the second, third and sixth overs to be 3 for 11. Mick Peters (69) and Scott Direen (36 not out) staged a brief recovery with a seventh wicket partnership of 64, but this merely delayed the ultimate result. Brighton was all out for 195, and for this the Clarence pace bowler Peter McPhee deserved much of the credit. McPhee took 8 wickets for 50, the best figures of his career.

Clarence

Batsman	How Out	Ttl
B Patterson	c Lenham b Gardner	33
P Schofield	b Wylie	5
G Shipperd	b Gardner	34
G Cooney	c Peters b Wylie	2
A de Winter	c and b Pears	18
A Dykes	b Conlan	64
D Hurd	c Paice b Conlan	83
M Lee	c Wylie b Conlan	10
G Campbell	not out	27
M Colegrave	c Lenham b Conlan	8
Sundries		17
Total		9 for 301

F/W: 10 65 83 85 110 232 259 268 297

Bowler	O	M	R	Wkts
D Gardner	31	10	81	2
W Wylie	27	7	71	2
R Pears	25	9	44	1
N Lenham	19	6	56	0
A Conlan	10	2	36	4

Brighton

Batsman	How Out	Ttl
N Lenham	c Campbell b McPhee	2
R Fehlberg	c de Winter b Colegrave	22
A Simpson	lbw b Campbell	2
P Rogers	c de Winter b McPhee	2
M Peters	lbw McPhee	69
R Pears	c Campbell b McPhee	14
R Paice	c Lee b McPhee	4
S Direen	not out	36
A Conlan	c Lee b McPhee	7
D Gardner	c Schofield b McPhee	14
W Wylie	b McPhee	0
Sundries		23
Total		195

F/W: 3 6 11 50 88 92 156 171 195 195

Bowler	O	M	R	Wkts
G Campbell	26	5	72	1
P McPhee	24	7	50	8
A de Winter	4	0	17	0
M Colegrave	19	5	49	1
A Dykes	1	0	1	0

Batting Averages—First Grade

Batsman	Inns	NO	Runs	Avge
Andrew Dykes (Clarence)	10	5	436	87.20
Alan Simpson (Brighton)	13	2	686	62.36
Roger Woolley (Clarence)	8	2	349	58.17
Don O'Connor (Sth Hobart-S Bay)	11	1	518	51.80
Glenn Cobern (Glenorchy)	13	3	517	51.70
Roger Hughes (Glenorchy)	14	1	659	50.69
Allister de Winter (Clarence)	9	0	430	47.78
Gavin Shaw (University)	14	2	561	46.75
Neil Lenham (Brighton)	11	0	492	44.73
Phillip Kingston (Kingborough)	14	2	497	41.42
Stuart Saunders (Sth Hobart-S Bay)	13	2	446	40.54

▶

Bowler	O	R	Wkts	Avge
Peter McPhee (Clarence)	268.3	648	35	18.51
Colin Jones (Sth Hobart-S Bay)	189.4	534	27	19.78
Mark Alexander (University)	185.4	439	22	19.99
Chris Broadby (Glenorchy)	205	497	23	21.61
Martin Bowerman (Glenorchy)	225.1	598	27	22.15
Tim Bower (Glenorchy)	199.4	539	24	22.46
Anthony Judd (North Hobart)	329.3	831	35	23.74
Geoff Rowlands (New Town)	202.2	481	20	24.05
Donald Gardner (Brighton)	324	799	32	24.97
Roland Hyatt (New Town)	211	518	20	25.90

NORTHERN TASMANIA CRICKET

FIRST GRADE

Launceston won the First Grade trophy for the second season in succession, after finishing only fourth on the points table at the end of the pennant matches. The season thus ended on a high note for Launceston, but on a most disappointing note for South Launceston, the club which dominated the competition throughout the season. Until it was beaten in the last of the pennant matches by Westbury, South Launceston had gone right through the season undefeated, and it easily topped the competition table, 11 points clear of the runner-up, Mowbray. But in the semi-final it came up against Launceston and was beaten easily. Mowbray won the other semi-final, defeating Westbury, only to go down to Launceston by 7 wickets in the final.

It was not by chance that Launceston found its best form when it did. The return to the side of Richard Bennett, who had been absent on Sheffield Shield duty for much of the season, certainly strengthened the batting, as Bennett demonstrated in the final. But perhaps the most important factor was the depth of experience of the Launceston players—especially‘former first-class players such as Bennett, Peter Faulkner, David Smith and Gary Goodman—which enabled them to perform at their best when it counted. In the semi-final match, Faulkner made a century and Smith 61, while in the final Goodman took 5 wickets for 32 with his off-spin and Bennett made 68, Smith 36 and Goodman 50 not out. Goodman was the side's most successful bowler during the season, taking 18 wickets at 18.00, while its most successful pace bowler was Paul McShane.

South Launceston's success was built on its strength of batting, the leading performers being Bruce Cruse, who easily topped the competition averages with 464 runs at 66.28, Michael Farrell, Robby Knight and Shaun Young. Young was the competition's outstanding all-rounder during the season, finishing third in the batting averages with 476 runs at 47.60 and, as a medium-fast bowler, fifth in the bowling averages with 24 wickets at 23.46. Accordingly, he won NTCA's best player award, finishing a long way ahead in the points list. He also won the prestigious 'Century Club Award'.

Mowbray had an effective bowling attack led by the fast bowler Troy Cooley, the runner-up in the competition's bowling averages, and the medium-fast bowler Scott Plummer, who was fourth in the averages. Its principal batsmen were Nick Hayes, Nick Sellers and Paul Barrow. Westbury was fortunate to have in its attack the most successful bowler of the competition, the medium-pacer Paul Goldberg, who topped both the aggregates and averages with 34 wickets at 12.68. Originally from Victoria, Goldberg bowled with skill and was consistently accurate. He was supported in the Westbury attack by the pace bowlers Shane Marsland and David Coe and the spinner Michael Claxton. One of three brothers in the Westbury team, Claxton was an outstanding all-rounder, finishing third in the points table for the best player award. He opened the batting with his brother Graeme, while the other brother, Paul, was a wicket-keeper-batsman. (A fourth brother, Steve, played as a batsman for Launceston.) Westbury's other leading batsman was Jeff Garwood, who scored 439 runs at an average of 48.78, finishing behind only South Launceston's Bruce Cruse in the competition batting averages.

First Grade Points Table

Club	Batting	Bowling	Win	Total
South Launceston	24.84	17.60	55.50	97.94
Mowbray	19.93	17.00	50.00	86.93
Westbury	18.86	20.60	42.00	81.46
Launceston	19.05	18.40	38.00·	75.45
Riverside	20.73	14.80	18.50	54.03
Old Scotch	21.36	14.80	10.00	46.16

SEMI-FINALS—FIRST GRADE

Mowbray 4/228 (P Barron 84*, C Laskey 45, M Sellers 24; S Marsland 2/34) defeated Westbury 166 (S Marsland 26, M Ewington 25; S Plummer 5/66, P Cunningham 2/45)

Launceston 5/310 (P Faulkner 115, D Smith 61, A Belsak 32, M Davy 32*, T Coyle 29*; D Castle 2/84) defeated South Launceston 146 (B Cruse 51, S Young 28, B Young 22; P McShane 4/26, W Squires 2/26)

FINAL—FIRST GRADE

Launceston v Mowbray
Launceston Cricket Ground, Launceston
March 10, 11 and 17, 1990
Toss: Mowbray
Result: Launceston won by 7 wickets

Mowbray's captain, Mick Sellers, won the toss and chose to bat on a pitch which seemed likely to play slowly. The openers, Sellers and Paul Barron, got the side off to a promising start, but the two departed in fairly quick succession, Sellers when the total was on 72 and Barron when it was 78 and thereafter Mowbray's batting seemed to lose its direction. The batsmen struggled against the accurate spin bowling of Gary Goodman, in particular. At stumps on the first day Mowbray was in trouble at 7 for 158. Because of overnight rain, play on the second day was delayed by 201 minutes and at stumps Mowbray had been dismissed for 181, a much smaller total than it seemed likely to compile earlier. Goodman's figures were a measure of his dominance over the batsmen—5 wickets for 32 runs in 46 overs. In reply Launceston had lost 1 for 86 with Richard Bennett not out on 33. On the third day play continued until Launceston had reached 3 for 192 at lunch when it was agreed by the two captains that there was no point in playing on. Richard Bennett batted steadily and was still there on 68 when Launceston levelled the scores at 181. Before the winning run was scored, however, he was ruled caught and bowled by Sellers. Gary Goodman was undefeated on 50, a fine performance on top of his outstanding bowling. Launceston thus won the match on the first innings by 7 wickets.

Mowbray
First Innings

Batsman	How Out	Ttl
P Barron	c Bennett b Goodman	25
M Sellers (c)	c Belsak b Goodman	45
P Smits	c Faulkner b Goodman	6
C Laskey	c Belsak b Palmer	15
N Hayes	lbw b Palmer	0
R Ponting	c Davy b Goodman	10
P Swindells	c and b Goodman	17
D Price	b McShane	30
S O'Byrne	b Faulkner	10
S Plummer	c Butler b Faulkner	4
P Cunningham	not out	6
Sundries: B2, LB8, W2, NB1		13
Total		181

F/W: 72 78 95 96 101 115 130 161 169 181

Bowler	O	M	R	Wkts
P Faulkner	32.3	11	50	2
P McShane	10	4	32	1
M Butler	11	6	15	0
G Goodman	46	29	32	5
S Palmer	27	10	42	2

Launceston
First Innings

Batsman	How Out	Ttl
R Bennett	c and b Sellers	68
S Claxton	c Sellers b Hayes	21
D Smith	b Sellers	36
G Goodman	not out	50
A Belsak	not out	2
Sundries: B9, LB2, W2, NB2		15
Total		3 for 192

F/W: 33 116 181

Bowler	O	M	R	Wkts
S Plummer	10	1	26	0
S O'Byrne	5	0	33	0
P Cunningham	26	11	40	0
N Hayes	16	2	52	1
M Sellers	18	8	17	2
D Price	3	1	13	0

Umpires P Griffin and P Clark

▶

Batting Averages—First-Grade *(pennant matches only)*

Batsman	Inns	NO	HS	Runs	Avge
B Cruse (South Launceston)	11	4	115°	464	66.28
J Garwood (Westbury)	11	2	122	439	48.78
S Young (South Launceston)	10	0	179	476	47.60
T Coyle (Launceston)	9	4	71	220	44.00
D Cash (Old Scotch)	10	0	100	418	41.80
R Bennett (Launceston)	7	0	103	290	41.43
P Faulkner (Launceston)	8	2	85°	234	39.00
M Claxton (Westbury)	11	0	85	426	38.73
P Freeland (Old Scotch)	12	1	121	399	36.27
N Hayes (Mowbray)	7	1	127°	213	35.50

Bowling Averages—First-Grade *(pennant matches only)*

Bowler	Best	Overs	Mdns	Runs	Wkts	Avge
P Goldberg (Westbury)	6/32	193	43	431	34	12.68
T Cooley (Mowbray)	7/34	139	24	324	24	13.50
G Goodman (Launceston)	5/54	159.1	38	360	20	18.00
S Plummer (Mowbray)	5/37	179.4	31	548	24	22.83
S Young (South Launceston)	4/74	200.3	42	563	24	23.46
P Martin (South Launceston)	5/45	194.5	46	555	21	26.43
R Heit (Old Scotch)	5/63	191.4	28	599	20	29.95

Examiner-Island State Credit Union Points—First-Grade

S Young (South Launceston)	194
B Cruse (South Launceston)	139
M Claxton (Westbury)	136
G Goodman (Launceston)	123
P Goldberg (Westbury)	117
P Faulkner (Launceston)	116
W Kirkman (Riverside)	115
T Cooley (Mowbray)	110
J Garwood (Westbury)	108
N Courtney (Riverside)	106
P Freeland (Old Scotch)	104
M Farrell (South Launceston)	103
D Cash (Old Scotch)	101

Highest Batting Aggregate—*First Grade:* S Young (South Launceston) 476

Highest Bowling Aggregate—*First Grade:* P Goldberg (Westbury) 34

Most Catches—*First Grade:* P Claxton (Westbury) 19

Most Stumpings—*First Grade:* P Claxton (Westbury) 2, M Quill (South Launceston) 2, T Coyle (Launceston) 2.

Centuries—First Grade

Batsman	Runs
S Young (South Launceston)	179
N Hayes (Mowbray)	127°
J Garwood (Westbury)	122
P Freeland (Old Scotch)	121
P Barron (Mowbray)	119
B Johncock (Riverside)	119
B Cruse (South Launceston)	115°
J Garwood (Westbury)	110°
P Smits (Mowbray)	104°
R Bennett (Launceston)	103
D Cash (Old Scotch)	100

SECOND GRADE

SEMI-FINALS
Old Scotch 143 (T Saunders 55; S Rose 5/33, D Williams 3/44) and
202 (S Dunstone 71, J Focken 55; D Williams 3/61, S Rose 3/63)
defeated Launceston 121 (S Palmer 38, S Rose 27°; J Humphreys
5/34, S Dunstone 2/24, D McLarty 2/47) and 6 for 50 (J Humphreys
2/17, D McLarty 2/19) on the first innings.

South Launceston 205 (T Styles 44, C Smith 44, R Jacobson 34, A
Gower 21; S Willox 3/37, S Pedder 2/36, T Veerman 2/44) defeated
Riverside 167 (M Town 61, D Sing 20; A Gower 4/44, C Shaw 4/45,
C Smith 2/38) on the first innings.

FINAL
Old Scotch v South Launceston, Coca Cola Ground, Launceston,
March 10, 11 and 17, 1989. Old Scotch 257 (T Saunders 110, J Wright
39, J Humphreys 31°; R Jacobson 6/26, C Shaw 2/67) and 236
(C Gifford 47, J Woolcock 46°, S Dunstone 41; S Evans 5/76, A Gower
4/80) defeated South Launceston 172 (D Lord 43, S Denmead 36,
A Gower 35; S Dunstone 4/43, J Humphreys 2/57, D McLarty 2/63)
and 265 (J Trueman 53, T Styles 53, S Denmead 47, R Jones 37;
S Dunstone 4/72, J Wicks 2/40) by 56 runs.

Batting Averages: S Dunstone (Old Scotch) 376 runs at 188.00, M Davy
(Launceston) 224 runs at 74.67, B Lynch (South Launceston) 282 runs
at 56.40, M Towns (Riverside) 209 runs at 41.80, D Santamaria (Old
Scotch) 235 runs at 39.17, S Palmer (Launceston) 302 runs at 37.75,
R Jones (South Launceston) 378 runs at 34.36.

Bowling Averages: C Smith (South Launceston) 20 wickets at 13.40,
L Walsh (Mowbray) 23 wickets at 14.09, A Gower (South Launceston)
22 wickets at 17.09, S Rose (Launceston) 26 wickets at 17.65, S
Matthews (Launceston) 24 wickets at 17.96, D Houise (Riverside)
20 wickets at 18.75.

NTCA Best Player Award: S Dunstone (Old Scotch) 149 points

THIRD GRADE

FINAL
Riverside White v Riverside Blue, Fosters Park, Launceston, March
10 and 17, 1989. Riverside Blue 9 for 337 (P Fulton 148, G McCulloch
48, J Stedman 46; I Lockett 3/67, M Cocker 3/71) defeated Riverside
White 143 (M Cocker 40, T Martin 29, A Norris 20; G McCulloch
5/65, P Galvin 3/22) on the first innings.

Batting Averages: G Blunderstone (Riverside Blue) 241 runs at 80.33,
D O'Byrne (Old Scotch) 405 runs at 67.50, B Robertson (Launceston)
301 runs at 50.17, G Clayton (Launceston) 281 runs at 46.83, T Walters
(Riverside White) 440 runs at 44.00, A Dillon (South Launceston)
452 runs at 41.00.

Bowling Averages: A Shaw (Riverside Blue) 21 wickets at 13.33, P Linger (South Launceston) 26 wickets at 13.42, S Bugg (South Launceston) 33 wickets at 14.27, B Lynch (Mowbray No. 2) 28 wickets at 16.25, M Jackson (Launceston) 31 wickets at 16.48.

NTCA Best Player Award: T Walters (Riverside White) 166 points.

NORTH-WESTERN TASMANIA CRICKET

Devonport was entitled to feel disappointed at not making the A grade final, for it had been on top of the competition table throughout the season. Wynyard defeated Devonport in one semi-final, and Sheffield defeated Ulverstone in the other. In the final, contested at Devonport in the final week of March, Sheffield defeated Wynyard by 21 runs in a low-scoring match, thereby winning its first premiership since the season of 1957-58.

For the first time, only six clubs competed in the competition, two fewer than in previous years. This was because, first, the East Devonport club had folded and, second, Burnie, the defending champion, had joined with Yeoman to form the club Burnie Yeoman. The amalgamation brought together two of the competition's most successful clubs. They had shared the premiership between them for the previous three years, and Yeoman had won it no fewer than seven times in the previous thirteen years. The disappearance of the East Devonport club, apparently because of a shortage of players, was regrettable, and it reflected the difficulty clubs experienced generally in maintaining the game at its previous levels. There was some cause for optimism in the fact that a junior coaching program was begun in schools in the north-west of the state in 1990. The program is being run by Warren Hegg, the Lancashire professional who has now had his third season with Sheffield.

Danny Buckingham of Burnie Yeoman topped the A grade batting averages with 840 runs at an average of 70.00. Baden Sharman, at fifty years the oldest registered player in the competition, topped the bowling averages, taking 18 wickets at 14.28. Wayne Stewart of Devonport had the best wicketkeeper's figures—19 catches and 10 stumpings for a total of 29 dismissals. He was followed by Warren Hegg—22 catches and 6 stumpings for a total of 28 dismissals.

Points Table

Club	
Devonport	191
Sheffield	171
Ulverstone	166
Wynyard	159
Burnie Yeoman	151
Latrobe	80

FINAL

Sheffield v Wynyard
Devonport Oval, Devonport
March 24-25 and 31, 1990
Result: Sheffield won outright by 21 runs

On a pitch of doubtful quality, both sides made low first innings scores on the opening weekend. Wynyard won the toss and asked Sheffield to bat, and its bowlers did all that was expected of them, dismissing Sheffield for 98. Only two batsmen reached double figures—Tim Irvine (15) and the captain, Baden Sharman (26). Wynyard's medium-pacer Brett Lee caused Sheffield its biggest problems, dismissing five of its top seven batsmen for 42 runs. Wynyard's batsmen, when they began their innings on the first afternoon, found the conditions just as difficult, and at stumps were 5 for 61. Next day, the collapse continued until Wynyard was all out for 96, the top scorer being Anthony Kinch with 18. The pace bowler Craig Boutcher finished with 6 for 49 and Dion Smith with 4 for 43. Sheffield batted again and by stumps on the second day was all out for 151, Tony Brown having held the batting together with a fine innings of 51, supported by Tim Irvine (24) and Terry Sharman (24). Thus, Wynyard began its second innings on the following weekend needing 154 to win. Wynyard lost its first wicket for 0, and although a partnership of 38 between Adrian Saltmarsh (19) and Anthony Kinch (13) revived its hopes briefly the loss of wickets continued, and Wynyard was all out for 132. Claye Young alone managed to resist for long, scoring 37 not out. Boutcher took 3 for 64 for a total of 9 wickets in the match, Dion Smith 4 for 54 and Gary Spillane 2 for 8. Sheffield thus won the match by 21.

In this keenly contested match there were incidents—one, the run out of the Wynyard batsman Kinch as he was backing up and the other a pushing incident which resulted in one player being reported.

Sheffield

Batsman	First Innings How Out	Ttl	Second Innings How Out	Ttl
T Irvine	b Lee	15	c Dixon b Kinch	24
S Wootton	b Lee	2	c Saltmarsh b Walker	3
W Hegg	c Hall b Kinch	9	lbw b Walker	2
T Brown	b Kinch	0	c Hall b Hills	51
J Maddox	c Kinch b Lee	9	c Dixon b Kinch	0
J Stevenson	b Young	4	c Allen b Young	6
T Sharman	b Lee	4	b Hills	24
B Sharman	c Young b Walker	26	c and b Hills	6
C Boutcher	c Walker b Young	1	not out	8
G Spillane	not out	7	b Hills	15
D Smith	b Lee	2	run out	0
Sundries		19		12
Total		98		151

F/W: 13 30 30 30 42 49 62 67 80 98 — F/W: 5 7 37 39 50 96 108 123 150 151

Bowler	O	M	R	Wkts	Bowler	O	M	R	Wkts
Young	17	4	25	2	Young	22	5	52	1
Lee	26	10	42	5	Lee	9	4	31	0
Kinch	4	1	10	2	Kinch	6	2	16	2
Walker	5	3	6	1	Walker	9	4	15	2
					Odgers	1	0	1	0
					Hills	13	6	30	4

Wynyard

First Innings				*Second Innings*		
Batsman	*How Out*		*Ttl*	*How Out*		*Ttl*
A Saltmarsh	b Smith		1	hit wkt b Smith		19
A Kinch	c Irvine b Boutcher		18	run out		13
J Kinch	c Hegg b Smith		0	lbw b Spillane		12
A Hall	c Hegg b Boutcher		10	b Smith		0
L Allen	c Hegg b Boutcher		17	lbw b Boutcher		7
S Hills	c. Irvine b Boutcher		0	c Hegg b Smith		1
C Young	b Boutcher		19	not out		37
S Walker	c Brown b Smith		1	c Irvine b Boutcher		17
B Lee	c Brown b Smith		0	b Boutcher		0
A Dixon	c. Hegg b Boutcher		11	c Hegg b Smith		0
D Odgers	not out		4	lbw b Spillane		5
Sundries			15			21
Total			96			132

F/W: 19 19 34 45 45 66 71 77 81 96

F/W: 0 38 54 56 62 74 96 106 108 132

Bowler	O	M	R	Wkts	Bowler	O	M	R	Wkts
Boutcher	26	10	49	6	Boutcher	19	3	64	3
Smith	24	9	43	4	Smith	15	2	54	4
Sharman	3	0	2	0	Spillane	3.5	0	8	2

Batting Averages 1989-90

Batsman	*Inns*	*NO*	*Runs*	*HS*	*Avge*
D Buckingham (Burnie Yeoman)	13	1	840	159	70.00
A Saltmarsh (Wynyard)	14	2	614	103*	51.17
J Pearce (Ulverstone)	15	1	624	122	44.57
L Allen (Wynyard)	14	3	477	93	43.36
W Hegg (Sheffield)	14	—	537	93	38.36
S Walker (Wynyard)	13	2	390	102	35.45
S Smith (Latrobe)	16	—	544	124	34.00
D Squibb (Devonport)	12	—	399	79	33.25
J Maddox (Sheffield)	13	2	357	76*	32.45
T Irvine (Sheffield)	14	1	418	100*	32.15

Bowling Averages 1989-90

Bowler	*O*	*M*	*R*	*Wkts*	*Avge*
B Sharman (Sheffield)	118.1	48	257	18	14.28
M O'Shea (Burnie Yeoman)	177.3	32	517	31	16.68
B Perry (Burnie Yeoman)	164	31	509	29	17.55
D Mullett (Devonport)	175.2	62	359	20	17.95
C Ayers (Devonport)	162	48	455	25	18.20
C Boutcher (Sheffield)	282.1	51	927	49	18.92
D Smith (Sheffield)	217	44	630	32	19.69
M Maney (Devonport)	206.2	48	511	25	20.44
P Mancell (Burnie Yeoman)	194.2	49	492	23	21.39
A Murphy (Ulverstone)	269.1	57	832	38	21.89

A RESERVE GRADE

Burnie Yeoman won the final against Ulverstone with unexpected ease, losing only three wickets while compiling the winning total of 300. The two teams, placed second and fourth respectively on the final points table, played the final at Latrobe over three days— March 24, 25 and 31. Ulverstone won the toss and chose to bat on a well-made pitch at Latrobe. It lost its first wicket when the score was 3, but S Platt (43), B Lyell (59) and Barry Beard (43) consolidated the innings, and later a fine innings of 71 not out by Scott Pearce enabled Ulverstone to compile 298, which at the time seemed possibly a winning total. Burnie Yeoman began its reply badly, losing its first wicket at 15, but by stumps on the second day Richard Ellings and David Bloomfield had advanced the score to 133 without further loss. There were still 166 runs to get, however, and Ulverstone appeared to be still in contention when the match resumed on the following Saturday. But Ellings and Bloomfield carried on where they had left off. Both made centuries, and when Ellings was eventually out Rod Jones came to the wicket and hit a brisk 57. At the end, Bloomfield remained 114 not out.

Burnie Yeoman 3 for 300 (D Bloomfield 114*, R Ellings 103, R Jones 57) defeated Ulverstone 298 (S Pearce 71*, B Lyell 59, S Platt 43, B Beard 43, D Clarke 19; S Johnstone 5/111, J Rubock 2/47)

Points Table

Club

Club	
Sheffield	185
Burnie Yeoman	156
Wynyard	147
Ulverstone	142
Devonport	118
Latrobe	86

Robert Ellings of Burnie Yeoman topped the batting averages by scoring 295 runs at 59.00, while Leon Duff of Sheffield headed the batting aggregates with 426 runs at 47.33. Don Pearce of Ulverstone headed the bowling averages with 21 wickets at 14.62. The leading wicket-taker was James Bramich of Latrobe, who took 25 wickets at 15.32.

WESTERN
AUSTRALIA

WESTERN AUSTRALIA WAS the Sheffield Shield's defending champion, and when the season got under way it had every reason to feel confident of winning the competition again. The Western Australians had had a successful Indian tour in September, and in late October they had beaten New South Wales in the opening inter-state match of the season, a one-day FAI Insurance Cup fixture. Yet from the opening of the Sheffield Shield season Western Australia was a side in trouble. As late as mid-February, it was running a bad last in the competition with just 2 points from seven matches—an extraordinary situation for a team to find itself after winning the Shield three seasons in a row. At this point, however, Western Australia suddenly regained its old strength and peeled off outright victories over the two teams which ultimately contested the final of the competition, Queensland and New South Wales. Then, at the end of March, it won the FAI Insurance Cup, easily defeating South Australia.

How had a team with so much obvious ability done so badly for so long? The controversy over the captaincy was cited as a destabilising factor, although it is impossible to say to what extent it affected the team's performances. Graeme Wood, who had led Western Australia to three consecutive Sheffield Shield victories, was captain again, but, in the words of a media release issued by the Western Australian Cricket Association, a 'deterioration in relations' between him and his players had arisen in the previous summer and had come to head this season. The upshot was that Wood was replaced as captain at the end of January and dropped from the team altogether two weeks later.

A more direct cause of the side's poor performance was the series of injuries which beset its bowlers. Chris Matthews, the side's key player in recent seasons, missed a large part of the season because of a number of muscle strains. Peter Capes, too, was recovering from a back injury and did not regain peak fitness until late in the season. Bruce Reid was the most severely affected of all; his back injury kept him out of the state side altogether, although he did play a few games for his club. Moreover, Western Australia was no less disadvantaged than other states by the loss of players to the Australian side. Terry Alderman, Geoff Marsh and Tom Moody were absent most of the season, and Mike Veletta missed several matches, too.

Matthews was the team's outstanding bowler. His figures in the last four Sheffield Shield matches were 3 for 56 and 3 for 35 against Tasmania, 3 for 49 and 3 for 54 against Queensland, 6 for 81 and 1 for 41 against New South Wales, and 0 for 64 and 1 for 29 against Victoria. The important thing about Matthews from the Western Australian viewpoint was not that he was a good, reliable bowler but that he was a potential match-winner—a bowler capable of turning a match around by suddenly taking a number of quick wickets—and he demonstrated this most dramatically in the match against Pakistan in late December, when he took 7 for 22 in 8.3 overs. Pakistan was dismissed for 75 in that innings, later losing the match by an innings, and no doubt some of the Pakistanis wondered afterwards why Matthews was not in stronger contention for the national side than he appeared to be.

Tom Hogan generally bowled well without achieving the results he would have liked, one of his problems being, apparently, that he tends not to perform at his best on his home ground in Perth. Bruce Yardley attracted a good deal of interest by his comeback to first-class cricket at the age of forty-two, but following some initial success, particularly in the match against New Zealand in November, in which he took 5 wickets, he was unable to hold his place in the side. Late in the season, against Tasmania in mid-February, the young pace bowler Chris Mack was brought back from the Cricket Academy in Adelaide to make his first-class debut. Mack took a wicket with the tenth ball he bowled, and in this and subsequent appearances for Western Australia showed sufficient promise to suggest he is likely to be a force in the Western Australian attack for seasons to come.

Geoff Marsh headed the batting averages for the season, although this was largely because of one innings—his 355 not out against South Australia at Perth in December. Marsh broke two records with this innings. His score was the highest ever made by a Western Australian in any first-class match, and his partnership of 431 with Mike Veletta, who scored 150, was the highest opening stand in Shield history. Taking the season as a whole, though, Wayne Andrews was certainly the team's most consistent producer of runs, even if his batting style often seemed unorthodox. Mike Veletta played several big innings, although it cannot be said he batted consistently. Of the younger batsmen, Mark McPhee and James Brayshaw batted well later in the season, McPhee making a century against Queensland in February and Brayshaw an 80 against Victoria in March, the last match of the season. Brendan Julian, who joined the team from the Cricket Academy in Adelaide for the fourth last match, did not have enough opportunity to make an impression. One player who did have a disappointing season with the bat was Tim Zoehrer, who showed poor form until the very last match of the season, when he made a century. Zoehrer's wicketkeeping, though, was generally of a high standard.

TOUR OF INDIA
September, 1989

The team for this brief tour was: G Wood (captain), T Moody, M Veletta, W Andrews, P Capes, C Matthews, T Hogan, K MacLeay, B Yardley, A Mullally, J Brayshaw, S Russell. Other members of the touring party were: Brian Kakich (manager), Daryl Foster (coach) and Anita Avery (physiotherapist).

Date	Venue	Opponent	Result
Sep 10*	Coimbatore	Tamil Nadu Cricket Asscn	Lost by 10 runs
Sep 12*	Bangalore	Karnataka State Cricket Asscn	Lost by 7 wkts
Sep 15	Madras	Tamil Nadu	Drawn
Sep 17*	Madras	Tamil Nadu	Won by 29 runs

* Denotes not first-class

Tamil Nadu Cricket Asscn v Western Australia
45-over Match
PSG Institute Ground, Coimbatore
Sep 10 1990
Toss: Tamil Nadu Cricket Asscn
Result: Tamil Nadu Cricket Asscn won by 10 runs

Having won the toss and chosen to bat, the home side scored 9 for 246, a large total for a 45-over match. VB Chandrasekhar was the highest scorer, playing an attacking innings of 83. The Western Australian batsmen thus faced a difficult task, which was not made easier by the fact that the clay pitch had been laid only a fortnight before. So they did well to make 6 for 236, thereby failing in their run chase by only 10 runs. Wayne Andrews played soundly for 69, and Graeme Wood made 42. Tom Moody and Mike Veletta both appeared to be on top of the bowling when they lost their wickets, Moody for 36 and Veletta for 28. The match was played in an athletics stadium used for soccer matches, and the fielding surface was uneven. The fieldsmen of both sides coped with the conditions well, especially James Brayshaw, who received a special fielding award.

Tamil Nadu Cricket Asscn	9/246	(VB Chandrasekhar 83, PC Prakash 63*)
Western Australia	6/236	(WS Andrews 69, GM Wood 42*, TM Moody 36, B Arun 3/50)

Karnataka State Cricket Asscn v Western Australia
40-over Match
Chinnaswamy Stadium, Bangalore
Sep 12 1989
Result: Karnataka won by 7 wkts

The match was reduced to 40 overs by rain, and the Western Australian batsmen failed to get going on a slow pitch in the shortened innings, finishing with 8 for 180. Mike Veletta, who batted down the order, played well for 45, while Tom Moody made 35 and James Brayshaw 27. The home side had little trouble making the necessary runs and was 3 for 184 after 37.1 overs.

Western Australia	8/180	(MRJ Veletta 45, TM Moody 35, JA Brayshaw 27, K Jeswant 3/38)
Karnataka	3/184	(C Saldanha 81*, VJ Raja 50*)

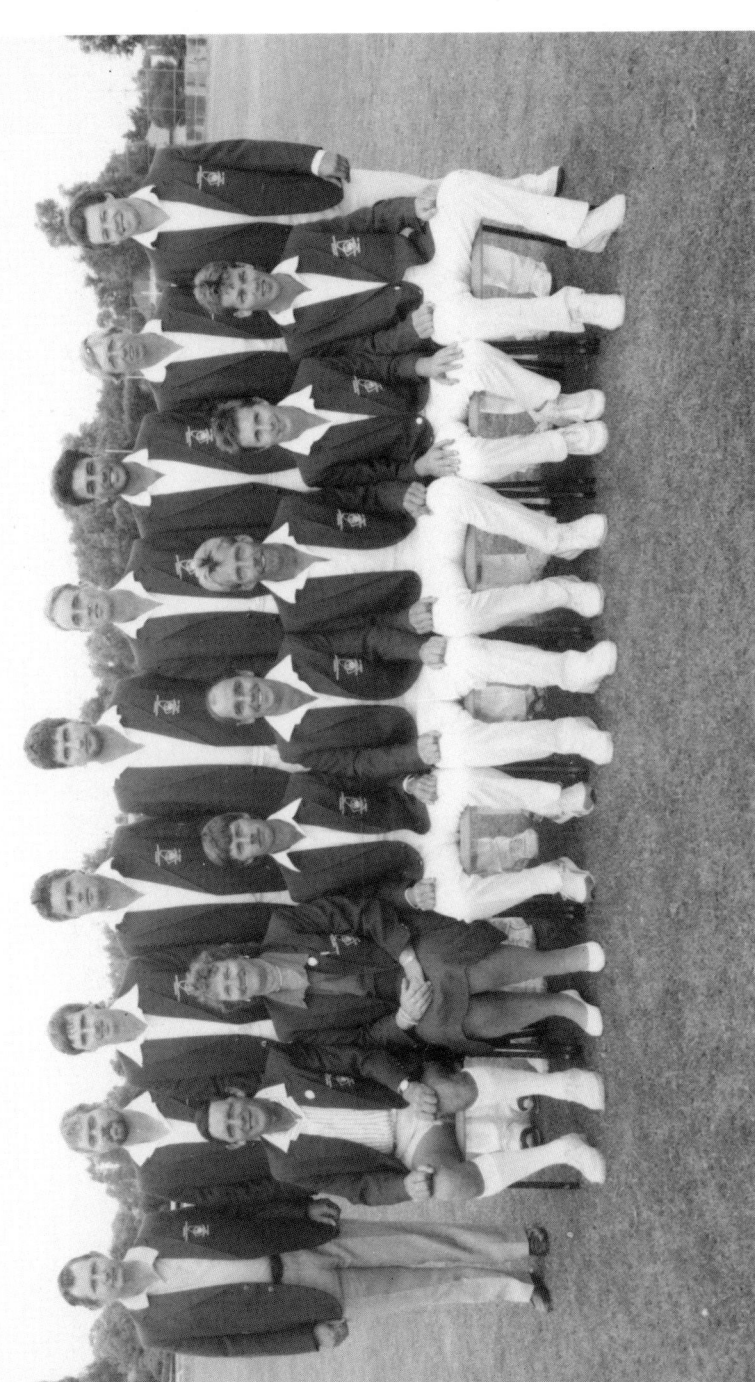

WESTERN AUSTRALIA, COUNTRY

Back Row, l to r: Leon White (Scorer), Ray Thompson, Peter Shine, Rod Walker, Miles Obst, Garry Morris, Richard Menasse, Max Johnson, Russell Waterman. Front Row, l to r: Bill & Audrey Bunker (Managers), Leith Bowyer, Terry Waldron (Captain), David Francis (Vice Captain), Mike Knuckey, Darryl Wyllie

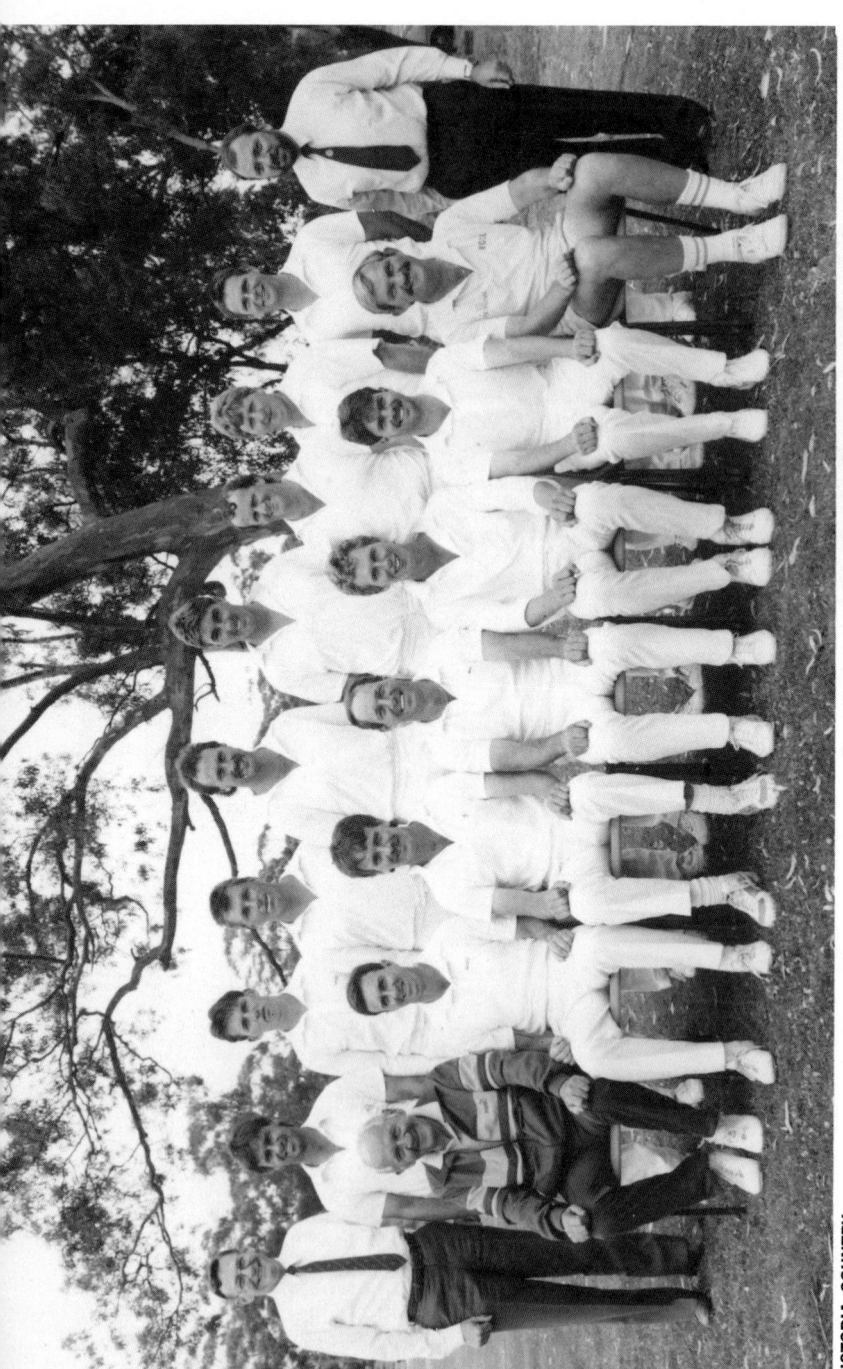

VICTORIA, COUNTRY

Back Row, l to r: Frank Fordyce (Scorer), Garry Tupper, Rodney Taylor, Graeme Bartholomew, Dean Benson, John Wrigley, Robert Scott, Geoff Banks, Robert Orr, Ed Parker (VCCL Secretary). Front Row, l to r: Keith Sherwill (Manager), David Lanyon, Russell Shultz, Wayne Walsh (Captain), Geoff Phillips, Graeme Beaumont, John Harris (Coach)

QUEENSLAND, COUNTRY

Back Row, l to r: Fred Jacobson (Assistant Manager), Andrew Walsh, Jim Wilson, Paul Hutchinson, Rod Petersen, Bevan Bauer, Bradley Spanner, Graeme Hogan, Clyde Veivers (Manager). Front Row, l to r: Brad Murphy, Errol Harris, Colin White, Lew Schulte, Sam Scuderi, Wayne Short, Terry Oliver

SOUTH AUSTRALIA, COUNTRY

Back Row, l to r: Justin Heyne, Paul Pasculli, Peter Lewis, Ian Kenny, Greg Williams, Allan Brooks, Anthony (Tony) Lowe, Robbie Ellis. Front Row, l to r: Don Woon (Public Relations), Mark Sommerfield, Barry Hutchins, Graham Madden (Captain), Peter Mattey, John Mitchell, Peter Haddrick (Manager)

KALLIS-CHEMPLAST TROPHY MATCH

Tamil Nadu v Western Australia
Chepauk Stadium, Madras
Sep 15, 16, 18, 19 (*No Play 19*) 1989
Result: Drawn

Rain interrupted and then finally washed out this four-day match before a result could be obtained. (There was one other interruption. Half-way through the match, on the Sunday, September 17, the two sides played a one-day match for the President's Cup, the details of which follow.) In hot and humid weather, Tamil Nadu set about compiling a large first-innings total. Vakkadai Chandrasekhar made a fine 119, Bharati Arun 104 and Pathamadi Prakash 90, and the last wicket did not fall until the morning of the third day. After spending two trying days in the field, the Western Australians were just as uncomfortable at the crease. They lost their first five wickets for 122, although they recovered later in the day to be 8 for 271 at stumps. Wayne Andrews (89), Tom Hogan (42) and Mike Veletta (41) were the principal scorers. Heavy rain overnight washed out the final day's play, which meant that, in the absence of a result, Western Australia retained the Kailis-Chemplast Trophy, thereby avoiding a dispute which at one time appeared likely to arise between the two teams' management over whether the match should be decided on the first innings. Tamil Nadu suggested the idea during the match, but it was rejected by the Western Australian camp, which insisted that the trophy-holder had to be beaten outright to lose it.

Tamil Nadu

First Innings

Batsman	How Out	Ttl
K Srikkanth (c)	b Matthews	23
VB Chandrasekhar	c Hogan b Yardley	119
PC Prakash	c Wood b MacLeay	90
AK Singh	c Capes b Yardley	0
V Sivaramakrishnan	b Capes	21
Robin Singh	c Veletta b MacLeay	33
B Arun	c Andrews b Capes	104
D Vasu	c Veletta b Andrews	43
MV Venkataramana	run out	44
S Subramaniam	c Moody b Mullally	3
M Sanjay (+)	not out	5
SUNDRIES: B. 4 LB. 7 W. 0 NB. 7		18
TOTAL	503	

F/W: 95 160 168 215 292 301 409 482 496 503

Bowler	O	M	R	Wkts
Mullally	19	4	81	1
MacLeay	10	1	66	2
Capes	15.2	1	62	2
Matthews	12	1	55	1
Hogan	26	6	74	—
Yardley	17	6	73	2
Andrews	9	—	35	1
Moody	8	1	15	—
Brayshaw	7	1	31	—
Overs:	123.2			

Western Australia

First Innings

Batsman	How Out	Ttl
JA Brayshaw	st Sanjay b Srikkanth	30
KH MacLeay	c Sanjay b Vasu	1
TM Moody	c Sanjay b Srikkanth	13
GM Wood (c)	c Chandrasekhar b Subramaniam	12
MRJ Veletta (+)	lbw Venkataramana	41
WS Andrews	b Venkataramana	89
CD Matthews	run out	19
TG Hogan	c (s)Madhavan b Srikkanth	42
PA Capes	not out	8
B Yardley	not out	1
AD Mullally	did not bat	
SUNDRIES: B. 8 LB. 1 W. 5 NB. 1		15
TOTAL	9 wkts for 271	

F/W: 2 52 56 63 122 172 246 262

Bowler	O	M	R	Wkts
Arun	5	—	13	—
Vasu	12	—	43	1
Srikkanth	26	8	61	3
Subramaniam	15	—	71	1
Venkataramana	26	3	74	2
Overs:	82.0			

PRESIDENT'S CUP MATCH

Tamil Nadu v Western Australia
Not First-Class—45-over Match
Chepauk Stadium, Madras
Sep 17 1989
Result: Western Australia won by 29 runs

The Western Australians won the toss for the first time in their three matches against Tamil Nadu and chose to bat first. Mike Veletta (30) and Wayne Andrews (26) got the side off to a strong start with an opening stand of 64 scored off only 11.3 overs. Graeme Wood (27) and Tom Moody (22) hurried the score along with brief but enterprising innings, and James Brayshaw carried on with a fine, undefeated innings of 55. Western Australia was 9 for 220 at the end of 45 overs, a big total yet one which was certainly within the range of the home side's batsmen. But Alan Mullally bowled with hostility on an easy-paced pitch, and Tamil Nadu suffered early setbacks from which it did not recover. It was ahead of the Western Australian scoring rate but it lost too many wickets, and in the end was dismissed in 39.3 overs for 191. It was a fine performance by the Western Australians—particularly since their leading bowler, Chris Matthews, injured his left shoulder in his second over and left the attack—and much credit had to go to the Western Australians' fine fielding. Western Australia thus retained the President's Cup.

Western Australia

Batsman	How Out	Ttl
WS Andrews	c Prakash b Robin Singh	26
MRJ Veletta (+)	lbw Srikkanth	30
TM Moody	c Chandrasekhar b Venkat	22
GM Wood (c)	c Srikkanth b Raman	27
JA Brayshaw	not out	55
KH MacLeay	lbw Venkataramana	8
CD Matthews	c Srikkanth b Raman	7
RS Russell	c Chandrasekhar b Srikkanth	12
TG Hogan	c Vasu b Robin Singh	6
PA Capes	run out	8
AD Mullally	not out	0
SUNDRIES: B. 5 LB. 9 W. 4 NB. 1		19
TOTAL	9 wkts for 220	

F/W: 64 113 122 135 160 190 206 220

Bowler	O	M	R	Wkts
Arun	6	—	38	—
Vasu	5	—	28	—
Robin Singh	7	—	29	2
Srikkanth	9	—	32	2
Venkataramana	9	—	36	2
Raman	9	—	43	2
Overs:	45.0			

Tamil Nadu

Batsman	How Out	Ttl
K Srikkanth (c)	c Veletta b Mullally	4
VB Chandrasekhar	c Russell b MacLeay	30
WV Raman	c Veletta b Mullally	4
PC Prakash	c Andrews b MacLeay	7
AK Singh	c Brayhaw b Matthews	3
Robin Singh	lbw Mullally	69
V Sivaramakrishnan	run out	31
B Arun	c Veletta b Russell	11
D Vasu	c & b Hogan	1
M Venkataramana	not out	20
M Sanjay (+)	run out	2
SUNDRIES: B. 1 LB. 2 W. 5 NB. 1		9
TOTAL		191

F/W: 4 20 42 49 51 134 153 154 170 191

Bowler	O	M	R	Wkts
Mullally	6.3	—	30	3
MacLeay	5	1	25	2
Matthews	1.3	—	7	1
Capes	4	1	15	—
Moody	5.3	—	25	—
Hogan	9	—	57	1
Russell	8	—	29	1
Overs:	39.3			

WESTERN AUSTRALIAN FIRST-CLASS RECORDS

Season 1989/90

Date	Venue	Opponent	Result for Western Australia
Oct 22*	Perth	New South Wales	Won by 4 wkts
Nov 1	Perth	Tasmania	Drawn
Nov 6*	Perth	Tasmania	Won by 4 wkts
Nov 8*	Perth	New Zealanders	Won by 8 wkts
Nov 10	Perth	New Zealanders	Drawn
Nov 17	St Kilda	Victoria	Drawn
Dec 15	Perth	South Australia	Drawn
Dec 27	Perth	Pakistanis	Won by an inns & 78 runs
Jan 6	Sydney	New South Wales	Drawn

Continued

355

Date		Venue	Opponent	Result for Western Australia
Jan	19	Brisbane	Queensland	Drawn
Jan	26	Adelaide	South Australia	Lost by an inns & 44 runs
Feb	2°	Perth	Sri Lankans	Lost by 4 wkts
Feb	4°	Perth	Sri Lankans	Won by 65 runs
Feb	9	Launceston	Tasmania	Lost by 85 runs
Feb	16	Perth	Queensland	Won by an inns & 177 runs
Mar	2	Perth	New South Wales	Won by 156 runs
Mar	9	Perth	Victoria	Drawn
Mar	17°	Perth	New South Wales	Won by 6 wkts
Mar	31°	Perth	South Australia	Won by 7 wkts
Apr	7°	Perth	Lancashire	Won by 3 runs

° Denotes not first-class

1989/90 Western Australia First-Class Averages

Batsman	M	Inn	NO	Runs	HS	50	100	Avrge	Ct/St
GR Marsh	5	8	2	434	355°	—	1	72.33	2
MRJ Veletta	12	19	2	846	228	3	3	49.76	17
GM Wood	9	13	4	440	125°	1	1	48.89	3
WS Andrews	12	18	—	759	103	6	1	42.17	5
JA Brayshaw	6	8	1	291	80	2	—	41.57	6
TM Moody	9	15	1	474	93	4	—	33.86	8
TG Hogan	9	12	3	286	58°	2	—	31.78	2
MW McPhee	6	11	1	311	113	—	1	31.10	3
KH MacLeay	7	9	3	177	53°	1	—	29.50	5
CD Matthews	9	12	2	259	53°	2	—	25.90	3
TJ Zoehrer	12	16	—	330	103	—	1	20.63	35/4
DJ Ramshaw	3	4	—	61	44	—	—	15.25	1
RS Russell	3	4	1	45	18	—	—	15.00	3
B Yardley	4	6	2	58	27	—	—	14.50	—
PA Capes	10	13	3	94	22	—	—	9.40	2
BP Julian	2	3	1	16	9	—	—	8.00	1
AD Mullally	6	6	1	38	34	—	—	7.60	3
TM Alderman	4	4	—	29	18	—	—	7.25	2
CD Mack	4	4	1	9	8	—	—	3.00	1

Bowler	M	Overs	Mdns	Runs	Wkts	Avrge	5wi	10m	NB	W	Best
GM Wood	9	0.4	—	0	1	0.00	—	—	—	—	1/0
GR Marsh	5	2	1	1	1	1.00	—	—	—	—	1/1
TJ Zoehrer	12	7	2	13	1	13.00	—	—	—	—	1/9
CD Matthews	9	304.3	77	806	42	19.19	3	—	15	10	7/22
TM Alderman	4	99.2	32	252	12	21.00	1	—	9	—	5/62
BP Julian	2	17.3	5	50	2	25.00	—	—	1	—	1/7
KH MacLeay	7	222.2	83	463	17	27.24	—	—	6	—	3/22
PA Capes	10	305	64	978	30	32.60	1	—	32	2	6/92
RS Russell	3	74	18	209	6	34.83	—	—	1	1	3/10
TG Hogan	9	248.3	70	641	18	35.61	1	—	—	—	5/60
WS Andrews	12	55	16	149	4	37.25	—	—	—	—	3/43
CD Mack	4	147.5	34	415	11	37.73	—	—	1	10	3/70
TM Moody	9	105.3	31	265	7	37.86	—	—	—	—	3/57
B Yardley	4	104	31	303	8	37.88	—	—	1	—	3/76
AD Mullally	6	239.4	55	648	11	58.91	—	—	9	20	3/74
JA Brayshaw	6	40.2	12	96	—	—	—	—	9	—	—

West Australian First-Class Records

Opponent	Venue	First Game	Games	W	L	D	T
Australian Rep. Teams							
Australian XI's	Perth	Mar 12 1926	11	—	5	6	—
Australian Services	Perth	Dec 24 1945	1	—	—	1	—
Total			12	—	5	7	—
England Teams	Perth	Oct 26 1907	22	1	9	12	—
Indians	Perth	Oct 17 1947	5	3	—	2	—
New Zealanders	Perth	Mar 5 1954	6	—	3	3	—

Continued

Opponent	Venue	First Game	Games	W	L	D	T
New South Wales	Perth	Mar 16 1907	44	16	14	14	—
	Fremantle	Mar 23 1907	1	1	—	—	—
	Sydney	Nov 9 1912	39	4	21	14	—
	Sydney SCG No 2	Nov 11 1966	1	—	—	1	—
	Canberra	Oct 26 1984	1	—	—	1	—
	Newcastle	Dec 2 1988	1	—	1	—	—
Total			87	21	36	30	—
Pakistanis	Perth	Nov 18 1972	5	4	—	1	—
Queensland	Perth	Mar 24 1894	40	20	6	14	—
	Brisbane	Feb 6 1948	38	6	9	23	—
Total			78	26	15	37	—
South Africans	Perth	Oct 22 1931	5	—	3	2	—
South Australia	Adelaide	Mar 17 1893	47	13	19	15	—
	Perth	Apr 3 1899	47	20	13	14	—
	Fremantle	Feb 3 1906	3	—	—	3	—
Total			97	33	32	32	—
Sri Lankans	Perth	Dec 31 1984	1	—	1	—	—
Tamil Nadu	Perth	Nov 4 1988	1	1	—	—	—
	Madras	Sep 15 1989	1	—	—	1	—
Total			2	1	—	1	—
Tasmania	Hobart TCA	Jan 24 1930	3	—	—	3	—
	Perth	Oct 29 1977	11	7	—	4	—
	Devonport	Jan 27 1979	4	3	1	—	—
	Launceston	Feb 17 1984	2	—	1	1	—
	Hobart Bel	Feb 6 1988	2	1	—	1	—
Total			22	11	2	9	—
Victoria	Melbourne	Apr 1 1893	41	8	15	18	—
	Perth	Feb 26 1910	46	11	14	21	—
	Fremantle	Mar 5 1910	1	1	—	—	—
	Fitzroy	Nov 6 1925	1	—	1	—	—
	St Kilda	Feb 10 1956	4	1	1	2	—
	Carlton	Nov 9 1984	1	—	—	1	—
Total			94	21	31	42	—
West Indians	Perth	Dec 14 1951	7	5	2	—	—
World XI	Perth	Dec 4 1971	1	—	1	—	—
Total for Western Australia			444	126	140	178	—

Most Appearances for Western Australia

Games	Player	Career	Games	Player	Career
119	RJ Inverarity	1962/63–1978/79	71	GAR Lock	1962/63–1970/71
111	GM Wood	1976/77–1989/90	71	R Edwards	1964/65–1974/75
101	IJ Brayshaw	1960/61–1977/78	68	G Shipperd	1977/78–1987/88
97	RW Marsh	1968/69–1983/84	67	KN Slater	1955/56–1967/68
89	TM Alderman	1974/75–1989/90	66	KJ Hughes	1975/76–1988/89
83	BK Shepherd	1955/56–1965/66	65	D Chadwick	1963/64–1971/72
81	GD McKenzie	1959/60–1973/74	64	BM Laird	1972/73–1983/84
81	GR Marsh	1977/78–1989/90	62	BL Buggins	1954/55–1962/63
87	KH MacLeay	1981/82–1989/90	61	WS Andrews	1982/83–1989/90
78	DK Lillee	1969/70–1983/84	58	B Yardley	1966/67–1989/90
78	AL Mann	1963/64–1983/84	54	DE Hoare	1955/56–1965/66
78	MRJ Veletta	1983/84–1989/90	53	TG Hogan	1981/82–1989/90
73	TJ Zoehrer	1980/81–1989/90	51	CS Serjeant	1976/77–1982/83
71	MT Vernon	1955/56–1967/68	50	TM Moody	1985/86–1989/90

Youngest Players on First-Class Debut for Western Australia

Player	Date of Birth	F/Class Debut	Opponent	Venue	Age on Years	Debut Days
AG Zimbulis	Feb 11 1918	Mar 23 1934	Australian XI	Perth	16	40
RJ Wilberforce	Jun 31 1910	Mar 26 1927	South Australia	Perth	16	238
KS Jeffreys	Jan 18 1921	Nov 17 1937	Victoria	Melbourne	16	303
FJ Bryant	Dec 7 1909	Mar 21 1927	South Australia	Perth	17	134
EH Bromley	Sep 2 1912	Jan 17 1930	Victoria	Melbourne	17	137
AEC Smith	Apr 10 1908	Mar 12 1926	Australian XI	Perth	17	159
L Pavy	Aug 21 1936	Feb 19 1954	Victoria	Perth	17	182
RO Doig	Jly 10 1909	Mar 26 1927	South Australia	Perth	17	259
AD Drew	Oct 30 1906	Oct 25 1924	MCC	Perth	17	361

Highest Innings Totals for Western Australia

Total	Opponent	Venue	Season
654	Victoria	Perth	1986/87
5d-615	Queensland	Brisbane	1968/69
8d-607	Queensland	Perth	1989/90
6d-594	New South Wales	Sydney	1968/69
6d-573	Queensland	Perth	1979/80
3d-565	South Australia	Perth	1989/90
7d-554	Queensland	Perth	1966/67
7d-553	Tasmania	Hobart TCA	1985/86
545	Pakistanis	Perth	1981/82
535	South Australia	Perth	1988/89
6d-533	Victoria	Melbourne	1988/89
8d-532	New South Wales	Perth	1957/58
531	Tasmania	Perth	1986/87
8d-529	Victoria	Melbourne	1986/87
527	Queensland	Brisbane	1985/86
520	West Indians	Perth	1975/76
8d-514	New South Wales	Perth	1986/87
9d-504	Tasmania	Devonport	1982/83
504	Tasmania	Perth	1984/85
2d-502	Tasmania	Hobart Bel	1988/89

Lowest Completed Innings Totals

Total	Opponent	Venue	Season
38	Victoria	Melbourne	1892/93
41	South Australia	Adelaide	1989/90
49	New South Wales	Perth	1922/23
50	New South Wales	Sydney	1951/52
51	New South Wales	Perth	1950/51
52	England XI	Perth	1978/79
54	Queensland	Brisbane	1972/73
57	MCC	Perth	1924/25
62	Australian XI	Perth	1935/36
63	South Australia	Perth	1931/32
63	South Africans	Perth	1931/32
69	MCC	Perth	1924/25
69	South Australia	Adelaide	1912/13
73	Australian XI	Perth	1937/38

Leading Batsmen for Western Australia

Batsman	Career	M	Inn	NO	Runs	HS	Avrge	100s
RJ Inverarity	1962/63–1978/79	119	207	21	7607	187	40.89	20
GM Wood	1976/77–1989/90	121	174	27	7077	186*	48.14	21
GR Marsh	1977/78–1989/90	81	139	10	5358	355*	41.53	15
BK Shepherd	1955/56–1965/66	83	141	14	5340	219	42.04	12
RW Marsh	1968/69–1983/84	97	156	12	5181	236	35.98	8
MRJ Veletta	1983/84–1989/90	76	126	15	4984	262	44.90	11
KJ Hughes	1975/76–1988/89	66	113	4	4587	183	42.08	13
R Edwards	1964/65–1974/75	71	122	15	4481	158	41.87	11
G Shipperd	1977/78–1987/88	68	117	16	4450	167*	44.05	10
IJ Brayshaw	1960/61–1977/78	101	161	25	4325	160	31.80	3
MT Vernon	1955/56–1967/68	71	121	4	4067	173	34.76	8
D Chadwick	1963/64–1971/72	65	118	10	3886	137	35.98	9
BM Laird	1972/73–1983/84	64	113	9	3759	171	35.44	7
KD Meuleman	1952/53–1960/61	48	75	9	3398	234*	57.48	11
TM Moody	1985/86–1989/90	50	81	3	3265	202	41.86	7
WS Andrews	1982/83–1989/90	61	88	9	3233	139	40.92	5

Continued

Batsman	Career	M	Inn	NO	Runs	HS	Avrge	100s
RS Langer	1973/74–1981/82	44	78	14	2756	150*	43.06	5
TJ Zoehrer	1980/81–1989/90	73	100	11	2673	168	30.03	5
CS Serjeant	1976/77–1982/83	51	86	16	2632	144*	37.60	6
RB Simpson	1956/57–1960/61	24	38	7	2470	236*	79.67	6
JW Rutherford	1952/53–1960/61	38	70	4	2383	167	36.10	5
AL Mann	1963/64–1983/84	76	114	17	2355	110	24.27	1
RI Charlesworth	1972/73–1979/80	47	82	5	2327	101*	30.22	1
AR Edwards	1946/47–1956/57	44	77	5	2325	105	32.29	3
KH MacLeay	1981/82–1989/90	87	108	18	2258	114*	25.09	2
KN Slater	1955/56–1967/68	67	110	11	2114	154	21.35	1
GC Becker	1963/64–1968/69	44	74	2	2062	195	28.63	2

Most Runs in a Season for Western Australia

Batsman	Season	M	Inn	NO	Runs	HS	50	100	Avrge
TM Moody	1988/89	13	20	1	1175	202	5	4	61.84
GM Wood	1987/88	12	18	3	1050	186*	5	3	70.00
MRJ Veletta	1986/87	12	19	6	971	262	6	2	74.69
MRJ Veletta	1988/89	12	19	2	933	166*	4	3	54.88
RB Simpson	1959/60	6	6	3	902	236*	3	3	300.66
GR Marsh	1988/89	10	15	1	865	223	3	3	61.79
PC Kelly	1965/66	8	15	1	856	132	3	3	61.14
MRJ Veletta	1989/90	12	19	2	846	228	3	3	49.76
C Milburn	1968/69	9	15	2	843	243	7	1	64.84
G Shipperd	1984/85	11	18	6	823	139	3	3	68.58
G Shipperd	1982/83	12	19	1	816	166	3	2	47.31
KJ Hughes	1982/83	8	13	—	811	130	4	3	62.38
G Shipperd	1983/84	12	19	3	811	167*	6	1	50.69

Highest Individual Innings for Western Australia

Score	Batsman	Opponent	Venue	Season
355*	GR Marsh	South Australia	Perth	1989/90
262	MRJ Veletta	Victoria	Perth	1986/87
243	C Milburn	Queensland	Brisbane	1968/69
236*	RB Simpson	New South Wales	Perth	1959/60
236	RW Marsh	Pakistanis	Perth	1972/73
234*	KD Meuleman	South Australia	Perth	1956/57
230*	RB Simpson	Queensland	Perth	1959/60
228*	MRJ Veletta	Queensland	Perth	1989/90
223	GR Marsh	Tasmania	Hobart Bel	1988/89
221*	RB Simpson	West Indians	Perth	1960/61
219	BK Shepherd	Victoria	Melbourne	1962/63
215*	BK Shepherd	Victoria	Perth	1964/65
212	BK Shepherd	Queensland	Perth	1961/62
209	GR Marsh	Tamil Nadu	Perth	1988/89
202	TM Moody	Victoria	Perth	1988/89
198	DK Carmody	South Australia	Perth	1947/48
195	GC Becker	Indians	Perth	1967/68
187	RJ Inverarity	New South Wales	Sydney	1978/79
186*	GM Wood	South Australia	Perth	1987/88
183	KJ Hughes	Tasmania	Perth	1984/85
182	J Irvine	South Australia	Perth	1968/69
180*	K Meuleman	South Australia	Adelaide	1958/59
177	RJ Inverarity	South Australia	Perth	1965/66
177	KS McEwan	Queensland	Perth	1979/80
176	GR Marsh	New South Wales	Sydney	1981/82

Leading Wicket-Takers for Western Australia

Batsman	Career	M	Runs	Wkts	Avrge	5wi	10m	Best
TM Alderman	1974/75–1989/90	88	8349	369	22.63	19	3	7/28
DK Lillee	1969/70–1983/84	76	8080	351	23.01	19	4	7/36
GAR Lock	1962/63–1970/71	71	7770	316	24.58	16	2	7/53
GD McKenzie	1959/60–1973/74	81	8142	254	32.05	7	—	6/100
KH MacLeay	1981/82–1989/90	87	6863	241	28.48	6	—	6/93
CD Matthews	1983/84–1989/90	45	4740	200	23.70	12	—	8/101
AL Mann	1963/64–1983/84	76	6592	196	33.63	5	—	6/94
DE Hoare	1955/56–1965/66	54	5075	194	26.15	10	1	8/98
IJ Brayshaw	1960/61–1977/78	101	4465	178	25.08	7	2	10/44
B Yardley	1966/67–1989/90	58	4473	173	25.86	12	2	7/44
MF Malone	1974/75–1981/82	42	4060	163	24.90	7	—	6/33
WM Clark	1974/75–1984/85	49	4641	150	30.94	4	—	6/39
CW Puckett	1939/40–1952/53	33	3796	149	25.47	13	2	6/35

Continued

Batsman	Career	M	Runs	Wkts	Avrge	5wi	10m	Best
TG Hogan	1981/82–1989/90	53	5117	147	34.81	3	—	6/57
RB Strauss	1952/53–1959/60	34	3036	128	23.71	8	—	7/59
LC Mayne	1961/62–1968/69	32	4090	125	32.72	5	—	7/75
KN Slater	1955/56–1967/68	67	5364	122	43.96	—	—	4/33
HG Bevan	1956/57–1963/64	40	3935	115	34.21	6	—	6/22
PA Capes	1985/86–1989/90	34	3299	114	28.94	4	1	6/92
RA Gaunt	1955/56–1959/60	29	2894	109	26.55	5	—	7/104
JB Gannon	1966/67–1978/79	37	3204	106	30.22	2	—	6/107

Most Wickets in a Season for Western Australia

Bowler	Season	M	Overs	Mdns	Runs	Wkts	Avrge	5wi	10m	Best
CD Matthews	1987/88	12	443.3	83	1277	57	22.40	3	—	8/101
GAR Lock	1966/67	8	398.4	105	1086	51	21.29	3	1	6/85
CD Matthews	1986/87	11	456.3	96	1269	51	24.88	3	—	6/46
GAR Lock	1968/69	9	356.2	62	1172	49	23.91	3	1	7/61
MF Malone	1977/78	9	261.4	60	784	45	17.42	4	—	6/33
GAR Lock	1967/68	9	261.6	59	725	44	16.47	4	—	5/36
DK Lillee	1972/73	6	207.2	38	778	44	17.68	3	—	6/30
TM Alderman	1979/80	10	398.0	99	1180	42	28.09	2	—	6/80
CD Matthews	1989/90	9	304.3	77	806	42	19.19	3	—	7/22
GAR Lock	1965/66	9	375.6	68	1017	41	24.80	3	—	5/61
TM Alderman	1988/89	10	362.0	99	836	41	20.39	2	—	5/26
GD McKenzie	1967/68	9	304.3	51	962	40	24.05	2	—	5/53
B Yardley	1980/81	9	376.5	109	968	40	24.20	3	1	7/62

Best Bowling in an Innings for Western Australia

Wkts	Bowler	Opponent	Venue	Season
10/44	IJ Brayshaw	Victoria	Perth	1967/68
8/28	RA Selk	Victoria	Fremantle	1909/10
8/56	HR Gorringe	Queensland	Perth	1952/53
8/71	RG Paulsen	West Indians	Perth	1975/76
8/98	DE Hoare	New South Wales	Perth	1964/65
8/101	CD Matthews	Queensland	Perth	1987/88
7/22	CD Matthews	Pakistanis	Perth	1989/90
7/28	TM Alderman	New South Wales	Perth	1981/82
7/36	DK Lillee	South Australia	Perth	1969/70
7/41	RG Paulsen	MCC	Perth	1974/75
7/41	DK Lillee	South Australia	Adelaide	1975/76
7/44	B Yardley	South Australia	Adelaide	1977/78
7/45	MU Herbert	Indians	Perth	1947/48
7/49	JM Hubble	Queensland	Perth	1972/73
7/49	TM Alderman	South Australia	Perth	1981/82
7/53	GAR Lock	Victoria	Melbourne	1962/63
7/59	RB Strauss	South Australia	Adelaide	1956/57
7/59	TM Alderman	New South Wales	Perth	1981/82
7/61	GAR Lock	Queensland	Brisbane	1968/69
7/62	B Yardley	Tasmania	Devonport	1980/81
7/75	RB Strauss	South Africans	Perth	1952/53
7/75	LC Mayne	New South Wales	Perth	1961/62
7/79	TE O'Dwyer	Queensland	Brisbane	1947/48
7/104	RA Gaunt	New South Wales	Sydney	1956/57
7/108	RA Selk	South Australia	Perth	1905/06
7/144	AH Christian	South Australia	Fremantle	1908/09

Best Bowling in a Match for Western Australia

Wkts	Bowler	Opponent	Venue	Season
14/87	TM Alderman	New South Wales	Perth	1981/82
13/77	RA Selk	Victoria	Fremantle	1909/10
12/90	IJ Brayshaw	Victoria	Perth	1967/68
12/113	DK Lillee	South Australia	Adelaide	1975/76
12/127	RA Selk	South Australia	Perth	1905/06
11/98	B Yardley	Tasmania	Devonport	1980/81
11/123	AH Christian	South Australia	Fremantle	1908/09
11/131	GAR Lock	Queensland	Brisbane	1968/69
11/134	CW Puckett	Indians	Perth	1947/48
11/138	HR Gorringe	Queensland	Perth	1952/53
11/200	AH Christian	South Australia	Fremantle	1908/09
10/70	DK Lillee	Queensland	Brisbane	1971/72
10/81	DK Lillee	South Australia	Perth	1976/77
10/84	JM Hubble	Queensland	Perth	1972/73
10/92	TM Alderman	South Australia	Perth	1981/82

Continued

Wkts	Bowler	Opponent	Venue	Season
10/102	IJ Brayshaw	Victoria	Perth	1977/78
10/105	B Yardley	Tasmania	Devonport	1982/83
10/117	RH Price	Queensland	Perth	1950/51
10/130	TM Alderman	England XI	Perth	1982/83
10/143	GAR Lock	Queensland	Perth	1966/67
10/144	TM Alderman	Queensland	Perth	1984/85
10/146	DK Lillee	Victoria	Perth	1976/77
10/153	DE Hoare	New South Wales	Perth	1964/65
10/164	PA Capes	Tasmania	Perth	1988/89
10/194	CW Puckett	Victoria	Perth	1949/50

Most Dismissals by a Wicket-Keeper for Western Australia

Wicket-Keeper	Career	M	Cght	Stmp	Total
RW Marsh	1968/69-1983/84	97	356	34	390
TJ Zoehrer	1980/81-1989/90	73	216	24	240
BL Buggins	1954/55-1962/63	62	143	19	162
KJ Wright	1974/75-1979/80	31	117	10	127
GC Becker	1963/64-1968/69	44	100	17	117

Most Dismissals in a Season for Western Australia

Wicket-Keeper	Season	M	Cght	Stmp	Total
TJ Zoehrer	1987/88	12	44	3	47
RW Marsh	1974/75	8	40	5	45
TJ Zoehrer	1988/89	13	41	4	45
RW Marsh	1975/76	9	37	4	41
TJ Zoehrer	1989/90	12	35	4	39
RW Marsh	1983/84	8	33	5	38
RW Marsh	1976/77	7	37	—	37
RW Marsh	1980/81	8	34	1	35
RW Marsh	1982/83	8	34	—	34
GC Becker	1965/66	9	27	6	33
RW Marsh	1969/70	8	23	8	31
RW Marsh	1970/71	9	27	3	30
R Edwards	1966/67	8	23	7	30

Most Dismissals in a Match for Western Australia

Ttl	Ct	St	Wicket-Keeper	Opponent	Venue	Season
11	11	—	RW Marsh	Victoria	Perth	1975/76
10	10	—	RW Marsh	South Australia	Perth	1976/77
9	8	1	GC Becker	Victoria	Melbourne	1965/66
9	9	—	DB Yagmich	Queensland	Perth	1973/74
9	9	—	RW Marsh	New South Wales	Perth	1974/75
9	9	—	TJ Zoehrer	South Australia	Adelaide	1987/88
8	8	—	RW Marsh	South Australia	Adelaide	1974/75
8	7	1	RW Marsh	Queensland	Perth	1975/76
8	8	—	RW Marsh	South Australia	Adelaide	1975/76
8	7	1	KJ Wright	Tasmania	Perth	1979/80
8	8	—	RW Marsh	New South Wales	Perth	1980/81
8	8	—	RW Marsh	South Australia	Perth	1981/82
8	8	—	KJ Wright	South Australia	Perth	1982/83

Most Dismissals in an Innings for Western Australia

Ttl	Ct	St	Wicket-Keeper	Opponent	Venue	Season
6	3	3	OI Lovelock	South Australia	Adelaide	1937/38
6	6	—	GC Becker	Victoria	Melbourne	1965/66
6	6	—	RW Marsh	New South Wales	Perth	1974/75
6	6	—	RW Marsh	Victoria	Perth	1975/76
6	6	—	RW Marsh	South Australia	Perth	1976/77
6	6	—	RW Marsh	Queensland	Brisbane	1979/80
6	6	—	RW Marsh	South Australia	Perth	1980/81
6	5	1	TJ Zoehrer	South Australia	Adelaide	1987/88
5	5	—	JKE Munro	South Australia	Perth	1951/52
5	5	—	BL Buggins	New South Wales	Perth	1958/59
5	2	3	BL Buggins	New South Wales	Perth	1959/60
5	5	—	BL Buggins	West Indians	Perth	1960/61
5	5	—	RW Marsh	Queensland	Brisbane	1969/70
5	4	1	RW Marsh	Queensland	Perth	1974/75
5	5	—	RW Marsh	Victoria	Perth	1975/76
5	5	—	KJ Wright	England XI	Perth	1978/79

Ttl	Ct	St	Wicket-Keeper	Opponent	Venue	Season
5	5	—	KJ Wright	New South Wales	Perth	1979/80
5	4	1	KJ Wright	Tasmania	Perth	1979/80
5	5	—	RW Marsh	New South Wales	Perth	1980/81
5	5	—	RW Marsh	South Australia	Perth	1980/81
5	5	—	RW Marsh	South Australia	Perth	1981/82
5	4	1	RW Marsh	Tasmania	Launceston	1983/84
5	3	2	TJ Zoehrer	Tasmania	Perth	1985/86
5	4	1	TJ Zoehrer	Tasmania	Perth	1987/88
5	3	2	TJ Zoehrer	New South Wales	Perth	1989/90

Most Catches by a Fieldsman for Western Australia

Fieldsman	Career	M	Catches
RJ Inverarity	1962/63–1978/79	119	156
IJ Brayshaw	1960/61–1977/78	101	108
MRJ Veletta	1983/84–1989/90	76	85
GAR Lock	1962/63–1970/71	74	84
GM Wood	1976/77–1989/90	121	80
TM Alderman	1974/75–1989/90	89	77
CS Serjeant	1976/77–1982/83	51	69
GR Marsh	1977/78–1989/90	81	62
BM Laird	1972/73–1983/84	64	61
KH MacLeay	1981/82–1988/89	87	60
BK Shepherd	1955/56–1965/66	83	56
MT Vernon	1955/56–1967/68	71	53

Most Catches in a Season for Western Australia

Catches	Fieldsman	M	Season
23	CS Serjeant	9	1981/82
18	RJ Inverarity	9	1968/69
17	IJ Brayshaw	9	1972/73
15	GAR Lock	9	1965/66
15	TM Alderman	7	1983/84
15	MRJ Veletta	12	1986/87
15	MRJ Veletta	8	1987/88
15	GR Marsh	10	1988/89
15	MRJ Veletta	12	1988/89
14	RJ Inverarity	9	1967/68
14*	MRJ Veletta	12	1989/90
13	RJ Inverarity	8	1972/73
13	GM Wood	12	1986/87
13	TM Alderman	10	1988/89

* MRJ Veletta took 4 further catches while wicket-keeping.

Most Catches in a Match for Western Australia

Ct	Fieldsman	Opponent	Venue	Season
6	CS Serjeant	Tasmania	Perth	1981/82
5	WP Dunn	New South Wales	Sydney	1949/50
5	D Chadwick	New South Wales	Perth	1963/64
5	RM Cowper	South Australia	Perth	1968/69
5	RJ Inverarity	New South Wales	Perth	1968/69
5	MRJ Veletta	New Zealanders	Perth	1987/88
5	GR Marsh	New South Wales	Perth	1988/89

Most Catches in an Innings for Western Australia

Ct	Fieldsman	Opponent	Venue	Season
5	MRJ Veletta	New Zealanders	Perth	1987/88
4	WP Dunn	New South Wales	Sydney	1949/50
4	RJ Inverarity	New South Wales	Perth	1968/69
4	RJ Inverarity	New South Wales	Sydney	1970/71
4	GR Marsh	England XI	Perth	1978/79
4	CS Serjeant	South Australia	Adelaide	1980/81
4	GR Marsh	New South Wales	Perth	1988/89
4	MRJ Veletta	Queensland	Brisbane	1989/90

Partnership Records for Western Australia

Wkt	Ttl	Batsmen	Opponent	Venue	Season
1st	431	MRJ Veletta, GR Marsh	South Australia	Perth	1989/90
2nd	254	MRJ Veletta, GR Marsh	Queensland	Brisbane	1985/86
3rd	330	GM Wood, GR Marsh	New South Wales	Sydney	1983/84
4th	260	GR Marsh, CS Serjeant	New South Wales	Sydney	1981/82
5th	301*	RB Simpson, K Meuleman	New South Wales	Perth	1959/60
6th	244	JT Irvine, R Edwards	New South Wales	Sydney	1968/69
7th	204	G Shipperd, TJ Zoehrer	New South Wales	Perth	1982/83
8th	160	GM Wood, KH MacLeay	South Australia	Perth	1987/88
9th	168*	KH Macleay, VJ Marks	South Australia	Adelaide	1986/87
10th	154	FR Buttsworth, JP Lanigan	Victoria	Perth	1921/22

Highest Partnerships for Western Australia

Wkt	Ttl	Batsmen	Opponent	Venue	Season
1st	431	MRJ Veletta, GR Marsh	South Australia	Perth	1989/90
1st	374	GR Marsh, MRJ Veletta	Tamil Nadu	Perth	1988/89
3rd	330	GM Wood, GR Marsh	New South Wales	Sydney	1983/84
1st	328	C Milburn, D Chadwick	Queensland	Brisbane	1968/69
1st	310	GR Marsh, MRJ Veletta	Tasmania	Hobart Bel	1988/89
5th	301*	RB Simpson, K Meuleman	New South Wales	Perth	1959/60
3rd	264	TM Moody, GM Wood	Victoria	Perth	1988/89
4th	260	GR Marsh, CS Serjeant	New South Wales	Sydney	1981/82
2nd	254	MRJ Veletta, GR Marsh	Queensland	Brisbane	1985/86
5th	251*	G Shipperd, RW Marsh	Victoria	Melbourne	1983/84
5th	248*	RW Marsh, RJ Inverarity	Pakistanis	Perth	1972/73
2nd	248	MRJ Veletta, G Shipperd	South Australia	Adelaide	1984/85
6th	244	JT Irvine, R Edwards	New South Wales	Sydney	1968/69
4th	242	RJ Inverarity, JT Irvine	New South Wales	Sydney	1967/68
2nd	238	FJ Bryant, WA McRae	Victoria	Perth	1927/28
2nd	234	MRJ Veletta, TM Moody	Tasmania	Perth	1987/88
2nd	233	IJ Brayshaw, RJ Inverarity	New Zealanders	Perth	1973/74
6th	231	TJ Zoehrer, TG Hogan	Victoria	Melbourne	1988/89
3rd	230	TM Moody, GM Wood	South Australia	Perth	1988/89
2nd	226	GR Marsh, TM Moody	South Australia	Perth	1988/89
3rd	223	BK Shepherd, RB Kanhai	South Australia	Adelaide	1961/62
4th	209	RJ Inverarity, R Edwards	Queensland	Perth	1970/71
3rd	205	RS Langer, KJ Hughes	New South Wales	Perth	1975/76
2nd	204	G Shipperd, RS Langer	Queensland	Perth	1979/80
7th	204	G Shipperd, TJ Zoehrer	New South Wales	Perth	1982/83
2nd	203	PC Kelly, MT Vernon	New South Wales	Perth	1965/66
1st	203	WJ Edwards, BM Laird	New South Wales	Sydney	1974/75

PERTH CRICKET

The results of Perth's 1989-90 first-grade competition seemed to support the view that the clubs with the most settled teams—that is, the teams least disturbed by the loss of players to the state side—tend to do best. The club which won the final, Claremont-Nedlands, fell into this category, for its only Sheffield Shield player was James Brayshaw, who played just six matches for the state. Moreover, the club which it beat in the final, Bayswater-Morley, had no current state players at all. (Bruce Reid played for Bayswater-Morley in the competition final, but did not represent Western Australia at all in 1989-90.) On the other hand, the club which won the competition in the previous season, Midland-Guildford, lost two players, Tom Moody and Tim Zoehrer, to state or international cricket for most of the season and it lost three to the Cricket Academy in Adelaide—Chris Mack, Brendan Julian and Matthew May. This no doubt had a lot to do with the club's indifferent performances during the season, which left it twelfth on the table.

The fact Claremont-Nedlands was playing its first season as a reconstituted club made its success seem all the more impressive. The club was the product of an amalgamation of the Claremont-Cottesloe club, which finished fifth in the competition in the previous season, and the Nedlands club, which finished tenth. Ironically, the two clubs had been at loggerheads and had strongly resisted the merger, although there is no doubt they have fared better jointly than they had independently. Claremont-Cottesloe had not won a first-grade premiership since 1973 and Nedlands not since 1963. This season, Claremont-Nedlands entirely dominated the competition, losing only one match in the entire season. As a result of the amalgamation, the number of clubs in the Perth competition decreased from sixteen to fifteen. Two players with experience of English county cricket played an important part in Claremont-Nedlands's success during the season—the Surrey player Ray Alikhan, who scored 625 runs at 52.06, and Dermot Reeve of Warwickshire, who finished second in the batting averages, scoring 628 runs at 62.80. Reeve had married and settled in the area, so his presence in the team did not breach the rule against having more than one overseas player. In the Claremont-Nedlands attack, the fast-medium bowler Keith Coughlan was consistently successful during the season, taking 50 wickets in the qualifying matches.

Claremont-Nedlands performed well throughout the season, finishing on top of the points table after the qualifying rounds. In the semi-finals it defeated Mt Lawley, while Bayswater-Morley defeated Fremantle. Although Bayswater-Morley was later beaten in the final, it has now established itself firmly as one of the most successful clubs in Perth, having made the finals consistently over the past eight years. Another club entitled to feel satisfied with its performance during the season was Gosnells, a relatively new club which had finished near the bottom of the table in its first two years. This year, only its third in the competition, it finished seventh.

Darrin Ramshaw, who opened the batting for Wanneroo, headed the batting averages, scoring 615 runs at 68.33. Ramshaw has played for Western Australia a few times without ever managing to hold down a place in the side, and his heavy scoring in grade cricket has certainly enhanced his reputation. The Claremont-Nedlands batsmen Ray Alikhan and Dermot Reeve were first and second in the aggregates list. Of the bowlers, the veteran pace bowler Ken Lilly topped the averages list, taking 51 wickets at 13.56 for North Perth.

Points Table—First-Grade

Claremont-Nedlands	163.34
Bayswater-Morley	155.24
Fremantle	148.41
Mount Lawley	146.06
Subiaco-Floreat	141.69
Wanneroo	131.21
Gosnells	130.47
University	127.47
North Perth	114.87
Perth	113.99

Willetton	112.61
Midland-Guildford	111.66
Scarborough	110.84
Melville	99.46
South Perth	96.52

SEMI-FINALS

Claremont-Nedlands 9 for 254 (D Reeve 125, K Coughlan 52; C McDonald 4/85, C Wilkinson 3/96) defeated Mt Lawley 243 (M Veletta 53, J Szeliga 38, C Matthews 25, P Moldrich 23, D Solly 23; R Alikhan 3/79, K Coughlan 3/90, S Cary 2/38) by 11 runs on the first innings.

Bayswater-Morley 7 for 141 (D Frame 35*, A Burress 29; S Russell 4/47, O Gibson 3/72) defeated Fremantle 131 (J Piromalli 75*, O Gibson 16, D Smith 14; B Reid 5/34, J Snadden 3/26, P Bagshaw 2/58) by 3 wickets on the first innings.

FINAL

Bayswater-Morley v Claremont-Nedlands
WACA Ground, Perth
March 24, 1990
Result: Claremont-Nedlands won on the first innings

The pitch was moist and grassy, and it was obvious the team which won the toss would have an important advantage. The toss was won by Claremont-Nedlands, which as expected sent Bayswater-Morley in and within an hour had taken a firm grip on the match. Its opening bowlers, Keith Coughlan and Sean Cary, broke through the top order batting so rapidly that Bayswater-Morley was at one point reduced to 5 for 24. Andre Burress alone held out against the Claremont-Nedlands bowlers, scoring 34 before he was run out. Bayswater-Morley was eventually dismissed for 95, Coughlan having taken 5 for 46 and Cary 3 for 36. It was clear that even on such a pitch Bayswater-Morley's bowlers would be hard-pressed to bowl their side to victory, but Bruce Reid made a determined attempt at it. Bowling with considerable hostility, he took three quick wickets, and at 3 for 22 it seemed Claremont-Nedlands might yet struggle to win. James Brayshaw and Craig Beveridge between them raised the total to 56, whereupon Reid took another couple of wickets, which seemed to revive Bayswater-Morley's hopes. But Brayshaw was now joined by David Lovell, and the pair saw their team through to a first innings lead and then carried on until stumps with an undefeated partnership of 121. Brayshaw was then 92 not out and Lovell 50 not out. Rain washed out play next day, Sunday, giving Claremont-Nedlands a win on the first innings and the premiership.

Bayswater-Morley—First Innings

Batsman	How Out	Ttl
G Healey	c Alikhan b Cary	9
I McRae	c Beveridge b Coughlan	1
A Burress	run out	34
G Ireland	c Lovell b Coughlan	4
C Kirkby	c Brayshaw b Cary	4
J Snadden	c Alikhan b Coughlan	1
D Frame	c Gorey b Coughlan	7
K McInerney	c Gorey b Cary	11
P Bagshaw	run out	0
B Mulder	not out	9
B Reid	c Brayshaw b Coughlan	8
Sundries		7
Total		95

F/W: 10 10 16 23 24 37 60 71 83 95

Bowler	O	M	R	Wkts
S Cary	19	7	36	3
K Coughlan	21.2	7	46	5
R Alikhan	2	0	5	0
J Brayshaw	2	1	1	0

Claremont-Nedlands—First Innings

Batsman	How Out	Ttl
R Alikhan	lbw b Reid	3
B Whiteaker	lbw b Reid	1
J Brayshaw	not out	92
C Beveridge	lbw b Reid	7
D Reeve	c Ireland b Reid	19
B Johnson	c McInerney b Reid	4
D Lovell	not out	50
Sundries		11
Total		5 for 187

F/W: 4 5 22 56 66

Bowler	O	M	R	Wkts
B Reid	14	3	47	5
P Bagshaw	8	0	38	0
J Snadden	12	2	50	0
D Frame	7	2	32	0
B Mulder	7	1	17	0

Batting Averages—First Grade

Batsman	Inns	NO	HS	Runs	Avge
D Ramshaw (Wanneroo)	11	2	104	615	68.33
D Reeve (Claremont-Nedlands)	14	4	125	628	62.80
D Harris (Gosnells)	13	3	120*	567	56.70
J Brayshaw (Claremont-Nedlands)	10	2	108	443	55.37
R Alikhan (Claremont-Nedlands)	15	3	177*	625	52.08
L Bott (University)	11	2	109	427	47.44
PJ Brindley (University)	12	3	102*	395	43.88
K MacLeay (University)	9	1	117	334	41.75
PA Brindley (Fremantle)	12	2	79*	417	41.70
R Leipold (Gosnells)	13	1	117	489	40.75

Batting Aggregates

Batsman	Agg.
D Reeve (Claremont-Nedlands)	628
R Alikhan (Claremont-Nedlands)	625
D Ramshaw (Wanneroo)	615
G Ireland (Bayswater-Morley)	580
D Harris (Gosnells)	567
J Langer (Scarborough)	494
R Leipold (Gosnells)	489

Continued

P Henderson (Scarborough)	487
J Brayshaw (Claremont-Nedlands)	443
S Frayne (Melville)	439
D Thompkins (Wanneroo)	439

Bowling Averages—First-Grade

Bowler	Runs	Wkts	Avge
K Lilly (North Perth)	692	51	13.56
B Raven (Subiaco-Floreat)	760	55	13.82
C Wilkinson (Mt Lawley)	639	44	14.52
V Greene (Wanneroo))	560	36	15.56
D Reeve (Claremont-Nedlands)	490	31	15.80
K Coughlan (Claremont-Nedlands)	984	58	16.96
C McDonald (Mt Lawley)	589	34	17.32
M Wasley (North Perth)	488	28	17.43
K Sheppard (Fremantle)	546	31	17.61
C Matthews (Mt Lawley))	501	28	17.89

Wicket Aggregates

Wicket-Keeper	Agg.
K Coughlan (Claremont-Nedlands)	58
B Raven (Subiaco-Floreat)	55
K Lilly (Nth Perth)	51
O Gibson (Fremantle)	46
C Wilkinson (Mt Lawley)	44
V Greene (Wanneroo)	36
C McDonald (Mt Lawley)	34
R Romeo (South Perth)	32
D Reeve (Claremont-Nedlands)	31
K Sheppard (Fremantle)	31

SECOND GRADE

Final: Melville 182 drew with Fremantle 1/45. Melville won the competition, having finished on top of the points table.

THIRD GRADE

Melville 243 drew with Scarborough, which did not bat. Melville won the competition, having finished on top of the points table.

FOURTH GRADE

North Perth 154 drew with Melville 1/14. Melville won the competition, having finished on top of the points table.

TOYOTA CUP

The 1989-90 competition resulted in a final between Wanneroo and Fremantle, played at the WACA Ground in Perth on April 1, 1990. Wanneroo batted first and at the end of its 50 overs had compiled the moderately good score of 7 for 198. None of the Wanneroo batsmen played a big innings, but three of them made valuable contributions—Darrin Ramshaw (48), David Fitzgerald (48) and Ian Herbert (33). Fremantle had no trouble scoring the necessary runs and passed the Wanneroo total with 9 wickets in hand and more than 5.3 overs to spare. Mark McPhee batted through the innings for 108 not out, sharing an opening stand of 104 with his fellow opener Geoff Marsh (65). At the end, Fremantle was 1 for 199, winning the match by 9 wickets.

SHELL COLTS

In the final of this competition, played at Stevens Reserve, Perth, on March 4, 1990, Melville (7 for 148) defeated Willetton (8 for 146).

COUNTRY CRICKET

COUNTRY WEEK

Nearly seventy country teams competed in the senior country carnival at various grounds in Perth from January 18 to 25. As usual, there were two divisions within each of the six sections, and the teams which topped the two divisions played off in a final. The top three sections played 60-over matches and the other three 50-over matches.

Mandurah-Rockingham won the A Section of the championship, comfortably defeating Busselton-Margaret River in the final. Mandurah-Rockingham does have an advantage over many other associations in the competition in that it is based on Perth's southern outskirts and so draws players from what is really a well populated metropolitan area, but considering that it is only a newly formed club its performance was certainly commendable. The defending champion, Albany, finished second to Mandurah-Rockingham in its division.

A SECTION
Division 1: Busselton-Margaret River 49.84, Narrogin 31.50, Mt Barker 30.96, Bunbury 29.39, Merredin 29.37, Central Great Southern 28.51.
Division 2: Mandurah-Rockingham 50.09, Albany 37.33, Wyalkatchem 35.09, Eastern Goldfields 31.34, Central Midlands 29.23, Bunbury No 2 13.81.

FINAL
Batting first, Busselton-Margaret River compiled 8 for 239 in its 50 overs, a substantial total but one which Mandurah-Rockingham was able to pass with more than 5 overs to spare.

Result: Mandurah-Rockingham defeated Busselton-Margaret River by 7 wickets

Busselton-Margaret River

Batsman	How Out	Ttl
B Skane	c Nock b D Wyllie	19
G Townsend	c Kot b Caparaso	17
C Coates	c Cullen b Caparaso	4
R Duggan	c J Wyllie b Caparaso	71
M Colthart	b D Wyllie	16
C Gibson	c Kot b MacIntosh	34
P Adams	b Caparaso	16
G Morris	b MacIntosh	18
N Smith	not out	11
B Devitt	not out	6
Sundries		27
Total		8 for 239

Bowler	O	M	R	Wkts
M Rowe	10	2	39	0
A Caparaso	26	5	76	4
D Wyllie	19	2	77	2
I MacIntosh	5	—	31	2

Mandurah-Rockingham

Batsman	How Out	Ttl
J Wyllie	not out	95
I MacIntosh	c Coates b Heselwood	4
R Kot	c Coates b Heselwood	0
B Nock	run out	70
D Wyllie	not out	55
Sundries		18
Total		3 for 242

Bowler	O	M	R	Wkts
G Morris	18	0	74	0
C Heselwood	7	0	32	2
B Devitt	6	0	29	0
P Adams	6	0	24	0
N Smith	2	0	10	0
C Gibson	13	2	47	0
M Colthart	1.5	0	8	0
R Duggan	1	0	5	0

B SECTION
Division 1: North Midlands 41.21, Port Hedland 35.96, Williams 35.85, Wickepin 35.53, Wongan-Ballidu 29.43, Mandurah-Rockingham No 2 13.57.
Division 2: Collie 43.94, Donnybrook Capel 43.53, Geraldton 43.41, Pingelly 29.46, Bruce Rock-Narembeen 20.96, West Pilbara 14.19.
Final: North Midlands 5 for 180 defeated Collie 9 for 176.

C SECTION
Division 1: South Midlands 42.95, Albany No 2 37.67, Karlgarin-Hyden 35.96, Esperance 29.00, East Avon 28.65, Northam 18.99.
Division 2: Lake Grace-Kukerin 39.58, Warren-Blackwood 33.35, Harvey-Murray 25.29, Central Great Southern No 2 24.78, Green Range 10.53.
Final: Lake Grace-Kukerin 227 defeated South Midlands 181.

D SECTION
Division 1: Broome 41.52, Geraldton No 2 40.34, Merredin No 2 33.52, Beverley-Brookton-York 27.92, Carnarvon 26.83, Wyalkatchem No 2 13.29.
Division 2: Busselton-Margaret River No 2 47.48, Yilgarn 34.91, Mt Barker No 2 34.39, Central Midlands No 2 29.03, Ravensthorpe 22.60, Kambalda 13.86.
Final: Broome 9 for 178 defeated Busselton-Margaret River No 2 171.

E SECTION
Division 1: Fortescue-Tom Price 44.65, Port Hedland No 2 35.92, North Midlands No 2 35.06, Mt Magnet 34.87, South Midlands No 2 27.50, Wongan-Ballidu No 2 12.78.

Division 2: Williams No 2 44.05, Kalgoorlie Friendly Society 43.04, Nor-West & Murchison 42.15, Karlgarin-Hyden No 2 28.96, Meekatharra 20.19, Narrogin No 2 14.43.
Final: Fortescue-Tom Price 3 for 150 defeated Williams No 2 146.

F SECTION
Lake Grace-Kukerin No 2 40.66, Warren-Blackwood No 2 33.56, Paraburdoo 24.85, New Norcia 15.66, Nor-West & Murchison No 2 9.50.
Final: Warren-Blackwood No 2 151 defeated Lake Grace-Kukerin No 2 112.

PRUDENTIAL CUP

Six of the state's seven country zones competed again in this knock-out championship, which culminated in a final between Central Great Southern and Merredin at the WACA Ground, Perth, on February 24, 1990. Merredin batted first and was all out for 241 in the last of its 50 overs. David Haines (53) and Rick Antonio (47) were the highest scorers, while Central Great Southern's pace bowlers Norm Herbert (4 for 31 in 9.4 overs) and Steve Gollan (2 for 32 in 8 overs) had the best bowling figures. Central Great Southern won the match with just two balls to spare, scoring 8 for 242. The opener P Evans retired hurt for 43, but Reece Edgley of Katanning saw his side through to victory with an innings of 65 not out. Central Great Southern's victory was consolation for its defeat by Bunbury in the final last year.

Result: Central Great Southern won by 2 wickets

Merredin

Batsman	How Out	Ttl
T Haines	lbw b Herbert	40
T Waterhouse	c Arnold b Gollan	1
D Beilken	c Byrne b Herbert	5
D Haines	c Byrne b Smith	53
N Caparosa	st Byrne b McGregor	0
R Antonio	c Evans b Willey	47
G McAuliffe	c and b McFarlane	37
G Douglas	c Smith b Herbert	31
N Bennett	c Herbert b Gollan	0
I Lane	c Byrne b Herbert	6
T Wilkey	not out	1
Sundries		20
Total		241

Bowler	O	M	R	Wkts
S Gollan	8	2	32	2
W Hams	10	2	26	0
N Herbert	9.4	1	31	4
A McFarlane	7	0	47	1
K McGregor	3	0	21	1
M Smith	6	0	33	1
G Willey	6	0	37	1

Batsman	How Out	Ttl
K McGregor	c Bennett b Douglas	18
P Evans	retired hurt	43
G Willey	c Caparosa b McAuliffe	13
N Herbert	c Waterhouse b Bennett	11
R Edgley	not out	65
W Hams	c and b McAuliffe	22
B Arnold	c Waterhouse b Bennett	27
M Smith	b Haines	13
W Byrne	run out	9
S Gollan	run out	1
A McFarlane	not out	1
Sundries		19
Total		8 for 242

Bowler	O	M	R	Wkts
I Lane	8	1	35	0
T Wilkey	10	1	45	0
G Douglas	9	0	56	1
N Bennett	9.4	1	42	2
G McAuliffe	10	0	41	2
D Haines	3	0	16	1

Combined Country

A Western Australian Combined Country team played Sri Lanka at
Brookton on February 6, 1990. The home side lost by 63 runs in
a low-scoring match. (For match details, see the section on the Sri
Lankan tour.) The Combined Country team chosen for this match
was: Terry Waldron—captain (Central Great Southern), David
Francis (Bunbury), Darryl Wyllie (Mandurah-Rockingham), Leith
Bowyer (Bunbury), Richard Menasse (Narrogin), Michael Knuckey
(Geraldton), Miles Obst (North Midlands), Russell Waterman
(Bunbury), Peter Shine (Bunbury), Gary Morris (Busselton-Margaret
River), Peter Rowe (Collie) and Brad Higgins (Mt Barker).

VICTORIA

AFTER A DISAPPOINTING SEASON in which it finished at the bottom of the Sheffield Shield table for the second year in a row, Victoria could console itself with the knowledge that at least it had performed better than in the season before. Whereas in 1988-89 Victoria lost four matches outright, in 1989-90 it did not lose one, and it gained at least first innings points in half the Shield matches it played. On the other hand, Victoria managed to win only one match outright itself, and it was this failure to gain full points more often which really explains why it ran last in the competition. Having lost on the first innings to Queensland in the opening fixture in October, Victoria had a run of success until early January. It finished ahead in four of five matches it contested in this period, winning one and gaining first innings points in the others.

It is probably significant that the slump in Victoria's fortunes in the second half of the season occurred after its captain, Simon O'Donnell, departed to join the national team. O'Donnell not only performed better as a player this season but he appeared to lead the team with more authority, and it is likely his improved captaincy was to some extent a consequence of his improved performance. His personal success appeared to help him perform his captain's duties with more confidence. The general point may be made that Victoria seemed to suffer more than other State sides from the loss of key players called up to the national side, which no doubt points to a lack of depth in Victoria's talent. The difference Dean Jones alone might have made to the team if he played for it regularly can only be imagined. Jones played for Victoria only four times—in three Sheffield Shield matches and against Pakistan—and he scored 363 runs at an average of 72.6. Similarly, Merv Hughes played for his State only four times.

In the absence of Hughes and O'Donnell, the Victorian attack was led by relatively inexperienced players. This is evident from the list of wicket-takers. Paul Reiffel, who topped the list with 31 wickets, was playing only his second full season for Victoria. The bowlers who finished second and third on the list, Damien Fleming with 28 wickets and Peter McIntyre with 27, were playing only their first full season for Victoria. The success of such young players must inspire hope for the future. Reiffel, who was 23, bowled off a short run but his pace was deceptively sharp. Although he was the leading wicket-taker, he might easily have taken many more wickets if luck had leant his way. Fleming was only 19 years old at the end of the season, so he must be considered a fine prospect. He bowled only 234 overs for his 28 wickets, which means he had the outstanding strike rate of 50.2. Fleming is originally from Western Australia but spent his formative years in Victoria. Bowling at fast-medium, he was able to swing the ball as well as move it off the pitch, and he has also developed an effective slower ball.

During the season, Peter McIntyre, the leg-spinner, attracted a good deal of media attention in other States as well as Melbourne. The Australian team was clearly in need of a quality leg-spinner, and in some quarters McIntyre was seen as a bowler with the potential to fill the vacancy. The prospect of McIntyre suddenly being summoned for Test duty is believed to have alarmed some of his admirers within Victoria's cricket fraternity, who believed such an advancement at the age of 23 would be premature and ultimately harmful to the young bowler's career. The call from the Australian selectors did not come, of course, and McIntyre continued to do good work for Victoria. He recorded his best figures in the match against Pakistan, in which he took 5 for 53 in Pakistan's second innings, so ensuring Pakistan's defeat. The Pakistanis themselves apparently rated McIntyre's bowling highly, yet the Victorian selectors chose to drop him in the next match, against New South Wales. This was done, it was said, in the interests of the team's balance. McIntyre took his 27 wickets at the generous average of 44.30. While he was initially a little quicker through the air than most leg-spinners, it seems that on certain advice he dropped his pace later in the season. Time will tell if the advice was sound or not.

The opener Gary Watts was often the mainstay of the Victorian innings, and he topped the batting aggregates with 940 runs at an average of 42.7. Jamie Siddons, who took over the captaincy in O'Donnell's absence, managed to score 793 runs at an average of 52.87, despite a hamstring injury which hampered him in the second half of the season. An interesting addition to the batting line-up in the last two matches of the season was Warren Ayres, a stylish young batsman who opened the innings and in these two matches scored 12, 134 not out, 93 and 23. If Victoria's batting had a weakness it was the failure of several capable batsmen down the order to score more runs than they did, most notably Michael Dimattina, who averaged only 11.25 for the season. The effect of this was to lengthen Victoria's tail. While he disappointed with the bat, however, Dimattina's wicketkeeping was as sound as ever.

Apart from the play, the Victorian season was notable for the fact that the Melbourne pitch played well throughout the season, so much so that it must now be regarded as one of the better pitches in the country. The season was also notable for the appointment of Bill Lawry as the Victorian Cricket Association's cricket manager, a position which gives him responsibility for the playing of the game at every level, from Sheffield Shield to junior. Part of the job's challenge, no doubt, will be to try to get Victoria off the bottom of the Shield table in 1990-91.

VICTORIAN FIRST-CLASS RECORDS

Season 1989/90

Date	Venue	Opponent	Result for Victoria
Oct 22*	Adelaide	South Australia	Won by 28 runs
Oct 25	Brisbane	Queensland	Drawn
Oct 29*	Queensland	Brisbane	Lost by 7 wkts
Nov 10	St Kilda	Tasmania	Drawn
Nov 17	St Kilda	Western Australia	Drawn
Nov 24	Sale	Sri Lankans	Won by an inns & 3 runs
Dec 1	Launceston	Tasmania	Drawn
Dec 8	Melbourne	South Australia	Won by 4 wkts
Dec 15	Albury	New South Wales	Drawn
Dec 22*	Melbourne	Sri Lankans	Won by 109 runs
Jan 6	Adelaide	South Australia	Drawn
Jan 26	Melbourne	Pakistanis	Won by 59 runs
Feb 9	Melbourne	New South Wales	Drawn
Mar 2	Melbourne	Queensland	Drawn
Mar 9	Perth	Western Australia	Drawn

* Denotes not first-class

1989/90 Victorian First-Class Averages

Batsman	M	Inn	NO	Runs	HS	50	100	Avrge	Ct/St
DM Jones	4	7	2	363	149	1	1	72.60	1
MG Hughes	4	5	3	122	60*	1	—	61.00	2
JD Siddons	10	17	2	793	159	3	3	52.87	15
SP O'Donnell	8	13	2	544	121	3	2	49.45	8
DA Harris	2	4	—	189	90	2	—	47.25	1
WG Ayres	4	8	1	310	134*	1	1	44.29	1
GM Watts	12	23	1	940	162*	5	3	42.73	10
WN Phillips	12	23	2	735	134	5	1	35.00	2
ID Frazer	9	16	1	415	90	4	—	27.67	6
CE Bradley	2	4	—	99	46	—	—	24.75	1
GR Parker	5	8	—	196	75	1	—	24.50	6
AIC Dodemaide	9	14	1	310	73	2	—	23.85	4
PR Reiffel	9	11	6	101	27	—	—	20.20	3
DW Fleming	8	10	3	113	63*	1	—	16.14	4
PW Jackson	3	3	2	15	14*	—	—	15.00	—
MGD Dimattina	12	19	3	180	32*	—	—	11.25	26/3
RCAM McCarthy	3	5	1	42	28	—	—	10.50	—
PE McIntyre	11	11	3	59	20	—	—	7.38	7
SS Prescott	2	4	—	29	10	—	—	7.25	3
PW Young	1	2	1	7	7	—	—	7.00	—
DJ Hickey	2	2	1	4	2*	—	—	4.00	1

Bowler	M	Overs	Mdns	Runs	Wkts	Avrge	5wi	10m	NB	W	Best
SP O'Donnell	8	1077	54	410	20	20.50	—	—	7	—	4/38
GR Parker	5	123	5	45	2	22.50	—	—	—	—	2/30
DW Fleming	8	1407	59	693	28	24.75	1	—	11	4	6/37
PW Young	1	54	—	26	1	26.00	—	—	—	—	1/26
PR Reiffel	9	1808	57	994	31	32.06	—	—	58	—	4/43
AIC Dodemaide	9	1714	67	750	21	35.71	—	—	11	—	4/54
PW Jackson	3	873	48	286	7	40.86	—	—	—	—	3/103
DJ Hickey	2	369	9	207	5	41.40	—	—	8	4	3/89
RCAM McCarthy	3	630	18	339	8	42.38	—	—	4	—	2/43
MG Hughes	4	840	38	350	8	43.75	—	—	1	—	3/68
PE McIntyre	11	2709	116	1196	27	44.30	1	—	—	—	5/53
DM Jones	4	132	7	60	1	60.00	—	—	—	—	1/25
WN Phillips	12	36	2	13	—	—	—	—	—	—	—
JD Siddons	10	24	1	16	—	—	—	—	—	—	—

Victorian First-Class Cricket Records

Opponent	Venue	First Game	Games	W	L	D	T
Australian Rep. Teams							
Australian XI's	Melbourne	Dec 7 1888	1	—	1	—	—
AIF Team	Melbourne	Jan 16 1920	1	—	1	—	—
Australian Services	St Kilda	Jan 4 1946	1	1	—	—	—
Total			3	1	2	—	—
Combined XIII	Melbourne	Dec 26 1872	1	—	1	—	—

Opponent	Venue	First Game	Games	W	L	D	T
England Teams	Melbourne	Feb 21 1879	57	9	30	17	1
Indians	Melbourne	Oct 30 1947	4	—	1	3	—
	Geelong	Jan 30 1981	1	—	1	—	—
Total			5	—	2	3	—
New South Wales	Melbourne	Mar 26 1856	110	51	34	25	—
	The Domain	Jan 15 1857	6	3	3	—	—
	Redfern	Mar 9 1871	4	2	2	—	—
	Sydney	Feb 22 1878	102	22	51	29	—
	Carlton	Dec 22 1945	1	—	—	1	—
	St Kilda	Dec 24 1955	4	1	1	1	1
	Newcastle	Dec 18 1982	2	—	1	1	—
	Albury	Dec 15 1989	1	—	—	1	—
Total			230	79	92	58	1
New Zealanders	Melbourne	Feb 17 1899	10	3	1	5	1
	Wellington	Mar 20 1925	1	1	—	—	—
	Christchurch	Mar 27 1925	1	—	—	1	—
Total			12	4	1	6	1
New Zealand Provinces							
Otago	Dunedin	Feb 20 1925	1	—	—	1	—
Canterbury	Christchurch	Feb 27 1925	1	—	—	1	—
Wellington	Wellington	Mar 6 1925	1	—	1	—	—
Auckland	Auckland	Mar 13 1925	1	—	—	1	—
Total			4	—	1	3	—
Pakistanis	Melbourne	Nov 24 1972	4	2	1	1	—
Queensland	Brisbane	Jan 31 1903	60	18	19	23	—
	Melbourne	Dec 16 1904	52	34	7	11	—
	Brisbane Ex	Jan 31 1920	5	2	1	2	—
	Carlton	Dec 14 1945	1	1	—	—	—
	St Kilda	Dec 9 1955	4	1	2	1	—
	Geelong	Feb 26 1981	2	—	1	1	—
	Wangaratta	Nov 21 1986	1	—	—	1	—
Total			125	56	30	39	—
Sri Lankans	Melbourne	Feb 6 1988	1	—	—	1	—
	Sale	Nov 24 1989	1	1	—	—	—
Total			2	1	—	1	—
South Australia	East Melbourne	Nov 12 1880	2	2	—	—	—
	Adelaide	Apr 1 1881	93	42	33	18	—
	Melbourne	Feb 3 1906	89	52	14	23	—
	St Kilda	Jan 21 1946	4	1	1	2	—
	Geelong	Mar 7 1981	2	—	—	2	—
Total			190	97	48	45	—
South Africans	Melbourne	Nov 11 1910	7	2	1	4	—
Tasmania	Launceston	Feb 11 1851	28	12	7	9	—
	South Yarra	Mar 29 1852	1	1	—	—	—
	Hobart LRG	Mar 4 1858	1	1	—	—	—
	Melbourne	Feb 12 1869	34	19	6	9	—
	East Melbourne	Jan 1 1889	1	1	—	—	—
	Hobart TCA	Jan 8 1890	25	13	6	6	—
	South Melbourne	Mar 15 1932	1	—	1	—	—
	Richmond	Mar 14 1933	1	1	—	—	—
	St Kilda	Jan 22 1957	4	1	—	3	—
	Geelong	Feb 19 1962	1	1	—	—	—
	Devonport	Jan 8 1983	4	1	—	3	—
	Carlton	Nov 15 1984	1	—	—	1	—
Total			102	51	20	31	—

Continued

Opponent	Venue	First Game	Games	W	L	D	T
Western Australia	Melbourne ————	Apr 1 1893	41	15	8	18	—
	Perth ————	Feb 26 1910	46	14	11	21	—
	Fremantle————	Mar 5 1910	1	—	1	—	—
	Fitzroy ————	Nov 6 1925	1	1	—	—	—
	St Kilda ————	Feb 10 1956	5	1	1	3	—
	Carlton ————	Nov 9 1984	1	—	—	1	—
Total			94	31	21	42	—
West Indians	Melbourne ————	Nov 28 1930	10	1	2	7	—
World XI	Melbourne ————	Nov 5 1971	1	—	—	1	—
Total for Victoria			847	334	252	258	3

Most Appearances for Victoria

Games	Player	Career	Games	Player	Career
114	RJ Bright	1972/73–1987/88	65	J Worrall	1883/84–1901/02
99	WM Lawry	1955/56–1971/72	64	RN Harvey	1946/47–1956/57
95	DF Whatmore	1975/76–1988/89	62	WJ Scholes	1968/69–1981/82
92	IR Redpath	1961/62–1975/56	62	AIC Dodemaide	1983/84–1989/90
87	GN Yallop	1972/73–1984/85	61	W Bruce	1882/83–1903/04
83	WW Armstrong	1989/99–1921/22	61	H Ironmonger	1913/14–1933/34
83	AN Connolly	1959/60–1970/71	60	CC McDonald	1947/48–1962/63
83	JD Higgs	1970/71–1982/83	60	DM Jones	1981/82–1989/90
81	J Potter	1956/57–1967/68	60	JD Siddons	1984/85–1989/90
80	J Ryder	1912/13–1931/32	59	GHS Trott	1885/86–1907/08
79	RC Jordon	1959/60–1970/71	59	WM Woodfull	1921/22–1933/34
78	F Laver	1891/92–1911/12	59	MG Hughes	1981/82–1989/90
77	IW Johnson	1935/36–1955/56	58	JM Wiener	1977/78–1984/85
77	SJE Loxton	1946/47–1957/58	56	WA Johnston	1935/36–1955/56
77	PA Hibbert	1974/75–1986/87	55	WH Ponsford	1920/21–1933/34
76	VS Ransford	1903/04–1927/28	55	GM Watts	1977/78–1989/90
76	RD Robinson	1971/72–1981/82	54	AE Liddicut	1911/12–1932/33
75	KR Stackpole	1959/60–1973/74	53	PA McAlister	1898/99–1910/11
73	BA Barnett	1929/30–1946/47	53	W Carkeek	1903/04–1914/15
73	AL Hassett	1932/33–1952/53	51	JH Stuckey	1891/92–1909/10
72	KE Rigg	1926/27–1938/39	51	JV Saunders	1899/00–1909/10
70	MHN Walker	1968/69–1981/82	51	LO Fleetwood-Smith	1931/32–1939/40
67	DT Ring	1938/39–1952/53	51	IS Lee	1931/32–1940/41
67	MGD Dimattina	1984/85–1989/90	51	TJ Laughlin	1974/75–1980/81
66	LV Maddocks	1946/47–1961/62	50	AG Hurst	1972/73–1980/81
66	RM Cowper	1959/60–1969/70	50	JK Moss	1976/77–1981/82

Youngest Players on First-Class Debut for Victoria

Player	Date of Birth	F/Class Debut	Opponent	Venue	Age on Years	Debut Days
LJ Junor	Apr 27 1914	Jan 17 1930	Western Australia	Melbourne	15	285
EF a'Beckett	Apr 16 1836	Mar 29 1852	Tasmania	South Yarra	15	348
P Shea	Mar 16 1896	Jan 24 1913	New South Wales	Sydney	16	314
IW Johnson	Dec 8 1918	Dec 31 1935	Tasmania	Launceston	17	23
JW Scaife	Nov 14 1909	Jan 25 1927	Tasmania	Melbourne	17	72
WB Wedgwood	Oct 23 1912	Jan 17 1930	Western Australia	Melbourne	17	86
GR Hazlitt	Sep 4 1888	Dec 29 1905	South Australia	Adelaide	17	116
RT Tuttle	Sep 11 1920	Feb 1 1938	Tasmania	Melbourne	17	143
D Campbell	Sep 18 1851	Feb 12 1869	Tasmania	Melbourne	17	147
LS Darling	Aug 14 1909	Jan 25 1927	Tasmania	Melbourne	17	164
KJ Schneider	Aug 15 1905	Feb 2 1923	Tasmania	Melbourne	17	171
M a'Beckett	Sep 26 1834	Mar 29 1852	Tasmania	South Yarra	17	185
GR Parker	Mar 31 1968	Dec 6 1985	England XI	Melbourne	17	250
G Cavenagh	Jun 16 1836	Mar 3 1854	Tasmania	Launceston	17	260
IS Lee	Mar 24 1914	Dec 18 1931	Queensland	Melbourne	17	269
RG Gregory	Feb 28 1916	Feb 15 1934	Western Australia	Melbourne	17	353

▶

Highest Innings Totals for Victoria

Total	Opponent	Venue	Season
1107	New South Wales	Melbourne	1926/27
1059	Tasmania	Melbourne	1922/23
793	Queensland	Melbourne	1927/28
724	South Australia	Melbourne	1920/21
699	South Australia	Melbourne	1907/08
697	South Australia	Adelaide	1945/46
660	Tasmania	Melbourne	1909/10
649	South Australia	Melbourne	1926/27
647	Tasmania	Melbourne	1951/52
8d-646	South Australia	Adelaide	1927/28
639	South Australia	Adelaide	1920/21
637	South Australia	Melbourne	1927/28
4d-633	Queensland	Melbourne	1962/63
626	Tasmania	Launceston	1908/09
620	South Australia	Adelaide	1921/22
6d-617	MCC	Melbourne	1922/23
614	South Australia	Melbourne	1910/11
609	South Australia	Melbourne	1983/84
605	South Australia	Melbourne	1919/20
604	South Australia	Melbourne	1925/26
602	New Zealanders	Melbourne	1898/99
7-601	West Indians	Melbourne	1984/85

Lowest Completed Innings Totals

Total	Opponent	Venue	Season
15	MCC	Melbourne	1903/04
28	New South Wales	Melbourne	1855/56
31	New South Wales	Sydney	1906/07
34	New South Wales	Melbourne	1875/76
35	New South Wales	Melbourne	1887/88
35	New South Wales	Sydney	1926/27
37	New South Wales	Redfern	1875/76
38	New South Wales	The Domain	1856/57
38	New South Wales	The Domain	1858/59
43	South Australia	Melbourne	1895/96
45	New South Wales	The Domain	1862/63
50	Tasmania	Tasmania	1853/54
50	MCC	Melbourne	1924/25
56	New South Wales	Melbourne	1859/60
56	New South Wales	Redfern	1872/73
57	Tasmania	Launceston	1850/51
58	New South Wales	The Domain	1866/67
59	New South Wales	Melbourne	1857/58
61	New South Wales	The Domain	1868/69
61	New South Wales	Sydney	1886/87
63	New South Wales	Melbourne	1855/56
63	New South Wales	The Domain	1856/57
65	Tasmania	Melbourne	1895/96
67	Tasmania	Hobart LRG	1857/58
68	New South Wales	The Domain	1860/61
68	New South Wales	Sydney	1886/87
68	A Shrewsbury's XI	Melbourne	1887/88
68	Tasmania	Melbourne	1933/34
70	New South Wales	Redfern	1874/75
71	New South Wales	The Domain	1860/61
71	New South Wales	Redfern	1874/75
73	Lord Sheffield's XI	Melbourne	1891/92
73	Western Australia	Melbourne	1971/72
74	New South Wales	The Domain	1866/67
75	A Shaw's XI	Melbourne	1881/82

Leading Batsmen for Victoria

Batsman	Career	M	Inn	NO	Runs	HS	Avrge	100s
WM Lawry	1955/56–1971/72	99	164	16	7618	266	51.47	20
WH Ponsford	1920/21–1933/34	55	87	7	6902	437	86.27	28
AL Hassett	1932/33–1952/53	73	121	13	6825	232	63.19	23
GN Yallop	1972/73–1984/85	87	156	14	6815	246	47.99	20
WW Armstrong	1898/99–1921/22	83	143	14	6732	250	52.18	23
IR Redpath	1961/62–1975/76	92	159	12	6103	261	41.51	13
J Ryder	1912/13–1931/32	80	137	13	5674	295	45.75	14
DF Whatmore	1975/76–1988/89	95	166	7	5545	170	34.87	10

Continued

377

Batsman	Career	M	Inn	NO	Runs	HS	Avrge	100s
WM Woodfull	1921/22–1933/34	59	94	21	5484	275*	75.12	18
J Potter	1956/57–1967/68	81	135	15	5101	221	42.50	13
RN Harvey	1946/47–1956/57	64	103	5	4914	209	50.14	12
PA Hibbert	1974/75–1986/87	77	132	10	4775	163	39.13	9
RM Cowper	1959/60–1969/70	66	101	14	4611	195*	53.00	10
KE Rigg	1926/27–1938/39	71	116	—	4582	167*	43.22	13
VS Ransford	1903/04–1927/28	76	123	13	4536	182	41.23	13
KR Stackpole	1959/60–1973/74	75	122	8	4483	145	39.32	8
DM Jones	1981/82–1989/90	60	100	6	4301	243	45.75	12
JD Siddons	1984/85–1989/90	60	100	7	4055	241*	43.60	11
AP Sheahan	1965/66–1973/74	47	78	11	3988	202	59.52	12
CC McDonald	1947/48–1962/63	60	101	8	3919	229	42.13	8
RD Robinson	1971/72–1981/82	76	121	26	3838	185	40.40	6
F Laver	1891/92–1911/12	78	141	15	3496	164	27.74	4
SJE Loxton	1946/47–1957/58	77	114	13	3492	232*	34.57	7
PA McAlister	1898/99–1910/11	53	99	3	3458	224	36.02	9
LS Darling	1926/27–1936/37	47	76	4	3451	188	47.93	10
IS Lee	1931/32–1940/41	51	86	2	3409	258	40.58	7
GM Watts	1977/78–1989/90	55	101	2	3405	176	34.39	8
JK Moss	1976/77–1981/82	50	84	7	3356	220	43.58	9
JM Wiener	1977/78–1984/85	58	108	4	3241	221*	31.16	7
WJ Scholes	1968/69–1981/82	62	112	8	3201	156	30.77	3

Most Runs in a Season for Victoria

Batsman	Season	M	Inn	NO	Runs	HS	50	100	Avrge
GN Yallop	1982/83	12	22	1	1418	246	6	4	67.52
WH Ponsford	1927/28	6	8	—	1217	336	1	4	152.12
WH Ponsford	1926/27	5	8	—	1091	352	2	5	136.37
JD Siddons	1987/88	11	18	2	1077	241*	5	4	67.31
AL Hassett	1950/51	9	16	3	1057	232	2	4	81.30
MD Taylor	1983/84	11	18	4	1010	172*	3	4	72.14
GM Watts	1989/90	12	23	1	940	162*	5	3	42.73
DF Whatmore	1989/90	11	19	1	912	170	7	2	50.67

Highest Individual Innings for Victoria

Score	Batsman	Opponent	Venue	Season
437	WH Ponsford	Queensland	Melbourne	1927/28
429	WH Ponsford	Tasmania	Melbourne	1922/23
352	WH Ponsford	New South Wales	Melbourne	1926/27
336	WH Ponsford	South Australia	Melbourne	1927/28
325*	HSTL Hendry	New Zealanders	Melbourne	1925/26
295	J Ryder	New South Wales	Melbourne	1926/27
275*	WM Woodfull	MCC	Melbourne	1928/29
275*	WH Ponsford	South Australia	Melbourne	1928/29
271	RI Maddocks	Tasmania	Melbourne	1951/52
266	WM Lawry	New South Wales	Sydney	1960/61
261	IR Redpath	Queensland	Melbourne	1962/63
258	IS Lee	Tasmania	Melbourne	1933/34
250	WW Armstrong	South Australia	Melbourne	1911/12
248	WH Ponsford	Queensland	Melbourne	1923/24
246	WM Lawry	South Australia	Melbourne	1964/65
246	GN Yallop	Queensland	Melbourne	1982/83
245	WW Armstrong	South Australia	Melbourne	1920/21
243	DM Jones	Western Australia	Perth	1984/85
242	J Ryder	South Australia	Melbourne	1921/22
241*	JD Siddons	South Australia	Adelaide	1987/88
236	WM Woodfull	South Australia	Melbourne	1925/26
234*	MD Taylor	West Indians	Melbourne	1984/85
232*	SJE Loxton	Queensland	Melbourne	1946/47
232	AL Hassett	MCC	Melbourne	1950/51
231	WW Armstrong	South Australia	Melbourne	1907/08
229	AL Hassett	South Australia	Melbourne	1951/52
229	CC McDonald	South Australia	Adelaide	1953/54
228	RL Park	South Australia	Melbourne	1919/20
226*	PJ Beames	Tasmania	Launceston	1938/39
224	PA McAlister	New Zealanders	Melbourne	1898/99
221*	JM Wiener	Western Australia	St Kilda	1981/82
221	J Potter	New South Wales	Melbourne	1965/66
221	KH Eastwood	South Australia	Adelaide	1970/71
220	NF Mitchell	Tasmania	Melbourne	1926/27
220	JK Moss	South Australia	Melbourne	1978/79
220	GN Yallop	Pakistanis	Melbourne	1983/84

Continued

Score	Batsman	Opponent	Venue	Season
218	GEJ Healy	Tasmania	Melbourne	1909/10
214	WH Ponsford	South Australia	Adelaide	1926/27
212°	WM Woodfull	Canterbury	Christchurch	1924/25
211	C McKenzie	Western Australia	Perth	1909/10
211°	AL Hassett	South Australia	Melbourne	1938/39
210	SO Quin	Tasmania	Melbourne	1933/34
209	ER Mayne	Queensland	Melbourne	1923/24
209	RN Harvey	New South Wales	Sydney	1956/57
207	CC McDonald	New South Wales	Sydney	1951/52
206°	KR Miller	New South Wales	Sydney	1946/47
206	FA Tarrant	New South Wales	Sydney	1907/08
206	KD Meuleman	Tasmania	Melbourne	1947/48
205	AL Hassett	Queensland	Brisbane	1948/49
204	AL Hassett	Queensland	Brisbane	1947/48
204°	GW Richardson	Queensland	Melbourne	1983/84
202°	WW Armstrong	Queensland	Melbourne	1913/14
202	WH Ponsford	New South Wales	Melbourne	1927/28
202	J Hallebone	Tasmania	Melbourne	1951/52
202	AP Sheahan	South Australia	Melbourne	1966/67
201°	KH Eastwood	New South Wales	Sydney	1970/71
200	WW Armstrong	Queensland	Melbourne	1904/05
200	AL Hassett	Queensland	Brisbane	1946/47
200°	JK Moss	Western Australia	Melbourne	1981/82
200	WH Ponsford	New South Wales	Sydney	1932/33

Leading Wicket-Takers for Victoria

Bowler	Career	M	Runs	Wkts	Avrge	5wi	10m	Best
AN Connolly	1959/60–1970/71	83	8925	330	27.04	12	4	9/67
H Ironmonger	1913/14–1933/34	61	6964	313	22.24	26	8	8/31
LO Fleetwood-Smith	1931/32–1939/40	51	7194	295	24.38	31	10	9/36
RJ Bright	1972/73–1987/88	114	9902	279	35.49	11	—	6/61
IW Johnson	1935/36–1955/56	77	6560	270	24.29	14	3	6/27
JD Higgs	1970/71–1982/83	83	8091	264	30.64	13	2	8/66
JV Saunders	1899/00–1913/14	51	6475	264	24.52	24	4	8/106
WW Armstrong	1898/99–1921/22	83	5587	248	22.52	7	—	6/66
MHN Walker	1968/69–1981/82	70	6999	248	28.22	11	—	6/49
DT Ring	1938/39–1952/53	67	7362	236	31.19	8	2	6/84
H Trumble	1887/88–1903/04	47	4832	229	21.10	15	6	8/39
AG Hurst	1972/73–1980/81	50	5047	199	25.36	7	1	8/84
WA Johnston	1945/46–1954/55	56	5496	192	28.62	9	3	8/52
MG Hughes	1981/82–1989/90	59	6106	185	33.00	7	2	7/81
GHS Trott	1885/86–1907/08	59	4520	181	24.97	12	2	8/63
I Meckiff	1956/57–1963/64	37	3802	164	23.18	7	1	5/41
AL Thomson	1968/69–1974/75	35	3906	160	24.41	12	3	8/87
IW Callen	1976/77–1982/83	41	4330	159	27.33	6	1	8/42
DD Blackie	1924/25–1932/33	33	3705	158	23.44	10	2	7/25
AIC Dodemaide	1983/84–1989/90	62	5676	158	35.92	4	—	5/43
F Laver	1891/92–1911/12	78	5086	154	33.02	3	—	6/17
J Ryder	1912/13–1931/32	80	4454	150	29.69	7	1	7/53
FB Collins	1899/00–1908/09	35	3730	145	25.72	11	—	7/61
SJE Loxton	1946/47–1957/58	77	3644	144	25.30	1	—	6/49
EL McCormick	1929/30–1938/39	43	3832	134	28.59	4	1	9/40
EA McDonald	1911/12–1921/22	22	2754	134	20.55	10	3	8/42
CE McLeod	1893/94–1904/05	41	3370	132	25.53	11	1	7/34
JC Hill	1945/46–1955/56	38	2896	125	23.16	5	—	7/51
AEV Hartkopf	1911/12–1928/29	40	3592	120	29.93	7	1	8/105
HI Ebeling	1923/24–1937/38	44	3647	117	31.17	2	1	7/33
AE Liddicut	1911/12–1932/33	54	3262	118	27.64	2	—	7/40
SP Davis	1983/84–1987/88	43	3957	116	34.11	5	—	7/104
LF Kline	1955/56–1961/62	31	3366	115	29.26	6	—	6/35
KR Stackpole	1959/60–1973/74	75	4115	112	36.74	2	—	5/38
JW Grant	1964/65–1968/69	43	3469	110	31.53	4	—	6/37
GE Palmer	1878/79–1894/95	19	1719	103	16.68	12	5	7/46
IW Quick	1956/57–1961/62	34	3360	102	32.94	4	—	7/47

Most Wickets in a Season for Victoria

Bowler	Season	M	Overs	Mdns	Runs	Wkts	Avrge	5wi	10m	Best
LO Fleetwood-Smith	1934/35	6	270.4	25	1137	60	18.95	8	3	8/113
I Meckiff	1962/63	10	353.7	62	1152	58	19.86	3	—	5/50
AL Thomson	1969/70	9	303.2	45	1031	55	18.74	6	2	8/87
AN Connolly	1967/68	9	325.4	80	961	52	18.48	4	1	7/61

▶

379

Best Bowling in an Innings for Victoria

Wkts	Bowler	Opponent	Venue	Season
9/2	G Elliott	Tasmania	Launceston	1857/58
9/36	LO Fleetwood-Smith	Tasmania	Richmond	1932/33
9/40	EL McCormick	South Australia	Adelaide	1936/37
9/45	GE Tribe	Queensland	Brisbane	1945/46
9/61	S Cosstick	Combined XIII	Melbourne	1872/73
9/67	AN Connolly	Queensland	Brisbane	1964/65
9/135	LO Fleetwood-Smith	South Australia	Melbourne	1937/38
8/20	FE Allan	New South Wales	The Domain	1868/69
8/21	S Cosstick	New South Wales	Redfern	1870/71
8/31	H Ironmonger	West Indians	Melbourne	1930/31
8/35	FE Allan	New South Wales	Melbourne	1871/72
8/39	H Trumble	South Australia	Melbourne	1898/99
8/42	EA McDonald	New South Wales	Sydney	1918/19
8/42	IW Callen	Queensland	Melbourne	1976/77
8/44	SAJ Smith	Tasmania	Hobart TCA	1933/34
8/52	WA Johnston	Queensland	Melbourne	1952/53
8/58	H Trumble	New South Wales	Melbourne	1898/99
8/63	GHS Trott	AE Stoddart's XI	Melbourne	1894/95
8/66	JD Higgs	Western Australia	Melbourne	1974/75
8/67	PH Wallace	Western Australia	Melbourne	1921/22
8/79	LO Fleetwood-Smith	Queensland	Melbourne	1936/37
8/84	EA McDonald	New South Wales	Sydney	1921/22
8/84	AG Hurst	Queensland	Melbourne	1977/78
8/87	AL Thomson	New South Wales	Melbourne	1969/70
8/105	AEV Hartkopf	MCC	Melbourne	1922/23
8/106	JV Saunders	South Australia	Adelaide	1902/03
8/110	H Trumble	South Australia	Adelaide	1889/90
8/111	LO Fleetwood-Smith	South Australia	Melbourne	1933/34
8/113	LO Fleetwood-Smith	New South Wales	Sydney	1934/35
8/129	H Trumble	South Australia	Adelaide	1898/99

Best Bowling in a Match for Victoria

Wkts	Bowler	Opponent	Venue	Season
15/96	LO Fleetwood-Smith	Queensland	Melbourne	1936/37
15/199	H Trumble	South Australia	Adelaide	1889/90
15/226	LO Fleetwood-Smith	New South Wales	Sydney	1934/35
14/85	LO Fleetwood-Smith	Tasmania	Richmond	1932/33
13/50	TW Antill	Tasmania	Launceston	1850/51
13/60	FE Allan	New South Wales	Melbourne	1871/72
13/118	H Ironmonger	West Indians	Melbourne	1930/31
13/128	AEV Hartkopf	MCC	Melbourne	1922/23
13/141	AL Thomson	New South Wales	Melbourne	1969/70
13/153	J Ryder	South Australia	Melbourne	1912/13
13/153	G Tribe	South Australia	Adelaide	1946/47
13/165	AN Connolly	South Australia	Adelaide	1967/68
13/181	H Ironmonger	South Australia	Melbourne	1914/15
13/195	JV Saunders	South Australia	Adelaide	1902/03
12/35	TWS Wills	Tasmania	Hobart LRG	1857/58
12/69	CA Reid	Tasmania	Melbourne	1870/71
12/79	RB Scott	New South Wales	Sydney	1938/39
12/79	J Carlton	Tasmania	Melbourne	1890/91
12/91	GHS Trott	Tasmania	Hobart TCA	1889/90
12/91	TJ Matthews	Tasmania	Launceston	1908/09
12/96	EL McCormick	South Australia	Adelaide	1936/37
12/99	S Cosstick	Combined XIII	Melbourne	1872/73
12/99	JD Higgs	Western Australia	Melbourne	1979/80
12/107	DDJ Blackie	MCC	Melbourne	1929/30
12/158	LO Fleetwood-Smith	South Australia	Melbourne	1933/34
12/171	GE Tribe	New South Wales	Sydney	1946/47
12/180	EA McDonald	South Australia	Melbourne	1918/19
12/181	IW Johnson	Queensland	Brisbane	1950/51
12/184	IW Johnson	South Australia	Adelaide	1953/54
12/195	H Ironmonger	South Australia	Adelaide	1930/31
12/262	JV Saunders	New South Wales	Sydney	1905/06
12/272	LO Fleetwood-Smith	South Australia	Melbourne	1937/38

Most Dismissals by a Wicket-Keeper for Victoria

Wicket-Keeper	Career	M	Cght	Stmp	Total
RD Robinson	1971/72–1981/82	76	235	30	265
RC Jordon	1959/60–1970/71	79	226	34	260
JL Ellis	1918/19–1929/30	72	146	56	202
MGD Dimattina	1984/85–1989/90	67	167	21	188
BA Barnett	1929/30–1946/47	73	126	50	176
LV Maddocks	1946/47–1961/62	66	129	43	172
IH McDonald	1948/49–1952/53	39	78	51	129
W Carkeek	1903/04–1914/15	53	67	32	99
JM Blackham	1874/75–1894/95	45	51	39	90
IL Maddocks	1977/78–1981/82	22	71	13	84
EA Baker	1935/36–1948/49	24	53	20	73
SO Quinn	1930/31–1937/38	24	34	25	59

Most Dismissals in a Season for Victoria

Wicket-Keeper	Season	M	Cght	Stmp	Total
IL Maddocks	1977/78	10	39	4	43
RC Jordon	1968/69	10	36	3	39
NM Carlyon	1969/70	10	31	6	37
RC Jordon	1962/63	10	36	—	36
MGD Dimattina	1985/86	11	34	2	36
RC Jordon	1970/71	8	33	2	35
RD Robinson	1976/77	9	31	4	35
RD Robinson	1972/73	9	31	2	33
RD Robinson	1973/74	9	28	5	33
IL Maddocks	1978/79	10	27	6	33
MGD Dimattina	1987/88	11	30	3	33
IH McDonald	1951/52	9	24	8	32
RD Robinson	1971/72	8	30	2	32
MGD Dimattina	1986/87	12	29	2	31
LV Maddocks	1956/57	7	26	4	30
RC Jordon	1964/65	8	24	6	30
MGD Dimattina	1984/85	10	24	6	30

Most Dismissals in a Match for Victoria

Ttl	Ct	St	Wicket-Keeper	Opponent	Venue	Season
10	9	1	RC Jordon	South Australia	Melbourne	1970/71
9	9	—	EA Baker	New South Wales	Melbourne	1946/47
9	2	7	EA Baker	New South Wales	Sydney	1946/47
9	8	1	RD Robinson	New South Wales	Melbourne	1973/74
9	8	1	RD Robinson	South Australia	Adelaide	1980/81
9	6	3	MGD Dimattina	South Australia	Melbourne	1985/86
8	7	1	LV Maddocks	New South Wales	Sydney	1956/57
8	8	—	LV Maddocks	Western Australia	Perth	1956/57
8	7	1	RC Jordon	South Australia	Melbourne	1964/65
8	8	—	RC Jordon	Queensland	Melbourne	1968/69
8	8	—	RD Robinson	New South Wales	Sydney	1972/73
8	7	1	RD Robinson	New South Wales	Melbourne	1975/76

Most Dismissals in an Innings for Victoria

Ttl	Ct	St	Wicket-Keeper	Opponent	Venue	Season
6	6	—	EA Baker	New South Wales	Melbourne	1946/47
6	1	5	EA Baker	New South Wales	Sydney	1946/47
6	6	—	RC Jordon	Queensland	Melbourne	1968/69
6	5	1	RD Robinson	Queensland	Brisbane	1974/75
6	6	—	MGD Dimattina	South Australia	Adelaide	1985/86
5	—	5	JM Blackham	Lord Harris's XI	Melbourne	1878/79
5	4	1	JE Monfries	New South Wales	Melbourne	1903/04
5	5	—	W Carkeek	New South Wales	Melbourne	1912/13
5	4	1	JL Ellis	South Australia	Melbourne	1920/21
5	4	1	BA Barnett	New South Wales	Sydney	1930/31
5	2	3	SO Quinn	Tasmania	Hobart TCA	1931/32
5	4	1	BA Barnett	South Australia	Melbourne	1932/33
5	3	2	SO Quinn	Western Australia	Melbourne	1937/38
5	2	3	IH McDonald	Queensland	Brisbane	1949/50
5	3	2	IH McDonald	New South Wales	Melbourne	1950/51
5	4	1	IH McDonald	South African	Melbourne	1952/53
5	4	1	LV Maddocks	New South Wales	Sydney	1956/57
5	5	—	LV Maddocks	Queensland	Melbourne	1958/59
5	4	1	LV Maddocks	South Australia	Melbourne	1959/60
5	4	1	RC Jordon	Queensland	Brisbane	1961/62

Continued

Ttl	Ct	St		Wicket-Keeper	Opponent	Venue	Season
5	5	—		RC Jordon	South Australia	Melbourne	1964/65
5	5	—		RC Jordon	South Australia	Melbourne	1970/71
5	4	1		RC Jordon	South Australia	Melbourne	1970/71
5	4	1		RD Robinson	New South Wales	Melbourne	1973/74
5	4	1		RD Robinson	Tasmania	Launceston	1976/77
5	5	—		IL Maddocks	Queensland	Melbourne	1978/79
5	5	—		RD Robinson	Queensland	Brisbane	1979/80
5	4	1		RD Robinson	South Australia	Adelaide	1980/81
5	5	—		GJ Miles	New South Wales	Melbourne	1982/83
5	5	—		PA Hyde	Western Australia	Perth	1983/84
5	5	—		MGD Dimattina	Tasmania	Carlton	1984/85
5	4	1		MGD Dimattina	Western Australia	Perth	1984/85
5	5	—		MGD Dimattina	Queensland	Melbourne	1985/86

Most Catches by a Fieldsman for Victoria

Fieldsman	Career	M	Catches
DF Whatmore	1975/76–1988/89	95	123
WW Armstrong	1898/99–1921/22	83	102
H Trumble	1887/88–1903/04	47	88
J Ryder	1912/13–1931/32	80	78
F Laver	1891/92–1911/12	78	75
KR Stackpole	1959/60–1973/74	75	74
RM Cowper	1959/60–1969/70	66	73
IR Redpath	1961/62–1975/76	92	72
GN Yallop	1972/73–1984/85	87	72
RJ Bright	1972/73–1987/88	114	71
J Potter	1956/57–1967/68	81	70
GHS Trott	1885/86–1907/08	59	69
AL Hassett	1932/33–1952/53	73	68
PA McAlister	1898/99–1910/11	53	64
DT Ring	1938/39–1952/53	67	62
IW Johnson	1935/36–1955/56	77	56
J Worrall	1883/84–1901/02	65	56
DM Jones	1981/82–1989/90	60	56

Most Catches in a Season for Victoria

Catches	Fieldsman	M	Season
17	JD Swanson	10	1969/70
17	DF Whatmore	11	1985/86
17	DF Whatmore	12	1986/87
17	PW Young	9	1987/88
15	DF Whatmore	11	1987/88
15	JD Siddons	10	1989/90
14	CN Compton	7	1957/58
14	DF Whatmore	10	1977/78
14	DF Whatmore	11	1978/79
13	H Trumble	4	1894/95
13	H Trumble	5	1897/98
13	GHS Trott	4	1892/93
13	WE Pearson	8	1937/38

Most Catches in a Match for Victoria

Ct	Fieldsman	Opponent	Venue	Season
7	H Trumble	South Australia	Melbourne	1900/01
5	OC Williams	New South Wales	Sydney	1870/71
5	GHS Trott	South Australia	Melbourne	1892/93
5	GHS Trott	New South Wales	Melbourne	1893/94
5	PA McAlister	South Australia	Melbourne	1901/02
5	J Ryder	MCC	Melbourne	1922/23
5	HSTL Hendry	Queensland	Brisbane	1926/27
5	CN Crompton	South Australia	Adelaide	1959/60
5	RM Cowper	Western Australia	Melbourne	1962/63
5	JD Swanson	Western Australia	Perth	1966/67
5	JD Swanson	South Australia	Melbourne	1969/70
5	WJ Scholes	Western Australia	St Kilda	1981/82

Most Catches in an Innings for Victoria

Ct	Fieldsman	Opponent	Venue	Season
5	H Trumble	South Australia	Melbourne	1900/01
5	PA McAlister	South Australia	Melbourne	1901/02
5	J Ryder	MCC	Melbourne	1922/23
4	J Carlton	New South Wales	Sydney	1892/93
4	GHS Trott	New South Wales	Sydney	1893/94
4	H Trumble	New South Wales	Sydney	1897/98
4	HSTL Hendry	Queensland	Brisbane	1926/27
4	HJ Plant	New South Wales	Melbourne	1935/36
4	WE Pearson	South Australia	Melbourne	1937/38
4	CN Crompton	South Australia	Adelaide	1959/60
4	RM Cowper	Western Australia	Melbourne	1962/63
4	JD Swanson	South Australia	Melbourne	1969/70
4	DF Whatmore	New South Wales	Sydney	1976/77
4	GN Yallop	Western Australia	Perth	1980/81
4	GN Yallop	Tasmania	St Kilda	1982/83
4	DF Whatmore	Tasmania	Devonport	1982/83

Partnership Records for Victoria

Wkt	Ttl	Batsmen	Opponent	Venue	Season
1st	456	WH Ponsford, ER Mayne	Queensland	Melbourne	1923/24
2nd	358	HHL Kortlang, C McKenzie	Western Australia	Perth	1909/10
3rd	390*	JM Wiener, JK Moss	Western Australia	St Kilda	1981/82
4th	424	IS Lee, SO Quin	Tasmania	Melbourne	1933/34
5th	343	RI Maddocks, J Hallebone	Tasmania	Melbourne	1951/52
6th	289	SJE Loxton, DT Ring	Queensland	Melbourne	1946/47
7th	187	PA McAlister, AW Murray	New Zealanders	Melbourne	1898/99
8th	215	WW Armstrong, RL Park	South Australia	Melbourne	1919/20
9th	146	TS Warne, A Facy	Tasmania	Launceston	1911/12
10th	211	M Ellis, TJ Hastings	South Australia	Melbourne	1902/03

Highest Partnerships for Victoria

Wkt	Ttl	Batsmen	Opponent	Venue	Season
1st	456	WH Ponsford, ER Mayne	Queensland	Melbourne	1923/24
4th	424	IS Lee, SO Quin	Tasmania	Melbourne	1933/34
3rd	390*	JM Wiener, JK Moss	Western Australia	St Kilda	1981/82
1st	375	WM Woodfull, WH Ponsford	New South Wales	Melbourne	1926/27
2nd	358	HHL Kortlang, C McKenzie	Western Australia	Perth	1909/10
5th	343	RI Maddocks, J Hallebone	Tasmania	Melbourne	1951/52
1st	337	CC McDonald, KD Meuleman	South Australia	Adelaide	1949/50
5th	336	WH Ponsford, HSB Love	Tasmania	Melbourne	1922/23
2nd	314	WH Ponsford, HSTL Hendry	Queensland	Melbourne	1927/28
4th	301	LPJ O'Brien, LS Darling	Queensland	Brisbane	1932/33
6th	289	SJE Loxton, DT Ring	Queensland	Melbourne	1946/47
3rd	281	KE Rigg, LS Darling	South Australia	Adelaide	1932/33
2nd	277	PA Hibbert, GW Richardson	Queensland	Melbourne	1983/84
2nd	271	MR Harvey, KR Miller	New South Wales	Melbourne	1946/47
5th	271	AJ Sieler, RP Rose	Queensland	Brisbane	1973/74
1st	270	KR Stackpole, AP Sheahan	Pakistanis	Melbourne	1972/73
5th	270	GN Yallop, DM Jones	Queensland	St Kilda	1982/83
5th	263	PLA Bedford, GD Watson	Western Australia	Melbourne	1969/70
6th	262	A Kenny, HHL Kortlang	Queensland	Brisbane	1909/10
4th	262	IS Lee, RG Gregory	MCC	Melbourne	1936/37
2nd	261	PA Hibbert, GN Yallop	South Australia	Geelong	1980/81
5th	255	GEJ Healy, F Vaughan	Tasmania	Melbourne	1909/10
6th	254	GN Yallop, RD Robinson	Western Australia	Melbourne	1976/77
2nd	252	WM Lawry, J Potter	New South Wales	Sydney	1960/61

MELBOURNE CRICKET

It was fitting that a 1st XI premiership closely contested throughout the season should have culminated in an exciting final, which was won by Richmond after several fluctuations in fortune by a mere 3 runs. It was a remarkable victory in many respects, one of them being that Richmond appeared to have lost its momentum as it approached the finals. Having begun the season with six wins in its first six matches, one of them an outright victory over North

Melbourne, Richmond went down in its last 3 and finished third on the points table. On the basis of recent form, therefore, it could not have been overly confident when it entered the finals. Clearly, the reappearance in the side of its state player Paul Reiffel made a big difference for Richmond, for Reiffel had an outstanding match in the final. Geoff Parker's return to form in the semi-final, after a generally disappointing season, was another important factor. Richmond's victory was its fourth in the 1st XI competition.

By contrast with Richmond, St Kilda sailed into the finals on a wave of success. Having at one stage looked unlikely to make the final four, St Kilda peeled off four wins in its last four games to finish at the top of the points table (indeed it won seven of its last eight) and at this stage it was certainly favoured to win the premiership. Moreover, its captain, Shaun Graf, who had had an indifferent season, regained his best form just at this point and produced marvellous performances in the semi-final and the final. Even so, St Kilda fell just short of victory. Darren Walker, a left-arm pace bowler, had a lot to do with St Kilda's success during the season and finished ninth in the competition bowling averages with 37 wickets at 18.91. He was St Kilda's outstanding bowler in the final, too, taking 5 wickets. Another St Kilda player, the all-rounder Warren Whiteside, won the Ryder Medal as the district player of the year for the second time. Whiteside, an attacking batsman and medium-pace bowler, made 606 runs at 37.87 and took 28 wickets at 20.14. He had previously won the Ryder Medal in 1986-87.

By finishing second on the points table behind St Kilda, South Melbourne continued the curious series of ups and downs it had begun three seasons before. Having been at a low ebb in 1986-87, it made the final in 1987-88 but finished down the ladder again in 1988-89. Now, in 1989-90, it was back near the top of the points table, and it owed much of its success to the wicket-taking capacity of its fast bowler Peter Smith, whose 53 wickets for the season were not only the highest aggregate in the competition but the highest since 1969-70, when the Essendon pace bowler John Grant took 66. At 22 years of age, Smith had only recently made the move from Geelong to Melbourne. He combined with the veteran leg-spinner Leigh Baker (32 wickets at 19.84) and the medium-pacer Geoff Van Vugt (31 wickets at 26.45) to form an effective attack. On the other hand, South Melbourne's batting was generally found wanting, so much so that the team managed to better 250 only once in the whole season.

Melbourne had led the competition after Christmas, but a succession of losses towards the end of the season reduced it to fourth place. Indeed, before the last round Melbourne was challenged on the points table by four other clubs—Carlton, Hawthorn, North Melbourne and Essendon—and if it had lost the match any of these four clubs might have replaced it in the final four. (The fact that Essendon, which eventually finished seventh, lost three leading players to the state side for much of the season—Simon O'Donnell, Jamie Siddons and Peter McIntyre—ought to be considered in any assessment of its performance.) Melbourne's premier batsman was

AUSTRALIAN INSTITUTE OF SPORT

Left to Right: Cameron Williamson, David Clarke, Michael Bevan, Chris Mack, Clint Auty, Jaimie Williams, James Bolton, Martin McCague, Michael Slater, Dene Hills, Craig White, Matthew May, Brenden Julian. Absent: Philip Alley, Ken Vowles, Gary Wright

BARCLAYS BANK – UNDER 19 CHAMPIONSHIP – NEW SOUTH WALES
Back Row, l to r: Tim Fraser, Simon Waddington, Brett Wheeldon, Richard Chee Quee, Warwick Adlam, Michael Beattie, Jason Gallian, John Wilson (Manager). Front Row, l to r: Jason Young, Kevin Roberts, Gavan Twining, Ted Cotton (Coach), Darrell Mann (Captain), Ben Saunders, Mark Pratt

BARCLAYS BANK – UNDER 19 AUSTRALIAN SQUAD
Back Row, l to r: Bradley Ruddell, Shane George, Jason Young, Greg Blewett, Damien Martyn, Darrell Conroy, Ken Vowles, Matthew Fraser, David Castle, Laurie Harper. Front Row, l to r: Darrell Mann, Stephen Cottrell, Michael Kasprowicz, Jason Gallian, Warwick Adlam, Stuart Oliver, Darren Gascoine

WOOL CORPORATION CHAMPIONSHIP – UNDER 17s, VICTORIA

Back Row, l to r: John Barry (Scorer), Paul Broster, Adam Mayhood, Ritchie Dodds, Jason Ferns, Troy Corbett, Jason Duff, Scott Duane, Paul Jones (Manager). Front Row, l to r: Adrian McCormack, Peter Webb, Michael Foster (Captain), John Harmer (Coach), Brett Montgomery (Vice Captain), Stuart Anderson, Kane Purcell

GILLETTE CUP WINNERS – CRAIGMORE HIGH SCHOOL
Back Row, l to r: Paul Rotolo, Richard Williams (Vice Captain), Scott Donaldson (Captain), Andrew Maher, Matthew Burton. Middle Row, l to r: Conrad Thorn, Matthew Castek, Chris Svetec, Matthew Blackwood. Front Row, l to r: Tim Mullen, Juy Foreman, Jamie Griffiths, Marc Lunt

VSCA UNDER 19 WINNERS – VICTORIA
Back Row, l to r: P Hetherington, T Paton, T Bean, J Rees (Vice Captain), C Nash, S Gross, Br John Laidlaw (Coach/Manager). Front Row, l to r: G Vimpani, J Bott, M Butler (Captain), A Bishop, A Cavigan, G Newman

the opener Craig Bustard, an attacking batsman who headed the competition's batting aggregates with 696 runs at 36.60. This was only 2 runs ahead of the veteran player Brendan McArdle of Waverley-Dandenong, who raised his aggregate to 694 by scoring 108 not out, 164 not out, 3, 88 and 99 not out in his last five innings. Melbourne's other leading batsmen were Warren Ayres, Craig Bradley and Glen Jansz, while its successful bowlers included Denis Hickey (36 wickets at 23.22) and the all-rounder Richard Herman, who took 26 wickets and scored 374 runs.

Other players to make a mark in the 1st XI premiership competition included: Steve Milosz of Ringwood, who was second in the wicket aggregates with 45—a fine performance by a leg-spinner; Brian Jende of Fitzroy-Doncaster, who made a century on debut; Brian Salmon of Essendon who scored a century in each innings against North Melbourne; Gary Watts of Fitzroy-Doncaster who played only three matches but topped the batting averages with 293 runs at 97.66; and Tony Dodemaide of Footscray, who took 20 wickets at 12.85, the best average in the competition.

South Melbourne won the club championship ahead of St Kilda, Richmond and Essendon respectively. South Melbourne teams contested the finals in all four grades but, curiously, did not win any of them.

Points Table 1st XI Premiership

Club	Bat	Bowl	Match	Pen	Total
St Kilda	33.32	46.20	66	0	145.52
South Melbourne	27.38	52.15	64	0	143.53
Richmond	33.96	47.25	58	0	139.21
Melbourne	40.10	43.40	48	0	131.50
Carlton	30.97	45.50	48	0	124.47
North Melbourne	33.42	46.90	42	0	122.32
Essendon	33.80	46.90	42	1	121.70
Hawthorn	28.99	48.65	42	0	119.64
University	31.54	44.45	42	0	117.99
Collingwood	29.20	45.15	40	0	114.35
Prahran	32.46	41.65	36	0	110.11
Fitzroy-Doncaster	30.91	39.20	36	0	106.11
Northcote	26.93	44.10	36	1	106.03
Ringwood	30.46	44.45	24	0	98.91
Waverley-Dandenong	34.40	38.85	24	0	97.25
Footscray	31.81	37.10	24	4	88.91

FINAL

St Kilda v Richmond
Junction Oval, Melbourne
March 30-April 1, 1990
Result: Richmond won by 3 runs

Sent in to bat on a greenish pitch, Richmond collapsed at once in startling fashion. At lunch, it was 7 for 38, and after lunch it slumped further to 8 for 54. It was a desperate situation which appeared to have been produced by a combination of factors—a pitch helpful to pace bowlers, fine bowling by Darren Walker, in particular, who took four of the 8 wickets, and indifferent batting. At this point, however, Richmond was rescued by a remarkable partnership of 142 between its number 9 and 10 batsmen, Paul Reiffel, who eventually made 79 not out, and Ray Bright, who was out early on the second day for 77. Richmond added another 18 runs for the last wicket to be all out for 215. In reply, St Kilda began almost as badly as Richmond on the previous day, losing its first five wickets for 69. Reiffel, who took four of these wickets, was the cause of most of its problems. By now, however, St Kilda's captain, Shaun Graf, was at the crease, and he proceeded to play a fighting innings which took St Kilda to within touching distance of victory. St Kilda reached 7 for 187, then fell back to 9 for 197. Graf was still there, however, and he passed the century as the St Kilda total steadily moved towards the winning target. It was just 4 runs short of the target when Graf flicked at a legside delivery and was caught behind, giving Richmond victory and the premiership. For his exceptional performance, with the ball as well as the bat, Graf was named man of the finals series, following on from his 53 and 6 for 39 in the semi-final against Melbourne.

Richmond

Batsman	How Out	Ttl
MB Quinn	c Jacoby b Walker	4
GJ Clarke	c Jacoby b Walker	0
PA Quinn	c and b Graf	0
DA Harris	c Jacoby b Walker	11
GR Parker	c Johnstone b Graf	2
PJ Davies	c Osborne b Whiteside	24
PW Jackson	c Jacoby b Walker	0
DJ Saker	c Jacoby b Cull	5
PR Reiffel	not out	79
BJ Bright	c Graf b Walker	77
GJ Holland	run out	3
SUNDRIES		10
Total		215

F/W: 1 4 10 12 24 24 38 54 197 215

Bowler	O	M	R	Wkts
DK Walker	28	10	57	5
SF Graf	25.2	8	50	2
WG Whiteside	16	7	36	1
GA Cull	18	6	33	1
SK Warne	12	5	24	0
M Osborne	10	5	10	0

St Kilda

Batsman	How Out	Ttl
DA Johnstone	c Davies b Reiffel	7
D Evans	c Saker b Reiffel	2
WG Whiteside	lbw b Reiffel	7
RB Gartrell	c Saker b Quinn	11
J Murphy	b Reiffel	19
SF Graf	c Holland b Saker	102
M Osborne	c Holland b Jackson	10
JR Jacoby	b Bright	21
GA Cull	c Holland b Saker	7
DK Walker	c Reiffel b Saker	1
SK Warne	not out	0
SUNDRIES		25
Total		212

F/W: 7 19 24 50 69 106 155 187 197 212

Bowler		O	M	R	Wkts
PR Reiffel		34	11	58	4
DJ Saker		37	12	73	3
PA Quinn		14	3	31	1
RJ Bright		13	7	11	1
GR Parker		4	1	13	0
PW Jackson		8	4	18	1

Batting Averages—1st XI Premiership

Batsman	M	Inns	NO	Runs	HS	Avrge
GM Watts (Fitzroy-Doncaster)	3	3	0	293	141	97.66
BJ McArdle (Waverley-Dandenong)	13	14	5	694	164*	77.11
B Jende (Fitzroy-Doncaster)	6	7	3	275	103*	68.75
DA Harris (Richmond)	14	15	4	608	112*	55.27
DA Emerson (Collingwood)	14	15	4	569	95	51.72
LJ Watts (Fitzroy-Doncaster)	14	15	3	606	113	50.50
M Brasher (Northcote)	6	7	0	328	100	46.85
M Drain (Essendon)	9	9	1	361	112	45.12
NR Buszard (Collingwood)	14	11	5	267	68	44.50
GJ Allardice (University)	14	16	3	572	110*	44.00

Bowling Averages—1st XI Premiership

Bowler	O	Mn	Runs	Wkts	Avrge
AIC Dodemaide (Footscray)	116.3	24	257	20	12.85
BN Wigney (Hawthorn)	272.5	69	631	39	16.17
RC McCarthy (North Melbourne)	276.4	63	714	43	16.60
PJ Smith (South Melbourne)	358.4	84	892	53	16.83
PE McIntyre (Essendon)	147.1	45	357	21	17.00
PF Watkin (Hawthorn)	247	71	620	35	17.71
CA Ingram (Collingwood)	140.1	28	406	22	18.45
SJ Milosz (Ringwood)	364.1	94	839	45	18.64
DK Walker (St Kilda)	317.5	92	700	37	18.91
RN Lane (Carlton)	309.2	91	719	38	18.92

2ND XI PREMIERSHIP

Points Table

Richmond	169.48
Essendon	149.78
South Melbourne	139.43
Footscray	137.07
Collingwood	133.56
St Kilda	130.12
Hawthorn	128.58
Melbourne	120.88
Fitzroy-Doncaster	118.26
Carlton	118.16
Prahran	114.94
University	110.68
Ringwood	105.83
Northcote	98.99
Waverley-Dandenong	98.39
North Melbourne	73.16

FINAL

Richmond 230 (Quarterman 47, Foster 45; Bakker 5/32, D. Wright 3/67) defeated South Melbourne 167 (Chisholm 55; Coloe 5/50, Wrigglesworth 3-35)

3RD XI PREMIERSHIP

South Melbourne	144.12
St Kilda	137.17
Melbourne	131.40
Collingwood	129.15
Essendon	125.48
Footscray	117.06
Fitzroy-Doncaster	108.72
Waverley-Dandenong	106.19
Ringwood	101.82
Prahran	98.64
University	91.57
Northcote	90.01
Richmond	88.36
Carlton	80.56
Hawthorn	71.10
North Melbourne	58.92

FINAL

Melbourne 7 for 300 (Main 89, Williams 61, Haig 56) defeated South Melbourne 9 for 254 (Langley 103*, Chernikeef 52; Henning 3/90)

4TH XI PREMIERSHIP

Points Table

Prahran	142.60
Collingwood	128.75
Hawthorn	122.96
South Melbourne	122.82
Essendon	119.47
Melbourne	118.04
Footscray	109.94
St Kilda	100.98
Richmond	90.92
University	87.64
Ringwood	86.99
Carlton	77.59
Waverley-Dandenong	75.77
North Melbourne	74.85
Fitzroy-Doncaster	67.86
Northcote	63.16

FINAL

Prahran 4 for 248 (Williams 81*, Gerdan 66, Happell 42*) defeated Collingwood 9 for 237 (Jarvis 56; Gerdan 5/57).

CLUB CHAMPIONSHIP

Club	1st XI	2nd XI	3rd XI	4th XI	Total
South Melbourne	717.65	418.29	288.24	122.82	1 547.00
St Kilda	727.60	390.36	274.34	100.98	1 493.28
Richmond	696.05	508.44	176.72	90.92	1 472.13
Essendon	608.50	449.34	250.96	119.47	1 428.27
Melbourne	657.50	362.64	262.80	118.04	1 400.98
Collingwood	571.75	400.68	258.30	128.75	1 359.48
Hawthorn	598.20	385.74	142.20	122.96	1 249.10
Prahran	550.55	344.82	197.28	142.60	1 235.25
Carlton	622.35	354.48	161.12	77.59	1 215.54
Footscray	444.55	411.21	234.12	109.94	1 199.82
University	589.95	332.04	183.14	87.64	1 192.77
Fitzroy-Doncaster	530.55	354.78	217.44	67.86	1 170.63
Ringwood	494.55	317.49	203.64	86.99	1 102.67
Northcote	530.15	296.97	180.02	63.16	1 070.30
Waverley-Dandenong	486.25	295.17	212.38	75.77	1 069.57
North Melbourne	611.60	219.48	117.84	74.85	1 023.77

COUNTRY CRICKET

KLEENEX CUP

Goulburn-Murray won the competition for the first time since 1977 when it defeated Central Highlands in convincing fashion in the final at Kyabram on December 16 and 17, 1989.

ROUND 1
Group A: Mallee 8 for 211 and 1 for 50 defeated North East 206.
Goulburn Murray 192 and 7 for 205 defeated Loddon 109.
Group B: Barwon 7 for 183 defeated Gippsland 88 and 3 for 165.
Mornington Peninsula 9 for 307 and 0 for 19 defeated South Gippsland 244.
Group C: Central Highlands 137 and 261 defeated Wimmera 104.
Corangamite 318 defeated Glenelg 253.

ROUND 2
Group A: Mallee 238 and 6 for 174 defeated Loddon 121.
Goulburn Murray 260 and 1 for 103 defeated North East 153.
Group B: Barwon 321 defeated South Gippsland 132 and 4 for 100.
Mornington Peninsula 9 for 147 defeated Gippsland 143.
Group C: Corangamite 202 defeated Wimmera 158 and 6 for 103.
Central Highlands 144 and 4 for 72 defeated Glenelg 63.

ROUND 3
Group A: Goulburn Murray 287 and 2 for 11 defeated Mallee 251.
North East 271 defeated Loddon 172.
Group B: Gippsland 8 for 277 defeated South Gippsland 235.
Barwon 144 and 4 for 139 defeated Mornington Peninsula 129.
Group C: Central Highlands 251 and 4 for 123 defeated Corangamite 155.
Glenelg 8 for 304 defeated Wimmera 238.

POINTS TABLE
Group A: Goulburn Murray 52.58, Mallee 39.64, North East 24.30, Loddon 12.62.
Group B: Barwon 51.27, Mornington Peninsula 36.82, Gippsland 23.93, South Gippsland 12.51.
Group C: Central Highlands 51.88, Corangamite 38.75, Glenelg 25.00, Wimmera 13.63.

Finalists: 1. Goulburn Murray, 2. Central Highlands, 3. Barwon, 4. Mallee.

SEMI FINALS

Goulburn Murray 7 for 295 (M Ryan 100, T Canobie 54*, M McMaster-Smith 38) defeated Mallee 294 (T Forster 133, D Hogarth 31, C Tomich 31; G Newman 6/89).
Central Highlands 188 (D Ward 56, G Davidson 35; G Wiese 5/44) defeated Barwon 108 (J O'Brien 41, D Duxson 35; M Marrow 4/17, D Wilson 3/43).

FINAL

Goulburn Murray v Central Highlands
Northern Oval, Kyabram
December 16-17, 1989
Result: Goulburn Murray won by 76 runs

Goulburn Murray

Batsman	How Out	Ttl
R D'Orria	c Davidson b Wilson	1
M McMaster-Smith	c Cairns b Wilson	76
P Stokes	b Ward	69
M Ryan	c Ward b Marrow	38
S Davidson	c Cole b Marrow	20
S Merkel	c Cole b Daly	11
T Canobie	b Daly	9
R Matthews	lbw b Cairns	37
R Taylor	not out	40
G McKenzie	not out	6
Sundries		18
Total		8 for 325

Bowler	O	M	R	Wkts
N Marrow	21	4	67	2
D Wilson	12	0	36	2
P Daly	21	1	65	2
P Cairns	16	0	70	1
A Bell	6	0	23	0
D Ward	26	4	59	1

Central Highlands

Batsman	How Out	Ttl
M Wood	c Taylor b Newman	3
M Skinner	st Taylor b Ryan	77
D Ward	b Newman	0
S Lynch	c & b Ryan	63
G Davidson	c Ryan b Trevaskis	4
P Cairns	c Taylor b Trevaskis	29
B Skinner	c Taylor b Trevaskis	7
D Cole	b Canobie	42
M Marrow	b Trevaskis	2
P Daly	not out	5
D Wilson	b McKenzie	4
Sundries		13
Total		249

Bowler	O	M	R	Wkts
G Newman	21	5	50	2
X Trevaskis	25	7	52	4
G McKenzie	8.2	0	45	1
M Ryan	20	6	50	2
M McMaster-Smith	11	1	36	0
T Canobie	3	0	10	1

The 1989-90 Kleenex Superteam, chosen after the Kleenex Cup matches, was: Matthew McMaster-Smith (captain) of Goulburn Murray, Darren Ward (vice-captain) of Central Highlands, Tim Baker of Loddon, Justin Bridgeman of Mornington Peninsula, Dwayne Duxson of Barwon, David Hogarth of Mallee, Anthony Matthews of South Gippsland, Paul Quick of North East, Geoff Stewart of Gippsland, Rodney Taylor of Goulburn Murray, Glen Wiese of Barwon and Andrew Wills of Barwon.

COUNTRY WEEK

A total of 56 teams competed in the 1990 championship, which was held, as usual, at various grounds in Melbourne in mid-February. Albury and Border won the Provincial division, thus completing a rapid rise through the divisions which it began two years before. In 1988, Albury and Border was the winner in Division 3 and, accordingly, was promoted in 1989 to Division 2. It won this division, too, so it was promoted to the Provincial division in 1990. Before the tournament began, much interest was centred on Warrnambool's chances of winning the Provincial division for the third year in a row, which, under the competition rules, would have entitled it to keep the Ewen Kirkton trophy. In fact, Warrnambool finished second last in the competition and so was relegated to Division 2.

PROVINCIAL DIVISION

DIVISION 1
Premiers: Albury and Border
Final: Albury and Border 9 for 212 defeated Bendigo 141.
Points Table: Albury and Border 63.33, Bendigo 50.87, Bairnsdale 39.38, Ballarat 38.31, Geelong 37.90, Kyabram 37.55, Warrnambool 23.82, Warragul 12.60.

DIVISION 2
Premiers: Mornington Peninsula
Final: Mornington Peninsula 8 for 191 defeated Sale-Maffra 136
Points Table: Mornington Peninsula 62.66, Sale-Maffra 50.39, Shepparton 50.24, Horsham 37.39, Traralgon 37.25, Leongatha 25.19, Sunraysia 25.17, Grampians 12.46.

DIVISION 3
Premiers: Wangaratta
Final: Wangaratta 5 for 223 defeated Central Gippsland 171.
Points Table: Central Gippsland 52.02, Wangaratta 50.87, Hamilton 49.14, Murray Valley 38.46, Echuca 38.11, South Gippsland 37.99, Yea-Ferntree Gully 24.97, Swan Hill 9.76.

DIVISION 4
Premiers: Benalla
Final: Benalla 1 for 106 defeated Alexandra-Mansfield 9 for 105.
Points Table: Benalla 60.06, Alexandra-Mansfield 51.95, Euroa 50.70, West Gippsland 39.12, Rochester 38.04, Maryborough 27.03, Portland 26.77, Geelong Southern 25.66.

DIVISION 5
Premiers: Geelong and District
Final: Geelong and District 9 for 198 defeated Yarra Valley 94.
Points Table: Yarra Valley 62.66, Geelong and District 60.94, Colac
53.60, Castlemaine 25.19, Hampden 24.95, Ovens and Kiewa 24.34,
Ouyen 24.17, Yarrawonga 14.92.

DIVISION 6
Premiers: Gisborne
Final: Gisborne 190 defeated Alberton 86.
Points Table: Gisborne 66.43, Alberton 57.17, Ranceby 52.11,
Wodonga 50.32, Seymour 29.41, Geelong Churches 23.81, Rutherglen
13.49, Timboon-Stoneyford 11.42.

DIVISION 7
Premiers: Leigh
Final: Leigh 9 for 158 defeated Hopkins-Nullawarre 9 for 157.
Points Table: Leigh 63.63, Hopkins-Nullawarre 60.01, Nathalia 59.05,
Robinvale 38.39, West Wimmera 36.07, Donald 34.93,
Upper Murray 11.87.

WOMEN'S CRICKET

NEW ZEALAND TOUR

AUSTRALIA MAINTAINED ITS DOMINANCE of trans-Tasman cricket on a four-week tour of New Zealand in January and February. Australia won the three-Test series by one match to nil, thus becoming the first winner of the new Southern Cross Trophy, which had been donated by the Australian Government during the season as a perpetual trophy for Australia-New Zealand Test series. Australia also won the Shell Rose Bowl series of one-day matches, defeating New Zealand by two matches to one. Australia's success was built around its batting, which had exceptional depth and resilience. Even when early wickets were lost, Australia could invariably count on two or three players getting runs. In fact, on only one occasion did its batting fail completely, and that was in the one-day match won by New Zealand. The depth of Australia's batting talent was illustrated by the fact that Joanne Broadbent, who made a century in the national titles, batted at number 10 or even 11 for Australia.

The Australian all-rounder Lyn Larsen was named Player of the Series at the end of the limited-overs tournament. In the first match, which Australia won, she scored 54 not out, and in the third and deciding match, also won by Australia, she took three wickets with her leg spin at a critical point. There was no award for the player of the Test series, but if there had been it might well have been won by the Australian fast bowler Debbie Wilson, who made deep inroads into the New Zealand batting in almost every innings. In the four innings in which she bowled, her figures were 4 for 58, 1 for 42, 4 for 50 and 5 for 42.

TEST SERIES

FIRST TEST

New Zealand v Australia
Cornwall Park, Auckland
January 18-21, 1990
Result: Match Drawn

Batting first, Australia was in some trouble at 7 for 157 when Sally Griffiths was joined by Debbie Wilson, batting at nine. Griffiths and Wilson shared in a partnership of 181, which enabled Australia to finish with a substantial total of 371. Griffiths made 133 and Wilson.

was not out 92 when the innings ended. With virtually no chance now of winning the match, New Zealand's priority was to avoid the follow-on, which meant it had to score 221. A determined innings of 126 not out by Debbie Hockley ensured that New Zealand passed this total—although only by 8 runs. In the time remaining, Australia barely had time to start its second innings.

Australia

First Innings

Batswoman	How Out	Ttl
B Haggett	lbw b Harris	13
K Raymont	lbw b Campbell	25
Z Goss	run out	40
D Annetts	lbw J Turner	19
S Griffiths	c Hockley b Campbell	133
A McCauley	lbw b Harris	8
K Brown	lbw b Harris	8
L Larsen (c)	c Kinsella b Legg	1
D Wilson	not out	92
C Matthews	c Kinsella b Campbell	3
J Broadbent	run out	8
SUNDRIES		21
TOTAL		371

F/W: 15 80 88 121 135 154 157 338 353 371

Second Innings

How Out	Ttl
not out	27
run out	22
not out	0
	3
1 for 52	

F/W: 49

Bowler	O	M	R	Wkts
J Turner	32.3	11	70	2
J Harris	33	7	84	2
B Legg	33	18	41	1
K Gunn	33	17	35	0
C Campbell	44	11	106	3
D Hockley	5	0	15	0

Bowler	O	M	R	Wkts
Turner	9	2	17	0
Harris	7	3	11	0
Legg	3	2	3	0
Gunn	11	8	3	0
Campbell	7	0	17	0

New Zealand

First Innings

Batswoman	How Out	Ttl
J Clark	c Matthews b Larsen	26
P Kinsella	c Raymont b Wilson	4
D Hockley	not out	126
L Murdoch (c)	lbw b Wilson	31
N Turner	b Wilson	0
I Jagersma	c Matthews b Wilson	8
K Gunn	b Brown	0
J Turner	b Brown	5
B Legg	c Matthews b Goss	1
C Campbell	b McCauley	5
J Harris	b Broadbent	2
SUNDRIES		21
TOTAL		229

F/W: 16 54 139 149 165 166 184 203 211 229

Bowler	O	M	R	Wkts
D Wilson	34	14	58	4
K Brown	27	13	27	2
J Broadbent	26.1	10	39	1
Z Goss	18	7	35	1
L Larsen	30	18	29	1
A McCauley	16	6	22	1

SECOND TEST

New Zealand v Australia
Basin Reserve, Wellington
January 26-29, 1990
Result: Match Drawn

The match ended in an inconsequential draw after rain washed out a day and a half's play. Batting first, the Australians showed consistency in the top order in scoring 9 declared for 325. Belinda Haggett made 70 and Denise Annetts 64. The New Zealanders seemed in some danger after losing 3 for 63, but the Australian bowlers ceased to make much headway after that, and New Zealand had no trouble avoiding the follow-on.

Australia

First Innings

Batswoman	How Out	Ttl
B Haggett	lbw b Legg	70
K Raymont	b Hockley	47
Z Goss	run out	38
D Annetts	b Harris	64
S Griffiths	lbw b J Turner	4
L Larsen	run out	26
K Brown	b J Turner	17
D Wilson	b Harris	17
C Matthews	run out	2
J Broadbent	not out	13
S Moffat	not out	10
SUNDRIES		17
TOTAL	9 dec for 325	

F/W: 88 145 182 198 260 281 298 301 302

Bowler	O	M	R	Wkts
J Turner	34	9	75	2
J Harris	28	11	53	2
B Legg	25	10	48	1
K Gunn	28	9	49	0
C Campbell	21	2	69	0
D Hockley	11	6	15	1

New Zealand

First Innings

Batswoman	How Out	Ttl
J Clark	b Larsen	31
P Kinsella	c Raymont b Broadbent	12
D Hockley	lbw b Brown	10
L Murdoch	lbw b Wilson	31
N Turner	not out	65
I Jagersma	c Matthews b Broadbent	5
K Gunn	b Larsen	25
J Turner	b Larsen	2
B Legg	not out	3
SUNDRIES		14
TOTAL	7 for 198	

F/W: 45 45 63 119 143 191 193

Bowler	O	M	R	Wkts
D Wilson	24	8	42	1
K Brown	20	11	18	1
J Broadbent	22	10	32	2
L Larsen	19	9	22	3
S Moffat	19	11	20	0
Z Goss	19	5	46	0
D Annetts	2	1	8	0

THIRD TEST

New Zealand v Australia
Hagley Oval, Christchurch
February 1-4, 1990
Result: Australia won by 8 wkts

New Zealand's opener Jackie Clark made 40 and Debbie Hockley a steady 77, but New Zealand compiled only the modest total of 9 declared for 197 in its first innings. Debbie Wilson, who took 4 for 50, was a renewed problem for the New Zealanders, none of whom played her with confidence. Australia made runs right down the list, Karen Brown top scoring with 65, and it declared its innings at 9 for 292, 95 ahead. In their second innings, the New Zealanders dug in on the last day to try to save the match, but they could not withstand the bowling of Debbie Wilson, who took 5 for 42. Wilson claimed the important wicket of Hockley, bowling her for a duck a few balls after striking her a painful blow on the elbow. Pacing themselves carefully, the Australians scored the 58 runs needed for victory with several overs to spare. The Australians owed their victory not only to their superior play but to the fact that not a minute's play was lost through rain.

New Zealand

First Innings			Second Innings	
Batswoman	How Out	Ttl	How Out	Ttl
J Clark	b Larsen	40	c Matthews b Wilson	14
L Murdoch	c Matthews b Brown	7	lbw b Wilson	1
D Hockley	lbw b Wilson	77	b Wilson	0
P Kinsella	lbw b Moffat	0	lbw b Brown	8
N Turner	b Wilson	6	c Larsen b Moffat	17
I Jagersma	c Wilson b Moffat	1	c Matthews b Brown	21
K Gunn	c Larsen b Wilson	37	b Larsen	23
B Legg	c Annetts b Wilson	0	b Wilson	26
J Turner	not out	11	c Haggett b Broadbent	1
C Campbell	b Goss	7	c Brown b Wilson	29
J Harris	not out	1	not out	1
SUNDRIES		10		11
TOTAL		9 dec for 197		152

F/W: 23 62 68 87 92 175 177 178 191

F/W: 16 16 20 30 61 67 96 97 143 152

Bowler	O	M	R	Wkts	Bowler	O	M	R	Wkts
D Wilson	27.2	10	50	4	Wilson	29.4	17	42	5
K Brown	20	10	30	1	Brown	20	5	36	2
J Broadbent	19	6	50	0	Broadbent	16	8	15	1
L Larsen	16	7	21	1	Larsen	26	18	14	1
S Moffat	16	10	12	2	Moffat	9	4	18	1
Z Goss	19	13	25	1	Goss	23	12	20	0

Australia

First Innings			Second Innings	
Batswoman	How Out	Ttl	How Out	Ttl
B Haggett	b J Turner	45	b J Turner	12
K Raymont	lbw b J Turner	25	b Gunn	23
Z Goss	lbw J Turner	0	not out	17
D Annetts	run out	38	not out	4

Continued

First Innings					Second Innings				
Batswoman	*How Out*			*Ttl*	*How Out*				*Ttl*
S Griffiths	c Jagersma b Legg			16					
L Larsen (c)	b Harris			10					
D Wilson	c Hockley b Campbell			26					
K Brown	c Jagersma b Legg			65					
C Matthews	lbw b Harris			14					
J Broadbent	not out			36					
S Moffat	not out			3					
SUNDRIES				14					2
TOTAL				9 dec for 292					2 for 58

F/W: 75 75 76 103 136 141 196 237 283   F/W 12 44

Bowler	*O*	*M*	*R*	*Wkts*	*Bowler*	*O*	*M*	*R*	*Wkts*
J Turner	28	10	62	3	J Turner	12	2	23	1
J Harris	20	6	57	2	J Harris	6	2	19	0
C Campbell	27	6	56	1					
B Legg	30	11	57	2					
K Gunn	22	7	47	0	K Gunn	5	2	14	1

SHELL ROSE BOWL LIMITED-OVERS TOURNAMENT

MATCH 1

New Zealand v Australia *60-over Match*
Lancaster Park, Christchurch
February 6, 1990
Result: Australia won by 3 wkts

Debbie Hockley and Karen Gunn both made half-centuries for New Zealand, and the home side was all out in the last over for 200. They would certainly have made more runs if they had judged their running better, for four of them were run out. The New Zealanders were entitled to feel optimistic after Australia lost 3 wickets for 21, but Denise Annetts (75) and Lyn Larsen (54 not out) saw the side out of its difficulties. Larsen, the captain, was still at the crease when Australia won the match in the 59th over with 3 wickets to spare.

New Zealand

Batswoman	*How Out*	*Ttl*
L Murdoch (c)	b Goss	14
J Clark	c Matthews b Brown	2
D Hockley	c Brown b Broadbent	56
K Bond	run out	25
P Kinsella	run out	1
K Gunn	run out	52
I Jagersma	c Haggett b Wilson	18
B Legg	lbw b Wilson	0
J Turner	b Wilson	0
C Campbell	run out	5
J Harris	not out	1
SUNDRIES		26
TOTAL		200

F/W: 3 43 101 102 115 171 177 177 199 200

Bowler	*O*	*M*	*R*	*Wkts*
D Wilson	12	2	24	2
K Brown	11	2	35	2
A McCauley	7	0	24	0
Z Goss	12	1	36	1
L Larsen	8	0	31	0
J Broadbent	10	1	34	1

▶

Australia

Batswoman	How Out	Ttl
B Haggett	c & b Legg	5
Z Goss	lbw b J Turner	4
D Annetts	st Jagersma b Hockley	75
M Papworth	run out	2
S Griffiths	lbw b Campbell	32
L Larsen	not out	54
K Brown	c J Turner b Legg	2
A McCauley	run out	7
D Wilson	not out	5
SUNDRIES		15
TOTAL		7 for 201

F/W: 6 18 21 58 170 175 188

Bowler	O	M	R	Wkts
J Turner	12	1	43	1
J Harris	12	4	20	0
B Legg	11.2	5	25	2
C Campbell	3	0	29	1
K Gunn	11	1	40	0
D Hockley	9	0	38	1

MATCH 2

New Zealand v Australia   60-over Match
Hutt Recreation Ground, Lower Hutt
February 10, 1990
Result: New Zealand won by 8 wkts

For once, Australia was let down badly by its batting. The Australians were dismissed in 54 overs for the modest total of 122, only Debbie Wilson (29 not out) offering much resistance. The pitch provided some help to the New Zealand bowlers, who were nevertheless entitled to take most of the credit for the Australians' demise. The New Zealanders had no trouble scoring the runs they needed for victory, losing only 2 wickets in the process. New Zealand's eight wicket victory squared the series at one all.

Australia

Batswoman	How Out	Ttl
B Haggett	c Harris b Gunn	13
Z Goss	c Hockley b Gunn	8
D Annetts	lbw b Gunn	5
H Papworth	c Jagersma b Campbell	18
S Griffiths	run out	9
J Broadbent	c Jagersma b J Turner	1
L Larsen (c)	run out	4
K Brown	c Jagersma b J Turner	9
D Wilson	not out	29
C Matthews	c Murdoch b Gunn	15
S Moffat	c and b Gunn	0
SUNDRIES		11
TOTAL		122

F/W: 22 25 30 52 55 61 70 92 122 122

Bowler	O	M	R	Wkts
J Turber	9	1	16	2
J Harris	12	7	15	0
B Legg	12	5	21	0
K Gunn	9	2	22	5
C Campbell	6	2	21	1
D Hockley	6	0	22	0

New Zealand

Batswoman	How Out	Ttl
J Clark	c Matthews b Brown	37
L Murdoch	not out	48
D Hockley	run out	11
K Bond	not out	16
SUNDRIES		11
TOTAL		2 for 123

F/W: 58 88

Bowler	O	M	R	Wkts
D Wilson	10	4	17	0
Z Goss	10	0	41	0
K Brown	9	4	12	1
L Larsen	8.4	5	20	0
S Moffat	12	2	28	0

MATCH 3

New Zealand v Australia   60-over Match
Hutt Recreation Ground, Lower Hutt
February 11, 1990
Result: Australia won by 57 runs

Batting first, the Australians did not score nearly as many runs as they would have liked and were all out (four of them by run outs) in the last over for a modest 168. Zoe Goss opened the batting and played a laboured innings, but in the end her 50 proved to be the salvation of her side. The Australian total was clearly within reach of the New Zealanders, who began their innings in determined fashion. Their total reached a promising 1 for 59 before the Australian leg-spinner Lyn Larsen took the first of a series of wickets which turned around the match. New Zealanders were dismissed at 59, 62, 63 and 64, and the Australian bowlers closed in to finish the innings off. New Zealand was all out for 111, which gave Australia victory by 57 runs and the series. Lyn Larsen finished with 3 for 19 and Karen Brown 2 for 23.

Australia

Batswoman	How Out	Ttl
K Raymont	lbw b Harris	2
Z Goss	c Jagersma b Legg	50
D Annetts	run out	7
L Larsen	run out	10
S Griffiths	run out	9
M Papworth	b Harris	19
K Brown	c N Turner b Gunn	10
D Wilson	b Legg	0
J Broadbent	c Murdoch b J Turner	18
C Matthews	run out	21
S Moffat	not out	4
SUNDRIES		18
TOTAL		168

F/W: 9 23 40 58 92 116 120 120 157 168

Bowler	O	M	R	Wkts
J Turner	11	1	24	1
J Harris	12	5	18	2
B Legg	12	2	25	2
K Gunn	12	4	35	1
C Campbell	9	2	32	0
D Hockley	4	1	21	0

▶

New Zealand

Batswoman	How Out	Ttl
J Clark	c and b Moffat	13
D Hockley	c and b Larsen	20
K Bond	b Larsen	26
N Turner	run out	14
K Gunn	c Wilson b Brown	1
I Jagersma	c and b Larsen	1
B Legg	c Annetts b Brown	17
J Turner	c Griffiths b Wilson	13
C Campbell	b Goss	0
J Harris	not out	0
L Murdoch	injured—did not bat	
SUNDRIES		6
TOTAL		9 for 111

F/W: 22 59 62 63 64 90 105 111 111

Bowler	O	M	R	Wkts
D Wilson	10	2	33	1
K Brown	12	2	23	2
Z Goss	9.2	1	13	1
S Moffat	12	5	21	1
L Larsen	12	4	19	3

Batting Averages—Tests

Batswoman	M	I	NO	HS	Runs	Avge
D Wilson	3	3	1	92*	135	67.50
J Broadbent	3	3	2	36*	57	57.00
S Griffiths	3	3	0	133	153	51.00
B Haggett	3	5	1	70	167	41.75
D Annetts	3	4	1	64	125	41.67
Z Goss	3	5	2	40	95	31.67
K Brown	3	3	0	65	90	30.00
K Raymont	3	5	0	47	142	28.40

Batting—Tour

Batswoman	M	I	NO	HS	Runs	Avge
Z Goss	8	9	3	91*	248	41.33
D Annetts	8	8	1	77	289	41.29
B Haggett	7	9	2	70	275	39.29
S Griffiths	7	6	0	133	203	33.83
M Papworth	5	5	2	33*	81	27.00
J Broadbent	8	5	2	36*	76	25.33
K Raymont	6	8	0	47	186	23.25
L Larsen	7	6	1	54*	105	21.00
K Brown	8	6	0	65	111	18.50
S Moffat	6	4	3	10*	17	17.00

Bowling Averages—Tests

Bowler	O	M	R	Wkts	Avge
D Wilson	114	49	192	14	13.71
L Larsen	91	52	86	6	14.33
S Moffat	44	25	50	3	16.67
K Brown	87	29	111	6	18.50
A McCauley	16	6	22	1	22.00
J Broadbent	83.1	34	136	4	34.00
Z Goss	79	37	126	2	63.00

400

Bowler	O	M	R	Wkts	Avge
D Wilson	146	57	266	17	15.65
K Brown	128	40	208	13	16.00
A McCauley	43	9	103	6	17.16
L Larsen	119.4	61	156	9	17.33
A Rowell	22	8	40	2	20.00
S Moffat	90	40	139	6	23.17
J Broadbent	115.1	39	228	8	28.50
Z Goss	123.2	42	241	6	40.17

NATIONAL CHAMPIONSHIP

New South Wales went through the tournament undefeated and so won the championship comfortably. The final placings were:

New South Wales	54.56
Victoria	51.23
South Australia	37.05
ACT	35.28
Western Australia	35.06
Queensland	22.78

New South Wales's success was not confined to the senior championship, for it won the two under-age competitions, too. Victoria, the defending champion in all three championships, finished runner-up to New South Wales in all three.

Sally Griffiths was named Player of the Series. Although Griffiths is better known for her fast bowling than her batting, she rescued her side from tough situations several times during the tournament. She topped both aggregates and averages with 182 runs at 45.50. Debbie Wilson was the leading wicket-taker with 24 wickets and Lyn Larsen (13 wickets at 6.77) led the averages.

MATCH 1
Victoria 155 (H Sattler 44; F Leonard 5/22) and 2 for 82 defeated Western Australia 96 (D Wilson 22; K Brown 4/33, C Fitzpatrick 4/27) by 59 runs on the first innings.

MATCH 2
New South Wales 146 (S Griffiths 44; K Hitchcock 3/35, B Calver 3/41) and 5 for 106 defeated ACT 90 (L Pepper 25; S Griffiths 4/19, S Moffat 3/15) by 56 runs on the first innings.

MATCH 3
South Australia 6 declared for 250 (J Broadbent 102*, A McCauley 64*, C Pickering 48; A Rowell 3/41) defeated Queensland 167 (I Tsakiris 4/23) and 4 for 85 by 83 runs on the first innings.

MATCH 4
Western Australia 9 declared for 222 (Z Goss 54, D Wilson 50, F Leonard 39) defeated Queensland 109 (K Raymont 49; D Wilson 5/32, Z Goss 4/20) and 6 for 110 (B Sigley 51*; D Wilson 4/35) by 113 runs on the first innings.

MATCH 5

New South Wales 144 (S Griffiths 40*; J Broadbent 5/42) defeated South Australia 130 (T Juhasz 33; S Moffat 3/22) and 5 for 121 (M Bradley 37*) by 14 runs on the first innings.

MATCH 6

Victoria 146 (M Papworth 43; B Calver 5/40, K Hitchcock 4/36) and 2 for 64 defeated ACT 124 (L Cook 62*; K Brown 4/19, C Fitzpatrick 4/39) by 22 runs on the first innings.

MATCH 7

Victoria 185 (M Papworth 55; A Rowell 5/33) and 2 declared for 77 defeated Queensland 111 (B Sigley 27; D Richey 4/22, K Brown 3/21) and 98 (K Raymont 20; S Gell 4/34, K Brown 3/12) outright by 53 runs.

MATCH 8

South Australia 209 (M Bradley 41, L Hunter 38; B Calver 3/40) and 3 for 43 defeated ACT 158 (B Calver 41*; L Fullston 3/28, J Broadbent 3/35) by 51 runs on the first innings.

MATCH 9

New South Wales 6 declared for 305 (M Brogan 99*, D Annetts 57, B Haggett 38; D Wilson 3/73) defeated Western Australia 73 (T Meintanis 25; B Mitchell 3/20) and 4 for 75 by 232 runs on the first innings.

MATCH 10

Western Australia 8 declared for 196 (T Meintanis 36, F Leonard 32, D Wilson 30) defeated South Australia 100 (L Fullston 30*; Z Goss 5/20, D Wilson 4/30) and 9 for 80 (L Hunter 28; Z Goss 6/24) by 96 runs on the first innings.

MATCH 11

ACT 183 (B Calver 50, R van der Zwet 31, H Drew 31; D Zipf 3/17) defeated Queensland 157 (M Ready 36, K Raymont 34, D Andrew 32; J Davis 4/45) and 1 for 5 by 26 runs on the first innings.

MATCH 12

New South Wales 253 (D Annetts 66, S Griffiths 61, B Haggett 41; K Saunders 4/42) and 2 for 33 defeated Victoria 158 (H Sattler 40; L Larsen 4/27, M Brogan 3/18) by 95 runs on the first innings.

MATCH 13

ACT 143 (L Cook 33; D Wilson 5/42) drew with Western Australia 9 for 134 (Z Goss 52, F Leonard 35; L Cook 4/40).

MATCH 14

New South Wales 122 (L Larsen 32; D Zipf 4/26, A Rowell 4/51) defeated Queensland 113 (M Stephenson 28) by 9 runs on the first innings.

MATCH 15
Victoria 9 for 171 (K Saunders 56*, C Fitzpatrick 34*, S Heywood 32; J Broadbent 6/23) defeated South Australia 154 (S Gell 3/35) by 17 runs on the first innings.

AUSTRALIAN UNDER 21 CHAMPIONSHIP

This tournament, conducted in Perth from January 14 to 25, was won by New South Wales. The final points table was: New South Wales 44, Victoria 36, Western Australia 26, Queensland 25, South Australia 20.

The Player of the Series was Sue Marsh of New South Wales. Helen Bancroft of Western Australia topped the batting aggregates with 207 runs and Deanna Thompson of New South Wales topped the batting averages with 66.0. T Langsford of New South Wales was the leading wicket-taker with 15 wickets, and Sue Marsh of New South Wales had the best bowling average, 9.50.

AUSTRALIAN UNDER 18 CHAMPIONSHIP

New South Wales won this limited-overs tournament, held in Sydney from December 11 to 15, 1989. The final placings were: 1. New South Wales, 2. Victoria, 3. President's XI, 4. South Australia. K Rolton of South Australia topped the batting aggregates with 108 runs and M Prouten of New South Wales topped the batting averages with 53.5. The leading wicket-takers were J Garey of New South Wales and J Walsh of Victoria with 8 wickets each, and S Whitehouse of Victoria had the best bowling average, 7.0.

ACT

THE ACT WAS GENERALLY SUCCESSFUL in the matches it played during the season, demonstrating again that at full strength its representative team is at least a match for state 2nd XIs. The ACT won the New South Wales Tooheys Limited Over Country Cup for the fifth time in seven seasons, and it finished second behind New South Wales in the Prudential national country championship. Two ACT players took the field for state teams in first-class cricket— Michael Bevan, who scored a century in his first first-class innings for South Australia, and Greg Rowell played one match for New South Wales. Their success provided further evidence of the ACT's growing strength as a cricketing entity and, accordingly, the ACT Cricket Association is continuing to seek inclusion in the FAI Insurance Cup competition. For the third time, Greg Irvine was named the ACT's representative player of the year. The grade player of the year was Steve O'Shaughnessy.

ACT v Newcastle Manuka Oval, Canberra, November 11-12, 1989

The ACT achieved an exciting victory over Newcastle in the final over of the match after its batsmen launched a furious assault on the bowling in the final session of play. Until tea on the second day, it seemed the match was destined to be an inconsequential draw. Sent in to bat on the opening day, Newcastle had batted without apparent purpose, reaching a total of 6 for only 218 at stumps. Tony Daley had batted steadily for 96, and Mark Curry had played a bright innings of 41. Newcastle pressed on next day, finally declaring at 8 for 272 at lunch. It was clear the ACT would be hard-pressed to score the runs in the time available, and its batting before tea suggested that it did not even intend to try. At tea the ACT was only 1 for 74, which meant it would have to make 199 runs at almost a run per ball. Michael Frost and Andrew Yates lifted the scoring rate after tea with brief but adventurous innings, but it was John Bull's appearance at the crease which ultimately proved decisive. With a spectacular display of hitting, Bull scored 62 runs in 47 minutes, striking 24 runs off just one over bowled by the left-arm spinner Greg McNeil. Darryle MacDonald and Ken Rooke carried on after Bull's departure, Rooke scoring the winning run in the final over.

ACT 7 for 273 (J Bull 62, G Woodbridge 42, M Frost 42, D MacDonald 31, A Yates 28, K Rooke 26*; M Christie 2/31, M Curry 2/44) defeated Newcastle 8 for 272 (A Daley 96, M Curry 41, G McNeil 31; G Irvine 2/32, K Bone 2/63, C Crouch 2/70) by three wickets.

ACT v AIS Cricket Academy Manuka Oval, November 28-30, 1989
Result: AIS won by 39 runs on the first innings
For details, see section on AIS.

ACT v Victoria 2nd XI Manuka Oval
December 5-7, 1989

Rain interruptions on the first two days virtually ruled out any chance of an outright result in this match, which was later awarded on the first innings to the ACT. Victoria's progress was hampered by rain interruptions, and it was only 2 for 47 at stumps on the first day. Eventually, it declared at 6 for 285. In reply, the ACT raced to a total of 4 for 287 in a little over five hours, thanks largely to an aggressive innings of 125 not out by Gordon Greenidge, who hit 13 fours. Earlier, Peter Solway had set the tone for the ACT innings by scoring 63 in an hour and a half. Warren Ayres played a fine innings of 137, in the course of which he shared a partnership of 143 with the AIS batsman Craig White, who made 77. Eugene Nix took 2 for 36.

ACT 4 for 287 (G Greenidge 125*, P Solway 63, G Woodbridge 36) defeated Victoria 2nd XI 6 for 285 (W Ayres 137, C White 77; E Nix 2/36) on the first innings.

ACT v New South Wales 2nd XI Manuka Oval, Canberra
December 19-21, 1989

ACT's bowlers set up an outright victory in this match by forcing New South Wales to follow on but then failed to press home the advantage, and in the end the ACT could claim merely a win on the first innings. Having won the toss and chosen to bat, the ACT was all out just before lunch on the second day for 338. Peter Solway batted in enterprising fashion for 101, hitting 13 fours, and while he and Neil Woods (64) were sharing a second-wicket partnership of 147 it seemed the ACT was likely to compile a really large total. New South Wales began promisingly enough, but Ken Macleod and Eugene Nix between them produced a middle-order collapse, in the course of which New South Wales lost 5 wickets for 61. New South Wales was 8 for 177 at stumps on the second day and was all out next morning for 186. Macleod took 4 for 51 and Nix 3 for 32. Scott Jacobson defied the ACT bowlers until the end with an innings of 66. ACT thus had nearly a whole day to bowl out New South Wales again, but in their second innings the visitors proved a much tougher proposition, and at the end had placed themselves well out of danger with a total of 3 for 267, Michael Slater having top scored with 139.

ACT 338 (P Solway 101, N Woods 64, G Greenidge 38, D Macdonald 30*; A Jones 4/66, T Shiner 2/66) defeated New South Wales 2nd XI 186 (S Jacobson 66, M Slater 32; L Macleod 4/51, E Nix 3/32) and 3 for 267 (M Slater 139, R Green 79; G Irvine 2/28) on the first innings.

ACT v Tasmania 2nd XI *50-over Match* **Kingston Oval, Canberra**
January 15, 1990

The ACT's team had not returned from the national country championships in Bendigo, so it was virtually a reserve team which took the field against Tasmania. Sent in, the Tasmanians scored so easily on the Kingston pitch that they were 7 for 259 at the end of their 50 overs. Michael Farrell, soon to make his debut for the state side, top scored with 78, scored off 144 balls. Steve O'Shaughnessy was the most successful of the home side's bowlers with 3 for 58. The ACT struggled from the outset to score at the required rate, and lost wickets steadily until it was all out in the 47th over for 206. O'Shaughnessy rounded off a personally successful match by top scoring with 40.

Tasmanian 2nd XI 7 for 259 (M Farrell 78, D Buckingham 48, B Cruse 45; S O'Shaughnessy 3/58, M Thornton 2/38) defeated ACT 206 (S O'Shaughnessy 40, S Smith 38, M Frost 29, J Bull 23; P McPhee 3/36, M Courtney 4/41) by 53 runs.

ACT v Tasmania 2nd XI   Manuka Oval, Canberra
January 16-18, 1990

Honours finished about even in this high-scoring match. The Tasmanians took so long to compile their huge first innings total of 613 that their bowlers had little hope of bowling the side to an outright victory. In the end the ACT batsmen denied the Tasmanians even a first-innings victory, and they gave the Tasmanian bowlers rough treatment while scoring 6 for 418. Having chosen to bat, the Tasmanians occupied the crease until 5pm on the second day. Michael Farrell again dominated the batting with a careful innings of 143. The ACT, still missing several leading players, lost 3 wickets before stumps, and the expectation was they would have to defend grimly on the final day to avoid defeat. Instead, the ACT batsmen batted with great fluency and in the final session, in particular, scored at a furious pace. The Lancashire player Nick Speak was the leading scorer with 107.

Tasmanian 2nd XI 613 (M Farrell 143, T Coyle 89, A de Winter 71, M Bowerman 70, D O'Connor 67, C Young 55, D Buckingham 43; S Smith 4/135) drew with ACT 6 for 418 (N Speak 107, J Williams 85°, G Woodbridge 76, G Irvine 63°; P McPhee 3/89).

ACTCA District Competition

The number of district clubs in the 1989-90 competition was reduced from ten to eight, the intention being to improve playing standards. One attraction of the first-grade competition was the appearance of the West Indian batsman Gordon Greenidge in the Canberra North-Daramalan team in the first half of the season. Greenidge also played several matches for the ACT's representative side. Steve O'Shaughnessy of Ginninderra was named the Canberra Times Grade Cricketer Of The Year, and he also won the DB Robin Medal.

FIRST GRADE

Tuggeranong Valley won the first-grade premiership, scoring an upset victory over Queanbeyan in the final. From the start of the season, Queanbeyan had dominated the competition and was a strong favourite to win the final. It had gone right through the season without once being defeated, finishing far ahead on the points table, and it had also won the Tooheys Twilight and Sunday League competitions. On the other hand, Tuggeranong Valley had made third place in the competition only in the final round. In the final, however, Tuggeranong Valley performed at its best with both bat and ball, winning the match by 81 runs on the first innings.

Points Table—First Grade

Club	Points
Queanbeyan	72
Can North-Dara	46
Tuggeranong	44
Ginninderra	42
South Canberra	40
Wests	36
Weston Creek	26
ANU	18

SEMI-FINALS

Queanbeyan 414 (M Frost 123, N Bulger 67, J Bull 48; P Leeson 5/88, I Holton 3/129) defeated Ginninderra 116 (J Bull 3/29, N Bulger 2/9, S Vidler 2/21) on the first innings.

Tuggeranong 9 for 304 (M Moore 68, K Rooke 65, B Jackson 62; M Tournier 4/67) defeated Canberra North-Daramalan 156 (S Smith 34; K Flaherty 3/29, B Jackson 3/55) on the first innings.

FIRST GRADE FINAL

Queanbeyan v Tuggeranong Valley
Manuka Oval, Canberra
March 23-25, 1990
Result: Tuggeranong Valley won by 81 runs on the first innings

Sent in to bat, Tuggeranong was in early trouble, losing its first four wickets for 71. Moreover, its young opener Paul Macpherson had to leave the field after being hit twice on the helmet and once on the elbow. But Barry Jackson, batting at five, led a middle order revival. Jackson made 55, and the three batsmen following him made valuable contributions—M Moore 20, G Weber 34 and P Nemes. In the meantime, Macpherson had returned to the crease at the fall of the fifth wicket and went on to make 58, the highest score of the innings. Tuggeranong was 7 for 230 at stumps on the first day, and next morning completed an innings total of 295. Of the Queanbeyan bowlers, Colin Crouch did the heaviest work and was also the most successful, taking 4 for 87 in 41 overs. In view of Queanbeyan's proven capacity for making large totals, 295 seemed well within its range. But having reached 26 without the loss of a

wicket, Queanbeyan collapsed in unexpected fashion, losing 6 wickets
for 50 runs. Tuggeranong's opening bowler Shaun McElhinney made
the early break, taking two wickets in successive overs, and then
Jackson took three cheap wickets with his medium pace. Neil Bulger
(64) and Chris Ball (42) fought back with a seventh wicket partnership
of 93, but after Ball went the fall of wickets began again, and
Queanbeyan was all out early on the third day for 214. Sound batting
by Tuggeranong in its second innings ended any hope Queanbeyan
might have had of gaining an outright win, and the match finished
in mid-afternoon.

Tuggeranong Valley

First Innings

Batsman	How Out	Ttl
T Kerr	c Solway b Bull	3
P Macpherson	c Bulger b Crouch	58
S Ball	b Vidler	7
G Lemin	c Carruthers b Vidler	4
K Rooke (c)	b Wynd	19
B Jackson	b Bulger	55
M Moore	c Carruthers by Crouch	20
G Weber	b Crouch	34
P Nemes	lbw b Bulger	50
S McElhinney	lbw b Crouch	14
K Flaherty	not out	2
Sundries		29
Total		295

F/W: 5 33 42 71 123 149 202 249 277 295

Second Innings

How Out	Ttl
b Vidler	8
c Vidler b Bulger	43
not out	27
not out	2
	8
	2 for 88

F/W: 21 83

Bowler	O	M	R	Wkts
C Crouch	41	19	87	4
J Bull	29	6	86	1
S Vidler	21	8	42	2
A Wynd	9	1	29	1
N Bulger	22	13	25	2
S McNamee	2	0	12	0

Bowler	O	M	R	Wkts
Crouch	10	6	10	0
Bull	5	1	11	0
Vidler	13	4	26	1
Wynd	8	3	25	0
Bulger	4	1	5	0
McNamee	3	1	7	0

Queanbeyan

First Innings

Batsman	How Out	Ttl
M Frost	c Moore b McElhinney	13
A Coles	c Macpherson b Flaherty	15
P Solway	b McElhinney	6
S McNamee	c Ball b Jackson	15
J Bull (c)	c Rooke b Jackson	10
M Carruthers	c Rooke b Jackson	5
C Ball	lbw b Moore	42
N Bulger	c Rooke b Jackson	64
A Wynd	b Moore	8
S Vidler	c Nemes b Jackson	16
C Crouch	not out	2
Sundries		18
Total		214

F/W: 26 38 38 59 71 76 169 189 199 214

Bowler	O	M	R	Wkts
S McElhinney	12	3	25	2
P Nemes	5	0	18	0
K Flaherty	19	5	46	1
B Jackson	23.3	4	58	5
M Moore	16	4	37	2
G Lemin	5	1	17	0

Batting Averages—First Grade (minimum 300 runs)

Batsman	Inns	HS	Runs	Avge
P Solway (Queanbeyan)	12	339	643	71.44
G Irvine (ANU)	8	91*	350	70.00
S O'Shaughnessy (Ginninderra)	13	118*	526	58.44
S Frost (Queanbeyan)	8	87	352	44.00
D MacDonald (Wests)	10	83	313	39.13
A Yates (South Canberra)	10	103	310	38.75
M Frost (Queanbeyan)	14	123	528	37.71
S Smith (Can North-Dara)	13	158	451	37.58
P Macpherson (Tuggeranong)	11	57	385	35.00
K Hanton (Ginninderra)	11	95*	313	34.78
N Speak (South Canberra)	12	76*	346	34.60
K Rooke (Tuggeranong)	11	65	305	33.89
G Woodbridge (South Canberra)	10	108	326	32.60
P Evans (Weston Creek)	11	69	323	29.36

Bowling Averages

Bowler	Overs	Runs	Wkts	Avge
S Broadbent (Wests)	95	306	24	12.75
P Leeson (Ginninderra)	180	510	36	14.17
P Nemes (Tuggeranong)	188	501	31	16.16
K McLeod (South Canberra)	139	392	24	16.33
C Crouch (Queanbeyan)	200	411	24	17.13
R Zocchi (Can North-Dara)	142	429	24	17.88
M Moore (Tuggeranong)	158	400	22	18.18
S O'Shaughnessy (Ginninderra)	198	487	26	18.73
J Bull (Queanbeyan)	180	453	21	21.57
S McElhinney (Tuggeranong)	180	457	20	22.85
S Smith (ANU)	170	662	21	31.52

SECOND GRADE

Premier: Queanbeyan.
Points Table: Weston Creek 60, Queanbeyan 50, South Canberra 48, Can North-Dara 40, Tuggeranong 40, Wests 38, Ginninderra 22, ANU 18.

THIRD GRADE

Premier: Can North-Dara.
Points Table: Can North-Dara 54, Weston Creek 54, ANU 48, South Canberra 48, Wests 38, Queanbeyan 36, Tuggeranong 24, Ginninderra 10.

FOURTH GRADE

Premier: Queanbeyan.
Points Table: South Canberra 61, Wests 58, Queanbeyan 52, ANU 44, Can North-Dara 37, Weston Creek 34, Ginninderra 22, Tuggeranong 10.

FIFTH GRADE

Premier: Can North-Dara.
Points Table: South Canberra 64, Can North-Dara 52, ANU 52, Queanbeyan 52, Weston Creek 40, Tuggeranong 32, Ginninderra 18, Wests 14.

Club Championship

Club	Points
Queanbeyan	1086
South Canberra	983
Can North-Dara	907
Weston Creek	854
Wests	760
Tuggeranong	654
ANU	626
Ginninderra	504

NORTHERN TERRITORY

THE DARWIN A-GRADE COMPETITION in 1989 was won by Tracy Village Easts for the fifth year in a row. In the final, played at Marrara Cricket Ground on September 16 and 17, Tracy Village Easts lost only 3 wickets while scoring its winning total of 3 for 211. Ashley Hammond, the son of the former Test player Jeff Hammond, scored 82 not out, and Kevin Major made 60. In Darwin's innings, the Melbourne batsman Gerard Clarke top-scored with 50, and Gary Stevens finished with the outstanding figures of 7 wickets for 99.

Darwin

Batsman	How Out	Ttl
S Prescott	c & b Stevens	8
S Smith	b Stevens	23
G Clarke	c Reeves b Stevens	50
D Kulmor	lbw Stevens	0
G Bicknell	lbw Miller	35
D Andrews	lbw Miller	4
D Campbell	b Stevens	8
G Dunne	c Hubbard b Stevens	5
C Widdowson	c & b Stevens	0
P Sheedy	not out	10
L Polkinghorne	not out	12
Sundries		14
Total		9/209

F/W: 19 36 39 125 129 138 173 173 188

Bowler	O	M	R	Wkts
G Stevens	39	2	99	7
J Hammond	14	7	18	0
W Hubbard	30	0	18	0
D Reeves	3	0	11	0
B Miller	29	9	30	2

Tracy Village Easts

Batsman	How Out	Ttl
N Allan	st Smith b Andrews	16
A Hammond	not out	82
D Reeves	b Andrews	32
K Major	lbw b Andrews	60
B Miller	not out	4
J Hammond	did not bat	
G Stevens	did not bat	
A Hubbard	did not bat	
D Davies	did not bat	
R Murry	did not bat	
Sundries		17
Total		3/211

F/W: 51 123 128

Bowler	O	M	R	Wkts
D Campbell	15	2	54	0
D Andrews	26	9	66	3
P Sheedy	1	0	1	0
C Widdowson	19	4	58	0
L Polkinghorne	2	0	12	0
G Clarke	4	1	12	0

Result: Tracy Village Easts won on the first innings

Batting Averages

Batsman	Inn	NO	Agg	Avrge	HS
S Smith (Darwin)	13	3	511	51.10	150
A Hammond (TV Easts)	12	2	462	46.20	103
B Rule (South. Dist.)	14	4	358	35.80	105
G Clarke (Darwin)	12	0	344	28.67	84
S Prescott (Darwin)	12	3	334	37.11	95
S Sinclair (N'cliff)	12	3	306	34.00	53
G McKenzie (South. Dist.)	11	1	297	29.70	86
C Hoffman (South. Dist.)	16	1	279	18.60	54
B Mappas (Pints)	12	0	274	22.83	87

Bowling Averages

Bowler	O	M	R	Wkts	Avge
S George (South. Dist.)	165	30	401	34	11.79
D Andrews (Darwin)	191	62	322	33	9.76
S McCarthy (Pints)	172	37	395	30	13.17
R Dempster (Univ.)	133	27	331	26	12.73
D Campbell (Darwin)	142	25	413	25	16.52
D Cruickshank (Pints)	121	17	341	24	14.21
G McKenzie (South. Dist.)	157	27	377	24	15.71
S Sinclair (N'cliff)	134	19	393	24	16.38
J Kelly (Waratah)	151	37	412	24	17.17
S de Kretser (Univ.)	147	36	377	23	16.39

Cricketer of the Year—Points Table

S Smith (Darwin)	846
S George (Southern Districts)	692
S Sinclair (Nightcliff)	671
G McKenzie (Southern Districts)	592

Darwin Beaufort International Best Player—Points Table

A Hammond (Tracy Village Easts)	16
S Sinclair (Nightcliff)	14
S Smith (Darwin)	12
G McKenzie (Southern Districts)	12
G Stevens (Tracy Village Easts)	11
S George (Southern Districts)	11

ALICE SPRINGS CRICKET ASSOCIATION

In the final of the 1989-90 competition, played at Anzac Oval, Alice Springs, on April 7 and 8, 1990, Railway Rovers easily defeated Federals on the first innings.

Railway Rovers

Batsman	How Out	Ttl
Hopkins	b Highman	0
Nickolai	lbw Highman	9
Bowden	c Osbourne b Highman	14
Kersten	b Highman	16
Murphy	run out	26
Connor	c Highman b Broomhall	19
Bowden	c Linehan b Broomhall	13
Trindle	c Schroeder b Broomhall	2
MacAllister	c Mackie b Mathwin	96
Weeks	c Gange b Highman	23
Snook	not out	5
Sundries		13
Total		236

F/W: 13 14 47 50 94 99 109 111 194 236

▶

Bowler	O	M	R	Wkts
Broomhall	17	0	67	3
Douglas	10	1	48	0
Mathwin	53	0	25	1
Highman	24	5	57	5
Murphy	9	2	28	0

Federals

Batsman	How Out	Ttl
Schroeder	b Kersten	1
Osbourne	b Snook	14
Mackie	lbw b Snook	7
Gange	b Kersten	9
Broomhall	c Connor b Snook	4
Leece	b Snook	6
Highman	c Weeks b Bowden	39
Linehan	c Kersten b Snook	2
Matthwin	c Nicholai b Bowden	0
Murphy	lbw b MacAllister	20
Sundries		10
Total		125

F/W: 4 20 35 39 41 56 64 68 99 125

Bowler	O	M	R	Wkts
Kersten	16	4	35	2
Bowden	11	5	18	2
Trindle	1	0	4	0
Snook	19	5	36	5
Weeks	6	0	21	0
MacAllister	0.2	0	3	1

PRUDENTIAL NATIONAL COUNTRY CRICKET CHAMPIONSHIP

NEW SOUTH WALES WON THE CHAMPIONSHIP for the second year in succession, but it was not until the fifth and final round that the outcome of the round-robin competition was decided. From the outset, the tournament was dominated by two teams, New South Wales and the ACT, which, as it happened, were not drawn to play each other until the final round. So both teams entered the final round undefeated, although the ACT was leading on points by virtue of its outright win over Queensland in the opening two-day match. So the two-day, 100-over match was to all intents and purposes a grand final. In the event, New South Wales won comfortably, thus retaining the title it has now won four times in the six years the championship has been contested. To some extent, New South Wales was open to the complaint that it was not really a country team, since no fewer than seven of the eleven players came from a large city—namely, Newcastle. The same could be said of the ACT, too. The problem really arises from the connotations of the term 'country'. If the championship had been called a provincial cricket championship, instead, the matter would not arise.

The New South Wales all-rounder Mark Curry, of Newcastle, was afterwards voted Berrivale Orchards Player of the Series. He polled twenty-one votes, ten more than the West Australian Leith Bowyer, of Bunbury, and the Queenslander Sam Scuderi, of Ingham, who were placed equal second, while Paul Evans of the ACT was a close fourth with nine votes. Curry, a consistent performer throughout the tournament, really showed his value in the all-important match against the ACT in the final round, scoring 68 and taking 3 for 66 off 25 overs. Sam Scuderi won the Sir Donald Bradman Trophy for his batting in the championship. His finest innings was his 187 not out against South Australia in the final round, which virtually won the match for Queensland. South Australia had scored the substantial total of 7 for 341 off its 100 overs, and Queensland was 1 for 24 when Scuderi came to the wicket and proceeded at once to attack the bowling. Even the opposing captain, Graeme Madden, described the innings as the finest he had seen. The Bill O'Reilly Trophy for bowling was won by Eugene Nix, the veteran fast-medium bowler from the ACT, who took 16 wickets in the tournament. It was Nix who set up the ACT's outright victory over Queensland in the opening match by taking 6 for 21 on the first day. The RM (Bob) Hooper Perpetual Trophy for the Victorian player of the tournament was won by the Geelong batsman Graham Beaumont.

Three days after the final round of the championship an Australian Country XI, chosen on the basis of performances during the tournament, played the Sri Lankans in a three-day match. (For details of the match see the section on the Sri Lankans' tour.) The Australian team was: Terry Waldron (captain), Western Australia; Sam Scuderi, Queensland; Colin Crouch, ACT; Graham Beaumont, Victoria; Paul Evans, ACT; Peter Gerhard, New South Wales; Mark Kelaher, New South Wales; Eugene Nix, ACT; Terry Oliver, Queensland; Geoff Phillips, Victoria; John Wrigley, Victoria.

Points Table

State	Points
New South Wales	69.63
ACT	66.00
Western Australia	42.38
Victoria	35.49
Queensland	32.49
South Australia	14.84

ROUND 1   January 6-7 1990
100-over matches

ACT 246 (G Irvine 55, M Carruthers 39, P Evans 32, E Nix 35; C White 4/52, R Petersen 3/33) defeated Queensland 59 (L Schulte 29; E Nix 6/21, C Crouch 4/36) and 133 (L Schulte 30°; C Crouch 4/46, D MacDonald 3/49) outright by an innings and 54 runs.

New South Wales 5 for 289 (M Kelaher 74, G Arms 70, M Curry 61°) defeated Western Australia 9 for 253 (T Waldron 67, R Waterman 58; D Willis 3/32, M Curry 3/51) by 36 runs on the first innings.

Victoria 7 for 312 (G Beaumont 84, G Tupper 73°, R Schultz 44; P Pasculli 2/61, I Kenny 2/63) defeated South Australia 281 (P Mattey 110, A Brooks 51; R Orr 4/65) by 31 runs on the first innings.

ROUND 2   January 8 1990
55-over matches

ACT 9 for 299 (P Evans 72, J Williams 70, G Irvine 52; P Pasculli 2/49, M Sommerfield 2/44) defeated South Australia 7 for 181 (J Mitchell 90°; E Nix 4/29) by 118 runs.

New South Wales 2/178 (G Arms 50, M Curry 48°) defeated Victoria 176 (G Phillips 42, J Wrigley 38; W McLennan 2/33, M Christie 2/27, P Gerhard 2/33) by eight wickets.

Western Australia 214 (L Bowyer 49, P Shine 36; W Short 3/22, G Hogan 3/48) tied with Queensland 9 for 214 (B Spanner 67, T Oliver 39, E Harris 38; R Menasse 3/40, M Orst 2/36, R Thompson 2/42).

414

ROUND 3   January 10-11 1990
100-over matches

ACT 8 for 403 (N Woods 168, P Evans 75, J Williams 73; R Orr 4/106, J Wrigley 2/70) defeated Victoria 184 (K Bartholomew 33; K Bone 4/49, C Crouch 4/56) and 0-2 by 219 runs on the first innings.

New South Wales 9 for 356 (J Frame 92, P Gerhard 71, G Arms 66; P Hutchinson 3/97, C White 2/39, E Harris 2/53) and 5 for 53 (J Frame 21, D Willis 20) defeated Queensland 280 (T Oliver 89, A Walsh 84; M Curry 3/92; G Hooper 2/19; P Gerhard 2/100) by 76 runs on the first innings.

Western Australia 8 for 245 (L Bowyer 71, R Waterman 43*, M Knuckey 33; P Pasculli 5/88) defeated South Australia 91 (B Hutchens 31; G Morris 5/27, R Menasse 2/18, R Thompson 2/22) and 5 for 171 (B Hutchens 44, P Mattey 36; R Menasse 2/30) by 154 runs on the first innings.

ROUND 4   January 12 1990
55-over matches

Victoria 248 (G Phillips 90, G Beaumont 76; G Hogan 2/38) defeated Queensland 179 (S Scuderi 72, C White 31; D Benson 5/19, J Wrigley 2/37) by 69 runs.

ACT 4 for 146 (A Yates 67, G Woodbridge 27; D Francis 2/22) defeated Western Australia 144 (R Walker 33, L Bowyer 21, R Waterman 20; K Bone 3/6, C Crouch 2/26) by 6 wickets.

New South Wales 3 for 151 (M Curry 62*, E Higgins 46*, G Arms 20) defeated South Australia 150 (B Hutchens 32, R Ellis 28, A Brooks 25; M Curry 4/15, C Hamilton 3/45) by 7 wickets.

ROUND 5   January 13-14 1990
100-over matches

Queensland 5 for 347 (S Scuderi 187*, B Spanner 63, A Walsh 39; J Heyne 2/101) defeated South Australia 7 for 341 (A Lowe 114*, P Mattey 70, J Mitchell 50, A Brooks 28; G Hogan 2/57) by six runs on the first innings.

Western Australia 8 for 340 (M Knuckey 81, R Waterman 78, P Shine 77, T Waldron 34; J Wrigley 3/53, D Lanyon 3/108) defeated Victoria 316 (G Beaumont 73, D Lanyon 51, D Benson 47, W Walsh 30; D Francis 4/66, R Menasse 4/125) by 24 runs on the first innings.

New South Wales 9 for 396 (M Kelaher 118, M Curry 68, E Higgins 57, G Arms 52, D Willis 47*; G Irvine 2/55) defeated ACT 281 (D MacDonald 81*, P Solway 63, P Evans 47, A Yates 32; P Gerhard 4/106, M Curry 3/66) by 115 runs on the first innings.

CRICKET ACADEMY

OF THE SIXTEEN YOUNG CRICKETERS enrolled full-time at the academy in the 1989-90 year, five played Sheffield Shield cricket and most of the others performed creditably in academy matches or Adelaide grade cricket. This was the academy's second year of operation, and it was noticeable that the cricketers in this year's intake were at least a year younger on average than those in the first intake, which appears to be consistent with the academy's long-term policy of offering places mainly to under-19 players.

Michael Bevan from Canberra probably made the biggest impact of all the academy players, batting so consistently for South Australia that by the end of the season he had established himself as one of the team's more valued players. At all levels of cricket, Bevan scored 1,835 runs during the season at an average of 59.2. Phil Alley played several games for South Australia, too, and he bowled with a fair measure of success. He took 3 for 78 against New Zealand at the start of the season, and against his home state, New South Wales, he took 4 for 98. There was another academy player in the South Australia-New Zealand match—the medium-fast bowler David Clarke. Not long afterwards, however, Clarke contracted pneumonia and was out of the game for virtually the whole of December. He recovered in time to join the academy's tour of New Zealand, where he distinguished himself by scoring 101 not out against the New Zealand youth side.

The other Sheffield Shield players were the Western Australians Chris Mack and Brendan Julian. Mack was the leading wicket-taker in the Adelaide grade competition until he was recruited for the Western Australian team half-way through the season. He produced several fine performances for Western Australia, taking 3 for 81 against Queensland and 3 for 70 against Tasmania. Brendan Julian's bowling was hampered by an injury for part of the season, but he showed he was a fine all-round cricketer. He batted well, scoring 136 for the academy against Western Australian Colts, and was extremely sharp in the field. In one match, against Young England, he managed to run out a batsman who merely backed up too far.

Dene Hills of Wynyard, Michael Slater of Wagga, Craig White of Bendigo and Michael Bevan of Canberra all played for State second XIs. Hills impressed those who saw him as a fine batting prospect. In all the matches he played, he made 1,251 runs at an average of 41.7, including 258 against Wellington on the New Zealand tour, a record for anyone batting for the academy. Slater was injured in a traffic accident and suffered ongoing problems as a result, yet he still managed to score 863 runs at an average of 45.4. White, from Bendigo, proved to be an extremely useful all-rounder, he bowled off-spin and batted with flair on occasions, as in the early match against South Australia, in which he made 115.

Other academy players who made their mark during the season included Ken Vowles from Darwin, who played in the Australian Under 19 side; Gary Wright who captained the South Australian Under 19 team; and James Bolton, who captained Queensland Colts.

TOUR OF NORTHERN TERRITORY AND NORTH QUEENSLAND

(In some matches members of the AIS touring party played for the opposition.)

Northern Territory v AIS *100-over Match*
Marrara Oval, Darwin   July 13-14, 1989
Result: Northern Territory won by 75 runs

AIS first innings 116 (B Julian 42, C Williamson 29; S George 3/19). Northern Territory first innings 191 (S George 38; C Williamson 5/37, M McCague 3/38). AIS second innings 222 (M May retired 72, C Williamson retired 63, D Hills 22).

Northern Territory Invitation XI v AIS *55-over Match*
Kahlin Oval, Darwin   July 16, 1989
Result: AIS won by 29 runs

AIS 9 for 196 (J Williams 42, D Hills 28, M Bevan 24). Northern Territory Invitation XI 9 for 167 (M McCague 3/16, B Julian 3/43).

Far North Queensland v AIS   Cairns No 2 Oval, Cairns
July 20-21, 1989
Result: Match Drawn

Far North Queensland first innings 131 (P Alley 4/29, D Clarke 3/30, C Auty 2/43). AIS first innings 236 (C White 78, G Wright 60, J Bolton 27, K Vowles 26). Far North Queensland second innings 7 for 217 (C Mack 2/34, D Clarke 2/51).

Atherton v AIS *55-over Match*
Loder Park, Atherton   July 23, 1989
Result: AIS won by 117 runs

AIS 8 for 284 (B Julian 84*, K Vowles 67, M May 45, G Wright 26). Atherton 167 (C White 56, C Auty 34; D Mann 3/22, M Bevan 3/5).

Innisfail v AIS *55-over Match*
Innisfail   July 25, 1989
Result: AIS won by 180 runs

AIS 5 for 300 (C White 100*, J Bolton 59, B Julian 43, M McCague 37*). Innisfail 9 for 120 (P Alley 3/11, C Auty 2/27).

Mid-North Queensland v AIS
Mackay   July 28-30, 1989
Result: AIS won by an innings and 54 runs

Mid-North Queensland first innings 150 (C Auty 6/33, P Alley 2/46). AIS first innings 363 (J Bolton 76, M Bevan 72, G Wright 70, M McCague 49, B Julian 35). Mid-North Queensland second innings 159 (C White 5/14).

Mid-North Queensland v AIS   *35-over Match*
Mackay   July 30, 1989
Result: AIS won by 75 runs

AIS 7 for 223 (C White retired 58, M May 34°). Mid-North Queensland 148 (K Vowles 45, M McCague 21; B Julian 3/59, D Mann 3/19, C Mack 2/11).

Rockhampton v AIS   *100-over Match*
RCG No 2, Rockhampton   August 3-4, 1989
Result: AIS won by 236 runs

AIS 4 for 438 (C White retired 100, J Bolton retired 100, M May 70°, B Julian 45). Rockhampton 202 (C Mack 6/44, C Auty 3/69).

QCA Development Squad v AIS   *100-over Match*
Boundary Street No 1, Brisbane   August 8-9, 1989
Result: AIS won by 167 runs

AIS first innings 9/282 (C White 62, J Bolton 36, D Mann 36°, J Williams 34, B Julian 33, M McCague 27). QCA first innings 115 (M McCague 3/17, B Julian 3/10, C White 3/58). AIS second innings 1 for 134 (M May 58°, M Bevan 41°, G Wright 26).

QCA Development Squad v AIS   *50-over Match*
Boundary Street No 1, Brisbane   August 10, 1989
Result: AIS won by 16 runs

AIS 9 for 233 (M Bevan 68, J Williams 56, D Mann 26, B Julian 22, J Bolton 22). QCA 7 for 217 (P Alley 4/29).

SACA XI v AIS   *50-over Match*
Adelaide Oval No 2, Adelaide   September 23, 1989
Result: SACA XI won by 98 runs

In this pre-season trial the academy team was disposed of for 118, Clint Auty of Perth top-scoring with 49. SACA did much better in reply and finished with 8 for 216, of which Paul Nobes made 75. Phil Alley took 3 for 32 and Auty 2 for 43.

SACA XI v AIS   *50-over Match*
Adelaide Oval No 2, Adelaide   September 24, 1989
Result: SACA XI won by 46 runs

The academy batsmen gave a better account of themselves in this second pre-season trial. A century by Paul Nobes (117) enabled the

SACA team to compile a total of 4 for 279. David Clarke bowled with exceptional economy, conceding only 18 runs in his 10 overs. The AIS replied with 8 for 233. Craig White made 57, Dene Hills 45 and Martin McCague 33 not out.

South Australian XI v AIS   *50-over Match*
Park 25, Adelaide   October 13, 1989
Result: AIS won by 41 runs

The AIS gave a fine all-round performance in defeating what was virtually the South Australian state side. Opening the batting for AIS, Craig White of Bendigo played an enterprising innings of 115, and the AIS made 5 for 244 by the end of its 50 overs, Michael Bevan finishing with 71 not out. The South Australians were thus set a difficult target, and they were all out for 203 striving to reach it. Andrew Hilditch top-scored with 72, while the off-spinner Clint Auty had the best bowling figures, 3 for 43. Brendan Julian, Phil Alley and Cameron Williamson each took 2 wickets.

ACT v AIS   Manuka Oval, Canberra, November 28-30, 1989
Result: AIS awarded the match on the first innings

Both sides scored too many runs to enable an outright result to be achieved in this three-day match. In the AIS's first innings of 377, which ended early on the second day, there were solid performances by a number of batsmen—Matthew May of Perth, who made a patient 79, Michael Slater (78), Cameron Williamson of Adelaide (53) and Craig White (31). The ACT replied with 338, the highest scorer being the academy batsman Michael Bevan (119). While Bevan was in the ACT seemed to have a good chance of gaining a first-innings lead, and the total rose to 3 for 208. But the ACT then lost five wickets in fairly rapid succession, three of them to the bowling of the off-spinner Clint Auty, and was in danger of being made to follow-on. But the ACT's tail-enders halted the collapse and had pushed the score to within 40 of the AIS's total when the last wicket fell. Clint Auty took 4 for 75 and Brendan Julian 3 for 81. The AIS had made 5 for 240 in its second innings when the match ended. Williamson (66) again batted well, and Dene Hills made 64.

Western Australian Colts v AIS
Melvista Oval, Perth   December 12-15, 1989
Result: Match Drawn

The AIS finished well on top in this drawn match. The Colts' first innings of 377 featured a century by Peter Brindley (119). Martin McCague took 4 for 129 and Clint Auty 3 for 76. Two AIS batsmen scored centuries in reply, Michael Slater (135) and Brendan Julian (136), enabling the AIS to compile the large total of 495. In the Colts' second innings, the bowlers got on top for the first time in the match, and the Colts were all out for 186. Chris Mack and Craig White each took 3 wickets, and Auty and Cameron Williamson each took two.

Western Australian Colts v AIS *50-over Match*
Melvista Oval, Perth   December 17, 1989
Result: AIS won by 65 runs

The highlight of AIS's winning performance was an exciting display of controlled hitting by Martin McCague, who scored 73 not out from only 45 balls, hitting 5 sixes and 4 fours. Adam Gilchrist of Lismore, brought in to replace Jamie Williams as wicketkeeper after Williams had his jaw broken, made 59 from 53 balls and Craig White made 47, with the result that the AIS finished with the impressive total of 8 for 257. In reply, the Colts were all out for 192. Chris Mack (3/31), Clint Auty (2/23) and Craig White (2/29) were the most successful of the bowlers.

Western Australian Colts v AIS
Wonthella Oval, Geraldton   December 19-20, 1989
Result: Match Drawn

For a change, the Colts had the better of the academy team in this two-day match. Innings of 93 by Doug Tompkins and 68 by Steve Russell helped the Colts to a first innings total of 290. Clint Auty was again successful with his off-spin, taking 4 for 88. The AIS responded with the meagre total of 161. James Bolton of Cairns made 50 and Dene Hills 32, but it was generally a poor batting performance. The Colts were 2 for 53 in their second innings when the match ended, Hills having taken both wickets.

AIS v Combined Service XI *Limited-overs Match*
Adelaide Oval No 2   October 25, 1989
Result: AIS won by 146 runs

This one-sided match was made memorable by an explosive innings by Jamie Williams of Sydney, who scored 75 from only 29 balls. The other leading scorers in the AIS innings of 8 for 248 were Gary Wright (49), Dene Hills (38) and Michael Bevan (37). The Combined Service XI could manage only 102 in reply, Cameron Williamson and David Clarke each taking 3 wickets.

AIS v Sri Lanka, Adelaide Oval *100-over Match*
Adelaide   January 11-12, 1990

In this match, shortened from three to two days, AIS (348) defeated Sri Lanka (103 and 1 for 117) by 245 runs on the first innings. For details, see the chapter on the Sri Lankan tour.

AIS v Young England
University Oval, Adelaide   January 30-31, 1990
Result: Match Drawn

The Young England side was outclassed in this two-day match and might well have been beaten by an innings if the match had gone to a third day. Young England could manage only 135 in its first innings, David Clarke (3 for 20), Brendan Julian (2 for 24) and Craig White (2 for 30) being the more successful bowlers. At stumps on the first day, Brendan Julian was not out on 74, having faced only 85 balls. Overnight, he was summoned to join the Western Australian team and so did not resume his innings next day. The academy team scored 7 for 320 before declaring, other leading scorers being Craig White (63), Cameron Williamson (59) and Matthew May (50). When the match ended, Young England was struggling in its second innings at 3 for 59, Clarke having taken two of the wickets.

AIS v Maharashtra Cricket Club   *50-over Match*
Argarna Park, Adelaide   February 7, 1990
Result: AIS won by 185 runs

The academy team was much too strong for the visitors, scoring 277 and then dismissing their opponents for 92. Dene Hills made 66, Gary Wright 62 and James Bolton 45. The most successful AIS bowler was Clint Auty, who finished with the impressive figures of 3 for 7.

TOUR OF NEW ZEALAND

Auckland XI v AIS
Cornwall Park, Auckland   February 15-16, 1990
Result: AIS won by 158 runs

The academy team batted first, and two batsmen, Dene Hills (91) and Jamie Williams (95), were out within a few runs of their centuries. But Cameron Williamson, batting at number seven, passed the 100 mark in a high-speed innings, in which he scored 140 not out off only 142 balls. The AIS was all out for 464, to which Auckland replied with 306, an innings which included a century by M Horne. The off-spinner Clint Auty was again a leading, if expensive, wicket-taker with 3 for 84 from 17 overs, but the most successful bowler was Brian McFadyen from Geelong, who took 4 for 73.

Hawkes Bay v AIS
Nelson Park No 1, Napier   February 18-19, 1990
Result: AIS won by 230 runs

The local team was no match for the academy players. Batting first, Hawkes Bay struggled to a total of 174 from nearly 85 overs. Phil Alley and David Clarke each took 3 wickets, and Craig White took two. The AIS made 404 in reply, an innings which included 113 by Matthew May and 54 by James Bolton. But the batsman who perhaps attracted most attention was Ken Vowles of Darwin, who raced to 65 off only 43 balls.

Wellington XI v AIS
Kilbirnie Oval, Wellington   February 22-24, 1990
Result: AIS won by 299 runs

Dene Hills, the left-handed batsman from Tasmania, was the leading performer in this match. Opening the batting for the AIS, he played an outstanding innings of 258, facing only 303 balls and hitting 46 fours. The other successful batsmen were James Bolton (72) and the number 11 batsman Brian McFadyen (64). The AIS made a total of 554, to which Wellington replied with 255 (M Lane 64), the leading wicket-takers being McFadyen (3 for 44), Cameron Williamson (2 for 46) and Ken Vowles (2 for 34). The AIS was 0 for 76 in its second innings when the match ended, Michael Slater having hit 41 not out off only 25 balls.

Wellington XI v AIS   *Limited-overs Match*
Kilbirnie Oval, Wellington   February 25, 1990
Result: AIS won by 209 runs

The AIS trounced Wellington, scoring 285 and then dismissing the home side for 76 within 22 overs. The successful AIS batsmen were Michael Slater (85 off 107 balls), James Bolton (54 off 41 balls) and Matthew May (47). Brian McFadyen headed the AIS attack with 5 for 37, while David Clarke and Ken Vowles each took 2 wickets.

New Zealand Youth v AIS
Burnside Park, Christchurch   February 27-March 2, 1990
Result: AIS won by 138 runs

Batting first, AIS was doing only moderately well at 6 for 267 when David Clarke came in and proceeded to play an outstanding innings, scoring 101 not out off 150 balls and hitting 11 fours and a six. He and Clint Auty (20 not out) had an unbeaten partnership of 86 for the last wicket and the AIS declared at 9 for 430. New Zealand Youth was all out for 269 (L Howell 89) and so trailed badly on the first innings. Brian McFadyen was again the leading wicket-taker with 4 for 36, while David Clarke and Phil Alley each took 2 wickets. The AIS lost wickets going for quick runs in its second innings but was able to declare at 6 for 192. The opening batsman Dene Hills scored 55 and Jamie Williams, batting at seven, scored 48 off 37 balls. New Zealand Youth was all out for 215 in its second innings, giving the AIS a comfortable victory. Brian McFadyen took 3 wickets, but it was Craig White, bowling his off-spin, who had the most success, finishing with the remarkable figures of 7 for 51 off 28 overs.

Canterbury v AIS   *50-over Match*
Burnside Park, Canterbury   March 5, 1990
Result: AIS won by 4 wkts

The academy team rounded off its highly successful New Zealand tour with a comfortable victory over Canterbury, which batted first and was bowled out for 121. Brian McFadyen, who had established himself as the team's most reliable wicket-taker, took 4 for 30 and Phil Alley 3 for 22. In reply, the AIS lost cheap wickets but won the match with a total of 6 for 123, Matthew May top-scoring with 40 not out.

LANCASHIRE TOUR
OF TASMANIA
AND WESTERN AUSTRALIA

IN LATE MARCH and early April 1990, Lancashire's county team made a two-week tour of Tasmania, which included one-day matches against various Tasmanian representative sides and a two-day and a one-day match against the Tasmanian state side. Tasmania has an old cricketing association with Lancashire through Jack Simmons, the Lancashire spin bowler who played an important part in the development of Tasmanian cricket in the 1970s. After leaving Tasmania, Lancashire played Western Australia in a one-day match in Perth.

North Western Tasmanian Cricket Assocn XI
v Lancashire *50-over Match*
Devonport Oval, Devonport   March 22, 1990

The home side, batting first, made 9 for 183 in its 50 overs, the opener Adrian Saltmarsh top scoring with 63. It was clearly only a moderate total, but the visitors did not overtake it until the first ball of their 50th over. For Lancashire, Steven Titchard (50) made the only substantial score, while C Young was the most effective of the home side's bowlers, taking 2 for 21 in 10 overs. Lancashire's total was 7 for 187.

Northern Tasmanian Cricket Assocn XI
v Lancashire *50-over Match*
NTCA Ground, Launceston   March 24

A high-powered innings of 147 by Launceston's Test batsman David Boon set up the NTCA XI's victory over Lancashire. Boon's century enabled the home side to score 5 for 265 from its 50 overs, to which Lancashire replied with only 8 for 206. Boon opened the batting with Richard Bennett, and for a time the pair played cautiously, scoring only 24 runs in the first 15 overs. From then on Boon began to hit out, and when he was out in the 38th over the total had risen to 187. He hit 17 fours and 5 sixes, several of them of enormous dimensions. None of the Lancashire batsmen really got set, and as a result the visitors could not match the home side's run rate. Michael Watkinson was the best of their batsmen, hitting a bright 55.

Tasmania v Lancashire   *50-over Match*
NTCA Ground, Launceston   March 25, 1990
Result: Tasmania won by 6 wkts

Batting first, Lancashire really needed a big innings by one of its batsmen to set the home side a challenging target, but in the event Neil Fairbrother (51) was the only batsman to better 30. At the end of its 50 overs, the visitors had scored 8 for 205, a total which the Tasmanians were able to pass in only 45.3 overs. David Boon made 71 and Michael Farrell 54.

Lancashire

Batsman	How Out	Ttl
G Mendis	b Oliver	20
G Fowler	lbw b Farrell	30
T Jesty	c Hughes b Pearce	6
N Fairbrother	b Hughes	51
M Watkinson	c Pearce b Farrell	25
I Austin	c Farrell b Boon	23
D Hughes (c)	not out	22
P Allott	c Young b Boon	2
J Simmons	b Hughes	15
Sundries		11
Total		8 for 205

F/W: 56 58 100 160 166 169 205

Bowler	O	M	R	Wkts
S Young	7	0	19	0
S Oliver	7	0	38	1
M Farrell	10	3	22	2
K Pearce	10	1	35	1
D Boon	8	0	45	2
R Hughes	8	0	41	2

Tasmania

Batsman	How Out	Ttl
D Boon	c Jesty b Simmons	71
M Farrell	c Martin b Hughes	54
D Wellham (c)	c Fairbrother b Hughes	12
J Cox	c Allott b Hughes	8
R Tucker	not out	28
D Buckingham	not out	26
Sundries		7
Total		4 for 206

F/W: 100 130 149 151

Bowler	O	M	R	Wkts
P Allott	10	1	33	0
P Martin	5	0	23	0
I Austin	8	1	45	0
M Watkinson	4.3	0	28	0
J Simmons	10	1	37	1
D Hughes	8	2	37	3

TCA Invitation XI v Lancashire *50-over Match*
New Town Ground, Hobart   March 27, 1990

Batting second, Lancashire had an easy victory, scoring 3 for 214 in 46.4 overs in reply to the home side's 5 for 212 in 50 overs. For Lancashire, Graham Lloyd made 64, Graeme Fowler 61 and Michael Watkinson 40 not out. The home side's most successful batsmen were R Wilson 56, J Cox 53 and G Cobern not out 36.

TCA Under 23 XI v Lancashire *50-over Match*
New Town Ground, Hobart   March 28, 1990

The home side was made to work hard for runs and at the end of its 50 overs had scored only 9 for 195. Bruce Cruse top-scored with a steady 75 while Dene Hills, who opened the batting, scored

36 off only 44 balls. Roni Irani was the most successful of the Lancashire bowlers, with 5 for 46 from 10 overs. Lancashire took only 46.1 overs to score the necessary runs for victory. The opener Graham Lloyd made 56, but it was Neil Fairbrother's high-speed century (110 off 115 balls) which really dominated the innings. Lancashire's final score was 5 for 201.

Tasmania v Lancashire *100-over Match*
NTCA Ground, Launceston   March 30-31, 1990
Result: Tasmania won on the first innings

Despite some solid scoring in the middle order, Lancashire occupied the crease for only 92.2 of its 100 overs and was all out on the first day for 294. The most successful of the Tasmanian bowlers was the leg-spinner Kevin Pearce, who took 4 for 104 in 32 overs and, more-over, dismissed several of the most in-form batsmen, including Michael Watkinson, who top scored with 45. In reply, Tasmania made 331 in 98.5 overs, thus inflicting upon the visitors their fourth defeat in six tour matches. Dene Hills was run out for 57, but Danny Buckingham top scored with 107. Kevin Pearce rounded off a personally successful match with a score of 44.

Lancashire

Batsman	How Out	Ttl
G Mendis	st Coyle b Castle	45
G Fowler	c Pearce b Castle	10
N Speak	c Cox b McPhee	1
T Jesty	c Oliver b Pearce	24
D Hughes	c Cox b Pearce	4
M Watkinson	c Coyle b Pearce	45
R Irani	c Pearce b Boon	42
G Yates	c Coyle b Pearce	39
I Folley	not out	42
P Martin	c Pearce b McPhee	17
J Stanworth	b McPhee	4
SUNDRIES: B.10 LB.7 NB.4 W.—		21
TOTAL		294

F/W: 36 45 75 86 146 154 224 234 284 294

Bowler	O	M	R	Wkts
P McPhee	19.2	6	38	3
S Oliver	14	3	51	0
D Castle	13	1	48	2
K Pearce	32	6	104	4
N Courtney	4	1	15	0
D Boon	10	4	21	1

Tasmania

Batsman	How Out	Ttl
D Boon	c and b Yates	14
D Hills	run out	57
P Coyle	c Watkinson b Yates	2
J Cox	c Lloyd (sub) b Martin	55
D Buckingham	c Lloyd (sub) b Martin	107
N Courtney	b Martin	16
K Pearce	lbw b Martin	44
S Young	b Watkinson	0
S Oliver	c Stanworth b Watkinson	5
P McPhee	b Irani	10
D Castle	not out	1
SUNDRIES: B.2 LB.4 NB.12 W.2		20
TOTAL		331

F/W: 48 57 102 187 227 294 301 307 319 331

▶

Bowler	O	M	R	Wkts
M Watkinson	18	2	42	2
P Martin	24	1	71	3
G Yates	36	5	100	3
I Folley	5	0	33	0
R Irani	11.5	0	65	1
D Hughes	4	0	14	0

Tasmanian XI v Lancashire   *50-over Match*
NTCA Ground, Launceston   April 1, 1990

Defending the meagre total of 181, the Tasmanians nevertheless won this low-scoring match, and its spin bowlers Kevin Pearce and David Castle, who contained the visitors with tight bowling, deserved much of the credit. Pearce took 2 for 18 in his 10 overs and Castle 1 for 20. Nick Courtney (89) was the only Tasmanian batsman to advance beyond the 20s, and after 50 overs the home side was 8 for 181. Paul Allott (3 for 27 in 10 overs) had the best bowling figures. Lancashire's batsmen made a promising start and the total was 71 before the second wicket fell, but later batsmen became tied down. At the end of 50 overs, Lancashire had made 8 for 171, its most successful batsmen being Trevor Jesty with 46 and Graham Lloyd with 40. Shaun Young (3 for 54 off 10 overs) took the most wickets for the Tasmanian XI, but he was relatively expensive.

Western Australia v Lancashire
Not First-Class
WACA Ground, Perth
April 7 1990
Toss: Lancashire
Result: Western Australia won by 3 runs

Lancashire just failed to overtake Western Australia in a hectic run chase which ended with the visitors at 6 for 234. Batting first, the Western Australians made 9 for 237, an innings highlighted by a high-speed innings of 80 by the young all-rounder Brendan Julian. Batting at six, Julian scored his runs off only 65 deliveries, hitting 7 fours and a straight six. The only other Western Australian to make a significant number of runs was the opener Mark McPhee, who scored 47 off 72 balls. Lancashire was given a sound start by its openers Graeme Fowler (53 off 90 balls) and Gehan Mendis (65 off 111 balls), who shared in a partnership of 110, but it failed to keep up with the required run rate. With 20 overs to go, Lancashire had to score at the rate of a run a ball to win—a difficult assignment which just proved too much for it in the end.

Western Australia

Batsman	How Out	Ttl	Balls	Mins	4s	6s
MW McPhee	c Hegg b Austin	47	72	90	6	—
D Martyn	b Austin	22	33	51	2	—
TM Moody	c Hegg b Watkinson	5	17	24	—	—
MP May	b Hughes	20	50	47	2	—

Batsman	How Out	Ttl	Balls	Mins	4s	6s
GR Marsh (c)	st Hegg b Hughes	23	29	56	3	—
BP Julian	not out	80	65	80	7	1
KH MacLeay	run out	8	19	18	—	—
TG Hogan	lbw Austin	11	12	16	—	—
CD Matthews	c Mendis b Allott	1	3	3	—	—
ME Palmer (+)	c Fowler b Watkinson	0	2	3	—	—
CD Mack	not out	8	7	10	1	—
SUNDRIES: B. 1 LB. 5 W. 5 NB. 1		12	309	203	21	1
TOTAL	9 wkts for 237					

F/W: 56 77 81 112 151 173 205 209 212

Bowler	O	M	R	Wkts	NB	W
Allott	9	—	45	1	—	—
Martin	9	—	42	—		5
Austin	10	—	37	3	1	—
Watkinson	10	3	32	2	—	—
Hughes	8	—	42	2	—	—
Jesty	4	—	33	—	—	—
Overs:	50.0					

Lancashire

Batsman	How Out	Ttl	Balls	Mins	4s	6s
GD Mendis	b Moody	65	111	135	4	—
G Fowler	c Marsh b Hogan	53	90	110	6	—
GD Lloyd	b Matthews	36	44	57	2	—
NH Fairbrother	c May b Matthews	30	33	42	2	—
TE Jesty	not out	18	14	29	—	—
M Watkinson	b MacLeay	12	8	10	—	1
ID Austin	c Palmer b MacLeay	0	1	1	—	—
WK Hegg (+)	not out	4	5	5	—	—
DP Hughes (c)	did not bat					
PJW Allott	did not bat					
P Martin	did not bat					
SUNDRIES: B. 1 LB. 12 W. 2 NB. 1		16	306	200	14	1
TOTAL	6 wkts for 234					

F/W: 110 146 193 204 227 227

Bowler	O	M	R	Wkts	NB	W
MacLeay	9	1	37	2	—	—
Mack	10	1	36	—	—	1
Matthews	10	—	38	2	—	1
Julian	5	—	33	—	1	—
Hogan	10	1	44	1	—	—
Moody	6	—	33	1	—	—
Overs:	50.0					

Umpires: W Reynolds & B Rennie

12th Men: J Langer (Western Australia) & I Folley (Lanchashire)

JUNIOR CRICKET

BARCLAYS UNDER 19 CHAMPIONSHIP

New South Wales won the tournament for the second year in a row with a resounding victory over Victoria in the final. Until then, however, it had not looked entirely convincing. It defeated South Australia in the first round, drew with Northern Territory in the second and lost to Queensland in the third. As a result, it finished only second in its group. But New South Wales defeated Western Australia in the semi-final and then overwhelmed Victoria in the final when its pace bowlers swept through the Victorian batting. Like New South Wales, Victoria had got into the final the hard way after finishing second in its group. It was the third successive year Victoria had made the final—and the third time it had been beaten. The 1989-90 tournament was played in Melbourne from December 11 to 22. The final team placings were: 1. New South Wales, 2. Victoria, 3. Western Australia, 4. Queensland, 5. Tasmania, 6. South Australia, 7. ACT, 8. Northern Territory.

The New South Wales all-rounder Jason Gallian was chosen as Player of the Carnival. Gallian scored 270 runs at an average of 54.00 and, bowling his medium pace, took 10 wickets at 13.50. He played an important part in New South Wales's victory in the final; taking 3 wickets and then scoring 102. Gallian was later chosen to captain the Australian Youth team in its series against the touring Young England team.

Damien Martyn of Western Australia, who made 289 runs at 57.80, was named Batsman of the Carnival, and the Bowler of the Carnival was Shane George of South Australia, who took 15 wickets at an average of 12.87.

FINAL

Victoria v New South Wales
Albert Ground, Melbourne   December 21-22, 1989
Result: New South Wales won on the first innings by 186 runs

Victoria

Batsman	How Out	Ttl
M Elliott	c Roberts b Adlam	11
J Kline	c Pratt b Adlam	5
D McLeod	run out	5
P Brown	c Pratt b Gallian	37
R Bartlett	c Pratt b Waddington	0
L Harper	c Mann b Gallian	3
C Parker	c Gallian b Adlam	21
R Harvey	c Mann b Adlam	0
A McGinty	lbw b Gallian	16
S Cottrell	c Pratt b Adlam	9
B Capuano	not out	1
SUNDRIES: B.4 LB.5 W.1 NB.6		16
TOTAL		124

F/W: 19 31 39 43 47 90 91 104 122 124

Bowler	O	M	R	Wkts
W Adlam	26	14	45	5
S Waddington	9	3	20	1
J Gallian	20.4	7	45	3
B Saunders	4	3	5	0

New South Wales

Batsman	How Out	Ttl
J Young	c Kline b McGinty	20
N Beattie	c Kline b Cottrell	6
R Chee Quee	c Kline b Harvey	5
J Gallian	c Bartlett b Harvey	102
K Roberts	run out	10
B Wheeldon	c Kline b Capuano	5
D Mann	c Brown b Harvey	12
B Saunders	c Kline b Harper	96
W Adlam	c Kline b Harvey	10
M Pratt	c Kline b Harper	26
S Waddington	not out	3
SUNDRIES: LB. 8 W.3 NB.4		15
TOTAL		310

F/W: 9 17 34 48 81 137 184 216 301 310

Bowler	O	M	R	Wkts
S Cottrell	23	5	73	1
B Capuano	17	6	29	1
B Harvey	27	5	86	4
A McGinty	22	6	56	1
L Harper	12.4	3	23	2
D McLeod	3	1	15	0
C Parker	3	0	20	0

BARCLAYS BANK 1990 YOUTH INTERNATIONAL SERIES
Australia v England (Under 19s)

Australia won this series of three four-day matches when it defeated England in the third match, after drawing the first two. Jason Young of Wagga was the leading batsman, scoring 295 runs at 59.00, including one century and two 60s. John Crawley of Lancashire batted with admirable consistency, scoring 210 at 42.00, with a highest score of only 52. Jeremy Hallett, a medium-pace bowler from Somerset, took the most wickets—16 at 16.31. Throughout the series he was never really mastered. He took two wickets or more in every innings with a best of 5/73 in the final game. Stephen Cottrell, a fast bowler from Prahran, took 10 for 100 in the final but proved costly in earlier games. David Castle, a Tasmanian off-spinner, and Darrell Mann, a leg-spinner from New South Wales, both proved extremely inexpensive. In fact, Castle conceded barely 1 run per over.

The relative strength of the two sides was illustrated by the fact that eight Australian batsmen, but only one Young England batsman, averaged 30 or more.

MATCH 1
North Sydney Oval, Sydney   Jan 14-17, 1990

Australia 6 declared for 410 (J Gallian 158*, B Ruddell 64, L Harper 61; D Gough 3/93) and 6 declared for 220 (D Martyn 71*, J Young

429

65; J Hallett 3/54) drew with England 319 (P Grayson 110, J Crawley 52; J Gallian 3/30, W Adlam 3/60) and 3 for 145 (K Butler 54*).

MATCH 2
Kardinia Park, Geelong Jan 25-28, 1990

England 279 (M Keech 49; J Gallian 4/46, D Mann 3/30) and 236 (J Crawley 48; D Castle 4/44) drew with Australia 288 (J Young 134, D Mann, 57; J Battey 5/60, J Hallett 3/47) and 3 for 64 (D Martyn 25*, J Hallett 3/22).

MATCH 3
WACA Ground, Perth Feb 6-9, 1990

Australia 345 (J Young 69, B Ruddell 68, L Harper 53; J Hallett 5/73) defeated England 71 (J Crawley 17; S Cottrell 6/40) and 272 (P Holloway 44; S Cottrell 4/60, S Oliver 4/95) by an innings and 2 runs.

LIMITED-OVERS SERIES

Australia made a clean sweep of the three-match, one-day series. The leading run-scorer was Piran Holloway of England, who scored 149 at 49.67. Piran has played for Warwickshire since 1988. Ken Vowles from Darwin was the leading bowler with 7 wickets at 14.71. Vowles also scored 140 runs at 70.00, including a dashing century in Melbourne, where he made 102.

MATCH 1
Manuka Oval, Canberra Jan 19, 1990

Australia 2 for 186 (D Martyn 69*) defeated England 184 (P Holloway 89; W Adlam 3/28).

MATCH 2
MCG, Melbourne Jan 23, 1990

Australia 3 for 239 (K Vowles 102, J Young 93) defeated England 7 for 238 (J Crawley 87, P Holloway 56).

MATCH 3
Stevens Reserve, Perth Feb 4, 1990

Australia 211 (D Mann 54) defeated England 134 (J Crawley 32; K Vowles 4/18).

THE AUSTRALIAN UNDER 19 SQUAD was: Jason Gallian (captain) of New South Wales, Laurie Harper of Victoria, Warwick Adlam of New South Wales, David Castle of Tasmania, Stephen Cottrell of Victoria, Matthew Fraser of Queensland, Justin Langer of Western Australia, Darrell Mann of New South Wales, Damien

Martyn of Western Australia, Stuart Oliver of Tasmania, Bradley Ruddell of Queensland, Ken Vowles of the Northern Territory and Jason Young of New South Wales.

WOOL CORPORATION UNDER 17 CRICKET CHAMPIONSHIP

Victoria easily won the Wool Corporation Under 17 Cricket Championship in Adelaide, thus compensating for the disappointment of finishing second in the Barclays Under 19 tournament. On the other hand, South Australia experienced a sharp downturn in fortune. Unbeaten a year earlier, it lost four games on its home turf. Bowlers tended to dominate the play more than in previous years, but eight centuries were still scored, two of them by Peter Webb of Victoria. Several excellent bowling analyses were recorded, and the best of them was by Troy Corbett of Victoria in the final, in which he ripped through the West Australian innings, taking 7 for 40. Corbett also took 7 for 55 against Queensland.

The first round featured high scoring by all winning teams. Queensland set a state record with 402 against Northern Territory. By batting on as long as it did, however, it possibly denied itself a chance in the finals, since an outright win would have earned it second place in its qualifying division. Forced to follow-on after a first innings score of 153, Northern Territory just held on at 9 for 108 in its second innings, still 141 runs behind.

The rain reduced the scores generally in round two. One match was abandoned and batting generally proved difficult. Shane Lee scored a century, a timely innings, as New South Wales won by only 13 runs against South Australia. Ian Connell set a Tasmanian match bowling aggregate record against the ACT yet finished on the losing side.

Both New South Wales and Victoria compiled 300-plus innings in the third round to guarantee their passage through to the semi-finals. Western Australia defeated the Northern Territory outright, dismissing it twice for less than 90.

Victoria advanced to the final when it easily defeated South Australia, Michael Foster hitting 152, and Western Australia qualified by narrowly defeating NSW. The final was a low-scoring game. Helped by 30 sundries, Victoria struggled to 176 from 86 overs. Peter Rodgers bowled 20 overs and took 4 for 29, and Paul Davies was equally economical, bowling 13 overs and taking 1 for 21. Western Australia was dismissed in 43 overs, Troy Corbett bowling unchanged and finishing with the outstanding figures of 7 for 40. David Fitzgerald top-scored for the match with 45, which represented nearly half of Western Australia's total of 101.

The Victorians dominated the averages and aggregates. Michael Foster made the highest score and had the highest batting aggregate and the highest average, and Troy Corbett took the most wickets and had the lowest bowling average. Scott Duane of Victoria was the most successful wicketkeeper with 13 wickets. Victoria was a strong batting side generally, and Michael Foster and Peter Webb were prominent in its line-up. Its bowlers, too, performed well, taking their wickets at a reasonable rate.

Western Australia's batting was disappointing at times, and David Fitzgerald was the only player to pass 50. It was, however, a strong bowling side, and its attack was led by Matthew Garnaut and Ray Muggeridge. It was unfortunate for Western Australia and Queensland that their game was washed out.

With three century-makers, Shane Lee, Anthony McQuire and Hamish Jamieson, New South Wales was well served by its batting. Lee proved a sound all-rounder, and Aaron Moseley took the most wickets.

Queensland had a three-pronged attack in Angus Cowan, Dene Rauchle and Ben Stackelberg, which was never easy to score from. Of its batsmen, Garth Stubbins scored two 50s and Dean Nye showed consistency with innings of 71, 57, 65 and 22.

Tasmania was an inconsistent batting side, although centuries were scored by Michael Di Venuto and Robert Ellings. The wicketkeeper, Todd Pinnington, also batted well at times. The bowlers Ian Connell and Robert Hodgson bowled conscientiously, but generally the Tasmanian bowlers found it hard to take wickets at a reasonable cost.

The Australian Capital Territory proved a weak batting side with no consistent scorers. Its medium pacers Paul Lawrence and Mark Thomas persevered, but they rarely had sufficient runs to play with.

Seven South Australian batsmen reached 50 but none made it to 75 or an aggregate of 200 runs. For bowling, the side relied heavily on the left arm medium pacer Ben Hook and the leg-spinner Greg Faull. Hook also batted capably.

The Northern Territory had a disappointing tournament, narrowly avoiding outright defeat in the first two games before going down in round three. Its leading batting average was only 15, which illustrates its batting problems. Its bowlers, too, took several batterings. Mathias Miller and Ben Southam were the best of them. Miller equalled the Northern Territory's match aggregate record when he took 7 for 105 against Tasmania.

ROUND 1
Victoria 351 (P Webb 107, M Foster 80; M Garnaut 4/44) defeated Western Australia 234 (J Seal 36*; A Mayhood 4/67).

New South Wales 302 (A McGuire 115, H Jamieson 55; M Thomas 3/54, P Lawrence 3/67) defeated ACT 227 (G Gregan 50; A Moseley 4/48).

Tasmania 368 (M Di Venuto 130, T Pinnington 81, M Harry 62; G Faull 4/89) defeated South Australia 270 (C Lanzoni 63, S Frost 56; I Connell 3/71) and 2 for 46 (C Lanzoni 32*).

Queensland 402 (G Stubbin 86, D Nye 71, A Walduck 60; M Miller 4/77) defeated Northern Territory 153 (P Miller 43; D Raulchle 3/26, J Colbourne 3/49) and 9 for 108 (M Miller 18*; B Stackelberg 4/17, D Raulchle 4/27).

ROUND 2
Victoria 210 (R Dodds 69, M Foster 54; B Southam 4/55) defeated Northern Territory 74 (B Southam 17; A Mayhood 4/16) and 7/124 (M Hatton 36, J Whitemore 36).

Western Australia v Queensland—match washed out.

New South Wales 211 (S Lee 102; B Hook 5/63, C Underwood 4/64) defeated South Australia 198 (R Kelly 54; S Lee 4/55).

ACT 140 (I Garrity 30; I Connell 4/32) and 9 for 95 (M Kavanagh 21, R Hodgson 4/22) defeated Tasmania 80 (R Jones 23; D Whitelum 3/30).

ROUND 3
Victoria 8 for 330 (P Webb 115, S Daune 76*; A Cowan 3/56) defeated Queensland 176 (D Nye 57; T Corbett 7/55).

Western Australia 7 for 268 (B Raynor 50) defeated Northern Territory 88 (J Whitemore 23; P Rodgers 4/15, R Muggeridge 4/40) and 85 (P Miller 26).

New South Wales 5 for 355 (H Jamieson 128, M Traill 61*, C Pearson 50) defeated Tasmania 136 (R Ellings 30; A Moseley 6/38).

South Australia 180 (G Faull 52; M Thomas 4/31) and 7 declared for 180 (M Yeen 73*, B Hook 51) defeated ACT 105 (S Maxwell 18; S Martin 4/59) and 2 for 36.

SEMI-FINALS
Western Australia 8/211 (D Fitzgerald 79) defeated New South Wales 207 (S Lee 49; M Garnaut 4/30).

Victoria 348 (M Foster 152; G Faull 6/67) defeated South Australia 215 (S Martin 54*; T Corbett 3/29).

OTHER MATCHES
Queensland 263 (D Muddle 66*; D Nye 65, D Whitelum 3/55) defeated ACT 112 (D Whitelum 33; A Cowan 3/19) and 3 for 44.

Tasmania 283 (R Ponting 75, M Harry 61, M Di Venuto 55; M Miller 5/75) and 3 declared for 187 (R Ellings 100*) defeated Northern Territory 61 (D Overall 12; A O'Hearne 6/20).

FINAL

Victoria v Western Australia
St Peter's College Adelaide
January 18, 1990
Result: Victoria won by 75 runs

Victoria

Batsman	How Out	Ttl
P Webb	c & b Rogers	13
B Montgomery	b Garnaut	23
M Foster (c)	lbw Rogers	0
S Flynn	c Muggeridge	1
J Duff	c Garnaut	1
S Anderson	lbw Davies	29
S Daune	b Rogers	37
P Broster	c Muggeridge	8
R Dodds	lbw Rogers	13
A Mayhood	run out	19
T Corbett	not out	2
SUNDRIES: B.1 LB.5 W.2 NB.22		30
TOTAL		176

F/W: 34 34 41 50 59 96 96 119 159 176

Bowler	O	M	R	Wkts
S Gibson	10	3	12	—
P Rodgers	20	6	29	4
A King	7	1	22	—
M Garnaut	17	2	38	2
P Davies	13	4	21	1
R Muggeridge	19	2	48	2

Western Australia

Batsman	How Out	Ttl
S Tobin	c Daune b Corbett	0
D Marsh	b Corbett	0
D Fitzgerald	c Daune b Mayhood	45
G Cananagh	c Webb b Corbett	0
S Gibson	b Corbett	2
A King	c Foster b Corbett	20
J Seal (c)	hit wkt b Corbett	6
R Muggeridge	c Flynn b Corbett	2
P Davies	c Mayhood b Montgomery	8
P Rogers	c Daune b Dodds	2
M Garnaut	not out	7
SUNDRIES: LB.6 W.3		9
TOTAL		101

F/W: 0 4 17 35 55 79 81 86 89 101

Bowler	O	M	R	Wkts
T Corbett	21	4	40	7
A Mayhood	13	2	40	1
B Montgomery	1.5	—	4	1
R Dodds	7	3	11	1

OTHER MATCHES

New South Wales 6/133 (C Pearson 29) defeated South Australia 129 (C Lanzoni 38; A Moseley 3/18).

Queensland 9/227 (G Stubbin 59) defeated Tasmania 172 (R Jones 48; A Cowan 4/38).

ACT 4 for 177 (I Garrity 70*, D Whitelum 56) defeated Northern Territory 172 (M Smith 36; P Lawrence 4/65).

Batting Averages (minimum 200 runs)

Batsman	Inn	NO	HS	Runs	Avge
M Foster (Vic)	5	0	152	296	59.20
D Nye (Qld)	4	0	71	215	53.75
P Webb (Vic)	5	0	115	254	50.80
H Jamieson (NSW)	5	0	128	232	46.40
A McQuire (NSW)	5	0	115	203	40.60

Bowling Averages (minimum 12 wickets)

Bowler	O	M	Wkts	R	Avge
T Corbett (Vic)	74	16	17	161	9.47
M Garnaut (WA)	68	19	14	140	10.00
A Cowan (Qld)	51	9	12	137	11.42
D Raulchle (Qld)	70	25	12	143	11.92
A Moseley (NSW)	78	29	13	159	12.23

Centuries

Michael Foster (Vic) 152, Peter Webb (Vic) 107 and 115, Shane Lee (NSW) 102, Anthony McQuire (NSW) 115, Hamish Jamieson (NSW) 128, Michael Di Venuto (Tas) 130, Robert Ellings (Tas) 100*.

Five wickets in an Innings

Troy Corbett (Vic) 7/40 and 7/55, Aaron Moseley (NSW) 6/38, Ben Hook (SA) 5/63, Greg Faull (SA) 6/67, Adam A'Herne (Tas) 6/20, Mathias Miller (NT) 5/75.

Leading Wicketkeepers

Scott Duane (Vic) 13 dismissals, Peter Richardson (SA) 12, Todd Pinnington (Tas) 11.

GILLETTE CUP AUSTRALIAN SCHOOLS CHAMPIONSHIP

Craigmore High School from Adelaide won the 1989 Gillette Cup in an exciting final match played at Essendon Grammar School in Melbourne in mid-December. The eight champion school teams from throughout Australia were divided into two pools of four, within which they played a round-robin competition. Craigmore High qualified for the finals by only 0.07 per cent. Wesley College of Perth also had to work hard to make the finals. In its last qualifying game it played Ipswich Grammar from Queensland. Wesley was sent in on a seaming wicket and was in trouble until the tail raised the score from 6 for 68 to 9 for 158. Ray Muggeridge made 43, and Duncan Begg took the first five wickets to finish with 5 for 25. The Muggeridge brothers then rocked Ipswich by dismissing three batsmen for only 2 runs. Darren Fowler provided lone resistance with 43. Although it had plenty of time, Ipswich lost wickets steadily and had to contend with rain and poor light. At the end, Wesley won narrowly by 6 runs.

In the final, Craigmore won the toss and batted on a sound wicket, but both its openers were out without scoring. The total had reached only 5 for 92 after 38 overs when Juy Foreman arrived at the crease and proceeded to hit out in crude but effective fashion. At the other end, Richard Williams batted responsibly, scoring ones and twos. Foreman was eventually out, swinging at a ball when well out of his crease, but his innings had been a crucial one, for he had helped add 59 for the seventh wicket.

Wesley had to bat for 20 minutes before lunch, and in this period Matthew Castek made life extremely difficult for the batsman. With the first ball of the innings he trapped Stagg lbw and with the second he had Brad Muggeridge caught in the gully. Wesley went to lunch at 2 for 12 but fought its way back into the match with some big hitting in the afternoon. The Craigmore players had backed each other up and generally given a fine exhibition of fielding and Scott Donaldson, the Craigmore captain, bowled 10 overs of his unorthodox medium pace for only 14 runs. But when Ray Muggeridge and Bernard Cregan continued to score rapidly, Craigmore began to mis-field. Wesley needed to make 30 runs off 5 overs, but its scoring rate slowed when Matthew Castek returned to the attack and took a vital wicket. At the start of the final over, Wesley needed 10 to win and, although Craigmore fielded with desperation, it succeeded in making 9—thus tying the scores. Craigmore was awarded the match, however, because it had lost fewer wickets.

Craigmore High School, located in the Elizabeth Plains area north of Adelaide, will keep the Gillette Cup until December 1990 when the competition is to be held in Canberra. It was a disappointing result for Wesley College. Although it was generally an efficient fielding combination, the team dropped four catches in the final and wasted runs with overthrows. It also gave the Craigmore batsmen an extra one and a half overs by bowling no-balls and wides.

Most teams managed to achieve something during the tournament. St Edmund's College from Canberra defeated St Virgil's and had a fine all-rounder in Michael Kavanagh. Oak Flats High School from New South Wales was unlucky not to make the finals, for it had two good wins, including an easy one over Craigmore, and went down only narrowly in its other game. Shane Lee played two fine innings for Oak Flats and Craig Bramble proved a consistent all-rounder. Casuarina Secondary College from the Northern Territory generally had to struggle, yet it almost won in the final round. Ipswich Grammar School was unfortunate to be in the same half of the draw as Wesley. It was a quality side, which only narrowly lost its final game. Andrew Bailey played two fine innings and Duncan Begg took 9 for 75 off 30 overs in three games. Andrew Cowan took 10 for 56 off 25 overs. Craigmore relied heavily on its captain, Scott Donaldson, a steady bowler who also batted well on occasions. St Virgil's College from Tasmania excelled itself on the last day by defeating Oak Flats. Damien Geason took 11 wickets with his fast-medium, and Michael Di Venturo twice passed 60. St Joseph's College from Victoria won in the rain on the last day but struggled at other times. Kane Purcell played a remarkable innings for 84 not out in a total of 109 on the first day but was then withdrawn from the competition to play in Victoria's under 17 side. Daniel Fanning bowled tight leg-spin which was admired by Tony Lock.

The finalists were: St Edmund's College of Canberra, Oak Flats High School of Wollongong, Casuarina Secondary College of Darwin, Ipswich Grammar School of Ipswich, Craigmore High School of Elizabeth, St Virgil's College of Hobart, St Joseph's College of Geelong and Wesley College of Perth.

RESULTS

ROUND 1 (December 11, 1989)
Wesley College 7 for 130 (J Stein 31; D Fanning 4/24) defeated St Joseph's College 8 for 129 (K Purcell 84*).
Craigmore High School 5 for 167 (S Donaldson 81*; D Geason 4/34) defeated St Virgil's College 166 (M Ferguson 50; M Blackwood 3/20).
Ipswich Grammar School 6 for 195 (A Bailey 55*, A Devereaux 54) defeated Casuarina Secondary College 114 (J Hatton 32; A Cowan 5/10, D Begg 3/22).
Oak Flats High School 6 for 101 (G Colliss 21*; D Swan 3/20) defeated St Edmund's College 100 (D Hall 33; G Chapman 4/23, M Atkinson 3/11).

ROUND 2 (December 12, 1989)
Wesley College 7 for 236 (B Muggeridge 58) defeated Casuarina Secondary College 103 (N Allen 42; J Stein 4/20, R Wheatley 3/9).
Oak Flats High School 216 (S Lee 83, C Bramble 63; K Hooker 4/34) defeated Craigmore High School 9 for 168 (A Maher 32; C Bramble 4/26).
St Edmund's College 195 (M Kavanagh 61) defeated St Virgil's College 143 (M Di Venuto 63; M Bugden 4/16, R Neill 3/23).
Ipswich Grammar School 7/221 (A Bailey 97) defeated St Joseph's College 117 (D O'Loughlin 34; A Cowan 4/22).

ROUND 3 (December 13, 1989)
Wesley College 9 for 158 (R Muggeridge 43, D Begg 5/25) defeated Ipswich Grammar School 152 (D Fowler 43; B Muggeridge 3/19).
St Joseph's College 7 for 193 (M Curtain 65) defeated Casuarina Secondary College 7 for 177 (A Hazeldine 52; M Slater 3/30).
Craigmore High School 135 (C Thorn 42; M Kavanagh 4/27) defeated St Edmund's College 99 (M Kavanagh 22; S Donaldson 5/20).
St Virgil's College 7 for 187 (S Kelly 67, M Di Venuto 60*) defeated Oak Flats High School 9 for 186 (A McColl 77, S Lee 52; D Geason 5/42).

FINAL

Craigmore High School v Wesley College
Essendon Grammar School, East Keilor   December 15, 1990
Result: Scores tied. Craigmore awarded the match as it lost fewer wickets

Craigmore High School

Batsman	How Out	Ttl
T Mullen	c Davies b B Muggeridge	0
C Thorn	c Davies b R Muggeridge	0
S Donaldson (c)	b Hilton	27
A Maher	c Stagg b Dudley	11
R Williams	not out	57
M Castek	c B Muggeridge b Stein	23
M Blackwood	c and b Stein	4
J Foreman	b R Muggeridge	28
P Rotolo	not out	1
SUNDRIES: B.3 LB.6 W.3 NB.6		18
TOTAL		7 for 169

F/W: 0 6 34 50 92 107 166

Bowler	O	M	R	Wkts
B Muggeridge	10	4	36	1
R Muggeridge	10	2	39	2
C Dudley	9	1	33	1
J Hilton	7	1	13	1
J Stein	10	1	26	2
S Willis	4	1	13	0

Wesley College

Batsman	How Out	Ttl
J Stagg	lbw b Castek	0
C Dudley	c Donaldson b Foreman	29
B Muggeridge (c)	c Williams b Castek	0
J Stein	b Castek	4
A Woodly-Page	lbw b Maher	34
R Muggeridge	c Svetec b Maher	20
S Willis	c Maher b Thorn	11
B Cregan	b Maher	24
G Davies	not out	21
R Wheatley	b Castek	8
J Hilton	not out	5
SUNDRIES: LB.11 W.2		13
TOTAL		9 for 169

F/W: 0 0 23 67 92 99 117 144 160

Bowler	O	M	R	Wkts
M Castek	10	2	25	4
M Blackwood	10	1	41	0
S Donaldson	10	5	14	0
J Foreman	5	1	32	1
A Maher	10	0	33	3
C Thorn	5	1	13	1

VICTORIAN SCHOOLS v
SOUTH AUSTRALIANS SCHOOLS

The annual three-day game for the Jack Woodruff Memorial Trophy was played at Melbourne Grammar School in mid-December. The Victorian captain, Mark Butler, won the toss and chose to bat on a well-prepared pitch. The first Victorian wicket fell in the eighth over before a solid second-wicket partnership between Andrew Bishop and Phil Hetherington added 62. Hetherington scored 54 before a minor collapse in which Victoria lost 3 for 33. Travis Bean and John Rees stabilised the innings, adding 52 for the sixth wicket, before Bean was run out. Victoria then batted quietly through to stumps.

Next morning Rees continued the innings with Ashley Cavigan, adding another 52 between them before Rees was run out. Rees top scored with a slow but valuable 76. The last 4 wickets fell for 46 and Victoria was all out, two overs short of the 95 overs set as the first-innings limit. Ben Johnson and Darren Hall gave South Australia a good start, scoring 44 for the first wicket. After Johnson was caught behind, Tim White joined Hall, and the pair added 50 for the second wicket to take South Australia to 2 for 94. The South Australian captain, David Nelson, was dismissed quickly, caught behind for a duck. Hall was batting freely at this time and he opened out in a fourth-wicket partnership of 122 with Richard Kelly. Both players were on top of the bowling, Kelly setting the pace with 7 fours and a six in his well-struck 61. Hall was on 99 when Kelly was dismissed by a smart stumping by wicketkeeper Bean. He moved carefully to his 100 before his next partner was dismissed for 3. These two quick wickets just before tea seemed to revive the Victorian attack, and the remaining 7 wickets fell for 56. Darren Hall compiled a patient 110, hitting only 5 fours in 78 overs, before being the sixth batsman out at 240. South Australia was all out for 276 with 8 overs left, 40 short of the Victorian total. Travis Paton took 3 for 50 in 22 overs, and the wicketkeeper, Travis Bean, had a hand in four dismissals. Because there was only a half-hour's play left and the light was poor, play was abandoned. Heavy overnight rain prevented further play on the third day. Victoria won by 40 runs on the first innings.

THE TEAMS WERE:

Victoria: Mark Butler (captain) of Peninsula School, John Rees of St Leo's College, Travis Bean of Hoppers Crossing Secondary College, Andrew Bishop of St Helena Secondary College, John Bott of Caufield Grammar, Ashley Cavigan of MacLeod High, Steven Gross of Peninsula School, Phillip Hetherington of Kangaroo Flat Technical School, Chris Nash of St Joseph's College at Ferntree Gully, Gareth Nash of Mooroopna High, Travis Paton of Gisborne Secondary College, and Graeme Vimpani of Carey Grammar. The manager-coach was Br John Laidlaw of St Kevin's College.

South Australia: David Nelson (captain) of Westminster School, Ben Smith of St Peter's College, Nick Dinan of Rostrevor College, Todd

Ferguson of Prince Alfred College, Mark Fuller of Marryatville High, Jeremy Gask of Pulteney Grammar, Daren Hall of Westminster School, Ben James of Prince Alfred College, Matthew Kelly of Rostrevor College, Richard Kelly of St Ignatius College, Ben Johnson of Prince Alfred College and Tim White of Rostrevor College. The coach was John Caulfield of Rostrevor College, and the manager Malcolm Jones of Scotch College.

Victoria *First Innings*

Batsman	How Out	Ttl
A Bishop	c Ferguson b James	54
G Vimpani	c Johnson b Dinan	11
P Hetherington	c Kelly b Gask	54
J Bott	b Kelly	27
M Butler (c)	run out	2
J Rees	run out	76
T Bean	run out	18
A Cavigan	c Johnson b Smith	28
S Gross	c White b Smith	20
T Paton	not out	7
C Nash	c and b Gask	6
SUNDRIES: B.7 LB.4 W.1 NB.1		13
TOTAL		316

F/W: 28 90 133 142 166 218 270 286 304 316

Bowler	O	M	R	Wkts
B Smith	25	1	88	2
N Dinan	11	1	39	1
J Gask	20.5	2	94	2
B James	8	1	19	1
M Kelly	21	3	52	1
D Nelson	3	1	6	0
T White	3	1	5	0
D Hall	1	0	2	0

South Australia *First Innings*

Batsman	How Out	Ttl
R Johnson	c Bean b Nash	25
D Hall	c Bott b Newman	110
T White	lbw b Newman	18
D Nelson (c)	c Bean b Newman	0
R Kelly	st Bean b Paton	61
J Gask	b Paton	3
M Fuller	not out	13
B Smith	c Hetherington b Paton	15
M Kelly	b Hetherington	1
T Ferguson	c Bean b Cavigan	9
B James	c Butler b Cavigan	0
SUNDRIES: B.7 LB.4 W.6 NB.4		21
TOTAL		276

F/W: 44 94 98 220 224 240 257 258 276 276

Bowler	O	M	R	Wkts
C Nash	19	2	62	1
G Newman	17	1	45	3
A Cavigan	17.2	3	49	2
T Paton	22	4	50	3
S Gross	3	0	24	0
P Hetherington	10	1	35	1

Result: Victoria won by 40 runs on the first innings

VICTORIAN SCHOOLS v
NEW SOUTH WALES SCHOOLS

The annual three-day under 19 game played for the Carbine Cup was held at Barker College, Hornsby, Sydney, in late December. The Victorian captain, Mark Butler, won the toss and chose to bat on an under-prepared pitch which suited spin bowling from the start. Victoria was dismissed in 59 overs for a lowly 125. Only Graeme Vimpani and John Bott offered much resistance as the New South Wales spinners, Hayden Smith and Neill Crotty, took control. Smith bowled sharply turning leg-breaks on a good length while Crotty bowled steady left-arm orthodox at the other end.

New South Wales had the pitch rolled before its innings, which seemed to settle it down. The New South Wales openers rattled up 50 in 13 overs before the Victorian spinners slowed the scoring rate. In a remarkable collapse, New South Wales slumped from 0 for 57 to 6 for 69—a loss of 6 wickets for 12 runs. The damage to the New South Wales innings was done by Travis Paton's left-arm orthodox spin and Steven Gross's off-spin. Duncan Gordon hung on for almost an hour for 3 runs and New South Wales finished the first day at 6 for 84. Next day, the seventh wicket fell quickly and although Shane Hadley batted adventurously against the spinners to score 50 off 59 balls, including 8 fours and a six, later batsmen dug in. The ninth-wicket pair, Duff and Moseley, batted for almost two hours to add 57 as New South Wales pushed on to 195 in 78 overs, which gave it a useful lead of 70. The two spinners shared the wickets, the other bowlers having proved generally ineffective.

Further rolling of the wicket improved it initially and gave the Victorians a chance to erase the first-innings deficit, which they did with the loss of 2 wickets. Andrew Bishop started aggressively, hitting 5 fours off 14 balls before being dismissed for 22 out of the first 23. Graeme Vimpani and John Bott settled down and batted responsibly, and Bott made 62 before being run out. The medium-pace bowler Shane Hadley destroyed Victoria's middle order, finishing with a personal double of 50 runs and 7 wickets for 54. The Victorians were 8 for 178 at stumps, but next day the two spinners, Gross and Paton, produced the best partnership of the match, adding 66 for the ninth wicket in over two hours.

New South Wales was set 161 to win in the 70 overs available. The pitch had settled down and the spinners were no longer the danger. In fact, the home side's batsmen gave them such rough treatment that they were removed from the attack. Jarrett and Stimson combined to add 116 for the second wicket before Jarrett scored the winning runs with a boundary.

Victoria

First Innings

Batsman	How Out	Ttl
G Vimpani	c J Smith b Crotty	28
A Bishop	b Moseley	8
P Hetherington	c Quint b H Smith	1
J Bott	b H Smith	29
M Butler (c)	b Crotty	0
J Rees	c Duff b Crotty	3
T Bean	c Moseley b H Smith	8
A Cavigan	c and b Hadley	21
S Gross	run out	5
T Paton	not out	4
M Fitzpatrick	c Hadley b H Smith	10
SUNDRIES: B.2 LB.3 W.1 NB.2		8
TOTAL		125

F/W: 13 16 68 68 76 76 95 110 112 125

Second Innings

How Out	Ttl
c Stimson b Crotty	2
lbw b Hadley	22
run out	6
run out	62
c Duff b Hadley	0
c H Smith b Hadley	5
lbw b Hadley	14
lbw b Hadley	9
b Hadley	27
c Duff b Hadley	31
not out	7
	20
	230

23 63 78 94 95 111 132 153 219 230

Bowler	O	M	R	Wkts
J Smith	6	1	9	1
Moseley	8	1	25	1
H Smith	21.3	8	43	3
Crotty	13	5	22	3
Gordon	3	1	8	0
Hadley	8	2	13	1

Bowler	O	M	R	Wkts
J Smith	10	2	37	0
Moseley	15	5	27	0
H Smith	19	7	45	0
Crotty	8	2	30	1
Gordon	4	1	6	0
Hadley	26.5	6	54	7
Quint	6	2	17	0

New South Wales

First Innings

Batsman	How Out	Ttl
G Hayne (c)	c and b Paton	20
J Jarrett	b Paton	27
M Stimson	c Bishop b Gross	6
D Gordon	b Paton	3
D Quint	c Bean b Paton	0
C Robberds	c Paton b Gross	0
J Smith	c Fitzpatrick b Gross	0
S Hadley	c Fitzpatrick b Gross	50
S Duff	c Butler b Gross	46
A Moseley	not out	18
H Smith	b Paton	2
SUNDRIES: B.8 LB.1 W.6 NB.8		23
TOTAL		195

F/W: 57 64 68 68 69 69 93 131 188 195

Second Innings

How Out	Ttl
lbw b Hetherington	14
not out	72
c and b Paton	67
not out	2
	9
2 for	164

F/W: 39 155

Bowler	O	M	R	Wkts
C Nash	3	0	22	0
M Fitzpatrick	11	6	22	0
A Cavigan	8	0	27	0
T Paton	28.1	12	75	5
S Gross	22	13	30	5
M Butler	3	1	8	0
A Bishop	3	1	2	0

Bowler	O	M	R	Wkts
Nash	6	1	19	0
Fitzpatrick	9	2	26	0
Cavigan	9	1	25	0
Paton	10	2	35	1
Gross	5	0	25	0
Bishop	4	1	17	0
Hetherington	11	5	9	1
Bott	1	0	4	0

Result: NSW won outright by 8 wkts

OBITUARIES

Desmond Morrah Brain *(died March 1, 1990)*. Des Brain had barely turned twenty-one when he scored 93 for Tasmania against Victoria in Melbourne, but Tasmanian cricket saw little of him thereafter. In fact, he played only three first-class matches for Tasmania, all in the 1930-31 season, scoring 156 runs at an average of 26.00. Afterwards, the bank he worked for posted him to the mainland, and his first-class career thereby came to a premature end. Known as 'Bulla' by his team-mates, Brain was a wristy right-handed batsman and a good fieldsman. He was born at Hobart on December 16, 1909, and played for South Hobart. After leaving Tasmania, he lived in Sydney and several towns in New South Wales, including Tumut, which is where he was living at the time of his death.

Richard John Bryant *(died August 17, 1989)*. Dick Bryant was a dominant figure in Western Australian cricket for more than sixty years, first as a player and later as an administrator. He was born at Perth on May 8, 1904, the son of a Western Australian gold prospector. Dick Bryant was the eldest of three brothers, all of whom were talented cricketers and all of whom represented the state. He made his debut for Western Australia at the start of the 1924-25 season, when he was twenty. He was primarily a batsman, and in the 29 matches he played for Western Australia he made 1,088 runs at an average of 22.66. He was also a useful medium-pace bowler, taking 20 first-class wickets in all. He was joined in the Western Australian team by his brother Frank, and later the third brother, Bill, played with them in one match—the first occasion on which three brothers appeared together in a first-class match in Australia. In the 1929-30 season Dick Bryant became captain of the state side. His appointment was followed by a distinct upturn in the side's fortunes, for which Bryant was given much of the credit. A high point of his career was the match against Victoria at Melbourne in 1933-34, in which both he and his brother Frank scored centuries in the first innings. Dick made 103, his only first-class century. He retired during the 1935-36 season, about the time he was admitted as a solicitor. By then, he had captained the state sixteen times.

Bryant's retirement as a player ended the first phase of his involvement in Western Australian cricket. The second began after World War II, when the Bryant brothers, Dick and Frank, became active in cricket administration. Dick Bryant was manager of the Western Australian team on its eastern tour in 1947-48, which concluded with Western Australia winning the Sheffield Shield at its first attempt. In the years which followed the Bryant brothers worked hard to build up Western Australian cricket to a point where it was treated as an equal by other states, and their efforts were rewarded in resounding fashion in the 1970s and 1980s, when Western Australia regularly fielded the strongest Sheffield Shield team in Australia. The contribution of the Bryant brothers to the development of West Australian cricket was acknowledged in 1981, when they were both named as recipients of the OAM in the Queen's Birthday Honours List.

Bernard Thomas Considine *(died June 4, 1989).* Bernie Considine was a tall, fast-medium bowler who played eight first-class games in all, six of them for Victoria and two for Tasmania. Born at Ararat on April 4, 1925, he played for Fitzroy in Melbourne before making his debut for Victoria against Tasmania in January 1950. He did not play for Victoria again that season, but made reappearances in 1951-52, when he played three games, and 1952-53, when he played two. In the latter season he took 6 for 85 against Western Australia, the best performance of his first-class career. After that, he moved to Tasmania, and played two games for that state in 1954-55. In all, Considine took 19 first-class wickets at an average of 29.44 and scored 19 runs at an average of 2.11. He also played football for Hawthorn.

Frank Alexander Easton *(died May 5, 1989).* For much of the 1930s Frank Easton stood in as New South Wales's wicketkeeper when Bert Oldfield was absent. Born in Sydney on February 19, 1910, he played 18 matches for New South Wales from 1933-34 to 1938-39, stumping sixteen batsmen and catching 28. In 1938-39, after Oldfield had retired, Easton kept wickets for New South Wales in its next four Sheffield Shield matches, but was afterwards replaced by Stan Sismey. He also performed creditably with the bat, making 619 runs at an average of 25.79. Easton was a neat wicketkeeper in the style of Oldfield, and he was remembered by his team-mates as a quiet man, yet a humorist.

Roy Higgins *(died February 24, 1990).* Roy Higgins was the last surviving member of the first Sheffield Shield side fielded by Queensland when it entered the Shield competition in 1926-27. Born in Brisbane on January 27, 1900, Higgins was himself the son of a first-class cricketer, James 'Larry' Higgins, who represented Queensland in the 1898-99 season. Higgins made his debut for Queensland in 1925-26 and played regularly for the state until 1931-32. He was an aggressive batsman, who could bat at any position and, in fact, sometimes opened the batting. In 20 matches for Queensland, he made 814 runs at an average of 23.94, took 3 catches and bowled a handful of overs without taking a wicket. He made his highest score, 179, in the 1927-28 season. Higgins retained a keen interest in the game until the end. He longed to see Queensland win the Shield, and in his later years he was fond of saying, 'I hope they hurry up and win it—I haven't got long to go.' He died in Brisbane on February 24, 1990, after being hit by a car in Gympie Road, Chermside.

Graeme Blake Hole *(died February 14, 1989).* Graeme Hole's record in Test cricket provides an inadequate measure of his talent. In 18 Tests between 1950-51 and 1954-55, Hole made 789 runs at an average of 25.45 and did not once score a Test century. Yet he was a fluent and elegant stroke-maker, who, when he first appeared in first-class cricket, was likened to stylists of the past such as Alan Kippax and

Archie Jackson. His failure to achieve more success at the Test level than he did is not easily explained. Some of his contemporaries felt that his high, flourishing backlift was often his undoing against top-class bowling, and it is also true that even as a young man he devoted much of his energy to his business career. Long after he retired from cricket, he told a journalist: 'I suppose I never had the dedication to reach the very top . . . I realised there were more important things to life than Test cricket.'

Born in Sydney on January 6, 1931, Hole attended North Sydney High School and played cricket for Mosman. He was a precociously talented batsman, and a few weeks after his nineteenth birthday he made his debut in first-class cricket for New South Wales in the last match of the 1949-50 season. Before the start of the next season, he had moved to Adelaide. It was a period in which New South Wales enjoyed a surplus of talent, and many promising young cricketers like Hole were welcomed by other states. In this first season with South Australia Hole impressed everyone by the quality of his batting, and he was chosen to play for Australia in the final Test of the 1950-51 series against England. England won the Test, its first victory over Australia since 1938, but Hole top-scored in Australia's second innings with 63.

Over the next three years Hole was a regular member of the Australian side, but the great promise he showed was never translated into performance. His 33 Test innings included scores of 63, 62, 59, 66, 53 and 57, yet somehow he did not ever manage to play a big innings. In the 1954-55 series against England, he was bowled three times in succession by Frank Tyson for low scores, after which he was dropped. He was not quite 24 years old then, but he never played for Australia again. He continued playing Sheffield Shield cricket, however, and captained South Australia. During a match against Victoria in Melbourne in January 1958, Hole ruptured his spleen while diving to take a catch, and for a time his life seemed in danger. He retired from first-class cricket after that, although he continued to bat in Adelaide grade cricket with distinction. In an interstate veterans' match in Sydney in September 1980, Hole scored 105 runs in 69 minutes for South Australia against Tasmania, hitting 13 fours and 4 sixes.

Hole was a fine slips fieldsman, with a flair for taking sharp catches. As an occasional off-spinner he took just 3 wickets in Tests at an average of 42.00, and one of them was the wicket of Len Hutton, whom Hole bowled in his maiden Test. As a bowler, he had an anonymous but loud-voiced admirer at the Gabba ground in Brisbane, who while Hole was on the field was often heard to chant: 'Give 'ole a bowl!' In all his 98 first-class matches, Hole scored 5,647 runs at an average of 36.66, including 11 centuries, and took 61 wickets at an average of 44.03. He maintained an active interest in cricket after his retirement from the game, serving on one of the South Australian Cricket Association's committees and coaching at his old club, Kensington. In his later years he ran an indoor cricket centre. Hole was a kindly man, who was regarded fondly by others in the cricket fraternity. His death at the age of 59 followed a long illness.

Raymond Sydney Holman *(died December 19, 1989).* Born on September 17, 1919, Ray Holman played for the Port Adelaide club as a right-handed batsman, and was promoted to the South Australian side for just one first-class match in 1940-41, in which he scored 4 runs in two innings. He also appeared as twelfth man for South Australia in Perth. Although he did not succeed at the first-class level, Holman was a fluent and talented batsman.

Tom Goodman *(died September 28, 1989).* For more than 30 years, from the 1930s to the 1960s, Tom Goodman was regarded as Sydney's premier sportswriter. Throughout this period he worked for the *Sydney Morning Herald*, covering cricket in the summer and Rugby League in the winter. In fact, he was capable of reporting on almost any sport, and in the late 1940s he was on assignment in Britain for more than a year covering four different sporting events—the cricket tour by Don Bradman's team, the Olympic Games in London, and tours by both the Australian Rugby League and Rugby Union teams. To judge from the extensive library of sports books which he kept at his home at Potts Point, however, cricket was his first love. Born at Parramatta in 1902, Goodman became a copy boy on the *Evening News* at the age of thirteen. As a boy, he saw Victor Trumper play, although in later years he regretted that his memory of the experience was faint. The first Test he attended as a working journalist was the Sydney Test of the 1920-21 series against England, but his job then was merely to phone through to his paper the over-by-over accounts of the play written by a more senior reporter. He remembered how Charlie Macartney's dynamic innings of 170 in that Test kept both of them busy. He joined the *Sydney Morning Herald* as a cricket writer in 1932, which meant that the first Test series he covered for that newspaper was the bodyline series. His reports on that eventful series were not by-lined, but his composed, controlled, unpretentious writing style is evident. Goodman never sought to attain literary heights, preferring, like a wise batsman, to perform successfully within the limits of his natural ability. He always wrote carefully and responsibly and, accordingly, was widely held in respect. He worked for the *Sydney Morning Herald* until his retirement in 1967, and was afterwards patron of the Australian Sportswriters' Association. A lifelong bachelor, he was a gentle-natured man who was regarded with fondness by almost everyone who knew him. Early in 1989 he broke his hip in a fall, and it was the illness which developed from this mishap which led to his death in a Sydney nursing home.

Gordon John Lethborg *(died August 31, 1989).* Gordon Lethborg was a right-handed batsman who played briefly for Tasmania in the late 1920s and early 1930s. By all accounts he was a better player than his first-class record suggests. He played three matches for Tasmania in 1929-30 and one match in 1932-33, scoring a total of only 47 runs at an average of 6.71. He was a stylish batsman, whose ability was respected by his contemporaries. He was also an accomplished slips fieldsman. Born at Scottsdale on November 23,

1907, he played variously for North Launceston, New Town and Tamar.

Allan Robert Charles McLean *(died November 9, 1989)*. Bob McLean was an outstanding all-round sportsman with a selfless devotion to sport. As a young man he represented South Australia at both cricket and Australian Rules football, and after his playing days were over he served as an administrator in both sports. Born on February 1, 1914, he began his career in senior cricket at the age of seventeen, bowling leg-spin for the East Torrens club, but, curiously, it was not until much later, when he was in his thirties, that he enjoyed his greatest success at the game. He played regularly for South Australia as 'an all-rounder from 1945-46 until 1950-51, scoring 897 runs at 28.94, including two centuries, and taking 65 wickets at 38.37. His highest innings was 213, scored against Queensland. After retiring, he remained active in the Port Adelaide club, and was the club's delegate to the South Australian Cricket Association for several years from 1978, becoming its chairman in 1981. McLean's son, Ian, was also a South Australian cricketer, from 1976-77 to 1982-83, and he, too, scored two first-class centuries. Ian McLean is the present chairman of the Port Adelaide club, the post once held by his father. Bob McLean was 193 cm (6 feet 4 inches) tall and solidly built, and he was widely known as Big Bob. He had a long and successful football career, playing for Norwood from 1934 until 1938 before moving to Port Adelaide in 1939. It was the start of a long association with that club. From 1949 until 1980 he was the club's secretary-general manager, and in 1983 he became its chairman. In that same year he was awarded the OBE for his services to Australian Rules football. His death followed a decline in health which began in 1986, when he suffered a stroke.

William Maurice Roberts *(died January 21, 1990)*. Maurie Roberts played for South Australia three times in a first-class career which spanned World War II. Born at Wallaroo Mines on August 26, 1916, Roberts made his debut in 1937-38 and played his last first-class match in 1946-47. A slow off-break bowler who could bat capably, he took a total of 9 wickets at an average of 25.89. His best figures were 4 for 35. Roberts played for Port Adelaide and was regarded as a fine team man..

Jack Tregoning *(died June 26, 1989)*. Jack Tregoning, a right-handed batsman and a useful right arm slow-medium bowler, had an unusual first-class career: he played only two matches for South Australia, and these were more than eight years apart. The first was against New South Wales in December 1939, when he was bowled by Bill O'Reilly for a duck and took 1 for 9. Long afterwards, Tregoning used to tell O'Reilly in jest that he had ruined his cricket career. Tregoning's other match was against Victoria in Melbourne in February 1948, when he made scores of 1 and 17. Born on June 13, 1919, Tregoning played for University Club in Adelaide. In his playing days he was a powerfully built man, who was a shot-putter as well as a cricketer.

Australian Test Players

Player	Test Career	Birthplace	State Representation						Tests	Runs	HS	100s	Avrge	Wkts	Avrge	Best	Ct/St
			NSW	Qld	SA	Tas	Vic	WA									
A'Beckett EL	1928/29–1931/32	Vic	—	—	—	—	4	—	4	143	41	—	20.43	3	105.67	1/41	4
Alderman TM	1981 –1989/90	WA	—	—	—	—	—	36	36	169	23	—	6.26	153	26.69	6/128	22
Alexander G	1880 –1884/85	Vic	—	—	—	—	2	—	2	52	33	—	13.00	2	46.50	2/69	2
Alexander HH	1932/33	Vic	—	—	—	—	1	—	1	17	17*	—	17.00	1	154.00	1/129	—
Allan FE	1878/79	Vic	—	1	—	—	—	—	1	5	5	—	5.00	4	20.00	2/30	—
Allan PJ	1965/66	Qld	—	1	—	—	—	—	1	—	—	—	—	2	41.50	2/58	—
Allen RC	1886/87	NSW	1	—	—	—	—	—	1	44	30	—	22.00	—	—	—	2
Andrews TJE	1921 –1926	NSW	16	—	—	—	—	—	16	592	94	—	26.91	1	116.00	1/23	12
Archer KA	1950/51–1951/52	Qld	—	5	—	—	—	—	5	234	48	—	26.00	—	—	—	—
Archer RG	1952/53–1956/57	Qld	—	19	—	—	—	—	19	713	128	1	24.59	48	27.46	5/53	20
Armstrong WW	1901/02–1921	Vic	—	—	—	—	50	—	50	2863	159*	6	38.69	87	33.60	6/35	44
Badcock CL	1936/37–1938	Tas	—	—	—	7	—	—	7	160	118	1	14.55	—	—	—	3
Bannerman AC	1878/79–1893	NSW	28	—	—	—	—	—	28	1108	94	—	23.08	4	40.75	3/111	21
Bannerman C	1878/79–1878/79	Eng	3	—	—	—	—	—	3	239	165*	1	59.75	—	—	—	—
Bardsley W	1909 –1926	NSW	41	—	—	—	—	—	41	2469	193*	6	40.48	—	—	—	12
Barnes SG	1938 –1948	NSW	13	—	—	—	—	—	13	1072	234	3	63.06	4	54.50	2/25	14
Barnett BA	1938	Vic	—	—	—	—	4	—	4	195	57	—	27.86	—	—	—	4/2
Barrett JE	1890	Vic	—	—	—	—	2	—	2	80	67*	—	26.67	—	—	—	1
Beard GR	1979/80	NSW	3	—	—	—	—	—	3	114	49	—	22.80	1	109.00	1/26	—
Benaud J	1972/73	NSW	3	—	—	—	—	—	3	223	142	1	44.60	2	6.00	2/12	—
Benaud R	1951/52–1963/64	NSW	63	—	—	—	—	—	63	2201	122	3	24.46	248	27.03	7/72	65
Bennett MJ	1984/85–1985	NSW	3	—	—	—	—	—	3	71	23	—	23.67	6	54.17	3/79	5
Blackham JM	1876/77–1894/95	Vic	—	—	—	—	35	—	35	800	74	—	15.69	—	—	—	36/24
Blackie DD	1928/29	Vic	—	—	—	—	3	—	3	24	11*	—	8.00	14	31.71	6/94	2
Bonnor GJ	1880 –1888	NSW	6	—	—	—	11	—	17	512	128	1	17.07	2	42.00	1/05	16
Boon DC	1984/85–1989/90	Tas	—	—	—	48	—	—	48	3186	200	8	39.33	—	—	—	49
Booth BC	1961 –1965/66	NSW	29	—	—	—	—	—	29	1773	169	5	42.21	3	48.67	2/33	17
Border AR	1978/79–1989/90	NSW	21	94	—	—	—	—	115	8701	205	23	53.38	29	35.24	7/46	125
Boyle HF	1878/79–1884/85	NSW	—	—	—	—	12	—	12	153	36*	—	12.75	32	20.03	6/42	10
Bradman DG	1928/29–1948	NSW	28	—	24	—	—	—	52	6996	334	29	99.94	2	36.00	1/08	31
Bright RJ	1977 –1986/87	Vic	—	—	—	—	25	—	25	445	33	—	14.35	53	41.13	7/87	13
Bromley EH	1932/33–1934	Vic	—	—	—	—	2	—	2	38	26	—	9.50	—	—	—	2
Brown WA	1934 –1948	NSW	22	—	—	—	—	—	22	1592	206*	4	46.82	—	—	—	14
Bruce W	1884/85–1894/95	Vic	—	—	—	—	14	—	14	702	80	—	29.25	12	36.67	3/88	12
Burge PJP	1954/55–1965/66	Qld	—	42	—	—	—	—	42	2290	181	4	38.17	—	—	—	23
Burke JW	1950/51–1958/59	NSW	24	—	—	—	—	—	24	1280	189	3	34.59	8	28.75	4/37	18
Burn EJK	1890	Tas	—	—	—	2	—	—	2	41	19	—	10.25	—	—	—	—
Burton FJ	1886/87–1888	Eng	2	—	—	—	—	—	2	4	2*	—	2.00	—	—	—	1/1
Callaway ST	1891/92–1894/95	NSW	2	—	—	—	—	—	3	87	41	—	17.40	6	23.67	5/37	—
Callen IW	1977/78	Vic	—	—	—	—	1	—	1	26	22*	—	—	6	31.83	3/83	1
Campbell GD	1989 –1988/89	Tas	—	—	—	4	—	—	4	10	6	—	2.50	13	38.69	3/79	1
Carkeek W	1912	Vic	—	—	—	—	6	—	6	16	6*	—	5.33	—	—	—	6
Carlson PH	1978/79	Qld	—	2	—	—	—	—	2	23	21	—	5.75	2	49.50	2/41	2
Carter H	1907/08–1921/22	Eng	28	—	—	—	—	—	28	873	72	—	22.97	—	—	—	44/21
Chappell GS	1970/71–1983/84	SA	—	74	14	—	—	—	88	7110	247*	24	53.86	47	40.70	5/61	122
Chappell IM	1964/65–1979/80	SA	—	—	76	—	—	—	76	5345	196	14	42.42	20	65.80	2/21	105
Chappell TM	1981	SA	—	—	3	—	—	—	3	79	27	—	15.80	—	—	—	2
Charlton PC	1890	NSW	2	—	—	—	—	—	2	29	11	—	7.25	3	8.00	3/18	—
Chipperfield AG	1934 –1938	NSW	14	—	—	—	—	—	14	552	109	1	32.47	5	87.40	3/91	15
Clark WM	1977/78–1978/79	WA	—	—	—	—	—	10	10	98	33	—	5.76	44	28.73	4/46	6
Colley DJ	1972	NSW	3	—	—	—	—	—	3	84	54	—	21.00	6	52.00	3/83	1
Collins HL	1920/21–1926	NSW	19	—	—	—	—	—	19	1352	203	4	45.07	4	63.00	2/47	13
Coningham A	1894/95	NSW	1	—	—	—	—	—	1	13	10	—	6.50	2	38.00	2/17	—
Connolly AN	1963/64–1970/71	Vic	—	—	—	—	30	—	30	260	37	—	10.40	102	29.23	6/47	17
Cooper BB	1876/77	Ind	—	—	—	—	1	—	1	18	15	—	9.00	—	—	—	2
Cooper WH	1881/82–1884/85	Eng	—	—	—	—	2	—	2	13	7	—	6.50	9	25.11	6/120	1
Corling GE	1964	NSW	5	—	—	—	—	—	5	5	3	—	1.67	12	37.25	4/60	—
Cosier GJ	1975/76–1978/79	Vic	—	9	9	—	—	—	18	897	168	2	28.94	5	68.20	2/26	14
Cottam JT	1886/87	WA	1	—	—	—	—	—	1	4	3	—	2.00	—	—	—	1
Cotter A	1903/04–1911/12	NSW	21	—	—	—	—	—	21	457	45	—	13.06	89	28.64	7/148	8
Couthard G	1881/82	Vic	—	—	—	1	—	—	1	6	6*	—	—	—	—	—	1
Cowper RM	1964 –1968	Vic	—	—	—	—	27	—	27	2061	307	5	46.84	36	31.64	4/48	21
Craig ID	1952/53–1957/58	NSW	11	—	—	—	—	—	11	358	53	—	19.89	—	—	—	2
Crawford WPA	1956 –1956/57	NSW	4	—	—	—	—	—	4	53	34	—	17.67	7	15.29	3/28	1
Darling J	1894/95–1905	SA	—	—	34	—	—	—	34	1657	178	3	28.57	—	—	—	27
Darling LS	1932/33–1936/37	Vic	—	—	—	—	12	—	12	474	85	—	27.88	—	—	—	8
Darling WM	1977/78–1979/80	SA	—	—	14	—	—	—	14	697	91	—	26.81	—	—	—	5
Davidson AK	1953 –1962/63	NSW	44	—	—	—	—	—	44	1328	80	—	24.59	186	20.53	7/93	42
Davis IC	1973/74–1977	NSW	15	—	—	—	—	—	15	692	105	1	26.62	—	—	—	9
Davis SP	1985/86	Vic	—	—	—	—	1	—	1	—	—	—	0.00	—	—	—	—
De Courcy JH	1953	NSW	1	—	—	—	—	—	3	81	41	—	16.20	—	—	—	3
Dell AR	1970/71	Eng	—	2	—	—	—	—	2	6	3*	—	—	6	26.67	3/65	—
Dodemaide AIC	1987/88–1988/89	Vic	—	—	—	—	8	—	8	171	50	—	19.00	28	28.71	6/58	6

Player	Test Career	Birth-place	NSW	Qld	SA	Tas	Vic	WA	Tests	Runs	HS	100s	Avrge	Wkts	Avrge	Best	Ct/St
Donnan H	1891/92–1896	NSW	5	—	—	—	—	—	5	75	15*	—	8.33	—	—	—	1
Dooland B	1946/47–1947/48	SA	—	—	3	—	—	—	3	76	29	—	19.00	9	46.56	4/69	3
Duff RA	1901/02–1905	NSW	22	—	—	—	—	—	22	1317	146	2	35.59	4	21.25	2/43	14
Duncan JRF	1970/71	Qld	—	1	—	—	—	—	1	3	3	—	3.00	—	—	—	—
Dyer GC	1986/87–1987/88	NSW	6	—	—	—	—	—	6	131	60	—	21.83	—	—	—	22/2
Dymock G	1973/74–1979/80	Qld	—	21	—	—	—	—	21	236	31*	—	9.44	78	27.13	7/67	1
Dyson J	1977/78–1984/85	NSW	30	—	—	—	—	—	30	1359	127*	2	26.65	—	—	—	10
Eady CJ	1896 –1901/02	Tas	—	—	—	3	—	—	2	20	10*	—	6.67	7	16.00	3/30	2
Eastwood KH	1970/71	NSW	—	—	—	—	1	—	1	5	5	—	2.50	1	21.00	1/21	—
Ebeling HI	1934	Vic	—	—	—	—	1	—	1	43	41	—	21.50	3	29.67	3/74	—
Edwards JD	1888	Vic	—	—	—	—	3	—	3	48	26	—	9.60	—	—	—	1
Edwards R	1972 –1975	WA	—	—	—	—	—	20	20	1171	170*	2	40.38	—	—	—	7
Edwards WJ	1974/75	WA	—	—	—	—	—	3	3	68	30	—	11.33	—	—	—	—
Emery SH	1912	NSW	4	—	—	—	—	—	4	6	5	—	3.00	5	49.80	2/46	2
Evans E	1881/82	NSW	6	—	—	—	—	—	6	82	33	—	10.25	7	47.43	3/64	5
Fairfax AG	1928/29–1930/31	NSW	10	—	—	—	—	—	10	410	65	—	51.25	21	30.71	4/31	15
Favell LE	1954/55–1960/61	NSW	—	—	19	—	—	—	19	757	101	1	27.04	—	—	—	9
Ferris JJ	1886/87–1890	NSW	8	—	—	—	—	—	8	98	20*	—	8.17	48	14.25	5/26	4
Fingleton JHW	1931/32–1938	NSW	18	—	—	—	—	—	18	1189	136	5	42.46	—	—	—	13
Fleetwood-Smith LO	1935/36–1938	Vic	—	—	—	—	10	—	10	54	16*	—	9.00	42	37.38	6/110	—
Francis BC	1972	NSW	3	—	—	—	—	—	3	52	27	—	10.40	—	—	—	1
Freeman EW	1967/68–1969/70	SA	—	—	11	—	—	—	11	345	76	—	19.17	34	33.18	4/52	5
Freer FW	1946/47	Vic	—	—	—	—	1	—	1	28	28*	—	—	3	24.67	2/49	—
Gannon JB	1977/78	WA	—	—	—	—	—	3	3	3	3*	—	3.00	11	32.82	4/77	3
Garrett TW	1876/77–1887/88	NSW	19	—	—	—	—	—	19	339	51*	—	12.56	36	26.94	6/78	7
Gaunt RA	1957/58–1963/64	WA	—	—	—	—	2	1	3	6	3	—	3.00	7	44.29	3/53	1
Gehrs DRA	1903/04–1910/11	SA	—	—	6	—	—	—	6	221	67	—	20.09	—	—	—	4
Giffen G	1881/82–1896	SA	—	—	31	—	—	—	31	1238	161	1	23.36	103	27.10	7/117	24
Giffen WF	1886/87–1891/92	SA	—	—	3	—	—	—	3	11	3	—	1.83	—	—	—	1
Gilbert DR	1985 –1986/87	NSW	9	—	—	—	—	—	9	57	15	—	7.13	16	52.69	3/48	—
Gilmour GJ	1973/74–1977	NSW	15	—	—	—	—	—	15	483	101	1	23.00	54	26.04	6/85	8
Gleeson JW	1967/68–1972	NSW	30	—	—	—	—	—	30	395	45	—	10.39	93	36.20	5/61	17
Graham H	1893 –1896	Vic	—	—	—	—	6	—	6	301	107	2	30.10	—	—	—	3
Gregory DW	1876/77–1878/79	NSW	3	—	—	—	—	—	3	60	43	—	20.00	—	—	—	—
Gregory EJ	1876/77	NSW	1	—	—	—	—	—	1	11	11	—	5.50	—	—	—	1
Gregory JM	1920/21–1928/29	NSW	24	—	—	—	—	—	24	1146	119	2	36.97	85	31.15	7/69	37
Gregory RG	1936/37	Vic	—	—	—	—	2	—	2	153	80	—	51.00	—	—	—	1
Gregory SE	1890 –1912	NSW	58	—	—	—	—	—	58	2282	201	4	24.54	—	—	—	25
Grimmett CV	1924/25–1935/36	NZ	—	—	37	—	—	—	37	557	50	—	13.93	216	24.22	7/40	17
Groube TU	1880	NZ	—	—	—	1	—	—	1	11	11	—	5.50	—	—	—	—
Gròut ATW	1957/58–1965/66	Qld	—	51	—	—	—	—	51	890	74	—	15.08	—	—	—	163/24
Guest CEJ	1962/63	Vic	—	—	—	—	1	—	1	11	11	—	11.00	—	—	—	—
Hamence RA	1946/47–1947/48	SA	—	—	3	—	—	—	3	81	30*	—	27.00	—	—	—	1
Hammond JR	1972/73	SA	—	—	5	—	—	—	5	28	19	—	9.33	15	32.53	4/38	2
Harry J	1894/95	Vic	—	—	—	—	1	—	1	8	6	—	4.00	—	—	—	1
Hartigan RJ	1907/08	NSW	2	—	—	—	—	—	2	170	116	1	42.50	—	—	—	1
Hartkopf AEV	1924/25	Vic	—	—	—	—	1	—	1	80	80	—	40.00	1	134.00	1/120	—
Harvey MR	1946/47	NSW	—	—	—	—	1	—	1	43	31	—	21.50	—	—	—	—
Harvey RN	1947/48–1962/63	Vic	27	—	—	—	52	—	79	6149	205	21	48.42	3	40.00	1/08	64
Hassett AL	1938 –1953	Vic	—	—	—	—	43	—	43	3073	198*	10	46.56	—	—	—	30
Hawke NJN	1962/63–1968	SA	—	—	27	—	—	—	27	365	45*	—	16.59	91	29.42	7/105	9
Hazlitt GR	1907/08–1912	NSW	7	—	—	—	2	—	9	89	34*	—	11.13	23	27.09	7/25	4
Healy IA	1988/89–1989/90	Qld	—	21	—	—	—	—	21	529	52	—	19.59	—	—	—	55/2
Hendry HSTL	1921 –1928/29	NSW	—	—	—	—	11	—	11	335	112	1	20.94	16	40.00	3/36	10
Hibbert PA	1977/78	Vic	—	—	—	—	1	—	1	15	13	—	7.50	—	—	—	1
Higgs JD	1977/78–1980/81	Vic	—	—	—	—	22	—	22	111	16	—	5.55	66	31.17	7/143	3
Hilditch AMJ	1978/79–1985/86	SA	9	—	9	—	—	—	18	1073	119	2	31.56	—	—	—	13
Hill C	1896 –1911/12	SA	—	—	49	—	—	—	49	3412	191	7	39.22	—	—	—	33
Hill JC	1953 –1954/55	Vic	—	—	—	—	3	—	3	21	8*	—	7.00	8	34.13	3/35	2
Hoare DE	1960/61	WA	—	—	—	—	—	1	1	35	35	—	17.50	2	78.00	2/68	2
Hodges JH	1876/77	Vic	—	—	—	—	2	—	2	10	8	—	3.33	6	14.00	2/07	—
Hogan TG	1982/83–1983/84	WA	—	—	—	—	—	7	7	205	42*	—	18.64	15	47.07	5/66	2
Hogg RM	1978/79–1984/85	Vic	—	—	32	—	4	—	38	439	52	—	9.76	123	28.48	6/74	7
Hohns TV	1988/99–1989	Qld	—	7	—	—	—	—	7	136	40	—	22.66	17	34.11	3/59	3
Hole GB	1950/51–1954/55	NSW	—	—	18	—	—	—	18	789	66	—	25.45	3	42.00	1/09	21
Holland RG	1984/85–1985/86	NSW	11	—	—	—	—	—	11	35	10	—	3.18	34	39.76	6/54	5
Hookes DW	1976/77–1985/86	SA	—	—	23	—	—	—	23	1306	143*	1	34.37	1	41.00	1/04	12
Hopkins AJY	1901/02–1909	NSW	20	—	—	—	—	—	20	509	43	—	16.42	26	26.77	4/81	11
Horan TP	1876/77–1884/85	Ire	—	—	—	—	15	—	15	471	124	1	18.84	11	13.00	6/40	6
Hordern HV	1910/11–1911/12	NSW	7	—	—	—	—	—	7	254	50	—	23.09	46	23.37	7/90	6
Hornibrook PM	1928/29–1930	Qld	—	6	—	—	—	—	6	60	26	—	10.00	17	39.06	7/92	7
Howell WP	1897/98–1903/04	NSW	18	—	—	—	—	—	18	158	35	—	7.52	49	28.71	5/81	12
Hughes KJ	1977 –1984/85	WA	—	—	—	—	—	70	70	4415	213	9	37.42	—	—	—	50

Continued

Player	Test Career	Birthplace	State Representation						Tests	Runs	HS	100s	Avrge	Wkts	Avrge	Best	Ct /St
			NSW	Qld	SA	Tas	Vic	WA									
Hughes MG	1985/86-1989/90	Vic	—	—	—	—	23	—	23	449	72*	—	19.52	88	30.56	8/87	8
Hunt WA	1931/32-1931/32	NSW	1	—	—	—	—	—	1	—	—	—	0.00	—	—	—	1
Hurst AG	1973/74-1979/80	Vic	—	—	—	—	12	—	12	102	26	—	6.00	43	27.91	5/28	3
Hurwood A	1930/31	Qld	—	2	—	—	—	—	2	5	5	—	2.50	11	15.45	4/22	2
Inverarity RJ	1968 -1972	WA	—	—	—	—	—	6	6	174	56	—	17.40	4	23.25	3/26	4
Iredale FA	1894/95-1899	NSW	14	—	—	—	—	—	14	807	140	2	36.68	—	—	—	16
Ironmonger H	1928/29-1932/33	Qld	—	—	—	—	14	—	14	42	12	—	2.63	74	17.97	7/23	3
Iverson JB	1950/51	Vic	—	—	—	—	5	—	5	3	1*	—	0.75	21	15.24	6/27	2
Jackson A	1928/29-1930/31	Scot	8	—	—	—	—	—	8	474	164	1	47.40	—	—	—	7
Jarman BN	1959/60-1968/69	SA	—	—	19	—	—	—	19	400	78	—	14.81	—	—	—	50/4
Jarvis AH	1884/85-1894/95	SA	—	—	11	—	—	—	11	303	82	—	16.83	—	—	—	9/8
Jenner TJ	1970/71-1975/76	WA	—	—	9	—	—	—	9	208	74	—	23.11	24	31.21	5/90	5
Jennings CB	1912	Vic	—	—	—	—	6	—	6	107	32	—	17.83	—	—	—	5
Johnson IW	1945/46-1956/57	Vic	—	—	—	—	45	—	45	1000	77	—	18.52	109	29.19	7/44	30
Johnson LJ	1947/48	Qld	—	1	—	—	—	—	1	25	25*	—	12.33	6	12.33	3/08	2
Johnston WA	1947/48-1954/55	Vic	—	—	—	—	40	—	40	273	29	—	11.38	160	23.91	6/44	16
Jones DM	1983/84-1989/90	Vic	—	—	—	—	34	—	34	2637	216	9	51.71	1	55.00	1/5	19
Jones E	1894/95-1902/03	SA	—	—	19	—	—	—	19	126	20	—	5.04	64	29.02	7/88	21
Jones SP	1881/82-1887/88	NSW	12	—	—	—	—	—	12	432	87	—	21.60	6	18.67	4/47	12
Joslin LR	1967/68	Vic	—	—	—	—	1	—	1	9	7	—	4.50	—	—	—	—
Kelleway C	1910/11-1928/29	NSW	26	—	—	—	—	—	26	1422	147	3	37.42	52	32.37	5/33	24
Kelly JJ	1896 -1905	Vic	—	—	—	—	36	—	36	664	46*	—	17.03	—	—	—	43/20
Kelly TJD	1876/77-1878/79	Ire	—	—	—	2	—	—	2	64	35	—	21.33	—	—	—	1
Kendall TK	1876/77	Eng	—	—	—	2	—	—	2	39	17*	—	13.00	14	15.36	7/55	2
Kent MF	1981	Qld	—	3	—	—	—	—	3	171	54	—	28.50	—	—	—	6
Kerr RB	1985/86	Qld	—	2	—	—	—	—	2	31	17	—	7.75	—	—	—	1
Kippax AF	1924/25-1934	NSW	22	—	—	—	—	—	22	1192	146	2	36.12	—	—	—	13
Kline LF	1957/58-1960/61	Vic	—	—	—	—	13	—	13	58	15*	—	8.29	34	22.82	7/75	9
Laird BM	1979/80-1982/83	WA	—	—	—	—	—	21	21	1341	92	—	35.29	—	—	—	16
Langley GRA	1951/52-1956/57	SA	—	—	26	—	—	—	26	374	53	—	14.96	—	—	—	83/15
Laughlin TJ	1977/78-1978/79	Vic	—	—	—	—	3	—	3	87	35	—	17.40	6	43.67	5/101	3
Laver F	1899 -1909	Vic	—	—	—	—	15	—	15	196	45	—	11.53	37	26.05	8/31	8
Lawry WM	1961 -1970/71	Vic	—	—	—	—	68	—	68	5234	210	13	47.15	—	—	—	30
Lawson GF	1980/81-1989/90	NSW	46	—	—	—	—	—	46	894	74	—	15.96	180	30.56	8/112	10
Lee PK	1931/32-1932/33	Qld	—	2	—	—	—	—	2	57	42	—	19.00	5	42.40	4/111	1
Lillee DK	1970/71-1983/84	WA	—	—	—	—	—	70	70	905	73*	—	13.71	355	23.92	7/83	23
Lindwall RR	1945/46-1959/60	NSW	47	14	—	—	—	—	61	1502	118	2	21.15	228	23.03	7/38	26
Love HSB	1932/33	NSW	1	—	—	—	—	—	1	8	5	—	4.00	—	—	—	3
Loxton SJE	1947/48-1950/51	Vic	—	—	—	—	12	—	12	554	101	1	36.93	8	43.63	3/55	7
Lyons JJ	1886/87-1897/98	SA	—	—	14	—	—	—	14	731	134	1	27.07	6	24.83	5/30	3
Macartney CG	1907/08-1926	NSW	35	—	—	—	—	—	35	2131	170	7	41.78	45	27.56	7/58	17
Mackay KD	1956 -1962/63	Qld	—	37	—	—	—	—	37	1507	89	—	33.49	50	34.42	6/42	15
Maclean JA	1978/79	Qld	—	4	—	—	—	—	4	79	33*	—	11.29	—	—	—	18
Maddocks LV	1954/55-1956/57	Vic	—	—	—	7	—	—	7	177	69	—	17.70	—	—	—	18/1
Maguire JN	1983/84	NSW	—	3	—	—	—	—	3	28	15*	—	7.00	10	32.30	4/57	2
Mailey AA	1920/21-1926	NSW	21	—	—	—	—	—	21	222	46*	—	11.10	99	33.92	9/121	14
Mallett AA	1968 -1980/81	NSW	39	—	—	—	—	—	39	430	43*	—	11.62	132	29.85	8/59	30
Malone MF	1977	WA	—	—	—	—	—	1	1	46	46	—	46.00	6	12.83	5/63	—
Mann AL	1977/78	WA	—	—	—	—	—	4	4	189	105	1	23.63	4	79.00	3/12	2
Marr AP	1884/85	NSW	1	—	—	—	—	—	1	5	5	—	2.50	—	—	—	—
Marsh GR	1985/86-1989/90	WA	—	—	—	—	—	36	36	2129	138	4	33.79	—	—	—	26
Marsh RW	1970/71-1983/84	WA	—	—	—	—	—	97	97	3633	132	3	26.52	—	—	—	343/12
Martin JW	1960/61-1966/67	NSW	8	—	—	—	—	—	8	214	55	—	17.83	17	48.94	3/56	5
Massie HH	1881/82-1884/85	Vic	—	—	—	—	9	—	9	249	55	—	15.56	—	—	—	5
Massie RAL	1972 -1972/73	WA	—	—	—	—	—	6	6	78	42	—	11.14	31	20.87	8/53	1
Matthews CD	1986/87-1988/89	WA	—	—	—	—	—	3	3	54	32	—	10.80	6	52.17	3/95	1
Matthews GRJ	1983/84-1986/87	NSW	21	—	—	—	—	—	21	1031	130	3	36.82	39	43.77	5/103	13
Matthews TJ	1911/12-1912	Vic	—	—	—	—	8	—	8	153	53	—	17.00	16	26.19	4/29	7
May TBA	1987/88-1988/89	SA	—	—	7	—	—	—	7	90	24	—	15.00	25	35.80	4/97	1
Mayne LC	1964/65-1969/70	WA	—	—	—	—	—	6	6	76	13	—	9.50	19	33.05	4/43	3
Mayne RE	1912 -1921/22	SA	—	—	2	—	2	—	4	64	25*	—	21.33	—	—	—	2
McAlister PA	1903/04-1909	Vic	—	—	—	—	8	—	8	252	41	—	16.80	—	—	—	10
McCabe SJ	1930 -1938	NSW	39	—	—	—	—	—	39	2748	232	6	48.21	36	42.86	4/13	42
McCool CL	1945/46-1949/50	NSW	14	—	—	—	—	—	14	459	104*	1	35.31	36	26.61	5/41	14
McCormick EL	1935/36-1938	Vic	—	—	—	—	12	—	12	54	17*	—	6.00	36	29.97	4/101	8
McCosker RB	1974/75-1979/80	NSW	25	—	—	—	—	—	25	1622	127	4	39.56	—	—	—	21
McDermott CJ	1984/85-1988/89	Qld	—	24	—	—	—	—	24	339	36	—	11.30	80	34.19	8/141	6
McDonald CC	1951/52-1961	Vic	—	—	—	—	47	—	47	3107	170	5	39.33	—	—	—	14
McDonald EA	1920/21-1921/22	Tas	—	—	—	11	—	—	11	116	36	—	16.57	43	33.28	5/32	3
McDonnell PS	1880 -1888	Eng	6	—	—	—	13	—	19	950	147	3	28.79	—	—	—	6
McIlwraith J	1886	Vic	—	—	—	—	1	—	1	9	7	—	4.50	—	—	—	1
McKenzie GD	1961 -1970/71	WA	—	—	—	—	—	61	61	945	76	—	12.27	246	29.79	8/71	34
McKibbin TR	1894/95-1897/98	NSW	5	—	—	—	—	—	5	88	28*	—	14.67	17	29.18	3/35	4
McLaren JW	1911/12	Qld	—	1	—	—	—	—	1	—	0*	—	—	1	70.00	1/23	—
McLeod CE	1894/95-1905	Vic	—	—	—	—	17	—	17	573	112	1	23.88	33	40.15	5/65	9

Player	Test Career	Birthplace	NSW	Qld	SA	Tas	Vic	WA	Tests	Runs	HS	100s	Avrge	Wkts	Avrge	Best	Ct/St
McLeod RW	1891/92-1893	Vic	—	—	—	—	6	—	6	146	31	—	13.27	12	32.00	5/55	3
McShane PG	1884/85-1887/88	Vic	—	—	—	—	3	—	3	26	12*	—	5.20	1	48.00	1/39	2
Meckiff I	1957/58-1963/64	Vic	—	—	—	—	18	—	18	154	45*	—	11.85	45	31.42	6/38	9
Meuleman KD	1945/46-1946/47	Vic	—	—	—	—	1	—	1	1	—	—	0.00	—	—	—	1
Midwinter WE	1876/77-1886/87	Eng	—	—	—	—	8	—	8	174	37	—	13.38	14	23.79	5/78	5
Miller KR	1945/46-1956/57	Vic	49	—	—	—	6	—	55	2958	147	7	36.98	170	22.97	7/60	38
Minnett RB	1911/12-1912	NSW	9	—	—	—	—	—	9	391	90	—	26.07	11	26.36	4/34	—
Misson FM	1960/61-1961	NSW	9	—	—	—	—	—	9	391	90	—	26.07	11	26.36	4/34	—
Moody TM	1989/90	WA	—	—	—	—	—	3	3	208	106	1	41.60	1	53.00	1/23	3
Moroney J	1949/50-1951/52	NSW	7	—	—	—	—	—	7	383	118	2	34.82	—	—	—	—
Morris AR	1946/47-1954/55	NSW	46	—	—	—	—	—	46	3533	206	12	46.49	2	25.00	1/05	15
Morris S	1884/85	Tas	—	—	—	1	—	—	1	14	10*	—	14.00	2	36.50	2/73	—
Moses H	1886/87-1894/95	NSW	6	—	—	—	—	—	6	198	33	—	19.80	—	—	—	1
Moss JK	1978/79	Vic	—	—	—	—	1	—	1	60	38*	—	60.00	—	—	—	—
Moule WH	1880	Vic	—	—	—	—	1	—	1	40	34	—	20.00	3	7.67	3/23	1
Murdoch WL	1876/77-1890	Vic	—	—	—	—	18	—	18	896	211	2	32.00	—	—	—	13/1
Musgrove H	1884/85	Eng	—	—	—	—	1	—	1	13	9	—	6.50	—	—	—	—
Nagel LE	1932/33	Vic	—	—	—	—	1	—	1	21	21*	—	21.00	2	55.00	2/110	—
Nash LJ	1931/32-1936/37	Vic	—	—	—	1	1	—	2	30	17	—	15.00	10	12.60	4/18	6
Nitschke HC	1931/32	SA	—	—	2	—	—	—	2	53	47	—	26.50	—	—	—	3
Noble MA	1897/98-1909	NSW	42	—	—	—	—	—	42	1997	133	1	30.26	121	25.02	7/17	26
Noblet G	1949/50-1952/53	SA	—	—	3	—	—	—	3	22	13*	—	7.33	7	26.14	3/21	1
Nothling OE	1928/29	Qld	—	1	—	—	—	—	1	52	44	—	26.00	—	—	—	—
O'Brien LPJ	1932/33-1936/37	Vic	—	—	—	—	5	—	5	211	61	—	26.38	—	—	—	3
O'Connor JDA	1907/08-1909	NSW	—	—	4	—	—	—	4	86	20	—	12.29	13	26.15	5/40	3
O'Donnell SP	1985 -1985/86	NSW	—	—	—	—	6	—	6	206	48	—	29.43	6	84.00	3/37	4
O'Keeffe KJ	1970/71-1977	NSW	24	—	—	—	—	—	24	644	85	—	25.76	53	38.08	5/101	15
O'Neill NC	1958/59-1964/65	NSW	42	—	—	—	—	—	42	2779	181	6	45.56	17	39.24	4/41	21
O'Reilly WJ	1931/32-1945/46	NSW	27	—	—	—	—	—	27	410	56*	—	12.81	144	22.60	7/54	6
Ogilvie AD	1977/78	Qld	—	5	—	—	—	—	5	178	47	—	17.80	—	—	—	5
Oldfield WAS	1920/21-1936/37	NSW	54	—	—	—	—	—	54	1427	65*	—	22.65	—	—	—	78/52
Oxenham RK	1928/29-1931/32	Qld	—	7	—	—	—	—	7	151	48	—	15.10	14	37.29	4/39	4
Palmer GE	1880 -1886	NSW	17	—	—	—	—	—	17	296	48	—	14.10	78	21.51	7/65	13
Park RL	1920/21	Vic	—	—	—	—	1	—	1	—	—	—	0.00	—	—	—	—
Pascoe LS	1977 -1981/82	WA	—	—	—	—	—	14	14	106	30*	—	10.60	64	26.06	5/59	2
Pellew CE	1920/21-1921/22	SA	—	—	10	—	—	—	10	484	116	2	37.23	—	—	—	4
Phillips WB	1983/84-1985/86	SA	—	—	27	—	—	—	27	1485	159	2	32.28	—	—	—	52
Philpott PI	1964/65-1965/66	NSW	8	—	—	—	—	—	8	93	22	—	10.33	26	38.46	5/90	5
Ponsford WH	1924/25-1934	Vic	—	—	—	—	29	—	29	2122	266	7	48.23	—	—	—	21
Pope RJ	1884/85	NSW	1	—	—	—	—	—	1	3	3	—	1.50	—	—	—	—
Rackemann CG	1982/83-1989/90	Qld	—	11	—	—	—	—	11	43	15*	—	5.38	39	26.36	6/86	2
Ransford VS	1907/08-1911/12	Vic	—	—	—	—	20	—	20	1211	143*	1	37.84	1	28.00	1/09	10
Redpath IR	1963/64-1975/76	Vic	—	—	—	—	67	—	67	4737	171	8	43.46	—	—	—	83
Reedman JC	1894/95	SA	—	—	1	—	—	—	1	21	17	—	10.50	1	24.00	1/12	1
Reid BA	1985/86-1987/88	WA	—	—	—	—	—	18	18	75	13	—	6.25	62	29.61	4/53	2
Renneberg DA	1966/67-1967/68	NSW	8	—	—	—	—	—	8	22	9	—	3.67	23	36.09	5/39	2
Richardson AJ	1924/25-1926	SA	—	—	9	—	—	—	9	403	100	1	31.00	12	43.42	2/20	1
Richardson VY	1924/25-1935/36	SA	—	—	19	—	—	—	19	706	138	1	23.53	—	—	—	24
Rigg KE	1930/31-1936/37	Vic	—	—	—	—	8	—	8	401	127	1	33.42	—	—	—	5
Ring DT	1947/48-1953	Tas	—	—	—	—	13	—	13	426	67	—	22.42	35	37.29	6/72	5
Ritchie GM	1982/83-1986/87	Qld	—	30	—	—	—	—	30	1690	146	3	35.21	—	—	—	14
Rixon SJ	1977/78-1984/85	NSW	13	—	—	—	—	—	13	394	54	—	18.76	—	—	—	42/5
Robertson WR	1884/85	NSW	—	—	—	1	—	—	1	2	2	—	1.00	—	—	—	—
Robinson RD	1977	Vic	—	—	—	—	3	—	3	100	34	—	16.67	—	—	—	4
Robinson RH	1936/37	NSW	1	—	—	—	—	—	1	5	3	—	2.50	—	—	—	1
Rorke GR	1958/59-1959/60	NSW	4	—	—	—	—	—	4	9	7	—	4.50	10	20.30	3/23	1
Rutherford JW	1956/57	WA	—	—	—	—	—	1	1	30	30	—	30.00	1	15.00	1/11	—
Ryder J	1920/21-1928/29	Vic	—	—	—	—	20	—	20	1394	201*	3	51.63	17	43.71	2/20	17
Saggers RA	1948 -1949/50	NSW	6	—	—	—	—	—	6	30	14	—	10.00	—	—	—	16/8
Saunders JV	1901/02-1907/08	Vic	—	—	—	—	14	—	14	39	11*	—	2.29	79	22.73	7/34	5
Scott HJH	1884 -1886	Vic	—	—	—	—	8	—	8	359	102	1	27.62	—	—	—	8
Sellers RHD	1964/65	India	—	—	1	—	—	—	1	—	—	—	0.00	—	—	—	1
Serjeant CS	1977 -1977/78	WA	—	—	—	—	—	12	12	522	124	1	23.73	—	—	—	13
Sheahan AP	1967/68-1973/74	Vic	—	—	—	—	31	—	31	1594	127	2	33.91	—	—	—	17
Shepherd BK	1962/63-1964/65	WA	—	—	—	—	—	9	9	502	96	—	41.83	—	—	—	2
Sievers MW	1936/37	Vic	—	—	—	—	3	—	3	67	25*	—	13.40	9	17.89	5/21	4
Simpson RB	1957/58-1977/78	NSW	46	—	—	—	—	16	62	4869	311	10	46.82	71	42.27	5/57	110
Sincock DJ	1964/65-1965/66	SA	—	—	3	—	—	—	3	80	29	—	26.67	8	51.25	3/67	2
Slater KN	1958/59	WA	—	—	—	—	—	1	1	1	1*	—	—	2	50.50	2/40	—
Sleep PR	1978/79-1989/90	SA	—	—	14	—	—	—	14	483	90	—	24.15	31	45.06	5/72	4
Slight J	1880	Vic	—	—	—	—	1	—	1	11	11	—	5.50	—	—	—	—
Smith DBM	1912	Vic	—	—	2	—	—	—	2	30	24*	—	15.00	—	—	—	—
Smith SB	1983/84	NSW	3	—	—	—	—	—	3	41	12	—	8.20	—	—	—	1
Spofforth FR	1876/77-1886/87	NSW	18	—	—	—	—	—	18	217	50	—	9.43	94	18.41	7/44	11

Continued

Player	Test Career	Birth-place	NSW	Qld	SA	Tas	Vic	WA	Tests	Runs	HS	100s	Avrge	Wkts	Avrge	Best	Ct/St
Stackpole KR	1965/66-1973/74	Vic					44		44	2807	207	7	37.43	15	66.73	2/33	46
Stevens GB	1959/60	SA			4				4	112	28	—	16.00	—	—	—	2
Taber HB	1966/67-1969/70	NSW	16						16	353	48	—	16.05	—	—	—	56/4
Tallon D	1945/46-1953	Qld		21					21	394	92	—	17.13	—	—	—	50/8
Taylor JM	1920/21-1926	NSW	20						20	997	108	1	35.61	1	45.00	1/25	11
Taylor MA	1988/89-1989/90	NSW	15						15	1618	219	6	64.72	—	—	—	16
Taylor PL	1986/87-1989/90	NSW	10						10	383	87	—	31.92	24	36.38	6/78	10
Thomas G	1964/65-1965/66	NSW	8						8	325	61	—	29.55	—	—	—	3
Thompson N	1876/77	Qld		2					2	67	41	—	16.75	1	31.00	1/14	3
Thoms GR	1951/52	Vic					1		1	44	28	—	22.00	—	—	—	1
Thomson AL	1970/71	Vic					4		4	22	12*	—	22.00	12	54.50	3/79	—
Thomson JR	1972/73-1985	NSW	50	1					51	679	49	—	12.81	200	28.01	6/46	20
Thurlow HM	1931/32	Qld		1					1	—	—	—	0.00	—	—	—	1
Toohey PM	1977/78-1979/80	NSW	15						15	893	122	1	31.89	—	—	—	9
Toshack ERH	1945/46-1948	NSW	12						12	73	20*	—	14.60	47	21.04	6/29	4
Travers JPF	1901/02	SA			1				1	10	9	—	5.00	1	14.00	1/14	1
Tribe GE	1946/47	Vic					3		3	35	25*	—	17.50	2	165.00	2/48	—
Trott AE	1894/95	Vic					3		3	205	85*	—	102.50	9	21.33	8/43	4
Trott GHS	1888-1897/98	Vic					24		24	921	143	1	21.93	29	35.14	4/71	21
Trumble H	1890-1903/04	Vic					32		32	851	70	—	19.79	141	21.79	8/65	45
Trumble JW	1884/85-1886	Vic					7		7	243	59	—	20.25	10	22.20	3/29	3
Trumper VT	1899-1911/12	NSW	48						48	3163	214*	8	39.05	8	39.63	3/60	31
Turner A	1975-1976/77	NSW	14						14	768	136	1	29.54	—	—	—	15
Turner CTB	1886/87-1894/95	NSW	17						17	323	29	—	11.54	101	16.53	7/43	8
Veivers TR	1963/64-1966/67	Qld		21					21	813	88	—	31.27	33	41.67	4/68	7
Veletta MRJ	1987/88-1988/89	WA						8	8	207	39	—	18.82	—	—	—	12
Waite MG	1938	SA			2				2	11	8	—	3.67	1	190.00	1/150	1
Walker MHN	1972/73-1977	Tas					34		34	586	78*	—	19.53	138	27.48	8/143	10
Wall TW	1928/29-1934	SA	18						18	121	20	—	6.37	56	35.89	5/14	11
Walters FH	1884/85	Vic					1		1	12	7	—	6.00	—	—	—	2
Walters KD	1965/66-1980/81	NSW	75						75	5357	250	15	48.26	49	29.08	5/66	43
Ward FA	1936/37-1938	NSW			4				4	36	18	—	6.00	11	52.18	6/102	1
Watkins JR	1972/73	NSW	1						1	39	36	—	39.00	—	—	—	1
Watson GD	1966/67-1972	Vic					3	2	5	97	50	—	10.78	6	42.33	2/67	1
Watson WJ	1954/55	NSW	4						4	106	30	—	17.67	—	—	—	2
Waugh SR	1985/86-1989/90	NSW	39						39	1983	177*	3	39.66	43	41.86	5/69	30
Wellham DM	1981-1986/87	NSW	6						6	257	103	1	23.36	—	—	—	5
Wessels KC	1982/83-1985/86	S Af		24					24	1761	179	4	42.95	—	—	—	18
Whatmore DF	1978/79-1979/80	Sri L					7		7	293	77	—	22.54	—	—	—	13
Whitney MR	1981-1988/89	NSW	4						4	8	4*	—	1.60	18	29.56	7/89	—
Whitty WJ	1909-1912	NSW	14						14	161	39*	—	13.42	65	21.12	6/17	4
Wiener JM	1979/80	Vic					6		6	281	93	—	25.55	—	—	—	4
Wilson JW	1956/57	Vic					1		1	—	—	—	—	1	64.00	1/25	—
Wood GM	1977/78-1988/89	WA						59	59	3374	172	9	31.83	—	—	—	41
Woodcock AJ	1973/74	SA			1				1	27	27	—	27.00	—	—	—	1
Woodfull WM	1926-1934	Vic					35		35	2300	161	7	46.00	—	—	—	7
Woods SMJ	1888	NSW	3						3	32	18	—	5.33	5	24.20	2/35	1
Woolley RD	1982/83-1983/84	Tas				2			2	21	13	—	10.50	—	—	—	7
Worrall J	1884/85-1899	Vic					11		11	478	76	—	25.16	1	127.00	1/97	13
Wright KJ	1978/79-1979/80	WA						10	10	219	55*	—	16.85	—	—	—	31/4
Yallop GN	1975/76-1984/85	Vic					39		39	2756	268	8	41.13	1	116.00	1/21	23
Yardley B	1977/78-1982/83	WA						33	33	978	74	—	19.56	126	31.63	7/98	31
Zoehrer TJ	1985/86-1986/87	WA						10	10	246	52*	—	20.50	—	—	—	18/1

Youngest Test Players on Debut

Player	Date of Birth	Test Debut	Opponent	Venue	Years	Days
ID Craig	12 Jun 1935	6 Feb 1953	South Africa	Sydney	17	239
TW Garrett	26 Jly 1858	15 Mar 1877	England	Melbourne	18	232
C Hill	18 Mar 1877	22 Jun 1896	England	Lord's	19	96
GR Hazlitt	4 Sep 1888	13 Dec 1907	England	Sydney	19	100
RG Archer	25 Oct 1933	6 Feb 1953	South Africa	Melbourne	19	104
RN Harvey	8 Oct 1928	23 Jan 1948	India	Adelaide	19	107
A Jackson	5 Sep 1909	1 Feb 1929	England	Adelaide	19	149
JT Cottam	5 Sep 1867	25 Feb 1887	England	Sydney	19	173
JJ Ferris	21 May 1867	28 Jan 1887	England	Sydney	19	248
CJ McDermott	14 Apr 1965	22 Dec 1984	West Indies	Melbourne	19	253
SJ McCabe	16 Jly 1910	13 Jun 1930	England	Nottingham	19	332
KD Walters	21 Dec 1945	10 Dec 1965	England	Brisbane	19	354
GD McKenzie	24 Jun 1941	22 Jun 1961	England	Lord's	19	363
LJ Joslin	13 Dec 1947	26 Jan 1968	India	Sydney	20	44
GB Hole	6 Jan 1931	23 Feb 1951	England	Sydney	20	48
A Cotter	3 Dec 1883	26 Jan 1904	England	Sydney	20	54

Player	Date of Birth	Test Debut	Opponent	Venue	Years	Days
DG Bradman	27 Aug 1908	30 Nov 1928	England	Brisbane	20	96
SE Gregory	14 Apr 1870	21 Jly 1890	England	Lord's	20	98
EH Bromley	2 Sep 1912	10 Feb 1933	England	Brisbane	20	161
IC Davis	25 Jun 1953	29 Dec 1973	New Zealand	Melbourne	20	187

Oldest Test Players on Debut

Player	Date of Birth	Test Debut	Opponent	Venue	Years	Days
DD Blackie	5 Apr 1882	14 Dec 1928	England	Sydney	46	254
H Ironmonger	7 Apr 1882	30 Nov 1928	England	Brisbane	46	238
NC Thomson	21 Apr 1838	15 Mar 1877	England	Melbourne	38	328
RG Holland	19 Oct 1946	23 Nov 1984	West Indies	Brisbane	38	35
EJ Gregory	29 May 1839	15 Mar 1877	England	Melbourne	37	290
HSB Love	10 Aug 1895	10 Feb 1933	England	Brisbane	37	184
J Harry	1 Aug 1857	11 Jan 1895	England	Adelaide	37	163
RE Oxenham	28 Jly 1891	29 Dec 1928	England	Melbourne	37	155
AJ Richardson	24 Jly 1888	19 Dec 1924	England	Sydney	36	149
JB Iverson	27 Jly 1915	1 Dec 1950	England	Brisbane	35	127
KH Eastwood	23 Nov 1935	12 Feb 1971	England	Sydney	35	81
JW Wilson	20 Aug 1921	26 Oct 1956	India	Bombay	35	68
AEV Hartkopf	28 Dec 1889	1 Jan 1925	England	Melbourne	35	4
TV Hohns	23 Jan 1954	26 Jan 1989	West Indies	Sydney	35	3
AA Mailey	3 Jan 1886	17 Dec 1920	England	Sydney	34	349
PA McAlister	11 Jly 1869	26 Jan 1904	England	Sydney	34	199
W Carkeek	17 Oct 1878	27 May 1912	England	Manchester	33	223
G Noblet	14 Sep 1916	3 Mar 1950	South Africa	Pt Elizabeth	33	170
CV Grimmett	25 Dec 1891	27 Feb 1925	England	Sydney	33	64
BB Cooper	15 Mar 1844	15 Mar 1877	England	Melbourne	33	0
TJD Kelly	3 May 1844	31 Mar 1877	England	Melbourne	32	332

Summary of Australian Test Cricket

Opponent	Played	Won	Lost	Drawn	Tied
England	270	101	88	81	—
West Indies	67	28	22	16	1
South Africa	53	29	11	13	—
India	45	20	8	16	1
Pakistan	34	12	9	13	—
New Zealand	26	10	6	10	—
Sri Lanka	4	3	—	1	—
Total	**499**	**203**	**144**	**150**	**2**

Australian Test Cricket – The Tests

Series	Toss	Australia 1st	Australia 2nd	Opponent	Opponents 1st	Opponents 2nd	Result	Captain
1876/77 in Australia								
Melbourne	Aus	9-245*	104	England	9-196	108	Aus by 45 runs	DW Gregory
Melbourne	Aus	122*	259	England	261	6-122	Eng by 4 wkts	DW Gregory
1878/79 in Australia								
Melbourne	Eng	256	0-19	England	113*	160	Aus by 10 wkts	DW Gregory
1880 in England								
The Oval	Eng	149	327	England	420*	5-57	Eng by 5 wkts	WL Murdoch
1881/82 in Australia								
Melbourne	Eng	320	3-127	England	294*	308	Drawn	WL Murdoch
Sydney	Eng	197	5-169	England	133*	232	Aus by 5 wkts	WL Murdoch
Sydney	Eng	260	4-66	England	188*	134	Aus by 6 wkts	WL Murdoch
Melbourne	Eng	300	—	England	309*	2-234	Drawn	WL Murdoch
1882 in England								
The Oval	Aus	63*	122	England	101	77	Aus by 7 runs	WL Murdoch
1882/83 in Australia								
Melbourne	Aus	291*	1-58	England	177	169	Aus by 9 wkts	WL Murdoch
Melbourne	Eng	114	153	England	294*	—	Eng by an inns & 27 runs	WL Murdoch
Sydney	Eng	218	83	England	247*	123	Eng by 69 runs	WL Murdoch
Sydney	Eng	262	6-199	England	263*	197	Aus by 4 wkts	WL Murdoch
1884 in England								
Manchester	Eng	182	—	England	95*	180	Drawn	WL Murdoch
Lord's	Aus	229*	9-145	England	379	—	Eng by an inns & 5 runs	WL Murdoch
The Oval	Aus	551*	—	England	346	2-85	Drawn	WL Murdoch
1884/85 in Australia								
Adelaide	Aus	243*	9-191	England	369	2-67	Eng by 8 wkts	WL Murdoch
Melbourne	Eng	279	126	England	401*	0-7	Eng by 10 wkts	TP Horan
Sydney	Aus	181*	165	England	133	207	Aus by 6 runs	HH Massie
Sydney	Eng	309	2-38	England	269*	77	Aus by 8 wkts	JM Blackham
Melbourne	Aus	163*	125	England	386	—	Eng by an inns & 98 runs	TP Horan
1886 in England								
Manchester	Aus	205*	123	England	223	6-107	Eng by 4 wkts	HJH Scott
Lord's	Eng	121	126	England	353*	—	Eng by an inns & 106 runs	HJH Scott
The Oval	Eng	68	149	England	434*	—	Eng by an inns & 217 runs	HJH Scott
1886/87 in Australia								
Sydney	Aus	119	97	England	45*	184	Eng by 13 runs	PS McDonnell
Sydney	Eng	84	150	England	151*	154	Eng by 71 runs	PS McDonnell
1887/88 in Australia								
Sydney	Aus	42	82	England	113*	137	Eng by 126 runs	PS McDonnell
1888 in England								
Lord's	Aus	116*	60	England	53	62	Aus by 61 runs	PS McDonnell
The Oval	Aus	80*	100	England	317	—	Eng by an inns & 137 runs	PS McDonnell

Series	Toss1st	Australia	2nd	Opponent1st	Opponents	2nd	Result	Captain
Manchester	Eng	81	70	England	172*	—	Eng by an inns & 21 runs	PS McDonnell
1890 in England								
Lord's	Aus	132*	176	England	173	3-137	Eng by 7 wkts	WL Murdoch
The Oval	Aus	92*	102	England	100	8-95	Eng by 2 wkts	WL Murdoch
1891/92 in Australia								
Melbourne	Aus	240*	236	England	264	158	Aus by 54 runs	JM Blackham
Sydney	Aus	145*	9-391	England	307	157	Aus by 72 runs	JM Blackham
Adelaide	Eng	100	169	England	499*	—	Eng by an inns & 230 runs	JM Blackham
1893 in England								
Lord's	Eng	269	—	England	334*	8d-234	Drawn	JM Blackham
The Oval	Eng	91	349	England	483*	—	Eng by an inns & 43 runs	JM Blackham
Manchester	Aus	204*	236	England	243	4-118	Drawn	JM Blackham
1894/95 in Australia								
Sydney	Aus	586*	166	England	325	437	Eng by 10 runs	JM Blackham
Melbourne	Aus	123	333	England	75*	475	Eng by 94 runs	G Giffen
Adelaide	Aus	238*	411	England	124	143	Aus by 382 runs	G Giffen
Sydney	Eng	284*	—	England	9-65	9-72	Aus by an inns & 147 runs	G Giffen
Melbourne	Aus	414*	267	England	385	4-298	Eng by 6 wkts	G Giffen
1896 in England								
Lord's	Aus	53*	347	England	292	4-111	Eng by 6 wkts	GHS Trott
Manchester	Aus	412*	7-125	England	231	305	Aus by 3 wkts	GHS Trott
The Oval	Eng	119	44	England	145*	84	Eng by 66 runs	GHS Trott
1897/98 in Australia								
Sydney	Eng	237	408	England	551*	1-96	Eng by 9 wkts	GHS Trott
Melbourne	Aus	520*	—	England	315	150	Aus by an inns & 55 runs	GHS Trott
Adelaide	Aus	573*	—	England	278	282	Aus by an inns & 13 runs	GHS Trott
Melbourne	Aus	323*	2-115	England	174	263	Aus by 8 wkts	GHS Trott
Sydney	Eng	239	4-276	England	335*	178	Aus by 6 wkts	GHS Trott
1899 in England								
Nottingham	Aus	252*	8d-230	England	193	7-155	Drawn	J Darling
Lord's	Eng	421	0-28	England	206*	240	Aus by 10 wkts	J Darling
Leeds	Aus	172*	224	England	9-220	0-19	Drawn	J Darling
Manchester	Eng	196	7d-346	England	372*	3-94	Drawn	J Darling
The Oval	Eng	352	5-254	England	576*	—	Drawn	J Darling
1901/02 in Australia								
Sydney	Eng	168	172	England	464*	—	Eng by an inns & 124 runs	J Darling
Melbourne	Eng	112*	353	England	61	175	Aus by 229 runs	J Darling
Adelaide	Eng	321	6-315	England	388*	9-247	Aus by 4 wkts	J Darling
Sydney	Eng	299	3-121	England	317*	99	Aus by 7 wkts	H Trumble
Melbourne	Aus	144*	255	England	189	178	Aus by 32 runs	H Trumble
1902 in England								
Birmingham	Eng	36	2-46	England	9d-376*	—	Drawn	J Darling
Lord's	Eng	—	—	England	2-102*	—	Drawn	J Darling
Sheffield	Aus	194*	289	England	145	195	Aus by 143 runs	J Darling
Manchester	Aus	299*	86	England	262	120	Aus by 3 runs	J Darling
The Oval	Aus	324*	121	England	183	9-263	Eng by 1 wkt	J Darling
1902/03 in South Africa								
Johannesburg	S Afr	296	7d-372	South Africa	454*	4-101	Drawn	J Darling
Johannesburg	Aus	175*	309	South Africa	240	85	Aus by 159 runs	J Darling
Cape Town	Aus	252*	0-59	South Africa	85	225	Aus by 10 wkts	J Darling
1903/04 in Australia								
Sydney	Aus	285*	485	England	577	5-194	Eng by 5 wkts	MA Noble
Melbourne	Eng	122	111	England	9-315*	9-103	Eng by 185 runs	MA Noble
Adelaide	Aus	388*	351	England	245	278	Aus by 216 runs	MA Noble
Sydney	Eng	131	171	England	249*	210	Eng by 157 runs	MA Noble
Melbourne	Aus	247*	133	England	61	9-101	Aus by 218 runs	MA Noble

▶

Series	Toss 1st	Australia 2nd	Opponent 1st	Opponents 2nd	Result	Captain
1905 in England						
Nottingham	Eng	9-221	9-188	England	196* 5d-426	Eng by 213 runs	J Darling
Lord's	Eng	181	—	England	282* 5-151	Drawn	J Darling
Leeds	Eng	195	7-224	England	301* 5d-295	Drawn	J Darling
Manchester	Eng	197	169	England	446* —	Eng by an inns & 80 runs	J Darling
The Oval	Eng	363	4-124	England	430* 6d-261	Drawn	J Darling
1907/08 in Australia						
Sydney	Eng	300	8-275	England	273* 300	Aus by 2 wkts	MA Noble
Melbourne	Aus	266*	397	England	382 9-282	Eng by 1 wkt	MA Noble
Adelaide	Aus	285*	506	England	363 183	Aus by 245 runs	MA Noble
Melbourne	Aus	214*	385	England	105 186	Aus by 308 runs	MA Noble
Sydney	Eng	137*	422	England	281 229	Aus by 49 runs	MA Noble
1909 in England						
Birmingham	Aus	74*	151	England	121 0-105	Eng by 10 wkts	MA Noble
Lord's	Aus	350	1-41	England	269* 121	Aus by 9 wkts	MA Noble
Leeds	Aus	188*	207	England	9-182 9-87	Aus by 126 runs	MA Noble
Manchester	Aus	147*	9d-279	England	119 3-108	Drawn	MA Noble
The Oval	Aus	325*	5d-339	England	352 3-104	Drawn	MA Noble
1910/11 in Australia						
Sydney	Aus	528*	—	South Africa	174 240	Aus by an inns & 114 runs	C Hill
Melbourne	Aus	348*	327	South Africa	506 80	Aus by 89 runs	C Hill
Adelaide	S Afr	465	339	South Africa	482* 360	S Afr by 38 runs	C Hill
Melbourne	S Afr	328*	578	South Africa	205 9-171	Aus by 530 runs	C Hill
Sydney	S Afr	364*	3-198	South Africa	160 401	Aus by 7 wkts	C Hill
1911/12 in Australia						
Sydney	Aus	447*	308	England	318 219	Aus by 146 runs	C Hill
Melbourne	Aus	184*	299	England	265 2-219	Eng by 8 wkts	C Hill
Adelaide	Aus	133*	476	England	501 3-112	Eng by 7 wkts	C Hill
Melbourne	Eng	191*	173	England	589 —	Eng by an inns & 225 runs	C Hill
Sydney	Eng	176	292	England	324* 214	Eng by 70 runs	C Hill
1912 in England						
Manchester	Aus	448*	—	South Africa	265 95	Aus by an inns & 88 runs	SE Gregory
Lord's	Eng	7-282	—	England	7d-310* —	Drawn	SE Gregory
Lord's	S Afr	390	0-48	South Africa	263* 173	Aus by 10 wkts	SE Gregory
Manchester	Eng	0-14	—	England	203* —	Drawn	SE Gregory
Nottingham	S Afr	219	—	South Africa	329* —	Drawn	SE Gregory
The Oval	Eng	111	65	England	245* 175	Eng by 244 runs	SE Gregory
1920/21 in Australia						
Sydney	Aus	267*	581	England	190 281	Aus by 377 runs	WW Armstrong
Melbourne	Aus	499*	—	England	9-251 9-157	Aus by an inns & 91 runs	WW Armstrong
Adelaide	Aus	354*	582	England	447 370	Aus by 119 runs	WW Armstrong
Melbourne	Eng	389	2-211	England	284* 315	Aus by 8 wkts	WW Armstrong
Sydney	Eng	392	1-93	England	204* 280	Aus by 9 wkts	WW Armstrong
1921 in England						
Nottingham	Eng	232	0-30	England	112* 147	Aus by 10 wkts	WW Armstrong
Lord's	Eng	342	2-131	England	187* 283	Aus by 8 wkts	WW Armstrong
Leeds	Aus	407*	7d-273	England	9-259 9-202	Aus by 219 runs	WW Armstrong
Manchester	Eng	175	—	England	4d-362* 1-44	Drawn	WW Armstrong
The Oval	Eng	389	—	England	8d-403* 2-244	Drawn	WW Armstrong
1921/22 in South Africa						
Durban	Aus	299*	7d-324	South Africa	232 7-184	Drawn	HL Collins
Johannesburg	Aus	450*	0-7	South Africa	243 8d-472	Drawn	HL Collins
Cape Town	S Afr	396	0-1	South Africa	180* 216	Aus by 10 wkts	HL Collins
1924/25 in Australia						
Sydney	Aus	450*	452	England	298 411	Aus by 193 runs	HL Collins
Melbourne	Aus	600*	250	England	479 290	Aus by 81 runs	HL Collins
Adelaide	Aus	489*	250	England	365 363	Aus by 11 runs	HL Collins
Melbourne	Eng	269	250	England	548* —	Eng by an inns & 29 runs	HL Collins
Sydney	Aus	295*	325	England	167 146	Aus by 307 runs	HL Collins

Series	Toss	Australia 1st	2nd	Opponent	Opponents 1st	2nd	Result	Captain
1926 in England								
Nottingham	Eng	—	—	England	0-32°	—	Drawn	HL Collins
Lord's	Aus	383°	5-194	England	3d-475	—	Drawn	HL Collins
Leeds	Eng	494°	—	England	294	3-254	Drawn	W Bardsley
Manchester	Aus	335°	—	England	5-305	—	Drawn	W Bardsley
The Oval	Eng	302	125	England	280°	436	Eng by 289 runs	HL Collins
1928/29 in Australia								
Brisbane Ex	Eng	9-122	8-66	England	521°	8d-342	Eng by 675 runs	J Ryder
Sydney	Aus	9-253°	9-397	England	636	2-16	Eng by 8 wkts	J Ryder
Melbourne	Aus	397°	351	England	417	7-332	Eng by 3 wkts	J Ryder
Adelaide	Eng	369	336	England	334°	383	Eng by 12 runs	J Ryder
Melbourne	Eng	491	5-287	England	519°	257	Aus by 5 wkts	J Ryder
1930 in England								
Nottingham	Eng	144	335	England	270°	9-302	Eng by 93 runs	WM Woodfull
Lord's	Eng	6d-729	3-72	England	425°	375	Aus by 7 wkts	WM Woodfull
Leeds	Aus	566°	—	England	391	3-95	Drawn	WM Woodfull
Manchester	Aus	345°	—	England	8-251	—	Drawn	WM Woodfull
The Oval	Eng	695	—	England	405°	251	Aus by an inns & 39 runs	WM Woodfull
1930/31 in Australia								
Adelaide	WI	376	0-172	West Indies	296°	249	Aus by 10 wkts	WM Woodfull
Sydney	Aus	369°	—	West Indies	9-107	9-90	Aus by an inns & 172 runs	WM Woodfull
Brisbane Ex	Aus	558°	—	West Indies	193	148	Aus by an inns & 217 runs	WM Woodfull
Melbourne	WI	8d-328°	—	West Indies	99	107	Aus by an inns & 122 runs	WM Woodfull
Sydney	WI	224	220	West Indies	6d-350°	5d-124	WI by 30 runs	WM Woodfull
1931/32 in Australia								
Brisbane	Aus	450°	—	South Africa	170	117	Aus by an inns & 163 runs	WM Woodfull
Sydney	S Afr	469	—	South Africa	153°	161	Aus by an inns & 155 runs	WM Woodfull
Melbourne	Aus	198°	554	South Africa	358	225	Aus by 169 runs	WM Woodfull
Adelaide	S Afr	513	0-73	South Africa	308°	274	Aus by 10 wkts	WM Woodfull
Melbourne	S Afr	9-153	—	South Africa	36°	45	Aus by an inns & 72 runs	WM Woodfull
1932/33 in Australia								
Sydney	Aus	360°	164	England	524	0-1	Eng by 10 wkts	WM Woodfull
Melbourne	Aus	228°	191	England	169	139	Aus by 111 runs	WM Woodfull
Adelaide	Eng	9-222	9-193	England	341°	412	Eng by 338 runs	WM Woodfull
Brisbane	Aus	340°	175	England	356	4-162	Eng by 6 wkts	WM Woodfull
Sydney	Aus	435°	182	England	454	2-168	Eng by 8 wkts	WM Woodfull
1934 in England								
Nottingham	Aus	374°	8d-273	England	268	141	Aus by 238 runs	WM Woodfull
Lord's	Eng	284	118	England	440°	—	Eng by an inns & 38 runs	WM Woodfull
Manchester	Eng	491	1-66	England	9d-627°	0d-123	Drawn	WM Woodfull
Leeds	Eng	584	—	England	200°	6-229	Drawn	WM Woodfull
The Oval	Aus	701°	327	England	8-321	9-145	Aus by 562 runs	WM Woodfull
1935/36 in South Africa								
Durban	S Afr	429	1-102	South Africa	248°	282	Aus by 9 wkts	VY Richardson
Johannesburg	S Afr	250	2-274	South Africa	157°	491	Drawn	VY Richardson
Cape Town	Aus	8d-362°	—	South Africa	102	182	Aus by an inns & 78 runs	VY Richardson
Johannesburg	S Afr	439	—	South Africa	157°	98	Aus by an inns & 184 runs	VY Richardson
Durban	S Afr	455	—	South Africa	222°	227	Aus by an inns & 6 runs	VY Richardson
1936/37 in Australia								
Brisbane	Eng	234	9-58	England	358°	256	Eng by 322 runs	DG Bradman
Sydney	Eng	9-80	324	England	6d-426°	—	Eng by an inns & 22 runs	DG Bradman
Melbourne	Aus	9d-200°	564	England	9d-76	323	Aus by 365 runs	DG Bradman
Adelaide	Aus	288°	433	England	330	243	Aus by 148 runs	DG Bradman
Melbourne	Aus	604°	—	England	239	165	Aus by an inns & 200 runs	DG Bradman

▶

Series	Toss	Australia 1st	2nd	Opponent 1st	Opponents 1st	2nd	Result	Captain
1938 in England								
Nottingham	Eng	411	6d-427	England	8d-658*	—	Drawn	DG Bradman
Lord's	Eng	422	6-204	England	494*	8d-242	Drawn	DG Bradman
Leeds	Eng	242	5-107	England	223*	123	Aus by 5 wkts	DG Bradman
The Oval	Eng	8-201	8-123	England	7d-903*	—	Eng by an inns & 579 runs	DG Bradman
1945/46 in New Zealand								
Wellington	NZ	8d-199	—	New Zealand	42*	54	Aus by an inns & 103 runs	WA Brown
1946/47 in Australia								
Brisbane	Aus	645*	—	England	141	172	Aus by an inns & 332 runs	DG Bradman
Sydney	Eng	8d-659	—	England	255*	371	Aus by an inns & 33 runs	DG Bradman
Melbourne	Aus	365*	536	England	351	7-310	Drawn	DG Bradman
Adelaide	Eng	487	1-215	England	460*	8d-340	Drawn	DG Bradman
Sydney	Eng	253	5-214	England	9-280*	9-186	Aus by 4 wkts	DG Bradman
1947/48 in Australia								
Brisbane	Aus	8d-382*	—	India	58	98	Aus by an inns & 226 runs	DG Bradman
Sydney	Ind	107	—	India	188*	7-61	Drawn	DG Bradman
Melbourne	Aus	394*	4d-255	India	9d-291	125	Aus by 233 runs	DG Bradman
Adelaide	Aus	674*	—	India	381	277	Aus by an inns & 16 runs	DG Bradman
Melbourne	Aus	8d-575*	—	India	331	67	Aus by an inns & 177 runs	DG Bradman
1948 in England								
Nottingham	Eng	509	2-98	England	165*	441	Aus by 8 wkts	DG Bradman
Lord's	Aus	350*	7d-460	England	215	186	Aus by 409 runs	DG Bradman
Manchester	Eng	9-221	1-92	England	363*	3d-174	Drawn	DG Bradman
Leeds	Eng	458	3-404	England	496*	8d-365	Aus by 7 wkts	DG Bradman
The Oval	Eng	389	—	England	52*	188	Aus by an inns & 149 runs	DG Bradman
1949/50 in South Africa								
Johannesburg	Aus	413*	—	South Africa	137	191	Aus by an inns & 85 runs	AL Hassett
Cape Town	Aus	7d-526*	2-87	South Africa	278	333	Aus by 8 wkts	AL Hassett
Durban	S Afr	75	5-336	South Africa	311*	99	Aus by 5 wkts	AL Hassett
Johannesburg	Aus	8d-465*	2-259	South Africa	352	—	Drawn	AL Hassett
Port Elizabeth	Aus	7d-549*	—	South Africa	158	132	Aus by an inns & 259 runs	AL Hassett
1950/51 in Australia								
Brisbane	Aus	228*	7d-32	England	7d-68	122	Aus by 70 runs	AL Hassett
Melbourne	Aus	194*	181	England	197	150	Aus by 28 runs	AL Hassett
Sydney	Eng	426	—	England	290*	9-123	Aus by an inns & 13 runs	AL Hassett
Adelaide	Aus	371*	8d-403	England	272	9-228	Aus by 274 runs	AL Hassett
Melbourne	Aus	217*	197	England	320	2-95	Eng by 8 wkts	AL Hassett
1951/52 in Australia								
Brisbane	WI	226	7-236	West Indies	216*	245	Aus by 3 wkts	AL Hassett
Sydney	Aus	517	3-137	West Indies	362*	290	Aus by 7 wkts	AL Hassett
Adelaide	Aus	82*	255	West Indies	105	4-233	WI by 6 wkts	AR Morris
Melbourne	WI	216	9-260	West Indies	272*	203	Aus by 1 wkt	AL Hassett
Sydney	Aus	116*	377	West Indies	78	213	Aus by 202 runs	AL Hassett
1952/53 in Australia								
Brisbane	Aus	280*	277	South Africa	221	240	Aus by 96 runs	AL Hassett
Melbourne	S Afr	243	290	South Africa	227*	388	S Afr by 82 runs	AL Hassett
Sydney	S Afr	443	—	South Africa	173*	9-232	Aus by an inns & 38 runs	AL Hassett
Adelaide	Aus	530*	3d-233	South Africa	387	6-177	Drawn	AL Hassett
Melbourne	Aus	520*	209	South Africa	435	4-297	S Afr by 6 wkts	AL Hassett
1953 in England								
Nottingham	Aus	249*	123	England	144	1-120	Drawn	AL Hassett
Lord's	Aus	346*	368	England	372	7-282	Drawn	AL Hassett
Manchester	Aus	318*	8-35	England	276	—	Drawn	AL Hassett
Leeds	Aus	266	4-147	England	167*	275	Drawn	AL Hassett
The Oval	Aus	275*	162	England	306	2-132	Eng by 8 wkts	AL Hassett

Series	Toss	Australia 1st	2nd	Opponent 1st	Opponents 2nd	Result	Captain
1954/55 in Australia							
Brisbane	Eng	8d-601°	—	England	190	257	Aus by an inns & 154 runs	IW Johnson
Sydney	Aus	228	184	England	154°	296	Eng by 38 runs	AR Morris
Melbourne	Eng	231	111	England	191°	279	Eng by 128 runs	IW Johnson
Adelaide	Aus	323°	111	England	341	5-97	Eng by 5 wkts	IW Johnson
Sydney	Aus	221	6-118	England	7d-371°	—	Drawn	IW Johnson
1954/55 in West Indies							
Kingston	Aus	9d-515°	1-20	West Indies	259	275	Aus by 9 wkts	IW Johnson
Port-of-Spain	WI	9d-600	—	West Indies	382°	4-273	Drawn	IW Johnson
Georgetown	WI	9-257	2-133	West Indies	182°	207	Aus by 8 wkts	IW Johnson
Bridgetown	Aus	668°	249	West Indies	510	6-234	Drawn	IW Johnson
Kingston	WI	8d-758	—	West Indies	357°	319	Aus by an inns & 82 runs	IW Johnson
1956 in England							
Nottingham	Eng	9-148	3-120	England	8d-217°	3d-188	Drawn	IW Johnson
Lord's	Aus	285°	257	England	171	186	Aus by 185 runs	IW Johnson
Leeds	Eng	143	140	England	325°	—	Eng by an inns & 42 runs	IW Johnson
Manchester	Eng	84	205	England	459°	—	Eng by an inns & 170 runs	IW Johnson
The Oval	Eng	202	5-27	England	247°	3d-182	Drawn	IW Johnson
1956/57 in Pakistan							
Karachi	Aus	80°	187	Pakistan	199	1-69	Pak by 9 wkts	IW Johnson
1956/57 in India							
Madras	Ind	319	—	India	161°	153	Aus by an inns & 5 runs	IW Johnson
Bombay	Ind	7d-523	—	India	251°	5-250	Drawn	RR Lindwall
Calcutta	Ind	177°	9d-189	India	136	136	Aus by 94 runs	IW Johnson
1957/58 in South Africa							
Johannesburg	S Afr	368	3-162	South Africa	9d-470°	201	Drawn	ID Craig
Cape Town	Aus	449°	—	South Africa	209	99	Aus by an inns & 141 runs	ID Craig
Durban	Aus	163°	7-292	South Africa	384	—	Drawn	ID Craig
Johannesburg	Aus	401°	0-1	South Africa	203	198	Aus by 10 wkts	ID Craig
Port Elizabeth	S Afr	291	2-68	South Africa	214°	144	Aus by 8 wkts	ID Craig
1958/59 in Australia							
Brisbane	Eng	186	2-147	England	134°	198	Aus by 8 wkts	R Benaud
Melbourne	Eng	308	2-42	England	259°	87	Aus by 8 wkts	R Benaud
Sydney	Eng	357	2-54	England	219°	7d-287	Drawn	R Benaud
Adelaide	Eng	476°	0-36	England	240	270	Aus by 10 wkts	R Benaud
Melbourne	Aus	351	1-69	England	205°	214	Aus by 9 wkts	R Benaud
1959/60 in Pakistan							
Dacca	Aus	225	2-112	Pakistan	200°	134	Aus by 8 wkts	R Benaud
Lahore	Pak	9d-391	3-123	Pakistan	146°	366	Aus by 7 wkts	R Benaud
Karachi	Pak	257	2-83	Pakistan	287°	8d-194	Drawn	R Benaud
1959/60 in India							
Delhi	Ind	468	—	India	135°	206	Aus by an inns & 127 runs	R Benaud
Kanpur	Ind	219	9-105	India	152°	291	Ind by 119 runs	R Benaud
Bombay	Ind	8d-387	1-34	India	289°	5d-226	Drawn	R Benaud
Madras	Aus	342°	—	India	149	138	Aus by an inns & 55 runs	R Benaud
Calcutta	Ind	331	2-121	India	194°	339	Drawn	R Benaud
1960/61 in Australia							
Brisbane	WI	505	232	West Indies	453°	284	Tied	R Benaud
Melbourne	Aus	348°	3-70	West Indies	181	233	Aus by 7 wkts	R Benaud
Sydney	WI	202	241	West Indies	339°	326	WI by 222 runs	R Benaud
Adelaide	WI	366	9-273	West ndies	393°	6d-432	Drawn	R Benaud
Melbourne	Aus	356	8-258	West Indies	292°	321	Aus by 2 wkts	R Benaud
1961 in England							
Birmingham	Eng	9d-516	—	England	195°	4-401	Drawn	R Benaud
Lord's	Eng	340	5-71	England	206°	202	Aus by 5 wkts	RN Harvey
Leeds	Aus	237°	120	England	299	2-62	Eng by 8 wkts	R Benaud

Continued

Series	Toss	Australia 1st	2nd	Opponent 1st	Opponents 1st	2nd	Result	Captain
Manchester	Aus	190*	432	England	367	201	Aus by 54 runs	R Benaud
The Oval	Eng	494	—	England	256*	8-370	Drawn	R Benaud
1962/63 in Australia								
Brisbane	Aus	404*	4d-362	England	389	6-278	Drawn	R Benaud
Melbourne	Aus	316*	248	England	331	3-237	Eng by 7 wkts	R Benaud
Sydney	Eng	319	2-67	England	279*	104	Aus by 8 wkts	R Benaud
Adelaide	Aus	393*	293	England	331	4-223	Drawn	R Benaud
Sydney	Eng	349	4-152	England	321*	8d-268	Drawn	R Benaud
1963/64 in Australia								
Brisbane	Aus	435*	1d-144	South Africa	346	1-13	Drawn	R Benaud
Melbourne	Aus	447	2-136	South Africa	274*	306	Aus by 8 wkts	RB Simpson
Sydney	Aus	260*	9d-450	South Africa	302	5-326	Drawn	RB Simpson
Adelaide	Aus	345*	331	South Africa	595	0-82	S Afr by 10 wkts	RB Simpson
Sydney	S Afr	311*	270	South Africa	411	0-76	Drawn	RB Simpson
1964 in England								
Nottingham	Eng	168	2-40	England	8d-216*	9d-193	Drawn	RB Simpson
Lord's	Eng	176*	4-168	England	246	—	Drawn	RB Simpson
Leeds	Eng	389	3-111	England	268*	229	Aus by 7 wkts	RB Simpson
Manchester	Aus	8d-656*	0-4	England	611	—	Drawn	RB Simpson
The Oval	Aus	379	—	England	182*	4-381	Drawn	RB Simpson
1964/65 in India								
Madras	Aus	211*	397	India	276	193	Aus by 139 runs	RB Simpson
Bombay	Aus	9-320*	9-274	India	341	8-256	Ind by 2 wkts	RB Simpson
Calcutta	Ind	174*	1-143	India	235	—	Drawn	RB Simpson
1964/65 in Pakistan								
Karachi	Pak	352	2-227	Pakistan	414*	8d-279	Drawn	RB Simpson
1964/65 in Australia								
Melbourne	Aus	448	2-88	Pakistan	287*	326	Drawn	RB Simpson
1964/65 in West Indies								
Kingston	WI	217	216	West Indies	239*	373	WI by 179 runs	RB Simpson
Port-of-Spain	Aus	516	—	West Indies	429*	386	Drawn	RB Simpson
Georgetown	WI	179	144	West Indies	355*	180	WI by 212 runs	RB Simpson
Bridgetown	Aus	6d-650*	4d-175	West Indies	9-573	5-242	Drawn	RB Simpson
Port-of-Spain	WI	294	0-63	West Indies	224*	131	Aus by 10 wkts	RB Simpson
1965/66 in Australia								
Brisbane	Aus	6d-443*	—	England	280	3-186	Drawn	BC Booth
Melbourne	Aus	358*	426	England	558	0-5	Drawn	RB Simpson
Sydney	Eng	221	174	England	488*	—	Eng by an inns & 93 runs	BC Booth
Adelaide	Eng	516	—	England	241*	266	Aus by an inns & 9 runs	RB Simpson
Melbourne	Eng	8d-543	—	England	9d-485*	3-69	Drawn	RB Simpson
1966/67 in South Africa								
Johannesburg	SAf	325	261	South Africa	199*	620	SAf by 233 runs	RB Simpson
Cape Town	Aus	542*	4-180	South Africa	353	367	Aus by 6 wkts	RB Simpson
Durban	Aus	147	334	South Africa	300*	2-185	SAf by 8 wkts	RB Simpson
Johannesburg	Aus	143*	8-148	South Africa	9d-332	—	Drawn	RB Simpson
Port Elizabeth	SAf	173*	278	South Africa	276	3-179	SAf by 7 wkts	RB Simpson
1967/68 in Australia								
Adelaide	Aus	335*	369	India	307	251	Aus by 146 runs	RB Simpson
Melbourne	Ind	529	—	India	173*	352	Aus by an inns & 4 runs	RB Simpson
Brisbane	Ind	379*	294	India	279	355	Aus by 39 runs	WM Lawry
Sydney	Ind	317*	292	India	268	197	Aus by 144 runs	WM Lawry
1968 in England								
Manchester	Aus	357*	220	England	165	253	Aus by 159 runs	WM Lawry
Lord's	Eng	9-78	4-127	England	7d-351*	—	Drawn	WM Lawry
Birmingham	Eng	9-222	1-68	England	409*	3d-142	Drawn	WM Lawry
Leeds	Aus	315*	312	England	302	4-230	Drawn	BN Jarman
The Oval	Eng	324	125	England	494*	181	Eng by 226 runs	WM Lawry

Series	Toss1st	Australia 1st	Australia 2nd	Opponent1st	Opponents 2nd	Result	Captain

1968/69 in Australia

Series	Toss1st	Aus 1st	Aus 2nd	Opponent 1st	Opp 2nd	Result	Captain
Brisbane	WI	284	240	West Indies 296*	353	WI by 125 runs	WM Lawry
Melbourne	Aus	510	—	West Indies 200*	280	Aus by an inns & 30 runs	WM Lawry
Sydney	WI	547	0-42	West Indies 264*	324	Aus by 10 wkts	WM Lawry
Adelaide	WI	533	9-339	West Indies 276*	616	Drawn	WM Lawry
Sydney	WI	619*	8d-394	West Indies 279	352	Aus by 382 runs	WM Lawry

1969/70 in India

Series	Toss1st	Aus 1st	Aus 2nd	Opponent 1st	Opp 2nd	Result	Captain
Bombay	Ind	345	2-67	India 271*	137	Aus by 8 wkts	WM Lawry
Kanpur	Ind	348	0-95	India 320*	7d-312	Drawn	WM Lawry
Delhi	Aus	296*	107	India 223	3-181	Ind by 7 wkts	WM Lawry
Calcutta	Aus	335	0-42	India 212*	161	Aus by 10 wkts	WM Lawry
Madras	Aus	258*	153	India 9-163	171	Aus by 77 runs	WM Lawry

1969/70 in South Africa

Series	Toss1st	Aus 1st	Aus 2nd	Opponent 1st	Opp 2nd	Result	Captain
Cape Town	SAf	164	280	South Africa 382*	232	SAf by 170 runs	WM Lawry
Durban	SAf	157	336	South Africa 9d-622*	—	SAf by an inns & 129 runs	WM Lawry
Johannesburg	SAf	202	178	South Africa 279*	408	SAf by 307 runs	WM Lawry
Port Elizabeth	SAf	212	246	South Africa 311*	8d-470	SAf by 323 runs	WM Lawry

1970/71 in Australia

Series	Toss1st	Aus 1st	Aus 2nd	Opponent 1st	Opp 2nd	Result	Captain
Brisbane	Aus	433*	214	England 464	1-39	Drawn	WM Lawry
Perth	Aus	440	3-100	England 397*	6d-287	Drawn	WM Lawry
Melbourne	Eng	—*	—	England —	—	Drawn	WM Lawry
Sydney	Eng	236	9-116	England 332*	5d-319	Eng by 299 runs	WM Lawry
Melbourne	Eng	9d-493*	4d-169	England 392	0-161	Drawn	WM Lawry
Adelaide	Eng	235	3-328	England 470*	4d-233	Drawn	WM Lawry
Sydney	Aus	264	160	England 184*	302	Eng by 62 runs	IM Chappell

1972 in England

Series	Toss1st	Aus 1st	Aus 2nd	Opponent 1st	Opp 2nd	Result	Captain
Manchester	Eng	142	252	England 249*	234	Eng by 89 runs	IM Chappell
Lord's	Eng	308	2-81	England 272*	116	Aus by 8 wkts	IM Chappell
Nottingham	Eng	315*	4d-324	England 189	4-290	Drawn	IM Chappell
Leeds	Aus	146*	136	England 263	1-21	Eng by 9 wkts	IM Chappell
The Oval	Eng	399	5-242	England 284*	356	Aus by 5 wkts	IM Chappell

1972/73 in Australia

Series	Toss1st	Aus 1st	Aus 2nd	Opponent 1st	Opp 2nd	Result	Captain
Adelaide	Pak	585	—	Pakistan 9-257*	214	Aus by an inns & 114 runs	IM Chappell
Melbourne	Aus	5d-441*	425	Pakistan 8d-574	200	Aus by 92 runs	IM Chappell
Sydney	Pak	334*	184	Pakistan 360	106	Aus by 52 runs	IM Chappell

1972/73 in West Indies

Series	Toss1st	Aus 1st	Aus 2nd	Opponent 1st	Opp 2nd	Result	Captain
Kingston	Aus	7d-428*	2d-260	West Indies 428	3-67	Drawn	IM Chappell
Bridgetown	Aus	324*	2d-300	West Indies 391	0-36	Drawn	IM Chappell
Port-of-Spain	Aus	332*	281	West Indies 9-280	9-289	Aus by 44 runs	IM Chappell
Georgetown	WI	341	0-135	West Indies 366*	109	Aus by 10 wkts	IM Chappell
Port-of-Spain	Aus	8d-419*	7d-218	West Indies 319	5-135	Drawn	IM Chappell

1973/74 in Australia

Series	Toss1st	Aus 1st	Aus 2nd	Opponent 1st	Opp 2nd	Result	Captain
Melbourne	Aus	8d-462*	—	New Zealand 237	9-200	Aus by an inns & 25 runs	IM Chappell
Sydney	Aus	162	2-30	New Zealand 312*	9d-305	Drawn	IM Chappell
Adelaide	Aus	477*	—	New Zealand 218	202	Aus by an inns & 57 runs	IM Chappell

1973/74 in New Zealand

Series	Toss1st	Aus 1st	Aus 2nd	Opponent 1st	Opp 2nd	Result	Captain
Wellington	Aus	6d-511*	8-460	New Zealand 484	—	Drawn	IM Chappell
Christchurch	NZ	223*	259	New Zealand 255	5-230	NZ by 5 wkts	IM Chappell
Auckland	NZ	221*	346	New Zealand 112	158	Aus by 297 runs	IM Chappell

1974/75 in Australia

Series	Toss1st	Aus 1st	Aus 2nd	Opponent 1st	Opp 2nd	Result	Captain
Brisbane	Aus	309*	5d-288	England 265*	166	Aus by 166 runs	IM Chappell
Perth	Aus	481	1-23	England 208*	293	Aus by 9 wkts	IM Chappell
Melbourne	Aus	241	8-238	England 242*	244	Drawn	IM Chappell
Sydney	Aus	405*	4d-289	England 295	228	Aus by 171 runs	IM Chappell
Adelaide	Eng	304*	5d-272	England 172	241	Aus by 163 runs	IM Chappell
Melbourne	Aus	152*	373	England 529	—	Eng by an inns & 4 runs	IM Chappell

▶

Series	Toss	Australia 1st	Australia 2nd	Opponent	Opponents 1st	Opponents 2nd	Result	Captain
1975 in England								
Birmingham	Eng	359*	—	England	101	173	Aus by an inns & 85 runs	IM Chappell
Lord's	Eng	268	3-329	England	315*	7d-436	Drawn	IM Chappell
Leeds	Eng	135	3-220	England	288*	291	Drawn	IM Chappell
The Oval	Aus	9d-532*	2-40	England	191	538	Drawn	IM Chappell
1975/76 in Australia								
Brisbane	WI	366	2-219	West Indies	214*	370	Aus by 8 wkts	GS Chappell
Perth	Aus	329*	169	West Indies	585	—	WI by an inns & 87 runs	GS Chappell
Melbourne	Aus	485	2-55	West Indies	224*	312	Aus by 8 wkts	GS Chappell
Sydney	Aus	405	3-82	West Indies	355*	128	Aus by 7 wkts	GS Chappell
Adelaide	Aus	418*	7d-345	West Indies	274	299	Aus by 190 runs	GS Chappell
Melbourne	Aus	351*	3d-300	West Indies	160	326	Aus by 165 runs	GS Chappell
1976/77 in Australia								
Adelaide	Pak	9-454	6-261	Pakistan	272*	466	Drawn	GS Chappell
Melbourne	Aus	8d-517*	8d-315	Pakistan	333	151	Aus by 348 runs	GS Chappell
Sydney	Pak	211*	180	Pakistan	360	2-32	Pak by 8 wkts	GS Chappell
1976/77 in New Zealand								
Christchurch	NZ	552*	4d-154	New Zealand	357	8-293	Drawn	GS Chappell
Auckland	Aus	377	0-28	New Zealand	229*	175	Aus by 10 wkts	GS Chappell
1976/77 in Australia								
Melbourne	Eng	138*	9d-419	England	95	417	Aus by 45 runs	GS Chappell
1977 in England								
Lord's	Eng	296	6-114	England	216*	305	Drawn	GS Chappell
Manchester	Aus	297*	218	England	437	1-82	Eng by 9 wkts	GS Chappell
Nottingham	Aus	243*	309	England	364	3-189	Eng by 7 wkts	GS Chappell
Leeds	Eng	103	248	England	436*	—	Eng by an inns & 85 runs	GS Chappell
The Oval	Aus	385	—	England	214*	2-57	Drawn	GS Chappell
1977/78 in Australia								
Brisbane	Aus	166*	327	India	153	324	Aus by 16 runs	RB Simpson
Perth	Ind	394	8-342	India	402*	9d-330	Aus by 2 wkts	RB Simpson
Melbourne	Ind	213	164	India	256*	343	Ind by 222 runs	RB Simpson
Sydney	Aus	131*	263	India	8d-396	—	Ind by an inns & 2 runs	RB Simpson
Adelaide	Aus	505*	256	India	269	445	Aus by 47 runs	RB Simpson
1977/78 in West Indies								
Port-of-Spain	WI	90*	9-209	West Indies	405	—	WI by an inns & 106 runs	RB Simpson
Bridgetown	WI	250*	178	West Indies	288	1-141	WI by 9 wkts	RB Simpson
Georgetown	WI	286	7-362	West Indies	205*	439	Aus by 3 wkts	RB Simpson
Port-of-Spain	Aus	290	94	West Indies	292*	290	WI by 198 runs	RB Simpson
Kingston	Aus	343*	3d-304	West Indies	280	9-258	Drawn	RB Simpson
1978/79 in Australia								
Brisbane	Aus	116*	339	England	286	3-170	Eng by 7 wkts	GN Yallop
Perth	Aus	190	161	England	309*	208	Eng by 166 runs	GN Yallop
Melbourne	Aus	258*	167	England	143	179	Aus by 103 runs	GN Yallop
Sydney	Eng	294	111	England	152*	346	Eng by 93 runs	GN Yallop
Adelaide	Aus	164	160	England	169*	360	Eng by 205 runs	GN Yallop
Sydney	Aus	198*	143	England	308	1-35	Eng by 9 wkts	GN Yallop
Melbourne	Aus	168	310	Pakistan	196*	9d-353	Pak by 71 runs	GN Yallop
Perth	Aus	327	3-236	Pakistan	277*	285	Aus by 7 wkts	KJ Hughes
1979/80 in India								
Madras	Aus	390*	7-212	India	425	—	Drawn	KJ Hughes
Bangalore	Aus	333*	3-77	India	5d-457	—	Drawn	KJ Hughes
Kanpur	Ind	304	125	India	271*	311	Ind by 153 runs	KJ Hughes
Delhi	Ind	298	413	India	7d-510*	—	Drawn	KJ Hughes
Calcutta	Aus	442*	6d-151	India	347	4-200	Drawn	KJ Hughes
Bombay	Ind	160	9-198	India	8d-458*	—	Ind by an inns & 100 runs	KJ Hughes
1979/80 in Australia								
Brisbane	WI	268*	6d-448	West Indies	441	3-40	Drawn	GS Chappell
Perth	Eng	244*	337	England	228	215	Aus by 138 runs	GS Chappell
Melbourne	Aus	156*	259	West Indies	397	0-22	WI by 10 wkts	GS Chappell

Series	Toss 1st	Australia 1st	Australia 2nd	Opponent 1st	Opponents 1st	Opponents 2nd	Result	Captain
Sydney	Aus	145	4-219	England	123°	237	Aus by 6 wkts	GS Chappell
Adelaide	Aus	203	165	West Indies	328°	448	WI by 408 runs	GS Chappell
Melbourne	Eng	477	2-103	England	306°	273	Aus by 8 wkts	GS Chappell
1979/80 in Pakistan								
Karachi	Aus	225°	140	Pakistan	292	3-76	Pak by 7 wkts	GS Chappell
Faisalabad	Aus	617°	—	Pakistan	2-382	—	Drawn	GS Chappell
Lahore	Aus	7d-407°	8-391	Pakistan	9d-420	—	Drawn	GS Chappell
1980 in England								
Lord's	Aus	5d-385°	4d-189	England	205	3-244	Drawn	GS Chappell
1980/81 in Australia								
Brisbane	Aus	305	0-63	New Zealand	225°	142	Aus by 10 wkts	GS Chappell
Perth	Aus	265	2-55	New Zealand	196°	121	Aus by 8 wkts	GS Chappell
Melbourne	N.Z	321°	188	New Zealand	317	6-128	Drawn	GS Chappell
Sydney	Ind	406	—	India	9-201°	201	Aus by an inns & 4 runs	GS Chappell
Adelaide	Ind	528°	7d-221	India	419	8—135	Drawn	GS Chappell
Melbourne	Aus	419	83	India	237°	9-324	Ind by 59 runs	GS Chappell
1981 in England								
Nottingham	Aus	179	6-132	England	185°	125	Aus by 4 wkts	KJ Hughes
Lord's	Aus	345	4-90	England	311°	8d-265	Drawn	KJ Hughes
Leeds	Aus	9d-401°	111	England	174	356	Eng by 18 runs	KJ Hughes
Birmingham	Eng	258	121	England	189°	219	Eng by 29 runs	KJ Hughes
Manchester	Eng	130	402	England	231°	404	Eng by 103 runs	KJ Hughes
The Oval	Eng	352°	9d-344	England	314	7-261	Drawn	KJ Hughes
1981/82 in Australia								
Perth	Pak	180°	8d-424	Pakistan	62	256	Aus by 286 runs	GS Chappell
Brisbane	Aus	9d-512	0-3	Pakistan	291°	223	Aus by 10 wkts	GS Chappell
Melbourne	Pak	293	125	Pakistan	8d-500°	—	Pak by an inns & 82 runs	GS Chappell
Melbourne	Aus	198°	222	West Indies	201	161	Aus by 58 runs	GS Chappell
Sydney	WI	267	4-200	West Indies	384°	255	Drawn	GS Chappell
Adelaide	WI	238°	386	West Indies	389	5-239	WI by 5 wkts	GS Chappell
1981/82 in New Zealand								
Wellington	Aus	1-85	—	New Zealand	7d-266°	—	Drawn	GS Chappell
Auckland	NZ	210°	280	New Zealand	387	5-109	NZ by 5 wkts	GS Chappell
Christchurch	NZ	353°	2-69	New Zealand	149	272	Aus by 8 wkts	GS Chappell
1982/83 in Pakistan								
Karachi	Aus	284°	179	Pakistan	9d-419	1-47	Pak by 9 wkts	KJ Hughes
Faisalabad	Pak	168	330	Pakistan	6d-501°	—	Pak by an inns & 3 runs	KJ Hughes
Lahore	Pak	316°	214	Pakistan	7d-467	1-64	Pak by 9 wkts	KJ Hughes
1982/83 in England								
Perth	Aus	9d-424	2-73	England	411°	358	Drawn	GS Chappell
Brisbane	Aus	341	4-190	England	219°	309	Aus by 7 wkts	GS Chappell
Adelaide	Eng	438°	2-83	England	216	304	Aus by 8 wkts	GS Chappell
Melbourne	Aus	287	288	England	284°	294	Eng by 3 runs	GS Chappell
Sydney	Aus	314°	382	England	237	7-314	Drawn	GS Chappell
1982/83 in Sri Lanka								
Kandy	Aus	4d-514°	—	Sri Lanka	271	205	Aus by an inns & 38 runs	GS Chappell
1983/84 in Australia								
Perth	Pak	9d-436°	—	Pakistan	129	298	Aus by an inns & 9 runs	KJ Hughes
Brisbane	Pak	7d-509	—	Pakistan	156°	3-82	Drawn	KJ Hughes
Adelaide	Aus	465°	7-310	Pakistan	624	—	Drawn	KJ Hughes
Melbourne	Pak	555	—	Pakistan	470°	7-238	Drawn	KJ Hughes
Sydney	Aus	6d-454	0-35	Pakistan	278°	210	Aus by 10 wkts	KJ Hughes
1983/84 in West Indies								
Georgetown	Aus	279°	9d-273	West Indies	230	0-250	Drawn	KJ Hughes
Port-of-Spain	WI	255°	9-299	West Indies	8d-468	—	Drawn	KJ Hughes
Bridgetown	WI	429°	97	West Indies	509	0-21	WI by 10 wkts	KJ Hughes
St John's	Aus	262°	200	West Indies	498	—	WI by an inns & 36 runs	KJ Hughes
Kingston	WI	199°	9-160	West Indies	305	0-55	WI by 10 wkts	KJ Hughes

▶

Series	Toss1st	Australia 1st	Australia 2nd	Opponent1st	Opponents 1st	Opponents 2nd	Result	Captain
1984/85 in Australia								
Perth	Aus	76	228	West Indies	416*	—	WI by an inns & 112 runs	KJ Hughes
Brisbane	WI	175*	271	West Indies	424	2-26	WI by 8 wkts	KJ Hughes
Adelaide	WI	284	173	West Indies	356*	7d-292	WI by 191 runs	AR Border
Melbourne	Aus	296	8-198	West Indies	479*	5d-186	Drawn	AR Border
Sydney	Aus	9d-471*	—	West Indies	163	253	Aus by an inns & 55 runs	AR Border
1985 in England								
Leeds	Aus	331*	324	England	533	5-123	Eng by 5 wkts	AR Border
Lord's	Aus	425	6-127	England	290*	261	Aus by 4 wkts	AR Border
Nottingham	Eng	539	—	England	456*	2-196	Drawn	AR Border
Manchester	Eng	257*	5-340	England	9d-482	—	Drawn	AR Border
Birmingham	Eng	335*	142	England	5d-595	—	Eng by an inns & 118 runs	AR Border
The Oval	Eng	241	129	England	464*	—	Eng by an inns & 94 runs	AR Border
1985/86 in Australia								
Brisbane	NZ	179*	333	New Zealand	1d-553	—	NZ by an inns & 41 runs	AR Border
Sydney	Aus	227	6-260	New Zealand	293*	193	Aus by 4 wkts	AR Border
Perth	NZ	203*	259	New Zealand	299	4-164	NZ by 6 wkts	AR Border
Adelaide	Aus	381*	0-17	India	520	—	Drawn	AR Border
Melbourne	Ind	262*	308	India	445	2-59	Drawn	AR Border
Sydney	Ind	396	6-119	India	4d-600*	—	Drawn	AR Border
1985/86 in New Zealand								
Wellington	NZ	435*	—	New Zealand	6-379	—	Drawn	AR Border
Christchurch	NZ	364*	7d-219	New Zealand	339	1-16	Drawn	AR Border
Auckland	Aus	314*	103	New Zealand	258	2-160	NZ by 8 wkts	AR Border
1986/87 in India								
Madras	Aus	7d-574*	5d-170	India	397	347	Tied	AR Border
Delhi	Aus	3d-207*	—	India	3-107	—	Drawn	AR Border
Bombay	Aus	345*	2-216	India	5d-517	—	Drawn	AR Border
1986/87 in Australia								
Brisbane	Aus	248	282	England	456*	3-77	Eng by 7 wkts	AR Border
Perth	Eng	401	4-197	England	8d-592*	8d-199	Drawn	AR Border
Adelaide	Aus	5d-514*	3d-201	England	455	2-39	Drawn	AR Border
Melbourne	Eng	141*	194	England	349	—	Eng by an inns & 14 runs	AR Border
Sydney	Aus	343*	251	England	275	264	Aus by 55 runs	AR Border
1987/88 in Australia								
Brisbane	Aus	305	1-97	New Zealand	186*	212	Aus by 9 wkts	AR Border
Adelaide	NZ	496	—	New Zealand	9d-485*	7-182	Drawn	AR Border
Melbourne	Aus	357	9-230	New Zealand	317*	286	Drawn	AR Border
Sydney	Eng	214	2-328	England	425*	—	Drawn	AR Border
Perth	Aus	455*	—	Sri Lanka	194	153	Aus by an inns & 108 runs	AR Border
1988/89 in Pakistan								
Karachi	Pak	165	116	Pakistan	9d-469*	—	Pak by an inns & 188 runs	AR Border
Faisalabad	Pak	321	3-67	Pakistan	316*	9d-378	Drawn	AR Border
Lahore	Aus	340*	3d-161	Pakistan	233	8-153	Drawn	AR Border
1988/89 in Australia								
Brisbane	Aus	167*	289	West Indies	394	2-63	WI by 8 wkts	AR Border
Perth	Aus	8d-395	9-234	West Indies	449*	9d-349	WI by 169 runs	AR Border
Melbourne	Aus	242	114	West Indies	280*	9d-361	WI by 285 runs	AR Border
Sydney	WI	401	3-82	West Indies	224*	256	Aus by 7 wkts	AR Border
Adelaide	Aus	515*	4d-224	West Indies	369	4-233	Drawn	AR Border
1989 in England								
Leeds	Eng	7d-601*	3d-230	England	430	191	Aus by 210 runs	AR Border
Lord's	Eng	528	4-119	England	286*	359	Aus by 6 wkts	AR Border
Birmingham	Aus	424*	2-158	England	242	—	Drawn	AR Border
Manchester	Eng	447	1-81	England	260*	264	Aus by 9 wkts	AR Border
Nottingham	Aus	6d-602*	—	England	255	167	Aus by an inns & 180 runs	AR Border
The Oval	Aus	468*	4d-219	England	285	5-143	Drawn	AR Border

Series	Toss1st	Australia 1st	Australia 2nd	Opponent1st	Opponents 1st	Opponents 2nd	Result	Captain
1989/90 in Australia								
Perth	NZ	9d-521*	—	New Zealand	231	7-322	Drawn	AR Border
Brisbane	SL	367*	6-375	Sri Lanka	418	—	Drawn	AR Border
Hobart	SL	224*	5d-513	Sri Lanka	216	348	Aus by 173 runs	AR Border
Melbourne	Pak	223*	8d-312	Pakistan	107	336	Aus by 92 runs	AR Border
Adelaide	Pak	341	6-233	Pakistan	257*	9d-387	Drawn	AR Border
Sydney	Aus	2-176	—	Pakistan	199*	—	Drawn	AR Border
1989/90 in New Zealand								
Wellington	Aus	110*	269	New Zealand	202	1-181	New Zealand by 9 wkts	AR Border

* Denotes team batting first

Results of All Test Series

Years	Opponent	Venue	Tests	Won	Australia Lost	Australia Drawn	Tied	Result of series
1876/77	England	Australia	2	1	1	—	—	Drawn 1-1
1878/79	England	Australia	1	1	—	—	—	Won 1-0
1880	England	England	1	—	1	—	—	Lost 1-0
1881/82	England	Australia	4	2	—	2	—	Won 2-0
1882	England	England	1	1	—	—	—	Won 1-0
1882/83	England	Australia	4	2	2	—	—	Drawn 2-2
1884	England	England	3	—	1	2	—	Lost 1-0
1884/85	England	Australia	5	2	3	—	—	Lost 3-2
1886	England	England	3	—	3	—	—	Lost 3-0
1886/87	England	Australia	2	—	2	—	—	Lost 2-0
1887/88	England	Australia	1	—	1	—	—	Lost 1-0
1888	England	England	3	1	2	—	—	Lost 2-1
1890	England	England	2	—	2	—	—	Lost 2-0
1891/92	England	Australia	3	2	1	—	—	Won 2-1
1893	England	England	3	—	1	2	—	Lost 1-0
1894/95	England	Australia	5	2	3	—	—	Lost 3-2
1896	England	England	3	1	2	—	—	Lost 2-1
1897/98	England	Australia	5	4	1	—	—	Won 4-1
1899	England	England	5	1	—	4	—	Won 1-0
1901/02	England	Australia	5	4	1	—	—	Won 4-1
1902	England	England	5	3	1	1	—	Won 3-1
1902	South Africa	South Africa	3	2	—	1	—	Won 2-0
1903/04	England	Australia	5	2	3	—	—	Lost 3-2
1905	England	England	5	—	2	3	—	Lost 2-0
1907/08	England	Australia	5	4	1	—	—	Won 4-1
1909	England	England	5	2	1	2	—	Won 2-1
1910/11	South Africa	Australia	5	4	1	—	—	Won 4-1
1911/12	England	Australia	5	1	4	—	—	Lost 4-1
1912	South Africa	England	3	2	—	1	—	Won 2-0
1912	England	England	3	—	1	2	—	Lost 1-0
1920/21	England	Australia	5	5	—	—	—	Won 5-0
1921	England	England	5	3	—	2	—	Won 3-0
1921/22	South Africa	South Africa	3	1	—	2	—	Won 1-0
1924/25	England	Australia	5	4	1	—	—	Won 4-1
1926	England	England	5	—	1	4	—	Lost 1-0
1928/29	England	Australia	5	1	4	—	—	Lost 4-1
1930	England	England	5	2	1	2	—	Won 2-1
1930/31	West Indies	Australia	5	4	1	—	—	Won 4-1
1931/32	South Africa	Australia	5	5	—	—	—	Won 5-0
1932/33	England	Australia	5	1	4	—	—	Lost 4-1
1934	England	England	5	2	1	2	—	Won 2-1
1935/36	South Africa	South Africa	5	4	—	1	—	Won 4-0
1936/37	England	Australia	5	3	2	—	—	Won 3-2
1938	England	England	5	1	1	2	—	Drawn 1-1
1945/46	New Zealand	New Zealand	1	1	—	—	—	Won 1-0
1946/47	England	Australia	5	3	—	2	—	Won 3-0
1947/48	India	Australia	5	4	—	1	—	Won 4-0
1948	England	England	5	4	—	1	—	Won 4-0
1949/50	South Africa	South Africa	5	4	—	1	—	Won 4-0
1950/51	England	Australia	5	4	1	—	—	Won 4-1
1951/52	West Indies	Australia	5	4	1	—	—	Won 4-1
1952/53	South Africa	Australia	5	2	2	1	—	Drawn 2-2
1953	England	England	5	—	1	4	—	Lost 1-0
1954/55	England	Australia	5	1	3	1	—	Lost 3-1
1954/55	West Indies	West Indies	5	3	—	2	—	Won 3-0

Continued

Years	Opponent	Venue	Tests	Won	Australia Lost	Drawn	Tied	Result of series
1956	England	England	5	1	2	2	—	Lost 2-1
1956/57	Pakistan	Pakistan	1	—	1	—	—	Lost 1-0
1956/57	India	India	3	2	—	1	—	Won 2-0
1957/58	South Africa	South Africa	5	3	—	2	—	Won 3-0
1958/59	England	Australia	5	4	—	1	—	Won 4-0
1959/60	Pakistan	Pakistan	3	2	—	1	—	Won 2-0
1959/60	India	India	5	2	1	2	—	Won 2-1
1960/61	West Indies	Australia	5	2	1	1	1	Won 2-1
1961	England	England	5	2	1	2	—	Won 2-1
1962/63	England	Australia	5	1	1	3	—	Drawn 1-1
1963/64	South Africa	Australia	5	1	1	3	—	Drawn 1-1
1964	England	England	5	1	—	4	—	Won 1-0
1964/65	India	India	3	1	1	1	—	Drawn 1-1
1964/65	Pakistan	Pakistan	1	—	—	1	—	Drawn 0-0
1964/65	Pakistan	Pakistan	1	—	—	1	—	Drawn 0-0
1964/65	West Indies	West Indies	5	1	2	2	—	Lost 2-1
1965/66	England	Australia	5	1	1	3	—	Drawn 1-1
1966/67	South Africa	South Africa	5	1	3	1	—	Lost 3-1
1987/68	India	Australia	4	4	—	—	—	Won 4-0
1968	England	England	5	1	1	3	—	Drawn 1-1
1968/69	West Indies	Australia	5	3	1	1	—	Won 3-1
1969/70	India	India	5	3	1	1	—	Won 3-1
1969/70	South Africa	South Africa	4	—	4	—	—	Lost 4-0
1970/71	England	Australia	7	—	2	5	—	Lost 2-0
1972	England	England	5	2	2	1	—	Drawn 2-2
1972/73	Pakistan	Australia	2	2	—	—	—	Won 2-0
1972/73	West Indies	West Indies	5	2	—	3	—	Won 2-0
1973/74	New Zealand	Australia	3	2	—	1	—	Won 2-0
1973/74	New Zealand	New Zealand	3	1	1	1	—	Drawn 1-1
1974/75	England	Australia	6	4	1	1	—	Won 4-1
1975	England	England	4	1	—	3	—	Won 1-0
1975/76	West Indies	Australia	6	5	1	—	—	Won 5-1
1976/77	Pakistan	Australia	3	1	1	1	—	Drawn 1-1
1976/77	New Zealand	New Zealand	2	1	—	1	—	Won 1-0
1976/77	England	Australia	1	1	—	—	—	Won 1-0
1977	England	England	5	—	3	2	—	Lost 3-0
1977/78	India	Australia	5	3	2	—	—	Won 3-2
1977/78	West Indies	West Indies	5	1	3	1	—	Lost 3-1
1978/79	England	Australia	6	1	5	—	—	Lost 5-1
1978/79	Pakistan	Australia	2	1	1	—	—	Drawn 1-1
1979/80	India	India	6	—	2	4	—	Lost 2-0
1979/80	West Indies	Australia	3	—	2	1	—	Lost 2-0
1979/80	England	Australia	3	3	—	—	—	Won 3-0
1979/80	Pakistan	Pakistan	3	—	1	2	—	Lost 1-0
1980	England	England	1	—	—	1	—	Drawn 0-0
1980/81	New Zealand	Australia	3	2	—	1	—	Won 2-0
1980/81	India	Australia	3	1	1	1	—	Drawn 1-1
1981	England	England	6	1	3	2	—	Lost 3-1
1981/82	Pakistan	Australia	3	2	1	—	—	Won 2-1
1981/82	West Indies	Australia	3	1	1	1	—	Drawn 1-1
1981/82	New Zealand	New Zealand	3	1	1	1	—	Drawn 1-1
1982/83	Pakistan	Pakistan	3	—	3	—	—	Lost 3-0
1982/83	England	Australia	5	2	1	2	—	Won 2-1
1982/83	Sri Lanka	Sri Lanka	1	1	—	—	—	Won 1-0
1983/84	Pakistan	Australia	5	2	—	3	—	Won 2-0
1983/84	West Indies	West Indies	5	—	3	2	—	Lost 3-0
1984/58	West Indies	Australia	5	1	3	1	—	Lost 3-1
1985	England	England	6	1	3	2	—	Lost 3-1
1985/86	New Zealand	Australia	3	1	2	—	—	Lost 2-1
1985/86	India	Australia	3	—	—	3	—	Drawn 0-0
1985/86	New Zealand	New Zealand	3	—	1	2	—	Lost 1-0
1986/87	India	India	3	—	—	2	1	Lost 2-0
1986/87	England	Australia	5	1	2	2	—	Lost 2-1
1987/88	New Zealand	Australia	3	1	—	2	—	Won 1-0
1987/88	England	Australia	1	—	—	1	—	Drawn 0-0
1987/88	Sri Lanka	Australia	1	1	—	—	—	Won 1-0
1988/89	Pakistan	Pakistan	3	—	1	2	—	Lost 1-0
1988/89	West Indies	Australia	5	1	3	1	—	Lost 3-1
1989	England	England	6	4	—	2	—	Won 4-0
1989/90	New Zealand	Australia	1	—	—	1	—	Drawn 0-0
1989/90	Sri Lanka	Australia	2	1	—	1	—	Won 1-0
1989/90	Pakistan	Australia	3	1	—	2	—	Won 1-0
1989/90	New Zealand	New Zealand	1	—	1	—	—	Lost 1-0
Total			499	203	144	150	2	

Summary of Test Matches at All Venues

Venue	Date of 1st Test	Tests	Won	Lost	Drawn	Tie
Melbourne	15 Mar 1877	83	43	26	14	—
Sydney	17 Feb 1882	76	40	24	12	—
Adelaide	12 Dec 1884	48	21	13	14	—
Brisbane	30 Nov 1928	34	17	9	7	1
Perth	11 Dec 1970	17	8	5	4	—
Hobart	16 Dec 1989	1	1	—	—	—
Total in Australia		**259**	**130**	**77**	**51**	**1**
The Oval	6 Sep 1880	30	5	13	12	—
Manchester	10 Jly 1884	26	6	7	13	—
Lord's	21 Jly 1884	30	12	5	13	—
Nottingham	1 Jun 1899	17	5	3	9	—
Leeds	29 Jun 1899	20	6	6	8	—
Birmingham	29 May 1902	8	1	3	4	—
Sheffield	3 Jly 1902	1	1	—	—	—
Total in England		**132**	**36**	**37**	**59**	
Madras	19 Oct 1956	6	4	—	1	1
Bombay	26 Oct 1956	6	1	2	3	—
Calcutta	2 Nov 1956	5	2	—	3	—
Delhi	12 Dec 1959	4	1	1	2	—
Kanpur	19 Dec 1959	3	—	2	1	—
Bangalore	19 Sep 1979	1	—	—	1	—
Total in India		**25**	**8**	**5**	**11**	**1**
Wellington	29 Mar 1946	5	1	1	3	—
Christchurch	8 Mar 1974	4	1	1	2	—
Auckland	22 Mar 1974	4	2	2	—	—
Total in New Zealand		**13**	**4**	**4**	**5**	
Karachi	11 Oct 1956	6	—	4	2	—
Dacca	13 Nov 1959	1	1	—	—	—
Lahore	21 Nov 1959	4	1	1	2	—
Faisalabad	6 Mar 1980	3	—	1	2	—
Total in Pakistan		**14**	**2**	**6**	**6**	
Johannesburg	11 Oct 1902	12	4	2	6	—
Cape Town	8 Nov 1902	7	6	1	—	—
Durban	5 Nov 1921	7	3	2	2	—
Port Elizabeth	3 Mar 1950	4	2	2	—	—
Total in South Africa		**30**	**15**	**7**	**8**	**—**
Kandy	22 Apr 1983	1	1	—	—	—
Total in Sri Lanka		**1**	**1**	**—**	**—**	**—**
Kingston	26 Mar 1955	6	2	2	2	—
Port-of-Spain	11 Apr 1955	8	2	2	4	—
Georgetown	26 Apr 1955	5	3	1	1	—
Bridgetown	14 May 1955	5	—	2	3	—
St John's	7 Apr 1984	1	—	1	—	—
Total in West Indies		**25**	**7**	**8**	**10**	**—**
Total in Australia		**259**	**130**	**77**	**51**	**1**
Total abroad		**240**	**73**	**67**	**99**	**1**
Total		**499**	**203**	**144**	**150**	**2**

467

Highest Innings Totals

Score	Opponent	Venue	Series
8d-758	West Indies	Kingston	1954/55
6d-729	England	Lord's	1930
701	England	The Oval	1934
695	England	The Oval	1930
674	India	Adelaide	1947/48
668	West Indies	Bridgetown	1954/55
8d-659	England	Sydney	1946/47
8d-656	England	Manchester	1964
6d-650	West Indies	Bridgetown	1964/65
645	England	Brisbane	1946/46
619	West Indies	Sydney	1968/69
617	Pakistan	Faisalabad	1979/80
604	England	Melbourne	1936/37
6d-602	England	Nottingham	1989
8d-601	England	Brisbane	1954/55
7d-601	England	Leeds	1989
600	England	Melbourne	1924/25
9d-600	West Indies	Port-of-Spain	1954/55
586	England	Sydney	1894/95
585	Pakistan	Adelaide	1972/73
584	England	Leeds	1934
582	England	Adelaide	1920/21
581	England	Sydney	1920/21
578	South Africa	Melbourne	1910/11
8d-575	India	Melbourne	1947/48
7d-574	India	Madras	1986/87
573	England	Adelaide	1897/98
566	England	Leeds	1930
564	England	Melbourne	1936/37
558	West Indies	Brisbane	1930/31
555	Pakistan	Melbourne	1983/84
554	South Africa	Melbourne	1931/32
552	New Zealand	Christchurch	1976/77
551	England	The Oval	1884
7d-549	South Africa	Port Elizabeth	1949/50
547	West Indies	Sydney	1968/69
8d-543	England	Melbourne	1965/66
542	South Africa	Cape Town	1966/67
539	England	Nottingham	1985
536	England	Melbourne	1946/47
533	West Indies	Adelaide	1968/69
9d-532	England	The Oval	1975
530	South Africa	Adelaide	1952/53
529	India	Melbourne	1967/68
528	South Africa	Sydney	1910/11
528	India	Adelaide	1980/81
528	England	Lord's	1989
7d-526	South Africa	Cape Town	1949/50
7d-523	India	Bombay	1956/57
9d-521	New Zealand	Perth	1989/90
520	England	Melbourne	1897/98
520	South Africa	Melbourne	1952/53
517	West Indies	Sydney	1951/52
8d-517	Pakistan	Melbourne	1976/77
516	West Indies	Port-of-Spain	1964/65
516	England	Adelaide	1965/66
9d-515	West Indies	Kingston	1954/55
515	West Indies	Adelaide	1988/89
4d-514	Sri Lanka	Kandy	1982/83
5d-514	England	Adelaide	1986/87
513	South Africa	Adelaide	1931/32
5d-513	Sri Lanka	Hobart	1989/90
9d-512	Pakistan	Brisbane	1981/82
6d-511	New Zealand	Wellington	1973/74
510	West Indies	Melbourne	1968/69
509	England	Nottingham	1948
7d-509	Pakistan	Brisbane	1983/84
506	England	Adelaide	1907/08
505	West Indies	Brisbane	1960/61
505	India	Adelaide	1977/78

468

Lowest Completed Innings Totals

Score	Opponent	Venue	Series
36	England	Birmingham	1902
42	England	Sydney	1887/88
44	England	The Oval	1896
53	England	Lord's	1896
58+	England	Brisbane	1936/37
60	England	Lord's	1888
63	England	The Oval	1882
65	England	The Oval	1912
66++	England	Brisbane	1928/29
68	England	The Oval	1886
70	England	Manchester	1888
74	England	Birmingham	1909
75	South Africa	Durban	1949/50
76	West Indies	Perth	1984/85
78	England	Lord's	1968
80	England	The Oval	1888
80+	England	Sydney	1935/36
80	Pakistan	Karachi	1956/57
81	England	Manchester	1888
82	England	Sydney	1887/88
82	West Indies	Adelaide	1951/52
83	England	Sydney	1882/83
83	India	Melbourne	1980/81
84	England	Sydney	1886/87
84	England	Manchester	1956
86	England	Manchester	1902
90	West Indies	Port-of-Spain	1977/78
91	England	The Oval	1893
92	England	The Oval	1890
94	West Indies	Port-of-Spain	1977/78
97	England	Sydney	1887/87
97	West Indies	Bridgetown	1983/84
100	England	The Oval	1888
100	England	Adelaide	1891/92

+ Denotes one man absent

Australia's Leading Test Run-Scorers

Batsman	M	Inn	NO	Runs	HS	50	100	Avrge	Eng	Ind	NZ	Pak	S Af	SL	WI
AR Border	115	199	36	8701	205	48	23	53.38	2834	1292	1130	1666	—	300	1479
GS Chappell	88	151	19	7110	247*	31	24	53.86	2619	368	1076	1581	—	66	1400
DG Bradman	52	80	10	6996	334	13	29	99.94	5028	715	—	—	806	—	447
RN Harvey	79	137	10	6149	205	24	21	48.42	2416	775	—	279	1625	—	1054
KD Walters	75	125	14	5357	250	33	15	48.26	1981	756	901	265	258	—	1196
IM Chappell	76	136	10	5345	196	26	14	42.42	2138	536	486	352	288	—	1545
WM Lawry	68	123	12	5234	210	27	13	47.15	2233	892	—	89	985	—	1035
RB Simpson	62	111	7	4869	311	27	10	46.82	1405	1125	—	316	980	—	1043
IR Redpath	67	120	11	4737	171	31	8	43.46	1512	475	413	299	791	—	1247
KJ Hughes	70	124	6	4415	213	22	9	37.42	1499	988	138	1016	—	—	774
RW Marsh	97	150	13	3633	132	16	3	26.52	1633	83	486	724	—	—	707
AR Morris	46	79	3	3533	206	12	12	46.49	2080	209	—	—	792	—	452
C Hill	49	89	2	3412	191	19	7	39.22	2660	—	—	—	752	—	—
GM Wood	59	112	6	3374	172	13	9	31.83	1063	287	393	550	—	4	1077
DC Boon	48	88	7	3186	200	14	8	39.33	906	648	800	172	—	131	529
VT Trumper	48	89	8	3163	214*	13	8	39.05	2263	—	—	—	900	—	—
CC McDonald	47	83	4	3107	170	17	5	39.33	1043	224	—	174	786	—	880
AL Hassett	43	69	3	3073	198*	11	10	46.56	1572	332	19	—	748	—	402
KR Miller	55	87	7	2958	147	13	7	36.98	1511	185	30	32	399	—	801
WW Armstrong	50	84	10	2863	159*	8	6	38.69	2172	—	—	—	691	—	—
KR Stackpole	44	80	5	2807	207	14	7	37.43	1164	368	197	37	441	—	600
NC O'Neill	42	69	8	2779	181	15	6	45.56	1072	416	—	218	285	—	788
GN Yallop	39	70	3	2756	268	9	8	41.13	709	568	—	882	—	98	499
SJ McCabe	39	62	5	2748	232	13	6	48.21	1931	—	—	—	621	—	196
DM Jones	34	59	8	2637	216	9	9	51.71	1157	371	171	291	—	261	386
W Bardsley	41	66	5	2469	193*	14	6	40.48	1487	—	—	—	82	—	—
WM Woodfull	35	54	4	2300	161	13	7	46.00	1675	—	—	—	421	—	204
PJP Burge	42	68	8	2290	181	12	4	38.17	1179	457	—	94	331	—	229
SE Gregory	58	100	7	2282	201	8	4	24.54	2193	—	—	—	89	—	—
R Benaud	63	97	7	2201	122	9	3	24.46	767	144	—	144	684	—	462

Continued

Batsman	M	Inn	NO	Runs	HS	50	100	Avrge	Eng	Ind	NZ	Pak	S Af	SL	WI
CG Macartney	35	55	4	2131	170	9	7	41.78	1640	—	—	—	491	—	—
GR Marsh	36	66	3	2129	138	9	4	33.79	837	341	371	299	—	53	227
WH Ponsford	29	48	4	2122	266	6	7	48.23	1558	—	—	—	97	—	467
RM Cowper	27	46	2	2061	307	10	5	46.84	686	604	—	99	255	—	417
MA Noble	42	73	7	1997	133	16	1	30.26	1905	—	—	—	92	—	—
SR Waugh	39	60	10	1983	177*	13	3	39.66	843	85	301	136	—	287	331
BC Booth	29	48	6	1773	169	10	5	42.21	824	112	—	72	531	—	234
KC Wessels	24	42	1	1761	179	9	4	42.95	754	—	73	256	—	141	537
GM Ritchie	30	53	5	1690	146	7	3	35.21	666	231	344	205	—	—	244
J Darling	34	60	2	1657	178	8	3	28.57	1632	—	—	—	25	—	—
RB McCosker	25	46	5	1622	127	9	4	39.56	977	—	198	228	—	—	219
MA Taylor	15	27	2	1618	219	8	6	64.72	839	—	18	330	—	304	67
AP Sheahan	31	53	6	1594	127	7	2	33.91	341	506	49	194	247	—	257
WA Brown	22	35	1	1592	206*	9	4	46.82	980	128	67	—	417	—	—
KD Mackay	37	52	7	1507	89	13	—	33.49	497	273	—	73	375	—	289
RR Lindwall	61	84	13	1502	118	5	2	21.15	795	173	—	29	107	—	398
WB Phillips	27	48	2	1485	159	7	2	32.28	350	67	312	362	—	—	394
WAS Oldfield	54	80	17	1427	65*	4	—	22.65	1116	—	—	—	221	—	90
C Kelleway	26	42	4	1422	147	6	3	37.42	874	—	—	—	548	—	—
J Ryder	20	32	5	1394	201*	9	3	51.63	1060	—	—	—	334	—	—
J Dyson	30	58	7	1359	127*	5	2	26.65	489	178	229	220	—	—	243
HL Collins	19	31	1	1352	203	6	4	45.07	1012	—	—	—	340	—	—
BM Laird	21	40	2	1341	92	11	—	35.29	162	—	147	492	—	—	540
AK Davidson	44	61	7	1328	80	5	—	24.59	750	109	—	130	127	—	212
RA Duff	22	40	3	1317	146	6	2	35.59	1079	—	—	—	238	—	—
DW Hookes	23	41	3	1306	143*	8	1	34.37	700	76	59	—	—	143	328
JW Burke	24	44	7	1280	189	5	3	34.59	676	183	—	14	389	—	18
G Giffen	31	53	—	1238	161	6	1	23.36	1238	—	—	—	—	—	—
VS Ransford	20	38	6	1211	143*	7	1	37.84	893	—	—	—	318	—	—
AF Kippax	22	34	1	1192	146	8	2	36.12	753	—	—	—	162	—	277
JHW Fingleton	18	29	1	1189	136	3	5	42.46	671	—	—	—	518	—	—
R Edwards	20	32	3	1171	170*	9	2	40.38	805	—	—	161	—	—	205
JM Gregory	24	34	3	1146	119	7	2	36.97	941	—	—	—	205	—	—
AC Bannerman	28	50	2	1108	94	8	—	23.08	1108	—	—	—	—	—	—
AMJ Hilditch	18	34	—	1073	119	6	2	31.56	428	313	12	135	—	—	185
SG Barnes	13	19	2	1072	234	5	3	63.06	846	172	54	—	—	—	—
GRJ Matthews	21	34	6	1031	130	4	3	36.82	236	282	395	97	—	—	21
IW Johnson	45	66	12	1000	77	6	—	18.52	485	124	7	13	117	—	254

Runs against each Test Nation (header spanning Eng, Ind, NZ, Pak, S Af, SL, WI)

Highest Aggregates in a Series

Batsman	Opponent	Venue	Series	M	Inn	NO	Runs	HS	50	100	Avrge
DG Bradman	Eng	Eng	1930	5	7	—	974	334	—	4	139.14
MA Taylor	Eng	Eng	1989	6	11	1	839	219	5	2	83.90
RN Harvey	S Af	Aus	1952/53	5	9	—	834	205	3	4	92.66
DG Bradman	Eng	Aus	1936/37	5	9	—	810	270	1	3	90.00
DG Bradman	S Af	Aus	1931/32	5	5	1	806	299*	—	4	201.50
DG Bradman	Eng	Eng	1934	5	8	—	758	304	1	2	94.75
DG Bradman	Ind	Aus	1947/48	5	6	2	715	201	1	4	178.75
GS Chappell	WI	Aus	1975/76	6	11	5	702	182*	3	3	117.00
KD Walters	WI	Aus	1968/69	4	6	—	699	242	2	4	116.50
AR Morris	Eng	Eng	1948	5	9	1	696	196	3	3	87.00
DG Bradman	Eng	Aus	1946/47	5	8	1	680	234	3	2	97.14
WM Lawry	WI	Aus	1968/69	5	8	—	667	205	2	3	83.38
VT Trumper	S Af	Aus	1910/11	5	9	2	661	214*	2	2	94.43
RN Harvey	S Af	S Af	1949/50	5	8	3	660	178	1	4	132.00
RN Harvey	WI	WI	1954/55	5	7	1	650	204	1	3	108.33
KR Stackpole	Eng	Aus	1970/71	7	12	—	627	207	2	2	52.25
GS Chappell	Eng	Aus	1974/75	6	11	—	608	144*	5	2	55.27
AR Border	Eng	Eng	1985	6	11	2	597	196	1	2	66.33
KJ Hughes	Ind	Ind	1979/80	6	12	2	594	100	5	1	59.40
WM Lawry	Eng	Aus	1965/66	5	7	—	592	166	2	3	84.57
IR Redpath	WI	Aus	1975/76	6	11	—	575	103	2	3	52.27
VT Trumper	Eng	Aus	1903/04	5	10	1	574	185*	3	2	63.77
W Bardsley	S Af	Aus	1910/11	5	9	—	573	132	5	1	63.67
WH Ponsford	Eng	Eng	1934	4	7	1	569	266	1	2	94.83
DM Jones	Eng	Eng	1989	6	9	1	566	157	3	2	70.75
HL Collins	Eng	Aus	1920/21	5	9	—	557	162	3	2	61.89
GN Yallop	Pak	Aus	1983/84	5	6	—	554	268	1	2	92.33
IM Chappell	WI	Aus	1968/69	5	8	—	548	165	3	2	68.50
IM Chappell	WI	WI	1972/73	5	9	2	542	109	3	2	77.43
JM Taylor	Eng	Aus	1924/25	5	10	—	541	108	4	1	54.10
RB Simpson	Ind	Aus	1977/78	5	10	—	539	176	2	2	53.90
J Darling	Eng	Aus	1897/98	5	8	—	537	178	—	3	67.13
AR Border	Eng	Eng	1981	6	12	3	533	123*	3	2	59.22

Batsman	Opponent	Venue	Series	M	Inn	NO	Runs	HS	50	100	Avrge
BC Booth	S Af	Aus	1963/64	4	7	1	531	169	3	2	88.50
NC O'Neill	WI	Aus	1960/61	5	10	—	522	181	3	1	52.20
AR Border	Ind	Ind	1979/80	6	12	—	521	162	3	1	43.42
AR Border	WI	WI	1983/84	5	10	3	521	100*	4	1	74.43
C Hill	Eng	Aus	1901/02	5	10	—	521	99	4	—	52.10
CC McDonald	Eng	Aus	1958/59	5	9	1	519	170	1	2	64.88
WA Brown	Eng	Eng	1938	4	8	1	512	206*	1	2	73.14
DM Jones	Eng	Aus	1986/87	5	10	1	511	184*	3	1	56.78
DG Bradman	Eng	Eng	1948	5	9	2	508	173*	1	2	72.57
SR Waugh	Eng	Eng	1989	6	8	4	506	177*	1	2	126.50
KC Wessels	WI	Aus	1984/85	5	9	—	505	173	4	1	56.11
AR Morris	Eng	Aus	1946/47	5	8	1	503	155	1	3	71.86

Century on Debut

In 1st innings

Batsman	1st inns	2nd inns	Opponent	Venue	Series
C Bannerman	165+	4	England	Melbourne	1876/77
H Graham	107	—	England	Lord's	1893
RA Duff	32	104	England	Melbourne	1901/02
RJ Hartigan	48	116	England	Adelaide	1907/08
HL Collins	70	104	England	Sydney	1920/21
WH Ponsford	110	27	England	Sydney	1924/25
A Jackson	164	36	England	Adelaide	1928/29
JW Burke	12	101*	England	Adelaide	1950/51
KD Walters	155	—	England	Brisbane	1965/66
GS Chappell	108	—	England	Perth	1970/71
GJ Cosier	109	—	West Indies	Melbourne	1975/76
DM Wellham	24	103	England	The Oval	1981
KC Wessels	162	46	England	Brisbane	1982/83
WB Phillips	159	—	Pakistan	Perth	1983/84

Highest Individual Test Innings

Batsman	Venue	Series	Eng	Ind	Opponent NZ	Pak	S Af	SL	WI
DG Bradman	Leeds	1930	334	—	—	—	—	—	—
RB Simpson	Manchester	1964	311	—	—	—	—	—	—
RM Cowper	Melbourne	1965/66	307	—	—	—	—	—	—
DG Bradman	Leeds	1934	304	—	—	—	—	—	—
DG Bradman	Adelaide	1931/32	—	—	—	—	299*	—	—
DG Bradman	Melbourne	1936/37	270	—	—	—	—	—	—
GN Yallop	Melbourne	1983/84	—	—	—	268	—	—	—
WH Ponsford	The Oval	1934	266	—	—	—	—	—	—
DG Bradman	Lord's	1930	254	—	—	—	—	—	—
KD Walters	Christchurch	1976/77	—	—	250	—	—	—	—
GS Chappell	Wellington	1973/74	—	—	247*	—	—	—	—
DG Bradman	The Oval	1934	244	—	—	—	—	—	—
KD Walters	Sydney	1968/69	—	—	—	—	—	—	242
GS Chappell	Faisalabad	1979/80	—	—	—	235	—	—	—
SG Barnes	Sydney	1946/47	234	—	—	—	—	—	—
DG Bradman	Sydney	1946/47	234	—	—	—	—	—	—
DG Bradman	The Oval	1930	232	—	—	—	—	—	—
SJ McCabe	Nottingham	1938	232	—	—	—	—	—	—
DG Bradman	Brisbane	1931/32	—	—	—	—	226	—	—
RB Simpson	Adelaide	1965/66	225	—	—	—	—	—	—
DG Bradman	Brisbane	1930/31	—	—	—	—	—	—	223
MA Taylor	Nottingham	1989	219	—	—	—	—	—	—
DM Jones	Adelaide	1988/89	—	—	—	—	—	—	216
VT Trumper	Adelaide	1910/11	—	—	—	—	214*	—	—
KJ Hughes	Adelaide	1980/81	—	213	—	—	—	—	—
DG Bradman	Adelaide	1936/37	212	—	—	—	—	—	—
WL Murdoch	The Oval	1884	211	—	—	—	—	—	—
WM Lawry	Bridgetown	1964/65	—	—	—	—	—	—	210
DM Jones	Madras	1986/87	—	210	—	—	—	—	—
KR Stackpole	Brisbane	1970/71	207	—	—	—	—	—	—
WA Brown	Lord's	1938	206*	—	—	—	—	—	—
AR Morris	Adelaide	1950/51	206	—	—	—	—	—	—
RN Harvey	Melbourne	1952/53	—	—	—	—	—	—	205
WM Lawry	Melbourne	1968/69	—	—	—	—	—	—	205
AR Border	Adelaide	1987/88	—	—	205	—	—	—	—
RN Harvey	Kingston	1954/55	—	—	—	—	—	—	204
GS Chappell	Sydney	1980/81	—	204	—	—	—	—	—

Continued

			Opponent						
Batsman	Venue	Series	Eng	Ind	NZ	Pak	S Af	SL	WI
HL Collins	Johannesburg	1921/22	—	—	—	—	203	—	—
SE Gregory	Sydney	1894/95	201	—	—	—	—	—	—
J Ryder	Adelaide	1924/25	201*	—	—	—	—	—	—
DG Bradman	Adelaide	1947/48	—	201	—	—	—	—	—
RB Simpson	Bridgetown	1964/65	—	—	—	—	—	—	201
GS Chappell	Brisbane	1981/82	—	—	—	201	—	—	—
DC Boon	Perth	1989/90	—	—	200	—	—	—	—

Australian Test Partnership Records

Wkt	Runs	Opponent	Batsmen	Venue	Series
1st	382	West Indies	WM Lawry, RB Simpson	Bridgetown	1964/65
2nd	451	England	WH Ponsford, DG Bradman	The Oval	1934
3rd	295	West Indies	CC McDonald, RN Harvey	Kingston	1954/55
4th	388	England	WH Ponsford, DG Bradman	Leeds	1934
5th	405	England	DG Bradman, SG Barnes	Sydney	1946/47
6th	346	England	DG Bradman, JHW Fingleton	Melbourne	1936/37
7th	217	New Zealand	KD Walters, CJ Gilmour	Christchurch	1976/77
8th	243	England	C Hill, RJ Hartigan	Adelaide	1907/08
9th	154	England	JM Blackham, SE Gregory	Sydney	1894/95
10th	127	England	JM Taylor, AA Mailey	Sydney	1924/25

Highest Wicket Partnerships

Wkt	Runs	Opponent	Batsmen	Venue	Series
2nd	451	England	WH Ponsford, DG Bradman	The Oval	1934
5th	405	England	SG Barnes, DG Bradman	Sydney	1946/47
4th	388	England	WH Ponsford, DG Bradman	Leeds	1934
1st	382	West Indies	WM Lawry, RB Simpson	Bridgetown	1964/65
6th	346	England	JHW Fingleton, DG Bradman	Melbourne	1936/37
4th	336	West Indies	WM Lawry, KD Walters	Sydney	1968/69
1st	329	England	GR Marsh, MA Taylor	Nottingham	1989
2nd	301	England	AR Morris, DG Bradman	Leeds	1948
2nd	298	West Indies	WM Lawry, IM Chappell	Melbourne	1968/69
3rd	295	West Indies	CC McDonald, RN Harvey	Kingston	1954/55
2nd	277	England	RB McCosker, IM Chappell	The Oval	1975
3rd	276	England	DG Bradman, AL Hassett	Brisbane	1946/47
2nd	275	England	CC McDonald, AL Hassett	Adelaide	1952/53
2nd	274	South Africa	WM Woodfull, DG Bradman	Melbourne	1931/32
3rd	264	New Zealand	IM Chappell, GS Chappell	Wellington	1973/74
6th	260*	Sri Lanka	DM Jones, SR Waugh	Hobart	1989/90
2nd	259	Pakistan	WB Phillips, GN Yallop	Perth	1983/84
4th	251	West Indies	GM Wood, CS Serjeant	Georgetown	1977/78
3rd	249	England	DG Bradman, SJ McCabe	Melbourne	1936/37
1st	244	England	RB Simpson, WM Lawry	Adelaide	1865/66
4th	243	England	DG Bradman, A Jackson	The Oval	1930
8th	243	England	RJ Hartigan, C Hill	Adelaide	1907/08
3rd	242	South Africa	C Kelleway, W Bardsley	Lord's	1912
2nd	236	India	SG Barnes, DG Bradman	Adelaide	1947/48
2nd	235	England	WM Woodfull, CG Macartney	Leeds	1926
4th	235	West Indies	AL Hassett, KR Miller	Sydney	1951/52
1st	233	South Africa	JHW Fingleton, WA Brown	Cape Town	1935/36
2nd	233	Pakistan	AP Sheahan, J Benaud	Melbourne	1972/73
2nd	231	England	WM Woodfull, DG Bradman	Lord's	1930
3rd	229	England	DG Bradman, AF Kippax	Leeds	1930
2nd	229	West Indies	WH Ponsford, DG Bradman	Brisbane	1930/31
3rd	225	West Indies	RM Cowper, DC Booth	Port—of—Spain	1964/65
2nd	224	South Africa	W Bardsley, C Hill	Sydney	1910/11
3rd	224	West Indies	RN Harvey, KR Miller	Kingston	1954/55
5th	223*	India	AR Morris, DG Bradman	Melbourne	1947/48
3rd	222	India	AR Border, KJ Hughes	Madras	1979/80
4th	221	England	GHS Trott, SE Gregory	Lord's	1896
5th	220	West Indies	KR Miller, RG Archer	Kingston	1954/55
2nd	220	England	IR Redpath, GS Chappell	Sydney	1974/75
1st	219	South Africa	WM Lawry, IR Redpath	Melbourne	1963/64
5th	219	England	RB Simpson, BC Booth	Manchester	1964
6th	219	England	IR Redpath, GS Chappell	Perth	1970/71
2nd	217	West Indies	WM Lawry, IM Chappell	Brisbane	1968/69
7th	217	New Zealand	KD Walters, CJ Gilmour	Christchurch	1976/77
4th	217	Pakistan	GS Chappell, GN Yallop	Faisalabad	1979/80
1st	217	India	DC Boon, GR Marsh	Sydney	1985/86
5th	216	England	AR Border, GM Ritchie	Lord's	1985
2nd	215	England	WM Woodfull, HSTL Hendry	Sydney	1928/29
1st	214	South Africa	AR Morris, JR Moroney	Johannesburg	1949/50

Wkt	Runs	Opponent	Batsmen	Venue	Series
4th	214	West Indies	DM Jones, AR Border	Adelaide	1988/89
5th	213	New Zealand	GM Ritchie, GRJ Matthews	Wellington	1985/86
3rd	212	England	WM Lawry, RM Cowper	Melbourne	1965/66
4th	210	West Indies	IR Redpath, KD Walters	Sydney	1968/69
3rd	209	South Africa	HL Collins, JM Gregory	Johannesburg	1921/22
3rd	209	England	KR Stackpole, KD Walters	Brisbane	1970/71
3rd	207	England	WL Murdoch, HJH Scott	The Oval	1884
3rd	207	India	RN Harvey, NC O'Neill	Bombay	1959/60
6th	206	West Indies	KR Miller, RG Archer	Bridgetown	1954/55
3rd	206	India	GN Yallop, KJ Hughes	Calcutta	1979/80
2nd	204	India	JW Burke, RN Harvey	Bombay	1956/57
3rd	203	Pakistan	GN Yallop, KJ Hughes	Melbourne	1983/84
3rd	202	South Africa	C Kelleway, W Bardsley	Manchester	1912
3rd	202	England	AR Morris, RN Harvey	Brisbane	1954/55
2nd	202	England	KR Stackpole, IM Chappell	Adelaide	1970/71
1st	201	England	WM Lawry, RB Simpson	Manchester	1964
3rd	201	England	IM Chappell, GS Chappell	The Oval	1972
5th	200	West Indies	GM Wood, SR Waugh	Perth	1988/89

Australia's Leading Test Wicket-Takers

Bowler	M	Balls	Mdns	Runs	Wkts	Avrge	5wi	10m	Best	Eng	Ind	NZ	Pak	S Af	SL	WI
DK Lillee	70	18467	652	8493	355	23.92	23	7	7/83	167	21	38	71	—	3	55
R Benaud	63	19108	805	6704	248	27.03	16	1	7/72	83	52	—	19	52	—	42
GD McKenzie	61	17684	547	7328	246	29.79	16	3	8/71	96	47	—	15	41	—	47
RR Lindwall	61	13642	419	5251	228	23.03	12	—	7/38	114	36	2	4	31	—	41
CV Grimmett	37	14513	736	5231	216	24.22	21	7	7/40	106	—	—	—	77	—	33
JR Thomson	51	10535	300	5602	200	28.01	8	—	6/46	100	22	6	10	—	—	62
AK Davidson	44	11587	431	3819	186	20.53	14	2	7/93	84	30	—	14	25	—	33
GF Lawson	46	11118	386	5501	180	30.56	11	2	8/112	97	—	10	33	—	1	39
KR Miller	55	10474	337	3905	170	22.97	7	1	7/60	87	9	2	2	30	—	40
WA Johnston	40	11048	372	3826	160	23.91	7	—	6/44	75	16	—	—	44	—	25
TM Alderman	36	9152	395	4083	153	26.69	13	1	6/128	84	—	16	23	—	5	25
WJ O'Reilly	27	10024	585	3254	144	22.60	11	3	7/54	102	—	8	—	34	—	—
H Trumble	32	8099	452	3072	141	21.79	9	3	8/65	141	—	—	—	—	—	—
MHN Walker	34	10094	380	3792	138	27.48	6	—	8/143	56	—	28	17	—	—	37
AA Mallett	39	9990	419	3940	132	29.85	6	1	8/59	50	28	19	13	6	—	16
B Yardley	33	8909	379	3986	126	31.63	6	1	7/98	29	21	13	21	—	7	35
RM Hogg	38	7633	230	3503	123	28.48	6	2	6/74	56	15	10	19	—	1	22
MA Noble	42	7109	361	3027	121	25.02	9	2	7/17	115	—	—	—	6	—	—
IW Johnson	45	8780	330	3182	109	29.19	3	—	7/44	42	19	—	4	22	—	22
G Giffen	31	6325	434	2791	103	27.10	7	1	7/117	103	—	—	—	—	—	—
AN Connolly	30	7818	289	2981	102	29.23	4	—	6/47	25	31	—	—	26	—	20
CTB Turner	17	5195	457	1670	101	16.53	11	2	7/43	101	—	—	—	—	—	—

Most Wickets in a Series

Bowler	Opponent	Venue	Series	M	Overs	Mdns	Runs	Wkts	Avrge	5wi	10m	Best
CV Grimmett	South Africa	South Africa	1935/36	5	346.1	140	642	44	14.59	5	3	7/40
TM Alderman	England	England	1981	6	325.0	76	893	42	21.26	4	—	6/135
RM Hogg	England	Australia	1978/79	6	217.4	60	527	41	12.85	5	2	6/74
TM Alderman	England	England	1989	6	269.2	68	712	41	17.37	6	1	6/128
DK Lillee	England	England	1981	6	311.4	81	870	39	22.31	2	1	7/89
WJ Whitty	South Africa	Australia	1910/11	5	232.3	55	632	37	17.08	2	—	6/17
AA Mailey	England	Australia	1920/21	5	244.1	27	946	36	26.28	4	2	9/121
GF Lawson	England	Australia	1982/83	5	230.4	51	687	34	20.21	4	1	6/47
G Giffen	England	Australia	1894/95	5	343.2	111	820	34	24.12	3	—	6/155
CV Grimmett	South Africa	Australia	1931/32	5	306.0	108	557	33	16.88	3	1	7/83
JR Thomson	England	Australia	1974/75	5	175.1	34	592	33	17.94	2	—	6/46
CV Grimmett	West Indies	Australia	1930/31	5	239.2	61	593	33	17.97	2	1	7/87
AK Davidson	West Indies	Australia	1960/61	4	173.7	25	612	33	18.55	5	1	6/53
MA Noble	England	Australia	1901/02	5	230.0	68	608	32	19.00	4	1	7/17
HV Hordern	England	Australia	1911/12	5	277.3	43	780	32	24.38	4	2	7/90
H Ironmonger	South Africa	South Africa	1931/32	4	221.5	112	296	31	9.55	3	1	6/18
DK Lillee	England	England	1972	5	249.5	83	548	31	17.68	3	1	6/66
R Benaud	England	Australia	1958/59	5	233.2	65	584	31	18.84	2	—	5/83

Continued

Bowler	Opponent	Venue	Series	M	Overs	Mdns	Runs	Wkts	Avrge	5wi	10m	Best
JV Saunders	England	Australia	1907/08	5	267.1	52	716	31	23.10	3	—	5/28
R Benaud	South Africa	South Africa	1957/58	5	242.1	56	658	30	21.93	4	—	5/49
GD McKenzie	West Indies	Australia	1968/69	5	206.1	27	758	30	25.27	1	1	8/71
CJ McDermott	England	England	1985	6	234.2	21	901	30	30.03	2	—	8/141

Three Wickets in Four Balls

Bowler	Opponent	Venue	Series
FR Spofforth	England	The Oval	1882
FR Spofforth	England	Sydney	1884/85
WH Howell	South Africa	Cape Town	1902/03
JM Gregory	England	Nottingham	1921
WJ O'Reilly	England	Manchester	1934
RR Lindwall	England	Adelaide	1946/47
R Benaud	West Indies	Georgetown	1954/55
JW Martin	West Indies	Melbourne	1960/61
KD Mackay	England	Birmingham	1961
GD McKenzie	West Indies	Port-of-Spain	1964/65
DK Lillee	England	Manchester	1972
DK Lillee	England	The Oval	1972
MG Hughes	West Indies	Perth	1988/89
CG Rackemann	Pakistan	Adelaide	1989/90

Best Innings Bowling Performance on Debut

Bowler	1st inns	2nd inns	Opponent	Venue	Series
TK Kendall	1/54	7/55	England	Melbourne	1876/77
WE Midwinter	5/78	1/23	England	Melbourne	1876/77
WH Cooper	3/80	6/120	England	Melbourne	1881/82
CTB Turner	6/15	2/53	England	Sydney	1886/87
JJ Ferris	4/27	5/76	England	Sydney	1886/87
RW McLeod	5/55	1/39	England	Melbourne	1891/92
AE Trott	-/9	8/43	England	Adelaide	1894/95
MA Noble	1/31	6/49	England	Melbourne	1897/98
JV Saunders	4/119	5/43	England	Sydney	1901/02
JDA O'Connor	3/110	5/40	England	Adelaide	1907/08
HV Hordern	3/39	5/66	South Africa	Melbourne	1910/11
CV Grimmett	5/45	6/37	England	Sydney	1924/25
TW Wall	3/123	5/66	England	Melbourne	1928/29
FA Ward	2/138	6/102	England	Brisbane	1936/37
I Meckiff	5/125	3/52	South Africa	Johannesburg	1957/58
GD McKenzie	1/81	5/37	England	Lord's	1961
DK Lillee	5/84	-/40	England	Adelaide	1970/71
RAL Massie	8/84	8/53	England	Lord's	1972
G Dymock	2/44	5/58	New Zealand	Adelaide	1973/74
MF Malone	5/63	1/14	England	The Oval	1977
RM Hogg	6/74	1/35	England	Brisbane	1978/79
TM Alderman	4/68	5/62	England	Nottingham	1981
TG Hogan	1/50	5/66	Sri Lanka	Kandy	1982/83
PL Taylor	6/78	2/76	England	Sydney	1986/87
AIC Dodemaide	1/48	6/58	New Zealand	Melbourne	1987/88

Best Match Bowling Performance on Debut

Bowler	Wkts	1st inns	2nd inns	Opponent	Venue	Series
RAL Massie	16/137	8/84	8/53	England	Lord's	1972
CV Grimmett	11/82	5/45	6/37	England	Sydney	1924/25
JJ Ferris	9/103	4/27	4/27	England	Sydney	1886/87
TM Alderman	9/130	4/68	5/62	England	Nottingham	1981
JV Saunders	9/162	4/119	5/43	England	Sydney	1901/02
WH Cooper	9/200	3/80	6/120	England	Melbourne	1881/82
JDA O'Connor	8/50	3/10	5/40	England	Adelaide	1907/08
AE Trott	8/52	-/9	8/43	England	Adelaide	1894/95
CTB Turner	8/68	6/15	2/53	England	Sydney	1886/87
LC Mayne	8/99	4/43	4/56	West Indies	Kingston	1964/65
HV Hordern	8/105	3/39	5/66	South Africa	Melbourne	1910/11
T Kendall	8/109	1/54	7/55	England	Melbourne	1876/77
WM Clark	8/147	4/46	4/101	India	Brisbane	1977/78
PL Taylor	8/154	6/78	2/76	England	Sydney	1986/87
I Meckiff	8/177	5/125	3/52	South Africa	Johannesburg	1957/58
TW Wall	8/189	3/123	5/66	England	Melbourne	1928/29
FA Ward	8/240	2/138	6/102	England	Brisbane	1936/37

Most Catches by a Fieldsman

Player	Tests	Catches	Eng	Ind	Opponent NZ	Pak	S Af	SL	WI
AR Border	115	125	45	9	25	22	—	6	18
GS Chappell	88	122	61	5	18	22	—	—	16
RB Simpson	62	110	30	21	—	3	27	—	29
IM Chappell	76	105	31	17	16	6	11	—	24
IR Redpath	67	83	29	17	1	8	6	—	22
R Benaud	63	65	32	5	—	2	15	—	11
RN Harvey	79	64	25	17	—	6	6	—	10
KJ Hughes	70	50	12	10	9	10	—	—	9

Most Catches in a Series

Player	Venue	Series	Tests	Ct	Eng	Ind	Opponent NZ	Pak	S Af	SL	WI
JM Gregory	Australia	1920/21	5	15	15	—	—	—	—	—	—
GS Chappell	Australia	1974/75	6	14	14	—	—	—	—	—	—
RB Simpson	South Africa	1957/58	5	13	—	—	—	—	13	—	—
RB Simpson	Australia	1960/61	5	13	—	—	—	—	—	—	13
DF Whatmore	India	1979/80	5	12	—	12	—	—	—	—	—
AR Border	England	1981	6	12	12	—	—	—	—	—	—
RB Simpson	Australia	1964/65	5	11	—	—	—	—	—	—	11
IM Chappell	Australia	1974/75	6	11	11	—	—	—	—	—	—
IR Redpath	Australia	1974/75	6	11	11	—	—	—	—	—	—
AR Border	England	1985	6	11	11	—	—	—	—	—	—

Most Catches in a Match

Player	Venue	Series	Eng	Ind	Opponent NZ	Pak	S Af	SL	WI
GS Chappell	Perth	1974/75	7	—	—	—	—	—	—
JM Gregory	Sydney	1920/21	6	—	—	—	—	—	—
VY Richardson	Durban	1935/36	—	—	—	—	6	—	—
RN Harvey	Sydney	1962/63	6	—	—	—	—	—	—
IM Chappell	Adelaide	1973/74	—	—	6	—	—	—	—
DF Whatmore	Kanpur	1979/80	—	6	—	—	—	—	—

Most Catches in an Innings

Player	Venue	Series	Eng	Ind	Opponent NZ	Pak	S Af	SL	WI
VY Richardson	Durban	1935/36	—	—	—	—	5	—	—
H Trumble	Lord's	1899	4	—	—	—	—	—	—
SJE Loxton	Brisbane	1950/51	4	—	—	—	—	—	—
GB Hole	Sydney	1952/53	—	—	—	—	4	—	—
RG Archer	Georgetown	1954/55	—	—	—	—	—	—	4
AK Davidson	Delhi	1959/60	—	4	—	—	—	—	—
RB Simpson	Sydney	1960/61	—	—	—	—	—	—	4
RN Harvey	Sydney	1962/63	4	—	—	—	—	—	—
RB Simpson	Bridgetown	1964/65	—	—	—	—	—	—	4
IM Chappell	Adelaide	1973/74	—	—	4	—	—	—	—
A Turner	Sydney	1976/77	—	—	—	4	—	—	—
DF Whatmore	Kanpur	1979/80	—	4	—	—	—	—	—
AR Border	Karachi	1979/80	—	—	—	4	—	—	—
KJ Hughes	Perth	1980/81	—	—	4	—	—	—	—
DC Boon	Karachi	1988/89	—	—	—	4	—	—	—

Australian Test Wicket-Keepers

Keeper	M	Inns Kept	Dis	Ct	St	Eng	Ind	Opponent NZ	Pak	S Af	SL	WI
RW Marsh	97	181	355	343	12	148	16	58	68	—	—	65
ATW Grout	51	97	187	163	24	76	20	—	17	—	—	41
WAS Oldfield	54	96	130	78	52	90	—	—	—	30	—	13
GRA Langley	26	50	98	83	15	37	3	—	3	14	—	41
H Carter	28	58	65	44	21	52	—	—	—	13	—	—
JJ Kelly	36	67	63	43	20	55	—	—	—	8	—	—
HB Taber	16	29	60	56	4	2	14	—	—	38	—	6
JM Blackham	35	56	60	36	24	60	—	—	—	—	—	—
D Tallon	21	41	58	50	8	42	14	2	—	—	—	—
IA Healy	21	38	57	55	2	14	—	7	20	—	4	12
BN Jarman	19	35	54	50	4	18	19	—	4	—	—	13
SJ Rixon	13	23	47	42	5	—	22	—	—	—	—	25

Continued

Keeper	M	Inns Kept	Dis	Ct	St	Eng	Ind	NZ	Pak	S Af	SL	WI
WB Phillips	27	27	43	43	—	11	8	7	—	—	—	17
KJ Wright	10	15	35	31	4	8	13	—	14	—	—	—
RA Saggers	6	10	24	16	8	3	—	—	—	21	—	—
GC Dyer	6	11	24	22	2	5	—	13	—	—	6	—
TJ Zoehrer	10	17	19	18	1	10	4	5	—	—	—	—
LV Maddocks	7	10	19	18	1	13	4	—	—	—	—	2
AH Jarvis	11	15	17	9	8	17	—	—	—	—	—	—
JA Maclean	4	7	18	18	—	18	—	—	—	—	—	—
RD Woolley	2	2	7	7	—	—	—	—	—	—	5	2
W Carkeek	6	8	6	6	—	2	—	—	—	6	—	—
BA Barnett	4	6	5	3	2	5	—	—	—	—	—	—
HSB Love	1	1	3	3	—	3	—	—	—	—	—	—
WL Murdoch	18	1	2	1	1	2	—	—	—	—	—	—
FJ Burton	2	1	2	1	1	2	—	—	—	—	—	—

Most Dismissals in a Series

Keeper	Venue	Series	Tests	Ct/St	Eng	Ind	NZ	Pak	S Af	SL	WI
RW Marsh	Australia	1982/83	5	28/-	28	—	—	—	—	—	—
RW Marsh	Australia	1975/76	6	26/-	—	—	—	—	—	—	26
ATW Grout	Australia	1960/61	5	20/3	—	—	—	—	—	—	23
RW Marsh	England	1972	5	21/2	23	—	—	—	—	—	—
RW Marsh	England	1981	6	23/-	—	—	—	—	—	—	—
SJ Rixon	Australia	1977/78	5	22/-	—	22	—	—	—	—	—
RA Saggers	South Africa	1949/50	5	13/8	—	—	—	—	21	—	—
GRA Langley	Australia	1951/52	5	16/5	—	—	—	—	—	—	21
ATW Grout	England	1961	5	20/1	21	—	—	—	—	—	—
RW Marsh	Australia	1983/84	5	21/-	—	—	—	21	—	—	—
D Tallon	Australia	1946/47	5	16/4	20	—	—	—	—	—	—
GRA Langley	West Indies	1954/55	4	16/4	—	—	—	—	—	—	20
ATW Grout	Australia	1958/59	5	17/3	20	—	—	—	—	—	—
HB Taber	South Africa	1966/67	5	19/1	—	—	—	—	20	—	—

Most Dismissals in a Match

Keeper	Venue	Series	Ct/St	Eng	Ind	NZ	Pak	S Af	SL	WI
GRA Langley	Lord's	1956	8/1	9	—	—	—	—	—	—
RW Marsh	Brisbane	1982/83	9/-	9	—	—	—	—	—	—
JJ Kelly	Sydney	1901/02	8/-	8	—	—	—	—	—	—
GRA Langley	Kingston	1954/55	8/-	—	—	—	—	—	—	8
ATW Grout	Lahore	1959/60	6/2	—	—	—	8	—	—	—
ATW Grout	Lord's	1961	8/-	8	—	—	—	—	—	—
HB Taber	Johannesburg	1966/67	7/1	—	—	—	—	8	—	—
RW Marsh	Melbourne	1975/76	8/-	—	—	—	—	—	—	8
RW Marsh	Christchurch	1976/77	8/-	—	—	8	—	—	—	—
RW Marsh	Sydney	1980/81	7/1	—	8	—	—	—	—	—
RW Marsh	Adelaide	1982/83	8/-	8	—	—	—	—	—	—
RA Saggers	Cape Town	1949/50	4/3	—	—	—	—	7	—	—
GRA Langley	Brisbane	1951/52	3/4	—	—	—	—	—	—	7
ATW Grout	Brisbane	1960/61	6/1	—	—	—	—	—	—	7
BN Jarman	Brisbane	1968/69	7/-	—	—	—	—	—	—	7
HB Taber	Johannesburg	1969/70	6/1	—	—	—	—	7	—	—
RW Marsh	Melbourne	1973/74	6/1	—	—	7	—	—	—	—
RW Marsh	Christchurch	1973/74	7/-	—	—	7	—	—	—	—
KJ Wright	Melbourne	1978/79	7/-	—	—	—	7	—	—	—
KJ Wright	Perth	1978/79	7/-	—	—	—	7	—	—	—
RW Marsh	Birmingham	1981	7/-	7	—	—	—	—	—	—
RW Marsh	Perth	1981/82	7/-	—	—	—	7	—	—	—
SJ Rixon	Adelaide	1984/85	7/-	—	—	—	—	—	—	7
IA Healy	Adelaide	1989/90	7/-	—	—	—	7	—	—	—

Most Dismissals in an Innings

Keeper	Venue	Series	Ct/St	Eng	Ind	NZ	Pak	S Af	SL	WI
ATW Grout	Johannesburg	1957/58	6/-	—	—	—	—	6	—	—
RW Marsh	Brisbane	1982/83	6/-	6	—	—	—	—	—	—
WAS Oldfield	Melbourne	1924/25	4/1	5	—	—	—	—	—	—
GRA Langley	Georgetown	1954/55	2/3	—	—	—	—	—	—	5
GRA Langley	Kingston	1954/55	5/-	—	—	—	—	—	—	5
GRA Langley	Lord's	1956	5/-	5	—	—	—	—	—	—
ATW Grout	Durban	1957/58	4/1	—	—	—	—	5	—	—

Keeper	Venue	Series	Tests	Ct/St	Eng	Opponent Ind	NZ	Pak	S Af	SL	WI
ATW Grout	Lahore	1959/60	5/-	—	—	—	—	5	—	—	—
ATW Grout	Brisbane	1960/61	4/1	—	—	—	—	—	—	—	5
ATW Grout	Lord's	1961	5/-	5	—	—	—	—	—	—	—
ATW Grout	Sydney	1965/66	5/-	5	—	—	—	—	—	—	—
HB Taber	Johannesburg	1966/67	5/-	—	—	—	—	—	5	—	—
HB Taber	Sydney	1968/69	5/-	—	—	—	—	—	—	—	5
HB Taber	Port Elizabeth	1969/70	5/-	—	—	—	—	—	5	—	—
RW Marsh	Manchester	1972	5/-	5	—	—	—	—	—	—	—
RW Marsh	Nottingham	1972	5/-	5	—	—	—	—	—	—	—
RW Marsh	Sydney	1973/74	5/-	—	—	5	—	—	—	—	—
RW Marsh	Christchurch	1973/74	5/-	—	—	5	—	—	—	—	—
RW Marsh	Melbourne	1975/76	5/-	—	—	—	—	—	—	—	5
RW Marsh	Christchurch	1976/77	5/-	—	—	5	—	—	—	—	—
JA Maclean	Brisbane	1978/79	5/-	5	—	—	—	—	—	—	—
KJ Wright	Melbourne	1978/79	5/-	—	—	—	5	—	—	—	—
RW Marsh	Brisbane	1979/80	5/-	—	—	—	—	—	—	—	5
RW Marsh	Sydney	1980/81	5/-	—	5	—	—	—	—	—	—
RW Marsh	Perth	1981/82	5/-	—	—	—	5	—	—	—	—
RW Marsh	Perth	1983/84	5/-	—	—	—	5	—	—	—	—
RW Marsh	Sydney	1983/84	5/-	—	—	—	5	—	—	—	—
WB Phillips	Kingston	1983/84	5/-	—	—	—	—	—	—	—	5
IA Healy	Adelaide	1989/90	5/-	—	—	—	5	—	—	—	—

Australian Test Captaincy Records

Captain	Tests as Captain	Eng	Ind	Opponent NZ	Pak	S Af	SL	WI	Won	Results Lost	Drawn	Tie	Won Toss
DW Gregory	3	3	—	—	—	—	—	—	2	1	—	—	2
WL Murdoch	16	16	—	—	—	—	—	—	5	7	4	—	7
TP Horan	2	2	—	—	—	—	—	—	—	2	—	—	1
HH Massie	1	1	—	—	—	—	—	—	1	—	—	—	1
JM Blackham	8	8	—	—	—	—	—	—	3	3	2	—	4
HJH Scott	3	3	—	—	—	—	—	—	—	3	—	—	1
PS McDonnell	6	6	—	—	—	—	—	—	2	5	—	—	4
G Giffen	4	4	—	—	—	—	—	—	2	2	—	—	3
GHS Trott	8	8	—	—	—	—	—	—	5	3	—	—	5
J Darling	21	18	—	—	—	3	—	—	7	4	10	—	7
H Trumble	2	2	—	—	—	—	—	—	2	—	—	—	1
MA Noble	15	15	—	—	—	—	—	—	8	5	2	—	11
C Hill	10	5	—	—	—	5	—	—	5	5	—	—	
SE Gregory	6	3	—	—	—	3	—	—	2	1	3	—	1
WW Armstrong	10	10	—	—	—	—	—	—	8	2	—	—	4
HL Collins	11	8	—	—	—	3	—	—	5	2	4	—	7
W Bardsley	2	2	—	—	—	—	—	—	—	—	2	—	1
J Ryder	5	5	—	—	—	—	—	—	1	4	—	—	2
WM Woodfull	25	15	—	—	—	5	—	5	14	7	4	—	12
VY Richardson	5	—	—	—	—	5	—	—	4	—	1	—	1
DG Bradman	24	19	5	—	—	—	—	—	15	3	6	—	10
WA Brown	1	—	—	1	—	—	—	—	1	—	—	—	—
AL Hassett	24	10	—	—	—	10	—	4	14	4	6	—	18
AR Morris	2	1	—	—	—	—	—	1	—	2	—	—	2
IW Johnson	17	9	2	—	1	—	—	5	7	5	5	—	6
RR Lindwall	1	—	1	—	—	—	—	—	—	1	—	—	—
ID Craig	5	—	—	—	—	5	—	—	3	—	2	—	3
R Benaud	28	14	5	—	3	1	—	5	12	4	11	1	11
RN Harvey	1	1	—	—	—	—	—	—	1	—	—	—	—
RB Simpson	39	8	10	2	—	9	—	10	12	12	15	—	19
BC Booth	2	2	—	—	—	—	—	—	—	1	1	—	1
WM Lawry	26	10	7	—	—	4	—	5	9	8	9	—	8
BN Jarman	1	1	—	—	—	—	—	—	—	—	1	—	1
IM Chappell	30	16	—	6	3	—	—	5	15	5	10	—	17
GS Chappell	48	15	3	8	9	—	1	12	21	13	14	—	29
GN Yallop	7	6	—	—	1	—	—	—	1	6	—	—	6
KJ Hughes	28	6	6	—	9	—	—	7	4	13	11	—	13
AR Border	52	18	6	11	6	—	3	8	7	14	19	1	26
Total	499	270	45	26	34	53	4	67	203	144	150	2	250

Most Consecutive Tests as Captain

Captain	Tests	Series
AR Border	52	1984/85 to 1989/90
IM Chappell	30	1970/71 to 1975
WM Lawry	26	1967/68 to 1970/71
WM Woodfull	25	1930 to 1934
R Benaud	19	1958/59 to 1961
RB Simpson	19	1963/64 to 1964/65
GS Chappell	17	1975/76 to 1977
GS Chappell	16	1979/80 to 1980/81
IW Johnson	15	1954/55 to 1956/57

Most Appearances by Australian Test Umpires

Umpire	Test Career	Tests	Eng	WI	NZ	Ind	Pak	S Af	SL
RM Crockett	1901/02–1924/25	32	27	—	—	—	—	5	—
CJ Egar	1960/61–1968/69	29	9	10	—	4	1	5	—
AR Crafter	1978/79–1989/90	29	7	7	5	2	7	—	1
RC Bailhache	1974/75–1988/89	27	12	6	3	2	3	—	1
LP Rowan	1962/63–1970/71	26	12	5	—	4	—	5	—
G Borwick	1930/31–1947/48	24	15	1	—	3	—	5	—
TF Brooks	1970/71–1978/79	24	14	4	1	2	3	—	—
MW Johnson	1979/80–1987/88	21	5	6	3	2	5	—	—
MG O'Connell	1970/71–1979/80	19	7	4	1	3	4	—	—
RA French	1977/78–1987/88	19	7	2	2	4	4	—	—
GA Hele	1928/29–1932/33	16	10	1	—	—	—	5	—
MJ McInnes	1951/52–1958/59	16	9	3	—	—	—	4	—
PJ McConnell	1983/84–1989/90	16	3	5	2	1	4	—	1

Australian Test Umpires

Umpire	Test Career	Tests	Eng	WI	NZ	Ind	Pak	S Af	SL
P Argall	1902/03–1907/08	7	7	—	—	—	—	—	—
H Armstrong	1930/31	1	—	1	—	—	—	—	—
RC Bailhache	1974/75–1988/89	27	12	6	3	2	3	—	1
C Bannerman	1887/88–1901/02	12	12	—	—	—	—	—	—
AN Barlow	1930/31–1951/52	11	4	3	—	4	—	—	—
G Borwick	1930/31–1947/48	24	15	1	—	3	—	5	—
TF Brooks	1970/71–1978/79	24	14	4	1	2	3	—	—
J Bryant	1884/85	1	1	—	—	—	—	—	—
R Callaway	1901/02	3	3	—	—	—	—	—	—
P Coady	1878/79	1	1	—	—	—	—	—	—
AF Cocks	1950/51	1	1	—	—	—	—	—	—
JR Collins	1972/73–1975/76	5	—	1	2	—	2	—	—
GC Cooper	1947/38–1950/51	2	1	—	—	1	—	—	—
WJ Copeland	1979/80	1	1	—	—	—	—	—	—
S Cosstick	1876/77	1	1	—	—	—	—	—	—
G Couthard	1878/79–1881/82	2	2	—	—	—	—	—	—
AR Crafter	1978/79–1989/90	29	7	7	5	2	7	—	1
RM Crockett	1901/02–1924/25	32	27	—	—	—	—	5	—
PM Cronin	1979/80	1	1	—	—	—	—	—	—
W Curran	1910/11–1911/12	2	1	—	—	—	—	1	—
G Downes	1891/92	1	1	—	—	—	—	—	—
CJ Egar	1960/61–1968/69	29	9	10	—	4	1	5	—
D Elder	1910/11–1928/29	14	12	—	—	—	—	2	—
EH Elliott	1882/83–1884/85	6	6	—	—	—	—	—	—
H Elphinston	1947/48–1952/53	10	3	3	—	1	—	3	—
PR Enright	1972/73–1973/74	3	—	—	2	—	1	—	—
RJ Evans	1988/89–1989/90	3	—	1	1	—	1	—	—
I Fisher	1884/85	1	1	—	—	—	—	—	—
T Flynn	1892/93–1894/95	4	4	—	—	—	—	—	—
RA French	1977/78–1987/88	19	7	2	2	4	4	—	—
WG French	1930/31	2	—	2	—	—	—	—	—
C Garing	1924/25	1	1	—	—	—	—	—	—
W Hannah	1907/08–1910/11	3	2	—	—	—	—	1	—
CE Harvey	1978/79–1979/80	2	—	1	—	—	1	—	—
GA Hele	1928/29–1932/33	16	10	1	—	—	—	5	—
JH Hodges	1884/85	1	1	—	—	—	—	—	—
C Hoy	1954/55–1960/61	9	4	5	—	—	—	—	—
RC Isherwood	1984/85–1985/86	3	—	1	1	1	—	—	—
AG Jenkins	1930/31	1	—	1	—	—	—	—	—
MW Johnson	1979/80–1987/88	21	5	6	3	2	5	—	—
AC Jones	1903/04–1920/21	6	6	—	—	—	—	—	—

Umpire	Test Career	Tests	Eng	WI	NZ	Ind	Pak	S Af	SL
LJ King	1988/89–1989/90	3	—	1	—	—	1	—	1
J Laing	1907/08	1	1	—	—	—	—	—	—
RR Ledwidge	1975/76–1976/77	3	—	2	—	—	1	—	—
J Lillywhite, jr	1881/82–1884/85	5	5	—	—	—	—	—	—
A Mackley	1962/63	1	1	—	—	—	—	—	—
BM Martin	1985/86	1	—	—	1	—	—	—	—
PJ McConnell	1983/84–1989/90	16	3	5	2	1	4	—	1
MJ McInnes	1951/52–1958/59	16	9	3	—	—	—	4	—
PG McShane	1884/85	1	1	—	—	—	—	—	—
MG O'Connell	1970/71–1979/80	19	7	4	1	3	4	—	—
JP Orr	1930/31	1	—	1	—	—	—	—	—
E Payne	1884/85	1	1	—	—	—	—	—	—
J Phillips	1884/85–1897/98	13	13	—	—	—	—	—	—
TA Prue	1988/89	2	—	2	—	—	—	—	—
SG Randell	1985/86–1989/90	7	2	1	1	2	—	—	1
H Rawlinson	1886/87	1	1	—	—	—	—	—	—
CA Reid	1976/77	1	1	—	—	—	—	—	—
J Richards	1930/31	1	—	1	—	—	—	—	—
LP Rowan	1962/63–1970/71	26	12	5	—	4	—	5	—
JD Scott	1936/37–1947/48	10	10	—	—	—	—	—	—
G Searcy	1894/95	1	1	—	—	—	—	—	—
W Smyth	1961/62–1965/66	4	3	—	—	—	1	—	—
JS Swift	1881/82–1886/87	8	8	—	—	—	—	—	—
RB Terry	1876/77	2	2	—	—	—	—	—	—
CD Timmins	1989/90	1	—	—	—	—	—	—	1
J Tooher	1891/92	1	1	—	—	—	—	—	—
L Townsend	1958/59	1	1	—	—	—	—	—	—
N Townsend	1972/73	1	—	—	—	—	1	—	—
J Travers	1884/85	1	1	—	—	—	—	—	—
GA Watson	1910/11–1911/12	2	1	—	—	—	—	1	—
DG Weser	1978/79–1980/81	3	2	—	1	—	—	—	—
RV Whitehead	1980/81–1982/83	4	1	—	—	3	—	—	—
WO Whitridge	1891/92	1	1	—	—	—	—	—	—
AP Williams	1924/25	1	1	—	—	—	—	—	—
R Wright	1947/48–1958/59	13	7	2	—	1	—	3	—
AE Wyeth	1930/31	1	—	1	—	—	—	—	—
EF Wykes	1962/63	1	1	—	—	—	—	—	—
W Young	1911/12	1	1	—	—	—	—	—	—

Most Appearances by Australian First-Class Umpires

Umpire	First-Class Career	Games	Sheffield Shield	Tests	Other
RM Crockett	1891/92–1929/30	127	56	39	32
RC Bailhache	1971/72–1989/90	90	47	16	27
CJ Egar	1956/57–1970/71	88	43	16	29
AN Barlow	1928/29–1953/53	86	45	30	11
MG O'Connell	1967/68–1989/90	85	50	16	19
EG Borwick	1927/28–1948/49	83	31	28	24
AR Crafter	1974/75–1989/90	82	40	13	29
TF Brooks	1967/68–1978/79	77	38	15	24
LP Rowan	1958/59–1971/72	75	38	11	26
WF Wykes	1956/57–1971/72	71	54	16	1
RA French	1975/76–1988/89	69	43	7	19
PJ McConnell	1977/78–1989/90	69	43	10	16
MW Johnson	1977/78–1987/88	67	34	12	21
AC Jones	1902/03–1930/31	62	26	30	6
RR Wright	1945/46–1960/61	61	29	19	13
WJ Smyth	1955/56–1971/72	59	42	13	4
N Townsend	1960/61–1973/74	56	43	12	1
GA Hele	1920/21–1934/35	56	24	16	16
SG Randell	1980/81–1989/90	54	38	9	7
C Bannerman	1886/87–1901/02	53	14	27	12
J Phillips	1883/84–1897/98	52	8	31	13
JD Scott	1932/33–1947/48	51	22	19	10
A Mackley	1951/52–1964/65	51	35	15	1

Australians First-Class Cricket Tours Abroad

Season	Touring Team	Country	Games	First-Class results				Captain
				W	L	D	T	
1878	Australia	England	15	7	4	4	—	DW Gregory
		North America	1	—	—	1	—	
1880	Australia	England	10	5	2	3	—	WL Murdoch

Continued

Season	Touring Team	Country	Games	W	L	D	T	Captain
				First-Class results				
1882	Australia	England	33	18	4	11	—	WL Murdoch
1883/84	Tasmania	New Zealand	4	—	3	1	—	JG Davis
1884	Australia	England	31	17	7	7	—	WL Murdoch
1886	Australia	England	37	9	7	21	—	HJH Scott
1888	Australia	England	37	17	13	7	—	PS McDonnell
1889/90	New South Wales	New Zealand	5	4	—	1	—	J Davis
1890	Australia	England	34	10	16	8	—	WL Murdoch
1893	Australia	England	31	14	10	7	—	JM Blackham
		North America	3	2	1	—	—	
1893/94	New South Wales	New Zealand	7	4	1	2	—	J Davis
1895/96	New South Wales	New Zealand	5	3	1	1	—	LT Cobcroft
1896	Australia	England	34	20	6	8	—	GHS Trott
		North America	3	2	1	—	—	
1896/97	Australia	New Zealand	5	3	1	1	—	OC Hitchcock
1899	Australia	England	35	16	3	16	—	J Darling
1902	Australia	England	38	22	2	14	—	J Darling
		South Africa	4	3	—	1	—	
1904/05	Australia	New Zealand	4	3	—	1	—	MA Noble
1905	Australia	England	35	15	3	17	—	J Darling
1909	Australia	England	37	11	4	22	—	MA Noble
1909/10	Australia	New Zealand	6	5	—	1	—	WW Armstrong
1912	Australia	England	36	9	8	19	—	SE Gregory
		North America	2	1	1	—	—	
1913	Australia	North America	5	4	—	1	—	A Diamond
1913/14	New South Wales	Ceylon	1	1	—	—	—	EF Waddy
1913/14	Australia	New Zealand	8	6	—	2	—	A Sims
1919	Australia	England	28	12	4	12	—	HL Collins
		South Africa	8	6	—	2	—	
1920/21	Australia	New Zealand	9	6	—	3	—	VS Ransford
1921	Australia	England	34	21	2	11	—	WW Armstrong
		South Africa	6	4	—	2	—	
1923/24	New South Wales	New Zealand	6	5	—	1	—	CG Macartney
1924/25	Victoria	New Zealand	6	1	1	4	—	ER Mayne
1926	Australia	England	33	9	1	23	—	HL Collins
1927/28	Australia	New Zealand	6	4	—	2	—	VY Richardson
1930	Australia	England	31	11	1	18	1	WM Woodfull
1934	Australia	England	30	13	1	16	—	WM Woodfull
1935/36	FA Tarrants XI	Ceylon	1	1	—	—	—	J Ryder
		India	16	9	3	4	—	
1935/36	Australia	South Africa	16	13	—	3	—	VY Richardson
1938	Australia	England	29	15	2	12	—	DG Bradman
1945	Australia	England	6	1	2	5	—	AL Hassett
		India	8	2	2	4	—	
		Ceylon	1	1	—	—	—	
1945/46	Australia	New Zealand	5	5	—	—	—	WA Brown
1948	Australia	England	31	23	—	8	—	DG Bradman
1949/50	Australia	South Africa	21	14	—	7	—	AL Hassett
1949/50	Australia	New Zealand	5	3	—	2	—	WA Brown
1953	Australia	England	33	16	1	16	—	AL Hassett
1954/55	Australia	West Indies	9	5	—	4	—	IW Johnson
1956	Australia	England	31	9	3	19	—	IW Johnson
		Pakistan	1	—	1	—	—	
		India	3	2	—	1	—	
1956/57	Australia	New Zealand	7	5	—	2	—	ID Craig
1957/58	Australia	South Africa	20	11	—	9	—	ID Craig
1959/60	Australia	Pakistan	4	3	—	1	—	R Benaud
		India	7	2	1	4	—	
1959/60	Australia	New Zealand	6	2	—	4	—	ID Craig
1961	Australia	England	32	13	1	18	—	R Benaud
1964	Australia	England	30	11	3	16	—	RB Simpson
		India	3	1	1	1	—	
		Pakistan	1	—	—	1	—	
1964/65	Australia	West Indies	11	3	2	6	—	RB Simpson
1966/67	Australia	South Africa	17	7	5	5	—	RB Simpson
1966/67	Australia	New Zealand	9	1	2	6	—	LE Favell
1968	Australia	England	25	8	3	14	—	WM Lawry
1969/70	Australia	Ceylon	1	—	—	1	—	WM Lawry
		India	10	5	1	4	—	
		South Africa	12	4	4	4	—	
1969/70	Australia	New Zealand	8	2	—	6	—	SC Trimble
1972	Australia	England	26	11	5	10	—	IM Chappell
1972/73	Australia	West Indies	12	7	—	5	—	IM Chappell
1973/74	Australia	New Zealand	7	2	1	4	—	IM Chappell
1975	Australia	England	15	8	2	5	—	IM Chappell
1976/77	Australia	New Zealand	6	5	—	1	—	GS Chappell

				First-Class results				
Season	Touring Team	Country	Games	W	L	D	T	Captain
1977	Australia	England	22	5	4	13	—	GS Chappell
1977/78	Australia	West Indies	11	5	3	3	—	RB Simpson
1979/80	Australia	India	11	—	3	8	—	KJ Hughes
1979/80	Australia	Pakistan	5	—	1	4	—	GS Chappell
1980	Australia	England	5	1	2	2	—	GS Chappell
1981	Australia	Sri Lanka	1	—	—	1	—	KJ Hughes
		England	16	3	3	10	—	
1981/82	Australia	New Zealand	5	1	1	3	—	GS Chappell
1982/83	Australia	Pakistan	6	—	3	3	—	KJ Hughes
1982/83	Australia	Zimbabwe	2	1	1	—	—	DM Wellham
1982/83	Australia	Sri Lanka	2	1	—	1	—	GS Chappell
1983/84	Australia	West Indies	10	1	3	6	—	KJ Hughes
1985	Australia	England	20	4	3	13	—	AR Border
1985/86	Australia	Zimbabwe	2	1	—	1	—	RB Kerr
1985/86	Australia	South Africa	10	2	2	6	—	KJ Hughes
1985/86	Australia	New Zealand	5	1	1	3	—	AR Border
1985/86	New South Wales	Zimbabwe	2	1	—	1	—	GC Dyer
1986/87	Australia	India	7	—	—	6	1	AR Border
1986/87	Australia	South Africa	12	2	3	7	—	KJ Hughes
1986/87	New South Wales	Zimbabwe	2	—	—	2	—	DM Wellham
1988/89	Australia	Pakistan	6	—	1	5	—	AR Border
1989	Australia	England	20	12	1	7	—	AR Border
1989/90	Western Australia	India	1	—	—	1	—	GM Wood
1989/90	Australia	New Zealand	1	—	1	—	—	AR Border
in England			941	398	133	409	1	
in New Zealand			135	71	13	51	—	
in South Africa			126	66	14	46	—	
in India			66	20	11	34	1	
in West Indies			53	21	8	24	—	
in Pakistan			23	3	6	14	—	
in North America			14	9	3	2	—	
in Ceylon/Sri Lanka			7	4	—	3	—	
in Zimbabwe			8	3	1	4	—	
Total			1373	595	189	587	2	

SHEFFIELD SHIELD

Most Appearances

Player	State	Career	Seasons	Games
RJ Inverarity	WA/SA	1962/63–1984/85	23	159
SC Trimble	Qld	1959/60–1975/76	17	123
LE Favell	SA	1951/52–1969/70	19	120
HN Dansie	SA	1949/50–1966/67	18	107
PR Sleep	SA	1976/77–1989/90	14	105
GS Chappell	SA/Qld	1966/67–1983/84	18	101
RJ Bright	Vic	1972/73–1987/88	16	101
KD Mackay	Qld	1946/47–1963/64	18	100
DW Hookes	SA	1975/76–1989/90	15	100
GM Wood	WA	1977/78–1989/90	13	97
TV Hohns	Qld	1972/73–1988/89	17	95
SJ Rixon	NSW	1974/75–1987/88	14	94
IJ Brayshaw	WA	1960/61–1977/78	18	91
KD Walters	NSW	1962/63–1980/81	19	91
IM Chappell	SA	1961/62–1979/80	19	89
AMJ Hilditch	NSW/SA	1976/77–1989/90	14	88
TJ Jenner	WA/SA	1963/64–1976/77	14	87
ATW Grout	Qld	1946/47–1965/66	20	86
JA Maclean	Qld	1968/69–1978/79	11	86
RW Marsh	WA	1968/69–1983/84	14	86
WM Lawry	Vic	1955/56–1971/72	17	85
DF Whatmore	Vic	1975/76–1988/89	14	85
JR Thomson	NSW/Qld	1972/73–1985/86	14	84
GM Ritchie	Qld	1980/81–1989/90	10	84

Continued

Player	State	Career	Seasons	Games
PJP Burge	Qld	1952/53–1967/68	16	83
GF Lawson	NSW	1977/78–1989/90	13	83
J Dyson	NSW	1975/76–1988/89	14	82
BC Booth	NSW	1954/55–1968/69	15	81
PH Carlson	Qld	1969/70–1980/81	12	81
G Shipperd	WA/Tas	1977/78–1989/90	11	81

Most Games for Each State

State	Player	Career	Seasons	Games
New South Wales	SJ Rixon	1974/75–1987/88	14	94
Victoria	RJ Bright	1972/73–1987/88	16	101
South Australia	LE Favell	1951/52–1969/70	19	120
Queensland	SC Trimble	1959/60–1975/76	17	123
Western Australia	RJ Inverarity	1962/63–1978/79	17	108
Tasmania	DC Boon	1978/79–1989/90	12	69

Highest Innings Totals

Total	Team	Opponent	Venue	Season
1107	Victoria	New South Wales	Melbourne	1926/27
918	New South Wales	South Australia	Sydney	1900/01
7d-821	South Australia	Queensland	Adelaide	1939/40
815	New South Wales	Victoria	Sydney	1908/09
807	New South Wales	South Australia	Adelaide	1899/00
805	New South Wales	Victoria	Melbourne	1905/06
802	New South Wales	South Australia	Sydney	1920/21
793	Victoria	Queensland	Melbourne	1927/28
786	New South Wales	South Australia	Adelaide	1922/23
770	New South Wales	South Australia	Adelaide	1920/21
8d-761	New South Wales	Queensland	Sydney	1929/30
6d-713	New South Wales	Victoria	Sydney	1928/29
724	Victoria	South Australia	Melbourne	1920/21
713	New South Wales	South Australia	Adelaide	1908/09
708	New South Wales	Victoria	Sydney	1925/26
705	New South Wales	Victoria	Melbourne	1925/26
699	Victoria	South Australia	Melbourne	1907/08
697	Victoria	South Australia	Adelaide	1945/46
690	New South Wales	South Australia	Adelaide	1919/20
687	Queensland	New South Wales	Brisbane Ex	1930/31
684	New South Wales	South Australia	Sydney	1923/24
681	New South Wales	South Australia	Sydney	1903/04
675	New South Wales	Victoria	Sydney	1913/14
673	South Australia	Tasmania	Adelaide	1987/88
8d-672	New South Wales	Victoria	Sydney	1933/34
661	New South Wales	Queensland	Brisbane	1963/64
654	Western Australia	Victoria	Perth	1986/87
649	Victoria	South Australia	Melbourne	1926/27
8d-646	Victoria	South Australia	Adelaide	1927/28
7d-644	South Australia	Queensland	Adelaide	1934/35
3d-643	South Australia	Tasmania	Adelaide	1986/87
642	New South Wales	South Australia	Sydney	1925/26
8d-642	South Australia	Queensland	Adelaide	1935/36
639	Victoria	South Australia	Adelaide	1920/21
639	New South Wales	Queensland	Sydney	1927/28
637	Victoria	South Australia	Melbourne	1927/28
4d-633	Victoria	Queensland	Melbourne	1962/63
624	New South Wales	South Australia	Adelaide	1903/04
620	Victoria	South Australia	Adelaide	1921/22
5d-615	Western Australia	Queensland	Brisbane	1968/69
614	Victoria	South Australia	Melbourne	1910/11
614	New South Wales	Victoria	Sydney	1924/25
6d-614	New South Wales	Queensland	Sydney	1933/34
613	Queensland	New South Wales	Brisbane	1963/64
610	New South Wales	South Australia	Adelaide	1930/31
610	South Australia	Victoria	Melbourne	1939/40
609	Victoria	South Australia	Melbourne	1983/84
8d-607	Western Australia	Queensland	Perth	1989/90
605	Victoria	South Australia	Melbourne	1919/20
604	Victoria	South Australia	Melbourne	1925/26
603	South Australia	New South Wales	Adelaide	1946/47
602	New South Wales	Queensland	Brisbane	1932/33
9d-601	New South Wales	South Australia	Adelaide	1964/65
8d-600	South Australia	New South Wales	Adelaide	1938/39

Highest for Tasmania

592	Tasmania	South Australia	Adelaide	1987/88

Lowest Completed Innings Totals

Total	Team	Opponent	Venue	Season
27	South Australia	New South Wales	Sydney	1955/56
31	Victoria	New South Wales	Melbourne	1906/07
35	Victoria	New South Wales	Sydney	1926/27
41	Western Australia	South Australia	Adelaide	1989/90
43	Victoria	South Australia	Melbourne	1895/96
49	Queensland	Victoria	Melbourne	1936/37
50	Western Australia	New South Wales	Sydney	1951/52
51	Western Australia	New South Wales	Perth	1950/51
52	Queensland	Western Australia	Perth	1982/83
54	Queensland	Victoria	Brisbane	1932/33
54	Western Australia	Queensland	Brisbane	1972/73
56	South Australia	Western Australia	Perth	1959/60
61	South Australia	New South Wales	Adelaide	1906/07
65	Queensland	Victoria	Melbourne	1957/58
65	Queensland	Victoria	Melbourne	1970/71
66	New South Wales	Victoria	Melbourne	1894/95
66	South Australia	Queensland	Brisbane	1965/66
68	South Australia	Victoria	Melbourne	1931/32
69	South Australia	New South Wales	Sydney	1979/80
71	New South Wales	Queensland	Brisbane	1976/77
72	South Australia	Queensland	Brisbane Ex	1930/31
73	South Australia	Victoria	Melbourne	1892/93
75	South Australia	Queensland	Brisbane	1953/54
77	Victoria	Queensland	Brisbane	1986/87
78	South Australia	Victoria	Adelaide	1961/62
78	Victoria	New South Wales	Newcastle	1985/86
79	South Australia	Victoria	Adelaide	1936/37
82	New South Wales	Queensland	Sydney	1962/63
83	New South Wales	Western Australia	Perth	1985/86
83	New South Wales	Queensland	Newcastle	1987/88
84	New South Wales	Victoria	Melbourne	1912/13
86	South Australia	Victoria	Adelaide	1976/77
87	South Australia	Victoria	Melbourne	1925/26
87	South Australia	New South Wales	Sydney	1966/67
87	South Australia	Western Australia	Adelaide	1975/76
89+	South Australia	New South Wales	Adelaide	1908/09
89	South Australia	Victoria	Melbourne	1974/75
89	South Australia	New South Wales	Adelaide	1980/81
89	Victoria	Tasmania	Hobart TCA	1983/84
90	New South Wales	Victoria	Sydney	1897/98
90	South Australia	Victoria	Melbourne	1922/23
90	South Australia	New South Wales	Sydney	1946/47
92	South Australia	New South Wales	Sydney	1892/93
92	New South Wales	Victoria	Melbourne	1897/98
92	New South Wales	South Australia	Sydney	1909/10
93	South Australia	Victoria	Melbourne	1950/51
93	New South Wales	Victoria	Sydney	1966/67
94	South Australia	New South Wales	Sydney	1935/36
94	South Australia	New South Wales	Sydney	1949/50
94	Western Australia	Victoria	Perth	1985/86
95	South Australia	New South Wales	Sydney	1967/68
96	South Australia	Queensland	Brisbane	1976/77
97+	South Australia	New South Wales	Adelaide	1908/09
97	New South Wales	Queensland	Brisbane	1974/75
97	South Australia	Queensland	Brisbane	1976/77
97	South Australia	Victoria	Melbourne	1978/79
98	South Australia	Victoria	Adelaide	1898/99
98	New South Wales	South Australia	Adelaide	1923/24
99	New South Wales	Victoria	Sydney	1892/93
99	New South Wales	Victoria	Melbourne	1894/95
99	New South Wales	Victoria	Melbourne	1898/99
100	New South Wales	Queensland	Sydney	1927/28
100	South Australia	New South Wales	Sydney	1929/30
100	New South Wales	Western Australia	Sydney	1972/73

+ Denotes 1 man absent

Lowest for Tasmania

102	Tasmania	Western Australia	Perth	1985/86

▶

483

Leading Run Scorers

Batsman	State	Seasons	M	Inn	NO	Runs	HS	50	100	Avrge
RJ Inverarity	WA/SA	23	159	275	32	9341	187	45	22	38.44
DG Bradman	NSW/SA	16	62	96	15	8926	452*	20	36	110.19
GS Chappell	SA/Qld	18	101	173	20	8762	194	42	27	57.27
SC Trimble	Qld	17	123	230	13	8647	252*	40	22	39.85
LE Favell	SA	19	121	220	4	8269	164	43	20	38.28
DW Hookes	SA	15	100	172	9	8211	306*	41	23	50.37
IM Chappell	SA	19	89	157	13	7665	205*	45	22	53.22
PJP Burge	Qld	16	83	138	12	7084	283	30	22	56.22
HN Dansie	SA	18	107	196	6	6692	185	32	17	35.22
WM Lawry	Vic	17	85	139	14	6615	266	38	17	52.92
RB Simpson	NSW/WA	26	78	133	21	6471	359	28	17	57.78
KD Mackay	Qld	18	100	162	22	6341	223	31	14	45.29
C Hill	SA	26	68	126	6	6274	365*	27	18	52.28
AMJ Hilditch	NSW/SA	14	88	158	8	6272	230	25	14	41.81
GM Wood	WA	13	97	152	25	6136	186*	29	18	48.31
AJ Kippax	NSW	17	61	95	8	6096	315*	14	23	70.07
AR Border	NSW/Qld	14	73	125	11	6023	200	32	15	52.83
VY Richardson	SA	19	77	146	7	6014	203	27	18	43.27
GN Yallop	Vic	13	76	136	9	5861	246	32	18	46.15
RN Harvey	Vic/NSW	17	75	122	6	5854	231*	13	16	50.46
J Dyson	NSW	14	82	150	16	5630	241	29	11	42.01
KD Walters	NSW	19	91	157	16	5602	253	24	16	39.73
AL Hassett	Vic	15	58	97	10	5535	232	25	19	63.62
GM Ritchie	Qld	10	84	137	10	5523	213*	32	13	43.49
WH Ponsford	Vic	14	43	70	5	5413	437	14	21	80.27
RB McCosker	NSW	11	70	124	15	5280	168	26	17	48.44
PR Sleep	SA	14	105	168	29	5265	146*	27	12	37.88
DF Whatmore	Vic	14	85	150	7	5235	170	31	10	36.60
IR Redpath	NSW	15	76	132	11	5222	261	26	11	43.16
G Shipperd	WA/Tas	11	81	136	18	5162	200*	24	13	44.50
DC Boon	Tas	12	69	122	4	5125	227	26	14	43.43
RB Kerr	Qld	9	79	135	7	5036	201*	24	15	39.34

Highest Run Scorer for Each State

State	Batsman	Seasons	M	Inn	NO	Runs	HS	50	100	Avrge
New South Wales	AJ Kippax	17	61	95	8	6096	315*	14	23	70.07
Queensland	SC Trimble	17	123	230	13	8647	252*	40	22	39.85
South Australia	LE Favell	19	121	220	4	8269	164	43	20	38.28
Tasmania	DC Boon	12	69	122	4	5125	227	26	14	43.43
Victoria	WM Lawry	17	85	139	14	6615	266	38	17	52.92
Western Australian	RJ Inverarity	17	108	188	18	6888	187	28	19	40.51

Most Runs in a Season

Season	Batsman	State	M	Inn	NO	Runs	HS	50	100	Avrge
1982/83	GN Yallop	Vic	10	18	—	1254	246	5	4	69.66
1927/28	WH Ponsford	Vic	5	8	—	1217	437	1	4	152.12
1970/71	BA Richards	SA	8	13	2	1145	356	3	4	104.09
1982/83	DM Wellham	NSW	11	20	5	1109	136*	10	3	73.93
1982/83	RB McCosker	NSW	11	21	3	1096	124	9	3	60.88
1926/27	WH Ponsford	Vic	5	8	—	1091	352	2	5	136.37
1939/40	DG Bradman	SA	6	10	2	1062	267	4	3	132.75
1977/78	AD Ogilvie	Qld	9	18	2	1060	194	2	6	66.25
1988/89	TM Moody	WA	11	18	1	1038	202	3	4	61.06
1981/82	KC Wessels	Qld	9	15	—	1015	220	2	5	67.66
1987/88	DW Hookes	SA	10	18	1	1014	132	7	3	59.65
1987/88	GM Wood	WA	11	16	3	1014	186*	5	3	78.00
1973/74	GS Chappell	Qld	7	13	2	1013	180	4	4	92.09
1983/84	J Dyson	NSW	10	18	3	1006	241	3	3	67.07
1957/58	NC O'Neill	NSW	8	14	2	1005	233	3	4	83.75

Most by a Tasmanian

Season	Batsman	State	M	Inn	NO	Runs	HS	50	100	Avrge
1983/84	BF Davison	Tas	10	18	4	955	171*	3	4	68.21

Highest Individual Innings

Total	Batsman	Team	Opponent	Venue	Season
452*	DG Bradman	New South Wales	Queensland	Sydney	1929/30
437	WH Ponsford	Victoria	Queensland	Melbourne	1927/28
365*	C Hill	South Australia	New South Wales	Adelaide	1900/01
359	RB Simpson	New South Wales	Queensland	Brisbane	1963/64
357	DG Bradman	South Australia	Victoria	Melbourne	1935/36

Total	Team	Opponent	Venue	Season
356 _____ BA Richards	South Australia	Western Australia	Perth	1970/71
355* _____ GR Marsh	Western Australia	South Australia	Perth	
352 _____ WH Ponsford	Victoria	New South Wales	Melbourne	1926/27
340* _____ DG Bradman	New South Wales	Victoria	Sydney	1928/29
336 _____ WH Ponsford	Victoria	South Australia	Melbourne	1927/28
325 _____ CL Badcock	South Australia	Victoria	Adelaide	1935/36
315* _____ AF Kippax	New South Wales	Queensland	Sydney	1927/28
306* _____ DW Hookes	South Australia	Tasmania	Adelaide	1986/87
295 _____ J Ryder	Victoria	New South Wales	Melbourne	1926/27
283 _____ PJP Burge	Queensland	New South Wales	Brisbane	1963/64
281 _____ MA Noble	New South Wales	Victoria	Melbourne	1905/06
277 _____ RB Simpson	New South Wales	Queensland	Sydney	1967/68
275* _____ WH Ponsford	Victoria	South Australia	Melbourne	1928/29
275* _____ FC Thomson	Queensland	New South Wales	Brisbane Ex	1930/31
271 _____ RA Duff	New South Wales	South Australia	Sydney	1903/04
271 _____ CE Pellew	South Australia	Victoria	Adelaide	1919/20
271* _____ AF Kippax	New South Wales	Victoria	Sydney	1925/26
271* _____ CL Badcock	South Australia	New South Wales	Adelaide	1938/39
267 _____ DG Bradman	South Australia	Victoria	Melbourne	1939/40
266 _____ WM Lawry	Victoria	New South Wales	Sydney	1960/61
264* _____ R Flockton	New South Wales	South Australia	Sydney	1959/60
263 _____ SB Smith	New South Wales	Victoria	Melbourne	1982/83
262 _____ MRJ Veletta	Western Australia	Victoria	Perth	1986/87
261 _____ IR Redpath	Victoria	Queensland	Melbourne	1962/63
260* _____ AF Kippax	New South Wales	Victoria	Melbourne	1928/29
260 _____ WB Phillips	South Australia	Queensland	Adelaide	1981/82
259* _____ GB Stevens	South Australia	New South Wales	Sydney	1958/59
258 _____ DG Bradman	New South Wales	South Australia	Adelaide	1930/31
253 _____ DG Bradman	New South Wales	Queensland	Sydney	1933/34
253 _____ CW Andrews	Queensland	New South Wales	Sydney	1934/35
253 _____ AR Morris	New South Wales	Queensland	Brisbane	1951/52
253 _____ KD Walters	New South Wales	South Australia	Adelaide	1964/65
252* _____ SC Trimble	Queensland	New South Wales	Sydney	1963/64
251 _____ GS Sobers	South Australia	New South Wales	Adelaide	1961/62
251* _____ DG Bradman	South Australia	New South Wales	Adelaide	1939/40
250 _____ WW Armstrong	Victoria	South Australia	Melbourne	1911/12

Highest Score by a Tasmanian

227 _____ DC Boon	Tasmania	Victoria	Melbourne	1983/84

Leading Bowlers

Bowler	State	Seasons	M	Balls	Runs	Wkts	Avrge	5wi	10wm	Best
CV Grimmett _____	Vic/SA	17	79	28465	12976	513	25.29	48	13	9/180
JR Thomson _____	NSW/Qld	14	84	16939	8591	355	24.20	18	3	7/27
DK Lillee _____	WA/Tas	17	75	17814	8086	338	23.92	18	4	7/36
TM Alderman _____	WA	16	77	15209	7426	328	22.64	16	3	7/28
GF Lawson _____	NSW	13	83	17543	7301	326	22.40	12	—	6/31
GAR Lock _____	WA	9	63	20107	7210	302	23.87	15	2	7/53
AN Connolly _____	Vic	12	71	18033	7745	297	26.00	12	4	9/67
JW Martin _____	NSW/SA	12	77	17078	8703	273	31.87	12	—	8/97
G Dymock _____	Qld	11	75	17110	7223	266	26.85	8	—	6/79
R Benaud _____	NSW	16	73	17948	7174	266	26.96	11	3	7/32
RJ Bright _____	Vic	16	101	22789	8833	252	35.05	10	—	6/61
AK Davidson _____	NSW	14	62	13423	5195	246	21.11	10	—	7/31
LO Fleetwood-Smith ___	Vic	9	40	11576	6034	246	24.52	25	8	9/135
AA Mallett _____	SA	14	77	20906	8173	244	23.76	19	2	7/57
RR Lindwall _____	NSW/Qld	14	66	14084	5518	244	22.61	11	1	7/45
JD Higgs _____	Vic	13	75	14961	7202	240	30.00	12	2	8/66
TJ Jenner _____	WA/SA	14	87	17010	8124	234	34.72	8	1	7/127
GD McKenzie _____	WA	15	73	16566	7322	232	31.56	7	—	6/100
PR Sleep _____	SA	14	105	16520	8405	222	37.86	6	—	8/133
H Ironmonger _____	Vic	17	44	14594	5290	215	24.60	16	4	7/13
E Jones _____	SA	11	39	12139	5508	209	26.35	19	4	8/157
WJ O'Reilly _____	NSW	13	33	10748	3472	203	17.10	18	7	9/41
JRF Duncan _____	Qld/VIC	9	62	14024	6025	202	29.82	9	1	8/55

▶

Leading Wicket-Takers for Each State

State	Bowler	Seasons	M	Balls	Runs	Wkts	Avrge	5wi	10wm	Best
New South Wales	GF Lawson	13	83	17543	7301	326	22.40	12	—	6/31
Queensland	JR Thomson	12	77	15166	7927	328	24.17	17	3	7/27
South Australia	CV Grimmett	17	78	28288	12878	504	25.55	46	13	9/180
Tasmania	PM Clough	4	28	6142	2913	102	28.56	5	—	8/95
Victoria	AN Connolly	12	71	18033	7745	297	26.00	12	4	9/67
Western Australia	TM Alderman	16	77	15209	7426	328	22.64	16	3	7/28

Most Wickets in a Season

Season	Bowler	State	M	Balls	Mdns	Runs	Wkts	Avrge	5wi	10wm	Best
1934/35	LO Fleetwood-Smith	Vic	6	2164	25	1137	60	18.95	8	3	8/113
1987/88	CD Matthews	WA	11	2553	81	1215	56	21.70	3	—	8/101
1982/83	J Garner	SA	8	2419	131	976	55	17.74	4	2	7/78
1989/90	CJ McDermott	Qld	10	1392	100	1375	54	25.46	4	—	8/44
1939/40	WJ O'Reilly	NSW	6	1766	48	705	52	13.55	6	2	8/23
1966/67	GRA Lock	WA	8	2392	104	1086	51	21.29	3	1	6/85
1934/35	CV Grimmett	SA	6	2214	35	1043	49	21.28	5	3	9/180
1939/40	CV Grimmett	SA	6	2478	33	1215	49	24.79	5	2	6/118
1969/70	AL Thomson	Vic	8	2104	42	876	49	17.87	5	2	8/87
1972/73	AA Mallett	SA	8	2551	89	893	49	18.22	3	—	5/41
1977/78	DW Hourn	NSW	9	2222	47	995	48	20.72	4	1	7/71
1962/63	I Meckiff	Vic	8	2207	45	922	47	19.61	2	—	5/50
1963/64	GS Sobers	SA	8	3034	49	1297	47	27.59	2	—	6/71
1983/84	JR Thomson	Qld	11	2099	59	1251	47	26.62	1	—	5/85
1986/87	CD Matthews	WA	10	3444	91	1216	47	25.87	3	—	6/46
1986/87	AK Zesers	SA	10	3776	155	1016	47	21.62	2	—	7/67
1934/35	HC Chilvers	NSW	6	1900	23	857	46	18.63	6	3	6/68
1949/50	JB Iverson	Vic	7	2357	58	764	46	16.60	5	—	7/77
1962/63	GS Sobers	SA	8	2515	45	1040	46	22.60	4	—	7/110
1963/64	RHD Sellers	SA	8	2503	43	1223	46	26.58	3	1	5/49
1966/67	AN Connolly	Vic	8	2533	41	1164	46	25.30	2	1	6/50
1967/68	AN Connolly	Vic	7	2116	62	752	46	16.34	4	1	7/61
1968/69	GRA Lock	WA	8	2674	59	1054	46	22.91	3	1	7/61
1987/88	D Tazelaar	Qld	11	2250	92	1036	46	22.52	3	—	6/52
1959/60	JW Martin	NSW	8	2403	37	1064	45	23.64	3	—	5/57
1971/72	AA Mallett	SA	7	2275	69	849	45	18.86	3	1	7/58
1979/80	AA Mallett	SA	8	2503	126	1013	45	22.51	2	—	5/67

Most by a Tasmanian

1985/86	RL Brown	Tas	10	2306	62	1365	41	33.29	1	1	7/80

Most Wickets in an Innings

Total	Bowler	Team	Opponent	Venue	Season
10/36	TW Wall	South Australia	New South Wales	Sydney	1932/33
10/44	IJ Brayshaw	Western Australia	Victoria	Perth	1967/68
10/61	PJ Allan	Queensland	Victoria	Melbourne	1965/66
9/30	JPF Travers	South Australia	Victoria	Melbourne	1900/01
9/40	EL McCormick	Victoria	South Australia	Adelaide	1936/37
9/41	WJ O'Reilly	New South Wales	South Australia	Adelaide	1937/38
9/50	WJ O'Reilly	New South Wales	Victoria	Melbourne	1933/34
9/52	WP Howell	New South Wales	Victoria	Melbourne	1902/03
9/67	AN Connolly	Victoria	Queensland	Brisbane	1964/65
9/77	DW Hourn	New South Wales	Victoria	Sydney	1978/79
9/83	RG Holland	New South Wales	South Australia	Sydney	1984/85
9/135	LO Fleetwood-Smith	Victoria	South Australia	Melbourne	1937/38
9/147	G Giffen	South Australia	Victoria	Adelaide	1892/93
9/180	CV Grimmett	South Australia	Queensland	Adelaide	1934/35
8/23	WJ O'Reilly	New South Wales	Queensland	Sydney	1939/40
8/31	ES White	New South Wales	South Australia	Sydney	1935/36
8/39	H Trumble	Victoria	South Australia	Melbourne	1898/99
8/41	LS Pascoe	New South Wales	Tasmania	Hobart TCA	1981/82
8/42	IW Callen	Victoria	Queensland	Melbourne	1976/77
8/44	CJ McDermott	Queensland	Tasmania	Brisbane	1989/90
8/50	RB Minnett	New South Wales	Victoria	Melbourne	1914/15
8/51	MA Polzin	Queensland	Victoria	Melbourne	1989/90
8/52	WA Johnston	Victoria	Queensland	Melbourne	1952/53
8/55	JRF Duncan	Queensland	Victoria	Melbourne	1970/71
8/56	AL Newell	New South Wales	Victoria	Sydney	1897/98
8/56	HR Gorringe	Western Australia	Queensland	Perth	1952/53
8/57	CV Grimmett	South Australia	New South Wales	Adelaide	1927/28
8/58	H Trumble	Victoria	New South Wales	Melbourne	1898/99

Total	Batsman	Team	Opponent	Venue	Season
8/61	NJN Hawke	South Australia	New South Wales	Sydney	1967/68
8/64	EW Freeman	South Australia	New South Wales	Adelaide	1970/71
8/66	TR McKibbin	New South Wales	South Australia	Sydney	1894/95
8/66	JN Crawford	South Australia	Victoria	Adelaide	1912/13
8/66	JD Higgs	Victoria	Western Australia	Melbourne	1974/75
8/74	TR McKibbin	New South Wales	South Australia	Adelaide	1896/97
8/77	G Giffen	South Australia	New South Wales	Adelaide	1894/95
8/79	LO Fleetwood-Smith	Victoria	Queensland	Melbourne	1936/37
8/81	AA Mailey	New South Wales	South Australia	Sydney	1920/21
8/84	EA McDonald	Victoria	New South Wales	Sydney	1921/22
8/84	AG Hurst	Victoria	Queensland	Melbourne	1977/78
8/86	CV Grimmett	Victoria	South Australia	Adelaide	1923/24
8/87	AL Thomson	Victoria	New South Wales	Melbourne	1969/70
8/93	TR McKibbin	New South Wales	Victoria	Melbourne	1895/96
8/95	PM Clough	Tasmania	Western Australia	Launceston	1983/84
8/97	JW Martin	New South Wales	Victoria	Sydney	1962/63
8/98	DE Hoare	Western Australia	New South Wales	Perth	1964/65
8/101	CD Matthews	Western Australia	Queensland	Perth	1987/88
8/106	JV Saunders	Victoria	South Australia	Adelaide	1902/03
8/109	G Giffen	South Australia	New South Wales	Adelaide	1894/95
8/110	H Trumble	Victoria	South Australia	Adelaide	1889/90
8/110	G Giffen	South Australia	Victoria	Adelaide	1902/03
8/111	TR McKibbin	New South Wales	Victoria	Sydney	1896/97
8/111	GM Pierce	New South Wales	South Australia	Adelaide	1892/93
8/111	LO Fleetwood-Smith	Victoria	South Australia	Melbourne	1933/34
8/113	LO Fleetwood-Smith	Victoria	South Australia	Melbourne	1933/34
8/129	H Trumble	Victoria	South Australia	Adelaide	1898/99
8/148	BJ Flynn	Queensland	New South Wales	Brisbane	1953/54
8/287	G Giffen	South Australia	New South Wales	Adelaide	1899/00

Most Wickets in a Match

Total	Bowler	Team	Opponent	Venue	Season
16/186	G Giffen	South Australia	New South Wales	Adelaide	1894/95
16/289	CV Grimmett	South Australia	Queensland	Adelaide	1934/35
15/96	LO Fleetwood-Smith	Victoria	Queensland	Melbourne	1936/37
15/125	TR McKibbin	New South Wales	South Australia	Adelaide	1896/97
15/185	G Giffen	South Australia	Victoria	Adelaide	1902/03
15/226	LO Fleetwood-Smith	Victoria	New South Wales	Sydney	1934/35
14/45	WJ O'Reilly	New South Wales	Queensland	Sydney	1939/40
14/86	TM Alderman	Western Australia	New South Wales	Perth	1981/82
14/98	WJ O'Reilly	New South Wales	South Australia	Adelaide	1937/38
14/189	TR McKibbin	New South Wales	South Australia	Sydney	1894/95
13/87	HV Hordern	New South Wales	Victoria	Sydney	1910/11
13/105	EW Freeman	South Australia	New South Wales	Adelaide	1970/71
13/110	PJ Allan	Queensland	New South Wales	Sydney	1968/69
13/111	WJ O'Reilly	New South Wales	Queensland	Brisbane	1933/34
13/122	AA Mallett	South Australia	Western Australia	Adelaide	1971/72
13/125	JRJ Duncan	Queensland	Victoria	Melbourne	1970/71
13/135	CV Grimmett	South Australia	Queensland	Brisbane	1932/33
13/141	AL Thomson	Victoria	New South Wales	Melbourne	1969/70
13/149	JC Reedman	South Australia	Victoria	Melbourne	1904/05
13/155	J Ryder	Victoria	South Australia	Melbourne	1912/13
13/165	AN Connolly	Victoria	South Australia	Adelaide	1967/68
13/181	H Ironmonger	Victoria	South Australia	Melbourne	1914/15
13/194	JV Saunders	Victoria	South Australia	Adelaide	1902/03
13/240	TR McKibbin	New South Wales	Victoria	Sydney	1896/97
13/265	GM Pierce	New South Wales	South Australia	Adelaide	1892/93

Best by a Tasmanian

Total	Bowler	Team	Opponent	Venue	Season
11/183	RL Brown	Tasmania	South Australia	Adelaide	

Leading Wicket-Keepers

Wicket-keeper	State	Seasons	M	Total	Ct	St
RW Marsh	WA	14	86	352	319	3?
JA Maclean	Qld	11	86	312	288	24
ATW Grout	Qld	20	86	276	214	62
SJ Rixon	NSW	14	94	260	219	41

Continued

487

Wicket-keeper	State	Seasons	M	Total	Ct	St
BN Jarman	SA	13	77	250	192	58
RD Robinson	Vic	11	68	238	212	26
RC Jordon	Vic	12	70	229	198	31
RB Phillips	NSW/Qld	8	71	226	214	12
TJ Zoehrer	WA	10	66	219	196	23
KJ Wright	WA/SA	10	63	213	195	18
HB Taber	NSW	10	64	211	179	32
D Tallon	Qld	15	69	207	146	61
CW Walker	SA	12	57	191	104	87
WAS Oldfield	NSW	14	51	180	109	71

Leading Fieldsman

Fieldsman	State	Seasons	M	Ct
RJ Inverarity	WA/SA	23	159	189
DW Hookes	SA	15	100	114
IM Chappell	SA	19	89	112
DF Whatmore	Vic	14	85	110
GS Chappell	SA/Qld	18	101	108
RB Simpson	NSW/WA	26	78	100
VY Richardson	SA	19	77	97
IJ Brayshaw	WA	18	91	95
R Benaud	NSW	16	73	92
RB McCosker	NSW	11	70	90
JW Martin	NSW/SA	12	77	83
GAR Lock	WA	9	63	81

Record Wicket Partnerships

Wkt	Ttl	Batsmen	Match	Venue	Season
1st	431	MRJ Veletta, GR Marsh	WA v SA	Perth	1989/90
2nd	378	LA Marks, KD Walters	NSW v SA	Adelaide	1964/65
3rd	390*	JM Wiener, JK Moss	Vic v WA	St Kilda	1981/82
4th	462*	DW Hookes, WB Phillips	SA v Tas	Adelaide	1986/87
5th	397	WW Bardsley, C Kelleway	NSW v SA	Sydney	1920/21
6th	332	NG Marks, G Thomas	NSW v SA	Sydney	1958/59
7th	335	CW Andrews, EC Bensted	Qld v NSW	Sydney	1934/35
8th	270	VT Trumper, EP Barbour	NSW v Vic	Sydney	1912/13
9th	232	C Hill, EA Walkley	SA v NSW	Adelaide	1900/01
10th	307	AF Kippax, JEH Hooker	NSW v Vic	Melbourne	1928/29

Highest Wicket Partnerships

Wkt	Ttl	Batsmen	Match	Venue	Season
4th	462*	DW Hookes, WB Phillips	SA v Tas	Adelaide	1986/87
1st	431	MRJ Veletta, GR Marsh	WA v SA	Perth	1989/90
5th	397	W Bardsley, C Kelleway	NSW v SA	Sydney	1920/21
3rd	390*	JM Wiener, JK Moss	Vic v WA	St Kilda	1981/82
1st	388	KC Wessels, RB Kerr	Qld v Vic	St Kilda	1982/83
2nd	378	LA Marks, KD Walters	NSW v SA	Adelaide	1964/65
1st	375	WM Woodfull, WH Ponsford	Vic v NSW	Melbourne	1926/27
3rd	363	DG Bradman, AF Kippax	NSW v Qld	Sydney	1933/34
3rd	345	W Bardsley, JM Taylor	NSW v SA	Adelaide	1920/21
1st	337	CC McDonald, KD Meuleman	Vic v SA	Adelaide	1949/50
7th	335	CW Andrews, EC Bensted	Qld v NSW	Sydney	1934/35
2nd	334	A Jackson, DG Bradman	NSW v SA	Adelaide	1930/31
6th	332	G Thomas, NG Marks	NSW v SA	Sydney	1958/59
1st	331	BA Courtice, RB Kerr	Qld v Tas	Brisbane	1984/85
3rd	330	GM Wood, GR Marsh	WA v NSW	Sydney	1983/84
1st	328	C Milburn, D Chadwick	WA v Qld	Brisbane	1968/69
5th	325	NC O'Neill, BC Booth	NSW v Vic	Sydney	1957/58
2nd	323	ID Craig, RN Harvey	NSW v Qld	Sydney	1960/61
1st	319	RB McCosker, J Dyson	NSW v WA	Sydney	1980/81
5th	315	MA Noble, SE Gregory	NSW v Vic	Sydney	1907/08
2nd	314	WH Ponsford, HSTL Hendry	Vic v Qld	Melbourne	1927/28
1st	310	GR Marsh, MRJ Veletta	WA v Tas	Hobart Bel	1988/89
2nd	308	BA Richards, IM Chappell	SA v WA	Perth	1970/71
1st	308	RB Simpson, G Thomas	NSW v WA	Sydney	1963/64
10th	307	AF Kippax, JEH Hooker	NSW v Vic	Melbourne	1928/29
3rd	304	KC Wessels, GM Ritchie	Qld v Tas	Devonport	1981/82
2nd	304	W Bardsley, MA Noble	NSW v Vic	Sydney	1908/09
4th	301	LPJ O'Brien, LS Darling	Vic v Qld	Brisbane	1932/33
5th	301*	RB Simpson, K Meuleman	WA v NSW	Perth	1959/60

Record Wicket Partnerships

New South Wales

Wkt	Ttl	Batsmen	Opponent	Venue	Season
1st	319	RB McCosker, J Dyson	Western Australia	Sydney	1979/80
2nd	378	LA Marks, KD Walters	South Australia	Adelaide	1964/65
3rd	363	DG Bradman, AF Kippax	Queensland	Sydney	1933/34
4th	325	NC O'Neill, BC Booth	Victoria	Sydney	1957/58
5th	397	WW Bardsley, C Kelleway	South Australia	Sydney	1920/21
6th	332	G Thomas, NG Marks	South Australia	Sydney	1958/59
7th	255	R Benaud, G Thomas	Victoria	Melbourne	1961/62
8th	270	EP Barbour, VT Trumper	Victoria	Sydney	1912/13
9th	226	C Kelleway, WAS Oldfield	Victoria	Melbourne	1925/26
10th	307	AF Kippax, JEH Hooker	Victoria	Melbourne	1928/29

Queensland

Wkt	Ttl	Batsmen	Opponent	Venue	Season
1st	388	KC Wessels, RB Kerr	Victoria	St Kilda	1982/83
2nd	243	GR Reynolds, JJ McLaughlin	South Australia	Adelaide	1957/58
3rd	304	KC Wessels, GM Ritchie	Tasmania	Devonport	1981/82
4th	295	PJP Burge, TR Veivers	South Australia	Brisbane	1962/63
5th	231	KD Mackay, RG Archer	Victoria	Brisbane	1953/54
"	231	AR Border, GS Trimble	Victoria	Brisbane	1987/88
6th	211	J Bratchford, TR Veivers	South Australia	Brisbane	1959/60
7th	335	CW Andrews, EC Bensted	New South Wales	Sydney	1934/35
8th	146	TV Hohns, G Dymock	Victoria	Melbourne	1978/79
9th	152*	ATW Grout, WT Walmsley	New South Wales	Sydney	1956/57
10th	105*	WT Walmsley, JE Freeman	New South Wales	Brisbane	1957/58

South Australia

Wkt	Ttl	Batsmen	Opponent	Venue	Season
1st	281	LE Favell, JP Causby	New South Wales	Adelaide	1967/68
2nd	308	BA Richards, IM Chappell	Western Australia	Perth	1970/71
3rd	253	DRA Gehrs, C Hill	Victoria	Adelaide	1909/10
4th	462*	DW Hookes, WB Phillips	Tasmania	Adelaide	1986/87
5th	281	CL Badcock, MG Waite	Queensland	Adelaide	1939/40
6th	255	GStA Sobers, BN Jarman	Western Australia	Perth	1963/64
7th	183	WC Alexander, J Rymill	Victoria	Melbourne	1925/26
8th	174	AK Zesers, DFG O'Connor	Victoria	Adelaide	1984/85
9th	232	C Hill, EA Walkley	New South Wales	Adelaide	1900/01
10th	104	L Michael, EI Pynor	Victoria	Adelaide	1949/50

Tasmania

Wkt	Ttl	Batsmen	Opponent	Venue	Season
1st	195	DC Boon, EJ Harris	Queensland	Brisbane	1986/87
2nd	166	G Shipperd, DC Boon	Queensland	Hobart, Bel	1989/90
3rd	181	N Jelich, GA Hughes	New South Wales	Newcastle	1986/87
4th	258	MD Taylor, DJ Buckingham	South Australia	Adelaide	1987/88
5th	176	RD Woolley, DJ Buckingham	South Australia	Adelaide	1985/86
6th	213	BF Davison, RD Woolley	South Australia	Adelaide	1980/81
7th	203*	BF Davison, PI Faulkner	Western Australia	Perth	1983/84
8th	148	BF Davison, PI Faulkner	South Australia	Adelaide	1983/84
9th	118	BF Davison, PI Faulkner	Queensland	Brisbane	1983/84
10th	120	SL Saunders, PM Clough	Western Australia	Perth	1981/82

Victoria

Wkt	Ttl	Batsmen	Opponent	Venue	Season
1st	375	WM Woodfull, WH Ponsford	New South Wales	Melbourne	1926/27
2nd	314	WH Ponsford, HSTL Hendry	Queensland	Melbourne	1927/28
3rd	390*	JM Wiener, JK Moss	Western Australia	St Kilda	1981/82
4th	301	LP O'Brien, LS Darling	Queensland	Brisbane	1932/33
5th	271	AJ Sieler, RP Rose	Queensland	Brisbane	1973/74
6th	289	SJE Loxton, DT Ring	Queensland	Melbourne	1946/47
7th	185	PA Hibbert, RJ Bright	New South Wales	Melbourne	1985/86
8th	215	WW Armstrong, RL Park	South Australia	Melbourne	1919/20
9th	143	GR Hazlitt, A Kenny	South Australia	Melbourne	1910/11
10th	211	M Ellis, TJ Hastings	South Australia	Melbourne	1902/03

▶

Western Australia

Wkt	Ttl		Batsmen	Opponent	Venue	Season
1st	431	_____	MRJ Veletta, GR Marsh	South Australia	Perth	1989/90
2nd	254	_____	MRJ Veletta, GR Marsh	Queensland	Brisbane	1985/86
3rd	330	_____	GM Wood, GR Marsh	New South Wales	Sydney	1983/84
4th	260	_____	GR Marsh, CS Serjeant	New South Wales	Sydney	1981/82
5th	301*	_____	RB Simpson, K Meuleman	New South Wales	Perth	1959/60
6th	244	_____	JT Irvine, R Edwards	New South Wales	Sydney	1968/69
7th	204	_____	G Shipperd, TJ Zoehrer	New South Wales	Perth	1982/83
8th	160	_____	GM Wood, KH MacLeay	South Australia	Perth	1987/88
9th	168*	_____	KH MacLeay, VJ Marks	South Australia	Adelaide	1986/87
10th	91	_____	IJ Brayshaw, JB Gannon	Queensland	Brisbane	1969/70

AUSTRALIAN INTERNATIONAL LIMITED-OVERS CRICKET

Game	Date	Venue	Australia Total	Opponent	Total	Result	Captain
1	5 Jan 1971	Melbourne	5-191	England	190*	Won by 5 wkts	WM Lawry
2	24 Aug 1972	Manchester	8-222*	England	4-226	Lost by 6 wkts	IM Chappell
3	26 Aug 1972	Lord's	5-240	England	9-236*	Won by 5 wkts	IM Chappell
4	28 Aug 1972	Birmingham	9-179*	England	8-180	Lost by 2 wkts	IM Chappell
5	30 Mar 1974	Dunedin	3-195	New Zealand	9-194*	Won by 7 wkts	IM Chappell
6	31 Mar 1974	Christchurch	5-265*	New Zealand	6-234	Won by 31 runs	IM Chappell
7	1 Jan 1975	Melbourne	190*	England	7-191	Lost by 3 wkts	IM Chappell
8	7 Jun 1975	Leeds	7-278*	Pakistan	205	Won by 73 runs	IM Chappell
9	11 Jun 1975	The Oval	5-328*	Sri Lanka	4-276	Won by 52 runs	IM Chappell
10	14 Jun 1975	The Oval	192*	West Indies	3-195	Lost by 7 wkts	IM Chappell
11	18 Jun 1975	Leeds	6-94	England	93*	Won by 4 wkts	IM Chappell
12	21 Jun 1975	Lord's	274	West Indies	8-291*	Lost by 17 runs	IM Chappell
13	20 Dec 1975	Adelaide	5-225	West Indies	224*	Won by 5 wkts	GS Chappell
14	2 Jun 1977	Manchester	9-169*	England	8-173	Lost by 2 wkts	GS Chappell
15	4 Jun 1977	Birmingham	70	England	171*	Lost by 99 runs	GS Chappell
16	6 Jun 1977	The Oval	8-246	England	242*	Won by 2 wkts	GS Chappell
17	22 Feb 1978	St. John's	7-181	West Indies	9-313*	Lost on run rate	RB Simpson
18	12 Apr 1978	Castries	8-140	West Indies	139*	Won by 2 wkts	RB Simpson
19	13 Jan 1979	Sydney	1-17*	England	—	No result	GN Yallop
20	24 Jan 1979	Melbourne	101*	England	3-102	Lost by 7 wkts	GN Yallop
21	4 Feb 1979	Melbourne	6-215	England	6-212*	Won by 4 wkts	GN Yallop
22	7 Feb 1979	Melbourne	4-95	England	94*	Won by 6 wkts	GN Yallop
23	9 Jun 1979	Lord's	9-159*	England	4-160	Lost by 6 wkts	KJ Hughes
24	13/14 Jun 1979	Nottingham	197	Pakistan	7-286*	Lost by 89 runs	KJ Hughes
25	16 Jun 1979	Birmingham	3-106	Canada	105*	Won by 7 wkts	KJ Hughes
26	27 Nov 1979	Sydney	5-196	West Indies	193*	Won by 5 wkts	GS Chappell
27	8 Dec 1979	Melbourne	9-207*	England	7-209	Lost by 3 wkts	GS Chappell
28	9 Dec 1979	Melbourne	8-191	West Indies	2-271*	Lost by 80 runs	GS Chappell
29	11 Dec 1979	Sydney	192	England	7-264*	Lost by 72 runs	GS Chappell
30	21 Dec 1979	Sydney	6-178*	West Indies	169	Won by 7 runs	GS Chappell
31	26 Dec 1979	Sydney	6-194*	England	6-195	Lost by 4 wkts	GS Chappell
32	14 Jan 1980	Sydney	163*	England	8-164	Lost by 2 wkts	GS Chappell
33	18 Jan 1980	Sydney	190*	West Indies	181	Won by 9 runs	GS Chappell
34	20 Aug 1980	The Oval	8-225	England	6-248*	Lost by 23 runs	GS Chappell
35	22 Aug 1980	Birmingham	5-273	England	8-320*	Lost by 47 runs	GS Chappell
36	23 Nov 1980	Adelaide	9-217*	New Zealand	7-219	Lost by 3 wkts	GS Chappell
37	25 Nov 1980	Sydney	3-289*	New Zealand	195	Won by 94 runs	GS Chappell
38	6 Dec 1980	Melbourne	142	India	9-208*	Lost by 66 runs	GS Chappell
39	7 Dec 1980	Melbourne	6-159	New Zealand	156*	Won by 4 wkts	GS Chappell
40	18 Dec 1980	Sydney	1-183	India	9-180*	Won by 9 wkts	GS Chappell
41	8 Jan 1981	Sydney	1-64	India	63*	Won by 9 wkts	GS Chappell
42	11 Jan 1981	Melbourne	3-193	India	5-192*	Won by 7 wkts	GS Chappell
43	13 Jan 1981	Sydney	7-219	New Zealand	8-220*	Lost by 1 run	GS Chappell
44	15 Jan 1981	Sydney	8-242*	India	8-215	Won by 27 runs	GS Chappell
45	21 Jan 1981	Sydney	180*	New Zealand	1-23	No result	GS Chappell
46	29 Jan 1981	Sydney	155	New Zealand	6-233*	Lost by 78 runs	GS Chappell
47	31 Jan 1981	Melbourne	3-130	New Zealand	126*	Won by 7 wkts	GS Chappell

Game	Date	Venue	Australia Total	Opponent	Total	Result	Captain
48	1 Feb 1981	Melbourne	4-235*	New Zealand	8-229	Won by 6 runs	GS Chappell
49	3 Feb 1981	Sydney	4-218	New Zealand	8-215*	Won by 6 wkts	GS Chappell
50	4 Jun 1981	Lord's	7-210*	England	4-212	Lost by 6 wkts	KJ Hughes
51	6 Jun 1981	Birmingham	8-249	England	247*	Won by 2 wkts	KJ Hughes
52	8 Jun 1981	Leeds	8-236*	England	165	Won by 71 runs	KJ Hughes
53	21 Nov 1981	Melbourne	9-209*	Pakistan	6-210	Lost by 4 wkts	GS Chappell
54	24 Nov 1981	Sydney	3-237	West Indies	8-236*	Won by 7 wkts	GS Chappell
55	6 Dec 1981	Adelaide	208*	Pakistan	8-170	Won by 38 runs	GS Chappell
56	17 Dec 1981	Sydney	6-222*	Pakistan	4-223	Lost by 6 wkts	GS Chappell
57	20 Dec 1981	Perth	9-188*	West Indies	2-190	Lost by 8 wkts	GS Chappell
58	20 Jan 1982	Melbourne	193	Pakistan	6-218*	Lost by 25 runs	GS Chappell
59	10 Jan 1982	Melbourne	146*	West Indies	5-147	Lost by 5 wkts	GS Chappell
60	14 Jan 1982	Sydney	5-230*	Pakistan	9-154	Won by 76 runs	GS Chappell
61	17 Jan 1982	Brisbane	9-185*	West Indies	5-186	Lost by 5 wkts	GS Chappell
62	19 Jan 1982	Sydney	7-168	West Indies	189*	Won on run rate	GS Chappell
63	23 Jan 1982	Melbourne	130	West Indies	8-216*	Lost by 86 runs	GS Chappell
64	24 Jan 1982	Melbourne	107	West Indies	9-235*	Lost by 128 runs	GS Chappell
65	26 Jan 1982	Sydney	8-214*	West Indies	168	Won by 46 runs	GS Chappell
66	27 Jan 1982	Sydney	9-216	West Indies	6-234*	Lost by 18 runs	GS Chappell
67	13 Feb 1982	Auckland	194	New Zealand	6-240*	Lost by 46 runs	GS Chappell
68	17 Feb 1982	Dunedin	4-160	New Zealand	9-159*	Won by 6 wkts	GS Chappell
69	9 Feb 1982	Wellington	2-75	New Zealand	74*	Won by 8 wkts	GS Chappell
70	20 Sep 1982	Hyderabad	9-170	Pakistan	6-229*	Lost by 59 runs	KJ Hughes
71	8 Oct 1982	Lahore	4-206	Pakistan	3-234*	Lost by 28 runs	KJ Hughes
72	22 Oct 1982	Karachi	—	Pakistan	1-44*	No result	KJ Hughes
73	9 Jan 1983	Melbourne	2-182	New Zealand	181*	Won by 8 wkts	KJ Hughes
74	11 Jan 1983	Sydney	180*	England	149	Won by 31 runs	KJ Hughes
75	16 Jan 1983	Brisbane	3-184	England	182*	Won by 7 wkts	KJ Hughes
76	18 Jan 1983	Sydney	179	New Zealand	8-228*	Lost by 47 runs	KJ Hughes
77	22 Jan 1983	Melbourne	9-188	New Zealand	6-246*	Lost by 58 runs	KJ Hughes
78	23 Jan 1983	Melbourne	5-217	England	5-213*	Won by 5 wkts	KJ Hughes
79	26 Jan 1983	Sydney	109	England	207*	Lost by 98 runs	KJ Hughes
80	30 Jan 1983	Adelaide	7-214	England	6-228*	Lost by 14 runs	KJ Hughes
81	31 Jan 1983	Adelaide	153	New Zealand	9-199*	Lost by 46 runs	KJ Hughes
82	6 Feb 1983	Perth	9-191*	New Zealand	164	Won by 27 runs	KJ Hughes
83	9 Feb 1983	Sydney	4-155	New Zealand	7-193*	Won by 6 wkts	KJ Hughes
84	13 Feb 1983	Melbourne	8-302*	New Zealand	153	Won by 149 runs	KJ Hughes
85	17 Mar 1983	Sydney	124	New Zealand	8-138*	Lost by 14 runs	KJ Hughes
86	13 Apr 1983	Colombo1	9-168*	Sri Lanka	8-169	Lost by 2 wkts	GS Chappell
87	16 Apr 1983	Colombo1	5-207*	Sri Lanka	6-213	Lost by 4 wkts	GS Chappell
88	20 Apr 1983	Colombo2	5-194*	Sri Lanka	—	No result	GS Chappell
89	30 Apr 1983	Colombo2	3-124*	Sri Lanka	—	No result	GS Chappell
90	9 Jun 1983	Nottingham	7-226	Zimbabwe	6-239*	Lost by 13 runs	KJ Hughes
91	11/12 Jun 1983	Leeds	9-151	West Indies	9-252*	Lost by 101 runs	KJ Hughes
92	13 Jun 1983	Nottingham	9-320*	India	158	Won by 162 runs	KJ Hughes
93	16 Jun 1983	Southampton	7-272*	Zimbabwe	240	Won by 32 runs	KJ Hughes
94	18 Jun 1983	Lord's	6-273*	West Indies	3-276	Lost by 7 wkts	KJ Hughes
95	20 Jun 1983	Chelmsford	129	India	247*	Lost by 118 runs	DW Hookes
96	8 Jan 1984	Melbourne	194	West Indies	7-221*	Lost by 27 runs	KJ Hughes
97	10 Jan 1984	Sydney	264*	Pakistan	9-230	Won by 34 runs	KJ Hughes
98	15 Jan 1984	Brisbane	0-15	Pakistan	6-184*	No result	KJ Hughes
99	17 Jan 1984	Sydney	9-195	West Indies	7-223*	Lost by 28 runs	KJ Hughes
100	21 Jan 1984	Melbourne	8-209*	Pakistan	166	Won by 45 runs	KJ Hughes
101	22 Jan 1984	Melbourne	226	West Indies	6-252*	Lost by 26 runs	KJ Hughes
102	25 Jan 1984	Sydney	8-244*	Pakistan	157	Won by 87 runs	KJ Hughes
103	29 Jan 1984	Adelaide	7-165*	West Indies	4-169	Lost by 6 wkts	KJ Hughes
104	30 Jan 1984	Adelaide	8-210*	Pakistan	140	Won by 70 runs	KJ Hughes
105	5 Feb 1984	Perth	8-211*	West Indies	197	Won by 14 runs	KJ Hughes
106	8 Feb 1984	Sydney	160*	West Indies	1-161	Lost by 9 wkts	KJ Hughes
107	11 Feb 1984	Melbourne	9-222	West Indies	5-222*	Tie	KJ Hughes
108	12 Feb 1984	Melbourne	8-212*	West Indies	4-213	Lost by 6 wkts	KJ Hughes
109	29 Feb 1984	Berbice	5-231*	West Indies	2-232	Lost by 8 wkts	KJ Hughes
110	14 Mar 1984	Port-of-Spain	6-194	West Indies	6-190*	Won by 4 wkts	KJ Hughes
111	19 Apr 1984	Castries	9-206*	West Indies	3-208	Lost by 7 wkts	KJ Hughes
112	26 Apr 1984	Kingston	7-209*	West Indies	1-211	Lost by 9 wkts	KJ Hughes
113	28 Sep 1984	New Delhi	9-220*	India	172	Won by 48 runs	KJ Hughes
114	1 Oct 1984	Trivandrum	1-29	India	175*	No result	KJ Hughes
115	3 Oct 1984	Jamshedpur	—	India	2-21*	No result	KJ Hughes

Continued

Game	Date	Venue	Australia Total	Opponent	Total	Result			Captain
116	5 Oct 1984	Ahmedabad	3-210	India	6-206*	Won by	7	wkts	KJ Hughes
117	6 Oct 1984	Indore	4-236	India	5-235*	Won by	6	wkts	KJ Hughes
118	6 Jan 1985	Melbourne	6-240*	West Indies	3-241	Lost by	7	wkts	AR Border
119	8 Jan 1985	Sydney	4-240	Sri Lanka	7-239*	Won by	6	wkts	AR Border
120	13 Jan 1985	Brisbane	191*	West Indies	5-195	Lost by	5	wkts	AR Border
121	15 Jan 1985	Sydney	5-200*	West Indies	5-201	Lost by	5	wkts	AR Border
122	19 Jan 1985	Melbourne	9-226*	Sri Lanka	6-230	Lost by	4	wkts	AR Border
123	20 Jan 1985	Melbourne	9-206	West Indies	7-271*	Lost by	65	runs	AR Border
124	23 Jan 1985	Sydney	7-242	Sri Lanka	6-240*	Won by	3	wkts	AR Border
125	27 Jan 1985	Adelaide	9-200*	West Indies	4-201	Lost by	6	wkts	AR Border
126	28 Jan 1985	Adelaide	2-323*	Sri Lanka	91	Won by 232	runs		AR Border
127	3 Feb 1985	Perth	1-172	Sri Lanka	171*	Won by	9	wkts	AR Border
128	6 Feb 1985	Sydney	6-247*	West Indies	221	Won by	26	runs	AR Border
129	10 Feb 1985	Melbourne	3-271*	West Indies	6-273	Lost by	4	wkts	AR Border
130	12 Feb 1985	Sydney	178*	West Indies	3-179	Lost by	7	wkts	AR Border
131	17 Feb 1985	Melbourne	3-215	England	8-214*	Won by	7	wkts	AR Border
132	24 Feb 1985	Melbourne	200	Pakistan	6-262*	Lost by	62	runs	AR Border
133	3 Mar 1985	Melbourne	163	India	2-165*	Lost by	8	wkts	AR Border
134	24 Mar 1985	Sharjah	8-178	England	8-177*	Won by	2	wkts	AR Border
135	29 Mar 1985	Sharjah	139*	India	7-140	Lost by	3	wkts	AR Border
136	30 May 1985	Manchester	7-220	England	219*	Won by	3	wkts	AR Border
137	1 Jun 1985	Birmingham	6-233	England	7-231*	Won by	4	wkts	AR Border
138	3 Jun 1985	Lord's	5-254*	England	2-257	Lost by	8	wkts	AR Border
139	9 Jan 1986	Melbourne	—	New Zealand	7-161*	No result			AR Border
140	12 Jan 1986	Brisbane	6-164	India	161*	Won by	4	wkts	AR Border
141	14 Jan 1986	Sydney	6-153	New Zealand	152*	Won by	4	wkts	AR Border
142	16 Jan 1986	Melbourne	161*	India	2-162	Lost by	8	wkts	AR Border
143	19 Jan 1986	Perth	6-161	New Zealand	6-159*	Won by	4	wkts	AR Border
144	21 Jan 1986	Sydney	6-292*	India	4-192	Won by 100	runs		AR Border
145	26 Jan 1986	Adelaide	8-262*	India	226	Won by	36	runs	AR Border
146	27 Jan 1986	Adelaide	70	New Zealand	7-276*	Lost by 206	runs		AR Border
147	29 Jan 1986	Sydney	7-239*	New Zealand	140	Won by	99	runs	AR Border
148	31 Jan 1986	Melbourne	7-235*	India	4-238	Lost by	6	wkts	AR Border
149	5 Feb 1986	Sydney	8-170*	India	159	Won by	11	runs	AR Border
150	9 Feb 1986	Melbourne	3-188	India	187*	Won by	7	wkts	AR Border
151	19 Mar 1986	Dunedin	156	New Zealand	6-186*	Lost by	30	runs	AR Border
152	22 Mar 1986	Christchurch	205	New Zealand	7-258*	Lost by	53	runs	AR Border
153	26 Mar 1986	Wellington	7-232	New Zealand	9-229*	Won by	3	wkts	AR Border
154	29 Mar 1986	Auckland	231*	New Zealand	9-187	Won by	44	runs	AR Border
155	11 Apr 1986	Sharjah	7-202*	Pakistan	2-206	Lost by	8	wkts	RJ Bright
156	7 Sep 1986	Jaipur	3-250*	India	3-251	Lost by	7	wkts	AR Border
157	9 Sep 1986	Srinagar	7-226	India	8-222*	Won by	3	wkts	AR Border
158	24 Sep 1986	Hyderabad	6-242*	India	1-41	No result			AR Border
159	2 Oct 1986	Delhi	6-238*	India	7-242	Lost by	3	wkts	AR Border
160	5 Oct 1986	Ahmedabad	141	India	193*	Lost by	52	runs	AR Border
161	7 Oct 1986	Rajkot	3-263	India	6-260*	Won by	7	wkts	AR Border
162	1 Jan 1987	Perth	235	England	6-272*	Lost by	37	runs	AR Border
163	2 Jan 1987	Perth	6-273*	Pakistan	9-274	Lost by	1	wkt	AR Border
164	4 Jan 1987	Perth	91	West Indies	8-255*	Lost by	164	runs	AR Border
165	18 Jan 1987	Brisbane	4-261*	England	9-250	Won by	11	runs	AR Border
166	20 Jan 1987	Melbourne	6-181*	West Indies	3-182	Lost by	7	wkts	AR Border
167	22 Jan 1987	Sydney	8-233*	England	7-234	Lost by	3	wkts	AR Border
168	25 Jan 1987	Adelaide	9-221	West Indies	5-237*	Lost by	16	runs	AR Border
169	26 Jan 1987	Adelaide	6-225*	England	192	Won by	33	runs	AR Border
170	28 Jan 1987	Sydney	194*	West Indies	158	Won by	36	runs	AR Border
171	1 Feb 1987	Melbourne	5-248*	England	139	Won by 109	runs		AR Border
172	6 Feb 1987	Sydney	8-195	West Indies	192*	Won by	2	wkts	AR Border
173	8 Feb 1987	Melbourne	8-171*	England	4-172	Lost by	6	wkts	AR Border
174	11 Feb 1987	Sydney	8-179	England	9-187*	Lost by	8	runs	AR Border
175	3 Apr 1987	Sharjah	9-176*	Pakistan	4-180	Lost by	6	wkts	AR Border
176	6 Apr 1987	Sharjah	6-176*	India	3-177	Lost by	7	wkts	GR Marsh
177	9 Apr 1987	Sharjah	9-219	England	6-230*	Lost by	11	runs	AR Border
178	9 Oct 1987	Madras	6-270*	India	269	Won by	1	run	AR Border
179	13 Oct 1987	Madras	9-235*	Zimbabwe	139	Won by	96	runs	AR Border
180	19 Oct 1987	Indore	4-199*	New Zealand	9-196	Won by	3	runs	AR Border
181	22 Oct 1987	New Delhi	233	India	6-289*	Lost by	56	runs	AR Border
182	27 Oct 1987	Chandigarh	8-251*	New Zealand	234	Won by	17	runs	AR Border
183	30 Oct 1987	Cuttack	5-266*	Zimbabwe	6-196	Won by	70	runs	AR Border
184	4 Nov 1987	Lahore	8-267*	Pakistan	249	Won by	18	runs	AR Border
185	8 Nov 1987	Calcutta	5-253*	England	8-246	Won by	7	runs	AR Border

Game	Date	Venue	Australia Total	Opponent	Total	Result	Captain
186	2 Jan 1988	Perth	7-249*	Sri Lanka	168	Won by 81 runs	AR Border
187	3 Jan 1988	Perth	231	New Zealand	9-232*	Lost by 1 run	AR Border
188	7 Jan 1988	Melbourne	216*	New Zealand	9-210	Won by 6 runs	AR Border
189	10 Jan 1988	Adelaide	6-289*	Sri Lanka	8-208	Won by 81 runs	AR Border
190	14 Jan 1988	Melbourne	8-243*	Sri Lanka	205	Won by 38 runs	AR Border
191	17 Jan 1988	Brisbane	5-177	New Zealand	5-176*	Won by 5 wkts	AR Border
192	19 Jan 1988	Sydney	7-189	Sri Lanka	9-188*	Won by 3 wkts	AR Border
193	20 Jan 1988	Sydney	8-221*	New Zealand	143	Won by 78 runs	AR Border
194	22 Jan 1988	Melbourne	2-180	New Zealand	177*	Won by 8 wkts	AR Border
195	24 Jan 1988	Sydney	4-169	New Zealand	5-168*	Won by 6 wkts	AR Border
196	4 Feb 1988	Melbourne	6-235*	England	8-213	Won by 22 runs	AR Border
197	14 Oct 1988	Lahore	8-229*	Pakistan	7-229	Lost—less wkts	AR Border
198	11 Dec 1988	Adelaide	1-178	Pakistan	177*	Won by 9 wkts	AR Border
199	13 Dec 1988	Sydney	8-219	West Indies	220*	Lost by 1 run	AR Border
200	15 Dec 1988	Melbourne	202	West Indies	236*	Lost by 34 runs	AR Border
201	2 Jan 1989	Perth	178	Pakistan	7-216*	Lost by 38 runs	AR Border
202	5 Jan 1989	Melbourne	226*	West Indies	8-218	Won by 8 runs	AR Border
203	8 Jan 1989	Brisbane	5-204	Pakistan	9-203*	Won by 5 wkts	AR Border
204	10 Jan 1989	Melbourne	4-258*	Pakistan	7-108	Won on run rate	AR Border
205	12 Jan 1989	Sydney	5-215*	West Indies	8-154	Won by 61 runs	AR Border
206	14 Jan 1989	Melbourne	9-204*	West Indies	9-202	Won by 2 runs	AR Border
207	16 Jan 1989	Sydney	185	West Indies	9-277*	Lost by 92 runs	AR Border
208	18 Jan 1989	Sydney	4-226*	West Indies	2-111	Lost on run rate	AR Border
209	25 May 1989	Manchester	136	England	9-231*	Lost by 95 runs	AR Border
210	27 May 1989	Nottingham	8-226	England	5-226*	Tied	AR Border
211	29 May 1989	Lord's	4-279	England	7-278	Won by 6 wkts	AR Border
212	19 Oct 1989	Hyderabad	3-242*	England	3-243	Lost by 7 wkts	AR Border
213	21 Oct 1989	Madras	6-241*	West Indies	142	Won by 99 runs	AR Border
214	23 Oct 1989	Bombay	139	Pakistan	8-205*	Lost by 66 runs	AR Border
215	25 Oct 1989	Goa	7-222*	Sri Lanka	194	Won by 28 runs	AR Border
216	27 Oct 1989	Bangalore	8-247*	India	7-249	Lost by 3 wkts	AR Border
217	26 Dec 1989	Melbourne	5-228*	India	198	Won by 30 runs	AR Border
218	30 Dec 1989	Perth	1-204	Sri Lanka	9-203*	Won by 9 wkts	AR Border
219	3 Jan 1990	Melbourne	3-162	Pakistan	161*	Won by 7 wkts	AR Border
220	4 Jan 1990	Melbourne	7-202*	Sri Lanka	129	Won by 73 runs	AR Border
221	11 Jan 1990	Brisbane	5-300*	Pakistan	233	Won by 67 runs	AR Border
222	13 Feb 1990	Sydney	8-165*	Pakistan	5-167	Lost by 5 wkts	AR Border
223	18 Feb 1990	Adelaide	3-159	Pakistan	158*	Won by 7 wkts	AR Border
224	20 Feb 1990	Sydney	9-218	Pakistan	8-220*	Lost by 2 runs	AR Border
225	23 Feb 1990	Melbourne	3-163	Pakistan	162*	Won by 7 wkts	AR Border
226	25 Feb 1990	Sydney	6-255	Pakistan	186*	Won by 69 runs	AR Border
227	3 Mar 1990	Christchurch	9-187*	India	169	Won by 18 runs	AR Border
228	4 Mar 1990	Christchurch	8-244*	New Zealand	94	Won by 150 runs	AR Border
229	8 Mar 1990	Hamilton	3-212	India	8-211*	Won by 7 wkts	AR Border
230	10 Mar 1990	Auckland	6-239*	New Zealand	2-167	Won on run rate	GR Marsh
231	11 Mar 1990	Auckland	2-164	New Zealand	162*	Won by 8 wkts	AR Border
232	26 Apr 1990	Sharjah	5-258*	New Zealand	7-195	Won by 63 runs	AR Border
233	30 Apr 1990	Sharjah	3-140	Bangladesh	8-134*	Won by 7 wkts	AR Border
234	2 May 1990	Sharjah	3-332*	Sri Lanka	218	Won by 114 runs	AR Border
235	4 May 1990	Sharjah	230	Pakistan	7-266*	Lost by 36 runs	AR Border

* Denotes batted first

Australian Limited-Overs Results

Opponent	First Game	Games	Won	Lost	N/R	Tied	Success Batting 1st	Success Batting 2nd
England	Jan 5 1971	47	21	24	1	1	34.78%	54.17%
New Zealand	Mar 30 1974	43	29	12	2	—	87.50%	55.56%
Pakistan	Jun 7 1975	33	15	16	2	—	61.11%	26.67%
Sri Lanka	Jun 11 1975	20	15	3	2	—	64.29%	100.00%
West Indies	Jun 14 1975	53	17	35	—	1	34.48%	29.17%
Canada	Jun 16 1979	1	1	—	—	—	—	100.00%
India	Dec 6 1980	33	18	12	3	—	47.06%	62.58%
Zimbabwe	Jun 9 1983	4	3	1	—	—	100.00%	0.00%
Bangladesh	Apr 30 1990	1	1	—	—	—	—	100.00%
Total		235					52.50%	49.57%

493

Opponent	First Game	Games	Won	Lost	N/R	Tied	Success Batting 1st	Success Batting 2nd
Games in Australia	Jan 5 1971	142	76	61	4	1	55.56%	51.43%
Games abroad	Mar 30 1974	93	44	42	6	1	47.92%	46.67%

Most wins in succession	9 games	(Jan 5 1988–Feb 4 1988)
Most losses in succession	5 games	(Mar 17 1983–Jun 11/12 1983)
	5 games	(Feb 8 1987–Apr 9 1987)

Summary of Limited-Overs Cricket for Australian Grounds

Venue	First Game	Games	Results Batting 1st	Batting 2nd	No Result	Tied
Melbourne	Jan 5 1971	65	29	34	1	1
Adelaide	Dec 20 1975	27	16	11	—	—
Sydney	Jan 13 1979	64	32	29	3	—
Brisbane	Dec 23 1979	21	7	13	1	—
Perth	Dec 9 1980	24	11	13	—	—
Hobart TCA	Jan 10 1985	1	—	1	—	—
Launceston	Feb 2 1986	1	1	—	—	—
Devonport	Feb 3 1987	1	1	—	—	—
Hobart Bel	Jan 12 1988	3	1	2	—	—
Total		207	98	103	5	1

Leading Run Scorers

Batsman	M	Inn	NO	Runs	HS	50	100	Avrge
AR Border	210	195	29	5263	127*	33	3	31.70
DM Jones	100	98	19	3857	121	28	6	48.82
GR Marsh	87	86	5	3147	126*	14	7	38.85
DC Boon	91	88	4	2965	122	17	2	35.30
CS Chappell	74	72	14	2331	138*	14	3	40.19
GM Wood	83	77	11	2219	114*	11	3	33.62
SR Waugh	96	84	21	2068	83*	10	—	32.83
KJ Hughes	97	88	6	1968	98	17	—	24.00
KC Wessels	54	51	3	1740	107	14	1	36.25
RW Marsh	92	76	15	1225	66	4	—	20.08
SP O'Donnell	75	57	14	1053	74*	7	—	24.49
GM Ritchie	44	42	7	959	84	6	—	27.40
SB Smith	28	24	2	861	117	8	2	39.14
WB Phillips	48	41	6	852	75*	6	—	24.34
DW Hookes	39	36	2	826	76	5	—	24.29
GN Yallop	30	27	6	823	66*	7	—	39.19
J Dyson	29	27	4	755	79	4	—	32.83
IM Chappell	16	16	2	673	86	8	—	48.07
BM Laird	23	23	3	594	117*	2	1	29.70
MA Taylor	16	15	—	516	76	5	—	34.40
KD Walters	28	24	6	513	59	2	—	28.50

Leading Wicket-Takers

Bowler	M	Balls	Mdn	Runs	Wkts	Avrge	5wi	Best
DK Lillee	63	3593	80	2145	103	20.83	1	5/34
SP O'Donnell	75	3738	42	2673	94	28.44	1	5/13
CJ McDermott	65	3549	36	2620	91	28.79	1	5/44
SR Waugh	96	3608	23	2687	88	30.53	0	4/33
GF Lawson	79	4259	94	2592	88	29.45	0	4/26
RM Hogg	71	3677	57	2418	85	28.45	0	4/29
TM Alderman	57	2951	67	1818	81	22.44	2	5/17
CG Rackemann	46	2480	47	1635	76	21.51	1	5/16
GS Chappell	74	3108	41	2096	72	29.11	2	5/15
PL Taylor	55	2721	24	1884	68	27.71	0	4/38
AR Border	210	2074	10	1601	55	29.11	0	3/20
JR Thomson	50	2696	37	1942	55	35.31	0	4/67
LS Pascoe	29	1568	21	1066	53	20.11	1	5/30
BA Reid	41	2190	33	1561	48	32.52	1	5/53
SP Davis	39	2016	46	1139	44	25.89	0	3/10
GRJ Matthews	46	2185	19	1553	43	36.12	0	3/27
MG Hughes	22	1052	12	716	27	26.52	0	4/44
TG Hogan	16	917	12	574	23	24.96	0	4/33
AIC Dodemaide	12	655	11	360	20	18.00	1	5/21
MHN Walker	17	1006	24	546	20	27.30	0	4/19

Highest Innings Totals

Total	Overs	Opponent	Venue	Season
6-332*	50.0	Sri Lanka	Sharjah	1989/90
5-328*	60.0	Sri Lanka	The Oval	1975
3-323*	50.0	Sri Lanka	Adelaide	1984/85
9-320*	60.0	India	Nottingham	1983
8-302*	50.0	New Zealand	Melbourne	1982/83
5-300*	50.0	Pakistan	Brisbane	1989/90
6-292*	50.0	India	Sydney	1985/86
3-289*	50.0	New Zealand	Sydney	1980/81
6-289*	50.0	Sri Lanka	Adelaide	1987/88
4-279	54.3	England	Lord's	1989
7-278*	60.0	Pakistan	Leeds	1975
274	58.4	West Indies	Lord's	1975
6-273*	60.0	West Indies	Lord's	1975
5-273	55.0	England	Birmingham	1980
6-273*	50.0	Pakistan	Perth	1986/87
7-272*	60.0	Zimbabwe	Southampton	1983
3-271*	50.0	West Indies	Melbourne	1984/85
6-270*	50.0	India	Madras	1987/88
8-267*	50.0	Pakistan	Lahore	1987/88
5-266*	50.0	Zimbabwe	Cuttack	1987/88
5-265*	35.0	New Zealand	Christchurch	1973/74
3-263	48.0	India	Rajkot	1986/87
8-262*	50.0	India	Adelaide	1985/86
4-261*	50.0	England	Brisbane	1986/87
4-258*	43.0	Pakistan	Melbourne	1988/89
6-255*	50.0	Pakistan	Sydney	1989/90
5-254*	55.0	England	Lord's	1985
5-253*	50.0	England	Calcutta	1987/88
8-251*	50.0	New Zealand	Chandigarh	1987/88
3-250*	47.0	India	Jaipur	1986/87

* Denotes batted first

Lowest Completed Innings Totals

Total	Overs	Opponent	Venue	Season
70	25.2	England	Birmingham	1977
70	26.3	New Zealand	Adelaide	1985/86
91	35.4	West Indies	Perth	1986/87
101*	33.5	England	Melbourne	1978/79
107	32.2	West Indies	Melbourne	1981/82
109	27.3	England	Sydney	1982/83
124	34.0	New Zealand	Sydney	1982/83
129	38.2	India	Chelmsford	1983
130	37.4	West Indies	Melbourne	1981/82
136	47.1	England	Manchester	1989
139*	42.3	India	Sharjah	1984/85
139	43.2	Pakistan	Bombay	1989/90
141	43.3	India	Ahmedabad	1986/87
142	42.1	India	Melbourne	1980/81
146	42.5	West Indies	Melbourne	1981/82

* Denotes batted first

Century Makers

Score	Batsman	Opponent	Venue	Season
138*	GS Chappell	New Zealand	Sydney	1980/81
127*	AR Border	West Indies	Sydney	1984/85
126*	GR Marsh	New Zealand	Chandigarh	1987/88
125*	GS Chappell	England	The Oval	1977
125	GR Marsh	India	Sydney	1985/86
125*	GR Marsh	Pakistan	Melbourne	1988/89
122	DC Boon	Sri Lanka	Adelaide	1987/88
121	DM Jones	Pakistan	Perth	1986/87
118*	AR Border	Sri Lanka	Adelaide	1984/85
117*	BM Laird	West Indies	Sydney	1981/82
117	SB Smith	New Zealand	Melbourne	1982/83
117*	DM Jones	Sri Lanka	Sharjah	1989/90
114*	GM Wood	England	Lord's	1985
111	DC Boon	India	Jaipur	1986/87
111*	GR Marsh	England	Lord's	1989
110	TM Chappell	India	Nottingham	1983
110	GR Marsh	India	Madras	1987/88

Continued

495

Score	Batsman	Opponent	Venue	Season
108	GS Chappell	New Zealand	Auckland	1981/82
108	GM Wood	England	Leeds	1981
107	KC Wessels	India	New Delhi	1984/85
107	DM Jones	New Zealand	Christchurch	1989/90
106	SB Smith	Pakistan	Sydney	1983/84
105*	AR Border	India	Sydney	1980/81
104*	GM Wood	West Indies	Adelaide	1984/85
104	GR Marsh	India	Jaipur	1986/87
104	DM Jones	England	Perth	1986/87
102*	DM Jones	New Zealand	Auckland	1989/90
101	A Turner	Sri Lanka	The Oval	1975
101	DM Jones	England	Brisbane	1986/87
101	GR Marsh	New Zealand	Sydney	1979/80

Best Individual Bowling Performance

Wkts	Bowler	Opponent	Venue	Season
6/14	GJ Gilmour	England	Leeds	1975
6/39	KH MacLeay	India	Nottingham	1983
5/13	SP O'Donnell	New Zealand	Christchurch	1989/90
5/15	GS Chappell	India	Sydney	1980/81
5/16	CG Rackemann	Pakistan	Adelaide	1983/84
5/17	TM Alderman	New Zealand	Wellington	1981/82
5/18	GJ Cosier	England	Birmingham	1977
5/20	GS Chappell	England	Birmingham	1977
5/21	AG Hurst	Canada	Birmingham	1979
5/21	AIC Dodemaide	Sri Lanka	Perth	1979/80
5/30	LS Pascoe	New Zealand	Sydney	1980/81
5/32	TM Alderman	India	Christchurch	1989/90
5/34	DK Lillee	Pakistan	Leeds	1975
5/44	CJ McDermott	Pakistan	Lahore	1987/88
5/46	DR Gilbert	New Zealand	Sydney	1985/86
5/48	GJ Gilmour	West Indies	Lord's	1975
5/53	BA Reid	India	Adelaide	1985/86

Record Wicket Partnerships

Wkt	Ttl	Batsmen	Opponent	Venue	Season
1st	212	Marsh GR, Boon DC	India	Jaipur	1986/87
2nd	178	Marsh GR, Jones DM	England	Brisbane	1986/87
3rd	224*	Jones DM, Border AR	Sri Lanka	Adelaide	1984/85
4th	173	Jones DM, Waugh SR	Pakistan	Perth	1986/87
5th	115*	Laird BM, Border AR	New Zealand	Dunedin	1981/82
6th	108*	Jones DM, O'Donnell SP	Sri Lanka	Melbourne	1989/90
7th	102*	Waugh SR, Dyer GC	India	Delhi	1986/87
8th	50*	Marsh RW, Hogg RM	Zimbabwe	Nottingham	1983
9th	52	O'Donnell SP, Wood GM	West Indies	Sydney	1984/85
10th	45	Laughlin TJ, Walker MHN	England	Sydney	1979/80

Highest Wicket Partnerships

Wkt	Ttl	Batsmen	Opponent	Venue	Season
3rd	224*	DM Jones, AR Border	Sri Lanka	Adelaide	1984/85
1st	212	DC Boon, GR Marsh	India	Jaipur	1986/87
1st	182	RB McCosker, A Turner	Sri Lanka	The Oval	1975
2nd	178	GR Marsh, DM Jones	England	Brisbane	1986/87
4th	173	DM Jones, SR Waugh	Pakistan	Perth	1986/87
4th	164	DM Jones, AR Border	England	Adelaide	1986/87
3rd	159	DC Boon, AR Border	England	Sharjah	1986/87
2nd	157*	SB Smith, WB Phillips	Sri Lanka	Perth	1984/85
4th	157*	RB Kerr, DM Jones	England	Melbourne	1984/85
1st	154	KC Wessels, J Dyson	New Zealand	Melbourne	1982/83
1st	154	MA Taylor, TM Moody	Pakistan	Brisbane	1989/90
1st	152	GR Marsh, DC Boon	India	Sydney	1985/86
2nd	151	J Dyson, GS Chappell	New Zealand	Sydney	1980/81
4th	150	AR Border, KJ Hughes	West Indies	Castries	1983/84

AUSTRALIAN DOMESTIC LIMITED-OVERS CRICKET RESULTS

State	Played	Won	Lost	No-Result	Tie
Western Australia	63	44	17	1	1
Victoria	53	22	29	1	1
Queensland	50	27	22	1	—
New South Wales	50	25	24	—	1
South Australia	50	19	30	—	1
Tasmania	42	11	30	1	—
*New Zealand	10	7	3	—	—

Total   159

* New Zealand did not compete after the 1974/75 season)

The Winners

Season	Winners	Runner-up
V & G Australiansian Knock-Out Competition		
1969/70	New Zealand	Victoria
1970/71	Western Australia	Queensland
Coca-Cola Australiansian Knock-Out Competition		
1971/72	Victoria	South Australia
1972/73	New Zealand	Queensland
The Gillette Cup		
1973/74	Western Australia	New Zealand
1974/75	New Zealand	Western Australia
1975/76	Queensland	Western Australia
1976/77	Western Australia	Victoria
1977/78	Western Australia	Tasmania
1978/79	Tasmania	Western Australia
McDonald's Cup		
1979/80	Victoria	New South Wales
1980/81	Queensland	Western Australia
1981/82	Queensland	New South Wales
1982/83	Western Australia	New South Wales
1983/84	South Australia	Western Australia
1984/85	New South Wales	South Australia
1985/86	Western Australia	Victoria
1986/87	South Australia	Tasmania
1987/88	New South Wales	South Australia
FAI Insurance Cup		
1988/89	Queensland	Victoria
1989/90	Western Australia	South Australia

AUSTRALIAN DOMESTIC LIMITED-OVERS CRICKET

	Date	Venue	Batted 1st		Batted 2nd		Result
THE V. & G. AUSTRALASIAN KNOCK-OUT COMPETITION							
1	Nov 22 1969	Melbourne	Tas	9-130	Vic*	2-131	Vic by 8 wkts
2	Nov 30 1969	Perth	WA*	8-188	SA	8-187	WA by 1 run
3	Dec 7 1969	Sydney	NSW	8-227	Qld*	195	NSW by 32 runs
4	Dec 30 1969	Sydney	NSW*	150	NZ	6-153	NZ by 4 wkts
5	Dec 30 1969	Melbourne	Vic	157	WA*	59	Vic by 98 runs
6	Jan 1 1970	Melbourne	Vic*	129	NZ	4-130	NZ by 6 wkts
7	Oct 18 1970	Adelaide	Vic*	9-199	SA	5-202	SA by 3 runs
8	Nov 1 1970	Brisbane	NSW	155	Qld*	3-156	Qld by 7 wkts
9	Nov 4 1970	Launceston	WA*	8-218	Tas	205	WA by 13 runs
10	Dec 6 1970	Adelaide	SA	6-261	Qld*	6-264	Qld by 3 runs
11	Jan 31 1971	Perth	NZ*	120	WA	7-123	WA by 3 wkts
12	Feb 6 1971	Melbourne	WA	170	Qld*	79	WA by 91 runs
THE AUSTRALASIAN (COCA-COLA) KNOCK-OUT COMPETITION							
13	Nov 14 1971	Adelaide	Tas*	124	SA	2-125	SA by 8 wkts
14	Nov 27 1971	Sydney	NSW*	205	WA	4-209	WA by 6 wkts

Continued

497

Date		Venue	Batted 1st		Batted 2nd		Result
15	Dec 5 1971	Brisbane	Qld°	161	Vic	7-162	Vic by 3 wkts
16	Dec 15 1971	Adelaide	WA°	6-211	SA	7-213	SA by 3 wkts
17	Feb 4 1972	Melbourne	Vic	7-232	NZ°	156	Vic by 76 runs
18	Feb 6 1972	Adelaide	SA	190	Vic°	2-192	Vic by 8 wkts
19	Oct 29 1972	Perth	SA	9-204	WA°	171	SA by 33 runs
20	Dec 31 1972	Brisbane	Qld	141	Tas°	111	Qld by 30 runs
21	Dec 17 1972	Melbourne	Vic	7-232	NSW°	9-233	NSW by 1 wkt
22	Jan 14 1973	Adelaide	NZ°	9-190	SA	137	NZ by 53 runs
23	Jan 14 1973	Brisbane	NSW	92	Qld°	1-94	Qld by 9 wkts
24	Jan 21 1973	Brisbane	NZ	9-170	Qld°	132	NZ by 38 runs

THE GILLETTE CUP

Date		Venue	Batted 1st		Batted 2nd		Result
25	Nov 11 1973	Perth	Vic	117	WA°	6-119	WA by 4 wkts
26	Dec 17 1973	Hobart	Tas	104	NSW°	5-105	NSW by 5 wkts
27	Jan 20 1974	Adelaide	Qld	230	SA°	5-233	SA by 5 wkts
28	Feb 2 1974	Sydney	NSW	9-262	WA°	6-263	WA by 4 wkts
29	Feb 2 1974	Adelaide	NZ	217	SA°	177	NZ by 40 runs
30	Feb 3 1974	Melbourne	NZ	150	WA°	3-151	WA by 7 wkts
31	Oct 19 1974	Perth	SA	8-180	WA°	4-182	WA by 6 wkts
32	Nov 3 1974	Brisbane	Qld	7-211	NSW°	210	Qld by 1 run
33	Nov 17 1974	Melbourne	Vic°	7-190	Tas	8-193	Tas by 2 wkts
34	Jan 12 1975	Perth	Qld	9-168	WA°	4-171	WA by 6 wkts
35	Jan 17 1975	Melbourne	Tas	8-176	NZ°	3-177	NZ by 7 wkts
36	Feb 2 1975	Melbourne	WA	76	NZ°	2-77	NZ by 8 wkts
37	Oct 26 1975	Perth	Vic	8-193	WA°	7-195	WA by 2 runs
38	Nov 23 1975	Adelaide	SA	195	NSW°	8-180	SA by 5 runs
39	Jan 1 1976	Hobart TCA	Qld	6-244	Tas°	158	Qld by 86 runs
40	Jan 11 1976	Brisbane	Qld	182	SA°	97	Qld by 85 runs
41	Feb 8 1976	Brisbane	Qld	7-236	WA°	232	Qld by 4 runs
42	Dec 4 1976	Adelaide	SA	6-207	WA°	6-211	WA by 4 wkts
43	Dec 5 1976	Brisbane	Tas	89	Qld°	5-93	Qld by 5 wkts
44	Dec 11 1976	Sydney	NSW	9-195	Vic°	6-199	Vic by 4 wkts
45	Dec 12 1976	Perth	WA	77	Qld°	62	WA by 15 runs
46	Jan 23 1977	Melbourne	Vic	164	WA°	9-165	WA by 1 wkts
47	Oct 30 1977	Brisbane	Qld	169	NSW°	4-170	NSW by 6 wkts
48	Jan 15 1978	Hobart TCA	Tas	184	SA°	7-167	Tas by 17 runs
49	Jan 21 1978	Perth	NSW	168	WA°	6-169	WA by 4 wkts
50	Jan 22 1978	Melbourne	Tas	9-224	Vic°	187	Tas by 37 runs
51	Feb 5 1978	Perth	Tas	9-184	WA°	3-185	WA by 7 wkts
52	Oct 28 1978	Brisbane	SA	101	Qld°	2-105	Qld by 8 wkts
53	Oct 29 1978	Sydney	NSW	6-156	Vic°	5-157	Vic by 5 wkts
54	Dec 10 1978	Brisbane	Qld	6-232	Tas°	9-236	Tas by 1 wkt
55	Dec 23 1978	Perth	WA	6-215	Vic°	7-214	WA by 1 run
56	Jan 14 1979	Hobart TCA	Tas	6-180	WA°	133	Tas by 47 runs

THE McDONALD'S CUP

Date		Venue	Batted 1st		Batted 2nd		Result
57	Nov 10 1979	Hobart TCA	Qld°	9-188	Tas	5-190	Tas by 5 wkts
58	Nov 10 1979	Adelaide	WA	9-219	SA°	184	WA by 35 runs
59	Nov 11 1979	Hobart TCA	NSW	4-191	Tas°	2-94	Tas on run rate
60	Nov 11 1979	Adelaide	SA	6-213	Vic°	7-215	Vic by 3 wkts
61	Nov 18 1979	Brisbane	Qld	167	NSW°	3-171	NSW by 7 wkts
62	Nov 18 1979	Perth	Vic	9-190	WA°	4-192	WA by 6 wkts
63	Nov 21 1979	VFL Park	Vic	6-242	Tas°	9-194	Vic by 48 runs
64	Nov 21 1979	Sydney	NSW	7-256	WA°	138	NSW by 118 runs
65	Nov 24 1979	Sydney	WA	8-209	Tas°	7-172	WA by 37 runs
66	Nov 25 1979	Melbourne	NSW	8-198	Vic°	6-199	Vic by 4 wkts
67	Nov 8 1980	Melbourne	Vic	5-121	Qld°	6-70	Vic by 51 runs
68	Nov 9 1980	Melbourne	Vic°	138	NSW	2-139	NSW by 6 wkts
69	Nov 20 1980	Perth	SA	7-176	WA°	3-178	WA by 7 wkts
70	Nov 21 1980	Sydney	NSW°	6-214	Qld	5-215	Qld by 5 wkts
71	Jan 16 1981	Hobart TCA	WA	9-203	Tas°	144	WA by 59 runs
72	Jan 30 1981	Hobart TCA	SA	8-218	Tas°	181	SA by 37 runs
73	Feb 14 1981	Perth	WA	8-214	Vic°	187	WA by 27 runs
74	Feb 15 1981	Adelaide	SA	9-218	Qld°	5-219	Qld by 5 wkts
75	Feb 21 1981	Adelaide	SA	209	Vic°	9-176	SA by 33 runs
76	Feb 22 1981	Brisbane	Qld°	9-188	WA	116	Qld by 72 runs
77	Nov 7 1981	Brisbane	Tas	7-225	Qld°	3-229	Qld by 7 wkts
78	Nov 8 1981	Brisbane	WA	8-148	Qld°	4-149	Qld by 6 wkts

Date			Venue	Batted 1st		Batted 2nd		Result
79	Nov	19 1981	Sydney	NSW•	2-260	Vic	8-213	NSW by 47 runs
80	Dec	3 1981	Sydney	NSW•	4-310	SA	199	NSW by 111 runs
81	Jan	1 1982	Adelaide	SA	5-249	Vic•	4-253	Vic by 6 wkts
82	Jan	7 1982	Perth	WA	3-215	Tas•	9-202	WA by 13 runs
83	Feb	6 1982	Brisbane	Qld	8-238	Vic•	7-217	Qld by 21 runs
84	Feb	7 1982	Perth	NSW	5-245	WA•	186	NSW by 59 runs
85	Mar	6 1982	St Kilda	Vic	8-171	WA•	8-172	WA by 2 wkts
86	Mar	7 1982	Sydney	Qld	8-224	NSW•	197	Qld by 27 runs
87	Nov	6 1982	Hobart TCA	Tas	147	Qld•	3-151	Qld by 7 wkts
88	Nov	7 1982	Hobart TCA	Vic	2-272	Tas•	7-169	Vic by 103 runs
89	Nov	18 1982	Sydney	NSW•	166	WA	4-167	WA by 6 wkts
90	Dec	8 1982	Sydney	SA•	9-195	NSW	2-197	NSW by 8 wkts
91	Dec	22 1982	Perth	SA	157	WA•	8-158	WA by 2 wkts
92	Jan	1 1983	Melbourne	Qld•	5-270	Vic	257	Qld by 13 runs
93	Mar	12 1983	Perth	Vic	112	WA•	7-115	WA by 3 wkts
94	Mar	13 1983	Brisbane	Qld	9-205	NSW•	8-206	NSW by 2 wkts
95	Oct	9 1983	Perth	NSW•	6-195	WA	6-198	WA by 4 wkts
96	Oct	15 1983	Brisbane	Tas	8-237	Qld•	194	Tas by 43 runs
97	Oct	15 1983	Perth	Vic	4-234	WA•	7-235	WA by 3 wkts
98	Oct	16 1983	Brisbane	NSW•	8-165	Qld	6-169	Qld by 4 wkts
99	Oct	16 1983	Perth	SA	6-136	WA•	3-112	WA on run rate
100	Nov	6 1983	Launceston	NSW•	7-237	Tas	9-166	NSW by 71 runs
101	Nov	6 1983	Adelaide	Vic	7-205	SA•	2-207	SA by 8 wkts
102	Dec	21 1983	Sydney	WA•	5-230	NSW	184	WA by 46 runs
103	Dec	21 1983	Launceston	Tas•	163	SA	5-167	SA by 5 wkts
104	Mar	4 1984	Adelaide	SA•	6-256	WA	9-248	SA by 8 runs
105	Oct	13 1984	Brisbane	Vic	202	Qld•	3-203	Qld by 7 wkts
106	Oct	13 1984	Perth	WA	5-218	Tas•	172	WA by 46 runs
107	Oct	14 1984	Brisbane	Qld	5-219	SA•	4-223	SA by 6 wkts
108	Oct	14 1984	Perth	NSW	203	WA•	189	NSW by 14 runs
109	Nov	3 1984	Devonport	NSW	190	Tas•	80	NSW by 90 runs
110	Nov	4 1984	Adelaide	SA	6-206	Vic•	4-209	Vic by 6 wkts
111	Dec	29 1984	Melbourne	Vic•	7-181	NSW	3-185	NSW by 7 wkts
112	Jan	5 1985	Adelaide	SA•	6-296	WA	173	SA by 123 runs
113	Feb	16 1985	Sydney	NSW•	7-278	SA	190	NSW by 88 runs
114	Oct	13 1985	Brisbane	Qld	8-235	Tas•	0-45	No result
115	Oct	13 1985	Adelaide	SA•	8-199	WA	8-200	WA by 2 wkts
116	Nov	28 1985	Melbourne	Vic	8-209	Tas•	7-201	Vic by 8 runs
117	Dec	5 1985	Sydney	NSW•	5-235	WA	7-234	NSW by 1 run
118	Dec	11 1985	Melbourne	Vic	170	Qld•	3-33	Qld by run rate
119	Dec	18 1985	Sydney	SA	8-203	NSW•	6-204	NSW by 4 wkts
120	Feb	15 1986	Sydney	NSW•	9-191	Vic	6-194	Vic by 4 wkts
121	Feb	16 1986	Brisbane	Qld•	212	WA	3-214	WA by 7 wkts
122	Mar	9 1986	Melbourne	WA	2-129	Vic•	—	No result
123	Mar	10 1986	Melbourne	WA	167	Vic•	148	WA by 19 runs
124	Oct	10 1986	Perth	WA•	7-248	Vic	8-174	WA by 74 runs
125	Oct	11 1986	Hobart TCA	Tas	7-231	Qld•	4-58	Tas on run rate
126	Oct	18 1986	Adelaide	SA•	5-226	Qld	1-193	Qld on run rate
127	Oct	19 1986	Adelaide	SA	5-245	Tas•	5-175	SA on run rate
128	Nov	2 1986	Perth	NSW	6-243	WA•	9-243	Tied
129	Nov	9 1986	Sydney	Vic	7-215	NSW•	214	Vic by 1 run
130	Feb	15 1987	Adelaide	SA•	7-222	Vic	6-222	Tied
131	Feb	15 1987	Perth	WA	5-266	Tas•	6-271	Tas by 4 wkts
132	Mar	15 1987	Hobart TCA	SA	6-325	Tas•	9-239	SA by 86 runs
133	Feb	19 1988	Perth	WA•	170	Vic	168	WA by 2 runs
134	Feb	21 1988	Brisbane	NSW•	7-287	Qld	134	NSW by 153 runs
135	Feb	28 1988	Launceston	Qld•	8-150	Tas	5-151	Tas by 5 wkts
136	Feb	28 1988	Adelaide	Vic•	232	SA	6-226	Vic by 6 runs
137	Mar	7 1988	Sydney	Tas	154	NSW•	6-123	NSW on run rate
138	Mar	7 1988	Perth	WA•	7-225	SA	6-229	WA by 4 wkts
139	Mar	12 1988	Adelaide	Tas	8-220	SA•	3-194	SA on run rate
140	Mar	13 1988	Sydney	Vic•	7-180	NSW	5-184	NSW by 5 wkts
141	Mar	27 1988	Sydney	NSW•	7-219	SA	6-196	NSW by 23 runs

THE FAI CUP

142	Feb	11 1989	Hobart TCA	Tas	121	WA•	2-125	WA by 8 wkts
143	Feb	12 1989	Brisbane	Vic•	7-216	Qld	114	Vic by 102 runs
144	Feb	19 1989	Adelaide	Qld•	3-258	SA	212	Qld by 46 runs
145	Feb	19 1989	Perth	NSW•	170	WA	7-173	WA by 3 wkts

Continued

Date			Venue	Batted 1st		Batted 2nd		Result
146	Feb	26 1989	Sydney	Tas	6-188	NSW*	1-189	NSW by 9 wkts
147	Feb	26 1989	Melbourne	SA*	185	Vic	3-186	Vic by 7 wkts
148	Mar	4 1989	Melbourne	Vic*	9-228	NSW	179	Vic by 49 runs
149	Mar	5 1989	Perth	Qld*	8-238	WA	6-222	Qld by 16 runs
150	Mar	19 1989	Melbourne	Qld*	4-253	Vic	90	Qld by 163 runs
151	Oct	21 1989	Adelaide	Qld*	6-210	SA	5-211	SA by 5 wkts
152	Oct	22 1989	Adelaide	Vic*	4-260	SA	9-232	Vic by 28 runs
153	Oct	22 1989	Perth	NSW*	5-248	WA	6-252	WA by 4 wkts
154	Oct	28 1989	Nth Sydney	NSW*	183	Tas	100	NSW by 83 runs
155	Oct	29 1989	Brisbane	Vic*	78	Qld	3-79	Qld by 7 wkts
156	Nov	6 1989	Perth	Tas*	6-249	WA	6-250	WA by 4 wkts
157	Mar	17 1990	Perth	Qld*	202	WA	4-203	WA by 6 wkts
158	Mar	18 1990	Adelaide	SA*	9-234	NSW	181	SA by 53 runs
159	Mar	31 1990	Perth	SA	87	WA*	3-88	WA by 7 wkts

* Denotes won toss

Most Appearances

Player	State	Career	Seasons	Games
GM Wood	WA	1977/78–1989/90	13	34
DW Hookes	SA	1975/76–1989/90	15	34
RW Marsh	WA	1969/70–1983/84	15	33
KH MacLeay	WA	1981/82–1989/90	9	30
JR Thomson	NSW/Qld	1972/73–1985/86	13	28
KJ Hughes	WA	1975/76–1984/85	10	28
RJ Inverarity	WA/SA	1969/70–1983/84	15	28
DK Lillee	WA/Tas	1969/70–1987/88	19	27
GS Chappell	SA/Qld	1969/70–1983/84	15	27
GF Lawson	NSW	1978/79–1989/90	12	27
WM Clark	WA	1973/74–1984/85	12	25
SJ Rixon	NSW	1974/75–1984/85	11	25
AR Border	NSW/Qld	1977/78–1989/90	13	25
DC Boon	Tas	1978/79–1989/90	12	25
TM Alderman	WA	1974/75–1989/90	16	25
GN Yallop	Vic	1974/75–1984/85	11	24
TM Chappell	SA/NSW	1972/73–1985/86	14	24
PR Sleep	SA	1978/79–1989/90	12	24
GM Ritchie	Qld	1980/81–1989/90	10	24
BM Laird	WA	1974/75–1983/84	10	23
G Dymock	Qld	1972/73–1981/82	10	23
PM Toohey	NSW	1974/75–1983/84	10	23
DM Jones	Vic	1981/82–1989/90	9	23
DM Wellham	NSW/Tas	1980/81–1989/90	10	23
AMJ Hilditch	NSW/SA	1977/78–1989/90	13	23
RD Woolley	Tas	1977/78–1986/87	10	22
B Yardley	WA	1973/74–1982/83	10	22
WB Phillips	SA	1977/78–1987/88	11	22
RJ Bright	Vic	1973/74–1986/87	14	22
DF Whatmore	Vic	1976/77–1987/88	12	22
RB McCosker	NSW	1973/74–1983/84	11	21
PH Carlson	Qld	1970/71–1980/81	11	20
JM Wiener	Vic	1977/78–1984/85	8	20
MG Hughes	Vic	1981/82–1989/90	9	20
MR Whitney	NSW	1980/81–1989/90	10	22
GRJ Matthews	NSW	1982/83–1989/90	8	20

Most Games For Each State

State	Player	Career	Seasons	Games
New South Wales	GF Lawson	1978/79–1989/90	12	27
Victoria	GN Yallop	1974/75–1984/85	11	24
South Australia	DW Hookes	1975/76–1989/90	15	34
Queensland	GM Ritchie	1980/81–1989/90	10	24
Western Australia	GM Wood	1977/78–1989/90	13	34
Tasmania	DC Boon	1978/79–1989/90	12	25

Highest Innings Totals—(Minimum 250 runs)

Total	Overs	Team	Opponent	Venue	Season
6-325*	50.0	South Australia	Tasmania	Hobart TCA	1986/87
4-310*	50.0	New South Wales	South Australia	Sydney	1981/82
6-296*	50.0	South Australia	Western Australia	Adelaide	1984/85
7-287*	50.0	New South Wales	Queensland	Brisbane	1987/88
7-278*	50.0	New South Wales	South Australia	Sydney	1984/85
2-272*	45.0	Victoria	Tasmania	Hobart TCA	1982/83
6-271	49.3	Tasmania	Western Australia	Perth	1986/87
5-270*	49.0	Queensland	Victoria	Melbourne	1982/83
5-266*	50.0	Western Australia	Tasmania	Perth	1986/87
6-264	39.0 +	Queensland	South Australia	Adelaide	1970/71
6-263	37.3 +	Western Australia	New South Wales	Sydney	1973/74
9-262*	40.0 +	New South Wales	Western Australia	Sydney	1973/74
6-261*	40.0 +	South Australia	Queensland	Adelaide	1970/71
2-260*	50.0	New South Wales	Victoria	Sydney	1981/82
4-260*	50.0	Victoria	South Australia	Adelaide	1989/90
3-258*	40.0	Queensland	South Australia	Adelaide	1988/89
257	48.4	Victoria	Queensland	Melbourne	1982/83
7-256*	50.0	New South Wales	Western Australia	Sydney	1979/80
6-256*	49.0	South Australia	Western Australia	Adelaide	1983/84
4-253	49.5	Victoria	South Australia	Adelaide	1981/82
4-253*	40.0	Queensland	Victoria	Melbourne	1988/89
6-252	49.5	Western Australia	New South Wales	Perth	1989/90
6-250	47.2	Western Australia	Tasmania	Perth	1989/90

Lowest Completed Innings Totals—(Minimum 100 runs)

Total	Overs	Team	Opponent	Venue	Season
59	21.3 +	Western Australia	Victoria	Melbourne	1969/70
62	20.3 +	Queensland	Western Australia	Perth	1976/77
76*	26.1 +	Western Australia	New Zealand	Melbourne	1974/75
77*	22.5	Western Australia	Queensland	Perth	1976/77
78*	42.1	Victoria	Queensland	Brisbane	1989/90
79	23.5 +	Queensland	Western Australia	Melbourne	1970/71
80	34.3	Tasmania	New South Wales	Devonport	1984/85
87*	34.5	South Australia	Western Australia	Perth	1989/90
89*	26.0 +	Tasmania	Queensland	Brisbane	1976/77
90	32.4	Victoria	Queensland	Melbourne	1988/89
92*	29.7 +	New South Wales	Queensland	Brisbane	1972/73
97	21.1 +	South Australia	Queensland	Brisbane	1975/76
100	38.5	Tasmania	New South Wales	North Sydney	1989/90

* Denotes batted 1st
+ Denotes 8 ball overs

Leading Run Scorers

Batsman	State	M	Inn	NO	Runs	HS	50	100	Avrge
DW Hookes	SA	34	34	1	1040	101	5	1	31.52
JM Wiener	Vic	20	20	2	1003	108*	10	1	55.72
GS Chappell	SA/Qld	27	27	1	891	92	9	—	34.26
RB McCosker	NSW	21	21	2	847	164	5	2	44.58
GM Ritchie	Qld	24	22	4	811	114	5	1	45.06
GM Wood	WA	34	33	3	794	108*	4	1	26.47
DC Boon	Tas	25	23	1	790	94	7	—	35.91
J Dyson	NSW	19	19	2	786	101	6	2	46.24
PR Sleep	SA	24	23	4	769	90	4	—	40.47
RW Marsh	WA	33	30	6	762	99*	5	—	31.75
GR Marsh	WA	18	18	4	758	105	4	2	54.14
AMJ Hilditch	NSW/SA	23	23	1	743	109	2	2	33.77
AR Border	NSW/Qld	25	25	6	714	97	7	—	37.58
KC Wessels	Qld	19	19	2	656	73	6	—	38.59
RJ Inverarity	WA/SA	28	26	6	655	90	5	—	32.75
DM Jones	Vic	23	21	3	655	139*	3	1	36.39
MRJ Veletta	WA	21	21	4	650	105*	5	1	38.24
RB Kerr	Qld	19	19	2	632	95*	7	—	37.18
GA Bishop	SA	19	18	1	589	119*	1	2	34.65
PM Toohey	NSW	23	22	5	586	82	5	—	34.47
GN Yallop	Vic	24	24	2	586	91	3	—	26.64
KJ Hughes	WA	28	28	1	560	69	4	—	20.74
GM Watts	Vic	16	16	—	537	85	5	—	20.74
DM Wellham	NSW/Tas	23	20	2	535	65*	6	—	29.72
CS Serjeant	WA	17	16	2	503	65	2	—	35.93

▶

Highest Run Scorer for Each State

State	Batsman	M	Inn	NO	Runs	HS	50	100	Avrge
New Zealand	BE Congdon	9	9	1	265	75	2	—	33.13
New South Wales	RB McCosker	21	21	2	847	164	5	2	44.58
Queensland	GM Ritchie	24	22	4	811	114	5	1	45.06
South Australia	DW Hookes	34	34	1	1040	101	5	1	31.52
Tasmania	DC Boon	25	23	1	790	94	7	—	35.91
Victoria	JM Wiener	20	20	2	1003	108*	10	1	55.72
Western Australian	GM Wood	34	33	3	794	108*	4	1	26.47

Most Runs in a Season

Season	Batsman	State	M	Inn	NO	Runs	HS	50	100	Avrge
1981/82	RB McCosker	NSW	4	4	1	346	164	1	2	115.33
1981/82	JM Wiener	Vic	4	4	1	288	108*	2	1	96.00
1981/82	J Dyson	NSW	3	3	—	279	101	1	2	93.00
1984/85	MD Haysman	S.A	4	4	2	249	100*	1	1	124.50
1988/89	GM Ritchie	Qld	4	4	—	241	114	1	1	60.25
1985/86	PW Young	Vic	5	4	1	240	97*	2	—	80.00
1986/87	GA Bishop	S.A	4	4	—	233	116	1	1	58.25
1979/80	JM Wiener	Vic	4	4	—	203	64	2	—	50.75
1986/87	GM Wood	W.A	3	3	1	203	96*	2	—	101.50

Highest Individual Innings

Total	Batsman	Team	Opponent	Venue	Season
164	RB McCosker	New South Wales	South Australia	Sydney	1981/82
139*	DM Jones	Victoria	New South Wales	Sydney	1986/87
119*	GA Bishop	South Australia	Western Australia	Perth	1987/88
116	GA Bishop	South Australia	Tasmania	Hobart TCA	1986/87
115	Majid Khan	Queensland	South Australia	Adelaide	1973/74
114	GM Ritchie	South Australia	Queensland	Adelaide	1988/89
112	RJ Crippin	New South Wales	Western Australia	Sydney	1973/74
111*	RB McCosker	New South Wales	Victoria	Sydney	1981/82
109	AMJ Hilditch	South Australia	Tasmania	Adelaide	1986/87
108*	WM Lawry	Victoria	South Australia	Adelaide	1972/73
108*	GM Wood	Western Australia	Tasmania	Perth	1977/78
108*	JM Wiener	Victoria	New South Wales	Sydney	1981/82
106	AMJ Hilditch	South Australia	Queensland	Adelaide	1988/89
105	BA Courtice	Queensland	Victoria	Melbourne	1982/83
105*	MRJ Veletta	Western Australia	Queensland	Brisbane	1985/86
105	GR Marsh	Western Australia	South Australia	Perth	1987/88
104*	GR Marsh	Western Australia	Tasmania	Perth	1984/85
102*	TM Moody	Western Australia	Tasmania	Perth	
101*	WM Darling	South Australia	Tasmania	Hobart TCA	1977/78
101	J Dyson	New South Wales	Western Australia	Perth	1981/82
101	DW Hookes	South Australia	Western Australia	Adelaide	1984/85
100*	MD Haysman	South Australia	Western Australia	Adelaide	1984/85
100	GW Goodman	Tasmania	Queensland	Brisbane	1978/79
100	J Dyson	New South Wales	South Australia	Sydney	1981/82
100	PE Cantrell	Queensland	South Australia	Adelaide	1988/89

Highest Score by New Zealand

75	BE Congdon	New Zealand	Queensland	Brisbane	1972/73

* Denotes not out

Leading Bowlers

Bowler	State	M	Balls	Mdns	Runs	Wkts	Avrge	5wi	Best
DK Lillee	WA/Tas	27	1559	32	811	48	16.89	—	4/21
KH MacLeay	WA	30	1542	26	951	46	20.67	1	5/30
G Dymock	Qld	23	1300	20	749	39	19.21	1	5/27
JR Thomson	NSW/Qld	28	1449	21	933	37	25.21	1	6/18
CG Rackemann	Qld	19	1045	21	628	35	17.94	1	7/34
TM Alderman	WA	25	1410	26	825	33	25.00	—	4/14
GS Chappell	SA/Qld	27	1189	15	698	32	21.81	—	4/35
GF Lawson	NSW	27	1421	33	783	32	24.47	—	4/31
MR Whitney	NSW	22	1230	19	766	28	27.36	—	4/34
TM Chappell	SA/NSW	23	1050	11	684	27	25.33	—	4/35
SF Graf	Vic/WA	18	965	16	650	26	25.00	—	4/15
WM Clark	WA	25	1405	22	849	24	35.38	—	4/20
MHN Walker	Vic	18	1098	18	583	24	24.29	—	4/37

Bowler	State	M	Balls	Mdns	Runs	Wkts	Avrge	5wi	Best
MF Malone	WA	17	946	24	506	24	21.08	—	4/30
GD Watson	Vic/NSW								
	/WA	14	680	9	416	23	18.80	1	5/20
MG Hughes	Vic	20	1038	20	758	23	32.96	—	4/34
AA Mallett	SA	15	881	9	589	23	25.61	—	3/43
SF Graf	Vic	15	815	14	537	22	24.41	—	4/15
IW Callen	Vic	12	680	9	445	21	21.19	—	4/47
JN Maguire	Qld	17	967	17	657	21	31.29	—	3/30
CD Matthews	WA	14	687	8	461	21	21.95	—	3/32
GRJ Matthews	NSW	20	930	11	584	21	27.81	—	3/29
RJ Bright	Vic	22	1168	4	765	20	38.25	—	3/30
DJ Baker	Tas/WA	12	619	4	387	20	19.35	—	4/35

Leading Wicket-Takers for Each State

State	Bowler	M	Balls	Runs	Wkts	Avrge	5wi	Best
Queensland	G Dymock	23	1300	749	39	19.21	1	5/27
New South Wales	GF Lawson	27	1421	783	32	24.47	—	4/31
New Zealand	HJ Howarth	5	247	109	11	9.91	1	5/22
South Australia	AA Mallett	15	881	589	23	25.61	—	3/43
Tasmania	J Simmons	11	613	280	14	20.00	—	4/17
Victoria	MHN Walker	18	1098	583	24	24.29	—	4/37
Western Australia	DK Lillee	26	1505	766	48	15.96	—	4/21

Most Wickets in a Season

Season	Bowler	State	M	Balls	Mdns	Runs	Wkts	Avrge	5wi	Best
1988/89	CG Rackemann	Qld	4	224	7	128	14	9.14	1	7/34
1979/80	DK Lillee	WA	4	240	3	150	11	13.64	—	4/30
1981/82	TM Chappell	NSW	4	234	4	159	10	15.90	—	4/35
1981/82	G Dymock	Qld	4	232	4	140	10	14.00	1	5/27
1982/83	DL Boyd	WA	4	210	9	95	10	9.50	1	5/15
1985/86	DJ Hickey	Vic	4	198	4	129	10	12.90	1	5/26

Most Wickets in an Innings

Wkts	Bowler	Team	Opponent	Venue	Season
7/34	CG Rackemann	Queensland	South Australia	Adelaide	1988/89
6/18	JR Thomson	Queensland	South Australia	Brisbane	1978/79
5/15	DL Boyd	Western Australia	Victoria	Perth	1982/83
5/20	GD Watson	Victoria	Western Australia	Melbourne	1969/70
5/22	HJ Howarth	New Zealand	New South Wales	Sydney	1969/70
5/23	RJ McCurdy	South Australia	Western Australia	Adelaide	1984/85
5/26	DJ Hickey	Victoria	Western Australia	Melbourne	1985/86
5/27	G Dymock	Queensland	New South Wales	Sydney	1981/82
5/28	LS Pasoce	New South Wales	Western Australia	Sydney	1979/80
5/29	MD Hill	Tasmania	Queensland	Brisbane	1985/86
5/30	KH MacLeay	Western Australia	Tasmania	Perth	1984/85
5/33	IH King	Queensland	New South Wales	Sydney	1969/70
5/36	AG Hurst	Victoria	Western Australia	Perth	1978/79
5/41	DW Hookes	South Australia	New South Wales	Adelaide	
5/49	LF Balcam	Queensland	Tasmania	Brisbane	1978/79

Record Wicket Partnerships

Wkt	Ttl	Batsmen	Team	Opponent	Venue	Season
1st	253	RB McCosker, J Dyson	New South Wales	South Australia	Sydney	1981/82
2nd	233	PE Cantrell, GM Ritchie	Queensland	South Australia	Adelaide	1988/89
3rd	172	G Shipperd, RS Langer	Western Australia	Tasmania	Perth	1981/82
4th	147°	J Dyson, Imran Khan	New South Wales	Victoria	Melbourne	1984/85
5th	133°	AMJ Hilditch, MD Haysman	South Australia	Queensland	Brisbane	1984/85
6th	100	GE Vivian, KJ Wadsworth	New Zealand	South Australia	Adelaide	1972/73
7th	111°	RW Marsh, B Yardley	Western Australia	New South Wales	Sydney	1973/74
8th	88°	RJ Inverarity, MF Malone	Western Australia	Victoria	Perth	1975/76
9th	73	RC Jordan, RK Rowan	Victoria	South Australia	Adelaide	1970/71
10th	36	KH MacLeay, PM Clough	Western Australia	New South Wales	Perth	1984/85

▶

Century Wicket Partnerships

1st Wicket

Ttl	Batsmen	Team	Opponent	Venue	Season
253	RB McCosker, J Dyson	New South Wales	South Australia	Sydney	1981/82
189	JM Wiener, GM Watts	Victoria	Tasmania	Hobart TCA	1982/83
178	RB Kerr, BA Courtice	Queensland	Victoria	Melbourne	1982/83
169	RB McCosker, J Dyson	New South Wales	Victoria	Sydney	1981/82
146	RB Kerr, TJ Barsby	Queensland	South Australia	Football Pk	1986/87
144	JM Wiener, GM Watts	Victoria	South Australia	Adelaide	1981/82
128	KC Wessels, RB Kerr	Queensland	Victoria	Brisbane	1984/85
128	SG Hookey, J Dyson	New South Wales	Queensland	Brisbane	1987/88
121	BM Laird, RW Marsh	Western Australia	Tasmania	Sydney	1979/80
118 +	RB McCosker, J Dyson	New South Wales	Western Australia	Perth	1981/82
115	KH Eastwood, KB Thomas	Victoria	Tasmania	Melbourne	1969/70
114	KR Stackpole, WM Lawry	Victoria	South Australia	Adelaide	1971/72
112	GM Watts, ID Frazer	Victoria	South Australia	Adelaide	1989/90
112	GM Watts, ID Frazer	Victoria	South Australia	Adelaide	1989/90
109	TJ Barsby, BA Courtice	Queensland	Victoria	Melbourne	1985/86
108	Sadiq Mohammad, BR Doolan	Tasmania	Victoria	Melbourne	1974/75
107	GM Wood, RI Charlesworth	Western Australia	Tasmania	Perth	1977/78
107	TM Moody, MRJ Veletta	Western Australia	Queensland	Brisbane	1985/86

2nd Wicket

Ttl	Batsmen	Team	Opponent	Venue	Season
233	PE Cantrell, GM Ritchie	Queensland	South Australia	Adelaide	1988/89
145	BA Richards, IM Chappell	South Australia	Queensland	Adelaide	1970/71
134	JM Buchanan, Ogilvie, AD	Queensland	Tasmania	Brisbane	1978/79
129	MRJ Veletta, G Shipperd	Western Australia	New South Wales	Sydney	1983/84
126	AJ Woodcock, IM Chappell	South Australia	Queensland	Adelaide	1973/74
120*	SB Smith, SR Waugh	New South Wales	Tasmania	Sydney	1988/89
118	GD Watson, RJ Inverarity	Western Australia	South Australia	Adelaide	1971/72
116	SB Smith, DM Wellham	New South Wales	Western Australia	Perth	1984/85
114	JM Wiener, GN Yallop	Victoria	Western Australia	Perth	1983/84
113	GA Bishop, DW Hookes	South Australia	Western Australia	Adelaide	1984/85
113	GM Wood, GR Marsh	Western Australia	New South Wales	Sydney	1985/86
106 +	J Dyson, IC Davis	New South Wales	Western Australia	Perth	1981/82
105	IR McLean, PR Sleep	South Australia	New South Wales	Sydney	1982/83
105	GR Marsh, TM Moody	Western Australia	Queensland	Perth	1988/89
103	RB McCosker, TM Chappell	New South Wales	South Australia	Sydney	1982/83
100	MRJ Veletta, TM Moody	Western Australia	Queensland	Perth	1989/90

3rd Wicket

Ttl	Batsmen	Team	Opponent	Venue	Season
172	G Shipperd, RS Langer	Western Australia	Tasmania	Perth	1981/82
152	GW Goodman, JH Hampshire	Tasmania	Queensland	Brisbane	1978/79
134	KJ Hughes, KS McEwan	Western Australia	Victoria	Perth	1979/80
133	GS Chappell, Majid Khan	Queensland	South Australia	Adelaide	1973/74
130	J Dyson, PS Clifford	New South Wales	South Australia	Sydney	1984/85
125	GS Chappell, AR Border	Queensland	Tasmania	Brisbane	1981/82
111	IM Chappell, GS Chappell	South Australia	Victoria	Adelaide	1971/72
108	RJ Crippin, KD Walters	New South Wales	Victoria	Melbourne	1972/73
107	KJ Hughes, CS Serjeant	Western Australia	Victoria	Perth	1978/79

4th Wicket

Ttl	Batsmen	Team	Opponent	Venue	Season
147*	J Dyson, Imran Khan	New South Wales	Victoria	Melbourne	1984/85
127	GN Yallop, JK Moss	Victoria	Western Australia	Perth	1978/79
125	GS Chappell, KG Cunningham	South Australia	Western Australia	Perth	1972/73
122	TW Graveney, PH Carlson	Queensland	South Australia	Adelaide	1970/71
117	GS Chappell, MF Kent	Queensland	Western Australia	Brisbane	1975/76
115*	BF Hastings, GP Howarth	New Zealand	Tasmania	Melbourne	1974/75
112	GS Chappell, GM Ritchie	Queensland	New South Wales	Brisbane	1982/83
104*	KC Wessels, AR Border	Queensland	Tasmania	Hobart TCA	1982/83
102	AMJ Hilditch, DS Lehmann	South Australia	Queensland	Adelaide	1988/89

5th Wicket

Ttl	Batsmen	Team	Opponent	Venue	Season
133*	AMJ Hilditch, MD Haysman	South Australia	Queensland	Brisbane	1984/85
112	PR Sleep, RJ Inverarity	South Australia	Victoria	Adelaide	1981/82
106	AMJ Hilditch, SC Wundke	South Australia	Tasmania	Adelaide	1986/87
100*	RW Marsh, IJ Brayshaw	Western Australia	South Australia	Perth	1974/75

6th Wicket

Ttl	Batsmen	Team	Opponent	Venue	Season
100	GE Vivian, KJ Wadsworth	New Zealand	South Australia	Adelaide	1972/73

7th Wicket

Ttl	Batsmen	Team	Opponent	Venue	Season
111*	RW Marsh, B Yardley	Western Australia	New South Wales	Sydney	1973/74
106*	JK Pyke, CM Killen	South Australia	Victoria	Adelaide	1987/88

+ Denotes in same innings

Record Wicket Partnerships

New South Wales

Wkt	Ttl	Batsmen	Opponent	Venue	Season
1st	253	RB McCosker, J Dyson	South Australia	Sydney	1981/82
2nd	120*	SB Smith, DM Wellham	Tasmania	Sydney	1988/89
3rd	130	J Dyson, PS Clifford	South Australia	Sydney	1984/85
4th	147*	J Dyson, Imran Khan	Victoria	Melbourne	1984/85
5th	88	GRJ Matthews, ME Waugh	Victoria	Sydney	1986/87
6th	83*	GRJ Matthews, GL Smith	Victoria	Sydney	1988/89
7th	73	GRJ Matthews, SJ Rixon	Tasmania	Launceston	1983/84
8th	50	DJ Colley, KJ O'Keeffe	South Australia	Adelaide	1975/76
9th	33	KJ O'Keeffe, SJ Rixon	Queensland	Brisbane	1976/77
10th	30	JW Gleeson, DA Renneberg	Queensland	Brisbane	1970/71

Queensland

Wkt	Ttl	Batsmen	Opponent	Venue	Season
1st	178	RB Kerr, BA Courtice	Victoria	Melbourne	1982/83
2nd	233	PE Cantrell, GM Ritchie	South Australia	Adelaide	1988/89
3rd	133	GS Chappell, Majid Khan	South Australia	Adelaide	1973/74
4th	122	TW Graveney, PH Carlson	South Australia	Adelaide	1970/71
5th	98	GM Ritchie, GS Trimble	South Australia	Brisbane	1984/85
6th	85	GM Ritchie, PW Anderson	South Australia	Adelaide	1989/90
7th	91	JN Langley, JA Maclean	South Australia	Brisbane	1975/76
8th	30	TV Hohns, JR Thomson	New South Wales	Brisbane	1977/78
9th	49*	AB Henschell, JN Maguire	Tasmania	Launceston	1987/88
10th	26	G Dymock, JR Thomson	New South Wales	Brisbane	1979/80

South Australia

Wkt	Ttl	Batsmen	Opponent	Venue	Season
1st	80	LE Nash, RJ Inverarity	Victoria	Adelaide	1979/80
2nd	145	BA Richards, IM Chappell	Queensland	Adelaide	1970/71
3rd	111	IM Chappell, GS Chappell	Victoria	Adelaide	1971/72
4th	125	GS Chappell, KG Cunningham	Western Australia	Perth	1972/73
5th	133*	AMJ Hilditch, MD Haysman	Queensland	Brisbane	1984/85
6th	88	PR Sleep, JK Pyke	New South Wales	Sydney	1987/88
7th	106*	JK Pyke, CM Killen	Victoria	Adelaide	1987/88
8th	48*	WM Darling, RM Hogg	Tasmania	Hobart TCA	1977/78
9th	61*	M Hendricks, AA Mallett	Western Australia	Perth	1974/75
10th	29	AA Mallett, W Prior	New South Wales	Adelaide	1975/76

Tasmania

Wkt	Ttl	Batsmen	Opponent	Venue	Season
1st	108	Sadiq Mohammad, BR Doolan	Victoria	Melbourne	1974/75
2nd	87	M Ray, DC Boon	Western Australia	Perth	1984/85
3rd	152	GW Goodman, JH Hampshire	Queensland	Brisbane	1978/79
4th	80	DC Boon, RD Woolley	Queensland	Hobart TCA	1983/84
5th	76	RJ Tucker, DFG O'Connor	Western Australia	Perth	1989/90
6th	91*	RD Woolley, RE Soule	South Australia	Adelaide	1986/87
7th	96*	TW Docking, J Siddons	Western Australia	Hobart TCA	1978/79

Continued

Wkt	Ttl	Batsmen	Opponent	Venue	Season
8th	39	RE Soule, RL Brown	South Australia	Hobart TCA	1986/87
9th	54	TW Docking, RJ McCurdy	South Australia	Hobart TCA	1980/81
10th	26	RJ McCurdy, PM Clough	South Australia	Hobart TCA	1980/81

Victoria

Wkt	Ttl	Batsmen	Opponent	Venue	Season
1st	189	JM Wiener, GM Watts	Tasmania	Hobart TCA	1982/83
2nd	114	JM Wiener, GN Yallop	Western Australia	Perth	1983/84
3rd	97	DM Jones, PW Young	New South Wales	Sydney	1985/86
4th	127	GN Yallop, JK Moss	Western Australia	Perth	1978/79
5th	88*	MD Taylor, SP O'Donnell	South Australia	Adelaide	1984/85
6th	79	TJ Laughlin, RD Robinson	South Australia	Adelaide	1979/80
7th	98*	TJ Laughlin, RJ Bright	New South Wales	Sydney	1976/77
8th	51	RD Robinson, MHN Walker	South Australia	Adelaide	1980/81
9th	73	RC Jordan, RK Rowan	South Australia	Adelaide	1970/71
10th	19	DW Fleming, PW Jackson	Queensland	Melbourne	1988/89

Western Australia

Wkt	Ttl	Batsmen	Opponent	Venue	Season
1st	121	RW Marsh, BM Laird	Tasmania	Sydney	1979/80
2nd	129	MRJ Veletta, G Shipperd	New South Wales	Sydney	1983/84
3rd	172	G Shipperd, RS Langer	Tasmania	Perth	1981/82
4th	97	RW Marsh, WJ Edwards	Queensland	Perth	1974/75
5th	100*	RW Marsh, IJ Brayshaw	South Australia	Perth	1974/75
6th	80	WS Andrews, MJ Cox	Victoria	Melbourne	1985/86
7th	111*	RW Marsh, B Yardley	New South Wales	Sydney	1973/74
8th	88*	RJ Inverarity, MF Malone	Victoria	Perth	1975/76
9th	48	RS Langer, MF Malone	New Zealand	Melbourne	1974/75
10th	36	KH MacLeay, PM Clough	New South Wales	Perth	1984/85

New Zealand

Wkt	Ttl	Batsmen	Opponent	Venue	Season
1st	44	GM Turner, GT Dowling	Western Australia	Perth	1970/71
2nd	76	GM Turner, MJF Shrimpton	South Australia	Adelaide	1973/74
3rd	61	BE Congdon, BF Hastings	Queensland	Brisbane	1972/73
4th	115*	BF Hastings, GP Howarth	Tasmania	Melbourne	1974/75
5th	24	BE Congdon, B Dunning	Queensland	Brisbane	1972/73
6th	100	GE Vivian, KJ Wadsworth	South Australia	Adelaide	1972/73
7th	58*	KJ Wadsworth, DR Hadlee	New South Wales	Sydney	1969/70
8th	22	B Dunning, DG Trist	Victoria	Melbourne	1971/72
9th	18	RJ Hadlee, RS Cunis	Queensland	Brisbane	1972/73
10th	20	JFM Morrison, BL Cairns	Western Australia	Melbourne	1973/74